ACCOUNTING

8TH EDITION

JOHN HOGGETT

JOHN MEDLIN
University of South Australia

LEW EDWARDS

MATTHEW TILLING
BDO Australia

EVELYN HOGG
Notre Dame University

WILEY

John Wiley & Sons Australia, Ltd

Eighth edition published 2012 by
John Wiley & Sons Australia, Ltd
42 McDougall Street, Milton Qld 4064

First edition published 1987
Second edition published 1990
Revised and updated second edition published 1992
Third edition published 1996
Fourth edition published 2000
Fifth edition published 2003
Sixth edition published 2006
Seventh edition published 2009

Typeset in 10/12pt Times LT Roman

National Library of Australia
Cataloguing-in-Publication data

Title:	Accounting / John Hoggett . . . [et al.].
Edition:	8th ed.
ISBN:	9781742466354 (pbk.)
Notes:	Includes index.
Subjects:	Accounting—Australia—Textbooks.
	Accounting—Australia—Problems, exercises. etc.
Other Authors/	
Contributors:	Hoggett, J. R. (John Robert), 1948–
Dewey Number:	657.0994

ISBN: 9781742466354 (pbk)
       9781118208182 (BRV)

Cover image: © Anelina/Shutterstock.com
Internal design images: © iStockphoto.com/Jamie Farrant and
© BigToto/Shutterstock.com

Typeset in India by Aptara

Printed in China by
1010 Printing International Ltd

10 9 8 7 6 5 4 3

About the authors

John Hoggett

John Hoggett, BCom (Hons), BTh, MFM (Qld), AAUQ, FCPA, has taught accounting at several different universities in Western Australia and Queensland during his 40 years as an academic. He has taught introductory accounting, corporate accounting and accounting theory to undergraduate and postgraduate students, and written books and monographs for a variety of organisations including CPA Australia and the Group of 100. He was also involved in secondary accounting education for several years with the Curriculum Council of Western Australia.

John Medlin

Dr John Medlin, PhD (UniSA), BEc (Adelaide), MEc (UNE), CA, is a senior lecturer in the School of Commerce at the University of South Australia. John began his career with Ernst & Whinney (now Ernst & Young) in the early 1980s. After a few years practical experience, John moved to accounting education where he has lectured in both financial and management accounting, accounting theory, economics and business finance. From 1998 until 2010, John coordinated a general first-year accounting subject with an enrolment in excess of 1000 students each year, 80% of whom were non-accounting majors. Since 2010, John has coordinated a second-year financial accounting subject. He has been recognised with teaching awards from the University of South Australia. His research interest is in the area of accounting education in which he has presented conference papers and been published.

Lew Edwards

Lew Edwards is Emeritus Professor of the School of Accounting, Queensland University of Technology. Lew's career includes over 25 years teaching financial and managerial accounting to undergraduate and postgraduate students. He was Head of School (Department) of Accountancy for 18 years. He is a both a chartered accountant and a CPA, and served for many years on education and technical standards committees (both state and national) of the professional accounting bodies. He has also served as a consultant to accounting firms, industry and government at both national and international levels. Lew is co-author (with John Hoggett) of the best selling Australian accounting texts *Financial Accounting in Australia* and *Accounting in Australia.* He has also published (as author and co-author) a wide range of manual and computerised accounting practice sets.

Matthew Tilling

Matthew Tilling, BCom (Flinders), is Manager, Learning and Development with BDO WA and a university lecturer in Perth. His roles straddle academic and professional issues around the understanding and implementation of accounting standards. He has also been involved with syllabus and exam design for high school accounting in Western Australia. Matt has published articles on accounting education and social environmental accounting in a range of international journals.

Evelyn Hogg

Evelyn Hogg, BCom, BAcc, CA, CA (SA), ACMA, is a senior lecturer in financial accounting and managerial accounting at the University of Notre Dame, Australia. She is a chartered accountant and a chartered management accountant. She has over 25 years of university teaching, commercial training and consulting experience in accounting and assurance services locally and overseas. She has a keen interest in the development of accounting education and training in secondary, tertiary and commercial environments.

Brief contents

Contents

Preface

Our main purpose in writing this book is to provide an introductory but comprehensive description of the purpose, practice and process of contemporary international financial and management accounting in an Australian context. With the increased emphasis on the globalisation of business, the material is ideal for the study of introductory accounting in a broad international context.

The book is designed for tertiary students interested in an accounting career and for those wanting a general understanding of the production and use of accounting information in the business sector. This eighth edition considers more fully the need for accounting knowledge by students undertaking business studies in areas other than accounting. The book is suited to a two-semester course at both the undergraduate level and the postgraduate level as it provides a general understanding of the role of financial and management accounting information systems in any business sector.

The eighth edition builds on the strengths of previous editions with a strong focus on the decision-making role of accounting as well as on a student's acquisition of generic skills such as communication, analysis and problem solving, critical thinking, judgement, and an appreciation of ethical issues. However, the authors believe that competency in the technical skills of accounting should remain as the core objective, and the book therefore continues to provide appropriate discussion of key technical issues. It is our belief that a person equipped with knowledge of technical material in accounting possesses a powerful tool for making economic decisions and for analysing and solving business problems. These technical skills are used in the book to provide clear and detailed explanations of the accounting concepts that form the basis of the practice of accounting. The use of the technical skills of accounting in teaching concepts gives students a practical foundation from which to build their understanding.

Significant changes from the previous edition

The most significant changes in the eighth edition result from the evolution of the international accounting standards and financial reporting standards issued by the International Accounting Standards Board (IASB) and their adoption in Australia since 1 January 2005. The AASB also modifies the standards so that they apply to the not-for-profit sector as well as the business sector. Newly adopted financial reporting standards since 2005, particularly in the area of presentation of financial statements, have caused major rewrites and changes in the financial reporting sections of the eighth edition. Where appropriate, the book refers to both the IASB and AASB accounting standards to encourage thinking at a global level in the field of accounting.

Significant amendments have also been made in the eighth edition to the material relating to the basic objectives of financial reporting, the qualitative characteristics of financial information and definitions of the elements of financial reports. These amendments are a result of the IASB and its American counterpart, the Financial Accounting Standards Board (FASB), jointly deliberating on the contents of the conceptual framework, in order to ensure that the IASB's *Conceptual Framework for Financial Reporting* reflects the contemporary thinking of accounting regulators globally. These proposed amendments to the framework will eventually be adopted in Australia.

As in the previous edition, the book provides an easy-to-use format for most introductory accounting courses at a tertiary level. The chapters on management accounting and decision making in business are introduced early in the book and have been simplified to provide a strong focus on the role of accounting in business decision making. We continue to believe that this is a more interesting approach to the teaching of an introductory accounting course. The coverage of regulatory issues and the application of accounting standards in an external reporting context are addressed at a later stage of the book. Hence, the focus is on coverage of management accounting and decision-making issues initially, with more emphasis on financial accounting issues later.

We believe that this structure helps students gain a greater appreciation of the contribution of accounting to the way businesses operate.

The book is organised in six parts as follows, with emphasis on decision making in a business enterprise before consideration of external reporting issues.

Part 1: Accounting for decision making (chapters 1–2)

Part 2: Accounting systems and processes (chapters 3–9)

Part 3: Financial planning, control and decision making (chapters 10–14)

Part 4: Equity in business (chapters 15–16)

Part 5: Accounting regulation of assets and liabilities (chapters 17–22)

Part 6: External reporting and performance evaluation (chapters 23–25).

Based on feedback from users of the previous editions of this book, there remains in the eighth edition a strong focus on:

1. service organisations operating in the business and not-for-profit sectors
2. the use of accounting information by non-accountants, both in text examples and in end-of-chapter activities
3. the impact of the goods and services tax (GST) on business records in a number of exercises and problems
4. the effect of accounting information on decisions made in business (segments in each chapter provide links to business activities, and each chapter contains a scene setter)
5. the effect on accounting systems of improvements in information technology
6. the impact of developments in the regulation of accounting standards at national and international levels.

We have continued to improve the readability of the book without compromising the integrity of its theoretical and practical content, and have continued the policy of including detailed learning objectives.

The major features of this eighth edition include the following:

- Material has been extensively rewritten in relation to the new regulatory arrangements for the development of accounting standards globally and in the Australian context.
- The text takes into account the impact of the newly adopted IASB standards, dealing with (a) the presentation of financial statements, especially in relation to the statement of profit or loss and other comprehensive income, statement of changes in equity, and statement of financial position, and (b) the statement of cash flows as a result of the preference for direct approach of reporting cash flows from operating activities in Australia.
- The text discusses new thinking on the conceptual framework's (a) objectives of general purpose financial reporting, (b) qualitative characteristics of financial information, (c) the reporting entity concept, (d) the definitions of elements, and (e) recognition criteria.
- Terminology has been updated to reflect the continued adoption of international accounting standards — e.g. the 'statement of profit or loss and other comprehensive income' will gradually replace the 'income statement' in external financial reports, the 'balance sheet' should be called the 'statement of financial position' in external financial reports and the 'cash flow statement' is now the 'statement of cash flows'.
- Many chapters provide a discussion of the impact of the GST on business, especially on small business. However, instructors can ignore the effects of the GST if they wish to pay attention to the other accounting issues in each chapter. An introductory coverage of the GST is provided as an appendix to chapter 3. Many exercises and problems permit lecturers to select where GST is included and where it is excluded. Those questions which incorporate GST throughout are marked with a GST icon.

- Material on basic accounting systems and computerised systems has been updated and rewritten to help students use computer packages such as the latest versions of MYOB and QuickBooks.
- The text continues to develop web-based activities for students in many chapters, in order to indicate the importance of the internet as an information tool for accounting practitioners.
- 'Scene setters' at the beginning of each chapter help students understand the relevance of the accounting material in that chapter to the issues faced by accountants in practice.
- Additional and new 'business knowledge' vignettes in each chapter show the relevance of accounting to the practical world of business.
- A list of 'key terms' with page numbers is provided at the end of each chapter, with full definitions of these terms (and their page numbers) listed in a glossary at the back of the book.
- The number of discussion questions, exercises and problems in many chapters has been increased to 15, and approximately half of the questions are new.
- Problems are graded using a star system, where one star indicates an 'easy' problem and three stars indicate a 'challenging' problem.
- In the end-of-chapter case material, several decision cases, critical thinking cases, communication and leadership activities and ethics and governance issues are either new or updated. Web-based activities are included in several chapters. In addition, the financial analysis is based on the latest JB Hi-Fi Limited annual report, which is available on its website, www.jbhifi.com.au.

Supplementary materials

Accounting 8th edition is supported with an extensive teaching and learning resources supplementary package.

- A solutions manual contains worked solutions to all end-of-chapter discussion questions, exercises, problems, case studies and activities. The solution manual has been thoroughly checked for accuracy and correctness.
- PowerPoint Presentation contains over 1000 slides with summaries of key concept and processes presented in the chapter.
- Computerised Test Bank contains over 2000 multiple-choice questions available with Respondus. The test bank is a fast and convenient resource for designing, preparing and delivering examinations.
- Blackboard, Moodle and WebCT resources are available for online teaching and learning designs supported by these systems. Your John Wiley & Sons sales consultant can provide instructors with a demonstration of the resources available to enhance course delivery and student learning.
- *WileyPLUS* is a research-based online environment for effective teaching and learning. With *WileyPLUS*, lecturers can prepare, assign and grade accounting activities simply and in a time efficient manner. *WileyPLUS* increases student confidence through an innovative design that allows greater engagement, which leads to improved learning outcomes. For more information, contact your John Wiley & Sons sales consultant or visit www.wileyplus.com.

Acknowledgements

We wish to express our appreciation of the following people and organisations who have contributed in some way to the development of the eighth edition of this book and to the refinement of our ideas. Particular appreciation is again extended to our very patient partners and to our families for their continued understanding, assistance with finding material for cases, business knowledge and profiles, and with proofreading, and for their tolerance of partners and parents who are buried in their studies for long hours at evenings and weekends.

Special appreciation is also extended to those who have contributed to the text as independent reviewers and preparers of the extensive teaching and learning resources associated with the textbook. We appreciate the contributions of Barbara Burns, Nila Latimer, Peter Baxter (University of the Sunshine Coast) and Jane Hamilton (LaTrobe University) who worked on various elements of the teaching and *WileyPLUS* resources, and Brian Perrin (Curtin University) for providing new content on computer accounting systems in chapter 7.

John Hoggett
John Medlin
Lew Edwards
Matthew Tilling
Evelyn Hogg
September 2011

How to use this book

Accounting 8th edition has been designed with you — the student — in mind. Improved learning features and a full-colour design represent our attempt to provide you with a book that both communicates the subject matter and facilitates learning. We have tried to accomplish these goals through the following elements.

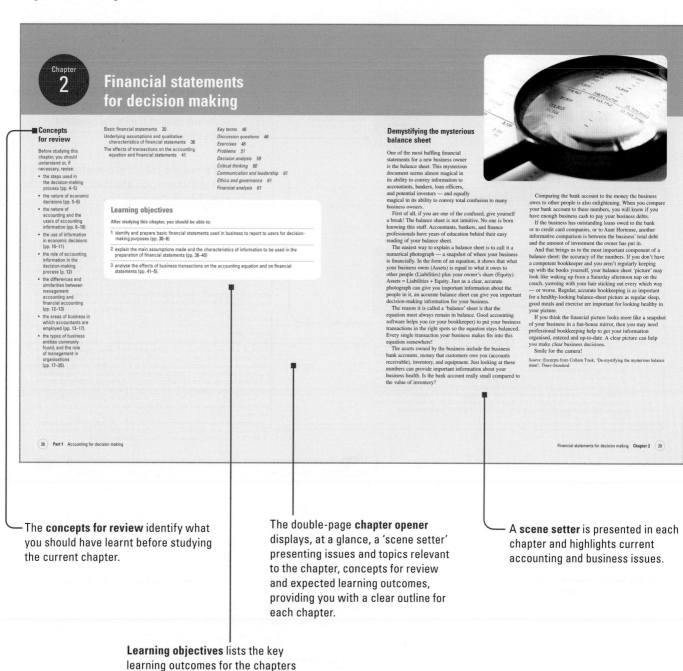

The **concepts for review** identify what you should have learnt before studying the current chapter.

The double-page **chapter opener** displays, at a glance, a 'scene setter' presenting issues and topics relevant to the chapter, concepts for review and expected learning outcomes, providing you with a clear outline for each chapter.

A **scene setter** is presented in each chapter and highlights current accounting and business issues.

Learning objectives lists the key learning outcomes for the chapters and aligns with each main section in the chapter.

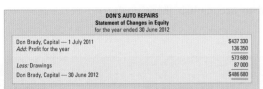

DON'S AUTO REPAIRS
Statement of Changes in Equity
for the year ended 30 June 2012

Don Brady, Capital — 1 July 2011	$437 330
Add: Profit for the year	136 350
	573 680
Less: Drawings	87 000
Don Brady, Capital — 30 June 2012	$486 680

Figure 2.4 Statement of changes in equity

The three statements illustrated above — balance sheet, income statement and statement of changes in equity — are related to one another. The balance sheet at the end of one period is the balance sheet at the beginning of the next period. The balance sheets at the beginning and end of a period are linked by the income statement and the statement of changes in equity as shown in figure 2.5.

Figure 2.5 Financial statements relationship

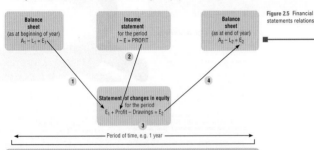

1. E_1 is shown in the beginning balance sheet and is the starting point for the statement of changes in equity.
2. Profit for the period is determined from the income statement and included in factors which alter the capital balance over the year.
3. Drawings made during the year (usually in cash) are recorded in the accounts and used in determining the equity at the end of the period E_2.
4. E_2 is shown on the ending balance sheet.

The statement of cash flows

Another important financial statement prepared by entities is a statement of cash flows. An entity's income statement does not report on the cash flows of the entity, but on its income and expenses (chapter 4 discusses this further). Income and expenses as defined above do not necessarily represent cash flows. Consequently, a **statement of cash flows** is prepared to report on the cash flows in and out of the entity. It is particularly useful in helping users to assess the sources and uses of an entity's cash, and the likely ability of the entity to remain solvent (i.e. able to pay its debts), so that the users can make informed decisions. The statement reports on the entity's performance in generating cash flows from operating activities, investing activities and financing activities as shown in figure 2.6 (p. 36) for Don's Auto Repairs. It is assumed that this business began its operations on 1 July 2011 when the owner, Don Brady, invested $437 330 cash in the business.

Financial statements, accounting flow charts and other **diagrams** enhance your understanding of the key accounting processes.

Key terms are bolded and printed in red in the text at first mention and then defined in the end-of-book glossary.

and immaterial for another. Thus, considerable judgement is needed by the accountant in assess which information is material and which is immaterial for the particular decision

rding to the *Conceptual Framework*, materiality must be considered in the context of the aracteristics, especially faithful representation. Materiality is viewed as a constraint on the tion to be included in an entity's financial statements rather than as a separate character-good information.

ts and costs

SB also states that the benefits of financial reporting information should jus- costs of providing and using it. The benefits of financial reporting information better investment, credit and similar economic decisions, which in turn result in more markets and greater benefits for the economy as a whole. But, the task of preparing l statements also imposes costs on both the preparers and the users of those statements, as on others such as auditors. Therefore, a major constraint on reporting the absolute ormation in a financial statement is the cost of generating that information and assuring s a faithful representation of the events it is supposed to represent. In other words, tion is costly to produce, and both the accountant and the user must be mindful of its and costs.

e assumptions and characteristics (and others as well) have been established by inter-national regulators of accounting standards. In a later chapter, we shall introduce the issue of regulation, and show how accounting standards have been developed in Australia.

'**Business Knowledge**' links accounting to current business events and highlights the application of accounting to a range of business environments.

BUSINESS KNOWLEDGE

Seeking sustainability

So how does a business prove its sustainability credentials?

'A starting point is always a greenhouse gas assessment which will give us the groundwork, the numbers, and ultimately reveal what the carbon footprint of the business is,' McIntosh, (the WA manager for Carbon Planet, a national carbon management company) says.

'Then there are emissions and sustainability planning. That involves risk analysis so you understand your exposure and the impact of a carbon price on your business.'

'So we might end up saying: "Well, 42 per cent of your expenses will be impacted by the price of carbon, causing an increase in the cost of doing business of nine per cent — or whatever" — and we can quantify that in the figures.'

He says the first aim is always to minimise emissions. After that might come risk mitigation strategies, buying credits to offset emissions and communication strategies so your staff, clients and suppliers know what you're doing and can track it.

'You'll never have a zero footprint,' McIntosh says. 'Everything you do in business causes an emission. But you can reduce it, and then you offset the remainder by buying credits.'

While legislation might be a major factor in Australian businesses becoming more carbon conscious, McIntosh says Europe already has an emissions trading scheme and business there has been keen on being green.

'The main driving force there has been corporate responsibility, they're not driven by government legislation. It's driven by the business community,' he says.

'Being seen as "clean and green — and offset" is seen as much a factor in doing business as OHS was when that came in, or even similarly with quality assurance.'

'If you weren't following those processes, then you'd start being left out of the supply chain.'

In Australia, peer pressure, corporate responsibility and public image — being seen to be green — are all playing a part.

'A lot of companies are going down this green path,' McIntosh says. 'The international ones were first, but a lot of the local ones are doing it as well. It's almost a case of "if we have to do it, we expect everyone we do business with to do it as well".'

'That's also coming through in tendering for government and big business jobs. Tender documents, for instance, are asking "how are you addressing your emissions or what are your sustainability practices?" And more and more weight is being given to those answers.'

'So companies who do a lot of business with government or overseas contracts have to address those factors, just for the sake of doing business.'

Source: Excerpts from Tony Malkovic, 'Seeking sustainability', *Charter*.

The **key terms** list the important terms presented in the chapter. Refer to the **end-of-book glossary** for definitions of these key terms.

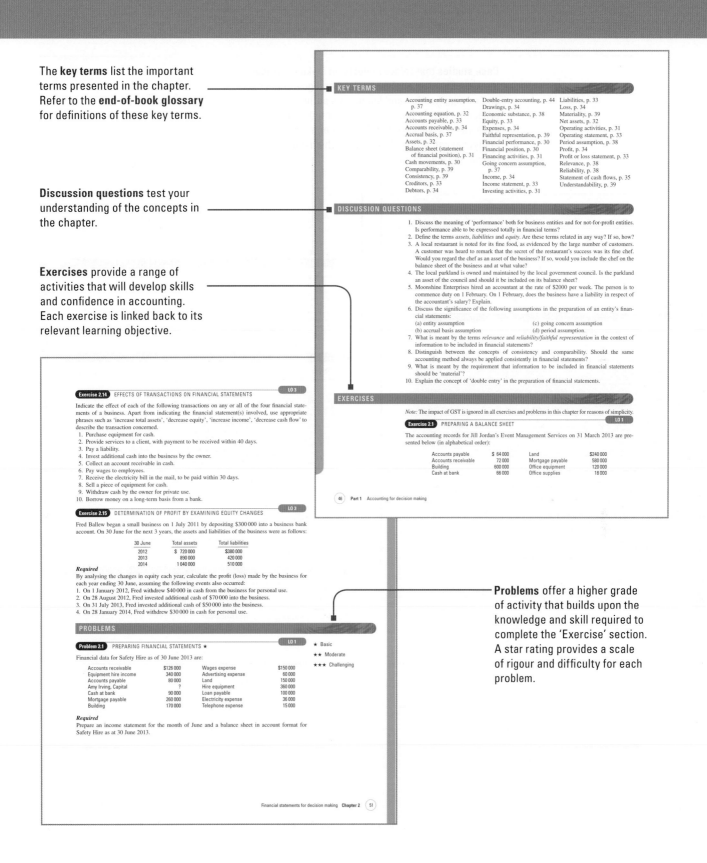

KEY TERMS

Accounting entity assumption, p. 37	Double-entry accounting, p. 44	Liabilities, p. 33
Accounting equation, p. 32	Drawings, p. 34	Loss, p. 34
Accounts payable, p. 33	Economic substance, p. 38	Materiality, p. 39
Accounts receivable, p. 34	Equity, p. 33	Net assets, p. 32
Accrual basis, p. 37	Expenses, p. 34	Operating activities, p. 31
Assets, p. 32	Faithful representation, p. 39	Operating statement, p. 33
Balance sheet (statement of financial position), p. 31	Financial performance, p. 30	Period assumption, p. 38
	Financial position, p. 30	Profit, p. 34
Cash movements, p. 30	Financing activities, p. 31	Profit or loss statement, p. 33
Comparability, p. 39	Going concern assumption, p. 37	Relevance, p. 38
Consistency, p. 39	Income, p. 34	Reliability, p. 38
Creditors, p. 33	Income statement, p. 33	Statement of cash flows, p. 35
Debtors, p. 34	Investing activities, p. 31	Understandability, p. 39

Discussion questions test your understanding of the concepts in the chapter.

DISCUSSION QUESTIONS

1. Discuss the meaning of 'performance' both for business entities and for not-for-profit entities. Is performance able to be expressed totally in financial terms?
2. Define the terms *assets, liabilities* and *equity.* Are these terms related in any way? If so, how?
3. A local restaurant is noted for its fine food, as evidenced by the large number of customers. A customer was heard to remark that the secret of the restaurant's success was its fine chef. Would you regard the chef as an asset of the business? If so, would you include the chef on the balance sheet of the business and at what value?
4. The local parkland is owned and maintained by the local government council. Is the parkland an asset of the council and should it be included on its balance sheet?
5. Moonshine Enterprises hired an accountant at the rate of $2000 per week. The person is to commence duty on 1 February. On 1 February, does the business have a liability in respect of the accountant's salary? Explain.
6. Discuss the significance of the following assumptions in the preparation of an entity's financial statements:
   (a) entity assumption   (c) going concern assumption
   (b) accrual basis assumption   (d) period assumption.
7. What is meant by the terms *relevance* and *reliability/faithful representation* in the context of information to be included in financial statements?
8. Distinguish between the concepts of consistency and comparability. Should the same accounting method always be applied consistently in financial statements?
9. What is meant by the requirement that information to be included in financial statements should be 'material'?
10. Explain the concept of 'double entry' in the preparation of financial statements.

Exercises provide a range of activities that will develop skills and confidence in accounting. Each exercise is linked back to its relevant learning objective.

EXERCISES

Note: The impact of GST is ignored in all exercises and problems in this chapter for reasons of simplicity.

Exercise 2.1   PREPARING A BALANCE SHEET   LO 1

The accounting records for Jill Jordan's Event Management Services on 31 March 2013 are presented below (in alphabetical order):

Accounts payable	$ 64 000	Land	$240 000
Accounts receivable	72 000	Mortgage payable	580 000
Building	600 000	Office equipment	120 000
Cash at bank	66 000	Office supplies	18 000

Exercise 2.14   EFFECTS OF TRANSACTIONS ON FINANCIAL STATEMENTS   LO 3

Indicate the effect of each of the following transactions on any or all of the four financial statements of a business. Apart from indicating the financial statement(s) involved, use appropriate phrases such as 'increase total assets', 'decrease equity', 'increase income', 'decrease cash flow' to describe the transaction concerned.
1. Purchase equipment for cash.
2. Provide services to a client, with payment to be received within 40 days.
3. Pay a liability.
4. Invest additional cash into the business by the owner.
5. Collect an account receivable in cash.
6. Pay wages to employees.
7. Receive the electricity bill in the mail, to be paid within 30 days.
8. Sell a piece of equipment for cash.
9. Withdraw cash by the owner for private use.
10. Borrow money on a long-term basis from a bank.

Exercise 2.15   DETERMINATION OF PROFIT BY EXAMINING EQUITY CHANGES   LO 3

Fred Ballew began a small business on 1 July 2011 by depositing $300 000 into a business bank account. On 30 June for the next 3 years, the assets and liabilities of the business were as follows:

30 June	Total assets	Total liabilities
2012	$ 720 000	$380 000
2013	890 000	420 000
2014	1 040 000	510 000

Required
By analysing the changes in equity each year, calculate the profit (loss) made by the business for each year ending 30 June, assuming the following events also occurred:
1. On 1 January 2012, Fred withdrew $40 000 in cash from the business for personal use.
2. On 28 August 2012, Fred invested additional cash of $70 000 into the business.
3. On 31 July 2013, Fred invested additional cash of $50 000 into the business.
4. On 28 January 2014, Fred withdrew $30 000 in cash for personal use.

PROBLEMS

Problem 2.1   PREPARING FINANCIAL STATEMENTS ★   LO 1

Financial data for Safety Hire as of 30 June 2013 are:

Accounts receivable	$126 000	Wages expense	$150 000
Equipment hire income	340 000	Advertising expense	60 000
Accounts payable	80 000	Land	150 000
Amy Irving, Capital	?	Hire equipment	360 000
Cash at bank	90 000	Loan payable	100 000
Mortgage payable	260 000	Electricity expense	36 000
Building	170 000	Telephone expense	15 000

★ Basic
★★ Moderate
★★★ Challenging

Required
Prepare an income statement for the month of June and a balance sheet in account format for Safety Hire as at 30 June 2013.

Problems offer a higher grade of activity that builds upon the knowledge and skill required to complete the 'Exercise' section. A star rating provides a scale of rigour and difficulty for each problem.

Case studies that relate to decision making, critical thinking, financial analysis, ethics and governance, and communication and leadership activity are presented in this section. It is expected that these case studies will assist in the development of your analytical and professional skills which will be relevant to your future careers.

Required

A. Using the information Gavin has provided, prepare an income statement and a balance sheet for the year ended 30 June 2013.
B. Discuss the elements of the financial statements you have prepared in part A above which the bank manager might be interested in when assessing whether or not to grant loan facilities to Gavin.
C. What information, in addition to the income statement and balance sheet, might the bank manager be interested in looking at before making a decision?

CRITICAL THINKING

Sporting glory — the great intangible

Read the following article from *Australian CPA*.

While rugby stars are heroes to many, when checking the books they become a complex intangible. Rosalind Whiting and Kyla Chapman investigate the merits of Human Resource Accounting in professional sport.

Australia, New Zealand and rugby union — a combination guaranteed to stir patriotic feelings across the Tasman! But what if we add accounting to this equation? Rugby players are the teams' most valuable assets, so should we be placing their value on the balance sheet? And if so, does it make any difference to the decisions that users of financial statements make?

Human resource accounting in professional sport

Professional sport has been prevalent in the United Kingdom and the United States for nearly 200 years. However, professional sport arrived later in Australia and New Zealand. In particular, the Kiwis only entered this arena in 1995 when the New Zealand Rugby Football Union (NZRFU) signed the Tri Nations sponsorship deal and removed all barriers preventing rugby union players being paid for their services. Player contract expenses in New Zealand now amount to over NZ$20 million annually, according to the NZRFU.

In the United Kingdom and the United States, the professional teams' financial accounts quite often incorporate human resource accounting (HRA). HRA is basically an addition to traditional accounting, in which a value for the employees is placed on the balance sheet and is amortised over a period of time, instead of expensing costs such as professional development.

There is debate about the merits of this process and the arguments are in line with those we have been hearing about intangibles in general. More recently, there has been worldwide movement towards recognising acquired identifiable intangible assets at fair value in the financial statements. So why not include an organisation's human resources? While (thankfully) most people agree that employees are valuable, there are accounting difficulties with the concept of ownership or control of the employees (asset definition) and the reliability of measurement.

Despite these concerns, one area where HRA does have some international acceptability is in accounting for professional sport, mainly because of the measurable player transfer costs. But there is still some variability in the reporting of human resource value, ranging from the capitalisation of signing and transfer fees through to player development costs or valuations.

To the authors' knowledge, HRA is not currently practised with Australia and New Zealand's professional sports teams. The absence of transfer fees between clubs when trading players may explain this.

Decision making

Accountants are required to provide information that assists users in assessing an organisation's financial and service performance and in making decisions about providing resources to, or doing business with, the firm.

The big question is whether HRA information is more useful to the decision maker than the alternative expensing treatment. Supporters of HRA argue that capitalised information is useful for strategic planning and management of employees, and provides a more accurate measure of the firm's status and total performance.

Those against HRA say it is too subjective to be useful and that it just imposes another cost on the organisation. Some detractors argue that it makes unprofitable organisations appear profitable simply because smart people work there. But those who believe in the efficiency of the market would argue that investors are not naive, and decisions would be unaffected by the way in which human resource information is presented.

Source: Excerpts from Rosalind Whiting and Kyla Chapman, 'Sporting glory — the great intangible', *Australian CPA*.

Required

Discuss whether rugby players are 'valuable assets' of a business, or an expense. Use the definitions of assets and expenses in this book to show which of the elements of the financial statements 'human resources' should be classified under.

COMMUNICATION AND LEADERSHIP

Preparing balance sheets

In groups of three or four, consider the following people and their situations:
● a student who has just completed secondary school and started at university and is living at home with parents
● an adult who works full time.

For each situation, prepare a list of assets the person would typically own, and estimate the cost of each asset in dollars. Then prepare a list of liabilities, and estimate the cost of each liability in dollars. Using the accounting equation, calculate the equity of each of the two people and draw up a balance sheet for each. Display them on overhead transparencies and compare them with those developed by other groups in the class.

ETHICS AND GOVERNANCE

Kickbacks

Read the following article and answer the questions.

COCA-COLA said today that two former employees of its Shanghai bottling company had been arrested for corruption.

The two employees worked for Shanghai Shenmei Beverage and Food Co, which was licensed to produce Coca-Cola in China and which was part-owned by the US soft drink giant, a Hong Kong-based spokesman for Coca-Cola said.

'We can confirm that two former employees at our Shanghai (Shenmei) bottling plant have been detained by the police,' said the spokesman.

Coca-Cola dismissed reports that the case involved bribes to government officials, saying the investigation focused on 'allegations that the former employees extracted kickbacks from suppliers and embezzled from our bottler'.

One employee left the company in early 2008, while the other left in May when the allegations surfaced, the spokesman said.

The bottler is cooperating with police in the investigation, he said.

Coca-Cola did not provide further details but the official Xinhua news agency reported that up to 10 million yuan ($1.69 million) could have been misappropriated.

Source: AFP, News.com.au.

Required

A. In the article, who are the stakeholders in this situation?
B. What ethical issues are involved?
C. If it is normal business practice to bribe government officials in a country that you are dealing with but not in your own country, do you believe it is ethical to do so?
D. Do you believe one country has the right to impose its values on another in this regard? Consider how you would feel if another country tried to impose its values on your country, and consider what overriding human rights issues might be relevant.

FINANCIAL ANALYSIS

Refer to the latest financial report of JB Hi-Fi Limited on its website, www.jbhifi.com.au. Answer the following questions using the directors' declaration, consolidated figures in the financial statements, and notes to the financial statements.
1. What does the directors' declaration state? What, if anything, does this declaration say about the going concern assumption?
2. What were the total assets at the end of the financial year?

Acknowledgements

The authors and publisher would like to thank the following copyright holders, organisations and individuals for their permission to reproduce copyright material in this book.

Images

• iStockphoto: **3** (top)/Andrew Penner, **275** (top right)/parema, **493** (top right)/René Mansi, **615** (top right)/ Will Selarep, **829** (top right)/Don Nichols, **867** (top right)/Skip O'Donnell, **907** (top right)/rukanoga, **977** (top right)/pamspix, **1055** (top) /Aurelio Scetta © iStockphoto.com. • Corbis Australia: **65** (top right) Corbis/ The Art Archive/ Alfredo Dagli Orti. • Photodisc: **177** (top right), **377** (top right), **539** (top right), **749** (top right) © Photodisc. • Shutterstock: **29** (top right)/Robyn Mackenzie, **123** (top)/Madis Uudam, **417** (top right)/ Aleksandr Bryliaev, **461** (top)/Paul Burdett, **785** (top right)/Yanik Chauvin, **945** (top)/Andy Dean Photography © Shutterstock.com. • Newspix: **229** (top), **581** (top), **649** (top right)/ Michael Potter © Newspix. • MYOB Australia: **309** (centre), **311** (bottom), **313** (top) Screen captures from MYOB reproduced with permission. Copyright © 2011 MYOB Technology Pty Ltd. • Reckon Ltd: **310** (centre), **312** (centre), **313** (bottom) Copyright © 2011 Intuit Inc. All rights reserved. • Photolibrary: **339** (top right)/Michael Steiner © Photolibrary. com. • Harvard Bus. School Publishing: **560** (top) Reprinted by permission of Harvard Business School Press. From 'The Balanced Scorecard' by Robert S. Kaplan and David P. Norton. Boston, MA, 1996, p. 9. Copyright ©) 1996 by the Harvard Business School Publishing Corporation; all rights reserved. • Financial Reporting Council: **704** (top) Financial Reporting Council — www.frc.gov.au. • AASB: **706** (top), **713** (top) © Commonwealth of Australia 2011. All legislation herein is reproduced by permission but does not purport to be the official or authorised version. It is subject to Commonwealth of Australia copyright. The *Copyright Act 1968* permits certain reproduction and publication of Commonwealth legislation. In particular, s.182A of the Act enables a complete copy to be made by or on behalf of a particular person. For reproduction or publication beyond that permitted by the Act, permission should be sought in writing from the Commonwealth available from the Australian Accounting Standards Board. Requests in the first instance should be addressed to the Administration Director, Australian Accounting Standards Board, PO Box 204, Collins Street West, Melbourne, Victoria, 8007

Text

• IDG Communications: **3** Reproduced with the permission of IDG Communications. • Copyright Agency Limited: **24** 'Business owners could 'plan to cover all futures' by Anthony Bell, *The Daily Telegraph*, 6/10/10, **26** 'Calling carbon to account' by Frances Stewart, *The Advertiser (Adelaide)*, 23/11/09, **26** 'Business owners need a plan for future survival' by Andrew Heaven, *The Daily Telegraph*, 2/7/10, **377** 'Surteco determined to be local hero' by Ben Woodhead, *The Australian*, 19/06/07, **535** 'Council's green strategy no longer a key area of failure' by Mahesh Sharma, *The Australian*, 26/1/10, **539** 'Skill is second to well-tuned feedback' by Dr Darryl Cross, *The Advertiser (Adelaide)*, 19/12/09, **589** 'Getting the green light' by Morris Kaplan, *The Sunday Tasmanian*, 8/11/09, **626** 'Macphersons shakes off suburban roots' by Chris Merritt, *The Australian*, 2/7/10, **749** 'Money too slow coming in' by Frances Stewart, *The Advertiser (Adelaide)*, 25/1/10, **907** '$200bn debt bomb ticking for Australian corporations' by Adele Ferguson, *The Daily Telegraph*, 27/7/09, **974** 'Coca-Cola Amatil backs out of Golden Circle takeover' by Kerrie Sinclair, *Herald Sun*, 6/10/07, **1064** 'Profit and revenue — the key difference' from www.news.com.au, 5/11/11, **1076** 'Payouts trail the good times' by Tim Boreham, *The Australian*, 19/7/10 © New Limited. • Ros Haniffa, Professor: **25** 'Time the boardroom learnt about ethics' by Ros Haniffa, *The Financial Times*, 30/11/09. Used with permission from Professor Ros Haniffa. • Colleen Trask: **29** 'De-mystifying the mysterious balance sheet' by Colleen Trask, for the *Times-Standard*, 31/10/10. • ICAA: **40** 'Seeking Sustainability' by Tony Malkovic, *Charter*, March 2010, pp. 32–6, **742** 'Invisible Assets' by Helen Tyzack, *Charter*, September 1998, pp. 72–3. • Rosalind Whiting: **60** 'Sporting glory — the great intangible' by Rosalind Whiting & Kyla Chapman, *Australian CPA*, Feb 2003, pp. 24–7. • AFP: **61** 'Coca-Cola says former China workers held over fraud' © AFP, 15/9/09. • Flyn Flesher: **65** 'Luca Pacioli: The Father of Accounting' by Flyn Flesher, see http://members.tripod.com/~FlynF/pacioli.htm. • Kath Walters: **155** 'I Did It My Way' by Kath Walters, *BRW*, November 12–18 2009, p. 18, **992** 'The Wolf at the Door' by Kath Walters, *BRW*, November 12–18 2009, pp. 40–1. • John Curtin Prime Ministerial: **177** from Pederson, A., 2001, 'Understanding society through its records' (online). Published by the John Curtin Prime Ministerial Library. Available: http://john.curtin.edu.au/society. • CPA Australia: **204** 'Malaysia moves to a GST' by Garry Addison, *InTheBlack*, March 2010, p. 49 © 2011. Reproduced with the permission of CPA Australia Ltd. • Eli Greenblat: **229** 'Target, Kmart buoy resilient Wesfarmers' by Eli Greenblat, courtesy of *The Sydney Morning Herald*, 19/2/10. • Emma Duncan: **250** from 'Here today, gone tomorrow' © Emma Duncan, *InTheBlack*, September 2008, p. 51. • ACP Publishing: **271** 'Liquid Assets' by Giles Parkinson, *The Bulletin*, 21/8/07, pp. 32–3. • CFO Publishing Corp.: **282** 'When in Doubt, Print It Out' by David Katz © CFO.com, dated 21/10/10.

• IHS iSuppli: **339** 'Mid-range iPad to generate maximum profits for Apple, iSuppli estimates' by Andrew Rassweiler, 10/2/10 © IHS iSuppli www.isuppli.com. • Mercedes-Benz: **358** Reproduced with permission. • ABC: **413** 'Catapult, Ask an Expert: Finding a manufacturer or designer', first published by *ABC Online*, is reproduced by permission of the Australian Broadcasting Corporation, ABC Online and the IDC. © 2011 ABC. All rights reserved. • Patrick Kissane: **417** Patrick Kissane, LLB, FCA, is a Chartered Accountant practising in Darwin, Australia. • Cumberland Newspapers: **437** 'Cash flow the culprit', *North Shore Times*, 20/6/07, p. 27. Reproduced with the permission of Cumberland Newspapers. • Susan Heron: **458** 'Managing the cash squeeze' © Susan Heron, *The Herald Sun*, 14/12/06, p. 90. Reproduced with the permission of Susan Heron. • Matthew O'Sullivan: **461** 'World's airlines stuck in time warp' by Matt O'Sullivan, courtesy of *The Sydney Morning Herald*, 9/1/10. • Maria Nguyen: **493** 'Use sense to stretch dollars' by Maria Nguyen, courtesy of *The Sun-Herald*, 10/5/09. • Julian Lee: **505** 'Budget shift to buying habits' by Julian Lee, courtesy of *The Sydney Morning Herald*, 4/6/09, Business, p. 26. • Martin Blake: **581** 'AFL has nine million reasons why their money was well spent at GWS' by Martin Blake, courtesy of *The Sydney Morning Herald*, 15/6/10, Sport, p. 22. • Australian Stock Report: **595** from article 'WACC', based on information from the Australian Stock Report, and published in the *Herald Sun*, 1/9/2007, Business, p. 102 © Australian Stock Report Ltd. • Richard Petty: **657–8** 'The sustainable accountant' by Richard Petty, originally published in *InTheBlack* magazine, February 2010. • West Australian Newspapers: **666** 'Port Bouvard rescue 'not fair but reasonable'' by Vivienne Ryan, 25/5/10, **833** 'Shopping Centres Rebound' by Marissa Lague, 1/9/10, p. 56, **882** 'Rio Faith in China revives $10bn Pilbara Expansion' by Peter Klinger, 12/2/10, p. 46, *The West Australian*. • Hugh Mackay Research: **701** Hugh Mackay is a social researcher and author. This is an extract from his newspaper column of 13 October 2001, which appeared in *The Sydney Morning Herald*, *The Age* and *The West Australian*. • Ramona Dzinkowski: **709** from 'Resistance is futile: IFRS in America' by Ramona Dzinkowski, *InTheBlack*, December 2007, pp. 37–8. • AASB: **713** © Commonwealth of Australia 2011. All legislation herein is reproduced by permission but does not purport to be the official or authorised version. It is subject to Commonwealth of Australia copyright. The *Copyright Act 1968* permits certain reproduction and publication of Commonwealth legislation. In particular, s.182A of the Act enables a complete copy to be made by or on behalf of a particular person. For reproduction or publication beyond that permitted by the Act, permission should be sought in writing from the Commonwealth available from the Australian Accounting Standards Board. Requests in the first instance should be addressed to the Administration Director, Australian Accounting Standards Board, PO Box 204, Collins Street West, Melbourne, Victoria, 8007. • Ben Power: **730** from 'Green profits' by Ben Power, *InTheBlack*, Feb 2010, pp. 28–29. • Anthony Black: **743** from 'Still on track', June 2010, **846–7** from 'Leading the Charge', September 2010, **887** from 'Wheeling and Dealing', November 2009. Originally published in *InTheBlack* magazine. These articles were written by the financial journalist Anthony Black who has extensive experience writing on corporate and financial matters. For enquiries on past articles refer to 'anthonyblack3@bigpond.com'. • Visa International: **764** 'Merchant Benefits' from www.visa-asia.com. Reproduced with permission from Visa. • Rachael Bolton: **785** 'New BlackBerry a response to rivals' by Rachael Bolton, courtesy of the *Australian Financial Review*, 5/8/10. • Ben Butler: **798** 'Consumers sever Bonds, change their underwear' by Ben Butler, courtesy of *The Age*, 26/8/10. • Carrie LaFrenz: **805** 'Harvey Norman falls short' by Carrie LaFrenz, courtesy of the *Australian Financial Review*, 27/7/10. • Thea O'Connor: **829** 'What a load of rubbish' by Thea O'Connor. Originally published in *InTheBlack* magazine, August 2009. • Carolyn Boyd: **867** 'Strike up the Brand' by Carolyn Boyd. Originally published in *InTheBlack* magazine, April 2010. • Global Accounting Alliance Ltd: **945** 'Making Financial Reporting Simpler and More Useful: The Way Forward', Global Accounting Alliance, 2009, p. 16. • James McCusker: **949** 'Pendulum swings back to the balance sheet wonks' from James McCusker's column in the *Snohomish County Business Journal*, 28/10/10. • Philip Bayley: **977** 'Lessons from the crisis' by Philip Bayley. Originally published in *InTheBlack* magazine, July 2010. • Ed Charles: **1006** 'The Cash Crash' by Ed Charles, Originally published in *InTheBlack* magazine, May 2010. • Luke Johnson: **1055** 'Don't be fooled by illusory numbers' by Luke Johnson, *The Financial Times*, 11/01/11. • John Collett: **1097** 'Turbocharged: ethical investments beat the market' by John Collett, courtesy of *The Sydney Morning Herald*, 13/10/10.

Every effort has been made to trace the ownership of copyright material. Information that will enable the publisher to rectify any error or omission in subsequent editions will be welcome. In such cases, please contact the Permissions Section of John Wiley & Sons Australia, Ltd who will arrange for the payment of the usual fee.

Part 1

Accounting for decision making

Decision making and the role of accounting

Learning objectives

After studying this chapter, you should be able to:

1 describe the decision-making process and the wide range of economic decisions made in the market place (p. 4)

2 explain the nature and dynamic environment of accounting and its main functions (pp. 6–8)

3 identify the potential users of accounting information (pp. 9–10)

4 identify and use information to make simple economic decisions and describe the role accounting information plays in the decision-making process (pp. 10–12)

5 distinguish between accounting for management and accounting for external users (pp. 12–13)

6 describe how the accounting profession is organised in Australia (pp. 13–14)

7 identify the different areas of the economy in which accountants work (pp. 14–17)

8 identify common types of business entities (pp. 17–18)

9 describe the functions carried out by managers (pp. 18–20)

10 explain the importance of ethics in business and accounting and identify ethical dilemmas and how to resolve them as part of the decision-making process (pp. 20–21).

Accountants looking for a new & exciting challenge

About our client

Are you looking to apply your accounting background to a new and refreshing career change? Do you enjoy working with like-minded, passionate and driven individuals? [We] are looking for part-qualified or newly qualified accountants who are excited about a career change into the recruitment industry. Our current Australian management team consists of a number of qualified accountants who began their career within the Big 4 firms, and have progressed internally by combining their accounting knowledge with consulting. Significant training and development is provided to enable this career change. [Our company] boasts a high profile client based that is well-established and we pride ourselves in delivering the highest quality outcome to our clients and candidates.

Job description

Working within a Brisbane CBD based team, your role will be to drive new sales and manage blue-chip accounts across Queensland. Key areas of responsibility will be:
- Procuring business
- Meeting new and existing clients
- Account and relationship management
- Training & development
- Client entertainment.

The successful applicant

This role demands high performers with a corporate image and articulate communication, with the ability to build strong long term relationships. Success will be borne from a team environment where your competitive spirit will drive you to reach your goals. As an accountant, you will be supported in your growth and development by a strong management team.

What's on offer

Our salary packages and bonus structure are competitive and dependent on experience and performance. In addition to this you will receive extensive on-going training, support from your mentor and manager whilst being a part of a young vibrant team-based culture that celebrates success. Down the track you will be open to exciting opportunities for career progression with the chance to work in locations such as New York, London, Tokyo and Rio de Janeiro.

Source: CFO World, www. cfoworld.com.au.

Chapter preview

Welcome to your journey into the field of accounting. Accountants are often colloquially referred to as the 'bean counters' or 'number crunchers' of an organisation, but in reality accountants play a major role in problem solving and decision making in many organisations, whether they be commercial organisations with a profit motive (such as JB Hi-Fi Ltd), not-for-profit entities (such as the Australian Red Cross), or government departments (such as the federal Department of Health and Ageing).

Accounting is a business language with its own terms, concepts and applications. Fluency in this language enables accountants to analyse and interpret an organisation's financial performance, and make decisions about the best way forward for the organisation.

Accounting, at times, can be full of politics and intrigue, and unethical accounting practices can lead to fraudulent financial reporting with often serious consequences for the organisation and its stakeholders.

Whether you are studying this subject to follow a career as a professional accountant, to equip yourself with skills to manage your own business, or to gain a basic understanding of the field as it relates to other areas of business, we hope that you find your study of the subject enjoyable, challenging and useful.

The recording of transactions for a business is usually called bookkeeping. Although a study of accounting requires a basic understanding of record keeping, it extends far beyond this to a deeper understanding of business events and how these link to financial results.

This book is designed for all students studying accounting for the first time at university level, whether as a major in accounting or as a complementary study to other majors, such as marketing, management, economics, information technology, law, engineering, the arts and sciences.

We begin the book by considering the decision-making process and the role of accounting in providing information for the decision-making process. Also in this chapter, we acquaint you with the types of activities that are carried out by a professional accountant working in business.

1.1 The decision-making process

Learning objective 1

Describe the decision-making process and the wide range of economic decisions made in the market place

We make many decisions every day — from minor decisions like what to eat for breakfast to major decisions like relocating to another country.

Decisions frequently involve making choices because it is not possible to do everything we might like to do as time and resources are usually limited. Some decisions can be made in no time at all with little thought such as putting on a coat if the weather is cold. Others, however, may require much thinking, planning and information gathering such as choosing a lifetime career, buying a house or a car, moving from one city to another, going on an overseas trip, choosing which subjects to study at university, and deciding when to retire from active employment.

The decisions we make shape our future, so it is important that we make decisions after careful consideration of all information available at the time.

Steps in decision making

In *simple* terms, a **decision** is the making of a choice between two or more alternatives. Every time a problem arises and we need to make a decision, we consciously or unconsciously follow four main steps, which can be framed as questions:

1. *What are we trying to achieve?* We must identify each situation in which a decision is needed and determine the goals we wish to achieve. The decision we make will be influenced by our values, motives and desires.
2. *What information do we need?* Information can help change our attitudes, beliefs or expectations. Information relevant to each decision helps us determine the alternatives available from which to choose given the time, resources and degree of effort that we are prepared to commit to making a choice.
3. *What are the consequences of different alternatives?* Having obtained information to help us determine the alternatives available, we then need to assess the consequences or outcomes of

these alternatives. Since the outcomes of each alternative lie in the future, every decision we make involves a degree of uncertainty, which means that there is an element of risk in achieving a desired outcome. For example, a decision to accept a job in a different city involves a degree of risk as we balance the potential opportunities of an exciting career with the risk of giving up the security of our current job and place of residence.

4. *Which course of action will we choose?* Finally, after consideration of the alternatives available and the consequences of those alternatives, we must choose a course of action which we hope will achieve the goals that we established in the first place.

The steps in the decision-making process are illustrated in figure 1.1.

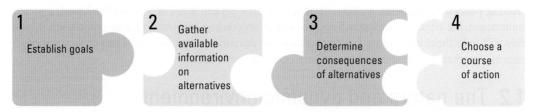

1 Establish goals

2 Gather available information on alternatives

3 Determine consequences of alternatives

4 Choose a course of action

Figure 1.1 Steps in the decision-making process

Once we have made a choice, we find eventually a set of actual outcomes or consequences. We may be satisfied or dissatisfied with these outcomes. If we are dissatisfied, we may need to make further decisions to achieve our ultimate goals. Hence, the outcomes or consequences of decisions commonly lead to further decisions, which in turn have further outcomes, and so on.

Economic decisions

Many of the decisions that we make involve the use of **economic resources**. These are resources that are traded in the marketplace at a price because they are in limited or scarce supply. Some decisions require economic resources for *consumption* purposes, such as choosing a particular brand of petrol. Other decisions are made for *investment* purposes. These decisions usually require major and longer-term commitment of resources, such as the decision to buy a car or a house. In business, some decisions require the investment or commitment of many millions of dollars for the purchase of large items of machinery. Still other decisions are related to finance; for example, if a business wants to make an investment decision to purchase an office building, a decision must also be made to find a suitable source of finance.

However, even though the economic aspects of decisions are very important, other factors must also be considered, and may be more important than economic factors in a particular circumstance:

- *personal taste* — our decision to buy a certain brand of toothpaste may be determined on the basis of preferred flavour or additives rather than price
- *social factors* — such as the impact on unemployment in the local community if a business decides to withdraw from that community
- *environmental factors* — such as the potential for air or water pollution
- *religious and/or moral factors* — our decision not to purchase particular types of meat may depend on religious beliefs
- *government policy* — such as the prohibition of trade in certain types of drugs.

Economic decisions usually involve a flow of money. We may purchase goods for immediate cash payment, on EFTPOS, or on credit, in which case the flow of money occurs at a later date than the flow of goods. The use of credit card facilities allows businesses to sell merchandise or provide services to us and to collect money from our bank, which then charges the cost to our account. Purchase of goods and services through the use of EFTPOS facilities or through the internet also allows a business to charge the cost to our bank account, which means that the flow of money may occur at a different time from the flow of goods and services.

Individuals and business entities make economic decisions in many different marketplaces. The marketplace with which we are all familiar is the retail market, where we make decisions as we buy groceries, cars, home furnishings and electrical goods. Then there is the wholesale market, where retailers decide to buy their supplies of goods in large quantities from various manufacturers for sale in their different retail outlets. Another popular market is the stock market, where individuals and business entities buy and sell shares, debentures and options. Even the flea market is a place where people make decisions to buy and sell merchandise, some of which they have hand-crafted, others of which are second-hand. Services also are traded in a marketplace.

Economic decisions may be made not only in the local marketplace but also in markets in different cities, states or countries. Many organisations have established places of business not only in their home country but also in overseas countries.

Hence, whenever an economic decision is to be made, there are many aspects and alternatives to consider, and this makes the decision-making process a fascinating study in itself. How do people in business organisations make decisions? What role does accounting play in the decision-making process? If decision makers are able to gain a certain level of accounting knowledge and understand the concepts and standards on which accounting information and reports are based, this will help them make more informed economic decisions, regardless of whether they are engineering, marketing, human resource, or any other business decision makers.

1.2 The nature and dynamic environment of accounting

Learning objective 2

Explain the nature and dynamic environment of accounting and its main functions

Accounting is a service activity. Its function is to provide and interpret financial information that is intended to be useful in making economic decisions. Business entities, government departments, charitable organisations and not-for-profit organisations, family units and individuals all engage in economic activity which involves making decisions about allocating available resources effectively. People need relevant information to be able to make sound economic decisions.

In a complex society, decision makers have to rely on data supplied by specialists in various fields. For example, lawyers provide information about the ramifications of existing and changing legislation, and medical practitioners offer advice about the possible effects of different healthcare decisions. Accounting as a profession has evolved in response to society's need for economic information to help people make economic decisions. The accountant's main role is to be involved in steps 2 and 3 of the decision-making process illustrated in figure 1.1 (p. 5), to offer advice regarding step 4, and to measure the outcomes or consequences of the decision-making process. However, as you will see once you have studied accounting more closely, much of the information needed to make an economic decision never makes its way into the accounting records, but exists outside of those records.

Accounting principles and practices have had to evolve as a result of social changes that have impacted the global business environment. Some of these changes include:
- the rapid development of information and communications technology including a move towards paperless transactions, electronic banking, and growing e-commerce business transactions
- the increasing demand by society for information of a non-financial nature, such as information about an entity's attention to health and safety issues, employment of people with disabilities, provision of childcare facilities and retirement packages, and efforts towards ensuring it embraces sustainable development
- the globalisation of business, which has placed increasing demands on organisations to be accountable for their corporate behaviour in foreign countries, including their impact on the society and the environment of those countries. Questions being asked include: How well does an organisation treat and pay its employees in developing countries? Is business being conducted in an ethical and responsible manner?
- the globalisation of regulations affecting business organisations, such as the development and adoption of international accounting standards.

One thing is certain: change will continue. In order to cope, accountants of the future will need to have skills in information systems and technology, critical thinking and strategy formulation, and possess strong communication and interpersonal skills to deal with cross-cultural business issues.

The scene setter at the start of this chapter sets out examples of the functions accountants can be responsible for, the skills they require to fulfill those responsibilities, and of the rewards offered for success.

The importance of understanding accounting information is not restricted to those engaged directly in business. Many people with little knowledge of accounting must interpret accounting data. For example, lawyers must often understand the meaning of accounting information if they are to represent their clients effectively, marketing consultants must be aware of the costs of developing advertising campaigns, and engineers and architects must consider cost data when designing new equipment and buildings. Thus, accounting plays a significant role in society and, in a broad sense, everyone is affected by accounting information.

Although accounting techniques are used in all types of economic units, in this book we concentrate mainly on accounting for business entities. Business owners and managers need information provided by the accounting system to plan, control and make decisions about their business activities. In addition, shareholders, creditors, government departments and not-for-profit organisations (such as clubs and societies) need financial information to help make investing, lending, regulatory and tax-related decisions.

Accounting defined

Accounting has been defined as the process of identifying, measuring, recording and communicating economic information to permit informed judgements and economic decisions by users of the information.

Identification involves observing economic events and determining which of those events represent economic activities relevant to a particular business. Selling goods to a customer, paying wages to employees and providing services to a client are examples of economic activities. Economic events of an entity are referred to by accountants as **transactions**, and are of two types, external and internal. Accountants use the single term *transaction* to refer to both internal and external transactions. Transactions constitute the inputs of the accounting information system.

External transactions (often called *exchange transactions*) are those that involve economic events between an entity and an outside party. When an entity purchases goods from a supplier, borrows money from a bank, or sells goods and services to customers, it participates in external or exchange transactions. *Internal transactions* are those economic events that take place entirely within one entity. For example, when a car component is transferred from the stores department to the assembly line in a car manufacturing business, the transfer must be accounted for, even if it is by simply transferring the cost of the component from the records of one department to those of the other. Similarly, the depreciation of machinery used in the production of goods must be accounted for, and since it does not concern an outside party, it is an internal transaction. Internal transactions may even involve such things as the growth of livestock or trees or grapevines held by the entity, because, under certain accounting standards, the increased value of these items must be recognised in the accounts of primary production companies.

Measurement must take place before the effects of transactions can be recorded. If accounting information is to be useful, it must be expressed in terms of a common denominator so that the effects of transactions can be combined. In our economy, business activity is measured by prices expressed in terms of money. *Money* serves as both a medium of exchange and as a measure of value, allowing us to compare the value or worth of diverse objects and to add and subtract the economic effects of various transactions. Accounting transactions are therefore measured and recorded in terms of some monetary unit, such as the dollar.

Recording provides a history of the economic activities of a particular entity. Recording is the process of systematically maintaining a file of all transactions which have affected the business entity after they have been identified and measured. Simply measuring and recording transactions, however, would provide information of limited use. The recorded data must be classified and summarised to be useful in making decisions.

- Classification allows thousands of transactions to be placed into more meaningful groups or categories. All transactions involving the sale of goods, for example, can be grouped into one total sales figure and all transactions involving cash can be grouped to report a single net cash figure.
- Summarisation of financial data is presented in reports and financial statements, which are provided for use by both internal management and outside users of accounting information. These

reports usually summarise the effects of all transactions occurring during some time period such as a month, a quarter or a year.

Communication is the final part of the accounting process. Identifying, measuring and recording economic activities are pointless unless the information contained in accounting records can be communicated in some meaningful form to the potential users of the information. Communication can be described as the process of preparing and distributing accounting reports to potential users of accounting information. Once the users of accounting reports have access to appropriate reports, they are able, after analysing and interpreting the reports, often with the assistance of professional advice, to make informed economic decisions. The most common forms of accounting reports are the financial statements, which are introduced in chapter 2.

The accounting process briefly overviewed above can be summarised diagrammatically as shown in figure 1.2.

Figure 1.2 The accounting process

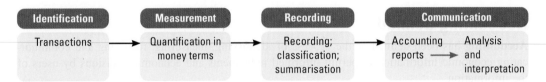

Many people with little knowledge of accounting tend to view it as being limited to the recording process and do not distinguish clearly between the recording and communicating of accounting data. The *recording* or *record-keeping process* involves measuring and recording business transactions which are usually recorded in a computerised system. Those systems range from simple spreadsheets to sophisticated integrated accounting software systems.

The *communication process* is a much broader function of accounting. It consists of placing accounting data that have been classified and summarised into financial reports, as well as preparing interpretive disclosures necessary to make the data understandable. The process requires extensive training, business experience and professional judgement.

Even though the recording phase of the accounting process is generally done electronically, a manual accounting process is presented in this book to develop an understanding of the processes performed by a computerised application system. An introduction to computerised accounting systems is given in chapter 7.

The communication process involves many potential users, and accountants who prepare reports must have a full appreciation of who the users of the reports are and their needs for accounting information in order to help them make economic decisions effectively. In this way, the accountant adds significant value to the running of the organisation.

BUSINESS KNOWLEDGE

Pair who worked for Devine Ltd jailed over $1 million fraud

Two high-flyers from construction firm Devine Ltd have been jailed for a brazen $1m fraud.

A court today heard the pair spent their forbidden booty on fast cars, overseas holidays, investments and an extravagant lifestyle that was brought to a shuddering halt by a curious accountant. They each pleaded guilty to a charge of employee fraud in excess of $30 000.

The pair set up a false company using their wives names called O & G Construction Services, and successfully invoiced their employer eight times for work their company never did. In all they netted $929 698. And they only came unstuck when a Devine

accountant noticed payments to O & G Construction were only authorised by the pair and not a third person, as per company policy.

The accountant then couldn't find a listing for O & G Construction until he checked the ASX website and was surprised to find O & G's female directors had the same first names as the fraudster's wives.

Court documents revealed the pair splashed out on an Audi TT Coupe, H3 Hummer, two Mercedes Benz C200s, Holden SS Ute, overseas holidays, furniture, investments and property.

The fraudsters repaid Devine the money they stole along with costs and interest, totalling $1.28m.

Source: Excerpts from James OLoan, 'Pair who worked for Devine Ltd jailed over $1 million fraud', *The Courier-Mail.*

1.3 Users of accounting information

Learning objective 3

Identify the potential users of accounting information

Although accountants are involved mainly in the analysis and interpretation of financial data when they serve as advisers to users of accounting information, the first objective of accounting is to provide information in reports which can be used by *internal* and *external* decision makers.

Managers (internal decision makers) must have financial data for planning and controlling the operations of the business entity as well as making decisions about the allocation of scarce resources, and hence need answers to such questions as:

- How much profit is being earned?
- What products should be produced?
- What resources are available?
- What is the most efficient production process?
- How much does it cost to reduce carbon emissions from the production process?
- What will be the effect of increasing or decreasing selling prices?
- How much is owing to outsiders?
- Will cash be available to pay debts as they fall due?
- What are the benefits of owning an asset as opposed to leasing it?

Providing data to help answer these and many other questions is an accounting function generally called *management accounting*. The data are presented to management in the form of **special-purpose financial reports**. These are prepared for users who have specialised needs and who possess the authority to obtain information to meet those needs. Apart from internal management, including marketing, production, finance, human resources, research and development, information systems and general managers, some external users such as banks and government agencies (e.g. the Australian Taxation Office (ATO)) also have the authority to command the type and nature of the information they require and hence can demand special-purpose reports.

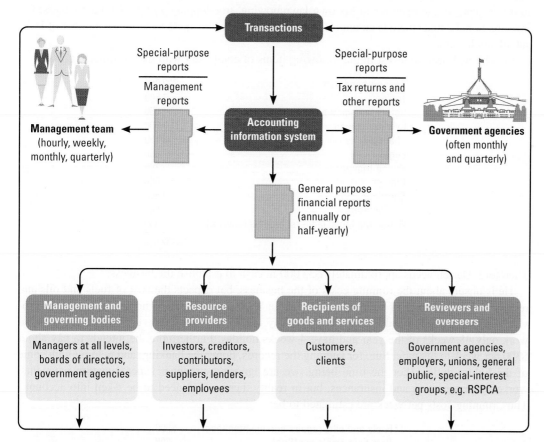

Figure 1.3 Financial reports and users

External decision makers such as resource providers (creditors, investors), recipients of goods and services (customers) and reviewers and regulators of business entities (employers, unions, government agencies) need accounting information for making decisions concerning granting credit, investing, purchasing goods and services, and complying with tax laws and other regulatory requirements. Questions raised by external users include:

- Should I invest money in this business?
- Am I likely to be paid my wages?
- Will the business be able to repay money lent to it?
- What are the company's earnings prospects?
- Is the business financially sound?
- Is the business providing products that are socially and environmentally friendly?

Reports prepared for external users include *financial statements* which generally consist of an income statement (also called a statement of profit or loss and other comprehensive income), a balance sheet (also called a statement of financial position), a statement of changes in equity and a statement of cash flows. These are often called **general purpose financial reports** because they provide general information for use by all external users.

General purpose financial reports are designed to meet the information needs of a wide range of users who are unable to command the preparation of reports tailored to satisfy their individual specific needs for information. Figure 1.3 (p. 9) illustrates the relationship between financial statements/reports and users of accounting information.

1.4 Using information in economic decisions

Economic decisions are made in business every day. To illustrate, consider the following business scenario.

Darren loves the outdoor life. After several years in an office behind a desk, he decides to accept a redundancy package from his employer and take on a new career. He now has the opportunity to work in the open air in his own lawnmowing, tree-lopping and gardening business. On investigation, he finds there is an opportunity to set up such a business to service a number of local suburbs in his area.

First he will need to invest in the following items of equipment with their estimated costs:

Second-hand van	$22 000
Trailer	1 500
Rotary lawnmower	950
Cylinder mower	1 600
Chainsaw	1 150
Edger	600
Hedge trimmer	700
Blower	1 000
Shredder	1 400
Brushcutters	800
Gardening tools, ladders, brooms (approx.)	850
	$32 550

Therefore, Darren needs approximately $33 000 in cash to establish the business.

He is unsure about the running costs of the business, but expects the cost of fuels and oils and repairs and maintenance of equipment to be about $500 per week. He is hoping to be able to provide services to about five different clients per day, and to work for 6 days each week. He wants to work only 48 weeks of the year and have 4 weeks holiday. Furthermore, he intends to pay about $300 per week to his wife, Sue, for keeping the records, doing the banking, and helping with some of the lighter duties. (For the time being, we are ignoring employer superannuation payments, workers compensation and insurances, but in reality these would need to be taken into account.) Thus, running costs per week are estimated to be:

Fuels and oils, repairs and maintenance	$500
Part-time employee (Sue)	300
	$800

In terms of charging for his services, Darren thinks he should be able to charge clients $45 per hour payable either in cash or, for large clients, on account. Initially, he expects to have the following numbers of clients for the various services he intends to provide:

Lawnmowing and trimming only (under a regular program)	60
Gardening, with shredding if necessary (under a regular program)	12
Tree-lopping and shredding (as requested)	20

Based on this client list, in each day he plans to mow five lawns, and to do gardening for one client. He expects that the lawnmowing and trimming will take, on average, 1 hour per client, gardening will take 2 hours per client, and tree-lopping will take about 3 hours per client. Hence, the approximate payment per client is:

Lawnmowing	$ 45
Gardening	$ 90
Tree-lopping	$135

In each week, the approximate amount of cash received, ignoring tree-lopping activities which are requested on an irregular basis, is expected to be:

5 lawns mowed for each of 6 days at $45 each	$1350
1 garden for each of 6 days at $90 each	$ 540
	$1890

This means that his gross annual turnover for the year's work of 48 weeks is equal to $1890 \times 48 = $90 720$, plus tree-lopping revenue. Because his annual turnover is greater than $75 000$, his accountant tells him that he will have to get an Australian business number (ABN) from the ATO and that he will be required to collect goods and services tax (GST) from each of his clients and forward the GST to the ATO at regular intervals. Also, the approximate cost he will pay to his accountant for preparing the annual tax return and GST documents is $2400. On a weekly basis over 48 weeks, this adds $50 per week ($2400 ÷ 48) for accounting services to the $800 per week calculated previously, a total of $850 per week. (Detailed consideration of the GST is covered in later chapters. It is assumed in this chapter that the figures quoted include the GST where applicable.)

Therefore, the expected weekly cash flow, excluding tree-lopping services, is $1890 less the weekly costs of $850, equalling $1040. Since Darren is in good health, after consultation with Sue he decides to proceed with the business. Thus, a decision is made after considering how much money he will need to contribute to set up the business (financing activity), the equipment he will need to buy (investing activity), the running costs of the business and the weekly cash inflow (operating activity).

Note that the decision is based on the steps illustrated in figure 1.1 — establishing goals (earning a living while working outdoors), collecting information about the proposed business, and considering the future consequences of conducting such a business. Of course, many of the factors considered in making such a decision are estimates of future events and, hence, there is a need to proceed with caution. Darren would be very wise to keep a careful eye on how well these cash flow estimates approximate reality.

Particularly important are the financial results. Will the actual weekly performance of Darren's business live up to the estimated performance? How much impact does the tree-lopping service have on the actual results? Is the lawnmowing service more profitable than the gardening service or the tree-lopping service? When does Darren plan to replace the assets he bought at the start? How will he account for the fact that these assets gradually wear out over time and through use? And how much income tax and GST will he have to pay? Darren may not have considered many of these aspects in making his decision, and much of this information can be provided by an accountant.

In the next four chapters, we shall consider other examples of service businesses — Don's Auto Repairs and Intellect Management Services — and consider how accounting information can help in the businesses' operations and decision making. We shall also return to Darren's lawnmowing business and ask further questions which accounting can help to answer.

Accounting information and decisions

From the example above, we can see that much financial information is needed before an economic decision is made. But how much of that information is accounting information? Since accounting is concerned mainly with identifying transactions and recording the financial history of the transactions of an entity, a major focus of accounting information is on actual financial events, not on future events. However, knowledge of information about actual events is useful in establishing relationships which are likely to hold in the future. In other words, for the purpose of decision making, past information is used often as a guide to future estimates of the consequences of different alternatives.

Accounting information is also very useful in providing decision makers with information about the outcomes or results of their decisions. Once these outcomes are known and investigated, decision makers are able to evaluate whether their decisions were correct or whether new decisions are required. The accountant can help significantly in investigating, interpreting and communicating these results for the guidance of decision makers. In this way, accountants can add value by pointing out to decision makers any areas needing attention, where new economic decisions become necessary.

The accountant in commerce is also heavily involved in the budgeting process for a business entity, and therefore in estimating the future outcomes for the entity. Thus, the work of the accountant in commerce is not restricted merely to recording a history of the entity's past. The accountant adds value by helping the owners and managers of a business in many ways, including developing strategies and plans for the future.

The information needs of managers are quite different from those of parties external to the entity. By definition, a manager is anyone in an organisation responsible for the work of other people who report to the manager for direction and support. The managers in a given organisation are collectively called its management. The senior management of a business is charged with the responsibility for implementing systems which are capable of producing reliable accounting information.

1.5 Management and financial accounting
What is management accounting?

Management accounting (also referred to as managerial accounting) is that area of accounting concerned with providing financial and other information to all levels of management in an organisation to enable them to carry out their planning, controlling and decision-making responsibilities. The accountants responsible for providing this information are known as management accountants. Management accounting is used in all forms of organisations — profit-seeking and not-for-profit undertakings; sole traders, partnerships and companies; retailing, manufacturing and service businesses; government; and charities.

Management accounting covers many activities, including cost estimation based on an analysis of cost behaviour, establishing an entity's break-even point, providing information for short-term tactical decisions, annual budgeting, strategic planning, performance measurement and capital budgeting, and producing segment margin reports.

What is financial accounting?

Financial accounting is concerned with reporting information to users external to an entity in order to help them to make sound economic decisions about the entity's performance and financial position. The financial accountant is heavily involved in the determination of an entity's overall financial performance (profits or losses), its financial position, financing and investing activities (which include raising and investing money), and information as to whether the entity is complying with the requirements of the law. The financial accountant must be well trained in the regulatory arrangements affecting various entities; such regulations include accounting standards, auditing standards, the law relating to corporations and other types of organisations, and the law relating to taxation (including income tax, fringe benefits tax and GST). Through financial accounting, an entity discharges much of its corporate governance responsibilities to the community at large.

Management accounting versus financial accounting

Management accounting can be distinguished from financial accounting in a number of ways: by reference to (1) the main *users* of the reports, (2) the *types of reports* produced, (3) the *frequency of reports*, (4) the *content and format of reports*, and (5) *external verification*. Table 1.1 summarises the differences between management accounting and financial accounting.

Table 1.1 Differences between management accounting and financial accounting

	Management accounting	**Financial accounting**
Users of reports	*Users are inside the entity and include:* • managers • chief executive officers • general managers • account managers	*Users are outside the entity and include:* • shareholders • lenders • potential investors • creditors • customers • government • interest groups
Types of reports	*Special-purpose reports for internal users including:* • financial budgets • sales forecasts • performance reports • cost-of-production reports • incremental analysis reports Do not have to comply with accounting standards	*General purpose financial reports for external users including:* • balance sheet/statement of financial position • income statement/statement of profit or loss and other comprehensive income • statement of changes in equity • statement of cash flows Required by regulatory authorities; must comply with accounting standards and other relevant legislation
Frequency of reports	On-demand reports — daily, weekly, monthly — as requested by management to help with decision making	Income tax legislation and accounting standards require reports at regular intervals
Content and format of reports	• Management establishes own guidelines for structure, content and type of information (financial and non-financial); structure and classification of reports are tailored to specific needs of decisions to be made • Reports can relate to particular segments of an entity or to a particular decision	• Structure and content dictated by accounting standards and legislation • Statements generally contain historical, verifiable data • Reflect the results of the entity as a whole, thus contain much summarisation and restricted classification • Based on the formal double-entry system (see chapters 3–7)
External verification	Special-purpose reports are not required to be audited, but management may want verification of the contents by internal auditors	General purpose financial reports of some entities must be audited by independent external auditors who verify that the statements provide a true and fair view of the performance and financial position of the entity

1.6 Accounting as a profession — Australian perspective

Learning objective 6

Describe how the accounting profession is organised in Australia

Accounting has developed as a profession over the past hundred years or so, attaining a status equivalent to that of law and medicine. The profession in Australia is predominantly self-regulating and is largely controlled by two major professional associations of accountants — CPA Australia and the Institute of Chartered Accountants in Australia (ICAA). However, there are certain legislative requirements that control accountants' activities. For example, it is necessary to register as a company auditor in order to practise auditing. People providing taxation services for a fee are required under taxation law to be registered as tax agents with the Tax Agents Registration Board, an agency of the Australian Government.

Entry to the two major professional accounting bodies requires a number of conditions to be satisfied. All people seeking entry must normally hold a degree or postgraduate qualification from a tertiary institution accredited for entry purposes by the particular professional body. Before full membership status is granted, a minimum of 3 years appropriate supervised work experience is required, as well as completion of the CPA Program of CPA Australia or the CA Program of the ICAA. A member is then referred to as a **certified practising accountant or CPA** in CPA Australia or as a **chartered accountant or CA** in the ICAA. CAs and CPAs are required to undertake a certain level of continuing professional development activities each year to maintain their level of membership. For further information on the CPA Program and the CA Program, visit the website of CPA Australia (www.cpaaustralia.com.au) and the ICAA's website (www.charteredaccountants.com.au).

Accountants generally practise in three main areas: public accounting, commercial accounting and not-for-profit accounting.

Learning objective 7

Identify the different areas of the economy in which accountants work

1.7 Public accounting versus commercial accounting

Public accounting

Public accountants run businesses which offer their professional services to the public for a fee. These vary from small businesses to very large international organisations with several thousand employees. Because of the complexity of today's business structure and increasing regulation by government, members of public accounting businesses tend to specialise in one of four general services: auditing and assurance services, taxation services, advisory services, and insolvency and administration.

Auditing and assurance services

Auditing has traditionally been the main service offered by most public accounting businesses. An **audit** is an independent examination of a business entity's financial statements, supporting documents and records in order to form an opinion as to whether they comply with certain levels of quality, as specified in accounting standards, and present a true and fair view of the entity's performance and financial position. Banks and other lending institutions often require an audit by an independent accountant before making a loan to a business. Companies that offer their shares for sale normally prepare a set of audited financial statements, and annual audited statements must be presented thereafter if the shares are traded through a stock exchange. External users who rely on financial statements in decision making place considerable emphasis on the auditor's report. It is essential, therefore, that auditors are independent observers in carrying out their duties.

The nature of audit services are likely to change — the role of the auditor is becoming one of providing a wider range of 'assurance services'. **Assurance services** are defined as 'independent professional services that improve the quality of information, or its context, for decision makers'.[1] This expanded role is driven largely by the availability of online real-time information which results in less demand for historical information. More emphasis is being placed on the detection of fraud and commenting on whether the entity is appropriately placed to remain as a going concern. The auditor is required to report on the 'reasonableness' of information provided by an entity through its published financial statements.

Examples of assurance services in which auditors are becoming involved include:

- *assessment of risk* — evaluates whether an entity has appropriate systems in place to effectively manage business risk and minimise fraud risk

---

1. This definition first appeared in the Report of the Special Committee on Assurance Services (the Elliott Report), prepared by the American Institute of Certified Public Accountants. It has since been adopted by the ICAA and CPA Australia. For further information, see Paul Coram, 'Towards assurance services — redefining the audit role', *Australian CPA*, November 1998, pp. 55–7.

- *business performance measurement* — evaluates whether an entity's accounting system contains measures to assess the degree to which an entity is achieving its goals and objectives, and how the entity's performance compares with its competitors
- *information systems reliability* — assesses whether the entity's accounting system provides reliable information for making economic decisions
- *electronic commerce* — assesses whether electronic commerce systems provide appropriate data integrity, security, privacy and reliability
- *health care and care of the elderly* — provides assurance on the effectiveness of health care and elderly care facilities provided by hospitals, nursing homes, and other carers.[2]

Taxation services

Few economic decisions are made without considering the tax consequences. Accountants provide advice concerning the tax consequences of business decisions. Individuals and business entities have to collect or pay various forms of taxes including income tax, capital gains tax, fringe benefits tax, goods and services tax, local government rates, and other taxes. Accountants are often engaged to help in tax planning to minimise the tax liability of the business, consistent with the rules and regulations established by taxing agencies. Accountants also are often called on to prepare tax returns, including business activity statements (BASs), required by law. To offer such services, accountants must be thoroughly familiar with tax laws and regulations. They must also keep up to date with changes in tax law and court cases concerned with interpreting tax law, which occur frequently. As many businesses now operate globally, detailed knowledge of the tax laws of many overseas countries is also useful.

Advisory services

Although audit and tax services have traditionally been the main activities of public accountants, advisory services are very important today. Accountants provide advice on overcoming detected defects or problems in a client's accounting system. Public accountants offer a wide range of advisory services, including advice on such events as installation of computer systems, production systems and quality control; installation or modification of accounting systems; budgeting, forecasting and general financial planning; design or modification of superannuation plans; company mergers and takeovers; personal financial planning; and advice for clients in managing deceased estates.

As a result of several well-publicised corporate collapses, it has been argued that public accountants provide too many advisory services to their clients. Hence, legislation and professional pronouncements have placed boundaries around non-assurance services that can be provided by a public accountant acting in a capacity as an auditor. Auditors are required by law to be independent of the client and must declare their independence annually. Furthermore, auditors of listed companies must be rotated every 5 years, and there must be a 2-year delay before a former auditor can become an officer of an audited client.[3]

Insolvency and administration

Public accountants are also employed in helping businesses with trading difficulties. Some businesses have difficulty in paying their short-term debts as they fall due, which means that they are becoming illiquid. If an entity cannot pay its long-term debts, the entity is said to be **insolvent**. Public accountants are employed to help businesses administer their recovery from trading difficulties or insolvency, if possible. However, if recovery is not possible, accountants then help in the winding-up of the business's affairs. In the case of the company form of business organisation, such a wind-up is referred to as **liquidation**.

Accountants in commerce and industry

Many accountants are employed in business entities. The entity's chief financial officer (CFO) has overall responsibility for directing the activities of accounting personnel. In a large company, the

---

2. Paul Coram, 'Towards assurance services', p. 56. See also Roger Debreceny, Michael Nugent & Glen Gray, 'A changing landscape', *Charter*, June 1997, pp. 62–4.
3. See CLERP Paper No. 9: CLERP (Audit Reform and Corporate Disclosure) Bill 2003. Available from the Treasury website, www.treasury.gov.au.

CFO may have several assistants, each with assigned responsibility for various accounting functions. These accountants are commonly referred to as management accountants.

General accounting

One function of the accountant in commerce and industry is to oversee the recording of transactions undertaken by the business entity and to prepare reports specially tailored for use by management in their planning, control and decision-making activities. The transaction data must be classified and summarised appropriately for the preparation of financial reports for external distribution. It is difficult to draw a clear line of distinction between general accounting and the other phases of commercial accounting because the accounting data recorded from transactions form the basic database from which other phases draw relevant information for planning, controlling, decision-making and reporting purposes.

Cost accounting

Cost accounting deals with the collection, allocation and control of the costs of producing specific products and services. Knowledge of the cost of each manufacturing process and each service activity is important in making sound business decisions. If management wants to know whether the production and sale of a product or service is profitable, it must know the cost of that product or service. Large manufacturing entities may employ several accountants in their cost accounting departments, but with the increased use of accounting packages in business, much of the routine work of capturing accounting information is now carried out by computerised information systems. The cost accountant's role has expanded to include many of the other functions mentioned here.

Accounting information systems

Commercial accountants also may be heavily involved in designing accounting information systems. Once systems have been designed and installed, their operation is constantly monitored for improvements and system maintenance. Developments have occurred in the design of accounting systems for e-commerce. Integrity of data and privacy issues are of paramount importance.

Budgeting

Budgeting is the phase of accounting that deals with the preparation of a plan or forecast for future operations. Its main function is to provide management with a projection of the activities necessary to reach established goals. Budgets are generally prepared for the business entity as a whole as well as for subunits. They serve as control devices when used in conjunction with performance reports, which measure actual results for the period. Budgets also are used in assessing the efficiency of operations.

Taxation accounting

Businesses are assessed for a variety of taxes — including income tax, capital gains tax, GST and fringe benefits tax — all of which require the preparation of periodic reports to the various taxing agencies. Tax effects must be considered in every investment and financing decision made by management. Although many businesses rely on public accountants for some tax-planning advice and tax-return preparation, many large companies also maintain a tax accounting department to deal with day-to-day tax accounting issues and problems.

Internal auditing and audit committees

To supplement the annual audit by the external auditor, many organisations also maintain an **internal audit** department. Its main function is to conduct ongoing reviews to make certain that established procedures and policies are being followed. Thus, any deficiencies can be identified and corrected quickly. An efficient internal audit process can also reduce the time required by the external auditors in conducting their annual audit, often producing significant cost savings.

As a result of an international demand for improvements in corporate governance within organisations, many large businesses have established audit committees. In Australia, any listed company in the S&P/ASX300 at the start of its financial year must establish an audit committee.

The Australian Securities Exchange (ASX) has issued guidelines to assist companies to set up effective audit committees. These guidelines include the following recommendations.

- The audit committee should report to the board.
- The audit committee's responsibilities should include:

  - assessment of whether external reporting is consistent with committee members' information and knowledge and is adequate for shareholder needs
  - assessment of the management processes supporting external reporting
  - procedures for the selection and appointment of the external auditor and for the rotation of external audit engagement partners
  - recommendations for the appointment or, if necessary, the removal of the external auditor
  - assessment of the performance and independence of the external auditors. Where the external auditor provides non-audit services, the report should state whether the audit committee is satisfied that provision of those services has not compromised the auditor's independence
  - assessment of the performance and objectivity of the internal audit function.[4]

Not-for-profit accounting

Another area of activity employing many accountants is not-for-profit accounting. City councils, shire councils, state governments and the federal government collect and spend large amounts of money annually. Elected and appointed officials have ultimate responsibility for the collection and efficient use of the resources under their control. Many of the problems and decisions faced by government officials are the same as those encountered in private industry, but accounting for not-for-profit entities may require a different approach in some respects because of the absence of a profit motive. Government accounting is concerned with the efficient use of its resources, consistent with the provisions of city, shire, state and federal laws. Other not-for-profit organisations (churches, hospitals, charities, clubs, private educational institutions) also have specialised accounting needs.

So far, this chapter has presented a basic introduction to decision making and to the nature of accounting, its purpose and its fields of specialisation. Accounting is applicable to all types of economic entities, including not-for-profit entities, which engage in making economic decisions. This text concentrates largely on accounting methods used for making economic decisions in business entities that have a profit motive. Nevertheless, throughout the book, selected exercises and problems applicable to not-for-profit entities are provided.

1.8 Types of business entities

Learning objective 8

Identify common types of business entities

Earlier in this chapter we introduced Darren's lawnmowing and gardening business. An important decision that Darren must make is how to structure his business. There are different types of business entities which may be formed. The three most common types for profit-seeking entities are sole traders (or single proprietorships), partnerships and companies.

A **single proprietorship** or **sole trader** is a business entity owned by one person. Many small service enterprises, retail stores and professional practices are operated as single proprietorships. The owner of a single proprietorship business supplies cash (or other assets) to the business, is entitled to all profits, and is legally liable for its debts. A sole trader is not a separate legal entity. From an accounting perspective, however, the business entity is treated as an entity separate from its owner, and accounting is done only for the affairs of the business entity. The owner's personal affairs and records are kept separate from those of the entity for accounting purposes.

A **partnership** is a business owned by two or more people acting as partners. No special legal requirements need be met to form a partnership. All that is necessary is an agreement among the people joining together as partners. Although the partnership agreement may be oral, a written agreement will help resolve disagreements which may arise between partners. The partners supply the resources and share the profits and losses.

---

4. See 'Corporate Governance Principles and Recommendations with 2010 Amendments — 2nd Edition' issued by the ASX Corporate Governance Council. Available from the ASX website, www.asx.com.au.

Partnerships are not separate legal entities. Consequently, the individual partners are personally liable for the debts of the partnership. From an accounting perspective, however, partnerships are treated as entities separate from their owners. Like single proprietorships, partnerships are widely used for small service enterprises, retail stores and professional practices. Partnerships are covered more fully later in this book.

A **company** or **corporation** is a separate legal entity formed under the *Corporations Act 2001*. Commonly, its owners are called **shareholders** and their ownership interests are represented by shares in the company. Because a company is a separate legal entity, shareholders in a limited company are not liable for the company's debts once the shares they hold have been paid for in full. This feature is known as **limited liability**, which simply means that the liability of a shareholder to contribute to the liabilities of the company is limited to the amount unpaid on the shares held in the company. The word 'limited' (abbreviated to Ltd) is required by law to appear in the company name if limited liability applies to shareholders of that company. Further discussion of companies is provided later in this book.

Darren thus has three organisation structures from which to choose when setting up his lawn-mowing and gardening business. He could conduct his business as a single proprietorship or sole trader, in which case he will be the sole recipient of any profits made by the business. Alternatively, he may choose to establish the business as a partnership with his wife, Sue. Partners normally provide cash or other resources for the business, and share any profits made from day-to-day operations. If Darren and Sue decide that the business should be formed as a company, then a small company can be registered with an appropriate name. Darren and Sue will then become shareholders providing cash or other resources to the business and receiving any dividends from the company if profits are made. To help make the decision, Darren would be wise to consult an accountant for advice, and he should make his decision carefully.

Although companies conduct the majority of business activity in Australia, sole traders are more numerous. Because of the relatively simple nature of the sole trader form, it is used as the basis for early discussion and illustrations in this book. Partnerships and companies and their special accounting problems are discussed later in this book.

Other forms of organisations include not-for-profit entities such as sporting clubs, trusts (family trusts or unit trusts), government commercial enterprises and government agencies. The structures appropriate to these entities are usually provided by the laws which lead to their establishment. Such laws can also impose special accounting and reporting requirements.

1.9 Management functions

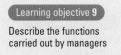

Describe the functions carried out by managers

As mentioned above, the most basic form of business enterprise is a one-person business or sole trader. Its management and information needs are simple because all decision-making responsibilities for such functions as purchasing, selling, performing services, accounting and financing rest with the individual owner-manager. This simple situation, where the owner is responsible for and does everything, seldom exists, and if it does, it normally is found only during the initial stage of a business's life cycle. As soon as the first employee is hired, a division of labour occurs and an organisation is born. An **organisation** is defined as a group of people who share common goals with a well-defined division of labour. The managers of an organisation need relevant information to integrate the activities of the various segments of the organisation and ensure that they are directed towards common goals. As an organisation develops in size and complexity, authority and responsibility for performance are delegated to a number of people. Consequently, the role of management becomes increasingly important. This is true for all service businesses, manufacturing businesses, banks, accounting businesses, hospitals, universities, retail stores, government departments or agencies, and charitable organisations.

Role of managers

A major goal of every business entity is to achieve satisfactory performance. The managers of a business are accountable to its owners for adequate profits as indicators of a successful operation.

Even not-for-profit organisations such as charities must be certain that their costs do not exceed their revenues in the long term. Every entity must accept the fact that its resources are limited and must be conserved if a satisfactory performance is to be achieved. Such factors as inflation, technological change, competition, government regulation, environmental and social issues, interest rates, increased power costs and declining productivity have an adverse effect on most entities' financial performance. Developing a good reputation ultimately attracts strong customer support for the business's products and services.

If an entity is to be successful, its management must be efficient and effective. **Efficiency** means maintaining a satisfactory relationship between an entity's resource inputs and its outputs of products or services (e.g. the number of labour hours required to process a loan application or to produce a product). **Effectiveness** refers to how well an entity attains its goals (e.g. the number of services provided to customers compared with the number planned). Efficiency and effectiveness are outcomes of the management process diagrammed in figure 1.4 and are essential to the overall success of any business. It is important to note that **management functions** are not always as sequentially dependent as figure 1.4 may suggest, since they often are performed concurrently and are constantly interacting with one another. The functions of the management decision process are examined below.

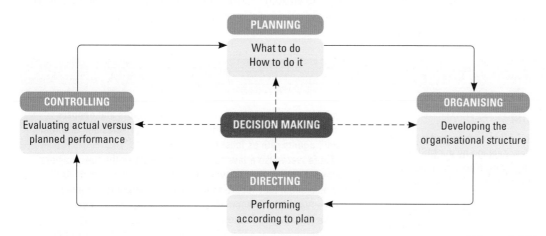

Figure 1.4 Management functions

Planning

A successful business entity plans for the future by carefully setting goals. Managers must decide what action the entity should take in the future and how it should be accomplished. Alternative courses of action are identified, their probable results are evaluated, and the course of action that will best achieve the entity's goals is selected. Planning is required so that managers can anticipate future events rather than react to circumstances once they are known. Much of management planning is concerned with the efficiency and effectiveness of future operations.

Organising

Plans are only words and numbers on paper until they are implemented. The organising function provides the resource structure or capacity within which management works to achieve its plans. The entity may be divided into segments (such as departments, divisions, plants and offices) to take advantage of the specialisation of skills and abilities. The right people are hired, trained and assigned to specific jobs. Well-defined lines of authority and responsibility are established. Sources of resources (such as raw materials, supplies and advertising) are selected, physical facilities (land, buildings, machinery and equipment) are obtained, and finance is arranged to fund the operations.

Directing

This function deals with the day-to-day management of the entity. Actions, decision making, communication and leadership are combined to carry out the planned activities within the organisational structure. Problems are solved, questions are answered, disagreements are resolved and the various segments are coordinated.

Controlling

Managers must be sure that the actual performance of the entity and its segments compares favourably with the goals established during the planning function. If managers are to be held accountable for their performance, they should know where and why actual results differ from those planned. Control is based on the concept of **management by exception**, which recognises that, since management time is a scarce resource, the main concern should be for any performance that deviates significantly from the plan. A performance report is a type of financial report issued periodically to inform management of any significant variations from the expected results, so action can be taken to improve the efficiency or effectiveness of future operations, whenever possible. Some businesses have established internal audit committees, as discussed earlier in this chapter to help management achieve its plans.

Learning objective 10

Explain the importance of ethics in business and accounting and identify ethical dilemmas and how to resolve them as part of the decision-making process

1.10 Ethics and accountants

The early 2000s in Australia saw the collapse of a number of large business and financial institutions, causing huge monetary losses and hardship to shareholders and policy holders. This has increased the pressure from the community to improve the ethics of all people working in business. Most professional bodies have laid down some form of code of ethical and moral behaviour. Such a code of ethics generally provides members of the profession with guidelines to establishing principles of ethical conduct.

BUSINESS KNOWLEDGE

In accountants we trust

According to a survey of 1112 business owners and members of the public in Australia and New Zealand by the MSI Global Alliance of Legal and Accounting Firms, New Zealanders rate accountants 9th on their country's 'most trusted' list. Australians place accountants 11th.

Respondents were asked to rate how much they trusted a range of 42 different people and organisations, from our political leaders and charity organisations to teachers and home cleaners. The survey results provide a clear picture of those we trust and those we have less faith in.

In a follow up survey from the previous year, Aussies and Kiwis agree most health professions continue to hold our trust with

ambulance drivers, nurses, pharmacists, doctors and dentists topping the list. Once again telemarketers, car salesmen and real estate agents rate as least trustworthy.

There were also a few notable differences as the Kiwi lawyers topped the trust ranking, while Aussie lawyers come in at 20. It would seem that Telstra took a dive for the worse dropping six places, while Telecom New Zealand gained six places on the New Zealand chart. However, there was a common understanding that accountants are trusted on both sides of the Tasman.

Source: Excerpts from MSI Global Alliance, 'Employers, public trust Malcolm Turnbull over Wayne Swan to manage their business, household expenses', www.msi-anz.net.

Ethics in business

Most businesses today appreciate the importance of ethical behaviour in all their business dealings. In order for a business entity to function effectively, all people working in the entity have to be honest, abide by the rules and 'do the right thing'. If managers, owners, employees and customers regularly deceived one another, told lies, falsified records and did not conform to the rules, the entity would eventually collapse and cease to exist. A high standard of ethical behaviour is thus in the long-term interest of business entities.

It is sound economic policy to have a business highly regarded by the whole business community for its reputation for honest and straight dealings, quality products and service. Most of the highly successful businesses today are noted generally for their high ethical standards of business. Financial statements are one of the many control mechanisms designed to assess the accountability of management and protect the interests of parties who have an interest in the performance of a particular business entity. The reports enable an evaluation to be made of a company's management performance, and provide information on the establishment of contracts, business dealings and resource allocations. The audit and assurance services function of accounting also represents a controlling influence in maintaining ethical behaviour in business entities.

Ethics and professional accounting bodies

The standing of the profession and individuals within the profession depends on the highest level of ethical conduct by members. The professional accounting bodies in Australia have recognised this, and in 2006 both CPA Australia and the Institute of Chartered Accountants established an independent body called the Accounting Professional & Ethical Standards Board (APESB) to set and maintain a code of ethics with which accountants who are members of these bodies must comply. More recently, the Institute of Public Accountants (IPA) has also joined the APESB. According to the website of the APESB (www.apesb.org.au) the vision of the APESB is:

> To be recognised by our stakeholders for our leading contribution in achieving the highest level of professional and ethical behaviour in the accounting profession. We will achieve this vision by:
> - Issuing professional and ethical standards that are integral to the Australian accounting profession
> - Being innovative in engaging our key stakeholders, including professional accountants and the public
> - Influencing the international standards agenda
> - Advocating for professionalism and ethical conduct to drive the behaviour of accountants

The code of ethics for professional accountants establishes the fundamental principles of professional ethics and provides a conceptual framework for applying those principles. Members of the profession are expected to adhere to various principles of ethical conduct, including integrity, objectivity, professional competence and due care, confidentiality and professional behaviour. For professional accountants, the code of ethics is contained in APES 110, issued by the APESB.

Ethics in practice

As a graduate, you will undoubtedly enter the business world as an accountant, an employee, a manager, a marketer, a consumer, or in some other capacity. As a future professional in the business world it is important that you appreciate the importance of ethical behaviour, have an appreciation of ethical issues and dilemmas that may arise, are able to analyse the consequences of unethical behaviour, can identify the stakeholders (i.e. those who are affected by the unethical behaviour), and can identify the correct course of action to follow.

The ability to choose the correct course of action always, and being seen to be 'doing the right thing' always, will not necessarily be easy. In the world of business, many personal and business pressures are experienced which make ethical behaviour a considerable challenge. There are no widely held, generally accepted codes of ethics or rules of ethical business behaviour. The resolution of ethical issues and dilemmas is greatly influenced by personal attitudes, personal problems and personal financial situations, pressure within the workplace (e.g. superior–subordinate relationships and peer pressure), and the pressure of meeting deadlines.

In order to provide practice in analysing, evaluating and resolving ethical issues that may arise in the workplace, an ethical case is included at the end of several chapters in this book. In analysing these cases, you will be required to identify the ethical issue(s) involved, resolve the issues by analysing the key elements involved, including who are the major stakeholders who stand to benefit or be disadvantaged by the situation, and then select the appropriate course of action. In some cases there will be one obvious correct resolution — in others there may be a number of ethical resolutions which may require further analysis to arrive at the most ethical outcome.

According to the results of a 2006 survey conducted by the Society of Human Resources Management (www.shrm.org), the following were considered to be the principal causes of pressures felt by 407 randomly selected HR professionals to compromise their organisation's standards of ethical conduct:

- Need to follow boss's directives — 47.50%
- Meeting overly aggressive financial/business objectives — 38.60%
- Meeting scheduled pressures — 28.00%
- Helping the organisation survive — 27.10%
- Wanting to be a team player — 22.90%
- Feeling peer pressure — 12.30%
- Rationalising that others do it — 10.60%
- Saving jobs — 10.60%
- Advancing boss's career interests — 10.20%
- Resisting competitive threats — 7.20%
- Advancing your own career — 1.70%.

Accounting, p. 7

Assurance services, p. 14

Audit, p. 14

Budgeting, p. 16

Certified practising accountant (CPA), p. 14

Chartered accountant (CA), p. 14

Company (or corporation), p. 18

Cost accounting, p. 16

Decision, p. 4

Economic resources, p. 5

Effectiveness, p. 19

Efficiency, p. 19

Financial accounting, p. 12

General purpose financial reports, p. 10

Insolvent, p. 15

Internal audit, p. 16

Limited liability, p. 18

Liquidation, p. 15

Management accounting, p. 12

Management by exception, p. 20

Management functions, p. 19

Organisation, p. 18

Partnership, p. 17

Special-purpose financial reports, p. 9

Shareholders, p. 18

Single proprietorship (sole trader), p. 17

Transactions, p. 7

DISCUSSION QUESTIONS

1. 'Accounting is irrelevant in decision making because the information it provides relates only to the past.' Discuss.
2. Discuss the difference between a special-purpose financial report and a general purpose financial report, and the nature of the users of each of these types of financial reports.
3. Distinguish between the work performed by public accountants and the work performed by accountants in commerce and industry and in not-for-profit organisations.
4. Should external auditors provide advisory services to a client at the same time as providing auditing services to that client? Why or why not?
5. How can accountants help small businesses?
6. 'When one examines the distinctive and different functions of financial and management accounting, it is obvious that to maximise the usefulness of the information derived, two systems of accounting are necessary. It does not matter how large or small the entity is, it is just common sense that one system cannot do the job.' (An assertion made by a recent management graduate.) Comment.
7. Explain the basic differences between a sole trader (or single proprietorship), a partnership and a company. What factors need to be considered in selecting an appropriate structure for Darren's lawnmowing business?
8. 'Good planning is useless without good control.' Discuss.
9. 'Ethical conduct on the part of a business is essential to its long-term survival.' Do you agree? Why or why not?
10. Why do professional accounting bodies in Australia require that their members act ethically? Should all other business and professional groups have similar requirements for their members? From your experience, how trustworthy do you believe accountants are?

EXERCISES

Exercise 1.1 INFORMATION FOR DECISIONS — LO 1, 4

Ashley Butler has been appointed as an accounts supervisor at a clothing manufacturer. A customer wants to open an account with the business and purchase goods on credit for export to Asia. Discuss six items of information Ashley should request from the prospective customer before opening an account for them. Classify the information Ashley should request as either 'economic' or 'other' (specify). Which do you consider to be more important?

Exercise 1.2 INFORMATION FOR DECISIONS — LO 4

Shannon Daniel's family lives in Perth, Western Australia. She has been accepted into a university course in Adelaide, and has to find accommodation in the city within walking distance of the university, or at least be close to public transport. She begins by perusing the 'to let' columns in *The Advertiser*. The first advertisement reads as follows:

Woodville   **$350 pw**
2 brms, unfurn villa, birs, 2 min train, very
handy location, ph 8123 4567 after 6 pm.

Required
A. Will this information help Shannon make a decision?
B. What extra information would she need before deciding whether to rent this villa?

Exercise 1.3 INFORMATION FOR DECISIONS   **LO 4**

Renee Carter has decided to study medicine at a university in Queensland. She has arranged to stay with a family on the north side of the city. In order to get to and from the university, she decides she will need to buy a car, costing a maximum of $10 000. She searches the classified ads in the local newspaper and finds the following advertisement which interests her:

HONDA 10yo, 3-speed man sedan,
immob, air con, tint winds, CD play,
power steer, $9800 ono, ph 3456 7890.

Required
A. How useful is this information in arriving at a decision?
B. What extra information would Renee need before deciding whether to buy this car?
C. Assume that Renee does purchase the car, and subsequently finds that the car has mechanical problems which will require $2000 to fix. What should she do, given that she does not have enough money to pay for the repairs?

Exercise 1.4 CHOOSING A UNIVERSITY MAJOR   **LO 1, 4**

You have just enrolled in a course in business at the Western University in Perth. There are several specialty areas, one of which you must choose — accounting, business law, economics, finance, management, marketing, information systems. The choice you make is important as it will affect your future; hence, you must give careful thought to this decision.

Required
A. Identify two possible specialty areas in business that interest you.
B. Set down your goals and personal preferences in selecting a business major. Identify the factors which will help you make this decision, and specify the factors which are most important to you.
C. Establish a set of criteria which must be met before making a decision about your appropriate specialty area.
D. Determine the sources of information you will need to make such a decision.

Exercise 1.5 MAKING AN ECONOMIC DECISION   **LO 1**

You have decided that now is the time to buy a new DVD recorder/player system. List the factors that are important in choosing a new system and gather relevant information from various sources about different models on the market. Given that you have a maximum of $1200 to spend, work out which system you would buy and discuss the reasons for your choice. Present your answer so as to illustrate the steps required in the decision-making process as discussed in this chapter.

Exercise 1.6 FACTORS IN MAKING A BUSINESS DECISION   **LO 1, 4**

Consult the business section of your local newspaper, or the *The Australian Financial Review*, or a business journal, such as *BRW* (*Business Review Weekly*), and find an appropriate article detailing an important business decision in the last month. Based on the article, determine the factors that were taken into account in arriving at the decision. Discuss the effects that such a decision will have on various interested parties or stakeholders.

Exercise 1.7 FACTORS IN MAKING A GOVERNMENT DECISION

Consult your local newspaper, or the *The Australian Financial Review*, or a business journal, such as *BRW*, and find an appropriate article detailing an important government decision in the last month. Based on the article, determine the factors that were taken into account in arriving at the decision. Discuss the effects that such a decision will have on various interested parties or stakeholders.

Exercise 1.8 ECONOMIC DECISIONS MADE BY MANAGEMENT

Accounting provides much information to help managers make economic decisions in their various workplaces.

Required

Provide examples of economic decisions that the following people would need to make with the use of accounting information:
- a manager in the sales department of a shoe store
- a factory manager
- the manager of a state cricket team
- the manager of an animal shelter which relies on donations for funding.

Exercise 1.9 SETTING UP A BUSINESS

John and Lynn Howard have decided to rent some newly built premises for the purpose of opening a discount fruit and vegetable market. They intend to provide a wide range of different products, from both tropical and temperate climates, and are planning to import certain exotic items from nearby countries to attract customers who have emigrated to Australia.

Required

As their accountant, discuss the types of economic decisions they will be required to make, and the information they will need to make those decisions. How much of this information do you think is 'accounting' information?

Exercise 1.10 THE SMALL BUSINESS OWNER

Read the following short article from *The Daily Telegraph* and answer the questions below.

Business owners could 'plan to cover all futures'

I'm branching out on my own and am about to draw up a business plan.

I see this more as a series of milestones of things I need to achieve by certain dates in order to fulfil my objectives. But my accountant said the plan should be about financial targets. Who is right?

The expert says:
Really you are both right. The business plan needs to cover a few areas, but essentially it needs to detail, among other things, what the business will be, what it will sell, who it will sell to, how it will reach its market and why it will succeed at doing it against its competition.

From that background you will derive your financial projections and budgets that demonstrate the financial viability of the business, including how you will fund it from the start up.

A strong business plan will be the blueprint for how the business will be set up and run. In saying that, it is not a static document and should be reviewed as the business develops and markets change.

A purely financial business plan will inevitably overlook the full nature of a business, and a business plan lacking projections and budgets will overlook many of the financial realities that a business owner must face up to, ideally before they start.

Source: Anthony Bell, *The Daily Telegraph.*

Required

What types of economic decisions would a person wishing to start their own small business be required to make? What types of non-financial decisions would they be required to make? How could an accountant assist in making these decisions?

Read the following extract from an article in the *Financial Times* and discuss the points that follow.

Time the boardroom learnt about *ethics*

The world's regulatory framework proved woefully inadequate when it came to preventing the global financial crisis.

We need to get the corporate elite in financial services to understand that protecting their professional integrity and maintaining high ethical standards will sometimes require taking less profit and bonus. The overall impact on the economy and society has to play a part in how the elite runs these businesses.

Business school faculty can have the greatest impact on the way the next generation of corporate leaders think, which will be more effective than any legislation. They need to be role models who can inspire and challenge business models. We have to move away from teaching business as a science devoid of moral or ethical considerations, as that results in managers who lack personal reflection and values.

Business schools should not approach teaching business ethics either as a stand-alone or integrated model, but should embrace it instead in the overall programme design.

How should we go about teaching ethics?

We must acquaint students with the various codes of ethics for critical evaluation, with examples of ethical challenges faced in the business world. Robust debate is needed, centred on overcoming business challenges within the highest ethical standards. This can partly be done with real-life cases in the classroom.

Students must be exposed to alternative business models and thinking, not just trained to resolve complicated financial problems through mathematical modelling. These tend to be detached from the real world and consideration of human elements. And we need to make students aware of the roles of various institutions, agencies and systems that can support or frustrate achieving socio-economic justice.

We also need to help businesses, through our research, to understand where they are vulnerable.

I have just completed research into how accountants manage ethical dilemmas, which is also relevant to businesses and banking. Nearly half of the 100-plus UK chartered accountants I surveyed, said their bosses were the drivers of ethical culture in their firms — none made reference to the professional code of ethics and only 15 per cent have had any training in how to apply codes of conduct in everyday situations.

Business schools need to help governments, regulatory bodies and businesses understand how to apply corporate governance frameworks in practice throughout an organisation. This includes training and debating ethical issues to ensure regulations are applied both in law and in spirit.

And we must encourage students to apply their contemporary thinking to mainstream business issues.

Source: Ros Haniffa, 'Time the boardroom learnt about ethics', *Financial Times*.

Required

1. Find out whether the university you are attending has a course on ethics in accounting or business. Also find out whether this ethics course (if it exists) is compulsory in your degree.
2. If such a course exists, find out the types of issues discussed in the course.
3. If you work in a business or other entity (full-time or casual), find out whether your business or other entity has a formal code of ethics.
4. Discuss how training in the application of a business's code of conduct in everyday situations, as suggested by the article, might help you in your role as an employee in the future.
5. Why do you think the author of the article believes that '[w]e need to get the corporate elite in financial services to understand that protecting their professional integrity and maintaining high ethical standards will sometimes require taking less profit and bonus'? Do you agree with the author? Why or why not?

DECISION ANALYSIS

Business owners need a plan for future survival

Read the article overleaf from *The Daily Telegraph*, and answer the questions that follow.

Required

What factors do you believe are important in deciding on a particular structure when going into business? Do you believe it may be advisable for a business to change its structure over time? Do you think the type of business structure chosen could influence customers' decisions about purchasing goods from the business, and if so, how?

People thinking about starting their own business know a business plan is essential and they've probably heard that businesses don't plan to fail, they fail to plan.

It's important for small business owners to think of themselves as a shareholder of their enterprise. They need to view their business as an investment and make all decisions on the basis that they will not destroy shareholder value, from the day-to-day running of the business to the people they employ.

Setting up a business is complex. People will most likely need a combination of accounting, legal and financial advice, in addition to government assistance.

So what are the keys to success people should address when contemplating the big leap into business?

Not only is a business plan vital to the day-to-day running of a business, it is nec-essary when applying for loans, fighting off competition and planning for the future. Business owners should prepare a financial plan outlining their expectations of what reward the business needs to deliver. All too often start-ups fail because what needs to be done to make the business sustainable hasn't been identified.

Structure it

One of the critical decisions a new small business owner will make is deciding on the most appropriate structure for the busi-ness. This can be a sole trader, a partner-ship, a trust (an entity that holds assets for the benefit of others) or a company, a legal entity separate from its shareholders. Each option has different tax and legal obli-gations so people should carefully consider the pros and cons of each before making a decision.

Registering the business

Depending on what type of business struc-ture is chosen, the registration process will differ. If a company structure is chosen, the business owner needs to register as a company. This gives people the advantage of having exclusive rights to their com-pany name across Australia. They can carry out business throughout Australia without having to register the name in each state. Sole traders, partnerships and trusts have to register their business name with the appro-priate state or territory. These requirements may not apply if the business is conducted under the name of the person involved. People should seek professional advice in this area.

Source: Andrew Heaven, 'Business owners need a plan for future survival', *The Daily Telegraph*.

CRITICAL THINKING

Calling carbon to account

Read the following article from *The Advertiser* and answer the question that follows.

As Federal Parliament debates emissions trading legislation, businesses are scram-bling to find out how to comply.

But according to enterprise software pro-vider TechnologyOne's general manager of business intelligence, Peter Gill, many organisations already capture much of the data required to report carbon emissions.

'In many cases, it is not necessary to rip systems out and start again or buy new carbon-accounting software,' he said.

South Australian customer relation-ship manager Monique Weiher has been working with the airport to implement the real-time monitoring of carbon emissions.

'When the team at Adelaide Airport was first looking to implement a carbon-accounting system, we worked very closely with them,' she said.

'They now have a system where they can measure, monitor and report on their carbon emissions, making Adelaide Air-port a leader in the industry. It certainly helps that the team was able to collect all the information it needed using existing systems. With the Business Intelligence software, the team can accurately measure, monitor and report as and when they need to, without needing to get another software application.'

Adelaide Airport general manager of corporate affairs John McArdle said the organisation began to measure and report carbon emissions late last year.

'The next step is to work with Tech-nologyOne so that we can start to extract additional reports and data out of the enter-prise suite,' he said.

'As soon as information comes in, we want to be able to enter it into the system and generate a real-time, accurate report of our carbon emissions. Hopefully, we'll be able to influence and change behaviours.'

Source: Frances Stewart, 'Calling carbon to account', *The Advertiser*.

Required

Assume you are a newly appointed accountant for a large company wishing to implement a 'green accounting' program. Prepare a draft report for the management team in which you discuss:

A. some of the issues you are likely to encounter in implementing a carbon accounting system. Consider issues around IT systems, willingness of the entity's management to report its carbon emissions to the public, and reliability of data gathered in the carbon accounting system.

B. some of the benefits the company might derive from implementing a good carbon accounting system

C. who should be responsible for designing, implementing and maintaining the carbon accounting system.

Exploring how professionals use accounting information

Within your tutorial group, organise yourselves into groups according to the professional majors that students are studying, such as groups of accounting, marketing, human resource management, economics and management students. Choose a local business from your profession, such as a marketing firm or recruitment company or government department, and list the types of accounting information that such a business would need to conduct its operations. If possible, make an appointment to talk to the manager of the business or the accountant to see whether there are crucial pieces of information that you have overlooked. Present a brief report of your findings to the class.

If the class is composed entirely of accounting/commerce students, organise groups of three or four students. Choose any non-accounting business and list the types of accounting information that such a business would need to conduct its operations.

ETHICS AND GOVERNANCE

Ethical practices among friends

Two friends, Mickey and Minnie, had just started university studies. Both intended to major in accounting. During the first week of lectures, Minnie, who had to go home for family reasons, asked Mickey to buy a copy of the prescribed accounting text for her from the university bookshop. She left Mickey $100 to cover the cost of the text currently selling in the bookshop for $80.

On the day Mickey visited the bookshop to buy the text, he noted that there were a number of copies that had been returned to the shop by students who had managed to get second-hand copies. These returned copies had been marked down to $65 and looked new. Unable to resist a bargain, Mickey bought a copy for $65.

Mickey then realised that Minnie would not know that the text he had bought was a return and had been bought at a special price, and that he could give Minnie change of $20 and keep the savings on the text of $15 for himself. He simply had to tell Minnie that he had lost the receipt, and given the crowds in the bookshop on the day the text was bought, Minnie could not possibly learn that he had not bought a new copy of the text for her.

Required

A. Who are the stakeholders in this situation?

B. What are the ethical issues involved?

C. What would you do if you were Mickey?

FINANCIAL ANALYSIS

Refer to the latest financial report of JB Hi-Fi Limited on its website, www.jbhifi.com.au. Browse through the chairman's and chief executive officer's reports, and the notes to the financial statements and answer the following questions:

1. What are the main activities and operations of the company?
2. Who are the chief executive officer and the chief financial officer for the company?
3. What are the key elements of the company's code of ethics as stated in the governance, environmental and social statements?
4. What are some of the initiatives taken by JB Hi-Fi Limited in looking after the environment?
5. Who has signed the directors' declaration for the year?
6. Examine the independent auditor's report on the company for the year and answer the following questions:
   (a) Who are the auditors of the company?
   (b) What have the auditors said in relation to the accounting information in the company's report?
7. Have the auditors received any money from the company for doing any work apart from conducting the audit? If so, how much was received for other services?

Financial statements for decision making

Concepts for review

Before studying this chapter, you should understand or, if necessary, revise:

- the steps used in the decision-making process (pp. 4–5)
- the nature of economic decisions (pp. 5–6)
- the nature of accounting and the users of accounting information (pp. 6–10)
- the use of information in economic decisions (pp. 10–11)
- the role of accounting information in the decision-making process (p. 12)
- the differences and similarities between management accounting and financial accounting (pp. 12–13)
- the areas of business in which accountants are employed (pp. 13–17).
- the types of business entities commonly found, and the role of management in organisations (pp. 17–20).

Learning objectives

After studying this chapter, you should be able to:

1 identify and prepare basic financial statements used in business to report to users for decision-making purposes (pp. 30–6)

2 explain the main assumptions made and the characteristics of information to be used in the preparation of financial statements (pp. 36–40)

3 analyse the effects of business transactions on the accounting equation and on financial statements (pp. 41–5).

Demystifying the mysterious balance sheet

One of the most baffling financial statements for a new business owner is the balance sheet. This mysterious document seems almost magical in its ability to convey information to accountants, bankers, loan officers, and potential investors — and equally magical in its ability to convey total confusion to many business owners.

First of all, if you are one of the confused, give yourself a break! The balance sheet is not intuitive. No one is born knowing this stuff. Accountants, bankers, and finance professionals have years of education behind their easy reading of your balance sheet.

The easiest way to explain a balance sheet is to call it a numerical photograph — a snapshot of where your business is financially. In the form of an equation, it shows that what your business owns (Assets) is equal to what it owes to other people (Liabilities) plus your owner's share (Equity). Assets = Liabilities + Equity. Just as a clear, accurate photograph can give you important information about the people in it, an accurate balance sheet can give you important decision-making information for your business.

The reason it is called a 'balance' sheet is that the equation must always remain in balance. Good accounting software helps you (or your bookkeeper) to put your business transactions in the right spots so the equation stays balanced. Every single transaction your business makes fits into this equation somewhere!

The assets owned by the business include the business bank accounts, money that customers owe you (accounts receivable), inventory, and equipment. Just looking at these numbers can provide important information about your business health. Is the bank account really small compared to the value of inventory?

Comparing the bank account to the money the business owes to other people is also enlightening. When you compare your bank account to these numbers, you will know if you have enough business cash to pay your business debts.

If the business has outstanding loans owed to the bank or to credit card companies, or to Aunt Hortense, another informative comparison is between the business' total debt and the amount of investment the owner has put in.

And that brings us to the most important component of a balance sheet: the accuracy of the numbers. If you don't have a competent bookkeeper and you aren't regularly keeping up with the books yourself, your balance sheet 'picture' may look like waking up from a Saturday afternoon nap on the couch, yawning with your hair sticking out every which way — or worse. Regular, accurate bookkeeping is as important for a healthy-looking balance-sheet picture as regular sleep, good meals and exercise are important for looking healthy in your picture.

If you think the financial picture looks more like a snapshot of your business in a fun-house mirror, then you may need professional bookkeeping help to get your information organised, entered and up-to-date. A clear picture can help you make clear business decisions.

Smile for the camera!

Source: Excerpts from Colleen Trask, 'De-mystifying the mysterious balance sheet', *Times-Standard*.

Chapter preview

In this chapter, we describe some of the basic financial statements prepared by the accountant, the assumptions made in preparing these statements, and the effects of transactions on the preparation of financial statements. Each financial statement shows a different aspect or view of the business — these different aspects will be explored in this chapter. The scene setter for this chapter explains that every transaction a business enters into affects the accounting equation — this will be illustrated through examples.

2.1 Basic financial statements

Accounting, as we have seen in chapter 1, may be viewed as an information system designed to communicate financial information to interested users for making economic decisions. The final outcome of the accounting process is the preparation of a set of financial statements which serve to communicate important information to users both within and external to the business.

Financial statements should provide information that is useful to existing and potential investors, lenders and other creditors. These users of financial statements make decisions about whether or not to provide resources to the entity in the form of invested funds, loans or other forms of credit. Such economic decisions require users to assess the ability of the entity to generate cash flows in the future which are sufficient and timely. Without the ability to generate cash, entities would not be in a position to pay their employees, creditors and providers of funds (whether through investment or loans). Many of these users rely on the financial statements of the entity as a basis for making their assessments. Financial statements also provide a mechanism for management and governing bodies to discharge their responsibility for the stewardship function they perform over the entity's resources.

In general, users may be interested in three types of information contained in financial statements to inform them about the entity: its financial performance, its financial position and its cash movements.

The entity's **financial performance** indicates the ability of the entity to utilise its assets efficiently and effectively to generate cash flows in the conduct of its activities, whether for profit or not for profit.

In order to assess performance, users need to be aware of the entity's overall objectives or goals. What is the entity trying to achieve? Is it trying to make profits for its shareholders or does it have a non-financial objective, such as providing shelter for homeless people? For a business entity, information about its ability to earn profits is an essential part of its financial statements; however, the achievement of its social and environmental goals should not be overlooked. For a not-for-profit entity, its performance in achieving its stated goals may have little to do with the profit motive. For example, clubs exist for the overall enjoyment and satisfaction of their members, and aid organisations exist to help people in need receive a better education and have a more comfortable social existence. Even though these entities do not have profit as their objective, they have to generate sufficient cash to continue to provide goods and services to their beneficiaries. Their financial performance will provide input into the evaluation of their ability to achieve this.

The **financial position** of an entity, as discussed in the *Conceptual Framework for Financial Reporting* (discussed in more detail later in this book, and hereafter referred to as the *Conceptual Framework*), deals with the economic resources controlled by an entity, its financial structure, its capacity to adapt to changes in its environment, and its liquidity and solvency. This information is useful in predicting the ability of the entity to generate cash flows in the future, and to meet its financial commitments as and when they fall due. The information that would help to assess these aspects includes the different types of assets held by the business, the amounts of money borrowed from other entities, the amount of cash or other assets supplied by the owner of the business, the time needed to repay borrowed money, the current state of repair of the entity's assets, the selling price of these assets, and the possible sources of finance available to the business in an emergency. All this information is desirable to help users make informed economic decisions about an entity.

The **cash movements** of an entity are made up of the cash inflows and outflows. According to the *Conceptual Framework*, information about the entity's cash flows is useful in order to assess the entity's operating, investing and financing activities. This provides a basis for assessing the ability of the entity to generate cash in the future to meet its objectives.

Operating activities are those associated with the provision of goods or services. Typical operating activities for a business entity include collecting cash for providing services or selling goods to customers, making payments for goods purchased for sale, paying suppliers amounts owing for goods or services purchased in the past, collecting outstanding debts owed to the entity from customers, paying wages to employees and paying income tax to the government. Some of these operating activities also arise in not-for-profit entities, and may be so reported in their financial statements.

Investing activities are those associated with the acquisition and disposal of long-term resources used in the entity's production, selling or administrative functions. For example, investing activities include purchasing or selling an office building, constructing a factory, purchasing or selling long-term investments, and purchasing or selling plant and machinery or delivery vehicles.

Financing activities are those which relate to the raising of funds for an entity to carry out its operating and investing activities. Examples of financing activities include raising capital by issuing shares to the public, receiving more funds from business owners to expand the business, borrowing money from a bank or other financial institution, and repaying these borrowed funds.

In Darren's lawnmowing and gardening business, introduced in chapter 1, operating activities consist of his lawnmowing, gardening and tree-lopping services and his costs for fuel, repairs and maintenance, and record keeping. Investing activities consist of the purchase of the vehicle, appropriate lawnmowers, the chainsaw and other gardening equipment. Financing activities include the cash contributed by Darren to the business out of his redundancy package.

The basic financial statements prepared by an entity for internal users are an income statement (also called a statement of profit or loss and other comprehensive income), a balance sheet (also called a statement of financial position), a statement of changes in equity and a statement of cash flows. For reporting to external users, all financial statements must be prepared in accordance with the requirements of accounting standards. Reporting to external parties is discussed in more detail later in this book.

The balance sheet

The **balance sheet (statement of financial position)** reports the financial position of an entity at a specific point in time. The financial position is reflected by the assets of the entity, its liabilities or debts owed, and the equity of its owners. Figure 2.1 (p. 31) shows a simple balance sheet for a single proprietorship involved in providing repair services for motor vehicles, Don's Auto Repairs, as at 30 June 2012.

The heading of the balance sheet indicates the name of the entity, the name of the statement and the date. The basic statement is divided into three main sections: assets, liabilities and equity. In figure 2.1, the assets are listed on the left-hand side and the liabilities and equity are listed on the right-hand side. Note that the two sides of the statement are equal. This equality must exist because the left-hand side lists the assets and the right-hand side shows the sources of the funds used to acquire the assets. Of the total assets of $968 440 controlled by the entity, $481 760 of them were funded by creditors (liabilities) and the remainder of $486 680 was funded by the owner, Don Brady.

Figure 2.1 Balance sheet (account format)

DON'S AUTO REPAIRS
Balance Sheet
as at 30 June 2012

ASSETS		LIABILITIES	
Cash at bank	$ 50 340	Accounts payable	$ 80 760
Accounts receivable	77 790	Mortgage payable	401 000
Repair supplies	14 610		481 760
Repair equipment	110 700		
Land	260 000	EQUITY	
Building	455 000	Don Brady, Capital	486 680
	$968 440		$968 440

Since the balance sheet must always show equality between the left-hand side and the right-hand side, a basic equation can be established to show this relationship.

The basic accounting model (**accounting equation**) for the balance sheet is:

$$\text{Assets} = \text{Liabilities} + \text{Equity}$$

All transactions of an entity can be analysed using this basic model, although we will see that better analyses can be made by expanding the equation to include the effect of the income statement.

The balance sheet shown in figure 2.1 follows the *account* form of presentation since, as will be seen in subsequent chapters, it resembles the structure of a T-shaped ledger account. The format of balance sheets varies considerably with assets, liabilities and equity arranged in various ways. For example, the *narrative* or *descriptive* form lists all of the elements of a balance sheet in one column. In Australia, no set format exists; however, the narrative format is most common in business practice for reporting by companies.

The basic accounting model (accounting equation) for the narrative form of balance sheet rearranges the equation shown above as follows:

$$\text{Assets} - \text{Liabilities} = \text{Equity}$$

Figure 2.2 illustrates the balance sheet presented in narrative format.

Figure 2.2 Balance sheet (narrative format)

DON'S AUTO REPAIRS
Balance Sheet
as at 30 June 2012

ASSETS	
Cash at bank	$ 50 340
Accounts receivable	77 790
Repair supplies	14 610
Repair equipment	110 700
Land	260 000
Building	455 000
TOTAL ASSETS	968 440
LIABILITIES	
Accounts payable	80 760
Mortgage payable	401 000
TOTAL LIABILITIES	481 760
NET ASSETS	$486 680
EQUITY	
Don Brady, Capital	$486 680
TOTAL EQUITY	$486 680

Balance sheets of organisations other than companies also may be presented in either account or narrative format, although the narrative style is more prevalent. Note that when liabilities are deducted from assets, the amount $486 680 is often called **net assets**, which equals equity.

Assets

Assets are resources controlled by the entity as a result of past events and from which future economic benefits are expected to flow to the entity.[1] They are economic resources which may be tangible (having physical characteristics, such as land, buildings and equipment) or intangible (assets without physical existence, such as legal claims or patent rights). It is a common practice for entities to list assets on the statement in the order of highest liquidity (cash and items easily converted to cash in the short term) to lowest liquidity, as a means of helping users to assess solvency. This is explained further in chapter 4.

---

1. Suggestions to amend the definition of an asset are discussed in chapter 17.

Liabilities

Liabilities are present obligations of an entity arising from past events, the settlement of which is expected to result in an outflow from the entity of resources embodying economic benefits.[2] They are the debts owed by an entity to outside parties called **creditors** and include amounts owed to suppliers for goods or services purchased on credit (**accounts payable**), amounts borrowed from banks or other lenders (*loans payable* and *mortgages payable*) and amounts owed to employees for wages and salaries that have not yet been paid (*wages and salaries payable*). Liabilities must be settled by the entity. This can occur by payment in cash, the transfer of other assets, or the performance of services to extinguish them.

Equity

Equity may be thought of as the owner's claim to (or the residual interest in) the assets of the entity after deducting all its liabilities. The basic accounting model introduced earlier (Assets = Liabilities + Equity) indicates that the total assets of the entity equal the total claims against those assets by creditors and owners. Creditors' claims take legal precedence over owners' claims and owners are the ultimate risk-takers in the entity; if the assets are sold, creditors must be paid before the claims of the owner(s) are recognised. Thus, equity is a residual (i.e. 'left over') claim on the assets, and the basic accounting model which expresses this idea clearly is:

$$\text{Assets} - \text{Liabilities} = \text{Equity}$$
$$or$$
$$\text{Net assets} = \text{Equity}$$

Other terms often used for equity are *proprietorship* and *capital*. Note that, in the case of government departments and government entities, equity is replaced by *accumulated surplus*. For not-for-profit entities, equity is usually represented by the term *accumulated funds*.

In summary, the two sides of the balance sheet in account format are always equal because they simply reflect two views of the same thing. In figure 2.1, the list of assets shows the resources controlled by the entity. The lists of liabilities and equity show the amounts of the resources provided in the past to the business by the creditors and the owners. Thus, all the assets are funded by either creditors or owners. Because creditors' claims take legal precedence, a business entity with a relatively large ratio of liabilities to equity is considered financially weaker (a greater risk) than an entity with a relatively large ratio of equity to liabilities. This emphasis on equity as a residual claim is shown in the narrative format in figure 2.2. As the scene setter to this chapter suggests, looking at and analysing the figures in the balance sheet can give some valuable insight into the business. The analysis and interpretation of financial statements is discussed in more detail in a later chapter.

The income statement

The **income statement** (sometimes called a statement of profit or loss and other comprehensive income, a **profit or loss statement**, or an **operating statement** in government and not-for-profit entities) reports the results of financial performance for a specific time period such as a month, half-year or year. Profit for the period is the excess of income over expenses for that time. If expenses for the period exceed income, a loss is incurred. Figure 2.3 shows a simple income statement for Don's Auto Repairs.

The heading identifies the entity being reported on — Don's Auto Repairs — the name of the statement and the time period covered by the statement. Identification of the time period covered is particularly important in an income statement because it indicates the length of time (here, 1 year) it took to earn the reported profit. The data in the income statement would have no meaning without a clear indication of the period covered.

---

2. Suggestions to amend the definition of a liability are discussed in chapter 17.

Figure 2.3 Income statement

DON'S AUTO REPAIRS
Income Statement
for the year ended 30 June 2012

INCOME		
Repair income		$642 500
EXPENSES		
Advertising expense	$ 20 250	
Repair supplies expense	133 710	
Salaries and wages expense	173 800	
Rent expense	110 260	
Telephone expense	20 190	
Light and power expense	47 940	
		506 150
PROFIT		$136 350

Income

Income represents an increase in the wealth of the owner(s). Income is defined in the *Conceptual Framework* as increases in economic benefits during the accounting period in the form of inflows or enhancements of assets or decreases of liabilities that result in increases in equity, other than those relating to contributions from equity participants. Income usually results from the sale of goods or the performance of services. It is commonly measured by the amount of cash or value of other assets received. Although income often is measured by the cash received, it may be measured by the receipt of other assets, such as promises by customers to pay in the future (**accounts receivable**, also called **debtors**) or the receipt of property from a customer. Regardless of the type of asset received, income usually results not only from the sale of goods and the performance of services, but also from other sources such as interest received, dividends received on shares owned, and rent. Note that any asset contributed to the entity by owners is not regarded as income, but as a different type of increase in the equity, referred to as a 'contribution by owners'. An entity cannot earn income or create wealth through transactions with its owners.

Expenses

Expenses are decreases in economic benefits during the accounting period in the form of outflows or depletions of assets or incurrences of liabilities that result in decreases in equity, other than those relating to distributions to equity participants. Expenses are measured by the amount of assets used up or the amount of liabilities incurred. They may arise through immediate cash payments, as for current wages and salaries, or through promises to pay cash in the future for services received, such as a liability for advertising. In some cases, cash may be paid out before the expense is incurred, such as payment for next month's or next year's rent. These prepayments represent assets until they are used. In figure 2.3, the total of all expenses incurred during 2012 by Don's Auto Repairs was $506 150. Subtracting these expenses from income produces a profit of $136 350. It is important to understand that the profit represents an increase in equity. Because income results in an increase in equity and expenses result in a decrease in equity, the difference between the two (where income exceeds expenses) — **profit** — must represent a net increase in equity. Similarly, a **loss** represents a decrease in equity. A loss arises where expenses exceed income.

The statement of changes in equity

The statement of changes in equity (figure 2.4) serves as a connecting link between the balance sheet and the income statement, and explains the changes that took place in equity during the period. For example, assuming that Don's capital balance on 1 July 2011 was $437 330 and that he withdrew $87 000 from the business for personal use during 2012 (referred to as **drawings**), the statement of changes in equity for 2012 would be as shown in figure 2.4.

Figure 2.4 Statement of changes in equity

DON'S AUTO REPAIRS
Statement of Changes in Equity
for the year ended 30 June 2012

Don Brady, Capital — 1 July 2011	$437 330
Add: Profit for the year	136 350
	573 680
Less: Drawings	87 000
Don Brady, Capital — 30 June 2012	$486 680

The three statements illustrated above — balance sheet, income statement and statement of changes in equity — are related to one another. The balance sheet at the end of one period is the balance sheet at the beginning of the next period. The balance sheets at the beginning and end of a period are linked by the income statement and the statement of changes in equity as shown in figure 2.5.

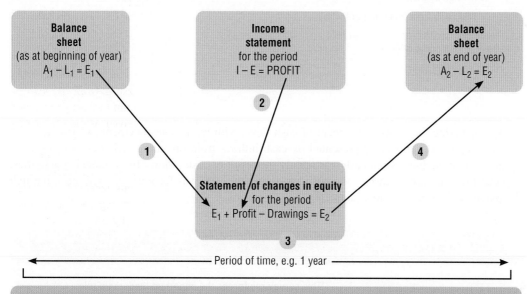

Figure 2.5 Financial statements relationship

1 E_1 is shown in the beginning balance sheet and is the starting point for the statement of changes in equity.

2 Profit for the period is determined from the income statement and included in factors which alter the capital balance over the year.

3 Drawings made during the year (usually in cash) are recorded in the accounts and used in determining the equity at the end of the period E_2.

4 E_2 is shown on the ending balance sheet.

The statement of cash flows

Another important financial statement prepared by entities is a statement of cash flows. An entity's income statement does not report on the cash flows of the entity, but on its income and expenses (chapter 4 discusses this further). Income and expenses as defined above do not necessarily represent cash flows. Consequently, a **statement of cash flows** is prepared to report on the cash flows in and out of the entity. It is particularly useful in helping users to assess the sources and uses of an entity's cash, and the likely ability of the entity to remain solvent (i.e. able to pay its debts), so that the users can make informed decisions. The statement reports on the entity's performance in generating cash flows from operating activities, investing activities and financing activities as shown in figure 2.6 (p. 36) for Don's Auto Repairs. It is assumed that this business began its operations on 1 July 2011 when the owner, Don Brady, invested $437 330 cash in the business.

Figure 2.6 Statement of cash flows

DON'S AUTO REPAIRS
Statement of Cash Flows
for the year ended 30 June 2012

CASH FLOWS FROM OPERATING ACTIVITIES		
Cash received from customers	$564 710	
Cash paid to suppliers and employees	(440 000)	
Net cash from operating activities		$124 710
CASH FLOWS FROM INVESTING ACTIVITIES		
Purchase of land and buildings	(715 000)	
Purchase of repair equipment	(110 700)	
Net cash used in investing activities		(825 700)
CASH FLOWS FROM FINANCING ACTIVITIES		
Amount borrowed under mortgage	401 000	
Investment by owner	437 330	
Drawings by owner	(87 000)	
Net cash from financing activities		751 330
Net increase (decrease) in cash held		50 340
Cash at beginning of year		—
Cash at end of year		$ 50 340

By comparing the entity's statement of cash flows with its income statement, we can see how well the reported profits are represented by cash inflows from operating activities. We see from figure 2.6 that the increase in cash was mainly the result of cash inflows from financing activities, and that the main use of cash in the business during the year was for investing activities, through the purchase of property and equipment.

BUSINESS KNOWLEDGE

Survey shows accountants number 1 with small business

The vast majority of Australian small businesses use the services of an accountant according to a survey of small business owners and managers released by software specialist Reckon Limited.

Over 400 small business owners/managers from across Australia took part in Reckon's *2010 Annual Australian Small Business Survey*. Nearly 90% of respondents indicated they use an accountant and 23% nominated their accountant as having the most influence over their decision making. Reckon's Business Division CEO Gavin Dixon says it's pleasing to see businesses valuing professional advice.

'This survey reinforces the important leadership role accountants play in communities and organisations. For small businesses, hiring an accountant is clearly about more than getting help with preparing their tax return,' said Dixon.

'This survey also highlights the importance of helping businesses through uncertainty with over half of the respondents concerned about the economy and changes to legislation that could impact their operation. Accountants, bookkeepers and other business professionals will play a key role in helping small businesses through the challenges they face in the months and years ahead,' says Dixon.

Source: Reckon's 2010 Annual Australian Small Business Survey.

Learning objective 2

Explain the main assumptions made and the characteristics of information to be used in the preparation of financial statements

2.2 Underlying assumptions and qualitative characteristics of financial statements

We have described accounting as a service activity, designed to identify, measure and record financial data of an entity, that provides useful information in making economic decisions. Over time, as accounting has evolved, questions have arisen concerning the method of identifying events, the principles of measurement to be used and the general guidelines to be followed in order to communicate financial data useful in decision making. Accountants have gradually produced responses to these questions and developed some underlying assumptions that are followed in present-day accounting reports. These assumptions are principles, concepts and practices that have developed and are assumed to be applied in the preparation of financial statements. Furthermore, financial statements should include qualitative characteristics to ensure that the information in them is meaningful. The assumptions and qualitative characteristics are discussed below.

Underlying assumptions of financial statements

The accounting entity assumption

If the transactions of an entity are to be recorded, classified and summarised into financial statements, the accountant must be able to identify clearly the boundaries of the entity being accounted for. Under the **accounting entity assumption**, the entity (Don's Auto Repairs, for example) is considered a separate entity distinguishable from its owner and from all other entities. It is assumed that each entity controls its assets and incurs its liabilities. The records of assets, liabilities and business activities of the entity are kept completely separate from those of the owner of the entity as well as from those of other entities. For example, the personal assets, debts and activities of Don Brady are not included in the records of Don's Auto Repairs because they do not constitute part of the activities of the business entity. A separate set of accounting records is maintained for each entity, and the financial statements prepared provide information on that entity only. This is done even if the business is not regarded as a separate legal entity (such as a sole trader).

The accounting entity assumption is important since it leads to the derivation of the accounting equation. Given this assumption, if the entity receives $50 000 cash from the owner as capital, the accountant for the entity records that it has an asset of $50 000 in the form of cash but also has to recognise that the entity is now indebted to the owner for $50 000.

Similarly, if the entity borrows cash from a lender, the asset (cash) increases, and the entity must acknowledge the debt to the lender for the cash borrowed.

The accrual basis assumption

The financial statements of an entity are assumed to be prepared on the **accrual basis** of accounting. According to the *Conceptual Framework*, under the accrual basis the effects of all transactions and events are recognised in accounting records when they occur, and not when the cash is received or paid. Hence, financial statements report not only on cash transactions but also on obligations to pay cash in the future and on resources that represent receivables of cash in future. It is argued in the *Conceptual Framework* that accounting on an accrual basis provides information about the transactions and other events that is most useful for decision making by both internal and external users of those statements. Further discussion of the accrual basis of accounting as opposed to the cash basis is provided in chapter 4.

The going concern assumption

According to the *Conceptual Framework*, financial statements are normally prepared on the assumption that the existing entity will continue to operate in the future — the **going concern assumption**. It is assumed that the entity will not be wound up in the near future but will continue its activities, and so the liquidation values (prices in a forced sale) of the entity's assets are not generally reported.

When management plans the sale or liquidation of the entity, the going concern assumption is set aside and the financial statements are prepared on the basis of estimated sales or liquidation values. The financial statements should then identify clearly the basis on which asset values are determined. In order for decision makers to understand information contained in financial statements, it is important that they know whether assets are valued at cost, at fair values, or on some other basis.

The period assumption

All entities need to report their results in the form of either profit or operating surplus. Profit is determined for particular periods of time, such as a month or a year, in order to get comparability of results. There are also statutory requirements for entities to determine periodic profit figures, such as for taxation. This division of the life of the entity into equal time intervals is known as the **period assumption**.

As a result of this assumption, profit determination involves a process of recognising the income for a period and deducting the expenses incurred for that same period.

Qualitative characteristics of financial statements

The characteristic of relevance

Since the purpose of presenting accounting information in financial statements is to provide information to users for making economic decisions, it is important that this information is relevant to users for decision making. **Relevance** means that the information can influence the economic decisions made by users. For example, the information may help users to predict future events, such as future cash flows, from the alternative courses of action under consideration. Furthermore, information is relevant if it is able to help decision makers evaluate past decisions. The information may confirm that a previous decision was correct, or it could show that the results of a previous decision were undesirable and that a new decision is necessary to correct or minimise the mistakes of the past. Thus, information that is relevant is said to have a predictive role and a confirmatory or feedback role.

A further aspect of relevance is that the information must be presented by the accountant to the user (internal or external) in time for a decision to be made. It is a waste of time and effort for the accountant to prepare detailed financial statements if they don't reach users before they make a decision. Users may be satisfied with receiving less detailed information as long as the information is provided on time. Thus, *timeliness* of information is an important factor in ensuring that information is relevant.

The characteristic of reliability/faithful representation

Just as important as relevance is reliability of information. **Reliability** means that the user is assured that the information presented represents faithfully, without bias or undue error, the underlying transactions and events being reported in the financial statements. Accountants require information to be reliable, which means that the information reported represents the facts as closely as possible. This is a major reason that accountants record assets in the financial records at their original historical cost. The cost of a resource acquired is determined on the basis of the exchange price negotiated between the buyer and the seller. For accountants to record current market values requires the use of estimates, appraisals or opinions, all of which are more unreliable, even though such information may be relevant to users for decision-making purposes.

In the past, users of accounting information were given the most reliable data available, that is, data were reported in terms of historical cost. However, it was argued that the accountant had sacrificed a degree of relevance so that information was reliable. Current market values are usually relevant in making decisions and, therefore, the reporting of cost data as the only reliable information is questionable. Balancing relevance with reliability in order to determine the content of financial statements for decision-making purposes by internal and external users is a constant challenge facing an accountant.

An additional aspect of reliability is that the economic substance of transactions and events should be given priority. **Economic substance** means that the accountant examines transactions and events in order to report on their economic reality as opposed to their legal form. Thus, it is common for the accountant to report assets on the entity's balance sheet even if those assets are not legally owned by the entity. Economic substance relates to the economic significance of the items to the entity, not to their legal ownership. Even though most items of economic significance to an entity are also legally owned by that entity, whenever there is a separation of economic substance from legal form, the accountant will report on the basis of the economic substance rather than on legal ownership.

For example, when an asset is leased by an entity on a long-term basis, the economic benefits and the risks of ownership often rest with the entity which has possession and use of the asset (lessee) and not with the legal owner (lessor). Thus, the long-term leased asset is reported on the balance sheet of the lessee rather than on the balance sheet of the lessor. The lessor is said to have 'sold' the asset to the lessee, even though, legally, the asset is still the property of the lessor. In order to accommodate the desire to report the economic substance of transactions and events, note that the accountant has defined an asset in terms of 'control' rather than 'ownership'.

In September 2010, the International Accounting Standards Board (IASB) amended its *Conceptual Framework* for the characteristics of information in financial statements by introducing the concept of 'faithful representation'. The IASB argues that, to be useful in making investment, credit and similar resource allocation decisions, information must be a **faithful representation** of the real-world economic phenomena that it purports to represent. The phenomena represented in financial reports are economic resources and obligations and the transactions and other events and circumstances that change them. To be a faithful representation of those economic phenomena, information must be *neutral* and *complete*. Further discussion is provided in chapter 17.

The characteristic of comparability (including consistency)

The revised *Conceptual Framework* issued by the IASB in September 2010 adopts the concept of comparability as an enhancing characteristic of accounting information. Comparability, including consistency, enhances the usefulness of financial reporting information in making economic decisions. **Comparability** is the quality of information that enables users to identify similarities in and differences between two sets of economic data. **Consistency** refers to use of the same accounting policies and procedures, either from period to period within an entity or in a single period across entities. The IASB argues that comparability is the goal and that consistency of policies and procedures is a means to an end that helps in achieving that goal. However, it is insufficient for policies and procedures to be applied consistently if the information they produce is no longer relevant or a faithful representation of economic reality.

The characteristic of understandability

A further characteristic of good information is that of understandability. According to the *Conceptual Framework*, **understandability** is the quality of information that enables users who have a reasonable knowledge of business and economic activities and financial accounting, and who study the information with reasonable diligence, to comprehend its meaning. It should be clear that, even though it is desirable for financial statements to be expressed in simple language, relevant information should not be excluded merely because it may be too complex or difficult for some users to understand. Understandability is enhanced when information is classified, characterised, and presented clearly and concisely.

The characteristic of materiality

To ensure that information in financial statements is useful for decision making, it is important that users are not overwhelmed with so much detail that they cannot clearly understand the message. Hence, it is desirable that users receive information about *significant* items for their decisions, with insignificant items either not shown separately or grouped together under appropriate headings. This ensures that financial statements focus on relevant information.

The concept of **materiality** relates to the extent to which information can be omitted, misstated or grouped with other information without misleading the statement users when they are making their economic decisions. Thus, the prices paid for insignificant items, such as for each piece of stationery, need not be shown separately in the financial statements because they are insignificant, or immaterial, in the overall context of the decision being made by the user. It is important, however, when assessing materiality, for the accountant to be aware of the particular decision being made by the user. The same information may be material for one decision and immaterial for another. Thus, considerable judgement is needed by the accountant in order to assess which information is material and which is immaterial for the particular decision at hand.

According to the *Conceptual Framework*, materiality must be considered in the context of the other characteristics, especially faithful representation. Materiality is viewed as a constraint on the information to be included in an entity's financial statements rather than as a separate characteristic of good information.

Benefits and costs

The IASB also states that the benefits of financial reporting information should justify the costs of providing and using it. The benefits of financial reporting information include better investment, credit and similar economic decisions, which in turn result in more efficient markets and greater benefits for the economy as a whole. But, the task of preparing financial statements also imposes costs on both the preparers and the users of those statements, as well as on others such as auditors. Therefore, a major constraint on reporting the absolute best information in a financial statement is the cost of generating that information and assuring that it is a faithful representation of the events it is supposed to represent. In other words, information is costly to produce, and both the accountant and the user must be mindful of its benefits and costs.

These assumptions and characteristics (and others as well) have been established by international regulators of accounting standards. In a later chapter, we shall introduce the issue of regulation, and show how accounting standards have been developed in Australia.

BUSINESS KNOWLEDGE

Seeking sustainability

So how does a business prove its sustainability credentials?

'A starting point is always a greenhouse gas assessment which will give us the groundwork, the numbers, and ultimately reveal what the carbon footprint of the business is,' McIntosh, [the WA manager for Carbon Planet, a national carbon management company] says.

'Then there are emissions and sustainability planning. That involves risk analysis so you understand your exposure and the impact of a carbon price on your business.'

'So we might end up saying: "Well, 42 per cent of your expenses will be impacted by the price of carbon, causing an increase in the cost of doing business of nine per cent — or whatever" — and we can quantify that in the figures.'

He says the first aim is always to minimise emissions. After that might come risk mitigation strategies, buying credits to offset emissions and communication strategies so your staff, clients and suppliers know what you're doing and can track it.

'You'll never have a zero footprint,' McIntosh says. 'Everything you do in business causes an emission. But you can reduce it, and then you offset the remainder by buying credits.'

While legislation might be a major factor in Australian businesses becoming more carbon conscious, McIntosh says Europe already has an emissions trading scheme and business there has been keen on being green.

'The main driving force there has been corporate responsibility, they're not driven by government legislation. It's driven by the business community,' he says.

'Being seen as "clean and green — and offset" is seen as much a factor in doing business as OHS was when that came in, or even similarly with quality assurance.'

'If you weren't following those processes, then you'd start being left out of the supply chain.'

In Australia, peer pressure, corporate responsibility and public image — being seen to be green — are all playing a part.

'A lot of companies are going down this green path,' McIntosh says. 'The international ones were first, but a lot of the local ones are doing it as well. It's almost a case of "if we have to do it, we expect everyone we do business with to do it as well".'

'That's also coming through in tendering for government and big business jobs. Tender documents, for instance, are asking "how are you addressing your emissions or what are your sustainability practices?" And more and more weight is being given to those answers.'

'So companies who do a lot of business with government or overseas contracts have to address those factors, just for the sake of doing business.'

Source: Excerpts from Tony Malkovic, 'Seeking sustainability', *Charter*.

2.3 The effects of transactions on the accounting equation and financial statements

Learning objective 3

Analyse the effects of business transactions on the accounting equation and on financial statements

The basic accounting model or accounting equation was expressed earlier as:

$$\text{Assets} = \text{Liabilities} + \text{Equity}$$

The sum of the assets of an entity is always equal to the total sources from which those assets came — liabilities plus equity. Transactions result in changes in assets, liabilities and equity. Even though the elements of the accounting equation change as a result of transactions, the basic equality of the accounting equation remains unchanged, which is illustrated using some transactions undertaken by the business of Darren's Lawn and Gardening Services, introduced in chapter 1.

Note that the impact of GST is not discussed in this example in order to focus on the basic accounting principles involved in recording the transactions for Darren's business. GST is introduced in chapter 3.

Transaction 1 Assume that Darren Jones decided to set up a business called Darren's Lawn and Gardening Services on 2 January 2012 by taking $35 000 from his personal savings account and depositing it in a business bank account he opened in the business name. This investment by Darren represents the first transaction (1) of Darren's Lawn and Gardening Services. After this initial investment, the new business has one asset (cash at bank), no liabilities and Darren's equity. Thus, the accounting equation for Darren's Lawn and Gardening Services is as shown below.

	Assets	=	Liabilities	+	Equity
	Cash at Bank				Darren Jones, Capital
(1)	$35 000	=			$35 000

The effect of this transaction is to increase assets by $35 000, with an equal increase in equity on the other side of the equation. (Remember that the equation relates only to the business entity.) Because of the accounting entity assumption, Darren's personal assets and debts are not part of the business and are therefore excluded from the equation.

Transaction 2 After making the initial investment, Darren, who also manages the business, purchased a vehicle and some lawnmowing and gardening equipment. The vehicle cost $21 000 and the list price of the equipment was $10 000, but after discussion on 3 January, the supplier agreed to sell the equipment to Darren's business for $9000 cash. The equation before this transaction, the effect of this transaction (2) on the equation, and the equation after the transaction are:

	Assets					=	Liabilities	+	Equity
	Cash at Bank	+	Lawn and Garden Equipment	+	Vehicle	=			Darren Jones, Capital
(1)	$35 000					=			$35 000
(2)	−30 000		+9 000		+21 000				
	5 000	+	9 000	+	21 000	=			35 000
			$35 000						

This transaction resulted in an exchange of one asset (cash) for two other assets (a vehicle, and lawn and garden equipment). No liabilities were incurred and Darren's equity remained unchanged. Note that the vehicle and equipment are recorded initially at their cost of $30 000; the list price of the equipment is irrelevant. Note that total assets of $35 000 are still equal to liabilities + equity.

Transaction 3 On 4 January, Darren purchased $2500 worth of fuel supplies from Adam Fuel Ltd on credit, with an agreement to pay for the supplies later. The effect of this transaction (3) is an increase in assets of $2500 and an increase in liabilities, accounts payable, of $2500:

	Cash at Bank	+	Lawn and Garden Equipment	+	Vehicle	+	Fuel Supplies	=	Accounts Payable	+	Darren Jones, Capital
				Assets				=	Liabilities	+	Equity
(1)	$35 000							=			$35 000
(2)	−30 000		+9 000		+21 000						
	5 000	+	9 000	+	21 000			=			35 000
(3)									+2 500		+2 500
	5 000	+	9 000	+	21 000	+	2 500	=	2 500	+	35 000
				$37 500						$37 500	

Darren's equity in the business did not change because assets and liabilities increased by equal amounts. The accounting equation is still in balance, with $37 500 in total assets and $37 500 of liabilities and equity.

One of the main objectives of a business is to engage in activities that will result in profit to its owners. As explained earlier, profit is the excess of income over expenses for a specific time period. Income for Darren's Lawn and Gardening Services is derived from charging fees for performing lawnmowing and gardening services for its customers. Because the assets received as income belong to the owner, income increases equity. Expenses for the business consist of such things as wages paid to Sue as an employee and fuel supplies used. Just as income increases equity, expenses decrease equity. The excess of income over expenses therefore results in an increase in the net assets and a net increase in equity. Of course, an excess of expenses over income (a loss) has the opposite effect.

Transactions 4 and 5 To illustrate the effect of income on the accounting equation, assume that up to 20 January Darren's Lawn and Gardening Services performed lawnmowing and gardening services for customers for the amount of $2200, which was received in cash — transaction (4). In addition, the business completed the removal of trees and rubbish for the local council and sent the customer an invoice for $550 — transaction (5). The effects of these transactions on the accounting equation are indicated in (4) and (5) below.

	Cash at Bank	+	Lawn and Garden Equipment	+	Vehicle	+	Fuel Supplies	+	Accounts Receivable	=	Accounts Payable	+	Darren Jones, Capital	
					Assets					=	Liabilities	+	Equity	
(1)	$35 000									=			$35 000	
(2)	−30 000		+9 000		+21 000									
	5 000	+	9 000	+	21 000					=			35 000	
(3)									+2 500		+2 500			
	5 000	+	9 000	+	21 000	+	2 500			=	2 500	+	35 000	
(4)	+2 200												+2 200	(Lawn and garden income)
	7 200	+	9 000	+	21 000	+	2 500			=	2 500	+	37 200	
(5)									+550				+550	(Tree-lopping income)
	7 200	+	9 000	+	21 000	+	2 500	+	550	=	2 500	+	37 750	
					$40 250							$40 250		

Note that the effect of transaction (4) is to increase the asset cash at bank and, because it represents a receipt for the performance of services (income), to increase equity by an equal amount. Transaction (5) introduces an important principle in accounting — that income under the accrual basis of accounting may be recognised before cash is received. The income is represented by an increase in an asset, in this case an account receivable, which is a right to collect cash in the future from a debtor.

Transactions 6 and 7   To see the effect of expenses on the accounting equation, assume that on 22 January Darren's business paid cash of $450 for wages to Sue, an employee — transaction (6). In addition, a count of the fuel supplies at 31 January showed that fuel supplies on hand amounted to $1700. The other $800 ($2500 − $1700) of fuel supplies had been used. Depletions of assets are recognised as expenses — transaction (7). The effects of these transactions on the accounting equation are shown in (6) and (7) below.

Note that expenses have an effect which is opposite to the recognition of income, with a decrease in assets and a decrease in equity. The basic principle in accrual accounting is that expenses are recognised in the period in which the consumption or loss of economic benefits has occurred and not when the cash is paid.

	Cash at Bank	+	Lawn and Garden Equipment	+	Vehicle	+	Fuel Supplies	+	Accounts Receivable	=	Accounts Payable	+	Darren Jones, Capital	
(1)	$35 000									=			$35 000	
(2)	−30 000		+9 000		+21 000									
	5 000	+	9 000	+	21 000					=			35 000	
(3)							+2 500				+2 500			
	5 000	+	9 000	+	21 000	+	2 500			=	2 500	+	35 000	
(4)	+2 200												+2 200	(Lawn and garden income)
	7 200	+	9 000	+	21 000	+	2 500			=	2 500	+	37 200	
(5)									+550				+550	(Tree-lopping income)
	7 200	+	9 000	+	21 000	+	2 500	+	550	=	2 500	+	37 750	
(6)	−450												−450	(Wages expense)
	6 750	+	9 000	+	21 000	+	2 500	+	550	=	2 500	+	37 300	
(7)							−800						−800	(Fuel supplies expense)
	6 750	+	9 000	+	21 000	+	1 700	+	550	=	2 500	+	36 500	

Assets = **Liabilities** + **Equity**

$39 000 = $39 000

In transaction (6), the benefits received from employees had been used by the time payment was made. Thus the payment represents expenses that reduced the asset cash at bank as well as equity by equal amounts of $450. The initial purchase of fuel supplies in transaction (3) resulted in the acquisition of an asset that will benefit several accounting periods. The measurement of fuel supplies at the end of the period indicated that $800 of the supplies had been used during the period and this is treated as an expense by decreasing fuel supplies and decreasing equity.

Transactions 8, 9 and 10   As one last illustration of the effect of transactions on the accounting equation, assume that on 31 January Darren's Lawn and Gardening Services collected the account receivable recognised in transaction (5) — transaction (8); and paid the amount due to Adam Fuel Ltd — transaction (9) — for the purchase of fuel supplies in transaction (3). In addition, Darren withdrew $200 from the business for his personal use — transaction (10). The effects of these transactions on the accounting equation are demonstrated in (8), (9) and (10) overleaf.

The effect of the collection of the account receivable in transaction (8) is to increase one asset (cash at bank) and decrease another asset (accounts receivable). There is no effect on total assets and no effect on liabilities or equity. The payment of the account payable in transaction (9) results in a decrease in cash at bank and an equal decrease in liabilities, with no effect on equity. The drawings by Darren in transaction (10) decrease cash at bank and equity by equal amounts.

	Assets					=	Liabilities	+	Equity	
	Cash at Bank	+ Lawn and Garden Equipment	+ Vehicle	+ Fuel Supplies	+ Accounts Receivable	=	Accounts Payable	+	Darren Jones, Capital	
(1)	$35 000					=			$35 000	
(2)	−30 000	+9 000	+21 000			=				
	5 000 +	9 000 +	21 000			=			35 000	
(3)				+2 500		=	+2 500			
	5 000 +	9 000 +	21 000 +	2 500		=	2 500 +		35 000	
(4)	+2 200								+2 200	(Lawn and garden income)
	7 200 +	9 000 +	21 000 +	2 500		=	2 500 +		37 200	
(5)					+550				+550	(Tree-lopping income)
	7 200 +	9 000 +	21 000 +	2 500 +	550	=	2 500 +		37 750	
(6)	−450								−450	(Wages expense)
	6 750 +	9 000 +	21 000 +	2 500 +	550	=	2 500 +		37 300	
(7)				−800					−800	(Fuel supplies expense)
	6 750 +	9 000 +	21 000 +	1 700 +	550	=	2 500 +		36 500	
(8)	+550				−550					
	7 300 +	9 000 +	21 000 +	1 700		=	2 500 +		36 500	
(9)	−2 500						−2 500			
	4 800 +	9 000 +	21 000 +	1 700		=			36 500	
(10)	−200								−200	(Drawings)
	4 600 +	9 000 +	21 000 +	1 700		=			36 300	
			$36 300						**$36 300**	

A review of this illustration brings out two important facts:
1. Every transaction affected at least two components of the equation. This dual recording process, known as **double-entry accounting**, is the method followed in the vast majority of accounting systems.
2. After the effects of each transaction were recorded, the equation remained in balance, with the sum of the assets equal to the sum of the liabilities and equity. Under double-entry accounting, this must always be the case.

Observe that, after all transactions have been recorded, Darren's equity (or capital) is $36 300, consisting of the $35 000 he invested to start the business plus $1500 profit, representing the excess of income ($2750) over expenses ($1250) for the period, minus the $200 drawings. In addition, total assets of the business are $36 300, and the business has no liabilities. Assets have therefore increased by $1300 during the period.

After taking the effects of the preceding transactions into account (the accounting period in this case is 1 month), we arrive at the financial statements for Darren's Lawn and Gardening Services shown in figure 2.7.

DARREN'S LAWN AND GARDENING SERVICES
Balance Sheet
as at 31 January 2012

ASSETS		EQUITY	
Cash at bank	$ 4 600	Darren Jones, Capital	$36 300
Fuel supplies	1 700		
Lawn and garden equipment	9 000		
Vehicle	21 000		
	$36 300		$36 300

Income Statement
for the month ended 31 January 2012

INCOME		
Lawn and garden income	$2200	
Tree-lopping income	550	$2750
EXPENSES		
Fuel supplies expense	$ 800	
Wages expense	450	
		1250
PROFIT		$1500

Statement of Changes in Equity
for the month ended 31 January 2012

Darren Jones, Capital — 2 January 2012	$35 000
Profit for the month	1 500
	36 500
Less: Drawings	200
Darren Jones, Capital — 31 January 2012	$36 300

Statement of Cash Flows
for the month ended 31 January 2012

CASH FLOWS FROM OPERATING ACTIVITIES		
Cash received from customers ($2200 + $550)	$ 2 750	
Cash paid to suppliers and employees ($2500 + $450)	(2 950)	
Net cash used in operating activities		$ (200)
CASH FLOWS FROM INVESTING ACTIVITIES		
Purchase of lawn and garden equipment	(9 000)	
Purchase of vehicle	(21 000)	
Net cash used in investing activities		(30 000)
CASH FLOWS FROM FINANCING ACTIVITIES		
Investment by owner	35 000	
Drawings by owner	(200)	
Net cash from financing activities		34 800
Net increase in cash held		4 600
Cash at beginning of month		—
Cash at end of month		$ 4 600

Figure 2.7 Financial statements for Darren's Lawn and Gardening Services

Accounting entity assumption, p. 37
Accounting equation, p. 32
Accounts payable, p. 33
Accounts receivable, p. 34
Accrual basis, p. 37
Assets, p. 32
Balance sheet (statement of financial position), p. 31
Cash movements, p. 30
Comparability, p. 39
Consistency, p. 39
Creditors, p. 33
Debtors, p. 34

Double-entry accounting, p. 44
Drawings, p. 34
Economic substance, p. 38
Equity, p. 33
Expenses, p. 34
Faithful representation, p. 39
Financial performance, p. 30
Financial position, p. 30
Financing activities, p. 31
Going concern assumption, p. 37
Income, p. 34
Income statement, p. 33
Investing activities, p. 31

Liabilities, p. 33
Loss, p. 34
Materiality, p. 39
Net assets, p. 32
Operating activities, p. 31
Operating statement, p. 33
Period assumption, p. 38
Profit, p. 34
Profit or loss statement, p. 33
Relevance, p. 38
Reliability, p. 38
Statement of cash flows, p. 35
Understandability, p. 39

DISCUSSION QUESTIONS

1. Discuss the meaning of 'performance' both for business entities and for not-for-profit entities. Is performance able to be expressed totally in financial terms?
2. Define the terms *assets*, *liabilities* and *equity*. Are these terms related in any way? If so, how?
3. A local restaurant is noted for its fine food, as evidenced by the large number of customers. A customer was heard to remark that the secret of the restaurant's success was its fine chef. Would you regard the chef as an asset of the business? If so, would you include the chef on the balance sheet of the business and at what value?
4. The local parkland is owned and maintained by the local government council. Is the parkland an asset of the council and should it be included on its balance sheet?
5. Moonshine Enterprises hired an accountant at the rate of $2000 per week. The person is to commence duty on 1 February. On 1 February, does the business have a liability in respect of the accountant's salary? Explain.
6. Discuss the significance of the following assumptions in the preparation of an entity's financial statements:
   (a) entity assumption
   (b) accrual basis assumption
   (c) going concern assumption
   (d) period assumption.
7. What is meant by the terms *relevance* and *reliability/faithful representation* in the context of information to be included in financial statements?
8. Distinguish between the concepts of consistency and comparability. Should the same accounting method always be applied consistently in financial statements?
9. What is meant by the requirement that information to be included in financial statements should be 'material'?
10. Explain the concept of 'double entry' in the preparation of financial statements.

EXERCISES

Note: The impact of GST is ignored in all exercises and problems in this chapter for reasons of simplicity.

LO 1

Exercise 2.1 PREPARING A BALANCE SHEET

The accounting records for Jill Jordan's Event Management Services on 31 March 2013 are presented below (in alphabetical order):

Accounts payable	$ 64 000	Land	$240 000
Accounts receivable	72 000	Mortgage payable	580 000
Building	600 000	Office equipment	120 000
Cash at bank	66 000	Office supplies	18 000

Required

A. Use these items to prepare a balance sheet in account format, similar to the one in figure 2.1. (*Note* that a major item is missing in the list.)

B. Use the items to prepare a balance sheet in narrative form, similar to the one in figure 2.2.

Exercise 2.2 INCOME STATEMENT AND ANALYSIS

LO 1

During the year ended 30 June 2013, Jenny's Sitters, a provider of professional baby-sitting services, had collected receipts from clients for a total value of $695 000. Wages of $504 000 had been paid to the baby sitters, rental of vehicles and electricity costs were $27 000 and $8550 respectively for the year, and salary paid to Jenny's personal assistant was $69 000.

Required

A. Prepare an income statement for the year for Jenny's Sitters.

B. Who made more out of the baby-sitting business — Jenny or her personal assistant? What action might Jenny take to increase the profitability of the business in the year ended 30 June 2014?

Exercise 2.3 ANALYSIS OF EQUITY

LO 1, 3

Cathy Oakes is a self-employed piano teacher operating her business from home. She keeps her accounting records for business activities completely separate from her records for personal activities. At 30 June 2013, Cathy had business assets and liabilities worth $75 000 and $42 000 respectively. At 30 June 2014, Cathy had business assets and liabilities worth $78 000 and $36 000 respectively.

Required

A. If Cathy did not contribute to or withdraw from the business during the year 2013–14, what was the profit/loss for the year?

B. If Cathy had withdrawn $24 000 during the year, calculate the profit/loss for the year.

C. If Cathy had contributed $30 000 and withdrawn $16 000, prepare a statement of changes in equity for the year ended 30 June 2014.

Exercise 2.4 DETERMINING PROFIT FROM EQUITY BALANCES

LO 1

Equity balances for Richard Burke appearing in the balance sheets of Burke's Financial Services as at 30 June 2012, 2013 and 2014 are set out below:

	30 June 2014	30 June 2013	30 June 2012
EQUITY			
Richard Burke, Capital	$136 500	$150 000	$140 000

During 2013–14, Richard withdrew $100 000 for personal use and also contributed additional capital of $45 000. During 2012–13, he withdrew $30 000 capital from the business, and withdrew $90 000 cash for his own use in anticipation of profits.

Required

Determine the profit/loss earned by the business in each of the 2 years ended 30 June 2013 and 30 June 2014.

Exercise 2.5 OPERATING, INVESTING AND FINANCING ACTIVITIES

LO 1

Classify each of the following activities as being either operating, investing or financing for the purpose of preparing a statement of cash flows. Indicate whether there is an inflow [I] or outflow [O] of cash:

(a) sale of plant and equipment for cash
(b) payment of rent for offices
(c) withdrawal of cash by the owner
(d) repayment of a bank loan
(e) cash purchase of a truck by a manufacturing company
(f) cash purchase of a fleet of motor vehicles by a car dealership
(g) borrowing of money from a finance company on a long-term basis
(h) cash collected from the customers of the business.

Exercise 2.6 ELEMENTS IN FINANCIAL STATEMENTS

A friend who has established a new tea house, T-Time, has asked you to give some advice as to the contents of financial statements. Specifically, you have been asked to indicate where, if at all, each of the following items will be reported in the financial statements of the business:

(a) contribution of cash by your friend to the business
(b) purchase of cake display cabinets on credit
(c) electricity costs paid
(d) cash received for tea and cake sold
(e) the owner's house
(f) hiring costs of a water cooler, paid in cash
(g) money withdrawn by your friend to pay a large medical bill for a member of the family
(h) cash held by the business at the end of the year
(i) money borrowed for purchase of shop fittings.

Required

Indicate whether these items would appear in T-Time's balance sheet, income statement, statement of changes in equity, and/or statement of cash flows. For those items included in the statement of cash flows, indicate whether the item relates to operating activities, investing activities, or financing activities. (*Hint:* Some items may appear in more than one financial statement.)

Exercise 2.7 ASSUMPTIONS AND CHARACTERISTICS OF INFORMATION

Identify by letter the assumption or characteristic of information which best represents the situations given.

A. Accounting entity assumption
B. Accrual basis assumption
C. Going concern assumption
D. Period assumption
E. Relevance
F. Reliability/faithful representation
G. Materiality
H. Comparability

_____ 1. The reporting of accounting information should be free from personal bias.
_____ 2. In a single proprietorship, the owner's house and car are not recorded in the records of the business.
_____ 3. The cost of stationery is not shown separately in the income statement.
_____ 4. Services provided by a business entity are recorded before the receipt of cash.
_____ 5. Machinery held by the business under a long-term lease arrangement is recorded by the business as its own asset.
_____ 6. An expense is recorded in the year in which an asset or benefit is consumed in the process of carrying on the entity's business.
_____ 7. Assets are not recorded at liquidation prices.
_____ 8. Consistent accounting policies and methods are used in the preparation of financial statements from one year to another.

Exercise 2.8 BUSINESS TRANSACTIONS

For each of the following, describe a transaction that would have the stated effect on the accounting equation:

1. Increase an asset and increase a liability
2. Increase one asset and decrease another asset
3. Decrease an asset and decrease equity
4. Increase an asset and increase equity
5. Decrease a liability and decrease an asset.

Exercise 2.9 PREPARATION OF A BALANCE SHEET

Month-end balance sheet amounts for the accounting practice of Nelson Pennock, an accountant, for 3 consecutive months of 2013 are shown below. The information is complete except for the balance in the Capital account.

	31 October	30 November	31 December
Cash at bank	$18 200	$ 7 800	$ 6 000
Accounts receivable	32 200	30 000	16 100
Prepaid insurance	1 400	3 600	3 200
Office equipment	59 600	59 400	78 600
Building	82 000	81 600	81 200
Land	6 000	6 000	6 000
Accounts payable	20 200	6 200	6 000
Wages payable	10 200	8 200	9 600
Mortgage payable	69 400	68 600	67 800
Nelson Pennock, Capital	?	?	?

Required
A. Determine the balance in Nelson Pennock's Capital account at the end of each month.
B. Assuming that Nelson made no additional investments and did not withdraw any money from the business during the 3 months, determine the profit for November and for December.
C. Prepare a balance sheet for the business at the end of December 2013. (The heading should read: Nelson Pennock, Accountant.)

Exercise 2.10 EXPLAINING ACCOUNTING TRANSACTIONS

The following schedule shows the effect of several transactions on the accounting equation of Bryan Kruse and the balance of each item in the equation after each transaction. Write a sentence to explain the nature of each transaction.

	Assets				=	Liabilities	+	Equity
	Cash at Bank	+ Accounts Receivable +	Office Equipment +	Office Supplies =		Accounts Payable +		Bryan Kruse, Capital
(1)	+$30 000				=			+$30 000
(2)	−10 500		+10 500					
	19 500		+ 10 500		=			30 000
(3)	+3 000							+3 000
	22 500		+ 10 500		=			33 000
(4)		+9 000						+9 000
	22 500 +	9 000 +	10 500		=			42 000
(5)				+4 500		+4 500		
	22 500 +	9 000 +	10 500 +	4 500 =		4 500 +		42 000
(6)	+6 000	−6 000						
	28 500 +	3 000 +	10 500 +	4 500 =		4 500 +		42 000
(7)	−12 000							−12 000
	16 500 +	3 000 +	10 500 +	4 500 =		4 500 +		30 000
(8)				−3 000				−3 000
	16 500 +	3 000 +	10 500 +	1 500 =		4 500 +		27 000
(9)	−4 500					−4 500		
	12 000 +	3 000 +	10 500 +	1 500 =		0 +		27 000

Exercise 2.11 RECORDING TRANSACTIONS

Jeff's Pool Repairs began operations on 1 August 2013 and completed the following transactions during the first month.

1. Jeff Drain deposited $50 000 of his personal funds in a current account at a bank opened in the name of the business.
2. Pool repair equipment was purchased at a cost of $30 000, of which $20 000 was paid in cash. A loan payable was given for the remainder of $10 000.
3. Jeff collected $6000 from customers for repair services performed.
4. Rent was paid for the month of August, $2400.
5. Supplies amounting to $2740 were purchased on credit.
6. Wages of $1000 were paid as well as an account for electricity, $540.
7. Jeff paid for the supplies purchased in (5) above.
8. Supplies used during August amounted to $1280.

Required

A. Prepare a schedule similar to that on page 41. List the following assets, liabilities and equity as column headings: Cash at Bank; Supplies; Equipment; Loan Payable; Accounts Payable; J. Drain, Capital.
B. Show the effects of each of the transactions on the accounts listed. Indicate totals after each transaction and complete the schedule as shown on page 44.
C. Prepare an income statement and a statement of changes in equity for the month ended 31 August 2013, and a balance sheet as at 31 August 2013.

Exercise 2.12 PREPARATION OF INCOME STATEMENT AND BALANCE SHEET

Peter and Anne Nesbit are the joint owners of Pebble Beach Caravan Park, which is near a swimming beach popular during the summer months. The park provides not only camping facilities for caravans and tents but also up-market cabins with kitchenettes and ensuites. For the year ended 30 June 2014, Peter and Anne determined the following financial information for their business:

Cash on hand	$ 20 000	Accounts payable	$ 87 000
Buildings purchased	420 000	Accounts receivable	8 000
Income — cabins	272 000	Income — camping	185 000
Salaries and wages	220 000	Supplies on hand	15 000
Supplies used	71 000	Other expenses	45 000
Other equipment purchased	63 000		

The market value of the buildings had risen to $500 000 by 30 June 2014.

Required

A. Prepare an income statement for Pebble Beach Caravan Park for the year ended 30 June 2014.
B. Prepare a balance sheet for the business as at 30 June 2014.
C. Explain why you have used a particular valuation for the buildings in the balance sheet.

Exercise 2.13 EFFECT OF TRANSACTIONS ON A BALANCE SHEET

The following events occurred during the month of September 2013 for the business of Joyce's Manicure Service:

Sept.	1	Joyce deposited $350 000 cash into the business bank account.
	2	Premises were purchased at a cost of $180 000 cash.
	4	Manicure equipment was purchased and installed at a cost of $60 000, $40 000 being paid in cash and the rest being borrowed from the local bank.
	6	Manicure services were provided to customers for $12 000 cash and $2000 on credit.
	7	Wages paid to an employee for the week amount to $1000 cash.

Required

Show the effects of business transactions on a balance sheet by preparing a new balance sheet for Joyce's Manicure Service after *each* transaction has occurred.

Exercise 2.14 EFFECTS OF TRANSACTIONS ON FINANCIAL STATEMENTS

Indicate the effect of each of the following transactions on any or all of the four financial statements of a business. Apart from indicating the financial statement(s) involved, use appropriate phrases such as 'increase total assets', 'decrease equity', 'increase income', 'decrease cash flow' to describe the transaction concerned.

1. Purchase equipment for cash.
2. Provide services to a client, with payment to be received within 40 days.
3. Pay a liability.
4. Invest additional cash into the business by the owner.
5. Collect an account receivable in cash.
6. Pay wages to employees.
7. Receive the electricity bill in the mail, to be paid within 30 days.
8. Sell a piece of equipment for cash.
9. Withdraw cash by the owner for private use.
10. Borrow money on a long-term basis from a bank.

Exercise 2.15 DETERMINATION OF PROFIT BY EXAMINING EQUITY CHANGES

Fred Ballew began a small business on 1 July 2011 by depositing $300 000 into a business bank account. On 30 June for the next 3 years, the assets and liabilities of the business were as follows:

30 June	Total assets	Total liabilities
2012	$ 720 000	$380 000
2013	890 000	420 000
2014	1 040 000	510 000

Required

By analysing the changes in equity each year, calculate the profit (loss) made by the business for each year ending 30 June, assuming the following events also occurred:

1. On 1 January 2012, Fred withdrew $40 000 in cash from the business for personal use.
2. On 28 August 2012, Fred invested additional cash of $70 000 into the business.
3. On 31 July 2013, Fred invested additional cash of $50 000 into the business.
4. On 28 January 2014, Fred withdrew $30 000 in cash for personal use.

PROBLEMS

Problem 2.1 PREPARING FINANCIAL STATEMENTS ★

★ Basic

★★ Moderate

★★★ Challenging

Financial data for Safety Hire as of 30 June 2013 are:

Accounts receivable	$126 000	Wages expense	$150 000
Equipment hire income	340 000	Advertising expense	60 000
Accounts payable	80 000	Land	150 000
Amy Irving, Capital	?	Hire equipment	360 000
Cash at bank	90 000	Loan payable	100 000
Mortgage payable	260 000	Electricity expense	36 000
Building	170 000	Telephone expense	15 000

Required

Prepare an income statement for the month of June and a balance sheet in account format for Safety Hire as at 30 June 2013.

Problem 2.2 PREPARING FINANCIAL STATEMENTS ★

Asset, liability, equity, income and expense amounts for Pam's Interior Decorating at 30 June 2012 are presented below:

Cash at bank	$ 45 600	Advertising expense	$ 72 000
Accounts receivable	235 200	Insurance expense	16 000
Supplies	52 800	Rent expense	66 000
Equipment	251 200	Supplies expense	25 200
Accounts payable	67 400	Telephone expense	24 400
Pam Jones, Capital	?	Electricity expense	34 000
Decorating services income	772 000	Wages expense	222 000

Required

A. Prepare an income statement for the business for the year ended 30 June 2012.

B. Prepare a balance sheet in narrative format as at 30 June 2012.

Problem 2.3 DETERMINING MISSING ELEMENTS IN ACCOUNTING EQUATION ★

Calculate the two missing amounts for each independent case below.

Case	Total assets	Total liabilities	Equity	Total income	Total expenses	Profit (loss)
A	$120 000	$69 000	?	$123 000	?	$57 000
B	$135 000	?	$85 500	$124 500	$96 000	?
C	?	$66 000	$85 500	$135 000	?	($15 000)
D	$ 75 000	?	$31 500	?	$34 500	($12 000)
E	?	$60 000	$84 000	?	$48 000	$36 000

Problem 2.4 IDENTIFYING TRANSACTIONS FROM BALANCE SHEET CHANGES ★★

During June 2012, Mark Fulcher started a new business, Mark's Cafe. After each June transaction, Mark prepared a balance sheet, as shown below.

(1)

MARK'S CAFE
Balance Sheet
as at 4 June 2012

ASSETS		EQUITY	
Cash at bank	$150 000	Mark Fulcher, Capital	$150 000

(2)

MARK'S CAFE
Balance Sheet
as at 13 June 2012

ASSETS		EQUITY	
Cash at bank	$ 92 000	Mark Fulcher, Capital	$150 000
Equipment	58 000		
	$150 000		$150 000

(3)

MARK'S CAFE
Balance Sheet
as at 18 June 2012

ASSETS		LIABILITIES AND EQUITY	
Cash at bank	$ 52 000	Loan payable	$ 80 000
Equipment	58 000	Mark Fulcher, Capital	150 000
Land	20 000		
Building	100 000		
	$230 000		$230 000

(4)

MARK'S CAFE
Balance Sheet
as at 26 June 2012

ASSETS		LIABILITIES AND EQUITY	
Cash at bank	$ 52 000	Accounts payable	$ 36 000
Food supplies	36 000	Loan payable	80 000
Equipment	58 000		116 000
Land	20 000	Mark Fulcher, Capital	150 000
Building	100 000		
	$266 000		$266 000

Required

Describe the nature of each of the four transactions that took place during June.

Problem 2.5 PREPARATION OF FINANCIAL STATEMENTS ★★   LO 1

Holman Industries began operations early in January 2013. On 31 December 2013, records showed the following asset, liability, equity, income and expense amounts:

Accounts receivable	$ 51 200	Alicia Holman, Capital	$?
Rent expense	27 000	Electricity expense	14 400
Cash at bank	20 500	Telephone expense	9 800
Supplies expense	10 500	Advertising expense	25 000
Accounts payable	19 000	Insurance expense	5 000
Service income	295 000	Wages expense	88 000
Supplies	22 000	Drawings	46 800
Equipment	96 000		

Required

A. Prepare an income statement for Holman Industries for the year ended 31 December 2013.
B. Prepare a balance sheet as at 31 December 2013.
C. Prepare a statement of changes in equity for 2013.

Problem 2.6 CORRECTION OF FINANCIAL STATEMENTS ★★   LO 1

A recently graduated accountant prepared the financial statements below for Tina's Tennis School at the end of the first year of operations.

TINA'S TENNIS SCHOOL
Income Statement
for the year ended 30 June 2012

INCOME		
Tennis coaching fees		$230 000
EXPENSES		
Tennis court rental	$36 000	
Wages expense	86 000	
Supplies expense	32 400	
Electricity expense	13 500	
T. Ball, Drawings	22 400	
Depreciation expense		
— vehicle	6 400	
— equipment	8 600	
		205 300
PROFIT		$ 24 700

(continued)

```
                        TINA'S TENNIS SCHOOL
                            Balance Sheet
                          as at 30 June 2012

ASSETS                                LIABILITIES
Cash at bank            $ 25 200      Accounts payable              $26 000
Equipment                 35 600
Vehicle                   41 400      EQUITY
                                      T. Ball, Capital               76 200

                        $102 200                                  $102 200
```

Additional analysis revealed the following:
1. Tennis coaching fees of $8000 (receivable from a customer) were unrecorded at 30 June.
2. Additional equipment of $9000 purchased on credit at the end of the month had not been recorded.
3. Supplies on hand at 30 June costing $13 200 were included in expenses.
4. Wages of $8200 were payable at 30 June.

Required
A. Prepare a corrected income statement for the year ended 30 June 2012.
B. Prepare a corrected balance sheet in narrative form as at 30 June 2012.
C. Prepare a statement of changes in equity for the year ended 30 June 2012.

Problem 2.7   PERFORMANCE ASSESSMENT FROM FINANCIAL STATEMENTS ★★   LO 1, 3

The Party Shop was established as a sole trader business, specialising in providing party hire services, on 1 January 2013. The owner, Claire Damico, contributed $150 000 in cash to the business and did not withdraw funds for the year.
    For the year ended 31 December 2013, the following events occurred in the business:
1. Received $420 000 cash for party hire services provided.
2. Paid cash expenses of $300 000 for office supplies and labour.
3. At the end of the year, the business purchased a vehicle for $48 000 cash and a new computer system for $75 000 cash.
4. The business leases premises as an office. Lease rental payments for the year amounted to $49 500.
5. The business purchased for $120 000 a block of land on which Claire hopes to build an office in the new year. To help pay for the land, the business had to borrow $45 000 from a bank.

Required
A. Prepare an income statement for The Party Shop for the year ended 31 December 2013.
B. Prepare a statement of cash flows for The Party Shop for the year ended 31 December 2013.
C. Can a business operate profitably and still have a net cash outflow for the year? Which do you believe is a better indicator of the entity's performance — profit or cash flow? Explain.

Problem 2.8   RECORDING TRANSACTIONS AND PREPARING FINANCIAL STATEMENTS ★★   LO 1, 3

Financial balances for the business of Matina Hana on 30 June 2013 are provided below in a table in accounting equation form similar to the chapter illustrations.

	Assets				=	Liabilities		+	Equity
	Cash at Bank	Accounts Receivable	Office Supplies	Equipment	=	Accounts Payable	Loan Payable	+	Matina Hana, Capital
Bal.	$22 000 +	$30 000 +	$3 000 +	$48 000	=	$7 000 +	$24 000 +		$72 000

During July, the business of Matina Hana entered into the following transactions:
1. Collected $16 000 of the accounts receivable.
2. Paid $3600 on accounts payable.
3. Purchased equipment for $16 200. Paid $6000 in cash and signed a loan agreement for $10 200 to pay for the remainder of the equipment.
4. Billed customers for services performed, $12 600.
5. Purchased supplies on credit, $750.
6. Paid expenses in cash, $5850 (wages, $3300; electricity $1650; advertising, $900).
7. The owner withdrew $4000 for personal use.
8. Used $1800 of supplies during the period.

Required
A. List the 30 June balances for assets, liabilities and equity in table form as shown on the previous page.
B. Record the effects of each transaction. Show the total of each column after recording each transaction.
C. Prepare an income statement, a statement of changes in equity and a statement of cash flows for the month ended 31 July 2013, and a balance sheet (account format) as at 31 July 2013.

Problem 2.9 CLASSIFYING ITEMS FOR FINANCIAL STATEMENTS ★★ **LO 3**

The following list of items relate to the business of Gary's Men's Wear:
1. cash paid into the business by Gary to begin operations
2. racks used to display merchandise to customers
3. building leased for 2 years, with rent payable monthly in advance
4. men's wear items obtained from a manufacturer
5. amount owing to the manufacturer for merchandise acquired
6. insurance premium on the merchandise paid in advance
7. cash withdrawn by Gary for personal use
8. wages paid to casual employee
9. amount borrowed long-term from the bank
10. sales of merchandise to customers
11. spare change kept in the cash register at the checkout counter.

Required
A. Select a suitable name to describe each of the listed items.
B. Classify each of the items as appropriate for inclusion in the balance sheet of the business.

Problem 2.10 RECORDING TRANSACTIONS AND PREPARING FINANCIAL STATEMENTS ★★ **LO 1, 3**

Financial balances for Xiu Miao, Solicitor, on 30 June 2013 are given below in a table in accounting equation form similar to the chapter illustrations.

	Assets				=	Liabilities		+	Equity
	Cash at Bank +	Accounts Receivable +	Office Supplies +	Office Equipment =		Accounts Payable +	Loan Payable +		Xiu Miao, Capital
Bal.	$16 000 +	$26 500 +	$2 000 +	$39 750 =		$4 850 +	$17 500 +		$61 900

During the early part of July, the business entered into the following transactions:
1. Paid $4720 on accounts payable.
2. Collected $14 800 of the accounts receivable.
3. Purchased office equipment for $12 400. Paid $3000 in cash and signed a loan agreement for $9400.
4. Billed customers for legal services performed, $11 640.
5. Purchased supplies on credit, $680.

6. Paid expenses in cash, $9300 (advertising, $1200; rent, $4000; wages, $4100).
7. Used $1440 of supplies during the period.
8. Collected $13 500 of accounts receivable.
9. The owner withdrew $1200 for personal use.

Required

A. List the 30 June balances for assets, liabilities and equity in table form as shown above.
B. Record the effects of each transaction. Show the total of each column after recording each transaction as illustrated in the text.
C. Prepare an income statement and a statement of changes in equity for the month and a balance sheet in narrative format as at 31 July 2013.

Problem 2.11 IDENTIFYING TRANSACTIONS FROM BALANCE SHEET CHANGES ★★   **LO 3**

Eva Brantley obtained registration to practise as a chiropractor, and spent the month of July 2013 setting up her business — E. Brantley, Chiropractor.

Eva prepared a new balance sheet after each transaction which occurred. During July, the following balance sheets were prepared.

(1)

E. BRANTLEY, CHIROPRACTOR
Balance Sheet
as at 1 July 2013

ASSETS		EQUITY	
Cash at bank	$170 000	E. Brantley, Capital	$170 000

(2)

E. BRANTLEY, CHIROPRACTOR
Balance Sheet
as at 8 July 2013

ASSETS		LIABILITIES AND EQUITY	
Cash at bank	$100 000	Loan payablo	$120 000
Land	50 000	E. Brantley, Capital	170 000
Building	140 000		
	$290 000		$290 000

(3)

E. BRANTLEY, CHIROPRACTOR
Balance Sheet
as at 15 July 2013

ASSETS		LIABILITIES AND EQUITY	
Cash at bank	$100 000	Accounts payable	$ 7 000
Office supplies	7 000	Loan payable	120 000
Land	50 000	E. Brantley, Capital	170 000
Building	140 000		
	$297 000		$297 000

(4)

E. BRANTLEY, CHIROPRACTOR
Balance Sheet
as at 22 July 2013

ASSETS		LIABILITIES AND EQUITY	
Cash at bank	$ 90 000	Accounts payable	$ 7 000
Office supplies	7 000	Loan payable	110 000
Land	50 000	E. Brantley, Capital	170 000
Building	140 000		
	$287 000		$287 000

(5)		E. BRANTLEY, CHIROPRACTOR		
		Balance Sheet		
		as at 31 July 2013		

ASSETS		LIABILITIES AND EQUITY	
Cash at bank	$ 82 000	Accounts payable	$ 7 000
Office supplies	7 000	Loan payable	110 000
Land	50 000	E. Brantley, Capital	162 000
Building	140 000		
	$279 000		$279 000

Required

Write an appropriate statement describing each of the five transactions that occurred during July 2013.

Problem 2.12 RECORDING TRANSACTIONS AND PREPARING FINANCIAL STATEMENTS ★★   LO 1, 3

Gerald's Shoe Repairs began operations on 1 August 2014 and completed the following transactions during the first month.

1. Gerald Hirst deposited $24 000 of his personal funds in a current account at a bank opened in the name of the business.
2. Shoe repair equipment was purchased at a cost of $16 000, of which $10 000 was paid in cash. A loan payable was given for the remainder of $6000.
3. Gerald collected $3000 from customers for repair services performed.
4. Rent was paid for the month of August, $1200.
5. Supplies amounting to $1700 were purchased on credit.
6. Wages of $500 were paid as well as an account for electricity, $250.
7. Gerald paid for the supplies purchased in (5) above.
8. Supplies used during August amounted to $280.

Required

A. Prepare a schedule similar to that on page 44. List the following assets, liabilities and equity as column headings: Cash at Bank; Supplies; Equipment; Loan Payable; Accounts Payable; G. Hirst, Capital.
B. Show the effects of each of the transactions on the accounts listed. Indicate totals after each transaction and complete the schedule.
C. Prepare an income statement, a statement of cash flows and a statement of changes in equity for the month ended 31 August 2014.
D. Prepare a balance sheet as at 31 August 2014.

Problem 2.13 CORRECTING ERRORS AND PREPARING FINANCIAL STATEMENTS ★★   LO 1

Baker's Bread Shop was established on 1 April 2013 with an initial investment of $100 000 by the owner. During the first few weeks of business, the owner employed a part-time record-keeper (with only a few months training in accounting) who listed the business's assets as follows:

Accounts payable	$ 37 100
Buildings	100 000
Cash at bank	31 000
Furniture	12 000
A. Baker, Capital	150 000
Baking supplies	5 600
Loan payable	20 700

The record-keeper also listed the business's liabilities and equity as follows:

Accounts receivable	$20 000
Land	43 200
Mortgage payable	40 000
Cash drawings by A. Baker	36 000

Required

A. Assuming that the amounts above are correct, prepare a corrected balance sheet in narrative form.
B. Determine the amount of profit (loss) made by the business during the period of its first few weeks of existence, assuming that the owner had invested an additional $20 000 into the business just before the above amounts were calculated by the record-keeper.
C. Prepare a statement of changes in equity for the period.

Problem 2.14 ANALYSING FINANCIAL STATEMENT ELEMENTS ★★★ **LO 3**

Dylan Andrews offers web design services to small businesses. He has set up a sole proprietorship business named DA Design. Dylan has collected the following information relating to his business activities at the end of the financial year:

Office supplies	$ 3 000	Accounts payable	$ 2 160
Office supplies expense	1 680	Cash at bank	16 890
Telephone expense	510	Computer equipment	16 500
Motor vehicle expense	660	Advertising expense	1 020
Accounts receivable	3 000	Web design income	19 500
Bank loan	15 000		

The following information was disclosed from examining Dylan's bank statement:

Web design receipts	$16 500	Payments to suppliers	$ 4 710
Initial contribution by Dylan	6 600	Repayment of loan	3 000
Bank loan received	18 000	Computer equipment purchase	16 500

Required

A. Without preparing formal financial statements, calculate the following:
  1. profit/loss for the year
  2. total assets at the end of the year
  3. total liabilities at the end of the year
  4. Dylan Andrews' capital balance at the end of the year
  5. net cash inflow/outflow for the year.
B. If Dylan had withdrawn $6000 in cash during the year, what effect would this have (increase, decrease, no change) on the figures you calculated in requirement A?

Problem 2.15 PREPARATION OF FINANCIAL STATEMENTS ★★★ **LO 1**

Ryan Stallard has just finished his training as a fitness instructor and personal trainer. He has been working part-time during his training program in a local gym, and has saved $15 000 over the past 2 years. Ryan decided he would like to open his own business as a personal trainer, and so he decided to open a business bank account in the name of Fit Pro and transferred all his savings from his personal bank account to the business account on 1 September 2013.

Ryan has been very busy in his new business, getting new clients, purchasing equipment and scheduling fitness sessions. Unfortunately Ryan has not had any accounting training, and so he has not kept formal financial records. He has deposited all the money he has received from his clients into the business bank account, and has paid all of his business expenses out of the business bank account. Ryan has also recorded in his diary all the fitness sessions he has delivered for which his clients still owe him money.

Ryan has printed out his bank statements for the first 6 months (1 September 2013 to 28 February 2014), has reviewed other invoices and bills he has received in that time period, and has prepared the following information:

1. The bank statements show that the total amount of money deposited into the account for the 6-month period was $24 000, which included the $15 000 transferred from Ryan's personal account.
2. There were payments made out of the bank account for the 6-month period which totalled $7500. Ryan has bills from suppliers that he has paid out of the bank account as follows:
    (a) Rent of small storeroom for storing his fitness equipment for 6 months, $750.
    (b) Electricity for the fitness studio for 6 months, $850.
    (c) Telephone accounts for 5 months from September 2013 to January 2014 amounting to $450.
    (d) Purchase of equipment, $4000.
    (e) Advertising flyers, $500.
    The remainder of the money taken out of the business bank account was used to pay Ryan's personal expenses.
3. Ryan has recorded in his diary that clients owe him $800 as at 28 February 2014 for fitness sessions he has already delivered.
4. Ryan has a few outstanding bills as follows:
    (a) Water bill for the 6 month period for $350.   (b) Telephone account for February 2014 for $110.

Required

A. Prepare an income statement for Fit Pro for the 6-month period from 1 September 2013 to 28 February 2014 from the information provided.
B. Prepare a balance sheet for Fit Pro as at 28 February 2014, and a statement of changes in equity for the 6-month period from the information provided.
C. Based on the financial statements prepared, do you believe Ryan should continue with his business venture? Why or why not?

DECISION ANALYSIS

Gavin Mackie financial statements

Gavin Mackie started a business as an engineering consultant a few years ago, and has been fairly successful in winning contracts and tenders. He would like to expand his business and employ a few graduate engineers to build his capacity and give the graduates an opportunity to gain valuable experience.

Gavin would like to purchase some vehicles and equipment as part of his expansion plans, but would need to borrow money from a bank to finance the purchases. He has approached a bank manager, who has requested some financial statements as a basis for assessing whether or not they will grant loan facilities.

Since Gavin has been focusing on his work, he has not had time to draw up a set of financial statements. He has managed to establish the following for the year ended 30 June 2013:

Cash in the business bank account at 30 June 2013	$ 3 000
Engineering consulting services billed to clients	400 000
Amounts customers owe Gavin at 30 June 2013 (already billed)	10 000
Cash paid to engineering subcontractors	120 000
Amounts owed to engineering subcontractors	20 000
Other engineering service expenses incurred and paid for	150 000
Motor vehicle	30 000
Equipment	25 000
Motor vehicle running expenses paid	5 000
Electricity and telephone expenses	4 000
Office rent for June 2013 still outstanding	2 500
Cash drawn out of the business bank account for personal use	8 000

Required

A. Using the information Gavin has provided, prepare an income statement and a balance sheet for the year ended 30 June 2013.

B. Discuss the elements of the financial statements you have prepared in part A above which the bank manager might be interested in when assessing whether or not to grant loan facilities to Gavin.

C. What information, in addition to the income statement and balance sheet, might the bank manager be interested in looking at before making a decision?

CRITICAL THINKING

Sporting glory — the great intangible

Read the following article from *Australian CPA*.

While rugby stars are heroes to many, when checking the books they become a complex intangible. Rosalind Whiting and Kyla Chapman investigate the merits of Human Resource Accounting in professional sport.

Australia, New Zealand and rugby union — a combination guaranteed to stir patriotic feelings across the Tasman! But what if we add accounting to this equation? Rugby players are the teams' most valuable assets, so should we be placing their value on the balance sheet? And if so, does it make any difference to the decisions that users of financial statements make?

Human resource accounting in professional sport

Professional sport has been prevalent in the United Kingdom and the United States for nearly 200 years. However, professional sport arrived later to Australia and New Zealand. In particular, the Kiwis only entered this arena in 1995 when the New Zealand Rugby Football Union (NZRFU) signed the Tri Nations sponsorship deal and removed all barriers preventing rugby union players being paid for their services. Player contract expenses in New Zealand now amount to over NZ$20 million annually, according to the NZRFU.

In the United Kingdom and the United States, the professional teams' financial accounts quite often incorporate human resource accounting (HRA). HRA is basically an addition to traditional accounting, in which a value for the employees is placed on the balance sheet and is amortised over a period of time, instead of expensing costs such as professional development.

There is debate about the merits of this process and the arguments are in line with those we have been hearing about intangibles in general. More recently, there has been worldwide movement towards recognising acquired identifiable intangible assets at fair value in the financial statements. So why not include an organisation's human resources? While (thankfully) most people agree that employees are valuable, there are accounting difficulties with the concept of ownership or control of the employees (asset definition) and the reliability of measurement.

Despite these concerns, one area where HRA does have some international acceptability is in accounting for professional sport, mainly because of the measurable player transfer costs. But there is still some variability in the reporting of human resource value, ranging from the capitalisation of signing and transfer fees through to player development costs or valuations.

To the authors' knowledge, HRA is not currently practised with Australia and New Zealand's professional sports teams. The absence of transfer fees between clubs when trading players may explain this.

Decision making

Accountants are required to provide information that assists users in assessing an organisation's financial and service performance and in making decisions about providing resources to, or doing business with, the firm.

The big question is whether HRA information is more useful to the decision maker than the alternative expensing treatment. Supporters of HRA argue that capitalised information is useful for strategic planning and management of employees, and provides a more accurate measure of the firm's status and total performance.

Those against HRA say it is too subjective to be useful and that it just imposes another cost on the organisation. Some detractors argue that it makes unprofitable organisations appear profitable simply because smart people work there. But those who believe in the efficiency of the market would argue that investors are not naive, and decisions would be unaffected by the way in which human resource information is presented.

Source: Excerpts from Rosalind Whiting and Kyla Chapman, 'Sporting glory — the great intangible', *Australian CPA*.

Required

Discuss whether rugby players are 'valuable assets' of a business, or an expense. Use the definitions of assets and expenses in this book to show which of the elements of the financial statements 'human resources' should be classified under.

Preparing balance sheets

In groups of three or four, consider the following people and their situations:

- a student who has just completed secondary school and started at university and is living at home with parents
- an adult who works full time.

For each situation, prepare a list of assets the person would typically own, and estimate the cost of each asset in dollars. Then prepare a list of liabilities, and estimate the cost of each liability in dollars. Using the accounting equation, calculate the equity of each of the two people and draw up a balance sheet for each. Display them on overhead transparencies and compare them with those developed by other groups in the class.

ETHICS AND GOVERNANCE

Kickbacks

Read the following article and answer the questions.

COCA-COLA said today that two former employees of its Shanghai bottling company had been arrested for corruption.

The two employees worked for Shanghai Shenmei Beverage and Food Co, which was licensed to produce Coca-Cola in China and which was part-owned by the US soft drink giant, a Hong Kong-based spokesman for Coca-Cola said.

'We can confirm that two former employees at our Shanghai (Shenmei) bottling plant have been detained by the police,' said the spokesman.

Coca-Cola dismissed reports that the case involved bribes to government officials, saying the investigation focused on 'allegations that the former employees extracted kickbacks from suppliers and embezzled from our bottler'.

One employee left the company in early 2008, while the other left in May when the allegations surfaced, the spokesman said.

The bottler is cooperating with police in the investigation, he said.

Coca-Cola did not provide further details but the official Xinhua news agency reported that up to 10 million yuan ($1.69 million) could have been misappropriated.

Source: AFP, News.com.au.

Required

A. In the article, who are the stakeholders in this situation?
B. What ethical issues are involved?
C. If it is normal business practice to bribe government officials in a country that you are dealing with but not in your own country, do you believe it is ethical to do so?
D. Do you believe one country has the right to impose its values on another in this regard? Consider how you would feel if another country tried to impose its values on your country, and consider what overriding human rights issues might be relevant.

FINANCIAL ANALYSIS

Refer to the latest financial report of JB Hi-Fi Limited on its website, www.jbhifi.com.au. Answer the following questions using the directors' declaration, consolidated figures in the financial statements, and notes to the financial statements.

1. What does the directors' declaration state? What, if anything, does this declaration say about the going concern assumption?
2. What were the total assets at the end of the financial year?

3. What were the total liabilities at the end of the financial year?
4. What was the total amount of equity?
5. State the accounting equation for JB Hi-Fi Limited in dollar figures at the end of the reporting period for the end and beginning of the last financial year.
6. Did the current assets increase or decrease over the year? By how much?
7. Did the current liabilities increase or decrease over the year? By how much?
8. Did non-current assets increase or decrease over the year? By how much?
9. What changes have occurred in the company's non-current liabilities over the year? Explain these changes.
10. Does the change in total assets equal the change in total liabilities plus the change in total equity? Explain.

Part 2

Accounting systems and processes

Recording transactions

Concepts for review

Before studying this chapter, you should understand or, if necessary, revise:

- the steps in the decision-making process (pp. 4–5)
- the nature of assets, liabilities, equity, income and expenses (pp. 32–4)
- the accounting equation, and its purpose (p. 32)
- the nature of the balance sheet, the income statement, the statement of changes in equity and the statement of cash flows (pp. 30–6)
- the assumptions made by accountants in the preparation of financial statements (pp. 36–40).

Learning objectives

After studying this chapter, you should be able to:

1 understand the nature and purpose of transactions (pp. 66–7)

2 understand the reason for the existence of source documents (pp. 67–8)

3 describe the basic accounting cycle used to record, classify and summarise transactions (pp. 68–9)

4 explain the purpose and basic format of ledger accounts and how to balance them (pp. 69–74)

5 explain the nature and purpose of the general ledger (pp. 74–5)

6 explain the purpose of a chart of accounts and how to develop one (pp. 75–7)

7 understand the rules of debit and credit used in double-entry accounting and how to apply these rules in analysing transactions (pp. 77–9)

8 explain the purpose and format of the general journal, record transactions in the general journal and transfer the information to the general ledger (pp. 79–99)

9 understand the purpose of a trial balance and how to prepare one (pp. 99–101)

10 correct errors made in the journal or ledger (p. 101).

Luca Pacioli: the father of accounting

Luca Pacioli was one of the greatest men of the Renaissance. He is also one of the least well known. This is surprising, for Luca Pacioli's manuscripts and ideas changed the way the world worked then, and continue to affect modern daily life.

Luca Pacioli was born in Sansepulcro, in Tuscany. He was probably born during 1445. His family was poor, and Pacioli's future seemed very unpromising. Pacioli joined a Franciscan monastery in Sansepulcro and became an apprentice to a local businessman. The young Pacioli had always loved mathematics though, and he soon abandoned his apprenticeship to work as a mathematics scholar...

The year 1494 is the only date during Pacioli's life that is absolutely certain. It was during this year that the 49-year-old Pacioli published his famous book *Summa de Arithmetica, Geometria, Proportioni et Proportionalita* (The Collected Knowledge of Arithmetic, Geometry, Proportion and Proportionality). Pacioli wrote the *Summa* in an attempt to redress the poor state of mathematics teaching in his time. One section in the book made Pacioli famous. The section was *Particularis de Computis et Scripturis*, a treatise on accounting ... Pacioli was the first person to describe double-entry accounting, also known as the Venetian method. This new system was state-of-the-art, and revolutionised economy and business. The *Summa* made Pacioli a celebrity and ensured him a place in history as 'The Father of Accounting'. The *Summa* was the most widely read mathematical work in all Italy, and became one of the first books published on the Gutenberg press.

Pacioli's important manuscript made him instantly famous, and he was invited to Milan to teach mathematics at the Court of Duke Lodovico Maria Sforzo. One of his pupils would be Leonardo da Vinci. During the 7 years Pacioli and da Vinci spent together, the two would help each other create two masterpieces that would withstand the test of time. Da Vinci illustrated Pacioli's next and second most important manuscript *De Divina Proportione* (Of Divine Proportions). Pacioli taught da Vinci perspective and proportionality. This knowledge allowed da Vinci to create one of his greatest masterpieces ... *The Last Supper*. The geometry Pacioli taught to da Vinci would occur in many of da Vinci's later works. Da Vinci mentions Pacioli many times in his notes.

Source: Excerpts from article by Flyn Flesher.

Chapter preview

This chapter examines the basic procedures used in a manual accounting system to analyse, record and summarise the effects of transactions on an entity in order to generate information for use in decision making. Transactions occur in all entities, whether they are business entities, government bodies, or not-for-profit organisations. The recording and summarising functions are performed today mainly by computers, as we shall see in chapter 7, but the data gathered and stored in a computerised system are based on an analysis similar to the manual one developed in this chapter. To be effective users of financial reports, it is essential that we understand the underlying accounting system, and this is most easily done by studying the procedures used in a manually operated system, developed originally by Pacioli in the fifteenth century (see the scene setter).

This chapter describes the basic procedures used to record the effects of transactions on an entity's financial position. The focus is on any entity that performs services for its customers/clients. Accounting for entities that engage in retailing and manufacturing operations is examined in later chapters.

3.1 Transactions

Types of transactions

External transactions. An entity may engage in transactions with outside parties that affect its financial statements. Examples include:

- the purchase of equipment
- the performance of services for others (e.g. medical, legal, cleaning, marketing, public relations)
- the provision by others of a service for the entity
- borrowing money from a bank
- the purchase of supplies (e.g. stationery, fuel).

These transactions are recorded by the accountant and are called **external transactions** because there is an exchange of economic resources and/or obligations between the entity and one or more outside parties. In other words, in an external transaction the entity gives up something and receives something in return.

Internal transactions. Other economic events that do not involve external transactions are recorded because they affect the internal relationships between the entity's assets, liabilities and equity. Use of office supplies by the entity's employees and of equipment to perform a service are examples of **internal transactions**. Other events, such as the destruction of an office building by fire, are also given accounting recognition because the entity's assets and equity are decreased. The term *transaction* is often used to refer to all events that are recorded in the accounting system.

Non-transaction events. Some events of importance to the entity are not usually recorded because there has not been an exchange of goods or services. Examples include:

- receiving an order from a customer
- signing a contract to purchase an asset in the future
- hiring an employee
- changing interest rates.

These situations are not captured by the accounting system because a transaction is not considered to have taken place at this point. In other words, initially such events do not affect the entity's recorded assets, liabilities or equity. These events will be recognised in the accounting system in the future if they result in a transaction.

Accounting is based on a set of rules for determining which events constitute accounting transactions. Two of the difficulties you will face in the study of accounting are (1) determining which events to record now and (2) deciding at what stage in the future an event should be recorded in the accounting system. Unfortunately, there are no simple rules.

Transactions of a business entity

Assets represent resources controlled by an entity which are expected to provide future economic benefits to the entity. The initial source of assets for any business is an investment by the owner(s). Although the investment may take various forms (such as cash at bank, land or equipment), the initial investment is often cash. Individuals invest in a business in the expectation of eventually being able to withdraw assets in excess of those invested. They expect that the business will operate at a profit and that they will receive a return on their investment.

However, the mere holding of cash invested by the owner(s) does not provide a return for the business. Cash is useful as a medium of exchange or as a measure of value, but it is essentially a non-productive asset. In order to generate income, the business acquires productive resources such as buildings, machinery and equipment. These non-cash resources are used to provide goods or services to customers in exchange for income in the form of cash or the customers' promises to pay cash in the future. Cash received from customers is then used to pay the expenses and obligations of the business. Any remaining cash may be held to pay future obligations, to finance future expansion, to invest, or to distribute to owners as a return on their investment.

Large and medium-sized entities are also required by government to capture data in relation to greenhouse gas emissions (e.g. kilotonnes of carbon dioxide emitted) in order to measure their carbon footprints. This information is required for each entity to prepare its sustainability report, as discussed briefly in chapter 1. Additional data must also be captured for each entity to prepare a social impact report that outlines, for example, non-financial contributions to the wellbeing of the townspeople in which the entity operates. This chapter, however, deals only with transactions that capture financial data.

3.2 Source documents

A **source document**, such as a tax invoice for the performance of services, purchase order, cash register tape, credit card slip or cheque, is prepared for every external transaction entered into by an entity and serves two basic purposes: (1) it provides written evidence of a transaction and is used by accountants as support for entries in the accounting records; (2) it serves as an important element in the control of the entity's resources. For each external transaction recognised by the accountant, there should be at least one supporting source document.

For example, figure 3.1 illustrates a typical tax invoice, which is regarded as evidence that an entity has performed services for a customer. From a copy of the tax invoice (the original is given to the customer), the entity can record the performance of the service, the name and address of the customer, details of payments to be received from the customer, and goods and services tax (GST) to be collected.

Learning objective 2

Understand the reason for the existence of source documents

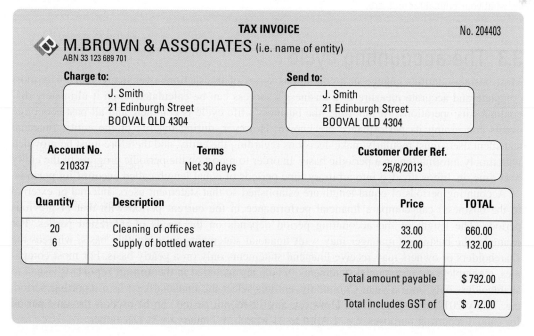

Figure 3.1 Typical tax invoice

On the tax invoice illustrated in figure 3.1, note that there is an item called 'ABN', followed by a number. ABN means **Australian business number**, a separate number given to all business entities which have registered with the Australian Taxation Office (ATO); it also covers the registration for the GST in Australia. At the bottom of the tax invoice is another line indicating that the $792 total of the invoice 'includes GST of $72'. In other words, the business of M. Brown & Associates will eventually collect $72 of GST from its customer, J. Smith. The business owes this amount to the ATO and will regularly pay the amount owing for GST. For further coverage of the basics of GST in Australia, refer to the appendix to this chapter (p. 102). A GST or similar retail tax is imposed in several countries.

Other commonly used source documents are:

- purchase order — when goods or services are ordered from a supplier
- tax invoice for purchases — invoice received from a supplier of goods/services
- cash register tapes — to record cash received for cash sales through a cash register
- credit card slips — to record sales made on credit cards
- cheque butts — to record payments made by cheque to creditors for goods and services.

Tax invoices can be prepared manually or by computer and are used subsequently for data entry in both manual and computerised accounting systems. In most modern computerised systems, the preparation of the invoice and the input of invoice data into the accounting system are done simultaneously, e.g. updating inventory records and recording amounts owed by customers. Increasingly, manually prepared source documents are being replaced by electronic source documents.

BUSINESS KNOWLEDGE

Lessons from Larry — the importance of records

One of the major lessons learnt from Cyclone Larry was that businesses need to think about securing their records, says Gerard Byrne FCPA from Queensland's Department of Primary Industries and Fisheries.

'What we found with [Cyclone] Larry is that people lost the computer, lost the power, lost their paper trail, lost their electronic trail. It is very hard to reconstruct records.

'We had that problem with accounting firms being out of action for some time. You need to know what your critical records are,

where are they stored, where are the backups and how quickly can you recapture the information?'

Byrne says in a disaster's aftermath insurance companies and the government will ask for records in order to assess relief.

One of the problems with Cyclone Larry was that accountants' clients all wanted their records reconstructed at the same time. 'If you are a small business and you have your records in place,' Byrne says, 'you can more quickly and easily get access to government assistance.'

Source: Excerpts from Ed Charles, 'Dealing with disaster', *InTheBlack.*

Learning objective 3

Describe the basic accounting cycle used to record, classify and summarise transactions

3.3 The accounting cycle

Most business entities engage in a continuous series of transactions over many years. The most complete and accurate measure of a business's success can be calculated when it ultimately discontinues its operations. At that time, the business's life cycle is complete and all past economic events concerning its performance are known. However, during the life of the entity, financial statement users must regularly make decisions regarding the entity, and therefore must be provided with timely information on a periodic basis. In order to report on the periodic progress of the entity over time, its life is divided into arbitrary time periods of equal length called **accounting periods**.

Accounting periods of equal length are established so that statement users (internal or external to the business) can compare financial performance in the current period with that of previous periods. The length of the accounting period depends on the needs of interested parties. For example, the business's manager may want financial statements on a monthly basis, whereas the shareholders or owners may receive financial statements only on a yearly basis. For most companies, a complete set of financial statements (which are included in the **annual report**) is issued to shareholders only once a year. Commonly, entities select the financial year as a reporting period, e.g. 1 July 2012 to 30 June 2013. However, any 12-month period can be used as the time period for annual reporting purposes, e.g. 1 April to 31 March, 1 January to 31 December.

Financial statements are used by creditors and other interested external parties to assess the entity's progress over time. The basic accounting period for which financial statements are presented is 1 year, but half-yearly and quarterly statements are sometimes required by external parties to provide more timely information on the activities of the entity. Many entities also prepare monthly or weekly statements for internal use by management. Statements prepared for external users before the end of the annual period are called **interim statements**.

During each period, steps and procedures are followed within the accounting function to ensure that all transactions are properly recorded, and records are kept to ensure that the financial statements can be prepared at the end of the accounting period. These steps and procedures, culminating in the preparation of financial statements, are referred to as the **accounting cycle**. The basic two-step accounting cycle is shown in figure 3.2.

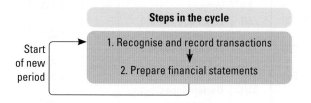

Figure 3.2 The basic accounting cycle

In practice, there are a number of additional steps or procedures which must occur between the recording of transactions and the preparation of financial statements. These are added progressively in this and later chapters.

3.4 The ledger account

Learning objective **4**

Explain the purpose and basic format of ledger accounts and how to balance them

Each transaction recorded results in an increase or decrease in one or more of the assets, liabilities, equity, income or expenses. A part of the accounting function is to classify the effects of transactions into these categories and to summarise the results in the entity's financial statements. To help in the collection of financial statement data, transactions are recorded in ledger accounts.

An **account** provides a record of increases and decreases in each item that appears in the financial statements. Thus, an entity typically has an account for each kind of asset, liability, equity, income and expense item. For example, a business maintains a separate account to record increases and decreases in cash, a separate account to record increases and decreases in accounts receivable, a separate account for accounts payable, another account for the owner's capital, and so on. All the accounts maintained by an entity to enable preparation of the financial statements are collectively called the **general ledger**.

Each account has three basic parts: (1) a title, which should be descriptive of the nature of the items being recorded in the account; (2) a place for recording increases; and (3) a place for recording decreases. Also, accounts typically provide space for recording an account number, the date of the transaction and an explanation of the transaction. One format, called a **T account** because of its similarity to the letter T, is shown below. Other formats are illustrated later in this chapter.

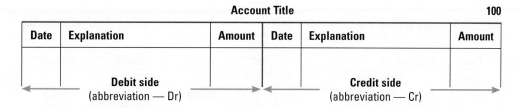

A T account has a left-hand side and a right-hand side, called respectively the **debit** side and **credit** side. An account is debited when an amount is entered on the left-hand side and credited when an amount is entered on the right-hand side. These terms have come down to us from Latin origins through Pacioli's original work on accounting (see the scene setter).

After the transactions are entered, including date, explanation (which describes the other accounts that are affected by the transaction) and amount, the **account balance** (the difference between the sum of its debits and the sum of its credits) can be calculated. If the sum of the debits exceeds the sum of the credits, the account has a debit balance. A credit balance results when the sum of the credits is greater than the sum of the debits. An account will have a zero balance if the sum of the debits equals the sum of the credits.

A summary of all increases and decreases in the account Cash at Bank for Darren's Lawn and Gardening Services can be presented in T-account form as illustrated below. Note that, for an asset, all increases are recorded as debits and all decreases as credits (see p. 77).

Cash at Bank

Date	Explanation	Post Ref*	Amount	Date	Explanation	Post Ref*	Amount
2013				2013			
2/1	Darren Jones, Capital		35 000	3/1	Vehicle		21 000
20/1	Lawn and Garden Income		2 200	3/1	Lawn and Garden Equipment		9 000
31/1	Accounts Receivable		550	22/1	Employee Wages Expense		450
				31/1	Accounts Payable		2 500
				31/1	Darren Jones, Drawings		200
					Balance c/d		4 600
			37 750				37 750
	Balance b/d		4 600				

*The purpose of the Post Ref column is discussed later in this chapter.

The entity's cash receipts or deposits are recorded on the debit (or left) side of the account and cash payments, disbursements or withdrawals are entered on the credit (right) side. Recording the receipts and payments separately helps determine the account balance. Cash receipts of $37 750 were deposited in the bank and exceeded the payments of $33 150, resulting in a debit balance of $4600. The balance to be carried down (c/d) is entered on the credit side which will then make the total on each side the same or 'in balance'. In a T account format the total is written on both sides on the same horizontal row and the balance is brought down (b/d) and inserted under the total on the debit side of the account. A balance sheet (also called the statement of financial position) prepared at this time would report $4600 in the Cash at Bank account as an asset.

Account formats

The T-account format is a convenient way to show the effects of transactions on individual accounts and is used commonly in accounting textbooks and in classroom illustrations. In practice, however, ledger accounts generally take the format shown in figure 3.3, known as a **running balance account**. This account format provides not only all the information shown in a T account but has the added advantage of showing a balance after each transaction.

Figure 3.3 A running balance account

ACCOUNT Cash at Bank						Account No. **100**
Date	Explanation	Post Ref*	Debit	Credit	Balance
2013					
Jan. 2	Darren Jones, Capital	1	35 000		35 000
3	Vehicle	1		21 000	14 000
3	Lawn and Garden Equipment	1		9 000	5 000
20	Lawn and Garden Income	1	2 200		7 200
22	Wages Expense	1		450	6 750
31	Accounts Receivable	1	550		7 300
31	Accounts Payable	1		2 500	4 800
31	Darren Jones, Drawings	1		200	4 600

*The purpose of the Post Ref column is discussed later in this chapter.

Note that in some computerised accounting systems an account could be a single-column account with the debits shown as positive amounts (with or without the + sign) and credit amounts shown as negative amounts. Alternatively, depending on the nature of the account, the credits may be shown as positive and the debits are shown as negatives. A description of the different types of accounts and the rules for debiting and crediting accounts are treated later in this chapter. An example of ledger accounts maintained in a computerised accounting system (MYOB in this case) is shown in figure 3.4.

Figure 3.4 Sample computerised accounts (MYOB)

```
DARREN'S LAWN AND GARDENING SERVICES
Hometown
                                        General Ledger [Detail]
                                          1/1/13 to 31/1/13                                    Page 1

                                                                                     Net        Ending
    ID#      Src    Date        Memo              Debit        Credit              Activity     Balance

 1-1100 Cash at Bank                                    Beginning Balance: $0.00

 GJ000001  GJ   2/1/13   Initial capital investment  $35 000.00                              $35 000.00
 GJ000002  GJ   3/1/13   Purchased vehicle for cash               $21 000.00                  14 000.00
 GJ000002  GJ   3/1/13   Purchased equipment for cash              9 000.00                    5 000.00
 GJ000004  GJ   20/1/13  Cash lawn and garden income   2 200.00                                7 200.00
 GJ000006  GJ   22/1/13  Drew cheque for wages                       450.00                    6 750.00
 GJ000008  GJ   31/1/13  Cash recd from customers        550.00                                7 300.00
 GJ000009  GJ   31/1/13  Paid a/cs payable                         2 500.00                    4 800.00
 GJ000010  GJ   31/1/13  Drawings by Jones                           200.00                    4 600.00

                                         Total:  $37 750.00    $33 150.00   $ 4 600.00   $ 4 600.00

 1-1200 Accounts Receivable                            Beginning Balance: $0.00

 GJ000005  GJ   20/1/13  Tree lopping income charged  $   550.00                          $   550.00
 GJ000008  GJ   31/1/13  Cash recd from customers                $   550.00                      0.00

                                                 $   550.00    $   550.00   $    0.00   $    0.00
```

As can be seen, much more detail can be shown in these accounts. Besides debit and credit entries and running balances, all debits and credits over a period are totalled and net activity is shown. This provides an additional check on the mathematical accuracy of the accounts. Note that at this stage the source of the entries is GJ for general journal (see p. 79) and an explanation for each entry is also shown in the 'Memo' column.

Accounts commonly used

The accountant establishes an account for each type of asset, liability, equity, income and expense to be reported in the financial statements. The number of accounts and specific account titles vary, depending on the nature and complexity of the entity's operations. For example, the accounts used to record transactions of a management consultancy firm differ significantly from those of a manufacturing business or a not-for-profit organisation. Note also that the same type of account is given different titles by different entities. In addition, the number of accounts can reflect the amount of information desired by the internal and external statement users. For example, although one account can be used for recording all expenses, it will generally not provide sufficient detail to monitor and control the entity's expenses.

The title or name given to a specific account should be descriptive of the items recorded in the account. Because some account titles consist of terms new to you or with special technical meaning in accounting, it will be helpful to look first at the nature of the accounts normally used by a service organisation before discussing the recording of transactions. Additional account types are introduced in later chapters.

Account titles commonly used for the preparation of the balance sheet and income statement are presented on the following pages.

Accounts: balance sheet

Asset accounts

Cash at bank. The Cash at Bank account is used to record deposits into and withdrawals from a bank account. This account is the bank account of the entity and withdrawals are made by electronic transfer or by cheque. Although an entity could have several accounts at the one bank and/or accounts at several banks, for simplicity in this book a single Cash at Bank account is used.

Accounts receivable. Accounts receivable are amounts owed to an entity by customers to whom the entity has provided goods or services on credit. An account receivable may be based on an oral agreement to pay, but is more commonly recognised when an invoice for goods sold or services rendered is issued. The Accounts Receivable account is often called the **Trade Debtors** account or simply **Debtors**.

Other receivables or debtors. At the end of the period, the entity may have receivables resulting from a variety of other transactions. For example, cash advances may have been made to employees, deposits may have been made with another entity for goods or services to be received in the future, GST may be receivable from the ATO as a result of input tax credits (see the appendix to this chapter), and a tenant may owe the entity rent. An entity normally establishes an individual account for each type of debtor.

Prepaid expenses. Prepaid expenses are goods or services that have been paid for in advance but not yet received or used. At the time of payment, an asset is recorded and subsequently expensed as the asset is used to earn income. Included in this category are advance payments of rent and insurance premiums. Each type of prepaid expense may be recorded in a separate account, e.g. Prepaid Rent, Prepaid Insurance.

Land. The Land account is used to record land controlled by the entity. Land is recorded in an account separate from any buildings on the land. (This is required by accounting standards.)

Buildings. The Buildings account is used to record buildings used by the entity in carrying out its activities.

Plant and equipment. Physical items used in the entity for a relatively long period of time are recorded in plant and equipment accounts. In general, these accounts include any item not permanently attached to land or buildings. The accounts are used to record acquisitions of delivery equipment, office furniture, computer equipment, factory equipment, machinery, motor vehicles, store and office fixtures, and store furniture. A separate account for each major type of equipment owned is usually established, e.g. Office Furniture, Store Furniture.

Land, buildings and equipment accounts are used for those items held for use in the operations of the entity.

Liability accounts

Accounts payable. An account payable is an obligation to pay an amount to an outside party — a creditor — for the purchase of goods, supplies or services on credit. The account is also commonly called **Trade Creditors** or simply **Creditors**.

Unearned income. Cash received from customers for goods yet to be delivered or services yet to be performed is not reported as income because the entity has a liability to the customer until the goods are delivered or the services are performed. When the goods are delivered or the services are performed, an amount is transferred from the unearned income account, a liability, to an income account. The income represents the reduction in the liability account. Examples are rent collected in advance from a tenant and a magazine subscription for 2 years received by a publisher. The use of unearned income accounts is discussed further in chapter 4.

Other current liabilities. At any given time, the entity may owe money to employees, the ATO, or other parties for services received. For example, many entities are required to collect GST on goods sold or services provided; a company may owe income tax; a telephone account may have been received for the quarter but not yet paid. It is not possible to list here all of the potential liabilities an entity may incur. The important fact at the moment is that an individual account can be used for each type of liability.

GST collections and outlays. As discussed in detail in the appendix to this chapter, any business which is registered for GST typically has two accounts:
- **GST Collections** for any GST received or receivable by the entity from its customers. This account represents the GST the entity owes to the ATO, and is a liability.
- **GST Outlays** for any GST paid or payable by the entity to its suppliers. This account represents the GST refundable to the entity by the ATO, and is an asset.

At the end of each reporting period, the GST Collections account (liability) is usually offset against the GST Outlays account (asset) to show a net liability or asset in the entity's balance sheet, depending on which account has the larger balance.

In the accounting records, all income and expenses and most assets are recorded in the accounts excluding the GST (i.e. net of GST). Receivables and payables are recorded with the GST component included.

Mortgage payable. This account is used to record a particular kind of liability for which the creditor has a claim secured by a mortgage deed against one or more of the entity's assets. A secured claim means that if the entity is unable to pay the obligation when due, the creditor may force the sale of the assets pledged as security to recover the debt.

Equity accounts

Four main types of transactions affect the owner's interest or equity in the entity: (1) investment of assets in the entity by the owner; (2) withdrawal of assets by the owner; (3) income derived; and (4) expenses incurred. Thus the equity part of the accounting equation may be expanded as follows:

> Assets = Liabilities + Equity
> Equity = Investment by the owner – Drawings by the owner + Income – Expenses

Separate accounts are maintained for each of these four categories as a convenient means of preparing the statement of changes in equity for the period.

Capital. Assets invested in the entity by the owner are recorded as an increase in assets and an increase in the capital account established in the name of the owner.

Drawings or withdrawals. The drawings account is used to record the withdrawal of assets, usually cash, from the entity by the owner. Thus, drawings are recorded as a reduction in both assets and equity. An owner of a sole trader business will often establish a fixed amount to be withdrawn at specific intervals for personal living expenses. Although the owner may think of these drawings as a salary, neither law nor tax codes recognise a single proprietor as an employee of the firm because the owner cannot hire himself. Consequently, recurring drawings made in the expectation of earning profit are considered as neither a salary nor an expense of the entity.

Occasionally, personal expenses of the owner may be paid directly from the bank account of the entity. Such payments are drawings by the owner and not expenses of doing business.

Equity accounts differ depending on the nature of the business organisation, e.g. sole trader or the company structure. Different equity accounts will be introduced throughout the book as appropriate.

Accounts: income statement

Income and expense accounts are subclassifications of equity. Because of the variety and volume of income and expense transactions, it is helpful in the preparation of the income statement to maintain separate accounts for each major type of income and expense item so that users of accounting information will know the amount and source of income and the expenses incurred. Relatively insignificant amounts are normally recorded in a Sundry Income or a Sundry Expenses account.

Income

Income represents increases in economic benefits during the period in the form of inflows or enhancements of assets or decreases in liabilities that result in increases in equity, other than contributions by the owners. In the *Framework for the Preparation and Presentation of Financial Statements*, two different types of income are identified, namely revenues and gains.

Revenues. **Revenue** represents income which arises in the course of the *ordinary activities* of an entity. Such revenues commonly occur in the performance of services by service organisations or in the sale of merchandise by retail and wholesale entities. Revenues are measured by the fair value of the assets received. The assets received for the goods or services are normally cash or a receivable. In the double-entry accounting system, revenues are recorded as both an increase in an asset (a debit) and an increase in equity (a credit). Each different revenue is reported in a separate equity account in order to show its particular source. Revenues are classified into many categories depending on their nature, e.g. commission revenue, cleaning services revenue, legal services revenue, gardening services revenue, consulting fees revenue, sales revenue.

Gains. A **gain** represents income which does *not* usually arise from the ordinary activities of an entity. An example is the gain from the sale of assets such as buildings or machinery which are used by the entity in carrying out its main activities. Gains may also arise if the entity has revalued upwards some of its assets, e.g. if an entity has revalued its share investments up to market value. In order to provide information to users of financial statements for making decisions, it is important to show gains as a separate category of income when preparing an income statement. However, the nature of gains and of revenue is essentially the same, and they are merely different categories of income.

Expenses

The cost of services and economic benefits consumed or lost or liabilities incurred during the period, other than a withdrawal of capital or profits by the owner, are called **expenses**. Expenses are recorded by decreasing an asset account (a credit) and increasing the appropriate expense account (a debit). If an expense has not been paid for, a liability is increased (a credit) rather than an asset being decreased. A number of expense accounts are normally reported in order to reflect the variety of expenses incurred by an entity, e.g. wages expense, fuel expense, telephone expense.

A distinction may be made between expenses arising from the normal activities of an entity and those arising outside those normal activities, e.g. from the sale of assets held for use by the entity, or by revaluing investments downwards. It is common to refer to expenses arising from normal activities as 'expenses' and to those outside the normal activities as 'losses'. Nevertheless, there is no difference in the nature of the two categories, and we shall refer to both as 'expenses' for the purpose of simplicity.

When total income (revenues and gains) exceeds total expenses, the difference is called **profit**. When total expenses exceed total income, the entity is said to incur a **loss**. An important function of accounting is to provide a measurement of a business entity's performance as revealed by the profit made or the loss incurred.

Learning objective 5

Explain the nature and purpose of the general ledger

3.5 General ledger

As previously defined, the collection of all the individual accounts for a particular business is referred to as a *general ledger*. In a manual system, each account is usually maintained on a separate card or on a separate sheet in a loose-leaf binder. In a computerised system, accounts are maintained on disks, tapes, CDs or DVDs. A computerised general ledger is generally referred to as the *general ledger master file*.

Accounts contained in the general ledger are usually organised in the order they appear in the balance sheet and the income statement, thus making it easier to find them and prepare financial statements. Each account has an identification number used for reference and for cross-referencing the transactions entered in a specific account.

3.6 Chart of accounts

Learning objective 6

Explain the purpose of a chart of accounts and how to develop one

A **chart of accounts** is a listing of the complete ledger account titles and their related numbers, and is maintained in both manual and computerised systems.

When analysing transactions, refer to the chart of accounts to identify specific accounts to be increased or decreased. A simple numbering system numbers all accounts consecutively starting with number 1 and continuing until all accounts are assigned a number. A better system, however, is one based on flexible numbering, which allows the addition of accounts as necessary. For example, all assets are assigned a three-digit number from 100 to 199, liabilities are 200 to 299, equity 300 to 399, income 400 to 499, and expenses 500 to 599. Some numbers are not assigned within each classification of accounts to permit the insertion of new accounts as they are needed. In computerised systems, the chart of accounts can use more complex numbering systems to facilitate processing by the computer. In these systems, a chart of accounts is essential. It is the first element of the system to be processed as it forms the basic framework under which the whole of the computerised accounting system functions.

A relatively simple chart of accounts used in this and later chapters to illustrate accounting procedures for Intellect Management Services is shown in figure 3.5.

The same chart of accounts produced by the MYOB computerised accounting system is shown in figure 3.6 (p. 76). Note the amount of extra detail which the program uses to record transactions and produce reports. Note also the use of levels of accounts (shown in the right-hand column in figure 3.6) which enables the computer to condense the amount of detail, e.g. level 2 accounts in a category can be totalled into a level 1 account. All level 1 accounts are headers in accounting reports.

INTELLECT MANAGEMENT SERVICES Chart of Accounts	
Assets (100–199)	
Cash at Bank	100
Accounts Receivable	104
Prepaid Insurance	110
Office Supplies	111
GST Outlays	120
Land	150
Building	160
Accumulated Depreciation – Building	161
Office Equipment	170
Accumulated Depreciation – Office Equipment	171
Liabilities (200–299)	
Accounts Payable	200
Salaries Payable	210
Loan Payable	214
Interest Payable	215
Electricity Account Payable	216
Unearned Appraisal Fees	220
GST Collections	250
Mortgage Payable	260
Equity (300–399)	
M. Mooney, Capital	300
M. Mooney, Drawings	310
	(continued)

Figure 3.5 A simple chart of accounts

Figure 3.5 *continued*

Income (400–499)	
Revenues	
Management Services Revenue	400
Appraisal Fees Revenue	401
Marketing Services Revenue	402
Expenses (500–599)	
Salaries Expense	500
Telephone Expense	510
Advertising Expense	520
Insurance Expense	521
Office Supplies Expense	530
Depreciation Expense – Office Equipment	540
Depreciation Expense – Building	541
Interest Expense	560
Electricity Expense	570
Profit or Loss Summary	600

Figure 3.6 Chart of accounts used in MYOB computerised accounting

INTELLECT MANAGEMENT SERVICES
Hometown
Chart of Accounts [Detail] Page 1

Account #	Account	Type	Normal Sign	Header/ Detail	Level
1-0000	ASSETS	Asset	Debit	Header	1
1-1100	Cash at Bank	Asset	Debit	Detail	2
1-2000	Accounts Receivable	Asset	Debit	Detail	2
1-3000	Prepaid Insurance	Asset	Debit	Detail	2
1-4000	Office Supplies	Asset	Debit	Detail	2
1-4500	GST Outlays	Asset	Debit	Detail	2
1-5000	Land	Asset	Debit	Detail	2
1-6000	Building	Asset	Debit	Detail	2
1-6500	Accum Deprec – Building	Asset	Debit	Detail	2
1-7000	Office Equipment	Asset	Debit	Detail	2
1-7500	Accum Deprec – Off Equip	Asset	Debit	Detail	2
2-0000	LIABILITIES	Liability	Credit	Header	1
2-2000	Accounts Payable	Liability	Credit	Detail	2
2-2500	GST Collections	Liability	Credit	Detail	2
2-3000	Salaries Payable	Liability	Credit	Detail	2
2-4000	Commissions Payable	Liability	Credit	Detail	2
2-5000	Loan Payable	Liability	Credit	Detail	2
2-6000	Interest Payable	Liability	Credit	Detail	2
2-7000	Electricity Payable	Liability	Credit	Detail	2
2-8000	Unearned Appraisal Fees	Liability	Credit	Detail	2
2-9000	Mortgage Payable	Liability	Credit	Detail	2
3-0000	EQUITY	Equity	Credit	Header	1
3-8000	M. Mooney, Capital	Equity	Credit	Detail	2
3-9000	M. Mooney, Drawings	Equity	Credit	Detail	2
4-0000	INCOME — Revenues	Income	Credit	Header	1
4-2100	Management Services Revenue	Income	Credit	Detail	2
4-2200	Appraisal Fees Revenue	Income	Credit	Detail	2
4-2300	Marketing Services Revenue	Income	Credit	Detail	2
5-0000	EXPENSES	Expense	Debit	Header	1
5-2100	Salaries Expense	Expense	Debit	Detail	2
5-2200	Commission Expense	Expense	Debit	Detail	2
5-2300	Telephone Expense	Expense	Debit	Detail	2
5-2400	Advertising Expense	Expense	Debit	Detail	2
5-2500	Insurance Expense	Expense	Debit	Detail	2
5-2600	Office Supplies Expense	Expense	Debit	Detail	2
5-2700	Deprec Exp – Off Equip	Expense	Debit	Detail	2
5-2750	Deprec Exp – Building	Expense	Debit	Detail	2
5-5000	Interest Expense	Expense	Debit	Detail	2
5-5200	Electricity Expense	Expense	Debit	Detail	2
6-0000	PROFIT OR LOSS SUMMARY	Equity	Credit	Header	1

A good chart of accounts reveals a great deal about the organisation. For example, it will tell you (a) whether the organisation is a sole trader business, a partnership, a company, a not-for-profit organisation or a government department, (b) whether the organisation is engaged in retailing, manufacturing or services, and (c) the different types of income derived and expenses incurred by the entity.

The chart of accounts is usually contained in the entity's **accounting manual**, which also typically contains such things as an overview of the accounting system, policies and procedures to be followed, sample source documents and sample financial statements. The manual is used as a guide for those involved in the operation of the accounting system.

3.7 Double-entry accounting

Learning objective 7

Understand the rules of debit and credit used in double-entry accounting and how to apply these rules in analysing transactions

In chapter 2, when recording the transactions for Darren's Lawn and Gardening Services, it was necessary to determine which assets, liabilities or equity items were affected and the amount by which each item increased or decreased. We noted that each transaction affected at least two financial statement items, and that the accounting equation always remained in balance. When accounts are used in the recording process, each transaction must also be analysed to determine what types of accounts are affected, and whether each account is increased or decreased so as to decide whether it is to be debited or credited. At least two accounts are affected by each transaction, hence the system is referred to as double-entry accounting.

Debit and credit rules

Accounts: balance sheet

As noted earlier, the *left-hand side* of a T account is called the *debit side* and the *right-hand side* is called the *credit side*. When accounts are maintained in the running balance format shown on page 69, 'debit' simply means the left-hand column and 'credit' means the right-hand column. Whether a debit or a credit is an increase or a decrease to the account balance depends on whether the account is an asset, a liability or an equity account.

In arriving at rules for debit and credit, an assumption is made that assets are of a debit nature. (This is just an accounting rule and is similar to the international road rules that a green light means go and a red light means stop.) From the accounting equation, it follows, then, that liabilities and equity are of a credit nature, and *total debits must equal total credits*. Increases and decreases are recorded in the three categories of accounts reported on the balance sheet as shown in T-account format below:

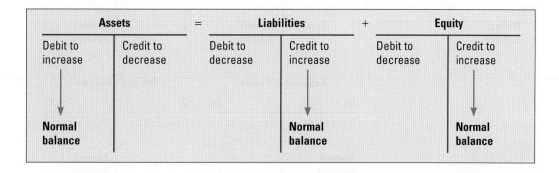

An increase in an asset account is recorded as a debit; an increase in a liability or equity account is recorded as a credit. A decrease in an asset account is recorded as a credit; a decrease in a liability or an equity account is recorded as a debit.

The procedure of recording increases to liability and equity accounts on the credit side and decreases on the debit side is opposite that of assets and permits an additional check for accuracy. Thus, not only must the accounting equation be in balance, but the sum of the debit balances must equal the sum of the credit balances.

Accounts: income statement

The debit/credit rules for income and expenses can be developed by examining the relationship of income and expense accounts to the equity account. As explained earlier, income increases equity and expenses decrease equity. Thus, increases in income are recorded as credits consistent with the recording of increases in equity. Increases in expenses are recorded as debits, because they decrease equity. Although a debit to an expense account is a reduction in equity, it is also an increase in an expense account.

Debit and credit rules for income statement accounts are shown below in T-account format:

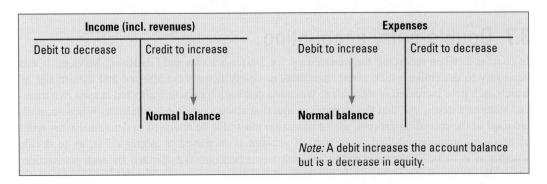

Understanding the rules of debit and credit is fundamental to understanding much of the material in the rest of this book. Because of the importance of understanding these rules, you should master them now. Remember that to debit (credit) an account simply means to enter the amount on the left-hand (right-hand) side of the account. A debit may increase or decrease the account balance, depending on the type of account being adjusted. The same is true for a credit. A summary of debit and credit rules is provided in figure 3.7.

Figure 3.7 Summary of debit/credit rules and the accounting equation

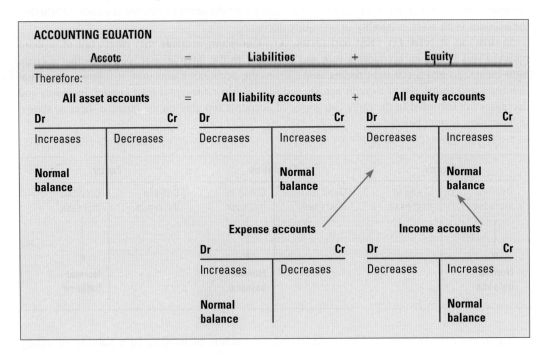

Normal account balances

It is helpful in finding ledger errors to know the normal balance for an account. In particular, if the running balance account format illustrated in figure 3.3 (p. 70) is used, the balance column does not indicate whether the amount is a debit or credit. As shown in figure 3.7, the **normal account balance** is the side on which increases to the account are recorded. The chart below summarises the normal balances for all accounts:

Account	Increases recorded on	Normal balance
Assets	Debit side	Debit
Liabilities	Credit side	Credit
Equity		
Investment in the entity by owner	Credit side	Credit
Drawings from the entity by owner	Debit side	Debit
Income: Revenues	Credit side	Credit
Expenses	Debit side	Debit

If an account has a balance different from its normal balance, it is likely that an error has been made. We would not expect to find a credit balance in an asset account or a debit balance in an income account. However, a credit balance in the Cash at Bank account could exist for a limited time if the bank account had been overdrawn, i.e. arrangements have been made with the bank to make use of overdraft facilities. Note that in computerised accounting, the system is usually designed to flag or highlight automatically any account which does not have a normal balance. Contrast this with a manual system where accounts with abnormal balances need to be discovered by visual inspection.

Expanded accounting cycle

Earlier, the accounting cycle was introduced and a very basic cycle was illustrated (figure 3.2, p. 69). We now introduce the general journal and the general ledger, so we need to expand the cycle to include the procedures of journalising transactions, posting the general journal to the general ledger, and preparing a trial balance. The cycle, taking these new steps into account, is shown in figure 3.8. (The accounting cycle will be expanded further in later chapters.)

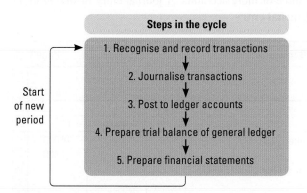

Figure 3.8 The expanded accounting cycle

3.8 General journal

Explain the purpose and format of the general journal, record transactions in the general journal and transfer the information to the general ledger

In a typical manual accounting system and in some computerised general ledger accounting systems, a transaction is analysed and recorded first in a book called a **journal** before the effects of the transaction are entered in the individual accounts in the ledger. The journal is the initial recording of a transaction from the entity's source documents. Although transactions could be entered directly into the accounts in the ledger, better control is achieved in a manual system by recording them first in a journal; then, when convenient, the debit and credit amounts can be recorded in the proper ledger accounts.

The journal provides in one place a complete record of all transactions as they occur in chronological order, i.e. by date. In the journal, the title and dollar amounts of each account to be debited or credited are listed for each transaction. Thus, the journal provides a detailed record of the full effect of a particular transaction on the entity. Since an individual transaction is recorded in two or more accounts in the ledger, no single account contains a complete record of each transaction.

In addition to providing a complete record of every transaction, the journal is a useful device for reducing and locating errors. If a transaction is recorded directly to ledger accounts, the effect of the transaction may inadvertently be recorded initially as two debits or two credits, or one side of a transaction may be omitted entirely, and such errors would be difficult to locate. However, in the journal the debit and credit information for each transaction is shown together in one place. The omission of a debit or a credit or the inclusion of two debits without an offsetting credit, for instance, would be evident. With a complete record of each transaction in the journal, some errors can be isolated by retracing the debits and credits to ledger accounts to ensure that the correct amounts were transferred to the proper accounts.

In computerised accounting systems, transactions are generally entered directly into the ledger accounts from various data input screens, and the system ensures that each transaction has an equal debit and credit recorded. Most computerised accounting systems do provide an option to print out a journal if required.

Recording transactions in a journal

The number of journals and the design of each vary from entity to entity, depending on the nature of operations and the frequency of a particular type of transaction. In this chapter, we are concerned with using the **general journal**, or the **two-column journal**, so called because it contains two columns for entering dollar amounts. Other types of journals are discussed in chapter 7.

The standard format for the general journal and the steps followed in recording a journal entry are shown in figure 3.9. Recording transactions in a journal is called **entering** or **journalising**, and each transaction recorded is a separate **journal entry**. Two transactions are illustrated in figure 3.9. The first journal entry records the receipt of cash for marketing services performed for a customer, plus GST collected. The second entry records the purchase of equipment with a part payment in cash and a loan payable for the balance. Most journal entries involve only two accounts; however, the entries illustrated in figure 3.9 involve three or more accounts. A journal entry involving more than two accounts is called a **compound journal entry**.

Figure 3.9 Example of a general journal (ringed numbers refer to the steps listed on the next page)

			General Journal			Page 1
	Date	Particulars	Post Ref	Debit	Credit	
(1)	2013 July 5	(2) Cash at Bank	(8) 100	(3) 15 400	(5)	
		Marketing Services Revenue (4)	402		14 000	
		GST Collections	250		1 400	
	(6)	(Marketing services rendered in exchange for cash)				
	10	(7) Office Equipment	170	62 000		
		GST Outlays	120	6 200		
		Cash at Bank	100		28 200	
		Loan Payable	214		40 000	
		(Purchased equipment for cash part-payment with a short-term loan for the balance)				

Before a transaction is entered in the journal, it is necessary to analyse the transaction for its effects on the various ledger accounts. Note that the principles of double-entry accounting are observed for each transaction:

- two or more accounts are affected by each transaction
- the sum of the debit amount(s) for every transaction equals the sum of the credit amount(s)
- the equality of the accounting equation is maintained.

Every page in the journal is numbered for future reference. Before an entry is made in the journal, the year and month are written at the top of the first column. The year and month are not repeated until the start of a new page or a new month. The process for journalising transactions is described below, and the steps in the process are keyed to the first entry in figure 3.9.

1. The date of each transaction is entered in the date column.
2. The name of the account(s) to be debited is entered against the left margin of the particulars column.
3. The amount to be debited to each account is entered in the debit amount column on the same line as the account name.
4. The name of the account(s) to be credited is entered on the line immediately below the account(s) to be debited and is indented to distinguish the account(s) credited from the account(s) debited.
5. The amount to be credited to each account is entered in the credit amount column on the same line as the account name.
6. A brief explanation of the transaction is entered on the line immediately below the journal entry. This explanation is referred to as a *narration*.
7. A single line is usually left blank between each journal entry or a line is drawn between each entry across the particulars column.
8. At the time the journal entry is recorded, the posting reference column is left blank until the account is posted to the ledger (see below). If an appropriate account title is not listed in the chart of accounts, the new account with a new appropriate number should be added to the chart of accounts.

Posting from journal to ledger

The process of transferring amounts entered in the journal to the proper ledger accounts is called **posting**. The aim is to classify the effects of all transactions on each individual asset, liability, equity, income and expense account.

The posting of one journal entry from figure 3.9 with one debit and two credits is shown in figure 3.10 (p. 82). The debit is posted in the first half of the figure and the credits are posted in the second half.

The steps involved in the posting process are:

1. Locate in the ledger the account to be debited.
2. Enter the date the transaction occurred as shown in the journal.
3. Enter in the explanation column the name of the other ledger account(s) to which the opposite side of the entry will be posted (i.e. cross-reference the debit and credit entries).
4. Enter the debit amount in the debit column of the ledger account.
5. Enter in the posting reference column of the ledger account the page number of the journal from which the entry is being posted.
6. Enter in the posting reference column of the journal the account number to indicate that the debit amount was posted.
7. If using running balance ledger accounts, insert the current balance in the account.
8–14. Repeat steps 1 to 7 for both credit parts of the entry.

Steps 5, 6, 12 and 13 (entries in the posting reference column) provide a cross-reference between the accounts in the ledger and the original journal entry. Cross-referencing is a convenient way to locate additional information relating to an amount recorded in an individual account in the ledger.

Note that steps 3 and 10 provide a cross-reference between two (or more) ledger accounts to which the entry is posted. From chapter 4 onwards, ledger cross-referencing is not always shown. A simplified T account is used instead. However, in practice, cross-referencing is always completed.

In computerised accounting systems, the posting process is carried out automatically by the computer. It is therefore essential that the data entered initially into the system are accurate. The computer provides a journal proof summary which totals the debits and credits of all data entered before posting takes place. This ensures that the general ledger remains in balance, i.e. debits equal credits. Most computerised systems automatically maintain the double-entry system of debits and credits. Running balance formats are used for ledger accounts in computerised systems.

Figure 3.10 Posting from the general journal to the general ledger (running balance format)

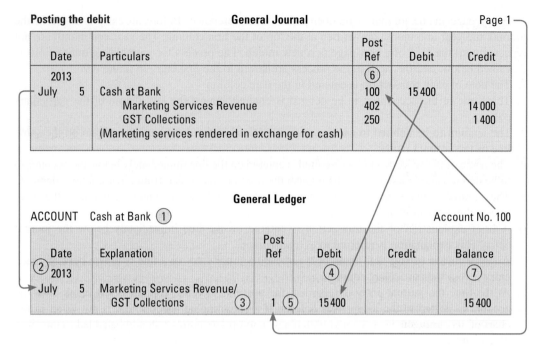

Posting the debit

General Journal — Page 1

Date	Particulars	Post Ref	Debit	Credit

2013 July 5	Cash at Bank
	    Marketing Services Revenue
	    GST Collections
	(Marketing services rendered in exchange for cash)
		⑥
		100
		402
		250
			15 400	
				14 000
				1 400

General Ledger

ACCOUNT   Cash at Bank ①   Account No. 100

Date	Explanation	Post Ref	Debit	Credit	Balance
② 2013 July 5	Marketing Services Revenue/ GST Collections ③	1 ⑤	④ 15 400		⑦ 15 400

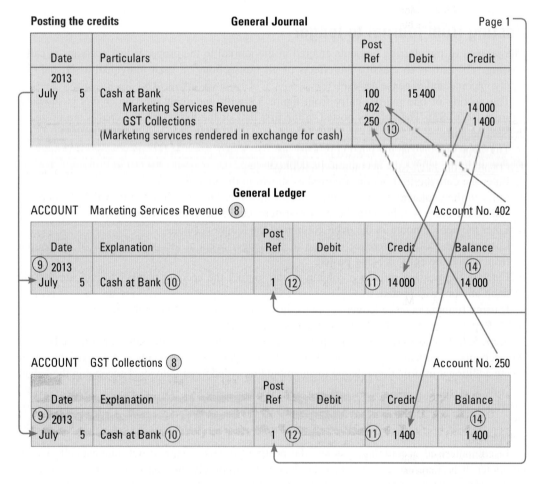

Posting the credits

General Journal — Page 1

Date	Particulars	Post Ref	Debit	Credit

2013 July 5	Cash at Bank
	    Marketing Services Revenue
	    GST Collections ⑬
	(Marketing services rendered in exchange for cash)
		100
		402
		250
			15 400	
				14 000
				1 400

General Ledger

ACCOUNT   Marketing Services Revenue ⑧   Account No. 402

Date	Explanation	Post Ref	Debit	Credit	Balance
⑨ 2013 July 5	Cash at Bank ⑩	1 ⑫		⑪ 14 000	⑭ 14 000

ACCOUNT   GST Collections ⑧   Account No. 250

Date	Explanation	Post Ref	Debit	Credit	Balance
⑨ 2013 July 5	Cash at Bank ⑩	1 ⑫		⑪ 1 400	⑭ 1 400

Illustrative example of journal and ledger

The June 2013 transactions for Intellect Management Services are used to illustrate the analysis of transactions and the sequence of steps to be followed in recording and summarising the transactions. GST transactions are shown as appropriate.

Step 1 involves an analysis of the transaction to identify which accounts are affected and whether an account needs to be increased or decreased. From the rules developed in the previous section it is then possible to determine whether to debit or credit the account involved. Note that each transaction affects two or more accounts with equal debits and credits so that, after posting, the accounting equation is still in balance. Having identified the accounts affected, it is possible to complete step 2. *Step 2* is the recording of the transaction in the general journal. This is the process of initial data entering. *Step 3* is the posting of the journal entry to the general ledger, presented in figure 3.12 on pages 96–9. For illustrative purposes, the T-account format is used and the accounts affected by each transaction are shown after posting has been completed. In the T accounts, the posting references to the journal are omitted at this stage for simplicity. Nevertheless, they must be present in practice, as illustrated later in the chapter.

The information accumulated in the general ledger in this chapter is used also in chapter 4 to prepare financial statements for the month of June. A time period of 1 month is used for illustrative purposes. However, as noted earlier, financial statements may be prepared at other intervals determined by management, such as every quarter, but they must be prepared annually at least.

1 June   Megan Mooney deposited $240 000 cash into an account opened for the management services business.

Analysis	The accounts affected are Cash at Bank and the Capital account of Megan Mooney (equity). The asset Cash at Bank is being increased and therefore is debited. M. Mooney, Capital account is being increased and therefore is credited. Capital transactions are exempt from GST.

Journal entry	General Journal				Page 1
	Date	Particulars	Post Ref	Debit	Credit

	2013 June 1	Cash at Bank
		      M. Mooney, Capital
		      (Cash deposited by owner into business bank account)
			100
			 300
				240 000	240 000

Ledger posting	**Cash at Bank**					**100**
	1/6	M. Mooney, Capital	240 000			

	M. Mooney, Capital					**300**
				1/6	Cash at Bank	240 000

1 June   Signed an agreement for the business to provide marketing services for a client for a monthly fee of $800 plus GST (10%) to be paid on the fifth day of the following month.

Analysis	Initially, signing the agreement does not create a recordable asset or income and therefore is not given accounting recognition. That is, the signing of the agreement does not normally constitute an accounting transaction. In the future, as the service is performed, the fee earned by the business plus GST is recognised as revenue in the accounts.
	There is no journal entry and hence no posting to the ledger.

2 June	Purchased land and office building for $300 000 plus GST (10%). The terms of the agreement provided for a payment by cheque of $90 000, the remainder to be financed with a 20-year mortgage bearing interest at 8% p.a. The purchase price is allocated $120 000 to land and $180 000 to the building.

Analysis	The land and building are both assets that are increased and are therefore debited. The GST paid is debited to the GST Outlays account. The Cash at Bank account is decreased by a credit. The unpaid portion of the purchase price is a claim against the business. A liability is therefore increased by a credit. Although this transaction involves more than two accounts (a compound entry), the sum of the dollar amounts debited equals the sum of the dollar amounts credited.

Journal entry	June	2	Land	150	120 000	
			Building	160	180 000	
			GST Outlays	120	30 000	
			Cash at Bank	100		90 000
			Mortgage Payable	260		240 000
			(Acquisition of land and buildings for cash and mortgage payable)			

Ledger posting

Cash at Bank   100

1/6	M. Mooney, Capital	240 000	2/6	Land/Building/ GST Outlays	90 000

GST Outlays   120

2/6	Cash at Bank/ Mortgage Payable	30 000			

Land   150

2/6	Cash at Bank/ Mortgage Payable	120 000			

Building   160

2/6	Cash at Bank/ Mortgage Payable	180 000			

Mortgage Payable   260

			2/6	Land/Building/ GST Outlays	240 000

3 June	A cash payment of $2112, representing $1920 for a 24-month fire and business liability insurance policy plus GST of $192, was made.

Analysis	The advance payment is recorded as a debit to an asset account, Prepaid Insurance. The asset acquired is insurance protection for 24 months, which will subsequently be expensed at some regular interval as insurance protection benefits are received and as a portion of the premium expires. Entries needed to adjust asset and liability accounts are covered in chapter 4. A payment decreases the asset Cash at Bank and is recorded as a credit in the account. The GST paid is recorded in the GST Outlays account.

Journal entry	June	3	Prepaid Insurance	110	1 920	
			GST Outlays	120	192	
			Cash at Bank	100		2 112
			(Purchase of a 24-month fire and business liability insurance policy)			

Ledger posting

Cash at Bank   **100**

| 1/6 | M. Mooney, Capital | 240 000 | 2/6 | Land/Building/ GST Outlays | 90 000 |
| | | | 3/6 | Prepaid Insurance/ GST Outlays | 2 112 |

Prepaid Insurance   **110**

| 3/6 | Cash at Bank | 1 920 | | | |

GST Outlays   **120**

| 2/6 | Cash at Bank/ Mortgage Payable | 30 000 | | | |
| 3/6 | Cash at Bank | 192 | | | |

---

5 June   Purchased office supplies for $1240 on credit, plus GST of $124.

| Analysis | This transaction increases an asset for office supplies, a liability for accounts payable, and the GST Outlays account for the GST. Increases in assets are recorded by debits and increases in liabilities are recorded by credits. |

Journal entry	June	5	Office Supplies	111	1 240	
			GST Outlays	120	124	
			Accounts Payable	200		1 364
			(Office supplies purchased on credit)			

Ledger posting

Office Supplies   **111**

| 5/6 | Accounts Payable | 1 240 | | | |

GST Outlays   **120**

2/6	Cash at Bank/ Mortgage Payable	30 000			
3/6	Cash at Bank	192			
5/6	Accounts Payable	124			

Accounts Payable   **200**

| | | | 5/6 | Office Supplies/ GST Outlays | 1 364 |

5 June Purchased office equipment for a price of $19 200 plus GST of $1920. Paid $11 920 in cash with the balance due in 90 days.

Analysis	The account Office Equipment is increased by a debit of $19 200 to record the purchase of the asset and GST Outlays records the GST paid. At the same time, Cash at Bank is decreased by a credit of $11 920 and Accounts Payable, a liability, is increased by a credit of $9200 to recognise a claim against the business.

Journal entry	June 5	Office Equipment	170	19 200	
		GST Outlays	120	1 920	
		Cash at Bank	100		11 920
		Accounts Payable	200		9 200
		(Office equipment purchased, paying cash and the balance due in 90 days)			

Ledger posting

Cash at Bank   **100**

1/6	M. Mooney, Capital	240 000	2/6	Land/Building/ GST Outlays	90 000
			3/6	Prepaid Insurance/ GST Outlays	2 112
			5/6	Office Equipment/ GST Outlays	11 920

GST Outlays   **120**

2/6	Cash at Bank/ Mortgage Payable	30 000			
3/6	Cash at Bank	192			
5/6	Accounts Payable	124			
5/6	Cash at Bank/ Accounts Payable	1 920			

Office Equipment   **170**

5/6	Cash at Bank/ Accounts Payable	19 200			

Accounts Payable   **200**

			5/6	Office Supplies/ GST Outlays	1 364
			5/6	Office Equipment/ GST Outlays	9 200

5 June Hired two management advisers and an office assistant.

Analysis	The hiring of employees is an important event to the business but is not recognised in the accounts since it is considered that an accounting transaction has not yet taken place. The new employees have, as yet, done nothing to alter the future economic benefits of the entity.
	There is no journal entry and hence no posting to the ledger.

6 June   Paid $264 (including $24 GST) in cash for radio commercials aired on 3 and 4 June.

Analysis	Advertising is an expense. The benefits were considered to be received when the radio announcements were made. The Advertising Expense account is increased by a debit. Expenses decrease equity (a debit), but a separate account, Advertising Expense, is established to facilitate preparation of the income statement. The Cash at Bank account is decreased by a credit, and the GST paid is recorded in the GST Outlays account.

Journal entry	June	6	Advertising Expense GST Outlays Cash at Bank (Radio commercials paid for, aired on 3 and 4 June)	520 120 100	240 24	 264

Ledger posting

Cash at Bank   100

1/6	M. Mooney, Capital	240 000	2/6	Land/Building/ GST Outlays	90 000
			3/6	Prepaid Insurance/ GST Outlays	2 112
			5/6	Office Equipment/ GST Outlays	11 920
			6/6	Advertising Expense/ GST Outlays	264

GST Outlays   120

2/6	Cash at Bank/ Mortgage Payable	30 000		
3/6	Cash at Bank	192		
5/6	Accounts Payable	124		
5/6	Cash at Bank/ Accounts Payable	1 920		
6/6	Cash at Bank	24		

Advertising Expense   520

6/6	Cash at Bank	240		

15 June   Performed management services for a customer. A fee of $9240 (including GST of $840) was receivable for the services, to be received on or before 30 June.

Analysis	Under accrual accounting, this is an income transaction (recorded as revenue in this case) even though no cash was received. The asset Accounts Receivable is therefore increased (a debit) to recognise the right to receive cash in the future. Income increases equity (a credit), but a separate account, Management Services Revenue, is established to facilitate preparation of the income statement. GST Collections is credited for the amount of GST receivable.

Journal entry	June	15	Accounts Receivable
			    Management Services Revenue
			    GST Collections
			(Revenue receivable on management
			services provided)
				104
				400
				250
					9 240	
						8 400
						840

Accounts Receivable						104
15/6	Management Services Revenue/GST Collections	9 240				

GST Collections						250
			15/6	Accounts Receivable	840	

Management Services Revenue						400
			15/6	Accounts Receivable	8 400	

19 June   Performed management services for a client. A fee of $10 800 was receivable, plus GST of $1080.

Analysis	Same as the income transaction on 15 June.				
Journal entry	June 19	Accounts Receivable	104	11 880	
		Management Services Revenue	400		10 800
		GST Collections	250		1 080
		(Fees for services rendered)			

Ledger posting

Accounts Receivable						104
15/6	Management Services Revenue/GST Collections	9 240				
19/6	Management Services Revenue/GST Collections	11 880				

GST Collections						250
			15/6	Accounts Receivable	840	
			19/6	Accounts Receivable	1 080	

Management Services Revenue						400
			15/6	Accounts Receivable	8 400	
			19/6	Accounts Receivable	10 800	

22 June   Paid salaries of $7600 to the office assistant and other employees for services rendered during the last two weeks.[1] (Deductions from the employees' salaries are ignored for now.) No GST is payable on wages and salaries.

Analysis	Analysis is similar to the transaction on 6 June. However, the transactions differ as to the kind of expense involved. A separate expense account is established for each significant expense category.

---

1. The term *salary* refers usually to fixed compensation paid on a regular basis for services received from employees. The term *wage* is used commonly to refer to compensation stated in terms of an hourly rate or a similar basis. Here, for convenience, the term *salary* applies to both.

Journal entry	June	22	Salaries Expense Cash at Bank (Salaries paid to employees)	500 100	7 600	7 600

Ledger posting				**Cash at Bank**			**100**

Cash at Bank   **100**

1/6	M. Mooney, Capital	240 000	2/6	Land/Building/ GST Outlays	90 000
			3/6	Prepaid Insurance/ GST Outlays	2 112
			5/6	Office Equipment/ GST Outlays	11 920
			6/6	Advertising Expense/ GST Outlays	264
			22/6	Salaries Expense	7 600

Salaries Expense   **500**

22/6	Cash at Bank	7 600			

23 June   Conducted a valuation of a customer's property and received a fee of $550 (including 10% GST) in cash.

Analysis	The performance of the service is an income transaction and the receipt of cash increases both asset (debited) and equity (credited). A separate revenue account is established to recognise this kind of income.

Journal entry	June	23	Cash at Bank Appraisal Fees Revenue GST Collections (Fee received for valuation)	100 401 250	550	500 50

Ledger posting

Cash at Bank   **100**

1/6
23/6
	M. Mooney, Capital
	Appraisal Fees
	  Revenue/GST
	  Collections
		240 000
		
		550
			2/6	Land/Building/
				  GST Outlays
					90 000

			3/6	Prepaid Insurance/ GST Outlays	2 112
			5/6	Office Equipment/ GST Outlays	11 920
			6/6	Advertising Expense/ GST Outlays	264
			22/6	Salaries Expense	7 600

GST Collections   **250**

			15/6	Accounts Receivable	840
			19/6	Accounts Receivable	1 080
			23/6	Cash at Bank	50

Appraisal Fees Revenue   **401**

			23/6	Cash at Bank	500

23 June   Mooney withdrew $1200 cash from the business bank account for her personal use.

Analysis	This transaction is a withdrawal of assets or a negative investment by the owner and is not an expense related to the earning of income. It does not attract GST. A debit is made to the Drawings account to reflect the decrease in capital, and the decrease in the Cash at Bank account is recorded by a credit.

Journal entry	June	23	M. Mooney, Drawings	310	1 200	
			Cash at Bank	100		1 200
			(Drawings of cash by owner)			

Ledger posting

Cash at Bank   100

1/6	M. Mooney, Capital	240 000	2/6	Land/Building/	
23/6	Appraisal Fees			GST Outlays	90 000
	Revenue/GST		3/6	Prepaid Insurance/	
	Collections	550		GST Outlays	2 112
			5/6	Office Equipment/	
				GST Outlays	11 920
			6/6	Advertising Expense/	
				GST Outlays	284
			22/6	Salaies Expense	7 600
			23/6	M. Mooney, Drawings	1 200

M. Mooney, Drawings   310

23/6	Cash at Bank	1 200			

27 June   Paid $1364 cash to creditors for office supplies purchased on credit on 5 June. No GST is recorded here as the GST was recorded on 5 June, and is recorded in the $1364 owing.

Analysis	The payment reduces a creditor's claim against the assets of the business. A decrease in liabilities is recorded by a debit and the asset Cash at Bank is decreased by a credit.

Journal entry	June	27	Accounts Payable	200	1 364	
			Cash at Bank	100		1 364
			(Payment for office supplies purchased on 5 June)			

Ledger posting

Cash at Bank   100

1/6	M. Mooney, Capital	240 000	2/6	Land/Building/	
23/6	Appraisal Fees			GST Outlays	90 000
	Revenue/GST		3/6	Prepaid Insurance/	
	Collections	550		GST Outlays	2 112
			5/6	Office Equipment/	
				GST Outlays	11 920
			6/6	Advertising Expense/	
				GST Outlays	264
			22/6	Salaries Expense	7 600
			23/6	M. Mooney, Drawings	1 200
			27/6	Accounts Payable	1 364

Accounts Payable						200
27/6	Cash at Bank	1 364	5/6	Office Supplies/ GST Outlays		1 364
			5/6	Office Equipment/ GST Outlays		9 200

29 June   Received cash of $616 for valuation appraisals to be performed in July, and banked the money. The money includes $56 for GST.

Analysis	Cash at Bank is increased by a debit. Since the service has not yet been performed, a liability, Unearned Appraisal Fees, is therefore recorded to reflect the obligation to perform the appraisal at some future date. The liability is increased and therefore is credited.

Journal entry	June	29	Cash at Bank	100	616	
			Unearned Appraisal Fees	220		560
			GST Collections	250		56
			(Cash received for appraisals to be performed in July)			

Ledger posting

Cash at Bank						100
1/6	M. Mooney, Capital	240 000	2/6	Land/Building/ GST Outlays		90 000
23/6	Appraisal Fees Revenue/GST Collections	550	3/6	Prepaid Insurance/ GST Outlays		2 112
29/6	Unearned Appraisal Fees/GST Collections	616	5/6	Office Equipment/ GST Outlays		11 920
			6/6	Advertising Expense/ GST Outlays		264
			22/6	Salaries Expense		7 600
			23/6	M. Mooney, Drawings		1 200
			27/6	Accounts Payable		1 364

Unearned Appraisal Fees						220
			29/6	Cash at Bank		560

GST Collections						250
			15/6	Accounts Receivable		840
			19/6	Accounts Receivable		1 080
			23/6	Cash at Bank		50
			29/6	Cash at Bank		56

30 June Paid the month's telephone bill of $160 plus $16 for GST.

Analysis	Analysis is similar to transaction on 6 June.				
Journal entry	June 30	Telephone Expense GST Outlays Cash at Bank (Telephone bill paid for June)	510 120 100	160 16	 176

Ledger posting							

Cash at Bank   100

1/6	M. Mooney, Capital	240 000	2/6	Land/Building/ GST Outlays	90 000

23/6	Appraisal Fees
	    Revenue/GST
	    Collections
		550	3/6	Prepaid Insurance/
				    GST Outlays
					2 112

29/6	Unearned Appraisal
	    Fees/GST
	    Collections
		616	5/6	Office Equipment/
				    GST Outlays
					11 920

			6/6	Advertising Expense/ GST Outlays	264
			22/6	Salaries Expense	7 600
			23/6	M. Mooney, Drawings	1 200
			27/6	Accounts Payable	1 364
			30/6	Telephone Expense/ GST Outlays	176

GST Outlays   120

2/6	Cash at Bank/ Mortgage Payable	30 000		
3/6	Cash at Bank	192		
5/6	Accounts Payable	124		
5/6	Cash at Bank/ Accounts Payable	1 920		
6/6	Cash at Bank	24		
30/6	Cash at Bank	16		

Telephone Expense   510

30/6	Cash at Bank	160		

30 June   An amount of $9240 was received for management services rendered and invoiced on 15 June, and was direct deposited into the business bank account. No GST is recorded here as the GST was recorded on 15 June.

Analysis	The increase in Cash at Bank is recorded by a debit. The receipt also reduces the claims against a debtor. A decrease in the asset Accounts Receivable is recorded by a credit. Note that this transaction increases one asset and decreases another. Recall that income (in the form of revenue) was recorded on 15 June, that is, when the services were rendered to the client rather than when the cash was collected.

Journal entry	June 30 Cash at Bank 100 9 240
	                    Accounts Receivable 104 9 240
	           (Cash received in relation to management
	           services on 15 June)

Ledger posting

Cash at Bank   100

1/6	M. Mooney, Capital	240 000	2/6	Land/Building/	
23/6	Appraisal Fees			GST Outlays	90 000
	Revenue/GST		3/6	Prepaid Insurance/	
	Collections	550		GST Outlays	2 112
29/6	Unearned Appraisal		5/6	Office Equipment/	
	Fees/GST			GST Outlays	11 920
	Collections	616	6/6	Advertising Expense/	
30/6	Accounts Receivable	9 240		GST Outlays	264
			22/6	Salaries Expense	7 600
			23/6	M. Mooney, Drawings	1 200
			27/6	Accounts Payable	1 364
			30/6	Telephone Expense/	
				GST Outlays	176

Accounts Receivable   104

15/6	Management Services		30/6	Cash at Bank	9 240
	Revenue/GST				
	Collections	9 240			
19/6	Management Services				
	Revenue/GST				
	Collections	11 880			

In summary, the complete general journal for the month of June 2013 is illustrated in figure 3.11.

Figure 3.11 General journal of Intellect Management Services

		General Journal			Page 1
Date	Particulars	Post Ref	Debit		Credit
2013					
June 1	Cash at Bank	100	240 000		
	M. Mooney, Capital	300			240 000
	(Cash deposited by owner into business bank account)				
2	Land	150	120 000		
	Building	160	180 000		
	GST Outlays	120	30 000		
	Cash at Bank	100			90 000
	Mortgage Payable	260			240 000
	(Acquisition of land and buildings for cash and mortgage payable)				
3	Prepaid Insurance	110	1 920		
	GST Outlays	120	192		
	Cash at Bank	100			2 112
	(Purchase of a 24-month fire and business liability insurance policy)				
5	Office Supplies	111	1 240		
	GST Outlays	120	124		
	Accounts Payable	200			1 364
	(Office supplies purchased on credit)				
5	Office Equipment	170	19 200		
	GST Outlays	120	1 920		
	Cash at Bank	100			11 920
	Accounts Payable	200			9 200
	(Office equipment purchased, paying cash and the balance due in 90 days)				
6	Advertising Expense	520	240		
	GST Outlays	120	24		
	Cash at Bank	100			264
	(Radio commercials paid for aired on 3 and 4 June)				
15	Accounts Receivable	104	9 240		
	Management Services Revenue	400			8 400
	GST Collections	250			840
	(Revenue receivable on management services provided)				

Figure 3.11 *continued*

			Post Ref	Debit	Credit
General Journal					Page 2
Date	Particulars				
2013					
June 19	Accounts Receivable		104	11 880	
	Management Services Revenue		400		10 800
	GST Collections		250		1 080
	(Fees for services rendered)				
22	Salaries Expense		500	7 600	
	Cash at Bank		100		7 600
	(Salaries paid to employees)				
23	Cash at Bank		100	550	
	Appraisal Fees Revenue		401		500
	GST Collections		250		50
	(Fee received for valuation)				
23	M. Mooney, Drawings		310	1 200	
	Cash at Bank		100		1 200
	(Drawings of cash by owner)				
27	Accounts Payable		200	1 364	
	Cash at Bank		100		1 364
	(Payment for office supplies purchased on 5 June)				
29	Cash at Bank		100	616	
	Unearned Appraisal Fees		220		560
	GST Collections		250		56
	(Cash received for appraisals to be performed in July)				
30	Telephone Expense		510	160	
	GST Outlays		120	16	
	Cash at Bank		100		176
	(Telephone bill paid for June)				
30	Cash at Bank		100	9 240	
	Accounts Receivable		104		9 240
	(Cash received in relation to management services on 15 June)				
				636 726	636 726

The general ledger for Intellect Management Services, showing the effects of the transactions on the accounts maintained by the business, is presented in figure 3.12 (pp. 96–9). In an actual manual accounting system, each account would be a separate page or card. The running balance format is used in figure 3.12 rather than the T-account form, which was used before, to illustrate the effects of the transactions on the accounts.

General Ledger

ACCOUNT **Cash at Bank**   Account No. **100**

Date		Explanation	Post Ref	Debit	Credit	Balance
2013						
June	1	M. Mooney, Capital	1	240 000		240 000
	2	Land/Building/GST Outlays	1		90 000	150 000
	3	Prepaid Insurance/				
		GST Outlays	1		2 112	147 888
	5	Office Equipment/				
		GST Outlays	1		11 920	135 968
	6	Advertising Expense/				
		GST Outlays	1		264	135 704
	22	Salaries Expense	2		7 600	128 104
	23	Appraisal Fees Revenue/				
		GST Collections	2	550		128 654
	23	M. Mooney, Drawings	2		1 200	127 454
	27	Accounts Payable	2		1 364	126 090
	29	Unearned Appraisal Fees/				
		GST Collections	2	616		126 706
	30	Telephone Expense/				
		GST Outlays	2		176	126 530
	30	Accounts Receivable	2	9 240		135 770

ACCOUNT **Accounts Receivable**   Account No. **104**

Date		Explanation	Post Ref	Debit	Credit	Balance
2013						
June	15	Management Services Revenue/				
		GST Collections	1	9 240		9 240
	19	Management Services Revenue/				
		GST Collections	2	11 880		21 120
	30	Cash at Bank	2		9 240	11 880

ACCOUNT **Prepaid Insurance**   Account No. **110**

Date		Explanation	Post Ref	Debit	Credit	Balance
2013						
June	3	Cash at Bank	1	1 920		1 920

ACCOUNT **Office Supplies**   Account No. **111**

Date		Explanation	Post Ref	Debit	Credit	Balance
2013						
June	5	Accounts Payable	1	1 240		1 240

Figure 3.12 *continued*

ACCOUNT **GST Outlays**   Account No. **120**

Date		Explanation	Post Ref	Debit	Credit	Balance
2013						
June	2	Cash at Bank/				
		Mortgage Payable	1	30 000		30 000
	3	Cash at Bank	1	192		30 192
	5	Accounts Payable	1	124		30 316
	5	Cash at Bank/				
		Accounts Payable	1	1 920		32 236
	6	Cash at Bank	1	24		32 260
	30	Cash at Bank	2	16		32 276

ACCOUNT **Land**   Account No. **150**

Date		Explanation	Post Ref	Debit	Credit	Balance
2013						
June	2	Cash at Bank/				
		Mortgage Payable	1	120 000		120 000

ACCOUNT **Building**   Account No. **160**

Date		Explanation	Post Ref	Debit	Credit	Balance
2013						
June	2	Cash at Bank/				
		Mortgage Payable	1	180 000		180 000

ACCOUNT **Office Equipment**   Account No. **170**

Date		Explanation	Post Ref	Debit	Credit	Balance
2013						
June	5	Cash at Bank/				
		Accounts Payable	1	19 200		19 200

ACCOUNT **Accounts Payable**   Account No. **200**

Date		Explanation	Post Ref	Debit	Credit	Balance
2013						
June	5	Office Supplies/				
		GST Outlays	1		1 364	1 364
	5	Office Equipment/				
		GST Outlays	1		9 200	10 564
	27	Cash at Bank	2	1 364		9 200

(continued)

Figure 3.12 *continued*

ACCOUNT **Unearned Appraisal Fees**   Account No. **220**

Date	Explanation	Post Ref	Debit	Credit	Balance
2013 June 29	Cash at Bank	2		560	560

ACCOUNT **GST Collections**   Account No. **250**

Date	Explanation	Post Ref	Debit	Credit	Balance
2013 June 15	Accounts Receivable	1		840	840
19	Accounts Receivable	2		1 080	1 920
23	Cash at Bank	2		50	1 970
29	Cash at Bank	2		56	2 026

ACCOUNT **Mortgage Payable**   Account No. **260**

Date	Explanation	Post Ref	Debit	Credit	Balance
2013 June 2	Land/Buildings/GST Outlays	1		240 000	240 000

ACCOUNT **M. Mooney, Capital**   Account No. **300**

Date	Explanation	Post Ref	Debit	Credit	Balance
2013 June 1	Cash at Bank	1		240 000	240 000

ACCOUNT **M. Mooney, Drawings**   Account No. **310**

Date	Explanation	Post Ref	Debit	Credit	Balance
2013 June 23	Cash at Bank	2	1 200		1 200

ACCOUNT **Management Services Revenue**   Account No. **400**

Date	Explanation	Post Ref	Debit	Credit	Balance
2013 June 15	Accounts Receivable	1		8 400	8 400
19	Accounts Receivable	2		10 800	19 200

Figure 3.12 *continued*

ACCOUNT	**Appraisal Fees Revenue**				Account No. **401**
Date	Explanation	Post Ref	Debit	Credit	Balance
2013 June 23	Cash at Bank	2		500	500

ACCOUNT	**Salaries Expense**				Account No. **500**
Date	Explanation	Post Ref	Debit	Credit	Balance
2013 June 22	Cash at Bank	2	7 600		7 600

ACCOUNT	**Telephone Expense**				Account No. **510**
Date	Explanation	Post Ref	Debit	Credit	Balance
2013 June 30	Cash at Bank	2	160		160

ACCOUNT	**Advertising Expense**				Account No. **520**
Date	Explanation	Post Ref	Debit	Credit	Balance
2013 June 6	Cash at Bank	1	240		240

BUSINESS KNOWLEDGE

Getting ready for sustainability reporting

'Crunch time' arrived for many large and medium-sized firms in Australia that had to start reporting on greenhouse gas activities under the *National Greenhouse and Energy Reporting (NGER) Act 2007*. If fact, hundreds of companies faced reporting for the first time if they emitted greenhouse gases, produced energy, or consumed energy at or above set levels.

Commentators at the time noted that issues surrounded data-capture processes that were typically set up for financial information. Many companies first reporting on their carbon footprint attempt to use existing data, which is not enough. Estimations were that two years are required to get to a robust set of greenhouse gas accounts. In most cases, new systems and staff retraining are required.

Source: Based on Deborah Tarrant, 'The root of the matter', *InTheBlack*.

3.9 Trial balance

Learning objective 9

Understand the purpose of a trial balance and how to prepare one

The double-entry accounting system requires, for every transaction, equal dollar amounts of debits and credits to be recorded in the accounts. The equality of debits and credits posted to the ledger accounts is verified by preparing a **trial balance** — a list of all of the accounts in the order in which they appear in the general ledger with their current balances. The dollar amounts of accounts with debit balances are listed in one column, and the dollar amounts of accounts with credit balances are listed in a second column. The totals of the two columns should be equal. When this occurs, the ledger is said to be 'in balance'. Figure 3.13 is a trial balance based on the accounts in the general ledger of Intellect Management Services (see figure 3.12).

Figure 3.13 Trial balance of Intellect Management Services

Account	Account no.	Debit	Credit
INTELLECT MANAGEMENT SERVICES Trial Balance as at 30 June 2013			
Cash at bank	100	$135 770	
Accounts receivable	104	11 880	
Prepaid insurance	110	1 920	
Office supplies	111	1 240	
GST outlays	120	32 276	
Land	150	120 000	
Building	160	180 000	
Office equipment	170	19 200	
Accounts payable	200		$ 9 200
Unearned appraisal fees	220		560
GST collections	250		2 026
Mortgage payable	260		240 000
M. Mooney, Capital	300		240 000
M. Mooney, Drawings	310	1 200	
Management services revenue	400		19 200
Appraisal fees revenue	401		500
Salary expense	500	7 600	
Telephone expense	510	160	
Advertising expense	530	240	
		$511 486	$511 486

Note that a trial balance may be prepared at any time to test the equality of debits and credits in the ledger. In a computerised accounting system, the computer will automatically produce a trial balance when requested by the user of the system.

Limitations of the trial balance

The fact that the sum of the debit column equals the sum of the credit column in the trial balance does not guarantee that errors have not been made. The trial balance is simply a verification that equal debits and credits have been recorded in the accounts. It also verifies that the account balances were calculated correctly, based on the recorded data. However, errors could be made that do not affect the equality of debits and credits. For example, a correct amount could have been posted to the wrong account, a journal entry might have been omitted, or an incorrect amount could have been posted to both of the correct accounts. The possibility of making such errors should serve to emphasise the need to exercise due care in entering and posting transactions.

Some errors are discovered by chance or during normal operations. For example, if an account receivable is overstated, the customer usually will point this out when the monthly accounts are sent. Other errors may be identified through procedures established by the business to check on the accuracy of its records. For example, as is discussed in a later chapter, a bank reconciliation is prepared each month to verify the balance in the Cash at Bank account.

A trial balance that does not balance is a clear indication of one or more errors in the accounts, or an error in preparing the trial balance. Although there is no one correct procedure for locating all types of errors, the following systematic approach will be helpful.

1. Check the accuracy of the trial balance totals by adding the columns again.
2. Calculate the difference between the totals. Certain types of errors may be identified by performing a couple of simple mathematical exercises. For example, the amount of the difference may be equal to a debit or credit that was omitted. If the difference between the trial balance totals is divisible by 2, this could indicate that a debit account balance is listed accidentally in the trial balance as a credit or vice versa. The trial balance and journal should first be reviewed for each of these amounts.

If the difference between the two trial balance totals is divisible by 9, it may be an indication of two common errors called **transpositions** and **slides**. To illustrate, assume that an expense account should have been debited for $4610. If the error is a transposition, the order of the digits in a number is altered, e.g. posting the amount as $4160. In a slide, the decimal point is shifted to the left or right, e.g. writing $461 instead of $4610. In both types of errors, the difference between the correct number and the incorrect number can be divided evenly by 9.

3. Compare the balances listed in the trial balance with the ledger accounts to verify that all account balances were included and copied correctly.
4. Recalculate the account balances.
5. Verify that the debits equal the credits for each entry in the journal.
6. Trace the entries as recorded in the journal to the ledger accounts, and place a small tick by each account in the journal and ledger as each posting is verified. Be alert for the posting of wrong amounts and debits posted as credits or vice versa. If the error is not found before this process is completed, review the journal and ledger, looking for amounts without a tick.

3.10 Correcting errors

Learning objective 10

Correct errors made in the journal or ledger

Once an error is located, it must be corrected. An error in a journal entry discovered before the amount is posted is corrected by crossing out the wrong amount with a single line and inserting the correct amount immediately above. An error in a ledger amount is corrected in the same way. Errors should not be erased or opaqued because this may give the impression that something is being concealed.

Journal entries that have been posted in the wrong accounts should be corrected by a journal entry. For example, assume that the receipt of cash for the performance of a service for a customer was entered in the journal and posted in the ledger to the following accounts:

Feb.	14	Accounts Receivable	946	
		Service Revenue		860
		GST Collections		86
		(Performance of a service on account)		

A correcting entry is needed to cancel the incorrect debit to Accounts Receivable and to record a correct debit to the Cash at Bank account.

March	10	Cash at Bank	946	
		Accounts Receivable		946
		(Correction of entry on 14 Feb. in which a cash receipt was debited to Accounts Receivable)		

Use of dollar signs and decimal points

Note that in the figures in this chapter dollar signs are not used in the journal or the ledger. Dollar signs are used, however, in the financial statements and other financial reports. A common practice in formal statements is to place a dollar sign before the first amount in a column of figures and also before the total amount. When dollar amounts are entered in the journal or ledger and the columns are ruled, decimal points are not necessary. The ruled columns serve to separate cents from dollars.

Introduction to the goods and services tax in Australia

A goods and services tax (GST) was introduced into Australia on 1 July 2000 as part of the Australian Government's tax reform package. The GST is a tax levied at the rate of 10% on the supply (sale) of most services and goods (referred to as 'taxable supplies' in the GST legislation). Businesses registered under the GST legislation collect the tax on behalf of the Australian Taxation Office (ATO), and remit the amounts collected to the ATO at regular intervals. With the GST comes the need to account for it in an entity's accounting records to enable the preparation of the necessary return, called a business activity statement (BAS), to be submitted to the ATO.

In order to avoid duplicating the GST at various levels of the production and supply chain, businesses are allowed to offset any GST they pay on buying services and goods ('creditable acquisitions' in the GST legislation) against the GST collected on supplies (services rendered or sales made). These offsets are referred to in the GST legislation as 'input credits'.

All supplies of services and goods are subject to GST unless they are non-taxable. There are two types of non-taxable supplies:
- 'GST-free' supplies
- 'input taxed' supplies.

GST-free supplies are services and goods that would normally attract GST but are exempted under the legislation, e.g. fresh food, educational courses, medical products and services, wages and salaries, capital contributions and withdrawals. If a supply is GST-free, then the supplier will not charge GST on the supply of services or goods to the consumer, but will still be able to claim an input tax credit for the GST paid on all things acquired to make the supply. If a supply is 'input taxed', then the supplier will not charge GST on the supply to the consumer, but will not be able to claim an input tax credit on the goods and services acquired in order to make the supply. Input taxed supplies include financial services such as bank fees and charges.

Non-current assets attract input tax credits when purchased, and GST when sold. The ATO requires separate reporting for non-current assets costing over $1000, and therefore a special note should be made of purchases and sales of these types of transactions.

A business with an annual turnover from supply of services or goods over $75 000 is required by law to register as a business responsible for collecting and remitting GST to the ATO. Such businesses are required to register with the ATO as a business and receive an eleven-digit Australian business number (ABN). This ABN is also the GST registration number. Currently, registered companies also require an Australian company number (ACN). These numbers must appear on all official documents (e.g. letterheads, invoices) relating to the business.

An ABN (and GST registration) is optional for businesses with annual turnover less than $75 000, but there are advantages in registering for an ABN. For example, an unregistered business cannot add GST to the services and goods it supplies, and without an ABN it cannot claim input credits for GST paid on acquisitions of services or goods.

Businesses with annual gross revenues less than $2 000 000 can choose to account for GST on either a cash or an accrual (invoice) basis. Businesses with annual gross revenues more than $2 000 000 must account for GST on the accrual (invoice) basis. Under the cash accounting system, GST collections are recorded at the time cash is received for supply of services and goods and GST outlays are recorded when cash is paid for services and goods. Under the accrual accounting system, GST collections and GST outlays are recorded when a tax invoice is issued/received (as in figure 3.1 on p. 67) or cash is received/paid, whichever event occurs first.

The GST in practice

To appreciate how the GST system of taxing the supply of services and goods (on 'taxable supplies') and allowing rebates ('input credits') for the GST outlays on the purchase of services and goods ('creditable acquisitions') works, consider the following example.

Example

In Australia, a steel merchant sells $2000 of steel to a furniture manufacturer. GST of 10% is charged, and the steel merchant must collect $200 GST from the furniture manufacturer, who is thus charged $2200 in total for the steel. The furniture manufacturer then uses the steel, along with other materials purchased from other suppliers and labour, to make furniture.

The manufacturer then sells the furniture to a retailer for $10 000, plus GST of $1000. Finally, the retailer sells the furniture to a consumer for $17 000, plus GST of $1700, making a total price of $18 700.

The final result of these transactions is as follows:

- The retailer (the end of the supply chain) collects $1700 from the customer on the taxable supply of furniture. This amount is payable by the retailer to the ATO, subject to any credits to which the retailer may be entitled.
- The retailer outlays $1000 for GST to the manufacturer on the manufacturer's taxable supply of furniture to the retailer. Since this represents a creditable acquisition, the retailer is entitled to claim an input tax credit of $1000 against the GST collected. This means that the retailer effectively pays no GST on the supply purchased from the manufacturer. In due course, the retailer has to pay $700 ($1700 − $1000) to the ATO.
- The manufacturer has collected $100 GST from the retailer, but is entitled to claim a credit for the $200 outlay for GST to the steel merchant. The manufacturer is entitled to claim an input tax credit of $200, thus paying no GST on the supply of the steel purchased from the steel merchant. In due course, the manufacturer has to pay $800 ($1000 − $200) to the ATO.
- The steel merchant has collected $20 from the furniture manufacturer. If we assume that the steel merchant pays no GST on inputs to manufacture the steel, the steel supplier is not entitled to claim an input tax credit from the government. Thus the steel supplier has to pay the full $200 GST collected to the ATO.

The flow of GST amounts in the above example is illustrated in figure A3.1.

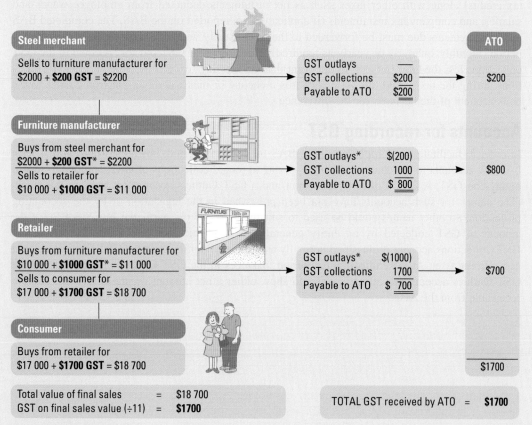

Figure A3.1 Flow of GST among entities and the ATO

It is assumed in this figure that the only transactions that occur in the current tax period are those mentioned. Furthermore, as explained previously, instead of each entity paying the gross amount of GST on a supply to the ATO, the amount of GST receivable as an input tax credit is netted off against the amount of GST payable. This information is supplied to the ATO on the entity's BAS. For example, the manufacturer pays a net amount of $800 ($1000 − $200) to the ATO, and the retailer pays a net amount of $700 ($1700 − $1000) to the ATO.

Each entity is required by law to show separately the amount of GST payable by its customers on the entity's tax invoice or sales docket. Each entity then records the flow of GST through its accounting records by means of the GST Collections and GST Outlays accounts.

Accounting for the GST

GST legislation requires businesses registered for GST (whether using the cash or accrual basis of accounting) to organise their accounting system so that records are made of the GST collected/collectable on taxable supplies of services and goods, and the GST paid/payable on creditable acquisitions of services and goods. GST-registered businesses are also required to design source documents so that they include all the information required under the GST legislation. Note that for the purposes of the GST legislation, for supplies of goods and services over $82.50 (including GST), a 'tax invoice' must be supplied if requested. Such invoices must meet the legislative requirements of a tax invoice, that is, they must be labelled as such, and must show the ABN of the business issuing the invoice and the GST-inclusive price of the goods and services being sold. Commonly, tax invoices also show the amount of GST included in the price of the goods and services. Additional requirements must be met under certain conditions.

The amounts of GST collections and outlays must be reported to the ATO on either a monthly, quarterly or yearly basis (the 'tax period') depending on turnover. In February 2001, the Treasurer of the Australian Government announced some relief for businesses with an annual turnover of less than $2 000 000 in that they can provide a BAS to the ATO on an annual basis. Nevertheless, tax payments must still be made quarterly by these businesses. GST collections and outlays (input tax credits) along with other taxes such as tax instalments deducted from employee wages and salaries, and company tax instalments (if applicable) are reported on the BAS. The completed BAS and any payments due must be forwarded to the ATO usually within 28 days of the end of the tax period (monthly, quarterly or yearly as required). The amount of GST payable is equal to the GST collections less the GST outlays. In the event that GST outlays exceed the amount of GST collections during the tax period, the ATO forwards a cheque or makes a direct electronic debit to the bank account of the business for the difference.

Accounts for recording GST

In order to facilitate the completion of the BAS for each tax period, businesses must add at least two new accounts to the chart of accounts — one to record collections of GST, and one to record outlays on GST. A GST Collections account and a GST Outlays account are used in this book. (The names for such accounts have not been prescribed in the legislation or by the accounting profession, so other names could be used to suit the needs of the particular business.) Since the amount of GST collected by an entity generally exceeds the GST paid each tax period, the GST Collections account is classified normally as a current liability, with the GST Outlays account as a current asset. At the end of the tax period, balances in the GST Collections account and the GST Outlays account are offset in order to show either a net amount owing to or a net amount receivable from the ATO.

Account, p. 69
Account balance, p. 69
Accounting cycle, p. 69
Accounting manual, p. 77
Accounting periods, p. 68
Annual report, p. 68
Australian business number (ABN), p. 68
Chart of accounts, p. 75
Compound journal entry, p. 80
Credit, p. 69
Creditors, p. 72
Debit, p. 69
Debtors, p. 72

Entering (journalising), p. 80
Expenses, p. 74
External transactions, p. 66
Gain, p. 74
General journal (two-column journal), p. 80
General ledger, p. 69
GST Collections, p. 73
GST Outlays, p. 73
Income, p. 74
Interim statements, p. 69
Internal transactions, p. 66
Journal (book of original entry), p. 79
Journal entry, p. 80

Loss, p. 74
Normal account balance, p. 78
Posting, p. 81
Profit, p. 74
Revenue, p. 74
Running balance account, p. 70
Slide, p. 101
Source document, p. 67
T account, p. 69
Trade creditors, p. 72
Trade debtors, p. 72
Transposition, p. 101
Trial balance, p. 99
Two-column journal, p. 80

DISCUSSION QUESTIONS

1. Indicate whether each of the following events is an internal transaction, an external transaction, or a non-transaction event. Explain your answer in each case:
   (a) Land is purchased.
   (b) Equipment is used to provide a service for a customer.
   (c) Money is borrowed from the Ballarat Bank.
   (d) Land owned by the business increased in value.
   (e) Received payment from a customer on account.
   (f) A prospective employee is interviewed and hired for a job.
   (g) Stationery supplies are used by an employee.

2. The owner of a very small, part-time business was not interested in keeping detailed accounts for the business. Recently, an accountant advised that the business should have its accounts recorded under the double-entry system. The owner argued that the system was too costly and too detailed for the needs of the business. What arguments could the accountant use to support the double-entry system? Do you agree with the owner?

3. One often hears the statement: 'Debits are bad and credits are good for the business.' Do you agree? Why or why not?

4. The detailed recording of transactions, as required in a general journal, is cumbersome and time consuming. Do you agree? Comment.

5. Why are journals required as part of the recording process? Would not a set of ledger accounts be sufficient?

6. Give an example of a transaction that results in:
   (a) an increase in one asset and an increase in a liability
   (b) a decrease in one asset but no change in the total assets
   (c) an increase in one asset and an increase in equity
   (d) a decrease in one asset and a decrease in a liability
   (e) a decrease in one asset and a decrease in equity
   (f) an increase in one asset, a decrease in another asset and an increase in one liability
   (g) a decrease in equity and an increase in a liability.

7. Recently, a new student of accounting was overheard making the following remarks: 'Why are we learning how to use the double-entry system of recording in the accounting cycle? Surely there are good computer packages available these days which can handle all of these details.' Provide a suitable reply.

8. Explain the fact that errors can exist even though the sum of the debit account balances may equal the sum of the credit account balances in the trial balance.

9. An antique dealer was in the habit of visiting local garage sales and flea markets in the hope of finding a bargain or two. On one occasion he purchased a china plate for $2, because he knew that the plate was rare and was worth at least twenty times that amount among antique collectors. In preparing the accounts for the antique dealer, what value should the dealer put on the plate? Why?

10. A goldmining company in Western Australia discovered an extremely rich seam of gold as a result of exploration activities, 50 kilometres away from its already existing mines. This information, when released to the public, caused the share price of the company to jump considerably. What entries (if any) should be made in the ledger of the company? Why?

EXERCISES

LO 4

Exercise 3.1 IDENTIFYING ACCOUNT CATEGORIES

The following is a list of ledger account titles extracted from the general ledger of P. Kettle, Upholsterer:

Accounts Receivable	Motor Vehicles
Interest	Rent
Cash at Bank	Mortgage Payable
P. Kettle, Capital	Upholstering Revenue
Accounts Payable	Wages and Salaries
Land (Under Mortgage)	Workshop Tools
Inventory, Fabrics	Inventory, Other Materials
Investments	

Required

A. Identify each of the above ledger accounts as either an asset, a liability, an income or an expense account. If you think that any of the accounts might fit into more than one of these categories, explain why.

B. For each of the accounts listed above, indicate (1) whether increases are recorded as debits or credits and (2) whether the normal balance is a debit or a credit.

LO 7

Exercise 3.2 TRANSACTION ANALYSIS

For each of the following transactions, indicate whether the accounts affected are an asset, a liability, an equity, an income or an expense. Also indicate whether the accounts are being increased or decreased and whether the increase or decrease is a debit or credit. Ignore GST.

Example: Paid for advertising.
Increase an expense (debit), decrease an asset (credit)

1. Owner invested cash.
2. Paid creditor by electronic transfer.
3. Cash payment made for insurance 6 months in advance.
4. Purchased supplies on credit.
5. Sold a vehicle for cash.
6. Invoiced a customer for services performed.
7. Owner withdrew money from business bank account for private use.
8. Received payment on an account receivable.
9. Paid some cash and took out a loan to purchase machinery.
10. Paid for an advertisement aired on television.

LO 7

Exercise 3.3 EFFECTS OF TRANSACTIONS ON FINANCIAL POSITION

The following transactions were undertaken by Loftus Computer Services during the month of April 2013. Ignore GST.

1. Paid current month's rent for office space, $3600.
2. Purchased on credit computers costing $70 000 from Doll Computers Ltd.

3. Invoiced M. Lyon for computer services provided, $4600.
4. Received $87 000 from clients for computer services provided in March.
5. Paid electricity account for April by cheque, $870.
6. S. Loftus invested a further $34 000 additional capital in the business.
7. Purchased on credit office equipment costing $17 400.
8. Paid Doll Computers Ltd for computers purchased in (2) above.
9. Invoiced G. Forrest for computer services provided in April, $6500.
10. Paid cash to Sunbright Insurance for insurance cover commencing in May, $2400.
11. Paid wages expenses of $5000.

Required

Indicate with the appropriate letter whether each of the above transactions resulted in:
(a) an increase in assets and a decrease in assets
(b) an increase in assets and an increase in liabilities
(c) an increase in assets and an increase in equity
(d) a decrease in assets and a decrease in liabilities
(e) a decrease in assets and a decrease in equity
(f) an increase in liabilities and a decrease in equity
(g) an increase in equity and a decrease in liabilities.

Exercise 3.4 NORMAL BALANCE AND CLASSIFICATION IN FINANCIAL STATEMENTS **LO 4**

The accounts below appear in the chart of accounts of Lightfoot Distribution Services. Show whether the normal balance is a debit or a credit. Indicate whether the account would appear in the balance sheet or in the income statement, and under what classification, e.g. liability, asset, equity, income or expense.

1. Telephone Expense
2. Unearned Service Fees
3. Prepaid Advertising
4. Repairs Expense
5. Accounts Receivable
6. Mortgage Payable
7. GST Collections
8. Delivery Vehicles
9. A. Lightfoot, Drawings
10. Interest Revenue
11. GST Outlays
12. Distribution Services Revenue
13. Office Supplies
14. A. Lightfoot, Capital
15. Accounts Payable

Exercise 3.5 RECORDING TRANSACTIONS IN GENERAL JOURNAL **LO 7, 8**
AND ANALYSIS

The chart of accounts of Lemon Squash Courts contained the following accounts: Cash at Bank; Accounts Receivable; Equipment; Accounts Payable; S. Ball, Drawings; Court Fees; Salaries Expense and Advertising Expense. Ignore GST.

The following transactions occurred during the month of November:

Nov. 1 S. Ball withdrew $1500 cash for personal use.
   5 Paid salaries of $970.
   9 Purchased new equipment for $1800. Paid $500 deposit with the balance to be paid within 60 days.
   14 Paid $470 to creditors for office supplies that had been purchased on credit in the previous month.
   18 Paid for advertising in the local newspaper, $510.
   22 Received $210 from players to reduce their account balances.
   30 $3000 in court fees was due during the month. Of this, 30% of the fees was collected in cash and 70% will be paid within 60 days.

Required

A. Prepare the general journal entries to record the above transactions.
B. For each transaction above, prepare an analysis similar to that shown in the illustrative example in the chapter (p. 83).

Exercise 3.6 ACCOUNT TITLES AND TYPE

Each of the following items describes aspects of the business of Jenny Linnehan, signwriter:

1. cash which Jenny Linnehan has withdrawn from the business for personal use
2. cash registers, fax machines and computers
3. amounts owing by the business to suppliers of materials used for signs
4. amounts owing by customers for jobs completed
5. tables, wall shelving and display cabinets for goods displaying signs
6. GST charged to clients for signwriting services
7. money borrowed from a bank
8. lease rental on premises which should have been paid 1 month ago
9. supplies held for future signwriting jobs
10. insurance premium paid in advance to cover the next 6 months.

Required

A. Suggest an account title for each item described above.
B. Classify the item as an asset, liability, equity, income or expense.

Exercise 3.7 CHART OF ACCOUNTS, POSTING TO T ACCOUNTS, AND TRIAL BALANCE

The general journal of Li Ong, Financial Adviser, contained the entries below for the month of March 2013. GST is ignored.

	General Journal			
Date	Particulars	Post Ref	Debit	Credit
2013				
Mar. 1	Cash at Bank		100 000	
	Li Ong, Capital			100 000
	(Cash invested by owner)			
8	Cash at Bank		38 000	
	Service Fees Revenue			38 000
	(Fees for services performed)			
16	Office Equipment		45 000	
	Cash at Bank			10 000
	Accounts Payable			35 000
	(Office equipment for cash and on credit)			
22	Service Fees Receivable		22 000	
	Service Fees Revenue			22 000
	(Services performed on credit)			
31	Cash at Bank		12 000	
	Service Fees Receivable			12 000
	(Cash received from client)			

Required

A. Post the transactions to T accounts. The chart of accounts for the business included the following accounts:

Cash at Bank	1–100
Service Fees Receivable	1–200
Office Equipment	1–300
Accounts Payable	2–100
Li Ong, Capital	3–100
Service Fees Revenue	4–100

B. Prepare a trial balance of the general ledger of Li Ong, Financial Adviser, as at 31 March 2013.

Exercise 3.8 RECORDING TRANSACTIONS IN GENERAL JOURNAL
AND ANALYSIS

The following accounts appear in the ledger of the Green Valley Gym: Cash at Bank; Accounts Receivable; Exercise Equipment; Accounts Payable; Brad Rawson, Drawings; Membership Fees Revenue; Salaries Expense; and Advertising Expense.

Required

A. Prepare the general journal entries to record the following transactions that occurred during May (ignore GST).

B. Explain why you have made each of the journal entries to account for the transactions.

May	1	Purchased exercise equipment for $21 000. Paid $3000 deposit and agreed to pay the balance in 60 days.
	3	Paid salaries of $7900.
	8	Brad Rawson withdrew $10 500 from the business for his personal use.
	14	Paid $4900 for radio commercials.
	19	Paid $3700 to creditors for supplies that had been purchased on credit.
	23	Received $1850 from customers to reduce the balance in their accounts.
	30	Earned $39 000 in membership fees during the month. Of these, 25% of the fees were collected in cash and 75% will be paid within 2 months.

Exercise 3.9 RECORDING TRANSACTIONS IN GENERAL JOURNAL
AND ANALYSIS

The following information relates to the business of Joel's Travel Agency for the month of June 2013:

June	1	Joel Brattsky invested $51 000 cash into the new business.
	2	The business set up an office by purchasing some office equipment for $14 000 cash.
	3	Joel hired an assistant to deal with customers for an annual salary of $36 000, payable in monthly amounts.
	6	The assistant books a holiday to Asia for a client, B. Idle, for a total cost of $28 000 (unpaid at this stage). The commission to be kept by the business is 10% of the total cost of the trip when B. Idle pays in full.
	15	B. Idle pays $18 000 to Joel's Travel Agency. Of this amount, $5500 represents the total cost of air fares, which will be forwarded to the airline concerned; and the remainder (excluding the travel agency's commission) is to be forwarded to a particular hotel chain to cover the client's accommodation.
	22	The business pays cash to the airline as payment for B. Idle's trip.
	25	The appropriate amount of cash is paid to the hotel chain for B. Idle's trip.
	30	The assistant is paid 1 month's wages in cash.

Required

A. Prepare general journal entries to record the above events, as appropriate, in the accounting records of Joel's Travel Agency. Ignore GST.

B. Explain why you have made each entry by providing analyses similar to those shown in the illustrative example in the chapter (p. 83)

Exercise 3.10 RECORDING TRANSACTIONS IN GENERAL JOURNAL
AND GENERAL LEDGER

The following transactions occurred in the business of Gardner's Gym for December 2013:

Dec.	2	Kevin Gardner invested $800 000 into the business of Gardner's Gym by purchasing a fully equipped gymnasium from an old friend. The gymnasium acquired consisted of the following assets and liabilities:

Land	$300 000
Building	200 000
Gymnasium equipment	250 000
Office equipment	90 000
Accounts payable	40 000

5   Purchased some new gym equipment on credit for $100 000.

6   Collected cash for gymnasium fees from clients for the month, $200 000.

12   Paid the accounts payable owing on 2 December when Kevin purchased the business.

14   Purchased an accident protection insurance policy for the new year for $3000 cash.

18   Purchased television advertising for the Christmas — New Year period for $15 000 to be paid for in 30 days.

23   Collected fees in cash from new clients for the Christmas — New Year period, amounting to $27 000.

30   Kevin withdrew $8000 cash in order to pay for private Christmas presents and parties.

Required

A. Prepare general journal entries for each of the above transactions and events.

B. Post the entries to ledger T accounts and balance the accounts as at 31 December 2013.

LO 8

Exercise 3.11   ANALYSING LEDGER ACCOUNTS

The following T accounts were taken from the ledger of Derdang's Environmental Services for June 2014:

	Cash at Bank		
2/6	90 000	3/6	6 000
		9/6	12 000
		10/6	48 000

	Garbage Collection Vehicle	
10/6	100 000	

	Office Supplies	
3/6	6 000	

	Office Equipment	
9/6	12 000	

	Loan Payable	
	10/6	52 000

	Ross Derdang, Capital	
	2/6	90 000

Required

Analyse the above accounts and describe in chronological order the transactions that have been recorded.

LO 10

Exercise 3.12   IDENTIFYING AND EXPLAINING ERRORS

The following errors were made in the recording process for the business of Ella's Fix-It Services:

(a) Collection of an account receivable for $5000 was recorded by a debit to Cash at Bank and a debit to the equity account of the owner.

(b) A $3500 payment for assorted handyman's tools was recorded as a debit to Equipment and a credit to Cash at Bank for $350.

(c) A cheque for $4000 issued to pay for an account payable was recorded as a debit to Accounts Payable and a credit to Accounts Receivable for $4000.

(d) Cash of $3000 withdrawn by the owner from the business was debited to Salaries Expense and credited to Cash at Bank.

(e) Office equipment purchased for $6500 cash was debited to Equipment and credited to Accounts Payable for an incorrect amount of $5600.

Required

A. Identify which of the above errors would cause unequal totals in a trial balance prepared at the end of the period.

B. Write a brief explanation for each error to indicate how it could be fixed in the accounting records.

Exercise 3.13 PREPARATION OF CORRECTED TRIAL BALANCE

The trial balance of Finney's Cleaning Services presented below does not balance. In examining the general journal and the general ledger you discover the following information. Ignore GST.

1. A purchase of cleaning supplies for a cheque of $210 was erroneously recorded as a purchase on credit.
2. The balance in the Mortgage Payable account is $2300.
3. The debits and credits to Accounts Receivable totalled $9400 and $6900 respectively.
4. A $790 payment for salaries was not posted to the Cash at Bank account.
5. The debit to record a withdrawal of $500 in cash by the owner was not posted.

	FINNEY'S CLEANING SERVICES **Trial Balance** **as at 31 March 2013**	
Account	Debit	Credit
Cash at bank	$ 2 400	
Accounts receivable		$ 2 480
Supplies	390	
Equipment	6 700	
Accounts payable		2 610
Salaries payable	310	
Mortgage payable		3 200
E. Finney, Capital		7 200
E. Finney, Drawings	3 920	
Service revenue		13 800
Salaries expense	5 100	
Rent expense	3 200	
Other expense	2 300	
	$24 320	$29 290

Required

Prepare a corrected trial balance.

Exercise 3.14 EFFECT OF ERRORS ON TRIAL BALANCE

A. For each of the following errors: (a) indicate whether the error would cause the trial balance to have unequal totals; (b) determine the amount by which the trial balance totals would differ; and (c) determine whether the error would cause the debit total or the credit total to be larger. Ignore GST.

1. A $21 debit to Cash at Bank was posted as a credit.
2. Receipt of a payment on account from a customer was recorded as a debit to Cash at Bank for $85 and a credit to Accounts Payable for $85.
3. A purchase of supplies for $78 was recorded as a debit to Supplies for $78 and a credit to Accounts Payable for $87.
4. A $117 credit to Service Revenue was not posted.
5. A $315 debit to the Drawings account was debited to the Capital account.
6. A $450 debit to Rent Expense was posted as a $45 debit.

B. How would each error be corrected? Give the correcting journal entry where appropriate.

LO 4, 6

Problem 3.1 IDENTIFYING TYPE OF ACCOUNT, DEBIT/CREDIT ANALYSIS AND NORMAL BALANCE ★

Listed below are the ledger accounts of Kathleen's Catering Services:

1. Cash at Bank
2. Land
3. Wages Expense
4. Kathleen Watts, Drawings
5. Sundry Revenue
6. Buildings
7. Mortgage Payable
8. Interest Revenue
9. Accounts Receivable
10. Supplies Used
11. Loan Payable
12. Insurance Expense
13. Supplies on Hand
14. Electricity Account Payable
15. Service Fee Revenue
16. Interest Receivable
17. Wages Payable
18. Prepaid Insurance
19. Accounts Payable
20. Maintenance Equipment
21. Unearned Revenue
22. Kathleen Watts, Capital
23. Interest Expense
24. Rent Revenue
25. GST Collections
26. GST Outlays

Required

A. For each account listed above, complete a solution form as shown below by placing a tick in the proper columns to indicate the type of account, the side of a T account on which increases are recorded, and the side on which normal balances are recorded.

Suggested solution form:

	Type of account			Increases		Normal balance	
Account	Asset	Liability	Equity (includes income and expenses)	Debit	Credit	Debit	Credit
1. Cash at Bank	✓			✓		✓	
(List remaining 25 accounts.)							

B. Prepare an appropriate chart of accounts for the business. Use the following digits for account classes: assets, 1; liabilities, 2; equity, 3; income, 4; expenses, 5. Within each category, assign a 3-digit code for each account.

LO 7, 8, 9

Problem 3.2 JOURNAL ENTRIES, POSTING TO LEDGER, AND TRIAL BALANCE ★

Gerry Munro opened a hairdressing salon on 1 July 2012. The following transactions occurred during the first month of operations (ignore GST):

July   2   Munro invested $30 000 in the business by depositing cash into a business cheque account with the NZA Bank.

      2   Paid $1200 for the first month's rent.

      3   Purchased equipment by issuing a cheque for $12 000 and signing a commercial loan agreement for $16 000.

      4   Purchased supplies for $1040.

      6   Paid advertising expense of $300.

    16   Recorded hairdressing revenue for the first half of the month of $1680 in cash and $250 on credit.

    20   Paid insurance expense for July of $560.

    23   Received a $150 payment from customers on credit.

28 Munro withdrew $440 cash for personal living expenses.
31 Recorded revenue for the second half of the month of $1760 in cash and $120 on credit.
31 Paid telephone account of $270 by electronic transfer.

Use the following account titles and numbers: Cash at Bank, 100; Accounts Receivable, 101; Supplies, 102; Equipment, 103; Loan Payable, 200; Gerry Munro, Capital, 300; Gerry Munro, Drawings, 301; Revenue, 400; Rent Expense, 500; Advertising Expense, 501; Insurance Expense, 502; Telephone Expense, 503.

Required
A. Prepare the general journal entries to record the transactions.
B. Post the entries from the general journal to the general ledger accounts (running balance format) and enter the posting references in the general journal.
C. Prepare a trial balance as at 31 July 2012.

Problem 3.3   PREPARING GENERAL LEDGER AND TRIAL BALANCE ★   LO 7, 9

The following transactions were for Flash Flights. Ignore GST.

July 1   Jenny Flash invested $120 000 into Flash Flights organised to provide flying services to remote parts of Australia.
2   Purchased equipment for $36 000 on credit from P. Ackland.
4   Gave P. Ackland a cheque for the amount owing.
5   Paid $1800 to R. Burton for two weeks rent to 14 July.
9   Charged White Cattle Station Ltd $10 000 for flying services.
10   Flash withdrew $6000 cash to meet personal expenses.
12   Paid $2400 for advertising on local radio.
12   Received $4800 from Outback Oil Ltd for flying services.
13   Charged Star Ltd $9600 and received $9000 from Hardie Ltd for flying services provided.
14   Received a cheque for $10 000 from White Cattle Station Ltd and deposited it into the business bank account.

Required
A. Record all transactions directly into ledger T accounts and prepare a trial balance.
B. Repeat requirement A, assuming that a GST of 10% needs to be added for all appropriate transactions.

Problem 3.4   PREPARING THE GENERAL JOURNAL ★   LO 8

Greg Parry opened The Wines Golf Club for business on 1 July. The following selected events and transactions occurred during the first month of operations:

July 1   The owner invested $600 000 cash into the business.
3   Acquired the business of Norman's Mini-Golf World for $375 000 cash. The price consisted of land $152 000, building $89 000, and equipment $134 000.
6   Advertised the opening of the golf course, paying advertising expenses of $10 000.
10   Paid cash $6000 for a 1-year insurance policy.
18   Purchased new golfing equipment for $9000 from Scott Ltd, payable in 30 days.
19   Received golf fees of $15 000 in cash.
25   Sold 200 coupon books for $90 each. Every book contains 10 coupons each of which entitles the holder to one round of golf.
27   Parry withdrew $7000 cash for personal use.
29   Paid wages of $8800.
30   Paid Scott Ltd in full.
31   Received $12 000 cash for golf fees.

Required
Prepare general journal entries for the month of July, using appropriate account titles. Ignore GST.

Problem 3.5 JOURNAL ENTRIES, ENTERING BEGINNING ACCOUNT BALANCES, POSTING TO T ACCOUNTS, AND TRIAL BALANCE ★★

The 31 May 2014 trial balance of Marcus Lee, Chiropractor, is shown below. Ignore GST.

MARCUS LEE, CHIROPRACTOR
Trial Balance
as at 31 May 2014

Account	Debit	Credit
Cash at bank	$ 96 300	
Accounts receivable	43 380	
Supplies	11 160	
Prepaid insurance	7 380	
Furniture and equipment	236 880	
Accounts payable		$ 8 820
Electricity account payable		8 600
Unearned revenue		2 640
M. Lee, Capital		286 240
M. Lee, Drawings	146 520	
Services revenue		120 000
Salary expense	154 840	
Electricity expense	8 600	
Rent expense	21 240	
	$726 300	$726 300

The following transactions were completed during June:

June 1 Purchased supplies on credit for $5230.
3 Received $22 200 from patients as payment on account.
6 Paid the electricity expense of $8600, previously recorded.
10 Performed services for $2000 that was recorded previously as unearned revenue.
14 Recorded revenue of $162 350 in cash and $12 450 on credit.
Paid salaries of $73 200.
20 Purchased furniture for $14 000 and paid by electronic transfer.
23 Paid creditors $6400.
24 Withdrew $80 000 from the business for personal use.
26 Purchased insurance policy for $4200 to cover business assets.
27 Received $12 000 from patients as payment on account.
29 Recorded revenue of $143 600 in cash and $21 000 on credit.
30 Paid rent of $24 500.

Required

A. Prepare journal entries to record each transaction.
B. 1. Open T accounts for the accounts shown in the trial balance.
   2. Enter the 31 May balance in each account.
   3. Post the journal entries to the T accounts.
C. Prepare a trial balance as at 30 June 2014.

Problem 3.6 JOURNAL ENTRIES FOR TWO CONSECUTIVE MONTHS ★★

The following transactions for Laserlite Installation Services occurred during April and May 2013:

April 1 Cash is received from a customer, D. Turnip, $12 400.
7 Installation services are provided on credit for $15 000 to M. Apples.
8 A bill for electricity consumed is received, $600.
11 Supplies are requisitioned from storage for use in the general office, $320.

15	A $6600 loan is taken out with Banana Loans Ltd. Interest is payable at 10% p.a.
18	A cheque is issued in payment of the electricity account received on 8 April.
23	Supplies are purchased on account from Cheap Supplies Ltd, $1200.
25	Supplies are requisitioned for use in the office, $560.
30	Prepaid insurance costs have been used to the extent of $300.

May	2	Owner contributes capital of $90 000, by an additional injection of cash.
	2	Rent for the month is paid by cheque, $1500.
	5	Installation equipment is purchased on account from Orange Suppliers, $27 000.
	12	Office fixtures are purchased from Knots Ltd for $5000. $1500 is paid immediately by cheque, the remainder is due in July.
	13	Installation services performed for clients for cash, $9200.
	14	Payment on account is made by cheque to Orange Suppliers, $27 000.
	19	A salary of $3000 is paid by cheque.
	31	Insurance expired, $300.

Required

A. Assuming that the accounting period is a calendar year, prepare general journal entries for Laserlite Installation Services during April and May 2013. Ignore GST.

B. At the end of May, interest is owing on the loan taken out on 15 April with Banana Loans Ltd. Should this interest be recorded by Laserlite Installation Services in its accounting records? Why or why not?

Problem 3.7   PREPARATION OF RUNNING BALANCE LEDGER ACCOUNTS AND TRIAL BALANCE ★★   **LO 7, 9**

James White decided to open White's Upholstery Repairs on 1 March 2013. He contributed for this purpose office equipment $10 000 and a commercial van $22 000, and deposited $10 000 cash in a business bank account. Transactions during March were as follows (ignore GST):

March	4	Took a 3-year lease on a shop and paid first month's rent $500.
	4	Purchased office supplies for $520, and issued a cheque for $200 in part payment for same.
	6	Cash received for minor repairs, $240.
		Revenue earned for repair work done for United Machinery Co. on credit, $700.
	7	Purchased an upholstery sewing machine, $3680, paying $800 cash and taking out a loan for the balance.
	8	Cash revenue earned, $460.
	11	Engaged an upholsterer at an agreed wage of $700 per week.
	12	Paid petrol $60, postage $20, and electricity bill $90.
	13	Cash of $400 received for over-the-counter repairs.
		Revenue of $900 accepted from a customer on credit.
	14	Paid for office supplies purchased on credit on 4 March.
	15	Withdrew $200 for own use.
	16	Office supplies purchased for $500 on credit.
	17	Cash revenue received, $730.
	18	Paid wages to employee.
	21	Revenue earned for repairs: cash $160; on account $340.
	23	United Machinery Co. paid the bill for services rendered on 6 March.
	24	Petrol expenses paid $40.
	25	Paid weekly wages to employee.
	28	Revenue earned for repair work $780, receiving $200 in cash and the remainder on credit.
	31	Office supplies used, $400.

Required

A. Prepare three-column running balance ledger accounts. Give each account a suitable account number.

B. Prepare a trial balance as at 31 March 2013.

Problem 3.8 POLICY DECISION, ANALYSIS AND CHART OF ACCOUNTS ★★

John Moulder decides to branch out on his own and set up his own private practice as a solicitor. Events occurring in March 2013 are as follows. Ignore GST.

March 1 Deposited $400 000 into a business bank account, set up under the business name of John Moulder, Solicitor.
  2 Hired an office secretary who commenced work immediately.
  3 Paid $8000 for the first month's rent of a suitable office.
  4 Purchased office equipment and furniture for a total of $28 800. An initial $12 800 is paid in cash immediately and the rest is to be paid in 3 month's time, with interest payable at 10% per annum.
  7 Paid $1200 for a 1-year insurance policy on the office equipment, effective from 1 March 2013.
  8 Paid $4000 in cash for office supplies.
  12 Sent invoices to a number of clients for services rendered for a total amount of $18 000.
  14 Moulder withdrew $12 000 cash from the business for personal use. Paid the office secretary $1300 for services rendered to the business.
  19 Received $14 000 in cash from clients billed on 12 March.
  24 Received $20 000 in cash from clients who paid immediately for services rendered. These clients were not invoiced previously.
  31 Paid $15 000 for sundry expenses and wages of $1300 to the office secretary for the previous fortnight's work.

Required

A. After analysing the events above, suggest a chart of accounts, with appropriate numbering, that would be satisfactory for the business. Explain why you have used particular numbering in the chart of accounts.
B. Prepare general journal entries as necessary for each of the events, using the chart of accounts that you have created.
C. Explain why you have made these journal entries by an analysis similar to that shown in the illustrative example in the chapter (p. 83).

Problem 3.9 JOURNAL ENTRIES, T ACCOUNTS AND ANALYSIS ★★

Shane's Car Rental began business operations on 1 January 2013. The capital of the business was $600 000 cash, which had all been contributed by Shane Dabrowski. He has asked you to be record-keeper for the business on a part-time basis, and you initially establish the need for the following accounts (and numbers). Additional accounts may need to be added in the near future. GST is ignored.

Cash at Bank	100
Accounts Receivable	110
Land	120
Building	130
Motor Vehicles	150
Office Equipment	170
Accounts Payable	220
Mortgage Payable	250
Shane Dabrowski, Capital	300
Shane Dabrowski, Drawings	310
Car Rental Income	320

The transactions undertaken by the business during January, including the initial investment by the owner, were as follows:

Jan. 1 Shane Dabrowski contributed $600 000 to the business.
  2 The business acquired land for $125 000 and a building on the land for $88 000. A cash payment of $110 000 was made and a mortgage loan with the Federal Bank was arranged for the balance owing.
  4 Purchased fifteen new vehicles at $25 000 each from City Auto Mart. The business paid $250 000 cash, and the remainder was due to be paid in 30 days.
  7 One of the vehicles was transferred from the business to the owner, Shane Dabrowski, for cost price.

10	One vehicle was found to be defective, and the business returned the vehicle to City Auto Mart. The amount due to the creditor was reduced by $25 000.
13	The business acquired some computer equipment for the main office at a total cost of $5000, paid in cash.
28	Car rental fees of $18 000 were received in cash.
29	Paid the remaining cash owing to City Auto Mart.
30	The business paid wages of $2500 to you for keeping the accounts.
31	Car rental fees of $12 000 were received in cash and an additional $5000 was owing by clients.

Required

A. Prepare general journal entries for the business for the month of January.

B. Post these entries to appropriate T accounts and determine their balances.

C. Provide an analysis of each transaction to explain each entry you have made in A above (see the illustrative example on page 83).

Problem 3.10   PREPARATION OF TRIAL BALANCE, BALANCE SHEET AND REPORT TO THE OWNER ★★   LO 1, 3, 9

Kerry's Management Services had been in business for several years. In September 2013, as a result of a dispute with the owner, the accountant of the business disappeared and took all the records with her.

You have been hired to reconstruct the accounting records, and with this in mind, you conduct a stocktake of all of the assets of the business. By checking with banks, counting the office equipment and supplies, and investigating the ownership of the buildings and equipment, you develop the following information as at 31 October 2013:

Account title	Balance
Land	$ 75 000
Office Equipment	125 000
Buildings	150 000
Accounts Receivable	50 000
Investments	25 000
Office Supplies	70 000
Cash at Bank	280 000

Statements from creditors and unpaid invoices found in the office indicate that $200 000 is owing to trade creditors. There is also $50 000 owing under a 30-year mortgage with the bank. The owner, Kerry Smith, has told you that she had contributed $150 000 cash to the business when it was established and that no further contributions had been made. There is no record of how much total profit(losses) had been earned in past years.

Required

A. Prepare a trial balance and balance sheet as at 31 October 2013 for the business.

B. Write a report to the owner suggesting a simple accounting system that could be used in future and why you recommend such a system.

Problem 3.11   JOURNAL ENTRIES, POSTING TO RUNNING BALANCE LEDGER ACCOUNTS, AND TRIAL BALANCE FOR 2 CONSECUTIVE MONTHS ★★   LO 7, 8, 9

Brad Kendrick opened Brad's Bowling Alley during July 2013 and completed the transactions below during its first month of operations. For the sake of simplicity, GST is ignored.

July	1	Invested $60 500 capital in the business.
	2	Purchased bowling balls and other equipment costing $65 000 for $25 000 cash and a loan for $40 000.
	4	Paid $300 for advertising.
	6	Purchased supplies on credit for $2600.
	15	Recorded cash revenue for the first half of the month of $4700.
	24	Withdrew $900 from the business bank account for personal use.
	31	Recorded cash revenue for the second half of the month of $5300.
	31	Paid wages of $1300.
	31	Paid rent for July, $900.

Use the following account titles and numbers:

Cash at Bank, 1–100
Supplies, 1–110
Equipment, 1–120
Accounts Payable, 2–100
Loan Payable, 2–110
B. Kendrick, Capital, 3–100

B. Kendrick, Drawings, 3–110
Revenue, 4–100
Rent Expense, 5–100
Advertising Expense, 5–110
Wages Expense, 5–120

Required

A. Prepare general journal entries to record the July transactions.
B. Post the entries from the general journal to running balance general ledger accounts and enter the posting references in the journal.
C. Prepare a trial balance as at 31 July 2013.

The following transactions took place in August:

Aug.	4	Paid $1200 of the amount owed for supplies.
	8	Paid $330 for advertisements in local newspaper.
	13	Brad withdrew $650 from the business for personal use.
	14	Recorded cash revenue for the first half of August of $4125.
	15	Paid wages of $1130 in cash.
	21	Purchased supplies on credit for $2100.
	31	Recorded cash revenue for the second half of August of $5610.
	31	Paid rent for August, $920.

Required

D. Prepare journal entries to record the August transactions.
E. Post the entries to the ledger.
F. Prepare a trial balance as at 31 August 2013.

Problem 3.12 JOURNAL ENTRIES, POSTING TO RUNNING BALANCE LEDGER ACCOUNTS, AND TRIAL BALANCE FOR 2 CONSECUTIVE MONTHS, INCLUDING GST ★★★

Using the data in problem 3.11, complete requirements A to F assuming the addition of GST of 10% where appropriate. Round your answers to the nearest dollar. Assume that, for the transaction on 2 July, the loan agreement remains at $40 000. Add two new accounts: GST Outlays 1–105 and GST Collections 2–150.

Problem 3.13 JOURNAL ENTRIES, POSTING TO RUNNING BALANCE LEDGER ACCOUNTS, AND TRIAL BALANCE ★★★ GST LO 7, 8, 9

Ang Majild opened a boat hire business in November 2012. The following transactions occurred during the first month of the business (ignore GST).

Nov.	1	Majild invested $15 000 in cash in the business, and the cash was deposited into a business bank account.
	3	Paid $590 for November rent of premises.
	4	Purchased equipment costing $7000 with $3000 cash and a $4000 commercial loan.
	5	Purchased supplies costing $250 on credit.
	15	Recorded revenue for the first half of the month of $1530 in cash and $70 on credit.
	18	Paid for supplies purchased on 5 November, $250.
	19	Paid insurance expense for November of $190.
	24	Received payment from customers on account of $40 and banked the receipts.
	27	Purchased supplies costing $70 on credit.
	29	Recorded revenue for the second half of the month of $1330 in cash and $60 on credit.
	30	Paid telephone expense of $60 in cash.

Use the following account titles and numbers:

Cash at Bank, 1–101	Accounts Payable, 2–101	Rent Expense, 5–110
Accounts Receivable, 1–102	Loan Payable, 2–110	Insurance Expense, 5–120
Supplies, 1–110	A. Majild, Capital, 3–101	Telephone Expense, 5–130
Equipment, 1–120	Revenue, 4–101	

Required

A. Journalise the above transactions.
B. Post the entries from the general journal to running balance general ledger accounts and enter the posting references in the general journal.
C. Prepare a trial balance as at 30 November 2012.
D. Repeat requirements A to C, adding a GST of 10% where necessary. Add two extra accounts:
   GST Outlays, 1–105
   GST Collections, 2–150
   Also assume the following:
   1. The cash paid 4 November was for $3700.
   2. The payment made on 18 November was $275.
   3. The receipt on 24 November was for $44.

Problem 3.14 CORRECTION OF ERRORS ★★★   LO 10

Your first assignment on your new job was to determine why the 31 December 2012 trial balance did not balance. In your review of the records you uncovered a number of errors described below:
1. A $1298 debit to Cash at Bank was posted as $1928.
2. A $280 credit to be made to the Services Revenue account was credited to the Accounts Receivable account instead.
3. A cash collection of $1200 from customers in partial settlement of their accounts was posted twice to the Cash at Bank account and the Accounts Receivable account.
4. The Accounts Payable account balance of $42 900 was listed in the trial balance as $49 200.
5. A $1450 credit to Services Revenue was posted as a $145 credit. The debit to Cash at Bank was for the correct amount.
6. A purchase of office supplies for $200 on credit was not recorded.
7. A purchase of a delivery truck for $30 000 cash was posted as a debit to the Cash at Bank account and a debit to the Equipment account.
8. The Drawings account balance of $28 000 was listed as a credit balance in the trial balance.
9. A $400 payment to employees for their weekly salaries was posted twice to the Wages Expense account. The credit to Cash at Bank was made only once.
10. The Sundry Expense account with a balance of $780 was omitted from the trial balance.
11. A payment of $550 on the telephone account payable was posted correctly to the Cash at Bank account, but was not posted to the Telephone Account Payable account.

Required

A. Indicate in the solution format shown below how each error would affect the trial balance totals. If the error does not cause the trial balance to be out of balance and you tick 'no' in the third column, write 'equal' in the 'Difference between trial balance totals' column. Each error is to be considered independently of the others.

Error	Would the error cause the trial balance to be out of balance?		Difference between trial balance totals ($)	Column having largest total	
	Yes	No		Debit	Credit
1.					
2.					
etc.					
to					
11.					

B. Prepare the journal entries necessary to correct errors number 2, 3 and 6 as listed above.

Abby's Pony Club

Abby Forbes owns and operates Abby's Pony Club. The club's main sources of income are riding fees and lesson fees, which are paid on a cash basis. In addition, the club boards a limited number of horses for owners, who are charged monthly for the boarding fees. The club owns six horses, a small riding yard, riding equipment and office equipment. The club employs several stable hands and an office employee, who receive weekly salaries. At the end of the month, accounts are received for advertising, electricity and veterinary services. The other major expense the club incurs is hay and feed for the horses.

Abby's Pony Club maintains the following general ledger accounts: Cash at Bank; Boarding Accounts Receivable; Hay and Feed Supplies; Horses; Building; Riding Yard; Riding Equipment; Office Equipment; Accounts Payable; Abby Forbes, Capital; Abby Forbes, Drawings; Riding Revenue; Lesson Revenue; Boarding Revenue; Salaries Expense; Advertising Expense; Electricity Expense; Veterinary Fees Expense; and Hay and Feed Expense.

Following the retirement of the club's accountant, Abby employed an inexperienced bookkeeper who has kept the records for the last month of operations and made 38 entries for the month. Abby is concerned the bookkeeper may have made some errors and has asked you to review the following eight general journal entries. In each case the narration is correct. GST is ignored.

General Journal				
Date	Particulars		Debit	Credit
2013				
June 1	Cash at Bank		30 000	
	Abby Forbes, Capital			30 000
	(Abby invested $30 000 cash in the business)			
5	Hay and Feed Expense		3 700	
	Cash at Bank			3 700
	(Purchased supply of hay and feed on account, $3700)			
8	Riding Equipment		1 600	
	Cash at Bank			1 600
	(Purchased office desk for $1600 cash)			
10	Cash at Bank		500	
	Lesson Revenue			500
	(Received $500 for lesson fees)			
12	Cash at Bank		1 200	
	Boarding Revenue			1 200
	(Received $1200 for boarding of horses billed last month)			
18	Salaries Expense		700	
	Cash at Bank			700
	(Issued cheque to Abby for personal expenses)			
20	Veterinary Fees Expense		270	
	Accounts Payable			270
	(Received an account for $270 from a veterinarian for services rendered)			
22	Cash at Bank		340	
	Riding Revenue			340
	(Received $340 for riding fees)			

Required

A. Decide which general journal entries are correct and which ones are incorrect.

B. For each general journal entry that is incorrect, prepare the correcting journal entry.

C. Which of the incorrect journal entries would prevent the trial balance from balancing?

D. What was the correct profit figure for June, assuming the bookkeeper originally had calculated profit to be $4500 after posting all the entries for the month?

E. What was the correct cash at bank balance at 30 June assuming the bookkeeper reported a balance of $5420 after posting all the entries for the month?

ETHICS AND GOVERNANCE

Big Business Tobacco Co. Ltd (BBT) is a large Australian producer of tobacco products including a market-leader brand of cigarettes. With the continuing development of Asian countries such as China and its move to a market-based economy, the company has made the decision to sell its cigarettes in this large market from the beginning of next month. The cigarettes will be sold in packs of 40.

Mary Bender, marketing manager, is discussing the design of the cigarette packet for the Asian market with Randall Hedges, the company's public relations manager. Having agreed on the basic design of the pack, Hedges raised the issue of whether to include the normal health warning on the pack, which has to be displayed under Australian law. He emphasised recent medical findings which predicted many hundreds of thousands of deaths from cigarette smoking in the next few years, particularly in the developing countries.

Mary Bender was strongly opposed to including a 'health hazard' warning on the packs destined for parts of the Asian market. She explained: 'In this business it is the bottom line (i.e. profits) which matters — we have to think of our shareholders. BBT stands to lose a considerable market share to competitors if it includes such a warning. Besides, it is not a legal requirement in many Asian countries to display a health warning on cigarette packs. If Asian law is subsequently amended then we will be one of the first to comply. Besides, the managing director supports me on this one.'

Hedges expressed a final opinion: 'The company could be better off in the long term by being seen to be acting with corporate responsibility, and demonstrating some concern for its consumers. Besides, such warnings have not been detrimental to the company's performance in Australia, where health warnings have been common for many years.'

Required

A. Who are the major stakeholders in the debate on the health warnings on cigarette packs?

B. What are the main ethical issues involved in the debate?

C. If you were Randall Hedges, what would you do?

FINANCIAL ANALYSIS

Refer to the consolidated financial statements in the latest financial report of JB Hi-Fi Limited on its website, www.jbhifi.com.au, and answer the following questions:

1. What is the total value in the consolidated financial statements for each of the following items at the end of the year?

Cash (and cash equivalents)	Interest expense (Financial Costs)
Inventories	Sales and marketing expenses
Sales revenue	Occupancy expenses
Other income	Trade and other payables
Plant and Equipment	Borrowings (non-current)

2. What is the normal balance for each of the accounts listed above? What side of the account, debit or credit, is affected in order to decrease each item?

3. What is the most likely other account(s) to be affected whenever each of the above items is increased?

Adjusting the accounts and preparing financial statements

Concepts for review

Before studying this chapter, you should understand or, if necessary, revise:

- the format for T accounts and running balance accounts, and the normal account balances for assets, liabilities, equity, income and expenses (pp. 69–74)

- the nature of double-entry accounting and the meaning of debit and credit (pp. 77–9)

- how to enter a transaction in the general journal (pp. 79–81)

- how to post transactions from the journal to the general ledger (pp. 81–2)

- how to prepare a trial balance (pp. 99–101).

Learning objectives

After studying this chapter, you should be able to:

1 describe the difference between the cash basis and the accrual basis of measuring profit (pp. 124–6)

2 explain the accounting cycle and the need for end-of-accounting-period adjusting entries (pp. 126–7)

3 identify the different types of adjusting entries (pp. 127–8)

4 prepare adjusting entries for prepaid or precollected items (pp. 128–35)

5 prepare adjusting entries for accruals or unrecorded items (pp. 136–40)

6 prepare and understand the purpose of an adjusted trial balance (pp. 140–2)

7 prepare financial statements from an adjusted trial balance (pp. 142–5)

8 describe the difference between current and non-current assets and liabilities (pp. 146–7)

9 use a worksheet to prepare the financial statements (pp. 148–54)

10 explain how financial statements are used in decision making (pp. 154–5).

Accrual accounting can help you save money and improve cash flow

Keeping track of your financial situation is one of the keys to a successful business — accrual accounting can not only help your business save money, it can improve cash flow. Find out how you can use this method to plan expenses, prepare monthly and yearly budgets and meet your tax obligations.

What is accrual accounting?

Accrual accounting involves recording transactions, either cash coming in or expenses going out, when they occur, regardless of when the cash arrives or departs, whereas cash accounting records income as it is received and expenses when they are paid. Accrual accounting gives a more accurate indication of the position and performance of your business.

Is accrual accounting appropriate for your business needs?

The simple answer is: ask an expert. Business owners or managers should seek advice from an accountant about whether accrual accounting is right for their specific industry and type of business. There could be variations within the

industry that might make the business suited to one form of accounting over another, but it requires advice from a professional who understands your business.

Accounting for size

The Australian Taxation Office will also help you with the decision. If your annual turnover exceeds $2 million, tax rules stipulate you must use accrual accounting. If you use a cash accounting system and later surpass the threshold, the ATO may consider a request to continue using this method, but approval is on a case-by-case basis. As a general rule, however, cash accounting will suit smaller operations, while accrual accounting will suit larger, more complex businesses.

Why use accrual accounting?

Accrual accounting will give your business a better understanding of when the cash is coming in. Money is as important as profit in smaller businesses, which don't always have access to adequate lending, so knowing your cash position helps you make sound decisions across every aspect of your business.

Source: Excerpts from 'Accrual accounting can help you save money and improve cash flow', www.improvemybusiness.com.au.

Chapter preview

The major objective of a business entity is to earn profits. All businesses must earn profits in the long term to survive. To accomplish this, most business entities engage in a continuous series of transactions and it is up to the business to ensure that these transactions are properly recorded. As discussed in chapter 2, in order to provide timely information to users of financial statements, the life of an entity is divided into relatively short intervals of equal length called accounting periods. One important function of accounting in a business entity is to measure the profit or loss during an accounting period. The amount of profit or loss is the difference between income and expenses. As mentioned in the scene setter, income and expenses are largely determined in business using accrual accounting. In this chapter we concentrate on how accountants define and determine profit, as well as how and why adjusting entries are made in the context of the accounting cycle for a business entity.

4.1 Measurement of profit

Learning objective 1

Describe the difference between the cash basis and the accrual basis of measuring profit

Profit for a period is determined by deducting expenses for the period from income for the period, i.e. Profit = Income − Expenses. The measurement of profit, therefore, is an outcome of the recognition and measurement of income and expenses. Income and expenses may be recognised on either a cash basis or an accrual basis; however, as discussed in chapter 2, most business systems are organised on the accrual basis.

Cash basis

Under the cash basis of accounting, income (including revenues) is recorded in the period in which cash is received and expenses are recorded in the period in which cash is paid. Profit is the excess of cash inflows from income over cash outflows for expenses. This method does not recognise income when goods are sold or services are performed on credit. In addition, the costs of goods and services consumed during the current period, but not paid for, are recognised as expenses in a subsequent period when cash is paid.

As discussed in the scene setter, although the cash basis approach is used by some small business entities and professionals who conduct most of their activities in cash, it is not satisfactory for most business entities that conduct a significant portion of their activities on credit. Nor is it considered satisfactory for use in government, which has switched to the accrual basis. The cash basis system can be justified only because it is simple to operate and only if it produces results essentially the same as those produced by accrual accounting.

Accrual basis

Under the accrual basis of accounting, income (including revenues) is recognised in the period in which the expected inflow of economic benefits can be measured in a faithful and verifiable manner, i.e. normally in the period in which a business sells goods or performs services under a contractual arrangement. Expenses are recognised when the consumption of goods or services is also capable of such measurement. A verifiable measurement which provides a faithful representation of these inflows and consumptions of economic benefits is an important challenge facing the accountant. Accrual basis profit for an accounting period is determined by subtracting expenses recognised during the period from income recognised in that period. To develop a more thorough understanding of accrual accounting, the important concepts of income and expense are discussed in more detail.

Income (including revenue)

Income represents increases in economic benefits during the period in the form of inflows or enhancements of assets or of decreases in liabilities that result in increases in equity, other than those relating to contributions by owners. As mentioned in chapter 3 (p. 74), revenue is regarded as a major part of income, i.e. that part which occurs in the ordinary activities of an entity, such as the performance of services or the sale of merchandise. Revenues are recognised at the fair value of assets received, if capable of verifiable measurement. Normally, the asset received is cash or the right to receive cash from customers in the future (an account receivable). Occasionally, an entity may receive property or services in payment for goods sold or services rendered, in which case the amount of revenue recorded is the fair value of the asset or service received. Thus, for a given accounting period, revenue is recognised as the sum of cash, accounts receivable and the fair value of other assets received from customers for the sale of goods or for the performance of services during that particular period.

To illustrate the accrual concept of revenue, assume that an entity began operations in 2012 and received $100 000 in cash for services rendered before the end of the year. Assume also that its clients were charged $20 000 for services completed in 2012 for which the cash is to be received in 2013. Revenue recognised in 2012 is $120 000, which is the sum of cash received ($100 000) and accounts receivable ($20 000) from customers for services rendered in 2012. Recall from chapter 3 that, when services are performed for customers on credit, both accounts receivable and revenue are increased. In 2013, the cash collection of $20 000 is not revenue but is recorded as an increase in the asset 'cash at bank' and a decrease in the asset 'accounts receivable'. Thus, revenue is recognised when it is capable of faithful and verifiable measurement, regardless of the period in which the resulting cash is collected.

Some entities perform services for their clients and charge a fee or commission for the services rendered. Examples are a real estate office, a law firm, an accounting firm, a public relations firm, an advertising agency, or an investment advisory service. Various account titles are used to describe the major sources of revenue, and the account titles should be descriptive of the nature of the revenue. For example, Management Services Fees Revenue and Tax Services Fees Revenue may be used by an accounting firm to account for major categories of revenue. Other firms, called retailers, generate revenue by selling goods. An account entitled Sales Revenue is commonly used by retail businesses to record revenue from the sale of merchandise.

Expenses

Costs are incurred as a necessary part of the revenue-generating process. The portion of a cost that is expected to provide economic benefits in a future period represents an **unexpired cost** and is reported as an asset in the balance sheet (also called the statement of financial position) at the end of the period. The costs of assets that have been consumed during the current period are reported in the income statement as expenses (sometimes called **expired costs**) and are deducted from income (revenues) in the determination of profit. In other words, expenses are the costs of services and assets consumed in the current period.

Under the accrual basis of accounting, expenses are recognised in the period in which the consumption of costs can be measured in a faithful, verifiable manner rather than in the period in which the cash is paid. For example, salaries earned by employees in this period are reported as a current expense because the amount of the salaries can be measured in a verifiable manner, even though payment may not be made until the next period. In other cases, such as the prepayment of rent for the next period and the purchase of office equipment for cash, cash is paid before an expense is incurred. These prepayments are accounted for as assets (unexpired costs) until the benefits of the rent or the office equipment are consumed by the entity, at which time they are transferred to expense accounts. In many cases, however, the expense and cash payment occur in the same period. Whatever the situation, it is important to realise that an expense incurred and the cash payment for it often do not occur in the same accounting period.

When a building is purchased, it is recorded as an asset as it will provide economic benefits over several periods. Allocating the cost of assets such as a building across time periods is based on estimates because of the accountant's inability to predict the future and to know the length of time over which an asset will be consumed. The need for timely information, however, takes precedence over the lack of precision involved in preparing accrual basis financial statements. Although the allocations are estimated as accurately as possible, the financial statements are only tentative, and the actual results can be determined accurately only at the time the entity ends its activities. Accrual estimates must be relevant if performance and financial position are to be assessed properly.

Despite the allocation problems, financial statements are prepared on the assumption that the entity will continue to operate in the future (the *going concern assumption*) unless there is evidence to the contrary. Going concern is the underlying basis for accrual accounting. If there were no need for periodic reports or if the entity were to liquidate in the near future, the cash basis would be satisfactory.

Although expenses decrease equity, not all decreases in equity are expenses. For example, a withdrawal of an asset by the owner decreases equity but is not an expense of the business.

Remember also that not all cash payments are expenses. Examples are the repayment of a loan, the cash purchase of office equipment (the cost will be expensed in future periods as the asset is used), and cash withdrawals by the owners.

Temporary (nominal) and permanent (real) accounts

Although income (including revenues) increases and expenses decrease equity, separate accounts are maintained for each major type of income and expense to provide detailed information about the dollar amount and sources of income and the dollar amount and types of expenses. This information is reported to interested parties, internal and external, via the income statement. Income statements are prepared for periods of equal length to enable statement users to make meaningful comparisons of current-period results with those of previous periods. To facilitate the preparation of the next period's income statement, all income and expense accounts are reduced to a zero balance at the end of the accounting period — a process called *closing the accounts* — by transferring these account balances to an equity account. (This step in the accounting cycle is described in the next chapter.) Because the income and expense accounts are reduced to a zero balance at the end of the accounting period, they are called **temporary** (or **nominal**) **accounts**. Accounts reported in the balance sheet are not closed; their ending balances of one period are carried forward and become the beginning balances of the next period. These accounts are called **permanent** (or **real**) **accounts**.

4.2 The accounting cycle — expansion to include adjusting entries

This chapter introduces the recording of end-of-period adjustments at the end of the accounting period. Because accounting has adopted the accrual basis assumption in the *Conceptual Framework*, end-of-period adjustments are very important to recognise the accruals needed at the end of the accounting period. These adjusting entries are recorded in the general journal, and then posted to the general ledger, and an adjusted trial balance is prepared to prove the general ledger is in balance after the adjusting entries have been posted to the relevant accounts. The use of an optional worksheet to enable the recording of adjustments outside the accounting records and to prepare financial statements also is illustrated. The worksheet is particularly helpful when managers wish to prepare end-of-month financial statements during the yearly accounting period.

The accounting cycle developed in chapter 3 (illustrated in figure 3.8, p. 79) is expanded to accommodate the additional steps introduced in this chapter (figure 4.1). Note that the cycle is repeated each accounting period.

Figure 4.1 The accounting cycle — expanded to include adjusting entries

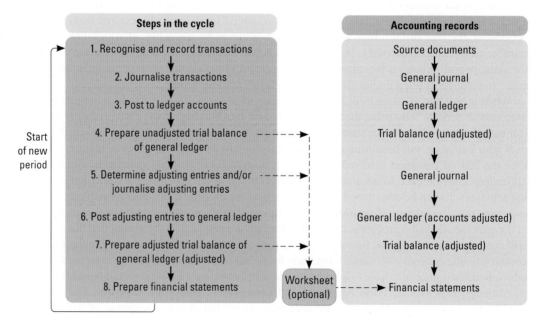

The need for adjusting entries

In many cases, the payment or receipt of cash coincides with the accounting period in which the expense or income is recognised. However, some transactions affect the entity's profits and financial position for two or more accounting periods. In these cases, the period in which the cash is paid or received does not coincide with the period in which the expense and income are recognised. As a result, some of the accounts must be adjusted as of the last day of the accounting period to provide for the correct recognition of income and expenses (inflows and outflows of economic benefits not reflected in cash receipts or cash payments) during the period in order to assess the entity's performance. In addition, adjusting entries are necessary to achieve an accurate reporting of asset and liability balances on the last day of the accounting period in order to assess the entity's financial position.

The adjusting process involves an analysis of the accounts and supporting documents to determine whether entries are needed to adjust account balances to their proper amounts for financial statement purposes. Once this analysis is completed, **adjusting entries** are entered, if necessary, in the journal and posted to the accounts.

Preparation of adjusting entries is an important step in the accounting cycle of a business. During the accounting year, if interim (end-of-month) financial statements are required, the adjusting entries commonly are not recorded in the entity's journal, but are shown on a worksheet (see later in this chapter). Adjusting entries are recorded in the entity's general journal only on the last day of the entity's accounting period.

4.3 Classification of adjusting entries

Learning objective 3

Identify the different types of adjusting entries

Adjusting entries are classified into two major categories, deferrals and accruals. **Deferrals** are expenses paid in advance (called 'prepaid expenses') or revenues received in advance (called 'unearned revenues') which need to be allocated over future accounting periods. **Accruals** are the recognition of expenses incurred but not yet paid for (called 'accrued expenses') or the recognition of revenue earned but for which cash has not yet been received (called 'accrued revenues'). Figure 4.2 summarises the types of adjusting entries.

Deferrals (prepayments)	Prepaid expenses Costs/expenses paid for before they are consumed, e.g. rent paid in advance, insurance premiums paid for protection in the future (initially recorded as *assets* and charged to expenses in subsequent periods as they are consumed)	Unearned revenues Revenues that have been collected or received in advance but not yet earned, e.g. magazine subscription fees received in advance, rent received in advance from a tenant (initially recorded as *liabilities* and recognised as revenue in subsequent periods as the revenue is earned)
Accruals (unrecorded expenses and revenues)	Accrued expenses Expenses incurred but not yet paid for or entered in the records, e.g. wages earned by employees but not yet paid, interest to be paid on a loan	Accrued revenues Revenue earned but not yet received in cash or entered in the records, e.g. sales commissions earned but not yet paid, interest accumulated on a receivable but not yet received

Figure 4.2 Types of adjustments

Since adjusting entries are made so that all income (revenues) and expenses are recognised in the appropriate accounting period, it follows that adjusting entries affect both the size of the entity's profit and its financial position. There are two rules for adjusting entries:

- One side of the entry affects an account reported in the income statement (expense or income (revenue)), and the other side of the entry affects an account reported in the balance sheet (asset or liability).
- The cash account is never adjusted as the cash flow occurs either before or after the end of the reporting period.

To demonstrate each of these types of adjusting entries, the illustration of Intellect Management Services developed in chapter 3 is continued. A trial balance on 30 June was prepared in chapter 3 and is shown again in figure 4.3. This trial balance is called an unadjusted trial balance because at this stage no adjustments to the accounts have been made. For illustrative purposes we shall assume that the financial year for Intellect Management Services ends on 30 June, i.e. only 1 month after commencing business, and therefore adjusting entries are prepared in the general journal.

Where an entity has operated for the whole 12 months of the financial year, formal adjusting entries are made in the general journal usually only at year's end. If interim (e.g. monthly) financial statements are prepared for internal management purposes, the adjusting entries are entered usually on a worksheet only, as illustrated later in the chapter.

Figure 4.3 Unadjusted trial balance of Intellect Management Services

INTELLECT MANAGEMENT SERVICES
Unadjusted Trial Balance
as at 30 June 2013

Account	Account no.	Account balance Debit	Account balance Credit
Cash at bank	100	$135 770	
Accounts receivable	104	11 880	
Prepaid insurance	110	1 920	
Office supplies	111	1 240	
GST outlays	120	32 276	
Land	150	120 000	
Building	160	180 000	
Office equipment	170	19 200	
Accounts payable	200		$ 9 200
Unearned appraisal fees	220		560
GST collections	250		2 026
Mortgage payable	260		240 000
M. Mooney, Capital	300		240 000
M. Mooney, Drawings	310	1 200	
Management services revenue	400		19 200
Appraisal fees revenue	401		500
Salaries expense	500	7 600	
Telephone expense	510	160	
Advertising expense	530	240	
		$511 486	$511 486

4.4 Adjusting entries for deferrals
Prepaid expenses

An entity often pays for certain items (such as rent, insurance and supplies) in advance of their use. Under the accrual basis of accounting, the payment of cash does not necessarily result in the recognition of an expense. Goods and services that are paid for in advance and are expected to provide benefits beyond the current period are *normally* recorded as assets at the time of payment. At the end of the accounting period, the portion of the cost that is associated with the goods that have been consumed or with services that have been received is transferred to an expense account. The remaining unexpired or unused portion of the cost is reported as an asset in the balance sheet, since it represents future economic benefits to be received in future periods. Thus, before the financial statements are prepared, the balance in the asset account is analysed and is apportioned between an asset and an expense.

Adjusting entries for prepaid expenses covered above are summarised in figure 4.4.

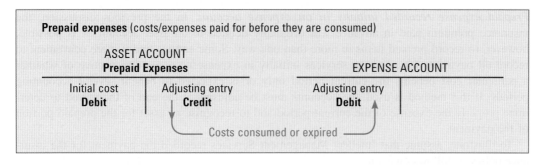

Prepaid insurance

On 3 June, a 24-month fire and business liability insurance policy was purchased by Intellect Management Services for $1920 plus GST of $192, as evidenced by a tax invoice of $2112. Insurance coverage began on 1 June. The transaction was initially recorded as follows:

June	3	Prepaid Insurance	110	1 920	
		GST Outlays	120	192	
		Cash at Bank	100		2 112
		(Purchase of a 24-month fire and business liability insurance policy)			

Recall that the account numbers are added to the posting reference column in the journal when postings are made to the ledger.

The balance in the Prepaid Insurance (asset) account remains the same until the end of the month, at which time the cost of the insurance protection for the month of June is calculated. The cost of the insurance protection per month is $80 ($1920 ÷ 24 months). The following adjusting entry is made on 30 June to record insurance expense and to reduce the Prepaid Insurance account. The GST has no effect on this internal transaction. (The adjusting entries are identified by letters in this illustration for reference purposes only.)

June	30	Insurance Expense	521	80	
(a)		Prepaid Insurance	110		80
		(Adjusting entry to record expiration of 1-month's insurance)			

After the adjusting entry is posted, the accounts appear as follows:

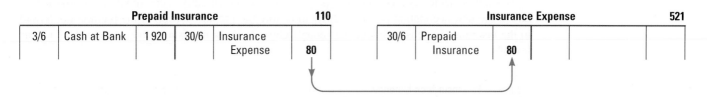

The adjusting entry reduces the Prepaid Insurance account *balance* to $1840 ($1920 − $80), which is the unexpired portion of the cost applicable to future periods, and is reported as an asset. The portion of the cost that is consumed in this period ($80) is properly shown as an expense for the month of June. If the adjusting entry were not made, profit, assets and equity would all be overstated.

In future periods, the $1840 balance is reduced by $80 each month as insurance protection is received by the entity, i.e. insurance expense is incurred. The costs of additional policies purchased are debited to the Prepaid Insurance account and allocated to expense following the same procedures.

Prepaid expense recorded initially in an expense account. In the previous discussion, the insurance premium paid in advance was originally debited to an asset account. It is possible, however, to record prepaid items in more than one way. Some entities find it more convenient to record all payments for goods or services initially in expense accounts, irrespective of whether a particular cost benefits the current period only or is expected to benefit several accounting periods. If this method is used, the accounts must be adjusted at the end of the period to determine properly the expense of the current period and to recognise an asset for the prepaid portion of the payment.

To illustrate, assume that Intellect Management Services recorded the payment for the insurance policy as follows on 3 June:

June	3	Insurance Expense	521	1 920	
		GST Outlays	120	192	
		Cash at Bank	100		2 112
		(Purchase of a 24-month fire and business liability insurance policy)			

At the end of the period, an adjusting entry is needed to remove the unexpired portion of the insurance coverage from the expense account.

June	30	Prepaid Insurance	110	1 840	
	(aa)	Insurance Expense	521		1 840
		(Adjusting entry to record portion of insurance policy unexpired)			
		[23 months × $80 per month]			

After these entries are posted, the two accounts appear as follows:

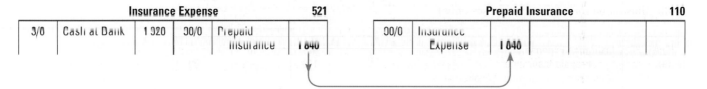

Note that the 30 June balances are the same (Prepaid Insurance, $1840; Insurance Expense, $80, i.e. $1920 − $1840) as when the insurance premium payment was made initially to the Prepaid Insurance (asset) account.

When this method is used to record prepayments, a journal entry is commonly made on the first day of the new accounting period (1 July) to restore the prepaid portion of the premium of $1840 to the Insurance Expense account. The entry, referred to as a reversing entry (see chapter 5), is as follows:

July	1	Insurance Expense	521	1 840	
		Prepaid Insurance	110		1 840
		(Reversing entry)			

Additional payments for insurance premiums are then added to the balance in the Insurance Expense account. At the end of the next reporting period, the account is analysed and the prepaid portion is removed again, as was done in entry (aa). The above treatment of prepaid expenses is summarised generally in figure 4.5.

The preferred treatment is to debit the Prepaid Insurance asset when the premium is paid. This approach correctly recognises an existing asset at the time and means that you don't have to make a reversing entry later.

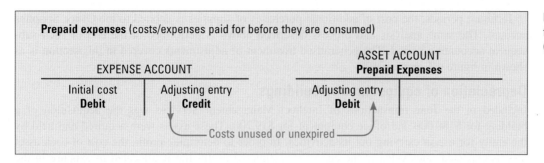

Office supplies

Intellect Management Services made the following journal entry on 5 June to record a tax invoice covering the purchase of office supplies:

June	5	Office Supplies	111	1 240	
		GST Outlays	120	124	
		Accounts Payable	200		1 364
		(Office supplies purchased on credit)			

The cost of unused office supplies is reported as an asset in the balance sheet. As the office supplies are consumed, their cost is transferred to an expense account. Normally, the recognition of the expense occurs at the end of the accounting period. In other words, no journal entry is made during the period to record the cost of supplies consumed because this information is not needed on a day-to-day basis. Before financial statements are prepared, an adjusting entry is made to remove the cost of the supplies consumed from the asset account and to recognise the cost of supplies consumed as an expense.

For control purposes, the supplies are normally kept in a central location and employees may be required to fill out a requisition when supplies are needed. The requisitions are then totalled to determine the cost of supplies consumed during the period. If a requisition system is not used, the cost of the supplies on hand is determined by counting the items on hand and costing them.

In the case of Intellect Management Services, assume that the cost of the supplies on hand at the end of June was determined to be $1080. The cost of supplies used this period is assumed to be $160, since a total of $1240 was available for use during the period. The following adjusting entry is made to record the supplies used:

June	30	Office Supplies Expense	530	160	
	(b)	Office Supplies	111		160
		(Adjusting entry to record supplies consumed in June)			

GST is not affected by the consumption of office supplies as this is an internal transaction. After the entry is posted, the accounts appear as follows:

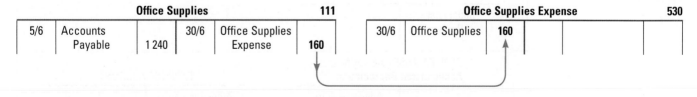

The $1080 balance left in the Office Supplies account is the cost of supplies available for use in future periods (an asset). The $160 balance in the Office Supplies Expense account is the cost of supplies consumed during June, which is charged against the income for this period in the income statement.

In future periods, the cost of additional purchases of supplies is debited to the Office Supplies account. The same analysis and process described above is performed at the end of each subsequent accounting period. The generalised treatment of adjustments covered in this section is as shown in figure 4.4 on page 129.

Depreciation of equipment and buildings

Included in the June transactions of Intellect Management Services was the acquisition of a building for $180 000 and office equipment for $19 200. These assets were acquired and held by the entity for use in carrying out its activities. In order to determine profit, the cost of each asset less its expected sales value at the end of its estimated useful life is allocated to expense in the current and future periods as the assets are consumed in producing income. **Useful life** is the estimated amount of time over which the asset is expected to be consumed by the entity. The portion of the asset's cost assigned to expense is called **depreciation**.

The adjusting entry to record depreciation is similar in concept to the entries made to allocate the cost of the insurance policy and office supplies described above. That is, an expense account is debited for the portion of the cost allocated to the current period and an asset is decreased. However, unlike the insurance policy and office supplies, which generally are used for one or two periods, items of equipment and buildings are used for long periods of time, sometimes up to 30 years or longer. It is often impossible for the accountant to know exactly the useful life of such assets or the sales values at the end of their useful lives. Consequently, amounts calculated for depreciation are by necessity based on estimates of the asset's useful life and expected sales value at the end of the asset's useful life. This expected sales value is called 'residual value' and is discussed further in a later chapter. Depreciation expense is an estimate only. There are no GST implications as depreciation is an internal transaction.

In making the adjusting entry for depreciation, a separate account entitled Accumulated Depreciation is credited for the cost associated with the period rather than making a direct credit to the asset account. The balance in the **Accumulated Depreciation** account reflects the portion of the cost that has been assigned to expense and accumulated since the item was purchased. The Accumulated Depreciation account is called a **contra account**. A contra account is reported as an offset to or a deduction from a related account. Thus, in the balance sheet, the Accumulated Depreciation account is reported as a deduction from the original cost as shown in the related asset account. Reporting both the original cost of the asset and the accumulated depreciation can provide useful information about the age of the asset to statement users. Adjusting for depreciation is summarised in figure 4.6.

To illustrate, assume the building has a useful life of 25 years, at which time it is expected to have a residual value of $30 000. The office equipment has an 8-year useful life and a zero residual value at the end of 8 years. The monthly depreciation expense for each asset is calculated as follows:

Office equipment

$$\frac{\$19\,200}{96\ \text{months}} = \$200 \text{ per month}$$

Building

$$\frac{\$180\,000 - \$30\,000}{300\ \text{months}} = \$500 \text{ per month}$$

Figure 4.6 Adjusting entries for prepaid expenses (non-current assets) — depreciation

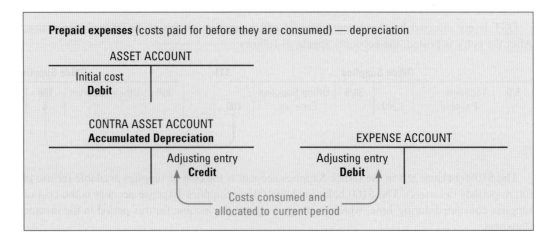

Prepaid expenses (costs paid for before they are consumed) — depreciation

ASSET ACCOUNT

Initial cost
Debit

CONTRA ASSET ACCOUNT
Accumulated Depreciation

EXPENSE ACCOUNT

Adjusting entry
Credit

Adjusting entry
Debit

Costs consumed and allocated to current period

The adjusting entries to record depreciation for the month of June are:

June	30	Depreciation Expense – Office Equipment	540	200	
	(c)	Accumulated Depreciation – Office Equipment	171		200
		(Adjusting entry to record depreciation of equipment)			
June	30	Depreciation Expense – Building	541	500	
	(d)	Accumulated Depreciation – Building	161		500
		(Adjusting entry to record depreciation of building)			

(Instead of preparing two entries, the adjustments could be accomplished in one combined entry.)

The accounts for depreciation of office equipment after posting appear as follows:

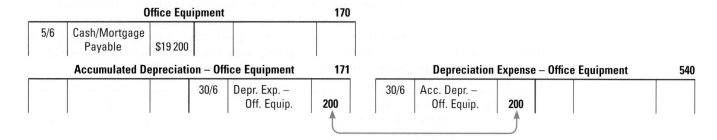

Depreciation is reported as an expense in the income statement. The Building and Office Equipment accounts will be shown in the balance sheet at the end of the first month as follows:

Building	$180 000	
Less: Accumulated depreciation – building	500	$179 500
Office equipment	19 200	
Less: Accumulated depreciation – office equipment	200	19 000

The difference between the original cost of the asset and its accumulated depreciation is called the **carrying amount** (or **book value**) of the asset and represents the unexpired cost of the asset.

As long as the assets are used, the same adjusting entries are made until the cost less expected sales value is fully assigned to expense. Thus, in successive balance sheets the Accumulated Depreciation – Office Equipment account increases $200 each month and the Accumulated Depreciation – Building account increases $500 each month. The original cost of the two assets remains in the Office Equipment and Building accounts and does not change. A more complete discussion of depreciation is provided in later chapters.

Precollected or unearned revenue

An entity may receive cash in advance for services that are to be performed in the future. Until the service is performed, a liability equal to the amount of the advance payment is reported in the balance sheet to reflect the obligation of the entity to perform future services. That is, recognition of the income (revenue) is postponed until the services are performed, at which time the entity's obligations are reduced. The adjusting process for unearned revenue is shown in figure 4.7 (p. 134).

To illustrate, recall from chapter 3 that Intellect Management Services issued a tax invoice and received a $560 advance payment plus GST of $56 on 29 June for a valuation appraisal to be completed on 2 July. The following entry was made to record the receipt of cash:

June	29	Cash at Bank	100	616	
		Unearned Appraisal Fees	220		560
		GST Collections	250		56
		(Cash received for appraisals to be performed in July)			

Figure 4.7 Adjusting entries for precollected or unearned revenues

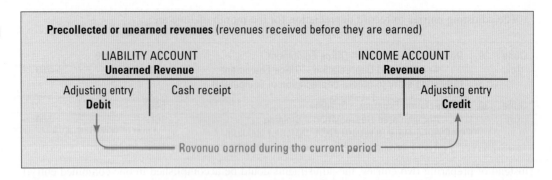

Since the appraisal will not be performed by 30 June, the credit is made to an *unearned revenue* account (a liability) at the time the cash is received. The income (revenue) of $560 will be recognised in July when the appraisal is performed for the client, thus reducing the entity's liabilities. Once the appraisal is completed on 2 July, an entry is made either at the time the obligation is reduced *or* at the end of the period as an adjusting entry when the accounts are reviewed, to transfer the appropriate portion of the advance payment to revenue as follows:

July	7	Unearned Appraisal Fees	220	560	
		Appraisal Fees Revenue	401		560
		(Appraisal fees earned in July)			

Note that the revenue is recognised in July, when the obligation is reduced, rather than in June, when the cash was received.

The receipt of cash for services to be performed in the future may have been recorded originally in a revenue account rather than a liability account. If so, an adjusting entry is needed at the end of the period to reduce the balance in the revenue account and to record a liability for the remaining portion representing services yet to be performed. The method illustrated above is preferred.

Another precollected or unearned revenue illustration (subscriptions)

The Intellect Management Services illustration contains one example of adjusting an unearned revenue account. In practice, other common precollected revenue items are rent received in advance, magazine subscriptions and advertising fees received in advance by a publisher, and deposits received from customers before merchandise is delivered.

To illustrate further the accounting for unearned revenue, another example *unrelated to Intellect's activities* is used. Assume that, on 8 September, the publishers of *People of the World*, a monthly magazine, receive $264, including $24 GST, for a 1-year subscription beginning with the October issue. The company makes the following entry upon receipt of the cash:

Sept.	8	Cash at Bank	264	
		Unearned Subscriptions Revenue		240
		GST Collections		24
		(Receipt of subscriptions in advance)		

On 31 December, the end of the financial year, the balance in the Unearned Subscriptions Revenue account includes 3 months (3/12) of the revenue for this period and 9 months (9/12) which will be reported as revenue in the next period. Therefore, the following adjusting entry must be made to remove $60 (3/12 × $240) from the liability account and to record the revenue in the current period:

Dec.	31	Unearned Subscriptions Revenue	60	
		Subscriptions Revenue		60
		(Adjusting entry to record subscriptions earned)		

After the two journal entries are posted, the accounts appear as follows:

Subscriptions Revenue								Unearned Subscriptions Revenue						
			31/12	Unearned Subscriptions Revenue	**60**			31/12	Subscriptions Revenue	**60**		8/9	Cash at Bank	240

The adjusting entry leaves a balance of $180 in the Unearned Subscriptions Revenue account, which is reported as a liability in the balance sheet; the subscriptions revenue of $30 appears as revenue in the income statement. In the next period, an adjusting entry for $90 will be made to transfer the liability balance to revenue, as the liability is reduced when each issue of the magazine is published and sent to the subscriber.

BUSINESS KNOWLEDGE

Small businesses on the rise

Small businesses could be the key drivers of economic recovery in some Asian economies, according to the CPA Australia *Asia-Pacific Small Business Survey 2009*.

This survey of small business operators in Hong Kong, Malaysia, Singapore and Australia also showed that Australian small business operators were the least likely to undertake even the most basic management activity such as stock and debtor control, and the least likely to seek additional funds.

'Many small business operators appear hesitant when it comes to obtaining extra funding or employing more staff,' says CPA Australia President Richard Petty 'What also emerged are correlations between business practice and business confidence, with businesses that are more meticulous in their management processes tending to be more optimistic about their growth prospects. On this measure, Australian small businesses appear to lag noticeably behind their Asia-Pacific counterparts.'

However, the reasons behind the Australian findings included: the fact that Australian small business operators tend to be in older age groups and thus took a more conservative approach; businesses are smaller in size than in the other countries; and they did not tend to access finance as readily.

Among the countries surveyed, Malaysian businesses were the most likely to have carried out business management activities.

Source: Excerpts from 'Small businesses on the rise', *InTheBlack*.

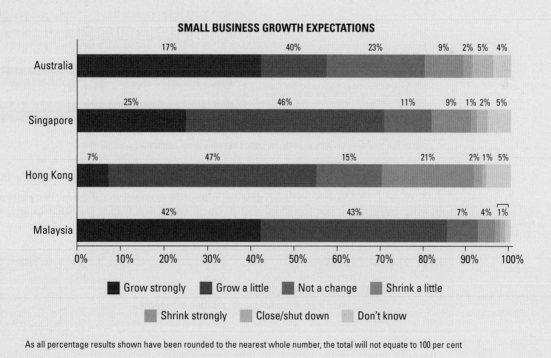

SMALL BUSINESS GROWTH EXPECTATIONS

As all percentage results shown have been rounded to the nearest whole number, the total will not equate to 100 per cent

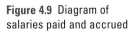

Learning objective **5**

Prepare adjusting entries for accruals or unrecorded items

4.5 Adjusting entries for accruals

Accrued or unrecorded expenses

During the period, most expenses are recorded when they are paid. At the end of the accounting period, there are usually some expenses that have been consumed but have not been recorded because payment has not yet been made. An adjusting entry is needed to recognise the expense in the period in which it is consumed rather than in the period of payment. An offsetting credit is made to a liability account to record the entity's obligation to pay for the goods or services that have been received. These items are called accrued expenses or accrued liabilities. See figure 4.8.

Figure 4.8 Adjusting entries for accrued and unrecorded expenses

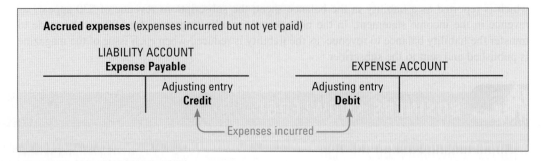

Accrued salaries (liability)

Intellect Management Services follows the practice of paying employees every 2 weeks. On Friday, 22 June, the employees were paid $7600 for the preceding 2 weeks of service. A diagram of the salaries earned between this payment and 30 June is presented in figure 4.9.

Figure 4.9 Diagram of salaries paid and accrued

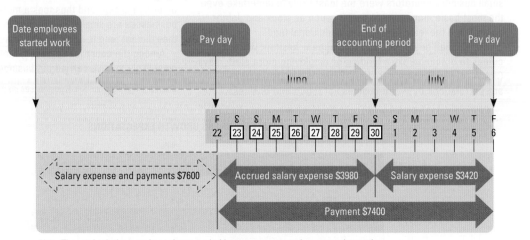

Note: The total salaries vary in each pay period because some employees work part time.

No particular problem was encountered on 22 June when salaries were paid for the period of 8 June to 22 June because both the payment and the expense occurred in the same period. The following entry was made to record that payment (note that wages and salaries are exempt from GST):

June	22	Salaries Expense	500	7 600	
		Cash at Bank	100		7 600
		(Salaries paid to employees)			
		[Deductions from the employees' salaries are ignored for now.]			

Because the end of the period, 30 June, occurs before the next salary payment date, 6 July, an adjusting entry is required to provide a correct determination of expenses consumed in June and to provide a record of liabilities at the end of June. Even though the employees are not paid until 6 July, a portion of the $7400 payment (some employees work part time and the office is open 7 days a week) is for employees' services that were received in June. The entry to accrue the unpaid salaries up to 30 June is:

June 30 (e)	Salaries Expense	500	3 980	
	Salaries Payable	210		3 980
	(Adjusting entry to record salaries payable from 23 June to 30 June)			

The accounts after the adjusting entry is posted are as follows:

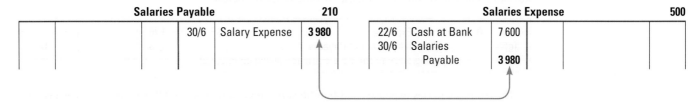

			Salaries Payable		**210**
			30/6	Salary Expense	**3 980**

		Salaries Expense		**500**
22/6	Cash at Bank	7 600		
30/6	Salaries Payable	**3 980**		

The adjusting entry records an expense ($3980) for the services received in June and reported in the June income statement along with the salaries previously paid ($7600). The credit of $3980 in the Salaries Payable account reflects *the amount owed* to the employees for services performed during the period 23 June to 30 June and is reported as a liability in the balance sheet. Failure to make the 30 June adjusting entry results in an understatement of expenses and an overstatement of profit for June; and in the balance sheet, liabilities would be understated and equity would be overstated.

The liability of $3980 is eliminated on 6 July, when the payment of $7400 is made to the employees. The $3420 earned by the employees in July is recorded as an expense, as shown in the following entry:

July 6	Salaries Payable	210	3 980	
	Salaries Expense	500	3 420	
	Cash at Bank	100		7 400
	(Payment for salaries earned from 23 June to 6 July)			

The effect of the above entries is to recognise the expense and liability in the period that an expense is incurred rather than in the period that payment is made to the employees.

Accrued interest (liability)

On 2 June, Intellect Management Services financed a portion of the land and building purchase with a 20-year, $240 000, 8% mortgage. An annual payment of $12 000 plus accrued interest is made on 2 June of each subsequent year. Interest expense accumulates daily. Therefore, Intellect must prepare an adjusting entry on 30 June to record the interest expense incurred in June and to recognise a liability for the unpaid interest. The entry is:

June 30 (f)	Interest Expense[1]	560	1 600	
	Interest Payable	215		1 600
	(Adjusting entry to record interest payable on mortgage for June)			

---

1. The formula for calculating interest is as follows:
    Principal $\times$ Rate $\times$ Time = Interest
  For this entry the interest is $1600 calculated for simplicity as follows:
    $240\,000 \times 8\% \times 1/12 = \$1600$

Note that only the $1600 additional liability for the accrued interest is recorded on 30 June. A Mortgage Payable account is already in the records as a result of making the 2 June entry to record the asset purchase. Interest expense is shown as an expense in the income statement for June, and interest payable is reported as a liability on the 30 June balance sheet. No GST outlays are necessary on interest payments. As the interest payable is an estimate and is not based on a statement from the financial institution, interest payable is credited rather than the Mortgage Payable account.

Accrued electricity (liability)

The electricity supplier invoices its customers after the service has been provided. Assume that Intellect Management Services makes an estimate of $420 for electricity used in June. The adjusting entry to record the expense in June is shown below:[2]

June 30 (g)	Electricity Expense	570	420	
	Electricity Account Payable	216		420
	(Adjusting entry to record electricity consumed in June)			

This entry increases expenses and liabilities by equal amounts. No GST is recorded because the electricity supplier has not yet issued a tax invoice for electricity. Note that even though the electricity bill may not be received until July or August, the adjusting entry on 30 June is made so that the expense and liability are properly reflected in the June financial statements. After this entry is posted, the accounts are as follows:

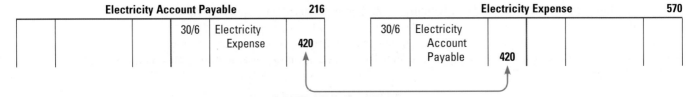

Unrecorded or accrued revenue

In most cases when a service is performed by the entity, an entry is made to recognise the transaction. Even if cash is not received immediately, an account receivable is established in order to maintain a record of amounts owed to the entity and to recognise revenue. No entry is required at the end of a period since the receivable and revenue have been recorded. There are occasions in most entities, however, when an increase in economic benefits has occurred as a result of revenue earned but not yet recorded.

Revenue that is unrecorded at the end of the period must be included in the accounting records by debiting a receivable and crediting a revenue account. Such items are often called accrued revenues or accrued receivables. The adjusting entry for accrued revenue is summarised in figure 4.10.

Figure 4.10 Adjusting entries for accrued revenues

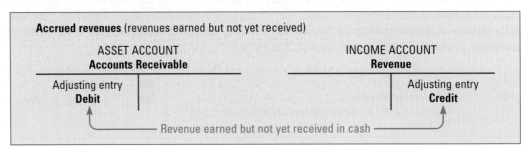

---

2. For simplicity, the entry provided ignores GST in that there is no tax invoice issued at this point by the electricity supplier. The tax invoice, showing GST to be paid, will be issued in the next accounting period. Nevertheless, a good conceptual argument exists for recognising a GST outlay in the adjusting entry in order to record the correct liability including the GST for electricity.

To illustrate, Intellect Management Services signed an agreement on 1 June to provide marketing services for a monthly fee of $800. Although the services fee represents an increase in economic benefits for the entity in one month, the agreement provides for the benefits (i.e. the fee) to be received on the fifth day of the following month. No entry was made on 1 June, when the agreement was made, because there was no increase or decrease in economic benefits. However, as services are performed, the benefits are gradually increased. By 30 June, the full fee of $800 is receivable (assuming that a tax invoice has not yet been issued) and is recorded by the entry below:[3]

June 30 (h)	Accounts Receivable Marketing Services Revenue (Adjusting entry to record marketing services fee receivable for June)	104 402	800	800

The account receivable is shown in the balance sheet as an asset, and the revenue account is reported in the income statement. GST is not recorded at this point as no tax invoice has been issued. The GST of $80 will be collected and recorded on 5 July.

Figure 4.11 summarises the four types of adjustments which may be necessary at the end of the accounting period. Included in this summary is a list of the consequences of not making adjusting entries.

Type of adjustment	Accounts affected	Adjusting entry		Results of making no adjustment
Prepaid expenses (deferrals)	Assets Expenses	**Expense account** **Asset account**	**Dr** **Cr**	Assets overstated Expenses understated
Unearned revenues (deferrals)	Liabilities Revenues	**Liability account** **Revenue account**	**Dr** **Cr**	Liabilities overstated Revenues understated
Accrued expenses (accruals)	Expenses Liabilities	**Expense account** **Liability account**	**Dr** **Cr**	Expenses understated Liabilities understated
Accrued revenues (accruals)	Assets Revenues	**Asset account** **Revenue account**	**Dr** **Cr**	Assets understated Revenues understated

Figure 4.11 Summary of end-of-period adjustments

The completed adjusting entries for Intellect Management Services are summarised in figure 4.12 (p. 140). The appropriate letter, e.g. (a), (b), is indicated in the figure to help you refer to earlier discussion in the chapter.

In computerised accounting systems, once adjusting entries have been entered, the computer is able to prepare the adjusted trial balance. With certain adjusting entries, such as depreciation, accrued interest and expired insurance, computer packages can calculate the correct amounts. In some packages, e.g. MYOB, end-of-period adjustments are called 'recurring transactions' and the computer automatically makes adjustments at period end, based on the instructions given to it.

---

3. For simplicity, the GST collection resulting from the marketing services is ignored in the entry as no tax invoice has yet been issued, and no GST is therefore payable for the current period. Nevertheless, a conceptual argument exists for recording the account receivable at the correct amount to be received, namely $880, including the GST, and recording the GST collection to be paid ($80), even though it is not payable at the end of the current period as no tax invoice has been issued. If a tax invoice had been issued, then the GST Collections account would also have been adjusted.

INTELLECT MANAGEMENT SERVICES
Summary of adjusting entries made

Date	Particulars	Post Ref	Debit	Credit
June 30 (a)	Insurance Expense	521	80	
	Prepaid Insurance	110		80
	(Adjusting entry to record portion of insurance consumed)			
30 (b)	Office Supplies Expense	530	160	
	Office Supplies	111		160
	(Adjusting entry to record supplies consumed in June)			
30 (c)	Depreciation Expense – Office Equipment	540	200	
	Accumulated Depreciation – Office Equipment	171		200
	(Adjusting entry to record depreciation of equipment)			
30 (d)	Depreciation Expense – Building	541	500	
	Accumulated Depreciation – Building	161		500
	(Adjusting entry to record depreciation of building)			
30 (e)	Salaries Expense	500	3 980	
	Salaries Payable	210		3 980
	(Adjusting entry to record salaries payable from 23 June to 30 June)			
30 (f)	Interest Expense	560	1 600	
	Interest Payable	215		1 600
	(Adjusting entry to record interest payable on mortgage for June)			
30 (g)	Electricity Expense	570	420	
	Electricity Account Payable	216		420
	(Adjusting entry to record electricity consumed in June)			
30 (h)	Accounts Receivable	104	800	
	Marketing Services Revenue	417		800
	(Adjusting entry to record marketing services fee receivable for June)			

4.6 Adjusted trial balance

Learning objective 6

Prepare and understand the purpose of an adjusted trial balance

The ledger accounts of Intellect Management Services (in T-account format) as they would appear after the adjusting entries are posted are shown in figure 4.13. The ledger accounts are then balanced, and a trial balance is prepared as the next step in the accounting cycle (see figure 4.1, p. 126). This trial balance is called an **adjusted trial balance**, and it seeks to verify the equality of debits and credits in the accounts *after* posting the adjusting entries. An adjusted trial balance taken from the ledger of Intellect Management Services on 30 June is presented in figure 4.14 (p. 142).

Figure 4.13 General ledger after adjusting entries are posted

ASSETS

Cash at Bank			100		Accounts Receivable		104
1/6	240 000	2/6	90 000	15/6	9 240	30/6	9 240
23/6	550	3/6	2 112	19/6	11 880		
29/6	616	5/6	11 920	30/6 (h)	800		
30/6	9 240	6/6	264				
		22/6	7 600				
		23/6	1 200		**Prepaid Insurance**		**110**
		27/6	1 364				
		30/6	176	3/6	1 920	30/6 (a)	80

Figure 4.13 *continued*

Office Supplies — 111

Debit		Credit	
5/6	1 240	30/6 (b)	160

GST Outlays — 120

Debit		Credit	
2/6	30 000		
3/6	192		
5/6	124		
5/6	1 920		
6/6	24		
30/6	16		

Land — 150

Debit		Credit	
2/6	120 000		

Building — 160

Debit		Credit	
2/6	180 000		

Accumulated Depr. – Bldg. — 161

Debit		Credit	
		30/6 (d)	500

Office Equipment — 170

Debit		Credit	
5/6	19 200		

Accum. Depr. – Off. Equip. — 171

Debit		Credit	
		30/6 (c)	200

LIABILITIES

Accounts Payable — 200

Debit		Credit	
27/6	1 364	5/6	1 364
		5/6	9 200

Salaries Payable — 210

Debit		Credit	
		30/6 (e)	3 980

Interest Payable — 215

Debit		Credit	
		30/6 (f)	1 600

Electricity Account Payable — 216

Debit		Credit	
		30/6 (g)	420

Unearned Appraisal Fees — 220

Debit		Credit	
		29/6	560

GST Collections — 250

Debit		Credit	
		15/6	840
		19/6	1 080
		23/6	50
		29/6	56

Mortgage Payable — 260

Debit		Credit	
		2/6	240 000

EQUITY

M. Mooney, Capital — 300

Debit		Credit	
		1/6	240 000

M. Mooney, Drawings — 310

Debit		Credit	
23/6	1 200		

Management Services Revenue — 400

Debit		Credit	
		15/6	8 400
		19/6	10 800

Appraisal Fees Revenue — 401

Debit		Credit	
		23/6	500

Marketing Services Revenue — 402

Debit		Credit	
		30/6 (h)	800

Salaries Expense — 500

Debit		Credit	
22/6	7 600		
30/6 (e)	3 980		

Telephone Expense — 510

Debit		Credit	
30/6	160		

Advertising Expense — 520

Debit		Credit	
6/6	240		

Insurance Expense — 521

Debit		Credit	
30/6 (a)	80		

Office Supplies Expense — 530

Debit		Credit	
30/6 (b)	160		

Depr. Exp. – Off. Equip. — 540

Debit		Credit	
30/6 (c)	200		

Depr. Exp. – Building — 541

Debit		Credit	
30/6 (d)	500		

Interest Expense — 560

Debit		Credit	
30/6 (f)	1 600		

Electricity Expense — 570

Debit		Credit	
30/6 (g)	420		

Figure 4.14 Adjusted trial balance

INTELLECT MANAGEMENT SERVICES
Adjusted Trial Balance
as at 30 June 2013

Account	Account no.	Account balance Debit	Account balance Credit
Cash at bank	100	$135 770	
Accounts receivable	104	12 680	
Prepaid insurance	110	1 840	
Office supplies	111	1 080	
GST outlays	120	32 276	
Land	150	120 000	
Building	160	180 000	
Accumulated depreciation – building	161		$ 500
Office equipment	170	19 200	
Accumulated depreciation – office equipment	171		200
Accounts payable	200		9 200
Salaries payable	210		3 980
Interest payable	215		1 600
Electricity account payable	216		420
Unearned appraisal fees	220		580
GST collections	250		2 026
Mortgage payable	260		240 000
M. Mooney, Capital	300		240 000
M. Mooney, Drawings	310	1 200	
Management services revenue	400		19 200
Appraisal fees revenue	401		500
Marketing services revenue	402		800
Salaries expense	500	11 580	
Telephone expense	510	160	
Advertising expense	520	240	
Insurance expense	521	80	
Office supplies expense	530	100	
Depreciation expense – office equipment	540	200	
Depreciation expense – building	541	500	
Interest expense	560	1 600	
Electricity expense	570	420	
		$518 986	$518 986

4.7 Preparation of financial statements

After the adjusting process is completed, the adjusted trial balance may be used to prepare financial statements. However, if the entity's accounting year finishes on 30 June, closing entries are made before preparing the statements. Discussion of closing entries is deferred until chapter 5.

Income statement

The income statement shown in figure 4.15 for Intellect Management Services was prepared from the adjusted trial balance in figure 4.14. Note that the heading shows the name of the entity, the type of financial statement, and the length of time it took to generate the reported profit or loss.

The income statement normally is prepared before the statement of changes in equity and the balance sheet because the profit or loss is needed to complete the equity section. For example, in this illustration a profit of $5560 is derived. This means the sum of the

Figure 4.15 Preparation of the income statement from adjusted trial balance

INTELLECT MANAGEMENT SERVICES Adjusted Trial Balance as at 30 June 2013			INTELLECT MANAGEMENT SERVICES Income Statement for the month ended 30 June 2013	

Account	Debit	Credit		
Cash at bank	$135 770			
Accounts receivable	12 680			
Prepaid insurance	1 840			
Office supplies	1 080			
GST outlays	32 276			
Land	120 000			
Building	180 000			
Accumulated depreciation – building		$ 500		
Office equipment	19 200			
Accumulated depreciation – office equipment		200		
Accounts payable		9 200		
Salaries payable		3 980		
Interest payable		1 600		
Electricity account payable		420		
Unearned appraisal fees		560		
GST collections		2 026		
Mortgage payable		240 000	INCOME	
M. Mooney, Capital		240 000	Revenues:	
M. Mooney, Drawings	1 200		Management services fees	$19 200
Management services revenue		19 200	Appraisal fees	500
Appraisal fees revenue		500	Marketing services fees	800
Marketing services revenue		800		20 500
Salaries expense	11 580		EXPENSES	
Telephone expense	160		Salaries expense	$11 580
Advertising expense	240		Telephone expense	160
Insurance expense	80		Advertising expense	240
Office supplies expense	160		Insurance expense	80
Depreciation expense – office equipment	200		Office supplies expense	160
Depreciation expense – building	500		Depreciation expense – office equipment	200
Interest expense	1 600		Depreciation expense – building	500
Electricity expense	420		Interest expense	1 600
	$518 986	$518 986	Electricity expense	420
				14 940
To fig. 4.16 ← PROFIT				$ 5 560

credit balances in the income accounts ($20 500) exceeds the sum of the debit balances in the expense accounts ($14 940) by $5560. The profit of $5560 must be added to equity to equalise the total liabilities and equity with the total assets. In other words, during the period there was an increase in net assets from earning a profit. This increase in net assets (assets minus liabilities) belongs to the owner and should be added to the capital account in the balance sheet. Details of movements in equity are shown in the statement of changes in equity.

Statement of changes in equity

Figure 4.15 presents the income statement of Intellect Management Services, showing a profit of $5560. The statement of changes in equity in figure 4.16 shows this profit added to the equity of the owner and any withdrawals of profits made by the owner to show the balance of the equity at the end of the period. This equity balance of $244 360 must then equal the net assets (assets minus liabilities) as reported in the balance sheet.

Figure 4.16 Preparation of the statement of changes in equity from equity accounts in the adjusted trial balance and the income statement

INTELLECT MANAGEMENT SERVICES Statement of Changes in Equity for the month ended 30 June 2013	
M. Mooney, Beginning capital	$240 000
Add: Profit for the month of June	5 560
Less: Drawings for the month of June	(1 200)
M. Mooney, Ending capital	$244 360

Balance sheet

In figure 4.17 (p. 145), the balance sheet for Intellect Management Services is prepared from the adjusted trial balance. The heading indicates the name of the entity, the title of the statement and the statement date. Recall that the statement reports the financial position on a specified date, 30 June in this illustration, whereas the income statement reports the flow of revenues and expenses during the month of June, and the statement of changes in equity shows the movement in the entity's capital account for the period.

There are three major categories of accounts reported in the balance sheet: assets, liabilities and equity. When a number of accounts are reported, statement users have found the information more useful if the assets and liabilities are further classified into several important subcategories:

Assets	Liabilities
Current assets	Current liabilities
Non-current assets:	Non-current liabilities
Investments	
Property, plant and equipment	
Intangible assets	
Other assets	

These categories facilitate the evaluation of financial data and are arranged in the statement so that important relationships between two subcategories are shown. For example, the **liquidity** of a business entity — its ability to satisfy short-term obligations as they fall due — is of primary concern to most statement readers. To help readers evaluate an entity's liquidity, assets and liabilities are classified as current (short-term) and non-current (long-term). The excess of current assets over current liabilities is called **working capital**. The use of these categories to analyse an entity's liquidity and to make relevant economic decisions is discussed in more detail in a later chapter.

In figure 4.17 two asset and liability categories are shown — current and non-current. These are discussed in the next section.

Figure 4.17 Preparation of the balance sheet from adjusted trial balance and statement of changes in equity in figure 4.16

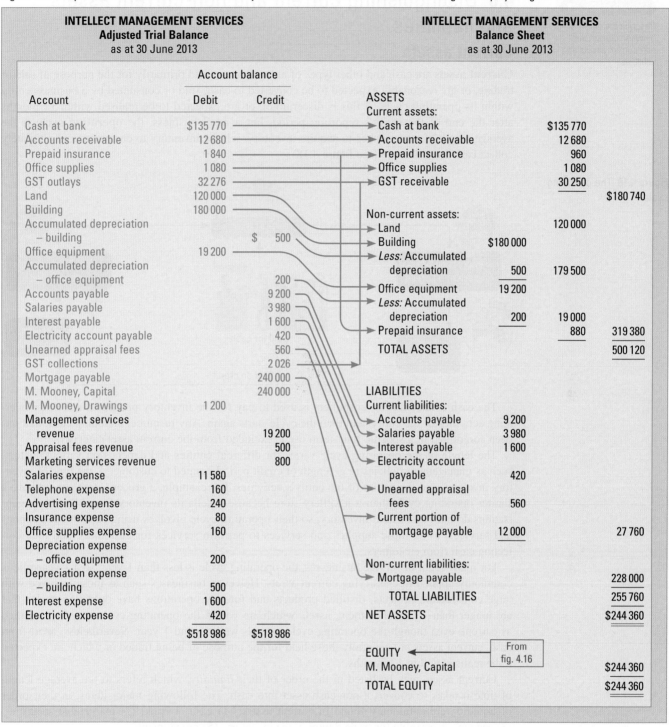

4.8 Distinguishing current and non-current assets and liabilities

Current assets

Current assets are cash and other types of assets that are held primarily for the purpose of sale or trading, or are reasonably expected to be converted to cash, sold or consumed by a business entity within its operating cycle (if this is discernible), or are expected to be realised within 12 months after the end of the entity's reporting period. For a retail business, the **operating cycle** is the average length of time it takes to acquire inventory, sell the inventory to customers and ultimately collect cash from the sale (see figure 4.18).

Figure 4.18 The operating cycle

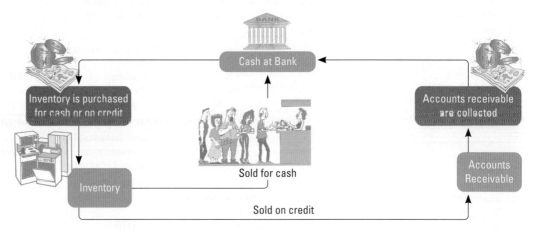

The cash collected from customers is used to pay for the inventory purchased and other operating activities of the entity, and then the cycle starts again. Any resource, including cash, that has been committed to a specific long-term use is excluded from the current asset category.

The length of the operating cycle varies for different entities and depends on various factors, such as management policies (e.g. length of credit period granted to customers), the type of inventory involved, and the nature of the entity's activities. For example, a grocery store should have a shorter operating cycle than a jewellery store because it sells its inventory faster. Service organisations do not buy or hold inventory, so their operating cycle involves using cash to buy supplies and services, using those supplies and services to perform services for customers, and then collecting cash from customers.

For many retail or service businesses, the operating cycle is less than 1 year, so a 1-year rule is commonly applied in classifying current assets. However, businesses such as those involved with large construction projects, distilled products and forestry operations have operating cycles that are longer than 1 year. For them, assets which are within the operating cycle may be classified as current, even though the operating cycle extends well beyond 1 year. Nevertheless, apart from cash, current assets are generally those held for the purpose of being traded or which are expected to be realised within 12 months.

Current assets may be listed in the order of their *liquidity*, which refers to the average length of time it takes to convert a non-cash asset into cash. The following major items, in their order of liquidity, are commonly found in current assets: (1) cash at bank, (2) marketable securities, (3) accounts receivable (or trade debtors), (4) inventory, (5) prepayments.

Marketable securities are investments that can be converted back into cash for use in conducting the short-term activities of the entity. Some prepaid assets may expire or be consumed over a number of years. Inclusion of these as current assets is supported to the extent that such prepayments will be consumed (expensed) within the next 12 months. Any prepayment to be consumed beyond the next 12 months generally should be classified as a non-current asset. Note that in figure 4.17 prepaid insurance has been split into its current ($960) element and non-current ($880) element, and GST collections have been offset against GST outlays to provide the GST receivable from the Australian Taxation Office (ATO).

Non-current assets

Investments. Assets classified as **investments** normally consist of shares and debentures and other long-term financial assets, land held for speculation, and cash or other assets set aside for specific long-term purposes such as a retirement fund for the entity's employees.

Property, plant and equipment. This category consists of assets of a physical nature (tangible) that are used in the normal activities of the entity to produce goods, sell goods or provide services to customers. Other terms are used occasionally for this classification, such as tangible assets and fixed assets. **Property, plant and equipment** are expected to be used by the business entity for a number of years and are not held for resale. Examples include land, buildings, machinery, motor vehicles, furniture, fixtures and computer equipment used in running the business.

Except for land, such assets have limited useful lives, and their costs are depreciated over their estimated useful lives. The depreciation recorded to date on an asset is shown in the *Accumulated Depreciation* account, which is deducted from the cost of the asset to reflect the asset's carrying amount. Because land has an unlimited life, it is not depreciated.

Intangible assets. An **intangible asset** is one that usually does not have a physical substance but is expected to provide future benefits to the entity. Intangibles derive their value from the rights that possession and use confer on their holder. Like property, plant and equipment, intangibles are recorded initially at cost or other faithfully representative measure, which is allocated to future periods over the asset's useful life. Examples are patents, copyrights, franchises, brand names and secret processes.

Other assets. The other assets category is used to report those assets that do not readily fit into one of the categories described previously. Some examples are plant and equipment no longer being used in the business but held for future disposal, and development expenditure in a mining operation.

Current liabilities

Current liabilities are obligations of the entity that are reasonably expected to be settled in the entity's normal operating cycle or held for the purpose of being traded, or are due to be settled within 12 months after the end of the reporting period. Most current liabilities will require payment in the short term, such as accounts payable (trade creditors), interest payable and other accrued liabilities. However, some current liabilities, such as cash advances received from customers, do not require the payment of cash but are settled by the delivery of goods or the performance of a service. Also included as a current liability is the portion of long-term debt that is due within 1 year.

To illustrate, recall that Intellect Management Services undertook a $240 000 mortgage payable to partly finance the purchase of certain assets. The contract required Intellect to make a $12 000 payment plus accrued interest on 2 June for the next 20 years. In figure 4.17, the $12 000 due within the next year is reported with the current liabilities of the business. The remaining $228 000 due beyond 12 months after the end of the reporting period is reported as a non-current liability.

Within the current liability section, in practice there is no agreed uniform order of presentation. One approach is to list the accounts from the largest amount due to the smallest. Another approach commonly used is to list the accounts payable first, followed by taxes payable, accrued liabilities and the current portion of long-term debt.

Non-current or long-term liabilities

Non-current liabilities are those obligations of the entity that do not require payment within the entity's operating cycle or within 12 months after the end of the reporting period. In other words, liabilities not classified as current are reported in this section.

In the case of Intellect Management Services, the only long-term debt is that portion of the mortgage due after 1 year. Note in figure 4.17 that only the interest that has accrued up to 30 June on the $240 000 outstanding debt is reported as interest payable. In other words, the total interest that will be paid over the life of the mortgage is not recognised as a liability at this time. Interest accrues with the passage of time and is not reported as a liability until it is accrued. The interest accrued on both the long-term and short-term portion of the debt is reported as a current liability because the interest payment is due on 2 June, which is 11 months after the end of the reporting period.

4.9 Preparing financial statements from a worksheet

To this point, adjusting entries have been made directly in the journal and then posted to the ledger, after which an adjusted trial balance and financial statements are prepared from the adjusted accounts. In practice, formal recording of adjusting entries does not occur except on the last day of the accounting period, i.e. end of financial year. Whenever financial statements are required for internal management purposes during the period, it is usual to prepare a worksheet, either manually or electronically, from which such statements can be prepared. The worksheet may still be used even at the end of the period.

The **worksheet** has a number of important functions.

* it assembles in one place all the information needed to adjust the accounts and prepare the financial statements
* it aids in the preparation of interim financial statements for internal use when adjusting and closing entries are not required in the formal accounting records
* it contains the information needed to close off the income and expense accounts (temporary accounts) at the end of the period. Closing entries are covered in chapter 5.

The worksheet does not replace the financial statements; it is simply a tool used to gather and organise the information needed to complete these steps of the accounting cycle. It is a convenient way of preparing interim financial statements for management and owners when adjusting and closing entries are not made.

Computerised accounting systems today can make the use of a worksheet unnecessary since all accounting reports can be kept up to date after processing transactions. Nevertheless, if worksheets are to be prepared, electronic spreadsheets can greatly speed up the process and increase reliability. Once all adjusting data have been entered, the adjusted trial balance, income statement and balance sheet columns are calculated automatically, and the financial statements are prepared automatically. Any errors made in entering adjustment data can be amended quickly.

Preparation of the worksheet

The basic format of a worksheet is shown in figure 4.19. The heading contains the name of the entity, the title of the document, i.e. 'worksheet', and the period it covers. The first column is used for the account titles. This column is followed by five sets of money columns for (1) the unadjusted trial balance, (2) adjusting entries, (3) the adjusted trial balance, (4) the income statement and (5) the balance sheet. Each set consists of a debit column and a credit column, making a total of ten columns for entering dollar amounts. The steps followed in preparing a worksheet are illustrated and described by using the information for Intellect Management Services.

Step 1. Enter the ledger account titles and balances in the account title and unadjusted trial balance columns. After all the transactions that occurred during the period are posted, a trial balance is prepared from the general ledger to verify the equality of debit and credit account balances, as shown in figure 4.19. This is an unadjusted trial balance because it is taken before any adjusting entries have been posted to the ledger.

Step 2. Enter the necessary adjusting entries in the adjustments columns. The adjusting entries are entered in the worksheet in the adjustments columns. After the worksheet is completed, the adjusting entries are recorded in the journal if financial statements are to be prepared at the end of the period. (If preparing interim financial statements, there is no need to record adjusting entries in the general journal.) To aid in journalising the entries and locating errors, each adjusting entry is identified by a separate letter so that the debit part of the entry can be cross-referenced to the credit part of the entry. The adjustments made in figure 4.20 (p. 150) are the same as those illustrated in figure 4.12 (p. 140) for Intellect Management Services. Adjustments were required for the following items:

Entry (a) Prepaid insurance expired, $80.
Entry (b) Office supplies used, $160.
Entry (c) Depreciation on office equipment, $200.
Entry (d) Depreciation on the building, $500.
Entry (e) Salaries earned but not paid, $3980.
Entry (f) Accrued interest on mortgage payable, $1600.

Figure 4.19 Worksheet format with unadjusted trial balance entered (step 1 in the preparation of a worksheet)

INTELLECT MANAGEMENT SERVICES
Worksheet
for the month ended 30 June 2013

Account	Unadjusted trial balance Debit	Credit	Adjustments Debit	Credit	Adjusted trial balance Debit	Credit	Income statement Debit	Credit	Balance sheet Debit	Credit
Cash at Bank	135 770									
Accounts Receivable	11 880									
Prepaid Insurance	1 920									
Office Supplies	1 240									
GST Outlays	32 276									
Land	120 000									
Building	180 000									
Accumulated Depreciation – Building										
Office Equipment	19 200									
Accumulated Depreciation – Office Equipment										
Accounts Payable		9 200								
Unearned Appraisal Fees		560								
GST Collections		2 026								
Mortgage Payable		240 000								
M. Mooney, Capital		240 000								
M. Mooney, Drawings	1 200									
Management Services Revenue		19 200								
Appraisal Fees Revenue		500								
Salaries Expense	7 600									
Telephone Expense	160									
Advertising Expense	240									
	511 486	511 486								

Entry (g) Electricity used but not paid for, $420.

Entry (h) Revenue not received from marketing services, $800.

When entering the adjustments, if an account already has a balance in the unadjusted trial balance columns, the adjusting amount is entered on the same line. The account titles required by adjusting entries that were not listed in the unadjusted trial balance columns are added on lines immediately below the trial balance account titles.

For example, in adjusting entry (a) the Insurance Expense account is debited and the Prepaid Insurance account is credited for $80. To enter the debit amount of this entry, it is necessary to add an Insurance Expense account on the line below the trial balance because the account had a zero balance before the adjusting entry and consequently was not included in the unadjusted trial balance. The $80 credit is entered in the adjustments credit column on the same line as the Prepaid Insurance account balance of $1920. Thus, in this entry it is necessary to add only one new account. However, in adjusting entry (f) (interest on mortgage), observe that both accounts affected by the entry must be entered below the unadjusted trial balance. The appropriate account titles were selected from the chart of accounts presented in chapter 3 on pages 75–6.

After all the adjustments are entered, the two adjustments columns are totalled to prove that the total debit adjustments equal the total credit adjustments.

Step 3. Prepare an adjusted trial balance. In this step, each account balance in the unadjusted trial balance columns is combined with the corresponding adjustments, if any, in the adjustments columns, and the resulting balance is extended on the same line to the appropriate adjusted trial balance column, as shown in figure 4.20. The combined amounts entered in these two columns will be the same as the ledger account balances after the adjusting entries are recorded in the journal and posted to the ledger. Combining the amounts entered on each line — that is, adding or subtracting across the worksheet horizontally — is called **crossadding**. The crossadding must be done very carefully because it is easy to make an error.

For those accounts unaffected by the adjustments, such as Cash at Bank, Accounts Payable and Management Services Revenue, the balance is simply extended directly to the appropriate debit or credit column in the adjusted trial balance columns. If an account has a debit balance in the unadjusted trial balance column, a debit adjustment will increase the balance (see the Salaries Expense account), whereas a credit adjustment will decrease the balance (see the Prepaid Insurance account). An account with a credit balance is increased by a credit adjustment and decreased

Figure 4.20 Adjusting entries entered in adjustments columns and account balances extended to the adjusted trial balance columns (steps 2 and 3 in the preparation of a worksheet)

	Unadjusted trial balance		Adjustments		Adjusted trial balance		Income statement		Balance sheet	
INTELLECT MANAGEMENT SERVICES **Worksheet** for the month ended 30 June 2013										
Account	Debit	Credit	Debit	Credit	Debit	Credit	Debit	Credit	Debit	Credit
Cash at Bank	135 770				135 770					
Accounts Receivable	11 880		(h) 800		12 680					
Prepaid Insurance	1 920			(a) 80	1 840					
Office Supplies	1 240			(b) 160	1 080					
GST Outlays	32 276				32 276					
Land	120 000				120 000					
Building	180 000				180 000					
Accumulated Depreciation – Building				(d) 500		500				
Office Equipment	19 200				19 200					
Accumulated Depreciation – Office Equipment				(c) 200		200				
Accounts Payable		9 200				9 200				
Unearned Appraisal Fees		500				500				
GST Collections		2 026				2 026				
Mortgage Payable		240 000				240 000				
M. Mooney, Capital		240 000				240 000				
M. Mooney, Drawings	1 200				1 200					
Management Services Revenue		19 200				19 200				
Appraisal Fees Revenue		500				500				
Salaries Expense	7 600		(e) 3 980		11 580					
Telephone Expense	160				160					
Advertising Expense	240				240					
	511 486	511 486								
Insurance Expense			(a) 80		80					
Office Supplies Expense			(b) 160		160					
Depreciation Expense – Office Equipment			(c) 200		200					
Depreciation Expense – Building			(d) 500		500					
Electricity Expense			(g) 420		420					
Salaries Payable				(e) 3 980		3 980				
Interest Expense			(f) 1 600		1 600					
Interest Payable				(f) 1 600		1 600				
Electricity Account Payable				(g) 420		420				
Marketing Services Revenue				(h) 800		800				
			7 740	7 740	518 986	518 986				

by a debit adjustment. In some cases, an account may not have a balance in the unadjusted trial balance columns, but an adjustment is made to the account. In such cases, the amount of the adjustment is extended directly to the adjusted trial balance column. Examples are those accounts added below the unadjusted trial balance. After all adjusted account balances have been determined, the equality of debits and credits is verified by totalling the two columns.

Step 4. Extend every account balance listed in the adjusted trial balance columns to its proper financial statement column. Every account balance listed in the adjusted trial balance columns is extended to either the income statement columns or the balance sheet columns, as shown in figure 4.21.

Figure 4.21 Account balances extended to financial statement columns and totals calculated (steps 4 and 5 in the preparation of a worksheet)

INTELLECT MANAGEMENT SERVICES
Worksheet
for the month ended 30 June 2013

Account	Unadjusted trial balance Debit	Unadjusted trial balance Credit	Adjustments Debit	Adjustments Credit	Adjusted trial balance Debit	Adjusted trial balance Credit	Income statement Debit	Income statement Credit	Balance sheet Debit	Balance sheet Credit
Cash at Bank	135 770				135 770				135 770	
Accounts Receivable	11 880		(h) 800		12 680				12 680	
Prepaid Insurance	1 920			(a) 80	1 840				1 840	
Office Supplies	1 240			(b) 160	1 080				1 080	
GST Outlays	32 276				32 276				32 276	
Land	120 000				120 000				120 000	
Building	180 000				180 000				180 000	
Accumulated Depreciation – Building				(d) 500		500				500
Office Equipment	19 200				19 200				19 200	
Accumulated Depreciation – Office Equipment				(c) 200		200				200
Accounts Payable		9 200				9 200				9 200
Unearned Appraisal Fees		560				560				560
GST Collections		2 026				2 026				2 026
Mortgage Payable		240 000				240 000				240 000
M. Mooney, Capital		240 000				240 000				240 000
M. Mooney, Drawings	1 200				1 200				1 200	
Management Services Revenue		19 200				19 200		19 200		
Appraisal Fees Revenue		500				500		500		
Salaries Expense	7 600		(e) 3 980		11 580		11 580			
Telephone Expense	160				160		160			
Advertising Expense	240				240		240			
	511 486	511 486								
Insurance Expense			(a) 80		80		80			
Office Supplies Expense			(b) 160		160		160			
Depreciation Expense – Office Equipment			(c) 200		200		200			
Depreciation Expense – Building			(d) 500		500		500			
Electricity Expense			(g) 420		420		420			
Salaries Payable				(e) 3 980		3 980				3 980
Interest Expense			(f) 1 600		1 600		1 600			
Interest Payable				(f) 1 600		1 600				1 600
Electricity Account Payable				(g) 420		420				420
Marketing Services Revenue				(h) 800		800		800		
			7 740	7 740	518 986	518 986	14 940	20 500	504 046	498 486
Profit for the period							5 560			5 560
							20 500	20 500	504 046	504 046

Income (revenue) accounts are extended to the income statement credit column, and expense accounts are extended to the income statement debit column. Asset, liability and equity accounts are extended to the proper balance sheet debit or credit column. In other words, accounts are sorted on the basis of their financial statement classification in this part of the process. The GST Collections account is shown in the credit column of the balance sheet, and the GST Outlays is shown in the debit column.

To avoid leaving out an account, the process should start by extending the first account listed, which is usually Cash at Bank, and then working vertically down the worksheet line by line. As a word of caution, the accounts listed in the unadjusted trial balance are in the order shown in the balance sheet and the income statement. However, the accounts added below the unadjusted trial balance must be analysed to determine whether the balance is to be extended to the balance sheet or income statement columns. Note that the balance of the Drawings account is extended to the balance sheet debit column rather than to the income statement debit column.

Step 5. Total the two income statement columns and the two balance sheet columns. Calculate the difference between the totals of the two income statement columns and enter this as a balancing amount in both the income statement and balance sheet columns. Calculate the four column totals again with the balancing amount included. After all the amounts have been extended to either the income statement or the balance sheet columns, the four columns are totalled and their amounts entered at the bottom of each column. The profit or loss for the period is determined by taking the difference between the totals of the two income statement columns as shown in figure 4.21. The calculation in our illustration is:

Total of the credit column	$20 500
Total of the debit column	14 940
Difference (= profit)	$ 5 560

In this illustration, the income (revenues) ($20 500) exceeded the expenses ($14 940), resulting in a profit of $5560. This difference is entered in the income statement debit column to balance the two columns and is also entered on the same line in the balance sheet credit column because profit for the period is an increase in equity. Extending the profit of $5560 in the balance sheet credit column updates the equity in the business to the end of the period. On the same line in the account title column, a caption 'Profit for the period' is entered to identify the nature of the item being entered in the two sets of columns.

The four columns are totalled again with the profit of $5560 included. If the debit and credit columns under the balance sheet heading are not equal, there is an error in extending the amounts from the adjusted trial balance columns.

If the income statement debit column had exceeded the credit column, a loss for the period would be indicated. In this case, the difference between the two columns would be captioned 'Loss for the period', and that difference entered in the income statement credit column and the balance sheet debit column.

Totalling the debit and credit columns as work proceeds across the worksheet does not ensure that an error has not been made. For example (as discussed in chapter 3), not all errors in the accounts are uncovered by the trial balance. Needed adjustments may have been omitted entirely or the wrong adjusting amounts may have been entered in the worksheet. In step 4, an amount may be extended to the wrong column — e.g. extending the credit balance in the Unearned Appraisal Fees account (a liability) to the income statement credit column. This will not destroy the equality of debits and credits, but it will result in an overstatement in revenues, an understatement in liabilities, and an overstatement in equity.

Preparation of financial statements

The completed worksheet is used at the end of the financial period to prepare the financial statements and can be used as a basis for journalising adjusting and closing entries.

Because account balances are already sorted between the income statement and the balance sheet in the worksheet, preparation of the financial statements is a relatively easy step. The income statement (figure 4.22) is prepared from account balances listed in the two income statement columns in figure 4.21. The statement of changes in equity (figure 4.23) and the balance sheet (figure 4.24, p. 154) are prepared from items contained in the balance sheet columns of figure 4.21.

Figure 4.22 Income statement

INTELLECT MANAGEMENT SERVICES
Income Statement
for the month ended 30 June 2013

INCOME		
Revenues:		
Management services revenue		$19 200
Appraisal fees revenue		500
Marketing services revenue		800
		20 500
EXPENSES		
Salaries expense	$11 580	
Interest expense	1 600	
Depreciation expense – office equipment	200	
Depreciation expense – building	500	
Telephone expense	160	
Advertising expense	240	
Office supplies expense	160	
Insurance expense	80	
Electricity expense	420	
		14 940
PROFIT		$ 5 560

Figure 4.23 Statement of changes in equity

INTELLECT MANAGEMENT SERVICES
Statement of Changes in Equity
for the month ended 30 June 2013

M. Mooney, Beginning capital	$240 000
Add: Profit for the month of June	5 560
	245 560
Less: Drawings for the month of June	1 200
M. Mooney, Ending capital	$244 360

Figure 4.24 Balance sheet

INTELLECT MANAGEMENT SERVICES
Balance Sheet
as at 30 June 2013

CURRENT ASSETS			
Cash at bank		$135 770	
Accounts receivable		12 680	
Prepaid insurance (current portion)		960	
Office supplies		1 080	
GST receivable*		30 250	$180 740
NON-CURRENT ASSETS			
Land		120 000	
Building	$180 000		
Less: Accumulated depreciation	500	179 500	
Office equipment	19 200		
Less: Accumulated depreciation	200	19 000	
Prepaid insurance (non-current portion)		880	319 380
TOTAL ASSETS			500 120
CURRENT LIABILITIES			
Accounts payable		9 200	
Salaries payable		3 980	
Interest payable		1 600	
Unearned appraisal fees		560	
Electricity account payable		420	
Current portion of mortgage payable		12 000	27 760
NON-CURRENT LIABILITIES			
Mortgage payable			228 000
TOTAL LIABILITIES			255 760
NET ASSETS			$244 360
EQUITY			
M. Mooney, Capital			$244 360
TOTAL EQUITY			$244 360

* GST outlays of $32 276 less GST collections of $2026.

4.10 Financial statements and decision making

This chapter introduced an expanded accounting cycle which includes adjustments to be made to the general ledger accounts at the end of the accounting period before financial statements are prepared. As always, the final output from the accounting cycle is the financial statements. Other reports derived from the accounting records for use by owners, internal management and external users are discussed in later chapters. At this point, the emphasis is on the income statement, balance sheet and statement of changes in equity.

Note that the financial statements are not ends in themselves. They are produced so that interested parties can evaluate the financial performance of the business over a period of time, and gauge its financial position at the end of the period. From the evaluation of these financial statements in association with other data, decisions can be made by owners and management about the future activities of the business and the interests that various other parties have in its future activities.

To gain some appreciation of the use that can be made of the financial statements by an owner, refer to Intellect Management Services' financial statements in figures 4.22 to 4.24 and to the case of Darren Jones in chapters 1 and 2 who set up a lawnmowing business. On examining the income statement for the period, Megan Mooney and Darren Jones could ask a number of questions and, based on the answers, make decisions about the future of their businesses. Some questions they might ask include:

- Has my business been profitable?
- Is the profit I have made satisfactory?
- How does the profit made compare with what I expected?
- How does my profit compare with similar businesses?
- How can I improve the profitability of my business, i.e. how can I increase revenues and decrease expenses?
- Should I expand my business?
- Am I getting sufficient financial return for the investment I have made?
- Do I continue with my current business or sell the business and use the proceeds in some alternative business venture or investment?

There are also a number of questions that could arise when Megan Mooney and Darren Jones look at the balance sheet and statement of changes in equity of their businesses. Some questions they could ask include:

- Is my business solvent, i.e. are my current assets sufficient to pay my current liabilities?
- Do I have enough cash to handle the day-to-day running of the business?
- Should I arrange with my bank to be able to overdraw my bank account if necessary?
- Should I contribute more capital to the business in order to expand?
- Have I financed my business by using too much long-term borrowing which incurs high interest charges and large cash repayments in the future?

Again, the answers to these and other questions will allow them to make decisions about their businesses and their continuing interests in their businesses.

It is important to appreciate that accounting exists to provide information for decision making, and the basic financial statements covered to this point are a source of information on which economic decisions can be made by those who have an interest in the operations of a business entity.

BUSINESS KNOWLEDGE

Murray James-Wallace
Managing Associate
Geraldton Medical Group
Health Services
Revenue 2008-09: $3.3 million (up 27 per cent)

The telephone call from the office of federal Minister for Health Nicola Roxon came as a big surprise to Murray James-Wallace, a managing associate of a fast-growing medical group in Geraldton, 400 kilometres north of Perth.

The minister toured the centre and chatted with doctors and staff on October 2. 'Our centre is really the model of the federal government's super clinics, but we were planning our expansion three years ago,' James-Wallace says. 'We're hoping we've shown that locally owned private enterprise can develop better integrated services quite independently of government.'

Notwithstanding the global financial crisis, the Geraldton Medical Group expanded into new premises in the past 12 months, adding ancillary services such as pathology and pharmacy and specialist nursing, and grew by 27 per cent over 2008-09.

Success came with a cost. 'Growth does not equal profit', James-Wallace says. 'We have expanded so rapidly and costs expanded as well. We had to watch where our pennies go. In the past, we always had so much money coming in, it didn't matter.'

Pushed to the limits of their management skills, James-Wallace and the two other doctors and practice owners watched in horror as costs 'skyrocketed'. They were stumped about how to rein them in. Profits have started to improve, and they will shortly appoint a chief executive.

James-Wallace found he had less time to spend with his patients as he managed recruiting (into remote areas), making strategic decisions, arranging finance and negotiating leases. 'We just didn't realise how long things take, and there is no point being impatient or you make mistakes.'

He says he is proud that the expansion has gone to plan. Ahead, the federal government's grand health reform plans are still unknown – a headache for planning.

Source: Excerpts from Kath Walters, 'I did it my way', *BRW*.

Accruals, p. 127	Current liabilities, p. 147	Permanent (real) accounts, p. 126
Accumulated depreciation, p. 132	Deferrals, p. 127	Property, plant and equipment, p. 147
Adjusted trial balance, p. 140	Depreciation, p. 132	
Adjusting entries, p. 127	Expired cost, p. 125	Temporary (nominal) accounts, p. 126
Carrying amount (book value), p. 133	Intangible assets, p. 147	
	Investments, p. 147	Unexpired cost, p. 125
Contra account, p. 132	Liquidity, p. 144	Useful life, p. 132
Crossadding, p. 150	Non-current liabilities, p. 147	Working capital, p. 144
Current assets, p. 146	Operating cycle, p. 146	Worksheet, p. 148

DISCUSSION QUESTIONS

1. How is profit determined under (a) the cash basis of accounting and (b) the accrual basis of accounting?

2. Explain why the purchase of supplies is usually recorded in an asset account rather than in an expense account. If supplies were expensed when purchased, which accounts should be debited and which credited at the end of the period in order to reflect the amount of supplies on hand?

3. During the year, the publishers of *Fishing for the Family*, a monthly magazine, received cash for a 3-year magazine subscription. A credit was made to the Unearned Subscriptions Revenue account.
   (a) Is the required adjusting entry made at the end of the period an example of accrual or a deferral?
   (b) What types of accounts will be affected by the required adjusting entry?
   (c) What effect will omission of the adjusting entry have on profit and on the balance sheet?

4. 'Why are adjusting entries necessary? Surely they cause too much delay in preparing financial statements, and the financial effect of any entries made is immaterial in the long run.' Respond to this criticism.

5. 'If adjusting entries are not recorded in the accounts at the end of each month but are included on a worksheet for interim financial statements, why do we need to record them in the accounts for the financial statements at the end of the financial year?' Discuss.

6. The owner of a business reviews the income statement prepared by you and asks, 'Why do you report a profit of only $30 000 when cash collections of $100 000 were received and cash payments for the period totalled only $50 000 for expenses?' How would you respond to the owner's question?

7. On 31 March, Padbury Publishers received a subscription of $240 for the supply of twelve monthly magazines, beginning in April. At the end of the reporting period, 30 June, the accountant suggested that the owner make an adjusting entry to defer the revenue on nine issues until the new year. The owner of the business was reluctant to do so, claiming that he had already received the subscriptions in cash and could see no reason for the delay in recognising the revenue. Do you agree with the owner or the accountant? Respond to the owner, explaining the accountant's position. Ignore GST.

8. The Claremont Cricket Club collects membership fees of $100 in advance from its members at the beginning of October each year for the summer season, which ends in April. This entitles members to free entry to all games played at the home ground for the season. The club's financial year ends on 31 December. Should the club make any adjusting entry in its accounts at the end of the year in relation to membership fees received? Why or why not? Explain.

9. 'Why would we bother classifying assets in order of their liquidity on a balance sheet? After all, the value placed on assets is not a true reflection of how much we could sell them for.' Discuss.

10. Describe the operating cycle. Is the operating cycle definition related in any way to the definitions of current and non-current assets? Explain.

Exercise 4.1 IDENTIFYING ADJUSTING JOURNAL ENTRIES **LO 3, 4, 5**

Match the end-of-financial-year adjustments (for each independent situation) to the appropriate journal entry.

Adjustments
1. Insurance expense which has not been used up (there is still future cover)
2. Portion of recognised revenue which is considered unearned
3. Revenue received in advance which is now earned
4. Portion of prepaid insurance which has now expired (been used up)
5. Revenue earned but not yet received
6. Expenses incurred but not yet paid

Journal entry
(a) Prepaid Insurance Dr, Insurance Expense Cr
(b) Unearned Revenue Dr, Revenue Cr
(c) Insurance Expense Dr, Prepaid Insurance Cr
(d) Revenue Dr, Unearned Revenue Cr
(e) Expenses Dr, Expenses Payable Cr
(f) Revenue Receivable Dr, Revenue Cr

Exercise 4.2 CASH VERSUS ACCRUAL BASIS OF ACCOUNTING **LO 1**

On 30 June 2013, the end of the first year of operations, Chloe Welsh, owner of Welsh Designers, engaged you to prepare yearly financial statements on that date, on both the cash basis and the accrual basis. The following data are a summary of selected transactions that occurred during the year. Ignore GST.
1. Fees of $82 000 were collected for services rendered during the year.
2. There were $6000 in receivables at 30 June 2013 for services performed on credit.
3. Cash payments of $54 000 were made for salaries, rent, insurance and other expenses *incurred* during the year.
4. Salaries owing but not yet paid amount to $7000.
5. On 15 June 2013, a client paid $3000 in advance for services to be rendered during the next financial year.
6. Expenses of $8000 were prepaid (not included in the $54 000) at 30 June.

Required
A. Calculate profit under both the cash basis and the accrual basis.
B. Explain how the following items would be reported in the business's balance sheet under the accrual basis:
1. the $6000 receivables
2. the unpaid salaries of $7000
3. the $3000 advance received on 15 June
4. the cash payment of $8000 for prepaid expenses.

Exercise 4.3 CASH VERSUS ACCRUAL ACCOUNTING **LO 1**

1. Raj Singh's business performed services in December for a specific customer for which the fee was $5000. Payment was received in the following January.
   (a) Was the revenue earned in December or January?
   (b) What account should be debited in (i) December and (ii) January?
2. During the month a business received $250 000 in cash and paid out $225 000 in cash. Does this indicate that the business earned $25 000 during the month? Explain.
3. Monster Ltd purchased a 3-year advertising contract on 1 August. The company debited the entire cost of $9000 to Advertising Expense. The financial year ends on 31 December. Under

the accrual system, what is the correct expense for the current year, and what entry would be made to correct the accounts? Under the cash basis of accounting, what is the correct expense and the correct adjusting entry (if any)?

LO 1, 2

Exercise 4.4 ACCRUAL BASIS INCOME STATEMENT

Stan Deer registered as a financial adviser several years ago. An income statement for the current period, prepared using cash accounting, is presented below. GST is ignored.

DEER'S FINANCIAL ADVISORY SERVICE
Income Statement
for the year ended 30 June 2014

Income: Fees revenue	$220 000
Less: Expenses	140 000
Profit	$ 80 000

Additional data
(a) Accrued salaries at 30 June 2013 and 2014 are $7000 and $7800, respectively.
(b) Depreciation expense of $20 000 is not included in the expenses.
(c) Fees for advice given for the year ended 30 June 2013 for $9000 were collected in the current year and are included above.
(d) Fees earned in the current year of $12 000 are expected to be collected in the following year. These have not been included above.
(e) Stan Deer withdrew $2200 per month to cover personal living expenses.

Required
A. Using the above information, prepare an income statement on the accrual basis. Show all calculations.
B. Briefly explain why the revised statement could be considered a better measure of performance.
C. Is it a correct accounting procedure to exclude drawings from expenses? Explain why.

LO 3, 4, 5

Exercise 4.5 JOURNALISING ADJUSTING ENTRIES

You are employed to investigate whether any accrual entries are needed in the business of Safe Security Services (SSS). On completion of your investigation on 30 June, you have discovered that the following items need attention:
1. Employee salaries owed but not recorded, $9200.
2. Prepaid insurance expired, $900.
3. Interest revenue accrued but not recorded, $10 000.
4. Unearned security services revenue now earned, $4600.
5. Depreciation not recorded, $16 000.

Required
A. Prepare the adjusting entries for items 1 to 5 at 30 June, the end of the accounting period.
B. Suppose the adjusting entries in requirement A were not made. Calculate the total overstatement or understatement of profit as a result of the omission of these adjustments.

LO 4, 5, 7

Exercise 4.6 ADJUSTING ENTRIES AND INCOME STATEMENT

The income statement of Jojo Ltd for the month of May 2013 shows a profit of $3300 based on:

Services revenue	$8 600
Wages expense	3 500
Supplies expense	1 050
Electricity expense	750

In reviewing the statement, you discover the following:
1. Insurance expired during May of $300 was omitted.
2. Supplies expense includes $540 of supplies that are still on hand at 31 May.
3. Depreciation on equipment of $250 was omitted.
4. Accrued wages at 31 May amounting to $400 were not included.
5. Services provided but unrecorded totalled $1250.

Required
Prepare a corrected income statement for the month of May 2013.

Exercise 4.7   ADJUSTING ENTRIES AND LEDGER ACCOUNTS   LO 3, 4, 5

The following information was extracted from the accounting records of the business of Cable's Suntanning Services:

Account balances at 1 July 2012:	
Rent accrued	$2000
Rates prepaid	1500
Insurance prepaid	1800

Payments made during the year ended 30 June 2013 were as follows:

2012			
Aug.	10	Rent, 3 months to 31 July 2012	$3000
Oct.	26	Insurance, 1 year to 31 October 2013	6000
Nov.	2	Rates, 6 months to 31 March 2013	3500
Dec.	12	Rent, 4 months to 30 November 2012	4000
2013			
April	17	Rent, 4 months to 31 March 2013	4000
May	9	Rates, 6 months to 30 September 2013	3500

Required
A. Write up and balance the Rent Payable, Prepaid Rates, and Prepaid Insurance accounts in the ledger of Cable's Suntanning Services for the year 1 July 2012 to 30 June 2013.
B. Show clearly any adjusting entries that may be required on 30 June 2013. Explain why these adjusting entries are necessary.

Exercise 4.8   ADJUSTING ENTRY FOR PREPAID INSURANCE   LO 4

Beautiful Bathrooms purchased a 1-year insurance policy on 1 October 2013. The entire premium of $5000 was recorded by debiting Prepaid Insurance. Ignore GST.

Required
A. Give the adjusting entry at 30 June for the year ending 30 June 2014.
B. What amount should be reported in the 30 June 2014 balance sheet for Prepaid Insurance?
C. If no adjusting entry were made on 30 June, by how much would profit be overstated or understated? Would assets be overstated or understated? Explain.
D. What would your adjusting entry in requirement A be if the premium of $5000 was recorded by debiting Insurance Expense?

Exercise 4.9   ADJUSTING ENTRY FOR UNEARNED REVENUE   LO 5

Everyday Rentals Ltd received 6 months rent in advance from tenants on 1 May 2012. The entire amount of $9600 was credited to the Unearned Revenue account at this date. Ignore GST.

Required
A. Give the adjusting entry at 30 June 2012.
B. What amount (if any) should be reported in the balance sheet at 30 June 2012?
C. If no adjusting entry were made on 30 June, by how much would profit be overstated or understated? Would liabilities be overstated or understated? Explain.
D. What would your adjusting entry be in requirement A if the amount of $9600 had been credited to Rental Revenue on 1 May 2012?

Exercise 4.10 EXTENSION OF ACCOUNT BALANCES TO PROPER
WORKSHEET COLUMNS

Listed below are ledger accounts that appear in the adjusted trial balance columns of a worksheet.

1. Cash at Bank
2. Wages Expense
3. Building
4. Sophie Kang, Capital
5. Service Revenue
6. Depreciation Expense
7. Accounts Receivable
8. Accumulated Depreciation
9. Equipment
10. Prepaid Insurance
11. Wages Payable
12. GST Collections
13. Interest Payable
14. Interest Receivable
15. Interest Expense
16. Interest Revenue
17. Office Supplies Expense
18. Office Supplies
19. GST Outlays
20. Sophie Kang, Drawings

Complete the tabulation shown below by entering a tick in the proper worksheet column in which the amount in each account would be extended in completing the worksheet.

Solution format

Account	Income statement		Balance sheet	
	Debit	**Credit**	**Debit**	**Credit**
1. Cash at Bank	_____	_____	✓	_____

Exercise 4.11 ADJUSTING ENTRIES FOR DEPRECIATION

Amy's Funeral Services purchased a new hearse on 1 July 2013 for $50 500. It was estimated to have a useful life of 8 years and a residual value at the end of that time of $2500.

Required

A. What is the depreciation expense for the year ended 30 June 2014?
B. What is the balance of the Accumulated Depreciation account at the end of June 2015?
C. What is the carrying amount of the hearse in the balance sheet at 30 June 2014 and at 30 June 2015?
D. Explain why an entry is made to the Accumulated Depreciation account rather than to the Hearse account.

Exercise 4.12 ADJUSTING ENTRIES

Selected accounts of Rikki's Real Estate are shown below at 30 June of the current year before any adjusting entries have been made.

	Debit	Credit
Prepaid Insurance	$ 1 200	
Supplies	550	
Office Equipment	6 000	
Unearned Rental Fees		$ 4 200
Salaries Expense	29 800	
Rental Fees Revenue		13 200

Additional information

(a) Prepaid insurance represents premiums for 1 year paid on 1 June.
(b) Supplies of $200 were on hand at 30 June.
(c) Office equipment, which had been purchased on 1 April, is expected to last 5 years.
(d) Rikki collected 4 months' rent in advance on 1 June from a number of tenants.
(e) Accrued salaries not recorded as at 30 June are $3500.

Required

Record in the general journal the necessary adjusting entries on 30 June.

Exercise 4.13 ADJUSTING ENTRIES — MISSING DATA

Selected T accounts for Jaques and Co. are shown below. Adjusting entries for the period have been posted.

Prepaid Insurance		
31/12 Bal.	725	

Insurance Expense		
31/12 Adj. ent.	495	

Supplies		
31/12 Bal.	290	

Supplies Expense		
31/12 Adj. ent.	260	

Rental Revenue Receivable		
1/1 Bal.	0	
31/12 Bal.	0	

Unearned Rental Revenue		
	31/12 Bal.	700

Rental Revenue		
	31/12 Bal.	9000

Required

A. The balance in the Prepaid Insurance account on 1 January was $650. Calculate the total cash payment made during the year for insurance premiums.
B. Supplies of $280 were purchased during the year. Calculate the 1 January balance in the Supplies account.
C. No balance existed in the Unearned Rental Revenue account on 1 January. Calculate the total amount of rental fees that were received in cash during the period.

Exercise 4.14 ADJUSTING ENTRIES

Design Graphics is a business providing art services for the advertising profession. On 30 April 2013, it completed its first year of operations. Some of the ledger account balances of the business, before any year-end adjustments, are given below:

Advertising Prepaid	$ 900
Fees Revenue	147 000
Rent Expense	7 200
Supplies Expense	5 100
Wages Expense	47 400
Electricity Expense	2 850

No adjusting entries have been made to these accounts at any time during the year. An analysis of the business records reveals:

1. The balance in Advertising Prepaid represents the amount paid for an advertisement in a professional journal for 1 year. The agreement with the publisher stipulates the same amount of space each month and covers the period 1 September 2012 to 31 August 2013.
2. The Electricity Expense ledger balance does not include the amount for April 2013. The account was received during May and amounted to $520.
3. All art supplies purchased during the year were charged to the Supplies Expense account. At 30 April 2013, unused supplies on hand amounted to $1200.
4. The wages are paid every Friday for a 5-day working week ending on the preceding Wednesday. In 2013, 30 April falls on a Thursday and the wages for the week ended 6 May 2013 amount to $3750. No overtime was worked and all employees worked the normal office hours during the 5-day week.
5. The firm's lease in respect of the premises stipulates a rent of $600 per month payable on the first day of each month, plus an annual amount equal to 0.5% of the annual fees earned. The extra rental is payable within 15 days of the financial year-end.

Required

Journalise the necessary adjusting entries.

Exercise 4.15 ADJUSTING ENTRIES AND EFFECT ON FINANCIAL STATEMENTS

Condensed financial statements for Weston Car Rental before adjusting entries were made are shown in the first column of the schedule presented below. The following items were not reflected in the statements:

1. Wages earned by employees but not paid at year-end, $3100.
2. Depreciation on vehicles not recorded, $8000.
3. Rental revenue earned but not collected or recorded, $840.
4. The company requires the first-day rental in advance as a deposit for making a reservation. The deposit is either deducted from the total rental charges or is forfeited. During the last week of December, deposits earned were not recorded as revenue, $550.

WESTON CAR RENTAL
Financial Statements

	Unadjusted balances	Adjustment	Adjusted balances
Income statement			
Rental revenue	$142 000		
Expenses:			
Depreciation expense	—		
Insurance expense	26 000		
Wages expense	78 000		
General expenses	12 000		
Profit	$ 26 000		
Statement of changes in equity			
Beginning capital	$ 50 000		
Add: Profit	26 000		
Less: Drawings	(40 000)		
Ending capital	$ 36 000		
Balance sheet			
Cash at bank	$ 26 000		
Accounts receivable	—		
Other receivables	6 000		
Vehicles	68 000		
Less: Accumulated depreciation	(32 000)		
	$ 68 000		
Wages payable	$ —		
Unearned rental revenue	4 000		
Loan payable	28 000		
Naomi Weston, Capital	36 000		
	$ 68 000		

Required

A. Prepare the necessary adjusting entries in general journal form.
B. Determine the effects of the adjustments on the financial statements by completing the schedule presented above.
C. 1. Did profit increase or decrease? By how much?
   2. What was the effect of the adjusting entries on total assets? total liabilities? total equity?

★ Basic

★★ Moderate

★★★ Challenging

Problem 4.1   ADJUSTING ENTRIES ★

The following transactions, relating to the business of Rhys Palmer, public accountant, occurred during June. Ignore GST.

June	1	Purchased office furniture for $7560. The furniture will be depreciated over a useful life of 9 years at which time it is expected to have a zero residual value.
	1	Purchased a 12-month fire insurance policy for $1800.
	2	Borrowed $10 000 from the State Bank on a short-term loan. The principal, plus 9% annual interest, will be repaid in 3 months. Interest of $75 accrued on the loan during June.
	11	Purchased supplies for $370. On 30 June, supplies worth $150 remained on hand.
	15	Paid $450 for 1 month's rent for the period 15 June to 15 July.
	18	Received a cheque from a client for $1200 as an advance payment for services to be performed. Only 10% of the work was completed by 30 June.
	28	Received an invoice for $350 for telephone and internet charges for the month.

Required

A. Prepare the journal entries to record each transaction and prepare any adjusting entries as at 30 June, the end of the accounting year.

B. Repeat requirement A assuming the addition of 10% GST where necessary. Assume the telephone and internet tax invoice for $385 was issued on 28 June.

Problem 4.2   ADJUSTING ENTRIES AND EFFECT ON FINANCIAL STATEMENTS ★

A. The financial year for Sharp Dry Cleaning Services ends on 30 June. Using the following information, make the necessary adjusting entries at year-end. Ignore GST.

1. On 15 April, Michelle Sharp's business borrowed $12 000 from Northern Bank at 10% interest. The principal and interest are payable on 15 October. Interest of $250 had accrued on the loan by 30 June.
2. Rent of $2400 for the 6-month period ending 31 July is due to be paid in August.
3. The annual depreciation on equipment is estimated to be $6200. The 1 July balance in the Accumulated Depreciation account was $18 600.
4. Sharp Dry Cleaning Services purchased a 1-year insurance policy on 1 April of the previous year for $420. A 3-year policy was purchased on 1 November of the current year for $1215. Both purchases were recorded by debiting Prepaid Insurance.
5. The business has two part-time employees who each earn $150 a day. They both worked the last 4 days in June for which they have not yet been paid.
6. On 1 May, the Heritage Resort paid the business $810 in advance for doing their dry cleaning for the next 3 months. This was recorded by a credit to Unearned Dry Cleaning Revenue.
7. Electricity for June of $2100 is unpaid and unrecorded.
8. The supplies account had a $170 debit balance on 1 July. Supplies of $640 were purchased during the year and $190 of supplies are on hand as at 30 June.

B. As you know, all adjusting entries affect one balance sheet account and one income statement account. Based on your adjusting entries prepared above:
1. Complete the schedule given below.
2. Calculate the increase or decrease in profit.
3. Calculate the increase or decrease in total assets, total liabilities and total equity.

Entry	Account	Balance in the account before adjustment	Dollar effect of adjusting entries	Balance reported in 30/6 balance sheet	Balance sheet classification*
1.	Interest Payable	_____	_____	_____	_____
2.	Rent Payable	_____	_____	_____	_____

(continued)

continued

3.	Accumulated Depreciation	_____	_____	_____	_____
4.	Prepaid Insurance	_____	_____	_____	_____
5.	Wages Payable	_____	_____	_____	_____
6.	Unearned Dry Cleaning Revenue	_____	_____	_____	_____
7.	Electricity Account Payable	_____	_____	_____	_____
8.	Supplies	_____	_____	_____	_____

* For each account, indicate whether it is an asset, liability or equity, and whether it is classified as a current or non-current asset or liability.

Problem 4.3   ADJUSTING ENTRIES FOR PREPAID INSURANCE, UNEARNED REVENUE AND PREPAID RENT AND LEDGER ACCOUNTS ★★   **LO 4**

The ledger of Local Publishing Services includes the following accounts: Subscription Revenue, Unearned Subscriptions Revenue, Prepaid Insurance, Insurance Expense, Prepaid Rent and Rent Expense.

The following transactions relating to subscriptions, insurance and rent occurred on the dates indicated. Ignore GST.

Subscriptions

1 July 2013. The Unearned Subscriptions Revenue account contained a credit balance of $18 345. Of this balance, $5220 is for subscriptions expiring at the end of September and $13 125 is for subscriptions expiring at the end of April.

1 October 2013. Local Publishing Services received $3525 for subscriptions lasting 6 months.

1 February 2014. Local Publishing Services received $8112 for subscriptions lasting 24 months.

1 May 2014. Local Publishing Services received $4170 for subscriptions lasting 6 months.

Insurance

1 July 2013. The Prepaid Insurance account contained a debit balance of $2850 in relation to the period 1 July to 31 March.

15 October 2013. Local Publishing Services paid $6450 for a 12-month policy beginning coverage on 15 October.

Rent

1 July 2013. The Prepaid Rent account contained a debit balance of $3094 for the period July to November inclusive.

1 December 2013. Local Publishing Services paid $5724 for 9 months rent.

Required

For each of the situations listed, enter the beginning balance in the proper ledger account and post the transactions directly to the accounts listed. Then record the necessary adjusting entry at 30 June 2014, the end of the financial year.

Problem 4.4   ADJUSTING ENTRIES AND CORRECTIONS ★★   **LO 4, 5, 7**

J. Stott submits to you draft accounts for the year ended 30 June 2013, and a balance sheet as at that date. Towards the end of the financial year his accountant resigned and he had completed the records himself. He thinks that errors have occurred and asks your help. An examination of the accounting records reveals the following:

1. Rent due from customers See and Els amounting to $800 is not included in the accounts.
2. A payment of $1300 for new office furniture has been incorrectly debited to the Sundry Expenses account. The furniture had been purchased late in June 2013.
3. Commission due to sales representatives for the month of June, $1400, has been overlooked.
4. Repairs to Stott's private motor vehicle, $840, have been debited to the Vehicle Expenses account.

5. A payment of $11 000 on 1 July 2012 for additions to buildings has been debited to Repairs and Maintenance.
6. A fire insurance policy covering buildings was taken out on 30 April 2013, the annual premium of $720 being paid in advance on this date and debited to the Prepaid Insurance account.
7. Interest of $600 on the investments held by the business was due, but has not been received.
8. No depreciation has been recognised for the year ending 30 June. The draft balance sheet shows the following:

Buildings (at cost)	$80 000*	
Accumulated depreciation	16 000	$64 000
Office furniture and equipment (at cost)*	10 500	
Accumulated depreciation	6 500	4 000

* Does not include additions to buildings in no. (5), nor adjustments for office furniture in (2) above.

Depreciation is to be calculated as follows:
Buildings: 2% on cost
Office furniture and equipment: 20% on cost.

Required
A. Ignoring GST, show the journal entries required to make the necessary adjustments listed.
B. Calculate the effect (increase or decrease) of each of the adjustments on the profit figure of $20 300 as shown in the draft accounts.

Problem 4.5 ADJUSTING ENTRIES AND ANALYSIS ★   LO 4, 5, 6

Lim Soo Chang's business, called Lim's Massage Services operates in the local shopping centre. The business prepared the following unadjusted and adjusted trial balances at 31 December 2013:

LIM'S MASSAGE SERVICES
Trial Balances
as at 31 December 2013

Account	Trial balance Debit	Trial balance Credit	Adjusted trial balance Debit	Adjusted trial balance Credit
Cash	$ 7 240		$ 7 240	
Accounts receivable	22 520		24 180	
Supplies	2 180		1 560	
Prepaid insurance	4 400		2 660	
Office furniture	43 260		43 260	
Accumulated depreciation		$ 16 440		$ 21 000
Accounts payable		12 620		12 620
Salaries payable				1 920
Interest payable				700
Loan payable		24 000		24 000
Unearned massage services revenue		2 880		1 920
Lim Soo Chang, Capital		26 020		26 020
Lim Soo Chang, Drawings	58 740		58 740	
Massage services revenue		145 780		148 400
Depreciation expense			4 560	
Supplies expense			620	
Electricity expense	9 920		9 920	
Salaries expense	53 320		55 240	
Rent expense	24 400		24 400	
Interest expense	1 760		2 460	
Insurance expense			1 740	
	$227 740	$227 740	$236 580	$236 580

Required

Prepare the adjusting entries that account for the differences between the two trial balances and explain the nature of each entry. The only account affected by more than one adjustment is Massage Services Revenue. Ignore GST.

Problem 4.6 ADJUSTING ENTRIES, POSTING TO T ACCOUNTS, AND EFFECT ON PROFIT ★★

At 30 June 2012, the trial balance of Kerry Parr, Architect, was as follows:

KERRY PARR, ARCHITECT
Unadjusted Trial Balance
as at 30 June 2012

Account	Debit	Credit
Cash at bank	$ 5 990	
Accounts receivable	16 700	
GST outlays	2 000	
Prepaid rent	2 100	
Prepaid insurance	2 600	
Office supplies	3 120	
Office equipment	9 400	
Accumulated depreciation — office equipment		$ 1 900
Accounts payable		210
Unearned fees		820
Loan payable — due 2015		7 000
GST collections		6 200
K. Parr, Capital		16 000
K. Parr, Drawings	40 000	
Fees revenue		106 180
Salaries expense	44 000	
Telephone expense	4 700	
Rent expense	7 700	
	$138 310	$138 310

Required

A. Using the following information, prepare adjusting entries. Use the accounts shown in the trial balance and these additional accounts: Salaries Payable, Interest Payable, Telephone Account Payable, Depreciation Expense, Office Supplies Expense, Insurance Expense, Interest Expense.
   1. A physical count of office supplies on 30 June shows $440 of unused supplies on hand.
   2. Depreciation of the office equipment this year is estimated to be $800.
   3. Half the amount in the Unearned Fees account had been earned by the end of the year.
   4. The amount in the Prepaid Rent account covers this June and the next 2 months.
   5. Of prepaid insurance, 60% expired this period.
   6. Salaries expense accrued for the last 4 days in June amounts to $1275.
   7. The telephone expense for June of $520 has not been recorded or paid. No tax invoice has been issued.
   8. Interest expense of $410 has accrued on the loan payable.
B. Open T accounts for the accounts shown in the trial balance and enter the 30 June balance in each account. Post the adjusting entries to the T accounts.
C. Prepare an adjusted trial balance, an income statement and a balance sheet.
D. Assuming that adjusting entries 1–8 in requirement A were not made, determine what the profit would have been. What is the difference between this figure and the profit derived in requirement C?

Problem 4.7 PREPARING A WORKSHEET ★★

The unadjusted trial balance of Catamaran Rentals is shown below:

CATAMARAN RENTALS
Unadjusted Trial Balance
as at 30 June 2013

Account	Debit	Credit
Cash at bank	$ 8 950	
Accounts receivable	6 915	
GST outlays	2 000	
Prepaid insurance	5 685	
Catamarans	121 500	
Accumulated depreciation — catamarans		$ 48 000
Office equipment	3 150	
Accumulated depreciation — office equipment		1 335
Accounts payable		8 895
Loan payable		37 500
Unearned rental revenue		1 260
GST collections		3 000
J. Kanaris, Capital		49 740
J. Kanaris, Drawings	12 450	
Rental revenue		54 405
Salaries expense	22 800	
Rent expense	3 945	
Repairs and maintenance expense	4 440	
Marine supplies expense	10 200	
Telephone expense	2 100	
	$204 135	$204 135

The following additional information is available at the end of June:
(a) Depreciation on the catamaran fleet for 1 year is $13 000. Depreciation on the office equipment is $600.
(b) Expired insurance amounted to $4950.
(c) The balance in the Unearned Rental Revenue account includes $253 received for services rendered on 27 June.
(d) Salaries earned but not paid amounted to $1720.
(e) Accrued interest on the loan payable is $3560.
(f) Repairs on one catamaran done in June for $850 have not yet been paid for or recorded. A tax invoice has been issued by the repairer.
(g) The June telephone costs of $275 have not been paid for or recorded at 30 June 2013. A tax invoice has been received.

Required
Prepare a 10-column worksheet for the year ended 30 June 2013.

Problem 4.8 WORKSHEET AND FINANCIAL STATEMENTS ★★

The adjusted trial balance columns of the worksheet for Michelle's Laundry Services are as shown on the next page.

MICHELLE'S LAUNDRY SERVICES
Worksheet (Partial)
for the month ended 28 February 2013

Account	Adjusted trial balance Debit	Adjusted trial balance Credit	Income statement Debit	Income statement Credit	Balance sheet Debit	Balance sheet Credit
Cash	$ 51 630					
Accounts Receivable	27 440					
Prepaid Rent	7 980					
Equipment	80 675					
Accumulated Depreciation		$ 16 595				
Loan Payable (due June 2013)		21 750				
Accounts Payable		19 580				
M. Stead, Capital		117 960				
M. Stead, Drawings	12 775					
Service Revenue		44 065				
Salaries Expense	34 440					
Rent Expense	2 660					
Depreciation Expense	2 350					
Interest Expense	200					
Interest Payable		200				
	$220 150	$220 150				
Profit for the period						

Required

Complete the worksheet and prepare an income statement, a statement of changes in equity and a classified balance sheet.

LO 4, 5, 7

Problem 4.9 ADJUSTING ENTRIES AND IMPACT ON FINANCIAL STATEMENTS ★★

Subiaco Rental Services ends its financial year on 30 June.

Required

A. Using the following information, make the necessary adjusting entries.
   1. Rent of office premises of $609 for the 3-month period ending 31 July is due to be paid in July.
   2. The telephone expense of $147 is unpaid and unrecorded at 30 June.
   3. The Supplies account had a $287 debit balance on 1 July of the preceding year. Supplies costing $1372 were purchased during the year, and $252 of supplies are on hand as at 30 June.
   4. Subiaco Rental Services borrowed $13 300 from ABC Bank on 15 February. The principal, plus 8% interest, is payable on 15 August. Accrued interest on 30 June has not been recorded.
   5. Annual depreciation on equipment is estimated to be $6580. The balance in Accumulated Depreciation at the beginning of the financial year was $9870.
   6. The office assistant earns $280 a day. He will be paid in July for the 5-day period ending 3 July.
   7. On 1 June, Subiaco Rental Services received 2 months rent in advance, totalling $896. This was recorded by a credit to Unearned Rental Revenue.

8. Subiaco Rental Services purchased a 6-month insurance policy for $567 on 1 November. A 24-month policy was purchased on 30 April for $1272. Both purchases were recorded by debiting Prepaid Insurance.

B. As you know, all adjusting entries affect one balance sheet account and one income statement account. Based on your adjusting entries prepared in requirement A:
1. calculate the increase or decrease in profit
2. calculate the increase or decrease in total assets, total liabilities and total equity.

LO 4, 5, 7

Problem 4.10   ADJUSTING ENTRIES AND IMPACT ON FINANCIAL STATEMENTS ★★

Megan Jackson established Jackson's Software Consulting Services in 2012 and kept her accounting records on a cash basis. During 2014, Megan decided to switch her accounting to the accrual basis and has asked you to help her convert the 2012 and 2013 financial statements to an accrual basis. Your analysis of the accounting records revealed the following data:

	2012	2013
Consulting fees revenue		
Cash collected for services performed during the year	$42 000	$43 500
Charged customers for services performed during the year,		
but cash was not received until the following year	12 000	15 000
Prepaid revenue collected in 2012 for services performed in 2013	2 250	
Expenses		
Cash paid for services received	24 000	25 500
Accrued expenses at end of the year paid for in the following year	10 500	10 950
Prepaid expenses:		
Cash paid during the year	6 000	9 000
Amount prepaid at the end of the year	4 500	10 500

Required
A. Using the data, complete abbreviated income statements in the form shown below for the years 2012 and 2013 for both the cash basis and accrual basis of accounting. Show supporting calculations in good form.

	Cash basis		Accrual basis	
	2012	2013	2012	2013
Consulting fees revenue	___	___	___	___
Expenses	___	___	___	___
Profit	___	___	___	___

B. Show the differences that would result in the 31 December 2013 balance sheet accounts from using the accrual basis instead of the cash basis.

LO 4, 5

Problem 4.11   ADJUSTING ENTRIES AND JUSTIFICATIONS ★★

After analysing the accounting records and other data for the business of Woody the Tree Lopper, the following information is made available for the year ended 30 June 2013:
1. The Office Supplies account has a debit balance of $3500. A physical count of office supplies on hand at 30 June gives a total of $1100.
2. The Prepaid Rent account has a debit balance of $5200. Included in this amount is $400 paid in June for the month of July 2013, and $4800 has expired.
3. The Prepaid Insurance account has a debit balance of $4140. It consists of the following policies purchased during the financial year ending 30 June 2013:

Policy number	Date of policy	Life of policy	Premium paid
ZX 5432	1 July 2012	2 years	$2880
ET 7890	1 October 2012	1 year	720
CQA 3120	1 February 2013	6 months	540

4. The Prepaid Advertising account has a debit balance of $12 000. Included in this amount is $2000 paid to the local newspaper for advertising space in their July and August 2013 papers.
5. At the end of the financial year, salaries and wages owing to employees amounted to $3500.
6. At the end of the year, the business had outstanding a long-term loan of $20 000 from one of Woody's friends. Interest of 7% p.a. is payable half-yearly on this loan, every 1 April and 1 October. The last interest payment made by the business was on 1 April 2013.
7. The Tree Lopping Services Revenue account had a credit balance of $72 000. Included in this amount was $4300 for services to be provided in July 2013.
8. The Equipment account has a debit balance of $23 000. The equipment has a useful life of 10 years and an estimated residual value of $3000. All equipment had been acquired when the business was established on 1 July 2010.
9. The Motor Vehicle account has a debit balance of $50 000. The vehicle was purchased on 1 January 2013 and has an estimated useful life of 5 years and an estimated residual value of $10 000.
10. Accrued council rates at 30 June 2013 were $3400.

Required

A. Prepare the end-of-period adjusting entries required on 30 June 2013. Show clearly your calculations

B. Provide reasons for your answers to items 2, 6 and 9 above.

Problem 4.12 ADJUSTING ENTRIES AND FINANCIAL STATEMENTS ★★★   LO 4, 5, 6, 7

The unadjusted trial balance of the general ledger of Jason's Electrical Repair Service on 31 December 2013 is presented below:

JASON'S ELECTRICAL REPAIR SERVICE Trial Balance as at 31 December 2013		
Account	Debit	Credit
Cash at bank	$ 9 200	
Investment in marketable securities	18 600	
Accounts receivable	48 500	
GST outlays	4 600	
Prepaid insurance	2 500	
Electrical equipment	90 000	
Accumulated depreciation – electrical equipment		$ 12 500
Accounts payable		45 000
Mortgage payable (due 31 December 2018)		15 000
GST collections		6 600
J. Dunstan, Capital		62 500
J. Dunstan, Drawings	5 500	
Electrical repairs revenue		106 000
Advertising expense	4 900	
Other selling expenses	7 500	
Electricity expense	5 000	
Sundry expenses	9 550	
Rent expense	4 800	
Wages expense	38 000	
Interest on mortgage expense	750	
Rent revenue		1 800
	$249 400	$249 400

Additional data for adjustment purposes

(a) Supplies on 31 December 2013 were:
   (i) advertising supplies (originally debited to Advertising Expense), $1700.
   (ii) store supplies (originally debited to Sundry Expenses), $900.
(b) On 1 July 2013, the business rented some electrical equipment to Jing's Cafe for 12 months and received a cheque for $1800 plus GST, representing the entire year's rental fee.
(c) Purchases of electrical equipment were as follows, net of GST:

Purchase date	Cost	Useful life
1 January 2008	$20 000	8 years
1 April 2013	$70 000	10 years

(d) The Prepaid Insurance account consists of the following, net of GST:

Policy number	Date of policy	Life of policy	Total premiums
37 457QL	1 January 2013	2 years	$1500
74 374NJ	1 July 2013	1 year	$1000

(e) Wages earned by employees but unpaid as at 31 December 2013 totalled $1230.
(f) Interest on the mortgage payable is $900 per year, paid in half-yearly instalments on 1 May and 1 November.

Required

A. Journalise adjustments in the general journal of the entity.
B. Prepare an income statement and a statement of changes in equity for the year ended 31 December 2013.
C. Prepare a balance sheet (properly classified in narrative form) as at 31 December 2013.
D. Present the Interest on Mortgage Expense account showing detailed entries for the year ended 31 December 2013 as it would appear after all adjustments have been made.

Problem 4.13   CASH AND ACCRUAL ACCOUNTING ★★★   LO 1, 7

John Grout is a tile contractor who specialises in laying kitchen and bathroom tiles. He began business in January 2013 but has not yet established a formal set of records. His son, Jeff, has prepared cash receipts and payments statements for each of the first 3 months of the year, but John Grout has become uneasy about relying on them. He asks you to prepare a 'proper' set of financial statements for the month of March.

By reviewing the bank statements, cheque butts, invoice files and other data, you derive a set of balance sheets at 1 March and 31 March. These are shown below, followed by a statement of cash receipts and payments for March. GST is ignored.

GROUT'S TILING SERVICE
Balance Sheets

	1 March 2013	31 March 2013
ASSETS		
Cash at bank	$ 2 160	$ 3 600
Accounts receivable	1 680	2 160
Supplies on hand	960	1 080
Equipment	14 400	18 000
Accumulated depreciation (credit)	(1 800)	(2 400)
	$17 400	$22 440
LIABILITIES AND EQUITY		
Salaries payable	$ 1 080	$ 1 800
Electricity account payable	—	360
J. Grout, Capital	16 320	20 280
	$17 400	$22 440

<table>
<tr><td colspan="3" align="center">**GROUT'S TILING SERVICE**
Statement of Cash Receipts and Payments
for March 2013</td></tr>
</table>

CASH RECEIPTS		
Received from credit customers	$6 480	
Contributed by J. Grout	4 800	
Total cash receipts		$11 280
CASH PAYMENTS		
Paid for supplies purchased	1 440	
Purchase of equipment	3 600	
Payment of salaries	1 560	
Paid for March rent	480	
Sundry expenses	360	
Cash withdrawn by J. Grout	2 400	
Total cash payments		9 840
Net increase in cash balance		$ 1 440

Required

A. From the information presented, prepare an income statement on the accrual basis for the month of March. *Hint:* You may wish to prepare (reconstruct) relevant accounts.

B. Illustrate the apparent correctness of your profit amount by preparing a statement of changes in equity for March 2013.

Problem 4.14 OPENING T ACCOUNTS, ADJUSTING ENTRIES AND PREPARING FINANCIAL STATEMENTS ★★★ GST LO 3, 4, 5, 6, 7

Macca's Party Hire hires out equipment and furniture for parties. The unadjusted trial balance of the business appears as shown below.

<table>
<tr><td colspan="3" align="center">**MACCA'S PARTY HIRE**
Unadjusted Trial Balance
as at 30 June 2013</td></tr>
</table>

Account	Debit	Credit
Cash at bank	$ 5 200	
Accounts receivable	2 400	
GST outlays	3 300	
Prepaid insurance	1 200	
Party equipment	31 400	
Accumulated depreciation – party equipment		$ 17 600
Furniture	47 300	
Accumulated depreciation – furniture		23 000
Accounts payable		6 800
GST collections		5 000
K. Maclean, Capital		18 710
K. Maclean, Drawings	18 310	
Hire fees revenue		74 700
Salaries expense	26 500	
Rent expense	5 700	
Maintenance expense	3 100	
Electricity expense	1 400	
	$145 810	$145 810

Additional information

(a) Expired insurance amounts to $850.

(b) June electricity costs of $300 have not been paid or recorded. No tax invoice has been received.

(c) Depreciation on the party equipment is $7850, and depreciation on the furniture is $9420.

(d) Hire fees of $1150 (plus GST of $115) were received in advance and were not considered to be revenue at balance date.

(e) The Rent Expense account contains $1320 paid for July 2013 rent.

(f) A hire fee of $264 received in cash (including $24 GST) was recorded by debiting Accounts Receivable.

(g) Salaries earned amounting to $810 will be paid in July and have not been recorded.

Required

A. Set up T accounts for the accounts listed in the trial balance.
   1. Enter the account balances from the trial balance into the T accounts.
   2. Post the adjusting information directly to the T accounts.

B. Prepare an adjusted trial balance.

C. Prepare an income statement and a statement of changes in equity for the year ended 30 June 2013.

D. Prepare a balance sheet as at 30 June 2013.

Problem 4.15   PREPARING A WORKSHEET AND FINANCIAL STATEMENTS ★★★   LO 4, 5, 6, 7, 9

The unadjusted trial balance of Everton Removalists is shown below:

EVERTON REMOVALISTS
Unadjusted Trial Balance
as at 30 June 2013

Account	Debit	Credit
Cash at bank	$ 8 140	
Accounts receivable	12 860	
GST outlays	1 500	
Office supplies	640	
Removal vans	93 600	
Accumulated depreciation – removal vans		$ 39 400
Office equipment	6 200	
Accumulated depreciation – office equipment		3 500
Accounts payable		10 800
Unearned removal fees		2 260
GST collections		3 240
G. Everton, Capital		76 600
G. Everton, Drawings	20 600	
Removal fees revenue		92 700
Insurance expense	8 180	
Wages expense	54 620	
Advertising expense	3 880	
Maintenance expense	7 600	
Fuel and oil expense	10 680	
	$228 500	$228 500

Additional information

(a) Depreciation for 1 year on the removal vans is $10 000. Depreciation on the office equipment is $1200.

(b) A physical count showed office supplies totalling $170 were still on hand at 30 June.

(c) The balance in the Unearned Removal Fees account includes $2000 received in May for removal services completed in June.

(d) The balance in the Advertising Expense account includes $700 prepayment (net of GST) for an advertising campaign beginning in July.

(e) Wages earned but not paid amounted to $2850.

(f) Petrol purchased on credit for $350 plus GST of 10% and used during the last week in June has not been paid for or recorded.

(g) The June insurance premium of $880 plus GST is overdue and has not been recorded. A tax invoice has been received.

Required

A. Prepare a 10-column worksheet for the year ended 30 June 2013.

B. Prepare the income statement for the business for the year ended 30 June 2013.

C. Prepare a statement of changes in equity for the year ended 30 June 2013.

D. Prepare a balance sheet as at 30 June 2013.

DECISION ANALYSIS

Home sewing business

Lana Priest set up a home sewing business on 1 July 2013. Usually, Lana collects $20 per hour for sewing on the completion of each day's work and pays for the maintenance of her machine with cash. Lana did an accounting subject at secondary school and so has kept her own accrual-based accounting records. At the end of the first year, Lana produced the following unadjusted trial balance:

Unadjusted Trial Balance as at 30 June 2014		
Account	Debit	Credit
Cash at bank	$ 2550	
Accounts receivable	40	
Sewing machines	3000	
Motor vehicle	24000	
Lana Priest, Capital		$19000
Lana Priest, Drawings	17570	
Sewing revenue		38400
Sewing supplies expense	4840	
Insurance	2300	
Repairs to machines	2560	
Sundry expenses	540	
	$57400	$57400

The following adjustments were required at the year-end:

● Sewing supplies on hand at year-end, $230.

● An account was received for repairs done to machines before year-end but not recorded, $270. Ignore the GST in your answers.

Required

A. Prepare an income statement for the year ended 30 June 2014 using accrual accounting.

B. Prepare an income statement for the year ended 30 June 2014 using cash accounting.

C. Lana was not sure whether she could use cash accounting rather than accrual accounting for her business records. From the information provided, decide whether Lana should use accrual or cash accounting, and explain to her the reasons for your decision.

End-of-period adjusting entries

In groups of three, select three companies and obtain a copy of their financial statements. Paper copies can be obtained from the companies, and electronic copies are available for most publicly listed companies on their websites. Alternatively, many university libraries have a copy of public company accounts in electronic form.

Required

A. For each of the three companies, find information on accruals and deferrals in the financial statements. These will usually be in the notes to the financial statements, and will include such things as depreciation expense, prepaid rent, unearned fees, salaries payable and interest payable. Compare the accruals and deferrals with the profit for each company to assess the impact of accrual accounting adjustments on the measures of profitability.

B. Prepare an overhead of your group's findings to present to the class.

ETHICS AND GOVERNANCE

The impact of a bonus incentive scheme on the financial statements

Lucia works as an accountant for a motor vehicle engine parts manufacturer called Vroom Ltd, owned by an international car firm. Her manager, Freda Chuse, is paid a bonus depending on the profitability of the company. If Vroom Ltd makes $1 million profit, Freda receives a bonus of $20 000 that increases progressively to $30 000 for a $3 million profit. If the profit of Vroom Ltd exceeds $3 million, Freda receives the maximum bonus of $30 000. Vroom Ltd currently receives a grant from the government of $100 000 per year to employ and train apprentice mechanics.

At the end of May, it appears that Vroom Ltd will make a profit of approximately $3.5 million for the year ending 30 June 2013. Freda approached Lucia and said that if the company made too much profit then the government may stop paying Vroom Ltd the grant for training apprentice mechanics, and it would lose the $100 000 tax-free cash inflow. Freda instructed Lucia to find ways of deferring recognition of as much revenue as possible until the following financial year, for which the forecasts for the industry were quite poor, and to accrue as many expenses as possible at the end of the current accounting period when it came to making the end-of-period adjustments. Although Lucia was not happy with this instruction, she did not want to risk her own opportunities for promotion by upsetting her manager.

Required

A. Who are the stakeholders in this situation?

B. Why do you believe Freda asked Lucia to do this?

C. What are the ethical issues involved?

D. Can Lucia defer revenues and accrue as many expenses as possible and still be ethical?

FINANCIAL ANALYSIS

Refer to the income (revenues) and expenses as shown in the notes in the latest financial report of JB Hi-Fi Limited on its website, www.jbhifi.com.au, and answer the following questions:

1. Which of these items, if any, would have been affected by adjusting entries for deferrals?

2. Which of these items, if any, would have been affected by adjusting entries for accruals?

3. What is the total amount of expense for depreciation of plant and equipment?

Completing the accounting cycle — closing and reversing entries

Learning objectives

After studying this chapter, you should be able to:

1 describe all the steps in the complete accounting cycle (pp. 178–9)

2 explain why temporary ledger accounts need to be closed (p. 179)

3 explain how to record adjusting entries from a worksheet (pp. 179–82)

4 describe the closing process, and enter closing entries in accounting records (pp. 182–98)

5 prepare a post-closing trial balance (pp. 198–9)

6 account for accrual items in subsequent periods (pp. 199–200)

7 explain reversing entries and how to record them (pp. 200–4)

8 prepare the equity accounts for a partnership and for a company (pp. 204–7).

Records at work — society's documentary glue

Records, old and new, come in many forms — paper, film, magnetic tape, optical disks, photographs, even multimedia — and, as the primary support for communication over space and time and means of proving identity and entitlements, records underpin all complex activity.

In the case of businesses or organisations, records are of critical importance. Such bodies cannot legitimately do business, hire staff, buy or sell property, goods and services until the appropriate records documenting their 'birth' and purposes as legal entities permit them to do so.

Individuals, businesses, organisations and government bodies make records to document accomplishments and to solve problems...

When people make and keep records, they do so because records 'work' to enable them to:

- establish or verify facts
- quantify and calculate possessions, resources, losses
- authorise, initiate, regulate actions
- endow and protect ownership, status, rights, entitlements
- act as reference points within a process to enable planning, reporting, evaluation of critical factors such as progress, productivity, achievement and risk
- trace and enforce accountability
- ensure continuity of management, operations, culture.

How many of the following records are important in your life? Perhaps all of them!

- Accounts/invoices
- Applications
- Certificates
- Contracts
- Conveyances
- Correspondence
- Identity records
- Inventories
- Licences
- Photographs
- Plans
- Receipts

Source: Excerpts from Ann Pederson, 'Understanding society through its records', John Curtin Prime Ministerial Library, http://john.curtin.edu.au/society/evidence/index.html.

Chapter preview

Record keeping is a vital activity in society (see the scene setter), and an essential part of the accounting cycle. In chapter 4, the accounting cycle was expanded to incorporate adjusting entries made at the end of an accounting period (the financial year) to adjust account balances before preparing the financial statements. Adjusting entries were journalised and then posted to relevant ledger accounts, and the adjusted ledger account balances were used to prepare the financial statements. Use of a worksheet to record adjustments outside the ledger accounts and for the preparation of interim financial statements as well as for the end-of-the-accounting-period statements was also illustrated.

During an accounting period, temporary accounts are used to accumulate income and expenses to enable preparation of the income statement for that period. At the end of each accounting period these temporary accounts need to be cleared so that entries for the new accounting period can be made. The process of clearing temporary accounts is referred to as the *closing process*, and represents the final step of the accounting cycle.

This chapter illustrates the closing process and the completion of the accounting cycle as shown in figure 5.1.

5.1 The complete accounting cycle

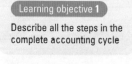

Learning objective **1**

Describe all the steps in the complete accounting cycle

The accounting cycle, that sequence of events or steps which leads from source documents to the final production of the financial statements, is completed usually once a year. The accounting cycle developed in chapter 4 is completed in this chapter by including the journalising and posting of closing entries, and the journalising and posting of reversing entries when they are required. The complete accounting cycle is summarised in figure 5.1.

Figure 5.1 The complete accounting cycle

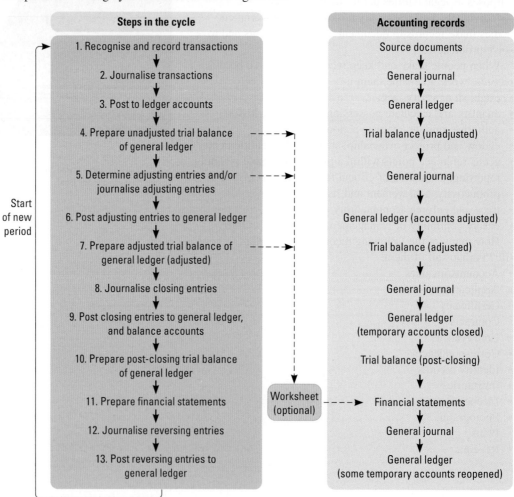

Steps 1 to 3 (preparing source documents, entering transactions in journals, and posting to ledger accounts) are carried out continuously during the year as transactions occur. Steps 4 to 13 are carried out only at the end of the accounting period (the financial year). If interim financial statements are prepared, steps 4, 5 and 7 are usually performed on a worksheet outside the accounting journals and ledger. From the worksheet, financial statements can be prepared without journalising adjusting and closing entries and posting these to general ledger accounts. Nevertheless, it is still quite common for accountants to prepare a worksheet even at the end of the financial year accounting period to help organise their work and minimise errors.

5.2 Closing temporary accounts

Learning objective 2

Explain why temporary ledger accounts need to be closed

The income statement reports income and expenses for a single accounting period. Data needed to prepare the statement are accumulated in the individual income and expense accounts. To help in the preparation of this statement for the *next* accounting period, all income and expense account balances are closed or cleared (reduced to a zero balance) by transferring their balances to another account in order to calculate profit. (Recall from chapter 4 that because income and expense accounts are closed each period, they are called *temporary* or *nominal* accounts.) This step in the accounting cycle is referred to as the closing process, and journal entries made to close the temporary accounts are called **closing entries**.

The closing process results in each income and expense account beginning the next period with a zero balance, which prepares them for accumulating information for that period's income statement. In addition, income increases and expenses decrease equity. Because they are recorded in separate temporary accounts rather than directly in the Capital account, journal entries are needed to transfer the net change in equity during the period to the Capital account.

In the closing process, a new temporary account called the *Profit or Loss Summary* account is established to summarise the balances in the income and expense accounts and to calculate profit (loss). This is the only time in the accounting process that this account is used. Closing entries are generally made in the following sequence:
1. The balance in each income account is transferred to the Profit or Loss Summary account.
2. The balance in each expense account is transferred to the Profit or Loss Summary account.
3. The balance in the Profit or Loss Summary account is transferred to the Capital account.
4. The Drawings account is transferred to the Capital account.

Note that the closing process closes only the temporary ledger accounts. The process is shown in figure 5.2 (p. 180) in T-account format, using the totals from the income statement columns in the worksheet presented in figure 4.21 (p. 151, repeated in figure 5.3, p. 181). When the closing entries are entered in the journal, the individual income and expense accounts are debited or credited.

5.3 Using the worksheet to record adjusting entries

Learning objective 3

Explain how to record adjusting entries from a worksheet

As we saw in chapter 4, a worksheet can gather together in the one place all the information needed to adjust account balances and prepare financial statements. It is also useful in preparing interim financial statements when adjusting entries are not recorded in the formal accounting records. The worksheet contains all the information necessary in the adjustments columns to record adjusting entries in the general journal and post to ledger accounts. Also, since all income and expenses are grouped in the income statement columns of the worksheet, all the information necessary to record closing entries in the general journal and post to ledger accounts is readily available.

The journalising of adjusting entries from a worksheet is illustrated on the following pages. For easy reference purposes, the worksheet for Intellect Management Services completed in the previous chapter is reproduced in figure 5.3 (p. 181).

It is common practice for an entity to prepare monthly financial statements for use by managers, and most large entities are required to issue quarterly and/or half-yearly statements to external statement users. Such statements are called **interim statements** because they are prepared between the annual reports issued at year-end. In the case of Intellect Management Services, it was assumed that monthly financial statements were to be prepared and that the accounting cycle,

Figure 5.2 Diagram of the closing process

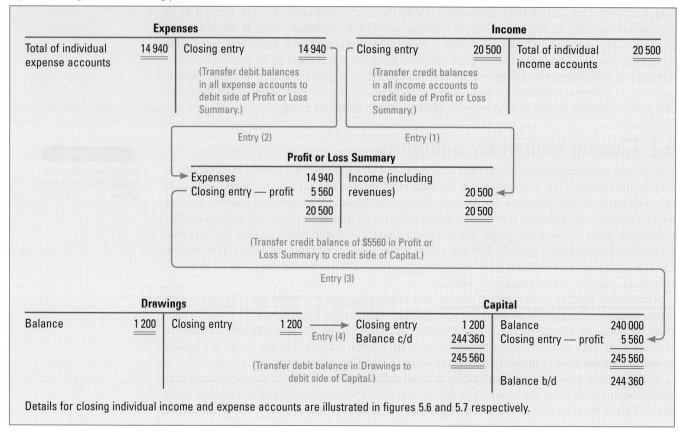

Details for closing individual income and expense accounts are illustrated in figures 5.6 and 5.7 respectively.

including entering and posting both adjusting and closing entries, was completed at the end of the month. However, many entities adjust and close their accounts at the end of the year only. Information needed to prepare interim financial statements is accumulated only in the worksheet. In other words, adjusting entries are made on the worksheet but are not entered in the accounting records except at the end of the accounting year. At that time the accounts are also closed.

Recording adjusting entries

From the worksheet shown in figure 5.3, formal adjusting entries may be entered in the general journal as shown in figure 5.4 (p. 182). The necessary information is available directly from the adjustments columns of the worksheet. Note that the entries are dated on the last day of the accounting period and generally the heading 'Adjusting entries' is written in the general journal to separate these entries from other transactions. After the adjusting entries are posted, as indicated by writing the account number in the 'post ref' column of the journal, the ledger account balances should agree with the balances reported in the worksheet.

Data for determining the entity's closing entries for the period are found in the income statement columns of the worksheet, as these contain the data for temporary income and expense accounts. The closing process is covered in the next section.

Figure 5.3 Completed worksheet for Intellect Management Services

INTELLECT MANAGEMENT SERVICES
Worksheet
for the month ended 30 June 2013

Account	Unadjusted trial balance Debit	Unadjusted trial balance Credit	Adjustments Debit	Adjustments Credit	Adjusted trial balance Debit	Adjusted trial balance Credit	Income statement Debit	Income statement Credit	Balance sheet Debit	Balance sheet Credit
Cash at Bank	135 770				135 770				135 770	
Accounts Receivable	11 880		(h) 800		12 680				12 680	
Prepaid Insurance	1 920			(a) 80	1 840				1 840	
Office Supplies	1 240			(b) 160	1 080				1 080	
GST Outlays	32 276				32 276				32 276	
Land	120 000				120 000				120 000	
Building	180 000				180 000				180 000	
Accumulated Depreciation – Building				(d) 500		500				500
Office Equipment	19 200				19 200				19 200	
Accumulated Depreciation – Office Equipment				(c) 200		200				200
Accounts Payable		9 200				9 200				9 200
Unearned Appraisal Fees		560				560				560
GST Collections		2 026				2 026				2 026
Mortgage Payable		240 000				240 000				240 000
M. Mooney, Capital		240 000				240 000				240 000
M. Mooney, Drawings	1 200				1 200				1 200	
Management Services Revenue		19 200				19 200		19 200		
Appraisal Fees Revenue		500				500		500		
Salaries Expense	7 600		(e) 3 980		11 580		11 580			
Telephone Expense	160				160		160			
Advertising Expense	240				240		240			
	511 486	511 486								
Insurance Expense			(a) 80		80		80			
Office Supplies Expense			(b) 160		160		160			
Depreciation Expense – Office Equipment			(c) 200		200		200			
Depreciation Expense – Building			(d) 500		500		500			
Electricity Expense			(g) 420		420		420			
Salaries Payable				(e) 3 980		3 980				3 980
Interest Expense			(f) 1 600		1600		1 600			
Interest Payable				(f) 1 600		1 600				1 600
Electricity Account Payable				(g) 420		420				420
Marketing Services Revenue				(h) 800		800		800		
			7 740	7 740	518 986	518 986	14 940	20 500	504 046	498 486
Profit for the period							5 560			5 560
							20 500	20 500	504 046	504 046

Figure 5.4 Recording adjusting entries

	General Journal				Page 3
Date	Particulars	Post Ref	Debit	Credit	
2013	**Adjusting entries**				
June 30 (a)	Insurance Expense Prepaid Insurance (Insurance expense for June)	521 110	80	80	
30 (b)	Office Supplies Expense Office Supplies (Office supplies used in June)	530 111	160	160	
30 (c)	Depreciation Expense – Office Equipment Accum. Depr. – Office Equipment (Depreciation for June on office equipment)	540 171	200	200	
30 (d)	Depreciation Expense – Building Accum. Depr. – Building (Depreciation for June on building)	541 161	500	500	
30 (e)	Salaries Expense Salaries Payable (Unpaid salaries at end of June)	500 210	3 980	3 980	
30 (f)	Interest Expense Interest Payable (Accrued interest on mortgage payable at end of June)	560 215	1 600	1 600	
30 (g)	Electricity Expense Electricity Account Payable (Unpaid electricity charges at end of June)	570 216	420	420	
30 (h)	Accounts Receivable Marketing Services Revenue (Revenue from marketing services receivable for June)	104 402	800	800	
			7 740	7 740	

BUSINESS KNOWLEDGE

Blue sky man

Jetstar, the successful offshoot of Qantas, has experienced record growth since its launch in 2004. Last October, CEO Bruce Buchanan predicted that passenger revenue will increase to A$2.6 billion in the 12 months to 30 June 2010, from around A$2.3 billion in the previous year. Meanwhile, AirAsia — voted best low-cost airline in the world in last year's prestigious Skytrax awards — dominates in the South-East Asian market. Analysts have called the alliance a 'killer proposition', where hundreds of millions of dollars will be saved through the joint purchase of aircraft and the sharing of ground operations and aircraft parts.

Jetstar and AirAsia are the two largest low-cost airlines (in revenue terms) in the Asia Pacific. Together they earned nearly A$3 billion in 2009. CEO Bruce Buchanan says: 'Jetstar is the number one in terms of revenue and RPKs [revenue passenger kilometres] and AirAsia's the number one in terms of passengers. Our long-haul network's a lot bigger. But we are both very profitable and growing much faster than the competition.'

Source: Excerpts from Jackie Blondell, 'Blue sky man', *InTheBlack*.

Learning objective 4

Describe the closing process, and enter closing entries in accounting records

5.4 The closing process

The closing process involves closing each income and expense account to the Profit or Loss Summary account, and the balance of this account (profit or loss) is then closed off to the Capital account. Any drawings made by the owner during the year are reflected in the Drawings account, which is also closed off to the Capital account. The closing of all temporary accounts is done by making compound general journal entries, and then posting to the relevant accounts. Closing entries are not shown on a worksheet, but the information necessary to make the general journal entries is available from the worksheet. The closing process is illustrated below.

The equity, income and expense account balances (in running balance format) after the adjusting entries are posted are shown for Intellect Management Services in figure 5.5. (These accounts were shown in figure 4.13 on pages 140–1 in T-account format.)

Figure 5.5 Equity accounts after adjusting entries and before closing entries

The Capital and Temporary Accounts of
INTELLECT MANAGEMENT SERVICES
after adjusting entries and *before* closing entries are posted

ACCOUNT **M. Mooney, Capital**   Account No. **300**

Date	Explanation	Post Ref	Debit	Credit	Balance
2013 June 1		1		240 000	240 000

ACCOUNT **M. Mooney, Drawings**   Account No. **310**

Date	Explanation	Post Ref	Debit	Credit	Balance
2013 June 23		2	1 200		1 200

ACCOUNT **Management Services Revenue**   Account No. **400**

Date	Explanation	Post Ref	Debit	Credit	Balance
2013 June 15		1		8 400	8 400
19		2		10 800	19 200

ACCOUNT **Appraisal Fees Revenue**   Account No. **401**

Date	Explanation	Post Ref	Debit	Credit	Balance
2013 June 23		2		500	500

ACCOUNT **Marketing Services Revenue**   Account No. **402**

Date	Explanation	Post Ref	Debit	Credit	Balance
2013 June 30	Adj. ent. (h)	3		800	800

ACCOUNT **Salaries Expense**   Account No. **500**

Date	Explanation	Post Ref	Debit	Credit	Balance
2013 June 22		2	7 600		7 600
30	Adj. ent. (e)	3	3 980		11 580

ACCOUNT **Telephone Expense**   Account No. **510**

Date	Explanation	Post Ref	Debit	Credit	Balance
2013 June 30		2	160		160

(continued)

Figure 5.5 *continued*

ACCOUNT **Advertising Expense**   Account No. **520**

Date	Explanation	Post Ref	Debit	Credit	Balance
2013 June 6		1	240		240

ACCOUNT **Insurance Expense**   Account No. **521**

Date	Explanation	Post Ref	Debit	Credit	Balance
2013 June 30	Adj. ent. (a)	3	80		80

ACCOUNT **Office Supplies Expense**   Account No. **530**

Date	Explanation	Post Ref	Debit	Credit	Balance
2013 June 30	Adj. ent. (b)	3	160		160

ACCOUNT **Depreciation Expense — Office Equipment**   Account No. **540**

Date	Explanation	Post Ref	Debit	Credit	Balance
2013 June 30	Adj. ent. (c)	3	200		200

ACCOUNT **Depreciation Expense — Building**   Account No. **541**

Date	Explanation	Post Ref	Debit	Credit	Balance
2013 June 30	Adj. ent. (d)	3	500		500

ACCOUNT **Interest Expense**   Account No. **560**

Date	Explanation	Post Ref	Debit	Credit	Balance
2013 June 30	Adj. ent. (f)	3	1 600		1 600

ACCOUNT **Electricity Expense**   Account No. **570**

Date	Explanation	Post Ref	Debit	Credit	Balance
2013 June 30	Adj. ent. (g)	3	420		420

ACCOUNT **Profit or Loss Summary**   Account No. **600**

Date	Explanation	Post Ref	Debit	Credit	Balance
2013					

Closing the income (including revenue) accounts

An income account normally contains a credit balance. Hence, to close the account, it must be debited for an amount equal to its credit balance. The offsetting credit is made to the Profit or Loss Summary account. The compound journal entry needed to close the income accounts is:

	General Journal			Page 4
Date	Particulars	Post Ref	Debit	Credit
2013	**Closing entries**			
June 30	Management Services Revenue	400	19 200	
	Appraisal Fees Revenue	401	500	
(1)	Marketing Services Revenue	402	800	
	Profit or Loss Summary	600		20 500
	(Closing the income accounts)			

In the journal, the adjusting entries are separated from the closing entries by the heading 'Closing entries'. For posting purposes, it is assumed that the closing entries are entered on page 4 of the general journal. Also, account numbers are entered in the posting reference column when the entry is posted to the ledger.

The effect of this entry is to reduce each of the income accounts to a zero balance for the start of the next period and transfer the sum of their credit balances to the credit side of the Profit or Loss Summary account, as shown in figure 5.6.

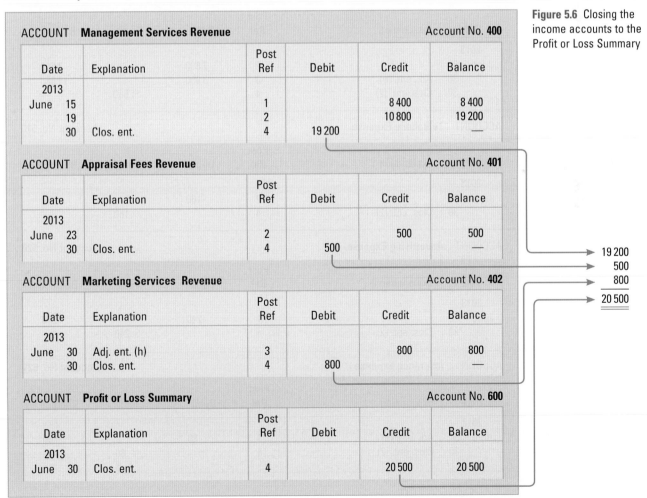

Figure 5.6 Closing the income accounts to the Profit or Loss Summary

ACCOUNT **Management Services Revenue** — Account No. **400**

Date	Explanation	Post Ref	Debit	Credit	Balance
2013					
June 15		1		8 400	8 400
19		2		10 800	19 200
30	Clos. ent.	4	19 200		—

ACCOUNT **Appraisal Fees Revenue** — Account No. **401**

Date	Explanation	Post Ref	Debit	Credit	Balance
2013					
June 23		2		500	500
30	Clos. ent.	4	500		—

ACCOUNT **Marketing Services Revenue** — Account No. **402**

Date	Explanation	Post Ref	Debit	Credit	Balance
2013					
June 30	Adj. ent. (h)	3		800	800
30	Clos. ent.	4	800		—

ACCOUNT **Profit or Loss Summary** — Account No. **600**

Date	Explanation	Post Ref	Debit	Credit	Balance
2013					
June 30	Clos. ent.	4		20 500	20 500

19 200
500
800
20 500

Closing the expense accounts

Expense accounts normally have debit balances. In order to close the expense accounts, each account is therefore credited for an amount equal to its balance, and the Profit or Loss Summary account is debited for the sum of the individual balances. The compound journal entry is entered on page 4 of the journal (underneath closing entry (1) shown on the previous page) as below:

June	30	Profit or Loss Summary	600	14 940	
		Salaries Expense	500		11 580
	(2)	Telephone Expense	510		160
		Advertising Expense	520		240
		Insurance Expense	521		80
		Office Supplies Expense	530		160
		Depreciation Expense – Office Equipment	540		200
		Depreciation Expense – Building	541		500
		Interest Expense	560		1 600
		Electricity Expense	570		420
		(Closing the expense accounts)			

As shown in figure 5.7, the entry reduces the expense accounts to a zero balance and transfers the total of $7470 as a debit to the Profit or Loss Summary account.

Figure 5.7 Closing the expense accounts to the Profit or Loss Summary

ACCOUNT   Salaries Expense   Account No. **500**

Date	Explanation	Post Ref	Debit	Credit	Balance
2013					
June 22		2	7 600		7 600
30	Adj. ent. (e)	3	3 980		11 580
30	Clos. ent. (2)	4		11 580	—

ACCOUNT   Telephone Expense   Account No. **510**

Date	Explanation	Post Ref	Debit	Credit	Balance
2013					
June 30		2	160		160
30	Clos. ent. (2)	4		160	—

ACCOUNT   Advertising Expense   Account No. **520**

Date	Explanation	Post Ref	Debit	Credit	Balance
2013					
June 6		1	240		240
30	Clos. ent. (2)	4		240	—

ACCOUNT   Insurance Expense   Account No. **521**

Date	Explanation	Post Ref	Debit	Credit	Balance
2013					
June 30	Adj. ent. (a)	3	80		80
30	Clos. ent. (2)	4		80	—

11 580
160
240
80
160
200
500
1 600
420

14 940

Figure 5.7 *continued*

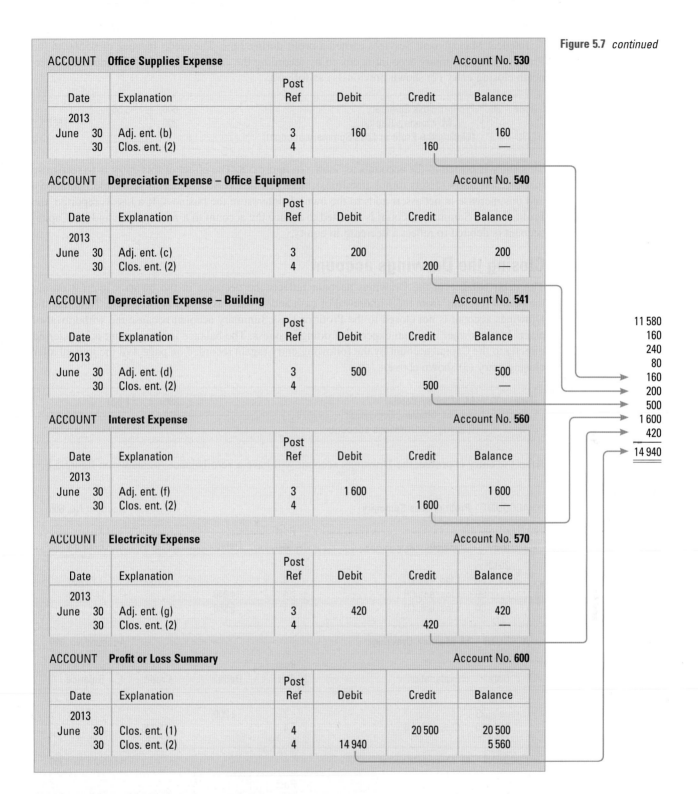

ACCOUNT **Office Supplies Expense** — Account No. **530**

Date	Explanation	Post Ref	Debit	Credit	Balance
2013					
June 30	Adj. ent. (b)	3	160		160
30	Clos. ent. (2)	4		160	—

ACCOUNT **Depreciation Expense – Office Equipment** — Account No. **540**

Date	Explanation	Post Ref	Debit	Credit	Balance
2013					
June 30	Adj. ent. (c)	3	200		200
30	Clos. ent. (2)	4		200	—

ACCOUNT **Depreciation Expense – Building** — Account No. **541**

Date	Explanation	Post Ref	Debit	Credit	Balance
2013					
June 30	Adj. ent. (d)	3	500		500
30	Clos. ent. (2)	4		500	—

ACCOUNT **Interest Expense** — Account No. **560**

Date	Explanation	Post Ref	Debit	Credit	Balance
2013					
June 30	Adj. ent. (f)	3	1 600		1 600
30	Clos. ent. (2)	4		1 600	—

ACCOUNT **Electricity Expense** — Account No. **570**

Date	Explanation	Post Ref	Debit	Credit	Balance
2013					
June 30	Adj. ent. (g)	3	420		420
30	Clos. ent. (2)	4		420	—

ACCOUNT **Profit or Loss Summary** — Account No. **600**

Date	Explanation	Post Ref	Debit	Credit	Balance
2013					
June 30	Clos. ent. (1)	4		20 500	20 500
30	Clos. ent. (2)	4	14 940		5 560

```
11 580
   160
   240
    80
   160
   200
   500
 1 600
   420
14 940
```

Closing the Profit or Loss Summary account

After the first two closing entries are posted, the balances formerly reported in the individual income and expense accounts are summarised in the Profit or Loss Summary account. If income exceeds expenses, a profit is recognised and the Profit or Loss Summary account will contain a credit balance. If expenses exceed income, a loss is indicated and the account will have a debit balance. In either case, the balance is transferred to the Capital account.

Intellect Management Services earned a profit during June. The credit balance of $5560 in the Profit or Loss Summary account is closed by recording the entry on page 4 of the journal (underneath closing entry (2) shown previously) as follows:

June 30	Profit or Loss Summary	600	5 560	
	M. Mooney, Capital	300		5 560
(3)	(Closing the Profit or Loss Summary account)			

This entry is posted to the accounts as shown in figure 5.8. The effect of this entry is to recognise that the net assets (assets minus liabilities) increased this period owing to profitable operations, and this increase in net assets adds to the owner's interest in the business. If a loss is reported, the Profit or Loss Summary account is credited to reduce the account to a zero balance and the Capital account is debited to reflect a decrease in equity.

Closing the Drawings account

The debit balance in the Drawings account reflects the decrease in the owner's interest during the period resulting from the withdrawal of cash and/or other assets for personal use. Note that the Drawings account is not closed to the Profit or Loss Summary account because the withdrawal of assets by the owner is not an expense of doing business. The balance in the account is transferred directly to the Capital account by the following entry (again recorded on page 4 of the journal after closing entry (3) shown above):

June 30	M. Mooney, Capital	300	1 200	
	M. Mooney, Drawings	310		1 200
(4)	(Closing the Drawings account)			

After the entry is posted, the Drawings account will have a zero balance, as shown in figure 5.8.

Figure 5.8 Closing the Profit or Loss Summary and Drawings accounts

ACCOUNT **Profit or Loss Summary**   Account No. **600**

Date	Explanation	Post Ref	Debit	Credit	Balance
2013					
June 30	Clos. ent. (1)	4		20 500	20 500
30	Clos. ent. (2)	4	14 940		5 560
30	Clos. ent. (3)	4	5 560		—

ACCOUNT **M. Mooney, Drawings**   Account No. **310**

Date	Explanation	Post Ref	Debit	Credit	Balance
2013					
June 23		2	1 200		1 200
30	Clos. ent. (4)	4		1 200	—

ACCOUNT **M. Mooney, Capital**   Account No. **300**

Date	Explanation	Post Ref	Debit	Credit	Balance
2013					
June 1		1		240 000	240 000
30	Clos. ent. (3)	4		5 560	245 560
30	Clos. ent. (4)	4	1 200		244 360

Account balances after the closing process

The detailed accounts for Intellect Management Services, after both the adjusting and closing entries have been posted, are presented in figure 5.9. Note that the income (revenue), expense and drawings accounts all have zero balances and are ready for recording transactions in the next period. The balances in the asset, liability and equity accounts are carried forward to the next period and are the only accounts that have balances. These balances are then reported in the balance sheet (also called the statement of financial position) (see later).

Figure 5.9 General ledger after the closing process (running balance accounts)

INTELLECT MANAGEMENT SERVICES

ACCOUNT Cash at Bank   Account No. **100**

Date		Explanation	Post Ref	Debit	Credit	Balance
2013						
June	1	M. Mooney, Capital	1	240 000		240 000
	2	Land/Building/GST Outlays	1		90 000	150 000
	3	Prepaid Insurance/GST Outlays	1		2 112	147 888
	5	Office Equipment/GST Outlays	1		11 920	135 968
	6	Advertising Expense/				
		GST Outlays	1		264	135 704
	22	Salaries Expense	2		7 600	128 104
	23	Appraisal Fees Revenue/				
		GST Collections	2	550		128 654
	23	M. Mooney, Drawings	2		1 200	127 454
	27	Accounts Payable	2		1 364	126 090
	29	Unearned Appraisal Fees/				
		GST Collections	2	616		126 706
	30	Telephone Expense/				
		GST Outlays	2		176	126 530
	30	Accounts Receivable	2	9 240		135 770

ACCOUNT Accounts Receivable   Account No. **104**

Date		Explanation	Post Ref	Debit	Credit	Balance
2013						
June	15	Management Services Revenue/				
		GST Collections	1	9 240		9 240
	19	Management Services Revenue/				
		GST Collections	2	11 880		21 120
	30	Cash at Bank	2		9 240	11 880
	30	Adj. ent. (h)	3	800		12 680

ACCOUNT Prepaid Insurance   Account No. **110**

Date		Explanation	Post Ref	Debit	Credit	Balance
2013						
June	3	Cash at Bank	1	1 920		1 920
	30	Adj. ent. (a)	3		80	1 840

ACCOUNT Office Supplies   Account No. **111**

Date		Explanation	Post Ref	Debit	Credit	Balance
2013						
June	5	Accounts Payable	1	1 240		1 240
	30	Adj. ent. (b)	3		160	1 080

(continued)

Figure 5.9 *continued*

ACCOUNT **GST Outlays**   Account No. **120**

Date	Explanation	Post Ref	Debit	Credit	Balance
2013					
June 2	Cash at Bank/Mortgage Payable	1	30 000		30 000
3	Cash at Bank	1	192		30 192
5	Accounts Payable	1	124		30 316
5	Cash at Bank/Accounts Payable	1	1 920		32 236
6	Cash at Bank	1	24		32 260
30	Cash at Bank	2	16		32 276

ACCOUNT **Land**   Account No. **150**

Date	Explanation	Post Ref	Debit	Credit	Balance
2013					
June 2	Cash at Bank/Mortgage Payable	1	120 000		120 000

ACCOUNT **Building**   Account No. **160**

Date	Explanation	Post Ref	Debit	Credit	Balance
2013					
June 2	Cash at Bank/Mortgage Payable	1	180 000		180 000

ACCOUNT **Accumulated Depreciation – Building**   Account No. **161**

Date	Explanation	Post Ref	Debit	Credit	Balance
2013					
June 30	Adj. ent. (d)	3		500	500

ACCOUNT **Office Equipment**   Account No. **170**

Date	Explanation	Post Ref	Debit	Credit	Balance
2013					
June 5	Cash at Bank/Accounts Payable	1	19 200		19 200

ACCOUNT **Accumulated Depreciation – Office Equipment**   Account No. **171**

Date	Explanation	Post Ref	Debit	Credit	Balance
2013					
June 30	Adj. ent. (c)	3		200	200

ACCOUNT **Accounts Payable**   Account No. **200**

Date	Explanation	Post Ref	Debit	Credit	Balance
2013					
June 5	Office Supplies/GST Outlays	1		1 364	1 364
5	Office Equipment/GST Outlays	1		9 200	10 564
27	Cash at Bank	2	1 364		9 200

Figure 5.9 *continued*

ACCOUNT   **Salaries Payable**   Account No. **210**

Date	Explanation	Post Ref	Debit	Credit	Balance
2013 June 30	Adj. ent. (e)	3		3 980	3 980

ACCOUNT   **Interest Payable**   Account No. **215**

Date	Explanation	Post Ref	Debit	Credit	Balance
2013 June 30	Adj. ent. (f)	3		1 600	1 600

ACCOUNT   **Electricity Account Payable**   Account No. **216**

Date	Explanation	Post Ref	Debit	Credit	Balance
2013 June 30	Adj. ent. (g)	3		420	420

ACCOUNT   **Unearned Appraisal Fees**   Account No. **220**

Date	Explanation	Post Ref	Debit	Credit	Balance
2013 June 29	Cash at Bank	2		560	560

ACCOUNT   **GST Collections**   Account No. **250**

Date	Explanation	Post Ref	Debit	Credit	Balance
2013 June 15	Accounts Receivable	1		840	840
19	Accounts Receivable	2		1 080	1 920
23	Cash at Bank	2		50	1 970
29	Cash at Bank	2		56	2 026

ACCOUNT   **Mortgage Payable**   Account No. **260**

Date	Explanation	Post Ref	Debit	Credit	Balance
2013 June 2	Land/Buildings/GST Outlays	1		240 000	240 000

ACCOUNT   **M. Mooney, Capital**   Account No. **300**

Date	Explanation	Post Ref	Debit	Credit	Balance
2013 June 1	Cash at Bank	1		240 000	240 000
30	Clos. ent. (3)	4		5 560	245 560
30	Clos. ent. (4)	4	1 200		244 360

(continued)

Figure 5.9 *continued*

ACCOUNT **M. Mooney, Drawings**   Account No. **310**

Date		Explanation	Post Ref	Debit	Credit	Balance
2013						
June	23	Cash at Bank	2	1 200		1 200
	30	Clos. ent. (4)	4		1 200	—

ACCOUNT **Management Services Revenue**   Account No. **400**

Date		Explanation	Post Ref	Debit	Credit	Balance
2013						
June	15	Accounts Receivable	1		8 400	8 400
	19	Accounts Receivable	2		10 800	19 200
	30	Clos. ent. (1)	4	19 200		—

ACCOUNT **Appraisal Fees Revenue**   Account No. **401**

Date		Explanation	Post Ref	Debit	Credit	Balance
2013						
June	23	Cash at Bank	2		500	500
	30	Clos. ent. (1)	4	500		—

ACCOUNT **Marketing Services Revenue**   Account No. **402**

Date		Explanation	Post Ref	Debit	Credit	Balance
2013						
June	30	Adj. ent. (h)	3		800	800
	30	Clos. ent. (1)	4	800		—

ACCOUNT **Salaries Expense**   Account No. **500**

Date		Explanation	Post Ref	Debit	Credit	Balance
2013						
June	22	Cash at Bank	2	7 600		7 600
	30	Adj. ent. (e)	3	3 980		11 580
	30	Clos. ent. (2)	4		11 580	—

ACCOUNT **Telephone Expense**   Account No. **510**

Date		Explanation	Post Ref	Debit	Credit	Balance
2013						
June	30	Cash at Bank	2	160		160
	30	Clos. ent. (2)	4		160	—

ACCOUNT **Advertising Expense**   Account No. **520**

Date		Explanation	Post Ref	Debit	Credit	Balance
2013						
June	6	Cash at Bank	1	240		240
	30	Clos. ent. (2)	4		240	—

Figure 5.9 *continued*

ACCOUNT **Insurance Expense**   Account No. **521**

Date		Explanation	Post Ref	Debit	Credit	Balance
2013						
June	30	Adj. ent. (a)	3	80		80
	30	Clos. ent. (2)	4		80	—

ACCOUNT **Office Supplies Expense**   Account No. **530**

Date		Explanation	Post Ref	Debit	Credit	Balance
2013						
June	30	Adj. ent. (b)	3	160		160
	30	Clos. ent. (2)	4		160	—

ACCOUNT **Depreciation Expense – Office Equipment**   Account No. **540**

Date		Explanation	Post Ref	Debit	Credit	Balance
2013						
June	30	Adj. ent. (c)	3	200		200
	30	Clos. ent. (2)	4		200	—

ACCOUNT **Depreciation Expense – Building**   Account No. **541**

Date		Explanation	Post Ref	Debit	Credit	Balance
2013						
June	30	Adj. ent. (d)	3	500		500
	30	Clos. ent. (2)	4		500	—

ACCOUNT **Interest Expense**   Account No. **560**

Date		Explanation	Post Ref	Debit	Credit	Balance
2013						
June	30	Adj. ent. (f)	3	1 600		1 600
	30	Clos. ent. (2)	4		1 600	—

ACCOUNT **Electricity Expense**   Account No. **570**

Date		Explanation	Post Ref	Debit	Credit	Balance
2013						
June	30	Adj. ent. (g)	3	420		420
	30	Clos. ent. (2)	4		420	—

ACCOUNT **Profit or Loss Summary**   Account No. **600**

Date		Explanation	Post Ref	Debit	Credit	Balance
2013						
June	30	Clos. ent. (1)	4		20 500	20 500
	30	Clos. ent. (2)	4	14 940		5 560
	30	Clos. ent. (3)	4	5 560		—

Figure 5.9 illustrates how running balance accounts of Intellect Management Services would appear in the ledger after adjusting and closing entries have been posted. If T accounts are prepared in the ledger, it is necessary formally to close off the temporary accounts at the end of the financial year by inserting totals, and to balance all the permanent accounts. Unlike the running balance accounts, T accounts do not show continuous balances. The ledger of Intellect Management Services based on T accounts is presented in figure 5.10.

Figure 5.10 General ledger after completion of the closing process (T-account format)

General Ledger

Cash at Bank — Account No. 100

2013				2013			
1/6	M. Mooney, Capital	(1)	240 000	2/6	Land/Building/ GST Outlays	(1)	90 000
23/6	Appraisal Fees Rev./ GST Collections	(2)	550	3/6	Prepaid Insurance/ GST Outlays	(1)	2 112
29/6	Unearned Appraisal Fees/GST Collections	(2)	616	5/6	Office Equipment/ GST Outlays	(1)	11 920
30/6	Accounts Receivable	(2)	9 240	6/6	Advertising Expense/ GST Outlays	(1)	264
				22/6	Salary Expense	(2)	7 600
				23/6	M. Mooney, Drawings	(2)	1 200
				27/6	Accounts Payable	(2)	1 364
				30/6	Telephone Expense/ GST Outlays	(2)	176
				30/6	Balance c/d		135 770
			250 406				250 406
1/7	Balance b/d		135 770				

Accounts Receivable — Account No. 104

2013				2013			
15/6	Man. Services Rev./ GST Collections	(1)	9 240	30/6	Cash at Bank	(2)	9 240
19/6	Man. Services Rev./ GST Collections	(2)	11 880				
30/6	Adj. ent. (h)	(3)	800	30/6	Balance c/d		12 680
			21 920				21 920
1/7	Balance b/d		12 680				

Prepaid Insurance — Account No. 110

2013				2013			
3/6	Cash at Bank/GST Outlays	(1)	1 920	30/6	Adj. ent. (a)	(3)	80
				30/6	Balance c/d		1 840
			1 920				1 920
1/7	Balance b/d		1 840				

Office Supplies — Account No. 111

2013				2013			
5/6	Accounts Payable	(1)	1 240	30/6	Adj. ent. (b)	(3)	160
				30/6	Balance c/d		1 080
			1 240				1 240
1/7	Balance b/d		1 080				

Figure 5.10 *continued*

GST Outlays					Account No. **120**
2013				2013	
2/6	Cash at Bank/			30/6 Balance c/d	32 276
	Mortgage Payable	(1)	30 000		
3/6	Cash at Bank	(1)	192		
5/6	Accounts Payable	(1)	124		
5/6	Cash at Bank/				
	Accounts Payable	(1)	1 920		
6/6	Cash at Bank	(1)	24		
30/6	Cash at Bank	(2)	16		
			32 276		32 276
1/7	Balance b/d		32 276		

Land					Account No. **150**
2013				2013	
2/6	Cash at Bank/				
	Mortgage Payable	(1)	120 000	30/6 Balance c/d	120 000
1/7	Balance b/d		120 000		

Building					Account No. **160**
2013				2013	
2/6	Cash at Bank/				
	Mortgage Payable	(1)	180 000	30/6 Balance c/d	180 000
1/7	Balance b/d		180 000		

Accumulated Depreciation – Building					Account No. **161**
2013				2013	
30/6	Balance c/d		500	30/6 Adj. ent. (d)	(3)	500
				1/7 Balance b/d		500

Office Equipment					Account No. **170**
2013				2013	
5/6	Cash at Bank/				
	Accounts Payable	(1)	19 200	30/6 Balance c/d	19 200
1/7	Balance b/d		19 200		

Accumulated Depreciation – Office Equip.					Account No. **171**
2013				2013	
30/6	Balance c/d		200	30/6 Adj. ent. (c)	(3)	200
				1/7 Balance b/d		200

Accounts Payable					Account No. **200**
2013				2013	
27/6	Cash at Bank	(2)	1 364	5/6 Office Supplies/GST Outlays	(1)	1 364
30/6	Balance c/d		9 200	5/6 Office Equipment/GST Outlays	(1)	9 200
			10 564			10 564
				1/7 Balance b/d		9 200

(continued)

Figure 5.10 *continued*

Salaries Payable — Account No. 210

2013				2013			
30/6	Balance c/d		3 980	30/6	Adj. ent. (e)		3 980
				1/7	Balance b/d		3 980

Interest Payable — Account No. 215

2013				2013			
30/6	Balance c/d		1 600	30/6	Adj. ent. (f)	(3)	1 600
				1/7	Balance b/d		1 600

Electricity Account Payable — Account No. 216

2013				2013			
30/6	Balance c/d		420	30/6	Adj. ent. (h)	(3)	420
				1/7	Balance b/d		420

Unearned Appraisal Fees — Account No. 220

2013				2013			
30/6	Balance c/d		560	30/6	Cash at Bank	(2)	560
				1/7	Balance b/d		560

GST Collections — Account No. 250

2013				2013			
30/6	Balance c/d		2 026	15/6	Accounts Receivable	(1)	840
				19/6	Accounts Receivable	(2)	1 080
				23/6	Cash at Bank	(2)	50
				29/6	Cash at Bank	(2)	56
			2 026				2 026
				1/7	Balance b/d		2 026

Mortgage Payable — Account No. 260

2013				2013			
30/6	Balance c/d	(1)	240 000	2/6	Land/Buildings/GST Outlays	(1)	240 000
				1/7	Balance b/d		240 000

M. Mooney, Capital — Account No. 300

2013				2013			
30/6	Clos. ent. (4)	(4)	1 200	1/6	Cash at Bank	(1)	240 000
30/6	Balance c/d		244 360	30/6	Clos. ent. (3)	(4)	5 560
			245 560				245 560
				1/7	Balance b/d		244 360

M. Mooney, Drawings — Account No. 310

2013				2013			
23/6	Cash at Bank	(2)	1 200	30/6	Clos. ent. (4)	(4)	1 200

Figure 5.10 *continued*

Management Services Revenue   Account No. **400**

2013				2013			
30/6	Clos. ent. (1)	(4)	19 200	15/6	Accounts Receivable	(1)	8 400
				19/6	Accounts Receivable	(2)	10 800
			19 200				19 200

Appraisal Fees Revenue   Account No. **401**

2013				2013			
30/6	Clos. ent. (1)	(4)	500	23/6	Cash at Bank	(2)	500

Marketing Services Revenue   Account No. **402**

2013				2013			
30/6	Clos. ent. (1)	(4)	800	30/6	Adj. ent. (h)	(3)	800

Salaries Expense   Account No. **500**

2013				2013			
22/6	Cash at Bank	(2)	7 600	30/6	Clos. ent. (2)	(4)	11 580
30/6	Adj. ent. (e)	(3)	3 980				
			11 580				11 580

Telephone Expense   Account No. **510**

2013				2013			
30/6	Cash at Bank	(2)	160	30/6	Clos. ent. (2)	(4)	160

Advertising Expense   Account No. **520**

2013				2013			
6/6	Cash at Bank	(1)	240	30/6	Clos. ent. (2)	(4)	240

Insurance Expense   Account No. **521**

2013				2013			
30/6	Adj. ent. (a)	(3)	80	30/6	Clos. ent. (2)	(4)	80

Office Supplies Expense   Account No. **530**

2013				2013			
30/6	Adj. ent. (b)	(3)	160	30/6	Clos. ent. (2)	(4)	160

Depreciation Expense – Office Equipment   Account No. **540**

2013				2013			
30/6	Adj. ent. (c)	(3)	200	30/6	Clos. ent. (2)	(4)	200

Depreciation Expense – Building   Account No. **541**

2013				2013			
30/6	Adj. ent. (d)	(3)	500	30/6	Clos. ent. (2)	(4)	500

(continued)

Figure 5.10 *continued*

Interest Expense							Account No. **560**	
2013					2013			
30/6	Adj. ent. (f)		(3)	1 600	30/6	Clos. ent. (2)	(4)	1 600

Electricity Expense							Account No. **570**	
2013					2013			
30/6	Adj. ent. (g)		(3)	420	30/6	Clos. ent. (2)	(4)	420

Profit or Loss Summary							Account No. **600**	
2013					2013			
30/6	Clos. ent. (2)	(4)	14 940		30/6	Clos. ent. (1)	(4)	20 500
30/6	Clos. ent. (3)	(4)	5 560					
			20 500					20 500

A computerised accounting system offers economy of time and effort when it comes to closing entries. The computerised system may be programmed to close off the temporary accounts in the general ledger whenever instructed to do so.

BUSINESS KNOWLEDGE

The business of poverty — are we there yet?

Companies are forming alliances to help alleviate the plight of the poor.

In September 2000, Australia, along with 188 other countries, signed the millennium declaration. It was a pledge by each signatory country to try to make eight goals — in the area of economy, health, human rights and environment — universal by 2015.

The millennium development goals (MDGs) are:
1. Halving extreme poverty and hunger.
2. Achieving universal primary education.
3. Achieving gender equality.
4. Reducing child mortality by two-thirds.
5. Reducing maternal mortality by three-quarters.
6. Reversing the spread of HIV/AIDS, malaria and other major diseases.
7. Ensuring environmental sustainability.
8. Creating a global partnership for development.

But World Vision Australia was startled to hear in late 2005 that when consulting firm The Allen Group asked CEOs from 20 of Australia's largest companies how they felt about MDGs, none had a clear idea what they were...

[I]n 2006, Tim Costello, World Vision Australia's CEO, [with others]...came up with the idea of the Business for Poverty Relief Alliance... The alliance's formal objectives state simply that companies should align their activities to meeting the MDGs. Costello would like them to go a bit further and describe — preferably in their annual reports — how they are doing it...

Some suggestions for getting started:
- Develop safe, affordable products for poor communities.
- Invest in local research and development.
- Ensure good working conditions in joint ventures.
- Ask suppliers about the wages and benefits they pay workers.

Source: Adapted from Prue Moodie, 'The business of poverty', *InTheBlack*.

Learning objective 5

Prepare a post-closing trial balance

5.5 The post-closing trial balance

After the closing entries have been posted, it is desirable to prepare a **post-closing trial balance** to verify the equality of debits and credits in the general ledger, and confirm that the ledger is 'in balance'. At this point, only the permanent accounts will have balances. It is these balances that are then used to prepare the end-of-period post-closing trial balance and the balance sheet. These balances are also the starting point for the next accounting period. A post-closing trial balance for Intellect Management Services is presented in figure 5.11.

INTELLECT MANAGEMENT SERVICES
Post-Closing Trial Balance
as at 30 June 2013

Account	Account no.	Account balance Debit	Account balance Credit
Cash at bank	100	$135 770	
Accounts receivable	104	12 680	
Prepaid insurance	110	1 840	
Office supplies	111	1 080	
GST outlays	120	32 276	
Land	150	120 000	
Building	160	180 000	
Accumulated depreciation – building	161		$ 500
Office equipment	170	19 200	
Accumulated depreciation – office equipment	171		200
Accounts payable	200		9 200
Salaries payable	210		3 980
Interest payable	215		1 600
Electricity account payable	216		420
Unearned appraisal fees	220		560
GST collections	250		2 026
Mortgage payable	260		240 000
M. Mooney, Capital	300		244 360
		$502 846	$502 846

Figure 5.11 Post-closing trial balance

5.6 Accrual entries in subsequent periods

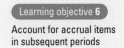

Learning objective 6

Account for accrual items in subsequent periods

As part of the adjusting process, entries must be made to recognise expenses that have been incurred but not yet paid for or recorded, and also revenues for services performed but not yet collected or recorded. Recall that such adjustments are collectively called accruals. Adjusting entries (e) to (h) illustrated in figure 5.4 are all examples of accruals. In subsequent periods, cash received or paid for accruals must be analysed to apportion the amount involved correctly between two or more periods.

For example, during June, $7600 in salaries was paid and $3980 in unpaid salaries was accrued at the end of June [adjusting entry (e)] to be paid on 6 July. The entry below is required on 6 July, assuming a $7400 payment is made for salaries earned from 23 June to 6 July:

July	6	Salaries Payable	210	3 980	
		Salaries Expense	500	3 420	
		Cash at Bank	100		7 400
		(Payment of salaries for the period 23 June to 6 July)			

After posting this entry, the Salaries Payable and Salaries Expense accounts appear as follows:

ACCOUNT Salaries Payable   Account No. **210**

Date	Explanation	Post Ref	Debit	Credit	Balance
2013					
June 30	Adj. ent. (e)	3		3 890	3 890
July 6	Cash at Bank/Salaries Expense	5	3 890		—

ACCOUNT	Salaries Expense					Account No. **500**
Date	Explanation	Post Ref	Debit	Credit		Balance
2013						
June 22		2	7 600			7 600
30	Adj. ent. (3)	3	3 980			11 580
30	Clos. ent. (2)	4		11 580		—
July 6	Salaries Payable/Cash at Bank	5	3 420			3 420

On 1 July, the Salaries Payable account has a credit balance of $3980, and the Salaries Expense account has a zero balance. The zero balance results from making an entry on 30 June to close all expense accounts. Because the $7400 payment is for salaries earned during two different accounting periods, the payment must be divided into two elements. First, the $3980 debit settles the liability for the salaries earned by employees in June that were reported as an expense in June. The second debit of $3420 properly recognises as an expense that portion of the payment made for salaries incurred in July. A similar analysis is required for the other accruals when a cash payment is made or cash is received after 30 June.

5.7 Reversing entries
Reversal of accrual entries

Learning objective 7

Explain reversing entries and how to record them

An alternative approach to the treatment of accrual entries in subsequent periods, as discussed in the previous section, is the preparation of **reversing entries**. This involves adding another step to the accounting cycle after the closing entries have been posted to the ledger (see step 12 in figure 5.1, p. 178). Reversing entries are dated as of the first day of the next accounting period and are so called because they reverse the effects of certain adjusting entries that were made on the last day of the preceding accounting period. Reversing entries are an accounting technique made to simplify the recording of regular transactions in the next period.

To illustrate reversing entries, we will continue with the accrued salaries adjustment for Intellect Management Services. Recall that $7600 in salaries was paid during June and that $3980 was accrued on 30 June. Salaries earned for the period 23 June to 6 July for the amount of $7400 are to be paid on 6 July. Throughout an accounting period, the normal entry to record the payment of salaries is to debit Salaries Expense and credit Cash at Bank. (Wages and salaries are exempt from GST.)

At the end of June, accrued salaries were recorded in the following *adjusting entry* (e):

June 30 (e)	Salaries Expense	500	3 980	
	Salaries Payable	210		3 980
	(Unpaid salaries at the end of June)			

At the end of the period, the balance of $11 580 in the Salaries Expense account is closed to the Profit or Loss Summary account and the Salaries Payable balance of $3980 is reported as a current liability in the balance sheet.

If the adjusting entry is not reversed, the following entry is made on 6 July to record payment (as illustrated in the previous section):

July 6	Salaries Payable	210	3 980	
	Salaries Expense	500	3 420	
	Cash at Bank	100		7 400
	(Payment of salaries for the period 23 June to 6 July)			

Note that this entry requires two debits, a variation from the normal entry of one debit to the Salaries Expense account. Thus, a change from the normal procedures is necessary and requires that the adjusting entry or the Salaries Expense account in the general ledger for the previous period be referred to in order to divide the payment between the two accounts.

If the adjusting entry is reversed on 1 July, this will simplify the 6 July entry. The reversing entry is:

July	1	Salaries Payable	210	3 980	
		Salaries Expense	500		3 980
		(Reversing the adjusting entry to accrue unpaid salaries at the end of the previous period)			

Compare this reversing entry with the adjusting entry on 30 June. Observe that the debit and credit amounts are the same in both entries, but the account debited (Salaries Expense) in the adjusting entry is credited in the reversing entry, and the account credited (Salaries Payable) in the adjusting entry is debited in the reversing entry. In other words, the reversing entry is the opposite of the adjusting entry.

The debit in the reversing entry transfers the liability to the expense account. This produces a temporary credit balance of $3980 in the expense account since it had a zero balance before the reversing entry as a result of the closing process. The business can now make the normal entry to record the payment on 6 July as follows, without having to refer to the previous period to find any accruals of salaries:

July	6	Salaries Expense	500	7 400	
		Cash at Bank	100		7 400
		(Payment of salaries for the period 23 June to 6 July)			

The debit of $7400 is partially offset by the credit of $3980 made in the reversing entry, leaving a debit balance of $3420 in the Salaries Expense account, which is the expense for July.

As shown in figure 5.12 (p. 202), the two approaches produce identical results. Salaries expenses for June and July are $11 580 and $3420 respectively, and a liability for $3980 is reported in the balance sheet on 30 June.

Reversing entries are also useful in relation to *accrued income* (*revenue*) items which have resulted in adjusting entries. For example, a bank may have thousands of outstanding loans. At the end of the period, interest earned but not received must be accrued in order to report correctly interest revenue and interest receivable in the financial statements. If a reversing entry is not made, each time an interest payment is received in the next period an employee must refer back to the list of accruals in order to divide the amount of the payment between the reduction in the receivable balance and the interest earned in the current period.

If the adjusting entry is reversed, however, the receipt of cash for interest is simply recorded as a debit to Cash at Bank and a credit to Interest Revenue. In this case, reversing entries result in saving a great deal of time since an employee does not have to allocate each interest payment between two periods.

As an additional example of accrued revenue where a reversing entry is useful, assume that Intellect Management Services normally receives $3200 (plus GST) on the fifteenth of each month for rent receivable in arrears on business premises in a shopping centre.

The following adjusting entry needs to be made on 30 June in order to recognise rent revenue receivable for the last 2 weeks of June (no tax invoice has yet been issued):

June	30	Rent Receivable	1 600	
		Rent Revenue		1 600
		(Revenue not received at end of June)		

Figure 5.12 Illustration of reversing entries

	Without reversing entry			With reversing entry		
1. *Payment of salaries*						
22/6	Salaries Expense	7 600		Salaries Expense	7 600	
	Cash at Bank		7 600	Cash at Bank		7 600
2. *Adjusting entry to accrue salaries*						
30/6	Salaries Expense	3 980		Salaries Expense	3 980	
	Salaries Payable		3 980	Salaries Payable		3 980
3. *Closing entry*						
30/6	Profit or Loss Summary	11 580		Profit or Loss Summary	11 580	
	Salaries Expense		11 580	Salaries Expense		11 580
4. *Reversing entry*						
1/7	No entry is made			Salaries Payable	3 980	
				Salaries Expense		3 980
5. *Payment of salaries*						
6/7	Salaries Payable	3 980		Salaries Expense	7 400	
	Salaries Expense	3 420		Cash at Bank		7 400
	Cash at Bank		7 400			

Without reversing entry

Salaries Payable				Salaries Expense			
6/7	3 980	30/6	3 980	22/6	7 600		
					3 980	30/6	11 580
					11 580		11 580
				6/7	3 420		

Cash at Bank			
		22/6	7 600
		6/7	7 400

With reversing entry

Salaries Payable				Salaries Expense			
1/7	3 980	30/6	3 980	22/6	7 600		
					3 980	30/6	11 580
					11 580		11 580
				6/7	7 400	1/7	3 980

Cash at Bank			
		22/6	7 600
		6/7	7 400

At the end of the period, the balance in the Rent Revenue account is closed to the Profit or Loss Summary, and Rent Receivable appears as an asset in the balance sheet.

If the adjusting entry is not reversed, the journal entry below needs to be made on 15 July to record receipt of cash.

July	15	Cash at Bank	3 520	
		Rent Receivable		1 600
		Rent Revenue		1 600
		GST Collections		320
		(Receipt of rent in arrears for the month from 16 June to 15 July)		

To avoid making a compound entry on 15 July and the need to refer back to the adjusting entry made on 30 June, a reversing entry may be made on 1 July to reverse the effects of the adjusting entry, as follows:

July	1	Rent Revenue	1 600	
		Rent Receivable		1 600
		(Reversing the adjusting entry)		

By making the reversing entry, the entry to record receipt of cash on 15 July is simplified and the normal entry is made as follows:

July	15	Cash at Bank		3 520	
		Rent Revenue			3 200
		GST Collections			320
		(Receipt of rent in arrears for the month from 16 June to 15 July)			

As with the Salaries Expense accrual illustrated in figure 5.12, the results for this Rent Revenue accrual are the same under both approaches. A reversing entry simplifies the entry made on 15 July to record the cash receipt, and avoids any necessity on 15 July to refer to the adjusting entries made at the end of the previous accounting period.

A thorough knowledge of reversing entries is not essential to the understanding of accounting concepts and procedures. It should be emphasised that they are optional and are made to facilitate the recording of routine transactions in future periods. Furthermore, only certain adjusting entries should be reversed if it is beneficial to do so. *A general rule is that adjusting entries for accruals can be reversed*, i.e. when the cash flow has not yet occurred.

Reversal of deferral entries

In relation to deferrals, adjusting entries are made for prepaid expenses and unearned or precollected revenue, as illustrated in figure 4.2 (p. 127). The need for reversing entries to reverse the effects of any adjusting entries depends on whether the initial recording of a transaction occurs in a permanent account, i.e. asset or liability. To illustrate, consider the purchase on 3 June of a 24-month fire and business liability insurance policy for $1920 plus $192 GST by Intellect Management Services. The entry to record this purchase was made to a permanent asset account, Prepaid Insurance, as follows:

June	3	Prepaid Insurance	110	1 920	
		GST Outlays	120	192	
		Cash at Bank	100		2 112
		(Purchase of a 24-month fire and business liability insurance policy)			

The adjusting entry (a) at 30 June for the expiration of 1 month's insurance was recorded as:

June	30	Insurance Expense	521	80	
(a)		Prepaid Insurance	110		80
		(Adjusting entry to record expiration of 1 month's insurance)			

In this circumstance, where the adjusting entry is merely recording the gradual expiration of the asset as time goes by, there is no need for any reversal of the adjusting entry in the new accounting period in order to facilitate the accounting procedure. All that needs to be done is to gradually reduce the value of the asset at the end of each accounting period by way of adjusting entries. Similarly, there is no need for reversing entries in relation to adjustments for supplies used or for depreciation expense, where the initial entry for purchase of the asset is placed in an asset account.

However, some entities, on initial purchase of an asset, make a debit entry to an expense account. For example, Intellect Management Services could have recorded the purchase of its insurance policy in the following entry, as previously discussed in chapter 4 (p. 129):

June	3	Insurance Expense	521	1 920	
		GST Outlays	120	192	
		Cash at Bank	100		2 112
		(Purchase of a 24-month fire and business liability insurance policy)			

If this initial entry is made, the adjusting entry (aa) at 30 June to record the portion of insurance premium unexpired is as follows:

June 30 (aa)	Prepaid Insurance Insurance Expense (Adjusting entry to record portion of insurance policy unexpired)	110 521	1 840	1 840

The adjusting entry in this case needs to recognise the existence of the Prepaid Insurance asset, and leaves only $80 in the expense account, as in the first case (see the previous page). The entity then has two options at the beginning of the new period:

1. Leave the amount of $1840 in the Prepaid Insurance account for the coming period and make adjusting entries at the end to write down the value of the asset, in the same way that adjusting entry (a) is made.
2. Make a reversing entry on the first day of the period to reverse adjusting entry (aa). In other words, the Insurance Expense account is reopened on the first day of the new period, and a further adjusting entry is necessary at the end of the period only if part of the Insurance Expense balance is still unexpired.

If option 2 is selected, then reversing entries are to be made also for all deferrals where the initial acquisition of the asset is recorded in an expense account. This particular procedure is not favoured by the authors, who believe that all assets should initially be recorded in asset accounts, as in the first case mentioned previously. If this procedure is followed, reversing entries for deferrals are unnecessary.

Applying similar reasoning, whenever precollected revenue is recorded in a liability account, e.g. subscriptions in advance, there is no need to apply reversing entries to any adjusting entries which are gradually reducing the liability over time. Nevertheless, if an entity initially records precollected revenue in an income (revenue) account, the entity may choose to use reversing entries for any adjusting entry made at the end of the period. As previously indicated, the authors favour the initial recognition of precollected revenue in a permanent account (liability), so there is no need for reversing entries in this situation.

In computerised accounting systems, reversing entries can be programmed to be done automatically on the first day of the new accounting period.

BUSINESS KNOWLEDGE

Malaysia moves to a GST

The Malaysian government has announced that it intends to implement a goods and services tax (GST) by mid-2011. The government first announced the move in 2004, but it was put on hold shortly thereafter. It is now set to debate the *Goods and Services Tax Bill* this month after it was presented for a first reading in the Malaysian parliament in December 2009.

The proposed GST is expected to replace the existing sales and services tax (SST) system, which the government believes is more costly for businesses and consumers. The GST is also designed to broaden the country's indirect tax base and is thus expected to raise an additional RM1.4 billion a year. At the same time, it is expected that the GST will provide businesses with savings of RM4 billion and exporters RM1.4 billion.

The GST will operate similarly to those in other countries with a GST or VAT (value added tax) system. There will be two rates with the main or standard rate expected to be 4 per cent and a zero rate applicable to most goods and services exported from Malaysia. This compares to GST rates in the closest neighbouring countries of 7 per cent in Singapore and Thailand and 10 per cent in Indonesia and Australia.

Source: Garry Addison, Malaysia moves to a GST, *InTheBlack*.

Learning objective 8

Prepare the equity accounts for a partnership and for a company

5.8 Accounting procedures applicable to a partnership or a company

In the preceding illustration, Intellect Management Services was owned by one person, who had elected to operate the business as a single proprietorship or sole trader. Although sole traders are the most numerous form of business organisation in Australia, the majority of business activity is conducted by the corporate form of business organisation. A company is a business entity incorporated under the *Corporations Act 2001* throughout Australia. Another common form of business organisation is the partnership, which is a business owned by two or more people acting as partners. Accounting and reporting for partnerships and companies are similar in most respects to accounting and reporting for sole traders. The financial statements are essentially the same for all three forms of business organisation except for transactions that directly affect the equity accounts. These differences are discussed briefly below. Special accounting problems associated with partnerships and companies are discussed more fully in later chapters.

Accounting for a partnership

In accounting for a partnership, separate Capital and Drawings accounts are maintained for each partner as a minimum. Any investment by a partner is credited to his or her Capital account, and a withdrawal of cash or other assets from the partnership is debited to his or her Drawings account. Any salary paid to a partner is normally regarded as drawings by that partner.

At the end of the accounting period, the Profit or Loss Summary account is closed by the balance, i.e. profit (loss), being allocated to each partner's Capital account in accordance with the partners' profit and loss sharing agreement. Each Drawings account is also closed to the appropriate Capital accounts so that the total of each partner's equity at the end of the period represents his or her capital contribution plus share of the profits as retained by him or her in the business.

Accounting for a company

The owners of a company are called shareholders because their ownership interests are represented by shares held in the company. The equity section of a company balance sheet (statement of financial position) is separated into two main account categories: (1) **share capital**, which represents the amount of assets invested in the company by the shareholders, and (2) **retained earnings** (or **accumulated losses**), which reflect the accumulated profits (or losses) earned by the company and retained in the business.

The investment of assets in a company is recorded by debits to the appropriate asset accounts and a credit to an account called the Share Capital account. When an investment is made in the company, the investors are given shares in the company as evidence of their ownership. For example, assume that Intellect Management Services was organised on 1 January 2013 as a company and initially issued 240 000 shares for $1 each. The simplified entry to record the issue is as follows:

2013				
Jan.	1	Cash at Bank	240 000	
		Share Capital		240 000
		(Issue of 120 000 shares for $1 each in cash)		

Just as the owner of a single proprietorship may periodically withdraw cash from the business in anticipation of profits, cash distributions called **dividends** may be made to the owners of a company. However, before a dividend can be paid, it must be 'declared'. Assume that on 1 December, Intellect Management Services Ltd declared a cash dividend out of retained earnings of 10c per share on the 240 000 shares issued. The dividend is to be paid on 20 December. Entries to record the declaration and payment are:

2013				
Dec.	1	Retained Earnings	24 000	
		Dividend Payable [liability]		24 000
		(Declared a dividend of 10c per share on the 240 000 shares issued)		
	20	Dividend Payable	24 000	
		Cash at Bank		24 000
		(Payment of the dividend liability)		

Dividends are considered a distribution or withdrawal of profits by the owners and are not a cost incurred for the purpose of producing income. Note that, because the dividend declared is debited directly to the Retained Earnings account, no closing entry is necessary (unlike the Drawings account in a sole trader or partnership). Further discussion of accounting for dividends is provided in a later chapter.

If profit for the year ending 31 December 2013 is $50 000, the Profit or Loss Summary account has a credit balance and is closed by the following closing entry:

2013			
Dec. 31	Profit or Loss Summary	50 000	
	Retained Earnings		50 000
	(Transfer of profits)		

At the end of the period, a company often prepares a statement of changes in equity similar to the following:

INTELLECT MANAGEMENT SERVICES LTD
Statement of Changes in Equity
for the year ended 31 December 2013

Share capital, 1 January 2013	$240 000
Share capital, 31 December 2013	240 000
Retained earnings, 1 January 2013	—
Add: Profit for the year	50 000
	50 000
Less: Cash dividends for the year	24 000
Retained earnings, 31 December 2013	$ 26 000

The Retained Earnings account for the year is shown as follows (in T-account format):

Retained Earnings

2013				2013		
1/12	Dividend Payable	24 000		31/12	Profit or Loss Summary	50 000
31/12	Balance c/d	26 000				
		50 000				50 000
				2014		
				1/1	Balance b/d	26 000

Based on the above entries, the equity section of the balance sheet appears as follows:

Balance Sheet (extract)
as at 31 December 2013

EQUITY	
Share capital, (240 000 shares issued for $1)	$240 000
Retained earnings	26 000
Total equity	$266 000

One important difference between the three forms of business organisation is the way income tax is determined. Although all three forms are recognised as separate business entities for accounting purposes, sole traders and partnerships are non-taxpaying entities. Sole traders or partners must include their share of business profit or loss in their own personal tax returns. Thus, income tax expense will not appear in the income statements for a sole trader or a partnership.

Companies, however, are separate taxable entities that must file tax returns and pay tax as assessed by the Australian Taxation Office (ATO). Therefore, in its financial statements, a company must show the amount of income tax expense incurred for the period and any unpaid amount of the tax as a liability. The amount of income tax to be paid each period is determined in accordance with the Income Tax Act. In this book, we use only simplified tax calculations, being the company's profit multiplied by the income tax rate.

KEY TERMS

Accumulated losses, p. 205	Interim statements, p. 179	Retained earnings, p. 205
Closing entries, p. 179	Post-closing trial balance,	Reversing entries, p. 200
Dividends, p. 205	p. 198	Share capital, p. 205

DISCUSSION QUESTIONS

1. In figure 5.1 (p. 178), the accounting cycle is illustrated. Explain the purpose and importance of each step in the cycle.
2. Compare and contrast the purposes of adjusting entries, closing entries and reversing entries.
3. For a sole trader, which accounts generally are involved in closing entries? Why are these accounts closed?
4. So far, we have heard of the existence of three trial balances — the unadjusted trial balance, the adjusted trial balance and the post-closing trial balance. Explain the purpose of each, and indicate the types of account balances that are contained in each.
5. You have been approached by a neighbour who is studying first-year accounting at university. He is very worried about reversing entries and can see no purpose for them. He also finds it very difficult to decide when a reversing entry would be helpful and when it would not. Discuss the major points to include in a suitable tutorial to overcome his concerns.
6. At the end of the preceding period, a company recorded accrued salaries payable of $3500. On 2 July, the second day of the new period, the company debited Salaries Expense and credited Cash at Bank for $4000.
   (a) If a reversing entry had not been made on 1 July, would the financial statements be in error for the month of July? Explain.
   (b) What entry should have been made on 2 July given that a reversing entry was not made?
   (c) If the company made reversing entries, what reversing entry should have been made on 1 July and what entry would then be made on 2 July?
7. The accountant in Bede Cameron's business has never worried about preparing reversing entries. However, a newly employed trainee accountant has strongly suggested to Bede that reversing entries are quite useful. Show, by way of a numerical example involving interest payable, how reversing entries can be used in the business accounts and discuss the benefits that reversing entries can provide.
8. Different equity accounts are used depending on the type of organisation. Illustrate and explain.
9. Explain the difference between the payment of cash dividends by a company and the withdrawal of cash by a sole trader. What is the effect of each on assets? on equity? on profit?
10. 'When preparing interim financial statements, certain steps in the accounting cycle may be omitted.' Discuss.

Exercise 5.1 CLOSING ENTRIES

The following accounts and account balances were taken from the adjusted trial balance columns of the worksheet of Rob's Petwashing Service for the year ended 30 June 2014.

Rob Leigh, Capital	$27 350	Rent Expense	$11 240
Rob Leigh, Drawings	18 000	Advertising Expense	8 316
Service Fees Revenue	77 265	Depreciation Expense	9 800
Interest Revenue	9 400	Sundry Expenses	3 900
Salaries Expense	42 150		

Required

Record the required closing entries for Rob's Petwashing Service.

Exercise 5.2 CLOSING ENTRIES AND EQUITY

The accounts below are taken from the ledger of Bogart Advertising on 30 June 2013, the end of the current financial year.

Required

A. Record the closing entries that affected the accounts.

B. Prepare a statement of changes in equity as at 30 June.

P. Bogart, Capital

30/6	16 230	1/7	8 940
		30/6	12 130

P. Bogart, Drawings

15/8	4 800	30/6	16 230
29/10	3 130		
18/11	2 900		
14/1	5 400		

Profit or Loss Summary

30/6	29 240	30/6	41 370
30/6	12 130		

Exercise 5.3 COMPLETION OF WORKSHEET, PREPARATION OF FINANCIAL STATEMENTS, AND CLOSING ENTRIES

The following unadjusted trial balance was taken from the ledger of Schubert Estate Agency on 31 December 2013.

Account	Debit	Credit
Cash at bank	$100 000	
Accounts receivable	80 000	
Prepaid insurance	20 000	
Equipment	200 000	
Accumulated depreciation – equipment		$ 80 000
Accounts payable		40 000
Karen Schubert, Capital		270 000
Karen Schubert, Drawings	50 000	
Service revenue		320 000
Wages expense	170 000	
Electricity expense	60 000	
Sundry expense	30 000	
	$710 000	$710 000

Required

A. Prepare a 10-column worksheet using the following additional information on 31 December 2013:
   1. Expired insurance, $9000.
   2. Accrued wages, $22000.
   3. Depreciation on equipment, $40000.
B. Prepare an income statement, a statement of changes in equity and a balance sheet.
C. Record the adjusting and closing entries in the general journal.

The adjusted trial balance columns of the worksheet for Johnson's Information Technology Services are as follows.

	JOHNSON'S INFORMATION TECHNOLOGY SERVICES Worksheet (Partial) for the year ended 30 June 2013						
	Adjusted trial balance		Income statement		Balance sheet	
Account	Debit	Credit	Debit	Credit	Debit	Credit
Cash at Bank	2 040					
Accounts Receivable	31 500					
Prepaid Rent	750					
Office Supplies	5 200					
Equipment	67 000					
Accumulated Depreciation		10 400				
Accounts Payable		15 000				
Salaries Payable		3 650				
Unearned Revenue		8 700				
D. Johnson, Capital		50 000				
D. Johnson, Drawings	13 000					
IT Services Revenue		91 520				
Salaries Expense	44 200					
Rent Expense	2 520					
Depreciation Expense	3 350					
Telephone Expense	1 670					
Office Supplies Expense	4 200					
Sundry Expenses	3 840					
	179 270	179 270				
Profit for the period						
Totals						

Required

A. Complete the worksheet.
B. Prepare the closing entries necessary at 30 June 2013, assuming that this date is the end of the entity's accounting period.

Anthony's Framing Services was founded by Anthony McIntosh on 1 January 2013. The adjusted trial balance at 31 December 2013 (the end of the financial year) is shown on page 210.

Required

A. Prepare closing entries to be made on 31 December 2013.
B. Prepare a post-closing trial balance as at 31 December 2013.

ANTHONY'S FRAMING SERVICES
Adjusted Trial Balance
as at 31 December 2013

Account	Debit	Credit
Cash at bank	$ 15 960	
Accounts receivable	25 200	
GST outlays	2 160	
Framing supplies	6 000	
Prepaid insurance	3 000	
Framing equipment	36 000	
Accumulated depreciation – framing equipment		$ 18 000
Accounts payable		6 000
Salaries payable		2 040
Interest payable		3 120
Mortgage payable		7 800
Unearned framing revenue		6 720
GST collections		3 600
Anthony McIntosh, Capital		18 000
Anthony McIntosh, Drawings	14 400	
Framing revenue		62 400
Commission revenue		1 800
Salaries expense	14 040	
Insurance expense	1 080	
Interest expense	600	
Depreciation expense	4 200	
Framing supplies expense	2 040	
Rent expense	4 800	
	$129 480	$129 480

LO 4, 8

Exercise 5.6   CLOSING ENTRIES FOR A COMPANY

The income statement of Eden Gardens Hire Ltd is presented below. During the year, directors declared and paid a dividend of $12 000.

EDEN GARDENS HIRE LTD
Income Statement
for the year ended 30 June 2013

INCOME		
Revenue:		
Hire fees – heavy equipment		$ 57 263
Hire fees – light equipment		46 052
		103 315
EXPENSES		
Salaries expense	$61 000	
Depreciation expense	16 595	
Insurance expense	5 208	
Repairs and maintenance expense	3 150	
Supplies expense	1 400	
Sundry expenses	1 326	
		88 679
PROFIT		$ 14 636

Required

Prepare the necessary general journal entries to close the accounts of the company.

Exercise 5.7 CLOSING ACCOUNTS AND PREPARING THE RETAINED EARNINGS
ACCOUNT FOR A COMPANY

On 1 January 2013, the equity of Brentwood Pty Ltd consisted of share capital of $550 000 and retained earnings of $308 000. During the period, the company declared and paid a cash dividend of $80 000. The general ledger contains only two income statement accounts — Revenues and Expenses. On 31 December 2013, the balance in the Revenues account was $840 000 and the balance in the Expenses account was $637 000.

Required
A. Prepare closing entries.
B. Show the Retained Earnings account at the end of 2013.
C. Calculate the total equity of the company as it would appear in the balance sheet at the end of 2013.

Exercise 5.8 REVERSING ENTRIES — ACCRUED EXPENSE

On 30 June 2014, the accountant for Bob the Mowerman calculated that 1 month's interest of $240 had accrued on a bank loan. An interest payment of $900 was made on 30 September 2014.

Required
A. Give the adjusting entry needed on 30 June 2014.
B. Give the closing entry.
C. Give the reversing entry that could be made on 1 July 2014 and the subsequent entry to record the payment of 30 September 2014.
D. Assuming that no reversing entry was made, give the entry to record the interest payment on 30 September 2014.

Exercise 5.9 ADJUSTING ENTRIES AND REVERSING ENTRIES

On 30 June 2014, the adjusted trial balance of Endless Car Rentals showed the following selected balances:

Rentals receivable	$ 52 000
Rental revenue	820 000
Interest expense	21 000
Interest payable	9 000

Both the Rentals Receivable and Interest Payable accounts had been recorded as a result of adjusting entries made on 30 June.

Required
A. Prepare the adjusting entries that would have been recorded on 30 June for both items.
B. Prepare any necessary reversing entries that would be made on 1 July.
C. Prepare the entries on 10 July assuming that cash of $52 000 had been received on the outstanding rentals and $9500 was paid in interest.
D. Assuming that any reversing entries in requirement B were not made, what entries would be made on 10 July for the cash receipt and cash payment?

Exercise 5.10 WORKSHEET, INCOME STATEMENT AND CLOSING ENTRIES

On the next page are the account balances taken from the trial balance and adjusted trial balance columns of the worksheet of Bloom Printing Services for the year ended 30 April 2014, the first year of operations.

Required
A. Reconstruct the 10-column worksheet for the year.
B. Prepare the income statement for Bloom Printing Services for the year ended 30 April 2014.
C. Prepare the closing entries required on 30 April 2014.

Account	Unadjusted trial balance	Adjusted trial balance
Cash at bank	$ 6 240	$ 6 240
Accounts receivable	10 400	10 400
Office supplies	9 100	2 600
Printing supplies	7 800	520
Prepaid insurance	9 360	3 120
Prepaid rent	12 480	3 120
Equipment	107 120	107 120
Accounts payable	36 400	36 400
D. Rose, Capital	102 180	102 180
D. Rose, Drawings	18 200	18 200
Printing revenue	80 600	80 600
Wages expense	28 600	28 964
General expense	9 880	9 880
Office supplies expense	—	6 500
Printing supplies expense	—	7 280
Insurance expense	—	6 240
Rent expense	—	9 360
Depreciation expense – equipment	—	10 400
Accumulated depreciation – equipment	—	10 400
Wages payable		364

LO 4

Exercise 5.11 CLOSING ENTRIES, INCOME STATEMENT AND STATEMENT OF CHANGES IN EQUITY

The accountant of S. Tromble, Solicitor, has posted adjusting entries (1) to (5) to the ledger accounts at 30 June 2013. All the income, expense and equity accounts of the entity are listed here in T-account form.

Accounts Receivable

11 500	
(5) 1 750	

Supplies

2 000	(1) 1 000

Salaries Payable

	(4) 750

S. Tromble, Capital

	24 700

S. Tromble, Drawings

26 200	

Service Revenue

	51 500
	(5) 1 750

Salaries Expense

14 000	
(4) 750	

Supplies Expense

(1) 1 000	

Depr. Expense – Buildings

(3) 3 000	

Accum. Depr. – Buildings

	11 500
	(3) 3 000

Accum. Depr. – Furniture

	2 500
	(2) 1 500

Depr. Expense – Furniture

(2) 1 500	

Required

A. Prepare the closing entries of the law firm at 30 June 2013.
B. Prepare the income statement and the statement of changes in equity for the year ended 30 June 2013.

LO 6, 7

Exercise 5.12 ADJUSTING AND REVERSING ENTRIES, JUSTIFICATION

The following information concerning the information technology consulting business of Shah and Singh is available at 30 June 2013, the end of the financial year.

1. Prepaid Insurance was debited for $1800 on 28 February to record the cost of a 6-month policy beginning on 1 March.

2. Interest earned but not received totals $3600.
3. Shah and Singh received $7488 in rent revenue on 1 May for the 3-month period beginning on that date. The transaction was recorded by a credit to Unearned Rent Revenue.
4. The June electricity account for $828 has not been paid or recorded.
5. Consulting fees owing to the business and unrecorded as at 30 June 2013 amounted to $7560.

Required

A. Prepare an adjusting entry for each item as at 30 June 2013.
B. Prepare reversing entries where appropriate. Justify why you have/have not prepared reversing entries for each adjustment.

Exercise 5.13   RECORDING CAPITAL TRANSACTIONS OF A COMPANY   **LO 8**

Prepare the general journal entries that are needed to record the transactions of Atlas Ltd.
1. Issued 10 000 shares for $10 000.
2. The board of directors declared a cash dividend of 10c per share.
3. The cash dividend declared in (2) above was paid.
4. Close the Profit or Loss Summary account which has a credit balance of $7800.

Exercise 5.14   REVERSING ENTRIES — ACCRUED REVENUE   **GST**   **LO 6, 7**

Payne Pty Ltd operates a telephone answering service. Its clients are charged $100 a month plus $10 GST for the service and tax invoices are prepared four times a year on 31 January, 30 April, 31 July and 31 October. Quarterly payments are due by the fifteenth of the month following the end of a quarter. The balance in the Answering Service Fees Revenue account was $27 000 on 31 December, the end of the period. Service fees for November and December not yet recorded were $4350.

Required

A. Prepare the adjusting entry in the general journal to record the fees revenue.
B. Assuming that reversing entries are not made, record the receipt of a $330 quarterly payment from a client on 12 February and the receipt of $220 on 13 February from a new client who had contracted for the service to start on 1 December.
C. Assuming that reversing entries are made to facilitate the record-keeping process, prepare the appropriate reversing entry, if any, and the receipt of cash on 12 and 13 February.

Exercise 5.15   REVERSING ENTRIES — UNEARNED REVENUE   **LO 6, 7**

During 2013, Shoreline Recreation Club received $170 000 for membership fees. The accountant credits Unearned Membership Fees, a liability account, for the full amount when cash is received. At 31 December 2013, it is determined that $52 100 of the membership fees are fees for the 2014 year. Ignore GST.

Required

A. What amount should be reported in the 2013 income statement for membership fees?
B. What amount should be reported in the 31 December 2013 balance sheet for unearned membership fees?
C. Prepare the adjusting entry needed at 31 December 2013.
D. What reversing entry, if any, would you make on 1 January 2014?
E. The record keeper could have recorded the receipt of cash initially in a revenue account. Prepare the adjusting entry, assuming that the Membership Fees Revenue account contains a credit balance of $170 000 at 31 December.
F. Compare the balances in the Unearned Membership Fees account and the Membership Fees Revenue account derived in requirement E with those calculated in requirements A and B.
G. What reversing entry, if any, would you make on 1 January 2014 to reverse the adjusting entry made in requirement E? Explain your answer.

★ Basic

★★ Moderate

★★★ Challenging

Problem 5.1 WORKSHEET, FINANCIAL STATEMENTS AND CLOSING ENTRIES ★

The unadjusted trial balance of Superquick Couriers is as follows:

SUPERQUICK COURIERS
Unadjusted Trial Balance
as at 31 December 2014

Account	Debit	Credit
Cash at bank	$ 4 725	
Office supplies	7 260	
Prepaid insurance	1 725	
Delivery vans	109 695	
Accumulated depreciation – delivery vans		$ 28 920
Bank loan payable (non-current)		30 000
B. Flash, Capital		42 075
B. Flash, Drawings	27 000	
Courier charges revenue		106 500
Salaries expense	40 965	
Advertising expense	2 250	
Repairs expense	1 260	
Fuel expense	7 200	
Electricity expense	3 405	
Telephone expense	660	
Interest on bank loan expense	1 350	
	$207 495	$207 495

The following additional information should be taken into account:
1. Office supplies unused at 31 December 2014 amount to $700.
2. Expired insurance at 31 December 2014 is $1540.
3. Delivery vans are to be depreciated by $11 550.
4. Salaries accrued but unrecorded on 31 December, $830.
5. Fuel costs accrued and unpaid, $1200.
6. On 31 December, telephone charges of $370 have accrued but are unrecorded and unpaid.
7. Interest accrued on bank loan at 31 December was $964.

Required
A. Prepare adjusting and closing entries
B. Prepare an income statement for the year ended 31 December 2014 and a balance sheet as at 31 December 2014. (A worksheet may be prepared to assist but it is not necessary.)

Problem 5.2 WORKSHEET, FINANCIAL STATEMENTS AND CLOSING ENTRIES ★

GST LO 1, 3, 4

Caroline Irving owns Job Locate, which provides employment placement services. The unadjusted trial balance on 30 June 2013 below was prepared by her accountant.

The following additional information is available at 30 June:
1. The Unearned Fees account includes $615 received for fees earned during June.
2. Unused supplies on hand on 30 June totalled $320.
3. Advertising costing $1350 was consumed during the year.
4. Estimated depreciation on the office equipment is $3150.

JOB LOCATE
Unadjusted Trial Balance
as at 30 June 2013

Account	Debit	Credit
Cash at bank	$ 6 090	
Accounts receivable	13 080	
GST outlays	1 200	
Prepaid advertising	1 880	
Office supplies	610	
Office equipment	15 580	
Accumulated depreciation – office equipment		$ 2 280
Accounts payable		11 670
Unearned fees		2 580
GST collections		3 220
C. Irving, Capital		9 270
C. Irving, Drawings	23 660	
Placement fees revenue		89 580
Rent expense	10 880	
Salaries expense	43 500	
Telephone expense	2 120	
	$118 600	$118 600

Required

A. Prepare a 10-column worksheet for the year ended 30 June 2013.

B. Prepare an income statement, a statement of changes in equity and a balance sheet.

C. Journalise the closing entries.

Problem 5.3 WORKSHEET ADJUSTING ENTRIES AND FINANCIAL STATEMENTS ★★ GST   LO 1, 3, 5

James Sheedy owns a massage and skin repair salon which conducts business in a large shopping complex in Adelaide. Presented below are selected (incomplete) data from the three trial balances at the end of the current year, 30 June 2014. Accounts are arranged alphabetically.

Account	Unadjusted	Adjusted	Post-closing
Accounts payable	$10 236	$ 10 236	$10 236
Accumulated depreciation	13 360		
Advertising expense		12 839	
Cash at bank	15 962		
Depreciation expense		3 645	
Electricity expense		19 000	
Equipment	41 640		41 640
J. Sheedy, Capital		81 545	
J. Sheedy, Drawings	19 085		
Skin repair supplies			17 350
Prepaid advertising			1 735
Prepaid rent	24 290		
Rent expense		20 820	
Skin repair supplies expense		45 110	
Massage fees earned		160 750	
Massage fees receivable	2 429		4 685
Wages expense	64 195		
Wages payable			2 082

During the period, adjustments were made to record massage fees receivable, skin supplies used expense, rent expense, advertising expense, depreciation expense and wages accrued.

Required

A. Prepare a worksheet in correct financial statement order, filling in the blank spaces where necessary. Note that the column totals for the trial balances are:

Unadjusted	$263 635
Adjusted	$271 618
Post-closing	$110 868

No additional accounts are required.

B. Prepare the income statement and balance sheet as at the date of the worksheet.

Problem 5.4 WORKSHEET, FINANCIAL STATEMENTS AND CLOSING ENTRIES ★★

The ledger of Michael Simpson, Financial Consultant, contains the following account balances on 30 June 2014.

Account	Debit	Credit
Cash at Bank	$ 6 000	
Accounts Receivable	9 260	
GST Outlays	800	
Office Supplies	1 140	
Land	25 600	
Building	146 000	
Accumulated Depreciation – Building		$ 43 800
Office Equipment	13 500	
Accumulated Depreciation – Office Equipment		6 420
Accounts Payable		7 960
Unearned Consulting Fees		1 560
GST Collections		2 000
Mortgage Payable		88 600
M. Simpson, Capital		42 070
M. Simpson, Drawings	52 780	
Consulting Fees Revenue		156 860
Insurance Expense	1 660	
Salaries Expense	87 940	
Electricity Expense	760	
Interest Expense	2 090	
Telecommunications Expense	1 740	
	$349 270	$349 270

The following additional account titles are included in the chart of accounts:

> Prepaid Insurance
> Telecommunications Expense Payable
> Office Supplies Expense
> Depreciation Expense
> Interest Payable

The following information is also available:

1. A physical count of office supplies reveals that supplies totalling $370 are on hand at 30 June.
2. The balance in the Unearned Consulting Fees account includes $240 earned for services rendered in the last week of June.
3. Estimated depreciation on the office equipment is $2140. Depreciation on the building is $8760.
4. A 12-month insurance policy was purchased on 1 April for $1000 plus GST.
5. The June monthly mortgage payment of $900 has not been paid or recorded. In each payment, $220 is attributable to interest.
6. The June telecommunications costs for $230 are unrecorded. No tax invoice has been received.
7. Salaries of $1240 were owing to employees at 30 June 2014.

Required

A. Prepare a 10-column worksheet for the year ended 30 June 2014.

B. Prepare the income statement, balance sheet and statement of changes in equity.

C. Journalise the closing entries.

Problem 5.5 PREPARATION OF WORKSHEET, FINANCIAL STATEMENTS AND CLOSING ENTRIES ★★

On 30 June 2013, the ledger of Goran Cilic, Veterinary Surgeon, contains the accounts and account balances shown below:

Account	Debit	Credit
Cash at Bank	$ 13 640	
Accounts Receivable	11 800	
Prepaid Insurance	1 680	
Land	69 200	
Building	196 000	
Accumulated Depreciation – Building		$112 880
Equipment	20 120	
Accumulated Depreciation – Equipment		8 800
Accounts Payable		16 040
Mortgage Payable		28 520
G. Cilic, Capital		103 840
G. Cilic, Drawings	127 360	
Fees Earned		227 920
Rent Revenue		14 400
Salaries Expense	63 600	
Telephone Expense	4 520	
Interest Expense	3 080	
Insurance Expense	1 400	
	$512 400	$512 400

The following account titles are included in the chart of accounts:

Interest Payable

Salaries Payable

Rates Payable

Unearned Fees

Depreciation Expense – Building

Depreciation Expense – Equipment

Rates Expense

The following information has not yet been recorded:

1. Rates owing at 30 June, $2120.
2. Depreciation on the equipment is $3240. Depreciation on the building is $9280.
3. An advance fee payment of $400 for minor surgery to be performed in July 2013 was credited to Fees Earned.
4. The mortgage contract provides for a monthly payment of $1000 plus accrued interest. The June payment was not made. Interest of $280 is accrued on the mortgage.
5. Prepaid insurance of $1240 has expired.
6. Salaries earned but not paid amount to $2360.

Required

A. Prepare a 10-column worksheet for the year ended 30 June 2013.

B. Prepare an income statement, a statement of changes in equity and a balance sheet.

C. Journalise the closing entries.

FINANCIAL STATEMENTS FROM AN ADJUSTED
TRIAL BALANCE; ADJUSTING AND CLOSING ENTRIES ★★

GST · LO 3, 4, 7

The adjusted trial balance of Bedrock Bowling Alley (owned by Bruce Rock) at 30 June 2014, the end of the entity's accounting year, follows:

BEDROCK BOWLING ALLEY
Adjusted Trial Balance
as at 30 June 2014

Account	Debit	Credit
Cash at bank	$ 15 660	
Accounts receivable	77 220	
Supplies	11 070	
Prepaid insurance	6 870	
GST outlays	6 470	
Bowling equipment	191 790	
Accumulated depreciation – bowling equipment		$ 85 290
Building	222 990	
Accumulated depreciation – building		54 780
Accounts payable		68 660
Interest payable		7 100
Wages and salaries payable		3 620
Unearned fees revenue		10 980
GST collections		15 020
Loan from ABC Bank Ltd (non-current)		233 700
B. Rock, Capital		138 600
B. Rock, Drawings	166 500	
Fees revenue		298 650
Depreciation expense – bowling equipment	20 100	
Depreciation expense – building	9 630	
Wage and salaries expense	89 400	
Insurance expense	17 040	
Interest expense	24 510	
Electricity expense	17 010	
Council rates expense	8 830	
Supplies expense	21 300	
	$906 390	$906 390

Additional data taken into account in the preparation of the above adjusted trial balance at 30 June 2014:
1. Supplies used during the year, $21 300.
2. Prepaid insurance expired during the year, $17 040.
3. Accrued interest expense, $7100.
4. Fees revenue earned but not received, $8100.
5. Depreciation for the year: bowling equipment, $20 100; building, $9630.
6. Accrued wages and salaries expense, $3620.
7. Unearned fees revenue earned during the year, $15 540.

Required
A. Prepare the income statement and statement of changes in equity for the year ended 30 June 2014 and a classified balance sheet as at 30 June 2014.
B. Record adjusting and closing entries in the general journal.
C. Prepare any suitable reversing entries on 1 July 2014.

Sunshine Tours is a travel agency operating in a suburban shopping centre in Noosa. Two trial balances prepared at different stages of the accounting cycle are presented below (account balances are all normal and GST is ignored):

Account	Trial balance at 30 June 2014	Adjusted trial balance at 30 June 2014
Cash at bank	$ 3 600	$ 3 600
Accounts receivable	6 000	7 500
Office supplies	5 250	1 500
Prepaid insurance	5 400	1 200
Prepaid rent on premises	7 200	1 800
Office equipment	61 800	61 800
Accumulated depreciation – office equipment	—	8 400
Accounts payable	21 000	21 200
Rachel Sayar, Capital	54 450	54 450
Rachel Sayar, Drawings	10 500	10 500
Commission revenue	46 500	48 000
Salaries expense	16 500	17 220
General expense	5 700	5 900
Office supplies expense	—	3 750
Insurance expense	—	4 200
Rent expense	—	5 400
Depreciation expense – office equipment	—	8 400
Salaries payable	—	720

Required

Show, in general journal format, the adjusting and closing entries that would have been made on 30 June 2014. Show also any suitable reversing entries on 1 July 2014.

Selected accounts taken from the general ledger of Baker and Son showed the following balances at 31 December.

Prepaid Insurance		Insurance Expense	
31/12 Bal. 1 720		31/12 Bal. 0	

Interest Receivable		Interest Revenue	
31/12 Bal. 0			31/12 Bal. 4 200

Wages Payable		Wages Expense	
	31/12 Bal. 0	31/12 Bal. 77 800	

Required

A. Prepare adjusting entries for the accounts based on the following data that are not yet recorded.
   1. Insurance expired during the year, $900.
   2. Wages earned by employees but not paid at year-end, $1420.
   3. Interest accrued but not yet received on a loan to employee, $370.
B. Open T accounts for each of the accounts listed. Enter the 31 December balances and the adjusting entries.

C. Enter in the appropriate accounts the closing entries that would be made at year-end.

D. Complete the following table:

Account	Balance before adjustment	Effects of adjusting entries	Balance after adjustments	Effects of closing entries	Balance after closing entries
Prepaid Insurance	$1 720	−$900	$820	0	$820
Insurance Expense					
Interest Receivable					
Interest Revenue					
Wages Payable					
Wages Expense					

E. Baker and Son follows the practice of making reversing entries. Prepare the reversing entries that would be made on 1 January of the next period.

F. Record the payment of $1840 in weekly wages on 3 January and the collection of $460 in interest on 18 January. What are the balances in the Wages Expense and Interest Revenue after these entries are posted?

G. Prepare the two entries given in requirement F, assuming the company did not prepare reversing entries.

Problem 5.9 ADJUSTING AND REVERSING ENTRIES ★★ LO 6, 7, 8

The records of Northam Ltd contain the following information at 31 December, the end of the year. Ignore GST.
1. Depreciation on the office equipment is $10 488.
2. Wages earned but not paid total $1656.
3. Interest of $600 has accrued on a loan payable.
4. On 15 September, the company paid $2880 for a 6-month advertising campaign beginning on that date. This transaction was recorded by debiting Prepaid Advertising. At the end of the year, advertising costing $2240 had been consumed.
5. Services performed for clients, but not yet recorded, amount to $6528.
6. The unearned revenue account has a balance of $1296, recorded when cash was received on 1 November. It was expected the $1296 would be earned equally over November, December and January.
7. The company decided to declare a dividend of $15 000 to its shareholders on 31 December.

Required
A. Prepare adjusting entries for items 1 to 7 above.
B. Prepare reversing entries where appropriate.

Problem 5.10 ADJUSTING AND REVERSING ENTRIES ★★ LO 6, 7

The following information concerning Kemp and Sons is available at 30 June, the end of the financial year:
1. Prepaid Insurance was debited for $924 on 28 February to record the cost of a 6-month policy beginning on 1 March.
2. Interest earned but not received totals $1350.
3. The June electricity bill for $253 has not been paid or recorded.
4. Kemp and Sons received $1716 rental revenue on 1 May for the 3-month period beginning on that date. The transaction was recorded by a credit to Unearned Rental Revenue.

Required
A. Prepare an adjusting entry for each item.
B. Prepare reversing entries where appropriate.

Problem 5.11 ADJUSTING ENTRIES, FINANCIAL STATEMENTS, CLOSING ENTRIES, REVERSING ENTRIES ★★

Daniella Floss operates a dental surgery in the suburbs, and the trial balance shown below summarises the year's activities.

DANIELLA FLOSS, DENTIST
Unadjusted Trial Balance
as at 30 June 2013

Account	Debit	Credit
Cash at bank	$ 7 000	
Fees revenue		$610 000
Accounts receivable	51 000	
Equipment	300 000	
Accumulated depreciation – equipment		95 000
Dental supplies	160 000	
Office supplies	8 000	
Daniella Floss, Capital		190 000
Daniella Floss, Drawings	140 000	
Accounts payable		20 000
Wages expense – nurse	100 000	
Rent expense	50 000	
Office expenses	29 000	
General expenses	70 000	
	$915 000	$915 000

The following additional information should be considered:
1. Inventory of dental supplies on hand at 30 June is $14 000; $3000 office supplies are on hand.
2. Depreciate equipment at the rate of 15% p.a. on cost ($300 000).
3. Rent of $4500 has been paid in advance and has been debited to rent expense.
4. Wages earned by the nurse but unpaid, $1500.

Required
A. Journalise the adjusting entries.
B. Journalise the closing entries.
C. Prepare an income statement, a statement of changes in equity and a balance sheet.
D. Journalise the reversing entries (if any).

Problem 5.12 THE COMPLETE ACCOUNTING CYCLE ★★★

Alexis Schubert owns Piano Tuning Service. The post-closing trial balance at 30 June 2013 is shown below. Ignore GST.

Account	Account number	Debit	Credit
Cash at bank	1100	$ 6 560	
Accounts receivable	1200	7 760	
Prepaid insurance	1300	380	
Supplies	1400	420	
Motor vehicle	1500	42 800	
Accumulated depreciation – motor vehicle	1510		$16 050
Accounts payable	2000		3 880
Interest payable	2100		880
Bank loan	2200		14 000
A. Schubert, Capital	3000		23 110
		$57 920	$57 920

Transactions completed during the year ended 30 June 2014 are summarised below:

1. Tuning fees of $57 000 were receivable during the year; $47 900 of this total was received in cash. The remainder consisted of transactions on credit.
2. Revenue from piano repairs was $48 700. Cash received totalled $33 500, and accounts receivable increased by $15 200.
3. Supplies costing $750 were purchased during the year on credit.
4. On 1 January 2014, Alexis Schubert paid $6000 off the bank loan plus interest of $1800. The interest payment consisted of $880 accrued up to 1 July 2013 and a further $920 which accrued for the period to 31 December 2013.
5. Petrol and oil for the vehicle cost $5300 in cash.
6. Insurance on the vehicle, paid in advance, was $1680.
7. Telephone expense of $4480 was paid.
8. Accounts receivable of $27 800 were collected, and $4000 was paid on accounts payable.
9. Alexis Schubert withdrew $65 000 cash from the business.

The following information relating to adjusting entries is available at the end of June 2014:

10. A physical count showed supplies costing $400 on hand at 30 June 2014.
11. Accrued interest on the bank loan is $420.
12. Insurance costing $1500 expired during the year.
13. Depreciation on the vehicle is $10 700.
14. The June telephone account for $380 has not been paid or recorded

Required

A. Open T accounts for the accounts listed in the post-closing trial balance and the accounts below. Insert beginning balances in the accounts as shown in the post-closing trial balance.

Account	Account number
Telephone Expense Payable	2300
A. Schubert, Drawings	3100
Profit or Loss Summary	3200
Piano Tuning Fees Revenue	4000
Piano Repair Fees Revenue	4100
Petrol and Oil Expense	5000
Telephone Expense	5100
Supplies Expense	5200
Insurance Expense	5300
Depreciation Expense – Vehicle	5400
Interest Expense	5500

B. Prepare journal entries to record the transactions (numbers 1–9) completed in the year to 30 June 2014.
C. Post the entries to T accounts.
D. Prepare a 10-column worksheet.
E. Prepare an income statement, a statement of changes in equity and a balance sheet.
F. Prepare and post the adjusting entries.
G. Prepare and post the closing entries.
H. Prepare a post-closing trial balance.

Problem 5.13 THE COMPLETE ACCOUNTING CYCLE ★★★

The post-closing trial balance at 30 June 2014 of Western Consulting Services is shown on the next page.

Transactions completed during the year ended 30 June 2015 are summarised below:

1. Collections on accounts receivable totalled $51 820.
2. Consulting fees of $55 720 plus GST of 10% were receivable during the year. Clients are invoiced after services are provided and are given 30 days in which to pay.
3. Rent paid in advance was $9120, plus GST.

WESTERN CONSULTING SERVICES
Post-Closing Trial Balance
as at 30 June 2014

Account	Account no.	Debit	Credit
Cash at bank	1100	$ 9 240	
Accounts receivable	1101	5 900	
Prepaid rent	1102	760	
GST outlays	1105	1 400	
Office supplies	1106	820	
Furniture and equipment	1110	17 950	
Accumulated depreciation – furniture and equipment	1111		$ 6 080
Accounts payable	2200		3 400
Salaries payable	2201		260
GST collections	2203		3 200
Amelie De Jong, Capital	3000		23 130
		$36 070	$36 070

4. Office supplies were purchased during the year for $240 plus GST in cash and $260 plus GST on credit.
5. De Jong withdrew $16 000 for private use.
6. Salary payments amounted to $19 960, of which $260 was for salaries accrued to the end of the year ending 30 June 2014.
7. Advertising totalling $2100 plus GST was purchased on credit.
8. Electricity expense of $2250 plus GST was paid.
9. Accounts payable of $1800 were paid.
10. GST collections of $5700 less GST outlays of $1500 were forwarded in cash during the year to the Australian Taxation Office.

The following additional information should be considered for adjusting entries:
11. Unused office supplies on hand at the end of the year totalled $480.
12. Depreciation on the furniture and equipment is $2900.
13. Salaries earned but not paid amount to $740.
14. Rent paid in advance in transaction 3. Rent for 6 months of $4560 plus GST was paid in advance on 1 August and 1 February.

Required
A. Prepare the ledger of Western Consulting Services by opening T accounts for the accounts listed in the post-closing trial balance and for the accounts listed below. Post the 30 June 2014 balances.

Account	Account number
Amelie De Jong, Drawings	3301
Profit or Loss Summary	3320
Consulting Fees Revenue	4400
Salaries Expense	5500
Electricity Expense	5503
Advertising Expense	5504
Depreciation Expense	5505
Rent Expense	5512
Office Supplies Expense	5513

B. Prepare journal entries to record the transactions numbered 1–10.
C. Post the entries to the T accounts.

D. Prepare a 10-column worksheet for the year ended 30 June 2015.

E. Prepare an income statement, a statement of changes in equity and a balance sheet.

F. Journalise and post the adjusting entries.

G. Journalise and post the closing entries.

H. Prepare a post-closing trial balance.

I. Prepare any suitable reversing entries on 1 July 2015.

Problem 5.14   COMPLETE ACCOUNTING CYCLE, RUNNING BALANCE ACCOUNTS ★★★   `LO 3, 4, 5, 7`

On 1 June 2014, Demis Doulos contributed $50 000 into a business bank account in order to establish the business of Doulos Cleaning and Gardening Services. The following transactions occurred in the month of June. Ignore GST.

June	1	Doulos signed a lease agreement to lease a suitable storage shed for a monthly rental of $1200. Rent for 3 months was paid in advance. He also hired an assistant to help him with cleaning and lawn mowing tasks. The assistant was to be paid casual wages.
	2	The business acquired suitable cleaning and gardening equipment for a total cost of $18 025. A deposit of $4000 was paid immediately and the balance was to be paid in 30 days. The equipment was expected to have a useful life of 7 years.
	2	Purchased a quantity of washing supplies for $480 cash. Purchased fuel and oil supplies for $790 cash.
	3	Signed a contract with Community Newspapers for 12 weeks of advertisements in its weekly, free newspaper delivered to local homes. The business paid $960 in advance for these advertisements.
	6	Received cash of $80 from a grateful client whose house had been cleaned by the business before the monthly rent inspection. Received cash of $1350 for several lawns that had been mowed for clients during the week.
	8	Signed a contract with the local shopping centre to provide cleaning services to its outside walls (including graffiti removal) for a monthly fee of $2000. The shopping centre paid for 2 months' services in advance.
	13	Received cash of $1400 for lawn mowing services provided to clients during the past week.
	14	Paid the assistant casual wages of $820 for services provided to the business during the past fortnight.
	21	Earned $730 for cleaning services from clients and $1270 for lawn mowing during the past week. All money was received in cash except for one client for cleaning services, who arranged to pay the business $300 in 3 weeks' time for services rendered.
	28	Received in cash the sum of $800 for cleaning services provided to clients and $1150 for lawn mowing and gardening services provided during the past week.
	28	Paid the assistant $760 for services provided to the business during the past fortnight.
	30	Doulos withdrew $2000 in cash from the business in order to pay for essential provisions for his family.

Additional information

The accounting period closed on 30 June 2014, and the following additional data was available.

1. Wages owing to the assistant on 30 June amounted to $280.

2. A physical count showed that only $120 of washing supplies and $340 of fuel and oil supplies were still on hand.

3. Four weeks of advertisements had appeared in the local community newspaper up to 30 June.

4. Cleaning services of $250 had been rendered to clients on 29 June but the invoice to bill these clients had not been prepared.

5. The business had provided cleaning services to its shopping centre client for 3 weeks of the first month (assumed to be 4 weeks long).

Required

A. Prepare journal entries to record the June 2014 transactions for Doulos Cleaning and Gardening Services and post these journal entries to suitable running balance ledger accounts. Provide appropriate account numbers and journal page numbers and record them in post ref. columns.

B. Prepare an unadjusted trial balance as at 30 June 2014.

C. Prepare adjusting entries and post them to the ledger accounts. Be careful to ensure that all adjusting entries have been recorded. Explain the reasons for each adjusting entry that you have made.

D. Prepare an adjusted trial balance.

E. Prepare closing entries, post them to the accounts and prepare a post-closing trial balance.

F. Prepare the income statement, the statement of changes in equity and the balance sheet as at 30 June 2014.

G. Prepare any suitable reversing entries on 1 July 2014 and post them to the accounts.

Problem 5.15 GST LO 1, 4, 6
INCOME STATEMENT, ADJUSTING AND CLOSING ENTRIES, ADVICE FOR CLIENT ★★★

Lara Knoffs, a qualified commercial artist, had worked as an employee of a large advertising agency for a number of years. She decided to resign her position and set up her own business which would be coordinated from the new home she and her husband had bought.

To establish the business, she invested $25 000 of her cash savings as capital. From this capital, she then purchased for the business equipment worth $15 000 with an expected life of 10 years and no residual value. Other specialist equipment cost $6600 (estimated life 6 years — expected residual value of $600). Lara charged competitive prices, produced quality work and built up a good clientele. Most customers paid a deposit before work started and bad debts had never been a problem.

Although there was a general feeling that the business was going well, Lara was concerned that she always seemed to have cash problems when trying to withdraw cash from the business at the same levels and above that she had earned as an employee. You have been asked by Lara to examine her business as she feels that it is not profitable.

An analysis of the Cash at Bank account for the financial year ended 30 June 2014 revealed the following:

Balance of cash at 1 July 2013		$ 3 100
Cash received from clients		88 750
		91 850
Cash payments.		
Accounts payable	25 750	
Insurance prepaid (2 years from 1 July 2013)	3 600	
Materials and stationery	10 000	
Electricity and telephone	5 500	
Drawings for personal use	31 000	
Sundry expenses	14 700	90 550
Balance of cash at 30 June 2014		$ 1 300

This analysis highlighted Lara's major concern in that the $31 000 she had withdrawn was several thousand dollars below the wage which she had earned as an employee of the advertising firm. She believed, given her assessment of the poor profitability of her business, that perhaps she should return to work as an employee.

Other enquiries reveal the following:

1. Cash received from clients ($88 750) included payments for work done in the financial year ended 30 June 2013 to the value of $6750 and also $8000 prepaid for work to be done in the next financial year.

2. Materials and stationery on hand at 30 June 2014 were costed at $4500.

3. $14 250 was yet to be collected from clients for work done during the year ended 30 June 2014.

Required

A. Prepare a report for Lara which discloses the profitability of her business. Produce figures to substantiate the report.

B. Prepare the closing entries that would be needed on 30 June 2014.

C. Advise Lara as to whether she should dispose of the business and return to the advertising firm as an employee.

Retain or sell a business

Lucy Chan owns an online financial services company called RightFinance.com. She has some idea about accrual accounting but is not very clear on what to do, so she has come to you for help. Lucy aims to achieve a profit margin on her business of 10%. That is, she expects profit divided by total revenue to be at least 10% or more. Lucy has provided the income statement below, which shows a profit margin of 7% ($29 000/$414 285). If the profit margin falls below 10%, Lucy intends to sell the business. Lucy knows that some accrual accounting adjustments need to be made and that is why she is seeking your help.

RIGHTFINANCE.COM
Income Statement
for the year ended 30 June 2013

INCOME		
Revenues:		$414 285
Fees revenue		
EXPENSES		
Salaries	$203 170	
Subcontracting expenses	57 815	
Council rates expense	2 600	
Insurance expense	7 000	
Advertising expense	12 500	
Rent expense	19 800	
Sundry expenses	2 400	
		385 285
PROFIT		$ 29 000

To determine the adjustments that need to be made, you have a long discussion with Lucy that reveals the following:

1. The fees revenue includes $900 for cash received but the services have not yet been provided to the customer.
2. A staff member went on holidays at the end of June and his July wages of $2300 are included in 'salaries'.
3. A prepayment of rent of $1400 for June is still shown in the balance sheet as an asset.
4. Depreciation expense of $6000 for the year has not yet been charged to the accounts.

Required

Should Lucy retain the business or sell it, given her requirement that the profit margin must be 10%? Explain the reason for your conclusion, showing calculations.

Accountability of aid organisations

Aid and development organisations, such as World Vision, have many different programs and campaigns to raise money for the purpose of emergency relief work in specific countries, and for large development projects. They are also involved in alleviating poverty around the world (see the business knowledge vignette on p. 198). Furthermore, World Vision has a program of child sponsorship in underdeveloped countries to provide a basic education for underprivileged children. It is important that World Vision (and other similar organisations) is accountable for the money collected, for the money spent, and for any government assistance received. In order for this to happen, the management requires monthly financial reports. Assume that it is your job to prepare these reports.

Required

A. Consider carefully the types of information that you would need to provide to management in order to satisfy their needs for accountability in relation to the above activities of the organisation.

B. What advantages (if any) would be provided by the use of worksheets in the preparation of this information?

COMMUNICATION AND LEADERSHIP

To reverse, or not to reverse

Form into groups of three or four. Half of the groups are to prepare a report on the advantages of not reversing adjusting entries at the beginning of the next financial year and the disadvantages of preparing reversing entries.

The other groups are to prepare a report on the disadvantages of not reversing adjusting entries at the beginning of the next financial year and the advantages of preparing reversing entries.

Then, alternating between arguments, the groups report back to the class.

FINANCIAL ANALYSIS

Refer to the consolidated financial statements in the latest financial report of JB Hi-Fi Limited on its website, www.jbhifi.com.au, and answer the following questions:

1. What are the different types of revenues generated by the consolidated group?
2. How are the group's assets classified?
3. What are the major categories listed among the group's equity? Have there been any shares issued during the past financial year? How many ordinary shareholders did JB Hi-Fi Limited have at the end of the financial year?
4. What is the group's current liability for dividends to ordinary shareholders? If you owned only 100 ordinary shares in JB Hi-Fi Limited, how much would you receive in dividends?
5. How do the dividends per share compare with the group's 'earnings' per share?

Chapter

6

Accounting for retailing

Concepts for review

Before studying this chapter, you should understand or, if necessary, revise:

- the steps in the accounting cycle (p. 126)

- how to prepare a worksheet (pp. 148–52)

- how to prepare adjusting and closing entries (pp. 128–40, 182–98)

- how to prepare financial statements from a worksheet (pp. 153–5)

- basic features of the goods and services tax and its impact on accounting in a service business (pp. 79–99, 102–4).

Learning objectives

After studying this chapter, you should be able to:

1 describe the nature of inventory and retailing operations (pp. 230–1)

2 describe the basic format of an income statement for retail businesses (p. 231)

3 describe the impact of GST legislation on retail businesses (pp. 231–4)

4 account for sales transactions of retail businesses registered for the GST, including the treatment of sales returns, cash discounts, trade discounts and freight costs (pp. 234–8)

5 account for purchases of inventory and cost of sales under both the perpetual and periodic inventory systems by retail businesses registered for the GST (pp. 238–50)

6 prepare worksheets and close the accounts for retail businesses for both the perpetual and periodic inventory systems (pp. 250–3)

7 prepare a detailed income statement for a retail business (pp. 253–4)

8 describe the net method of recording purchases and sales whenever there are settlement discounts (pp. 255–6)

9 perform a brief analysis of profitability in a retail business for decision-making purposes (pp. 256–7).

Target, Kmart buoy resilient Wesfarmers

Wesfarmers has pulled off one of the big surprises of the earnings season to date, revealing that Target and Kmart had recorded double-digit earnings leaps in the first half to drive the conglomerate's profit well ahead of estimates. The company also delighted investors concerned about the long-promised turnaround of its Coles food and liquor business, as the division showed tangible results from the massive investment by Wesfarmers in the group, with revenue and earnings before interest and tax growing strongly.

Its chief executive, Richard Goyder, now sits atop an empire worth $30.76 billion engaged in a diverse range of sectors including retail, hardware, resources, insurance and chemicals. Yesterday he said the company was well placed to benefit from any further upturn in the Australian and global economies.

Wesfarmers yesterday posted a 0.9 per cent increase in net profit for the six months to December 31, to $879 million, as group revenue drifted slightly higher to $26.53 billion.

Although the profit was flat for the half, analysts had pencilled in interim profit to plunge by as much as 25 per cent, as well as recording a heavy loss in its resources operation, to generate a profit result of closer to $760 million. Some estimates had been even more dire.

Mr Goyder said the first-half result again laid out the benefits of a diversified business model, given that the company's resources division was hit hard by a fall in coal prices. The division's EBIT plunged to $2 million, from $664 million.

The market rewarded the profit outperformance, sending Wesfarmers' shares 95c higher, or 3.2 per cent, to close at $30.60.

Coles, the biggest contributor to the pre-tax earnings, reported EBIT of $486 million, up 12.8 per cent, as like-for-like store sales revenue lifted to 6 per cent from 2.6 per cent.

Total revenue drawn from Coles supermarkets was up 7.5 per cent to $12.03 billion.

However, margins rose by only 20 basis points. Analysts had been tipping as much as a 70 basis point lift, as the Coles management invested more capital in refurbishments, discounting and promotions to win over customers from its arch rival Woolworths and from other independents.

'We're seeing good volume growth and we're getting more customers as well,' Mr Goyder said.

The most impressive return was posted by its merchandise businesses, Target and Kmart, at a time when higher interest rates and belt tightening caused many consumers to pull back their spending on clothes, toys and electronics.

Target had EBIT of $279 million, up 29.8 per cent for the period, while Kmart had EBIT of $154 million, up 105.3 per cent.

Wesfarmers declared a fully-franked interim dividend of 55c per share, up 10 per cent.

Source: Eli Greenblat, 'Target, Kmart buoy resilient Wesfarmers', *The Sydney Morning Herald.*

Chapter preview

In previous chapters, an entity that provided personal services to customers and clients was used to illustrate the accounting cycle. Service businesses make up a significant part of our economy and provide a wide range of important service products. Such businesses include law firms, accounting firms, medical and dental practices, management services, motels, hairdressers, airlines, real estate, travel agencies, golf clubs, cinemas, photographic studios, shire and city councils, and government departments.

The main activity of many other businesses centres on goods rather than on services. *Manufacturing businesses* purchase raw materials and component parts for conversion into finished products for sale. *Retailing businesses*, which often distribute at both the wholesale and retail levels, purchase goods that are in a form ready to be sold to their customers. *Wholesale businesses* normally buy commodities in bulk from manufacturers/producers and then distribute in smaller lots or units to *retail businesses*, which in turn sell to the final consumer.

Several large firms operate in the retail market in Australia and New Zealand. For example, David Jones and Myer run well-known department stores around Australia and countless other organisations conduct business in the retail sector, many of which franchise out their operations — Wesfarmers (which owns Bunnings hardware, Coles, Kmart and Target stores) (see the scene setter), Harvey Norman, The Warehouse, JB Hi-Fi, Angus and Robertson, Lowes Menswear, Woolworths and Hungry Jacks, to name a few. The distribution of goods throughout Australia and New Zealand is thus a highly complex and expensive operation for large decentralised retailers, and they are constantly seeking ways to efficiently track the movement of goods among stores and within retail outlets. Retailers have always made use of the latest technology to help with this problem. The retail sector is also characterised by a large number of small and medium-sized enterprises (often referred to as SMEs).

The accounting principles and methods described in earlier chapters apply to retail businesses, but a number of additional accounts and procedures are used to record inventory transactions. This chapter considers these.

6.1 Inventory

Learning objective 1

Describe the nature of inventory and retailing operations

The term **inventory** is used in a retail operation to mean goods or property purchased and held for sale in the operating cycle of a business. Other assets held for future sale but not normally sold as part of regular business activities, such as an item of used office equipment that is no longer needed, are not included in the inventory category. Nor are stationery supplies regarded as inventory because they are not held for sale in the operating cycle of the business.

Stock and *stock in trade* are commonly used terms for inventory. In conformity with accounting standard IAS 2/AASB 102 *Inventories*, the term 'inventory' is used in this text.

Retail business operations

The operating cycle for a retail business is the average length of time it takes for the business to acquire inventory, sell that inventory to its customers and collect cash from those customers. At the time of purchase, inventory is recorded at cost. The cost of inventory available for future sale is reported in the balance sheet as a current asset. When sales are made, both assets and revenues are recorded for an amount equal to the sales price. In the income statement, the cost of inventory sold during the current period is charged against the income (revenue) received from selling it.

Determination of profit is, in fact, a major objective of accounting for inventory. It involves determining the amount of the total inventory cost to be deducted from sales in the current period and the amount to be carried forward as an asset to be expensed in some future period. One of the major problems in accounting for inventory concerns the allocation of the costs of inventory over goods sold during a period and the goods held at the end of a period for sale in a future period.

Inventory is one of the most active assets in a retail business. It is continually being acquired, sold and replaced. Inventories can also make up a significant part of a business's total assets. The cost of sales for a given period is often the business's largest expense, sometimes exceeding the total of all other expenses. For these reasons, the control and safeguarding of inventory is essential for efficient and profitable operations. Target, Kmart and Coles, as discussed in the scene setter, would all have considerable inventories across a whole range of goods.

6.2 Condensed income statement for a retailer

Learning objective 2

Describe the basic format of an income statement for retail businesses

A simplified income statement for The Fashion Shop Ltd, a retail business, is shown in figure 6.1.

A comparison of this statement with the one prepared for Intellect Management Services (p. 153) reveals several differences:

- Income (revenue) is the first item reported in both cases, but for a retail business the most important revenue is **sales** (net sales revenue).
- A major difference is the inclusion of the **cost of sales**, which shows the total cost of the inventory that was sold during the period. The cost of sales is subtracted from net sales revenue to arrive at an intermediate amount called **gross profit (or gross margin) on sales**.
- After adding any other income, expenses are subtracted to determine the profit (or loss) for the period. Although many of the expenses incurred by a service business are also incurred by a retail business, there are other expenses that relate to buying and selling inventory. Expenses are normally grouped by function. **Selling and distribution expenses** result from efforts to sell the inventory and include storage costs, advertising, sales salaries and commissions, and the cost of delivering goods to customers. **Administrative expenses** are expenses associated with operating the general office, accounting systems and personnel. A third category, **finance expenses**, represents expenses of financing the business's operations, collecting debts and running the credit department, e.g. interest, bad debts, and cash discounts allowed for prompt payment by debtors. Any other expenses are then usually added to finance expenses and reported under the category 'finance and other expenses'.

Figure 6.1 Simplified income statement for a retail business

THE FASHION SHOP LTD
Income Statement
for the year ended 31 December 2013

INCOME		
Revenue:		
Net sales revenue		$ 692 890
Less: Cost of sales		470 490
GROSS PROFIT		222 400
Other income		5 260
		227 660
EXPENSES		
Selling and distribution	$100 270	
Administrative	78 850	
Finance and other	4 260	183 380
PROFIT (before income tax)		$ 44 280

6.3 Retailing and the goods and services tax

Learning objective 3

Describe the impact of GST legislation on retail businesses

The goods and services tax (GST) is introduced in the appendix to chapter 3, where the features of the GST legislation as it applies to the purchase and supply of services are explained. This chapter focuses on retail businesses that purchase goods for resale as well as the services (e.g. electricity) required to carry on business. Under GST legislation, retail businesses have to register for an Australian business number (ABN) and hence GST if their gross taxable supplies (sales of goods) exceed $75 000 per year. Given the threshold, the GST affects most retail businesses unless they deal exclusively in GST-free supplies. In order for a retail business to claim input credits on its purchases of inventories and services, the suppliers of such inventories and services must also be registered for GST and must quote their ABN on supply documents, e.g. tax invoices. Retail businesses are required to issue tax invoices when goods subject to the GST are sold, and adjustment notes (credit notes) when adjustments are necessary. These relevant source documents are illustrated below.

Retail businesses must ensure that adequate records of GST collections and GST outlays are kept. As illustrated in earlier chapters, the two accounts used in this book for this purpose are GST Collections and GST Outlays. It is assumed that the accrual basis of accounting is used in all cases. The guiding principles for accounting for the GST are contained in Interpretation 1031 *Accounting for the Goods and Services Tax (GST)*, issued by the Australian Accounting Standards Board (AASB). In relation to retailing, the effect of Interpretation 1031 is that all revenue, costs and expense amounts are recorded exclusive of GST, and receivables and payables are recorded inclusive of GST.

Tax invoices

For all sales in excess of $75, a retail business has to issue a **tax invoice** that complies with the GST legislation. Requirements for tax invoices vary depending on whether the total amount payable on the invoices is $1000 or more. Requirements common to all tax invoices are:

- the words 'tax invoice' stated prominently on the invoice
- the ABN of the entity issuing the invoice
- the date of issue of the invoice
- the name of the supplier
- a brief description of the items being supplied
- if the invoice is for a taxable supply *and* either a GST-free or input-taxed supply, the invoice must show each supply, the GST payable on each supply, and the total amount payable on the invoice as a whole.

For tax invoices where the total payable is less than $1000, there is another requirement in addition to those above — where the GST payable is exactly 1/11 of the total price, either the statement 'the total price includes GST' must appear on the invoice, or alternatively the GST amount on the supply can be shown separately.

For tax invoices where the total payable is more than $1000, the requirements in addition to those shown above are:

- the name of the recipient of the invoice
- the ABN or the address of the recipient
- the quantity of the goods or extent of the services being supplied.

Where the total GST amount is exactly 1/11 of the total price, the invoice amount should show either a statement such as 'the total price includes GST' or the amount of GST. A tax invoice for a total amount less than $1000 is illustrated in figure 6.2 (assuming a cash sale), and an invoice for a total amount of $1000 or more is illustrated in figure 6.3 (assuming a credit sale with the offer of a cash settlement discount for prompt payment).

Figure 6.2 Tax invoice, less than $1000 — cash sale

TAX INVOICE

EEE **Eliza's Electrical Emporium**

ABN: 23 123 123 123

15 March 2013

321 Homebush Road
Homebush NSW 2140

Description	Total
1 only Panasonic home theatre system	$528.00
Total price including GST	**$528.00**

Figure 6.3 Tax invoice, more than $1000 — credit sale

TAX INVOICE
Eliza's Electrical Emporium
ABN: 23 123 123 123

15 March 2013

321 Homebush Road
Homebush NSW 2140

TO: Joe's Coffee Bar
111 Olympic Avenue
Homebush NSW 2140

Terms: 2/10, net 30 days

Qty	Description	Unit Price	Total Price	GST	Total
2	Toshiba 68 cm 3D TV	$1400	$2800	$280	$3080
1	Panasonic Blu-ray player	350	350	35	385
				Total	**$3465**

Total price includes GST of $315

In practice, it is normal for a business to issue invoices with a common format, i.e. the invoice format as shown in figure 6.3 is often used for all transactions whether the total amount of the invoice is greater than $1000 or not. The format shown in figure 6.2 can be used only when all sales are less than $1000 in total.

Adjustment notes

When goods sold are later returned by the customer, or an allowance is given, it is a legislative requirement for the seller to give the customer an **adjustment note** detailing amendments to the GST amount for all adjustments totalling more than $50. The adjustment note represents notification that the amount of the debt owing by the customer is reduced, and includes a write-back of any GST charged in the original sale. An adjustment note is essentially a 'negative invoice'. The **adjustment** usually results in an increase (decrease) in the net GST amount payable (refundable) for a tax period. An adjustment note can arise when:

- all or part of the goods sold are returned
- an allowance, including the granting of a cash discount (but see other options below) is made
- the price of a supply or acquisition is changed
- part of, or the full amount owing, has to be written off
- the retailer cannot pay a debt.

These types of adjustment notes represent credit advices, and could be described as adjustment credit notes.

Similarly, when a retailer returns goods previously acquired, or receives an allowance, or otherwise is entitled to an adjustment on which GST has been outlaid, the original supplier is required to issue an adjustment credit note. The receipt of the adjustment note by the retailer is then used as the basis for an adjustment of the GST that arose on the original purchase.

The legislative requirements for adjustment notes are essentially the same as for invoices, including the $1000 cut-off. A typical adjustment note is illustrated in figure 6.4 (p. 234) (note that the amount exceeds $1000).

Adjustment notes — other options

The GST legislation allows a valid tax invoice to serve both as a tax invoice and as an adjustment note. The most obvious application of this in practice arises where a customer or client accepts a discount offered for prompt payment. The supplier of the goods or services would not have to issue

Figure 6.4 Adjustment note

ADJUSTMENT CREDIT NOTE
Eliza's Electrical Emporium
ABN: 23 123 123 123

16 March 2013

321 Homebush Road
Homebush NSW 2140

TO: Joe's Coffee Bar
111 Olympic Avenue
Homebush NSW 2140

Qty	Description	Unit Price	GST	Total
1	Toshiba 68 cm 3D TV — returned, surplus to requirements	$1400	$140	$1540
	Tax invoice date: 15 March 2013			
		Total amount credited		$1540

Total amount credited includes GST of $140

an adjustment note in this situation. All that is required is that the tax invoice includes the terms of settlement for prompt payment discount. Such terms are illustrated on the invoice in figure 6.3.

For those businesses that issue monthly statements, the statement can replace adjustment notes for returns, refunds, allowances and discounts provided certain requirements are met. Such a monthly statement must show all the details required for a valid tax invoice, and a separate amount must be shown for each adjustment.

In this chapter and throughout the book, tax invoices are issued for all supplies, and adjustment notes are issued for all adjustments except for cash settlement discounts. It is assumed that the terms of any cash settlement discounts offered are stated on the invoice. If the customer or client pays within the discount period, the invoice is assumed to be a combined invoice/adjustment note.

Note that even when the business collects GST on its sales and pays GST on goods purchased, GST does not affect the income statement. This reflects the principle stated above that income and expenses are recorded in the accounts at amounts excluding the GST.

6.4 Accounting for sales transactions

Learning objective 4

Account for sales transactions of retail businesses registered for the GST, including the treatment of sales returns, cash discounts, trade discounts and freight costs

A sales transaction is generally recorded by the retailer when inventory is transferred from the business to the customer. The sales revenue is recognised and recorded at the point of delivery and does not depend on when the cash for the sale is received. To record the sale, an asset account is debited and the Sales account is credited. The asset recorded in exchange for the inventory is normally Cash at Bank or Accounts Receivable. If the business is registered for the GST, the asset account (Cash or Accounts Receivable) is debited for the price of the goods plus the GST, the Sales account is credited for the net sales price (i.e. excluding GST), and the GST Collections account is credited for the GST included in the sale. The GST amount is received from the customer at the time of the cash sale or, in the case of a credit sale, when the customer pays the amount owing. The entry to record a credit sale including GST to Ray Stevens is:

Aug.	5	Accounts Receivable*	1 980	
		Sales		1 800
		GST Collections		180
		(Sold merchandise to Ray Stevens on credit)		

* Cash at Bank account is debited if the sale was for cash.

At the end of the accounting period, the balance in the Sales account shows the total amount of cash and credit sales made during the period excluding GST. When a sale is made on credit, the cash may be received in a subsequent period. As a result, there may be a significant difference between cash collections from sales and the balance accumulated in the Sales account. Cash collections from customers are shown in an entity's statement of cash flows, whereas the period's sales appear in the income statement. Future amounts to be collected are recorded as an asset, Accounts Receivable, in the balance sheet. Note that the Accounts Receivable balance includes GST.

Sales returns and allowances

In order to maintain good customer relations and to meet warranty agreements, most businesses permit a customer to return unsatisfactory goods. Goods may be regarded as unsatisfactory if they are damaged in transit, or are different from the goods ordered (e.g. wrong size, wrong colour). Alternatively, the customer may agree to keep the goods in exchange for a reduction in the sales price. The return of goods or an adjustment to the sales price (allowance) is a reduction in the amount of recorded sales, and either a cash refund is made to the customer, or the customer's account receivable is credited. If GST is included in the original sale, it is necessary to write back the GST included in the return against the GST collections amount recorded as a result of the sale. This requires a debit to the GST Collections account that was credited when the sale was made. A credit note is issued to the customer to confirm that a credit will be recorded for the return or allowance. If the business is GST-registered, then a valid adjustment credit note has to be issued if the total credited exceeds $50.

Handling returned merchandise is time-consuming and results in increased costs. For these reasons, management must look for the cause of excessive returns and correct the problem whenever possible. To provide information on the volume of returns and allowances, a contra sales account called Sales Returns and Allowances is debited as follows:

Aug.	8	Sales Returns and Allowances	300	
		GST Collections	30	
		Accounts Receivable		330
		(Nay Stevens returned unsatisfactory merchandise sold on 5 Aug for credit)*		

* Making only one journal entry at this time assumes use of the periodic inventory system, discussed in a later section of this chapter.

Note that the Sales Returns and Allowances account is debited for an amount excluding GST. **Sales returns and allowances** are subtracted from sales in the income statement in order to show *net* sales revenue, as in figure 6.1 (p. 231).

Cash (settlement) discounts

The parties involved in an inventory transaction may agree that payment is to be made immediately on transfer of the goods as in a cash sale, or payment may be delayed for some specific length of time called the **credit period**. The length of the credit period varies among businesses.

When inventory is sold on credit, the terms of payment, called the **credit terms**, agreed to by the buyer and seller should be clear about the amount due and the credit period. The terms of payment normally appear on the invoice issued by the seller (as in figure 6.3). The credit period is often expressed in the following format: 'net 30 days' or 'n/30'. In this case, the invoiced amount is due and payable within 30 days after the invoice date and no discount is offered.

To provide an incentive for the buyer to make payment before the end of the credit period, the seller may grant a **cash discount** called **discount allowed** by the seller and **discount received** by the buyer. A cash discount entitles the buyer to deduct a specified percentage of the sales price if payment is made within a given time span, the **discount period**. Cash discounts are also known as *settlement discounts*. A Discount Allowed account is used by the seller to record the amounts of sales discount granted to customers. To the seller, a discount allowed represents a reduction in the selling price and therefore should be deducted from sales revenue to determine net sales.

The purchaser, on the other hand, records the purchases discount in an account called Discount Received. In accordance with IAS 2/AASB 102, the Discount Received account should be deducted against Purchases (if the periodic inventory system is used) or against Cost of Sales (if the perpetual inventory system is used) (see later in the chapter). If the terms are quoted as '2/10, n/30' (read 'two ten, net thirty'), then the buyer has two payment options. If payment is made within 10 days of the invoice date, the buyer may deduct 2% from the amount of the invoice. If payment is not made within the 10-day discount period, the full amount is due 30 days from the invoice date.

For GST-registered businesses, if customers take advantage of a settlement discount, they are in effect paying less of the total amount due. The reduced amount consists of a normal sales price component and the GST charged on those goods. The total GST on the original sales price needs to be reduced and the amount originally recorded in the GST Collections account has to be written back.

To illustrate, assume that goods were sold to A. Jones for $1000 plus GST of $100. The tax invoice for this transaction states a cash settlement discount of 2% will be allowed if the debt is paid within 15 days. If Jones pays within the discount period, the reduction in the amount that has to be paid is 2% of $1100 or $22. This adjustment to the debt consists of $20 on the normal sale price of the goods, plus $2 of GST ($22 × 1/11). The general journal entry to record the receipt of the money within the discount period is:

Aug.	10	Cash at Bank	1 078	
		Discount Allowed	20	
		GST Collections	2	
		Accounts Receivable — A. Jones		1 100
		(Payment of account within the discount period)		

If sales returns and settlement discounts have both occurred, then any GST included in the discount amount must be adjusted on the net amount receivable, i.e. after the sales return has been recorded. To illustrate, assume that the credit terms were 2/10, n/30 on the original $1980 sale (including GST of $180) to Ray Stevens recorded previously (p. 234). The entry to record the collection within the discount period, *after allowing for the $330 return* (see entry on p. 235), which reduces the net sales to $1500 (i.e. $1800 − $300), is:

Aug.	15	Cash at Bank	1 617	
		Discount Allowed ($1500 × 2%)	30	
		GST Collections ($150 × 2%)	3	
		Accounts Receivable ($1980 − $330)		1 650
		(Received payment from Ray Stevens within		
		the discount period)		

From the seller's point of view, the purpose of offering cash discounts is to encourage early payment for the goods. The earlier payment may tend to reduce losses from uncollectable accounts receivable. To the buyer, taking advantage of the discount results in a favourable return for the use of the money, which can be shown by converting the discount rate to an annual rate. For example, with terms of 2/10, n/30 on a $300 invoice, the added cost of waiting 20 days to make payment at the end of the credit period is $6 ($300 × 2%). This is equivalent to an effective annual interest rate of 37.2%, i.e.

$$\frac{\$6}{\$294} \times \frac{365}{20} \times 100\% = 37.2\%$$

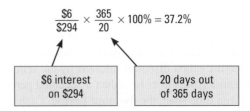

$6 interest on $294

20 days out of 365 days

Obviously, buyers would be keen to take advantage of discounts offered unless they have a more profitable use for the discount money forgone. Any discount received is recorded by the buyer in an account called Discount Received, which represents an item of income to the purchasing entity.

The ledger accounts after the general journal entries for all sales transactions with Ray Stevens have been posted appear as set out in figure 6.5. Follow each of the postings from the journal entries for Ray Stevens's transactions (beginning on p. 234) to the appropriate ledger account to appreciate the full double-entry effects of each transaction.

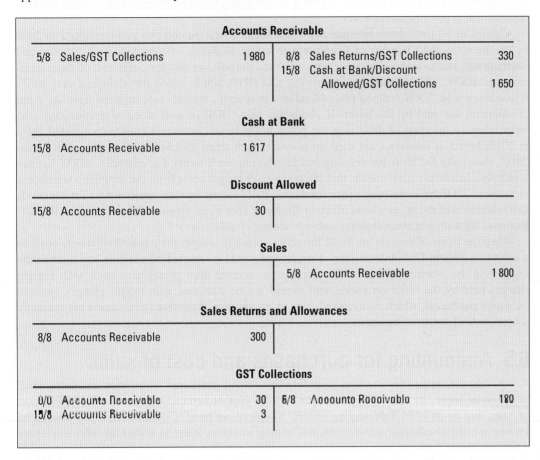

Figure 6.5 Accounts used for credit sales, after allowances and settlement discounts

	Accounts Receivable				
5/8	Sales/GST Collections	1 980	8/8	Sales Returns/GST Collections	330
			15/8	Cash at Bank/Discount Allowed/GST Collections	1 650

	Cash at Bank	
15/8	Accounts Receivable	1 617

	Discount Allowed	
15/8	Accounts Receivable	30

	Sales				
			5/8	Accounts Receivable	1 800

	Sales Returns and Allowances	
8/8	Accounts Receivable	300

	GST Collections				
8/8	Accounts Receivable	30	5/8	Accounts Receivable	180
15/8	Accounts Receivable	3			

Trade discounts

A **trade discount** is a percentage reduction granted to a customer from the normal list price. In contrast to a cash discount, a trade discount is not related to early payment but is used in determining the actual invoice price to the customer. Trade discounts enable the business to print one price list but nevertheless vary prices in dealing with different customers.

Trade discounts are not recorded in the accounts by either the buyer or the seller, and are disclosed as reductions in the list price on the sales invoice. For example, assume that a wholesaler quotes a list price of $200 per item but grants a trade discount of 30% to retailers if they purchase in quantities of ten or more. The entry to record the sale of ten units is (assuming GST of 10%):

July	10	Accounts Receivable	1 540	
		Sales ($200 × 10 units × 70%)		1 400
		GST Collections		140
		(Sale of inventory on credit, subject to a 30% trade discount)		

The buyer records a purchase of inventory for the amount of $1400, and a GST outlay of $140. If included in the terms of the sale, a cash discount is calculated on the $1400 sales price less any subsequent returns or allowances.

Freight outwards

In the process of selling and buying goods (including exporting and importing), a variety of costs are incurred in moving the goods from the seller's place of business to that of the buyer. These costs include postage, freight, insurance and customs duty. They can be significant, and the issue of who bears the costs is important. The obligations of the seller and/or buyer in relation to these costs are stated on the invoice issued by the seller. Certain abbreviations used on invoices indicate which party bears the costs.

A series of 13 three-letter international commercial terms (Incoterms) was developed in 2000 by the International Chamber of Commerce to cover all forms of transport, both national and international, and to standardise trade terms. For the purposes of this text, only two of these terms are used: **EXW**, which stands for 'ex works', and **DDP**, which stands for 'delivered duty paid'. If goods are sold 'EXW [named place of seller's business]', freight costs incurred from the point of shipment are paid by the buyer. If goods are sold 'DDP [named place of destination]', the seller bears all the costs of delivering the goods to the buyer. Incoterms have been updated again in 2010; hence, if Incoterms are used on invoices, such terms should be followed by 'Incoterms 2010', indicating the basis for defining and interpreting such terms. For example, 'EXW Sydney warehouse Incoterms 2010' means that the buyer pays freight costs from the supplier's warehouse in Sydney; 'DDP Brisbane head office Incoterms 2010' means that the supplier pays for the goods to be delivered to the buyer's head office in Brisbane. (For more detail on Incoterms, visit the ICC Business Bookstore at the following website: www.iccbooks.com.)

When the terms of the sale are DDP, the seller normally records the payment of freight costs as a debit to a Freight Outwards account. **Freight outwards** is reported as a selling and distribution expense in the income statement. The expense is incurred after goods have been sold. Freight charges paid by the seller on goods sold should not be confused with freight charges incurred on goods purchased, which is discussed later in the chapter. Note that freight costs are normally subject to GST for retail businesses.

6.5 Accounting for purchases and cost of sales

Accounting for inventories involves recording the cost of purchased inventories and being able, as the need arises, to determine which parts of the cost of inventories can be allocated to cost of sales and to an asset representing ending inventory on hand. Cost of sales must always be known in order to calculate gross profit, and ending inventory must be known in order to prepare a balance sheet.

Two distinctly different inventory systems, perpetual and periodic, can be used to determine the amounts reported for ending inventory and cost of sales. The system adopted by a business entity largely depends on the type of inventory held and the sophistication of the computer system used to keep records of inventory on hand. The perpetual inventory system has become more common especially for businesses using computerised inventory systems.

Perpetual inventory system

A **perpetual inventory system** involves keeping a current and continuous record of all inventory transactions on a separate computer record or inventory card for each type of inventory item held. Each record or card shows the quantity, unit cost and total cost for each purchase and each sale, and the inventory balance, as illustrated in figure 6.6. Note that the record or card is concerned only with recording unit and total *costs*, even for the sales columns. The sales columns disclose *cost* of sales and the balance columns show *cost* of inventory on hand. When each item is different, as with vehicles that have different options and costs, a separate inventory record is maintained for each type of item. Figure 6.6 is an example of an inventory record for a certain type of refrigerator sold by Fridge Town. The total dollar value of all inventory held by the business on any given date is represented by an aggregate of all the balances of the individual detailed inventory records.

A perpetual inventory system is commonly used in practice because it provides more timely information to managers for decisions relating to controlling and planning inventory. In the past, however, many businesses that sold a large number of items with a low unit cost found that the

Figure 6.6 Inventory record

FRIDGE TOWN

Item	Refrigerator	Location		Minimum Stock	4
Code	C350	1 unit showroom Remainder — Warehouse		Maximum Stock	17

Date	Explanation	Purchases			Sales			Balance		
		Units	Unit cost	Total cost	Units	Unit cost	Total cost	Units	Unit cost	Total cost
1/1	Beginning balance							4	650	2600
15/1	Purchases	10	650	6500				14	650	9100
21/1	Sales				3	650	1950	11	650	7150
23/1	Purchases returns	(1)	650	(650)				10	650	6500
24/1	Sales returns				(1)	650	(650)	11	650	7150

cost of maintaining a manual perpetual inventory system was prohibitive. So the perpetual inventory system was used more by businesses selling inventory of high unit value such as vehicles, airconditioning units, pianos and whitegoods.

However, with the introduction of *computer-based inventory systems*, more and more businesses have found it feasible to use the perpetual inventory system for planning and controlling their investments in inventory. Most retail businesses now use optical-scan cash registers to read product bar codes. They not only record the sales price of the item but also enter the item sold for inventory purposes. The cash registers are, in effect, data input computer terminals entering transactions into the accounting and inventory records at the point of sale. Entities adopt the perpetual system because they believe the benefits obtained from detailed inventory records outweigh the cost of maintaining the system. Computer packages such as MYOB and QuickBooks also automatically track GST collections and GST outlays. They also facilitate the preparation of the business activity statement.

Illustration of a perpetual inventory system

In a retail business that uses the perpetual inventory system, a single account — Inventory — is maintained in the general ledger to record all inventory transactions. Supporting details are entered in individual inventory cards or records for each type of inventory held. The balance in the general ledger account should equal the sum of the dollar amounts of balances shown on all the inventory cards or records. Entries for inventory transactions are made to both the Inventory account and the appropriate inventory records. A purchase of inventory is entered as an increase and hence debited; as goods are sold, the cost of sales is entered as a decrease and hence credited. To determine the dollar cost of each sale, the accountant refers to the individual inventory record of the item sold. An item sold must therefore be identified so that the unit and related cost may be removed from the appropriate inventory record and the cost removed from the Inventory account in the general ledger.

To illustrate the entries required under a perpetual inventory system, assume that Fridge Town, which is registered for the GST, sells large electrical appliances. The entries that follow are based on the transactions shown on the inventory record illustrated in figure 6.6.

The Inventory account in the general ledger of Fridge Town at the beginning of the period in T-account form is:

Inventory

1/1	Bal. b/d (4 units @ $650)	2 600		

(In practice, the balance in this account would be much larger and would show the total cost of *all* types of appliances held at the beginning of the period rather than the cost of the refrigerators only.)

Entries to record the transactions for January for Fridge Town are presented on the following pages.

Transaction 1 ***Recording purchases on credit:*** Fridge Town purchased 10 refrigerators @ $650 per unit plus GST on credit from the manufacturer, Fridge King Ltd.

Jan.	15	Inventory	6 500	
		GST Outlays	650	
		Accounts Payable		7 150
		(Purchased 10 refrigerators at $650 plus GST per unit on credit from Fridge King Ltd. Terms 2/10, n/30. Invoice date: 15 Jan.)		

Since the business is registered for the GST, the asset account (Inventory) is debited for the cost of the goods excluding the GST, the GST Outlays account is debited for the GST included in the purchase, and the Accounts Payable account is credited for the total amount owing (purchase price plus GST). (The GST outlay represents an input credit that can be offset against the GST Collections account to reduce the GST payable to the Australian Taxation Office (ATO).) The above assumes that a valid tax invoice is received as evidence of the purchase and that the purchase is a creditable acquisition under the GST legislation. For a retailing business, this is normally the case as the goods are meant for resale. At the same time, the details of the purchase are entered in the relevant perpetual inventory record (net of GST) and a new balance for inventory is calculated (see figure 6.6 — transaction of 15/1).

Transaction 2 ***Recording freight costs:*** Fridge Town paid freight cost of $420 plus GST on inventory shipped EXW supplier's warehouse.

The cost of inventory includes the invoice price plus freight charges and other costs directly related to acquiring the goods net of any GST. If several different items are included on the one tax invoice, freight costs are listed separately on the invoice and are normally recorded in a **Freight Inwards** or **Transportation-in** account. This is done because it is difficult to allocate freight cost to individual units when several different inventory items are included in a single shipment. Furthermore, in most cases the allocation of freight cost would not significantly change the financial statements of the business. The entry by Fridge Town to record payment of the freight on 17 January is:

Jan.	17	Freight Inwards	420	
		GST Outlays	42	
		Cash at Bank		462
		(Paid freight cost on goods purchased EXW supplier's warehouse)		

Note that no entry for freight appears on the inventory record shown in figure 6.6. In the income statement of Fridge Town, the freight inwards for the period is generally added as a separate item in the cost of sales or is combined directly into the amount reported as the cost of sales. Under IAS 2/AASB 102, freight inwards should be included as part of the cost of inventories and hence cost of sales.

The business responsible for paying the freight cost is directed to pay the carrier under conditions set out on the invoice. Goods can be shipped 'freight collect' when the terms are EXW and 'freight prepaid' when the terms are DDP destination. As a matter of convenience, the business not responsible for the freight costs may be directed to pay the costs on behalf of the other. When this happens, the seller and the buyer will make the necessary adjustment when receiving or paying for the goods.

To illustrate the impact of freight charges, assume Brisbane Lighting Co. Ltd sells $1000 worth of goods plus GST on credit to Sydney Supply Co. Ltd on terms EXW, 2/10, n/30, but the freight charges of $100 plus GST are paid by Brisbane Lighting Co. Ltd. (Note that under the terms of shipping, freight cost is to be borne ultimately by Sydney Supply Co. Ltd.) Brisbane Lighting Co. Ltd will add the freight cost to the invoice price, invoicing the goods at a total GST-inclusive cost of $1210. In the accounting records of Sydney Supply Co. Ltd, the freight cost and the GST are separated out and $100 recorded as freight inwards.

In these circumstances, the buyer is not entitled to claim discount on the full $1210 as this amount includes $110 in freight cost and GST thereon. If Sydney Supply Co. Ltd paid for the goods within the discount period, the amount to be paid would be:

Invoice amount ($1100 + $110 freight)	$1 210
Less: Discount received (2% of $1000)	20
GST outlays (2% of $100)	2
Amount paid	$1 188

If the terms were DDP (seller normally pays) but the buyer paid the freight cost initially to the carrier on a separate tax invoice, the buyer deducts the amount of freight when paying for the goods. Using the above figures, except that the freight cost of $100 + $10 GST was paid by Sydney Supply Co. Ltd, the amount to be forwarded by the business if paying within the discount period is:

Invoice amount (excluding freight)	$1 100
Less: Discount received (2% of $1000)	20
GST outlays (2% of $100)	2
	1 078
Less: Freight and GST paid to carrier on behalf of Brisbane Lighting Co. Ltd	110
Amount paid to Brisbane Lighting Co. Ltd	$ 968

Transaction 3 **Recording sales on credit:** Fridge Town sold 3 refrigerators for $1050 per unit plus GST on credit; cost $650 per unit.

Jan.	21	Accounts Receivable	3 465	
		Sales		3 150
		GST Collections		315
		(Sold 3 refrigerators on credit: [$1050 + $105 GST] × 3 units = $3465)		
	21	Cost of Sales	1 950	
		Inventory		1 950
		(Removing the cost of refrigerators sold from the Inventory account, $650 × 3 units)		

When a perpetual inventory system is used, each sale requires two entries. One entry records the revenue from the sale. A second entry records the cost of the items sold as a debit in the Cost of Sales account and reduces the Inventory account, which is credited. Thus, reductions are made to the Inventory account and to the individual inventory record each time a sale occurs. Note carefully that the sales entry is based on the sales price amount, whereas the amount of the inventory entry is based on the total cost of the units sold as shown on the inventory record (see figure 6.6 — transaction of 21/1).

Transaction 4 **Recording purchases returns:** Fridge Town returned to the manufacturer, Fridge King Ltd, a defective unit, which cost $650 + $65 GST.

Jan.	23	Accounts Payable	715	
		Inventory		650
		GST Outlays		65
		(Defective unit returned to Fridge King Ltd for credit on account)		

When the buyer and seller agree that an item is to be returned for credit, the buyer's Inventory account and the inventory record are both reduced to show that the item is no longer being held, as illustrated in figure 6.6 — transaction of 23/1. Note that on the inventory record the item returned is shown as a negative item in the 'Purchases' columns. The GST of $65 is written back against the GST Outlays previously debited when the unit was purchased. This reduces the amount of the input credit that can be claimed against GST Collections.

Transaction 5   Recording payment of creditors within discount period: Fridge Town paid for purchases made on 15 January within the discount period, after purchases returns on 23 January.

Accounting for discount allowed by the seller and the notation (2/10, n/30) used to describe the credit terms have already been discussed. Recall that a cash discount entitles the buyer to deduct a specified amount from the invoice price if payment is made within a specified time period. As is the case when discount is allowed to a customer, the GST included in the amount of the reduction for prompt payment of the total debt must be adjusted and written back to the GST Outlays account. In this case, the reduction for prompt payment is $129 (2% × [$7150 − $715 return]). Of this amount, $117 ($129 × 10/11) is allocated to a reduction in the amount owing, and $12 ($129 × 1/11) to GST adjustment.

The entry to record the payment made by Fridge Town within the discount period is:

Jan.	24	Accounts Payable ($7150 − $715)	6 435	
		Cash at Bank		6 306
		Discount Received ($6435 × 2% × $^{10}/_{11}$)		117
		GST Outlays ($6435 × 2% × $^{1}/_{11}$)		12
		(Paid for inventory purchased on 15 Jan.)		

Note that returns were deducted to determine the amount subject to adjustment for discount and the GST. If the payment was not made within the discount period, the credit to Cash at Bank in the entry would be for $6435. The Discount Received account has a credit balance, and is deducted from cost of sales in the income statement. Note that this transaction has no impact on the inventory record shown in figure 6.6.

Transaction 6   Recording sales returns and allowances: A refrigerator that was sold by Fridge Town on 21 January for $1050 plus GST is returned by a customer for credit. The unit cost $650.

Jan.	24	Sales Returns and Allowances	1 050	
		GST Collections	105	
		Accounts Receivable		1 155
		(A refrigerator sold on 21 Jan. was returned by customer)		
	24	Inventory	650	
		Cost of Sales		650
		(Returned refrigerator was placed back in inventory)		

An item returned by a customer also requires two entries in order to reverse the effects of the two entries made to record the original sale. The first entry records the sales return. Because it is assumed that the unit is still suitable for sale, a second entry is necessary to eliminate the cost of sales previously recorded and restore the unit to the Inventory account. Note that the first entry is based on the original sales price of $1050 plus GST, whereas in the second entry the inventory is recorded only at its cost, $650. The unit returned is also entered on the inventory record (see figure 6.6 — transaction of 24/1) by recording it as a negative item in the 'Sales' columns for its cost price, $650.

If the inventory returned was unfit for resale, the debit to Inventory in the second journal entry above would be replaced by a debit to Inventory Loss or some other similar expense account.

The ledger accounts for Fridge Town after the above general journal entries for a perpetual inventory system have been posted appear in figure 6.7 (p. 243). For each general journal entry, follow

Perpetual Inventory System

LEDGER OF FRIDGE TOWN

Accounts Receivable

21/1	Sales/GST Collections	3 465	24/1	Sales Returns/GST Collections	1 155

Accounts Payable

23/1	Inventory/GST Outlays	715	15/1	Inventory/GST Outlays	7 150
24/1	Cash at Bank/Discount Received/GST Outlays	6 435			

Cash at Bank

			17/1	Freight Inwards/GST Outlays	462
			24/1	Accounts Payable	6 306

Cost of Sales

21/1	Inventory	1 950	24/1	Inventory (Return)	650

Sales

			21/1	Accounts Receivable	3 150

Freight Inwards

17/1	Cash at Bank	420	

GST Collections

24/1	Accounts Receivable	105	21/1	Accounts Receivable	315

GST Outlays

15/1	Accounts Payable	650	23/1	Accounts Payable (Return)	65
17/1	Cash at Bank	42	24/1	Accounts Payable	12

Inventory

1/1	Balance	2 600	21/1	Cost of Sales	1 950
15/1	Accounts Payable	6 500	23/1	Accounts Payable	650
24/1	Cost of Sales (Return)	650			

Discount Received

			24/1	Accounts Payable	117

Sales Returns and Allowances

24/1	Accounts Receivable	1 050	

Figure 6.7 Ledger of Fridge Town, showing January purchases and sales — perpetual inventory system

each of the postings to the appropriate ledger account to appreciate the full double-entry effects of each transaction.

Note that the balance in the Inventory account in figure 6.7 agrees with the balance on the inventory record (see figure 6.6). All amounts recorded in the Inventory account exclude GST. By maintaining a continuous inventory record, it is not necessary to take a physical count of the inventory on hand to determine an inventory balance. Entities using a perpetual inventory system nevertheless must undertake a physical inventory count at least once a year to verify the accuracy of the inventory records. A **physical inventory count** or **stocktake** involves (1) counting all inventory units on hand, (2) determining the unit cost of items in stock from purchase invoices, and (3) multiplying unit cost by units of inventory to determine the total cost of inventory. In a computerised inventory system, once the items have been counted and entered into the system, the computer performs all of the calculations to determine cost.

Differences between the physical count and inventory records can result from clerical error, theft of goods, breakage and obsolescence. Causes of large discrepancies should be identified and eliminated if at all possible. In some cases, the difference may result from natural causes such as evaporation or shrinkage. Performing a stocktake is discussed in more detail in a later chapter.

At the end of the year, if the physical inventory and the Inventory account balances differ, a journal entry is made to bring the account balance into agreement with the physical count. Assuming that the physical inventory showed that the cost of inventory on hand was $5850, the entry to reduce the Inventory account by $1300 is:

Dec.	31	Inventory Shortage Expense	1 300	
		Inventory		1 300
		(Adjusting the Inventory account to the physical count)		

The Inventory Shortage Expense account is for management information only. Normally the account is included with the cost of sales in the income statement. This will result in the same cost of sales if the periodic inventory system is used.

Periodic inventory system

Businesses that sell a large number of low-cost items often find the maintenance of perpetual inventory records for all types of inventory too costly and time-consuming to be practical, unless they have access to a computerised inventory system. Such businesses include fruit shops, newsagents, butchers and coffee shops. A store operating with high volume may conveniently record the amount of each sale, but would find it difficult to trace the cost of each item sold back to detailed inventory records. Entities that do not use a perpetual inventory system use a **periodic inventory system**.

Illustration of a periodic inventory system

In a periodic inventory system, the beginning balance in the Inventory account does not change until the end of the accounting period. The costs of additional inventory purchased during a period are recorded in a Purchases account rather than in the Inventory account. When inventory is sold, only one entry is made and that is to record the sales at selling price. Since no record of the particular goods sold is maintained during the period, it is necessary to physically count the units on hand and multiply the number of units by the cost per unit to determine the cost of inventory on hand. Once this is completed, the cost of sales is calculated as:

Cost of beginning inventory	$2 600
Add: Net cost of goods purchased during the current period	6 153*
Cost of goods available for sale	8 753
Less: Cost of ending inventory (from physical stocktake)	5 850
Cost of sales	$2 903

* ($6500 + $420 freight − $650 returns − $117 discount received)

Figure 6.8 Cost of sales (periodic inventory system)

A
Beginning inventory
$2600

B
Net cost of purchases
$6153

Cost of goods available for sale = $8753

C
Cost of sales
$2903

D
Ending inventory
$5850

Note: If A, B and D are known, C can be calculated.

The **ending inventory** for the current period becomes the **beginning inventory** for the following period. The process of adjusting the Inventory account to its end-of-year balance is discussed later in this chapter.

A periodic inventory system is illustrated using the same data for Fridge Town in the perpetual inventory system above, so that you can compare the two systems. In practice, remember, the periodic system is used when large volumes of low-priced items are sold. Note that no detailed inventory records (as illustrated in figure 6.6) are maintained. The Inventory account at the beginning of the period for Fridge Town is:

Inventory

1/1	Bal. b/d (4 units @ $650)	2 600	

The beginning inventory of $2600 is the ending inventory of the previous period established by a physical stocktake conducted on the last day of the preceding period.

Transaction 1 *Recording purchases on credit:* Fridge Town purchased 10 refrigerators @ $650 per unit plus GST on credit from the manufacturer, Fridge King Ltd.

Jan.	15	Purchases	6 500	
		GST Outlays	650	
		Accounts Payable		7 150
		(Purchased 10 refrigerators at $650 plus GST per unit on credit from Fridge King Ltd. Terms 2/10, n/30. Invoice date: 15 Jan.)		

The **Purchases** account is a temporary account used to accumulate the cost (excluding GST) of all merchandise acquired for resale during the period. This account is used to record only inventory purchases. Other acquisitions of assets, e.g. equipment, are recorded in appropriate asset accounts. Because the balance is closed at the end of each accounting period, the account balance reflects the total purchases to date for the current period.

Transaction 2 *Recording freight costs:* Fridge Town paid freight cost of $420 plus GST on inventory purchased EXW supplier's warehouse.

Jan.	17	Freight Inwards	420	
		GST Outlays	42	
		Cash at Bank		462
		(Paid freight cost on goods purchased EXW supplier's warehouse)		

Freight inwards is reported as an additional cost of purchases, as is required under IAS 2/ AASB 102.

Transaction 3 *Recording sales on credit:* Fridge Town sold 3 refrigerators for $1050 per unit plus GST on credit.

Jan.	21	Accounts Receivable	3 465	
		Sales		3 150
		GST Collections		315
		(Sold inventory on credit: [$1050 + $105 GST] × 3 = $3465)		

At the time of sale, only one entry is made to record the sale. A second entry is not made to record the cost of sales as is the case in the perpetual inventory system.

Transaction 4 ***Recording purchases returns:*** Fridge Town returned to the manufacturer, Fridge King Ltd, a defective unit, which cost $650 + $65 GST.

Jan.	23	Accounts Payable	715	
		Purchases Returns and Allowances		650
		GST Outlays		65
		(Defective unit returned to Fridge King Ltd for credit)		

There is a cost to the business to order merchandise, receive and inspect the merchandise, and to repack it for return to the seller. To provide relevant information to management concerning the total amount of goods returned, the return is recorded in a contra purchases account, **Purchases Returns and Allowances** (net of GST), rather than directly as a credit to the Purchases account. The entry is the same if the goods are kept by the buyer and a downward adjustment or allowance is made to the invoice cost.

Transaction 5 ***Recording payment of creditors within discount period:*** Fridge Town paid for purchases made on 15 January within the discount period, after purchases returns on 23 January.

Jan.	24	Accounts Payable ($7150 − $715)	6 435	
		Cash at Bank		6 306
		Discount Received ($6435 × 2% × $^{10}/_{11}$)		117
		GST Outlays ($6435 × 2% × $^{1}/_{11}$)		12
		(Paid for inventory purchased on 15 Jan.)		

Note that this entry is the same as the one made under the perpetual inventory system. Furthermore, discounts received are reported as a reduction of cost of sales, as in the perpetual system.

Transaction 6 ***Recording sales returns and allowances:*** A refrigerator that was sold by Fridge Town on 21 January for $1050 plus GST is returned by a customer for credit.

Jan.	24	Sales Returns and Allowances	1 050	
		GST Collections	105	
		Accounts Receivable		1 155
		(A refrigerator sold on 21 Jan. was returned by customer)		

When a periodic inventory system is used, only one entry is needed to record the merchandise returned. A second entry, to reverse the cost of sales, is not needed here because the cost of sales was not recorded on the date of sale.

The ledger accounts after the above general journal entries for a periodic inventory system have been posted appear as set out in figure 6.9 (p. 247). For each general journal entry, follow each of the postings to the appropriate ledger account to appreciate the full double-entry effects of each transaction.

Perpetual and periodic inventory systems contrasted

The basic differences between the perpetual and periodic inventory systems for Fridge Town are illustrated by the entries shown in figure 6.10 (p. 248). First, under the perpetual inventory system the balance in the Inventory account provides a continuous and current record of inventory on hand. Second, a perpetual system provides for an accumulation of the cost of sales during the period. In contrast, a physical stocktake must be taken to determine the inventory on hand and the cost of sales when a periodic inventory system is used. A physical inventory count is taken under the perpetual system only to verify the accuracy of the recorded ending inventory. Note also that a Purchases account is used in a periodic inventory system, whereas a Cost of Sales account is maintained with a perpetual inventory system.

Periodic Inventory System

LEDGER OF FRIDGE TOWN

Accounts Receivable

21/1	Sales/GST Collections	3 465	24/1	Sales Returns/GST Collections	1 155

Accounts Payable

23/1	Purchases Returns/GST Outlays	715	15/1	Purchases/GST Outlays	7 150
24/1	Cash at Bank/Discount Received/GST Outlays	6 435			

Cash at Bank

			17/1	Freight Inwards/GST Outlays	462
			24/1	Accounts Payable	6 306

Purchases Returns and Allowances

			24/1	Accounts Payable	650

Sales

			21/1	Accounts Receivable	3 150

Freight Inwards

17/1	Cash at Bank	420	

GST Collections

24/1	Accounts Receivable	105	21/1	Accounts Receivable	315

GST Outlays

15/1	Accounts Payable	650	23/1	Accounts Payable (Return)	65
17/1	Cash at Bank	42	24/1	Accounts Payable	12

Purchases

15/1	Accounts Payable	6 500	

Discount Received

			24/1	Accounts Payable	117

Sales Returns and Allowances

24/1	Accounts Receivable	1 050	

Figure 6.9 Ledger of Fridge Town, showing January purchases and sales — periodic inventory system

It is also instructive to compare the general ledger accounts under the two systems illustrated in figures 6.7 and 6.9.

Figure 6.10 Comparison of entries to record inventory transactions under the perpetual and periodic inventory systems

Data:		
	Cost per unit	$ 650
	Selling price per unit	$1050 (plus GST of 10%)
	Beginning inventory	4 units

Perpetual Inventory System   Periodic Inventory System

FRIDGE TOWN

Inventory account — beginning of the period

Inventory				Inventory		
4 units	2 600			4 units	2 600	

1. *Purchased 10 units of merchandise on credit. Terms 2/10, n/30; EXW warehouse.*

Inventory (10 × $650)	6 500		Purchases	6 500	
GST Outlays	650		GST Outlays	650	
Accounts Payable		7 150	Accounts Payable		7 150

2. *Paid freight cost.*

Freight Inwards	420		Freight Inwards	420	
GST Outlays	42		GST Outlays	42	
Cash at Bank		462	Cash at Bank		462

3. *Sold 3 units to customers on credit.*

Accounts Receivable	3 465		Accounts Receivable	3 465	
Sales (3 × $1050)		3 150	Sales		3 150
GST Collections		315	GST Collections		315
Cost of Sales	1 950				
Inventory (3 × $650)		1 950			

4. *Returned 1 unit to the supplier for credit on account.*

Accounts Payable	715		Accounts Payable	715	
Inventory (1 × $650)		650	Purchases Returns		
GST Outlays		65	and Allowances		650
			GST Outlays		65

5. *Paid for purchases within discount period.*

Accounts Payable	6 435		Accounts Payable	6 435	
Cash at Bank		6 306	Cash at Bank		6 306
Discount Received		117	Discount Received		117
GST Outlays		12	GST Outlays		12

6. *Customer returned 1 unit for credit on account.*

Sales Returns and			Sales Returns and		
Allowances	1 050		Allowances	1 050	
GST Collections	105		GST Collections	105	
Accounts Receivable		1 155	Accounts Receivable		1 155
Inventory (1 × $650)	650				
Cost of Sales		650			

Inventory account — end of the period

Inventory					Inventory			
1/1 Balance b/d	2 600	21/1 Cost of Sales	1 950		Balance b/d	2 600		
15/1 Accounts Payable	6 500	24/1 Accounts Payable	650					
24/1 Cost of Sales	650	Balance c/d	7 150					
	9 750		9 750					

Based on the six transactions recorded in figure 6.10, income statements are prepared in figure 6.11 for both systems. It is assumed that a physical stocktake taken at the end of the period confirmed that 11 units were on hand. The dollar amount is calculated to be $7150 (11 units × $650). Note that the net sales, cost of sales and gross profit are the same in both statements.

Figure 6.11 Partial income statements, perpetual and periodic inventory systems

FRIDGE TOWN
Income Statement
for the month ended 31 January

Perpetual Inventory System

Sales revenue	$3 150
Less: Sales returns and allowances	1 050
Net sales revenue	2 100
Cost of sales*	1 603
GROSS PROFIT	$ 497

* $1603 = $1950 − $650 + $420 − $117
Freight inwards and discount received are combined with cost of sales.

Periodic Inventory System

Sales revenue		$3 150
Less: Sales returns and allowances		1 050
Net sales revenue		2 100
Cost of sales:		
Cost of beginning inventory		$2 600
Add: Cost of purchases	$6 500	
Freight inwards	420	
	6 920	
Less: Purchases returns and allowances	650	
Discount received	117	
Cost of net purchases		6 153
Cost of goods available for sale		8 753
Less: Cost of ending inventory		7 150
Cost of sales		1 603
GROSS PROFIT		$ 497

Some relationships shown in statement format for the *periodic* inventory system are summarised below:
1. Net sales revenue = Sales revenue − Sales returns and allowances − Discount allowed
2. Gross profit = Net sales revenue − Cost of sales
3. Cost of sales = Cost of beginning inventory + Cost of net purchases − Cost of ending inventory
4. Cost of net purchases = Cost of purchases + Freight inwards − Purchases returns and allowances − Discount received

Familiarity with these relationships will help you to understand the characteristics of the periodic inventory system and make it easier for you to determine the effect of inventory errors.

Under the periodic inventory system, the cost of sales is a residual amount after deducting the ending inventory from the cost of all goods available for sale. As a result, losses of inventory from causes such as theft, shrinkage, breakage and clerical error are difficult to identify. Techniques used to determine any large inventory losses are examined in a later chapter.

BUSINESS KNOWLEDGE

Ship pop-up shops and sustainability

Market research was one of the objectives for the Australian fashion designer and retailer, Lisa Gorman, when she erected an environmentally sustainable pop-up shop in the carpark at the 2008 Australian Fashion Week. Rather than a runway show, Gorman used a sparsely fitted shipping container to promote her organic range to media and buyers. Samples in all sizes were displayed and orders were made online. Clothing was complemented with organic tea and snacks. "The ship-shop as we called it, was really about reiterating to the consumer that not only are we making (sustainable clothing), we are choosing to retail it in a responsible way," Gorman says.

For Gorman, the pop-up is part of a broad philosophical and organisational shift towards sustainability. The container was made from recycled wood, minimally furnished and operated on one power point. She is implementing carbon-minimising practices across her business and is planning an environmentally friendly tour of the ship-shop around Australia. "Using a different medium to promote the range generated a great response," she says. "Our sales in the organic range are up 500 per cent. While I can't contribute that solely to the ship-shop, it was definitely a factor."

It seems that if you're smart enough, pop-up can turn a profit. It's power is psychological, says retail analyst and author Paco Underhill in *Why We Buy: The Science of Shopping:* "If you approach a store with the knowledge that it's got a limited life span it becomes a different set of values." he says. "It becomes a news item."

But unlike most trends, it is a positive when we say it's here today and gone tomorrow.

Source: Excerpt from Emma Duncan, 'Here today, gone tomorrow', *InTheBlack.*

Learning objective 6

Prepare worksheets and close the accounts for retail businesses for both the perpetual and periodic inventory systems

6.6 End of period processes

Illustration of worksheets in retail businesses

At the end of the accounting period, after all the year's transactions have been posted to the ledger, a worksheet can be used to organise the information needed to prepare financial statements and closing entries. Worksheets for a perpetual and a periodic inventory system are presented in figures 6.12 and 6.13 for The Fashion Shop Ltd. In practice, however, it is most likely that The Fashion Shop Ltd would use a perpetual inventory system.

In both figures 6.12 and 6.13, the first two columns (unadjusted trial balance) contain a listing of the account balances taken from the general ledger of the company. For simplicity, the various types of selling and administrative expense accounts have been combined into one item for each category.

The adjustments columns are for the end-of-year adjustments based on the following information:

(a) Accrued salaries: Sales   \$ 2 200
           Administrative   1 050
(b) Depreciation of store equipment   7 600
(c) Depreciation of office equipment   3 200
(d) Prepaid insurance expired during the year   610
(e) Income tax expense for the current period   10 470

Based on a physical inventory taken on 31 December each year, the ending inventory was determined to be \$53 260 at the end of the current period and was \$58 400 at the end of the previous period.

The worksheets (in figures 6.12 and 6.13) prepared for a business organised as a company are essentially the same as the one illustrated in chapter 4 for a sole trader. In the trial balance columns there are new equity accounts — Share Capital (\$50 000 credit) and Retained Earnings (\$20 000 credit) — that appear in place of the owner's Capital account. These new accounts are extended to the appropriate balance sheet columns. In addition, the income tax expense for The Fashion Shop Ltd is calculated to be \$10 470 in respect of the year ended 31 December 2013. This requires payment in the following period to the ATO, but is an expense of doing business in the current period. Hence, an adjusting entry [entry (e)] is made in the adjustments column to debit Income Tax Expense and to credit the Current Tax Liability account. The Income Tax Expense account is extended to the income statement debit column, and the Current Tax Liability is extended to the balance sheet credit column to be reported as a current liability. Note that GST Collections represents the amount of GST collected on behalf of the ATO. After the total of GST Outlays is offset against this amount (as GST input credits), the net amount is payable to the ATO when the next business activity statement is lodged.

Figure 6.12 Worksheet based on perpetual inventory system

THE FASHION SHOP LTD
Worksheet
for the year ended 31 December 2013

Account	Unadjusted trial balance Debit	Credit	Adjustments Debit	Credit	Adjusted trial balance Debit	Credit	Income statement Debit	Credit	Balance sheet Debit	Credit
Cash at Bank	50 170				50 170				50 170	
Accounts Receivable	98 710				98 710				98 710	
Inventory	53 260				53 260				53 260	
Prepaid Insurance	1 910			(d) 610	1 300				1 300	
GST Outlays	63 200				63 200				63 200	
Store Equipment	72 000				72 000				72 000	
Accumulated Depreciation – Store Equipment		46 600		(b) 7 600		54 200				54 200
Office Equipment	26 400				26 400				26 400	
Accumulated Depreciation – Office Equipment		13 300		(c) 3 200		16 500				16 500
Accounts Payable		107 610				107 610				107 610
GST Collections		69 200				69 200				69 200
Share Capital		50 000				50 000				50 000
Retained Earnings		20 000				20 000				20 000
Sales		714 280				714 280		714 280		
Sales Returns and Allowances	21 390				21 390		21 390			
Discount Allowed	3 260				3 260		3 260			
Rent Revenue		2 400				2 400		2 400		
Cost of Sales	464 280				464 280		464 280			
Freight Inwards	6 210				6 210		6 210			
Discount Received		2 860				2 860		2 860		
Selling and Distribution Expenses	90 470		(a) 2 200 (b) 7 600		100 270		100 270			
Administrative Expenses	73 990		(a) 1 050 (c) 3 200 (d) 610		78 850		78 850			
Interest Expense	1 000				1 000		1 000			
	1 026 250	1 026 250								
Salaries Payable				(a) 3 250		3 250				3 250
Income Tax Expense			(e) 10 470		10 470		10 470			
Current Tax Liability				(e) 10 470		10 470				10 470
			25 130	25 130	1 050 770	1 050 770	685 730	719 540	365 040	331 230
Profit							33 810			33 810
							719 540	719 540	365 040	365 040

Perpetual inventory system

Referring to the worksheet in figure 6.12, when a perpetual inventory system is used to account for the flow of goods, the balance in the Inventory account is the ending inventory amount. This balance is extended to the balance sheet debit column. The cost of sales, freight inwards and discounts received are extended along with the other temporary accounts to the proper income statement columns. The rest of the worksheet is completed in the manner illustrated in chapter 4. In a computerised system, such a worksheet can be prepared using an appropriate spreadsheet package, or preparation of worksheets may be avoided completely.

Figure 6.13 Worksheet based on periodic inventory system

THE FASHION SHOP LTD
Worksheet
for the year ended 31 December 2013

Account	Unadjusted trial balance Debit	Unadjusted trial balance Credit	Adjustments Debit	Adjustments Credit	Adjusted trial balance Debit	Adjusted trial balance Credit	Income statement Debit	Income statement Credit	Balance sheet Debit	Balance sheet Credit
Cash at Bank	50 170				50 170				50 170	
Accounts Receivable	98 710				98 710				98 710	
Inventory	58 400				58 400		58 400	53 260	53 260	
Prepaid Insurance	1 910			(d) 610	1 300				1 300	
GST Outlays	63 200				63 200				63 200	
Store Equipment	72 000				72 000				72 000	
Accumulated Depreciation – Store Equipment		46 600		(b) 7 600		54 200				54 200
Office Equipment	26 400				26 400				26 400	
Accumulated Depreciation – Office Equipment		13 300		(c) 3 200		16 500				16 500
Accounts Payable		107 610				107 610				107 610
GST Collections		69 200				69 200				69 200
Share Capital		50 000				50 000				50 000
Retained Earnings		20 000				20 000				20 000
Sales		714 280				714 280		714 280		
Sales Returns and Allowances	21 390				21 390		21 390			
Discount Allowed	3 260				3 260		3 260			
Rent Revenue		2 400				2 400		2 400		
Purchases	472 620				472 620		472 620			
Freight Inwards	6 210				6 210		6 210			
Purchases Returns and Allowances		13 480				13 480		13 480		
Discount Received		2 860				2 860		2 860		
Selling and Distribution Expenses	90 470		(a) 2 200 (b) 7 600		100 270		100 270			
Administrative Expenses	73 990		(a) 1 050 (c) 3 200 (d) 610		78 850		78 850			
Interest Expense	1 000				1 000		1 000			
	1 039 730	1 039 730								
Salaries Payable				(a) 3 250		3 250				3 250
Income Tax Expense			(e) 10 470		10 470		10 470			
Current Tax Liability				(e) 10 470		10 470				10 470
			25 130	25 130	1 064 250	1 064 250	752 470	786 280	365 040	331 230
Profit							33 810			33 810
							786 280	786 280	365 040	365 040

Closing entries based on the income statement columns are presented in figure 6.14 (p. 253). Except for the new accounts introduced in this chapter, the closing process for a retail business is similar to that illustrated for a service business. For comparison purposes, the closing entries based on the periodic inventory system are also shown.

Periodic inventory system

Under a periodic inventory system (see worksheet in figure 6.13), the inventory balance of $58 400 listed in the unadjusted trial balance debit column is the beginning inventory amount. This amount is extended to the income statement debit column because it is added to the cost of net purchases to determine the cost of goods available for sale. The accounts that affect the cost of net purchases — Purchases, Purchases Returns and Allowances, Discount Received, and Freight Inwards — are also extended to the income statement columns. The ending inventory of $53 260 is entered directly in the income statement credit column since it is a deduction from the cost of goods available for sale when calculating the cost of sales. The amount is also entered in the balance sheet debit column because the ending inventory is an asset, and because it is necessary to enter an equal debit to maintain the equality of debits and credits in the worksheet.

At the end of the period, it is necessary to remove the beginning inventory balance and record the ending inventory in the Inventory account. There are several ways of doing this, and each method produces the same cost of sales amount. The approach adopted in this text is to adjust the Inventory account during the closing process at the same time the other income statement accounts are closed. This approach is illustrated in figure 6.14 for The Fashion Shop Ltd. The credit to the Inventory account of $58 400 in the first closing entry removes the beginning inventory balance and transfers it to the Profit or Loss Summary account. The ending inventory balance of $53 260 is recorded in the second closing entry. Before this second entry is made and posted, the ending inventory is not reported in any ledger accounts.

	Perpetual		Periodic	
	Debit	Credit	Debit	Credit
Profit or Loss Summary	685 730		752 470	
Inventory (beginning)		—		58 400
Sales Returns and Allowances		21 390		21 390
Cost of Sales		464 280		—
Purchases		—		472 620
Freight Inwards		6 210		6 210
Selling and Distribution Expenses		100 270		100 270
Administrative Expenses		78 850		78 850
Discount Allowed		3 260		3 260
Income Tax Expense		10 470		10 470
Interest Expense		1 000		1 000
(Closing temporary debit balances)				
Sales	714 280		714 280	
Purchases Returns and Allowances	—		13 480	
Discount Received	2 860		2 860	
Rent Revenue	2 400		2 400	
Inventory (ending)	—		53 260	
Profit or Loss Summary		719 540		786 280
(Closing temporary credit balances and inserting ending inventory balance)				
Profit or Loss Summary	33 810		33 810	
Retained Earnings		33 810		33 810
(Closing profit to retained earnings)				

Figure 6.14 Closing entries, perpetual and periodic inventory systems

6.7 Detailed income statement for a retailer

Learning objective 7

Prepare a detailed income statement for a retail business

A detailed income statement for The Fashion Shop Ltd is presented in figure 6.15 (p. 254). In this figure, for illustrative purposes only, we assume that the company uses a periodic inventory system and therefore reports a detailed cost-of-sales section. In a perpetual inventory system, cost of sales is shown on one line, as in figure 6.11 for Fridge Town. Expenses are classified by function into three categories: selling and distribution, administrative, and finance and other expenses.

In the figure, individual types of expenses and amounts are assumed within each category for illustrative purposes. Note the items included in finance and other expenses, especially the discount allowed. Discount received is shown as an item of other income. A detailed listing of individual expenses was not included in the worksheet.

Figure 6.15 Income statement for a retail business — periodic inventory system

THE FASHION SHOP LTD
Income Statement
for the year ended 31 December 2013

INCOME			
Revenue:			
Sales revenue			$714 280
Less: Sales returns and allowances			21 390
Discount allowed			3 260
Net sales revenue			689 630
Cost of sales:			
Inventory 1/1/13		$ 58 400	
Add: Purchases	$472 620		
Freight inwards	6 210		
	478 830		
Less: Purchases returns and allowances	13 480		
Discount received	2 860		
Net cost of purchases		462 490	
Cost of goods available for sale		520 890	
Less: Inventory 31/12/13		53 260	
Cost of sales			467 630
GROSS PROFIT			222 000
Other income:			
Rent revenue			2 400
			224 400
EXPENSES			
Selling and distribution expenses:			
Sales salaries and commission expense		61 040	
Freight outwards		6 210	
Advertising expense		8 420	
Rent expense — store space		17 000	
Depr. expense — store equipment		7 600	
		100 270	
Administrative expenses:			
Office salaries expense		63 040	
Rent expense — office space		12 000	
Depr. expense — office equipment		3 200	
Insurance expense		610	
		78 850	
Finance and other expenses:			
Interest expense		1 000	
			180 120
PROFIT BEFORE INCOME TAX			44 280
Less: Income tax expense			10 470
PROFIT			$ 33 810

6.8 Net price method and settlement discounts

Learning objective 8

Describe the net method of recording purchases and sales whenever there are settlement discounts.

Purchases and sales were recorded at the gross invoice price in the preceding illustrations. Under the gross price method, inventory purchases are recorded at the gross, or full, invoice price, and any discount received is not recorded unless payment is made within the discount period. Any discounts lost are not separately reported for use by management and become a part of the inventory cost. In effect, the gross price method assumes initially that discounts will not be taken; they are recorded later in the accounts only when the discounts are taken by the seller or buyer.

However, if one assumes that discounts are normally taken, then a discount received could be seen as reducing the initial unit cost of the inventory purchased. If the subsequent payment is not made within the discount period, the discount is lost and could be reported as interest expense. Thus, it could be argued that use of the gross price method overstates inventory costs and understates interest expense.

In the accounting records of the seller, when the gross price method is used, a sale is recorded for the full invoice price and a Discount Allowed account is recorded if the customer pays within the discount period. If a discount is not taken, it is not separately reported and the amount of the discount is included in the Sales account. However, it could be argued that a discount not taken is an added charge to the customer for permitting the deferral of the payment and should be reported as a separate item of other revenue.

An alternative procedure to the gross price method, namely the net price method, could be used. Under the net price method, a buyer of inventory debits purchases of inventory (credits sales in the case of the selling business) for the net invoice amount (invoice price less the expected cash discount) when recording the initial transaction, on the assumption that all discounts on offer will be taken. This would be more in line with the requirement of IAS 2/AASB 102 to record inventory at the net cost of purchases.

To illustrate the net price method (and ignoring GST), assume the purchase of goods for $5850 on terms of 2/10, n/30, and a settlement of the account balance within the discount period. The entries for both the buying and selling business, assuming both use the periodic inventory system, are as follows:

		Buying business		Selling business	
Jan.	15	Purchases	5 733	Accounts Receivable	5 733
		Accounts Payable	5 733	Sales	5 733
		(Invoice price of $5850 less 2% discount of $117 = $5733.)			
Jan.	24	Accounts Payable	5 733	Cash at Bank	5 733
		Cash at Bank	5 733	Accounts Receivable	5 733

If payment is not made within the discount period, the full invoice price of $5850 must be paid since the cash discount is lost. The entry is as follows:

Buying business			Selling business		
Accounts Payable	5 733		Cash at Bank	5 850	
Discount Lost	117		Discount Earned		117
Cash at Bank		5 850	Accounts Receivable		5 733

Note that the Accounts Payable (Accounts Receivable) account must be reduced by $5733 to offset the initial credit (debit) of $5733 made to the account on 15 January even though cash of $5850 was eventually paid (received). The difference of $117 is the discount. Discount Lost is a financial expense that results from delaying payment and is reported along with interest expense in the income statement. Discount Earned is considered interest revenue and is reported in the income statement as other revenue.

The net method is considered by the authors as conceptually preferable because the cost of the asset purchased (or sales revenue recognised) is recorded in terms of the net cash price. This method also results in reporting the amounts of discount lost and discount earned as separate items for use by management in evaluating financial management practices since discounts should normally be taken. Nevertheless, the gross method is commonly used in practice because it avoids the practical problem of allocating the discount to individual units when a physical inventory is taken and when the amounts are entered on individual inventory records under the perpetual inventory system. In addition, the discount amounts involved are often immaterial. In this text, the gross price method of recording purchases will be used.

6.9 Profitability analysis for decision making

The income statement for a business engaged in retailing is illustrated in summary form in figure 6.1 (p. 231), and in detail in figure 6.15. This statement is structured to present a picture of the main items of income and expense associated with retail operations. This structure enables management to assess the profitability of operations, by monitoring over time the relationships that exist among sales, cost of sales, gross profit, expenses and profit. For example, if cost of sales rises faster proportionately than sales, then gross profit will decline. Overall profit, however, could remain stable if there are compensating savings in expenses.

These relationships are commonly expressed in the form of percentages or ratios, and are monitored over time to ascertain trends. Comparison with those ratios of similar business entities or industry averages (if available) can aid in interpreting ratios to assess profitability performance. These common ratios are gross profit ratio, profit margin (or return on sales ratio), expenses to sales and inventory turnover. Note that these ratios are not affected by GST as all amounts used in their calculation exclude GST.

Gross profit ratio

The **gross profit ratio** expresses gross profit as a percentage of net sales, and represents the portion of the sales dollar that is reflected in gross profit. It is calculated by:

$$\frac{\text{Gross profit}}{\text{Net sales}} \times 100\%$$

This ratio is considered informative because it expresses gross profit in relation to sales. This ratio also indirectly reflects the relationship of cost of sales to sales. A decline in the ratio over time could be caused by selling price reductions or increased cost of sales. Any decline is carefully monitored to determine whether the trend is temporary or long term requiring management action to correct the trend if possible.

Profit margin

The **profit margin** reflects the portion of each sales dollar that ends up as final profit. It is calculated by:

$$\frac{\text{Profit (after tax)}}{\text{Net sales}} \times 100\%$$

Again, this ratio is considered more informative than simply stating profit in absolute terms, because it expresses profit as a proportion of sales. Adequacy of the profit margin depends on the industry in which the entity is involved. For example, it would be expected that a large supermarket chain would have a low profit margin, compensated by a large volume of sales, whereas a jewellery store would generally have a high profit margin, offset by a low sales volume. Again, the trend in this ratio over time is more relevant to managers, and remedial action needs to be taken if a long-term unfavourable trend becomes apparent.

Expenses to sales ratio

Expenses to sales ratio reflects the portion of each sales dollar that is needed to meet the entity's expenses other than cost of sales. It is calculated by:

$$\frac{\text{Expenses}}{\text{Net sales}} \times 100\%$$

Similar to the other ratios above, this ratio is considered more informative than simply stating expenses in absolute terms because it shows the relationship between expenses and sales. Reducing costs has been heavily pursued by businesses in Australia in recent years, greatly enhancing their profit performance. Of course, there is a limit to just how far costs can be cut without service declining, which can lead to loss of customers and hence loss of income.

Inventory turnover

Another important ratio used to assess performance in a retail business is the **inventory turnover**. This ratio indicates the number of times average inventory has been sold during a period, and is calculated as follows:

$$\frac{\text{Cost of sales}}{\text{Average inventory}}$$

Since cost of sales represents an 'average' of the cost of all items sold during an accounting period, the ratio uses the 'average' inventory for the period in order to assess more accurately the number of times the inventory has been sold during that period. Average inventory is usually calculated as the mean of the beginning and ending inventories for the period. The higher the ratio, the higher the turnover of inventory and, usually, the higher the profitability of the business. However, the inventory turnover ratio can vary significantly from industry to industry; for example, a retailer of spare parts for motor vehicles will always have a lower inventory turnover than a retailer selling fruit and vegetables. Hence, it is always wise to interpret the ratio by relating it to the industry average and to trends in the ratio for that particular business for previous years.

Even though high inventory turnover generally is considered to be a desirable trait of good management, this is not always the case. For example, a very high inventory turnover may also indicate that the business is holding too little inventory, and that the business may be losing sales as a result of insufficient inventory on hand. Management is always faced with the challenge of having enough inventory to serve customers but not too much that it has large amounts of money tied up in inventory.

Ratios illustrated

For illustration purposes, the following data are assumed for a retail business:

	2013	2014
Net sales	$320 000	$350 000
Cost of sales	208 000	238 000
Gross profit	112 000	112 000
Expenses	32 000	42 000
Profit	80 000	70 000
Inventory ($43 000 in 2009)	47 000	53 000

Using the above figures, the profitability ratios discussed previously are:

Gross profit ratio	35%	32%
Profit margin	25%	20%
Expenses to sales	10%	12%
Inventory turnover	4.6 times	4.8 times

As can be seen from the ratios, profitability has declined from 2013 to 2014. Both profit ratios have declined sharply because of increasing costs of purchases and/or declining mark-ups. Management must look at increasing prices and/or seek alternative cheaper supplies of merchandise. Nevertheless, the business has managed to increase its inventory turnover. This seems to suggest that the rising costs of merchandise have not been passed on to customers and that management could improve profitability with an increase in selling prices. This, of course, may result in a fall in inventory turnover in the future. Expenses as a proportion of sales also have risen sharply, and management must take action to reduce costs, if profit margins are to be preserved.

Adjustment (GST), p. 233

Adjustment note, p. 233

Administrative expenses, p. 231

Beginning inventory, p. 245

Cash discount, p. 235

Cost of sales, p. 231

Credit period, p. 235

Credit terms, p. 235

DDP (delivered duty paid), p. 238

Discount allowed, p. 235

Discount period, p. 235

Discount received, p. 235

Ending inventory, p. 245

Expenses to sales ratio, p. 256

EXW (ex works), p. 238

Finance expenses, p. 231

Freight inwards (transportation-in), p. 240

Freight outwards, p. 238

Gross profit (or gross margin) on sales, p. 231

Gross profit ratio, p. 256

Inventory, p. 230

Inventory turnover, p. 257

Periodic inventory system, p. 244

Perpetual inventory system, p. 238

Physical inventory count (stocktake), p. 244

Profit margin, p. 256

Purchases, p. 245

Purchases returns and allowances, p. 246

Sales, p. 231

Sales returns and allowances, p. 235

Selling and distribution expenses, p. 231

Stocktake, p. 244

Tax invoice, p. 232

Trade discount, p. 237

Transportation-in, p. 240

DISCUSSION QUESTIONS

1. Define the term 'inventory' as used in the accounting standard AASB 102/IAS 2 *Inventories*. Are office supplies included in inventory? Why or why not?

2. Discuss the purpose and content of source documents used by a business registered for GST to record the purchase and sale of inventory. How would your answer differ if the business was not GST-registered?

3. Discuss how gross profit on sales is calculated for a retail entity. Why are sales returns and allowances and purchases returns and allowances recorded in contra accounts to sales and purchases respectively? Why is freight inwards added to purchases but freight outwards treated as an expense?

4. What is a cash discount? What are the benefits to the seller of allowing cash discounts? Distinguish between a cash discount and a trade discount.

5. What is the meaning of the terms DDP and EXW? Discuss the impact of such terms on the buyer's and seller's accounting system. Give an example to illustrate.

6. 'The perpetual inventory system is superior to the periodic system.' Discuss.

7. With the growing importance of computerised accounting systems, which inventory system (perpetual or periodic) has become more popular? Explain why. Is this desirable? Why?

8. Why do businesses that use a perpetual inventory system continue to perform a physical stocktake at least once a year?

9. Having examined the income statements for the last 2 years, the manager of a small business noticed that, in spite of the prosperous result for the current year, the income items recognised as 'discount received' had fallen sharply from the previous year. Upon investigation, she found that the new employee appointed to look after payment of the accounts had not paid several invoices within the discount period, giving the reason that it was not worth the effort because the discount to be received was only 1% on some invoices, and 2% on others, if paid within 10 days. Discuss the importance (or otherwise) of paying creditors' accounts within the discount period.

10. Describe the ratios that may be used by management to assess the profit performance of a retail business. Explain the factors that could contribute to adverse trends developing in these ratios.

Exercise 6.1 JOURNAL ENTRIES FOR BOTH BUYER AND SELLER — PERIODIC INVENTORY SYSTEM

A. Prepare general journal entries to record the following transactions (a) for Aesop Ltd and (b) for Fable Ltd. Both companies use a periodic inventory system. (Assume neither is registered for GST.)

June 3 Aesop Ltd sold merchandise to Fable Ltd for $1340 with terms 2/10, n/30, EXW supplier's warehouse.
     5 Fable Ltd paid the freight cost of $50.
     7 Fable Ltd returned merchandise worth $160.
     8 Fable Ltd paid Aesop Ltd the amount due.

B. Indicate how each relevant account balance should be reported in the financial statements of Aesop Ltd and Fable Ltd.

Exercise 6.2 JOURNAL ENTRIES — PERPETUAL INVENTORY SYSTEM

LO 4, 5

Using the perpetual inventory system, record the following transactions in the general journal of Celtic Ltd (assume GST does not apply):
1. Purchased 80 units for $150 each on credit.
2. Returned 9 units to the supplier.
3. Sold 25 units for $240 each on credit.
4. Purchased office supplies for $360 cash.
5. Customer returned 5 of the units sold in (3).
6. Sold 22 units for $240 each on credit.
7. The physical inventory count at the end of the period consisted of 3 fewer units than the inventory account balance.

Exercise 6.3 JOURNAL ENTRIES — PERPETUAL INVENTORY SYSTEM

 LO 3, 4, 5

Using the perpetual inventory system, record transactions (1) to (7) in exercise 6.2 in the general journal, assuming the business is registered for the GST, and that GST has to be added to the figures given.

Exercise 6.4 JOURNAL ENTRIES — PERIODIC INVENTORY SYSTEM

LO 4, 5

Using the periodic inventory system, prepare general journal entries for the following transactions of Labels Ltd (assume no GST):
1. Purchased inventory on credit for $26 000.
2. Sold inventory for $8400 in cash and $7470 on credit.
3. A customer returned goods she had bought on credit for $820.
4. Purchased a computer to be used in the business for $1400 cash.
5. Returned inventory for credit that was previously purchased for $470.
6. Purchased inventory on credit with $6200 list price. A 25% trade discount applies.
7. Sold inventory for $3400 on credit.

Exercise 6.5 JOURNAL ENTRIES — PERIODIC INVENTORY SYSTEM

 LO 3, 4, 5

Using the periodic inventory system, prepare general journal entries to record transactions (1) to (7) in exercise 6.4, assuming the business is registered for the GST, and that GST has to be added to the figures given.

Exercise 6.6 JOURNAL ENTRIES FOR BUYER AND SELLER — PERPETUAL
INVENTORY SYSTEM

The following are selected transactions of Barwick Stores:

May	20	Sold goods on account to Now Discounters for $800, terms 2/10, n/30. The cost of the goods sold was $500.
	27	Forwarded a credit note for $80 to Now Discounters covering part of the goods sold on 20 May, which cost $50, that were returned by Now Discounters as inappropriate. The goods returned were not defective.
	29	Received from Now Discounters a cheque in full settlement of the above transactions.

Required

Assuming that neither business is registered for GST, record the above transactions in the general
journal of (1) Barwick Stores and (2) Now Discounters.

Exercise 6.7 JOURNAL ENTRIES — PERPETUAL INVENTORY SYSTEM
WITH GST

Refer to the information in exercise 6.6 and assume now that both businesses are registered for
GST.

Required

Record the transactions in the general journal of (1) Barwick Stores and (2) Now Discounters.

Exercise 6.8 DISCOUNTS AND RETURNS

Dean's Furniture Importers sells furniture with credit terms of 4/15, n/45. A trade discount of 35%
is given to purchases made by wholesalers. On 4 April 2013, Harper's Wholesalers purchased
furniture with a list price of $242 000 from Dean's Furniture Importers. The furniture had cost the
business $110 000 to import from Malaysia. Ignore GST.

Required

A. Determine the amount of the trade discount given to Harper's Wholesalers.
B. Assume that Harper's Wholesalers returned furniture with an original list price of $8000, and a
   cost of $3200. What source documents would be used by each business to note the transaction?
   Prepare journal entries to record the return in the accounting records of both entities.
C. What is the discount period? If Harper's Wholesalers pays on the last day of the discount
   period, how much is the sales discount recorded by Dean's Furniture Importers? (Don't forget
   the return.) Record the journal entry made by both entities.
D. If Harper's Wholesalers does not pay within the discount period, when is the net amount due?
   What would be the effective annual interest rate assuming that Harper's Wholesalers pays on
   the day the net amount is due?

Exercise 6.9 JOURNAL ENTRIES — FREIGHT COSTS AND DISCOUNTS

The Wonderful World of Glass (WWG) operates its business in Margaret River and buys fine
glassware manufactured by many different glassblowers around the country. WWG always purchases glassware from various suppliers on the terms EXW (place of seller's business) and usually
sells to customers on the basis of cash over the counter. Assume the use of a periodic inventory
system and ignore GST.

The following events occurred in the first week of May 2014 for WWG:

May	2	Purchased fine glassware for $22 000 on credit, terms 1/10, n/30, EXW Pemberton, from David Flute, a glassblower operating in Pemberton. Freight costs were $400.
	4	WWG sold and delivered glassware to the head office of WA Mining Ltd in Perth for $35 000 cash. The freight cost was $750. Freight terms were DDP Perth.
	5	WWG sold some fine glassware for $13 000 cash to Bunbury Gifts. Freight costs were $500 cash, and the terms were EXW Margaret River.
	7	WWG paid David Flute for the glassware purchased on 2 May.

Required

Record the transactions above in the general journal of WWG.

Exercise 6.10   INCOME STATEMENT — PERIODIC INVENTORY SYSTEM

Use the following information from the records of Narrabri Ltd to prepare an income statement under the periodic inventory system for the year ended 30 June 2014.

Purchases	$133 250
Inventory, 1 July 2013	9 900
Inventory, 30 June 2014	13 130
Selling and distribution expenses	32 452
Sales	192 760
Purchases returns and allowances	3 156
Sales returns and allowances	4 440
Administrative expenses	11 760
Freight inwards	2 270
Finance expenses	1 440

Exercise 6.11   INCOME STATEMENT — PERPETUAL INVENTORY SYSTEM

The account balances below are taken from the records of Moree Retail Ltd. Prepare an income statement under the perpetual inventory system for the year ended 30 June 2013.

Cost of sales	$120 740
Inventory, 30 June 2013	14 200
Selling and distribution expenses	37 330
Sales	192 720
Sales returns and allowances	4 560
Administrative expenses	12 650
Freight inwards	2 370
Finance expenses	1 600

Exercise 6.12   COMPLETION OF WORKSHEET — PERIODIC INVENTORY SYSTEM

Selected accounts and a section of a worksheet for Sunblest Stores Pty Ltd are shown below:

	Worksheet (section only)					
	Adjusted trial balance		Income statement		Balance sheet	
Account	Debit	Credit	Debit	Credit	Debit	Credit
Inventory	?					
Sales		258 000				
Sales Returns and Allowances	5 000					
Discount Allowed	3 780					
Purchases	151 200					
Purchases Returns and Allowances		2 520				
Discount Received		2 010				
Freight Inwards	1 510					
Income Tax Expense	10 580					
Current Tax Liability		10 580				

Required

The beginning and ending inventory were $35 200 and $40 320 respectively. Enter the beginning and ending inventory amounts in the appropriate columns and extend the other account balances listed to their appropriate columns.

Exercise 6.13 CLOSING ENTRIES — PERIODIC INVENTORY SYSTEM

The following information is taken from the trial balance of Peta's Pet Parlour.

	Debit	Credit
Inventory, 1 July 2013	$ 26 400	
Peta Portas, Drawings	22 400	
Sales		$391 875
Sales returns and allowances	4 910	
Discount allowed	1 980	
Purchases	236 280	
Purchases returns and allowances		1 720
Discount received		1 510
Freight inwards	3 820	
Selling and distribution expenses	75 075	
Administrative expenses	61 470	

Required

Given that the cost of the inventory on 30 June 2014 is $27 500, prepare the closing entries on 30 June 2014.

Exercise 6.14 CLOSING ENTRIES — PERPETUAL INVENTORY SYSTEM

The trial balance of Nature's Nursery contains the following account balances at 30 June.

	Debit	Credit
Inventory	$ 174 400	
Josie Potts, Drawings	106 300	
Sales		$2 715 600
Sales returns and allowances	49 700	
Discount allowed	8 800	
Cost of sales	1 737 450	
Freight inwards	31 230	
Discount received		6 090
Selling and distribution expenses	433 125	
Administrative expenses	265 240	
Other finance expenses	50 500	

Required

Prepare the closing entries under the perpetual inventory system.

Exercise 6.15 MISSING DATA AND PROFITABILITY ANALYSIS

Summary financial information for two independent companies is presented below:

	Morgan Ltd	Riley Ltd
Sales	350 000	?
Sales returns	?	15 000
Net sales	330 000	420 000
Cost of sales	190 000	?
Gross profit	?	140 000
Expenses	85 000	?
Profit	?	65 000

Required

A. Calculate the missing amounts.
B. Calculate the gross profit ratio, profit margin and expenses to sales ratio for each company.
C. Compare and comment on the two companies' ratios you calculated in requirement B.

Problem 6.1 JOURNAL ENTRIES — PERPETUAL INVENTORY SYSTEM ★ GST LO 4, 5

★ Basic

★★ Moderate

★★★ Challenging

Robertson Retailers carried out the following transactions relating to a single product in March:

March	3	Purchased 120 units for $50 each on credit.
	8	Returned 4 units which were unsuitable.
	11	Sold 95 units for $70 each on account.
	21	A customer returned 5 units sold on 11 March.
	27	Sold 42 units for $70 each on account.

Required

A. Prepare general journal entries to record the transactions, assuming that a perpetual inventory system is used. The beginning inventory on 28 February consisted of 75 units at $50 cost each. Ignore GST.

B. Prepare general journal entries to record the transactions, assuming the business is registered for the GST.

C. Assuming that the business closes its records at the end of the month, prepare entries to close the Profit or Loss Summary accounts based on the data in requirements A or B (or both), assuming that expenses for March were $2400.

Problem 6.2 JOURNAL ENTRIES FOR BOTH BUYER AND SELLER — PERIODIC INVENTORY SYSTEM ★ LO 4, 5

The following transactions relate to the businesses of B. Butcher and N. Naylor. Both businesses use a periodic inventory system.

May	9	Butcher sold goods to Naylor for $4250. Terms were 2/15, n/30.
	17	Naylor paid Butcher the net amount due.
	21	Butcher sold goods to Naylor for $2250. Terms were 2/15, n/30.
	28	Naylor paid for the goods.

Required

A. Prepare general journal entries to record the transactions, ignoring GST.

B. Prepare general journal entries to record the transactions, assuming both businesses are registered for the GST.

Problem 6.3 JOURNAL ENTRIES — PERPETUAL INVENTORY SYSTEM ★★ LO 4, 5

On 31 December 2013, Brisbane-based entity, ReadiBike Ltd, had inventory of 570 bicycles at a total cost of $51 300. The company maintains a perpetual inventory system. The following transactions occurred during January 2014:

Jan.	1	Purchased 330 bicycles on credit for $90 each from Mountain Bikies, DDP Brisbane, terms 2/10, n/30. Mountain Bikies also made a cash payment of $150 for freight on this date.
	4	Sold 435 bicycles on credit to Ride Don't Drive for $140 each.
	7	Received $720 credit for 8 damaged bicycles returned to Mountain Bikies.
	10	Paid Mountain Bikies in full, less discount.
		Received payment in full from Ride Don't Drive.
	17	Sold 50 bicycles on credit to Bayside Fitness for $150 each; terms 2/10, n/30.
	19	Purchased 70 bicycles on credit for $90 each from Watlow Manufacturing, EXW Toowoomba, terms 2/15, n/30. Watlow Manufacturing also made a cash payment of $120 for freight on this date.
	23	Received payment in full from Bayside Fitness, less discount.
	25	Paid Watlow Manufacturing in full, less discount.
	29	Sold 110 bicycles on credit to Wild Ride Ltd for $150 each.
	31	Granted Wild Ride Ltd $2250 credit for 15 bicycles returned, which cost $1350.

ReadiBike Ltd's chart of accounts contained the following accounts: Cash at Bank, Sales, Accounts Receivable, Discount Allowed, Inventory, Sales Returns and Allowances, Accounts Payable, Cost of Sales, Discount Received.

Required

Prepare journal entries for the above transactions for the month of January 2014 for ReadiBike Ltd.

Problem 6.4 JOURNAL ENTRIES — PERPETUAL AND PERIODIC INVENTORY SYSTEMS ★★ **LO 4, 5**

Assume that Musonda's Markets had an inventory balance of $13 860 at the close of the last accounting period. The following sales and purchase transactions are for the current period:
1. Purchased goods on account for $11 570.
2. Returned part of the above purchase that had an original purchase price of $670.
3. Paid for the balance of the purchase in time to receive a discount of 1% of the purchase price.
4. Sold goods costing $10 600 for $21 200. Cash of $9800 was received, with the balance due on account.
5. Goods sold on credit for $860 (cost $430) were returned.

Required

A. In two columns, prepare general journal entries (ignoring GST) assuming:
   1. a periodic inventory system is used
   2. a perpetual inventory system is used.
B. Same as for requirement A, except that GST is to be added to the figures where appropriate.
C. Suppose that a physical count of the inventory at the end of the current period shows inventory of $13 200 to be on hand. Present the entries (if any) required under each inventory system to adjust for any discrepancy.
D. Comment on which system would best disclose any discrepancy.

Problem 6.5 JOURNAL ENTRIES, DISCOUNTS, CLOSING ENTRIES AND INCOME STATEMENTS — BOTH PERPETUAL AND PERIODIC INVENTORY SYSTEMS ★★★ **LO 4, 5, 6, 7**

Starbright Lighting buys lamps for $40 each and sells them for $70 each. On 1 April 2013, 24 lamps were in inventory. Starbright Lighting completed the transactions below during April.

April	3	Purchased 40 lamps on account. Terms: 2/10, n/30, EXW supplier's warehouse.
	4	Paid freight cost of $60 on 3 April purchase.
	5	Sold 22 lamps on account. Terms: 3/10, n/30, DDP acquirer's warehouse. Paid freight cost of $30.
	9	Returned 10 of the lamps purchased on 3 April and paid the amount due on the lamps retained in stock.
	10	A customer returned 3 of the lamps sold on 5 April. The lamps were not defective and were returned to stock.
	13	Purchased 20 lamps on credit. Terms: 2/10, n/30, EXW supplier's warehouse.
	14	Received payment from customer for the amount due on 5 April sale.
	19	Sold 39 lamps for cash at $60 each.
	20	Four of the lamps sold on 19 April were returned by the customer for a cash refund. The lamps were not defective.
	22	Paid the supplier the amount owed for the 13 April purchase.

A physical inventory count taken on 30 April 2013 showed 20 lamps in stock.

Required

A. In two columns and ignoring GST, prepare general journal entries to record the transactions assuming:
   1. a perpetual inventory system is used
   2. a periodic inventory system is used. Narrations are not required.
B. Repeat requirement A but assume the business is registered for the GST.
C. Assuming Starbright closes its accounts at month-end, prepare relevant entries to close the accounts under both inventory systems.

D. Prepare two separate income statements showing gross profit and profit for April, assuming that:
1. the perpetual inventory system was used
2. the periodic inventory system was used.

Problem 6.6 JOURNAL ENTRIES INVOLVING DISCOUNTS, CLOSING ENTRIES AND INCOME STATEMENT — PERPETUAL INVENTORY SYSTEM ★★

Montana Ltd sells handheld video games for $50 each. It buys the games for $30 each. On 1 April 2014, 40 games are in inventory. Montana Ltd completed the following transactions during April (ignore GST):

April	1	Sold 10 games for cash.
	2	Paid the supplier for 20 games purchased on 6 March. Terms: 2/10, n/30.
	4	Purchased 25 games on credit. Terms: 2/10, n/30, EXW supplier's warehouse.
	5	A customer returned 4 of the games sold on 1 April and received a cash refund. The games were not defective in any way.
	8	Paid $30 in freight charges on 4 April purchase.
	10	Returned 5 of the games purchased on 4 April for credit.
	12	Sold 20 games on credit. Credit terms: 2/10, n/30.
	14	Paid the supplier the amount due on the 4 April purchase.
	23	A customer returned 5 games sold on 12 April and included a cheque for the amount due on the other 15 games. The games were not defective and were returned to inventory.
	24	Purchased 30 games on credit. Terms: 2/10, n/30, EXW supplier's warehouse.
	29	Paid the supplier for the 24 April purchase.

A physical inventory count taken on 30 April disclosed that 64 games were on hand.

Required
A. Prepare general journal entries to record the transactions, assuming that a perpetual inventory system is used. Ignore GST.
B. Assuming that Montana Ltd completes the closing process at the end of each month, prepare entries to close the accounts.
C. Prepare an income statement for the month of April 2014.

Problem 6.7 JOURNAL ENTRIES INVOLVING GST, DISCOUNTS, CLOSING ENTRIES AND INCOME STATEMENT — PERPETUAL INVENTORY SYSTEM ★★

Complete all of the requirements of problem 6.6, assuming that Montana Ltd is registered for the GST. Assume that dollar figures quoted in problem 6.6 are ex GST. Hence, the selling price of games is now $55 including GST, the purchase price is now $33 including GST and the freight charge paid on 8 April is now $33 including GST.

Problem 6.8 PERPETUAL INVENTORY SYSTEM AND GST ★★

Jimmy Hayes opened a football souvenir store on 1 June 2013. The business trades under the name of The Footy Emporium and uses a perpetual inventory system to account for its inventory. The business was registered for GST. All credit sales are made on the following terms: 2/10, n/30.
    Transactions for the business in June 2013 were as follows:

June	1	Hayes invested $160 000 cash and $42 000 of store equipment into the business. The store equipment is to be depreciated evenly over 7 years.
	2	Purchased an inventory of souvenir footy shirts from B. Judd on credit for $48 000 plus GST; terms: 2/15, n/30.
	3	Paid $1600 rent for June 2013.
	4	Purchased additional inventory of footy shirts from Hall Enterprises on credit for $33 000 plus GST; terms: n/30.
	5	Sold some merchandise to J. Cousins on credit for $12 000 plus GST. Cost of this merchandise was $8000.
	6	Purchased stationery supplies for cash from G. Bartel for $9900, which included GST.
	8	Purchased a supply of souvenir footballs from Voss Ltd, for $8700 cash, plus GST.

10	Sold merchandise costing $16 000 to Lockyer Ltd on credit for $24 000 plus GST.
12	Purchased footy souvenirs from N. Giteau on credit for $20 000 plus GST; terms were 2/10, n/30.
14	Paid B. Judd for 2 June purchase.
15	Received payment from J. Cousins in payment of the account. The discount had been taken by Cousins.
18	Sold merchandise costing $12 000 to W. Scarlet on credit for $20 000 plus GST.
18	Received payment from Lockyer Ltd in payment of its account, less discount.
21	Sold merchandise costing $10 000 to Slater Ltd on credit for $16 000 plus GST.
21	Paid N. Giteau for 12 June purchase.
22	Purchased additional merchandise from B. Judd on credit for $25 000 plus GST; terms: 2/15, n/30.
23	Sold for cash, merchandise costing $7500 to eager footy fans, for $13 000 plus GST.
25	Returned defective goods that cost $6600 including GST back to B. Judd.
28	Sold merchandise costing $25 000 to T. Black on credit for $36 000 plus GST.
29	Purchased inventory from K. Langer on credit for $8000 plus GST; terms: 1/10, n/30.
30	Paid month's salary to sales assistant, $2500.

At the end of the month, Jimmy Hayes undertook a physical stocktake and calculated that inventory worth $56 800 was still on hand and that stationery supplies of $7500 were still in storage. He also estimated that electricity usage for the month was $300 and that telephone usage for the month was $260. No tax invoices had been received from either supplier by 30 June.

Required

A. Prepare general journal entries for June 2013 for the above transactions, including any adjusting entries at the end of the month.
B. Calculate the profit for the business for the month of June 2013.
C. Explain how the entries in A would differ if the business had used the periodic inventory system.

Problem 6.9 WORKSHEET AND COMPLETION OF ACCOUNTING CYCLE — PERPETUAL INVENTORY SYSTEM ★★ LO 6, 7

A trial balance for Fiona's Fashions Pty Ltd is shown below.

FIONA'S FASHIONS PTY LTD
Unadjusted Trial Balance
as at 30 June 2014

Account	Debit	Credit
Cash at bank	$ 17 457	
Accounts receivable	18 667	
Inventory	24 530	
Supplies	341	
GST outlays	500	
Store equipment	39 105	
Accumulated depreciation – store equipment		$ 8 734
Accounts payable		3 960
Loan payable		11 000
GST collections		1 000
Share capital		36 597
Retained earnings		8 872
Sales		125 609
Sales returns and allowances	1 133	
Discount received		1 072
Cost of sales	72 842	
Freight inwards	1 204	
Discount allowed	495	
Sales salaries expense	20 570	
	$196 844	$196 844

Required

A. Prepare a worksheet for Fiona's Fashions Pty Ltd. Use the following information to make adjusting entries:
1. Supplies on hand at 30 June, $110.
2. Depreciation on the store equipment, $3465.
3. Interest accrued on the loan payable, $820.
4. Income tax expense and payable for the year, $8100.

B. Prepare an income statement, a statement of changes in equity and a balance sheet for the year ended 30 June 2014.

C. Prepare closing entries.

Problem 6.10 JOURNAL ENTRIES, T ACCOUNTS, CLOSING ENTRIES — PERPETUAL INVENTORY SYSTEM ★★ `LO 4, 5, 6`

The following transactions relating to paint brand Sheen-2, sold by Master Painters, occurred in July. The beginning inventory on 1 July consisted of 150 tins at $27 each.

July	1	Purchased 302 tins for $27 each on credit.
	7	Returned 8 tins that were defective.
	12	Sold 190 tins for $55 each on account.
	24	A customer returned 11 tins sold on 12 July.
	25	Sold 64 tins for $55 each on account.
	31	A physical inventory count shows 201 tins on hand at a total cost of $5427.

Required

A. Prepare journal entries to record the transactions, assuming that a perpetual inventory system is used.

B. Post the entries to T accounts, assuming no beginning balances in the cash, receivables and payables accounts.

C. Assuming that the business closes its accounting records each month, prepare entries to close the income statement accounts based on the above data and assuming that all other expenses for July amounted to $7420.

Problem 6.11 INCOME STATEMENT AND RATIOS — PERIODIC INVENTORY SYSTEM ★★ `LO 7, 9`

The following selected information is available for Thurston Wholesale Ltd for March 2013.

Purchases	$ 84 000
Sales	155 000
Freight inwards	1 800
Discount received	1 400
Beginning inventory, 1 March 2013	60 000
Ending inventory, 31 March 2013	36 400
Purchases returns and allowances	1 200
Sales returns and allowances	3 000
Freight outwards	620
Rent expense	1 500
Sales salaries expense	12 800
Discount allowed	3 200
Depreciation expense — office equipment	120
Office supplies expense	360
Office salaries expense	11 600
Advertising expense	2 200
Insurance expense	280

Required

A. Prepare the detailed income statement for Thurston Wholesale Ltd for the month ended 31 March 2013.

B. Calculate the ratio of gross profit to net sales and express as a percentage.

C. Calculate the ratio of profit to net sales and express as a percentage.

D. What might these ratios indicate?

Problem 6.12 WORKSHEET AND COMPLETION OF ACCOUNTING CYCLE —
PERIODIC INVENTORY SYSTEM ★★

The unadjusted trial balance of Plaza Office Equipment Pty Ltd is shown below.

PLAZA OFFICE EQUIPMENT PTY LTD
Unadjusted Trial Balance
for the year ended 30 June 2014

Account	Debit	Credit
Cash at bank	$ 21 900	
Accounts receivable	26 230	
Inventory (1 July 2013)	59 170	
Prepaid insurance	2 400	
Store equipment	39 060	
Accumulated depreciation – store equipment		$ 11 560
Delivery van	9 800	
Accumulated depreciation – delivery van		4 100
Accounts payable		12 780
Loan payable		15 000
Share capital		57 120
Retained earnings		21 500
Dividends	21 780	
Sales		357 960
Sales returns and allowances	14 610	
Discount received		1 070
Purchases	199 570	
Purchases returns and allowances		12 800
Freight inwards	4 120	
Sales salaries expense	43 100	
Freight outwards	2 000	
Discount allowed	1 800	
Interest expense	2 130	
Office salaries expense	46 220	
	$493 890	$493 890

Required

A. Prepare a worksheet for Plaza Office Equipment Pty Ltd. Use the following information to make the year-end adjustments.
1. Prepaid insurance expired during the year, $1700.
2. Depreciation on the store equipment, $4100; and on delivery van, $2030.
3. Accrued interest on the loan payable, $980.
4. Total income tax expense for the period of $11 500 to be recorded

The ending inventory determined by physical count was $47 930.

B. Prepare an income statement, a statement of changes in equity and a balance sheet for the year ended 30 June 2014.

C. Prepare adjusting and closing entries.

D. Prepare a post-closing trial balance.

Problem 6.13 PROFITABILITY ANALYSIS ★★

The following data have been extracted from the income statement of Eclipse Electronics Store Ltd, retailers in South Yarra, Victoria.

	2014	2013
Net sales	$613 000	$532 700
Cost of sales	373 184	315 700
Profit	115 000	128 600
Inventory (ending)	84 000	70 000

Required

A. Calculate the gross profit ratio, profit margin, and expenses to sales ratio for the years 2013 and 2014.

B. Assuming that the inventory at the beginning of 2013 is $56 000, calculate the inventory turn-over for 2013 and 2014.

C. Advise management on any trends in these ratios, and any actions you consider necessary.

Problem 6.14 CORRECTION OF ERRORS ★★★ LO 4, 5, 7

The accountant of Thursday Plantation Ltd prepared the income statement below from the accounting records at 31 December 2013. This statement showed a significant improvement over the preceding year when the profit for the year ended 31 December 2012 was $442 000.

On 28 January 2014, while reviewing inventory records, the accountant noticed that incoming shipments of goods received near the annual closing dates had been handled as follows:

1. Purchases in transit on 31 December 2012, amounting to $38 000, had not been included in the ending inventory for that year although the invoice for the goods had been entered in the accounting records on 29 December 2012 and the goods had been shipped on 28 December from the supplier (i.e. ownership of the merchandise had passed on that date).

2. Goods on hand at 31 December 2013, amounting to $21 000, were not included in the ending inventory at that date. They had been omitted because the purchase invoice for this shipment had not been received and the employee supervising the physical stocktake believed that the goods were not the property of the business until the invoice was received. The invoice in question arrived by mail late on 31 December 2013, but no entry was made for it before closing the accounts for 2013. The invoice was recorded on 6 January 2014 as a January transaction.

THURSDAY PLANTATION LTD
Income Statement
for the year ended 31 December 2013

INCOME			
Sales revenue			$7 484 000
Less: Sales returns and allowances			58 000
Net sales revenue			7 426 000
Cost of sales:			
Inventory, 1 January		$1 700 000	
Add: Purchases	$4 176 000		
Freight inwards	54 000		
	4 230 000		
Less: Purchases returns and allowances	34 000		
Net cost of purchases		4 196 000	
Cost of goods available for sale		5 896 000	
Less: Inventory 31 December		302 000	
Cost of sales			5 594 000
GROSS PROFIT			1 832 000
EXPENSES			1 320 000
PROFIT			$ 512 000

Required

A. Calculate the corrected final profit for the years 2012 and 2013. State the effect of the errors on the profit for the year 2014.

B. Indicate which items, if any, were incorrectly stated in the income statement for 2013, and in the balance sheet prepared at 31 December 2013. Indicate also whether the items were under-stated or overstated, and the amount of the error in dollar terms.

C. Prepare any correcting journal entries necessary on 28 January 2014.

Steve's Home Improvements had the following balances in its ledger at 30 June 2013.

Cash at bank	$ 35 688	Sales revenue	$961 400
Accounts receivable	102 528	Sales returns and allowances	13 232
Inventory	187 200	Cost of sales	549 744
Prepaid insurance	6 552	Discount received	11 232
Office supplies on hand	4 368	Freight inwards	12 480
Furniture and fixtures	53 040	Sales salaries expense	91 104
Accumulated depreciation –		Delivery expense	24 336
furniture and fixtures	15 912	Advertising expense	35 880
Delivery equipment	62 400	Rent expense	38 064
Accumulated depreciation –		Office salaries expense	45 000
delivery equipment	24 960	Electricity expense	13 344
Accounts payable	36 036	Discount allowed	9 048
Loan payable (long-term)	156 000	GST collections	94 817
Steve Unwin, Capital	88 296	GST outlays	67 205
Steve Unwin, Drawings	37 440		

Steve's Home Improvements' financial year ends on 30 June. During the year the accountant prepared monthly statements using worksheets, but no adjusting entries were made in the journals and ledgers. Data for the year-end adjustments are as follows:

1. Prepaid insurance, 30 June 2013	$ 2 808
2. Office supplies on hand, 30 June 2013	1 872
3. Depreciation expense for year, furniture and fixtures	5 304
4. Depreciation expense for year, delivery equipment	12 480
5. Sales salaries payable but unrecorded	3 000
6. Office salaries payable but unrecorded	1 680

Required

A. Prepare a worksheet for the year ended 30 June 2013.
B. Prepare an income statement for the year ended 30 June 2013.
C. Prepare a balance sheet as at 30 June 2013.
D. Make the necessary adjusting entries.
E. Make the closing entries.
F. Make any necessary reversing entries.

DECISION ANALYSIS

Bookshop inventory records

The UniBooks Store maintains its inventory records manually, keeping a separate card for each book title in store. Every time a book is purchased or sold, the card for that title is adjusted. Once a year, staff count the inventory of books and compare the amount with the cards. Appropriate alterations are made for differences between inventory on hand and the cards. Nadia Duglosz is in charge of the shop and she has decided that it is time to install a computer-based system. She has heard that there are two ways to account for inventory but she is not sure which method she has been using and which method to use if she computerises the inventory records. You are an accounting student working part time in the shop, so Nadia approaches you for help.

Required

Explain the main differences between the two methods of accounting for inventory and how each method works. Which method of inventory has the UniBooks Store been using? Which inventory method would you recommend when the computerised accounting system is installed, and why?

Liquid assets

Read the following article and answer the questions that follow.

Privatising water is being floated as a solution to the shortage — but it's not all free flow

Should governments own the nation's water infrastructure? Now that air is to become a tradeable commodity in the form of carbon credits, should water utilities be sold to private investors and companies in the hope that the ability to make a profit would guarantee a clean and plentiful supply?

Some economists think so. This month, the world's biggest banking group, Citi, released a report looking at a market-based water-pricing model for Australia framed around the premise that private companies would compete as wholesale suppliers, pipeline owners and retail suppliers, just as they do for gas and electricity in some states.

Citi economist Shane Lee argues that Australians living in cities have been paying only the cost of water. 'Water should move away from a cost recovery approach to an approach based on pricing water on its scarcity;' he says.

Lee says that state governments have been slow to respond to the water crisis that has struck most of the mainland capitals in the past year, as a result of their obsession with trying to balance budgets. He's convinced that private enterprise, allowed to reap a similar return on assets as other privatised utilities — about 6.5% — would have been quicker to respond with projects such as desalination plants, aquifers, new dams or water-recycling schemes.

The states are already taking tentative steps towards bringing private investment into water supply. It has already occurred with desalination projects in NSW, Queensland and Western Australia. Lee says there has been strong interest in his competitive pricing model from several state government authorities since the release of the Citi report in late July. Many countries are heading down the same path, although none has a market-based model quite as comprehensive as Citi's. Many water utilities have already been privatised. Macquarie Bank owns London's retail water supply; Hastings Funds Management — a unit of Westpac — supplies water to much of south-east England; the Commonwealth Bank and industry super fund IFS are majority owners of the water utility in north-east England.

Huge water utility companies have emerged from Europe, including the French giants Veolia and Suez and Germany's RWE.

'We are at the cusp of the development of a water industry,' notes Lee. Indeed, some say the world's water assets could be worth more than $1 trillion to governments short of cash to invest in infrastructure.

Not everyone is pleased, however. Efforts to privatise water infrastructure for cash-strapped developing nations in Africa and South America have been met with riots in countries where government regulation of the privatised assets has been poor and where the population can ill afford steep price rises.

Lee says that under his model, an independent market regulator would super-vise the market, but a sharp rise in the price of water in Australia is inevitable, whatever the ownership structure. Despite the scarcity here, capital city prices are relatively inexpensive compared with capital cities elsewhere and are not sustainable.

A recent CSIRO report suggested that the price of water could rise threefold by 2032 if there was sufficient investment in facilities such as desalination and recycling plants and stormwater harvesting. A failure to invest would result in a tenfold increase in water prices because of its potential scarcity. 'We need new supplies of water to put downward pressure on price,' Lee says. 'That can't be achieved under the current pricing model.'

Indeed, consumers risk paying higher water prices in more ways than one. Apart from the direct cost of consumption, the increased price will flow through to the cost of fresh food, fruit juices and other products, according to a recent report by another leading investment bank, JP Morgan. Woolworths and Coles would be able to easily pass on the cost to the consumer, the bank says, while soft drink companies and wine groups would not.

It could even be a triple-whammy. Because power stations rely on water for cooling, energy costs could rise, pushing up inflation and adding another layer of cost for the consumer.

Source: Giles Parkinson, 'Liquid assets', *The Bulletin.*

Required

A. Would private companies need to keep inventory records for water?
B. What type of inventory system would you recommend for privatised water companies?
C. When would entries be made in accounting records for water?
D. Would a physical stocktake be needed for water inventories at the end of the financial year?

Revenue recognition issues

A large wholesale business in Melbourne's northern suburbs has run into difficulties in the past few years due to a fall in demand from retailers for certain product lines. The CEO of the business and other senior managers, including the sales manager, were appointed on the basis that they will be paid bonuses at the end of the financial year depending on the level of profits made by the business. In recent times, these bonuses have been reduced somewhat and the sales manager has had difficulty meeting some of her private financial commitments. Just before the end of the financial year, a large order was received from a retailer for the supply of merchandise. The order was placed on the terms of DDP to the warehouse of the retailer, and hence revenue is to be recognised once the merchandise has been delivered to the retailer. Shipment of the order was not possible until 2 weeks into the new financial year. The sales manager, knowing that the entity's profits, and her bonus and that of the other managers, would be increased if the sale was recognised in the current financial year, has approached you, the accountant, to make an entry in the current period to recognise the revenue from this order prior to the goods being shipped.

Required

A. Who are the stakeholders in this situation?

B. What are the ethical issues involved as a result of the sales manager's request?

C. If you were the accountant of this organisation, what action (if any) would you take? Why?

FINANCIAL ANALYSIS

Refer to the consolidated financial statements in the latest financial report of JB Hi-Fi Limited on its website, www.jbhifi.com.au, and answer the following questions:

1. List the subsidiary companies in the JB Hi-Fi Group.
2. What is the value of the group's sales revenue for the current and previous years? What has been the percentage change in sales revenue for the current year?
3. What is the group's final profit (after income tax) for the current and previous years? What has been the percentage change in profit (after income tax) for the current year?
4. Compare the percentage change in (2) with the percentage change in (3). What information does this comparison provide?
5. What is the total value of inventories on hand for both current and previous years? What is the percentage change in inventory levels? How does this compare with the percentage change in sales revenue calculated in question (2)? Comment on any differences.
6. Calculate appropriate profitability ratios for the most recent 2 years in order to assess the profit performance of JB Hi-Fi Limited.

Concepts for review

Before studying this chapter, you should understand or, if necessary, revise:

- each of the steps in the accounting cycle (p. 178)

- how to record the sales transactions (including returns) of a retail business registered for the GST (pp. 234–8)

- the difference between the perpetual and periodic inventory systems and how the GST affects inventory transactions for businesses registered for the GST (pp. 238–49)

- how to prepare an income statement for a retail business (pp. 253–4).

Learning objectives

After studying this chapter, you should be able to:

1 outline how an accounting system operates (pp. 276–7)

2 describe the three phases involved in the development of accounting systems, and identify the important considerations in developing accounting systems (pp. 277–9)

3 identify the principles of internal control and the limitations of internal control systems (pp. 280–3)

4 Explain why subsidiary ledgers and special journals make an accounting system more efficient (p. 283)

5 record appropriate transactions in subsidiary ledgers, and reconcile each subsidiary ledger with the appropriate control account in the general ledger (pp. 283–5)

6 record transactions for sales, purchases, cash receipts and cash payments in special journals and describe the purpose and use of the general journal when special journals are used (pp. 285–307)

7 identify some of the basic features of accounting software through exposure to MYOB and QuickBooks (pp. 307–10)

8 compare how transactions are entered into accounting software using MYOB and QuickBooks (pp. 311–14)

9 describe the advantages and disadvantages of computerised accounting systems (p. 314)

10 describe how the accounting cycle works in manual and computerised systems (p. 315).

Evolution of accounting systems

In early accounting systems, all recording, processing, analysis and report preparation were done manually. This system was acceptable when businesses were small and had a limited number of transactions. As businesses grew in size and complexity, the large volume of transactions and the repetitive nature of accounting tasks led to the use of machines to increase the speed and accuracy of processing. Special functional machines called accounting machines were introduced as part of the process. Accounting machines eventually made way for accounting systems based on punched card machines. Finally, electronic computers were introduced to the accounting system, and today constitute an essential element of all accounting systems.

Today's accountants must have knowledge of computer systems, because the accounting system is now only one component of an organisation's total integrated management information system.

As a result of these developments, methods of recording, processing and preparing reports have changed over time. Data entry has progressed from handwritten source documents to direct entry via computer terminals or product code scanners. The processing of data has undergone changes with the result that output can now be produced the instant data are entered into the system. Records are now maintained and stored electronically. Today, accounting systems usually involve a combination of some manual, but mostly computerised processing. The drivers of the evolution of accounting systems continue to be technological advancement and economic advancement (including world population growth, industrialisation, globalisation, competition, and legal and accounting regulation). Increasing volumes and complexity of transactions require increasingly sophisticated technology to produce timely and meaningful information.

Chapter preview

In earlier chapters, we saw that the effects of various business transactions are *identified*, *measured*, *recorded* and *reported* within an entity's accounting system. This chapter describes accounting systems used for efficient and dependable processing of financial data. An **accounting system** is a collection of source documents, records, procedures, management policies and data processing methods used to transform data about economic transactions and events into information useful for decision making and evaluating past decisions. Accounting systems can take many forms, ranging from simple manual systems to sophisticated computerised systems.

We have limited the consideration of an accounting system in earlier chapters to one that is both *simple* and *manually operated* in order to introduce and illustrate basic accounting procedures. Such a system may be satisfactory for a small business entity with a limited number of transactions. In most cases, however, even relatively small businesses require a more sophisticated accounting system, even if largely manual, for two reasons:

- The procedures described earlier may be too time-consuming for rapid data processing and timely reporting. The volume of transactions may be so great that the accounting staff cannot process the data manually in a cost-effective and timely manner.
- Many of the transactions are so repetitive that they can be handled more efficiently by classifying them into related groups. Special journals can be used for such repetitive transactions as sales, purchases, cash receipts and cash payments instead of the less efficient general journal, as illustrated in previous chapters.

This chapter initially concentrates on refinements to the manual system of accounting. Computerised accounting systems are introduced in the latter part of the chapter. Even though most organisations use computerised accounting systems, we discuss manual systems to explain the basic processes that all computerised systems follow.

7.1 Operation of an accounting system

The operation of an accounting system has three basic phases: *input*, *processing* and *output*. Transactions are recorded as they occur on numerous source documents such as sales invoices, purchase invoices, cheque butts and bank deposit slips. Source documents serve as input entered into journals, which become a chronological record of the transactions. Periodically, these journals are posted to a general ledger (the processing phase), which represents a permanent record of assets, liabilities, equity, income and expenses. Financial statements are prepared from the data in the general ledger and become the output from the system. The statements provide useful information for decision making and evaluation of the entity by parties outside the entity (such as shareholders, creditors, customers and the taxation authorities) and by insiders, e.g. owners, managers and employees. Consequently, both financial and management accounting information is produced in the same system. Figure 7.1 illustrates the variability of accounting systems, and the relationship between input, processing and output.

Converting data to information

In the conversion of input to output, data are transformed into information. Although the two terms *data* and *information* are often used synonymously, a useful distinction between them can be made. *Data* are recorded facts; *information* is data that have been processed in some prescribed manner so as to be more useful to a potential user. For example, sales data are collected chronologically on invoices, processed through the accounting system, and reported as sales information (revenue) in the income statement. The transformation of raw data into useful information in an accounting system occurs as we proceed through the accounting cycle as shown in figure 7.2.

Manual accounting systems are acceptable when the system is small with a limited number of transactions. But with a large volume of transactions, the repetitive nature of the task lends itself to using computers to increase the speed and accuracy of processing. Data entry has progressed from handwritten source documents to direct entry via computer terminals or product code scanners, and output can be produced the instant data are entered. Records are stored electronically on hard disks, optical disks, including CDs and DVDs, or tapes.

Figure 7.1 The variability of accounting systems, and the relationship between input, processing and output

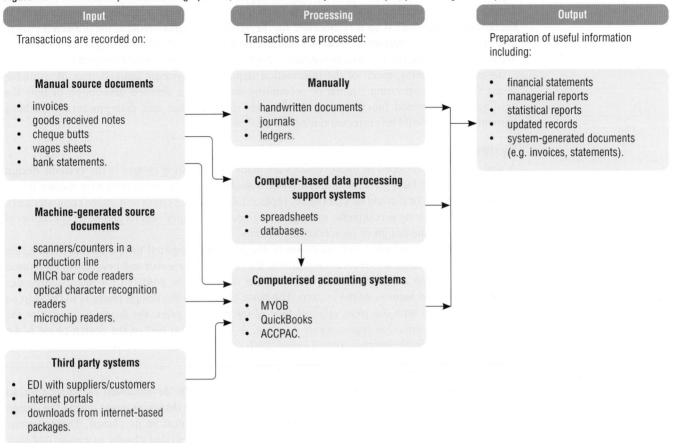

Figure 7.2 Conversion of accounting data to accounting information

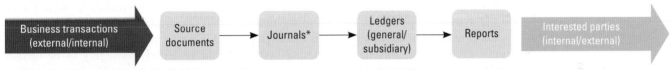

*Computerised accounting systems will generate automatically.

7.2 Development of an accounting system

One of the essential steps in the establishment of any business is the development of a dependable accounting system. In some instances, the system is designed in-house and installed by a member of the entity's own accounting department, although the system may be developed by an outside source such as a public accounting firm or management consultant. More commonly, a commercially available accounting software package may be purchased. Whichever approach is taken, the development of an accounting system must be based on a thorough understanding of the business and the industry in which it operates.

As the business grows and engages in different activities, a review of the accounting system may show that it needs to be revised or even replaced to accommodate a larger volume of transactions and changes in the nature of those transactions. The installation and/or revision of an accounting system consists of three phases: (1) systems analysis, (2) systems design, and (3) systems implementation and review.

Systems analysis

The objective of the **systems analysis** phase is to gather facts that provide a thorough understanding of a business's *information requirements* and the *sources of information*. A study of the organisation and how it functions is performed to determine the best combination of personnel, forms, records, procedures and equipment. Such questions as these must be considered: How is the business organised? Who is responsible for the various activities? What is the projected growth and direction of the business? What are management's plans for future changes in operations? What source documents, records, procedures, reports and equipment should be used?

In existing systems, much of the information required for systems analysis may be available in the form of an operating manual or accounting manual — a detailed description of how the existing system should function. Any deficiencies in procedures and data-processing methods currently in use should be corrected during the analysis phase.

Systems design

A new system is developed or improvements are made to an existing system in the **systems design** phase based on the facts gathered through systems analysis. An existing system may require minor amendments only, or it could be completely replaced with a new system (e.g. more computerised). A team approach using accountants, managers, engineers, computer experts and other specialists is often required in the design of an accounting system.

The design must include a consideration of the *personnel* required to operate the system, the *source documents* needed to record transactions, the *accounting records* and *procedures* to be used to process data, *job descriptions* for personnel, the *reports* to be prepared for interested parties and *any automated features* of the system. The basic concern in the design phase is to develop an *accounting system with the most efficient flow of information, given the funds committed to the system and the information requirements involved*. A fundamental part of the design phase is the development of reliable internal control (see p. 280).

Systems implementation and review

Systems implementation and review is the final phase in the development or revision of an accounting system. This step involves the implementation of the decisions made during the design phase. The source documents, records and equipment chosen must be purchased. The personnel needed to operate the system must be selected, trained and supervised closely to ensure that they understand how the system should function. An accounting manual should be prepared as a formalised description of the procedures required to transform economic data into useful information.

When an existing system is being revised or replaced, one of two approaches is taken. Either the old system is operated in parallel to the new one until management is certain that the new system is reliable, or the new system is thoroughly tested in a pilot phase to ensure the expected results are achieved. Any new accounting system should be tested thoroughly to be certain that its output is compatible with the desired results, and modifications made when necessary. Major reviews are usually accomplished gradually rather than all at once to help ensure reliable data flows.

The phases in developing an accounting system are summarised in figure 7.3.

Figure 7.3 Phases in the installation or revision of an accounting system

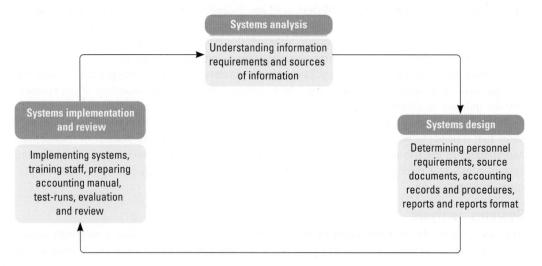

Important considerations in developing an accounting system

When developing a new accounting system or expanding an existing one, whether it is a relatively small system or a large sophisticated one, there are a number of important system considerations for management and those responsible for the implementation of the system. These considerations are discussed below.

Costs versus benefits

The value of the benefits that will flow from the established system *must* exceed the costs of designing, implementing and maintaining the system. The major benefit comes from the output of the system, which provides timely, reliable and relevant information to managers to ensure that they are able to make business decisions — planning (preparation of budgets), reviewing and controlling operations. The ability to centralise, outsource, automate and/or combine processing functions within the organisation and across organisational boundaries may also be a significant benefit. Other benefits are the capacity to report to owners, and to meet the reporting requirements of legislative authorities.

Apart from the obvious development costs of systems analysis and design, and the everyday operating costs of the system including personnel, any system has the potential to incur intangible costs such as those that result from poor managerial decisions flowing from inadequate information, e.g. lost revenues and growth opportunities.

At all times management must ensure that the appropriate balance between system benefits and costs is maintained. In some cases the existing system may no longer be sustainable due to outdated technology and/or lack of support from the developer.

Compatibility

An accounting system must be compatible with the organisational and personnel characteristics of the business. The system should be appropriate to the size and nature of the business operations, e.g. the system used by a mining company would not be compatible with the system requirements of a small service partnership, nor would the accounting system used by JB Hi-Fi Limited be appropriate for a small retail operation. Similarly, a system used by a single-product local business would not be appropriate for a multiproduct business operating interstate and/or overseas.

All accounting systems must be compatible with the qualifications, competencies, and behavioural characteristics of the personnel responsible for the day-to-day operation of the system. Those responsible for recruiting staff must ensure that people have appropriate qualifications and experience, and are appropriately trained and supervised. Dedication and commitment of staff are essential ingredients for the ongoing success of any business.

Flexibility/adaptability

Businesses do not stay the same over time. Either they experience success and growth or they cease to operate. Most big businesses today were once smaller successful businesses. The life cycle of a business is one of constant change. Growing businesses develop and offer new products, expand into new markets, take over existing businesses, dispose of parts of the business, and restructure. The accounting system must adapt to these changes. Flexibility within an accounting system allows these structural changes to take place without major disruptions to business operations.

Internal control

An accounting system must have adequate controls built into the system. The system must provide mechanisms for the protection of the assets of the business and ensure that information provided by the system is timely, reliable and relevant to the decision-making needs of management and external users. Such a system is known as a system of internal control — this is discussed more fully in the next section.

7.3 Internal control systems

The efficient use and protection of an entity's assets (physical assets as well as data and information) is a primary management function. One of the ways this is achieved is through the implementation of a risk management system. Risk management involves the identification and mitigation of all risks faced by a business. An **internal control system** is an important aspect of this risk management process. In a sole trader business, the owner often has direct involvement in all business activities, and achieves control through this personal involvement. As the business grows, however, the owner must place increasing reliance on others to help manage and control operations, requiring a more formal and sophisticated system of internal controls.

Internal control systems defined

All policies and procedures adopted by an entity to control its activities and protect its assets are described collectively as a system of internal control.

At this point, it is important to appreciate the relationship of internal control to an accounting system. One of the main objectives of internal control is to ensure the *reliability* of accounting information. As we have seen, financial data are transformed into information with a number of accounting procedures such as preparing source documents, analysing transactions, recording transactions, posting to ledger accounts, and generating financial reports. A sound system of internal control ensures that these accounting procedures are performed correctly so that the resulting information is relevant and provides a faithful representation of the entity's underlying economic events.

A system of internal control consists of all the measures used by a business:
- to safeguard its resources against waste, misappropriation and inefficient use
- to promote the reliability of accounting data
- to encourage compliance with business policies and government regulations
- to maintain the sustainability of the business with regard to its impact on the environment and its resource consumption now and in the future
- to ensure business is conducted in an ethical manner in its dealings with its stakeholders.

There are two aspects to internal control: (1) administrative controls and (2) accounting controls. *Administrative controls* are those established to provide operational efficiency and adherence to prescribed policies, such as a written directive identifying the standards to be followed in hiring new employees, manuals identifying purchasing and sales procedures, and various performance reports required from employees.

Accounting controls are the methods and procedures used to protect assets and ensure the reliability of accounting records, such as procedures for the authorisation of transactions and the separation of record-keeping duties from custodianship of the entity's assets. Accounting controls are designed to provide reasonable assurance that:
- transactions are carried out in accordance with management's general or specific authorisation
- transactions are recorded as necessary (a) to permit preparation of financial statements that conform with appropriate accounting standards and (b) to maintain accountability for assets
- access to assets is permitted only in accordance with management's authorisation
- the accounting records for assets are compared with the physical assets at reasonable intervals and appropriate action is taken with respect to any differences.

Principles of internal control systems

In systems of internal control, several important principles are followed to achieve adequate administrative and accounting controls. Some of these important principles are discussed below.

Organisational culture and clearly established lines of responsibility

Control ultimately involves people, since individuals carry out business transactions, record the transactions and handle the assets resulting from those transactions. Thus the cornerstone of a good internal control system is the employment of competent personnel and assignment of responsibilities to them. This starts with the knowledge, skills and attitude of senior management, which are integral to the organisational culture and should guide behaviour and accountability throughout the business. Responsibility should be commensurate with ability and authority, and employees should have a clear understanding of their responsibilities.

Responsibility must be assigned so that there are no overlapping or undefined areas. If two or more employees share the same responsibility and something goes wrong, it is very difficult to determine who is at fault and therefore difficult to take corrective action. If two or more employees use the same cash register, for example, each should be assigned a separate drawer and register key or PIN so that any errors or cash shortages can be identified with individuals on a daily basis.

Responsibilities and duties should be rotated among employees periodically so that they can become familiar with the entire system. Rotation of duties also tends to discourage deviation from prescribed procedures since employees know that other employees may soon be taking over their duties and reviewing their activities.

Separation of record keeping and custodianship

Whenever possible, responsibility for initiating business transactions and for custody of the entity's assets should be separated from responsibility for maintaining the accounting records. This helps avoid the misappropriation or misuse of assets. The person with custody of an asset is unlikely to misappropriate or misuse it when a record of the asset is kept by another employee. A theft of the asset and falsification of records to cover up the theft would therefore require collusion between the two employees.

Division of responsibility for related transactions

To minimise the possibility of errors, fraud and theft, responsibility for a series of related transactions should be divided among two or more employees or departments so that the work of one employee acts as a check on the work of another. For example, if one employee orders goods, receives the goods and pays the supplier, that employee might be tempted to order goods for personal use, have the goods delivered to his or her home and pay for them from business funds.

To avoid such potential abuses, authority for ordering goods should be placed with a purchasing department, the goods should be physically received by a separate receiving department, and payment for the order should be performed by a third department or employee. Documents (purchase orders, receiving reports, invoices) showing the work done by each department or employee are then sent to the accounting department for recording purposes. In this way, the work of each employee acts as a check on the work performed by others.

Mechanical and electronic devices

Mechanical and electronic devices designed to protect assets and to improve the accuracy of the accounting process, although not infallible, should be used wherever feasible. Such devices can be programmed to minimise the likelihood of errors, both intentional and unintentional, occurring in the accounting records. Cash registers provide an accurate record of cash sales, produce a receipt for the customer and protect the cash received. A safe or vault protects cash on hand and important documents. Measuring devices such as those used to measure metres of cloth and litres of fuel sold are other examples of devices used to strengthen internal control. Product code readers at checkout points in supermarkets are also designed to minimise errors.

Adequate insurance

Adequate insurance over an entity's assets ensures that, in the event of loss, theft or damage, the entity will be able to recover losses and replace assets.

Internal auditing

Many large entities have internal auditors who are employees of the entity and who are responsible for, amongst other things, a continuing review of the internal control system. Non-compliance with established procedures and suggestions for improving the system are reported to top management. Internal auditors are an important element of corporate governance.

Programming controls

In computerised accounting systems, programming controls are usually built into the system. The system can confirm that processing of data has been carried out in correct sequence, highlight where transaction debits do not equal credits, and provide proof of mathematical calculations. One of the great challenges facing computer programmers today is to build in controls that limit unauthorised and unintentional interference in the system. Computer hackers, viruses and spyware continue to pose a real threat to the integrity of an entity's internal control system.

Physical controls

Physical controls relate to the safeguarding of physical assets, such as a safe to hold cash and other valuable documents, lockable buildings and storage areas, external fencing, and employee identification cards. An entity may employ security staff during business hours, and engage security firms to provide property surveillance after hours.

Other controls

Other control measures include the use of prenumbered documents, the rotation of employees over a range of jobs, and requiring all employees to take annual leave. The prenumbering of documents, such as cheques and sales invoices, enables all documents to be accounted for and prevents the same document from being used more than once. Daily banking of cash received reduces the risk of theft.

BUSINESS KNOWLEDGE

When in doubt, print it out

Effective fraud risk management is a matter of going back to basics, a forensic accountant contends.

For the past six months, Stephen Pedneault has been on a soapbox, decrying technology's negative effects on the detection, prevention, and resolution of accounting and financial fraud. 'When it comes to internal controls, we need to go back to basics,' he proclaims.

Not exactly a Luddite, Pedneault, a forensic accountant and investigator for 23 years, thinks the automation of controls isn't itself the problem; instead, it's the complacency with which executives have greeted it.

One example of the problem stems from changes in how payroll-services vendors make client reports available, says Pedneault. Instead of dispatching couriers once a week with packages of papers for review, vendors may send CDs containing the reports — but executives tend to throw the CDs in their desk drawers without looking at their contents.

Ten or 15 years ago, he observes, frauds were caught more swiftly. In that less-automated time and in relatively small companies, one employee would be responsible for collecting and photocopying all the checks and recording them on a deposit slip before the funds were deposited in a bank. That employee would then give the income information to a colleague, who would post it in the company's accounting records. Later, executives would receive a report derived from the records that said how much money was posted for the day.

It was hard to steal cash receipts, says Pedneault, because they wouldn't be posted to the accounting records if a theft occurred. In the case of repeated thefts of a single customer's payments, the customer's balance would get noticeably bigger and older. Eventually, an executive following up on accounts receivable would see the gap and request customer payments. The customer would then offer proof that a payment was indeed made, and the fraud would be detected.

Source: Excerpts from David M. Katz, 'When in doubt, print it out', www.cfo.com.

Limitations of internal control systems

All systems of internal control are generally established to provide a high level of assurance that the assets of an entity are safeguarded and that the accounting data are reliable. All systems of internal control have limitations, including the following:

- It is not possible to obtain absolute assurance that assets are safeguarded and accounting data are reliable because the costs of establishing such a system would exceed the benefits expected to be derived. For example, in an effort to reduce shoplifting, it is not cost-effective to have security staff search all customers as they leave the premises — such a procedure could draw a negative reaction from customers, leading to significant loss of business. Instead, large retail stores have resorted to other methods to improve security, such as signs saying 'bags may be examined' and that 'shoplifters will be prosecuted', electronic sensing devices at shop exits, and supervision of customer activity by store detectives and/or security staff.

- The size of the entity's operations can influence the effectiveness of internal controls. For example, it is not cost-effective, or indeed possible, for a small corner store operation to have the same internal control system as a large company such as JB Hi-Fi Limited. Many of the principles of internal control have to be compromised in smaller operations.
- Good internal control systems can also break down because of tiredness, indifference to work, or carelessness on the part of employees.
- Since most systems of internal control rely heavily on the segregation of duties of employees, the controls can be negated by collusion of two or more employees. In the short term at least, this could result in the misappropriation of assets and the accompanying adjustment of records to conceal the crime.
- Computer fraud is prevalent in computerised accounting systems. Such frauds are usually perpetrated by people within the system itself and do not involve other employees of the business. Such negating of the inbuilt system controls is thus very difficult to discover. It is generally conceded today that, for each computer fraud exposed, many more go undetected.

7.4 Efficient accounting systems — subsidiary ledgers and special journals

Learning objective 4

Explain why subsidiary ledgers and special journals make an accounting system more efficient

This chapter has emphasised so far the importance of reliable accounting records and how good internal controls help to achieve reliability.

In earlier chapters, we illustrated basic accounting procedures by recording each transaction with an entry in a general journal and later posting each debit and credit from the general journal to the appropriate general ledger accounts. Most businesses have several types of repetitive classes of transactions — such as sales, purchases, cash receipts and cash payments. The journal entries required for each transaction within the same class of transactions are essentially the same. We will consider how an accounting system can be enhanced to be more streamlined and efficient, and thus reduce the amount of duplication that would occur if only a general journal were used to record all transactions.

Most accounting systems today are at least partly computerised, and the design, structure and operation of both manual and computerised accounting systems are essentially the same. A working knowledge of the manual accounting process is essential in order to operate a computerised accounting system effectively. For example, if a data entry operator has incorrectly coded transactions, an accountant needs to know what entries need to be recorded to correct the coding errors.

Non-accountants who understand the accounting system are more likely to recognise errors in computer-generated accounting reports they are using if they understand the relationship between the transactions they are responsible for and how the accounting system will process them.

Although we describe the systems of subsidiary ledgers and special journals in a manual accounting system context, similar subsidiary ledgers are used in computerised systems and similar special journals may be produced. Some computerised accounting systems do not require the use of special journals at all, but such journals can be produced for transaction summary purposes if required.

7.5 Manual accounting systems — subsidiary ledgers and control accounts

Learning objective 5

Record appropriate transactions in subsidiary ledgers, and reconcile each subsidiary ledger with the appropriate control account in the general ledger

The coverage so far of a ledger as an essential part of an accounting system has been limited to one general ledger. For more timely and efficient processing, the use of subsidiary ledgers and control accounts in the general ledger is more appropriate.

To illustrate, assume that a business sells goods on credit to 5000 customers. If the entity used only one general ledger Accounts Receivable or Trade Debtors account — as we have done for illustrative purposes so far — it would not provide adequate detail concerning the amounts of inventory sold to individual customers, amounts of money received from them, and amounts still owed by them. Consequently, the entity needs to establish a separate receivable account for each customer. If this is done in the general ledger, 5000 accounts will have to be established and combined with the other assets, liabilities, equity, income and expenses. As a result, the general ledger will be unwieldy, and the likelihood of errors will be high. The trial balance prepared from such a large general ledger will also be very long and difficult to work with. This is complicated further by the fact that other general ledger accounts, such as Accounts Payable (or Trade Creditors) and Inventory (perpetual system), require the same detailed information.

When a large amount of detailed information about a certain general ledger account must be kept, a separate ledger called a **subsidiary ledger** is used. With this, the detailed information is recorded *outside* the general ledger in a group of individual accounts, the total of the balances of which should equal the balance of the related **control account** in the general ledger. One Accounts Receivable Control account (a summary of all receivables transactions) can be used in the general ledger and an individual receivable account can be established for each customer (5000 in the case above) in one subsidiary ledger. Unlike the general ledger where the double-entry recording system is used and the sum of the debit entries must equal the sum of the credit entries, the subsidiary ledger provides detailed memoranda on the receivables and there is no need for the equality of debits and credits.

The principle of control accounts and subsidiary ledgers is used for a number of other general ledger accounts such as Accounts Payable, Inventory (where a perpetual system is used), Marketable Securities, Plant and Equipment, and Investments. Accounts Receivable is used here to demonstrate this principle.

To illustrate the relationship between Accounts Receivable as a control account and its subsidiary ledger, consider figure 7.4, which summarises the November sales and cash receipts activities of an entity with only three customers, given their beginning-of-the-month account balances.

Figure 7.4 Relationship between general ledger and subsidiary ledger

General Ledger
Accounts Receivable Control

Date	Debit	Credit	Balance
Nov. 1			6 500
Nov. 30	5 100		11 600
Nov. 30		6 900	4 700

Schedule of Accounts Receivable as at 30 November

P. Able	$1 800
R. Baker	2 400
D. Cane	500
	$4 700

Subsidiary Ledger
P. Able

Date	Debit	Credit	Balance
Nov. 1			3 200
Nov. 8	1 800		5 000
Nov. 16		3 200	1 800

R. Baker

Date	Debit	Credit	Balance
Nov. 1			1 100
Nov. 3		1 100	—
Nov. 20	2 400		2 400

D. Cane

Date	Debit	Credit	Balance
Nov. 1			2 200
Nov. 12	900		3 100
Nov. 28		2 600	500

The accounts receivable subsidiary ledger is an alphabetical file with a separate account for each customer. Note that at the beginning and end of November the totals of the subsidiary ledger accounts are in agreement with the Accounts Receivable Control account in the general ledger.

Note the following features of the illustration in figure 7.4, which apply regardless of the number of accounts in the subsidiary ledger:

1. The opening balance on 1 November of the Accounts Receivable Control account ($6500) is the total of all the opening balances of the individual accounts receivable accounts ($3200 + $1100 + $2200).
2. The total debit of the Accounts Receivable Control account ($5100) is the total of all the debits (e.g. credit sales) made in the individual accounts receivable accounts ($1800 + $2400 + $900).
3. The total credit of the Accounts Receivable Control account ($6900) is the total of all the credits (e.g. cash received) made in the individual accounts receivable accounts ($3200 + $1100 + $2600).
4. The closing balance on 30 November of the Accounts Receivable Control account ($4700) is the total of all the closing balances of the individual accounts receivable accounts ($1800 + $2400 + $500).

Note also that debit and credit postings in the control account are end-of-month summary postings, whereas the debit and credit postings to the individual accounts receivable accounts are detailed postings done daily throughout the month. Since these postings are done by different accounting personnel, reconciling the subsidiary ledger balances with the balance of the control account provides an element of control within the system. Furthermore, a schedule of accounts receivable balances is prepared at a certain date and compared with the balance of the Accounts Receivable Control account as part of the reconciliation process. A computerised accounting system automatically ensures that the subsidiary ledger is in agreement with the control account, and the preparation of a schedule is not required.

The use of a subsidiary ledger has three major advantages: (1) it relieves the general ledger of a mass of detail; (2) it allows a division of labour among accounting staff in maintaining the ledgers; and (3) it provides effective internal control through periodic comparison of the total of the schedule of the subsidiary ledger with the balance in the appropriate control account.

Thus, although a business has only one general ledger, it can have a large number of subsidiary ledgers.

7.6 Manual accounting systems — special journals

Learning objective 6

Record transactions for sales, purchases, cash receipts and cash payments in special journals and describe the purpose and use of the general journal when special journals are used

The general journal described in earlier chapters can be used to record all types of transactions — sales, purchases, cash receipts, cash payments, sales returns and allowances, and purchases returns and allowances. The universal nature of the general journal imposes some limitations that will adversely affect the efficiency of processing data. These are:

- each debit and credit recorded in the general journal must be posted individually, requiring a large amount of posting time, and this can make it difficult to provide accounting information on a timely basis
- only one person at a time can record the effects of transactions and post debits and credits to the ledger accounts, since all entries are recorded in one journal
- the general journal needs narrations to describe every transaction.

To avoid these limitations, transactions are grouped into categories according to the most common business transactions and a **special journal** is set up for each category. Most of the transactions of a retail business fall into four categories, which allows the use of four special journals:

Category of transaction	Special journal
Sales of inventory on credit	Sales journal
Purchases of inventory on credit	Purchases journal
Receipts of cash (all sources including cash sales)	Cash receipts journal
Payments of cash (all payments including cash purchases)	Cash payments journal

Special journals may also be used for returns and allowances of sales and purchases if they are sufficiently numerous. In this text, however, all returns and allowances will be processed through the general journal.

The combination of the four journals listed, together with a general journal for all other types of transactions, represents a much more efficient way to process data than the use of a general journal alone. The time required to journalise entries is reduced, and totals rather than individual entries can be posted to general ledger accounts in many cases, thus reducing the cost of accounting labour. The journals allow all necessary detail to be entered in subsidiary ledgers.

Also, duties can be efficiently divided by assigning different journals to different employees so that work can be performed concurrently. Several selected transactions involving Baldwin Video Equipment during the month of January illustrate the four special journals in this section. The formats used for the four special journals are typical but not unique. The nature of a given entity determines the exact formats required. For example, use of a perpetual inventory system rather than the periodic requires additional columns in most of the special journals.

Some computerised accounting systems do not require the use of special journals, as the computer can classify and enter data directly to the ledger. Transaction summaries that resemble special journals in appearance and content may be printed out.

Sales journal

A **sales journal** such as the one shown in figure 7.5 is used solely for recording sales of inventory on credit. (Cash sales are recorded in the cash receipts journal, and sales of non-current assets on credit are recorded in the general journal, as we shall see later.) As each credit sale occurs, several copies of a sales invoice are prepared to document the transaction. For GST-registered businesses, these must be tax invoices (see chapter 6).

The information shown on a sales invoice includes the customer's name, date of sale, invoice number (usually prenumbered), amount of the sale and the credit terms. One copy of the invoice is used by the seller to record the sale in the sales journal. In figure 7.5, eight sales to five different customers have been recorded. All credit sales are made on the basis of 2/10, n/30.

Other columns can be added to the sales journal to satisfy the needs of a specific entity. If credit terms vary among customers, an additional column can be added to the sales journal to identify the terms of each sale.

The sales journal illustrated in figure 7.5 is suitable for use in an entity that maintains a periodic inventory system. For those entities using a perpetual inventory system, where two entries are made every time a sale is recorded (see chapter 6, p. 241), an additional column entitled 'cost of sales' is added to the journal. This column records the cost of sales at the same time as the credit sale is recorded (at selling price). It is assumed that Baldwin Video Equipment has an ABN and is registered for the GST.

Advantages of a sales journal

The sales journal shown in figure 7.5 has these time-saving advantages:

1. Each sales transaction is recorded on a *single line*. All credit sales are alike in that they result in a debit to Accounts Receivable, a credit to Sales, and a credit to GST Collections (if applicable). Record-keeping efficiency is achieved by simply identifying the customer who is the debtor, instead of entering all the account titles — Accounts Receivable, Sales, and GST Collections — when the transaction is recorded in the general journal. In a perpetual inventory system, an additional column is used to record the cost of sales and reduction of the inventory balance.
2. The entries in the sales journal do not require a narration because (a) all the transactions involved are the same, and (b) the detailed information of each sale is documented on an invoice that is referenced in the second column of the sales journal. If more information concerning a particular sale is required, you can simply identify the invoice number or customer and refer to the details shown on the invoice.
3. Only the totals of sales, GST collections and amounts receivable from customers are posted to the general ledger. Note in figure 7.5 that the amount for total credit sales (including GST)

Figure 7.5 Relationship of sales journal and ledger accounts

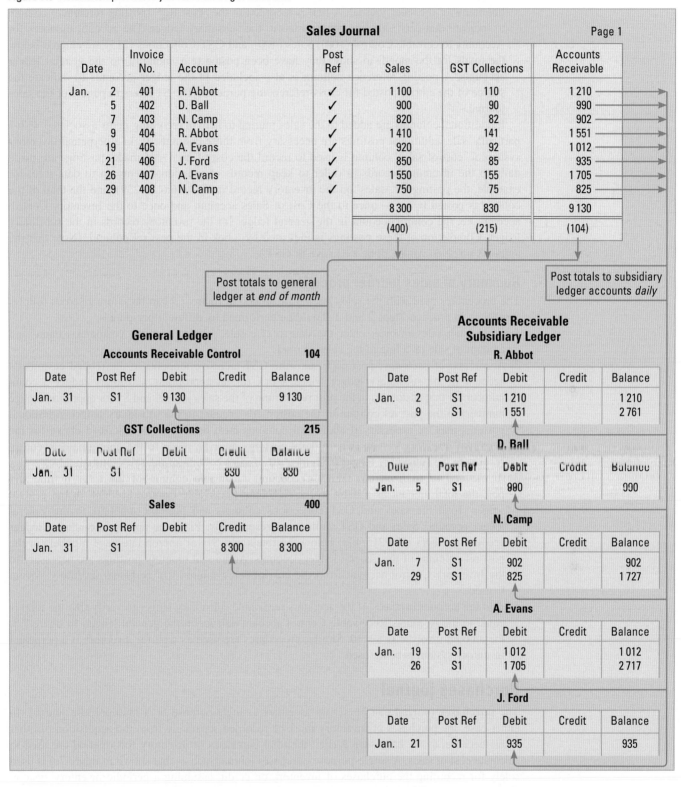

Sales Journal

Page 1

Date	Invoice No.	Account	Post Ref	Sales	GST Collections	Accounts Receivable
Jan. 2	401	R. Abbot	✓	1 100	110	1 210
5	402	D. Ball	✓	900	90	990
7	403	N. Camp	✓	820	82	902
9	404	R. Abbot	✓	1 410	141	1 551
19	405	A. Evans	✓	920	92	1 012
21	406	J. Ford	✓	850	85	935
26	407	A. Evans	✓	1 550	155	1 705
29	408	N. Camp	✓	750	75	825
				8 300	830	9 130
				(400)	(215)	(104)

Post totals to general ledger at *end of month*

Post totals to subsidiary ledger accounts *daily*

General Ledger

Accounts Receivable Control   104

Date	Post Ref	Debit	Credit	Balance
Jan. 31	S1	9 130		9 130

GST Collections   215

Date	Post Ref	Debit	Credit	Balance
Jan. 31	S1		830	830

Sales   400

Date	Post Ref	Debit	Credit	Balance
Jan. 31	S1		8 300	8 300

Accounts Receivable Subsidiary Ledger

R. Abbot

Date	Post Ref	Debit	Credit	Balance
Jan. 2	S1	1 210		1 210
9	S1	1 551		2 761

D. Ball

Date	Post Ref	Debit	Credit	Balance
Jan. 5	S1	990		990

N. Camp

Date	Post Ref	Debit	Credit	Balance
Jan. 7	S1	902		902
29	S1	825		1 727

A. Evans

Date	Post Ref	Debit	Credit	Balance
Jan. 19	S1	1 012		1 012
26	S1	1 705		2 717

J. Ford

Date	Post Ref	Debit	Credit	Balance
Jan. 21	S1	935		935

of $9130 is posted to the Accounts Receivable Control account, total sales (exclusive of GST) is posted to the Sales account, and the total GST added to sales is posted to the GST Collections account. (The GST amounts are removed for businesses not registered for GST.) This procedure eliminates posting separate debits and credits during the month. The sales information needed for each customer in the accounts receivable subsidiary ledger is posted daily from the line items of the sales journal. A tick is recorded in the 'Post Ref' (posting reference) column to indicate that each sale has been posted to the subsidiary ledger. The account numbers for Accounts Receivable Control (104), Sales (400), and GST Collections (215) are entered below the totals for the month to show they have been posted (e.g. monthly) to the general ledger accounts. A posting reference column is also included in the ledger accounts to indicate the source of the entries posted for cross-referencing purposes. The S1 refers to page 1 of the sales journal.

If additional columns are added to the sales journal to help in recording items associated with a particular sale, additional postings are necessary from those columns. If, in a perpetual inventory system, a 'cost of sales' column is used to record the cost of each sale made, postings are made daily to the inventory records in order to keep records of individual items up to date (see, for example, the posting for 'sales' on the inventory record in figure 6.6, p. 239), and the total of the column is posted twice — once to the Cost of Sales account, and once to the Inventory Control account, i.e. the control account in the general ledger for the inventory records in the subsidiary ledger. Completion of these postings is indicated by a tick in the post ref column. (Note that the amounts involved would all be exclusive of GST.)

Summary of sales journal procedures

The procedures used with the sales journal illustrated in figure 7.5 can be summarised as follows (note that, in practice, steps 2 and 3 should be performed by different personnel):

1. From each sales invoice, enter the date of the sale, invoice number, customer's name and amount of sale on a line in the sales journal.
2. *At the end of each day*, post each sale (the GST-inclusive amount) to the related customer's account in the subsidiary ledger. Place a tick (or an appropriate subsidiary ledger account number for that customer) in the post ref column of the sales journal and S1 (or appropriate page number) in the post ref column of the customer's account in the subsidiary ledger. Additional postings may be necessary if additional columns have been used as described above for the perpetual inventory system, where daily postings must be made to the appropriate inventory records in the subsidiary ledger from the cost of sales column of the sales journal.
3. *At the end of each month*, total the accounts receivable column of the sales journal and post the total amount as a debit to the Accounts Receivable Control account, in the general ledger. Total the sales and GST collections columns and post the amounts to the general ledger accounts Sales and GST Collections respectively. Place the appropriate general ledger account numbers (104/215/400) below the totals and S1 (or appropriate page number) in the post ref columns of the general ledger accounts. Additional monthly postings are necessary to the Inventory Control account from the cost of sales column if a perpetual inventory system is used.
4. Add the account balances of the accounts receivable subsidiary ledger to verify that the total is equal to the Accounts Receivable Control account balance in the general ledger. In figure 7.5, the amount involved is $9130. Similar procedures are used as well for inventory if a perpetual inventory system is being used.

Purchases journal

The **purchases journal** can be set up as either a single-purpose or a multipurpose journal. In either case, the purchases of inventory must be recorded separately from the acquisition of other assets because, as we have seen earlier, the total purchases of inventory for a period are used to calculate cost of sales. A single-purpose purchases journal such as that shown in figure 7.6 is used solely for recording the purchases of inventory on credit, assuming a periodic inventory system. Cash purchases of inventory are recorded in the cash payments journal, as discussed later. Other purchases, such as the acquisition of a motor vehicle or a computer, are recorded in some other journal, determined by the means of payment involved. If such assets are acquired for cash, the transactions are recorded in the cash payments journal; if purchased on credit, they are recorded in the general journal.

Figure 7.6 Relationship of purchases journal and ledger accounts

Purchases Journal
Page 1

Date Recorded	Date of Invoice	Account	Terms	Post Ref	Purchases	GST Outlays	Accounts Payable
Jan. 3	Jan. 2	Kirby Ltd	n/30	✓	1 900	190	2 090
6	Jan. 4	Risk Ltd	n/30	✓	1 200	120	1 320
8	Jan. 8	Dunn Supply	n/30	✓	1 410	141	1 551
13	Jan. 12	Dunn Supply	n/30	✓	1 820	182	2 002
20	Jan. 18	CSR Ltd	2/10, n/30	✓	820	82	902
24	Jan. 24	Cooper Ltd	2/10, n/30	✓	900	90	990
27	Jan. 26	Risk Ltd	2/10, n/30	✓	2 810	281	3 091
30	Jan. 29	CSR Ltd	n/30	✓	900	90	990
					11 760	1 176	12 936
					(510)	(160)	(210)

Post totals to general ledger at *end of month*

Post totals to subsidiary ledger accounts *daily*

General Ledger

GST Outlays   160

Date	Post Ref	Debit	Credit	Balance
Jan. 31	P1	1 176		1 176

Accounts Payable Control   210

Date	Post Ref	Debit	Credit	Balance
Jan. 31	P1		12 936	12 936

Purchases   510

Date	Post Ref	Debit	Credit	Balance
Jan. 31	P1	11 760		11 760

Accounts Payable Subsidiary Ledger

Cooper Ltd

Date	Post Ref	Debit	Credit	Balance
Jan. 24	P1		990	990

CSR Ltd

Date	Post Ref	Debit	Credit	Balance
Jan. 20	P1		902	902
30	P1		990	1 892

Dunn Supply

Date	Post Ref	Debit	Credit	Balance
Jan. 8	P1		1 551	1 551
13	P1		2 002	3 553

Kirby Ltd

Date	Post Ref	Debit	Credit	Balance
Jan. 3	P1		2 090	2 090

Risk Ltd

Date	Post Ref	Debit	Credit	Balance
Jan. 6	P1		1 320	1 320
27	P1		3 091	4 411

The advantages of and procedures required for a single-purpose purchases journal are similar to those described earlier for a sales journal. Recall from the discussion in chapter 6 that the purchase of inventory on credit with a periodic inventory system is recorded with a debit to Purchases and a credit to Accounts Payable. A periodic inventory system is illustrated in figure 7.6. If a perpetual inventory system is used, the debit for purchases goes to the Inventory Control account and individual inventory records in the subsidiary ledger are updated daily.

The account credited on each line item of a purchases journal is an account payable with a particular creditor to whom the business has an obligation. A subsidiary ledger is maintained to provide the detailed information concerning each individual account payable. An Accounts Payable Control account also is established in the general ledger. The procedures used with a single-purpose purchases journal, as illustrated in figure 7.6 for a periodic inventory system, can be summarised as follows (note that steps 2 and 3 would normally be performed by different personnel):

1. From the tax invoice received from the supplier, enter the recording date, invoice date, supplier's name, credit terms if applicable, and the dollar amounts of the purchase and GST on a single line of the journal.
2. *At the end of each day*, post each purchase for the full amount owing, including GST, to the related supplier's account in the subsidiary ledger. Place a tick (or an appropriate subsidiary ledger account number for that supplier) in the post ref column of the purchases journal and P1 (indicating page 1 of the purchases journal in this case) in the post ref column of the creditor's account in the subsidiary ledger. These posting reference marks indicate that the journal entry has been posted and identify the source of the entry.
3. *At the end of each month*, total the amount columns of the purchases journal and post the total of the accounts payable column as a credit to the Accounts Payable Control account in the general ledger. Post the totals of the purchases and GST outlays columns as debits to the general ledger accounts Purchases and GST Outlays respectively. Place the general ledger account numbers (510/160/210) below the relevant totals and P1 in the post ref columns of the general ledger accounts.
4. Add the account balances of the accounts payable subsidiary ledger to verify that the total is equal to the Accounts Payable Control account balance in the general ledger. In figure 7.6, the total amount is $12 936.

A single-purpose purchases journal can be expanded to a multipurpose format such as the one shown in figure 7.7. This journal has a single credit column for accounts payable and several debit columns for purchases of inventory (periodic inventory system), purchases of store supplies, and other debits. The 'other debits' column can be used to record such things as the acquisition of equipment or freight inwards charges.

Figure 7.7 Multipurpose purchases journal

| Date | Account | Post Ref | Purchases Debit | Stores Supplies Debit | GST Outlays Debit | Other Debits | | | Accounts Payable Credit |
						Account	Post Ref	Amount	
Jan. 3	Hull Co. Ltd	✓	1 900		190				2 090
10	Kirk Ltd	✓	2 800		280				3 080
14	Deckers Ltd	✓		810	81				891
19	Short Co. Ltd	✓		460	46				506
24	Zinn Co. Ltd	✓			115	Office Equipment	170	1 150	1 265

All the transactions recorded in this journal will involve credit rather than cash because of the single accounts payable credit column. The recording and posting procedures with a multipurpose purchases journal are similar in principle to those described for the cash journal covered on the following pages.

Cash receipts journal

The **cash receipts journal** is used to record all transactions involving the receipt of all forms of cash (a debit to Cash at Bank). Typical sources of cash are the sale of goods for cash, the collection of accounts receivable, capital invested by owners, and borrowings.

Daily banking of cash receipts is important for internal control. All receipts for a day are checked against appropriate documents, deposit slips are prepared, and the deposits are taken to the bank or placed in a night-safe. A common source of receipts is accounts receivable, and a discount is often allowed. The typical cash receipts journal therefore has at least two money columns, one to record the daily receipts and deposits to the bank and one to record discount allowed to customers. The totals of these columns are debited to the Cash at Bank and Discount Allowed accounts respectively. If the business is registered for the GST, an additional column for GST collections is required to record the write-back of the GST included in the allowance for prompt payment (see chapter 6 for details).

Since the totals of the cash at bank, discount allowed, and GST collections columns are debited to accounts in the general ledger, corresponding credits for the amount of the total of these three debits must be made in general ledger accounts. These credits can be posted individually from the account column of the journal (see figure 7.8, overleaf). Where the receipts from a particular source are numerous, such as cash sales, GST collections on cash sales, and accounts receivable, processing is made more efficient by having additional columns in which receipts relating to particular activities can be recorded.

The following cash receipts transactions for Baldwin Video Equipment provide the basis for the entries in figure 7.8 (note that for simplicity all figures have been rounded to the nearest $1):
1. The owner of the business, Barbara Baldwin, invested $10 000 of her own cash on 3 January, and this was deposited in the bank account of the business as capital (GST-free).
2. Video equipment was sold for $280 (plus GST) cash on 8 January.
3. Received payment from R. Abbot for an 8-day-old account receivable of $1210 less a 2% discount of $24 (includes $2 GST) on 10 January, i.e. $1186 cash was received. Credit terms were 2/10, n/30 and the cash was received within 10 days.
4. Received payment from D. Ball for a 15-day-old account receivable of $990 on 20 January. No discount was involved since the cash was not received within 10 days.
5. Video equipment was sold for $220 (plus GST) cash on 20 January.
6. The proceeds of a bank loan of $2500 were received on 31 January (GST-free).

At the end of the period, the totals of the columns in the journal can be credited to the appropriate accounts, so there is no need to post each receipt individually. This principle should become clear from the illustration. In the typical situation, four columns are used for the credit part of the posting process. These are sales, GST collections, accounts receivable and other accounts. The first three credit columns are used to record collections from cash sales, GST, and accounts receivable. All other sources of cash are entered in the fourth credit column.

Additional columns may be used to meet the needs of a particular entity if there are a sufficiently large number of debit postings to be made to particular accounts. Note that the order and arrangement can vary among entities. The three debit columns and four credit columns of the cash receipts journal shown in figure 7.8 (p. 292) are used as described below.

Debits

Cash at bank. The cash at bank column is used in *every* entry because *only* cash receipts transactions are recorded in the cash receipts journal. Each amount appearing in this column also represents the amount of cash received on the date shown and hence deposited to the business bank account. The entries on each day therefore correspond with daily bank deposits. Note in figure 7.8 that, on 20 January, two amounts were received. These are recorded in the appropriate credit columns and in the cash at bank column. The total banking for that day can easily be determined by adding the two amounts: $990 + $242 = $1232.

Discount allowed. This column is used to record the discount allowed to customers for prompt payment. Note that on 10 January a 2% discount ($0.02 \times \$1210 = \$24$) was given to R. Abbot because the payment was made within 10 days in accordance with the credit terms. This amount consists of $22 discount allowed plus an adjustment of the GST collections of $2 ($22 ÷ 11) recorded at the time of the sale. Total debits to cash at bank ($1186), discount allowed ($22), and GST collections write-back of $2 are equal to the $1210 accounts receivable.

GST collections. This column records the write-back of the GST included in any discount for prompt payment.

Figure 7.8 Relationship of cash receipts journal and ledger accounts

Cash Receipts Journal | Page 1

Date	Account	Post Ref	Debits — Cash at Bank	Debits — Discount Allowed	Debits — GST Collections	Credits — Sales	Credits — GST Collections	Credits — Accounts Receivable	Credits — Other Accounts
Jan. 3	B. Baldwin, Capital	300	10 000						10 000 →
8	Sales		308			280	28		
10	R. Abbot	✓	1 186	22	2			1 210	
20	D. Ball	✓	990					990	
20	Sales		242			220	22		
31	Bank Loan	205	2 500						2 500 →
			15 226	22	2	500	50	2 200	12 500
			(100)	(511)	(215)	(400)	(215)	(104)	(x)

Post totals to general ledger at *end of month*

Post other accounts and accounts receivable *daily*

General Ledger

Cash at Bank 100

Date	Post Ref	Debit	Credit	Balance
Jan. 31	CR1	15 226		15 226

Accounts Payable Control 104

Date	Post Ref	Debit	Credit	Balance
Jan. 31	S1	9 130		9 130
31	CR1		2 200	6 930

Bank Loan 205

Date	Post Ref	Debit	Credit	Balance
Jan. 31	CR1		2 500	2 500

GST Collections 215

Date	Post Ref	Debit	Credit	Balance
Jan. 31	S1		830	830
31	CR1		50	880
31	CR1	2		878

B. Baldwin, Capital 300

Date	Post Ref	Debit	Credit	Balance
Jan. 3	CR1		10 000	10 000

Sales 400

Date	Post Ref	Debit	Credit	Balance
Jan. 31	S1		8 300	8 300
31	CR1		500	8 800

Discount Allowed 511

Date	Post Ref	Debit	Credit	Balance
Jan. 31	CR1	22		22

Accounts Receivable Subsidiary Ledger

R. Abbot

Date	Post Ref	Debit	Credit	Balance
Jan. 2	S1	1 210		1 210
9	S1	1 551		2 761
10	CR1		1 210	1 551

D. Ball

Date	Post Ref	Debit	Credit	Balance
Jan. 5	S1	990		990
20	CR1		990	—

(Other subsidiary accounts totalling $5379 not shown)

Credits

Sales. All cash sales are recorded in the sales column at GST-exclusive prices. Most entities use cash registers to account for daily cash sales. At the end of a day, sales tapes showing the total cash sales are removed from the cash registers and a summary of these tapes is used to make the entry in the sales column. Cash registers and barcode readers can automatically track any GST involved.

GST collections. This column records the GST applicable to the cash sales recorded in the sales column.

Accounts receivable. This column is used to record collections from customers. The name of the customer is written in the account column to identify the proper account to be credited in the subsidiary ledger. Note that amounts entered in this column represent the gross amount of debt discharged by the amount received. For January, $2176 ($1186 + $990) was received in cash, and accounts receivable were allowed $24 discount under the terms of credit and the GST of $2 in the discount was written back. Hence, the Accounts Receivable Control account is credited for the full amount of $2200 (cash, discount allowed and GST).

Other accounts. This column is used for all cash collections other than from cash sales and accounts receivable. The title of the specific account to be credited is identified in the account column. For example, Barbara Baldwin's Capital account is credited on 3 January for the $10 000 investment of capital.

Summary of posting procedures for cash receipts journal

The procedures required to post the entries in the cash receipts journal can be summarised as follows (note that, in practice, steps 1–3 would be performed by different personnel):

1. The entries in the accounts receivable column are *posted daily* to the subsidiary ledger. A tick (or an appropriate subsidiary ledger account number for that customer) is placed in the post ref column of the cash receipts journal, and CR1 (representing in this case page 1 of the cash receipts journal) is entered in the post ref columns of the subsidiary ledger accounts.
2. The credits in the other accounts column are posted *daily or at other frequent intervals* during the month. The number of the account involved is recorded in the post ref column as the entries are posted to show that the posting has been done. In addition, CR1 is entered in the post ref column of each account to indicate the source of each entry
3. *At the end of the month*, the entries in each column are totalled. The sum of the debit columns is compared with the sum of the credit columns to verify that the debits and credits are equal. This procedure is called cross-adding, which gives the following results, using the totals of the journal columns:

Debit columns		**Credit columns**	
Cash at bank	$15 226	Sales	$ 500
Discount allowed	22	Accounts receivable	2 200
GST collections	2	GST collections	50
		Other accounts	12 500
Total debits	$15 250	Total credits	$15 250
		Cross-added totals	

After the totals have been cross-added, the following six column totals are posted:

Cash debit column. Posted as a debit to the Cash at Bank account. The account number (100) is entered below the total to indicate that the posting has been done, and CR1 is recorded in the post ref column of the Cash at Bank account.

Discount allowed debit column. Posted as a debit to the Discount Allowed account. The account number (511) is placed below the total to show that the posting has been done, and CR1 is entered in the post ref column in the Discount Allowed account.

GST collections debit column. Posted as a debit to the GST Collections account. The account number (215) is placed below the total to show that the posting has been done, and CR1 is entered in the post ref column of the GST Collections account.

Sales credit column. Posted as a credit to the Sales account. The account number (400) is entered below the total as an indication that the posting has taken place, and CR1 is recorded in the Sales account.

GST collections credit column. Posted as a credit to the GST Collections account. The account number (215) is placed below the total to show that the posting has been done, and CR1 is entered in the post ref column of the GST Collections account.

Accounts receivable credit column. Posted as a credit to the Accounts Receivable Control account. The account number (104) is recorded below the total, and CR1 is entered in the control account.

The total of the other accounts column *is not posted at the end of the month* because each entry was posted individually during the month. A special symbol — such as (x) — is used at the bottom of the column to indicate that it is not posted as a total.

As discussed previously with the sales journal, additional columns may be added to the cash receipts journal to record items associated with a particular cash receipt. If so, additional postings are necessary from those columns. In a *perpetual inventory system*, a 'cost of sales' column is added to the cash receipts journal to record the cost of each cash sale made, and postings must be made daily to the inventory records in order to keep records of individual items up to date (see the posting for 'sales' on the inventory record in figure 6.6, p. 239). Furthermore, at the end of the month, the total of the 'cost of sales' column is posted twice — once to the Cost of Sales account, and once to the Inventory Control account, i.e. the control account in the general ledger for the inventory records in the subsidiary ledger. Completion of these postings is indicated by a tick in the post ref column in the cash receipts journal.

Cash payments journal

The **cash payments journal**, also called the cash disbursements journal, is used to record all transactions involving payments of cash — cash purchases of inventory, payment of accounts payable, payments for expenses, and repayment of bank loans.

Cash is a very valuable asset and can easily be misappropriated. As we shall see in the chapter on cash management and control, adequate controls are essential to safeguard this asset. We have already noted that all cash received (in whatever form) is banked daily. In all entities using a sound system of internal control, all payments are made through the bank account of the entity.

The two most common means used by an entity to make payments are cheques drawn on the entity's bank account or payments made via direct transfers by the bank under the authority of the entity. In this chapter, we shall assume that all payments, after proper authorisation, are made by cheque or electronic transfer unless otherwise stated. Small or minor payments can be made from petty cash held in the form of notes and coins.

The cash payments journal must have at least three money columns — one to record the amount of each payment, i.e. each cheque written, another to record the discount received when accounts payable are paid, and another to adjust the GST outlays. Writing cheques against the entity's bank account reduces the balance of the Cash at Bank account, or increases the overdraft if the bank account is overdrawn. In either case, the Cash at Bank account is credited. Again, since an entity earns income by receiving discounts, the Discount Received account is credited. Note that the GST Outlays account is credited for any GST adjustments.

Other columns are added to improve the posting process for the accounts to be debited as a result of each payment. Two common ones are for purchases of inventories and accounts payable. An 'other accounts' column can then be used for all other accounts to be debited. As can be seen from figure 7.9, four debit columns (other accounts, accounts payable, purchases and GST outlays) are used along with three credit columns (cash at bank, discount received and GST outlays).

Figure 7.9 Relationship of cash payments journal and ledger accounts

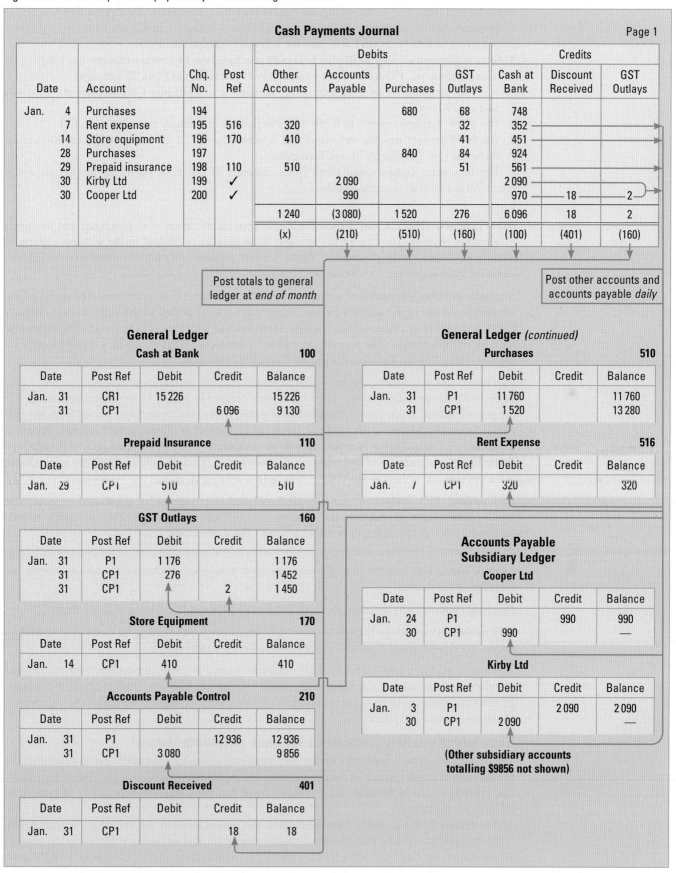

The following transactions for Baldwin Video Equipment are used to illustrate the cash payments journal (note that for simplicity all figures have been rounded to the nearest $1):

1. Inventory costing $680 plus GST was purchased on 4 January (cheque no. 194).
2. Store rent of $320 plus GST was paid on 7 January (cheque no. 195).
3. Store equipment costing $410 plus GST was purchased on 14 January (cheque no. 196).
4. Issued cheque no. 197 for inventory costing $924 (includes GST) on 28 January.
5. A 1-year premium for an insurance policy amounting to $510 plus GST (cheque no. 198) was paid on 29 January.
6. The $2090 account payable to Kirby Ltd was paid on 30 January by cheque no. 199.
7. The $990 account payable to Cooper Ltd was paid less a 2% discount of $20 on 30 January. A cheque (no. 200) for $970 was forwarded.

The four debit columns and three credit columns of the cash payments journal shown in figure 7.9 are used as described below.

Debits

Other accounts. This column is used for all cash payments *except* cash purchases and payments of accounts payable. The title of the account to be debited is entered in the account column to identify the reason for the payment. In figure 7.9, rent expense and prepaid insurance were paid for along with the acquisition of store equipment.

Accounts payable. Payments of accounts payable are entered in this column. The name of the supplier is written in the account column so the entry can be posted to the appropriate subsidiary ledger account. Note that a similar position exists here as with the accounts receivable column in the cash receipts journal. The accounts in figure 7.9 are recorded gross, i.e. they represent the total amount owing that has been discharged by forwarding payment.

Purchases. The purchases column is used to record all cash purchases of inventory (net of GST) when using the periodic system. The total of this column is posted to the Purchases account in the general ledger. When posted, the amount is added to the credit purchases posted from the purchases journal to determine the total purchases for the period. If the perpetual inventory system is used, the purchases column is replaced with an 'inventory' column, the total of which is debited to the Inventory Control account representing cash purchases, and daily postings are necessary to inventory records in the inventory subsidiary ledger.

GST outlays. This column records any GST included in payments for goods and services. The total of this column is posted to the debit of the GST Outlays account. This account's balance represents input credits that can be offset against GST Collections.

Credits

Cash at bank. This column must be used for *each* transaction because *only* cash payments are recorded in the journal.

Discount received. Any discount received for prompt payment is recorded in this column.

GST outlays. This column is used to record any adjustments that need to be made to GST outlays previously recorded, e.g. if an allowance is made for prompt payment.

The format used in figure 7.9 for the cash payments journal is a typical one. However, the number of columns used, and the order and arrangement of columns, can vary from business to business. In practice, there could be separate columns for all frequently occurring expenses, e.g. wages, electricity, repairs and telephone.

Summary of posting procedures for cash payments journal

The posting procedures required with the cash payments journal are the two types discussed earlier for the cash receipts journal — *postings during the month* and *postings at the end of the month*. The procedures can be summarised as follows (note that steps 1–3 would normally be performed by different personnel):

1. The entries in the accounts payable column are posted *daily* to the subsidiary ledger. A tick (or an appropriate subsidiary ledger account number for that supplier) is placed in the post ref column of the cash payments journal, and CP1 (representing in this case page 1 of the cash

payments journal) is entered in the post ref columns of the subsidiary ledger accounts. In a perpetual inventory system, daily postings are made also to inventory records in the subsidiary ledger for any cash purchases recorded in the 'inventory' column.

2. The debits in the other accounts column are posted *daily or at other frequent intervals* during the month. The number of each account involved is recorded in the post ref column as the entries are posted to indicate that the posting has been done. CP1 is entered in the post ref column of each account to show the source of each entry.

3. *At the end of the month*, the dollar amounts entered in each column are totalled and cross-added to verify that the debits and credits are equal, as shown below:

Debit columns		Credit columns	
Other accounts	$1 240	Cash at bank	$6 096
Accounts payable	3 080	Discount received	18
Purchases	1 520	GST outlays	2
GST outlays	276		
Total debits	$6 116	Total credits	$6 116
		Cross-added totals	

4. The column totals for accounts payable, purchases (or inventory), cash at bank and discount received are posted *at the end of the month* to their respective accounts in the general ledger. The account numbers are entered below the column totals, and CP1 is recorded in the post ref columns of the general ledger accounts. The total of the other accounts column is *not* posted at the end of the month because the individual entries were posted earlier. An (x) can be placed below the column total to indicate that it is not posted at the end of the month.

BUSINESS KNOWLEDGE

The numbers of life

In a manual accounting system, posting is done using appropriate account descriptions or names. But computers are able to process data in response to numerical input much faster than if descriptive names are used. Hence, in today's computerised environment, numbers dominate our lives — tax file numbers, Medicare numbers, bank account numbers, personal identification numbers (PINs), credit card numbers, employee numbers and so on. So it is with accounting.

Use of the general journal

Despite the inefficiency of a general journal for repetitive transactions such as sales, purchases, cash receipts and cash payments, it is an essential part of every accounting system. A *limited number* of infrequent transactions (such as sales returns and allowances, purchases returns and allowances, and the purchase or sale of equipment on credit) are recorded in the general journal *during* an accounting period. If a particular transaction cannot be recorded effectively in one of the special journals, it should be entered in the general journal.

The general journal is also used for all *adjusting* and *closing* entries at the end of the accounting period. The procedures used to record entries in the general journal and to post them daily to ledger accounts have already been described in previous chapters. In addition, the general journal is used to record *correcting entries* or adjustments to the accounts that must be made either during the accounting period or after special journals have been posted.

As we have seen in the description of special journals, the ledger accounts should indicate the journal from which each debit and credit is posted. The symbol GJ typically is used in the ledger accounts for postings from the general journal; GJ1 refers to page 1 of the general journal. The following symbols can be used to identify the sources of entries posted from the five journals discussed so far:

S1 — page 1 of the sales journal
P1 — page 1 of the purchases journal
CR1 — page 1 of the cash receipts journal
CP1 — page 1 of the cash payments journal
GJ1 — page 1 of the general journal

To illustrate the use of the general journal, assume that Barbara Baldwin agreed to give A. Evans a $77 (including GST of $7) allowance because of a faulty component in video equipment sold on 19 January. The sales allowance is recorded in the general journal as shown in figure 7.10. Note that the GST included in the allowance ($77 ÷ 11) is written back against the GST recorded in the GST Collections account when the goods were originally sold. Both the Accounts Receivable Control account and the customer's subsidiary ledger account must be credited; otherwise the control account will not be in balance with the subsidiary ledger. The number of the Accounts Receivable Control account (104) and a tick (or an appropriate subsidiary ledger account number for that customer) are recorded in the post ref column to indicate that both postings have been made.

Figure 7.10 Relationship of general journal and ledger accounts

General Journal Page 1

Date	Particulars	Post Ref	Debit	Credit
Jan. 31	Sales Returns and Allowances	402	70	
	GST Collections	215	7	
	Accounts Receivable Control, A. Evans	104/✓		77
	(Sales allowance given because of faulty equipment)			

General Ledger

Accounts Receivable Control   104

Date	Post Ref	Debit	Credit	Balance
Jan. 31	S1	9 130		9 130
31	CR1		2 200	6 930
31	GJ1		77	6 853

GST Collections   215

Date	Post Ref	Debit	Credit	Balance
Jan. 31	S1		830	830
	CR1		50	880
	CR1	2		878
	GJ1	7		871

Sales Returns and Allowances   402

Date	Post Ref	Debit	Credit	Balance
Jan. 31	GJ1	70		70

Accounts Receivable Subsidiary Ledger

A. Evans

Date	Post Ref	Debit	Credit	Balance
Jan. 19	S1	1 012		1 012
26	S1	1 705		2 717
31	GJ1		77	2 640

To illustrate the use of the general journal for the purpose of correcting entries that have already been posted to the accounts, assume that the accountant for Barbara Baldwin had posted the payment of $475 for repairs to office equipment to the debit side of the Office Equipment account. To correct this error, it is necessary to cancel the debit entry in the Office Equipment account and debit an account such as Equipment Maintenance and Repairs Expense. The correcting entry is shown in figure 7.11.

Note that if errors are discovered in the journals *before postings have been made*, the errors can simply be corrected by ruling through the incorrect figure and inserting the correct one.

Figure 7.11 Use of general journal for correcting entries

General Journal — Page 1

Date	Particulars	Post Ref	Debit	Credit
Sept. 12	Equipment Maintenance and Repairs Expense	560	475	
	Office Equipment	134		475
	(Correction of debit to incorrect account)			

Note: It is assumed that no entry was made in the subsidiary ledger for office equipment.

General Ledger

Office Equipment 134

Date	Post Ref	Debit	Credit	Balance
Sept. 1	—	—	—	10 000
7	CP1	475		10 475
12	GJ1		475	10 000

Equip. Maintenance and Repairs Exp. 560

Date	Post Ref	Debit	Credit	Balance
Sept. 12	GJ1	475		475

Abnormal balances in subsidiary ledgers

From time to time it is possible that temporary abnormal balances will arise in the accounts receivable and accounts payable subsidiary ledgers. For example, in placing an order for inventory, a deposit may be required to be paid on the goods. At the time of payment, this could result in a debit to an account in the accounts payable subsidiary ledger before the purchase of the goods. During the accounting period, this temporary abnormal balance will cause no problems and the account will revert to a normal credit balance on receipt of an invoice for the inventory purchased.

However, if the accounts payable account has a debit balance at the end of the accounting period, this should not be offset against the total accounts payable. It should be added to the accounts receivable balances for the purposes of end-of-period reporting. A similar situation could arise in relation to the accounts receivable subsidiary ledger.

Note that abnormal balances can be flagged automatically in a computerised system, and can easily be added to the appropriate classification, e.g. credit balances in accounts receivable would be added automatically to accounts payable for reporting purposes.

Account set-offs

Selling to a customer and buying from the same customer is another situation that may arise. For example, a business selling computer equipment to a customer could, in turn, buy stationery from the same customer. Under normal trading conditions, this causes no problems. For example, if

$5000 worth of equipment was sold on credit to Ace Supplies, and before payment was received $1500 of stationery was purchased on credit from the same business, an account for Ace Supplies would appear in both the accounts receivable and accounts payable subsidiary ledgers. These accounts normally would be discharged by receiving a cheque for $5000 from Ace Supplies and forwarding a separate cheque for $1500 to Ace Supplies.

It may arise, however, that in settlement of its debt of $5000 Ace Supplies offsets the amount to be paid by the $1500 owing to it, and forwards a cheque for the net amount of $3500. This leads to a balance of $1500 in Ace Supplies' account in both the receivable and payable subsidiary ledgers. A general journal entry is required to remove the $1500 in both accounts from the subsidiary ledgers.

To illustrate the principle involved, the ledger accounts and general journal are set out below:

Accounts before payment:

Accounts Receivable Ledger					**Accounts Payable Ledger**				
Ace Supplies					**Ace Supplies**				
Date	Post Ref	Debit	Credit	Balance	Date	Post Ref	Debit	Credit	Balance
	S1	5 000		5 000		P1		1 500	1 500

Accounts after payment:

Accounts Receivable Ledger					**Accounts Payable Ledger**				
Ace Supplies					**Ace Supplies**				
Date	Post Ref	Debit	Credit	Balance	Date	Post Ref	Debit	Credit	Balance
	S1	5 000		5 000		P1		1 500	1 500
	CR1		3 500	1 500					

The general journal entry below needs to be made and, after posting, the accounts in the subsidiary ledgers would appear as shown.

General Journal				
Date	Particulars	Post Ref	Debit	Credit
	Accounts Payable Control, Ace Supplies	201/✓	1 500	
	Accounts Receivable Control, Ace Supplies	104/✓		1 500
	(Accounts offset)			

Accounts Receivable Ledger					**Accounts Payable Ledger**				
Ace Supplies					**Ace Supplies**				
Date	Post Ref	Debit	Credit	Balance	Date	Post Ref	Debit	Credit	Balance
	S1	5 000		5 000		P1		1 500	1 500
	CR1		3 500	1 500		GJ1	1 500		—
	GJ1		1 500	—					

Note that the general journal entry also requires a debit to be made to the Accounts Payable Control account and a credit to the Accounts Receivable Control account. Both these accounts are in the general ledger and are not shown here.

Demonstration problem

The following demonstration problem illustrates the use of the general journal, the four special journals introduced here, and the general ledger with two subsidiary ledgers.

Sidney Carton began business on 1 July 2012, specialising in the purchase and supply of packaging materials. Carton obtained the necessary ABN (99 111 222 333) and registered for the GST. An accounting system was designed and a chart of accounts was established:

101	Cash at Bank	158	Office Equipment	405	Discount Received
113	Accounts Receivable Control	201	Accounts Payable Control	501	Purchases
		202	Bank Loan	503	Purchases Returns and Allowances
117	Prepaid Insurance	240	GST Collections		
118	Office Supplies	251	Mortgage Payable	601	Salaries Expense
120	GST Outlays	301	S. Carton, Capital	611	Delivery Expense
151	Land	401	Sales	621	Office Expenses
154	Buildings	403	Sales Returns and Allowances	631	Sundry Expenses
156	Store Furniture			633	Discount Allowed

The following transactions occurred during July 2012. The applicable rate of GST is 10%. All calculations are rounded to the nearest dollar.

2012

July 1   S. Carton invested $60 000 cash in the new business (GST-free).

     1   Purchased land and buildings of an existing retail store (GST-free in this case) for $100 000 of which $30 000 is considered land cost. Paid $30 000 by cheque no. 101 for the land and buildings and signed a mortgage payable for the balance.

     2   Purchased store furniture on credit from Cooma Ltd for $7480 including GST, terms n/60.

     5   Purchased inventory on credit from Tumut Co. Ltd, $4000 plus GST; invoice date 6 July, terms 2/10, n/60.

     6   Purchased a 3-year fire insurance policy for $792 including GST, cheque no. 102.

     8   Purchased inventory for $5500 including GST, cheque no. 103.

     9   Returned unsatisfactory goods to Tumut Co. Ltd and received an adjustment note (credit note) for $880, including GST adjustment

   13   Sold inventory to B. Miller on account, $8200 plus GST; invoice no. 1, terms 1/10, n/30.

   15   Paid Tumut Co. Ltd cheque no. 104 for amount due.

   15   Cash sales for period to 15 July were recorded today, $3740 including GST.

   16   Sold inventory to M. Owen on account, $4700 plus GST; invoice no. 2, terms 1/10, n/30.

   16   Paid salaries for period to 15 July totalling $2650, cheque no. 105 (GST-free).

   20   Purchased inventory on credit from Lockwood Ltd, $5390 including GST; invoice date 20 July, terms 1/10, n/30.

   22   Received account for $143 including GST from P. Mason for items chargeable to Office Expenses, terms n/30.

   23   Received inventory returned by M. Owen, and issued adjustment note (credit note) no. 1 for $2200 including GST adjustment.

   23   Received cheque from B. Miller for invoice no. 1, less discount.

   26   Received cheque from M. Owen for balance due on invoice no. 2, less discount.

   29   Sold inventory worth $4000 plus GST on credit to B. King; invoice no. 3, terms 1/10, n/30.

   29   Paid $237 including GST for sundry expenses, cheque no. 106.

   29   Paid Lockwood Ltd for the invoice dated 20 July, less discount, cheque no. 107.

   31   Cash sales from 16 July to 31 July were $2145 including GST.

   31   Paid salaries for period 16–31 July totalling $2850, cheque no. 108 (GST-free).

   31   Received account from J. Bond for $106 including GST, for delivery expenses for the month.

   31   Purchased a printer for use in the business office at a cost of $825 including GST using a short-term bank loan.

   31   Purchased office supplies for $330 including GST, cheque no. 109.

Required

A. Record the transactions in a general journal, a cash receipts journal, a cash payments journal, a sales journal and a purchases journal.

B. Show the accounts receivable and accounts payable subsidiary ledgers as they would appear at the end of July, and prepare schedules of balances.

C. Post all journals to the general ledger accounts (running balance).

D. Prepare a trial balance of the general ledger as at 31 July 2012.

Solution to demonstration problem

A.

		General Journal			
Date		Particulars	Post Ref	Debit	Credit
2012 July	1	Buildings	154	70 000	
		Mortgage Payable	251		70 000
		(Purchase of store buildings and land)			
	2	Store Furniture	156	6 800	
		GST Outlays	120	680	
		Accounts Payable Control, Cooma Ltd	201/✓		7 480
		(Purchase of furniture, terms n/60)			
	9	Accounts Payable Control, Tumut Co. Ltd	201/✓	880	
		Purchases Returns and Allowances	503		800
		GST Outlays	120		80
		(Returned goods, adjustment note received)			
	22	Office Expenses	621	130	
		GST Outlays	120	13	
		Accounts Payable Control, P. Mason	201/✓		143
		(Purchase of office supplies, terms n/30)			
	23	Sales Returns and Allowances	403	2 000	
		GST Collections	120	200	
		Accounts Receivable Control, M. Owen	113/✓		2 200
		(Return of goods sold. Issued adjustment note 1)			
	31	Delivery Expense	611	96	
		GST Outlays	120	10	
		Accounts Payable Control, J. Bond	201/✓		106
		(Account received for delivery expenses)			
	31	Office Equipment	158	750	
		GST Outlays	120	75	
		Bank Loan	202		825
		(Purchase of printer)			
				81 634	81 634

		Purchases Journal						Page 1
Date Recorded	Date of Invoice	Account	Terms	Post Ref	Purchases	GST Outlays	Accounts Payable	
2012 July 5	6 July	Tumut Co. Ltd	2/10, n/60	✓	4 000	400	4 400	
20	20 July	Lockwood Ltd	1/10, n/30	✓	4 900	490	5 390	
					8 900	890	9 790	
					(501)	(120)	(201)	

Sales Journal — Page 1

Date	Invoice No.	Account	Terms	Post Ref	Sales	GST Collections	Accounts Receivable
2012							
July 13	1	B. Miller	1/10, n/30	✓	8 200	820	9 020
16	2	M. Owen	1/10, n/30	✓	4 700	470	5 170
29	3	B. King	1/10, n/30	✓	4 000	400	4 400
					16 900	1 690	18 590
					(401)	(240)	(113)

Cash Receipts Journal — Page 1

Date	Account	Post Ref	Debits Cash at Bank	Discount Allowed	GST Collections	Credits Sales	GST Collections	Accounts Receivable	Other Accounts
2012									
July 1	S. Carton, Capital	301	60 000						60 000
15	Sales		3 740			3 400	340		
23	B. Miller	✓	8 930	82	8			9 020	
26	M. Owen	✓	2 940	27	3			2 970	
31	Sales		2 145			1 950	195		
			77 755	109	11	5 350	535	11 990	60 000
			(101)	(633)	(240)	(401)	(240)	(113)	(x)

Cash Payments Journal — Page 1

Date	Account	Chq. No.	Post Ref	Debits Other Accounts	Accounts Payable	Purchases	GST Outlays	Credits Cash at Bank	Discount Received	GST Outlays
2012										
July 1	Land	101	151	30 000				30 000		
6	Prepaid insurance	102	117	720			72	792		
8	Purchases	103				5 000	500	5 500		
15	Tumut Co. Ltd	104	✓		3 520			3 450	64	6
16	Salaries expense	105	601	2 650				2 650		
29	Sundry expenses	106	631	215			22	237		
29	Lockwood Ltd	107	✓		5 390			5 336	49	5
31	Salaries expense	108	601	2 850				2 850		
31	Office supplies	109	118	300			30	330		
				36 735	8 910	5 000	624	51 145	113	11
				(x)	(201)	(501)	(120)	(101)	(405)	(120)

B.

Accounts Receivable Subsidiary Ledger

B. King

Date	Post Ref	Debit	Credit	Balance
2012 July 29	S1	4 400		4 400

B. Miller

Date	Post Ref	Debit	Credit	Balance
2012 July 13	S1	9 020		9 020
23	CR1		9 020	—

M. Owen

Date	Post Ref	Debit	Credit	Balance
2012 July 16	S1	5 170		5 170
23	GJ1		2 200	2 970
26	CR1		2 970	—

Schedule of Accounts Receivable
as at 31 July 2012

B. King	$4 400
	$4 400

Accounts Payable Subsidiary Ledger

J. Bond

Date	Post Ref	Debit	Credit	Balance
2012 July 31	GJ1		106	106

Cooma Ltd

Date	Post Ref	Debit	Credit	Balance
2012 July 2	GJ1		7 480	7 480

Lockwood Ltd

Date	Post Ref	Debit	Credit	Balance
2012 July 20	P1		5 390	5 390
29	CP1	5 390		—

P. Mason

Date	Post Ref	Debit	Credit	Balance
2012 July 22	GJ1		143	143

Tumut Co. Ltd

Date	Post Ref	Debit	Credit	Balance
2012 July 5	P1		4 400	4 400
9	GJ1	880		3 520
15	CP1	3 520		—

Schedule of Accounts Payable
as at 31 July 2012

J. Bond	$ 106
Cooma Ltd	7 480
P. Mason	143
	$7 729

C.

General Ledger

Cash at Bank 101

Date	Post Ref	Debit	Credit	Balance
2012 July 31	CR1	77 755		77 755
31	CP1		51 145	26 610

Accounts Receivable Control 113

Date	Post Ref	Debit	Credit	Balance
2012 July 23	GJ1		2 200	(2 200)
31	S1	18 590		16 390
31	CR1		11 990	4 400

Prepaid Insurance 117

Date	Post Ref	Debit	Credit	Balance
2012 July 5	CP1	720		720

Office Supplies 118

Date	Post Ref	Debit	Credit	Balance
2012 July 31	CP1	300		300

GST Outlays 120

Date	Post Ref	Debit	Credit	Balance
2012 July 2	GJ1	680		680
9	GJ1		80	600
22	GJ1	13		613
31	GJ1	10		623
31	GJ1	75		698
31	P1	890		1 588
31	CP1	624		2 212
31	CP1		11	2 201

Land 151

Date	Post Ref	Debit	Credit	Balance
2012 July 1	CP1	30 000		30 000

Buildings 154

Date	Post Ref	Debit	Credit	Balance
2012 July 1	GJ1	70 000		70 000

Store Furniture 156

Date	Post Ref	Debit	Credit	Balance
2012 July 2	GJ1	6 800		6 800

Office Equipment 158

Date	Post Ref	Debit	Credit	Balance
2012 July 31	GJ1	750		750

Accounts Payable 201

Date	Post Ref	Debit	Credit	Balance
2012 July 2	GJ1		7 480	7 480
9	GJ1	880		6 600
22	GJ1		143	6 743
31	GJ1		106	6 849
31	P1		9 790	16 639
31	CP1	8 910		7 729

Bank Loan 202

Date	Post Ref	Debit	Credit	Balance
2012 July 31	GJ1		825	825

GST Collections   **240**

Date	Post Ref	Debit	Credit	Balance
2012				
July 23	GJ1	200		(200)
31	S1		1 690	1 490
31	CR1		535	2 025
31	CR1	11		2 014

Note: GST outlays exceed collections because of purchase of non-current assets. In the normal course of business, collections will exceed outlays for a business of this type.

Mortgage Payable   **251**

Date	Post Ref	Debit	Credit	Balance
2012				
July 1	GJ1		70 000	70 000

S. Carton, Capital   **301**

Date	Post Ref	Debit	Credit	Balance
2012				
July 1	CR1		60 000	60 000

Sales   **401**

Date	Post Ref	Debit	Credit	Balance
2012				
July 31	S1		16 900	16 900
31	CR1		5 350	22 250

Sales Returns and Allowances   **403**

Date	Post Ref	Debit	Credit	Balance
2012				
July 23	GJ1	2 000		2 000

Discount Received   **405**

Date	Post Ref	Debit	Credit	Balance
2012				
July 31	CP1		113	113

Purchases   **501**

Date	Post Ref	Debit	Credit	Balance
2012				
July 31	P1	8 900		8 900
31	CP1	5 000		13 900

Purchases Returns and Allowances   **503**

Date	Post Ref	Debit	Credit	Balance
2012				
July 9	GJ1		800	800

Salaries Expense   **601**

Date	Post Ref	Debit	Credit	Balance
2012				
July 16	CP1	2 650		2 650
31	CP1	2 850		5 500

Delivery Expense   **611**

Date	Post Ref	Debit	Credit	Balance
2012				
July 31	GJ1	96		96

Office Expenses   **621**

Date	Post Ref	Debit	Credit	Balance
2012				
July 22	GJ1	130		130

Sundry Expenses   **631**

Date	Post Ref	Debit	Credit	Balance
2012				
July 29	CP1	215		215

Discount Allowed   **633**

Date	Post Ref	Debit	Credit	Balance
2012				
July 31	CR1	109		109

D.

S. CARTON Trial Balance as at 31 July 2012		
Account	Debit	Credit
Cash at bank	$ 26 610	
Accounts receivable control	4 400	
Prepaid insurance	720	
Office supplies	300	
GST outlays	2 201	
Land	30 000	
Buildings	70 000	
Store furniture	6 800	
Office equipment	750	
Accounts payable control		$ 7 729
Bank Loan		825
GST collections		2 014
Mortgage payable		70 000
S. Carton, Capital		60 000
Sales		22 250
Sales returns and allowances	2 000	
Discount received		113
Purchases	13 900	
Purchases returns and allowances		800
Salaries expense	5 500	
Delivery expense	96	
Office expenses	130	
Sundry expenses	215	
Discount allowed	109	
	$163 731	$163 731

7.7 Accounting software

Learning objective 7

Identify some of the basic features of accounting software through exposure to MYOB and QuickBooks

The computer software used by accountants falls generally into two categories — electronic spreadsheets and general ledger software. These are discussed below.

Electronic spreadsheets

An **electronic spreadsheet** is a grid of cells formed by the intersection of rows and columns into which data and formulas are entered. The spreadsheet can be used to analyse business data and solve everyday business problems. The spreadsheet market is currently dominated by Excel.

Spreadsheets can be used to develop business budgets and offer the facility to experiment with the budget data and budget outcomes by allowing an analysis of 'what if?' alternative budget scenarios and outcomes. The alternative outcomes of the various 'what if?' scenarios are instantaneously available. Other applications commonly handled by spreadsheets include inventory records (including price lists), depreciation schedules, accounts receivable accounting, payroll processing and record keeping.

General ledger programs

Most businesses use some type of computerised accounting system and these systems are collectively referred to as **general ledger software** or general ledger packages. Although some businesses still use accounting software developed in-house (usually as a component of a wider management information system), a wide range of general ledger software is commercially available and some of the best known packages are ACCPAC, Attache, MYOB, QuickBooks and Sybiz.

The software consists of a series of modular programs covering each of the major functional areas of accounting — sales (accounts receivable), purchases (accounts payable), cash receipts and banking, cash payments and banking, inventory, and payroll.

Other specialist modules are also available, e.g. time billing and product costing. The separate modules or programs are integrated and collectively access and provide input to the general ledger module, which is central to all packages, just as it is in manual systems of accounting.

Data input for each of the modules is obtained from source documents (handwritten or computer produced), and is processed by the software of the integrated modules. All output, including special and general reports, is produced on demand by the program. All programs are available in various configurations or 'packages', each tailored to the particular needs of businesses based on business size, nature and number of employees, and determined by the range of the accounting functions or modules required. For example, a service business has no need to purchase a package providing accounting modules for inventory and product costing.

To cater for the varying needs of businesses, MYOB Australia Ltd, for example, offers a variety of accounting software programs for the Windows platform — MYOB BusinessBasics, which includes basic accounting for a small business with no inventory or payroll (MYOB FirstEdge is available for businesses using the Mac system); MYOB AccountRight, AccountRight Plus, AccountRight Premier and AccountRight Enterprise, which include a range of features that may be required for different types and sizes of businesses. MYOB AccountEdge is designed for Mac users. Quicken (marketers of QuickBooks software) also offers a similarly packaged range of accounting software products for Windows — including QuickBooks EasyStart, QuickBooks Accounting, QuickBooks Plus, QuickBooks Pro, QuickBooks Premier and QuickBooks Enterprise. The structure of a typical integrated software package, based on the structure of MYOB AccountRight Plus (version 19) is illustrated in figure 7.12.

Figure 7.12 General ledger integrated software — based on MYOB AccountRight Plus (version 19)

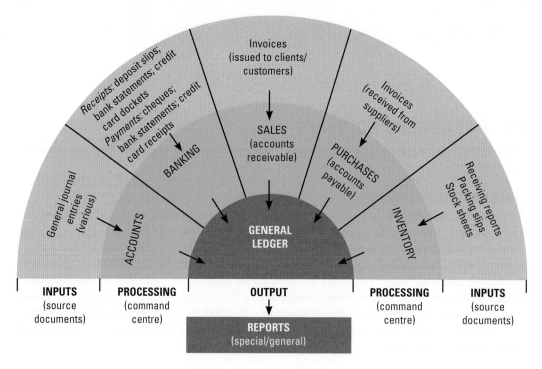

Note that all accounting software programs follow the same principles and procedures as the manual accounting system covered earlier in this chapter. Data recorded in the computerised system are obtained from the same source documents as used in the manual system. The programs make use of a general ledger containing control accounts for accounts receivable, accounts payable, inventory and payroll (if available in the program) in a similar way as in manual accounting. Although special journals are not used as the basis of entry to the general ledger, they are available in summary form for analysis within the system and can be viewed and/or printed out if required.

An introduction to MYOB and QuickBooks

Accounting software marketed by MYOB and Quicken is designed around a user-friendly graphical interface that makes the software easy to use under both the Windows and Mac platforms. The interface uses a combination of menus and associated drop-down submenus together with pictorial symbols or buttons referred to as icons. Using the mouse to click on a particular button/icon activates a further graphical interface until ultimately a graphical depiction of a data entry form, e.g. an invoice form, is presented on-screen. Data can be entered directly into the data entry screen to be subsequently recorded in the accounting system. If preferred, the user can access all functions of the software through traditional menu bars on the screen, or use a combination of icons and menu bars.

The MYOB AccountRight Plus interface

With the MYOB AccountRight Plus (version 19) software, access to the various accounting functions—once the company has been created and set up—is gained via a number of command centres. A command centre is available for Accounts, Banking, Sales, Time Billing, Purchases, Payroll, Inventory and Card File (this is a database of information about customers, suppliers, employees and inventory items that can be accessed by any of the other command centres).

Figure 7.13 shows an example of the Sales Command Centre.

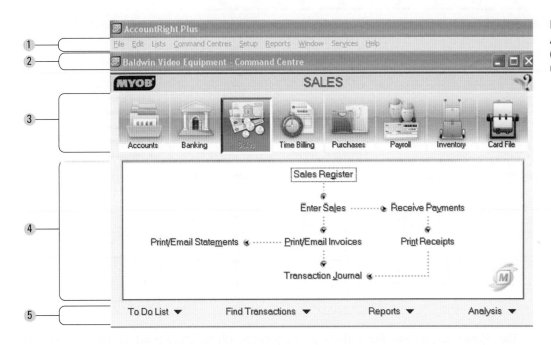

Figure 7.13 MYOB AccountRight Plus (version 19) Sales Command Centre screen

The Sales Command Centre has the following components (these correspond to the numbers in figure 7.13):

1. *Main menu bar.* This is the traditional menu bar with drop-down lists that provide access to all functions within MYOB, including command centres. Some actions/commands that are not available through the command centres can be accessed via the main menu bar.
2. *Title bar.* This indicates the current accounting data field (company) that is loaded in the program.
3. *Command centre icons/buttons bar.* Clicking on one of these command centre icons gives access to the accounting functions available under that command centre that appear as text-based flowcharts, as described below.
4. *Flowchart.* The flowchart, which differs for each command centre, provides text-based icons that, when selected, provide access to commands and actions relevant to that command centre. Figure 7.13 shows the sales command centre flowchart, which is used for a number of

accounting functions including entering sales, creating invoices for emailing or printing, creating statements for printing or emailing, receiving payments from customers, printing receipts, or posting journals related to sales.

5. *Quick access toolbar*. Clicking on the down-arrow for each of these alternatives presents a drop-down list of options giving quick access to other useful functions, including reminders, account information, commonly used reports and analysis of operations, that provide information required for everyday operations and control of the business.

The QuickBooks Premier interface

With QuickBooks, the graphical user interface similar to the one shown in figure 7.14 will be active on the computer screen (Windows). Centres are the QuickBooks equivalent to MYOB's command centres. To illustrate, QuickBooks Premier Student Edition V19 screenshots are shown. This student edition has the features of the full QuickBooks Premier product, but with a limited number of transactions that can be entered for each company set up.

In figure 7.14, the Home Centre interface is shown. In the Customers section of this centre, the content and function is similar to that shown in figure 7.13 for the MYOB Sales Command Centre.

Figure 7.14 QuickBooks Premier Student Edition V19 Home screen

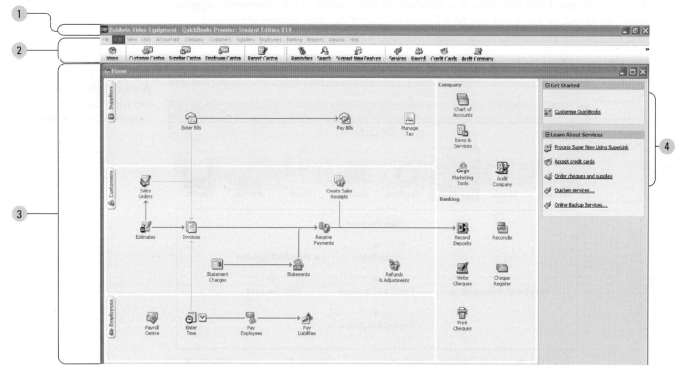

The Home screen has the following components (these correspond to the numbers in figure 7.14):

1. *Title bar*. This indicates the current accounting data file loaded in the program.
2. *Main menu bar and menu icons bar*. The traditional main menu bar with drop-down lists provides access to all functions within QuickBooks including all functional areas of accounting. Some commands/actions that cannot be accessed through the centres are available through these menus. The menu icons bar provides quick access to some of the more commonly used functions.
3. *The Home centre flowchart with icons for all centres and functions*. This page presents all icons available for this company, and represents the major accounting functions for Company, Suppliers (purchases and accounts payable), Customers (sales and accounts receivable), Employees (payroll) and Banking (receipts and payments). The customer accounting functions can be accessed either by first entering the Customer centre, or by clicking on the relevant icon on the Home page.
4. *Quick access icons*. These icons link to other functions which allow you to customise the settings for each company, and provide links to other services available.

7.8 Recording transactions in MYOB and QuickBooks

Learning objective 8

Compare how transactions are entered into accounting software using MYOB and QuickBooks

In the preceding section the graphical user interfaces for both MYOB AccountRight Plus (version 19) and QuickBooks Premier student edition (version 19) were illustrated and the essential components explained. These user interfaces are used to enter accounting data into these accounting packages. Data are entered into the system via one of two main approaches, depending on the nature of the transaction and its documentation:

1. Information is extracted from traditional source documents and entered into the accounting system using an entry screen in a form similar to the source document being recorded. For example, the details on a purchases invoice received from a supplier are entered into the fields of an on-screen purchase invoice.

2. Data are entered and a source document is generated in the one process. In this approach, data are entered into the accounting system using an entry screen in the form of the source document being generated. For example, the details of a sale to a customer are entered into the fields of an on-screen sales invoice, and the sales data are then recorded in the system. The sales invoice can then be printed out at that time or later to provide the traditional hard copy of the invoice.

To illustrate the second of these approaches, we will consider how some of the transactions in the demonstration problem in this chapter (Sidney Carton, on page 301) would be processed using both MYOB and QuickBooks.

We will consider firstly the transaction dated 13 July 2012, in which inventory was sold to B. Miller on account for $8200 plus GST, invoice no. 1, terms 1/10, n/30.

Both MYOB and QuickBooks have facilities to create new customers at several points in the processing of a transaction, including at the point where the invoice is created.

If using MYOB AccountRight Plus, the sales invoice will be created via the Sales Command Centre, which can be accessed by clicking on the Enter Sales icon. A blank invoice screen will appear, which can be completed with the relevant details.

Figure 7.15 shows what the completed invoice would look like. The on-screen invoice format can be customised, and then printed in the same format as that shown on the screen. The invoice details are posted to the ledger accounts by clicking the Record button on the bottom right of the screen.

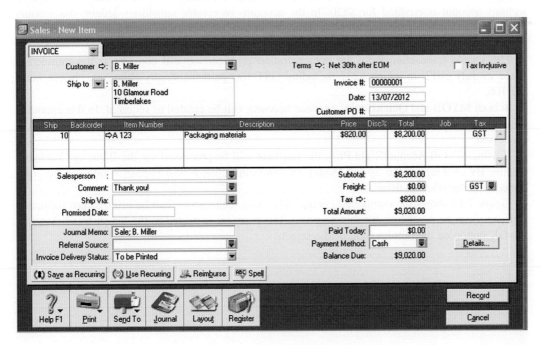

Figure 7.15 MYOB AccountRight Plus (version 19) completed invoice screen

If QuickBooks Premier is used, the same principles apply. A sales invoice can be created by clicking on the Invoices icon in the Customers section of the Home page. Using the same transaction as that for the MYOB example, the invoice to be issued to B. Miller will appear as shown in figure 7.16. The invoice details are posted to the ledger by clicking either on the Save & Close button (which processes the invoice and then exits the sales function) or Save & New button (which processes the invoice and then provides a new blank invoice for processing the next sales transaction) on the bottom right of the screen.

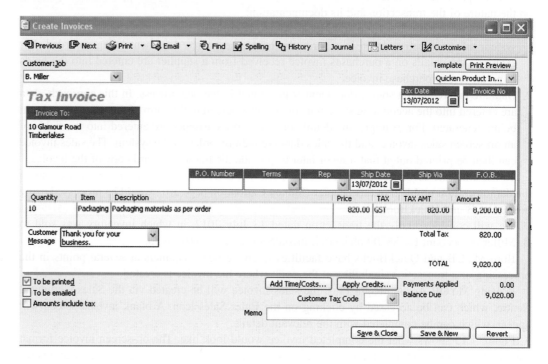

In terms of accounting, the procedures described above for both MYOB and QuickBooks result in the same entries being made in the ledgers. In the general ledger, the Accounts Receivable Control account is debited for $9020, the sales account is credited for $8200, and the GST Collections account is credited for $820. In the accounts receivable subsidiary ledger, the account of B. Miller is debited for $9020. Note that all commercially available packages handle the processing of GST automatically based on the GST codes established by the user.

The second transaction from the demonstration problem we will consider is the transaction dated 29 July 2012, in which $237 including GST was paid for sundry expenses, cheque number 106.

In both MYOB and QuickBooks, expense accounts can be created as required. In this example, an expense account called Sundry Expenses has been created, and the details of the payment processed.

If using MYOB AccountRight Plus, the payment will be processed via the Banking Command Centre. By clicking on the Spend Money icon, a blank cheque will appear, which can be completed with the relevant details.

Figure 7.17 shows the completed cheque. The on-screen cheque can be printed (pre-formatted stationery can be purchased for this purpose). The payment is posted to the ledger by clicking on the OK button on the bottom right of the screen.

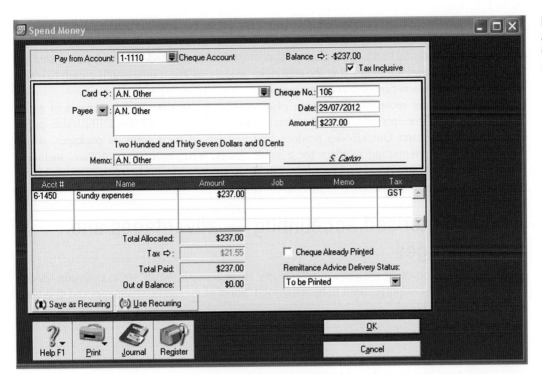

Figure 7.17 MYOB AccountRight Plus (version 19) completed cheque screen

If using QuickBooks Premier, the payment will be processed via the Banking section on the Home page. By clicking on the Write Cheques icon, a blank cheque will appear, which can be completed with the relevant details.

Figure 7.18 shows the completed cheque. As with MYOB, the cheque can be printed using pre-formatted stationery. The cheque payment is recorded in the ledger by clicking on either the Save & Close or Save & New button on the bottom right of the screen.

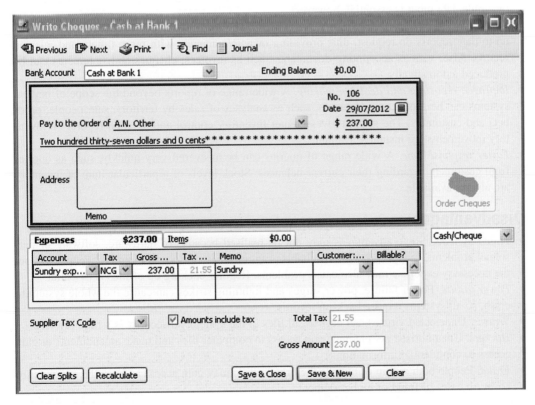

Figure 7.18 QuickBooks Premier student edition (version 19) completed cheque screen
Copyright © 2011 Intuit Inc. All rights reserved

In terms of accounting, the procedures described above for both MYOB and QuickBooks result in the same entries being made in the ledgers. In the general ledger, the Sundry Expenses account is debited for $215.45, GST Outlays is debited for $21.55, and Cash at Bank is credited for $237.00. No entries are required in the subsidiary ledgers, as this transaction is a cash payment for expenses and does not involve accounts payable.

The procedures for recording other types of accounting transactions (e.g. purchases of goods and services, cash receipts and general journal entries) are similar to those illustrated previously. Both MYOB and QuickBooks produce trial versions of their software packages, which are available from computing retailers for a small charge. Versions of the software, including documentation, demonstrations and tutorials, can be downloaded from the respective marketers' websites: www.myob.com.au and www.quicken.com.au.

Learning objective 9

Describe the advantages and disadvantages of computerised accounting systems

7.9 Computerised accounting — advantages and disadvantages

A computerised accounting system can offer many advantages; however, some problems associated with the use of computers need to be recognised. Some of the major advantages and disadvantages are described below.

Advantages

- *Reduction in processing costs.* The low cost of hardware and software and the availability of user-friendly packages such as MYOB and QuickBooks give computerised accounting systems a cost advantage over manual systems.
- *Speed of processing.* Thousands of transactions can be processed at high speed, and high-speed printers enable output at thousands of lines per minute.
- *Error reduction.* Once programmed, the computer is virtually error-free compared with manual systems, which are much more prone to human error. But control procedures must exist to ensure accuracy of data input. Input processing is facilitated by computer help and interactive feedback.
- *Automatic posting.* All posting is performed automatically at high speed and virtually error-free (accurate data input is essential, however).
- *Automatic production of documents and reports.* The system can be programmed to produce up-to-date reports on request, thus providing owners/managers with more timely and relevant reports. Also, various accounting documents such as invoices, cheques and statements can be produced automatically.
- *Improved reporting and decision making.* A wide range of reports beyond the scope of manual systems can be produced in seconds, such as analyses of sales by territory, salespeople, products and customers. The system gives greater inventory control and detailed reports on inventory movements are instantly available.
- *Faster response time.* A wide range of queries can be answered very quickly, such as queries from customers regarding their current balances. Stock levels of a particular item of inventory are always available.

Disadvantages

- *Failed systems.* Some advantages may not be realised because of hardware, software or personnel problems. Inappropriate or unsuitable programs may cause system failure. People without the necessary expertise may also cause problems. Regular backing up of files is essential.
- *Power failure.* Power failure, power surges and lightning strikes can cause the whole system to crash, so all systems require back-up records.
- *Viruses.* Undetected viruses can destroy all files in the system, so security is a high priority.
- *Hackers.* Unauthorised people may gain access to computer files and make amendments or gain access to confidential information.
- *Fraud.* People both within or outside the organisation may gain access and use the computer to cover up cases of fraud or embezzlement.

7.10 Accounting cycle — manual and computerised

Learning objective 10

Describe how the accounting cycle works in manual and computerised systems

This chapter has presented in some detail the procedures used to record common business transactions in a manual system of accounting, as well as an overview of computerised accounting systems. The steps in the accounting cycle depicted in figure 5.1 (p. 178) are carried out differently under manual and computerised systems. Apart from the analysis and recognition of transactions, and the input of data, computerised systems perform all steps automatically. Table 7.1 presents a comparison of how the steps in the accounting cycle are performed under manual and computerised accounting systems.

Table 7.1 Accounting cycle — manual versus computerised

	Steps in the accounting cycle	Manual system	Computerised system
1.	Recognise transactions	Manual	Manual
2.	Journalise transactions	Manual	Manual data entry (including manual and electronic coding for data entry)
3.	Post to ledger accounts	Manual	Automatic
4.	Prepare unadjusted trial balance	Manual	Automatic
5.	Journalise adjusting entries Prepare worksheet	Manual	Manual — some automatic Unnecessary
6.	Post adjusting entries	Manual	Automatic
7.	Prepare adjusted trial balance	Manual	Automatic
8.	Journalise closing entries	Manual	Automatic
9.	Post closing entries	Manual	Automatic
10.	Prepare post-closing trial balance	Manual	Automatic
11.	Prepare financial statements	Manual	Automatic
12.	Journalise reversing entries	Manual	Automatic
13.	Post reversing entries	Manual	Automatic

KEY TERMS

Accounting system, p. 276
Cash payments journal, p. 294
Cash receipts journal, p. 290
Control account, p. 284
Electronic spreadsheet, p. 307

General ledger software, p. 307
Internal control system, p. 280
Purchases journal, p. 288
Sales journal, p. 286
Special journal, p. 285

Subsidiary ledger, p. 284
Systems analysis, p. 277
Systems design, p. 278
Systems implementation and
    review, p. 278

DISCUSSION QUESTIONS

1. 'Accountants should not concern themselves too much with elaborate administrative and accounting controls, since any system is only as good as the human element in the system.' Do you agree? Explain your answer.
2. What is an internal control system? Discuss the principles involved in establishing a good internal control system. Discuss also the limitations of internal control systems.
3. 'Since all necessary detail is recorded in subsidiary ledgers, the control accounts in the general ledger could be dispensed with.' Do you agree? Explain your answer.
4. During the month of October, credit sales for a business actually amounted to $963 534. However, an error of $10 000 had been made in totalling the sales column of the sales journal. When and how will this error be discovered?

5. Identify the major sources of cash receipts recorded in a cash receipts journal. Identify the major transactions that involve cash payments in the cash payments journal.

6. An inventory purchase on credit of $10 000 plus GST was correctly recorded in the purchases journal of a business. However, when postings were made to the accounts payable in the subsidiary ledger, the purchase was incorrectly recorded as $1100; however, the correct amount was posted to the inventory subsidiary ledger. When and how will this error be discovered?

7. Consider and discuss any differences that are required in the structure of special journals as a result of using the perpetual inventory system instead of the periodic inventory system.

8. Which journal(s) are used to record the following transactions? The business is registered for GST.
   (a) The introduction of cash and office equipment by the owner on establishment of the business.
   (b) The cash payment of rent in advance.
   (c) The purchase of inventory on credit.
   (d) The purchase of office supplies on credit.
   (e) The sale of inventory on credit.
   (f) The sale of some pieces of office equipment on credit.
   (g) The collection of cash from a customer.
   (h) The return of part of the inventory purchased previously on credit from a supplier.
   (i) The adjusting entry for rent that is still prepaid at the end of the accounting period.
   (j) The adjusting entry for unused office supplies.
   (k) The closing entry for expenses at the end of the period.

9. Explain the treatment of abnormal balances in the financial statements if they arise in subsidiary ledgers.

10. 'Since nearly all accounting functions today are computerised, there is really no need for accountants to have an understanding of manual accounting systems.' Do systems designers need to understand manual accounting systems? Discuss.

EXERCISES

LO 5

Exercise 7.1 SUBSIDIARY LEDGER AND CONTROL ACCOUNT

J. Carmen uses subsidiary ledgers and special journals in her accounting system. The accounts in the accounts payable subsidiary ledger for the most recent month are shown below:

G. Parisi			
CP	2 500	Bal. (b/d)	0
		P	3 300

J. Traylor			
CP	3 000	Bal. (b/d)	3 000
		P	4 200
		P	3 500

P. Ledoux			
CP	3 500	Bal. (b/d)	7 500
		P	3 900

L. Chen			
CP	2 800	Bal. (b/d)	2 800
		P	4 400

Required
A. Prepare the Accounts Payable Control account showing the final balance of the account, assuming that all transactions are reflected in the above accounts.
B. Prepare a schedule of accounts payable to reconcile the subsidiary ledger with the control account.

LO 5

Exercise 7.2 RECONCILING A CONTROL ACCOUNT AND A SUBSIDIARY LEDGER

Assume that Marvin Kozak sold merchandise to three customers — Adair, Bruce and Casper, — during May on credit, as shown in the Accounts Receivable Control account on the next page.

General Ledger
Accounts Receivable Control

Date	Explanation	Post Ref	Debit	Credit	Balance
1/5	Balance				10 000
5/5		GJ8		890	9 110
31/5		S9	14 150		23 260
31/5		CR6		9 800	13 460

Subsidiary Ledger

Adair

1/5 Bal.	3 900		5/5 GJ8		980
9/5 S9	5 800		10/5 CR6		3 900

Bruce

1/5 Bal.	3 300		17/5 CR6		3 300
15/5 S9	3 500				

Casper

1/5 Bal.	2 800		24/5 CR6		2 800
27/5 S9	2 150				

Required

Explain why the control account and related subsidiary ledger are not in balance. All postings to the subsidiary ledger were correct. Prepare the corrected control account.

Exercise 7.3 RECONCILING A CONTROL ACCOUNT AND A SUBSIDIARY LEDGER

Assume that Ruggles Footwear bought merchandise from three suppliers — Sills, Thomas and Unwin — during March on credit, as shown in the Accounts Payable Control account.

General Ledger
Accounts Payable Control

Date	Explanation	Post Ref	Debit	Credit	Balance
1/3	Balance				19 500
6/3		GJ		218	19 718
10/3		GJ		412	20 130
14/3		GJ	780		19 350
31/3		P		10 350	29 700
31/3		?	?		7 200

Subsidiary Ledger

Sills

		31/3 Bal.	3 600

Thomas

		31/3 Bal.	2 100

Unwin

		31/3 Bal.	?

Required

A. Determine the missing amount (?) in the control account and insert the correct posting reference in the post ref column.

B. Determine the ending balance in the account of Unwin.

Exercise 7.4 RECONCILING A CONTROL ACCOUNT AND A SUBSIDIARY LEDGER

Katie Fleur operates Gorgeous Dried Flowers, using the periodic inventory system and balancing her books at month-end. At 30 April 2012, the balances of the Accounts Receivable Control and Accounts Payable Control accounts were $42 900 and $26 600 respectively. Ignore GST.

A summary of her dealings with customers and suppliers for May 2012 follows:

Customers	Bal. b/d 1/5/12	Credit sales	Sales returns (unpaid goods)	Cash received	Discount allowed
Able & Co.	$11 100	$3 500	(9 May) $80	$ 9 016	$184
R. Wilson	4 500	2 000	(11 May) 60	4 500	—
Omicron Sales	8 600	4 400	—	7 840	160
Kewdale Traders	15 200	1 600	—	11 700	300
Wales Wholesalers	1 500	1 950	(16 May) 90	1 500	—
Subiaco Sales	1 400	3 300	—	1 200	—
Beautiful Ltd	600	1 210	—	588	12
Petunia Ltd	—	1 520	—	—	—

Suppliers	Bal. b/d 1/5/12	Credit purchases	Purchases returns (unpaid goods)	Cash paid	Discount received
Aster Suppliers	$15 000	$3 800	(8 May) $180	$10 780	$220
Pekoe Products	—	1 900	—	—	—
Petunia Ltd	10 700	5 900	(18 May) 220	8 820	180
R. Katspaw	900	1 400	—	882	18

The following additional information is available:
1. At Petunia Ltd's request, on 31 May, Katie Fleur offset the amount owed by Petunia Ltd against the amount owing to it.
2. Gorgeous Dried Flowers paid Petunia Ltd on 3 May, sold goods to Petunia Ltd on 10 May, and purchased goods from Petunia Ltd on 13 May.

Required

A. Prepare the Accounts Receivable Control and Accounts Payable Control ledger accounts for the month of May 2012.
B. Prepare Petunia Ltd's accounts payable subsidiary ledger account for the month of May 2012 in the accounting records of Gorgeous Dried Flowers.
C. Prepare schedules of accounts receivable and accounts payable as at 31 May 2012.

Exercise 7.5 MATCHING TRANSACTION TYPES WITH JOURNALS

Gloria Bartlett uses a purchases journal, a cash payments journal, a sales journal, a cash receipts journal and a general journal. Indicate in which journals the following transactions are most likely to be recorded:
1. Issue of shares for cash.
2. Cash purchase of inventories (cheque no. 2001).
3. Purchase of inventories on credit.
4. Sale of inventory on credit.
5. Sale of marketable securities (shares in another company held as an investment) for cash.
6. Receipt of payment of a customer's account.
7. Withdrawel of cash by the owner.
8. Receipt of credit note for defective goods, which were purchased on credit and returned to the supplier.

9. Withdrawal of inventory by the owner for personal use.
10. Payment of monthly rent by cheque.
11. Cash refund to a customer who returned inventory.
12. Year-end closing entries.

LO 6

Exercise 7.6 MATCHING LEDGER ACCOUNTS WITH JOURNALS

Ballew Ltd has an accounting system that uses a general journal and special journals for sales, purchases, cash receipts and cash payments.

	Cash at Bank	110			Discount Received	450
(a)	15 240	(g)	11 832		(i)	276

	Accounts Receivable Control	120			Purchases	510
(c)	46 800	(e)	13 800	(h)	1 320	
				(k)	16 800	

	Accounts Payable Control	210			Purchases Allowances	515
(j)	11 100	(l)	16 800		(m)	210

	Sales	410			Discount Allowed	520
	(b)	46 800		(f)	204	
	(d)	2 970				

Required

A. What journal would be the most probable source of the postings in the accounts?
B. Which of the above accounts would be affected if GST was recorded?

LO 6

Exercise 7.7 RECORDING TRANSACTIONS IN PURCHASES AND SALES JOURNALS

Halpin Ltd's accounting system uses special journals and subsidiary ledgers. The following transactions occurred during May 2013 (GST to ignored). All sales are n/30.

May	3	Purchased inventory from T. Tallis, $1800, terms 2/15, n/30.
	11	Sold goods to M. Lockyer on credit, invoice 236, $1300.
	13	Purchased office furniture on credit from R. Parker, terms n/30, $9500.
	18	Paid T. Tallis for goods purchased on 3 May.
	24	Purchased goods from K. Kelly, $1700, terms 2/15, n/30.
	27	Sold inventory to C. Carroll for cash, $1900.

Required

A. Ignoring GST, enter the appropriate transactions into the purchases and sales journals for May, and explain how each would be posted to accounts in the ledgers.
B. Assuming that the company is registered for the GST, enter the appropriate transactions into suitably ruled purchases and sales journals, and explain how each would be posted to accounts in the ledgers.

LO 5, 6

Exercise 7.8 JOURNALS, SUBSIDIARY LEDGERS AND CONTROL ACCOUNTS

The Accounts Receivable Control account in the general ledger of Boston and Associates on 1 April was $19 728. The subsidiary ledger contained the following accounts receivable accounts and balances at the same date: Clark $2592, Hayden $4752, Johnson $3708, Hussey $8676. At 30 April, a summary of entries made in the journals shown were:

General journal: Hussey returned goods for a credit of $198.

Sales journal: Recorded credit sales were: Hussey $1440, Clark $2430, Ponting $1854, Johnson $1980.

Cash receipts journal: Cash amounts received from accounts receivable were (no discounts were allowed):

Hussey $4140, Ponting $738, Johnson $2358, Hayden $3240, Clark $2232.

Required

A. Enter the opening balances of the control account and subsidiary ledger accounts and post the April entries and totals in the three journals to the accounts (ignore GST).

B. Prepare a schedule of accounts receivable at 30 April and reconcile the total with the control account in the general ledger.

LO 5, 6

Exercise 7.9 RELATING SALES AND CASH RECEIPTS JOURNALS TO THE SUBSIDIARY LEDGER

The sales and cash receipts journals of Tandem Ltd for the month of June are presented below. The accounts receivable subsidiary ledger is reconciled with the general ledger account each month. On 1 June, the subsidiary ledger had four accounts: M. Lemon — $960; J. Good — $1160; T. Potts — $1400; C. Ladd — $1000.

Sales Journal			Page 18
Date	Invoice	Account	Amount
1/6	2302	A. Smith	760
5/6	2303	M. Lemon	440
7/6	2304	J. Good	720
16/6	2305	T. Potts	400
26/6	2306	M. Harmon	640

Cash Receipts Journal			Page 12
Date	Account	Cash	Accounts Receivable
3/6	M. Lemon	480	480
12/6	J. Good	1 000	1 000
22/6	T. Potts	700	700
25/6	C. Ladd	1 000	1 000

Required

A. Establish a T account for each customer's account in the subsidiary ledger and an Accounts Receivable Control account. Post the amounts to the accounts receivable subsidiary ledger and the general ledger using the information in the journals shown.

B. Prepare a schedule of the accounts in the subsidiary ledger and compare its total with the balance in the control account.

LO 5, 6

Exercise 7.10 RELATING PURCHASES, CASH PAYMENTS AND THE GENERAL JOURNAL TO THE SUBSIDIARY LEDGER AND CONTROL ACCOUNT

At 1 June, the following information was extracted from the records of Edith Yu (assume no GST):

Schedule of Accounts Payable
as at 31 May 2013

A. Green	$ 500
Jones Ltd	5 000
Close Ltd	12 340
	$17 840

Extracts from the purchases, cash payments and general journals for June are presented below:

Purchases Journal		Page 1
Date	Account	Amount
3/6	A. Green	1 000
10/6	Jones Ltd	4 050
12/6	Peter Ltd	2 550
21/6	G. Galway	2 340

Cash Payments Journal			Page 1
Date	Account	Chq. No.	Accounts Payable
5/6	Jones Ltd	003	5 000
18/6	A. Green	004	1 500
31/6	Close Ltd	005	5 880

General Journal			Page 1
Date	Particulars	Debit	Credit
17/6	Accounts Payable Control, Close Ltd	400	
	Purchases Returns and Allowances		400
	(Returned goods, adjustment credit note received)		

Required

A. Establish running balance ledger accounts for each supplier in the subsidiary ledger and an Accounts Payable Control account in the general ledger. Post the above amounts from the journals to the subsidiary ledger and control accounts.

B. Prepare a schedule of accounts payable as at 30 June and compare the total with the balance in the control account.

LO 5, 6

Exercise 7.11 ACCOUNTING WITH SEVERAL JOURNALS

Starlight uses sales, purchases, cash receipts, cash payments and a general journal (ignore GST). The following column totals were taken from the entity's journals at the end of June:

1. Sales journal $12 960
2. Purchases journal   6 912
3. Cash receipts journal:
   (a) Cash   10 716
   (b) Accounts receivable   8 985
   (c) Sales   1 815
   (d) Discounts allowed   84
4. Cash payments journal:
   (a) Cash $10 194
   (b) Accounts payable   8 640
   (c) Discounts received   174
   (d) Purchases   1 728

The balance in the Accounts Receivable Control account on 1 June was $5184 and the Accounts Payable Control account balance was $7344.

Required

A. At the end of June, the total amount from the sales journal should be posted to what account or accounts?

B. At the end of June, the total amount from the purchases journal should be posted to what account or accounts?

C. For each column total in the cash receipts and the cash payments journals, specify whether it would be posted to the general ledger as a debit or a credit, and to which account.

D. After the amounts in the journals have been posted to the general ledger for June, what would be the balances in the Accounts Receivable Control and the Accounts Payable Control accounts?

LO 5, 6

Exercise 7.12 ACCOUNTING WITH SEVERAL JOURNALS

Shirley & Co. uses sales and purchases journals in its accounting system. The following transactions took place during March (ignore GST):

March	2	Purchased inventory on credit from Dye Ltd, invoice 408, $420, terms 2/10, n/30.
	6	Purchased inventory on credit from R. Rider, invoice 606, $600, terms 2/10, n/30.
	11	Sold inventory on credit to R. Jetty, invoice 228, $1140.
	14	Sold inventory on credit to Dynamics Ltd, invoice 229, $990.
	19	Purchased inventory on credit from D. Donnelly, invoice 1614, $510, 2/10, n/30.
	23	Sold inventory on credit to Dockey Ltd, invoice 230, $780.
	28	Sold inventory on credit to G. Peck, invoice 231, $600, 2/10, n/30.

Required

A. Establish all necessary general ledger accounts, accounts receivable subsidiary ledger accounts, and accounts payable subsidiary ledger accounts. Use the following account numbers: Accounts Receivable Control, 104; Accounts Payable Control, 201; Sales, 400; Purchases, 500.

B. Enter the March transactions in the appropriate journals.

C. Post the data from the journals to the appropriate general ledger and subsidiary ledger accounts.
D. Develop a schedule of accounts receivable and a schedule of accounts payable as at 31 March to prove the subsidiary ledger balances against the control accounts.

Exercise 7.13 RELATING JOURNALS TO THE ACCOUNTS PAYABLE CONTROL ACCOUNT

LO 5, 6

Rusko and Sons use purchases, cash payments and general journals with their accounting system. They also maintain an accounts payable subsidiary ledger, which contains the following accounts at 31 May:

K. Barron

Date	Explanation	Post Ref	Debit	Credit	Balance
1/5	Balance				4 500
12/5		CP6	3 750		750

H. Colley

Date	Explanation	Post Ref	Debit	Credit	Balance
1/5	Balance				3 320
20/5		CP6	2 000		1 320

J. Gardner

Date	Explanation	Post Ref	Debit	Credit	Balance
6/5		P7		3 400	3 400
21/5		P7		1 100	4 500
28/5		CP6	3 400		1 100

H. Chow

Date	Explanation	Post Ref	Debit	Credit	Balance
1/5	Balance				3 800
15/5		CP6	960		2 840
22/5		P7		760	3 600

Y. Tan

Date	Explanation	Post Ref	Debit	Credit	Balance
1/5	Balance				5 300
15/5		GJ5	900		4 400
21/5		CP6	4 400		—

Required

A. Prepare an Accounts Payable Control account assuming all postings for the month of May have been made, showing the appropriate posting references.
B. Explain how each of the amounts that appear in the Accounts Payable account were obtained.

Exercise 7.14 RELATING JOURNALS TO THE ACCOUNTS RECEIVABLE CONTROL
ACCOUNT

Landsdale and Gnangara uses sales, cash receipts and general journals in its accounting system.
The firm also maintains an accounts receivable subsidiary ledger, which contained the following
accounts on 30 June:

L. Engels

Date	Explanation	Post Ref	Debit	Credit	Balance
1/6	Balance				3 750
9/6		CR4		2 970	780

G. Gilbert

Date	Explanation	Post Ref	Debit	Credit	Balance
6/6		S9	1 900		1 900
18/6		S9	1 600		3 500
21/6		CR4		1 320	2 180

M. Jacobs

Date	Explanation	Post Ref	Debit	Credit	Balance
11/6		S9	1 820		1 820
20/6		CR4		620	1 200

P. Parkes

Date	Explanation	Post Ref	Debit	Credit	Balance
1/6	Balance				2 556
10/6		CR4		1 056	1 500
23/6		S9	528		2 028

Sanders and Son

Date	Explanation	Post Ref	Debit	Credit	Balance
1/6	Balance				3 800
19/6		GJ5		1 028	2 772
30/6		CR5		2 772	—

Required

A. Prepare an Accounts Receivable Control account after all postings for the month of June have
been made with the necessary posting references.
B. Explain how all the amounts that appear in the Accounts Receivable Control account were
obtained.

Exercise 7.15 DETECTING ERRORS IN AN ACCOUNTING SYSTEM

Carrie Myles has an accounting system that uses sales, purchases, cash receipts and cash payments
journals and a general journal. At various times during the year, the following errors have occurred.

1. The amount column in the purchases journal was incorrectly totalled.
2. A credit purchase for $800 was posted as $80 in the accounts payable subsidiary ledger.
3. The sales journal was incorrectly totalled.

4. The amount of a bank loan entered in the 'other accounts' column of the cash receipts journal was posted as a debit to loans payable.
5. A subtraction error was made in determining a customer's account balance in the accounts receivable subsidiary ledger.
6. An error was made in totalling the cash column in the cash payments journal.
7. A sales allowance for goods sold on credit was entered in the general journal. The entry was posted to only two accounts — the accounts receivable subsidiary account and to Sales Returns and Allowances.
8. A purchases return, journalised in the general journal, was posted to the Accounts Payable Control account and to the Purchases Returns and Allowances account but was not posted to the accounts payable subsidiary ledger.
9. Discount allowed was not entered in the cash receipts journal. The amount of the customer's invoice was entered in the accounts receivable column and the net amount of the cheque was entered in the cash at bank column.
10. A cheque to a supplier was posted from the cash payments journal as a credit to the accounts payable subsidiary ledger, a debit to the accounts payable control account, and a credit to cash at bank in the ledger.

Required

Specify a procedure that would detect each error.

PROBLEMS

★ Basic

★★ Moderate

★★★ Challenging

LO 6

Problem 7.1 ACCOUNTING WITH SALES JOURNAL AND PURCHASES JOURNAL ★

Apex Construction Ltd uses sales and purchases journals in its accounting system. The following transactions occurred during June 2012.

June	5	Purchased merchandise on account from Jason Ltd, invoice 207, $2400, terms 2/10, n/30.
	8	Purchased merchandise on account from Ross Ltd, invoice 787, $1680, terms 2/10, n/30.
	10	Sold merchandise on account to E. Mears, invoice 226, $4560.
	16	Sold merchandise on account to Benz Ltd, invoice 227, $3960.
	19	Purchased merchandise on account from J. Henley, invoice 828, $1160, terms 2/10, n/30.
	26	Sold merchandise on account to A. Alberts, invoice 228, $3120.
	29	Sold merchandise on account to Benz Ltd, invoice 229, $2400.

Required

A. Complete the requirements below, assuming the business is not registered for the GST.
  1. Establish all necessary general ledger accounts, accounts receivable subsidiary ledger accounts, and accounts payable subsidiary ledger accounts. Use the following account numbers: Accounts Receivable, 1200; Accounts Payable, 2200; Sales, 4100; Purchases, 5100.
  2. Enter the transactions for June in the appropriate special journals.
  3. Post the data from the journals to the general ledger and subsidiary accounts.
  4. Prepare a schedule of the accounts receivable subsidiary ledger and the accounts payable subsidiary ledger as at 30 June to prove that their totals reconcile with the balances of the control accounts.
B. Complete sections 1–4 of requirement A, assuming the business is registered for the GST. Add the accounts 1300 GST Outlays and 2300 GST Collections to the accounts list in requirement A.1. Assume the amounts given are exclusive of GST.

LO 1, 5, 6

Problem 7.2 DETERMINING AN APPROPRIATE ACCOUNTING SYSTEM ★

Go-Go Wheels sells go-karts on both a credit and cash basis. A full range of spare parts and accessories is stocked to cater for the enthusiast. The business also employs a full-time mechanic who carries out servicing and repairs on go-karts — those sold by Go-Go Wheels and those purchased from other suppliers.

Prenumbered invoices are issued for all sales and services provided. Terms are strictly n/30 and no discounts are offered. Total revenues last financial year amounted to $400 000 — $240 000 from the sale of go-karts, $70 000 for parts and accessories, and $90 000 for servicing and repairs. All receipts are banked daily, and a petty cash system is in operation. Cash discounts are offered by all suppliers, and the business ensures that all discounts on offer are taken. All payments are made by cheque with frequent payments made to suppliers, transport companies for delivery costs on purchases, sponsorships and advertising. The mechanic is paid on every second Friday. The office manager is paid an annual salary for managing the office, and for performing the manual accounting duties.

The business currently has a manual system of accounting using special journals and subsidiary ledgers. Paula Speedie, the owner of Go-Go Wheels, is considering implementing a tried and tested integrated accounting package.

Required

A. Identify the subsidiary ledger or ledgers that would be used in the current system.

B. Identify the special journals that would be appropriate in the current system, and suggest appropriate columns that would be used in each of them.

C. Should a computer-based accounting system be implemented? Explain the reasons for your decision.

LO 5

Problem 7.3 CONTROL ACCOUNTS FOR RECEIVABLES AND PAYABLES ★

Preston Trading uses the periodic inventory system and has control accounts and subsidiary ledgers for trade receivables and payables. The general ledger control account balances at 1 December 2013 were:

Accounts receivable control	$146 800
Accounts payable control	172 000

The following transactions took place during December:

Credit inventory sales for the month	$191 100
Cash inventory purchases for the month	138 000
Credit inventory purchases for the month	96 300
Cash payments to creditors for the month	190 000
Discount received for the month	4 500
Discount allowed for the month	3 600
Cash receipts from customers for the month	194 000
Cash inventory sales for the month	14 100
Dec. 10: Goods (unpaid) returned by customer	14 100
12: Bill payable accepted by creditor in respect of balance of account	4 120
18: Goods (paid for) returned to supplier	10 700
20: Offset of accounts receivable and payable recorded	14 000
23: Goods (paid for) returned by customer	9 900
27: Goods (unpaid) returned to supplier	13 000

Required

Prepare the Accounts Receivable Control and Accounts Payable Control ledger accounts for the month of December 2013.

LO 5

Problem 7.4 RECONCILING MONTHLY STATEMENT — ACCOUNTS PAYABLE ★★

As the person responsible for the accounts payable ledger of Weems Ltd, you are concerned that the statement of account for the month ending 31 May 2012 received from Jay Ltd does not agree with the records shown for Jay Ltd in the accounts payable subsidiary ledger. Weems Ltd is a valued customer of Jay Ltd, and receives a trade discount of 10% off the marked price of all goods purchased. In addition, a 2% discount is allowed for payments made within 15 days of the statement date. Ignore GST.

Jay Ltd records all sales to Weems Ltd net of trade discount. The statement dated 31 May shows that the amount of $16 000 is owing to Jay Ltd. An examination of the account of Jay Ltd in the subsidiary ledger and other records reveals the following discrepancies:

1. The cash discount of $550, which had been deducted when making the April payment, had been disallowed by Jay Ltd because the payment was received after the discount date.

2. Because of a clerical error, the credit side of the account of Jay Ltd had been overstated by $475.

3. Invoice no. K773 for a gross amount (before trade discount) of $880 had been correctly entered on the statement but no records of the invoice had been recorded in the books of Weems Ltd even though the goods had been received.

4. Invoice no. K785 for a gross amount (before trade discount) of $660 had been entered on the statement twice.

5. Adjustment (credit) note no. G221 for $100 received from Jay Ltd had not been entered in the subsidiary ledger, and had been entered on the statement as an invoice.

6. Invoice no. K794 for $120 had been incorrectly debited on the statement as $210, and this invoice had not been entered in the purchases journal or the subsidiary ledger as the goods had not yet been received.

Required

Prepare a reconciliation memo that reconciles the amount owing on the statement of account from Jay Ltd to the amount that Weems Ltd actually owes at 31 May. Assuming that payment will be made on 12 June 2012, what is the amount of the cheque that will be sent to Jay Ltd to pay the amount owing?

Problem 7.5 ACCOUNTING WITH SALES, CASH RECEIPTS AND GENERAL JOURNALS ★★ **LO 5, 6**

Myrtle Ltd uses a sales journal, a cash receipts journal, a general journal and an accounts receivable subsidiary ledger within a periodic inventory system. The terms of all credit sales are 2/10, n/30. Where necessary, round amounts to the nearest dollar.

The accounts receivable subsidiary ledger balances on 31 May 2013 were:

R. Dikes	$ —
D. Freward	5 940
S. Samson	1 120
R. Robson	4 950
T. Sheeny	4 752
T. Jennings	2 970
	$19 732

The trial balance as at 1 June included, among others, the following accounts:

Account no.	Account title	Account balance
1-1100	Cash at Bank	$ 26 800
1-1150	Marketable Securities	45 500
1-1200	Accounts Receivable Control	19 732
1-1300	Bills Receivable	—
2-2200	Bills Payable	3 600
4-4100	Sales	309 000
4-4150	Sales Returns and Allowances	3 840
4-4200	Dividend Revenue	1 500
4-4300	Interest Revenue	1 350
4-4400	Gain on Sale of Marketable Securities	420
5-5200	Discount Allowed	2 880

The following transactions during June were recorded in the sales, cash receipts or general journals (ignore GST):

June 2 Issued an adjustment note to T. Jennings for defective goods sold on credit during April for $260.

3 Sold inventory on credit to R. Dikes, $2880, invoice 324.

8 Received a cheque from S. Samson for payment of a May purchase, $1120.

10 Sold inventory on credit to R. Robson, $400, invoice 325.

12 Sold inventory on credit to D. Freward, $640, invoice 326.

13 Received payment from R. Dikes for invoice 324.

16 Received payment in full from T. Jennings.

20 Borrowed $20 000 cash from the bank for 3 months at 10%. Issued a bill payable in favour of the bank to cover the loan.

21 Sold inventory for cash, $440.

23 Sold marketable securities that had been held as a short-term investment for $18 000 cash. The securities were originally purchased for $18 000.

June	25	Received a 60-day promissory note (bill receivable) from R. Robson in settlement of his account receivable balance.
	26	Received a cheque from D. Freward for $6580, for payment on his account.
	27	Sold inventory on credit to S. Samson, $1080, invoice 327.
	30	Received payment from S. Samson for invoice 327.

Required

A. Record the June transactions in the appropriate journals. Make all postings to the appropriate general ledger accounts and to the accounts receivable subsidiary ledgers.

B. Reconcile the subsidiary ledger with the Accounts Receivable Control account in the general ledger.

Problem 7.6 **LO 5, 6**

ACCOUNTING WITH SALES, CASH RECEIPTS AND GENERAL JOURNALS ★★

Refer to the details and data presented in problem 7.5, and assume further that Myrtle Ltd and its suppliers are registered for the GST. The following additional accounts are in the general ledger and appear in the trial balance — 2-2300 GST Outlays and 1-1300 GST Collections. Assume both accounts had a zero opening balance.

Required

A. Record the June transactions in the appropriate journals. Make all postings to the appropriate general ledger accounts and to the accounts receivable subsidiary ledgers.

B. Reconcile the Accounts Receivable subsidiary ledger with the Accounts Receivable Control account in the general ledger.

Problem 7.7 **LO 5, 6**

ACCOUNTING FOR TRANSACTIONS WITH SEVERAL JOURNALS ★★

A. Mota started business on 1 June 2012. The accounting system includes a sales journal, a purchases journal, a cash receipts journal, a cash payments journal and a general journal. The chart of accounts shows the following titles:

100	Cash at Bank		410	Sales Returns and Allowances
110	Accounts Receivable Control		420	Discount Received
115	Prepaid Insurance		500	Purchases
150	Office Equipment		503	Purchases Returns
201	Accounts Payable Control		510	Discount Allowed
210	Loan Payable		550	Rent Expense
300	T. Friday, Capital		560	Insurance Expense
400	Sales		570	Sundry Expenses

During June, the transactions were as follows (ignore GST):

June	1	A. Mota deposited $26 000 capital in the business bank account.
	3	Paid rent for June, $2800, cheque no. 101.
	4	Borrowed $25 000 from the Rural Bank.
		Purchased inventory on credit from Georgio Ltd, $5400, invoice 834, terms 2/10, n/60.
	6	Purchased inventory on credit from Love Ltd, $2100, invoice 202, terms 1/10, n/30.
	9	Purchased office equipment, $1200, cheque no. 102.
		Sold inventory on credit to McHenry Ltd, $2200, terms 2/10, n/30, invoice 301.
	10	Paid for inventory purchased from Georgio Ltd, invoice 344, cheque no. 103.
	12	Received an adjustment (credit) note from Love Ltd for inventory returned, $120.
	12	Forwarded cheque no. 104 to Love Ltd for balance owing on invoice 202.
	13	Sold inventory for cash, $750.
	16	Paid for a 12-month insurance policy, $1500. The effective date of the policy was 1 June. Issued cheque no. 105.
	17	Purchased inventory on credit from O. Caine, $3200, invoice 766, terms n/60.
	20	Purchased inventory on credit from C. Clavel, $1760, invoice 406, terms 2/10, n/30.
	23	Sold inventory on credit to B. Beres, $1500, invoice 302, terms 2/10, n/30.
	24	Received payment from McHenry Ltd in full settlement of invoice 401.

June 25 Sold inventory on credit to Hand Ltd, invoice 303, $2500, terms 2/10, n/30.
Paid C. Clavel in full for goods purchased on 20 June, cheque no. 106.
30 Issued cheque no. 107, $240, for sundry expenses.
Issued an adjustment (credit) note to Hand Ltd for defective goods sold on 25 June, $125.
30 Received payment from B. Beres in settlement of invoice 302.

Required

Record the transactions in the appropriate journals. Indicate how the postings would be made from the journals by entering the relevant posting references.

Problem 7.8 JOURNALISING TRANSACTIONS, POSTING, AND PREPARATION OF A TRIAL BALANCE ★★ **LO 5, 6**

Peart Ltd uses sales, purchases, cash receipts, cash payments and a general journal along with subsidiary ledgers for accounts receivable and accounts payable. The post-closing trial balance as at 30 April 2012 and schedules of balances of the subsidiary ledgers are presented below.

PEART LTD
Post-closing Trial Balance
as at 30 April 2012

1-100	Cash at bank	$17 100	
1-110	Accounts receivable control	9 900	
1-150	Inventory	16 200	
1-170	Office equipment	34 000	
1-175	Accumulated depreciation – office equipment		$ 5 000
2-200	Accounts payable control		13 200
3-300	Share capital		40 000
3-350	Retained earnings		19 000
4-400	Sales		—
4-405	Sales returns	—	
4-410	Discount received		—
5-500	Purchases	—	
5-505	Purchases returns		—
5-512	Discount allowed	—	
5-530	Rent expense	—	
5-540	Sundry expenses	—	
5-550	Commissions expense	—	
		$77 200	$77 200

Schedule of Accounts Receivable
as at 30 April 2012

Lossett Ltd	$2 310
Keo Ltd	4 620
South Ltd	2 970
	$9 900

Schedule of Accounts Payable
as at 30 April 2012

Newitt Ltd	$ 4 620
C. Rams	3 300
Tall Timbers Ltd	5 280
	$13 200

The following transactions occurred in May 2012:

May 1 Received a cheque from Lossett Ltd for payment on account, $2310.
2 Paid rent for May, $2400, cheque no. 201.
4 Sold inventory to Blue Ltd on credit, invoice 620, $2700, terms 2/10, n/30.
5 Purchased inventory on credit from E. East, $3140, invoice 423, terms 2/10, n/30.

May	8	Paid C. Rams for inventory purchased previously (no discount), $3300, cheque no. 202.
		Received payment from Blue Ltd for full settlement of invoice 620.
	10	Received an adjustment note from E. East for inventory returned, $140.
	11	Paid E. East in full for invoice 423 by issuing cheque no. 203.
	12	Paid sales commissions, $6140, by cheque no. 204.
	15	Received a cheque from Keo Ltd in part payment of the account, $2310, no discount applicable.
	16	Paid $9000 for new office equipment, cheque no. 205.
	18	Cash sales, $1680.
	19	Sold inventory on credit to Lossett Ltd, $2840, invoice 621, terms 2/10, n/30.
	19	Sold inventory on credit to G. Garson, $1400, invoice 622, terms 2/10, n/30.
	23	Paid Tall Timbers Ltd for inventory purchased in February, $5280, cheque no. 206.
	25	Cash sales, $1800.
	26	Issued cheque no. 207 to pay sundry expenses, $820.
	30	Received a cheque from South Ltd, $2970, for payment of account.
	30	Received a cheque from G. Garson in payment of invoice 622.

Required

A. 1. Journalise the transactions in the appropriate journals.
   2. Make all necessary postings for the month.
   3. Prepare a trial balance of the general ledger as at 31 May 2012, and reconcile subsidiary ledgers with their control accounts.
B. Rework requirements A.1, A.2 and A.3 assuming that recording of GST is required. Add 1-800 GST Outlays and 2-250 GST Collections to the post-closing trial balance (assume both accounts have zero balances and the transaction amounts given are exclusive of GST).

Problem 7.9 SPECIAL JOURNALS, SUBSIDIARY LEDGERS, PERPETUAL INVENTORY SYSTEM ★★ LO 5, 6

Victor Strawn uses sales, purchases, cash receipts, cash payments and general journals along with subsidiary ledgers for accounts receivable and accounts payable in the accounts of his business. The business has adopted the perpetual inventory system. The post-closing trial balance as at 31 May 2013 and the subsidiary ledger schedules follow. Ignore GST.

Post closing Trial Balance
as at 31 May 2013

	Debit	Credit
Cash at bank	$10 800	
Accounts receivable control	5 400	
Inventory	9 000	
Equipment	18 000	
Accumulated depreciation – equipment		$ 1 800
Accounts payable control		7 200
V. Strawn, Capital		34 200
	$43 200	$43 200

Schedule of Accounts Receivable
as at 31 May 2013

Gourd Ltd	$1 620
Melon Ltd	2 520
D. Taylings	1 260
	$5 400

Schedule of Accounts Payable
as at 31 May 2013

Cantaloupe Ltd	$1 800
P. Pumpkin	2 520
Rocky Ltd	2 880
	$7 200

The following transactions took place during June 2013:

June 1 Received a cheque from D. Taylings for payment on account, $1260.
2 Sold inventory to Cabbage Ltd on credit, invoice 604, $1620, terms 2/10, n/30. The inventory sold had cost $900.
3 Paid rent for June, $1350 (cheque no. 621).
5 Paid Cantaloupe Ltd for goods purchased previously, $1800 (cheque no. 622).
6 Purchased inventory on credit from E. Caulie, $1890, invoice 883, terms 2/10, n/30.
8 Received payment from Cabbage Ltd for full settlement of invoice 604.
10 Received a credit note from E. Caulie for inventory returned, $90.
11 Paid E. Caulie the amount due on invoice 883 by issuing cheque no. 623.
12 Paid sales commissions, $3690 (cheque no. 624).
13 Received a cheque from Melon Ltd in part payment of the account, $1260.
16 Issued cheque no. 625 for new office equipment, $5400.
18 Cash sales, $1008. Cost of the goods sold was $700.
19 Sold inventory on credit to D. Taylings, $1710, invoice 605, terms 2/10, n/30. Cost of the inventory sold amounted to $1000.
22 Sold inventory on credit to Aubergine Ltd, $810, invoice 606, terms 2/10, n/30. Cost of sales, $640.
23 Paid Rocky Ltd for goods purchased in May, $2880 (cheque no. 626).
26 Cash sales, $1125. Cost of the goods sold amounted to $745.
27 Issued cheque no. 627 to cover sundry expenses, $495.
30 Received a cheque from Gourd Ltd, $1620, for payment on account.
Received a cheque from Aubergine Ltd for payment of account.

Required

A. Enter the transactions in the appropriate journals.
B. Make all necessary postings for the month to both the general and subsidiary ledgers.
C. Prepare schedules of accounts receivable and accounts payable as at 30 June 2013.
D. Prepare the trial balance as at 30 June 2013.

Problem 7.10 SPECIAL JOURNALS, PERIODIC INVENTORY SYSTEM, GST ★★ **LO 5, 6**

Davidia Shorten began her business on 1 March 2012. The business balances its books at month-end and uses special journals and the periodic inventory system. Transactions for March 2012 were as follows:

March 1 Davidia Shorten invested $16 000 cash and $10 000 office equipment into the business.
2 Purchased inventory from B. Wigg on account for $4000 plus GST; terms 2/15, n/30.
Paid March rental of $1600 plus GST; cheque no. 001.
4 Purchased inventory from Big Ltd on account for $3200 plus GST; terms n/30.
5 Sold inventory to S. Slap on account for $1000 plus GST; terms 2/10, n/30.
Received March rental of $400 plus GST for space sublet to Hobart Services.
7 Purchased stationery supplies for cash, $900 plus GST; cheque no. 002.
8 Purchased inventory for cash, $860 plus GST; cheque no. 003.
10 Sold inventory to Dash Ltd on account for $2000 plus GST; terms 2/10, n/30.
12 Purchased inventory from C. Cliff on account for $2500 plus GST; terms 2/10, n/30.
14 Paid B. Wigg for 2 March purchase; cheque no. 004.
15 Received $1078 from S. Slap in payment of her account.
18 Sold inventory to W. Williams on account for $2000 plus GST; terms 2/10, n/30.
Received $2156 from Dash Ltd in payment of its account.
21 Sold inventory to Paddy Ltd on account for $1600 plus GST; terms 2/10, n/30.
Paid C. Cliff for 12 March purchase; cheque no. 005.
22 Purchased inventory from B. Wigg on account for $2400 plus GST; terms 2/15, n/30.
23 Sold inventory for cash, $1300 plus GST.
25 Returned defective inventory that cost $600 to B. Wigg.
28 Sold merchandise to W. Ratson on account for $3600 plus GST; terms 2/10, n/30.
29 Purchased merchandise from A. Fie on account for $800 plus GST; terms 1/10, n/30.
30 Paid month's salary of office assistant, $1400; cheque no. 006.

Required

A. Prepare journal entries for March 2012, using appropriate journals.

B. Prepare the following ledger accounts (T format) for March 2012:

1. Accounts Receivable Control
2. Accounts Payable Control
3. Cash at Bank
4. Purchases.

Problem 7.11 SPECIAL JOURNALS AND FINANCIAL STATEMENTS ★★ LO 5, 6

Andrew Jones began trading as a hardware merchant on 1 March 2013. His transactions for the month of March 2013 were as follows (ignore GST):

March	1	Jones transferred $10 000 from his personal savings to his business bank account.
	1	Purchased shop fittings for cash: paid by cheque no. 100, $3800.
		Paid March rent by cheque no. 101, $750.
	2	Purchased goods for resale on credit from A Co. Ltd, $2500.
	3	Banked cash sales totalling $860.
	4	Sold goods on credit to A. Adam: invoice no. 001, $380.
	5	Purchased goods for resale: paid by cheque no. 102, $850.
	6	Banked cash sales totalling $410.
	8	Purchased goods for resale on credit from B Co. Ltd, $1200.
	9	Sold goods on credit to B. Brown: invoice no. 002, $490.
	10	Purchased office stationery: paid by cheque no. 103, $120.
	11	Banked cheque for return of defective goods that had been purchased for cash, $95.
	12	Banked cash sales totalling $900.
	15	Issued cheque no. 104 for miscellaneous expenses, $180.
	16	Refunded a customer for a cash sale returned: paid refund by cheque no. 105 for $170.
	17	Purchased goods for resale on credit from C Co. Ltd, $3000.
	18	Paid freight on goods purchased from C Co. Ltd: cheque no. 106, $65.
	19	Sold goods on credit to C. Charles: invoice no. 003, $530.
	20	Banked cash sales totalling $1060.
	22	Issued cheque no. 107 to A Co. Ltd in full settlement of its account, less a cash discount of 3%.
	23	Banked cheque received from A. Adam in full settlement of his account, less a 2% cash discount.
	24	Issued cheque no. 108 to Andrew Jones as personal drawings, $600.
		Banked cash sales totalling $1200.
	26	Paid March salaries: cheque no. 109 in favour of A. Harmer, $650; cheque no. 110 in favour of A. Chiswell, $560.
	30	Paid March electricity: cheque no. 111, $75.
		Paid March telephone: cheque no. 112, $56.
	31	Banked cash sales totalling $1400.

The following additional information is available:

1. A physical inventory count held at the close of business on 31 March 2013 revealed that the cost price of inventory on hand amounted to $3000.
2. The March salary of a part-time sales representative amounting to $800 was not paid until 2 April 2013.
3. Depreciation on shop fittings for the month of March amounted to $38.

Required

A. Record the above transactions in the appropriate journals for the business of Andrew Jones.

B. Post the entries in the journals to the general ledger as well as to the debtors and creditors subsidiary ledgers.

C. Prepare the trial balance of Andrew Jones at 31 March 2013.

D. Prepare schedules of debtors and creditors at 31 March 2013, and reconcile the totals with the balances of the related control accounts in the trial balance.

E. Prepare the income statement of Andrew Jones for the month ended 31 March 2013.

F. Prepare the balance sheet of Andrew Jones at 31 March 2013.

Problem 7.12 CORRECTION OF ERRORS ★★★

Patty Morel, the accountant for Phoenix Fashions, was unable to complete the trial balance of the business's general ledger. The total of the credit column was less than the total of the debit column by $6950. In addition, the balance of the Accounts Receivable Control account in the general ledger was less than the total of the schedule of accounts receivable by $4346, and the schedule of accounts payable was more than the credit balance of the Accounts Payable Control account by $750.

Patty's analysis identified the following errors:

1. There was an error of addition in the debit column in the trial balance, which resulted in the total of the debits being $750 more than it should be.
2. A purchase invoice for $1440 was recorded in the purchases journal as $540. The purchase was duly posted to the ledgers.
3. An error of addition had occurred in the sales journal that resulted in the total of the sales journal being recorded and posted as $83 170 instead of the correct figure of $83 710.
4. An allowance of $1528 on a sale to a customer was correctly recorded in the general journal and correctly posted to the general ledger. However, the amount was posted to the debit side of the customer's account in the accounts receivable ledger, instead of being credited.
5. Interest revenue of $3820 had been correctly recorded in the cash receipts journal, but had been posted as $2380 to the debit of the Interest Expense account.
6. A major supplier, James Kyte, had also bought goods to the value of $750 during the last week of the financial year. A general journal entry to off-set the $750 against the amount owing by Kyte was recorded in the general journal and correctly posted to the general ledger subsidiary ledger control accounts. However, the set-off was not recorded in the subsidiary ledgers.

Required

A. Patty believes that after the above are taken into account, the trial balance will balance. Show your calculations to verify that she is correct.
B. Which of errors 1–6 need to be corrected for the reconciliation of the schedules of accounts receivable and accounts payable to their respective control accounts? Explain, showing calculations, how the adjustments for the errors will achieve reconciliation.

Problem 7.13 DETECTING ERRORS IN AN ACCOUNTING SYSTEM ★★★

On 31 May 2012 the following information appeared in the accounting records of Usher and Childs:

Balance of Accounts Receivable Control account, $5478
Total of schedule of accounts receivable, $2896
Balance of Accounts Payable Control account, $7368
Total of schedule of accounts payable, $4034

Because the schedules and control account balances do not agree, an investigation was carried out. The following errors and omissions were discovered.

1. The schedule of accounts payable was understated by $800 because of error in addition.
2. The balance of a debtor was accidentally left out of the schedule of accounts receivable, $36.
3. The total of the accounts payable column in the cash payments journal is overstated by $300 because of an addition error.
4. $160 owed by a debtor was written off as uncollectable. The write-off was recorded in the general journal, but the entry was never posted.
5. The total payment of $2875 made to creditors was debited to the Accounts Receivable Control account in error.
6. The sales journal was incorrectly added and posted as $3146. The total should have been $3416.
7. A credit note given for $40 was recorded as $60 in the general journal and posted as such.
8. An invoice for $175 was recorded correctly in the purchases journal but posted to the creditor's account as $157.
9. A cheque received from a debtor for $59 was dishonoured. To record the dishonoured cheque, an entry was made in the cash payments journal but included in the accounts payable column in error. The posting to the debtor's account in the subsidiary ledger was done correctly.

Required

Rule columns as shown below. Indicate how the errors and omissions should be corrected by inserting the amounts in the correct columns. Obtain totals for the columns and reconcile the control totals to the respective schedule totals.

No.	Accounts Receivable Control		Schedule of Accounts Receivable		Accounts Payable Control		Schedule of Accounts Payable	
	Dr	Cr	Dr	Cr	Dr	Cr	Dr	Cr

LO 1, 5, 6

Problem 7.14 COMPREHENSIVE ACCOUNTING SYSTEM ★★★

Forrest Resort uses a sales journal, purchases journal, cash receipts journal, cash payments journal and a general journal. The business also maintains subsidiary ledgers for accounts receivable and accounts payable, in addition to the related control accounts (ignore GST). The relevant account balances as of 31 December 2012 were as follows:

Account no.	Account title	Account balance	
		Debit	Credit
100	Cash at Bank	$ 21 600	
120	Accounts Receivable	26 400	
140	Inventory	38 000	
200	Equipment	500 000	
300	Accounts Payable		$ 22 000
330	Bank Loan		240 000
400	L. Yeung, Capital		324 000
500	Sales		—
510	Sales Returns and Allowances	—	
520	Discount Received		—
600	Purchases	—	
610	Discount Allowed	—	
		$586 000	$586 000

The accounts receivable and accounts payable subsidiary ledger balances were as follows:

Accounts receivable		Accounts payable	
J. Dicks	$ 5 280	D. J. Ltd	$ 4 400
K. Moorehead	3 520	Concepts-R-Us	4 400
A. Piccioli	8 800	NR Stores	13 200
R. Robbie	6 600	Total	$ 22 000
D. Roberts	2 200		
	$26 400		

The following transactions occurred during the first quarter of 2013:

Jan. 3   K. Moorehead took advantage of the 2% sales discount and paid off her account.
      11   Sold a $4000 item to D. Roberts on account, invoice 401.
      15   Purchased $12 000 of inventory from Concepts-R-Us on credit. The terms were 2/10, n/30.
      18   Received $2400 from J. Dicks on his account. No discount was allowed.
      20   Paid $4400 to Concepts-R-Us on its previous account balance. No discount was taken.
      25   Paid $12 000 owing to Concepts-R-Us, taking advantage of the 2% discount.
Feb. 10   A cash sale of $8000 was made to a new customer, J. Faraday.
      14   A. Piccioli paid $4400 on his account, outside the discount period.
      23   Sold a $2000 item to D. Roberts on account, invoice 402.
      28   Paid $8800 on the NR Stores account. No discount was received.

Mar.	4	Purchased $16 000 in inventory from D. J. Ltd on credit. Terms were n/30.
	16	Sold a $200 item to R. Robbie on account, invoice 403.
	22	Paid $8800 on the D. J. Ltd account.
	27	A $200 sales allowance was given to R. Robbie, due to a defective product.

Required

A. Enter the first quarter's transactions in the appropriate journals.

B. Open the necessary general ledger accounts, the accounts receivable subsidiary ledger accounts, and the accounts payable subsidiary ledger accounts.

C. Post the data from the journals to the appropriate general ledger and subsidiary ledger accounts.

D. Prepare a schedule of accounts receivable and accounts payable as at 31 March 2013, to confirm the balances in the control accounts.

E. Prepare a trial balance as at 31 March 2013.

Problem 7.15 COMPREHENSIVE PROBLEM (INCLUDING GST) ★★★   **LO 1, 5, 6**

The post-closing trial balance of Pollack Ltd as at 1 November 2012 contained the following normal balances:

Account no.	Account title	Account balance
1100	Cash at Bank	$120 000
1120	Accounts Receivable	14 540
1130	Bills Receivable	1 500
1140	Inventory	160 000
1150	Prepaid Insurance	—
1160	GST Outlays	4 000
1210	Delivery Vehicle	80 000
1215	Accumulated Depreciation – Delivery Vehicle	8 000
1220	Office Equipment	48 000
1225	Accumulated Depreciation – Office Equipment	8 000
2110	Accounts Payable	11 560
2120	Bills Payable	—
2150	GST Collections	7 000
3110	Share Capital	384 000
3120	Retained Earnings	9 480
4110	Sales	—
4115	Sales Returns and Allowances	—
4120	Discount Received	—
5110	Purchases	—
5115	Purchases Returns and Allowances	—
5120	Discount Allowed	—
5130	Rent Expense	—
5140	Electricity Expense	—
5150	Salaries Expense	—

Subsidiary ledger balances at 31 October 2012 were:

Accounts Receivable

Customer	Date of sale	Terms	Amount
D. Draper	28 October	2/10, n/30	$4 200
C. Hand	30 October	2/10, n/30	4 620
T. Tremble	18 October	2/10, n/30	5 720

Accounts Payable

Creditor	Date of purchase	Terms	Amount
Laws Ltd	19 October	1/30, n/60	$3 280
M. Merlow	10 October	n/30	5 300
Lenny Ltd	23 October	1/15, n/30	2 980

Transactions for the month of November 2012 were:

Nov. 1 Bought inventory from M. Merlow on credit, $4800 plus GST; terms n/30.
Purchased 1 year's insurance cover for $1800 plus GST, cheque no. 400.

3 Inventory sold to C. Hand last month was returned. Issued an adjustment note for the amount of $110 (including GST).
Received a cheque from D. Draper to cover the sale made on 28 October.

4 Paid Lenny Ltd cheque no. 401 for purchase of 23 October.
Purchased inventory from Laws Ltd on credit, $4800 plus GST; terms 1/10, n/60.

5 Issued cheque no. 402 for $3300 to M. Merlow on account, and issued a 60-day 10% bill payable for the balance due on the purchase of 10 October.

8 Paid November rent of premises $1080 plus GST, cheque no. 403.
Paid Laws Ltd for the purchase of 19 October, cheque no. 404.

10 Sold inventory on account to A. Arnott, $9000 plus GST; terms 2/10, n/30.
Received cash for the issue of additional share capital, $60 000 (GST-free).

11 Received cheque for $2860 from T. Tremble in part payment of the sale made on 18 October, together with a bill receivable for the balance due.

12 Sold merchandise to D. Draper on account, $9600 plus GST; terms 2/10, n/30.

13 Purchased goods on credit from Lenny Ltd, $7920; terms 1/15, n/30 (including GST).

14 Paid fortnightly salaries by cheque no. 405, $2400.
Cash sales from 1 November to 14 November, $18 400 plus GST.

18 Sold goods to T. Tremble on account, $9300 plus GST; terms 2/10, n/30.
Received an adjustment note from Lenny Ltd for $154 for defective goods returned (includes GST).

19 Forwarded cheque no. 406 to ATO to cover GST owing from previous month, $3000.

20 A. Arnott forwarded a cheque for $2640 on account; no discount was allowed.
Purchased goods for cash. Issued cheque no. 407 for $10 800 plus GST.

21 Received a cheque from D. Draper for $1320 and a promissory note (bill receivable) for the balance of his account; no discount was allowed.

26 T. Tremble forwarded a cheque for the goods sold on 18 November.

27 Paid Lenny Ltd for the purchase made on 13 November, cheque no. 408.

28 Paid fortnightly salaries with cheque no. 409, $2400 (GST-free).

30 Electricity account paid by cheque no. 410, $420 plus GST.
Cash sales from 15 November to 30 November, $18 000 plus GST
Purchased inventory on credit from Lenny Ltd, $7260; terms 1/15, n/30 (includes GST).

Required

A. Record the November transactions (round amounts to the nearest dollar) in appropriate special journals and the general journal.

B. Open running balance accounts in the subsidiary ledgers and their control accounts in the general ledger, and enter the opening details of these accounts.

C. Post relevant data from the journals to the appropriate running balance subsidiary ledger accounts.

D. Prepare schedules of accounts receivable and accounts payable as at 30 November 2012, and reconcile to the appropriate subsidiary ledger control accounts in the general ledger.

E. Prepare the GST Collections and GST Outlays accounts as they would appear at 30 November 2012.

DECISION ANALYSIS

Designing an accounting system

Silvertail Petroleum Ltd is a distributor of a range of petroleum products including petrol, oils and grease in a rural area of Australia from its depot based at Gubbo. Petrol is stored in bulk storage tanks at the depot and these tanks are refilled twice weekly by bulk tankers from the refinery. At each refuelling, a receiving report is prepared and sent to the accounting department. Other bulk supplies are replenished as required. The refinery sells on the basis of net 30 days and does not allow discount.

Silvertail Petroleum Ltd operates several delivery trucks that travel to customers in the surrounding district to deliver supplies of fuel and other products. For each delivery a sales docket is prepared on which is recorded the number of litres delivered at each drop. These sales dockets are returned to the accounting department at the end of each day, invoices are prepared by pricing quantities shown on the dockets, and these are mailed to customers. Customers are allowed a discount for payment within 10 days.

The business has twelve employees who are paid on the fifteenth and the last day of each month. Supplies and other expenses are charged to Silvertail Petroleum Ltd as they are incurred.

Required

You have been asked for an opinion on the accounting system that would be most suited to the needs of this company. Give your response to the following queries:

A. Should the company use a sales journal? Why or why not? If a sales journal is used, what procedures would you recommend to record entries in it and to send invoices to customers as soon as possible after deliveries?
B. Is a purchases journal needed, or can all purchases be recorded in the general journal? Explain.
C. Should the company use a cash receipts journal, considering that some 30 to 50 cheques are received by mail each week? If so, what special columns would you use?
D. Should the company use a cash payments journal? Explain.

CRITICAL THINKING

Using technology to improve business information

Jenny Morrison owns and manages a business which offers web design services. She started the business five years ago from home. The business has grown fairly quickly, and two years ago Jenny decided to employ two graduates to help her cope with the demand for the services she offers. At that stage she also decided to rent a small office on the outskirts of the city. Most of the work carried out is charged at an hourly rate, and there are several clients that retain Jenny's services on an ongoing basis to help with the maintenance of their websites. When the business first started, Jenny used to keep a manual diary of all the hours she worked, and then used to send bills out at the end of each month. When she got really busy, she would sometimes forget to diarise her hours, resulting in missing or inaccurate invoices. On average, the business has around 50 clients. Jenny is now considering whether she should try and set up a simple spreadsheet-based accounting system, or whether she should consider purchasing an off-the-shelf accounting package.

Required

A. What advice would you give Jenny regarding setting up an accounting system? In what ways would a computerised accounting package help Jenny make better decisions about her business?
B. What source documents do you think Jenny should use as input into the new accounting system? What sort of data should be captured on these source documents to improve the accuracy of the accounting information produced?

ETHICS AND GOVERNANCE

Computerised shipping documents

Fremantle Fisheries (FF) operates a fleet of fishing boats out of three ports in Western Australia — Fremantle, Bunbury and Geraldton. Each port has its own fishing fleet and all seafood caught is sold through the Fish Marketing Board, a board established by the state government. The accounting procedures for all sales to the Board are centralised and handled by a computerised accounting system at FF's head office in Perth. The majority of the company's employees work on the fishing boats, and are paid bonuses from head office, depending on the volume, type and quality of seafood caught. This means that head office must be able to identify the source of each shipment sent to the Board.

John Dorey, who was originally based in Geraldton and handled the accounting procedures at Geraldton before computerisation, is now based in Perth as manager of the computerised accounting system. His father and two sisters are still based in Geraldton and work for the company on the fishing boats, as do many friends of the family.

Shipping documents are sent to the Perth head office from all three ports, and the source of the shipment is clearly marked in the top right-hand corner of the documents. Occasionally, however, details of the source are missing, and it is not easy to trace the source quickly. Dorey, in his capacity as manager of the system, is keen to keep the system fully operational and up to date, and has instructed the keyboard operator to insert any one of three Geraldton source codes, namely those of his father and two sisters, whenever the source code is missing from the shipping document. The keyboard operator knows that the codes given are those belonging to his boss's family, but nevertheless complies with the request for fear that non-compliance may lead to his own dismissal.

Required
A. Who are the stakeholders in this situation?
B. What are the ethical issues involved here as a result of Dorey's request and the action taken by the keyboard operator?
C. If you were the keyboard operator, what action (if any) would you take to prevent this situation occurring? Why?

FINANCIAL ANALYSIS

Refer to the latest financial report of JB Hi-Fi Limited on its website, www.jbhifi.com.au, and answer the following questions:
1. JB Hi-Fi Limited is one of Australia's major home entertainment retail organisations. After reviewing the financial report, what types of different accounting journals would you expect the company to use?
2. From the statement of cash flows, name the journal(s) or journal summaries in which you would expect to find the following transactions recorded:
   (a) receipts from customers
   (b) payments to suppliers and employees
   (c) dividends paid to members of the parent entity
   (d) payments for property, plant and equipment.
3. From the financial statements and notes in relation to revenues and expenses, name the journal(s) or journal summaries in which you would expect to find the following transactions recorded:
   (a) cost of sales expense
   (b) sales and marketing expenses
   (c) other income
   (d) occupancy expenses.
4. In general journal format, provide entries that could be made by the company to account for all of the items in (2) and (3) above.

Chapter

8

Accounting for manufacturing

Concepts for review

Before studying this chapter, you should understand or, if necessary, revise:

- the users of accounting information and the different types of financial statements (pp. 142–5)

- the calculation of cost of sales using a periodic inventory system (pp. 244–6)

- the role of adjusting and closing entries in the accounting cycle for a retail business (pp. 126–40, 182–98)

- the use of a worksheet in preparing the financial statements for a retail business (pp. 148–54).

Learning objectives

After studying this chapter, you should be able to:

1 describe three ways in which costs are used by management for decision making (p. 340)

2 describe the nature of manufacturing operations (pp. 340–3)

3 define and identify the three manufacturing cost elements — direct materials, direct labour and factory overhead (pp. 343–6)

4 explain the basic nature of absorption costing and a cost allocation based on cost behaviour (pp. 346–7)

5 identify the essential differences in the financial statements for retail and manufacturing entities (pp. 347–9)

6 describe the additional accounts and accounting procedures required for a manufacturing entity, including the completion of a worksheet (pp. 349–57)

7 understand how designing for sustainability contributes to minimising and controlling manufacturing costs (pp. 357–8).

Mid-range iPad to generate maximum profits for Apple, iSuppli estimates

The mid-range, 3G-wireless version of Apple Inc.'s upcoming iPad is expected to carry a combined Bill of Materials (BOM) and manufacturing cost of $287.15, making it the most profitable member of the iPad product line on a percentage basis, according to a virtual teardown generated in part by leveraging iSuppli Corp.'s Mobile Handset Cost Model tool.

The mid-priced version of the iPad equipped with 32Gbytes of NAND flash memory and 3G wireless capability will contain $275.95 worth of components and other materials, iSuppli estimates. This version of the device will cost $11.20 to manufacture. Note these cost estimates account only for hardware and manufacturing costs and do not include other expenses such as software, royalties and licensing fees.

'At a BOM and manufacturing cost of $287.15, and a retail price of $729, the 32Gbyte/3G version is expected to generate the highest profit of any member of the iPad line on a percentage basis,' said Dr. Jagdish Rebello, senior director and principal analyst for iSuppli. 'The 32Gbyte versions of the iPad cost only $29.50 more to produce than the 16Gbyte versions, but their retail pricing is $100 higher. This shows that Apple believes the highest-volume opportunity for the iPad resides in the mid range of the product line.'

The 32Gbytes of NAND flash in the mid-range iPad costs an estimated $59, compared to $29.50 for the 16Gbtyes in the low-end version, accounting for the cost differential.

Touch and feel

At a combined cost of $80 for all models, the iPad's display and touch-screen interface represents the most expensive segment of the system, accounting for 29 percent of the BOM of the mid-range 3G model, according to Vinita Jakhanwal, principal analyst for iSuppli.

The display employs In-Plane Switching (IPS) technology which supports a wider viewing angle and better picture quality in terms of presentation of color than conventional LCDs. While the iPad's display probably is sourced from three suppliers, LG Display and Innolux are the two most likely suppliers of the iPad's IPS LCD, Jakhanwal said.

Precious memory

The NAND flash memory is expected to be the second most expensive item in the iPad's BOM, regardless of the model. In the mid-range 3G model, the 32Gbytes of NAND accounts for 21.4 percent of the total BOM.

PA inside

The applications processor and DRAM are expected to carry a combined cost of $28.90, representing 10.5 percent of the mid-range 3G model's total BOM, making them the third most expensive line item in the mid-range iPad.

The A4 processor in the iPad is expected to carry a $17 cost. iSuppli believes the processor integrates an ARM RISC architecture microprocessor and a graphics processing unit. For memory support for the A4, the iPad is expected to include 512Mbytes of DRAM, costing $11.90.

Wireless expense

For the 3G-enabled versions of the iPad, the cost of the wireless subsystem — comprising the baseband IC, the radio frequency components, the power amplifier and other parts — is estimated at $24.50, equal to 8.5 percent of the BOM of the mid-range version.

Supply side

Other notable components in the iPad include:
- The user interface components — including an accelerometer, compass, audio codec and other components — are estimated at $10.20.
- The wireless LAN, Bluetooth and FM functionality is likely supported by a Broadcom Corp. device also seen in the iPod Touch and the Google Nexus One. This Broadcom device probably is integrated into a module supplied by Murata, but there remains a possibility that Texas Instruments could supply this chip. iSuppli estimates the cost of this device at $8.05.
- In line with previous Apple products, the GPS chip in the iPad probably is supplied by Infineon. iSuppli estimates the cost of the chip at $2.60.

Source: Excerpts from 'Mid-range iPad to generate maximum profits for Apple, iSuppli estimates', www.isuppli.com.

Chapter preview

A **manufacturing business** is more complex than retailing because it involves production as well as selling and administration. In accounting for manufacturing operations, the emphasis is on the gathering of costs and the recording of expenses.

The case in the scene setter of the Apple Inc. iPad highlights the importance of accounting for and understanding the nature of manufacturing costs, particularly the direct costs of materials and their relationship to sales and profit margins. This is of particular interest to marketing personnel as well as the accountants.

To most people, the terms *cost* and *expense* mean the same thing. However, to an accountant, these terms are technically different. A **cost** is when an economic sacrifice of resources is made in exchange for a product or service. This may or may not result in a decrease in equity. An **expense** is the consumption or loss of resources and will result in a decrease in equity.

Accountants classify costs in many ways: they may be classified as direct costs or indirect costs, as variable costs or fixed costs, or as controllable costs or uncontrollable costs, depending on which classification best suits the decision maker's purpose at the time. The important point is that *different costs will be used for different purposes*. Once the purpose of the cost information is known, managers and accountants choose the cost classification that is most relevant to their decision. This chapter provides an introduction to accounting for and reporting manufacturing costs.

8.1 Costs and decision making

Learning objective 1

Describe three ways in which costs are used by management for decision making

Some of the main reasons managers need to know about the costs of manufacturing for decision making include:

- *Inventory valuation.* The cost of manufacturing finished goods and goods still in production needs to be determined so that these costs can be used in preparing the income statement and balance sheet (statement of financial position). As these goods are not simply purchased but are manufactured, this is not as straightforward as indicated in chapter 6.
- *Profit determination.* Calculation of cost of sales is not possible without first determining the cost of inventory. The cost of manufacturing goods needs to be determined before a price can be set. Marketing may set the price according to what the market may bear but the cost of manufacturing must be covered and there must be sufficient mark-up on cost to cover other expenses and to provide a profit.
- *Management decision-making applications.* These include pricing and planning. Past costs are useful for future planning when adjusted to changes in circumstances. Costs of alternative methods of production are useful in planning the most efficient method of production. Costs of alternative options for a product suggested by market research are necessary to determine whether it is profitable. As shown in the scene setter, Apple Inc. has considered the costs of different versions of the iPad and priced what it believes will be the most popular version to also be the most profitable.

8.2 Nature of manufacturing operations

Learning objective 2

Describe the nature of manufacturing operations

Manufacturers convert raw materials into finished products. A phone manufacturer, like Apple Inc., purchases casings, screens, communication chips and component parts and converts them through a production process into phones that are sold to retailers. In contrast, retailers buy completed phones and sell them to the public. A manufacturing entity uses most of the accounting procedures discussed earlier, but requires extra procedures for the collection, reporting and control of production costs.

Manufacturing entities and the GST

As with service and retail entities, manufacturing entities with gross annual turnover in excess of $75 000 are required to register for an ABN and for the GST. The GST of 10% is added by the manufacturer to the price of all goods supplied to wholesalers and retailers. Manufacturers must therefore issue 'tax invoices'. In addition, manufacturing entities are entitled to offset any GST outlaid on the purchase of goods (e.g. raw materials) and services (e.g. electricity charges) against GST collections on finished goods sold. Manufacturing entities are also required to lodge a business activity statement (BAS). To illustrate the GST process for a manufacturer, refer to figure A3.1 (p. 103) which shows the GST outlays and collections for a furniture manufacturer.

In accordance with the principles set out in earlier chapters for accounting for the GST, income, costs and expenses are recorded exclusive of GST, whereas amounts relating to accounts receivable and accounts payable are recorded inclusive of GST.

Production flows

To understand what manufacturing is all about, consider the production flow of Fast Fones Industries Pty Ltd, a maker of mobile phones, shown in figure 8.1. There are two production departments, assembly and packaging. Skilled labour and a highly automated production process are combined to make a phone that is sold to a retailer. Raw materials (such as the casing, phone display and communications chip) are purchased from outside suppliers, kept in the stores department, and issued when needed to the assembly department. In the assembly department, each phone is put together and then transferred to the packaging department, where the product is finished.

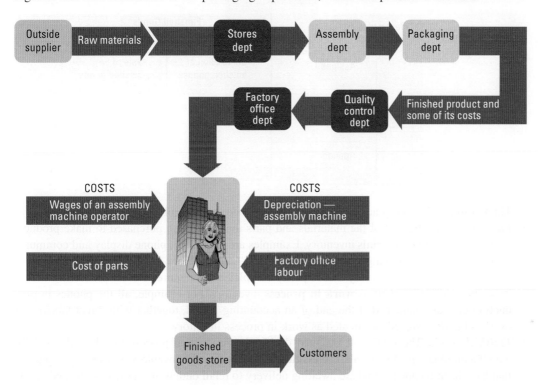

Figure 8.1 Simplified production flow of Fast Fones Industries

Managers at all levels must be able to account for the costs incurred in the production of phones to make decisions about pricing the finished product and evaluating the profitability of the operation. Production occurs only in the two production departments, assembly and packaging, even though there are five departments in the manufacturing process. The other three departments — stores, quality control, and factory office — are called service or support departments because they support the two production departments. For example, the factory office department provides services such as accounting, payroll, personnel and purchasing. Next we consider the accounting processes that record the manufacturing operation.

Inventories — manufacturing and non-manufacturing

Manufacturing and non-manufacturing business entities engage in many of the same selling and administrative activities such as marketing, granting credit, clerical work and general management. However, the valuation of a manufacturing entity's inventories introduces some accounting practices that are different from those of a service entity that does not have any inventory, or a retail entity that buys finished goods ready for resale. A comparison of the inventory cost flows of a retail entity and a manufacturing entity, as reflected in the ledger accounts, is shown in figure 8.2 (p. 342).

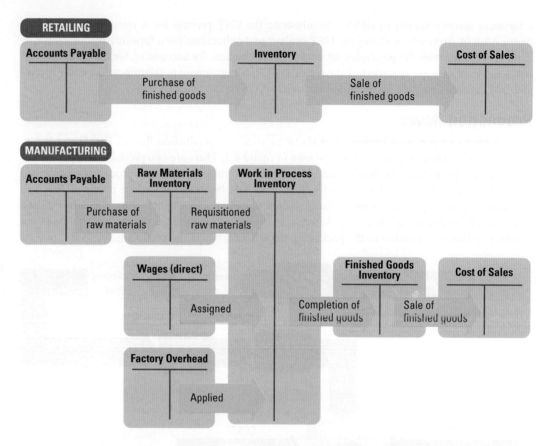

Figure 8.2 Retailing and manufacturing entities' inventory cost flows

Three different inventory accounts must be maintained by a manufacturing entity:

- *Raw materials.* The cost of the materials and parts that have been purchased to make products is classified as **raw materials** inventory. Examples are the casing, phone display and communications chip used in making a phone.
- *Work in process.* The inventory that is partly completed but requires further processing before it can be sold is classified as **work in process** inventory. For example, all the phones in production that are unfinished at the end of an accounting period, together with direct labour and overhead costs assigned, are treated as work in process inventory.
- *Finished goods.* The total cost assigned during the production process to all products fully manufactured and ready for sale is classified as **finished goods** inventory. For example, phones that have been completed and are awaiting delivery to retail outlets are shown as finished goods inventory.

At the end of any accounting period, the balances in the three inventory accounts are reported as current assets on the balance sheet (also called the statement of financial position). In contrast, a retail entity uses a single inventory control account. A proper measure of income and expenses depends on the accuracy with which the costs of the three inventories are accumulated during the production process.

Product and period costs

It was noted earlier that managers and accountants classify costs in many ways. We also noted that a cost is classified as an asset as long as it has future economic benefits controlled by the entity. Expired costs are reported in the income statement as expenses because they no longer have future economic benefits.

The terms *product cost* and *period cost* are particularly important in the development of a manufacturing entity's income statement. An accurate *calculation of expenses* must be based on a well-defined distinction between product and period costs, because the period in which the benefit of any cost is received is the period in which the cost should be treated as an expense.

Product costs are integral to producing the product as they are necessary for its physical existence. They are included in the cost of inventories as assets until the products are sold. At that point, the product costs have been consumed or their benefit received so they are expensed on the income statement of the period as cost of sales.

Period costs are identified with a specific time interval because they are not directly required to produce a product. Therefore, they are not added to inventory costs and are charged as expenses in the period in which they are incurred.

The flows of product costs and period costs through the financial statements are illustrated in figure 8.3 using wages and salaries of factory and non-factory staff.

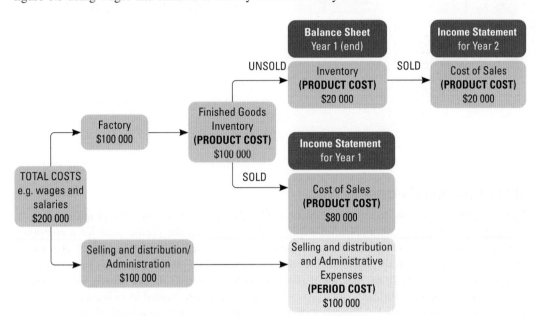

Figure 8.3 Flows of product costs and period costs

Note that product costs are included in inventory until the inventory is sold. Then they are charged to the period of sale. Period costs are treated as expenses of the accounting period in which they are incurred.

Product costs for wholesalers and retailers will consist only of purchase costs because the inventory purchased is ready for resale. The purchase costs are kept in an inventory account until they are expensed as cost of sales. All other costs, including labour, are charged to a specific period as selling and distribution, administrative or finance and other expenses. Service entities, such as accounting practices, real estate agents or consulting practices, *do not have product costs* as they do not maintain an inventory for resale. As a result, all costs are period costs because they are expensed in the period in which they are incurred.

In a manufacturing entity, *all* the manufacturing cost elements related directly to the product as it is being produced are treated as product costs until the product is sold. Then the costs are transferred to the cost of sales expense in the income statement. The non-product, or period, costs are classified as selling and distribution, administrative, or finance and other expenses according to their functional nature and are expensed. For example, advertising expense and managers' salaries would be treated as period costs. The next consideration is the identification of the manufacturing cost elements that are included in inventory as product costs.

8.3 Manufacturing cost elements

The inventory cost flow of a manufacturing entity, illustrated in figure 8.2, can be expanded to the more complete manufacturing cost flow shown in figure 8.4 (p. 344). The flow of **manufacturing cost elements** corresponds to the *physical flow of products* through the production process. The accounting process must record the manufacturing cost elements as they are incurred so they can be accumulated as assets and then expensed once the related products are sold. The cost of a

Learning objective 3

Define and identify the three manufacturing cost elements — direct materials, direct labour and factory overhead finished product consists of three basic cost elements — *direct materials cost, direct labour cost* and *factory overhead cost*.

Figure 8.4 The flow of manufacturing costs

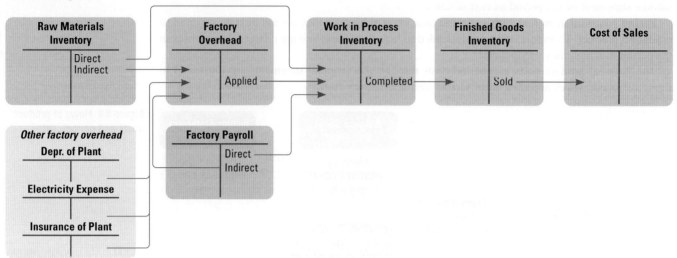

Direct materials cost

The cost of raw materials directly traceable to the finished product is called **direct materials cost**. The display screen and communications chip used for a phone, the plastic used for a computer, the crude oil used for petrol and the steel used for a motor vehicle are examples of direct materials. Since direct materials physically become part of a finished product, they can be traced to the product or, in some situations, batches of products. Direct materials do not usually include small, low cost items, such as lubricants, glue, screws or nails, which are treated as indirect materials and included in factory overhead. Although such items are an integral part of a finished product, it may not be possible or cost-effective to trace such items to the products.

Direct labour cost

The wages paid to employees whose time and costs can be traced to the products are classified as **direct labour cost**. As long as the employees perform tasks that can be identified specifically with the conversion of direct materials into finished goods, the labour is a direct cost. An example is the wages paid to carpenters in the construction of a house. Other labour is required to support the production process but cannot be traced directly to finished products. The wages or salaries paid to cleaners, maintenance personnel, production supervisors, and materials handlers are classified as indirect labour costs and included in factory overhead costs (see below). In manufacturing, the total of the direct labour costs and direct materials costs is referred to as **prime cost** because of their direct association with the finished product.

Factory overhead cost

All manufacturing costs except direct materials and direct labour are included in **factory overhead cost**. Factory overhead costs are incurred in both **production** and **service departments**. (Other terms used for factory overhead cost are indirect manufacturing cost, manufacturing overhead, factory burden, or simply overhead.) Indirect materials, indirect labour, electricity, maintenance, insurance, rent, depreciation and rates are examples of factory overhead costs. Three issues that must be resolved in accounting for factory overhead are discussed below.

Allocation of common costs. Several costs such as rent, depreciation, insurance and rates *may be applicable in part* to manufacturing and *in part* to selling and administrative functions. They are common costs because they are incurred for all three activities. Methods must be devised to allocate these common costs to the manufacturing, selling and administrative functions.

Assignment of service departments costs. Service departments provide support to the production departments with activities such as maintenance, production control, inspection, stores and engineering. The service departments overhead costs must be allocated in some way to the production departments so they can be included in the product cost.

Assignment of factory overhead costs. The indirect nature of factory overhead costs prevents them from being traced to the products as direct materials costs and direct labour costs are. They include indirect materials, indirect labour, rent, rates, insurance and electricity. Without these costs, manufacturing could not take place. A manufacturing entity must develop a reliable method to allocate overhead costs to the product. Instead of tracing factory overhead costs to the production process, the costs are applied on some basis that closely relates the costs incurred with the work performed. Common bases for the application of factory overhead costs are direct labour cost, direct labour hours or units produced.

An **overhead application rate** is developed by using the following steps.
1. Calculate the total expected factory overhead cost. For example, assume this is $200 000.
2. Calculate the expected total of the item used to measure normal production capacity. For example, assume total direct labour hours are *expected* to be 50 000.
3. Calculate the *overhead application* rate by dividing the projected factory overhead costs by the projected direct labour hours:

$$\$200\,000 \div 50\,000 = \$4$$

4. Apply factory overhead costs to the product costs using the overhead application rate. For example if each product takes 2 direct labour hours to produce then the factory overhead allocated to each unit of production is $2 \times \$4 = \$8$ per product.

It is important to note that an overhead application rate is usually a predetermined rate based on future estimates of both factory overhead cost and production activity, rather than actual results. Therefore, applied overhead and actual overhead are often different. This difference and how it is interpreted and handled are covered in the next chapter.

BUSINESS KNOWLEDGE

The mix of production costs

Although the three elements of production costs are still raw materials, direct labour and factory overhead, there have been significant shifts in the mix of these elements over the past 50 years. In the 1950s, direct labour was generally the largest element of production costs, and would typically constitute some 40% of total manufacturing costs. Direct materials costs were around 35% of total manufacturing costs, and factory overhead costs were some 25%. In other words, direct costs could constitute some 75% of total production costs.

With the improvement in production techniques and the advent of computerised production systems and robotics, significant shifts have occurred in the mix of the components of manufacturing costs. Today, indirect costs of factory overheads can reach or exceed 50% of total manufacturing costs, with direct costs dropping to about 50% of total manufacturing costs. The diagrams emphasise the shift that has had far-reaching consequences for the decision processes of all levels of management in manufacturing businesses.

Direct materials 35%	Direct labour 40%	Factory overheads 25%

1950s

Direct materials 40%	Direct labour 10%	Factory overheads 50%

2000s

Source: Adapted from B. Needles, M. Powers & S. Crossen, *Principles of accounting*, Houghton Mifflin, Boston.

With automation and computerisation, factory overhead costs have grown to the point where they can constitute a higher proportion of total cost than direct labour does. This has placed increased importance on the application rate used to assign costs to products. Both direct labour costs and overhead costs are seen as necessary to convert the raw materials into finished products and are therefore commonly referred to as **conversion costs**. This subject is discussed in more detail in the next chapter.

8.4 Absorption costing and cost behaviour

Learning objective 4

Explain the basic nature of absorption costing and a cost allocation based on cost behaviour

Two product costing methods available to a manufacturing entity are absorption costing and direct costing. With **absorption costing**, all manufacturing costs are treated as product costs regardless of whether they vary with production levels. Therefore, all direct materials costs, direct labour costs and factory overhead costs are treated as product costs. In contrast, **direct costing**, sometimes called variable costing or marginal costing, *only* recognises as product costs those manufacturing costs that vary with production levels. Costs that are fixed across different levels of production are treated as period costs and are therefore expenses. We limit our coverage of product costing to absorption costing, as accounting standard IAS 2/AASB 102 *Inventories* allows only the use of absorption costing for general purpose financial reports prepared for external users. Managers can use direct costing for internal reporting purposes.

Managers, such as marketing or production managers, must often evaluate the effect of changes in sales or production volume on the profits of the entity as demonstrated in the scene setter. One of the most widely used ways to classify costs is by their **cost behaviour**. This describes how a cost will react to changes in the level of business activity. Although we are concerned at this point with the cost behaviour of manufacturing costs, the same concepts can be applied to costs/expenses in service and retail businesses.

Variable costs

Variable costs in the production process are defined as costs that vary directly, or nearly directly, *in total* with the volume of production. Direct materials cost, direct labour cost and certain factory overhead items such as the electricity cost for machinery operation are variable costs. For example, assume that the cost of a phone display was estimated at $840 for each phone — the direct materials cost of phone displays increases and decreases proportionately with the number of phones produced, as illustrated in the following schedule:

Number of phones produced	Direct materials cost of phone display per unit	Total direct materials cost of phone displays
1	$40	$ 40
25	40	1 000
50	40	2 000
100	40	4 000

Although the direct materials rate per unit is constant, the *total* direct materials cost varies with the level of production. Variable costs are defined in terms of their total cost in relation to production/output levels, not their per unit cost.

Fixed costs

Fixed costs in the production process are defined as those costs that remain relatively constant *in total*, within the normal range of operations, irrespective of variations in the volume of production. In a manufacturing operation, a fixed cost is *the same* in terms of its total amount regardless of the units of production completed during the period. Examples are depreciation of factory equipment, rent, rates and supervisory salaries. Although a fixed cost remains constant in total regardless of the level of activity, its unit cost varies inversely with volume. For example, a $500 monthly depreciation charge for production equipment is constant regardless of the production level, but changes in terms of cost per unit as follows:

Number of units produced	Monthly depreciation	Depreciation per unit
1	$500	$500
25	500	20
50	500	10
100	500	5

Since variable and fixed costs are not generally segregated in product costing under absorption costing, cost behaviour information is not readily available from the accounting system.

8.5 Financial statements — retailing and manufacturing

Learning objective 5

Identify the essential differences in the financial statements for retail and manufacturing entities

When the financial statements of a manufacturing entity are compared with those of a retail entity, it is apparent that the major differences relate to cost of sales in the income statement and inventories in the current assets section of the balance sheet.

Cost of sales

The major difference between accounting for a retailer and a manufacturer is the *calculation of cost of sales*. As we saw in chapter 6, a retailer calculates cost of sales as follows:

$$\begin{array}{c}\text{Beginning}\\\text{inventory}\end{array} + \begin{array}{c}\text{Net purchases}\\\text{of inventory}\end{array} - \begin{array}{c}\text{Ending}\\\text{inventory}\end{array} = \begin{array}{c}\text{Cost of}\\\text{sales}\end{array}$$

In contrast, a manufacturing entity determines cost of sales in the following way:

$$\begin{array}{c}\text{Beginning finished}\\\text{goods inventory}\end{array} + \begin{array}{c}\text{Cost of goods}\\\text{manufactured}\end{array} - \begin{array}{c}\text{Ending finished}\\\text{goods inventory}\end{array} = \begin{array}{c}\text{Cost of}\\\text{sales}\end{array}$$

The cost of goods manufactured results from the conversion of raw materials to finished goods and replaces the net purchases of inventory in a retail enterprise. A manufacturing entity makes rather than buys its stock of goods for sale. This difference is reflected in the presentation of an income statement.

Income statement

In figure 8.5 (p. 348), the difference in the cost of sales calculations in the income statements prepared for retail and manufacturing entities is shown. Sales revenue, selling and distribution expenses, administrative expenses, finance and other expenses, and income tax are treated the same. Again, we see that the cost of goods manufactured replaces the purchases of the retail business. The next step is to identify what constitutes the cost of goods manufactured.

Cost of goods manufactured statement

The cost of goods manufactured can be calculated as:

$$\begin{array}{c}\text{Cost of goods}\\\text{manufactured}\end{array} = \begin{array}{c}\text{Direct}\\\text{materials}\\\text{used}\end{array} + \begin{array}{c}\text{Direct}\\\text{labour}\end{array} + \begin{array}{c}\text{Factory}\\\text{overhead}\end{array} + \begin{array}{c}\text{Beginning}\\\text{work in}\\\text{process}\\\text{inventory}\end{array} - \begin{array}{c}\text{Ending}\\\text{work in}\\\text{process}\\\text{inventory}\end{array}$$

A **cost of goods manufactured statement** is prepared to show the calculations for the cost of goods manufactured reported in the income statement. In figure 8.5, the cost of goods manufactured

Figure 8.5 Comparison of income statements

A RETAIL ENTITY Income Statement for the year ended 30 June 2013			A MANUFACTURING ENTITY Income Statement for the year ended 30 June 2013		
INCOME			INCOME		
Net sales revenue		$1 000 000	Net sales revenue		$1 000 000
Less: Cost of sales:			*Less:* Cost of sales:		
Beginning inventory	$150 000		Beginning finished goods inventory	$150 000	
Net purchases	710 000		Cost of goods manufactured (figure 8.6)	710 000	
Goods available	860 000		Goods available	860 000	
Ending inventory	160 000		Ending finished goods inventory	160 000	
Cost of sales		700 000	Cost of sales		700 000
GROSS PROFIT		300 000	GROSS PROFIT		300 000
EXPENSES			EXPENSES		
Selling and distribution	90 000		Selling and distribution	90 000	
Administrative	120 000		Administrative	120 000	
Finance and other	20 000		Finance and other	20 000	
		230 000			230 000
PROFIT BEFORE TAX		70 000	PROFIT BEFORE TAX		70 000
Income tax expense		28 000	Income tax expense		28 000
PROFIT		$ 42 000	PROFIT		$ 42 000

is shown as $710 000, and the purpose of the statement in figure 8.6 is to provide a detailed explanation of that amount. The total cost of the direct materials used, the direct labour and the factory overhead represents the manufacturing costs for the period. The direct materials of $142 000 are determined by adding the purchases of the period ($141 000) to the beginning materials ($48 000) and subtracting the ending materials ($47 000). The direct labour cost of $355 000 and the factory overhead cost of $208 000 are recorded during the period. Consequently, the total manufacturing costs for the period are $705 000.

The individual factory overhead items are listed and totalled on the statement. The beginning work in process inventory of $35 000 represents costs that have been incurred in the previous period. They are added to the manufacturing costs of the current period. Since the ending work in process of $30 000 consists of costs associated with products that will be finished later, it must be subtracted to obtain the cost of goods manufactured for the period. The cost of goods manufactured of $710 000 represents the production cost of the products that have been completed and transferred to finished goods inventory during the period.

Balance sheet

The balance sheet of a retail entity shows only one type of inventory, finished goods, since the entity is in the business of buying and selling finished goods. For a manufacturing entity, the balance sheet usually shows three inventory items:

1. *Raw materials inventory* shows the cost of raw materials that have been purchased but have not yet been placed into production at the date of the statement.
2. *Work in process inventory* shows the costs of materials, labour and overheads assigned to products being manufactured that remain incomplete at the date of the statement.
3. *Finished goods inventory* represents the cost of goods that have been completed during the reporting period and that remain unsold at the date of the statement.

In figure 8.7, the differences in the current assets section of the balance sheets of a retail and a manufacturing entity are shown.

Figure 8.6 Cost of goods manufactured statement

A MANUFACTURING ENTITY
Cost of Goods Manufactured Statement
for the year ended 30 June 2013

Direct materials:		
Beginning raw materials	$ 48 000	
Net purchases of raw materials	141 000	
	189 000	
Ending raw materials	47 000	
Direct materials used		$142 000
Direct labour		355 000
Factory overhead:		
Indirect labour	56 000	
Supplies	5 000	
Electricity	42 000	
Rent	22 600	
Insurance	18 000	
Rates and taxes	28 400	
Depreciation	32 000	
Miscellaneous	4 000	
Total factory overhead		208 000
Manufacturing costs for the period		705 000
Beginning work in process		35 000
Total work in process		740 000
Ending work in process		30 000
COST OF GOODS MANUFACTURED		$710 000

Figure 8.7 Comparison of balance sheets (current assets section)

A RETAIL ENTITY Balance Sheet as at 30 June 2013		**A MANUFACTURING ENTITY** Balance Sheet as at 30 June 2013	
CURRENT ASSETS		CURRENT ASSETS	
Cash at Bank	$ 50 000	Cash at Bank	$ 50 000
Accounts receivable	100 000	Accounts receivable	100 000
Inventories*	160 000	Inventories:	
Other	50 000	Finished goods	160 000
TOTAL CURRENT ASSETS	$360 000	Work in process	30 000
		Raw materials	47 000
		Other	50 000
		TOTAL CURRENT ASSETS	$437 000

* All finished goods

8.6 Accounting systems considerations

Learning objective 6

Describe the additional accounts and accounting procedures required for a manufacturing entity, including the completion of a worksheet

A manufacturing entity's accounting system is more complex than one used by a non-manufacturing entity because of the manufacturing cost flow illustrated in figure 8.4. The basic accounts used for assets, liabilities, equity, income and expenses in service and retail entities are also needed in a manufacturing entity. Additional asset accounts are required in manufacturing to calculate the cost of sales and to provide management with reliable product cost information.

A manufacturing entity must decide between a periodic and perpetual inventory system in accounting for the manufacturing costs. The essential features of periodic and perpetual inventory systems are introduced in chapter 6. In this chapter, we illustrate the use of a periodic inventory system and then extend these procedures to a perpetual inventory system in the next chapter.

Periodic inventory system for a manufacturing entity

Small manufacturing businesses may be able to use a periodic inventory system if a single product or a few similar products are produced. As such, the manufacturing accounting is performed within the general accounting system by extending the basic procedures used for retail accounting. The additional accounts required with a periodic inventory system in a manufacturing operation are:

1. raw materials inventory
2. raw materials purchases
3. work in process inventory
4. finished goods inventory
5. manufacturing plant and equipment
6. factory payroll
7. factory overhead
8. manufacturing summary

Many of these accounts are set up as control accounts supported by the detailed information in a subsidiary ledger. For example, the balance in the Factory Overhead account is the sum of the amounts recorded in subsidiary ledger accounts for such items as indirect labour, supplies, electricity and rent.

The Manufacturing Summary account is used at the end of an accounting period to summarise the costs incurred and to determine the cost of goods manufactured. Note that beginning balances are carried in the three inventory accounts (raw materials, work in process and finished goods) during an accounting period when a periodic inventory system is used. At the end of each accounting period, a physical count of raw materials, work in process and finished goods must be made and costs assigned to inventory. Consequently, the manufacturing cost flow shown in figure 8.4 is not accounted for as it takes place, but the inventory cost information is made available through the closing of the accounts at the end of the period. For example, the Manufacturing Summary account is prepared by a manufacturing entity to generate the information already shown in figures 8.5 and 8.6.

Manufacturing Summary

2013			2013		
30/6	Beginning raw materials	48 000	30/6	Ending raw materials	47 000
30/6	Purchases of raw materials	141 000	30/6	Ending work in process	30 000
30/6	Factory payroll	355 000	30/6	Cost of goods manufactured	
30/6	Factory overhead	208 000		(to Profit or Loss Summary)	710 000
30/6	Beginning work in process	35 000			
		787 000			787 000

Profit or Loss Summary

2013			2013		
30/6	Beginning finished goods	150 000	30/6	Ending finished goods	160 000
30/6	Cost of goods manufactured	710 000	30/6	Balance c/d (cost of sales)	700 000
		860 000			860 000
30/6	Balance b/d (cost of sales)	700 000			

The $700 000 balance shown in the Profit or Loss Summary account before the income, expenses and income tax accounts are closed represents the cost of sales and coincides with the amount shown in figure 8.5. After the income and other expenses accounts are closed to the Profit or Loss Summary account, a credit balance of $42 000 remains as the profit for the period.

The profit of $42 000 is closed to equity (or retained earnings) as a final step in the closing process. The cost of goods manufactured under a periodic inventory system is usually calculated on a manufacturing worksheet, similar to the one introduced in chapter 6 for a retail business. A description of a manufacturing worksheet and a more complete illustration of accounting for a manufacturing business with a periodic inventory system follow.

Worksheet for a manufacturing entity

The worksheet of a non-manufacturing entity can be adapted easily for use by a manufacturing entity. Two additional columns are required to record the financial data reported in the cost of goods manufactured statement. The **manufacturing worksheet** of Fast Fones Industries Pty Ltd, a manufacturer of mobile phones whose flow of product was presented earlier, is presented in figure 8.8 (p. 352). The balances of the general ledger accounts are listed as a trial balance in the first two columns. The end-of-period adjustments are made in the adjustments columns, and the cost of goods manufactured information is recorded in the manufacturing columns. Income statement and balance sheet columns are used for the data needed to prepare the two basic financial statements. As we saw in earlier chapters, a worksheet is used by a business to organise financial information in a systematic manner and to *prepare* the financial statements. It is especially important for a manufacturing operation because of the complexities of the production process and the additional financial data involved.

Once the trial balance data are entered on the worksheet, the end-of-period adjustments must be made. Fast Fones Industries Pty Ltd has identified the following adjustments that are required at 30 June 2013:

1. Expired insurance on manufacturing equipment currently recorded as a prepaid expense is $1700.
2. Accrued wages amount to $8200: $7000 direct labour, $1200 indirect labour.
3. Interest expense to be accrued on the loan payable is $280.
4. Lease rental on equipment to be accrued is $574.
5. Depreciation on the machinery used in manufacturing is $10 750.
6. Depreciation on the factory fittings is $6400.
7. Amortisation (i.e. depreciation) of patents is $1100.
8. Income tax expense amounts to $32 040.
9. An inventory of the small tools used in manufacturing was taken on 30 June 2013. Small tools amounting to $10 800 were on hand compared with the $14 100 shown in the small tools account. Consequently, $3300 is written off as an expense in 2013.

The debits and credits associated with the adjustments are in balance at $64 344. The amounts in the adjustments columns are combined with the amounts in the trial balance columns and the results are transferred, as appropriate, to the manufacturing columns and financial statements columns. Those items that will appear on the cost of goods manufactured statement are shown in the manufacturing columns. All items except the ending work in process and raw materials inventories are debits because they are expensed. The beginning work in process and raw materials inventories of $49 000 and $67 200 respectively are entered as debits in the manufacturing section.

The ending work in process and raw materials inventories amounting to $50 700 and $71 500 respectively are entered in the manufacturing credit column because they are deducted on the cost of goods manufactured statement. They are then extended to the balance sheet debit column to be reported as assets. The $956 780 figure required to balance the debits and credits in the manufacturing columns is the cost of goods manufactured for the period, which is transferred to the income statement debit column.

The beginning finished goods inventory of $210 000 is entered in the income statement debit column since it represents an addition in determining cost of sales. The ending finished goods inventory of $201 500 is entered in the income statement credit column because it will be subtracted from goods available in determining cost of sales. The figure also is entered in the balance sheet debit column to be reported as an asset. The sales of $1 400 000 are recorded in the income statement credit column. All expenses are recorded in the income statement debit column. The debit of $77 320 needed to balance these columns is profit, which is closed to retained earnings. All asset, liability and equity items are carried forward to the balance sheet columns. Formal statements prepared by Fast Fones Industries Pty Ltd from the worksheet are presented in figures 8.9, 8.10, 8.11 and 8.12 (pp. 353–4).

In computerised accounting systems for manufacturers, the computer automatically produces cost reports and various cost analyses, plus financial statements. This means that a manufacturing worksheet as presented in figure 8.8 is not needed.

Figure 8.8 Worksheet for a manufacturing entity

FAST FONES INDUSTRIES PTY LTD
Worksheet
for the year ended 30 June 2013

Account	Unadjusted trial balance Debit	Credit	Adjustments Debit	Credit	Manufacturing Debit	Credit	Income statement Debit	Credit	Balance sheet Debit	Credit
Cash at Bank	24 500								24 500	
Accounts Receivable	110 100								110 100	
Inventories:										
Finished Goods	210 000						210 000	201 500	201 500	
Work in Process	49 000				49 000	50 700			50 700	
Raw Materials	67 200				67 200	71 500			71 500	
Prepaid Expenses	2 600			(1) 1 700					900	
GST Outlays	40 000								40 000	
Manufacturing Machinery	86 000								86 000	
Acc. Depr. – Machinery		26 000		(5) 10 750						36 750
Factory Fittings	32 000								32 000	
Acc. Depr. – Fittings		11 000		(6) 6 400						17 400
Small Tools	14 100			(9) 3 300					10 800	
Patents	11 800								11 800	
Acc. Amort. – Patents		2 200		(7) 1 100						3 300
Accounts Payable		20 200								20 200
GST Collections		140 000								140 000
Lease Rent Payable		1 400		(4) 574						1 974
Loan Payable (long-term)		28 000								28 000
Share Capital		50 000								50 000
Retained Earnings		224 336								224 336
Sales		1 400 000						1 400 000		
Raw Materials Purchases	194 600				194 600					
Freight Inwards	2 800				2 800					
Direct Labour	490 000		(2) 7 000		497 000					
Indirect Labour	77 200		(2) 1 200		78 400					
Supplies Expense	8 726				8 726					
Electricity Expense	58 800				58 800					
Rent of Property Expense	31 640				31 640					
Insurance Expense	22 120		(1) 1 700		23 820					
Lease Rent Expense	39 270		(4) 574		39 844					
Other Manuf. Expenses	5 600				5 600					
Advertising Expense	20 800						20 800			
Sales Salaries Expense	121 520						121 520			
Other Selling Expenses	11 680						11 680			
Admin. Salaries Expense	156 800						156 800			
Other Admin. Expenses	11 200						11 200			
Interest Expense	3 080		(3) 280				3 360			
	1 903 136	1 903 136								
Wages Payable				(2) 8 200						8 200
Interest Payable				(3) 280						280
Depr. Exp. – Machinery			(5) 10 750		10 750					
Depr. Exp. – Fittings			(6) 6 400		6 400					
Amortis. Exp. – Patent			(7) 1 100		1 100					
Income Tax Expense			(8) 32 040				32 040			
Current Tax Liability				(8) 32 040						32 040
Small Tools Used			(9) 3 300		3 300					
Cost of Goods Manufactured						956 780	956 780			
			64 344	64 344	1 078 980	1 078 980	1 524 180	1 601 500	639 800	562 480
Profit after tax							77 320			77 320
							1 601 500	1 601 500	639 800	639 800

FAST FONES INDUSTRIES PTY LTD
Cost of Goods Manufactured Statement
for the year ended 30 June 2013

Direct materials:		
Beginning raw materials	$ 67 200	
Purchases	194 600	
Freight inwards	2 800	
	264 600	
Ending raw materials	71 500	
Direct materials used		$ 193 100
Direct labour		497 000
Factory overhead:		
Indirect labour	78 400	
Supplies	8 726	
Electricity	58 800	
Rent of property	31 640	
Insurance	23 820	
Lease rent of equipment	39 844	
Other expenses	5 600	
Depreciation expense (machinery and fittings)	17 150	
Small tools used	3 300	
Patent amortisation expense	1 100	268 380
Total manufacturing costs for the period		958 480
Beginning work in process		49 000
Total work in process		1 007 480
Ending work in process		50 700
COST OF GOODS MANUFACTURED		$ 956 780

Figure 8.9 Cost of goods manufactured statement

FAST FONES INDUSTRIES PTY LTD
Income Statement
for the year ended 30 June 2013

INCOME			
Sales revenue			$1 400 000
Less: Cost of sales:			
Beginning finished goods inventory		$ 210 000	
Cost of goods manufactured (figure 8.9)		956 780	
Goods available for sale		1 166 780	
Ending finished goods inventory		201 500	
Cost of sales			965 280
GROSS PROFIT			434 720
EXPENSES			
Selling and distribution expenses:			
Advertising	$ 20 800		
Sales salaries	121 520		
Other selling expenses	11 680	154 000	
Administrative expenses:			
Administrative salaries	156 800		
Other administrative expenses	11 200	168 000	
Finance and other expenses:			
Interest expense		3 360	325 360
PROFIT BEFORE TAX			109 360
Income tax expense			32 040
PROFIT			$ 77 320

Figure 8.10 Income statement

Figure 8.11 Statement of
changes in equity

FAST FONES INDUSTRIES PTY LTD
Statement of Changes in Equity
for the year ended 30 June 2013

Share capital	
Share capital, 1 July 2012	$ 50 000
Movement in share capital	—
Share capital, 30 June 2013	50 000
Retained earnings	
Retained earnings, 1 July 2012	224 336
Add: Profit for the year	77 320
Retained earnings, 30 June 2013	301 656
Total equity, 30 June 2013	$351 656

Figure 8.12 Balance sheet

FAST FONES INDUSTRIES PTY LTD
Balance Sheet
as at 30 June 2013

CURRENT ASSETS			
Cash at bank		$ 24 500	
Accounts receivable		110 100	
Inventories:			
Finished goods	$201 500		
Work in process	50 700		
Raw materials	71 500	323 700	
Prepaid expenses		900	
TOTAL CURRENT ASSETS			$459 200
NON-CURRENT ASSETS			
Machinery	86 000		
Accumulated depreciation	(36 750)	49 250	
Factory fittings	32 000		
Accumulated depreciation	(17 400)	14 600	
Small tools		10 800	
Patents	11 800		
Accumulated amortisation	(3 300)	8 500	
TOTAL NON-CURRENT ASSETS			83 150
TOTAL ASSETS			542 350
CURRENT LIABILITIES			
Accounts payable		20 200	
GST payable*		100 000	
Lease rent payable		1 974	
Wages payable		8 200	
Interest payable		280	
Current tax liability		32 040	
TOTAL CURRENT LIABILITIES			162 694
NON-CURRENT LIABILITIES			
Loan payable			28 000
TOTAL LIABILITIES			190 694
NET ASSETS			$351 656
EQUITY			
Share capital			$ 50 000
Retained earnings			301 656
TOTAL EQUITY			$351 656

* GST collections $140 000 – GST outlays $40 000

Closing entries for a manufacturing entity

In the general ledger, the account balances that are used to determine the cost of goods manufactured are closed to the Manufacturing Summary account, which is then closed to the Profit or Loss Summary account. The general journal entries to close the account balances shown on the worksheet in figure 8.8 are shown below.

	Date		Particulars	Debit	Credit
			General Journal		
	2013				
1.					
	June	30	Manufacturing Summary	1 078 980	
			Raw Materials Inventory		67 200
			Work in Process Inventory		49 000
			Raw Material Purchases		194 600
			Freight Inwards		2 800
			Direct Labour		497 000
			Indirect Labour		78 400
			Supplies Expense		8 726
			Electricity Expense		58 800
			Rent of Property Expense		31 640
			Insurance Expense		23 820
			Lease Rent Expense		39 844
			Other Manufacturing Expenses		5 600
			Depreciation Expense – Machinery		10 750
			Depreciation Expense – Fittings		6 400
			Amortisation Expense – Patent		1 100
			Small Tools Used		3 300
			(Closing manufacturing accounts with debit balances)		
2.					
	June	30	Raw Materials Inventory	71 500	
			Work in Process Inventory	50 700	
			Manufacturing Summary		122 200
			(Ending raw materials and work in process inventories)		
3.					
	June	30	Profit or Loss Summary	1 524 180	
			Finished Goods Inventory		210 000
			Advertising Expense		20 800
			Sales Salaries Expense		121 520
			Other Selling Expenses		11 680
			Administrative Salaries Expense		156 800
			Other Administrative Expenses		11 200
			Interest Expense		3 360
			Income Tax Expense		32 040
			Manufacturing Summary		956 780
			(Closing the income statement accounts with debit balances)		
4.					
	June	30	Finished Goods Inventory	201 500	
			Sales	1 400 000	
			Profit or Loss Summary		1 601 500
			(Establishing the ending finished goods inventory and closing the Sales account)		
5.					
	June	30	Profit or Loss Summary	77 320	
			Retained Earnings		77 320
			(Closing profit to Retained Earnings)		

Note that all of the account balances used in the closing process are taken directly from the worksheet. The first entry includes all debit balances in the manufacturing section of the worksheet. The second entry sets up the ending raw materials and work in process inventories, which are shown as credits in the manufacturing section of the worksheet. The balance left in the Manufacturing Summary account after the second closing entry is $956 780, which is the cost of goods manufactured for the period. The $956 780 balance is closed along with the other debit balances of the income statement section of the worksheet in the third closing entry. In the fourth entry, the ending finished goods inventory is established and the sales for the year are closed to profit or loss summary. The credit balance left in the Profit or Loss Summary account is $77 320, which is the annual profit. The final closing entry transfers the profit to the Retained Earnings account.

Valuation of inventories in manufacturing

When a periodic inventory system is used in a manufacturing entity such as Fast Fones Industries Pty Ltd, the three types of inventory must be valued using a physical stocktake at the end of an accounting period before the financial statements can be prepared. The worksheet shown in figure 8.8 indicates that the ending balances of raw materials, work in process and finished goods are $71 500, $50 700 and $201 500 respectively. Remember that a periodic inventory system requires that the inventory items must be counted and costed to determine the value of the ending inventories. The valuation of the raw materials inventory is relatively straightforward because it is very similar to the procedures used for inventory in a retail business. A count is made and the cost is determined from original purchase invoices.

The valuation of work in process and finished goods with a periodic inventory approach is more complex. As figure 8.1 (p. 341) illustrates, the production flow used to convert raw materials to finished goods is a constant process. Yet we must 'freeze' the process at the end of a period for accounting purposes to count and place a value on the ending inventories without the benefit of detailed records concerning the costs incurred during production. Because of the addition of direct labour costs and factory overhead costs during the period, the ending work in process and finished goods inventories are in different forms from how they were at the beginning of the manufacturing process.

The question is: 'How much of the total manufacturing costs incurred should be assigned to the ending inventories and how much should be charged to the cost of goods manufactured?'

A manufacturing entity using a periodic inventory system must rely on the judgement of the accountant and the production manager to estimate the value of the ending work in process and finished goods inventories. The amount of direct materials costs applicable to the ending inventory normally can be found by referring to the product specifications for the units in work in process and finished goods. Each finished product will require a certain amount of direct materials compatible with its quality level and selling price. The same product specifications will indicate how much labour cost should be required to complete a product. Based on the percentage of completion for the various products in the ending inventories, managers can assign an approximate amount of labour that *should* have been used.

As factory overhead cost is not traceable directly to the products manufactured, a predetermined overhead application rate is used to assign factory overhead costs to inventories. When a periodic inventory system is used, a common practice is to express factory overhead cost as a percentage of direct labour costs. The use of this predetermined overhead application rate is based on the assumption that the ratio of factory overhead costs to direct labour costs is the same for all products produced during the period. The overhead rate is multiplied by the direct labour cost estimated for the ending work in process and finished goods inventories so that factory overhead cost can be charged to each of the inventories.

In the Fast Fones Industries Pty Ltd example, factory overhead costs of $268 380 and direct labour costs of $497 000 were incurred. The overhead application rate is, therefore, $268 380 ÷ $497 000 or 54% of direct labour cost. Consequently, 54 cents of factory overhead cost will be assigned as product costs for every dollar of direct labour cost.

We assume that the procedures discussed in this section have been used to value Fast Fones Industries Pty Ltd's ending inventories. The amounts of direct materials cost, direct labour cost and factory overhead cost assigned to work in process and finished goods are the following — based on management's estimates of the direct costs incurred and the use of the 54% overhead application rate:

	Direct materials	Direct labour	Factory overhead	Total
Work in process	$24 674	$ 16 900	$ 9 126	$ 50 700
Finished goods	46 345	100 750	54 405	201 500

Limitations of a periodic inventory system

We must emphasise that only a small manufacturing entity can use a periodic inventory system. Even then, the results may not be adequate to satisfy the cost information needs of management. Product costs are calculated in manufacturing for three basic purposes: (1) *inventory valuation*, (2) *profit determination*, and (3) *management decision-making applications* such as product pricing by marketing staff, cost control by production managers or engineers, product profitability analysis by accountants and resource allocation by senior management. As we can see in the Fast Fones Industries Pty Ltd example, the cost information will be available only at the end of an accounting period after physical stocktakes and estimates have been made for raw materials, work in process and finished goods. The cost information from a periodic inventory system will not be sufficiently timely, reliable and detailed to serve the day-to-day needs of management except in extremely simple situations.

Counting and pricing an ending inventory is very time-consuming — particularly for work in process and finished goods inventories. Consequently, a complete inventory is usually taken only at the end of the financial year despite the fact that management needs the information for decisions that must be made regularly throughout the period. We noted in the Fast Fone Industries Pty Ltd example that rough approximations may be the only measures possible for the ending work in process and finished goods inventories. Any errors made with the estimates will have a direct effect on the profit reported for the period and the management decision-making process.

In addition, management may have trouble controlling costs over time because the cost results are not adequately detailed. Since unit costs for each product are not calculated, it will be difficult to evaluate the effect of changes in costs between periods. Management typically needs to relate the cost information to products and to responsibility centres.

The deficiencies of a periodic inventory system increase with the number of products and producing departments. A cost accounting system is used by many manufacturing entities to correct the deficiencies of a periodic inventory system. Cost accounting provides management with the cost information necessary to plan, control and evaluate the performance of the production function. Perpetual inventories are maintained so the cost information is timely, reliable and detailed. The emphasis of cost accounting is on unit cost determination for each type of product rather than the total cost of goods manufactured during the period. The two types of cost accounting systems, job order costing and process costing, are discussed in the next chapter.

8.7 Sustainable manufacturing

Learning objective 7

Understand how designing for sustainability contributes to minimising and controlling manufacturing costs

Increasingly, manufacturing entities are concerned about the sustainability of their operations. Not only is this a general social issue of interest to customers and, therefore, potentially part of entities' marketing strategies, but it is also a practical way in which to control and minimise costs. That is, a focus on the environmental impact and sustainability of the manufacturing process can lead to improved efficiencies in production and cost savings.

Companies are increasingly trying to improve sustainability through changes in product design and manufacturing processes. This is considered necessary for long-term survival as the costs of non-renewable resources continue to escalate. Therefore, where possible, non-renewable resources based on products such as oil may be redesigned to be manufactured with renewable inputs. For example, synthetic materials for clothing are increasingly being replaced with material made from products such as bamboo and even banana plants. By-products of food production are being used for making cloth. This becomes economically more viable as the cost of oil-based products rises.

As a part of designing, or redesigning, manufacturing processes to reduce environmental impacts and costs, strategies such as reduction, recycling and remanufacturing are considered.[1] Reduction is related to waste minimisation and must be considered in the design phase of a product. For example, shoes may be designed to maximise the number of parts that may be cut from a piece of leather and, therefore, minimise waste. Reduction in wastage also involves minimising the number of defective products in the manufacturing process and, therefore, the number of products scrapped rather than sold to customers. This helps minimise manufacturing costs. Recycling can be on two levels: reuse within the entity of resources from the production process. For example, reusing water within a manufacturing process rather than always using fresh water can reduce costs where water has to be paid for. Recycling can also occur after production by using materials that can be recycled at the end of the product's useful life. Remanufacturing involves disassembling products to recycle the materials from the after-market of the products. Increasingly, manufacturers are considering making as many parts of products reusable or recyclable as possible. In Australia, it now usually costs customers to dispose of products such as computers and television sets when they take them to recycling depots.

The case of Mercedes-Benz in the business knowledge vignette is a good example of the relationship between manufacturing costs and designing and manufacturing for sustainability. For Mercedes-Benz, manufacturing for sustainability began with implementing 'Design for Environment' (DfE) to ensure that all environmental issues were considered at the earliest phase of development. This included eco-balancing, disassembly and recycling planning, materials and process engineering, design and production. This use of DfE is good for the environment and sustainability. As well as any goodwill generated, DfE is also likely to improve profitability through cost control and minimisation over the life cycle of the vehicles Mercedes-Benz manufactures.

While traditionally ignored, it is now essential that in developing products, reduction, recycling and remanufacturing are incorporated in manufacturing planning to minimise and control manufacturing costs. Not only does this approach provide the immediate benefits of lowering costs through reducing waste, but as resources become scarce, recycling and remanufacturing will increasingly become the more cost-effective solutions to manufacturing.

BUSINESS KNOWLEDGE

New Mercedes-Benz E-Class awarded environmental certificate

The environmental compatibility of the all-new Mercedes-Benz E-Class has now been confirmed by the independent examiners at the German organisation TÜV Süd. The E-Class received the much sought-after environmental certificate according to ISO standard 14062 on 'International Environment Day 2009'. This award honours the commitment of the Daimler group to comprehensive environmental protection, which is firmly embedded in the operating guidelines for the entire corporation.

In the development on the all-new E-Class, environmental certification of this model involved the examination of more than 40 000 individual, environment-related processes, which were analysed, quantified and assessed to produce an all-round eco-profile.

For the E-Class this work began with the environmentally compatible product development process known as 'Design for Environment' (DfE). Integrating 'DfE' into the development process ensured that all environment-related aspects were already taken into account during the very earliest development phase.

Special 'DfE' teams made up of engineers from a wide range of specialist departments ensured compliance with the declared environmental aims, for example in the areas of eco-balancing, disassembly and recycling planning, materials and process engineering, design and production.

Chief Environmental Officer of Daimler AG, Professor Herbert Kohler: 'Daimler AG is an environment-oriented automobile company, and therefore considers itself to have particular responsibilities in this regard. We analyse the environmental compatibility of our models over their entire life cycle — from production and many years of use right up to eventual recycling and disposal'.

Source: Excerpts from Mercedes-Benz Australia, 'New Mercedes-Benz E-Class Awarded Environmental Certificate', www2.mercedes-benz.com.au.

1. Joseph Sarkis, 'Manufacturing's role in corporate environmental sustainability: concerns for the new millennium', *International Journal of Operations & Production Management,* vol. 21, no. 5/6, 2001, pp. 666–86.

Absorption costing, p. 346
Conversion costs, p. 346
Cost, p. 340
Cost behaviour, p. 346
Cost of goods manufactured statement, p. 347
Direct costing, p. 346
Direct labour cost, p. 344
Direct materials cost, p. 344
Expense, p. 340

Factory overhead cost, p. 344
Finished goods, p. 342
Fixed costs, p. 346
Manufacturing business, p. 340
Manufacturing cost elements, p. 343
Manufacturing worksheet, p. 351
Overhead application rate, p. 345

Period costs, p. 343
Prime cost, p. 344
Product costs, p. 343
Production departments, p. 344
Raw materials, p. 342
Service departments, p. 344
Variable costs, p. 346
Work in process, p. 342

DISCUSSION QUESTIONS

1. Many people confuse the terms *cost* and *expense*. Using an example, explain the difference between a cost and an expense.

2. 'Accounting for cost of sales in a manufacturing entity creates no more problems than those encountered in a retail entity.' Discuss.

3. As the new marketing manager for Phones 'R' Us, a company that manufactures mobile phones, you need to learn about the accounting system for the business. Why is it important that marketing managers have some understanding of the accounting processes in the manufacturing business for which they work?

4. 'Variable costs can be distinguished from fixed costs if one keeps in mind that unit cost is fixed in the case of variable costs and is variable for fixed costs.' Discuss.

5. The senior management of a manufacturing entity decided to overhaul its approach to managerial performance evaluation. Paul Tyler, manager in charge of production, is informed that as a result of the new policy he will be held responsible 'only for controllable costs, i.e. the direct costs of production'. Tyler is upset at this decision by senior management. Whose position would you support as a fellow manager? Explain.

6. As a graduate accountant, one of the first things you have been asked to do by your employer, Smart Manufacturing Systems Pty Ltd, is to write a memo to senior management explaining the difference between absorption and direct costing. Write the memo and explain which one is required by the accounting standard on inventories.

7. Medal Manufacturers Pty Ltd is a small manufacturing business that houses its manufacturing operations, selling activities and administration activities in the one building. The insurance premium on this building is $1800 for the reporting period concerned. Recommend how this cost should be assigned to production costs, selling costs and administrative activities.

8. 'Accounting for inventories for a manufacturer is rather pointless if the periodic system of inventory is used. Only by using the perpetual inventory system can meaningful information for management decision making become available.' Discuss.

9. You are the new accountant for Ted Cowpitt, who runs his own small pottery manufacturing business. Ted says, 'I can't see why it is so difficult to work out the value of my pottery inventory. Surely you just need to know roughly how much clay is used in each one and multiply that by the cost of clay?' Explain to Ted how his pottery inventories would need to be valued and why it is more complicated than just the cost of the clay used.

10. There are differences between the inventories of a manufacturing entity and a retail entity. Do these differences have any effects on the financial statements of the two types of entities? Explain.

LO 2

Exercise 8.1 PRODUCT OR PERIOD COSTS

Classify the following items as either product costs or period costs:

1. depreciation on a vehicle used by the entity's general manager
2. containers used to package finished goods
3. salaries of workers handling inventory during production
4. rent on the premises
5. lease payments on a motor vehicle used by sales representatives
6. superannuation contributions for production workers by the entity.

LO 2

Exercise 8.2 PRODUCT AND PERIOD COSTS

As the Human Resources manager for Beautiful Bottles Pty Ltd, bottle manufacturers for the food industry, you have been asked by the accountant to help reduce the product costs of each bottle. You have compiled the following information to help with the decision:

Number of bottles produced each year	3 300 000
Production supervisor's salary	$120 000
Senior production staff wages (2 staff @ $70 000 each)	$140 000
Junior production staff wages (10 staff @ $40 000 each)	$400 000

You are considering two options. The first option is to replace one of the senior production staff with a junior staff member. This option will reduce the amount of quality control checks that the company can perform. The second option is to not replace two of the junior staff when they resign. This will reduce the number of bottles produced by 300 000 bottles per year.

Required

A. Explain what some of the qualitative factors are that may arise from each of the two options being considered and whether these may favour one option over the other.
B. Calculate the direct labour cost per bottle under the current conditions and each of the two proposed options.
C. Using the qualitative factors from requirement A and the quantitative factors from requirement B, explain which option you would consider the best for Beautiful Bottles Pty Ltd.

LO 4

Exercise 8.3 BASIC COST BEHAVIOUR

Goode Computers Pty Ltd produces laptops. Each computer contains a rechargeable battery and LCD screen, which is purchased from an outside supplier for $96 and $150 each, respectively. The production process is highly automated with an annual depreciation charge of $720 000.

Required

A. What are per computer and total costs of the rechargeable batteries and LCD screens for 10 computers, 100 computers, 1000 computers and 10 000 computers?
B. What is the depreciation charge per computer if 1000 computers are produced each year? What would it be for 10 000 computers?
C. What kind of cost behaviour is evident in requirements A and B?

LO 3

Exercise 8.4 ALLOCATION OF OVERHEAD

As the marketing manager for Fast Fones Industries Pty Ltd you have asked the accountant what it costs to make the FFI2020 model as you want to set a price for the phone. A similar phone produced by a competitor sells for $420. Your usual pricing policy is to set the price of phones at the cost of manufacturing plus 100%.

The accountant has given you the following costs:

Direct materials	$192
Direct labour	3
Factory overhead per phone if allocated on direct labour hours	16
Factory overhead per phone if allocated on labour costs	20
Factory overhead per phone if allocated on machine hours	10

Required

Calculate the cost and the price of the FFI2020 using each of the factory overhead rates that the accountant has supplied. How do the different allocation methods for factory overhead affect the pricing of the FFI2020 compared with the price of the competition, and what are the likely implications of this for the marketability of the phone?

LO 5

Exercise 8.5   INCOME STATEMENT

Listed below are selected financial data from the accounting records of Large Ltd for the year ended 30 June 2013.

Cost of goods manufactured	$ 676 000
Ending finished goods	90 000
Income	1 760 000
Beginning finished goods	72 000
Selling and administrative expenses	400 600

Required

Prepare an income statement for the year ended 30 June 2013.

LO 5

Exercise 8.6   COST OF GOODS MANUFACTURED STATEMENT AND ANALYSIS

Listed below are selected financial data extracted from the accounting records of Lee Yew Tan Manufacturing Pty Ltd for the year ended 30 June 2013.

Beginning raw materials	$ 93 600
Ending raw materials	90 720
Beginning work in process	72 000
Ending work in process	63 360
Direct labour	603 300
Factory overhead	359 436
Purchases of raw materials	248 304

Required

A. Prepare a cost of goods manufactured statement for the year ended 30 June 2013.
B. Calculate ratios of each of the major manufacturing costs to the total manufacturing costs for the period.
C. Using your answers to part B and the business knowledge vignette on page 345, explain whether the mix of costs reflects a 1950s production technique or one from the 2000s. How could the mix of costs be changed to modernise production techniques?

LO 5

Exercise 8.7   COST OF GOODS MANUFACTURED STATEMENT AND ANALYSIS

Below is selected financial data extracted from the accounting records of Wilson Manufacturing Pty Ltd for the year ended 30 June 2014.

Beginning work in process	$ 362 600
Ending work in process	452 200
Beginning raw materials	263 600
Ending raw materials	195 400
Indirect materials	342 000
Purchases of raw materials	1 546 000
Direct labour	403 550
Indirect labour	123 800
Sundry factory overhead	1 551 950

Required

A. Prepare a cost of goods manufactured statement for the year ended 30 June 2014.
B. Calculate ratios of each of the major manufacturing costs to the total manufacturing costs for the period.
C. Using your answers to part B and the business knowledge vignette on page 345 explain whether the mix of costs reflects a 1950s production technique or one from the 2000s.

Exercise 8.8 WORK IN PROCESS

Information from the records of Paddy & Co. for the year ended 30 June 2013 is given below.

Factory overhead, 200% of direct labour cost	$240 000
Raw materials inventory, 1 July 2012	24 000
Cost of goods manufactured	620 800
Raw materials inventory, 30 June 2013	25 500
Work in process inventory, 30 June 2013	50 500
Raw materials purchased during the year	210 000

Required

Calculate the cost of work in process inventory on 1 July 2012.

Exercise 8.9 WORK IN PROCESS

Information from the records of Oscar & Co. for the year ended 30 June 2014 is given below.

Factory overhead, 150% of direct material cost	$?
Direct labour	120 000
Raw material inventory, 1/7/13	65 000
Cost of goods manufactured	2 198 750
Raw materials inventory, 30/6/14	72 300
Work in process inventory, 1/7/13	243 500
Raw materials purchased during the year	820 000

Required

Calculate the ending work in process inventory on 30 June 2014.

Exercise 8.10 DIFFERENT COSTS FOR DIFFERENT PURPOSES

Management uses different costs for different purposes in decision making. Included in the different costs are product costs, period costs, variable costs and fixed costs.

Required

As a manager, choose the concept of cost mentioned above that best describes the cost involved in each of the following situations:

1. Depreciation for printing equipment used for this book is a _____ cost on the income statement. It is a _____ cost in terms of cost behaviour.
2. The paper used to produce this book is a _____ cost on the income statement. It is also a _____ cost in terms of cost behaviour.
3. A commission paid to the sales representative who sold this book is a _____ cost on the income statement.
4. A _____ cost could be called an inventoriable cost because this type of cost is treated as an asset on the balance sheet unless the related item is sold.
5. The costs of operating a service department are classified as _____ costs as far as the products produced are concerned.
6. Depreciation for the delivery vehicle used by the sales representative is a _____ cost on the income statement. In terms of cost behaviour, it is a _____ cost.

Exercise 8.11 VALUATION OF MANUFACTURING INVENTORIES

During the year ended 30 June 2014, Amila Ltd incurred the following costs of manufacture.

Direct labour	$ 652 800
Direct materials	890 500
Factory overhead	1 827 840

The company charges factory overhead costs to work in process inventory and finished goods inventory, using an overhead application rate based on direct labour costs.

Required

A. Determine the company's overhead application rate.
B. If the company's ending finished goods inventory of $128 420 included $18 600 of direct materials costs, determine the inventory's labour and overhead costs.

Exercise 8.12 VALUATION OF MANUFACTURING INVENTORIES

During the year ended 30 June 2014 Bishop Ltd incurred the following costs of manufacture.

Direct labour	$ 375 600
Direct material	1 427 800
Factory overhead	3 426 720

The company charges factory overhead costs to work in process inventory and finished goods inventory using an overhead application rate based on direct materials costs.

Required
A. Determine the company's overhead application rate.
B. If the company's ending finished goods inventory of $420 800 included $12 800 of direct labour costs, determine the inventory's material and overhead costs.

Exercise 8.13 MANUFACTURING STATEMENT WITH MISSING DATA

For each company below, fill in the missing data. Each company is independent.

Income Statement

	Company X	Company Y	Company Z
Sales	?	$154 400	$80 300
Beginning finished goods	?	36 300	8 500
Cost of goods manufactured	$ 96 200	?	32 600
Ending finished goods	38 000	50 800	?
Cost of sales	88 000	?	35 300
Gross profit	106 600	?	?
Expenses	?	61 200	21 000
Profit	70 000	?	?
Beginning work in process	25 800	28 400	?
Direct labour	36 500	50 800	12 500
Raw materials used	22 000	42 800	11 800
Factory overhead	28 800	36 600	13 400
Ending work in process	?	72 600	14 200

Exercise 8.14 MANUFACTURING STATEMENT WITH MISSING DATA

For each company below, fill in the missing data. Each company is independent.

Income Statement

	Company A	Company B	Company C
Sales	$640 000	?	$240 000
Beginning finished goods	?	$ 24 500	15 600
Cost of goods manufactured	395 400	?	122 700
Ending finished goods	48 000	13 100	?
Cost of sales	?	392 000	120 000
Gross profit	256 000	168 000	?
Operating expenses	?	117 600	?
Profit	76 800	?	84 000
Beginning work in process	38 600	16 200	?
Direct labour	?	128 000	84 300
Raw materials used	37 500	62 000	12 300
Factory overhead	319 500	192 900	27 800
Ending work in process	43 200	?	11 200

Exercise 8.15 USE OF RAW MATERIALS

Precision Balls Ltd produces and sells high-quality lawn bowls sets. Each set of balls is contained in a wooden carrying case, which is purchased from an outside supplier. The wooden cases are held as raw materials inventory until they are placed into production and combined with the lawn bowls. The production and purchasing departments have provided the following information for the month of March.

1. Beginning raw materials inventory of wooden cases was 760 at a cost of $19 000.
2. The company purchased 1600 additional cases at $25 each.
3. 1800 cases were transferred to production.
4. 120 cases were given to managers of possible retail outlets for promotional purposes.

Of the cases placed into production, 65% were combined with lawn bowls sets, which were then transferred to finished goods. Of the cases transferred to finished goods during March, 70% had been sold by the end of the month. There was no beginning inventory of wooden cases in finished goods or in work in process.

Required
Determine the cost of the wooden cases that would be included in the following accounts as at 31 March:

1. raw materials
2. work in process
3. finished goods
4. selling expense
5. cost of sales.

PROBLEMS

★ Basic

★★ Moderate

★★★ Challenging

Problem 8.1 COST OF GOODS MANUFACTURED STATEMENT ★

Juang Ltd's accountant recently prepared the following data from the company's accounting records for the year ended 30 June 2013:

Sales	$1 200 300
Inventories at 1 July 2012:	
Raw materials	75 600
Work in process	53 800
Finished goods	94 500
Inventories at 30 June 2013:	
Raw materials	72 300
Work in process	51 400
Finished goods	97 200
Direct labour	114 000
Purchases of raw materials	324 000
Selling expenses	118 300

Factory overhead is applied at the rate of 240% of direct labour cost.

Required
A. Prepare a cost of goods manufactured statement for the year ended 30 June 2013.
B. What was the company's cost of sales for the year ended 30 June 2013?
C. What was the company's gross profit for the year ended 30 June 2013?

During the year ended 30 June 2013, Krakatoa Manufacturing Pty Ltd incurred the following costs in connection with its production activities.

Raw materials purchases	$195 000
Factory electricity	35 500
Indirect labour	45 000
Direct labour	41 375
Depreciation on manufacturing equipment	32 500
Plant rent	28 000
Supplies used in production	11 500
Repairs to manufacturing equipment	13 000

The beginning and ending inventory values were:

	Beginning inventory	Ending inventory
Raw materials	$14 200	$11 800
Work in process	26 200	31 000
Finished goods	43 250	37 500

Required

A. Calculate the relationship between factory overhead costs and direct labour cost.

B. Prepare a cost of goods manufactured statement for the year ending 30 June 2013.

C. Prepare closing entries using the Manufacturing Summary account.

D. Prepare the general journal entry to close the Manufacturing Summary account.

As the marketing manager for Fancy Fones Industries Ltd, you have asked the accountant what it costs to make the fFone2000 model because you want to set a price for the phone. A similar phone produced by a competitor sells for $600. Your usual pricing policy is to set the price of phones at twice the cost of manufacturing them. The accountant has not been entirely helpful in giving you the following costs:

Direct materials	$90
Direct labour	15
If allocated on direct labour hours (DLH) factory overhead per phone is $760 per DLH and each phone takes ¼ DLH to manufacture.	
If allocated on labour costs factory overhead per phone is 10 times direct labour costs.	
If allocated on machine hours (MH) factory overhead per phone is $400 per MH and each phone take ½ MH to manufacture.	

Required

A. Assuming that the total factory overhead to be allocated to the various phone models produced by Fancy Fones Industries Ltd is $2 400 000, what are the implications of allocating too much, or too little, factory overhead to the cost of each fFone2000?

B. Calculate the cost and the price of the fFone2000 using each of the factory overhead rates that the accountant has supplied. How do the different allocation methods for factory overhead affect the pricing of the fFone2000 compared with the price of the competition, and what are the likely implications of this for how well the phone does in the phone market?

Problem 8.4 MISSING DATA FOR MANUFACTURING ENTITIES ★★

Incomplete information concerning the financial performance of two manufacturing companies is presented below.

	Company A	Company B
Work in process, 1/7/12	$ 10 500	$ 23 500
Work in process, 30/6/13	(a)	23 800
Direct materials used	35 800	41 250
Direct labour	18 500	(e)
Factory overhead	250 000	224 300
Sales income	314 650	417 000
Accounts receivable, 1/7/12	54 150	61 800
Accounts receivable, 30/6/13	46 800	58 050
Cost of sales	(b)	302 500
Finished goods, 1/7/12	23 500	17 500
Finished goods, 30/6/13	(c)	16 750
Gross profit	15 850	(f)
Cost of goods manufactured	303 500	(d)

Required

Determine the answers to (a) to (f) for the two companies.

Problem 8.5 INCOME STATEMENT FROM CLOSING ENTRIES ★★

Bigwood's Manufacturing Ltd uses a periodic inventory system and closes its accounts on 30 June each year. The company's closing entries made on 30 June 2013 were as shown below.

June	30	Manufacturing Summary	405 060	
		Raw Materials Inventory		10 200
		Work in Process Inventory		26 400
		Raw Materials Purchases		80 630
		Freight Inwards		2 450
		Direct Labour		20 060
		Factory Overhead		265 320
	30	Raw Materials Inventory	12 400	
		Work in Process Inventory	29 750	
		Manufacturing Summary		42 150
	30	Profit or Loss Summary	523 510	
		Finished Goods Inventory		32 000
		Selling and Distribution Expenses		61 800
		Administrative Expenses		54 300
		Finance and Other Expenses		12 500
		Manufacturing Summary		362 910
	30	Finished Goods Inventory	28 400	
		Sales	680 500	
		Profit or Loss Summary		708 900
	30	Profit or Loss Summary	185 390	
		Retained Earnings		185 390

Required

A. Prepare a cost of goods manufactured statement for the year ended 30 June 2013.
B. Prepare an income statement for the year ended 30 June 2013.

Problem 8.6   MISSING DATA FOR MANUFACTURING ENTITIES ★★

Two cases of data concerning production costs, other expenses and sales are presented below:

	Case 1	Case 2
Beginning work in process	28 000	(h)
Ending work in process	(b)	51 500
Direct materials cost	108 500	(g)
Direct labour	36 500	33 000
Factory overhead	283 500	167 500
Total manufacturing costs	(a)	348 000
Cost of goods manufactured	431 000	334 000
Sales income	523 100	(l)
Beginning finished goods inventory	(c)	57 750
Ending finished goods inventory	35 000	41 250
Cost of goods available for sale	463 500	(j)
Cost of sales	(d)	(k)
Gross profit	(e)	118 000
Expenses	58 750	(i)
Profit	(f)	38 000

Required

A. Calculate the missing amounts for the letters (a) to (l).

B. Using the data in Case 1, prepare a cost of goods manufactured statement.

C. Using the data in Case 1, prepare an income statement.

D. Using the data in Case 2, and additional data consisting of cash at bank $70 000, accounts receivable $200 000, raw materials inventory $9900 and prepaid expenses $800, prepare the current assets section of the balance sheet.

Problem 8.7   COST OF GOODS MANUFACTURED SCHEDULE ★★

An analysis of the accounts of Maloney Manufacturing reveals the following manufacturing cost data for the month ended 30 June 2013.

	Beginning	Ending
Inventories:		
Raw materials	$ 7 000	$11 100
Work in process	5 000	9 000
Finished goods	8 000	6 000
Costs incurred:		
Raw materials purchases	$64 000	
Direct labour	50 000	
Manufacturing overhead	30 000	
Specific overhead costs:		
Indirect labour	$15 600	
Factory insurance	4 000	
Machinery depreciation	4 000	
Machinery repairs	1 800	
Factory utilities	3 100	
Miscellaneous factory costs	1 500	

Required

A. Prepare the cost of goods manufactured schedule for the month ended 30 June 2013.

B. Show the presentation of the ending inventories on the 30 June 2013 balance sheet.

Problem 8.8 COST OF GOODS MANUFACTURED AND INCOME STATEMENTS ★★

The following accounts and amounts (balances are normal balances) were taken from the records of Prider Manufacturers Ltd at 30 June 2014:

Advertising expense	$ 60 000	Administrative office rent	$ 30 000
Sales travel expense	18 300	Office salaries	211 200
Depreciation – factory machinery	19 200	Rates – factory	24 000
Depreciation – office equipment	7 200	Discounts received on raw materials	4 000
Direct labour	195 000	Raw materials inventory, 1/7/13	57 600
Factory power	18 000	Raw materials inventory, 30/6/14	62 400
Factory rent	120 000	Raw materials purchases	640 000
Factory supplies	148 000	Sales revenue	1 900 000
Finished goods, 1/7/13	130 000	Sales returns	31 400
Finished goods, 30/6/14	125 000	Sales commissions	57 300
Freight inwards (materials)	8 700	Work in process, 1/7/13	27 000
Indirect labour	64 000	Work in process, 30/6/14	30 000
Machinery repairs	38 900		

Note: All amounts exclude GST.

Required

A. Prepare a cost of goods manufactured statement for the year ended 30 June 2014.

B. Prepare an income statement for the year ended 30 June 2014.

C. The industry average for gross profit margin is 30%, and the profit margin is 10%. Explain how Prider Manufacturers Ltd's financial performance compares with the industry average.

Problem 8.9 COST OF GOODS MANUFACTURED SCHEDULE ★★   LO 6

The following data were taken from the records of Manik Manufacturing Ltd for the year ended 31 December 2013.

Raw materials inventory, 1/1/13	$ 40 000	Freight-in on raw materials purchased	$ 3 900
Raw materials inventory, 31/12/13	44 200	Factory utilities	15 900
Finished goods inventory, 1/1/13	85 000	Office utilities expense	8 600
Finished goods inventory, 31/12/13	72 800	Sales	495 000
Work in process inventory, 1/1/13	9 500	Sales discounts	3 500
Work in process inventory, 31/12/13	8 000	Plant manager's salary	40 000
Direct labour	145 100	Factory rent	61 000
Indirect labour	19 100	Factory repairs	800
Accounts receivable	27 000	Raw materials purchases	64 600
Factory insurance	5 400	Cash	28 000
Factory machinery depreciation	7 700		

Required

A. Prepare the cost of goods manufactured schedule for the year ended 31 December 2013.

B. Prepare an income statement for the year ended 31 December 2013 as far as gross profit.

C. Prepare the current assets section of the balance sheet as at 31 December 2013.

Problem 8.10 MANUFACTURING WORKSHEET ★★   LO 6

You are provided with the worksheet shown on page 369 for Norman Pty Ltd for the year ended 30 June 2014. The adjustments have already been made and the worksheet begins with the adjusted trial balance.

Assume all insurance relates to the factory. Closing inventory balances at 30 June 2014 were $54 000 for finished goods, $16 400 for work in process and $8500 for raw materials.

Required

Complete the worksheet for Norman Pty Ltd.

NORMAN PTY LTD
Worksheet
for the year ended 30 June 2014

Account	Adjusted trial balance		Manufacturing		Income statement		Balance sheet	
	Debit	Credit	Debit	Credit	Debit	Credit	Debit	Credit
Cash at Bank	20 500							
Accounts Receivable	32 600							
Finished Goods	60 000							
Work in Process	14 000							
Raw Materials	16 800							
Prepaid Insurance	8 000							
Machinery and Equipment	360 500							
Accum. Depr. – Machinery & Equipment		150 000						
Accounts Payable		28 600						
Loan Payable		120 000						
Share Capital		60 500						
Retained Earnings		65 000						
Sales		804 500						
Purchases – Raw Materials	252 000							
Direct Labour	62 800							
Indirect Labour	27 000							
Factory Supplies	52 000							
Depreciation Expense – Factory	25 700							
Depreciation Expense – Office	3 600							
Electricity	4 300							
Rent	96 000							
Insurance	64 000							
Rates & Taxes	12 600							
Selling & Distribution Expenses	53 600							
Administrative & Office Expenses	32 800							
Sales Commissions	12 200							
Interest Expense	17 600							
	1 228 600	1 228 600						
Cost of Goods Manufactured								
Profit								

Problem 8.11   CLOSING ENTRIES FOR A MANUFACTURING ENTITY ★★   **LO 6**

You are provided with the cost of goods manufactured statement and income statement for Hossain Manufacturing Pty Ltd.

Required

Prepare the closing entries for Hossain Manufacturing Pty Ltd.

HOSSAIN MANUFACTURING PTY LTD
Cost of Goods Manufactured Statement
for the year ended 30 June 2013

Direct materials:		
Beginning raw materials	$ 53 800	
Purchases	155 680	
Freight inwards	2 500	
	211 980	
Ending raw materials	57 200	
Direct materials used		$154 780
Direct labour		398 000
Factory overhead:		
Consumables	2 560	
Depreciation expense (plant and equipment)	14 800	
Electricity	46 200	
Indirect labour	62 800	
Insurance	24 000	
Rent of factory	54 200	
Sundry expenses	3 400	
Supplies	7 650	215 610
Total manufacturing costs for the period		768 390
Beginning work in process		39 200
Total work in process		807 590
Ending work in process		40 560
COST OF GOODS MANUFACTURED		$767 030

HOSSAIN MANUFACTURING PTY LTD
Income Statement
for the year ended 30 June 2013

INCOME			
Sales revenue			$1 100 000
Less: Cost of sales:			
Beginning finished goods inventory		$160 000	
Cost of goods manufactured		767 030	
Goods available for sale		927 030	
Ending finished goods inventory		162 000	
Cost of sales			765 030
GROSS PROFIT			334 970
EXPENSES			
Selling and distribution expenses:			
Advertising	$ 16 600		
Sales salaries	98 000		
Other selling expenses	9 340	123 940	
Administrative expenses:			
Administrative salaries	125 500		
Other administrative expenses	9 000	134 500	
Finance and other expenses:			
Interest expense		3 600	262 040
PROFIT BEFORE TAX			72 930
Income tax expense			22 000
PROFIT			$ 50 930

Problem 8.12 MANUFACTURING WORKSHEET AND MANUFACTURING COST
STATEMENT ★★★

The unadjusted trial balance of Gremlins Pty Ltd on 30 June 2013 is presented below:

GREMLINS PTY LTD
Unadjusted Trial Balance
as at 30 June 2013

	Debit	Credit
Cash at bank	$ 60 000	
Trade debtors	85 120	
Finished goods inventory, 1/7/12	145 000	
Work in process, 1/7/12	80 000	
Raw materials inventory, 1/7/12	37 500	
Prepaid insurance	12 000	
Machinery and equipment	400 000	
Accumulated depreciation – machinery and equipment		$ 140 000
Trade creditors		83 750
Loan payable		120 000
Share capital		300 000
Retained earnings		98 780
Sales		3 513 600
Purchases – raw materials	1 645 000	
Direct labour	420 000	
Indirect labour	105 000	
Factory supplies	140 700	
Electricity	102 250	
Rent	180 000	
Insurance	80 600	
Rates and taxes	37 500	
Selling and distribution expenses	154 500	
Administrative and office expenses	210 000	
Sales commissions	351 360	
Interest expense	9 000	
	$4 256 130	$4 256 130

The following additional information is available:
1. The inventories as of 30 June 2013 were:

Raw materials	$32 000
Work in process	82 000
Finished goods	163 750

2. The Machinery and Equipment account comprises $250 000 of factory machinery and the balance of office equipment. All machinery and equipment is depreciated using the straight-line method over an 8-year life. There were no plant and equipment acquisitions or disposals during 2012–13.
3. On 1 May 2013 the company paid $12 000 for 12 months insurance cover on the factory. Prepaid Insurance was debited at the time of the transaction.
4. Accrued expenses at year-end but not yet recorded: direct labour, $10 000; indirect labour, $3500; selling and distribution expenses, $20 000.
5. All electricity, rent, rates and taxes, and insurance are charged to factory operations.
6. An additional stationery expense payable of $1500 is to be recorded and treated as an administrative expense. No invoice has been received.
7. Ignore income tax.

Required

A. Prepare a worksheet including pairs of columns for unadjusted trial balance, adjustments, manufacturing, and the financial statements.
B. Prepare a cost of goods manufactured statement for the year ended 30 June 2013.
C. Prepare the closing entries assuming use of a Manufacturing Summary account.
D. Calculate the relationship between overhead and direct labour costs. Using that relationship, calculate the labour and overhead included in the ending inventories if work in process ending inventory contains $25 200 of raw materials and $38 000 of raw materials is included in the finished goods ending inventory.

Problem 8.13   MANUFACTURING WORKSHEET ★★★   **LO 6**

The listing of the ledger accounts (unadjusted) of Papayianis Manufacturing Co. Ltd at 30 June 2013 is presented below. All ledger balances are normal balances.

PAPAYIANIS MANUFACTURING CO. LTD
Unadjusted List of Accounts
as at 30 June 2013

	Balance
Cash at bank	$ 22 050
Accounts receivable	55 450
Finished goods inventory, 1/7/12	34 500
Work in process, 1/7/12	11 250
Raw materials inventory, 1/7/12	5 550
Prepaid rent	81 000
Machinery and equipment	294 000
Accumulated depreciation	52 500
Accounts payable	27 000
Loan payable	112 500
Share capital	70 000
Retained earnings	55 500
Sales	1 290 000
Direct labour	324 000
Raw materials purchases	307 500
Indirect labour	106 500
Factory supplies	27 000
Electricity and gas	84 000
Insurance	24 450
Factory rent	47 250
Selling and distribution expenses	48 000
Administrative expenses	100 500
Interest expense	34 500

Additional information relating to the company is as follows:

1. The inventories as of 30 June 2013 were:

Raw materials	$ 4 650
Work in process	13 050
Finished goods	37 500

2. On 1 January 2013, the company paid $81 000 for the next 12 months factory rent. Prepaid rent was debited at the time of the transaction.
3. The Machinery and Equipment account consists of $220 500 of factory machinery and $73 500 of office equipment. All machinery and equipment is depreciated using a 7-year life.
4. Expenses incurred as of year-end but not yet recorded are: direct labour, $6000; indirect labour, $1800; administrative expenses, $1050.
5. The electricity and gas, rent and insurance costs are related to factory operations.
6. Allow for company income tax expense at 30% of profit before tax.

Required

A. Prepare a worksheet including a pair of columns for unadjusted trial balance, adjustments, manufacturing, and the financial statements.
B. Prepare a cost of goods manufactured statement.
C. Prepare the closing entries.
D. Calculate the relationship between factory overhead costs and direct labour costs. Using that relationship, calculate the labour and overhead included in the ending inventories if work in process ending inventory contains $3600 of raw materials and $6000 of raw materials is included in the finished goods inventory.

LO 6

Problem 8.14   RECONSTRUCTION OF ACCOUNTS ★★★

Catastrophic Chemicals Ltd produces a highly flammable chemical product. The company experienced a flood on 1 April 2014 that destroyed its entire work in process inventory but did not affect the raw materials or finished goods inventories because they were located elsewhere. The insurance company wants to determine the cost of work in process inventory at the time of the flood. The company uses a periodic inventory system so perpetual records are not available.

A periodic inventory taken after the flood indicated that raw materials were valued at $89 200 and finished goods at $116 000. The company's accounting records show that the inventories as at 1 January 2014 were:

Raw materials	$ 29 600
Work in process	88 800
Finished goods	136 800

In addition, the accounting records indicate that the costs recorded during the first quarter of 2014 amounted to:

Purchase of raw materials	$160 000
Direct labour	42 000

In the past, factory overhead costs have amounted to 350% of direct labour cost.

Sales for the first quarter of 2014 amounted to $600 000. The company's gross profit has been 40% of sales for a long time.

Required

Determine the following amounts:
1. the cost of sales for the first quarter of 2014
2. the cost of goods manufactured for the first quarter of 2014
3. the work in process inventory as at 31 March 2014, broken down into direct materials, direct labour and factory overhead.

LO 6

Problem 8.15   VALUATION OF INVENTORIES IN MANUFACTURING ★★★

Moore Manufacturing Pty Ltd makes refrigerators and is trying to determine the cost of its ending work in process. The accountant has put together the following data for the year ended 30 June 2014.

Factory overhead costs for the year	$360 000
Direct labour costs for the year	$600 000
Machine hours for the year	24 000
Direct material allocated to ending work in process	$18 000

Each refrigerator uses $300 of direct materials, $60 of direct labour and 2.4 machine hours. Direct material is all added in the first third of the production process, direct labour is used equally throughout the entire production and machine hours are used equally throughout the first 80% of the production process. In the past, Moore Manufacturing Pty Ltd has allocated the factory overhead costs on the basis of direct labour but the accountant and the chief executive officer (CEO) are considering whether machine hours used would better reflect the way in which factory overhead costs are incurred. The accountant needs to estimate the percentage of completion of the ending work in process and whether to use direct labour or machine hours to calculate the overhead rate. The CEO is paid a significant bonus if the profit for the year exceeds $10 000 000.

The accountant estimates that the work in process is 50% complete and that the company should continue to use direct labour to allocate factory overhead and this will result in a profit for the year of $9 998 000.

The CEO is not happy with this and argues that the work in process is 80% complete and that machine hours should be used to allocate factory overhead.

Required

A. Give possible reasons for the CEO preferring her method of calculating the value of ending work in process rather than using the accountant's method.
B. Calculate the value of ending work in process using both the accountant's approach and the CEO's method and the resulting change in profit to see whether your explanation in requirement A is reasonable.

DECISION ANALYSIS

Pricing computers for a manufacturer

Creative Computers Pty Ltd began manufacturing inexpensive computers for the student market on 1 July 2012. The variable costs of manufacturing each computer are as follows:

Direct materials	$120
Direct factory labour	10
Variable factory overhead	20

During the year ended 30 June 2013, the following fixed costs were incurred:

Factory overhead	$1 200 000
Administration	84 000
Marketing	120 000

At the end of the year there was no work in process and 10 000 computers had been produced and sold during the year. Inventory was costed at the average cost of production per computer. The computers were priced so that a profit mark-up of $300 over manufacturing costs was obtained from each computer sold.

Required

A. Determine the selling price of each computer over the past year.
B. Creative Computers Pty Ltd wants to increase sales by 25% in the next year. Management is not sure whether to increase the price of the computers by up to 25%, keep the price the same, or even reduce the price. Assuming that the policy of a $300 mark-up on cost will continue, decide on a price to recommend to the managers of Creative Computers Pty Ltd.

GREEN ACCOUNTING

Design for the environment

Sustainable manufacturing is increasing in importance as consumers and governments become more aware of the long-term impacts of the production of the products we use. On page 358 the concept of Design for Environment (DfE) is outlined and the business knowledge vignette explains how Mercedes-Benz put this concept into action.

Required

A. With reference learning objective 7 of this chapter and the Powerhouse Museum website, what are nine principles of DfE? (*Hint:* access the website at www.powerhousemuseum.com, then search on 'design for the environment'.)
B. There are many benefits to manufacturers of pursuing DfE. Outline at least four benefits of DfE.
C. Research three companies, other than Mercedes-Benz, that incorporate DfE into their manufacturing processes and provide a brief summary of how they believe DfE reduces their manufacturing costs.

Manufacturing cost elements

The three major inputs into the manufacturing process are direct materials, direct labour and factory overheads. If the costs of any of these are not controlled, they may inflate the cost of manufacturing. If the selling price of the final output is determined by the market for the product and cannot be increased, the profit margin will be reduced.

Required

A. Organise the class into three groups. Group 1 is to discuss ways in which a business can ensure that direct material costs could be controlled. Group 2 is to discuss ways in which direct labour costs can be controlled. Group 3 is to discuss control of overhead costs.
B. Each group should prepare a written summary of its discussion and give a copy to the other groups.

Cost allocation for a manufacturing firm

Toolkit Pty Ltd manufactures high-quality tools for sale to tradespeople. The company produces two major lines of products — spanners and hammers. Trevor is the manager of spanner production and Helmut is the manager responsible for hammer production. The direct materials for the spanners and hammers are different as they are made with different metal alloys and the hammers also have a rubber handle supplied by a rubber manufacturer. The direct labour for each product line is also usually separate as different skills are required for making spanners than for making hammers. Occasionally, one of the hammer manufacturers, Leanne, does a few hours work per week on making spanners as she has had some experience in making both lines of tools. The factory overhead is divided between spanners and hammers based on the number of each produced. Both Trevor and Helmut receive bonuses based on how much they can minimise the production costs of their products.

Maria is the accountant for Toolkit and is responsible for allocating all costs to manufactured goods. Trevor and Maria are engaged and Trevor's bonuses will be helpful in meeting the costs of the wedding. After much discussion, Trevor has convinced Maria that, as no record is kept of Leanne's time spent making spanners instead of hammers, it would be easier just to charge all of Leanne's wages to direct labour for hammers. Usually an estimate is made of Leanne's time spent on spanners. Trevor also convinced Maria that rather than allocating the factory overhead based on the number of spanners and hammers produced, it would be better to use the hours of production of each. This meant that instead of spanners receiving 60% of factory overhead they would receive only 50%.

Required

A. Who are the stakeholders in this situation?
B. Are there any ethical issues involved? If so, what are they?
C. What would you do if you were Maria?

Refer to the latest financial report of JB Hi-Fi Limited on its website, www.jbhifi.com.au, and answer the following questions:
1. What inventories are carried by JB Hi-Fi Limited in the consolidated statement? If only one class of inventories is carried, suggest why any classification used is necessary.
2. Can you identify a product cost in the annual report? If so, what is it?
3. Identify three period costs, and explain why they are period costs even for a retail entity such as JB Hi-Fi Limited.
4. Can you identify any entities within the group which might carry out some manufacturing operations? If so, give examples.

Concepts for review

Before studying this chapter, you should understand or, if necessary, revise:

- how inventories are accounted for using a perpetual inventory system (pp. 238–44)

- the difference between product and period costs (pp. 342–3)

- the three cost elements of manufacturing costs (pp. 343–6)

- how to prepare a cost of goods manufactured statement (pp. 347–9).

Learning objectives

After studying this chapter, you should be able to:

1 explain the nature of cost accounting (p. 378)

2 describe the flow of costs in a job order cost accounting system (pp. 379–81)

3 explain the accounting procedures used in job order cost systems (pp. 381–7)

4 describe the flow of costs in a process cost accounting system and explain the nature and role of a cost of production report (pp. 387–91)

5 explain the accounting procedures used in process costing systems (pp. 391–3)

6 compare the characteristics of job order and process costing systems (pp. 393–4)

7 understand how costing and cost accounting are applied in service businesses (pp. 394–5)

8 understand the basic principles of a just-in-time processing system (pp. 395–6)

9 understand the basic principles of activity-based costing (pp. 396–8).

Surteco determined to be local hero

Plastics maker Surteco Australia has turned to technology to pursue its vision for sustainable, onshore manufacturing in the face of stiff price competition from rivals in low-cost centres throughout Asia.

The company, which is the domestic subsidiary of €400 million ($636 million) a year German concern Surteco AG, has bucked recent trends towards offshore manufacturing with a deliberate decision seven years ago to build some of its products in Australia.

It spent $20 million on a manufacturing facility in 2000 and is now involved in a complete overhaul of its information infrastructure in a project that its managing director expects to demonstrate the local industry's ability to compete with rivals manufacturing in lower cost countries.

'The key for Australian industry is that we can be very competitive in manufacturing in Australia,' Surteco Australia boss Marc Taylor says 'It is not true that we can't be, What is required is good investment in technology and good investment in people.'

Taylor says Surteco has already made considerable investments in people and technology to cut its operating costs by 50 per cent over the last few years. The moves have also dramatically improved productivity in the business.

'We've gone from being the worst in the world in productivity to the best in our group,' Taylor says. 'That has been achieved really by investment in technology and in training our people. The next step is that we have to automate totally our IT processes throughout our operation.

'We're trying to integrate everything from customer input right through to production, secondary processing, logistics,

warehousing and distribution, so it works as one package with total traceability through our plants and warehouses...

'We're also putting in a full materials resource planning [MRP] system because we want to reduce our costs by making sure our materials are more just-in-time and that they're in the right quantities, rather than what we think the right quantities might be,' he says.

'We're putting in what we call advance production planning as well, which helps us to change over our machines for different tasks more quickly, which is something a traditional MRP system can't do.'

Source: Excerpts from Ben Woodhead, 'Surteco determined to be local hero', *The Australian.*

Chapter preview

Chapter 8 demonstrated the difficulties in calculating the cost of manufacturing each unit of output. However, every business entity must know what it costs to produce a good or service so management can make decisions, particularly marketing managers when setting a selling price for each product or service. Cost accounting systems provide this information. This chapter presents the essential features of cost accounting systems that are integrated into the accounting systems developed in earlier chapters.

The plastics manufacturer Surteco (in the scene setter) has managed to reduce its operating costs by 50% by understanding what it costs to produce plastics and adapting its manufacturing processes through better technology and training for its staff. In plastics manufacture, because the total costs of each product must be known in order to calculate the cost per item, a system known as process costing is used. Job order costing is an alternative costing system. Both systems are covered in this chapter. Surteco is also using just-in-time processes for ordering materials, and this is covered later in this chapter.

9.1 Cost accounting

Learning objective 1

Explain the nature of cost accounting

Cost accounting is a specialised type of accounting used to accumulate, or gather, product costs as production takes place or services are provided. Both total cost and unit costs can be determined. A **cost accounting system** records cost data in separate ledger accounts in the general ledger.

The cost information, developed through cost accounting, serves two basic purposes:
1. Product costs are used to value a manufacturing entity's work in process and finished goods inventories as well as to determine its profit. Product costing is based on a perpetual inventory system, which eliminates the need for the rough estimates of ending inventory values used in the periodic inventory system illustrated in chapter 8.
2. Management requires regular reliable cost information for making decisions on such things as planning a business's financial performance, product pricing, profitability analysis, production cost control such as that by Surteco (in the scene setter), resource allocations, and quoting potential customers.

Job order costing and process costing

The two basic types of cost accounting systems used in manufacturing entities are *job order costing* and *process costing*. The system used depends on how goods are manufactured. Job order costing is used by service organisations and manufacturers that provide activities or manufacture products in response to customer orders and specifications. For example, a plastics manufacturer like Surteco makes special plastic parts for a motor vehicle manufacturer. A job order is a request from a customer to provide a given quantity of specifically designed made-to-order products. Costs can be accumulated for each specific job order.

Process costing is appropriate for manufacturers of large quantities of homogeneous (standard) products on a continuous production line, such as paints, soft drinks, bricks and paper. Under process costing, costs are collected by production process, department or activity rather than for each unit produced. Total production costs are divided by the total units produced to calculate the unit cost. Both costing systems are explained in detail below.

Cost accounting in non-manufacturing entities

The principles of cost accumulation and assignment used in a manufacturing business are just as applicable in many non-manufacturing businesses such as hospitals, banks, retail stores, insurance companies, accounting and other service-based practices. Non-manufacturing entities use cost accounting procedures to determine the costs of performing services or activities rather than producing products — for example, a bank costing its credit card service, an insurance company costing the policies written by its agents, a recruiting firm costing recruitment of various levels of employees for clients, a hospital costing a medical procedure, an accounting practice costing the preparation of a tax return for a company, and a university costing the delivery of a subject. Costing for service entities is discussed in more detail later in this chapter.

9.2 Job order costing

Learning objective 2

Describe the flow of costs in a job order cost accounting system

Job order costing is most appropriate when products are manufactured according to customers' orders or specifications and the identity of each job can be kept separate. Costs can then be allocated to each job. The technique can be used to accumulate the costs of a single product (e.g. a large ship being produced) or a group of identical or similar products (e.g. several custom-designed dining-room tables being manufactured). Such industries as commercial printing, aviation, shipbuilding and heavy machinery typically rely on job order costing to determine product costs. It is also used by construction companies, hospitals, marketing firms, tourism management, human resource management, management consulting firms and film companies.

An entity engaged in manufacturing may calculate production costs using the general accounting system as described in chapter 8, or by incorporating a cost accounting system. The two systems differ in the methods of determining and controlling costs.

If the general accounting system is used, the cost of goods manufactured is determined by assembling appropriate account balances in a manufacturing summary account. As we saw in chapter 8, this account summarises the detail contained in a cost of goods manufactured statement. This requires estimates of ending inventory values to be made (via stocktakes) in keeping with a periodic inventory system. The problem with this approach is that the cost of each job, unit of product, or process is not able to be determined — only total overall costs can be determined periodically after stocktakes of inventories have been performed. The use of a periodic inventory system also does not provide an efficient way of controlling the cost of raw materials and other inventories, whereas a perpetual inventory system provides such control.

To overcome the problems with the general accounting approach, a cost accounting system is integrated into the general accounting system. This chapter is based on the use of the perpetual inventory system with the cost accounting system incorporated into the general accounting system.

Cost flows in a job order cost system

A job order cost system involves the use of the perpetual inventory approach to accumulate costs, and provides for a system of inventory control through general ledger control accounts with subsidiary cost ledgers. As production costs are incurred, they are recorded in general ledger control accounts for Raw Materials Inventory, Factory Wages and Salaries, and Factory Overhead. These costs are subsequently assigned to production:

- Materials costs are assigned to Work in Process Inventory (direct materials) and to Factory Overhead (indirect materials) when materials are placed into production.
- Labour costs are assigned from Factory Wages to Work in Process (direct labour) and to Factory Overhead (indirect labour) as labour costs are incurred.
- Factory Overhead costs are applied to production periodically on the basis of a predetermined factory overhead rate as briefly outlined in chapter 8.

On completion of production, the total accumulated costs are transferred to Finished Goods Inventory. When the finished goods are sold, the cost of the finished goods sold is transferred to Cost of Sales, which will be transferred by a closing entry to the Profit or Loss Summary at the end of the accounting period. The accumulation and assignment of cost flows in a job order cost system are summarised diagrammatically in figure 9.1 (p. 380).

In this recording and assignment of production costs, the distinction between *product costs* and *period costs* is important. As we saw in chapter 8, product costs are initially reflected as assets in the form of inventories. These costs become expenses only when they are 'consumed' on the sale of the inventories. Sales salaries and all selling and distribution and administrative costs are *period costs* and are treated as expenses in the period in which they are incurred. Factory wages and all other costs of manufacturing, on the other hand, are initially unexpired *product costs* (assets, not expenses) in the form of work in process and finished inventories. When the finished product is sold, these costs become expired costs or *period costs*, and are reflected in the cost of sales expense in the period in which the jobs/products are sold.

Figure 9.1 Cost flows in a job order cost system (numbers relate to general journal entries illustrated later in this chapter)

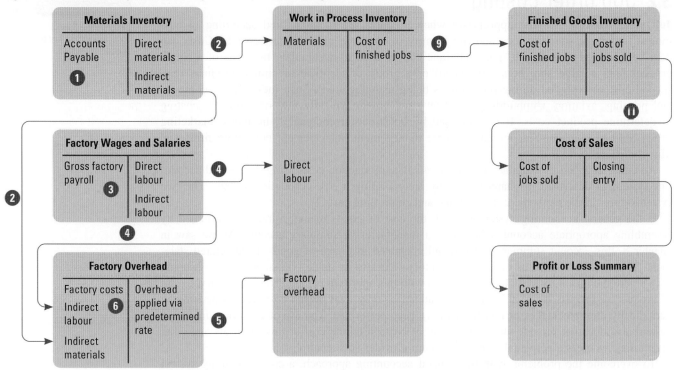

Each of the cost accumulation accounts shown in figure 9.1 is a control account with a corresponding subsidiary ledger. The subsidiary ledger consists of the job cost orders, which are used to accumulate direct materials, direct labour and factory overhead costs for each job. In manual accounting systems, these are called 'job cost sheets', but with computerisation of the accounting process the costs are usually accumulated by the customer's order number. On completion of production, the cost orders are used as the subsidiary ledger for finished goods and costs of sales. The cost accumulation control accounts and their corresponding subsidiary ledgers are summarised below:

Control account	Subsidiary ledger
Work in Process Inventory	Job Cost Orders (for jobs incomplete)
Finished Goods Inventory	Job Cost Orders (for jobs completed)
Cost of Sales	Job Cost Orders (for jobs sold)
Factory Wages and Salaries	Job Cost Orders (for direct labour assigned)
Factory Overhead	Job Cost Orders (for overheads applied)

Job cost order

A control account and subsidiary ledger are required with a job order costing system to accumulate the production costs and report the results to management. In job order costing, the job itself is the focal point for accumulating product costs. The subsidiary ledger used in job order costing, a **job cost order**, provides an *itemised listing* of all direct materials, direct labour and factory overhead costs charged to a job. A job cost order is illustrated in figure 9.2. The information recorded on the job cost order is explained below.

A control number is assigned to each job started and is recorded on the job cost order. Information about the customer and product description is also entered in the job cost order and all job cost orders initially represent the work in process subsidiary ledger. The job cost order in figure 9.2 indicates that Cottage Manufacturing Co. Ltd, which produces custom furniture, started Job 691 on 12 January and finished it on 19 January. One hundred dining-room tables were produced for the customer, J. Chan. The cost order subsidiary ledger consisting of cost orders for all jobs being produced is controlled by the Work in Process Inventory account while production takes place. The reference columns show the original sources of data recorded in the job cost order (e.g. a specific labour time ticket). When direct materials are requisitioned from the storeroom for a specific job, their cost is recorded in the materials column of the job cost order. The direct labour cost required to convert raw materials to finished goods is recorded in the labour column, and an appropriate amount of factory overhead is applied using the predetermined overhead rate and recorded in the overhead column.

Figure 9.2 Job cost order

Job no. __691__

JOB COST ORDER
COTTAGE MANUFACTURING CO. LTD

Customer ___J. Chan___

Product ___L-100___   Quantity ___100___

Date started ___12/1___   Date finished ___19/1___

Labour			Materials			Overhead	
Date	Reference	Amount	Date	Reference	Amount	Direct labour hours	1350
12/1	12-30	$1920	12/1	1126	$6000	Overhead rate	$4.50
13/1	13-30	1920	19/1	1198	1500	Overhead applied	$6075
14/1	14-30	1920					
15/1	15-30	1920				**Summary (on completion)**	
16/1	16-30	1920				**Direct labour**	$11 520
19/1	19-17	1920				**Direct materials**	7 500
						Factory overhead	6 075
						Total cost	25 005
						Unit cost	$250.05

When the job is completed, its total cost can be determined by adding the costs recorded in the three columns and summarised in the cost order. As noted above, completed cost orders are the subsidiary ledgers for Finished Goods Inventory and Cost of Sales control accounts.

9.3 Job order costing procedures

Learning objective 3

Explain the accounting procedures used in job order cost systems

The preceding section provides a general overview of the flow of costs through the cost control accounts in the general ledger. We now look at the detailed accounting procedures required to perform job order costing. Cottage Manufacturing Co. Ltd's January performance is used to illustrate the procedures. General journal entries are numbered and these numbers are shown in figures 9.1 and 9.5 to allow the entries to be traced to the accounts.

Accounting for materials

All raw materials are kept in a storeroom under the supervision of a stores manager and are issued to work in process when a **materials requisition**, such as the one shown in figure 9.3, is prepared or entered into the computer by an authorised person. It identifies the specific material required and shows the job or factory overhead account to which it is to be charged as direct or indirect materials. When the materials are transferred to production, the accounting records are updated. Figure 9.3 (p. 382) indicates that 250 units of raw materials were charged to Job 691 at a total cost of $6000 on 12 January.

Figure 9.3 Materials requisition

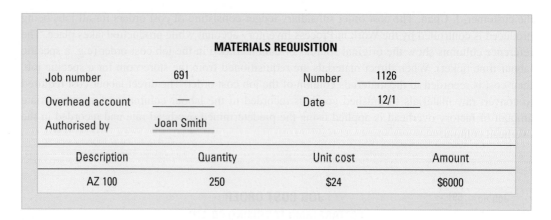

MATERIALS REQUISITION

Job number	691	Number	1126
Overhead account	—	Date	12/1
Authorised by	Joan Smith		

Description	Quantity	Unit cost	Amount
AZ 100	250	$24	$6000

Materials ledger records such as the one presented in figure 9.4 are maintained for each type of material used and serve as the subsidiary ledger for the Raw Materials Inventory account. This method is also used to record purchases of inventory in a retail entity using the perpetual inventory system (as illustrated in figure 6.6 for Fridge Town, p. 239).

Figure 9.4 Materials ledger record

MATERIALS LEDGER RECORD

Item: AZ 100

		Received			Issued			Balance		
Date	Reference	Quantity	Unit cost	Total cost	Quantity	Unit cost	Total cost	Quantity	Unit cost	Total cost
6/1	1820	300	$24	$7200				300	$24	$7200
12/1	1126				250	$24	$6000	50	$24	$1200

The materials ledger records provide perpetual inventory control with columns for receipts, issues and a current balance. The raw materials requisitioned during an accounting period are recorded as direct materials in the job cost orders or as indirect materials charged to factory overhead by the accounting department. The $6000 of materials requisitioned to Job 691 have been deducted in figure 9.4 to maintain a current balance of materials on hand. The costs also must be charged to the control accounts established for Work in Process Inventory and Factory Overhead. We assume that Cottage Manufacturing Co. Ltd makes all entries to the general ledger accounts at the end of the month, although they may be recorded throughout the month. The entries in the materials ledger records should be made continuously during the period. The company purchased raw materials amounting to $42 500, including $7200 for the materials in figure 9.4, in January, so the following entry is required (the number in parentheses relates to figure 9.1, and GST of 10% is included):

Jan.	31	Raw Materials Inventory	42 500	
		GST Outlays	4 250	
(1)		Accounts Payable		46 750
		(Raw materials purchased during January)		

Five jobs, including Job 691, were worked on during the month and each has a separate job cost order. We consider only the one for Job 691. As we saw in figure 9.2, raw materials totalling $7500 were requisitioned for Job 691 during January. This includes $6000 for material item AZ 100. The total raw materials requisitioned for the five jobs amounted to $36 550 and those charged to factory overhead as indirect materials were $1680. The following is a summary of the general journal entries that occurred in January:

Jan.	31	Work in Process Inventory	36 550	
		Factory Overhead	1 680	
	(2)	Raw Materials Inventory		38 230
		(Raw materials requisitioned to jobs during January)		

Accounting for labour

With job order costing, employees book on and off job numbers on computers to accumulate labour costs. The computer records the time spent by each employee on a specific job (direct labour) or an overhead assignment (indirect labour). Any time an employee is not logged on to a job is idle time and this is accumulated as overhead. Each employee is required to clock in when work begins and clock out at the end of the day.

Each labour hour recorded on the computer is multiplied by the appropriate rate and the total cost is charged either to jobs as direct labour or to factory overhead as indirect labour. During each day, employees must log on to the computer as they change from one job or overhead assignment to another. Since labour cannot be assigned to inventories like raw materials, the entire factory payroll must be distributed each period as direct or indirect labour. Based on the computer records, Cottage Manufacturing Co. Ltd incurred a total payroll cost of $100 000 during January. Factory wages and salaries amounted to $48 200. The labour computer records indicate that the company's direct labour was $42 000 (including $11 520 for Job 691) and indirect labour amounted to $6200. The following entries are made (detailed payroll deductions, which are discussed in a later chapter, are ignored for simplicity) to record total and factory payroll for January:

Jan.	31	General Wages and Salaries	51 800	
		Factory Wages and Salaries	48 200	
	(3)	Payroll Deductions Payable (various)		30 000
		Wages Payable		70 000
		(Payroll for January)		
Jan.	31	Work In Process Inventory	42 000	
		Factory Overhead	6 200	
	(4)	Factory Wages and Salaries		48 200
		(Direct and indirect labour assigned for January)		

Accounting for factory overhead

The accumulation of the direct costs of materials and labour was basically straightforward, because the costs could be traced directly to production from a materials requisition or labour computer records. Accounting for factory overhead is more complicated because of its indirect nature and the need to accumulate costs as production occurs.

The challenge is to relate the overhead cost to production output, i.e. each job, on some reliable basis. Since factory overhead is a common cost incurred for the benefit of all products, it cannot be traced directly to individual products. Instead, it must be related to the jobs on some production activity basis that closely relates the cost to the work performed. Examples of bases used are direct labour hours, direct labour cost, machine hours or units produced. This approach assumes that there is a relationship between the overhead costs and the activity base chosen.

With a perpetual inventory system, an entity cannot wait until the end of an accounting period to allocate the factory overhead actually incurred, because management needs the product cost information for decision-making purposes on an ongoing basis. Also, fluctuations in the amount of factory overhead or the level of production activity between short time periods such as months may produce inconsistent results if actual costs and actual production activity are used.

For example, assume that a highly automated toy manufacturer has a monthly depreciation charge for its machinery of $50 000, which must be included in the product cost. Also assume that production activity is seasonal and 25 000 units are produced in January and 100 000 units are manufactured in September. If actual factory overhead and actual production activity are used, the unit cost for depreciation will be $2.00 for January and $0.50 for September. In months of high production the unit cost will be low, whereas in months of low production the unit cost will be high, despite the fact that the products and the manufacturing process are identical from month to month.

In order to avoid these accounting problems, a predetermined overhead rate is used to apply the cost to jobs as they are worked on. A **predetermined overhead rate** can be calculated for the coming year based on the following formula:

$$\frac{\text{Estimated annual factory overhead cost}}{\text{Estimated annual level of production activity}} = \frac{\text{Predetermined}}{\text{overhead rate}}$$

For example, assume that Cottage Manufacturing Co. Ltd forecast factory overhead of $270 000 for the year and expected to work 60 000 direct labour hours. Its predetermined overhead rate is:

$$\frac{\$270\,000}{60\,000} = \$4.50 \text{ per direct labour hour}$$

Since 1350 direct labour hours were incurred for Job 691, the factory overhead applied is $6075 (1350 hours × $4.50), as shown in figure 9.2. The amounts charged to the various job cost orders for all jobs are totalled and recorded in the Work in Process Inventory account with an entry as follows (assuming a total of 5280 direct labour hours were worked in January):

Jan.	31	Work in Process Inventory	23 760	
		Factory Overhead Applied		23 760
	(5)	(Factory overhead applied during January: 5280 hours at $4.50)		

The applied factory overhead is credited to the Factory Overhead Applied account. The actual factory overhead incurred is debited to the Factory Overhead account and to subsidiary ledger accounts established for the individual overhead items such as depreciation, rent, insurance, rates, electricity, indirect materials and indirect labour. Cottage Manufacturing Co. Ltd already has recorded $1680 for indirect materials and $6200 for indirect labour (see entries (2), (3) and (4) on the previous page). Assume additional factory overhead charges for the month of January were:

Rates	$ 600
Rent	2 200
Electricity	3 470
Costs subject to GST	6 270
Depreciation	8 200
Insurance (prepaid)	850
	$15 320
GST ($6270 × 10%)	$ 627

The total actual factory overhead for January was $23 200 ($15 320 + $1680 from entry (2) + $6200 from entry (4)), and the entry shown below is required to record the additional actual charges:

Jan.	31	Factory Overhead	15 320	
		GST Outlays	627	
	(6)	Rent Payable		2 420
		Electricity Account Payable		3 817
		Accumulated Depreciation		8 200
		Rates Payable		660
		Prepaid Insurance		850
		(Additional actual factory overhead for January)		

Overapplied and underapplied overhead

The actual factory overhead and the applied factory overhead are rarely the same for any given month. If the Factory Overhead Applied account balance exceeds the balance in the Factory Overhead account, the overhead will be **overapplied**. This means that more overhead was charged to work in process than was actually incurred. When the Factory Overhead account balance exceeds that of Factory Overhead Applied, the overhead is **underapplied**.

In the Cottage Manufacturing Co. Ltd example, factory overhead was overapplied by $560, since $23 760 was applied to the jobs but only $23 200 was actually incurred. Ideally, the estimates used for the predetermined overhead rate will be accurate and any difference in the balances in the Factory Overhead account and Factory Overhead Applied account will be small — particularly at the end of an annual period.

Assuming the preparation of interim monthly accounts, the Factory Overhead Applied account is closed off to the Factory Overhead account at month-end. In the Cottage Manufacturing Co. Ltd example, the general journal entry made at the end of the month of January is:

Jan.	31	Factory Overhead Applied	23 760	
		Factory Overhead		23 760
(7)		(Overhead applied transferred to overhead account)		

This creates a credit balance in the Factory Overhead account of $560, which is the amount by which overhead was overapplied during the month of January. At the end of each month, the balance remaining in the Factory Overhead account is transferred to a Factory Overhead Under/Overapplied account as illustrated below:

Jan.	31	Factory Overhead	560	
		Factory Overhead Under/Overapplied		560
(8)		(Overapplied overhead transferred)		

A similar journal entry is made at the end of each month throughout the year, and it is expected that the amount will vary from month to month. In some months the overhead will be overapplied and in other months underapplied. This reflects the seasonal fluctuations of business activity and its impact when accounting is done on a monthly basis. Normally, at the end of the year, the overapplied amounts and the underapplied amounts that occurred during each month tend to offset each other, and the resulting yearly difference is small.

Because of the seasonality of business activity and the resulting under- or overapplied overhead, the monthly differences between actual and applied overhead are not charged or credited to cost of sales at month-end but are carried forward on the monthly balance sheet (also called the statement of financial position). At year-end, the net effects of the monthly variations are normally closed off to the Cost of Sales account by the entry below (assuming a final debit balance in the account to be $820, representing underapplied overhead):

Jan.	31	Cost of Sales	820	
		Factory Overhead Under/Overapplied		820
		(Underapplied overhead for the year transferred to cost of sales)		

Limitation of direct labour as a cost driver

As manufacturing entities automate their operations, labour is replaced by equipment. Computerised machinery in manufacturing reduces labour costs, increases capacity and improves product quality, as demonstrated in the scene setter concerning Surteco. Direct labour costs, which often used to represent 40% to 50% of production costs, can now amount to as little as 10%. The decline in labour costs has been accompanied by a significant increase in factory overhead. As such, a variable cost (direct labour) has been replaced by fixed costs such as depreciation of equipment and the write-off of costs incurred to develop the computer software needed to control the automated production operations. To fully use the high level of fixed capacity, many companies produce a variety of products with different production requirements. If labour cost is such a small part of the overall cost structure, the use of direct labour hours or direct labour costs in overhead application can produce inaccurate predetermined overhead rates and result in distorted product costs.

The key question is: Which products require which factory overhead costs? Managers must carefully identify the best 'cost driver' for the application of overhead. A **cost driver** is a measure of business activity that incurs overhead cost. Cost drivers are identified with the kinds of transactions that create the need for the overhead. Examples in highly automated operations are machine hours, computer time, the number of parts in the products and the number of production schedule changes (resulting in set-up costs) required. The use of cost drivers enables managers to differentiate more accurately between the overhead costs required for the various products. As a result, the application of factory overhead can become more complex, well beyond the direct labour base used in the above illustration. If the impact of automation on overheads is ignored, the overhead cost allocation can lead to wrong conclusions about which products are profitable and which are not. The problems caused by using direct labour as a cost driver have been overcome partly by the use of activity-based costing (ABC) (see later in the chapter).

Accounting for the completion of a job

When a job is completed, its costs are totalled on the job cost order and transferred from Work in Process Inventory to Finished Goods Inventory. The job cost order in figure 9.2 is moved from the work in process subsidiary ledger to the finished goods subsidiary ledger. In order to record the completion of Job 691, Cottage Manufacturing Co. Ltd makes the following entry:

Jan.	31	Finished Goods Inventory	25 095	
		Work in Process Inventory		25 095
(9)		(Completion of Job 691 transferred to finished goods inventory)		

Accounting for the sale of a job

Since perpetual inventories are maintained with job order costing, the total costs accumulated for each job are known at the point of completion. As we see in figure 9.2, Job 691 consisted of 100 tables produced at a total cost of $25 095. This information is important to management for making decisions on product pricing, evaluating production performance, analysing profitability, forecasting future operations, and controlling costs. Job order costing also permits the recording of the cost of sales at the time of sale. For example, if Job 691 is sold on credit for $39 000 plus GST, the transaction is recorded as follows:

Jan.	31	Accounts Receivable	42 900	
		Sales		39 000
(10)		GST Collections		3 900
		(Sale of Job 691)		
Jan.	31	Cost of Sales	25 095	
		Finished Goods Inventory		25 095
(11)		(Cost of sale of Job 691)		

The job cost order for Job 691 is moved from the finished goods subsidiary ledger to the cost of sales subsidiary ledger as the final step in the job order costing flow. Note that the difference between the selling price of Job 691 ($39 000) and the cost of sales ($25 095) is the job's gross profit ($13 905).

A summary of the job order costing flows of Cottage Manufacturing Co. Ltd is presented on the next page in figure 9.5 by tracing the various transactions through T accounts in order to see their interrelationships. The numbers (1) to (11) refer to the journal entries recorded earlier in the chapter, starting with the purchase of raw materials and ending with the sale of Job 691 (GST accounts are not shown).

Accounts Receivable		
(10)	42 900	

Raw Materials Inventory		
(1)	42 500	(2)	38 230

Work in Process Inventory		
(2)	36 550	(9)	25 095
(4)	42 000		
(5)	23 760		

Finished Goods Inventory		
(9)	25 095	(11)	25 095

Prepaid Insurance		
1/1 Bal.	10 200	(6)	850

Accumulated Depreciation		
		(6)	8 200

Accounts Payable		
		(1)	46 750

Electricity Payable		
		(6)	3 817

Rent Payable		
		(6)	2 420

Rates Payable		
		(6)	660

Factory Wages and Salaries		
(3)	48 200	(4)	48 200

Factory Overhead		
(2)	1 680	(7)	23 760
(4)	6 200		
(6)	15 320		
(8)	560		

Factory Overhead Applied		
(7)	23 760	(5)	23 760

Factory Overhead Under/Overapplied		
		(8)	560

Sales		
		(10)	39 000

Cost of Sales		
(11)	25 095	

9.4 Process costing

Process costing is used by manufacturing entities with the *continuous production flows* usually found in mass-production industries. The homogeneity of the production output means units or groups of units cannot be identified like they are in job order costing. The technique can also be used to accumulate costs for a number of non-manufacturing activities such as the services performed by a power station, mail sorting in a post office, and cheque-clearing in a bank. The focal point of process costing is the **processing centre** in which the work is performed during a specified period of time. A process costing centre can be a department, a work station, a factory assembly line or a division. Output usually is measured in such units as litres, kilograms, tonnes, barrels or square metres. Unit costs are calculated for raw materials and conversion costs in each processing centre.

Conversion costs consist of the total of the direct labour and factory overhead costs incurred by a processing centre in converting raw materials into finished goods. In its most basic form, process costing produces an average unit cost calculated as:

$$\frac{\text{Total processing centre costs for a period}}{\text{Total processing centre output for a period}} = \text{Average unit cost}$$

This deceptively simple calculation becomes more complicated in most cases for the following reasons:

- When a processing centre has work in process at the beginning or at the end of a period, its output cannot be measured just in terms of whole units actually completed. Costs will have been incurred for any partly completed units that are part of the centre's output despite the fact they are not finished.

- The manufacturing cost elements will not usually be incurred uniformly during the production process. For example, the conversion costs that consist of direct labour and factory overhead typically are consumed continuously during the production process, whereas raw materials are normally added at specific points in time, e.g. at start of production. Consequently, a work in process inventory may be at different stages of completion for different cost elements. It is therefore necessary to calculate a separate unit cost for the materials cost and conversion costs.

Process costing — cost flows

Figure 9.6 shows the flow of costs for two departments — blending and packaging — in the production of Shower Magic bathroom cleaner using process costing. Actual costs of materials, labour and factory overheads are recorded in the same way as for job order costing. Then the costs of raw materials, direct labour and factory overhead are accumulated within each processing centre using procedures similar to those discussed earlier for job order costing.

A Work in Process Inventory account is established for each processing centre and is debited for the materials, labour and overhead costs for a given period. When multiple processing centres are involved, the output of a given centre becomes the input of the following centre, costed with the total unit cost accumulated up to the point of transfer. The receiving centre's Work in Process account is debited and the transferring centre's account is credited for the total cost transferred. Once the amount of each manufacturing cost is known, a total unit cost can be calculated.

Figure 9.6 Cost flows in a process costing system

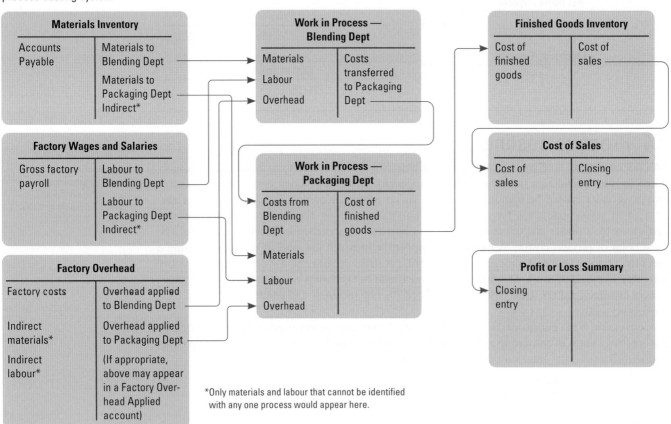

*Only materials and labour that cannot be identified with any one process would appear here.

The total unit cost of the production output of each processing centre is calculated by dividing the costs accumulated for each cost element by its respective number of equivalent completed units and adding the results. When the production process is completed, a Finished Goods Inventory account is debited and the final processing centre's Work in Process Inventory account is credited.

Cost of production reports (discussed below) are prepared for each processing centre's periodic performance to monitor the physical flow of the production and the costs to be accounted for.

The absence of jobs simplifies the accounting significantly since all costs are accumulated by processing centres instead of separate jobs. Costs are accounted for over a period such as a month rather than over the life of each job. Many of the employees work in only one department, so the labour time reporting requirements are minimal. For example, a departmentalised payroll register may provide all the information required to distribute labour costs without the detail of labour computer records. Also, the distinction between direct and indirect costs (materials and labour) required in job order costing is not necessary since the cost focus is now on a processing centre. All of the material and labour costs are considered as being direct to the processing centre. In some situations where factory overhead and production output are relatively constant from month to month, actual overhead may be used for costing purposes rather than using a predetermined overhead rate.

Equivalent units

Equivalent units are the key to process costing. Unfinished work in process inventory at the end of a period requires additional work and costs in the next period. These partly completed units are not the same as whole units and so equivalent units must be calculated. They represent the number of units that would have been produced if all the work and costs had been applied to produce completed units. In other words, any partly processed inventories must be *restated* to the equivalent number of finished units they would represent. For example, 500 units that are 50% completed are the equivalent of 250 units that are 100% finished. Since no additional work is required for fully completed units, they automatically become equivalent units. Consequently, the equivalent units for a particular period will be a measure of how many whole units of production are represented by the units finished plus the units partly finished.

Calculating equivalent units of production

The stage of completion for each manufacturing cost element (materials, labour, overhead) must be calculated separately when working out the equivalent units except in the rare case where all the manufacturing costs are incurred uniformly. To illustrate the most basic form of equivalent units, *assume no beginning inventory* (i.e. no partly finished processing) and 108 000 units are started in the production process. During the period, 90 000 units are finished and 18 000 are left in the ending work in process inventory, 100% complete for materials but only one-third finished as far as conversion costs are concerned.

The equivalent units for materials cost would be 108 000 (i.e. 90 000 + 18 000), and the equivalent units for conversion costs would be 96 000 (i.e. 90 000 units completed plus one-third of the 18 000 still in process). Assuming that all the raw materials are added at the beginning of the production process at a cost of $216 000, and since the equivalent units are 108 000, the unit cost for materials is $2.00. If the conversion costs for the period are $336 000 and the equivalent units are 96 000, the unit conversion cost is $3.50. This is summarised below:

	Physical units	Equivalent units	
		Materials	Conversion costs
Work in process at beginning	—		
Production units started	108 000		
Units to account for	108 000		
Production units completed	90 000	90 000	90 000
Work in process at end	18 000	18 000	6 000 (18 000 × ¹/₃)
Units accounted for	108 000	108 000 (a)	96 000 (a)
Production costs for period		$216 000 (b)	$336 000 (b)
Cost per equivalent unit (b ÷ a)		$2	$3.50

The *existence of a beginning inventory* of units in work in process can complicate the calculation of equivalent units because, on completion, costs will have been incurred for the current period as well as for the previous period. In calculating equivalent unit cost, the costs assigned to the beginning inventory of work in process are combined with the current period's costs of production, and the degree of completion of the beginning units is ignored. This approach relies on the averaging of current and past costs over the equivalent units completed, and is known as the weighted average cost method of dealing with beginning inventory of work in process. Other methods are available but are not considered in this book.

To illustrate, assume that the beginning work in process inventory consists of 10 000 units 100% complete as to materials and at the 40% stage of completion for conversion costs, 108 000 units are started, 100 000 units are completed during the period, and 18 000 units are one-third finished for conversion costs in the ending inventory as before.

Using the weighted average method, we have 118 000 (i.e. 100 000 + 18 000) equivalent units for materials and 106 000 (i.e. 100 000 + 18 000 × ¹/₃) equivalent units for the conversion costs. The percentage of completion for the beginning inventory is ignored since the units and costs of the previous periods are combined with the current period. If the materials costs in the beginning work in process are $20 000 and the materials costs of the current period are $216 000, the total of $236 000 is divided by 118 000 to give a unit cost for materials of $2.

If the conversion costs in the beginning work in process inventory are $30 000 and those of the current period are $336 000, the total of $366 000 is divided by 106 000 to give a unit conversion cost of $3.45. Details of the above example are summarised below:

	Physical units	Equivalent units	
		Materials	Conversion costs
Work in process at beginning	10 000		
Production units started	108 000		
Units to account for	118 000		
Production units completed	100 000	100 000	100 000
Work in process at end	18 000	18 000	6 000 (18 000 × ¹/₃)
Units accounted for	118 000	118 000 (a)	106 000 (a)
Production costs for period		$236 000 (b)	$366 000 (b)
Cost per equivalent unit (b ÷ a)		$2	$3.45

Cost of production report

A **cost of production report** serves as the subsidiary ledger account in process costing because it is used to account for the costs charged to a processing centre during a specified time period. A cost of production report such as the one shown in figure 9.7 has three sections:

1. A *physical flow schedule* shows the number of production units for which a processing centre is responsible, their stage of completion and where they are at the end of the period.
2. A *costs to be accounted for* section identifies the manufacturing cost elements for which the processing centre is accountable, the equivalent units for each cost element and the unit costs calculated.
3. A *costs accounted for* section indicates what happened to the cost elements for which the processing centre is responsible in terms of finished units and those left in process at the end of the period. This section must be reconciled with (2) above.

The cost of production report summarises production quantities and costs for each processing department. The data in the report are obtained from materials requisitions, payroll summaries and predetermined application rates, as in the case of a job order cost system.

Figure 9.7 Cost of production report — blending department

CHAPLIN CHEMICALS LTD
Blending Department
Cost of Production Report
for the month ended 31 January 2013

Physical flow schedule

Work in process, 1 January	8 000 litres ($1/2$ complete)
Units started	106 000 litres
Units finished	108 000 litres
Work in process, 31 January	6 000 litres ($1/3$ complete)

Costs to be accounted for

Cost element	Beginning	Current	Total	Equiv. units*	Unit cost
Raw materials	$12 000	$159 000	$171 000	114 000	$1.50
Conversion costs	16 000	424 000	440 000	110 000	4.00
	$28 000	$583 000	$611 000		$5.50

Costs accounted for

Units transferred to finishing department		
(108 000 litres × $5.50)		$594 000
Work in process, 31 January:		
Raw materials (6000 litres × $1.50)	$9 000	
Conversion costs (6000 litres × $1/3$ × $4.00)	8 000	17 000
		$611 000

* Equivalent units

	Raw materials	Conversion costs
Units completed	108 000	108 000
Work in process	6 000	2 000 (6000 × $1/3$)
	114 000	110 000

9.5 Process costing procedures

To illustrate process costing procedures, assume Chaplin Chemicals Ltd produces a single product, Stayclean, used for swimming-pool maintenance. Two departments, blending and finishing, are operated as processing centres with the output of the blending department becoming the input of the finishing department. Raw materials in chemical powder form are issued at the start of the production process in the blending department and at the end of the processing in the finishing department. Conversion costs (direct labour and factory overhead) are incurred uniformly throughout the processing in each of the departments. The data summarising the January 2013 performance of the two departments are shown below:

Beginning work in process data

	Blending department	Finishing department
Units in beginning inventory	8000 litres	10 000 litres
Raw materials costs	$12 000	—
Conversion costs	$16 000	$14 500
Cost from preceding department (blending)	—	$55 000

January processing data

	Blending department	Finishing department
Units started	106 000 litres	108 000 litres
Units finished	108 000 litres	100 000 litres
Units in ending inventory	6 000 litres	18 000 litres
Raw materials costs	$159 000	$160 000
Conversion costs	$424 000	$292 900
Cost from preceding department (blending)	—	$594 000

The beginning and ending work in process inventories of the blending department are a half and one-third complete respectively in terms of the conversion costs of that department. The same stages of completion prevail for the beginning and ending work in process inventories of the finishing department. The January cost of production reports for the two departments are shown in figures 9.7 and 9.8 respectively. Essentially the same procedures and concepts are required to prepare either report so we shall concentrate on the cost of production report for the finishing department in figure 9.8.

Figure 9.8 Cost of production report — finishing department

CHAPLIN CHEMICALS LTD
Finishing Department
Cost of Production Report
for the month ended 31 January 2013

Physical flow schedule

Work in process, 1 January	10 000 litres ($1/2$ complete)
Units started	108 000 litres
Units finished	100 000 litres
Work in process, 31 January	18 000 litres ($1/3$ complete)

Costs to be accounted for

Cost element	Beginning	Current	Total	Equiv. units*	Unit cost
Raw materials	$ 0	$ 160 000	$ 160 000	100 000	$ 1.60
Conversion costs	14 500	292 900	307 400	106 000	2.90
Cost from preceding department	55 000	594 000	649 000	118 000	5.50
	$69 500	$1 046 900	$1 116 400		$10.00

Costs accounted for

Units transferred to Finished Goods (100 000 litres × $10.00)		$1 000 000
Work in process, 31 January:		
Raw materials	$ 0	
Conversion costs (18 000 litres × $1/3$ × $2.90)	17 400	
Cost from preceding department (18 000 litres × $5.50)	99 000	116 400
		$1 116 400

* Equivalent units

	Materials	Conversion costs	Costs from previous department
Units completed	100 000	100 000	100 000
Work in process	0	6 000 (18 000 × $1/3$)	18 000
	100 000	106 000	118 000

The physical flow schedule shows the units (litres) for which the finishing department is accountable as well as what happens to them. A total of 118 000 units are involved, with 100 000 completed and 18 000 remaining in the ending inventory — one-third complete. The 'costs to be accounted for' section identifies the costs incurred for the various cost elements, their equivalent units, and the average unit cost calculations. The weighted average method is used for inventory costing. All units are finished as far as the preceding department (blending) costs are concerned, so their equivalent units amount to 118 000. *Since the raw materials are not added until the end of the process*, they are not in the ending inventory and the equivalent units are equal to those actually finished, or 100 000.

The equivalent units for the conversion costs are the total of the finished units plus one-third of those in process at the end of January, or 106 000. The percentage of completion for the beginning inventory is irrelevant because the weighted average method is used.

Unit costs are calculated by dividing the total costs accumulated for each element by their number of equivalent units. The total unit cost after both departments are finished with production is $10. The unit cost of $5.50 incurred in the blending department (figure 9.7) is applied to each of the units transferred to the finishing department, as shown on both cost of production reports.

The final section of the report shows the accountability for the departmental cost performance. The finishing department has costs of $1 116 400 for which it is accountable. The units transferred to finished goods are costed at $1 000 000, and $116 400 is left in the ending inventory to be completed in February. Separate calculations must be made for the various cost elements in the ending inventory because of the different equivalent units and unit costs. The ending work in process inventory of $116 400 will be shown as a current asset on the balance sheet at 31 January 2013, along with the $17 000 from the blending department.

It is assumed that 80 000 litres of Stayclean are sold by Chaplin Chemicals Ltd on credit at a price of $18 per litre plus GST of 10%. The remaining 20 000 litres produced during January will be left in finished goods inventory at a cost of $200 000. Essentially the same general journal entries shown earlier for job order costing are made to record the work in process costs of each department. The journal entries to transfer units from the blending to the finishing department, to record the finished goods and to record the sales for January are as shown below:

Jan.	31	Work in Process – Finishing	594 000	
		Work in Process – Blending		594 000
		(Transfer of inventory from the blending department to the finishing department)		
	31	Finished Goods Inventory	1 000 000	
		Work in Process – Finishing		1 000 000
		(Finished goods inventory recorded)		
	31	Accounts Receivable	1 584 000	
		Sales		1 440 000
		GST Collections		144 000
		(Sale of 80 000 litres of product)		
	31	Cost of Sales	800 000	
		Finished Goods Inventory		800 000
		(Cost of litres sold recorded: $10 × 80 000)		

BUSINESS KNOWLEDGE

Costing systems coexist

Modern computerised production processes now allow for job order and process costing systems to be run simultaneously. Thus costing can be done for production runs of mass-produced products where process costing procedures are appropriate, and for one-off custom-made products where job order costing procedures are appropriate. Examples of this exist in motor vehicle manufacture where custom-made vehicles can be produced along with the mass-produced stock models.

9.6 Comparison of job order and process costing

Learning objective 6

Compare the characteristics of job order and process costing systems

In the discussion of cost accumulation systems above, the characteristics of job order costing and process costing were explained. In many ways, the two systems are similar, but there are differences. Table 9.1 (p. 394) presents a comparison of the more important characteristics of job order and process costing systems.

Table 9.1 Comparison of job order costing and process costing

Characteristic	Job order costing	Process costing
Basic purpose	Accumulate production costs	Same as job order costing
Cost flows	Raw materials to work in process to finished goods to cost of sales	Same as job order costing
Type of production	Heterogeneous	Homogeneous
Examples of entities using the method	Custom-built furniture, heavy equipment, printing, construction	Chemicals, oil, flour, plastics, paint
Focal point for costs	Job	Processing centre
Control document	Job cost order	Cost of production report
Reporting period	Life of a job	Time period such as a month
Unit cost calculation	By job	By processing centre/department
Flow of products	Separated by jobs	Continuous
Measure of output	Number of jobs produced	Equivalent units
Direct versus indirect costs	Separation based on jobs as cost objectives	Direct as to the processing centres only
Manufacturing costs to be reported	All costs incurred for a job	All costs incurred for a processing centre/department
Record keeping required	Very detailed	Less detailed than job order costing

9.7 Cost accounting in service entities

Learning objective 7

Understand how costing and cost accounting are applied in service businesses

Managers in non-manufacturing businesses need cost information to enable them to prepare budgets, determine the fees (prices) to be charged for services provided, quote on potential jobs or activities for clients, and analyse the profitability of services provided.

To illustrate the principles involved, consider the advertising business of Global Marketing Pty Ltd, owned and managed by Luci Tenurae. The business specialises in the development of advertising campaigns for its wide range of clients (providing services). In order to be able to quote for particular jobs, and to bill clients for professional services performed, the manager needs to have all relevant cost information available.

For such a business, the major costs involved are the cost of labour for the advertising specialists assigned to each client, general overhead costs of occupying business premises, and administration. In this situation, costs have to be accumulated and assigned to particular clients for jobs or activities performed. Some costs that can be identified with a particular client (e.g. telephone calls and printing, hours spent with the client) can be assigned directly to that client. Other overhead costs that cannot be directly identified with particular clients have to be applied using an overhead application rate. These other overhead costs represent the indirect labour, indirect materials and other common overheads such as electricity, rates and rent of buildings that cannot be associated with particular clients. The same procedures used in manufacturing businesses to develop a predetermined overhead application rate are applied.

In summary, service-type businesses determine the total costs to be assigned to particular clients by adding any direct costs that can be directly assigned, and then assigning indirect common overheads by means of a predetermined overhead application rate.

Illustrative example

Luci's costing and pricing procedures involve assigning to each client or job (a) costs based on the hours spent by each marketing specialist and (b) overheads using a predetermined application rate based on the labour hours charged to the client or job. The fees charged to each client are determined by adding a 50% mark-up to the total costs associated with the job performed for that client.

There are four specialist marketing consultants, including Luci. At 1 July 2013, it is expected that all consultants will work for 40 hours a week for 48 weeks of the year. Not all hours worked can be charged to particular clients (jobs), as the consultants engage in training, research and other activities that cannot be associated with particular clients (jobs). Hourly charge-out rates are determined for each consultant based on the expected annual total salaries cost and the budgeted annual chargeable hours. Details relating to a senior consultant, James Cox, are that his expected chargeable hours in 2013–14 will be 1680, and 240 hours will not be directly chargeable to clients. His total annual labour cost is $153 600. Total estimated chargeable hours for the year for all consultants are expected to be 7000. Budgeted overheads for the 2013–14 financial year are:

Non-chargeable time of four consultants	$ 80 000
Occupancy expenses	180 000
Office staff salaries	90 000
Legal and accounting advice	80 000
Depreciation of equipment	20 000
Other overheads, e.g. electricity	75 000
Total overheads	$525 000

Developing cost application rates

Two cost application rates must be determined — one for the assignment of direct labour costs, and one for applying general overheads to all jobs.

To determine the rate at which direct labour costs are applied to a particular job, a labour cost per hour is developed for each marketing consultant employed. This is achieved by dividing the total costs of employing a consultant by the number of chargeable hours it is estimated the consultant will work in a year. James Cox's chargeable hourly labour cost in the next year will be:

$$\frac{\$153\,600}{1680 + 240} = \$80 \text{ per hour}$$

This means that for each hour Cox spends with a particular client on a particular job, $80 will be charged as direct labour cost. The cost of his non-chargeable time ($80 × 240 hours) is classified as an indirect labour cost and will be included with other overheads when calculating the overhead application rate.

To determine the rate at which indirect costs are applied to jobs, an overhead application rate is developed in the same manner as for a manufacturing business. Total overheads for the year must be estimated, and then divided by the application base chosen. In this case chargeable direct labour hours are used. If the total estimated chargeable hours are 7000, the overhead application rate is $75 per chargeable hour ($525 000/7000 hours).

Assigning costs to jobs and setting a price

To determine the costs to be charged to a particular job, assume that James Cox, who had sole responsibility for the job, spent 50 hours on an advertising job for Ajax Printers Ltd. This job would be charged at $4000 ($80 × 50) for the directly chargeable hours, and overhead assigned would be $3750 ($75 × 50). Total costs of the job are thus $7750. Global Marketing Pty Ltd adds a 50% mark-up on costs to provide a profit and so Ajax Printers Ltd would be invoiced for $11 625 ($7750 + 50% mark-up) plus GST of 10%, making the total price charged $12 788.

Most service businesses adopt a similar approach to that outlined above. Note again that the principles involved are very similar to those used by businesses that manufacture products rather than sell services.

9.8 Just-in-time processing

Learning objective 8

Understand the basic principles of a just-in-time processing system

An alternative production and costing system is **just-in-time (JIT) processing**. JIT is aimed at eliminating the holding of excess inventories, thus saving the significant costs of carrying inventories of raw materials, work in process and finished goods. An example of this is Surteco in the scene setter at the beginning of this chapter where Marc Taylor says, 'We're also putting in a full materials resource planning system because we want to reduce our costs by making sure our materials are more just-in-time and that they're in the right quantities.'

Traditional costing systems have been based on the *just-in-case* principle. Raw materials and manufactured component parts are held 'just in case' there is an interruption to supply or some materials prove faulty, and finished goods are completed and stored 'just in case' customers require urgent supply of finished goods. This principle reflects a *push* approach to production as goods are pushed through the production process in expectation of sales. A consequence of this approach is that large inventories are carried by a manufacturing entity.

Under JIT, as raw materials arrive at the manufacturing plant, they are put into production immediately, and finished goods are shipped immediately on completion to customers. Hence, the only inventory held in an ideal JIT processing plant is work in process. Of course, JIT requires strict quality control and a processing plant that can rely on a steady, reliable supply of raw materials and labour, and a steady demand from customers to purchase the finished goods. JIT requires efficiency in supplier ordering, production design, production processes and production scheduling, and an efficient system of processing customer orders. All these are achieved by use of computer systems that integrate all the processes and are also used to perform most of the production activities.

JIT requires a high degree of automation and a multiskilled workforce. JIT is based on the principle that raw materials should be received just in time to be put into production, manufactured component parts are completed just in time to be included in production, and finished goods are completed just in time to be supplied to customers. JIT reflects a *pull* approach to manufacturing in that raw materials and manufactured components are pulled through the production processes in instantaneous response to customer demand. Such an approach to manufacturing can result in significant savings for an organisation in that inventory levels at all stages of production are eliminated or reduced to a minimum.

In traditional costing systems, the costs of raw materials, work in process and finished goods are accumulated in inventory accounts as we have shown in this chapter. However, under JIT, any raw materials purchased can be entered directly into a single Materials and Work in Process Inventory account or a Raw and In-Process Inventory account, and on completion of production the cost of such materials may be transferred to Finished Goods Inventory, if one is maintained. Direct labour can be regarded as another factory overhead cost. Factory overhead costs (including direct labour) can be applied at the end of the accounting period directly to the Cost of Sales account.

JIT processes are covered in advanced management accounting texts and are not considered further here.

9.9 Activity-based costing (ABC)

Traditional cost accounting systems assign costs of manufacturing to products using a job order cost system or process cost system. Costs are assigned to cost objects (the job or process) directly in the case of direct materials and direct labour, and by an overhead application rate in the case of indirect costs such as factory overhead. Traditionally, overhead costs have been applied to products on the bases of direct labour hours or direct labour costs.

The development of computerised and automated production systems has seen a decrease in the role played by labour in modern manufacturing processes, with labour costs continually falling to a small proportion of total costs and a compensating increase in overhead costs. This fact, together with situations where a manufacturing entity produces a large number of products that vary in both volume and complexity of production, has led to the conclusion that applying overheads on a single basis of labour hours or costs can produce distorted and inaccurate unit costs.

Activity-based costing has been developed as a means of overcoming these problems and increasing the accuracy of overhead allocation and hence unit cost of products.

Activity-based costing (ABC) is a system in which the production processes have been analysed and broken down into *activities*. An activity is any event or act that causes the costs to increase. Costs associated with these activities are assigned to products on the basis of *cost drivers* appropriate to these activities. Under ABC, the final cost of a product is the sum of the costs of all the activities that have contributed to producing the product or service. Examples of these activities include machine set-ups, materials purchasing, processing production orders, receipt of materials, machine time and computer hours logged. Cost drivers have to be determined as a means of assigning costs to products depending on how they consume these activities. Examples of activities and possible cost drivers that would be used to assign costs to products are set out below:

Activity	Cost driver
Machine set-ups	Set-up hours
Materials purchasing	Number of orders
Production orders	Number of orders
Materials receipts	Number of receipts
Machine usage	Number of hours used
Computer usage	Computer hours logged

ABC is a refinement of process costing. Rather than accumulating costs by production processes and using one cost driver, such as direct labour hours, costs are accumulated by activities. For each activity for which costs are accumulated, there is usually a different cost driver. Whereas process costing may have only a few production departments to accumulate costs, ABC has many activities for which to accumulate costs. Some ABC systems have dozens of activities each with its own cost driver used to apply those costs to production. This refinement of process costing leads to far more accurate costing of the final product or service.

To appreciate how ABC can reduce the degree of distortion that can result from inappropriate overhead application, consider a company that produces two products, A and B. Product A is a high-volume item requiring little machine set-up time, few purchase and production orders, and little computer time. Product B, on the other hand, is a low-volume item that requires numerous machine set-ups, many purchase and production orders to be processed, and relatively high usage of computer time. If the direct labour hours worked for both products are the same, overhead costs associated with the activities highlighted would lead to an equal amount of overhead being allocated to A and B. Assigning the costs of the activities on the basis of the cost driver for each activity would invariably lead to a different overhead cost amount being allocated in line with the product's demand on those activities. ABC is sometimes referred to as *transaction costing*, because it improves the accuracy with which costs are traced or assigned to units of production.

The same problems that arise from the use of a single overhead application rate arise in service-type businesses. There may be advantages to be gained by such businesses adopting the principles of ABC to improve the accuracy of the cost of jobs and activities.

BUSINESS KNOWLEDGE

Life cycle accounting

Life cycle accounting (LCA) refers to a product's full life cycle, from raw materials to end-products (and disposal), including all upstream and downstream activities and impacts. This is broken down into direct activities — those at the production site and thus under the entity's control — and indirect activities, beyond the site.

The appeal of the product-focus approach is that it provides a way to assess, measure, and manage sustainability impacts and competitive opportunities. However, reporting that focuses on a product's economic, environmental, and social impacts needs to be a supplement to entity reporting — it can't stand alone.

That said, product-based assessment is worthwhile as an adjunct to a more widely accepted corporate perspective describing a business's non-financial elements.

Where LCA gets tricky is in the different use of direct and indirect management accounting applications. For instance, some activities are considered direct because they are controlled, but their costs would be treated as indirect under activity-based costing.

Product LCA allows a company to identify and co-ordinate a wider range of effects as part of continuous improvement. And, by introducing the notion of measurable indirect economic, social, and environmental impacts throughout the supply chain, the externalities of economic activity can be better recognised.

Source: Excerpts from John Purcell, 'Sharpening the edge — sustainability can sustain the bottom line', *The Age Business Supplement.*

Although ABC has received a large amount of attention and application in several countries, particularly the United States, adoption of this approach to overhead application has been slow in other countries. The main reason could be the higher costs of introducing an ABC system without fully appreciating the benefits to management decision making. However, ABC is increasingly being used in service organisations. ABC is a specialist topic appropriately studied in more advanced courses.

KEY TERMS

Activity-based costing (ABC), p. 396

Conversion costs, p. 387

Cost accounting, p. 378

Cost accounting system, p. 378

Cost driver, p. 386

Cost of production report, p. 390

Equivalent units, p. 389

Job cost order, p. 380

Job order costing, p. 379

Just-in-time (JIT) processing, p. 395

Materials requisition, p. 381

Overapplied factory overhead, p. 385

Predetermined overhead rate, p. 384

Process costing, p. 387

Processing centre, p. 387

Underapplied factory overhead, p. 385

DISCUSSION QUESTIONS

1. The production of 100 cartons of cans of soft drink could be costed as part of a job order costing system or a process costing system. Do you agree? Explain.

2. Marko is studying for a marketing degree at university and when he graduates he would like to work for an international marketing firm. Explain to Marko how an understanding of cost accounting would help him to succeed in his intended career.

3. 'Both a job order costing system and a process costing system enable the calculation of the unit cost of a product. However, process costing provides a more accurate unit cost.' Discuss.

4. 'If you order a vehicle with special features from a large motor vehicle manufacturer, then it is possible to track the production of your vehicle online so that you know when the manufacturer began building it, where it is roughly in the production process and when it is being finished off. With the special order you can have features that are not on the standard vehicles, although there is only a set range of options — such as colour of paint, type of air-conditioning, engine specifications and seat material — from which you can choose the individualised features.'

   To what extent would the costing of these special-order vehicles use job order costing and process costing?

5. 'With process costing, the need to distinguish between direct and indirect materials and labour is not as important as in a job order costing system.' Discuss.

6. 'It is difficult to understand how costs can be assigned to equivalent units when such units do not really exist in a physical form.' Discuss.

7. When your motor vehicle is serviced, the account you receive lists such things as labour, part numbers of parts used, consumables, GST and who performed the service. What type of cost accounting system does this suggest is used for motor vehicle servicing, and under what cost heading are the service centre overhead costs likely to be included?

8. 'In service businesses, the principles of costing services are the same as for producing physical products and the same problems exist.' Do you agree? Explain.

9. With Surteco Australia, the plastics manufacturer in the scene setter, would direct labour be the most appropriate cost driver to allocate overhead given its recent changes to manufacturing?

10. A managing director was heard to remark: 'Activity-based costing may offer some entities advantages, but given our situation I do not think the cost of implementing such a system can be justified.' Is this stance reasonable? Discuss.

LO 3

Exercise 9.1 JOB COSTS

Fine Furniture Ltd, which specialises in the manufacture of custom-built furniture, uses a job order costing system. On 1 March, the company had no beginning work in process inventory. During March, the following costs were recorded:

Direct materials	$81 300
Direct labour (4200 hours)	75 600
Actual factory overhead	33 000

Factory overhead is applied using a predetermined overhead rate of $7.20 per direct labour hour. No jobs were finished during March.

Required

Determine work in process inventory on 31 March.

LO 7

Exercise 9.2 PREDETERMINED OVERHEAD RATE FOR SERVICE INDUSTRY

As a graduate of a tourism and hospitality course you have been asked by your employer, Hyend Hotels, to determine the overhead rate applicable to each night's accommodation in one of the hotel's rooms. The hotel has 150 rooms and achieves an 80% occupancy rate on average over the 365 days of the year. You have determined the overhead costs that cannot be charged direct to each room are as follows:

Depreciation	$206 400
Gardening and pool maintenance	201 600
Insurance	230 400
Maintenance	268 800
Rates	67 200
Electricity	93 600
Sundry expenses	150 000
Indirect salaries	528 000

Required

A. Calculate the overhead rate applicable to each room night for the hotel.
B. What are some of the direct labour and direct expenses that are likely to be applicable to a hotel room that will also need to be included in pricing the room rate?

LO 3

Exercise 9.3 PREDETERMINED OVERHEAD RATES

The expected costs and operating data for two manufacturers are presented below:

	Aloe Ltd	Basil Ltd
Units produced	52 000	41 980
Factory overhead costs	$249 600	$444 080
Direct labour hours	75 800	82 000
Direct labour cost	$498 000	$401 800

Aloe Ltd applies factory overhead on the basis of units of production, whereas Basil Ltd uses direct labour hours. During the last financial year, Aloe Ltd produced 54 800 units and incurred factory overhead costs of $264 000, and Basil Ltd's overhead costs were $430 000, using 87 000 direct labour hours.

Required

A. Calculate the predetermined factory overhead rate for each company.
B. Indicate whether factory overhead was overapplied or underapplied for each company, and by how much.

Exercise 9.4 JOB ORDER COSTING PROCEDURES

Job order cost data for Jobs 125 to 134 are shown below. The costs were incurred by Beejay Ltd during March and April, the company's first 2 months of operations.

Job order no.	Costs at 1 April	April production costs
125	$ 7 820	
126	10 500	
127	8 960	$ 2 400
128	12 100	1 200
129	9 800	5 800
130	6 500	9 500
131		12 600
132		15 320
133		4 600
134		2 275

Jobs 125 and 126 were completed in March.
Jobs 127, 128, 129, 130 and 131 were completed in April.
Jobs 132, 133 and 134 were incomplete at 30 April.
Jobs 125, 127, 128, 130 and 131 were sold during April.

Required
Calculate the following:
1. work in process inventory, 1 April
2. work in process inventory, 30 April
3. finished goods inventory, 1 April
4. finished goods inventory, 30 April
5. cost of sales for April.

Exercise 9.5 JOB ORDER COSTING PROCEDURES

Esjay Ltd uses a job order costing system. The September cost data were as follows:

Raw materials purchased on credit	$ 354 000
Direct labour costs	366 600
Raw materials issued to production	329 400
Actual factory overhead costs	
(including depreciation of $27 240)	275 000
Cost of goods manufactured	944 600
Sales (all credit)	1 040 200

Machine hours for September were 55 700 hours, and the business applies factory overhead to production at a rate of $5.60 per machine hour. The beginning raw materials inventory was $40 000. The beginning work in process inventory was $66 800. The beginning and ending finished goods inventories were $99 000 and $128 000 respectively. Ignore GST.

Required
A. Prepare general journal entries to record the September transactions.
B. Was overhead overapplied or underapplied for the month of September?
C. Calculate the ending balances of raw materials and work in process. (*Hint:* Prepare T accounts for inventories.)

Exercise 9.6 JOB ORDER COSTING PROCEDURES

Complete the requirements of exercise 9.5, but include 10% GST on raw materials, actual factory overhead costs and sales.

Exercise 9.7 JOB ORDER COSTING PROCEDURES FOR SERVICE INDUSTRY

PUBLCT Pty Ltd, a marketing firm, uses a job order costing system to charge its clients. The firm specialises in marketing work for small local businesses in Melbourne such as tradespeople and small shops that are not associated with national franchises. The cost data for March were as follows:

Labour charged direct to jobs	$80 600
Stationery and consumables charged direct to jobs	38 750
Office overhead costs	70 000

PUBLCT Pty Ltd applies office overhead costs to advertising jobs at 90% of the direct labour charge. Once the total cost of a job is determined, the firm marks up the costs by 40% to calculate the amount charged to the client.

Required
A. Calculate the total amount charged to clients' accounts during March.
B. Were office overhead costs overapplied or underapplied for the month of March?
C. What factors could cause an over- or underapplication of overhead costs during a particular month?

Exercise 9.8 JOB ORDER COSTING PROCEDURES

Ben's Beds Ltd had a balance in its Work in Process Inventory account on 1 October 2013 of $6800 made up of two jobs: Job 730, $3200; and Job 731, $3600. At the end of October, costs assigned to production summarised by the source documents are presented below:

Job no.	Materials requisitions	Labour time records
730	$ 2 940	$ 3 200
731	3 180	3 850
732	5 080	7 900
Factory overhead (actual)	1 310	2 060
	$12 510	$17 010

Factory overhead is applied to jobs at the rate of 100% of direct labour costs. Job 730 was the only job completed during October.

Required
A. Show the general journal entries to record the costs as revealed by the source documents and the application of factory overhead.
B. Prepare the Work in Process Inventory account for the month of October.

Exercise 9.9 EQUIVALENT UNITS WITH BEGINNING WORK IN PROCESS

Delish Ltd produces a dishwashing liquid. At the beginning of January, 126 000 litres of liquid cleaner were in process, 100% complete as to raw materials and 40% complete as to conversion costs. During the month, 920 000 litres of raw materials were placed into production. At the end of the month, 80 000 litres of dishwashing liquid were in work in process inventory, 100% completed as to raw materials and 50% completed in terms of conversion costs.

Assume that the following costs were recorded by Delish Ltd for the beginning work in process and the production performance for January:

Beginning inventory:	
Raw materials costs	$ 48 000
Conversion costs	38 400
January production costs:	
Raw materials costs	368 000
Conversion costs	761 600

Required

A. Prepare a schedule of equivalent units for January (weighted average method).
B. Calculate the unit cost for each litre of liquid cleaner.
C. Determine the total costs of the litres of liquid cleaner finished during January. What is the balance of the ending work in process inventory?

Exercise 9.10 EQUIVALENT UNITS WITH BEGINNING WORK IN PROCESS

Pizza Cheese Ltd produces cheese topping for the fast pizza industry. At the beginning of April, 20 000 kilograms of cheese topping was in process, 100% complete as to raw materials and 60% complete as to conversion costs. During the month, 460 000 kilograms of raw materials were placed into production. At the end of the month, 40 000 kilograms of cheese topping was in work in process inventory, 80% completed as to raw materials and 40% completed in terms of conversion costs.

Assume that the following costs were recorded by Pizza Cheese Ltd for the beginning work in process and the production performance for April:

Beginning inventory:	
Raw materials costs	$ 12 000
Conversion costs	4 800
April production costs:	
Raw materials costs	271 200
Conversion costs	177 600

Required

A. Prepare a schedule of equivalent units for April (weighted average method).
B. Calculate the unit cost for each kilogram of cheese topping.
C. Determine the total costs of the kilograms of cheese topping finished during April. What is the balance of the ending work in process inventory?

Exercise 9.11 COST OF PRODUCTION REPORT

Thomas Oliphant Pty Ltd produces a single product, using two production departments — Construction and Packaging. The June cost and operating data for the Construction Department is:

Beginning work in process inventory	—
Units started in Construction Department	40 500
Units transferred to Packaging Department	38 200
Raw materials costs	$351 340
Conversion costs	$295 125

The work in process inventory in the Construction Department on 30 June is half complete as to conversion costs and three-quarters complete as to materials.

Required

Prepare a cost of production report for the June production of the Construction Department.

Exercise 9.12 COST OF PRODUCTION REPORT WITH OPENING WORK IN PROCESS

North Point Pty Ltd produces a single product in three departments: Construction, Finishing and Packaging. The April cost and operating data for the Construction Department is:

Beginning work in process inventory	3 000
Units started in Construction Department	42 000
Units transferred to Finishing Department	42 500
Beginning work in process:	
Raw material costs	$13 800
Conversion costs	$17 280
Current period costs:	
Raw material costs	$190 325
Conversion costs	$297 720

The work in process inventory in the Construction Department on 1 April is 80% complete as to conversion costs and 100% complete as to materials. At 30 April the work in process inventory in the Construction Department is half complete as to conversion costs and three-quarters complete as to materials.

Required

Prepare a cost of production report for the April production of the Construction Department.

LO 7

Exercise 9.13 CHARGE-OUT RATE

Green Consultants Pty Ltd specialise in consulting on landscape design. The company developed a predetermined charge-out rate based on hours for each of its consultants on 1 July 2013 to assign the cost of labour directly associated with each client job for the coming year. The company employs four consultants who each work 40 hours per week for 48 weeks of the year; 20% of each consultant's total yearly labour time is not directly chargeable to client jobs. The budgeted total labour cost for one of the consultants, G. Wuurm, is $92 160.

Required

Determine the hourly charge-out rate to be assigned as labour cost to all client jobs on which G. Wuurm works to 30 June 2014. (Ignore GST.) If Wuurm worked for 1500 hours for clients during the year, what is the total labour cost charged for Wuurm?

LO 7

Exercise 9.14 CHARGE-OUT RATE

Refer to the information provided in exercise 9.13. The following additional information is available. The total labour costs for all consultants employed for the year is budgeted to be $400 000. Budgeted overhead costs for the year, excluding the costs of non-chargeable hours of the consultants, is $319 360.

Required

A. Calculate the overhead application rate based on chargeable hours to be used to allocate overhead costs to client jobs for the year ended 30 June 2014. (Ignore GST.)
B. If G. Wuurm is the only consultant to work for 80 hours on job number 2468 completed during the year, calculate the total costs that would have been assigned to this job.

LO 7

Exercise 9.15 CHARGE-OUT RATE

Professionals Pty Ltd is a firm that offers a wide variety of professional services such as marketing, employment of professionals for other firms and accounting services. The firm has the following annual overhead costs:

Office rent	$ 104 000
Secretarial staff wages	210 000
Cleaning costs	7 800
Depreciation of office equipment	260 000
Lease of office furniture	83 200
Floral arrangements	2 600
Stationery costs not chargeable to clients	31 200
Office manager's salary and on-costs	84 000
Advertising	41 600
Sundry overhead cost	174 000

The firm has six professionals with total salary plus on-costs of $1 248 000. The owners of the firm have invested $1 797 120 in the firm and expect a return on this investment of 25%. Alice is one of the six professionals and her total salary plus on-costs is $104 000. It is assumed by the firm that each professional will charge 40 hours per week for 48 weeks of the year. Professionals are expected to work as many hours as it takes each week to enable them to charge out 40 hours so that there is no cost to the firm of non-chargeable hours.

Required

Calculate the hourly charge out rate for Alice's services by allocating the office overhead costs and return on owners' investment on the basis of total salary plus on-costs for each professional.

★ Basic

★★ Moderate

★★★ Challenging

LO 3

Problem 9.1 JOB ORDER COSTING AND FACTORY OVERHEAD ★

Giles Products Ltd uses a job order costing system to control costs in its two production departments. Factory overhead is applied on the basis of machine hours in the Construction Department and on the basis of direct labour cost in the Finishing Department. The company prepared the following estimates for its production.

	Construction Department	Finishing Department
Machine hours	6 800	7 125
Direct labour cost	$240 000	$380 000
Direct labour hours	13 000	24 000
Factory overhead	$408 000	$570 000

The accounting records for Job 431 reveal the following:

	Construction Department	Finishing Department
Machine hours	40	50
Direct labour cost	$1 640	$1 800
Direct labour hours	90	100
Raw materials	$1 300	$1 420

Required
A. Calculate the predetermined overhead rate for each department.
B. Calculate the total cost of Job 431.
C. If the actual direct labour cost in the Finishing Department was $375 800 and the actual factory overhead was $560 000, was the overhead overapplied or underapplied?

LO 3

Problem 9.2 JOB ORDER COSTING AND ALTERNATIVE FACTORY OVERHEAD ★★

Giles Products Ltd from problem 9.1 has just employed an accountant who is reviewing the overhead allocations in the two production departments.

Required
A. The new accountant has reviewed the costs in the Finishing Department and believes that rather than allocating factory overhead using direct labour costs it would be more accurate to apply the overhead on the basis of machine hours. What factors may have led the accountant to decide that machine hours is a more accurate method of allocating factory overhead in the Finishing Department?
B. Calculate the predetermined overhead rate for both departments using machine hours.
C. Calculate the total cost of Job 431 using machine hours to allocate overhead for both of the departments.
D. The price of each job is calculated by adding a 30% margin to the total costs of a job. How much would the price of Job 431 change if the Finishing Department factory overhead is allocated using machine hours rather than direct labour costs?

LO 3

Problem 9.3 JOB ORDER COSTING ★★

The April 2013 transactions of Jackson Productions Ltd, which uses a job order costing system, are shown below. (Ignore GST.)
1. Raw materials purchased, $342 000.
2. Raw materials issued to production, $320 000 direct and $42 000 indirect.
3. Factory payroll included $498 000 of direct labour and $96 000 of indirect labour.

4. Other overhead costs incurred were:

Rates	$52 000
Supplies	40 500
Insurance	48 000
Gas	76 800

5. Depreciation of manufacturing equipment, $57 000.
6. Factory overhead is applied at 80% of direct labour cost.
7. Jobs completed and transferred to finished goods at cost, $1 170 000.
8. Jobs with a cost of $1 100 000 were sold for $1 375 000 cash.
9. Beginning inventories were:

Raw materials	$ 43 500
Work in process	122 000
Finished goods	105 000

Required

A. Prepare the general journal entries to record the transactions.
B. Calculate the ending balances in work in process, raw materials and finished goods.
C. Was overhead underapplied or overapplied in April? By what amount?

LO 5

Problem 9.4 PROCESS COSTS, EQUIVALENT UNITS AND COST OF PRODUCTION
REPORT ★★

Abbott Ltd produces a chemical used to clean showers in a single process in the Production Department. Raw materials in the form of chemicals are added at the beginning of the process, and a litre container is added at the end. The conversion costs (direct labour and factory overhead) are incurred uniformly throughout the process. The following cost and production data are available for the month of October 2013.

Beginning work in process inventory:	
Units	15 000 litres
Cost of chemicals added	$12 000
Cost of containers added	
Conversion costs added	$4 500
October operating data:	
Units started	300 000 litres
Units finished	290 000
Cost of chemicals added	$240 000
Cost of containers added	$43 500
Conversion costs	$361 500

The ending work in process inventory was 60% complete as to conversion costs.

Required

A. Determine equivalent units for both raw materials and conversion costs.
B. Prepare a cost of production report for the October 2013 production.

LO 3

Problem 9.5 JOB ORDER COSTING ★★

Eatern and Sons Ltd accounts for its manufacturing costs using a job order costing system and has provided the following production data during June 2013.
- Job Z241 was in process as of 1 June with a cost of $22 000.
- The purchases of raw materials on credit during the month amounted to $72 000. Raw materials requisitioned were charged to the following:

Job Z241	$17 500
Job Z242	15 000
Job Z243	23 500
Indirect materials	9 000

- Payroll of $78 000 was incurred. Each worker earns $12.00 per hour. Ignore income tax and other payroll deductions.
- The factory payroll was distributed as follows:

Job Z241	$21 000
Job Z242	25 500
Job Z243	22 500
Indirect labour	8 500

- Additional factory overhead costs incurred during the month were $11 200 (assume that accounts payable was credited for $8600 and the rest was for accumulated depreciation of factory equipment).
- Factory overhead is applied at $4.60 per direct labour hour.
- Jobs Z241 and Z242 were completed and transferred to finished goods.
- Job Z241 was sold at a mark-up of 50% over cost.
- The beginning raw materials were $22 200.

Required

A. Prepare the general journal entries to record the June 2013 transactions.
B. Determine the balances of the Raw Materials Inventory and Work in Process Inventory accounts at the end of June 2013.

Problem 9.6 PROCESS COSTS, EQUIVALENT UNITS AND COST OF PRODUCTION REPORT ★★   **LO 5**

Mexican Chocolates Ltd produces blocks of chocolate. Raw materials in the form of cocoa solids, milk and sugar are added at the beginning of the process, flavouring, fruit and nuts are added halfway through the process and a cardboard box is added at the end. The conversion costs (direct labour and factory overhead) are incurred uniformly throughout the process. The following cost and production data are available for the month of June 2014.

Beginning work in process inventory:	
Units	60 000 blocks of chocolate
Cost of cocoa etc. added	$36 000
Cost of flavouring etc. added	—
Cost of boxes added	—
Conversion costs added	$12 000
June operating data:	
Units started	600 000 blocks of chocolate
Units finished	620 000 blocks of chocolate
Cost of cocoa etc. added	$360 000
Cost of flavouring etc. added	$124 000
Cost of boxes added	$62 000
Conversion costs	$306 000

The ending work in process inventory was 40% complete as to conversion costs.

Required

A. Determine equivalent units for both raw materials and conversion costs.
B. Prepare a cost of production report for the June 2014 production.

Problem 9.7 COSTING FOR A PUBLIC ACCOUNTING FIRM ★★   **LO 7**

Newbery and Newstead is a public accounting firm specialising in auditing local medium-sized businesses. Fees charged for each audit are determined on the basis of identifiable hours worked on an audit by each one of the accountants in the firm, an allocation of general overheads via a predetermined rate per chargeable hour, plus a mark-up of 40% on the cost of chargeable hours for the accountants working on the audit. The hourly charge rate for one of its accountants, Michael, set for the year ending 30 June 2014, is $120. The following budgeted information was used at the beginning of the year to determine the overhead application rate per chargeable hour to be assigned to all audit jobs during the year ending 30 June 2014.

Total budgeted chargeable hours of all accountants in the firm were 10 800 hours. Estimated overheads were:

Accountants' indirect (non-chargeable) time	$ 14 000
Secretarial services	64 000
Computer services/support	36 000
Printing, telephone, postage, stationery	18 000
Professional indemnity, and other insurance	120 000
Legal support	60 000
Other overheads (including depreciation)	12 000

Required
A. Calculate the application rate for the firm's overheads. (Ignore GST.)
B. If Michael was the only accountant to work on the annual audit of APT Ltd, and he recorded 90 hours on this audit, determine the total costs (labour and overheads) to be charged to this client.
C. Determine the total professional fees charged for this audit, after adding GST.

LO 7

Problem 9.8 COSTING FOR A HUMAN RESOURCE MANAGEMENT FIRM ★★

EmployUs Pty Ltd is a human resource management firm that specialises in employing middle to senior management staff on behalf of other firms. The charge to employ a person is set at 50% of the first year's remuneration package for the person being employed. To work out the profitability of each job, EmployUs Pty Ltd charges direct labour, advertising costs, travel costs and any other costs directly traceable to the job. The firm also allocates its overhead costs to jobs based on the first year's remuneration of the person being employed.

EmployUs Pty Ltd expects to successfully employ 200 managers on behalf of its clients in the coming year with an average remuneration package of $150 000.

Estimated overheads are:

Human resource staff indirect time	$280 000
Secretarial services	120 000
Information technology costs	60 000
Printing, telephone, postage, stationery	30 000
Advertising EmployUs	40 000
Insurance	115 000
Legal support	105 000
Other overheads	75 000

Required
A. Calculate the application rate for the firm's overheads. (Ignore GST.)
B. Brianna has just successfully employed a new executive manager for Carbone Ltd on a first year's remuneration package of $200 000. Brianna is on an $80 000 salary plus 30% on-costs and she estimates that she has spent the equivalent of 3 months employing the new executive. Calculate the profit that EmployUs Pty Ltd will attribute to this job.
C. During the year EmployUs Pty Ltd employed managers for clients with total remuneration packages of $25 million. Will EmployUs Pty Ltd have overapplied or underapplied overhead for the year?

LO 5

Problem 9.9 COST OF PRODUCTION REPORT FOR ONE DEPARTMENT ★★★

Chiu Ltd prepares bulk supplies of Singapore noodles using two departments, a Blending Department and a Packaging Department. The finished product is sold in large quantities to retailers that package it and sell it with their own labels.

Raw materials (ingredients) are added at the beginning of each department's process, and conversion costs are incurred uniformly throughout. The noodles flow from the Blending Department to the Packaging Department and then to finished goods inventory when all the work is completed.

Production data in kilograms for the month of August with completed percentages for the conversion costs were as follows:

	Beginning inventory	% complete	Units started	Ending inventory	% complete
Blending Department	30 000	40	280 000	40 000	30
Packaging Department	36 000	60	?	84 000	50

Beginning work in process inventory costs on 1 August were as follows:

	Blending Department	Packaging Department
Previous department costs	—	$252 000
Raw materials	$114 000	64 800
Conversion costs	28 800	36 000

Production costs incurred during August were the following:

	Blending Department	Packaging Department
Raw materials	$1 064 000	$360 000
Conversion costs	648 000	486 000

Required

Prepare a cost of production report for August for the blending department. (Ignore GST.)

Problem 9.10 PROCESS COSTING — JOURNALISING TRANSACTIONS ★★★   **LO 5**

Hotbox Ltd produces pizza boxes using two processes — cutting and packaging. The production budget for the year ending 30 June 2013 estimated raw materials use of $400 000, factory overhead of $270 000, direct labour costs of $190 000 and 168 750 machine hours. (Ignore GST.)

During April 2013, the following transactions were recorded:

1. Raw materials transferred to cutting, $21 600.
   Raw materials transferred to packaging, $28 000.
2. Direct labour costs incurred by cutting, $15 800.
   Direct labour costs incurred by packaging, $20 200.
3. Machine hours used by cutting, 13 800 hours.
   Machine hours used by packaging, 17 600 hours.
4. Other production costs for April were:
Factory supplies	$25 400
Depreciation	16 500
Repairs	6 200
Insurance	1 700
5. Product with an assigned cost of $61 400 was transferred from cutting to packaging.
6. Overhead was applied in each department based on machine hours used. (A predetermined rate based on estimated overheads and total machine hours over both departments is to be calculated.)
7. Raw material purchases were $56 000.
8. Goods with an assigned cost of $136 000 were transferred from packaging to finished goods.
9. Finished goods with an assigned cost of $140 000 were sold on credit for $162 000.
10. Beginning inventory as at 1 April comprised the following amounts:
Raw materials	$17 500
Work in process — cutting	18 400
Work in process — packaging	21 800
Finished goods	14 000

Required

A. Prepare journal entries to record the April transactions. Assume all expenses were paid in cash. Use Factory Overhead and Factory Overhead Applied accounts.

B. Calculate ending work in process and finished goods balances in each process.

C. Was overhead underapplied or overapplied in April? By what amount?

LO 5

Problem 9.11 PROCESS COSTING — CHOICE OF COST ACCOUNTING SYSTEM ★★★

Refer to the Hotbox Ltd production process details in problem 9.10.

Required

Explain in detail, using the facts from problem 9.10, why it is most appropriate for Hotbox Ltd to use a process costing system rather than a job order costing system. Your answer should be no less than 250 words and should relate to the steps evident in the construction of cardboard pizza boxes.

LO 5

Problem 9.12 UNIT COSTS AND TOTAL COSTS — PROCESS COSTING ★★★

Internet Inhand Ltd began producing netbooks on 1 July 2013. A unit of production passes through two processes — manufacturing and finishing. Production data for the month of July are presented below:

	Manufacturing	Finishing
Units started in process during July	98 000	—
Units received from previous process during July	—	82 000
Total	98 000	82 000
Costs of production		
Materials	$7 840 000	—
Direct labour	450 000	387 500
Factory overhead	5 400 000	4 030 000
Units completed in July and transferred out	82 000	70 000
Units in process, all materials added 31 July		
½ complete for labour and overhead	16 000	
¼ complete for labour and overhead		6 000

Required

Prepare a cost of production report for July for each department, showing the unit cost on completed units for each process assuming that materials are added at the beginning of the process, and conversion costs are incurred continuously. The company uses the average cost method.

LO 5

Problem 9.13 UNIT COSTS AND TOTAL COSTS — PROCESS COSTING ★★★

Cakemix Ltd produces cakes. Production is carried out in three processes — mixing, baking and packaging. The work in process accounts for the three processes for the month of April are set out below:

Work in Process – Mixing

April	30	Materials	62 000	April	30	WIP – Baking	105 000
		Labour	18 000				
		Factory Overhead	29 600				

Work in Process – Baking

April	1	Balance	4 800	April	30	WIP – Packaging	129 600
	30	Labour	4 000				
		Factory Overhead	15 800				
		WIP – Mixing	105 000				

Work in Process – Packaging

April	1	Balance	3 136*	April	30	Finished Goods	?
	30	Materials	28 800				
		Labour	14 956				
		Factory Overhead	21 060				
		WIP – Baking	129 600				

* Conversion costs included — $320

Cost and production data for the final two processes are set out below:

	Baking	Packaging
Inventory, 1 April	4000 units (40% complete)	3200 units (50% complete)
Inventory, 30 April	nil	3800 units (60% complete)
Units transferred out	180 000	179 400

Required

A. Calculate the unit materials cost, unit conversion cost, and total manufacturing cost per equivalent unit for the packaging process.
B. Calculate the costs assigned to units transferred out and units in ending work in process for April for baking and packaging.

Problem 9.14 COSTING FOR ARCHITECTURAL CONSULTANTS ★★★ — LO 7

Tsoulos, Tsoulakis and Associates is a small firm of architectural consultants. At 1 July 2012, three architects other than the principals, Tony Tsoulos and Maria Tsoulakis, are employed. The following information is relevant for the 2012–13 financial year.

It is expected that each of the five architects in the firm will work an average of 46 weeks, working a 40-hour week. All hours worked on client jobs are charged at a charge-out rate determined for each architect. Only 70% of the total hours worked by the principals and 85% of the total hours worked by others are assigned directly to client jobs.

The total labour costs of all five architects for the year ended 30 June 2013 are $530 000 (Tsoulos and Tsoulakis $300 000, other architects $230 000). Expected overheads of the firm for the year (except for the labour costs of architects not directly charged to clients) are:

Secretarial services	$71 740
Labour fringe benefits	55 000
Computer services	14 500
Legal services	22 000
Insurances	23 000
Staff training	17 000
Office administration expenses	35 000
Other overheads (including depreciation)	37 000

During the year, the firm completed a consultancy for one of its regular clients, Superior Homes Ltd. Tony Tsoulos and one other architect, Tung Thanh Tran, worked on this particular job. Tony charges his time to clients at $100 per hour. Tung Thanh's gross salary and other costs amount to $93 840. Tony worked on the job for 20 hours and payroll time sheets showed that Tung Thanh had spent 60 hours on the job.

Required

A. Determine the costs to be charged to Superior Homes Ltd for labour and overheads.
B. If the firm has a mark-up of 25% on total costs charged to a job in determining gross fees, what was the total professional fee (including GST) shown on the tax invoice sent to Superior Homes Ltd?

Problem 9.15 ACTIVITY-BASED COSTING ★★★ — LO 9

Melaleuca Manufacturing Ltd produces timber felling machines for the forestry industry around the world. Its two machines are the Tree Toppler, which cuts down trees and clears undergrowth, and the Melaleuca Muncher that pulps the timber into woodchips.

The costs, volumes and cost drivers for the year ended 30 June 2013 are as follows:

	Tree Toppler	Melaleuca Muncher	Total
Sales and production (units)	320	280	600
Direct materials cost	$86 000	$72 000	$47 680 000
Direct labour hours	48.75	32	24 560
Machine hours	66.75	54	36 480
Direct labour cost	$1 755	$1 152	$875 520
Number of production runs	14	16	30
Number of deliveries	320	280	600
Number of receipts of materials	19 200	13 440	32 640
Number of production orders	160	112	272

Overhead costs	$
Set-up costs	720 000
Machine maintenance and depreciation	2 918 400
Receiving and warehousing	1 958 400
Preparing for shipment and freight	5 160 000
Engineering for production orders	1 523 200
Total	$12 280 000

Required

A. Calculate the unit cost of each machine if all overhead costs are allocated on the basis of direct labour hours.

B. Calculate the unit cost of each machine using activity-based costing.

C. Which machine is likely to be overpriced using the single overhead allocation method of direct labour hours and which machine is likely to be underpriced?

DECISION ANALYSIS

Allocation of factory overheads

Macquarie Manufacturing Ltd prepared the following planned production data for the forthcoming year ending 30 June 2014:

Direct materials costs	$648 000
Direct labour costs	$324 000
Factory overheads	$1 296 000
Direct labour hours required	20 250 hours
Machine hours required	432 000 hours
Units of completed production	1 800 000 units

Required

A. Prepare a table showing the predetermined factory overhead rate based on each of the following: direct materials cost, direct labour cost, direct labour hours, machine hours, and units of production.

B. The following data relate to Job 6543, which was completed during the year: materials costs $280, direct labour costs $720, direct labour hours 45, machine hours used 1200. Job 6543 consisted of 400 identical units. Prepare a table summarising the amount of factory overhead that would have been assigned to Job 6543 using each of the bases given in requirement A. Calculate the cost per unit for Job 6543 using each of the factory overhead bases.

C. Which overhead rate is the most appropriate and why?

D. Management is considering introducing an activity-based costing (ABC) system. How would such a system affect the way the cost of Job 6543 is determined? Should management introduce an ABC system? Explain your answer.

Costing procedures for Hardwood Furniture Ltd

Hardwood Furniture Ltd produces standard dining-room tables and chairs on a production line that includes a cutting department, a shaping department, a construction department and a finishing department. This dining-room furniture is sold to mid-priced retailers around the country. They are a standard product and over 25 000 dining-room settings are produced and sold each year.

Hardwood Furniture Ltd also takes special one-off orders for custom-built dining-room settings that are produced to the customer's specifications in consultation with the company's master carpenter. This furniture is hand-finished and French-polished, and is not made on the company's production line.

Required

A. Should the company use the same costing procedures for materials used in the production of both products? Would this always be necessary?

B. Should the company use the same costing procedures for factory wages and salaries in the production of both products? Is this necessary in all circumstances?

C. Why would the company use a predetermined overhead application rate for costing the production of custom-built dining-room settings?

D. When would it be necessary to use a predetermined overhead application rate in costing the production of the standard dining-room settings? Would there be some circumstances where actual overhead costs could be used rather than a predetermined overhead application rate? Explain.

Allocation of costs to overheads

Tom Shanks, production manager for Innovative Products Ltd, had just finished his annual performance appraisal with the managing director, May Martin. May had indicated that, although Tom's performance as production manager was satisfactory, she and other senior managers were concerned with the continuing high levels of production costs. As a result, Tom was informed that he would receive a smaller bonus this year as compared with the past. In this regard, May had remarked: 'You will need to pay close attention to production costs over the next quarter. I am confident that your production costs will improve. You obviously need to get costs down a little. Why don't you talk to the management accountant and work something out? If things improve we might be able to do something about that bonus.'

Tom approached the management accountant, Jerry Flynn, and explained his position in the following manner: 'Jerry, I have just had lengthy discussions with May and we agreed that I should get together with you and work out ways of reducing production costs. I suggested several options, and May was very supportive. I have carefully examined costs assigned to production, and research and development costs and rent on the factory part of the total building complex cause me some concern. Both of these costs, which are fairly significant, are currently included in factory overheads and applied as production costs. Research and development is an ongoing cost but should be regarded as a period cost — likewise rent of the factory. I therefore propose that for the coming quarter these costs be excluded from overheads and be written off against revenues.'

Jerry responded that given the nature of the business and its emphasis on innovative products, he believed that research and development costs should be included in overheads. Likewise, he believed that factory rent was a product cost. He thought that perhaps he should discuss the proposal with May.

Tom then said: 'I appreciate your position, Jerry, but, as I have said, May is supportive of my suggestions to reduce costs of production. She is very upset about this whole issue, and I would caution you about raising this subject with her again. It's up to you to do your job as management accountant. I'm positive it will be okay.'

Required

A. Who are the stakeholders in this situation?

B. Discuss the ethical issue or issues involved in this situation.

C. What would you do if you were Jerry Flynn?

The following extract is an answer provided on the ABC's *Catapult* show's website on 'Where can I find a manufacturer?'.

If you've already undertaken some of the preliminary areas of commercialising an innovation such as patent searching and market research, the next step is to find a manufacturer.

Outsourcing to South East Asia has become extremely popular in recent times driven by the perception of cheaper manufacturing costs, however in reality this is not always the case, particularly for smaller or start-up businesses.

If you're considering manufacturing in China it's important to take into account the additional costs you may incur such as:

- Identifying and qualifying manufacturers including time and travel
- Email, mail and telephone costs
- Transport and logistics, both land and sea
- Cost of inventory while in transit
- Quality issues, warranties and the cost of returning non-conforming products
- Currency value fluctuations

Other factors worth considering may also include:

- Potential increased risk of intellectual property infringement
- Potential increased competition
- Possible quality perception by Australian consumers
- Different business processes such as payment terms

However, there are opportunities for considerable savings in China particularly for products that have a high labour component or for bulk orders where the sheer size of the order makes the costs outlined above less significant.'

Source: T. White, 'Where can I find a manufacturer?: ask an expert', *Catapult*, ABC Online, www.abc.net.au/catapult/askexpert/s1452071.ht.

Required

A. Why has outsourcing manufacturing to South-East Asia become so popular?
B. For which type of business does the article suggest that the reason given in answer to requirement A may not be true?
C. What are some of the additional costs that may be incurred in manufacturing in China?
D. Where would the costs listed in the article be included in the costing process of goods manufactured?

Refer to the latest financial report of JB Hi-Fi Limited on its website, www.jbhifi.com.au, and answer the following questions.

1. Is it likely that JB Hi-Fi Limited would have to confront such questions as to how to design a job cost order? a cost of production report? Explain your conclusion.
2. Would JB Hi-Fi Limited be able to avail itself of the advantages offered by just-in-time processing? Why or why not?
3. Could activity-based costing principles have any applicability within JB Hi-Fi Limited? Explain.

Part 3

Financial planning, control and decision making

Cash management and control

Learning objectives

After studying this chapter, you should be able to:

1 define the term *cash* as it is used in accounting (p. 418)

2 explain internal control procedures relevant to the control of cash receipts and cash payments (pp. 418–21)

3 identify the purpose and control features in maintaining a bank account (pp. 422–4) and prepare a bank reconciliation statement (pp. 424–30)

4 explain the purpose of a petty cash fund, understand how one operates, and account for petty cash (pp. 430–3)

5 identify the purpose and control features of a cash budget and prepare a cash budget (pp. 433–6)

6 explain the essential principles of cash management (pp. 436–7)

7 understand and interpret measures of cash adequacy (p. 437).

Understanding your books

In recent years the Australian Taxation Office has carried out 'record-keeping audits' in selected geographic areas, and found that more than 80% of small businesses need to make some improvement.

If your claims can't be substantiated, your tax return may be amended and subjected to financial penalties. Therefore businesses need to keep all supporting documentation such as car log books, receipts, invoices, statements, bank statements, cash register tapes and deposit books for five years.

So if it is your responsibility to keep the books, should you attend night-classes in double-entry bookkeeping?

Probably not. Double-entry bookkeeping is difficult to learn and, in practice, only professional accountants make use of it.

But if you are a business that does not have a full-time accountant or bookkeeper, you may follow the following basic accounting rules:

- *Separate accounts.* Keep separate bank accounts for business and private purposes — or at least keep personal cheques to a minimum. Pay personal expenditure as far as possible in cash and pay all business expenditure by cheque.
- *Bank everything.* Bank all monies received intact, preferably daily ... This means you don't take out any cash to pay business expenses or wages.
- *Don't pay bills with cash.* Pay all expenses by cheque or online bank transfer. If you use cash, you will often forget to record the amount, and will thus pay too much tax ...
- *Business plan and cashflow record.* Don't fly blindly. Your business plan should show your forecast gross income and expenses, expected net profit and tax payable. You should also prepare a cash flow forecast for 3 months in advance throughout the year so you know you've got enough to pay wages and suppliers.
- *Retain all records.* Hand the following to your accountant at the end of the year: (1) cheque book butts, (2) bank deposit book, (3) bank statements, (4) finance company agreements and (5) vehicle log books.

Source: Extracts from Patrick Kissane, 'Understanding your books'. Patrick Kissane, LLB, FCA is a practising Chartered accountant in Darwin.

Chapter preview

Cash is the one common asset with which all businesses begin, and is the basis for measuring and accounting for all business transactions. Cash is the most liquid asset in a business and can be transferred easily from one person to another and easily transported and converted into other assets. Hence, cash is the asset that is most commonly the subject of theft or fraud.

The chapter scene setter focuses on the importance of managing and controlling cash and maintaining adequate business records.

Most businesses have a large volume of cash transactions daily, and so the recording of cash transactions has the potential for many errors. Effective control of cash is essential to safeguard it and ensure accuracy of recording transactions. Therefore, two of the most important functions of accounting are accurate *accounting for cash* and *control of cash*. The survival of any business requires careful management of cash inflows and outflows. An essential management tool in achieving this is the cash budget, which forms an essential part of any cash management strategy.

10.1 Cash defined

Learning objective 1

Define the term *cash* as it is used in accounting

Cash is a term used in accounting to identify money, duplicates of credit card and electronic funds transfer at point of sale (EFTPOS) sales, and any other negotiable instrument, such as a cheque or postal note, that a bank or financial institution will normally accept as a deposit to an account. Cash does not include accounts receivable or bills receivable. 'Cash' must be readily available to pay liabilities as they fall due, and therefore cannot be subject to any restrictions, contractual or otherwise.

Practically every transaction eventually results in an inflow or outflow of cash. In normal operations, cash refers to cash held in the entity (including petty cash), cash lodged in night safes of financial institutions (e.g. banks), and cash deposits with financial institutions. The sum of all the cash items is reported generally as a single item in the current assets section of the balance sheet. Users of financial statements are interested in the current cash position of an entity because it helps them evaluate the ability of the entity to meet both short-term and long-term obligations falling due for payment in the immediate future.

The control and proper use of cash is an important management function. Cash in hand is, however, an unproductive asset because it produces no income. Effective management of cash should include the following:

- Any cash accumulated that is not needed for current use should be invested, even temporarily, in some type of income-producing activity. Cash funds must be continually monitored and controlled by management, who need to make decisions about how best to use the cash.
- Cash must be adequately protected by controlling access to it and its use by employees.
- Internal control systems for cash receipts and payments should be established.
- The preparation of cash budgets and investment planning are also highly desirable.
- The statement of cash flows is a financial statement that allows decision makers to analyse the sources of cash inflows over a period, and how cash was used over the same period. The classification of cash flows into operating, investing and financing activities can also help decision makers, both internal and external, to evaluate past cash positions and use and to predict future cash flows.

The first four of these points are discussed in more detail in the rest of this chapter. Cash flows are discussed in a later chapter.

10.2 Control of cash

Learning objective 2

Explain internal control procedures relevant to the control of cash receipts and cash payments

Cash is the asset most subject to theft, and it is therefore important to set up a good internal control system for handling cash and recording cash transactions. Such a system must contain procedures for protecting cash on hand as well as for handling both cash receipts and cash payments. Three particularly important principles of an internal control system for cash are:

- the separation of responsibility for handling and custodianship of cash from responsibility for maintaining the records about cash — prevents misappropriation of cash and falsification of accounting records unless there is collusion among employees
- the banking intact of each day's cash receipts — prevents the cashier from borrowing the funds for a few days and replacing them before they are deposited

- making all payments by electronic transfer to a bank account of another person or entity or by cheque — requires authorisation by designated personnel; the bank record of all cash transactions is a cross-check on the accuracy of the internal cash records of the entity.

Because the details of a system of internal control for cash vary with the size and type of entity, we consider aspects of a general system that might be used. Internal control procedures used to build a system of internal control for cash can be illustrated best by considering cash receipts and cash payments separately.

Control of cash receipts

Cash receipts may come from a variety of sources, the most common being cash sales, cash in the form of cheques received from customers through the mail, interest and dividends received from investments, cash borrowings, and the sale of non-current assets. Each type of receipt has its own characteristics, and internal control procedures appropriate to the particular receipt must be developed. The discussion below concentrates on internal control aspects of cash receipts.

Cash received through the mail

Procedures for the control of cash received in the mail are based heavily on the separation of record keeping and custodianship. The employee who opens the mail, and who should be supervised by another employee, prepares a list of the amounts received. One copy is sent to the cashier along with the cash amounts (usually cheques, credit card authorisations, notes and coins). These amounts are combined with those from the cash registers in preparing the daily bank deposit. Another copy of the list is forwarded to the accounting department for preparing entries in the cash receipts journal and in customers' accounts. Again, neither the mail clerk nor the cashier has access to the accounting records, and accounting department personnel have no access to cash. Thus, fraud is generally avoided unless there is collusion by two or more employees.

Cash receipts from cash sales

Use of a cash register

Cash received from cash sales, on EFTPOS or on credit cards should be rung up on a cash register located in a position that permits the customer to see the amount recorded. The register prints a receipt that is given to the customer. Registers are usually linked directly to computers used by the accounting department or have a locked-in tape on which each cash sale is recorded. The basis for internal control here is the principle of separation of record keeping from custodianship (discussed more fully in chapter 7).

The register supervisor who collects the cash should not have access to the accounting department computers or to the tape in the register. The cash in the register plus EFTPOS and credit card slips are counted and recorded on a preprinted form that is sent to the accounting department. The cash and slips are then forwarded to the cashier for deposit, and the tape, along with any difference noted, is sent to the accounting department, where it is used to prepare appropriate accounting entries. In this way, neither the register supervisor nor the cashier has access to the accounting records, and the accounting department personnel have no access to cash.

Cash short and over

When several individual cash sales are recorded, it is inevitable that, in spite of internal control measures, some errors are made by cash register operators and customers are given the wrong change. As a result, a cash shortage or cash surplus is discovered when the actual cash in the cash register is compared with the register tape. For example, assume that the cash register records on 4 April shows that total sales were $1397 ($1270 plus $127 GST), and the cash in the register amounted to $1390. The cash shortage is recorded when the daily sales are recorded as follows (in general journal format):

April	4	Cash at Bank	1 390	
		Cash Short and Over	7	
		Sales		1 270
		GST Collections		127
		(The day's cash sales recorded)		

If the cash count exceeds the amount of sales recorded, the Cash Short and Over account is credited for the difference.

The Cash Short and Over account is closed to the Profit or Loss Summary account at year-end as part of the normal closing process. If the account has a debit balance (shortages exceed cash overs), it is reported as sundry expenses on the income statement. If the account has a credit balance (cash overs exceed shortages), it is normally reported as an item of other income on the income statement.

The above entry is in general journal form for illustration purposes. If special journals are used, the entry is recorded in the cash receipts journal as shown below (selected columns only):

		Debits		Credits		
		Cash at Bank	Discount Allowed		Accounts Receivable	GST Collections
Date	Account			Sales		
April 4	Sales	1 390		1 263		127

Cash Receipts Journal

As well as the above entry in the cash receipts journal, an entry also needs to be made in the general journal for the amount of cash shortage. The general journal entry is:

April	4	Cash Short and Over	7	
		Sales		7
		(Cash shortage on cash sales)		

Throughout the remainder of this book, we illustrate many cash entries in general journal form; but the reader should remember that the entry can be made in the appropriate special journal if such journals are used.

A summary of how some of the concepts that characterise a good system of internal control, as discussed in chapter 7, can be applied to cash receipts is shown in table 10.1. The application examples are not exhaustive.

Table 10.1 Internal control and cash receipts

Internal control concepts	Cash receipts application
Clear lines of responsibility	Only designated people act as cashiers
Separation of record keeping and custodianship	People who handle cash do not bank cash or record receipts in the accounts
Division of responsibility for related transactions	Mail clerk records receipts through the post while another person supervises
Mechanical and electronic devices	Use of cash registers and EFTPOS equipment
Internal control	One senior staff member records cash receipts daily; another compares total receipts with daily deposits
Physical controls	Use of safe on premises for temporary cash storage, and night safe for deposits
Other	Prenumbered sales dockets and receipt forms if done manually; all employees take holidays; all receipts banked intact each day

Control of cash payments

Payments are made to cover a wide range of obligations — to pay for cash purchases, to pay suppliers for goods and services, to cover withdrawals by owners, to pay interest and other expenses, to repay loans, and to purchase non-current assets. Determining appropriate procedures for authorisation of electronic payments and the issue of cheques is an essential part of internal control over cash payments. Consider the payment of invoices received from suppliers for purchases made. These procedures are supported by a division of responsibility for the approval and payment of invoices, and involve the following:

- *Approving invoices for payment.* Employees designated to approve invoices for payment should have no responsibility for preparing cheques or other payment instruments. They should verify that the goods or services represented by the invoice were properly ordered and actually received before authorising payment, which is generally indicated by placing an approval stamp on the invoice.
- *Signing cheques and approving electronic transfers.* Employees responsible for signing cheques or approving electronic transfers of cash should have no invoice approval or accounting responsibilities. Cheques should be signed only on receipt of a properly approved invoice. At the time cheques are signed, the related invoices should be cancelled by placing a *paid* stamp or an appropriate computer imprint on them to prevent the possibility of the invoices being presented for payment a second time. Cheques should be prenumbered, so that all cheques can be accounted for.

Approved invoices and copies of the cheques and approved electronic transfers are sent to the accounting department, where appropriate entries are made to record payments. The combination of these procedures makes it difficult for a fraudulent payment to be made without collusion by two or more employees.

Two key elements of effective control of cash payments are:

- use of a business bank account to enable all major payments to be made by cheque or electronic transfer
- use of a petty cash fund to cover small incidental cash payments.

These and their control elements are considered in the following sections.

The same concepts of internal control used in table 10.1 are again used in table 10.2 to illustrate some examples of the application of the concepts to cash payments.

Table 10.2 Internal control and cash payments

Internal control concepts	Cash payments application
Clear lines of responsibility	Designated people authorise payments; only authorised people sign cheques or other payment instruments
Separation of record keeping and custodianship	People who sign payment instruments are not involved with recording payments in accounting records
Division of responsibility for related transactions	Person who authorises payments does not sign the cheques or make the electronic funds transfer
Mechanical and electronic devices	Use of cheque printing machines to prevent changing of amounts
Internal control	Reconcile cheques issued and electronic payments with records kept by bank as shown on bank statement Random checks on petty cash fund balance
Physical controls	Use of safe to store unused blank cheques
Other	Sequentially prenumbered cheques; use of imprest petty cash system

Learning objective 3

Identify the purpose
and control features in
maintaining a bank account
and prepare a bank
reconciliation statement

10.3 Bank accounts and reconciliation
Cheque accounts

An essential element of internal control of cash is the requirement that each day's cash receipts are to be deposited intact into a bank account and that all payments are made by cheques drawn on that account or by properly authorised electronic funds transfer. Internal control is strengthened because the bank record of deposits received, cheques paid and transfers provides an independent cross-check on the internal cash records of the entity. Deposits of cash receipts are made by preparing a deposit slip (see figure 10.1 for a handwritten example). This is prepared electronically in some computerised accounting systems. Any cheque deposited is identified by the drawer and the bank on which the cheque is drawn. The deposit slip is prepared in duplicate; one copy is retained by the bank and the other copy is retained by the depositor.

Cheques are legal instruments and are defined in the *Cheques Act 1986* as an unconditional order in writing addressed by one person to another person (being a financial institution), signed by the person giving it and requiring the financial institution to pay on demand a certain sum in money. Figure 10.2 shows a copy of a typical cheque.

Note that cheques are not legal tender, i.e. they do not have to be accepted if offered in payment of a debt. However, they are commonly accepted in business. Although a significant proportion of business payments are made by cheque, electronic funds transfer are gradually replacing cheques.

Figure 10.1 A completed deposit slip

DEPOSIT SLIP

EAST COAST BANK

MELBOURNE, VIC.
ABN 99 123 123 123

4 June 2013

			Notes	126	00
ACCOUNT IDENTIFICATION No. (Branch No.) 9076 (Account No.) 430607	AGENT No. (if applicable)		Coins	7	80
Cheques etc. while accepted for credit will not be available until cleared.			Chqs etc.	691	35
			Less stamp duty	–	–
PAID IN BY (signature) *P. Edwards*	TELLER		TOTAL	$825	15

FOR CREDIT OF

Robert Robson and Son

PARTICULARS OF CHEQUES, ETC. (To be completed by customer)

DRAWER	BANK	BRANCH	$	¢
W. Bloggs	ANZ	Canberra	86	23
S. Keyes	Nat.	Ipswich	214	25
ILX Ltd	Com.	Melbourne	74	56
P.H.B Co. Ltd	ANZ	Geelong	316	31
			$691	35

Figure 10.2 A completed cheque

Cheques, as with other forms of currency, are subject to misappropriation, and every effort should be made to protect the interests of all parties to a cheque. Therefore, unless cheques are to be cashed they should be 'crossed' (two parallel straight lines drawn across the face of the cheque) and the words 'not negotiable' placed within the crossing. Some cheques issued are open or bearer cheques, which the issuing bank will honour regardless of who presents the cheque for payment. Cheques can be made payable to 'order' by deleting the word 'bearer' and including the words 'only' or 'order only' on the face of the cheque.

Use of electronic funds transfer

The cost of processing cheques through the banking system is high. Considerable delays of up to 5 working days exist in the clearing process for cheques. With electronic funds transfer (EFT), money is transferred from one location to another almost instantaneously using computers. This not only speeds up the transfer of money but also helps reduce the cost by reducing the amount of documentation (cheques and deposit slips, etc.) and labour required. EFT is now widespread with such common uses as the payment of employee wages by electronic transfer to bank accounts nominated by employees. EFT opens up the possibility of a 'chequeless society'. However, given the small number of people involved in such a system, internal control becomes more difficult. It opens up many new possibilities for fraud and error because the process is highly automated and transfers, which happen quickly, are sometimes difficult to monitor. For example, in 2009–10 an Australian university cashier siphoned $27 million into his own accounts using electronic transfers. He used his own password and that of a casual staff member who was away when the frauds were perpetrated.

Banks also have made available and encourage the use of facilities for electronic banking by customers. Customers are given access to software, software instructions and access codes for use with a personal computer and they are then able to operate their accounts, including accounts payable, via the internet. Banks also provide customers with phone banking facilities. Internet banking has increased security risk and users must make sure their online access details are protected by using a firewall, anti-spyware and anti-virus software.

The bank statement

Each month (or as arranged) the bank sends the entity a **bank statement** detailing the activity that has taken place in the account during the month. A list of bank transactions can also be downloaded from the bank's website directly into accounting packages such as MYOB, MSMoney or Quicken. The bank statement is a statement of the bank's liability to the entity rather than a statement of the entity's asset, as commonly assumed. The statement shows the balance in the account at the beginning of the month, the individual deposits received (credited by the bank as they increase the bank's liability to the entity), cheques that have been presented and paid and electronic payments made during the month (debited by the bank as they decrease the bank's liability to the entity), any other adjustments made during the month, and the account balance at month-end. The balance in the account normally represents a liability on the part of the bank and is therefore reflected in the bank's records by a credit balance. An example of a bank statement is shown in figure 10.3.

Note that the bank statement is nothing more than a running balance account. If the opening balance is in credit, debit entries reduce the running balance, and credit entries increase the running balance. If the opening balance is in debit, i.e. the business bank account is overdrawn or in overdraft, debit and credit entries will have the opposite effect.

The most common entries in the credit column are the deposits made to the account. Other credit entries are those that normally increase the depositor's balance, and include collections made by the bank on behalf of the business, other third-party deposits paid directly to the bank, and direct-deposit electronic transfers. Particulars of the source of the deposit appear in the 'Particulars' column. The most common entries in the debit column are cheques and EFTs that have been paid by the bank as evidenced by cheque and EFTs numbers in the 'Particulars' column. Other debits arise from direct payments authorised to be made by the bank (payment authorities) and other charges made against the account. Common charges seen on bank statements include account-keeping fees and transaction fees.

Another common debit made by the bank is to cover **dishonoured cheques** — cheques that were included in a customer's deposit but were not paid by the drawer's bank because of some irregularity or lack of sufficient funds to cover the cheque. Dishonoured cheques are charged back to the depositor's account and the depositor is notified. An entry is made in the cash receipts journal with the amount recorded as a negative amount to offset the original deposit, as demonstrated in the illustrative example beginning on page 427. Generally, GST will not appear on bank statements since financial transactions are exempt from the GST.

It is important to realise, especially for the discussion in the following section, that theoretically the bank statement should reflect exactly the same transactions and events as those that are recorded in the cash journals and the Cash at Bank account of the related business. Assuming that an entity has not withdrawn more than it has deposited into the bank account, the opening balance is a debit in the Cash at Bank account in the ledger (an asset to the entity) but appears as a credit in the bank statement (liability to the bank). The same applies to the ending balance. If the entity has arranged with its bank to overdraw its current account (i.e. it has an overdraft), the nature of the balances in the two sets of records is reversed.

Deposits made by the entity are entered in the cash receipts journal and ultimately debited to the Cash at Bank account (increasing an asset of the entity), and the same deposits appear as credits in the bank statement (increasing the liability of the bank). Withdrawals made by the entity from its bank account by cheques and other arrangements with the bank are entered in the cash payments journal and ultimately credited to the Cash at Bank account (decreasing an asset of the entity), and the same withdrawals appear as debits in the bank statement (decreasing a liability of the bank). In practice, however, differences do arise in an entity's records of its transactions with its bank and the records maintained by the bank. This aspect is discussed fully in the next section.

Bank reconciliation

As indicated before, the Cash at Bank account balance at a particular date rarely agrees with the balance shown on a bank statement of the same date. To prove the accuracy of both records it is necessary to compare them, identify factors that have caused a variation in the balances, and satisfy oneself that if these factors are taken into account the two sets of records agree. This process is referred to as reconciling the bank's balance as disclosed on the bank statement to the balance shown in the Cash at Bank account of the depositor. For effective control, this process should be carried out at least once a month. To formalise this process of reconciliation, a special statement called a **bank reconciliation statement** is prepared.

The reconciliation process is concerned with identifying the transactions and entries that cause the balances in the Cash at Bank account and the bank statement to differ at a particular date. There are three main reasons that the two records may disagree over the same period of time.

Figure 10.3 A bank statement

STATEMENT OF ACCOUNT WITH

EAST COAST BANK

MELBOURNE, VIC.

ABN 99 123 123 123

NAME OF ACCOUNT	ACCOUNT NO.
R. Robson and Son	801055

DATE OF ISSUE	PAGE
31 JULY 2013	30

DATE	PARTICULARS	DEBIT	CREDIT	BALANCE
July 1	Balance			312.40 Cr
2	1910	5.15 ✓		307.25 Cr
	Card entry St Kilda branch		119.50 ✓	426.75 Cr
	1899	56.00 ✓		370.75 Cr
	Card entry St Kilda branch		305.78 ✓	676.53 Cr
4	1911	298.30 ✓		378.23 Cr
5	1912	25.50 ✓		352.73 Cr
	Standing Order Autopay	275.00 ✓		77.73 Cr
	1914	25.00 ✓		52.73 Cr
	Direct transfer Hayden Ltd		60.00 ✓	112.73 Cr
8	1913	49.18 ✓		63.55 Cr
	Direct transfer F. Perry & Son		310.50 ✓	374.05 Cr
12	1915	112.15 ✓		261.90 Cr
	Standing Order Autopay	275.00 ✓		13.10 Dr
	Card entry Camberwell branch		391.95 ✓	378.85 Cr
14	1917	15.00 ✓		363.85 Cr
	1918	30.75 ✓		333.10 Cr
15	Direct entry D. Logovic		111.15 ✓	444.45 Cr
16	1916	32.80 ✓		411.45 Cr
19	1919	94.10 ✓		317.35 Cr
	Standing Order Autopay	275.00 ✓		42.35 Cr
	Card entry Camberwell branch		305.00 ✓	347.35 Cr
25	Card entry Camberwell branch		265.68 ✓	613.03 Cr
26	Standing Order Autopay	275.00 ✓		338.03 Cr
	1920	16.90 ✓		321.13 Cr
	Ret	25.00 ✓		296.13 Cr
29	1921	38.32 ✓		257.81 Cr
	Account fees	11.00 ✓		246.81 Cr
	External BPay-ATO	42.60 ✓		204.21 Cr
	Card entry St Kilda branch		204.39 ✓	408.60 Cr
	Transaction fees	9.50 ✓		399.10 Cr

TOTAL DEBITS	TOTAL CREDITS	BALANCE
1987.25	2073.95	399.10 CR

Note: Ticks have been added as part of the reconciliation procedure in the illustrative example beginning on page 427.

1. *Some items recorded in the entity's cash journals in the period covered are not recorded by the bank on the bank statement for the same period.* These include:
    (a) **unpresented or outstanding cheques** drawn by the entity — these are entered in the entity's cash payments journal when drawn and may not have been presented to the paying bank for recording by the date the bank statement is completed
    (b) outstanding or late deposits, or deposits in transit — the entity may show cash receipts on the last day of the month recorded in its cash receipts journal but this deposit may have to be held over to the following day for banking and hence recording by the bank.
2. *Some items originate in the bank statement.* These include bank fees and charges and interest, dishonoured (Ret for 'returned') cheques and bills of exchange or promissory notes forming all or part of a previous deposit or lodgement, any deposits made directly to the entity's bank account, and electronic transfers. The first indication the entity receives of these transactions is normally the bank statement.
3. *Errors may have been made either by the entity in the cash journals or by the bank in the entity's account and bank statement.* For example, a cheque for $89 payable to A.B. Motors Ltd could be incorrectly shown in the cash payments journal as $98. This would cause a discrepancy of $9 between the two records. Again the bank may in error have debited the amount of a cheque drawn by another entity to this particular entity's business account, or the bank may have recorded an amount incorrectly in the account of the entity.

Reconciliation procedure

To prepare a bank reconciliation statement, the following is required:
- the last bank reconciliation statement prepared
- cash receipts and cash payments journals covering the period since the last reconciliation
- the opening balance of the Cash at Bank account for the period beginning with the preparation of the last reconciliation statement
- the bank statement covering the period since last reconciliation.

The procedures to be followed in the preparation of the bank reconciliation statement are outlined below.

Step 1. Check that outstanding items and errors included in the last reconciliation statement now appear in the bank statement for the current period. Any items not adjusted for in the current bank statement must be noted and again included in the current reconciliation statement when prepared.

Step 2. Compare the entries in the cash receipts journal with the entries in the credit column of the bank statement, and the entries in the cash payments journal with the debit column of the bank statement. Entries that appear in both the cash journals and the bank statement should be ticked or otherwise marked. These items will not be responsible for any variations between the entity's and bank's records, including the ending balances. Unticked entries will then fall into the following categories:
(a) outstanding or late deposits
(b) unpresented cheques
(c) items on the bank statement that have been initiated by the bank
(d) errors made in entering items in the cash journals and/or errors made in the preparation of the bank statement by the bank.

Entries under (a) appear only in the cash receipts journal, and entries under (b) appear only in the cash payments journal. Initially, entries under (c) appear only in the bank statement. Entries under (d) could appear in either set of records.

Step 3. Enter all the items that appear under item (c) in step 2 in the appropriate cash journals. Once these items have been entered into the cash journals they can be ticked, since they are now common to both sets of records, and hence of no further concern in the reconciliation process.

Step 4. Adjust the cash journals for any errors that exist in these journals. Once these errors have been adjusted, the entries should agree with the bank statement entries and can be ticked off. Note that errors appearing in the bank statement can be corrected only by the bank. The bank should be notified of these errors so that it can correct them. These items therefore must remain unticked and will appear in the bank reconciliation statement. The error should be corrected in the subsequent bank statement.

Step 5. The cash journals should now be totalled and crossadded and the appropriate totals posted to the Cash at Bank account in the general ledger. This account can then be balanced to give the final adjusted balance as recorded by the entity.

Step 6. Prepare the bank reconciliation statement. Note that at this stage the only normal entries that cause a difference to exist between the final balance of the Cash at Bank account and the final balance shown on the bank statement are those items that appear in the cash journals but not in the bank statement — items (a) and (b) in step 2. These items represent outstanding deposits and unpresented cheques. Errors made in the preparation of the bank statement also need to be taken into account. Any outstanding items in the previous reconciliation statement that are still outstanding need to be included in the current reconciliation statement.

A typical reconciliation statement is shown below:

R. ROBSON AND SON
Bank Reconciliation Statement
as at . . . 2013

Balance as per bank statement Cr (or Dr)		$xxx
Add (or deduct) outstanding deposits		xxx
		xxx
Deduct (or add) unpresented cheques	xx	
	xx	
	xx	xxx
Balance as per Cash at Bank account (Dr or Cr)		$xxx

The following example illustrates the procedure outlined above.

Illustrative example

The bank statement of R. Robson and Son up to 31 July 2013 is shown in figure 10.3 (p. 425). Figure 10.4 (p. 428) and figure 10.5 (p. 429) show the cash payments journal and the cash receipts journal respectively up to 31 July 2013. The bank reconciliation statement *for the previous month* is set out in figure 10.6 (p. 429). Requirements are to reconcile the two sets of records and prepare a bank reconciliation statement after making any necessary adjustments in the cash journals and Cash at Bank account. It is assumed in this example that there are no errors made by the bank. The procedure follows the general steps outlined previously.

Step 1. A check is made on the reconciliation statement prepared at 30 June to see whether items outstanding at that time appear in the current bank statement. The outstanding deposit has been recorded by the bank and therefore can be ticked off in both records. Similarly, cheque number 1899 for $56 unpresented at 30 June has been paid by the bank. The $56 can be ticked off in both records.

Step 2. Compare the deposits recorded in the cash receipts journal (figure 10.5) with the entries shown in the credit column of the bank statement (figure 10.3). All entries agree (e.g. for 2 July, $305.78 = $110.60 + $195.18) except for the deposit of $219.40 recorded in the cash receipts journal as having been banked on 31 July. Since the deposit does not appear in the bank statement it is marked o/s (i.e. outstanding). This item must appear in the bank reconciliation statement. Note that the cheque received from R. Richards and banked on 19 July has been returned on 27 July. Because this is entered in both records, it will not appear in the bank reconciliation statement. Cheques and electronic transfers recorded in the cash payments journal are then compared with the debit column of the bank statement, and items common to both are ticked off. Cheques 1922

Figure 10.4 Cash payments journal of R. Robson and Son

				Debits		Credits
Date	Account	Chq. No.	Post Ref	Accounts Payable	Other	Cash at Bank
2013						
July 1	Office Supplies	1910	116		5.15	✓ 5.15
	Wm. Prince and Co. Ltd	1	✓	298.30		✓ 298.30
4	Advertising Expense	2	560		25.50	✓ 25.50
5	R. Bill and Co.	3	✓	49.18		✓ 49.18
	Standing Order Autopay-Wages and Salaries		550		275.00	✓ 275.00
	Petty Cash	4	105		25.00	✓ 25.00
8	L. Edwards and Son	5	✓	112.15		✓ 112.15
12	Truck Maintenance	6	545		31.80	✓ 31.80
	Standing Order Autopay-Wages and Salaries		550		275.00	✓ 275.00
14	Travel Expenses	7	532		15.00	✓ 15.00
16	Commission Expense	8	520		30.75	✓ 30.75
18	Wm. Prince and Co. Ltd	9	✓	94.10		✓ 94.10
19	Standing Order Autopay-Wages and Salaries		550		275.00	✓ 275.00
24	Light and Power	20	540		16.00	✓ 16.00
26	Standing Order Autopay-Wages and Salaries		550		275.00	✓ 275.00
27	J. Norton	1	✓	38.32		✓ 38.32
	External BPay-ATO		570		42.60	✓ 42.60
29	Donation — Red Shield	2	575		10.00	o/s 10.00
	L. Edwards and Son	3	✓	77.40		o/s 77.40
31	Freight Inwards	4	510		22.05	o/s 22.05
	P. Perkins	5	✓	82.56		o/s 82.56
				752.01	1 324.75	2 076.76
	Account fees	B/S	569		11.00	✓ 11.00
	Transaction fees	B/S	569		9.50	✓ 9.50
	Truck maintenance (error adjustment cheque no. 1916)	B/S	545		1.00	✓ 1.00
				752.01	1 346.25	2 098.26
				(210)	(x)	(100)

Note: Ticks, o/s in the cash at bank column, and B/S are added as part of the reconciliation process. The last three items in the cash payments journal are added once the journal is compared with the bank statement (B/S) in figure 10.3.

to 1925 have not been presented for payment since they are absent from the bank statement. These cheques are marked o/s and therefore will be included in the bank reconciliation statement.

Step 3. Step 2, apart from identifying a number of outstanding cheques, also uncovers a number of items initiated by the bank, e.g. transaction and account keeping fees and an error made in recording cheque 1916 in the cash payments journal. These items can be entered into the cash payments journal (see bottom of the cash payments journal in figure 10.4), and can therefore be ticked off in both sets of records since they now appear in both. Note that at this stage all amounts appearing in the bank statement should be ticked except for any errors made by the bank. As there are no errors made by the bank, all amounts are ticked.

Step 4. Adjust errors in the cash journals if there are any. In this illustration, there is one in relation to cheque 1916 as uncovered in the bank statement in step 3.

Step 5. The cash journals are then totalled, crossadded and posted. The Cash at Bank account can now be balanced to give the balance of the bank account according to business records (figure 10.7, p. 430).

Figure 10.5 Cash receipts journal of R. Robson and Son

			Debits			Credits	
						Accounts	
		Post	Discount			Accounts	
Date	Account	Ref.	Allowed		Cash at Bank	Receivable	Sales
2013							
July 2	M. Mason	✓		✓	110.60	110.60	
	Sales			✓	195.18		195.18
5	Hayden Ltd	✓		✓	60.00	60.00	
8	F. Perry & Son	✓		✓	310.50	310.50	
12	Sales			✓	136.20		136.20
	H. Lawson	✓		✓	85.00	85.00	
	W. Wentworth	✓		✓	170.75	170.75	
15	Sales			✓	111.15		111.15
19	R. Richards	✓		✓	25.00	25.00	
	Morley Co-op	✓		✓	280.00	280.00	
25	Sales			✓	77.18		77.18
	M. Mason	✓		✓	140.00	140.00	
	Hayden Ltd	✓		✓	48.50	48.50	
27	R. Richards (dishonoured cheque)	✓		✓	(25.00)	(25.00)	
29	Sales			✓	204.39		204.39
31	Sales			o/s	219.40		219.40
					2 148.85	1 205.35	943.50
					(100)	(110)	(400)

Note: Ticks and o/s in the cash at bank column are added as part of the reconciliation process.

R. ROBSON AND SON
Bank Reconciliation Statement
as at 30 June 2013 (previous month)

Balance as per bank statement	$312.40 Cr
Add: Outstanding deposits	119.50
	431.90
Less: Unpresented cheque no. 1899	56.00
Balance as per Cash at Bank account	$375.90 Dr

Note: Ticks are added as part of the reconciliation process.

Figure 10.6 Bank reconciliation statement for previous month

Step 6. The bank reconciliation statement can be prepared (figure 10.7) using the unticked items that appear in the cash journals (see figures 10.4 and 10.5).

The bank reconciliation statement in figure 10.7 could be interpreted in the following way. The depositor's or entity's records of depositing into and withdrawing from the bank are as up to date as is possible, having incorporated all transactions originating within the entity and within the bank. The bank statement is also as up to date as the bank can make it, but the bank has not been able to record a deposit made on the last day, nor can it record the payment of cheques from the account if the cheques have not yet been presented for payment.

The reconciliation statement has been prepared with the following question in mind: 'What would the bank's balance be if the bank was able to include those items that appear in the entity's records but not in the bank statement?' In the illustration, it can be seen that if the balance as shown in the bank statement is adjusted for those items not able to be recorded by the bank at 31 July, then the bank statement balance will be in agreement with the balance arrived at from records kept by the entity. As noted above, this reconciliation of the bank statement balance to the balance in the entity's Cash at Bank account provides an important control technique by verifying the entity's records of deposits to and withdrawals from the bank account with independently kept records of the same transactions.

Cash at Bank

2013					2013				
July	1	Balance		375.90	July	31		CP15	2 098.26
	31		CR16	2 148.85			Balance c/d		426.49
				2 524.75					2 524.75
Aug.	1	Balance b/d		426.49					

Bank Reconciliation Statement
as at 31 July 2013

Balance as per bank statement		$399.10 Cr
Add: Outstanding deposit		219.40
		618.50
Less: Unpresented cheques		
1922	$10.00	
1923	77.40	
1924	22.05	
1925	82.56	192.01
Balance as per Cash at Bank account		$426.49 Dr

Note that the bank statement was the source of evidence for recording, in the cash payments journal, transaction fees, $9.50, the error in cheque no. 1916, $1.00, and account fees, $11.00.

BUSINESS KNOWLEDGE

Computers and reconciliation

The method of bank reconciliation used in computerised accounting systems differs from one system to another. A common approach used in MYOB Accounting is to compare the bank statement with receipts and payments in a manner similar to the manual method described. Items on the bank statement are checked on the computer screen and items on the bank statement not already entered are recorded. The program then produces a reconciliation report.

It is now possible to download statement data from the bank to further simplify the reconciliation process.

10.4 The petty cash fund

As emphasised earlier, a basic principle of internal control is that all payments should be made by cheque or electronic transfer. However, to avoid the expense and inconvenience of writing many cheques to cover minor or petty expenses for things like postage stamps and miscellaneous supplies, most entities establish a **petty cash fund** — a specified amount of cash, placed under the control of a specific employee (the petty cashier) — for making small payments.

Establishing the fund

The petty cash fund is established by writing a cheque to be given to the petty cashier, who cashes the cheque and places the proceeds in a lockable box to which only they have access. The fund is generally established for a round amount, such as $100 or $200, expected to be sufficient to handle petty cash payments for a relatively short period such as a month. The cheque is recorded by a debit to a Petty Cash account and a credit to the Cash at Bank account. For example, assuming a fund of $100 is established on 2 January, the journal entry (in general journal format) is:

Jan.	2	Petty Cash	100	
		Cash at Bank		100
		(Petty cash fund established)		

If special journals are being used, the entry to record the establishment of the petty cash fund is made in the cash payments journal. Petty Cash is entered in the account column and the amount of $100 is entered in the cash at bank and other accounts columns. After posting, the effect is the same as for the general journal entry, i.e. the Petty Cash account in the general ledger is debited and the Cash at Bank account is credited.

Making payments from the fund

As cash payments are made from the fund, the recipient signs a **petty cash voucher** or **receipt** prepared by the petty cashier. The voucher shows the amount paid, the purpose of the payment and the date paid. A voucher is prepared for every payment made from the fund and is placed in the petty cash box. Outlays on most of the expenses and minor assets covered by petty cash payments will include GST. The petty cashier must ensure that expenses are recorded at GST-exclusive amounts, and that adequate records are made of any GST outlays associated with these expenses. Thus, at all times the total of the vouchers plus cash in the fund should be equal to the amount originally placed in the fund, $100 in our illustration. Figure 10.8 shows an example of a petty cash voucher.

PETTY CASH VOUCHER

No. 2
DATE 15 January 2013   AMOUNT $13.53
PURPOSE Miscellaneous office supplies
GST included $1 23
DEBIT TO Office Expenses
APPROVED BY   J.B.Small
                               Petty cashier

Figure 10.8 A petty cash voucher

Reimbursing the fund

Because payments from the fund will gradually decrease the cash available, the petty cashier must be reimbursed periodically by writing a cheque equal to the amount of the sum of the vouchers in the fund. Each voucher is stamped *paid* by the cashier (or printed as being paid when processed by the computer system). The cheque is cashed by the cashier of the fund and the proceeds are placed in the petty cash box. Various expense accounts are debited as indicated by the petty cash vouchers, the GST Outlays account is debited for the GST, and Cash at Bank is credited for the amount needed to reimburse the fund. For example, the petty cash box had vouchers and cash at the end of the first month of operations as shown below:

Voucher no.	Purpose	GST	Amount	Total
1	Postage stamps	$3.00	$30.00	$ 33.00
2	Office supplies	1.23	12.30	13.53
3	Postage	2.65	26.47	29.12
4	Stationery	1.52	15.22	16.74
	Cash in box	—	—	7.61
		$8.40	$83.99	$100.00

Because the cash in the fund is low, the petty cashier is reimbursed and the following entry (in general journal format) is made:

Jan.	31	Stationery Expense	15.22	
		Office Supplies Expense	12.30	
		Postage Expense	56.47	
		GST Outlays	8.40	
		Cash at Bank		92.39
		(Petty cash fund reimbursement)		

Since the petty cash vouchers are supplementary records, this entry is needed so that the expenses are properly recorded and posted to general ledger accounts. Thus, expense accounts and the GST Outlays account are debited when the fund is replenished. Note that the Petty Cash account is not affected by the reimbursement entry. The Petty Cash account is debited only when the fund is initially established, and no other entries are made to the Petty Cash account unless a decision is made to increase or decrease the size of the fund. The petty cash fund is normally included with other cash amounts and reported as a single amount on the balance sheet.

The petty cash fund is also reimbursed at the end of an accounting period, even if the amount of cash in the fund is not running low, in order to have the expenses represented by the vouchers in the fund plus the GST outlayed recorded during the current accounting period. If the fund is not reimbursed, cash will be overstated in the balance sheet and expenses will be understated in the income statement for the period.

On occasion, the petty cashier may forget to obtain a signed voucher for a payment from the fund, in which case the fund will be short. When this occurs, the Cash Short and Over account is debited for the shortage when the fund is replenished.

If special journals are being used, the above entry for reimbursement of the petty cash fund is entered in the cash payments journal. Reimbursement is done by drawing a cheque for the total amount of the petty cash vouchers used (i.e. cash spent) during the period, and this cheque has to be recorded in the cash payments journal along with all other cheques written. When the reimbursement is recorded in a payments journal, the entry is as shown below (selected columns only):

Cash Payments Journal								
					Debits		Credits	
Date	Account Debited	Chq. No.	Post Ref	Accounts Payable	GST Outlays	Other	Cash at Bank	Discount Received
Jan. 31	Stationery Exp.		530		1.52	15.22		
	Office Supplies Exp.		515		1.23	12.30		
	Postage Exp.	140	572		5.65	56.47	92.39	

Note that the effect on the general ledger accounts is exactly the same as that for the general journal — the appropriate expense accounts are debited, GST Outlays is debited for the total of $8.40, and the Cash at Bank account is credited.

The system of operating petty cash just described is known as the **imprest system**. The essential features of the imprest system are:
● the determination of a fixed sum, which becomes the imprest amount
● at all times cash remaining in the fund together with the total of the vouchers for cash spent will equal the imprest amount
● reimbursement is always for the amount spent (as evidenced by the vouchers) to bring the balance remaining up to the imprest amount.

Sometimes the petty cashier keeps a record of cash received and expended in a petty cash book. In this book all money received into the fund and all payments made from the fund are recorded. The source documents for the book are the cheques received to establish or vary the imprest amount of the fund and to reimburse the fund, and the vouchers that are the authorisations for expenditure from the fund. The petty cash book usually has a number of expenditure analysis columns to enable the expenditure to be analysed into the various accounts that will be debited. A petty cash book incorporating the entries referred to in the simple illustration above is similar to the example shown below:

Petty Cash Book								
Date	Particulars	Vchr No.	Receipts	Payments	Postage Expense	Office Supp. Exp.	Stationery Expense	GST Outlays
Jan. 2	Cheque 100		100.00					
10	Stamps	1		33.00	30.00			3.00
15	Office supplies	2		13.53		12.30		1.23
20	Postage	3		29.12	26.47			2.65
25	Stationery	4		16.74			15.22	1.52
				92.39	$56.47	$12.30	$15.22	$8.40
31	Balance c/d			7.61				
			$100.00	$100.00				
31	Balance b/d		7.61					
	Reimbursement							
	cheque 140		92.39					

As we saw above, the use of a bank account and an imprest system of petty cash provides a strong basis for internal control over cash payments. These controls incorporate many of the concepts of internal control we discussed earlier in the chapter.

10.5 Cash budgeting
Need for cash budgeting

Learning objective 5

Identify the purpose and control features of a cash budget and prepare a cash budget

The coverage of control over the asset cash was based on establishing controls within the recording process. As noted in the scene setter, an important aspect of control over cash is planning cash inflows and outflows. Any entity must be concerned not only with recording cash flows but also with ensuring that the entity has sufficient cash to be able to make *future* payments such as payments of accounts payable to obtain available discounts, wages and salaries of employees and other expenses, and for the purchase of non-current assets.

Although it is essential to provide cash for future use, excessive cash funds lying idle in non- or low-interest-bearing deposits should be avoided. It is essential for management to plan and control future cash flows. This type of control is obtained by the preparation of a cash budget.

A **cash budget** is a projection of expected future cash receipts and cash payments. Only cash items are included and non-cash items such as depreciation are excluded. The preparation of a cash budget ensures that:

- an entity is able to meet its commitments as they fall due
- as a result of paying on time, the reputation and credit standing of the entity is maintained
- all proposed expenditures are carefully assessed and wasteful cash outlays are discouraged
- the use of borrowed funds is kept to a minimum and hence interest and other charges are reduced
- cash funds are not left lying idle and can be put to use, generating income from interest and dividends.

Preparation of a cash budget

Cash budgets are usually prepared on a monthly basis although this varies depending on the needs of the particular entity. The period of time covered by the cash budget varies from 3 to 6 months, although this period can be longer. However, the longer the time period involved, the more diffi-cult it is to predict the future cash flows accurately. The cash budget is a forecast of the probable amounts of cash receipts and payments over a period of time, and the cash balance expected at the end of that period. This budget is, in effect, a forecast of cash flows based on an analysis of past activities and an examination of possible future cash inflows and possible future cash require-ments. The illustrative example below shows the preparation of a cash budget.

Illustrative example

The following information relates to the expected cash receipts and payments of City Enterprises, which requires a cash budget prepared for the months of November and December 2013. All income and expenses amounts include GST except for the GST-exempt items of wages and per-sonal drawings.

Sales usually consist of 50% cash sales and the credit sales are collected on the following pattern — 80% in the month following the month of sale and the remainder in the second month after the sale. Purchases are all on credit and are paid for in the month following the month of purchase to take advantage of the 2% discount offered. City Enterprises estimates that it will have the following cash commitments during the budget period: wages $16 000 per month; rent payable $4620 (including GST) per month; advertising payable $3300 (including GST) in November (same as October) and $4400 (including GST) in December; and personal drawings by the owner, Terry Duncan, of $900 per month. A new colour printer costing $900 plus GST will be purchased for cash in November. The balance in the entity's bank account at 1 November was $800. Details of sales and purchases (GST is included in all amounts) relevant to the preparation of the budget are:

	Sales	Purchases
September (actual)	$61 600	$35 200
October (actual)	70 400	37 400
November (estimated)	72 600	39 600
December (estimated)	77 000	44 000

The steps in the preparation of the budget are:
1. Prepare a schedule of estimated cash collections from credit sales — these amounts will include the GST component.
2. Prepare a schedule of estimated cash payments for credit purchases — these amounts will include the GST component.
3. Prepare a schedule of estimated GST collections and outlays from sales and purchases of goods and services to determine the estimated cash payments to be made to the Australian Taxation Office (ATO).
4. Prepare the cash budget.

The first step in the preparation of the cash budget is to ascertain the expected cash collections from credit sales. A schedule of estimated cash collections from credit sales is prepared for this purpose, and is set out below:

Schedule of Estimated Cash Collections from Credit Sales for two months ending 31 December 2013				
Month	Credit sales*		November	December
September	$30 800		$ 6 160	
October	35 200		28 160	
November	36 300			$ 7 040
December	38 500			29 040
			$34 320	$36 080

* 50% of total sales.

Using a similar analysis, the schedule of payments for credit purchases is as follows:

Schedule of Estimated Cash Payments from Credit Purchases for two months ending 31 December 2013		November	December
Month	Credit purchases	November	December
September	$35 200	$36 652	
October	37 400*		
November	39 600**		$38 808
December	44 000		
		$36 652	$38 808

* $37 400 less discount $748 (i.e. 2%) = $36 652
   (discount includes $68 GST to be written back — affects December cash flows)

** $39 600 less discount $792 (i.e. 2%) = $38 808
   (discount includes $72 GST to be written back — affects January cash flows)

Because City Enterprises is registered for the GST, it is required to pay to the ATO the difference between the GST collections recorded using the accrual basis and GST outlays recorded using the accrual basis. For this purpose, it is necessary to prepare an estimate of the amount payable. Assuming that City Enterprises submits its BAS monthly, the amount payable in any month will be based on the recorded collections and outlays for the previous month. Any write-back of GST for discounts received will affect the cash flows to the ATO 2 months after the month of purchase, e.g. GST outlays recorded on September purchases will affect October cash flows, but any GST in discounts received when the account is paid in October will affect December GST cash flows to the ATO. A schedule setting out estimated GST collections and GST outlays, and the resulting estimated amount payable to the ATO, can now be drawn up, as shown below. The cash budget can now be prepared and appears in figure 10.9 (p. 436).

Note that in the preparation of the cash budget the cash at bank balance at the end of one month becomes the opening balance for the next month. The same principles as outlined above are followed if a budget covering 3 or 6 months is prepared.

Note also that if City Enterprises had a policy of maintaining a cash position of $10 000 at the end of each month, it would need to borrow $3386 at the end of November and could afford to pay it back at the end of December.

Schedule of Estimated Cash Payments for GST for two months ending 31 December 2013		November	December
Estimated GST collections			
Sales in October	$70 400 × 1/11	$6400	
Sales in November	72 600 × 1/11		$6600
		$6400	$6600
Estimated GST outlays			
Purchases* in October	$37 400 × 1/11	$3400	
Purchases* in November	39 600 × 1/11		$3600
Expenses (including GST):			
Rent	Oct. $4620 × 1/11	420	
	Nov. $4620 × 1/11		420
Advertising	Oct. $3300 × 1/11	300	
	Nov. $3300 × 1/11		300
Write-back (discount received)*		−64	−68
Purchase of printer	Nov. $990 × 1/11		90
		$4056	$4342
GST payable to ATO		$2344	$2258

* Discount on September purchases $35 200 × 2% = $704 × 1/11 = $64
   Discount on October purchases $37 400 × 2% = $748 × 1/11 = $68

Figure 10.9 Cash budget

	November	December
CITY ENTERPRISES **Cash Budget** for two months ending 31 December 2013		
Cash at bank, beginning of month	$ 800	$ 6 614
Expected cash collections from sales:		
Cash	36 300	38 500
Credit (from schedule)	34 320	36 080
Total from sales	70 620	74 580
Total cash available	$71 420	$81 194
Estimated cash payments:		
Purchases (from schedule)	$36 652	$38 808
Wages	16 000	16 000
Rent	4 620	4 620
Advertising	3 300	4 400
Purchase of printer	990	
GST payable (from schedule)	2 344	2 258
T. Duncan, drawings	900	900
Total expected payments	$64 806	$66 986
Cash at bank, end of month	$ 6 614	$14 208

Although the cash budget is a key element of control in the cash management of an entity, other factors such as changing economic conditions, credit policy in relation to receivables and inventory turnover rates must be considered. Some of these important factors are covered in this book, and others outside the scope of this book can be found in financial management texts.

Learning objective **6**

Explain the essential principles of cash management

10.6 Cash management

The development of a good system of internal control over cash receipts and cash payments and the preparation of cash budgets are essential ingredients in effective control over the asset cash. These activities are, however, only a part of any total cash management strategy. Cash management strategies are determined to a large extent by the size and nature of the activities of a business entity. However, there are basic principles that can be followed to ensure adequate management of cash. Most of these principles can be derived from an appreciation of the role of cash flows in the operating cycle discussed in chapter 4.

Referring to figure 4.18 (p. 146), it is apparent that there is a need to collect cash from accounts receivable as quickly as possible, in order to be able to pay accounts payable. It therefore follows that tying up cash in receivables and inventory should be avoided as much as possible. In addition to demands for cash generated by the operating cycle, cash surpluses must be built up to help finance non-current assets, and any cash surplus to requirements should be invested to increase overall cash inflows. The broad principles of good cash management are set out below.

Principles of cash management

Reduce collection time for accounts receivable. Money owed by accounts receivable represents money that cannot be used by the business. The business needs to develop a collections policy to speed up the collection of money owing, i.e. reduce the average collection time for receivables. However, management must ensure that the policy does not put customers off and lead to the loss of their business.

Postpone payments to accounts payable. There are due dates for all payables and payment should be delayed until those due dates. This allows the business to have use of funds that would otherwise be unavailable. This policy should take advantage of any discounts on offer, and ensure that the business's credit rating is not threatened by late payment.

Keep inventory levels to a minimum. Although there is a need to keep adequate levels of inventory to meet the demands of customers, remember that inventories tie up cash and incur costs of storage and insurance. It is therefore sound cash management policy to keep inventory levels to a minimum.

Invest surplus cash. As already noted, cash is in itself a non-productive asset. Good cash management ensures that any cash surplus to immediate requirements is invested in appropriate ways to produce a return in the form of additional cash, or savings in cash outlays. Many forms of investment enable quick return of the cash if the need arises.

Plan for capital expenditures. The acquisition of non-current assets, which can involve large amounts of cash, is an important and ongoing decision all business entities have to make. These decisions require careful long-term planning to ensure that cash surplus to requirements can be used to help finance these large expenditures whenever possible, thus reducing reliance on external financing and its associated costs.

10.7 Analysing adequacy of cash flows

Learning objective **7**

Understand and interpret measures of cash adequacy

The previous discussion considers principles to be followed in managing cash, particularly in relation to the operating cycle. An important requirement for any business, however, is to remain solvent. Decision makers will always be keen to assess an entity's **solvency**, that is, the ability of an entity to pay its debts as and when they fall due. An important component in assessing solvency is the amount of cash generated by the entity's operating activities. The statement of cash flows is a financial statement which provides decision makers with details of cash inflows and outflows, a major component of which is cash flows from operating activities. Cash flows from operating activities can be used to monitor whether cash generated from operations is sufficient to meet both current and non-current liabilities. Two ratios that can be helpful to management in assessing solvency are (1) short-term cash flow adequacy ratio, and (2) cash flow adequacy ratio.

The short-term cash flow adequacy ratio is calculated by relating cash flow from operating activities to current liabilities. This ratio shows the ability of the entity to meet its current liabilities with cash generated from operating activities. The cash flow adequacy ratio relates cash flow from operating activities to total liabilities, thereby indicating the ability of the entity to meet its obligations to all its creditors. Both these ratios are important tests of an entity's solvency. As with all ratios, the trend in these ratios over time provides more information for decision making than the ratio itself.

BUSINESS KNOWLEDGE

Why does my business keep running short of cash?

While businesses may generate an acceptable profit, the first sign of possible financial problems is usually a cash flow problem... Cash-flow management is usually the culprit...

Cash-flow management or planning is a critical discipline in every business; keeping creditors happy actually allows you to remain in business.

Continual and frequent monitoring of cash inflow and outflow are essential for maintaining an adequate cash balance for trading.

The objective of cash-flow management is to smooth out the peaks and troughs of cash movement over a specified business period so you don't have any cash supply crises.

Every business owner should prepare a cash-flow forecast that shows what cash will be received and spent each month. To do this you need to analyse your history of cash use.

The objective is obviously to remain cash positive all the time, and if there are any major cash outlays predicted in the future (holiday pay, advertising, stock) your business must plan to have the cash resources available for these outlays. Your own cash costs you nothing!...

It is far better to prepare a forecast using 'best knowledge', and update that forecast every month from your bank reconciliation. Then, if the business gets into a tight cash spot, you can show the bank how much you need and for how long, i.e. until the business becomes cash-positive again...

It cannot be stressed too strongly that the cash flows for a period do not equal the sum of revenues and expenses shown in your P&L for that period. The P&L period will reflect the business transaction record, not the actual timing or value of receipts and payments. Non-cash items from other periods, such as depreciation values for assets, will also appear in the P&L report.

Source: 'Cash flow the culprit', *North Shore Times.*

Bank reconciliation statement, p. 424

Bank statement, p. 423

Cash, p. 418

Cash budget, p. 433

Dishonoured cheques, p. 424

Imprest system, p. 432

Petty cash fund, p. 430

Petty cash voucher or receipt, p. 431

Solvency, p. 437

Unpresented cheques or outstanding cheques, p. 426

DISCUSSION QUESTIONS

1. Explain the limitations of balance sheets, income statements and statements of cash flows in anticipating future cash flow issues.

2. Many people think of cash as coins and notes. In accounting, cash has a broader meaning. What type of assets are defined as cash in accounting?

3. Internal control of cash is strengthened by requiring that each day's receipts are deposited intact and that all payments are made by cheque or electronic transfer. Do you agree? Why or why not?

4. 'Although the process of bank reconciliation provides a measure of control over cash in a business entity, bank reconciliation is useless unless it operates within a framework that incorporates essential elements of a good internal control system.' Discuss.

5. Mark has done the accounts for his local basketball club for a number of years. You joined the club in the last year and because you have studied some accounting Mark has asked you to help him with the accounts. You note that when doing a bank reconciliation Mark changes the accounts of the basketball club so that they show the same month-end cash balance as the bank statement, even though there are outstanding deposits and cheques. Mark believes this approach is best as the bank must be correct so he needs to agree with its balance. Explain to Mark why the basketball club's cash balance may be different from the bank statement and yet be the correct balance.

6. After reading about the concepts of a good system of internal control over cash covered in this chapter, the owner of a small business was concerned that his internal control was not good. He counted the daily cash takings and prepared the deposit slip, and banked the takings intact each day. He also approved payments and signed all cheques. To overcome his problem, he decided he would have to hire more staff, so that he would be able to ensure adequate division of responsibility. Would this solve his problem? Explain.

7. A manager of a small online business believes that because most of the transactions take place using electronic transfer of funds rather than cash or cheques, the business no longer needs to do a bank reconciliation each month. Explain to the manager why a bank reconciliation is still necessary for the business.

8. 'The principle that receipts should be banked daily and all payments made by cheque or electronic transfer provides a sound basis for internal control over cash. But it breaks down immediately when cash is given to a junior employee to spend through the petty cash fund.' Discuss.

9. A manager of a small business made the following comment when a friend suggested that his business could benefit if he were to prepare cash budgets: 'Some people think they are all right but I run only a small business and don't want to waste my time preparing budgets, which, after all, are just best-guessing the future. I am more interested in what actually happens, not what I think might happen.' Discuss.

10. Using the Business Knowledge 'Why does my business keep running short of cash?' on the previous page explain why it is important to manage cash flow and what a business can do to manage its cash flow.

Exercise 10.1 CASH FLOW MANAGEMENT

LO 2

Benjamin runs a cheese shop at the local shopping centre. Some months Benjamin seems to have more than enough cash to pay his bills when they are due. Other months Benjamin struggles to pay bills on time as he runs short of cash in the business's bank account and has to use money from his personal account to pay business expenses.

Required

Advise Benjamin on ways he can overcome his cash flow management issues.

Exercise 10.2 COMPOSITION OF CASH

LO 1

On 30 June, Sophisticated Coffee had the following on its premises:
1. 18 blank cheque forms
2. a cheque for $275 received from a customer on 28 June but dated 1 July
3. cheques dated 28–30 June for the total amount of $2164 received from customers on 30 June.
4. postage stamps to the value of $12.10
5. a $300 IOU from an employee representing a short-term loan
6. currency and coin, $672

Required

A. What total dollar amount should be included in 'cash' at 30 June?
B. Explain how any items not included in 'cash' should be reported on a balance sheet prepared on 30 June.

Exercise 10.3 CASH INTERNAL CONTROL PROCEDURES

LO 2

Explain briefly the significance of each of the following in a comprehensive system of control over cash transactions:
1. the segregation of cashier's duties from other functions
2. the daily banking principle
3. the bank reconciliation statement
4. the imprest system of petty cash
5. cash budgets
6. statements of cash flows.

Exercise 10.4 CASH SHORT AND OVER

LO 2

Hassam runs a fruit stall at the local market and at the end of each day he banks the cash in the cash register. The cash register records each sale and can provide a total for each day but Hassam believes that often the staff are too busy and do not always enter the sales in the register but simply put the cash in the till. The total from the cash register is produced each month for the business's accountant to prepare financial statements. Recently, Hassam employed a university student to work on weekends and he is concerned that soon after this the daily amount banked seems to have decreased even though Hassam feels that sales have not really changed. The student often talks about how he spends his evenings at the casino in the hope of winning enough to pay for his university studies so that he doesn't have to work every weekend.

Required

A. Explain to Hassam what controls he could put in place to minimise the risk of one of his employees stealing cash.
B. After Hassam put in place the controls that you suggested, he found that for the first week the cash register showed sales of $7150, including GST, and the amount banked was $6800. Record the cash short or over.
C. The second week after the new controls were implemented the student resigned and the cash register showed sales of $6930, including GST, and the amount banked was $7200. Record the cash short or over.

Exercise 10.5 CASH INTERNAL CONTROL PROCEDURES

Five principles of internal control are listed below:

Internal control principle	Cash receipts	Cash payments
Physical controls		
Mechanical/electronic devices		
Separation of record keeping and custodianship		
Clear lines of authority		
Division of responsibilities		

Required

Complete the table by inserting at least one example of how each principle is applied in the control of cash receipts and cash payments.

Exercise 10.6 BANK RECONCILIATION

The following information has been extracted from the accounting records and bank statement of Pete's Pancakes Ltd at 30 June 2013:

Closing balance shown on the bank statement	$12 620 Cr
Cash receipts of 30 June which were deposited on 30 June did not appear on the bank statement	$ 6 350
Cheques recorded in the cash payments but not yet presented for payment to the bank	$ 4 720

Required

A. Prepare a bank reconciliation statement as at 30 June 2013 disclosing the closing balance of the Cash at Bank account.
B. Assume the same data as above, but assume further that the closing balance shown on the bank statement is $12 620 Dr (i.e. the bank account is overdrawn). Prepare a bank reconciliation statement as at 30 June 2013 disclosing the closing balance of the Cash at Bank account.

Exercise 10.7 BANK RECONCILIATION

Sandy Poglase, owner of Sandy's Sandwiches, wants a bank reconciliation statement to be prepared for the month ended 31 March 2013 using the following information:
1. Final balance in the Cash at Bank account in the ledger of Sandy's Sandwiches (after all entries arising from the bank statement had been entered) was $13 204.26 Dr.
2. Balance shown by the bank statement at 31 March was $13 155.10 Cr.
3. Cheques recorded in the cash payments journal but not presented to the bank for payment were:

Cheque no.	41	$339.30
	43	262.64
	46	423.90
	51	195.10

4. A deposit of $1270.30 appears as a deposit in the cash receipts journal but had not been recorded by the bank at the date of the statement.

Required

Prepare the bank reconciliation statement at 31 March 2013.

Exercise 10.8 BANK RECONCILIATION

The following information relates to the cash position of Cathy Fraser, loan broker:
1. Cash at Bank account balance as at 30 June 2013: $45 451 debit.
2. Bank statement balance as at 30 June 2013: $47 512 credit.

3. 30 June receipts amounting to $1820 have not been deposited.
4. Cheques issued but not presented total $3468.
5. A $312 cheque was returned marked 'dishonoured'. The cheque had been received from J. Simms, a new customer.
6. A $750 deposit made by L. Richards was incorrectly credited to the bank account of Cathy Fraser.
7. The bank statement shows that the bank has charged the business's account with fees and charges of $25.
8. Items 4, 5 and 6 have not yet been entered in the cash journals.

Required
Prepare a bank reconciliation at 30 June 2013, assuming that items 4, 5 and 6 are already recorded in the cash journals.

LO 3

Exercise 10.9 BANK RECONCILIATION — BANK ACCOUNT OVERDRAWN

Cathy's Consulting collected its latest bank statement on 1 July 2013. All entries appearing in the bank statement that had not been entered into the cash journals were entered therein. The cash journals were posted and the resulting balance of the Cash at Bank account in the ledger at 30 June was $15 136.50 Cr. The balance shown on the bank statement at 30 June was $17 016.62 Dr.

The following items recorded in the cash journals did not appear in the bank statement:
1. A deposit made on 30 June of $2627.12.
2. Cheques written during June that had not been presented for payment were:

Cheque no.	841	$325.30
	845	212.45
	846	227.25

A cheque written for $24 appeared incorrectly in the bank statement as $42.

Required
Prepare the bank reconciliation statement at 30 June 2013.

LO 4

Exercise 10.10 PETTY CASH FUND TRANSACTIONS

On 1 July, David and Irene, insurance agents, established a $300 petty cash fund. Cheque no. 432 was received by the petty cashier and duly cashed. On 31 July, the petty cash box contained the following cash and expense vouchers:

Cash			$47

Expense vouchers (all amounts include GST which is shown in parentheses)

Voucher no.	Date		Purpose	Amount
0214	July	7	Office supplies	$99.00 (9.00)
0215		13	Stationery	55.00 (5.00)
0216		20	Newspapers	33.00 (3.00)
0217		23	Customer refund	44.00 (4.00)
0218		28	Taxi fare	22.00 (2.00)

Required
A. Show the cash payments journal entry that was made to establish the petty cash fund on 1 July.
B. Show the cash payments journal entry needed on 31 July to reimburse the petty cash fund (cheque no. 883). (Taxi and newspaper expenditures should be charged to Sundry Expenses.)
C. Assume that a decision was made to increase the petty cash fund to $400 from 1 August (cheque no. 894). Show the cash payments journal entry to do so.
D. Prepare a petty cash book, with appropriate analysis columns, to incorporate the transactions of the fund shown above.

Exercise 10.11 BUDGETED CASH RECEIPTS FROM SALES, EXCLUDING GST

Hannah's Handbags Pty Ltd is preparing a budget for the quarter ended 30 June 2013. Hannah estimates that approximately 70% the handbag sales will be for cash and the rest will be on credit. Of the credit sales, 20% of the money will be received in the month of sale, 40% will be received the following month and 38% will be received 2 months after sale. Approximately 2% of credit sales are never collected and are written off.

The actual sales for the previous quarter ended 31 March 2013 were as follows:

January	$33 620
February	34 770
March	40 180

The budgeted sales for the June quarter are as follows:

April	$42 640
May	43 950
June	45 920

Required

Calculate budgeted cash receipts for the quarter ended 30 June 2013.

Exercise 10.12 BUDGETED CASH RECEIPTS FROM SALES, INCLUDING GST

Kay's Hardware Ltd's budgeted monthly sales for January to June 2013 are given below. About 70% of the monthly sales are expected to be on credit. Approximately 60% of the credit sales are collected in the month of sale, 30% in the month following the sale, and 5% in the second month following the sale; 5% are never collected and are written off.

The budgeted gross sales including GST of 10% by month are:

January	$115 000
February	162 000
March	139 000
April	125 000
May	150 000
June	130 000

Required

Prepare a schedule of expected cash receipts from sales for April, May and June 2013.

Exercise 10.13 BUDGETED CASH PAYMENTS FOR PURCHASES

The accountant for Schulz Ltd compiled the following figures in order to estimate budgeted cash payments for March and April 2013:

Purchases for December	$312 000
Purchases for January	298 000
Purchases for February	317 400
Ending inventory — 28 February	262 800
Budget sales: March	496 800
April	446 000
May	530 000
June	480 000

Schulz Ltd uses the following assumptions when preparing budgets. The cost of sales is 60% of sales. The company pays for 60% of its purchases in the month after purchase, 30% in the second month, following the purchase and 10% in the third month following the purchase. No discounts are received. It is business policy to maintain a month-end inventory balance sufficient to meet the projected sales requirement for the following month.

Required

A. Calculate the budgeted purchases for March and April 2013. Ignore GST.

B. Prepare a schedule of expected cash payments for purchases for March and April 2013.

Exercise 10.14 PRINCIPLES OF CASH MANAGEMENT

Bill has been running his local homewares store for 4 decades and has built up a large following of loyal customers. Bill believes that the key to developing a loyal customer base is to be generous in giving credit, to let customers pay when they have the money, and have plenty of stock so that customers don't have to wait for him to order in what they want. Bill also prides himself in minimising his debts by paying his accounts as soon as he receives them — to do this he likes to keep at least $30 000 in his store's cheque account. While you are studying at university, you work part-time for Bill and are aware of his approach to customers and bill paying. Bill has expressed his concern that he does not think he will have enough saved for when he retires in a few years.

Required

Explain to Bill how the principles of cash management can help him increase his savings so that he has more funds set aside for his retirement.

Exercise 10.15 ANALYSING ADEQUACY OF CASH FLOWS

Overton Pty Ltd is a private company that runs a coffee shop. Its owner, Carl, is concerned that the cash flows for the past year have deteriorated and has provided the following abridged versions of Overton Pty Ltd's balance sheet and statement of cash flows.

OVERTON PTY LTD
Balance Sheet
as at 30 June

	2014	2013
Current assets	$ 310 000	$ 320 000
Non-current assets	1 880 000	1 890 000
Total assets	2 190 000	2 210 000
Current liabilities	190 000	160 000
Non-current liabilities	1 560 000	1 580 000
Total liabilities	1 750 000	1 740 000
Net assets	$ 440 000	$ 470 000
Equity	$ 440 000	$ 470 000

OVERTON PTY LTD
Statement of Cash Flows
for the years ended 30 June

	2014	2013
Cash flows from operations	$110 000	$180 000
Cash flows from investing	(30 000)	(20 000)
Cash flows from financing	(20 000)	(25 000)
Net increase in cash	60 000	135 000
Beginning cash	160 000	25 000
Ending cash	220 000	160 000

Required

Calculate the short-term cash flow adequacy ratio and the cash flow adequacy ratio for 2013 and 2014 and comment on Overton Pty Ltd's ability to meet its current and overall obligations to creditors.

★ Basic

★★ Moderate

★★★ Challenging

LO 2

Problem 10.1 CASH RECEIPTS ★

During the week ended 12 September 2014 the daily sales for Calum's Chocolaterie were as follows:

	Total sales (including GST)	Sales on account	Banked
September 2014			
Monday 8	$1 562	$88	$1 474
Tuesday 9	1 518	55	1 443
Wednesday 10	1 694	66	1 633
Thursday 11	1 892	77	1 815
Friday 12	1 848	55	1 763

Required

Record the transactions for the week ended 12 September in the cash receipts journal of Calum's Chocolaterie, set out as below, and prepare a general journal entry for cash short and over if necessary.

CALUM'S CHOCOLATERIE
Cash Receipts Journal

		Debits		Credits		
Date	Account	Cash at Bank	Discount Allowed	Sales	Accounts Receivable	GST Collections
Sept. 8						

LO 2

Problem 10.2 CASH RECEIPTS ★

The daily sales for Sunny Fruit & Vegetable Shop during the week ended 5 April 2013 were as follows:

	Total sales (including GST)	Sales on account	Banked
April 2013			
Monday 1	$2 456	$421	$2 052
Tuesday 2	2 522	443	2 078
Wednesday 3	2 643	465	2 178
Thursday 4	2 784	496	2 175
Friday 5	3 035	527	2 542

Required

Record the transactions for the week ended 5 April 2013 in the cash receipts journal of Sunny Fruit & Vegetable Shop, set out as below, and prepare a general journal entry for cash short and over if necessary.

SUNNY FRUIT & VEGETABLE SHOP
Cash Receipts Journal

		Debits		Credits		
Date	Account	Cash at Bank	Discount Allowed	Sales	Accounts Receivable	GST Collections
Apr. 1						

Problem 10.3 OUTSTANDING DEPOSITS AND UNPRESENTED CHEQUES ★

The following information has been extracted from the cash records of Wheeler Ltd and shows four independent situations. Assume there were no direct bank debits or credits on the bank statement and that all outstanding deposits and unpresented cheques in one month appeared on the bank statement in the following month.

1. The total of outstanding deposits on the 30 April bank reconciliation statement was $1875. During May, the company made deposits of $40 200 to its bank account but the bank statement showed that only $39 840 was deposited during the month.
2. The total of unpresented cheques on the 30 April bank reconciliation statement was $1440. During May, the total of cheques issued was $29 175 but the bank statement showed that only $27 720 in cheques were presented during the month.
3. During July, deposits recorded on the bank statement totalled $46 200, but deposits according to the company's records were $43 950 and outstanding deposits at 31 July were $4125.
4. In July, cash payments according to Wheeler Ltd's records were $40 800, cheques presented and shown on the bank statement were $43 000 and unpresented cheques at 31 July were $3960.

Required
A. In situation 1, what were the outstanding deposits at 31 May?
B. In situation 2, what were the unpresented cheques at 31 May?
C. In situation 3, what were the outstanding deposits at 30 June?
D. In situation 4, what were the unpresented cheques at 30 June?

Problem 10.4 BANK RECONCILIATION ★

Information about the cash position for Cavanagh's Charter Tours Pty Ltd for the month of June is presented below:

1. The general ledger Cash at Bank account had a balance of $6300 on 31 May.
2. The cash receipts journal showed total cash receipts of $22 898 for June.
3. The cash payments journal showed total cash payments of $24 576 for June.
4. The June bank statement reported a bank balance of $4033 on 30 June.
5. Outstanding cheques at the end of June were: no. 864, $60; no. 866, $73; and no. 870, $112.
6. Cash receipts of $1200 for 30 June were placed in the bank's night safe on 30 June and were not included in the June bank statement.
7. Comparison of the presented cheques with the entries in the cash payments journal disclosed that cheque no. 842 for $354, for rent expense, had been wrongly recorded as $345.
8. Included on the bank statement were:
   (a) a total credit for $734, indicating an electronic transfer of $680 plus interest earned, which the bank had credited to the account
   (b) a dishonoured cheque written by Vinko Ltd, a client, for $327
   (c) account and transaction fees, $32.

Required
A. Set up cash receipts and cash payments journals with the totals shown above, enter the necessary adjustments, and complete the journals for June.
B. Post the journals in requirement A to the Cash at Bank account and balance the account.
C. Prepare a bank reconciliation statement as at 30 June.
D. What is the amount of cash that should be reported on the 30 June balance sheet?

Problem 10.5 BANK RECONCILIATION ★

Information about Bond Ltd's cash position for the month of December is presented below:

1. The general ledger Cash at Bank account had a balance of $10 600 on 30 November.
2. The cash receipts journal showed total cash receipts of $146 352 for December.
3. The cash payments journal showed total cash payments of $132 546 for December.
4. The December bank statement reported a bank balance of $20 592 on 31 December.

5. Outstanding cheques at the end of December were: no. 3456, $724; no. 3457, $42; no. 3460, $35 and no. 3462, $205.
6. Cash receipts of $5045 for 31 December were placed in the bank's night safe on 31 December and were not included in the December bank statement.
7. Comparison of the presented cheques with the entries in the cash payments journal disclosed that cheque no. 3442 for $423, for purchases expense, had been wrongly recorded as $432.
8. Included on the bank statement were:
   (a) a dishonoured cheque written by James Ltd, a client, for $68
   (b) a credit for an electronic transfer from a customer of $320 and a credit for interest earned of $22
   (c) account and transaction fees, $60.

Required

A. Set up cash receipts and cash payments journals with totals shown above, and enter the necessary adjustments, and complete the journals for December.
B. Post the journals in requirement A to the Cash at Bank account and balance the account.
C. Prepare a bank reconciliation statement at 31 December.
D. What is the amount of cash that should be reported on the 31 December balance sheet?

Problem 10.6   BANK RECONCILIATION ★   LO 3

The following information was available from records and the bank statement of Baldacchino Services Ltd, on 31 May.

The date and the amount of each deposit as recorded during May were as follows:

Date		Amount		Date		Amount
May	2	$1357.00		May	18	$1111.50
	5	1647.40			23	1487.16
	8	1897.96			25	1516.20
	11	1257.36			28	1636.60
	14	1341.20			31	1285.80

The number and amount of each cheque written during the month were recorded in the cash payments journal as follows:

Cheque no.	Amount	Cheque no.	Amount	Cheque no.	Amount
329	$ 966.66	335	$1546.80	341	$ 277.40
330	1163.80	336	801.30	342	402.80
331	1270.26	337	996.90	343	330.00
332	2015.00	338	960.20	344	1000.20
333	1017.50	339	1297.60	345	348.00
334	165.00	340	241.20		

The bank statement obtained on 31 May is as shown below:

Bank Statement				
April 30 Balance				$17 554.10
Date		**Debits**	**Credits**	
May 1	328	242.00	1 437.60	
	320	938.16		
2	329	966.66		
	330	1 163.80	1 357.00	
5	331	1 270.26	1 647.40	
6	334	165.00		
7	333	1 017.50		
8	332	2 015.00	1 897.96	
11	339	1 297.60	1 257.36	
14	335	1 546.80	1 341.20	
18	336	810.30	1 111.50	
	337	996.90		
	338	960.20		
23	340	241.20	1 487.16	
	341	277.40		
	343	330.00		
25			1 516.20	
28			1 636.60	
29	344	1 000.20		
31		268.00 Dishon. Cheque		
		32.00 Account Fees	1 250.00	
Totals		15 538.98	15 939.98	
May 31 Balance				$17 955.10

On 31 May, the bank debited the account for $268.00 for a customer cheque (deposited in April) returned because of insufficient funds, and for $32.00 for account fees. On 31 May, the bank also credited the account for $1250.00 for the proceeds of a non-interest-bearing note receivable that it had collected on behalf of the company.

Outstanding cheques at the last statement date, 30 April, were: no. 320 for $938.16, no. 328 for $242.00, and no. 326 for $813.00; outstanding deposits were $1437.60.

The accountant discovered that cheque no. 336 (in payment for the purchase of office equipment) was correctly issued for $810.30 but incorrectly recorded in the cash payments journal as $801.30.

The balance in the Cash at Bank account in the company's records on 1 May was $16 998.54.

Required

A. Complete the cash journals and post the totals to the Cash at Bank account. Show the Cash at Bank account (T-account form) after it has been balanced on 31 May.
B. Prepare a bank reconciliation statement as at 31 May.

Problem 10.7 BANK RECONCILIATION ★★

The bank reconciliation statement of Feng Zhen Liu on 21 June 2013 was as shown below.

FENG ZHEN LIU Bank Reconciliation Statement as at 21 June 2013		
Balance as per bank statement		$11 572 Dr
Add: Unpresented cheques:		
No. 172	$732	
177	406	
178	27	1 165
		12 737
Less: Deposit not credited by bank		10 125
Balance as per Cash at Bank account		$ 2 612 Cr

The cash receipts and cash payments journals for the week ending 28 June were as follows:

Cash Receipts Journal			
Date	Particulars	Details	Cash at Bank
2013			
June 24	Y. Luo	625	
	A. Zho	372	
	K. H. Tan	452	
	Sales	968	2 417
25	Sales	1 372	1 372
26	L. Jiang	28	
	Sales	1 421	1 449
27	Sales	1 762	1 762
28	R. Chen	321	
	Sales	1 854	2 175
			9 175

Cash Payments Journal			
Date	Particulars	Cheque no.	Cash at Bank
2013			
June 24	Y. Du	179	241
	Sundry expenses	180	89
25	J. Liang	181	322
	Wages	182	1 220
26	Rent	183	432
	M. Choi	184	376
27	D. Tsu	185	825
	Insurance	186	457
28	Purchases	187	328
	N. Ma	188	2 016
			6 306

Feng Zhen Liu's bank statement at 28 June is shown below.

		Bank Statement			
Date		Particulars	Debits	Credits	Balance
2013					
June	24	Balance			$11 572 Dr
				$10 125	1 447 Dr
				2 417	970 Cr
		177	$ 406		564 Cr
		Account fees	60		504 Cr
		180	89		415 Cr
	25	172	732		317 Dr
				1 372	1 055 Cr
		179	241		814 Cr
		182	1 220		406 Dr
		Returned cheque (H. Tsui)	430		836 Dr
	26			1 449	613 Cr
		184	376		237 Cr
		Interest on bonds		420	657 Cr
	27			1 762	2 419 Cr
		181	322		2 097 Cr
		Payment Auth. (to B. Chang)	948		1 149 Cr
		Transaction fees	12		1 137 Cr
	28	187	328		809 Cr
		Account Fees	60		749 Cr
		Interest on O/D	422		327 Cr
		TOTAL DEBITS $5646		TOTAL CREDITS $17 545	

Required

A. Complete, where necessary, the cash journals starting with the totals shown.
B. Open a Cash at Bank account with the correct balance on 21 June 2013 and post the totals of the cash journals. Balance the account at 28 June 2013.
C. Prepare a statement reconciling the Cash at Bank balance to the balance as shown by the bank statement as at 28 June 2013.

LO 3

Problem 10.8 BANK RECONCILIATION ★★

The March 2013 bank statement of Tong's Toyworld has just been received from its bankers. The following information is available:

1. The March bank column totals of the cash receipts and cash payments journals are, respectively, $21 546 and $24 108 before taking into account any of the items appearing on the bank statement.
2. The following items appear on the March bank statement but not in the cash journals for the same month:
   A deposit on 1 March 2013 of $2100.
   Cheque no. 253 for $248.20 and no. 257 for $417.40.
   A debit of $300 to correct an error.
   A dishonoured cheque (received from K. Matthews) for $294.
   A deposit of $400 by owner Penelope Tong to her personal bank account held at the same bank.
   Rent of $420 from a tenant who sublets space was deposited directly.
   A standing transfer order of $350 for insurance premiums.
   Interest on overdraft $48, account fees $30.

3. The following items appear in the cash journals but not on the bank statement:

Cheque no. 284 was stopped for payment because the amount written on the cheque was wrong. The cheque was given to NW Minerals Ltd for goods, $1500.

Cheque no. 288 for $632 and no. 293 for $342.

A deposit on 31 March for $1720.

A post-dated cheque no. 289 for $1000 given to Simpson Pty Ltd.

4. Additional information:

On 31 March 2013 the bank statement showed a debit balance of $2342.80.

Cheque no. 193 for $60 was drawn on 17 December 2011 as a donation to the Scouts Association (cheque is now a stale cheque).

Cheque no. 285 for $228 appears twice on the bank statement.

Cheque no. 296 was entered correctly as $360 in the cash journal but appeared in the bank statement as $560.

5. Bank reconciliation statement on 28 February 2013:

Balance as per bank statement		$ 839.20 Dr
Add: Cheques not debited by bank:		
No. 193	$ 60.00	
253	248.20	
257	417.40	
261	719.20	
Bank error — deposit to incorrect account	300.00	1744.80
		2584.00
Less: Outstanding deposit		2100.00
Balance as per Cash at Bank account		$ 484.00 Cr

Required

A. Prepare and balance the Cash at Bank account in the general ledger for March 2013.

B. Prepare the bank reconciliation statement at 31 March 2013.

C. What conclusions can be drawn regarding control over cash payments after preparation of the reconciliation statement?

LO 3

Problem 10.9   BANK RECONCILIATION ★★

As accountant for J. Stojanovic & Son, you are required to perform a bank reconciliation at the end of June 2013. The bank reconciliation statement for the previous month is set out below:

Bank Reconciliation Statement as at 31 May 2013	
Balance as per bank statement	$343.64 Cr
Add: Outstanding deposit	131.45
	475.09
Less: Unpresented cheque no. 1008	61.60
Balance as per Cash at Bank account	$413.49 Dr

Abridged cash receipts and cash payments journals before finalisation and posting are:

Cash Receipts Journal

Date		Account	Cash at Bank
2013			
June	2	R. Wike	121.66
	5	Sales	270.36
		Langer Ltd	66.00
	9	C. Nunn	341.55
	12	Sales	149.82
		J. Byron	93.55
		S. Banks	187.78
	16	Sales	122.26
	22	R. Ricketts	27.50
		Cowra Cannery Ltd	308.00
	27	Sales	84.89
		R. Wike	154.00
		Langer Ltd	53.40
	28	R. Ricketts — dishon. cheque	(27.50)
	29	Sales	224.83
	30	Sales	241.34
			2419.44

Cash Payments Journal

Date		Account	Cheque no.	Cash at Bank
2013				
June	2	Stationery	1010	35.75
	3	Royal Ltd	1011	328.13
	5	Advertising	1012	28.05
	6	J. Brown Ltd	1013	54.10
		Wages and salaries	1014	302.50
		Petty cash	1015	27.50
	9	Riley and Sons	1016	123.36
	11	Vehicle expenses	1017	36.08
		Wages and salaries	1018	302.50
	13	Travel — sales staff	1019	16.50
	16	Sales commission	1020	33.82
	17	Royal Ltd	1021	105.51
	18	Wages and salaries	1022	302.50
	20	Electricity expense	1023	118.59
	25	Wages and salaries	1024	297.00
	26	R. Banco	1025	42.15
		Austral Motors	1026	46.86
		Donation — Red Cross	1027	11.00
	28	Riley and Sons	1028	85.14
	30	Freight inwards	1029	24.25
		P. Minecello	1030	90.82
				2412.11

The following is a copy of the bank statement for the month of June 2013.

BANK STATEMENT

DATE	PARTICULARS	DEBIT	CREDIT	BALANCE
2013				
June 1	Balance			343.64 Cr
2	1010	35.75		307.89 Cr
			131.45	439.34 Cr
			121.66	561.00 Cr
5	1008	61.60		499.40 Cr
			336.36	835.76 Cr
6	1011	328.13		507.63 Cr
7	1012	28.05		479.58 Cr
	1014	302.50		177.08 Cr
	1015	27.50		149.58 Cr
9	1013	54.10		95.48 Cr
			341.55	437.03 Cr
12	1016	123.36		313.67 Cr
	1018	302.50		11.17 Dr
			431.15	442.32 Cr
15	1019	16.50		425.82 Cr
	1020	33.82		392.00 Cr
16			122.26	514.26 Cr
19	1017	36.08		478.18 Cr
22	1021	105.51		372.67 Cr
			335.50	708.17 Cr
	1022	302.50		405.67 Cr
27			292.29	697.96 Cr
28	1024	302.50		395.46 Cr
	1023	118.59		276.87 Cr
	Returned cheque	27.50		249.37 Cr
30	1025	42.15		207.22 Cr
	Account and transaction fees	22.50		184.72 Cr
	1026	46.86		137.86 Cr
			224.83	362.69 Cr

TOTAL DEBITS	TOTAL CREDITS	BALANCE
2318.00	2337.05	362.69 CR

Required

A. Complete the cash journals, amending or adding to them as necessary, and post the cash at bank totals to the Cash at Bank account.

B. Prepare the Cash at Bank account showing the final balance at 30 June 2013.

C. Prepare the bank reconciliation statement as at 30 June 2013.

BANK RECONCILIATION ★★

As the accountant for Sam & Ben Ice cream you are required to perform a bank reconciliation at the end of June 2015. The bank reconciliation statement for the previous month is set out below:

Bank Reconciliation Statement as at 31 May 2015			
Balance as per bank statement			$5 634.58
Add: Outstanding deposit			432.67
			6 067.25
Less: Unpresented cheques:			
Cheque no.	4578	$ 67.35	
	4579	134.89	
	4581	287.34	489.58
Balance as per Cash at Bank account			$5 577.67

Abridged cash receipts and cash payments journals before finalisation and posting are:

Cash Receipts Journal		
Date	Account	Cash at Bank
2015 June 1	Sales	599.54
2	M. Fraser	56.98
	Sales	515.90
4	P. Bartel	64.00
	Sales	602.78
5	Sales	548.70
8	C. Mason	98.00
	I. Ellis	45.68
	Sales	555.60
9	Sales	525.00
12	J. Rasheed	34.65
	Sales	502.40
15	Sales	519.56
17	J. Botten	35.40
	J. Greenhalgh	22.20
	Sales	440.86
19	J. Rasheed — dishon. cheque	(34.65)
	Sales	498.90
22	Sales	548.65
26	M. Fraser	34.50
	Sales	536.00
29	Sales	506.80
30	Sales	480.65
		7 738.10

Cash Payments Journal			
Date	Account	Cheque no.	Cash at Bank
2015			
June 1	Love Ltd	4582	345.67
2	Bishop Ltd	4583	189.60
4	Wages and salaries	4584	880.00
5	Petty cash	4585	54.65
	D. Elliot	4586	125.60
8	Taylor & Sons	4587	54.90
9	PB Petrol Bowsers	4588	95.00
	Accommodation	4589	235.40
11	G. Warner & Partner	4590	584.30
12	Electricity Ltd	4591	720.89
15	Big Gas Corporation	4592	220.54
	Telephone Company	4593	325.90
17	Advertising	4594	220.00
18	Wages and salaries	4595	880.00
19	Donation – Sallies Army	4596	50.00
22	Freight	4597	80.00
24	Purchases	4598	2 080.90
25	PB Petrol Bowsers	4599	56.80
26	S. Bartel	4600	125.00
29	Petty cash	4601	42.05
30	K. Turner	4602	38.70
			7 405.90

The following is a copy of the bank statement for the month of June 2015.

Bank Statement				
Date	Particulars	Debit	Credit	Balance
2015				
June 1	Balance			5 634.58 Cr
2	4579	134.89		5 499.69 Cr
	Deposit		432.67	5 932.36 Cr
	Deposit		599.54	6 531.90 Cr
3	Deposit		572.88	7 104.78 Cr
4	4582	345.67		6 759.11 Cr
	4583	189.60		6 569.51 Cr
	4584	880.00		5 689.51 Cr
	Deposit		666.78	6 356.29 Cr
5	4585	54.65		6 301.64 Cr
	Deposit		548.70	6 850.34 Cr
6	4581	287.34		6 563.00 Cr
8	Deposit		699.28	7 262.28 Cr
9	4588	95.00		7 167.28 Cr
	Deposit		520.00	7 687.28 Cr
12	4586	125.60		7 561.68 Cr
	4589	235.40		7 326.28 Cr
	Deposit		537.05	7 863.33 Cr
15	4590	584.30		7 279.03 Cr
	4587	54.90		7 224.13 Cr
	4592	220.54		7 003.59 Cr
	Deposit		519.56	7 523.15 Cr
17	4593	325.90		7 197.25 Cr
	Deposit		498.46	7 695.71 Cr
18	4595	880.00		6 815.71 Cr

(continued)

		Bank Statement			
Date		**Particulars**	**Debit**	**Credit**	**Balance**
2015					
June	19	4591	720.89		6 094.82 Cr
		4594	230.00		5 864.82 Cr
		Deposit		498.90	6 363.72 Cr
		Returned cheque	34.65		6 329.07 Cr
	22	4597	80.00		6 249.07 Cr
		Deposit		548.65	6 797.72 Cr
	26	4596	50.00		6 747.72 Cr
		4598	2 080.90		4 666.82 Cr
		Deposit		570.50	5 237.32 Cr
	29	4599	56.80		5 180.52 Cr
		4601	42.05		5 138.47 Cr
	30	Deposit		506.80	5 645.27 Cr
		Account fees	60.00		5 585.27 Cr

TOTAL DEBITS 7 769.08	TOTAL CREDITS 7 719.77	**BALANCE 5 585.27 CR**

Required

A. Complete the cash journals, amending or adding to them as necessary, and post the cash at bank totals to the Cash at Bank account.
B. Prepare the Cash at Bank account showing the final balance at 30 June 2015.
C. Prepare the bank reconciliation statement as at 30 June 2015.

LO 4

Problem 10.11 PETTY CASH TRANSACTIONS ★★

The following transactions and events relate to the petty cash fund (imprest amount $400) of Honshu Ltd (all amounts include GST):

1. Paid $55 delivery charges on inventory purchased.
2. Paid $88 (part payment) for the repair of computer scanner.
3. Purchased office supplies, $63.80.
4. Paid $40 for postage (GST-free).
5. Paid $33 for newspapers.
6. The petty cashier exchanged the vouchers in the petty cash box for a cheque to reimburse the fund and to increase the size of the fund from $400 to $500.
7. Paid Post Express $88 for delivery of urgently needed supplies.
8. Paid $66 for office window cleaning.
9. Reimbursed an employee $35.20 for taxi fares for business-related trip.
10. Paid $25.50 for coffee and supplies for the staffroom.
11. Refunded $59.40 for petrol purchased by driver for business delivery vehicle.
12. Paid $66 for dry-cleaning an office curtain.

Required

Note: GST can be ignored in this question by treating all amounts as excluding GST.
Show the entries in the cash payments journal to:

1. establish the petty cash fund for the amount of $400 (cheque no. 0137)
2. reimburse the fund after transaction (5) and increase its size to $500 with cheque no. 0146 (delivery charges and express delivery payments are to be debited to Freight Inwards; expenses unrelated to motor vehicles, office supplies and postage should be debited to Sundry Expenses).
3. reimburse the fund after transaction (12) (cheque no. 0155).

LO 5

Problem 10.12 CASH BUDGET ★★

Brockbank Builders Ltd is preparing a cash budget for May and June of 2013. Past records reveal that 20% of all credit sales are collected during the month of sale, 60% in the month following the sale, 10% in the second month following the sale and 10% in the third month following the sale.

The company pays for 75% of purchases in the month after purchase, and the balance is paid in the month following that.

Selling expenses amount to $6600 per month plus 15% of monthly sales. Administrative expenses are estimated to be $13 200 per month, which includes $4800 of depreciation expense. Finance expenses are $1200 per month. All selling and distribution, administrative, and finance and other expenses (except depreciation) are paid for when incurred.

It is planned to purchase equipment during May 2013 at a cost of $6600. A $9000 loan payable will be repaid during June 2013. The interest due at maturity will be $1650. The company's expected Cash at Bank balance at 1 May 2013 is $13 500.

Estimated sales and purchases data are as follows:

	Sales	Purchases
2013		
February	$75 000	$38 500
March	66 000	33 000
April	88 000	55 000
May	60 500	27 500
June	71 500	38 500

Required
Ignoring GST, prepare a cash budget for May and June 2013, by month and in total.

LO 3

Problem 10.13 BANK RECONCILIATION AND INTERNAL CONTROL ★★★

The owner of Hatzidimitriou Hardware has completed a bank reconciliation and cannot get the bank's records to agree with the cash records of his business. He concludes that internal control has somehow failed and cash is being misappropriated. He asks you to check the records and confirm or otherwise his suspicions. He supplies the reconciliation statement at the end of last month, his cash records, and the most recent bank statement.

Last month's reconciliation statement is presented below.

Bank Reconciliation Statement	
as at 31 May 2013	
Balance per bank statement 31 May 2013	$ 4328.90 Cr
Add: Outstanding deposit	1224.50
	5553.40
Less: Unpresented cheques	223.70
Balance per Cash at Bank account at 31 May 2013	$ 5329.70 Dr

The total of the cash receipts journal for June is $64 776.30 and the total of the cash payments journal is $63 265.60. The current bank statement shows that cheques presented and paid amount to $59 725.10, and total deposits amount to $64 780.60. There are also additional debits on the statement for a dishonoured cheque for $210, and account fees for $20.

An examination of the records reveals that all reconciling items at 31 May 2013 appear in the bank statement for June, unpresented cheques at 30 June total $7154.40, and the 30 June deposit of $1950.40 has not been credited by the bank. Your check of the cash journals reveals that addition errors have been made by the clerks responsible. Receipts should total $65 766.30 and payments should total $63 185.60.

Required
A. Recalculate and present the general ledger Cash at Bank account balance as it should be at 30 June 2013.
B. Prepare the bank reconciliation statement at 30 June 2013.
C. Advise the owner of Hatzidimitriou Hardware whether cash is being misappropriated, assuming that the records maintained by the bank are accurate.

Problem 10.14   CASH BUDGET ★★★

Prickly Pear Ltd wishes to prepare a cash budget for the first quarter of 2013. In response to your request for past and projected financial data, you receive the following:

Projected sales (excludes GST):	November 2012	$144 000
	December 2012	147 000
	January 2013	198 000
	February 2013	190 000
	March 2013	288 000
	April 2013	216 000
	May 2013	216 000

Of sales, 70% of sales are on credit, with 65% collected during the month of sale, 30% collected during the month following the sale, and 5% during the second month after the sale; 30% of the projected sales are for cash. Ignore GST. Since all suppliers require substantial lead time, purchases of inventory are made 2 months in advance of sale and are paid for 1 month in advance of sale. The cost of sales is 50% of the selling price. Other regular monthly cash payments (ignoring GST) are:

Salaries and wages	$6600
Sales commissions (on credit sales only)	10%
General and administrative expenses	$14 850
Insurance	$16 500
Delivery expenses	3% of total sales

A special advertising campaign is planned that will require a cash payment of $16 650 on 1 March. An interim dividend of $13 500 is planned for payment on 16 February.

On 1 January 2013, there was an outstanding bank debt of $90 000 that must be paid off in 5 months by making principal repayments of $18 000 at the end of each month. Interest is payable at the end of each month at 1% per month on the balance outstanding at the beginning of the month. The cash balance on 1 January is estimated to be $112 500.

Required
Prepare the cash budget of Prickly Pear Ltd covering January, February and March 2013.

Problem 10.15   CASH BUDGET ★★★

Ken Dunlop of Dunlop's Dishes wishes to prepare a cash budget for the 6 months ending 30 June 2014 so he can arrange for overdraft drawings facilities, if required. The following information is available:

1. The business has consistently marked up its goods so as to realise a gross margin of 40% on sales (excluding GST). Policy is to have sufficient inventory on hand at the end of each month to cover the next 2 months sales. This was the situation at 31 December 2013, when the inventory was $160 500 (cost).
2. All sales are on credit and are subject to GST. Debtors pay their accounts 50% in the month of sale and 50% in the following month.
3. All creditors are paid in the month following purchase.
4. The bank overdraft on 31 December 2013 was $10 800. Purchases in December of goods for resale amounted to $86 400.
5. Estimated quarterly payments of GST to the ATO are to be made in January for $14 000 and in April for $6900.
6. Sales in November and December 2013 were $72 000 and $86 000 respectively. A growth of $14 000 per month (before GST) is expected over the next 6 months. (GST has yet to be added to these amounts.)
7. The estimated payments for expenses are:
    Salaries $10 800 per month (GST-free)
    Administration $3300 per month (includes GST)
    Rent $19 800 (including GST) for the year to 31 December 2010; this is to be paid as a lump sum in January 2014.

8. On 1 January 2014, a new machine costing $90 000 plus GST is to be purchased and paid for. It is expected that this machine will last 10 years and have no resale value. All existing plant was scrapped during December 2013.

Required

A. Prepare a separate cash budget for each of the 6 months, January to June 2014.

B. Prepare the projected income statement for the 6 months ending 30 June 2014.

C. Explain the reasons for the difference between the projected profitability and the projected liquidity for the period.

DECISION ANALYSIS

Improving cash flows for Exquisite Hotels Pty Ltd

Your friend Ninette Nobis was a tourism management student when you were at university together and is now a manager of an upmarket hotel in the Exquisite Hotels chain. Because of the impact of an economic downturn on her customers, Ninette is concerned about the cash flow of the hotel she manages. Ninette needs advice on how to improve the business's cash flow. You begin your research by reading the article below.

Required

Based on the *Herald Sun* article, how would you help Ninette decide on ways to improve the cash flow of the hotel?

Cash is king, especially for busy, growing companies. But many businesses say they have noticed that customers are increasingly paying their bills later and later. And they are not alone.

A recent Dun & Bradstreet study showed that on average Australian businesses are being paid more than three weeks over the standard 30-day payment term, putting a squeeze on cash flow.

Good cash flow management is the solution to the gap between the time you have to pay your suppliers and employees and the time you collect from your customers.

The first step is to prepare cash flow projections for the next year, the next quarter, even the next month. Start by adding cash on hand with cash to be received. What cash will we get in, from who and when?

Then have a line item for everything you must pay out, such as rent, salaries, equipment, and advertising. Now you have an idea of exactly where you stand.

Next, look at how you can improve payment. Offer discounts to customers who pay bills quickly, issue invoices more promptly and follow up firmly if they're late even by a few days, ask new customers for a deposit when an order is taken, and avoid slow-paying customers.

At the same time, manage your suppliers and payables. Take full advantage of payment terms, using electronic banking to make payments on the last day they are due. Also look at your costs carefully and make cuts where you can.

Finally, anticipate the worst. There might well be a day when you find you are short on cash. Speak to your bank now, when business is good, about a line of credit. You might never need it but your bank will be more receptive when your business is fundamentally sound than if you have to go cap in hand one day.

Also speak to your suppliers. If you have been a good customer they will want to see you stay in business and might give you extended terms of payment.

Source: Susan Heron (CEO, AIMVT), 'Managing the cash squeeze', *Herald-Sun.*

CRITICAL THINKING

Internal controls over cash receipts

The Leaning Tower of Metropolis is a tall structure attached to the top of the highest building in the city with a lift in the centre to take paying customers to a viewing platform at the top of the tower. On payment of the appropriate fee for an adult, concession or child customer, the cashier in the ticket booth enters the details into the computer system, which then prints out a cardboard ticket. The ticket includes the price paid and whether the customer is an adult, concession or child.

The customer then takes the ticket to the attendant who stands ouside the lift. The attendant collects the tickets and is supposed to tear them in half and put them in a bin.

At the end of the day, the manager counts the money in the ticket booth and compares this with what has been entered into the computer to produce the tickets. At the end of each month the accountant compares the deposits per the bank statement with the daily takings compiled by the computer system.

Required

A. What are the most important internal control principles and procedures being used by the Leaning Tower of Metropolis to ensure control over cash receipts? Does the Tower have an adequate system of internal control?

B. Is it possible for the ticket seller and lift attendant to misappropriate cash through collusion? If so, how could the system be improved to overcome this possibility?

ETHICS AND GOVERNANCE

Maintaining a cash balance

You are the assistant accountant at Krispies Co. Ltd, a distributor of snack foods. Krispies has a large loan from a bank, and part of the loan agreement stipulates that the company must maintain a Cash at Bank account balance of at least $75 000, reviewed monthly by the bank manager. At 31 March you report to the accountant, Naomi Kidman, that the cash balance is only $50 000.

Naomi is concerned and instructs you to keep the cash receipts records open for one more day. She explains that if Krispies reports this cash balance to the bank, the company will default on the loan agreement and the bank may foreclose on the loan. The company could be forced into liquidation and all employees will lose their jobs. Naomi's friend Brian Sheen is the accountant at Freers Foods, one of Krispies' largest customers. She says she will ring Brian and get him to send through a cheque for $35 000 (in part payment of Freers Foods' account) dated 30 March, which you will receive tomorrow, 1 April.

Naomi instructs you to include this cheque in the cash balance that will place Krispies in the clear with the bank.

Required

A. Who are the stakeholders in this situation?

B. What do you think are the ethical issues involved here?

C. List the courses of action you might take and the consequences of each.

FINANCIAL ANALYSIS

Refer to the latest financial report of JB Hi-Fi Limited on its website, www.jbhifi.com.au, and answer the following questions.

1. How is 'cash' defined in the financial statements?

2. Did the total of cash held by JB Hi-Fi Limited increase or decrease over the period? By how much?

3. Is the balance of cash as shown in the balance sheet at the end of the year different from the figure for cash at end of period as shown in the statement of cash flows? If so, how and why? (*Hint:* Refer to the notes to the statement of cash flows for the explanation.)

4. Is there any reference in the report to aspects of internal control used by JB Hi-Fi Limited?

5. Does JB Hi-Fi Limited have an internal audit department? If it has, what are the major functions of such a department?

Cost–volume–profit analysis for decision making

Concepts for review

Before studying this chapter, you should understand or, if necessary, revise:

- the difference between product and period costs (pp. 342–3)
- the three manufacturing cost elements (pp. 343–6)
- the distinction between variable and fixed costs (pp. 346–7)
- the contents of a cost of goods manufactured statement and income statement for a manufacturing entity (pp. 347–9).

Learning objectives

After studying this chapter, you should be able to:

1 distinguish between variable, fixed and mixed expenses behaviour, and describe the basic assumptions of cost–volume–profit (CVP) analysis (pp. 462–6)

2 define contribution margin and discuss the benefits of a contribution margin-based income statement (pp. 466–8)

3 explain how CVP analysis can be used by management for profit planning (pp. 468–9)

4 explain break-even point and identify the three methods of determining the break-even point (pp. 469–71)

5 understand the application of a margin of safety in break-even analysis (p. 471) and use break-even analysis to determine target sales and target profit (pp. 471–2)

6 understand how changes in certain factors affect profits (pp. 472–5)

7 explain how CVP analysis is used with multiple products (pp. 475–6)

8 explain variations between planned and actual contribution margins using sales price, sales volume and variable expense variances (pp. 476–7).

World's airlines stuck in time warp

It might have been one of the most severe downturns in the aviation industry's history — a shock bigger than September 11 and the SARS virus because of its duration — but dysfunctional airlines still fly and mega-mergers across national borders remain a pipe dream.

More than a year since the collapse of Lehman Brothers sent markets into a near-death spiral, the ensuing travel downturn has bottomed out but airlines remain cautious about forecasting a sustained recovery in demand this year.

The shadow of rising fuel prices hangs over an industry which cannot forget all-time highs of $US182 a barrel in July 2008.

Airlines found a saviour in a sharp fall in fuel prices from record highs in 2008. Cheaper input costs can make all the difference, especially when jet fuel prices can make up to a third of an airline's total outlay.

'If the oil price had stayed over $US100 a barrel I don't know how many carriers would have survived,' a former senior Qantas executive says. 'It saved their bacon. Who knows where things may have ended up if oil had stayed at a very high level.'

US airlines, which account for half the world's air traffic, were also better placed to counter the global downturn following major surgery in the aftermath of September 11 and the SARS crisis.

But the surgery needed worldwide remains as unlikely as ever. Consolidation is confined within countries or borderless economic blocks such as the European Union — where British Airways and Spain's Iberia finally cleared the way for a merger late last year — because of foreign ownership restrictions and, ultimately, national pride. AirAsia's tie up

with Jetstar is still light years from a fully fledged union however much it was talked up by the two sides this week.

Full-service airlines such as Singapore Airlines, Cathay Pacific and Japan Airlines are suited to long-haul routes because they have the necessary networks, hubs and larger aircraft. These are crucial to long-haul airlines but not low-cost carriers flying from point-to-point destinations.

In the absence of fundamental change, the airlines have had to resort to gnawing away at any excess fat to carry them through the downturn. And after investing heavily in high-end ancillary services, long-haul airlines have been forced to heavily discount tickets to fill seats and reconsider their finer product offerings. The luxuries have included in-flight showers and bathrooms for first-class passengers on some A380 super-jumbos.

The other response has been resorting to alliances in an attempt to shred costs. Take the planned joint venture between Virgin Blue's [now trading as Virgin Australia] long-haul offshoot, V Australia, and Delta Air Lines for flights between Australia and the US, or the proposed tie-up between British Airways and American Airlines for flights across the Atlantic.

In Australia, the short-haul market is regarded as unique. Qantas is one of the few legacy airlines to successfully maintain a low-cost offshoot. Qantas has avoided the failed experiments of other full-service airlines such as British Airways (which sold low-cost subsidiary Go to easyJet after just four years), Delta (Song), United Airlines (TED) and Air New Zealand (Freedom) in setting up low-cost subsidiaries.

'The only reason it worked in Australia was because Qantas was so powerful.'

Source: Matt O'Sullivan, 'World's airlines stuck in time warp', *The Sydney Morning Herald*.

Chapter preview

The scene setter raises issues that managers and marketing staff constantly face when making decisions concerning *selling prices*, *sales volume*, *sales mix* and *costs* in the search for the combination of these factors that will produce acceptable if not maximum profits. The airline industry in recent years has become divided between full-service airlines and low-cost airlines. These airlines not only target different parts of the market but are established with a different mix of fixed and variable costs. Full-service airlines use larger planes and have a higher fixed-cost structure while the low-cost airlines rely on fewer facilities and therefore have lower fixed costs to reduce their overheads. To find the right combination to test their market niche, a manager must be able to evaluate the effect on profit of interrelationships among the four factors. **Cost–volume–profit (CVP) analysis** is an important technique used to determine how costs and profits are affected by changes in the level of business activity in all types of businesses.

When the cost behaviour concepts introduced in chapter 8 are combined with information concerning selling prices, sales volume and sales mix, the effect of a change in the level of business activity can be evaluated effectively with CVP analysis. Thus, knowledge about cost behaviour patterns is an important part of CVP analysis.

11.1 Cost behaviour and assumptions of cost–volume–profit analysis

Chapter 8 introduced the concept of **cost behaviour**, which is the measure of how cost will respond to changes in the level of business activity. Several types of cost behaviour are possible, but the three most important ones for CVP analysis are variable costs, fixed costs and mixed costs. Recall that a variable cost changes in total with the level of some activity or volume such as sales dollars, products produced, fees charged or labour hours, whereas a fixed cost remains constant in total over a wide range of activity. A third type of cost behaviour is a **mixed cost** (sometimes called a semi-variable cost), which contains both fixed and variable cost components. The cost of operating a mobile phone is a good example of this type of cost. Monthly access fees are fixed regardless of the number of calls made. The cost of a call varies with how many calls are made and the duration of each call. Even the cost of a call is not all variable, since the flagfall is a fixed amount regardless of the length of the call.

The management accountant must be able to evaluate each cost incurred to determine the cost function that best describes the item's cost behaviour. In its most basic form, a **cost function** is a relationship between cost as a dependent variable and some measure of activity or volume as an independent variable.

An important aspect of CVP analysis is that all cost functions are assumed to be linear (i.e. a straight line) so the rate of change is constant and easy to predict. The cost function used in CVP analysis can be expressed as a linear equation, as follows:

$$y = a + bx$$

where: y = the total cost (dependent variable)
a = the y intercept or the fixed portion of the total cost
b = the slope of the cost function or the variable cost rate
x = the measure of activity or volume such as sales dollars, fees charged, units produced or labour hours (independent variable)

The three basic cost functions can be graphed as shown in figure 11.1. Many entities experience some costs that are not exactly variable and others that are not exactly fixed over the entire range of business activity possible. In order to understand how management accountants treat the more complex cost behaviour patterns in the application of CVP analysis, we must first consider some of the complications associated with variable and fixed cost behaviour.

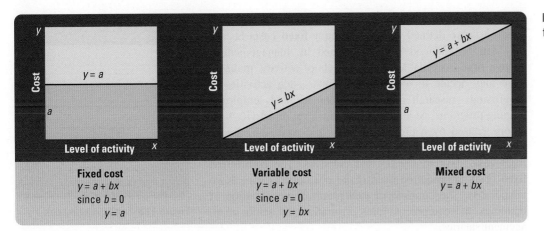

Figure 11.1 Three basic cost functions

Variable cost behaviour

Few variable costs behave exactly as linear functions with constant slopes over all levels of activity. Two notable exceptions, a *curvilinear function* and a *step function*, are found in many businesses. A graphic version of these cost functions is shown in figure 11.2. The curvilinear variable cost shown in graph (a) is the result of what economists describe as economies and diseconomies of scale. At extremely low levels of activity, an entity does not have sufficient volume to take advantage of such factors as automation and the specialisation of labour. So the variable cost function increases at an increasing rate. When unusually high levels of activity are achieved, inefficiencies and bottlenecks occur so a variable cost again increases at an increasing rate. Within the darker area of graph (a), the cost function is approximately linear because the rate of increase is relatively constant. This area of the graph is called the **relevant range**, which is the range of activity within which an entity normally operates. The relevant range concept is important for CVP analysis because it permits a **linearity assumption** for curvilinear variable costs within the usual range of activity.

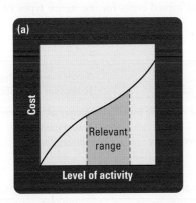 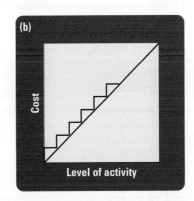

Figure 11.2 Curvilinear and step cost functions

A step cost function such as the one shown in graph (b) in figure 11.2 will be incurred for some variable cost items because they cannot be purchased in divisible units. For example, each worker's wage represents a step in the cost function shown in graph (b). The cost function increases abruptly as each additional worker is hired to satisfy the needs of a higher level of activity. Again, the management accountant converts the step function into a linear function, as shown in graph (b), by connecting the points representing the highest level of activity for each step. The justification for the conversion is that the business will want to fully use the labour cost for any given step by attaining the highest level of activity possible.

Fixed cost behaviour

The relevant-range concept also permits management to assume that the total fixed costs will remain constant over a range of activity. In reality, the total fixed costs may change over a complete range of activity in wide steps, as shown in figure 11.3. Many fixed costs are defined as **discretionary fixed costs** because they can be changed or discontinued by management if enough time is available. At low levels of activity, management may decide to reduce or eliminate such activities as advertising, research and development, and employee training programs. At an extremely low level of activity such as one caused by a prolonged economic recession, drastic measures may be necessary to eliminate all but the committed fixed costs through layoffs and cutbacks. The **committed fixed costs** are required even if the operation is shut down temporarily. They consist of such items as depreciation of buildings and equipment, rates, insurance and senior management salaries.

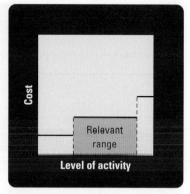

Figure 11.3 Fixed cost function

At an extremely high level of activity, added capacity will be necessary to satisfy the market demand for the entity's products or services, so fixed costs such as depreciation and managerial salaries will increase. Again, the relevant-range concept permits management to ignore the low and high levels by concentrating on the normal range of operation. Within the relevant range, fixed costs will remain constant in total.

Mixed cost behaviour

As we can see in figure 11.1, a mixed cost contains both fixed and variable components. Consequently, a mixed cost increases or decreases linearly with changes in activity but has a positive amount even at zero activity. The fixed portion of a mixed cost represents the minimum cost of obtaining a service, and the variable element is the result of a change in activity. For example, the rental of a motor vehicle is a mixed cost when a fixed amount per day and a certain rate per kilometre are charged. Other examples of mixed costs in some cases are electricity charges, telephone charges, maintenance, sales salaries and office machine rentals.

Table 11.1 sets out examples of variable, fixed and mixed costs for the major types of business organisations.

Table 11.1 Examples of variable, fixed and mixed costs

Type of costs	Manufacturer (motor mowers)	Retailer (designer clothes)	Service organisation (computer consultant)
Variable	Direct materials Direct labour Indirect labour Factory supplies Paint finish	Purchases of goods for resale Sales commissions	Wages of consultants Travel costs Parking fees
Fixed	Salaries of supervisors Depreciation of machinery Depreciation of factory Council general rates Insurance premiums	Depreciation of premises Salaries Insurance Council general rates	Depreciation of office furniture Insurance premiums Salaries of staff Rent/lease of premises
Mixed	Electricity Telephone Water rates	Electricity Telephone Water rates	Electricity Telephone Internet usage

For mixed costs to be planned and controlled, they must be divided into their fixed and variable components. A number of techniques based on the equation $y = a + b$ can be used for the separation of mixed costs. The three most popular techniques are:
- visual fit of a scatter diagram
- high–low method
- linear regression analysis.

All three techniques are based on the collection of historical data that represent the mixed costs incurred at different levels of activity. The aim is to develop a cost function that best reflects the cost behaviour pattern of the mixed costs. Assume that a manufacturing entity has experienced the following maintenance costs and machine hours during the past 12 months of the financial year ended 30 June:

Month	Maintenance costs	Machine hours
July	$27 550	2920
August	28 600	3625
September	31 680	4380
October	33 350	4752
November	36 000	5986
December	37 700	7250
January	41 760	8640
February	38 610	7150
March	36 250	6525
April	34 560	5720
May	30 030	5005
June	29 930	4350

Visual fit

The monthly maintenance costs can be plotted as a function of machine hours, as shown in figure 11.4. The visual fit of a scatter diagram method is applied by drawing a straight line through the relationships of the dependent and independent variables. The straight line through the points representing the various relationships of maintenance costs and machine hours is chosen as the best visual fit, with approximately the same number of observations above and below the line. This means that the differences between the scatter points and the straight line are minimal compared with other lines that might be drawn through the scatter diagram. The fixed portion of maintenance costs is determined by extending the line to the vertical axis and amounts to approximately $20 000.

The variable costs can be found for any given number of machine hours by subtracting the fixed costs of $20 000 from the total costs related to that level of activity. For example, total maintenance costs of $35 000 are estimated for 6000 machine hours, so the variable costs are $15 000 ($35 000 less $20 000). In turn, the variable cost rate is approximately $2.50 ($15 000 ÷ 6000). Consequently, the maintenance cost function is equal to $20 000 plus $2.50 per machine hour. Although the visual fit method provides a useful estimation technique, it depends on the judgement of the person performing the analysis and is subject to significant error.

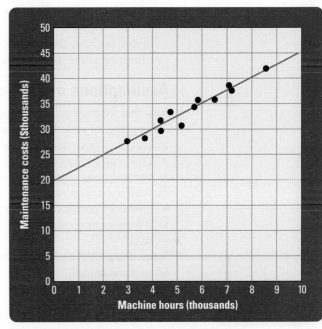

Figure 11.4 Scatter diagram — maintenance costs

High–low method

The high–low method is a quantititive technique that can be used to estimate a mixed cost function. As long as the costs at the highest level of activity and those at the lowest level are representative of the straight line that best describes a cost function, they provide useful information for cost estimation. The high–low method is based on the procedure used to determine the slope of any linear function because it compares the cost at the highest level of activity with the cost at the lowest level. The difference in cost caused by variable costs is divided by the difference in activity to find the variable cost rate. Once the variable costs for a given level of activity are known, they can be subtracted from the total costs to determine the fixed costs. This method must be used with caution as the high and low points may not represent the true cost function. The high–low method can be applied to the maintenance cost data as shown below:

	Maintenance cost	Machine hours
High	$41 760	8640
Low	27 550	2920
Difference	$14 210	5720

Variable cost rate = $14 210 ÷ 5720 = $2.484 per hour
Fixed costs   = $41 760 − ($2.484 × 8640)
             = $20 298

Linear regression

The results of using the visual fit technique and high–low method in this case are approximately the same. The weaknesses of these two cost estimation approaches can be eliminated by applying linear regression analysis to find the straight line that best fits the points on a scatter diagram. This can be automatically calculated by a range of computer programs, including Excel. The technique is beyond the scope of this text but is described in introductory statistics textbooks. If linear regression analysis had been used, the estimated cost function would have been:

$$\text{Maintenance costs} = \$19\,645 + (\$2.568 \times \text{Machine hours})$$

In this example, the two less accurate estimation techniques produced approximately the same cost function as the more sophisticated one, but this will not always be the case.

Assumptions of cost–volume–profit analysis

Now that we have considered cost behaviour, we must also appreciate that CVP analysis is based on a number of underlying assumptions:
- Unit sales price remains constant.
- Costs can be identified as variable or fixed with some degree of accuracy.
- Variable costs change proportionately with volume.
- Total fixed costs remain constant over the relevant range.
- Efficiency remains relatively unchanged.
- Whenever more than one product is sold, total sales are in some predictable proportion or sales mix.

When using CVP analysis, it is essential that any conclusions drawn are interpreted in light of the above assumptions.

Learning objective 2

Define contribution margin and discuss the benefits of a contribution margin-based income statement

11.2 Cost behaviour and income statement

The main concern in CVP analysis is an expectation of future profits. To project a future earnings performance, management must be able to evaluate how *costs and profits will fluctuate* with changes in sales volume. The conventional income statement discussed in earlier chapters is of limited value in predicting cost–volume–profit relationships. In a conventional statement, costs are classified by business function (manufacturing, selling and distribution, administrative, and finance and other) without consideration of whether the costs are fixed, variable or mixed. Although such a statement may provide the historical profit performance of a specific period, it does not indicate what should happen to costs and profits with a different sales volume in the future. For example, consider the conventional income statement of Butler Enterprises shown in figure 11.5.

Butler Enterprises earned profit of $120 000, which was 12% of sales. Suppose management expects sales to increase by $200 000, or 20%, to $1 200 000 in 2013–14 because more units will be sold, and wants to predict the related profit. Can management simply multiply the projected sales revenue of $1 200 000 by the profit margin of 12% to predict a 2013–14 profit of $144 000 (which would also be a 20% increase)? The answer is *no*; many of the costs involved are fixed and do not change with the increase in sales volume as long as the level of activity remains within the relevant range. We know that the selling and distribution, administrative, and finance and other expenses typically will be both fixed and variable. Even if Butler Enterprises were a manufacturing business, it would be expected that all its expenses would be partly fixed and partly variable. Our discussion of costing in chapter 8 showed that fixed factory overhead costs are included in the cost of sales section of the income statement because they are assigned to the products during the production operation.

Figure 11.5 Income statement

BUTLER ENTERPRISES
Income Statement
for the year ended 30 June 2013

	Amount	Percentage
INCOME		
Sales revenue	$1 000 000	100
Less: Cost of sales	520 000	52
GROSS PROFIT	480 000	48
EXPENSES		
Selling and distribution expenses	200 000	20
Administrative expenses	140 000	14
Finance and other expenses	20 000	2
	360 000	36
PROFIT	$ 120 000	12

Contribution margin

To make a conventional income statement more useful for decision making, many businesses construct the statement on the basis of cost behaviour. Here, the emphasis is on the **contribution margin** — sales revenue less all variable costs. The **contribution margin ratio** is found by dividing the contribution margin by sales. The contribution margin represents the amount of sales revenue available to cover the fixed costs and then to contribute towards profit. Since only the variable costs are deducted to calculate the contribution margin, it will vary directly as a fixed percentage with sales volume. Before an income statement emphasising the contribution margin can be prepared, each cost item must be analysed carefully with the procedures discussed earlier in this chapter to determine its cost behaviour pattern. We assume that the cost behaviour classifications shown in figure 11.6 (p. 468) have been developed for Butler Enterprises — a retailer. A manufacturing business would also include fixed manufacturing expenses in fixed costs.

The information contained in the revised statement in figure 11.6 will enable managers to evaluate the effect on profit of a change in sales volume. If sales of $1 200 000 are expected, the resulting profit can be calculated as follows:

Projected contribution margin ($1 200 000 × 0.4)	$480 000
Fixed expenses	280 000
Profit	$200 000
Profit as a percentage of sales	16.7

The profit projected for 2013–14 is $200 000 and is a higher percentage of sales than that of the previous year because the fixed costs remain at $280 000. Only the variable costs have increased on the basis of 60% of sales. Thus, the contribution margin in dollars increases from $400 000 to $480 000, but as a percentage of sales it remains constant at 40%. Alternatively, the increase in profit of $80 000 can be calculated by multiplying the sales increase of $200 000 by the contribution margin rate of 0.40.

An income statement that emphasises the contribution margin is used for internal purposes only and provides a basis for CVP analysis.

Figure 11.6 Income statement showing contribution margin

BUTLER ENTERPRISES Income Statement for the year ended 30 June 2013		
	Amount	Percentage
INCOME		
Sales revenue	$1 000 000	100
Variable cost of sales	400 000	40
Variable selling and other expenses	200 000	20
CONTRIBUTION MARGIN	400 000	40
Fixed expenses		
Selling and distribution	120 000	12
Administrative	140 000	14
Finance and other	20 000	2
	280 000	28
PROFIT	$ 120 000	12

BUSINESS KNOWLEDGE

Flying costs

An understanding of cost structures and capacity per aircraft provides airlines, such as Qantas in the scene setter, with the ability to maximise profitability on each flight by offering discount airfares. Airline companies have very high fixed costs (e.g. cost or lease of each aircraft and salaries of cabin crew) relative to the variable costs of operating a flight. The additional variable costs of adding an extra passenger to a flight are quite small. If

a traveller can be induced by a reduced fare to occupy a seat that would otherwise be empty, the airline increases its revenue per flight and hence overall profitability. Airlines realise that they can charge 'normal' high prices for a certain proportion of the available seating on each flight, and can therefore afford to reduce the price of seats that are unlikely to sell. Airlines have refined their pricing structures to achieve maximum seating per flight, and hence maximise overall profitability.

11.3 Profit planning with CVP analysis

Learning objective 3

Explain how CVP analysis can be used by management for profit planning

As indicated earlier, CVP analysis is used by managers to evaluate the interrelationships of selling price, sales volume, sales mix and costs to plan future profits. Profit goals are established during the budgeting process (see chapter 12) and are evaluated continuously during the budget period. In order to plan profits, managers must estimate the selling price of each product, the variable costs required to produce and sell it, and the fixed costs expected for a given period. This information is combined with estimates concerning the expected sales volume and sales mix. Cost–volume–profit analysis can help answer such questions as:

- What is the entity's break-even point, i.e. the sales level at which the business will make neither a profit nor a loss?
- What will be the impact on sales volume and profit of increasing advertising costs?
- What level of sales must be achieved to earn a desired level of profit?
- If selling prices are increased or decreased, what will be the effect on sales volume and the break-even point?
- If a variable cost (such as labour) is eliminated and replaced with a fixed cost (such as machinery depreciation), what would be the impact on profits?
- What additional sales volume is required to offset an increase in purchasing cost?
- If additional plant capacity is acquired and increases fixed factory overhead cost, what will happen to profit?
- What is the most profitable sales mix?

The coverage of CVP analysis that follows refers to the financial performance of Sunshine Stabilisers Ltd, which began manufacturing a single model of grass ski on 1 July 2012 in a northern New South Wales plant. A condensed income statement showing contribution margin for the company's first year of operation is shown below.

SUNSHINE STABILISERS LTD Condensed Income Statement for the year ended 30 June 2013		
	Amount	Percentage
INCOME		
Sales revenue (8000 units @ $50)	$400 000	100.0
Less: Variable cost of sales	240 000	60.0
Manufacturing margin	160 000	40.0
Other variable expenses	40 000	10.0
Contribution margin	120 000	30.0
Fixed expenses		
Factory overhead	110 000	27.5
Other fixed expenses	40 000	10.0
PROFIT (LOSS)	$ (30 000)	(7.5)

11.4 Break-even analysis

Learning objective 4

Explain break-even point and identify the three methods of determining the break-even point

Break-even analysis is the typical starting point for CVP analysis. The **break-even point** is the sales volume at which revenues and total costs are equal, and so no profit or loss is made. Profit arises above the break-even point; a loss is incurred below it. Both the variable and fixed costs are covered by sales revenue at the break-even point. Although a break-even point is not a desired performance target because of the lack of profit, it does indicate the level of activity necessary to avoid a loss. As such, the break-even point represents a target of the minimum sales volume that must be achieved by a business. Also, break-even analysis provides valuable information concerning the impact of cost behaviour patterns at different sales levels.

Break-even equation

The break-even point can be determined mathematically or graphically and can be expressed in either sales units or sales dollars. Mathematically, the basic contribution margin income statement format can be stated as:

Sales revenue = Variable expenses + Fixed expenses + Profit

At the break-even point, the profit is zero. To illustrate the use of the equation, consider the financial data presented earlier for Sunshine Stabilisers Ltd. The company operated below its break-even point in 2012–13 because it incurred a loss of $30 000. Note that fixed expenses were $150 000 and the variable expense was $35 per unit ($280 000 ÷ 8000). The break-even sales (S) can be determined as:

$$\$50S = \$35S + \$150\,000$$
$$\$50S - \$35S = \$150\,000$$
$$\$15S = \$150\,000$$
$$S = 10\,000 \text{ units}$$

The break-even sales in units can be converted to sales dollars of $500 000 by multiplying 10 000 units by the selling price of $50. The analysis indicates that Sunshine Stabilisers Ltd must increase its sales level by 25% to $500 000 or 10 000 pairs of grass skis in order to break even.

Contribution margin approach

Recall that the contribution margin is found by subtracting unit variable cost from unit sales price. The contribution margin ratio or percentage is calculated by dividing the contribution margin by sales. The contribution margin ratio is used in the absence of unit sales price and when unit variable costs are not available. The contribution margin is shown on the left side of the above equation. In the equation, $15S is the contribution margin as a dollar amount. The use of the contribution margin measured as dollars resulted in a break-even point in sales units. Instead of using the equation, a contribution margin approach can be used as:

$$\frac{\text{Break-even}}{\text{sales in units}} = \frac{\text{Fixed expenses}}{\text{Unit contribution margin}} = \frac{\$150\,000}{\$15} = 10\,000 \text{ units}$$

Graphic approach

For visual purposes, the break-even point can be plotted on a **cost–volume–profit chart** such as the one shown in figure 11.7 for Sunshine Stabilisers Ltd. In addition to the break-even point, the profitability of various revenue and expense relationships over a range of volume can be evaluated.

Figure 11.7 Sunshine Stabilisers Ltd cost–volume–profit chart

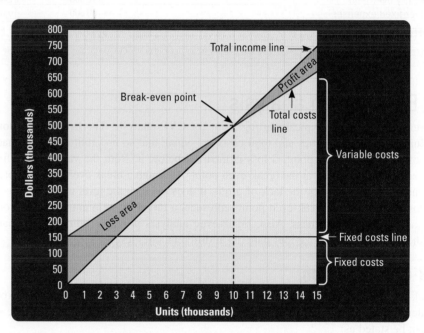

The vertical axis of the chart represents dollars of income and costs in thousands, and the volume of units in thousands is measured along the horizontal axis. The steps used to prepare this cost–profit–volume chart are:

1. Plot the income line, which begins at the origin (0, 0) and increases at the rate of $50 per unit.
2. Plot the fixed costs line, which begins at $150 000 and runs parallel to the horizontal axis. This indicates that it is assumed that fixed costs are constant at $150 000 for all the given levels of production units.
3. Plot the total costs line, starting at $150 000 on the vertical for zero production (where variable costs would be zero), increasing at the rate of $35 per unit on top of fixed costs. At a total output of 5000 units, the total costs are $150 000 plus $35 × 5000 = $325 000. At an output of 10 000 units, the total costs are $150 000 plus $35 × 10 000 = $500 000. The gap between the fixed costs line and the total costs line therefore represents the variable costs applicable to each level of output.

The chart indicates that Sunshine Stabilisers Ltd's break-even point is $500 000 in sales or 10 000 units. This is the point where the total cost line intersects with the total income line. The profit or loss expected for any sales volume can be found on the chart. If the company does not achieve sales of $500 000, it will incur a loss (the dark blue area). A profit will be earned when sales exceed $500 000 (the pale pink area). By comparing the variable expenses with revenue, the contribution margin in dollars also can be determined at any sales volume from the cost–volume–profit chart. For example, the contribution margin at the break-even point of 10 000 units is $150 000 (sales of $500 000 less variable costs of $350 000). Note that at the break-even point, the contribution margin must equal the total fixed expenses.

11.5 Margin of safety and target sales

Determining a margin of safety

Learning objective 5

Understand the application of a margin of safety in break-even analysis and use break-even analysis to determine target sales and target profit

An important extension of break-even analysis is its use in determining an entity's **margin of safety** — the amount by which sales can decrease before a loss occurs. The margin of safety is the excess of actual or expected sales over break-even sales. A large margin of safety is an indication that a business can absorb a significant decline in sales volume without incurring a loss. For example, assume that the management of Sunshine Stabilisers Ltd expects sales of $600 000 for the year ended 30 June 2014 without any change in its break-even point of $500 000. Its margin of safety for 2014 would be $100 000, or 2000 units.

Determining target sales and profit

The basic procedures of break-even analysis can also be used to determine the sales volume needed to *earn a desired profit*. A profit goal can be expressed as a fixed amount of profit or as a percentage of sales. Either way, the basic income statement equation presented earlier is used to find the sales volume required for the desired profit. Assume that management of Sunshine Stabilisers Ltd wants to earn a profit before tax of $60 000 in 2013–14 and expects the same selling price and costs as those experienced in 2012–13. The necessary sales target can be calculated as:

$$S = \text{Sales target}$$
$$S = \text{Variable expenses} + \text{Fixed expenses} + \text{Target profit before tax}$$
$$\$50S = \$35S + \$150\,000 + \$60\,000$$
$$\$15S = \$210\,000$$
$$S = 14\,000 \text{ units [or } \$700\,000 \text{ (i.e. } \$50 \times 14\,000)]$$

With sales of $700 000, the following analysis shows that profit before tax is $60 000:

Sales revenue (14 000 units @ $50)	$700 000
Variable expenses (14 000 @ $35)	490 000
Contribution margin	210 000
Fixed expenses	150 000
Profit before tax	$ 60 000

Alternatively, assume that management's goal is to achieve before-tax profits that are 10% of sales. The equation required to determine the sales target is:

$$S = \text{Sales target}$$
$$\$50S = \$35S + \$150\,000 + \$5S$$
$$\$10S = \$150\,000$$
$$S = 15\,000 \text{ units [or } \$750\,000 \text{ (i.e. } \$50 \times 15\,000)]$$

Again, a profit and loss analysis can be prepared to prove that a sales level of $750 000 will produce a before-tax profit equalling 10% of sales:

Sales revenue (15 000 units @ $50)	$750 000	
Variable expenses (15 000 @ $35)	525 000	
Contribution margin	225 000	
Fixed expenses	150 000	10%
Profit before tax	$ 75 000	

Many entities choose to define their profit target as profit after tax, in which case an additional calculation is required to determine the before-tax profit. To do so, the after-tax profit is divided by the factor (1 − tax rate). For example, assume that Sunshine Stabilisers Ltd's profit goal for 2013–14 is to earn after-tax profit of $42 000 with a tax rate of 30%. The required sales volume can be calculated as follows:

$$S = \text{Variable expenses} + \text{Fixed expenses} + \text{Target before-tax profit}$$
$$\$50S = \$35S + \$150\,000 + [\$42\,000/(1 - 0.3)]$$
$$\$15S = \$150\,000 + \$60\,000$$
$$\$15S = \$210\,000$$
$$S = 14\,000 \text{ units (or } \$700\,000)$$

Alternatively, the profit before tax can be calculated as follows:

$$X = \text{Profit before tax}$$
$$0.3X = \text{Tax}$$
$$X - 0.3X = \text{Profit after tax}$$
$$X - 0.3X = \$42\,000$$
$$0.7X = \$42\,000$$
$$X = \$60\,000$$

Then the $60 000 can be inserted into the equation to solve for *S*, the sales volume required to earn an after-tax profit of $42 000.

11.6 Analysing CVP relationships for profit planning

Learning objective 6

Understand how changes in certain factors affect profits

Once the CVP relationships are known, management can use the information to find the combination of revenue and expenses that will produce acceptable profits. CVP analysis is particularly important to management during the budgeting process, when various alternative strategies regarding future financial performance must be evaluated. Effective profit and marketing planning must be concerned with the impact on profits of:
- changes in selling prices
- changes in sales volume
- changes in sales mix
- changes in variable expenses
- changes in fixed expenses.

To illustrate the CVP analysis used to evaluate potential changes, we continue to use the 30 June 2013 financial data of Sunshine Stabilisers Ltd shown on page 469. Management is dissatisfied with the first-year financial results because a loss of $30 000 occurred. Assume that the initial version of the 2013–14 budget has been prepared with the 2012–13 selling prices and costs, but sales volume is expected to increase by 2000 units to 10 000 units. As a result, the following profit and loss analysis is prepared assuming no additional changes:

Sales revenue (10 000 units @ $50)	$500 000
Variable expenses (10 000 @ $35)	350 000
Contribution margin	150 000
Fixed expenses	150 000
Profit before tax	$ 0

Although the projected performance is better than the results of 2012–13, it is still not acceptable to management because the company will operate only at break-even sales. Consequently, the company is considering a number of changes and will apply CVP analysis to evaluate the impact of these changes on profits. We consider each of these changes independently, although they would be evaluated concurrently in a real-life situation.

Change in selling price

The sales manager of Sunshine Stabilisers Ltd estimates that a price reduction of 10% (to $45) will increase the budgeted number of units sold by 20%, from 10 000 units to 12 000 units. If this happens, the impact on break-even sales is:

$$S = \text{Break-even sales}$$
$$\$45S = \$35S + \$150\,000$$
$$\$10S = \$150\,000$$
$$S = 15\,000 \text{ units or } \$675\,000$$

Profit analysis based on the proposed change (i.e. increase sales units from 10 000 to 12 000) is:

Sales revenue (12 000 × $45)	$ 540 000
Variable expenses (12 000 × $35)	420 000
Contribution margin	120 000
Fixed expenses	150 000
Profit (loss)	$ (30 000)

Despite the fact that sales revenue would increase by $40 000 ($540 000 − $500 000) with this proposal, the company would still incur a loss of $30 000 instead of operating at break-even. The reason is the $5 loss of contribution margin per unit, which is not offset by selling 2000 additional units. The break-even point also increases from $500 000 to $675 000, so this change would not produce favourable results.

Change in variable costs

The production manager believes changes in the manufacturing process will make labour use more efficient and reduce variable costs by $5 per unit. The impact on the break-even sales is:

$$S = \text{Break-even sales}$$
$$\$50S - \$30S + \$150\,000$$
$$\$20S = \$150\,000$$
$$S = 7500 \text{ units or } \$375\,000$$

Profit analysis based on the proposed change (i.e. variable costs reduced from $35 to $30 per unit) is:

Sales revenue (10 000 units @ $50)	$500 000
Variable expenses (10 000 units @ $30)	300 000
Contribution margin	200 000
Fixed expenses	150 000
Profit before tax	$ 50 000

The improved efficiency increases profits from $0 to $50 000 because the contribution margin per unit is $20 instead of $15. Also, the break-even point reduces from 10 000 to 7500 units.

Change in fixed and variable costs

Management is considering changing the bonus scheme applicable to the sales representatives, whose 2013 salaries were based on a commission of 10% of sales. Instead of the commission, management is proposing to pay the sales representatives a fixed sum of $40 000 per year. Without the commission, the variable costs will be 60% (i.e. 70% less 10%) or $30 ($50 × 60%) and the contribution margin will be 40%. The effect on the company's break-even point is:

$$S = \text{Break-even sales}$$
$$\$50S = \$30S + \$190\,000$$
$$\$20S = \$190\,000$$
$$S = 9500 \text{ units [or } \$475\,000 \text{ (i.e. } 50 \times 9500)]$$

Profit analysis based on the proposed change (i.e. variable costs down from $35 to $30 and fixed costs increase by $40 000) is:

Sales revenue (10 000 units @ $50)	$500 000
Variable expenses (10 000 units @ $30)	300 000
Contribution margin	200 000
Fixed expenses	190 000
Profit before tax	$ 10 000

The profit is increased from $0 to $10 000 with this proposed change because the total contribution margin increases by $50 000 (10 000 units times $5 per unit) and the fixed expenses increase by only $40 000.

Change in fixed costs and sales volume

Another proposal being considered by the management of Sunshine Stabilisers Ltd is an advertising campaign that would cost the company $30 000 per year. Management estimates that sales will increase by 30%, from 10 000 units to 13 000 units, as a result of the additional advertising. The new break-even point is:

$$S = \text{Break-even sales}$$
$$\$50S = \$35S + \$180\,000 \text{ [i.e. } \$150\,000 + \$30\,000 \text{ advertising]}$$
$$\$15S = \$180\,000$$
$$S = 12\,000 \text{ units or } \$600\,000$$

Profit analysis based on the proposed change (i.e. fixed costs increase by $30 000 and sales increase from 10 000 units to 13 000 units) is:

Sales revenue (13 000 units @ $50)	$650 000
Variable expenses (13 000 units @ $35)	455 000
Contribution margin	195 000
Fixed expenses	180 000
Profit before tax	$ 15 000

The break-even point would increase by 2000 units because an additional contribution margin of $30 000 (2000 units @ $15 per unit) is necessary to cover the proposed advertising expenditures. Since the sales are expected to increase by 3000 units, the projected profit will be $15 000 — the result of earning a contribution margin of $15 for each of the 1000 units above the break-even point.

Break-even analysis can be performed successfully with the aid of computer graphics packages, which can provide colourful graphs representing cost–volume–profit charts. The packages can also help to show the effects of assumption changes in the decision-making process, e.g. what would be the break-even point for Sunshine Stabilisers Ltd if the selling price per unit rose from $50 to $53 and the company could sell only 7000 units? Such 'what if?' questions fed into a graphics package can help considerably in the planning process.

CVP and motor vehicle manufacturing

Building motor vehicles involves large fixed-cost investments in plant and equipment, particularly with the use of modern robotics in the manufacturing process. If a manufacturer is not making a profit, then CVP analysis can provide insights into how to solve the problem. The market for motor vehicles largely determines the selling price, and only minimal changes can be made to this. Sales volume can be improved through more appealing car design and marketing, but this is done in competition with other vehicle manufacturers who are also attempting to increase their market share.

Eliminating excess capacity (if any) can reduce fixed costs. Variable costs can be reduced by sourcing cheaper direct materials or by helping suppliers make their manufacturing more efficient and sharing the savings. Alternatively, some variable costs such as labour may be replaced with fixed costs through the use of robots.

The effect of these alternatives can be modelled using CVP analysis, which, along with CVP graphs, presents the information to management in a way that can be easily understood.

11.7 Using CVP analysis with multiple products

Learning objective 7

Explain how CVP analysis is used with multiple products

In the Sunshine Stabilisers Ltd illustration, we considered cost–volume–profit analysis with only one product. Earlier we stated as a basic assumption of CVP analysis that total sales must be in *some predictable proportion or sales mix* whenever more than one product is sold. CVP analysis is performed by a multiproduct business using a weighted average contribution margin for an assumed constant sales mix. For example, assume that Sunshine Stabilisers Ltd can produce and sell two models of grass skis with the following data:

	Standard model	Deluxe model
Selling price	$50	$80
Variable expenses	35	48
Contribution margin	$15	$32
Contribution margin ratio	30%	40%

The fixed costs are $184 000 and the company's expected product mix is four standard models for each deluxe model. The weighted average contribution margin per unit is $18.40, calculated as follows:

Total contribution margin for 5 units of product	
($15 × 4) + ($32 × 1)	= $92.00
Divided by number of units	5
Average contribution margin per unit	$18.40

Alternatively, it can be calculated using the assumed mix of 4:1:

$$^4/_5(\$15) + ^1/_5(\$32) = \$18.40$$

Thus, the break-even sales with the two products is:

S = Break-even sales

$$S = \frac{\text{Fixed costs}}{\text{Weighted average contribution margin per unit}}$$

$$S = \frac{\$184\,000}{\$18.40}$$

$S = 10\,000$ units

Since the sales mix is four standard models for one deluxe model, the 10 000 units are divided into 8000 standard models and 2000 deluxe models ($^4/_5 \times 10\,000 = 8000$ standard models and $^1/_5 \times 10\,000 = 2000$ deluxe models). The break-even profit and loss analysis is:

	Standard model	Deluxe model	Total
Sales — units	8 000	2 000	10 000
Sales revenue — dollars	$400 000	$160 000	$560 000
Variable expenses	200 000	90 000	370 000
Contribution margin	$120 000	$ 64 000	184 000
Fixed expenses			184 000
Profit			$ 0

This same weighted average contribution margin approach can be used to determine break-even sales or to plan profits in any multiproduct business as long as the sales mix can be predicted reliably.

11.8 Contribution margin variance analysis

Learning objective 8

Explain variations between planned and actual contribution margins using sales price, sales volume and variable expense variances

Another important use of the contribution margin in management accounting is to evaluate why an entity's planned profit performance was not achieved during a particular period. Earlier in the chapter, the contribution margin was used to project a future profit performance, which involves the planning phase of management. We now consider the application of **contribution margin variance analysis**, which helps managers analyse actual profit results compared with those planned. The difference between actual and planned results is called a **variance**. When expected profits are not achieved, management needs to know the causes so that it can decide who and what are responsible, and take steps to correct any problems, thereby exercising control over operations.

Since the contribution margin is the difference between sales and the variable expenses, any change in it will be due to one or a combination of the following:

- a variation of selling price per unit sold
- a variation of the number of units sold
- a variation of the mix or combination of units sold
- a variation of the variable costs of producing and selling each unit.

To illustrate the fundamentals of contribution margin variance analysis, we consider an entity that sells only one product. This means that there can be no sales mix variance, a subject left to more advanced accounting texts. Assume that the management of Sunshine Stabilisers Ltd decided that sales of 15 000 units, a selling price of $50 and variable costs of $35 should be budgeted for the year ended 30 June 2013. As a result, the budgeted contribution margin is $225 000 (i.e. 15 000 units × $15). Assume that after the year ended 30 June 2013 is over, the company reported the performance presented below showing the actual contribution margin earned compared with the one budgeted (planned).

	Budget	Actual	Variance
Sales — units	15 000	16 000	1 000 F
Sales — dollars	$750 000	$752 000	$ 2 000 F
Variable expenses	525 000	592 000	67 000 U
Contribution margin	$225 000	$160 000	$65 000 U

F indicates a favourable variance, since actual results were better than budgeted.
U indicates an unfavourable variance, since actual results were worse than budgeted.

Management wants an explanation of why the actual contribution margin was $65 000 less than the budgeted contribution margin, even though the actual number of units sold exceeded those budgeted for by 1000 and actual sales dollars were $2000 more than the amount budgeted. Three separate variances — sales price, sales volume and variable expenses — must be calculated to determine the causes of the unfavourable contribution margin variance of $65 000. Only one factor (sales price, sales volume or variable expenses) is considered at a time, while the other two factors are held constant as follows.

Sales price variance

The budgeted selling price was $50 per unit ($750 000/15 000 units), but the actual selling price was only $47 per unit ($752 000/16 000 units). The selling price variance is unfavourable and is calculated by multiplying the difference of $3 per unit by the 16 000 units actually sold. The 16 000 units actually sold are used to eliminate the effect of sales volume, and the result is an unfavourable sales price variance of $48 000 (16 000 units × $3).

Sales volume variance

A favourable sales volume variance was incurred because the actual units sold (16 000) were 1000 units more than those budgeted (15 000). The additional units will cause both sales revenue and the variable expenses to increase, so the net result is a higher contribution margin. To eliminate the effect of changes in selling price or variable expenses from the amounts planned, we use the budgeted contribution margin of $15 (budgeted selling price of $50 less budgeted variable expenses of $35, or $225 000/15 000 units) to calculate the sales volume variance for the 1000 additional units. As a result, the favourable sales volume variance was 1000 units × $15, or $15 000.

Variable expense variance

The budgeted variable expenses for each unit sold were $35 ($525 000/15 000 units), whereas the actual unit variable expenses were $37 ($592 000/16 000). As a result, the actual variable expenses per unit were $2 higher than expected. The $2 per unit deviation is multiplied by the 16 000 units sold (again holding sales volume constant at the actual units sold) to calculate an unfavourable variable expense variance of $32 000.

The algebraic summation of the three variances should equal the unfavourable contribution margin variance of $65 000. The unfavourable variances for sales price ($48 000) and variable expenses ($32 000), less the favourable sales volume variance ($15 000), equal $65 000. These variances are reported to the managers responsible for the related financial performances so that corrective action can be taken wherever possible to improve future profitability.

KEY TERMS

Break-even point, p. 469
Committed fixed costs, p. 464
Contribution margin, p. 467
Contribution margin ratio, p. 467
Contribution margin variance analysis, p. 476

Cost behaviour, p. 462
Cost function, p. 462
Cost–volume–profit (CVP) analysis, p. 462
Cost–volume–profit chart, p. 470
Discretionary fixed costs, p. 464

Linearity assumption, p. 463
Margin of safety, p. 471
Mixed cost, p. 462
Relevant range, p. 463
Variance, p. 476

DISCUSSION QUESTIONS

1. It is reasonable to assume variable expenses approximate a straight line over the relevant range of operations (even if the overall variable expense line is curved). Discuss.
2. Fixed costs are not usually constant over all volumes of output. What are some of the factors that are likely to mean that fixed costs change over all volumes? Give an example.
3. Discuss the difficulties that would arise in CVP analysis if each of the six assumptions that underlie the analysis was totally unrealistic.
4. In predicting the future profitability of a business, there is a basic limitation in the standard form of income statement. Discuss.
5. What type of cost behaviour describes the cost of operating a mobile phone?

6. Discount airfares have become a feature of the pricing policies of Australian airlines leading to substantial discounts off normal fares. How can these actions be justified on the basis of cost–volume–profit relationships?

7. The owner-manager of a small business was heard to make the following remark: 'Break-even analysis has little relevance for my business. I am not in business to break even, but to make profits.' Do you agree? Explain your position.

8. As the marketing manager for a mobile phone company, explain how CVP analysis could be useful in determining the best mix of price, volume, sales mix and advertising.

9. Imagine you are the manager of a hotel. What are some of the fixed, variable and mixed costs of running the hotel and how could you use CVP relationships for profit planning?

10. 'Break-even analysis is all right if you have a one-product business, but it falls down badly if you want to derive a break-even point for several products.' Discuss.

EXERCISES

Exercise 11.1 LINEARITY ASSUMPTION OF A STEP COST FUNCTION   LO 1

Gavini's Café is run by Alex and Lara Gavini. They usually run the business with three staff and this is sufficient when there are up to 30 customers in the café. When the bookings for an evening are higher than 30 customers, the Gavinis hire an extra staff member for each extra 10 customers they expect, up to the café's limit of 90 customers. For example, if between 31 and 40 customers book for the evening, one extra staff member is employed. It costs the café $80 per staff member for an evening, not including the Gavinis.

Required

A. Determine the variable cost function for the extra staff employed to cater for customer numbers between 30 and 90.

B. The Gavinis would like to save some money and are considering employing extra staff at the rate of one for every 15 extra customers. What is the new cost function and what other qualitative factors should they consider in their decision?

Exercise 11.2 HIGH–LOW METHOD AND COST BEHAVIOUR   LO 1

Tania's Legal Services rents a photocopier. The company is charged a fixed annual rental plus a per-copy charge. If the company makes 120 000 copies per year, the overall per-copy cost is estimated to be $0.12. If 90 000 copies are made during a year, it is estimated that the cost per copy is $0.14.

Required

A. Using the high–low method, estimate the variable rate per copy and the fixed annual rental fee.

B. What would be the total cost if 140 000 copies are made during a year?

C. If the variable rate per copy falls by $0.01 each time another 20 000 copies are made over and above 120 000 copies, can Tania's Legal Services approximate the cost of photocopying with a straight line?

Exercise 11.3 REASONABLENESS OF THE HIGH–LOW METHOD   LO 1

Lucerne Ltd sells feather quilts and has never used CVP analysis in its 4-year history. The manager provides you with the following sales and cost data for the first 4 years of operation:

Year	Costs of manufacturing	Number of quilts
2011	$2 384 000	42 000
2012	$2 795 000	47 000
2013	$3 236 000	54 000
2014	$3 580 000	65 000

Required

A. Using the high–low method, estimate the cost function for the manufacture of quilts by Lucerne Ltd.

B. Check whether the cost function you calculated in requirement A would represent the actual costs of manufacturing for 2012 and 2013. What does this tell you about the high–low method of estimating a cost function?

LO 1

Exercise 11.4 CVP ANALYSIS USING CHARTS

Begin by drawing up a hypothetical CVP chart showing where the break-even point is. Treat each of the following cases as independent.

Required

A. Show what would happen to the CVP chart if the selling price of the goods reflected in the total income line were to increase. Does the break-even point occur at a higher or lower volume of activity than before?

B. Show what would happen to the CVP chart if the fixed costs increased. Does the break-even point occur at a higher or lower volume of activity than before?

C. Show what would happen to the CVP chart if the variable cost per unit were to decrease. Does the break-even point occur at a higher or lower volume of activity than before?

D. Show what would happen if the selling price increased, the fixed costs increased and the variable costs per unit decreased. What happens to the break-even point?

LO 1

Exercise 11.5 MIXED COSTS WITH THE HIGH–LOW METHOD

Adam Leeman Ltd has determined total factory overhead costs at both minimum and maximum levels of production — 100 000 machine hours and 150 000 machine hours respectively. The total factory overhead, made up of variable costs, mixed costs and fixed costs, was $398 000 for 150 000 machine hours and $323 000 for 100 000 machine hours. At an activity level of 100 000 machine hours, the total factory overhead consists of the following components:

Fixed costs	$115 000
Variable costs	110 000
Mixed costs	98 000
	$323 000

Required

A. Determine the fixed and the variable portion (rate per machine hour) of the mixed costs.

B. What should be the total factory overhead cost for 120 000 machine hours?

LO 2

Exercise 11.6 CONTRIBUTION MARGIN INCOME STATEMENT

RingTone Pty Ltd produces phones. The company prepared the following budgeted income statement:

Sales		$2 560 000
Cost of sales		1 028 000
Gross profit		1 532 000
Expenses		
Selling expenses	$260 000	
Administrative expenses	110 000	370 000
Profit		$1 162 000

The owner, Rhing Thonn, wants to use this income statement as the basis of projecting the profits for the forthcoming year. He needs to know what the projected profit will be if the unit sales of phones increase by 20%. The following relevant information is available:

Selling price per phone	$320
Variable manufacturing costs per phone	$96
Annual fixed manufacturing costs	$260 000
Percentage of selling expenses that are variable	20%
Annual fixed administrative expenses	$120 000

Required

A. Restructure the previous year's income statement to present it in contribution margin format.
B. What is the contribution margin for each phone?
C. Assuming the selling price and all costs remain unchanged, what will be the projected profit for the forthcoming year?

Exercise 11.7   CONTRIBUTION MARGIN — INTERPRETIVE SKILLS   LO 2

Energy Experiences Pty Ltd runs camps for school children and sporting clubs that provide 3 days of canoeing, horseriding, abseiling and skiing. As a graduate with a sports and recreation degree, you have eventually worked your way up to managing the camps. The accountant has presented you with the following income statement and wants to work with you to improve the company's financial position so that it may continue in business.

	Amount	Percentage
Sales revenue (2500 campers)	$750 000	100
Variable cost of sporting activities	375 000	50
Variable promotional and other expenses	150 000	20
Contribution margin	225 000	30
Fixed expenses:		
Selling and site maintenance	150 000	20
Administrative	75 000	10
Finance and other	75 000	10
	300 000	40
Loss	$ (75 000)	(10)

Required

A. Taking into account the nature of the activities provided by Energy Experiences Pty Ltd, what costs are likely to be fixed regardless of the number of campers and what costs are likely to vary in total with the number of campers?
B. Suggest specific ways in which the company could make a profit by changing its pricing, reducing fixed costs and reducing variable costs.

Exercise 11.8   CONTRIBUTION MARGIN — CALCULATIONS   LO 2

Use the same information for Energy Experiences Pty Ltd in exercise 11.7. The accountant can't make decisions on the future of the company without your authority as manager, so he believes it is important to work through the possible solutions together so that you understand what you are authorising.

Required

A. Using the contribution margin income statement from exercise 11.7, calculate the CVP equation for the operations of Energy Experiences Pty Ltd.
B. What is the break-even number of campers for Energy Experiences Pty Ltd?
C. You believe that the maximum number of campers that the camp site can accommodate in a year is 3000. What would you suggest to change the CVP equation for Energy Exercises Pty Ltd so that you can make a profit with this number of campers?

Exercise 11.9 CVP ANALYSIS

Big Beef BBQ Ltd sells a single product, a gas barbecue. The barbecue sells for $960 per unit. Annual fixed costs are $1 536 000, and the contribution margin rate is 40%.

Required
A. What are the variable costs per unit?
B. How many units must the company sell to break even?
C. What is the break-even point in sales dollars?
D. If the company wants to earn a before-tax profit of $768 000, how many units must be sold? What sales dollar level is required? What is the company's margin of safety at this sales level?
E. If the company wants to earn a before-tax profit of 20% of sales, how many units must be sold? What are the sales dollars?
F. Prepare a CVP chart for the company.

Exercise 11.10 CVP ANALYSIS WITH CHANGES

Warner Ltd sells its only product at a price of $200 per unit. Variable costs are $160 per unit and total fixed costs are $208 000. Current annual sales are 6500 units.

Required
A. What is the company's break-even point in sales units? What is the break-even point in sales dollars?
B. What is the company's margin of safety?
C. Calculate the company's profit under the following situations. Treat each case as independent of the others.
  1. Variable costs increase 10%.
  2. Sales volume decreases 20%.
  3. Fixed costs increase 10%.
  4. Sales price increases 15%.
  5. Sales price increases 20%, sales volume decreases 20%, variable costs increase 20%, and fixed costs decrease 20%.

Exercise 11.11 CVP RELATIONSHIPS

Information for three independent companies is presented below.
1. Delta Ltd has annual fixed costs of $120 000. The variable costs are $5 per unit and the break-even point is 40 000 units. What is the selling price per unit?
2. Epsilon Ltd has a product that sells for $120 and is produced at a variable cost of $72 per unit. The variable costs can be reduced 12% by installing a new piece of equipment. Installation of the new equipment will increase fixed costs from the present level of $432 000 to $453 120. Calculate the present break-even point and the new break-even point if the equipment is installed.
3. Zeta Ltd incurs variable costs of $42 per unit for a product that has a selling price of $72. If the break-even point is $216 000 of annual sales, what are the company's annual fixed costs?

Exercise 11.12 COST–VOLUME–PROFIT ANALYSIS WITH TWO PRODUCTS

Flaherty Ltd sells two types of shoes, men's shoes and women's shoes. During the financial year ended 30 June 2013, fixed costs were $230 400 and sales were in the ratio of three units (pairs) of men's shoes to one unit (pair) of women's shoes. Men's shoes sell for $90 per pair, and the variable costs are $58 per pair. Women's shoes sell for $150 per pair, and the variable costs are $102 per pair.

Required
A. Calculate the break-even point in total units and the number of units of each type of shoe that must be sold at the break-even point.
B. How many pairs of men's shoes and how many pairs of women's shoes must the firm sell to achieve a profit of $28 800?

Exercise 11.13 COST–VOLUME–PROFIT ANALYSIS WITH TWO PRODUCTS

LO 7

Aussie Sporting Company Pty Ltd produces two types of sporting balls: basketballs and footballs. During the year ended 30 June 2014 it sold the balls in the proportion of three basketballs for every two footballs sold. The basketballs are high-quality balls and sell for $120 each and the variable costs per ball are $80. The footballs sell for $110 each and the variable costs per ball are $55. The fixed costs for Aussie Sporting Company are $432 400 per year.

Required
A. Calculate the break-even point in total units and the number of units of each type of ball that must be sold.
B. How many basketballs and how many footballs must the firm sell to achieve an after-tax profit of $579 600 if the tax rate is 30%?

Exercise 11.14 CONTRIBUTION MARGIN VARIANCE ANALYSIS

LO 8

SJM Ltd has prepared the following income statement information showing the actual contribution margin earned from the sale of its only product, and the planned contribution margin.

	Budget	Actual
Sales — units	3 200	3 000
Sales — dollars	$480 000	$468 000
Variable expenses	256 000	255 000
Contribution margin	$224 000	$213 000

Required
Calculate the sales price variance, the sales volume variance and the variable expense variance. Report to your manager on what is revealed in the analysis.

Exercise 11.15 CONTRIBUTION MARGIN VARIANCE ANALYSIS — INTERPRETIVE SKILLS

LO 8

Assume you are marketing manager for SJM Ltd in exercise 11.14, and the accountant explains that when the actual results were compared with budget results he found a favourable sales price variance, an unfavourable sales volume variance and an unfavourable variable expense variance.

Required
A. For which of these three variances would it be reasonable for the accountant to expect you, as marketing manager, to take responsibility?
B. Explain what could have caused the sales price variance, the sales volume variance and the variable expense variance.

PROBLEMS

★ Basic

★★ Moderate

★★★ Challenging

Problem 11.1 COST BEHAVIOUR ANALYSIS USING HIGH–LOW METHOD ★

LO 1

The factory overhead of TJD Ltd has fluctuated significantly from year to year in relation to the direct machine hours. The average costs at the average high and low levels of activity during the past 3 years are as follows:

	Level of activity	
	High	Low
Factory overhead	$1 680 000	$1 200 000
Direct machine hours	240 000	160 000

Factory overhead consists of indirect materials, repairs and maintenance, rates and taxes, and power. The company has analysed these costs at the low level of activity and determined that the costs are incurred as follows at that level:

Indirect materials (variable)	$ 416 000
Repairs and maintenance (mixed)	360 000
Rates and taxes (fixed)	92 000
Power (variable)	192 000
Total	$1 060 000

Required
A. Determine the cost function for factory overhead using the format $y = a + bx$.
B. If direct machine hours of 150 000 are expected for the next year, what is the estimate of factory overhead?
C. Calculate how much of the factory overhead is maintenance cost at the high activity level of 240 000 direct machine hours.

LO 4

Problem 11.2 CVP ANALYSIS ★★

Slip Shod Ltd has provided the following production and sales information for each pair of its dress shoes:

Direct materials	$ 22
Direct labour	35
Variable factory overhead	15
Selling price	180
Sales commissions	10% of the selling price

The fixed costs for the period are $1 125 000.

Required
A. Calculate the break-even point.
B. Calculate the number of pairs that must be sold to achieve a profit of $63 000. What is the margin of safety at this sales level?
C. Would it be better to sell 16 000 pairs at a selling price of $180 each or 19 000 pairs at a selling price of $160?
D. If an additional $63 270 is spent on fixed advertising costs, what level of dollar sales must be attained to earn a new profit of $36 000? Assume that there has been no change in the sales price.
E. Assume an income tax rate of 30%. Using the given information, how many pairs of shoes need to be sold to earn an after-tax profit of $37 800?

LO 5

Problem 11.3 CVP ANALYSIS OF PROFITABILITY ★★

Move On Marketing (MOM) Pty Ltd produces television advertisements for local businesses. The contribution margin income statement for the company is as follows:

Marketing fees (52 television advertisements)	$624 000
Variable expenses	249 600
Contribution margin	374 400
Fixed expenses	324 000
Profit	$ 50 400

The company is supposed to achieve a 15% profit margin (profit ÷ marketing fees) and as the CEO of the company you have to sign off on any actions taken to meet this target. This requires you to understand each of the possible alternative actions.

Required
A. With the current level of fees, what is the required profit to achieve the target profit margin?
B. What is the CVP equation for MOM Pty Ltd and the break-even number of television advertisements per year?
C. With the current pricing and variable cost structure, what level of sales are required to meet the company's profit target?

Problem 11.4 CVP ANALYSIS WITH CHANGES ★★

AEK Ltd has prepared its income statement, summarised below, for the year ended 30 June 2013:

Sales revenue (40 000 units)	$256 000
Variable expenses	192 000
Contribution margin	64 000
Fixed expenses	40 000
Profit	$ 24 000

The company is evaluating three independent situations and has asked for your assistance.

Required

A. If the company hires a new salesperson at a salary of $36 000, how much must sales increase in terms of dollars to maintain the company's current profit?

B. If sales units increase 25% in the next year and profit increases 50%, would the management perform better or worse than expected in terms of profit? Assume that there would be adequate capacity to meet the increased volume without increasing fixed costs. Comment on the variable cost per unit.

C. If a new marketing method would increase variable expenses (by an amount you should calculate), increase sales units 10%, decrease fixed costs 10%, and increase profit by 20%, what would be the company's break-even point in terms of dollar sales if it adopts this new method? Assume that the sales price per unit would not be changed. Round your answer to the nearest whole number.

Problem 11.5 CVP ANALYSIS IN A MEDICAL CENTRE ★★

The accountant of Pearl Coast Medical Centre is evaluating ways to increase revenues. The financial objective of the centre is to operate at or just above its break-even point. The centre currently refers approximately 8000 patients each year to a nearby laboratory for a standard blood test. The laboratory charges $100 for each test. The equipment needed to perform the test can be leased by the centre for $80 000 per year, and a technician would have to be hired at an annual salary of $60 000. Other fixed annual costs for the tests are expected to be $24 000. The accountant estimates that the direct costs of performing each test (e.g. supplies) would be $20.

Required

A. If the centre charges $100 per test, how many tests must be performed each year to break even on the service?

B. Prepare a CVP graph based on a fee of $100 per test.

C. If the centre can perform 8000 tests per year, how much should be charged for each test to break even?

D. Assume that the centre wants to offset losses of $32 000 from another department with profit from the blood tests. If $100 per test is charged, how many patients must be treated annually?

Problem 11.6 CVP ANALYSIS IN A SERVICE BUSINESS ★★

XYZ Childcare Ltd plans to open a day care centre at the beginning of next year. A building has been leased and the company has estimated that the following annual costs will be required:

Salaries — three qualified staff	$128 000
Salaries — two assistants	64 000
Lease rental (building)	62 400
Electricity	4 800
Sundry expenses (all fixed)	21 600
Supplies	780 per child
Meals and snacks	2 080 per child

Based on available space and qualified staff, management believes that the maximum number of children that can be cared for at the day care centre is 120.

Required

A. Assume that the day care centre can attract 120 children when it opens. Determine the annual fee per child that must be charged to break even financially.

B. If the company charges $5980 per child annually, how many children must be enrolled to break even?

C. Prepare a CVP graph based on a charge of $5980 per child.

D. If management wants to earn an annual profit of $62 400 from the day care centre and can charge $5980 per child, how many children must be enrolled?

E. If the day care centre can attract 120 children, how much must be charged per child to earn a profit of $60 000?

F. If the day care centre can attract 120 children, how much must be charged per child to earn a profit of $60 000 plus 15% of annual fees?

Problem 11.7 CVP ANALYSIS WITH MULTIPLE SERVICES ★★   LO 7

Copeland Hotels Ltd provide three levels of rooms in their hotels. The following planning data are provided for the year ended 31 December 2013:

	Deluxe Suite	Superior Suite	Presidential Suite
Rate per night	$240	$360	$600
Direct room maintenance costs	$80	$100	$140
Variable hotel overhead	$20	$30	$40
Variable marketing expenses	$20	$30	$60
Room nights in 2012	60 000	36 000	24 000
Planned 2013 room nights	64 000	56 000	40 000

Fixed hotel overhead costs are $12 180 000 per year, and the annual fixed marketing and administrative costs are $5 100 000.

As a graduate of a tourism management course, you are part of the planning process for 2013 and need to understand what is happening in the process.

Required

A. Calculate the break-even point for 2012 and 2013 in total room nights and the number of room nights of each type of room that must be sold at the break-even point.

B. Calculate the number of room nights of each type of room that will have to be sold in 2013 to earn an after-tax profit of $9 744 000. Assume a tax rate of 30%.

Problem 11.8 CVP ANALYSIS WITH MULTIPLE PRODUCTS ★★   LO 7

A to Z Pty Ltd has provided the following planned per-unit cost and sales data for the year ended 30 June 2014:

	A	B	C
Selling price	$90	$100	$80
Direct labour cost	18	24	16
Direct materials cost	28	24	12
Variable factory overhead	10	12	8
Variable selling expenses	4	6	4
Units sold in 2013	24 000	24 000	32 000
Planned 2014 unit sales	31 500	36 000	22 500

Fixed factory overhead costs are $1 056 000 per year, and the annual fixed selling and administrative costs are $352 000.

Required

A. Calculate the break-even point for 2013 and 2014 in total units and the number of units of each product that must be sold at the break-even point.
B. Calculate the number of units of each product that would have had to be sold in 2013 to earn an after-tax profit of $246 400. Assume a tax rate of 30%.
C. Calculate the number of units of each product that would have to be sold in 2014 to earn an after-tax profit of $255 640.

Problem 11.9 BREAK EVEN ANALYSIS ★★   LO 6

Long Weekend Ltd suffered a severe drop in sales and profit performance for the year ended 30 June 2013. The income statement revealed that net sales were $1 500 000 with a profit of $310 000. Unit sales were 300 000, and total costs were $1 190 000. A breakdown of costs and expenses is presented below:

	Fixed	Variable	Total
Cost of sales (includes manufacturing costs)	$350 000	$600 000	$ 950 000
Selling expenses	108 000	36 000	144 000
Administration expenses	72 000	24 000	96 000
Total	$530 000	$660 000	$1 190 000

In response to the bad result, management is considering a number of options for the year ending 30 June 2014 to try to improve performance. Independent policy options being considered are set out below:

1. Update factory machinery and production methods to adjust the mix of fixed and variable cost of sales (which includes manufacturing costs) to 40% fixed and 60% variable.
2. Increase the selling price by 15%, with no changes to costs and expenses but unit sales will decrease 10%.
3. Change the manner in which sales staff are remunerated. It is proposed to pay sales staff on the basis of a base salary of $32 000 plus a 5% commission on net sales. The current policy is to pay fixed total salaries of $105 000.

Required

A. Calculate the break-even point in dollars of sales for the year ended 30 June 2013.
B. Calculate the break-even point and profit for each of the options being considered by management.
C. What action should be recommended to management? Explain why.

Problem 11.10 ALTERNATIVES WITH CVP ANALYSIS ★★★   LO 6

Details of BJM Pty Ltd's income statement for the past year are:

Sales (22 000 units)		$1 320 000
Cost of sales:		
Direct materials	$440 000	
Direct labour	396 000	
Variable factory overhead	88 000	
Fixed factory overhead	60 000	984 000
GROSS PROFIT		336 000
Variable selling expenses	132 000	
Fixed selling and administrative expenses	30 000	162 000
PROFIT BEFORE TAX		174 000
Income tax expense (30%)		52 200
PROFIT		$ 121 800

Required

Consider each of the following independent situations.

1. Determine the company's break-even point in units and sales dollars. What is the margin of safety?
2. If the company wants to make an after-tax profit of $109 200, what is the dollar level of sales necessary to reach its goal?
3. If the sales volume is 15 000 units, what is the selling price needed to achieve an after-tax profit of $109 200?
4. If the company's sales volume increases by 10% as a result of increasing fixed selling expenses by $30 000 and variable selling expenses by $0.60 per unit, what is the company's after-tax profit?
5. If direct material costs increase 10%, direct labour costs increase 15%, variable overhead costs increase 10%, and fixed overhead increases by $10 000, how many units must be sold to earn an after-tax profit of $89 600? Round your calculations to the next highest unit.

LO 6

Problem 11.11   IMPACT OF CHANGE WITH CVP ANALYSIS ★★★

TMP Human Resource Consulting had the following contribution margin income statement for the year ended 2013:

Employment services fees (1500 employed)	$36 000 000
Variable expenses	14 400 000
Contribution margin	21 600 000
Fixed expenses	12 240 000
Profit	$ 9 360 000

Required

Answer each of the following independent situations:

1. Explain how an understanding of CVP analysis would improve the performance of the manager of a human resource consulting firm like TMP Human Resources Consulting.
2. As a graduate of a human resource management course you have finally become the manager of TMP Human Resource Consulting. In setting your salary at $500 000, you need to calculate what the service fees need to increase by to maintain the company's profit equal to at least 25% of total service fees.
3. You employ a friend who graduated with a degree in marketing and she believes that by increasing variable expenses by $1200 per client and fixed advertising expenses by $300 000 the firm will increase the number of clients by 100 per year. Would your marketing friend's suggestions improve profitability? Explain why or why not.

LO 6

Problem 11.12   IMPACT OF CHANGE WITH CVP ANALYSIS AND TAX ★★★

Kids Sports Consulting Pty Ltd is a company set up by sports and recreation management students to gain experience in running their own business. It had the following contribution margin income statement data for the year ended 2014:

Sporting event fees (48 events)	$ 24 000
Variable expenses	9 600
Contribution margin	14 400
Fixed expenses	8 160
Profit before tax	6 240
Tax (at 30%)	1 872
Profit after tax	$ 8 112

Required

Answer each of the following independent situations:

A. Explain how an understanding of CVP analysis would improve the performance of the manager of a sports and recreation firm like Kids Sports Consulting Pty Ltd.

B. As a student in a sports and recreation management degree you are required to act as the manager of Kids Sports Consulting Pty Ltd. In setting your salary at $10 000, calculate the increase in service fees to maintain the company's profit after tax equal to at least 25% of total service fees.

C. You employ a friend who is studying for a marketing degree. They believe that by increasing variable expenses by $50 per client and fixed advertising expenses by $1500 the company will increase the number of clients by 10 per year. Would your marketing friend's suggestions improve profitability after tax? Explain why the suggestion will, or will not, increase the company's profit.

Problem 11.13   IMPACT OF CHANGE WITH CVP ANALYSIS ★★★   **LO 6**

Lawsistan Ltd has prepared the following draft profit analysis for the current year.

Sales (150 000 units)	$1 200 000
Variable expenses	690 000
Contribution margin	510 000
Fixed expenses	217 600
Profit	$ 292 400

Required
Answer each of the following four independent situations:

1. If the company's manager is considering increasing his salary by $42 500, how much must dollar sales increase to maintain the company's current profit?

2. If the company changes its marketing approach, it is expected that variable expenses will increase 10%, fixed expenses will decrease 15% and sales units and dollars will increase 20%. Calculate the company's break-even point in terms of sales dollars if the new strategy is adopted. Assume that the sales price per unit will not be changed. Round your answer to the nearest dollar.

3. If the company decreases sales commissions, variable expenses will decrease by 10%. The company believes that unit sales will decrease 5% because of the loss of sales representatives, even though the company plans to increase its advertising budget by $25 000. Should the company decrease the sales commissions?

4. If the company's profit increases 100% next year because of a 35% increase in sales, will performance be better or worse than expected? Assume adequate capacity exists to meet the increased volume without increasing fixed costs.

Problem 11.14   IMPACT OF CHANGE WITH CVP ANALYSIS AND TAX ★★★   **LO 6**

Richards Ltd has prepared the following draft profit analysis for the current year:

Sales	$600 000
Variable expenses	345 000
Contribution margin	255 000
Fixed expenses	108 800
Profit before tax	146 200
Tax (at 30%)	43 860
Profit after tax	$102 340

Required
Answer each of the following four independent situations:

A. If the company's manager is considering increasing his salary by $34 000, how much must dollar sales increase to maintain the company's current after-tax profit?

B. If the company changes its marketing approach, it is expected that variable expenses will increase 10%, fixed expenses will decrease 15%, and sales units and dollars will increase 20%. Calculate the company's break-even point in terms of sales dollars if the new strategy is adopted. Assume that the sales price per unit will not change. Round your answer to the nearest dollar.

C. If the company decreases sales commissions, variable expenses would decrease by 10%. The company believes that unit sales would decrease 5% due to the loss of sales representatives, even though the company plans to increase its advertising budget by $25 000. Should the company decrease sales commissions?

D. If the company's profit increases 100% next year due to a 35% increase in sales, would performance be better or worse than expected? Assume adequate capacity exists to meet the increased volume without increasing fixed costs.

Problem 11.15 CONTRIBUTION MARGIN VARIANCE ANALYSIS ★★★ | LO 8

The manager of Fritz Fabricators Ltd has just reviewed the income statement for the previous quarter and is concerned by the profit earned. Her main concern is the significant difference between the planned contribution margin and the one actually achieved. The company sells only one product. A summary of contribution margins is shown below:

	Actual	Budget
Sales — units	32 000	33 000
Sales — dollars	$217 600	$221 100
Variable expenses	121 600	130 350
Contribution margin	$ 96 000	$ 90 750

Required
Calculate the sales price, sales volume, and variable expense variances for the quarter. Explain the variation in contribution margin to the manager.

CRITICAL THINKING

Costing backpacks

Jemma Simpkins began her own business manufacturing backpacks 10 years ago under the brand name Drop Dead. These are popular with secondary school and university students as they have a secure pocket for mobile phones and a hidden compartment that parents can't find. As Jemma's accountant, you have been responsible for determining the cost of the backpacks. Demand has been so great that Jemma has not worried about the accounting side of the business and has focused on the creative and marketing aspects.

But fashions change, and students are no longer happy with floppy backpacks and now want neon-coloured briefcases with designer graffiti printed all over them. Jemma has been wondering whether she could compete by reducing the price of the Drop Dead backpacks. Jemma decided to look through your accounting files to see what she could work out for herself, but she was confused. She can't understand why you have been telling her that the backpacks cost $30 to make when the cost of direct material is only $8 and the cost of direct labour is $7. 'Where did the other $15 come from and why can't I reduce the price of the bags by $15?' she asks.

Required
A. Explain, in non-accounting terms, about the nature of manufacturing costs and costing products.
B. Why can't Jemma simply reduce her price by $15 and cover only the variable costs of production? What would you suggest Jemma should do to combat the new competition?

Using CVP analysis when applying for a loan

Jill owns and operates a business that makes hand-crafted rocking chairs. The business is expanding but the increasing costs of raw materials and labour, and the GST, have badly affected profitability. Jill believes that if she buys some wood-turning equipment that is more modern she could reduce her use of labour and wastage of wood and this would make her business profitable again. The price of the equipment that Jill wishes to install is $15 000, which she will have to borrow from the bank. Jill has done a CVP analysis under her existing structure and also for the new structure if she buys the new wood-turning equipment. Although the new equipment would reduce the direct costs of labour and material, the fixed costs would increase so much that the break-even point of output would still exceed the likely level of rocking chair sales. Jill is passionate about her business and, although the CVP analysis doesn't support the purchase of the new equipment, she is determined to buy the equipment no matter what.

In making her presentation to the bank for the loan of $15 000, Jill uses CVP analysis to show how the new equipment would reduce the direct costs of labour and materials but does not show the fixed manufacturing costs as increasing.

Required

A. Who are the stakeholders in this situation?
B. Is there an ethical issue in this situation? If so, explain.
C. What would you have done if you were in Jill's position?

To convert, or not to convert

Not only is switching a motor vehicle from petrol to gas better for the environment, producing less green house gases, it also has financial benefits for firms and individuals. The following extract from the LPG Autogas website illustrates the type of savings that a business could expect to make:

> Make the switch to LPG Autogas and keep more money in your pocket.
>
> — Autogas is typically at least 50 per cent cheaper than other automotive fuels, meaning you will save money at the pump from day one.
>
> For example, if over the course of a year Autogas averaged 65 cents per litre, while unleaded petrol averaged $1.40 per litre, a Holden Commodore driver traveling 28 000 kilometres a year on Autogas would save $2020 – the equivalent of $38 per week.
>
> — Using the same comparative fuel prices, a Toyota HiAce van travelling 40 000 kms a year on Autogas would save its owner $2886 a year or $55 a week.
>
> *Source:* Excerpt from the LPG Autogas website, www.lpgautogas.com.au.

Required

Go to the LPG Autogas Australia website, www.lpgautogas.com.au, and using the savings calculator enter the current price of petrol and LPG in your area and how much you currently spend on petrol each week. Calculate the annual savings of changing a car from petrol to LPG. If you do not have a car, assume that you spend $80 per week on petrol. If a gas conversion costs $3000 on a used car and the government will give you a $2000 rebate, how long will it take for the savings to pay off the conversion? What other factors might influence your decision to convert a car from petrol to LPG?

Refer to the latest financial report of JB Hi-Fi Limited on its website, www.jbhifi.com.au, and answer the following questions:

1. Would JB Hi-Fi Limited be able to make use of cost–volume–profit analysis within its business operations?

2. Examine the note on 'Segmentation information'. Look at the 'Total segment revenue' for each of the segments and the 'Segment results'. Compare the trend over the last 3 years.

Budgeting for planning and control

Learning objectives

After studying this chapter, you should be able to:

1 explain the role of budgeting in the planning and control functions of management (p. 494)

2 understand the importance of organisational structure in an effective budgeting system (pp. 494–5)

3 understand the importance of management participation in and acceptance of budget preparation (pp. 495–6)

4 describe the benefits of budgeting (pp. 496–7)

5 define a master budget and distinguish between operating budgets and financial budgets (pp. 497–500)

6 explain the significance of the income/sales forecast in budgeting (pp. 500–1)

7 prepare and interpret a set of operating and financial budgets within a master budget for a service entity (pp. 501–6)

8 prepare and interpret a set of operating and financial budgets within a master budget for a retail or manufacturing entity (pp. 506–18)

9 explain the use of budgets for performance reporting and financial control (pp. 518–19).

Use sense to stretch dollars

One of the first lessons is budgeting, writes Maria Nguyen.

University is often the first time young adults need to manage their finances and maintain a budget. And the challenges associated with balancing the costs of studying, socialising and day-to-day living can come as quite a shock.

'The broke uni student is such a cliché but I really didn't expect to have to budget as much as I do,' says 19-year-old Melissa Tweedie, now into the second year of a psychology degree at Macquarie University.

'I've become stingy. I didn't realise how much all these costs would compromise my life because it affects your social life and extracurricular activities.'

It's a far cry, she notes, from the relatively sheltered life of a high school student.

'It's the first time the Government doesn't pay for your transport, paying for food at the shops is more expensive than the school canteen and not having a school uniform means I've never spent so much on clothes,' Tweedie says.

'And even with my mobile phone, before I make a call, I now think, 'How much is this going to cost me?'

Similarly, for Louise Treloar, a 19-year-old live-in student at Charles Sturt University, learning to budget in order to maintain a healthy social life and pay for basic living and studying costs hasn't been easy.

'This is the first time I've lived away from home and things like groceries I didn't realise how much basics actually cost,' Treloar says.

'You buy some meat and cheese and it's $100! But I'm getting a job this year to help with my finances.'

For many students like Treloar, the first taste of freedom and independence often comes with the reality check of having to juggle finances and learning to prioritise the endless burst of attractive, and costly, options that come with campus life: partying with new friends, involvement with sporting activities and social clubs.

This, along with the day-to-day expenses of uni life such as tuition, textbooks, rent, transport, groceries, petrol, internet and mobile phones means students can easily lose track of their budget. It's little wonder then that sticking to one poses a major challenge.

Annette Cairnduff, the head of Equity Support Services at Sydney University, says the big costs are rent, transport and food.

'Rent is such a huge cost, especially in the metro areas, and $150 to $200 a week is not unusual,' she says. 'It's a shock, especially if you're moving out of home or moving from a rural or regional area.'

However, many universities do provide financial assistance, such as loans and bursaries, Cairnduff says, 'so students should find out how their uni can help'.

Annette Cairnduff's top five budgeting tips:

- Seek help early from your university. If you're struggling, don't allow yourself to fall behind in your rent or debt repayments.
- Be realistic when developing a budget. Make sure that you factor in socialising and little things such as lunch, snacks, newspapers — the real costs can add up quickly.
- Don't rely too much on credit cards.
- Put some money away for the year ahead. Save $500 to be used as emergency funds.
- Find out what types of financial assistance your university provides: for example, interest-free loans, bursaries and grants.

Source: Maria Nguyen, 'Use sense to stretch dollars — mid-year enrolments', *Sun-Herald*.

Chapter preview

The scene setter highlights the importance to tertiary students of budgeting while they are studying so that they can achieve their goals. Similarly, for business, budgeting is an essential management tool that ensures a business keeps track of its income and expenses so that it can achieve its goals. Budgeting is an important part of the accounting objectives of helping with decision making and promoting accountability.

A formal **budget** is a detailed written financial plan that shows how resources are expected to be acquired and used during a specified time period to achieve an organisation's goals. Virtually every person, family and organisation (government or business) uses some form of budget to identify the resources they need to support their expenditures.

Sometimes we do this in our personal lives without even recognising it as a formal application of budgeting. For example, assume that we are considering enrolling in a university to study a business degree. Whether we actually write down the expected financial impact of this decision, or simply estimate the costs in our minds, we are involved in a budgeting process. We must determine what fees we will incur and how they will be paid. We must determine whether we need to borrow money or whether the fees can be deferred to a later date. We need to estimate what our textbooks will cost and the costs of accommodation if we have to move to another city or country. We also need to consider how much we can earn by working while we are studying. This situation requires the preparation of a relatively simple budget to make sure that we can afford to study without running into financial difficulties.

Although the main emphasis of this chapter is on budgeting for a business entity, many of the concepts and procedures are useful in non-business activities as well.

Learning objective 1

Explain the role of budgeting in the planning and control functions of management

12.1 The nature of budgetary planning and control

Although all budgets serve the same basic purpose, a budget prepared by a business is more detailed than one used by an individual. Budgeting is an essential step in managing a business efficiently and effectively.

A budget, as a management tool, is similar to the architectural drawings used by a contractor to build a house. If the contractor is to build the house efficiently (with the correct amount of resources in the form of labour and materials) and effectively (so that the results are compatible with the predetermined specifications), the contractor must follow the blueprint drawings carefully to guide the building process from beginning to end. A budget serves management in much the same way, by providing a formal plan of an entity's future course of action according to well-defined goals.

Initially, management determines the entity's goals for the **budgeting period**. The budget then expresses these goals in the form of financial and operating targets. These targets provide the direction for the entity's activities and transactions, which are normally expected to lead to satisfactory financial results. Then, as actual performance occurs, it is monitored and checked against the related budget targets for control purposes. When significant differences (called variances) between actual and planned performances are found, they are investigated and corrected whenever possible. Budgeting and performance evaluation are closely related, since the budget provides many of the performance targets that must be achieved by management.

Learning objective 2

Understand the importance of organisational structure in an effective budgeting system

12.2 Organisational structure and budgeting

Successful budgeting depends on an organisational structure in which the individual manager's authority and responsibility are clearly defined. This is achieved by structuring the organisation into responsibility centres such as divisions and departments. Dividing an entity into well-defined components or specialised segments, called business segmentation, helps the business to accomplish more than it otherwise could. The choice of segments depends on such things as the size of the organisation, nature of the business activity, management philosophy and geographic location.

For example, a motor vehicle dealership might be segmented into two divisions that each have three departments: new car sales, used car sales, leasing, repairs, body shop, and spare parts, as shown in figure 12.1.

Figure 12.1 Motor vehicle dealership organisation chart

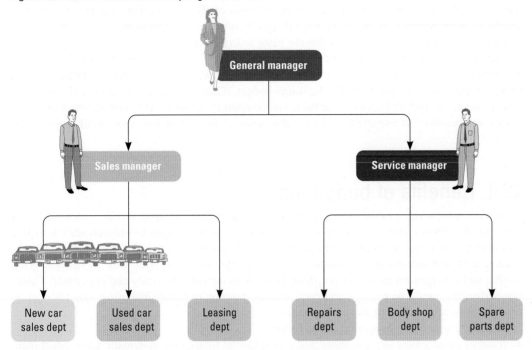

Once the choice of specific business segments is made, a manager is assigned to each of them. In figure 12.1, a manager is appointed to manage each of the departments shown. Each manager is given authority to make decisions and take whatever action is necessary to accomplish departmental goals. In turn, the manager is held responsible for the department's performance. This is called responsibility accounting and is described in detail in chapter 13. Ideally, both efficiency and effectiveness measures (see chapter 1, p. 19) are used to evaluate this performance. This means that resource inputs, outputs in the form of products or services, and the goals of the department are considered in the evaluation process. Each department has its own budget that is used in setting departmental targets and in performance evaluation.

Even service businesses divide their activities into well-defined segments. An accounting firm typically is structured into departments such as management advisory services, assurance services and taxation.

12.3 Management participation and acceptance

Learning objective 3

Understand the importance of management participation in and acceptance of budget preparation

A budget is a financial plan for each segment of the organisation. For the budget to work as an effective planning and controlling device, the plans expressed in the written budget must be accepted by all levels of management.

When all levels of management, e.g. division heads, department heads and supervisors within departments, participate in the preparation of the budget, the budget has a greater chance of acceptance. Managers at all levels generally will endorse and support a budget if they have participated in its preparation. To increase the probability of acceptance, the preparation of the budget is best approached from the bottom up rather than from the top down, i.e. having the budget imposed by senior management.

Budget data are reviewed and consolidated as the data flow up from the lowest levels in the organisation to the top level of management. It is essential that each manager believes the targets expressed in the budget are achievable. If this is the case, managers will be motivated to accept responsibility for achieving the targets. If managers consider the targets to be unreasonable or unachievable, they will not be motivated to achieve those targets.

How employees respond to the budgeting process can have some influence on the success of the budget. The budgeting process should encourage **goal congruence** within an organisation so that the employees act in a way that advances the goals of the organisation as a whole as well as satisfying their personal goals. *Budgeting always involves a negotiation process as the various departments within an entity compete for the same scarce resources.*

The final consolidated budget must be acceptable to senior management and, if not, data are returned to the lower levels of management for review, acceptance and resubmission until senior management is happy with the final budget. Once finalised and accepted by senior management, the budget becomes the basis for comparing actual results with the budgeted outcomes and becomes an important tool in performance evaluation of managers at all levels of the organisation.

12.4 Benefits of budgeting

Learning objective 4

Describe the benefits of budgeting

Achieving satisfactory profits in a competitive and uncertain business world is not easy. For example, for many companies in Australia the average profit margin is only about 5%, which means that these companies have approximately *5 cents out of every sales dollar* to pay dividends, redeem debt and reinvest in the business. There is little room for error with these tight profit results, and management must do everything possible to operate efficiently and effectively. Financial performance must be planned and controlled as thoroughly as possible using sound budgeting procedures to achieve acceptable profit results.

The major benefits of budgeting are as follows:

- *It forces management to plan ahead* and anticipate the future on a systematic basis. Most managers are very busy with their day-to-day activities and may resist formalised planning unless budgeting is part of their job. An annual budgeting cycle means that at least once a year managers have to consider the future direction of the business.
- *It provides management with realistic performance targets* with which actual results can be compared. Management can identify significant variances that require correction. Consequently, the budget plays an important role in controlling and allocating scarce resources within an organisation.
- *It coordinates the various segments of the organisation* and makes each manager aware of how the different activities fit together. Every organisation must ensure that all its segments work towards the overall goals set by management. Since the performances of the various segments are interrelated in many ways, segment managers must know not only their own roles, but also how they interact with the rest of the organisation. For example, the accounting, finance, marketing, personnel, production and purchasing functions of a manufacturing entity must be coordinated. The same is true for the agencies of a government, the services of a bank, or the departments of a hospital. Otherwise, inefficiency and ineffectiveness will develop in the allocation and use of resources.

  Without a formal coordination system, individual managers tend to operate in their own best interests rather than those of the organisation. This problem becomes greater as an organisation grows and management responsibility is delegated to more people. The various activities of a business must be planned and controlled with the full participation and support of the managers responsible for them.

  Goal congruence occurs when the personal and corporate goals of the managers of an entity are consistent with the goals of the organisation. Goal congruence can be achieved by the unifying effect budgeting has on an organisation — particularly when it is combined with responsibility accounting (as discussed in the next chapter).

- *It serves as a communication device* with which the various managers can exchange information concerning goals, ideas and achievements. Since direct contact will decrease as an organisation increases in size, a formal communication network is essential. Budgeting enables the managers to interact and develop an awareness of how each of their activities contributes to the entity's overall operation. The budgeting process in an organisation is a way of communicating and coordinating management goals and financial targets.

The budget also clearly communicates top management's priorities for the organisation. For example, as a marketing exercise, management may state that the customers are the most important priority to the organisation. However, if the budget shows that resources are being reduced in the customer service area and transferred to management remuneration, then this will reveal the true priorities of management.

- *It furnishes management with motivation* by providing goals to be achieved. Few people work just for the fun of it; most people need some form of stimulus to work hard and maintain an enthusiastic attitude towards their jobs. A properly constructed budget is a motivating device that provides performance targets against which actual results can be evaluated. An improperly prepared budget may have an adverse effect on the motivation of managers, who may criticise the process as being unrealistic and unfair.

Managers will be more highly motivated if they have participated in setting budget estimates than if the estimates have been established entirely by someone at a higher level in the organisation. However, managers cannot be given sole responsibility for setting their budget targets as they may set them at a level that can be too easily achieved.

Two key aspects of a correct application of budgeting are:
- the budgeted level of performance should be attainable with a reasonably efficient amount of effort
- the managers who will be evaluated with the budget data should participate actively in budget development.

12.5 The master budget

Learning objective 5

Define a master budget and distinguish between operating budgets and financial budgets

The main objective of the financial planning phase of budgeting is to identify how management intends to acquire and use the entity's resources to achieve organisational goals during a budget period. A *master budget* consisting of several interrelated budgets provides the basis for financial planning. The major steps in developing a master budget are:

1. Management identifies the organisational goals for the budget period, including those that are financially oriented such as desired profit, profit margins, return on investment, liquidity, market share and financial position.
2. The managers of the various responsibility centres participate in the development of the parts of the master budget for which they are accountable.
3. Income/sales for the budget period are forecast.
4. Expenses for the budget period are estimated for all entities including service, not-for-profit and government organisations, and cost of sales figures are also estimated for retail and manufacturing entities.
5. Capital expenditures for the budget period are identified.
6. Accrued accounting data are converted to a cash basis to determine cash receipts and payments. Any financial sources or applications of cash (such as the sale of shares, issue of debentures or notes, payment of dividends or redemption of debt) are considered.
7. A set of budgeted financial statements is prepared based on the initial version of the financial performance projections.
8. The estimated financial performance results (e.g. profit) are compared with the organisational goals, and revisions are made wherever necessary to make the final version of the budget compatible with the overall goals.

The **master budget** is a set of interrelated budgets representing a comprehensive plan of action for a specified time period. It is typically prepared for a 1-year period that coincides with an entity's reporting period. The budget for the year is subdivided into shorter periods such as months or quarters to allow timely comparisons of actual results and budgeted figures. Alternatively, the budget may be developed for a continuous period of 12 months or more by adding a month or quarter in the future as the month or quarter just ended is eliminated. The budgeted targets are usually revised as the year progresses and new information concerning the business and its environment becomes available.

The master budget consists of two major parts: day-to-day operating budgets and financial budgets. **Operating budgets** are detailed descriptions of the income and costs of projected activities required to achieve satisfactory profit results. **Financial budgets** show the funding needed for the planned operations and the projected financial position. The two parts consist of separate but inter-related budgets, such as those shown in figure 12.2 for a typical service entity.

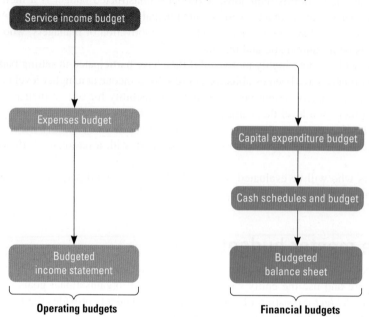

Figure 12.2 Master budget interrelationships for a service entity

Service organisations

In entities that provide services to customers, e.g. financial institutions, legal practices, accounting practices, financial advisory services, public relations firms, and businesses engaged in tourism and hospitality, comprehensive budgets are prepared. Even small service businesses, such as Darren's Lawn and Gardening Services illustrated in chapter 1 and Intellect Management Services illustrated in chapters 3–5, benefit greatly from using budgets.

The key element or starting point is the budgeted income (including revenues) to be obtained from selling services. For example, a legal practice estimates total income from fees it expects to receive over the budgetary period and then uses this figure to determine budgeted expenses and other costs. Alternatively, projected income can be determined by taking the expected billable hours of services to be performed and multiplying this by the appropriate charge-out rates for employees. The critical planning components are then determining the appropriate level and numbers of professional and support staff that need to be employed during the budgetary period. Other overheads and expenses can be budgeted once these key elements have been determined. Other components of a comprehensive budgetary system are then finalised.

Retail entities

In retail entities, the preparation of the budget closely follows that used in a service entity, with a sales forecast being the starting point of the process. As goods need to be purchased for resale in a retail entity, a **purchases budget** is necessary. A purchases budget shows the budgeted volume and cost of goods that need to be purchased during the budget period to meet the level of projected sales. If the retail entity is departmentalised, then separate sales, purchases and expense budgets can be prepared for each department. Other aspects of the budgetary process are the same as for service businesses.

Manufacturing entities

Budgeting for manufacturing entities is more complicated than for any other type of organisation because it involves more budgets. Like service and retail entities, a manufacturing entity's master budget begins with a sales budget. Like a retail entity, a manufacturing entity must budget for the cost of sales. But unlike retail entities that simply purchase goods for resale, a manufacturing entity produces its own goods for sale and this involves extra budgets, such as materials, labour and overheads budgets. The interrelated budgets for a typical manufacturing entity are shown in figure 12.3 (p. 500).

The manufacturing entity follows essentially the same budgeting cycle as a service or retail entity but in addition the process involves budgeting for production costs. This requires the purchases budget of a retail entity to be replaced by a production budget. This then leads to the need to budget for raw materials, direct labour and factory overhead.

The budgets normally prepared as part of a master budget for service, retail and manufacturing entities are compared in table 12.1.

Table 12.1 Budgets included in the master budgets for service, retail and manufacturing entities

	Service entity	Retail entity	Manufacturing entity
Operating budgets			
Service income/sales budget	✓	✓	✓
Purchases budget (finished goods)		✓	
Purchases budget (raw materials)			✓
Production budget			✓
Direct materials budget			✓
Direct labour budget			✓
Factory overhead budget			✓
Cost of sales budget		✓	✓
Selling and distribution expenses budget	✓	✓	✓
Administrative expenses budget	✓	✓	✓
Finance and other expenses budget	✓	✓	✓
Budgeted income statement	✓	✓	✓
Financial budgets			
Capital expenditure budget	✓	✓	✓
Cash budget	✓	✓	✓
Budgeted balance sheet	✓	✓	✓

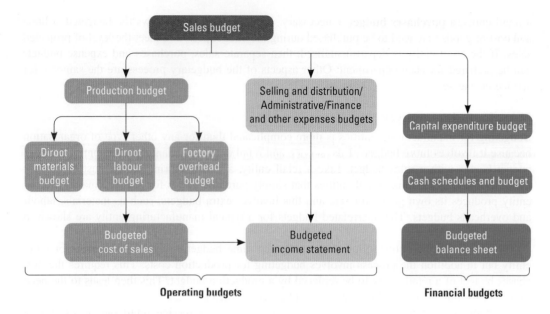

Figure 12.3 Master budget interrelationships for a manufacturing entity

Not-for-profit organisations

Budgeting is just as important in not-for-profit entities such as sporting bodies and clubs, but the emphasis is generally placed on cash flows and final cash position rather than on income and expenses. In budgeting for an expected cash outcome for a period, emphasis is usually placed on expenditures planned for the forthcoming period. When the total expenditures have been determined, the entity then focuses on ensuring that cash receipts are at least sufficient to cover planned expenditure. Planned expenditures will be cut if budgeted income is not sufficient.

Government entities

Budgets also constitute an integral part of the activities of entities at all levels of government. Such budgets are approved by the relevant federal or state parliament and local government councils. Again, the emphasis in preparing budgets for government departments is on expenditure. Once programs have been costed, attention then focuses on obtaining the appropriate income through taxation and other revenue-raising procedures. This involves a balancing process of weighing up the potential to increase income via taxation and the political impact of reducing expenditure on government-funded programs.

12.6 Income/sales forecast

Learning objective 6

Explain the significance of the income/sales forecast in budgeting

An accurate income or sales revenue forecast is the cornerstone of successful budgeting because virtually everything else depends on it. The forecast in hours of services provided or in units sold provides the basis for preparing an income/sales budget, predicting cash receipts and constructing a variety of expense budgets. These forecasts are usually subject to more uncertainty than any other aspect of budgeting. Unless a business entity has a large number of unfilled orders that guarantee a highly consistent demand for its products or services, forecasting is complicated by the uncertainties of the future. The general economy, industry conditions, effect of proposed advertising, actions of competitors, consumer buying habits, population changes, natural disasters and technological developments are factors that influence the reliability of a sales forecast.

A combination of several methods can be used to forecast income/sales. The most common methods are: predictions by members of the marketing staff; estimates prepared by senior management; statistical or mathematical techniques.

The marketing staff generally is aware of current market conditions and should participate actively in the preparation of the income/sales forecast. Field surveys can be conducted to predict income by products or services, geographical areas, customers and marketing representatives. In large businesses, market research staff may be available to conduct the field studies of consumer demand and develop a sales volume forecast.

All members of the senior management team — including production, finance, purchasing and administrative officers — should collectively develop their own estimates of expected sales volume based on their knowledge of the total business and the environment in which the entity operates. In addition, a number of statistical and mathematical techniques beyond the scope of this book are available. The basic reason for using alternative forecasting methods is that they provide a check on each other and produce a compromise representing management's best estimate of income.

12.7 Operating and financial budgets for service entities

Learning objective 7

Prepare and interpret a set of operating and financial budgets within a master budget for a service entity

Operating budgets for service entities

The preparation of a master budget for a service entity is illustrated with reference to Mark Ting Ltd, a marketing company. Preparing operating budgets for service entities is simpler than for retail or manufacturing entities because service entities need to calculate only budgeted service income. There is no need to prepare a cost of sales or manufacturing budget. The remainder of the master budgeting process, including expense budgets, capital expenditure budgets, cash budgets and budgeted financial statements, is similar for all entities regardless of their function.

In the following illustration, we are concerned with the steps taken by Mark Ting Ltd in the preparation of the master budget. The master budget illustrated is prepared for the financial year and is subdivided into quarters.

Income budget

The levels of activity included in the income forecasts must be as accurate as possible, since the remainder of the master budget depends on these. Detailed information concerning activity levels and charge-out rates are presented in the **service income budget**. Mark Ting Ltd has used the forecasting methods discussed earlier to determine the level of activity for the service income budget shown in figure 12.4.

Figure 12.4 Service income budget for a service entity

MARK TING LTD Service Income Budget for the year ending 30 June 2014					
	Quarter				Annual total
	Sept.	Dec.	Mar.	June	
Graduate staff					
Budgeted chargeable hours	1 300	1 400	1 200	1 200	5 100
Budgeted charge rate	$60	$60	$60	$60	$60
BUDGETED SERVICE FEES	$ 78 000	$ 84 000	$ 72 000	$ 72 000	$ 306 000
Marketing executives					
Budgeted chargeable hours	1 000	1 000	900	900	3 800
Budgeted charge rate	$120	$120	$120	$120	$120
BUDGETED SERVICE FEES	$120 000	$120 000	$108 000	$108 000	$ 456 000
Senior management					
Budgeted chargeable hours	1 000	1 100	900	900	3 900
Budgeted charge rate	$180	$180	$180	$180	$180
BUDGETED SERVICE FEES	$180 000	$198 000	$162 000	$162 000	$ 702 000
TOTAL BUDGETED SERVICE FEES	$378 000	$402 000	$342 000	$342 000	$1 464 000
Budgeted expenses charged to clients	130 000	140 000	120 000	130 000	520 000
TOTAL SERVICE INCOME	**$508 000**	**$542 000**	**$462 000**	**$472 000**	**$1 984 000**

Mark Ting Ltd bases its service income budget on the number of hours it estimates will be charged to clients in the budget period. This is a common method of budgeting for service entities. The charge rate per hour is based on the salary of the staff involved for each client multiplied by 3 to cover the indirect costs of running the business, such as rent and electricity, and to provide a profit. Expenses that can be directly related to clients' work, such as typing, media, printing, supplies and travel, are also charged to them. An estimate of these direct expenses, based on past experience, is shown in figure 12.4 as 'Budgeted expenses charged to clients'.

Mark Ting Ltd has three levels of staff and their salaries per hour and charge-out rates per hour are as follows:

	Salary per hour	Charge-out rate	
Graduate staff	$20	$60	($20 × 3)
Marketing executives	$40	$120	($40 × 3)
Senior management	$60	$180	($60 × 3)

GST is ignored in this example so that it does not detract from the focus of understanding the budgeting process.

Expenses budget

For a service entity, the budget is not usually broken down into the categories of selling and distribution, administrative, and finance and other expenses. The management of Mark Ting Ltd needs to budget for expenses carefully to ensure that they are good estimates for the budget period. If expenses look as if they may be too high, management must consider whether it can reduce the expenses or increase the charge-out rates to cover them. In this illustration we assume that all the expenses for Mark Ting Ltd are fixed except for employee commissions, which are calculated at 10% of total fees revenue. The expenses budget is shown in figure 12.5.

Figure 12.5 Expenses budget for a service entity

MARK TING LTD
Expenses Budget
for the year ending 30 June 2014

	Quarter				Annual total
	Sept.	Dec.	Mar.	June	
Salaries	$130 000	$130 000	$130 000	$130 000	$ 520 000
Clerical salaries	25 000	25 000	25 000	25 000	100 000
Commissions (10% of service revenues)	50 800	54 200	46 200	47 200	198 400
Depreciation	28 000	30 500	31 300	31 800	121 600
Electricity	1 500	1 500	1 500	1 500	6 000
Entertainment	2 000	2 000	2 000	2 000	8 000
Insurance	3 000	3 000	3 000	3 000	12 000
Media-related expenses	80 000	70 000	75 000	85 000	310 000
Printing	50 000	50 000	50 000	50 000	200 000
Rent	1 000	1 000	1 000	1 000	4 000
Supplies	2 000	2 000	2 000	2 000	8 000
Travel	5 000	5 000	5 000	5 000	20 000
TOTAL EXPENSES	**$378 300**	**$374 200**	**$372 000**	**$383 500**	**$1 508 000**

Budgeted income statement

The budgeted income statement shown in figure 12.6 is developed from the service income and expenses budgets. An estimate is made of the income tax expense, assuming a company tax rate of 30%. The statement may appear to be the result of simply combining the previous two budgets. However, remember that the basic idea of budgeting is to plan a financial performance level that is acceptable to management. The control feature of the budgeted income statement is exercised when management compares the actual results with the budget.

Figure 12.6 Budgeted income statement for a service entity

MARK TING LTD
Budgeted Income Statement
for the year ending 30 June 2014

	Quarter				Annual total
	Sept.	Dec.	Mar.	June	
SERVICE INCOME (figure 12.4)	$508 000	$542 000	$462 000	$472 000	$1 984 000
Less: EXPENSES (figure 12.5)	378 300	374 200	372 000	383 500	1 508 000
PROFIT BEFORE TAX	129 700	167 800	90 000	88 500	476 000
Income tax expense (30%)	38 910	50 340	27 000	26 550	142 800
PROFIT	$ 90 790	$117 460	$ 63 000	$ 61 950	$ 333 200

Regardless of whether top-down or bottom-up budgeting is used, the process begins with top management establishing certain guidelines within which the business will plan its financial performance. These guidelines relate to such goals as profit margin, return on assets and investment, financial position and productivity.

Financial budgets for service entities

Once preparation of the operating budgets is completed, the financial budgets (capital expenditure budget, cash budget and the budgeted balance sheet) within the master budget can be prepared. These budgets are illustrated below.

Capital expenditure budget

The capital expenditure budget included in the master budget shows the acquisition of facilities and equipment planned for the period. Capital expenditures represent investments that are expected to provide benefits over many years. Most businesses prepare long-term capital expenditure budgets for periods of 5 or more years. The amounts shown in figure 12.7 represent only the capital expenditure for the next financial year. (Capital budgeting is discussed in chapter 14.) Mark Ting Ltd will finance capital expenditure of $80 000 from internal sources during the year ending 30 June 2014. In this example it is assumed that all capital expenditure is paid for in the quarter in which it is incurred.

Figure 12.7 Capital expenditure budget for a service entity

MARK TING LTD
Capital Expenditure Budget
for the year ending 30 June 2014

	Quarter				Annual total
	Sept.	Dec.	Mar.	June	
Photocopier	$50 000				$50 000
Office equipment		$10 000		$5 000	15 000
Computer equipment		6 000	$9 000		15 000
TOTAL CAPITAL EXPENDITURE	**$50 000**	**$16 000**	**$9 000**	**$5 000**	**$80 000**

Cash budget

The service income and expenses budgets must be translated into cash receipts and cash payments from operations for financial planning purposes. The goal is to make sure that the business has enough liquidity to pay its debts as they fall due. The **cash budget** (figure 12.10, p. 505) is used to ensure an adequate, but not excessive, cash balance exists throughout the period. Cash earns a low rate of return and excess cash can be used more efficiently by investing in productive assets. Although cash budgeting is covered in chapter 10, it is included here to show how it fits into the master budget.

A satisfactory income statement does not guarantee sufficient liquidity because of the time lag caused by the difference between accrual and cash accounting. An estimate of the time lag between service revenues recognised and cash collections as well as the lag associated with costs and expenses charged and cash payments must be considered carefully. In addition, any non-cash expenses (such as depreciation and bad debts) must be eliminated in the preparation of the cash budget.

To simplify the preparation of the cash budget it is useful to firstly prepare schedules of (1) estimated cash collections of service income and (2) estimated cash payments for expenses. Mark Ting Ltd has analysed its previous experience with cash receipts and believes that 60% of each quarter's income should be collected in the current quarter and 40% in the following quarter. Bad debts are negligible, so they are ignored. Using this information, Mark Ting Ltd can prepare a schedule of estimated cash collections from service income as shown in figure 12.8.

Figure 12.8 Schedule of estimated cash collections from service income

MARK TING LTD
Schedule of Estimated Cash Collections from Service Income
for the year ending 30 June 2014

Quarter	Revenues	Cash collections			
		Sept.	Dec.	Mar.	June
June 2010	$550 000	$220 000			
September (figure 12.4)	508 000	304 800[a]	$203 200[b]		
December	542 000		325 200	$216 800	
March	462 000			277 200	$184 800
June	472 000				283 200
CASH COLLECTIONS FROM SERVICE INCOME		$524 800	$528 400	$494 000	$468 000

(a) $508 000 × 60% = $304 800.
(b) $508 000 × 40% = $203 200.

The next step is to prepare a schedule of estimated cash payments for expenses. The depreciation expense of $121 600 is ignored in the cash budget since it is a non-cash expense. The business calculates commissions at the end of each quarter and pays them in the following quarter. Media expenses are paid for 80% in the quarter in which they are incurred and the remaining 20% in the following quarter. Media expenses for the June quarter 2013 were $72 000. All other expenses are paid for in the quarter in which they are incurred. Using this information, Mark Ting Ltd can now prepare a schedule of estimated cash payments for expenses as illustrated in figure 12.9.

Figure 12.9 Schedule of estimated cash payments for expenses in a service entity

MARK TING LTD
Schedule of Estimated Cash Payments for Expenses
for the year ending 30 June 2014

	Quarter				Annual total
	Sept.	Dec.	Mar.	June	
Total budgeted expenses (figure 12.5)	$378 300	$374 200	$372 000	$383 500	$1 508 000
Less: Depreciation (non-cash expense)	(28 000)	(30 500)	(31 300)	(31 800)	(121 600)
Less: Commissions (current quarter, paid next quarter)	(50 800)	(54 200)	(46 200)	(47 200)	(198 400)
Add: Commission (previous quarter)	55 000[a]	50 800	54 200	46 200	206 200
Less: 20% of media-related expenses payable paid in following quarter	(16 000)[b]	(14 000)	(15 000)	(17 000)	(62 000)
Add: 20% of media-related expenses payable from previous quarter	14 400[c]	16 000[b]	14 000	15 000	59 400
BUDGETED EXPENSE PAYMENTS	$352 900	$342 300	$347 700	$348 700	$1 391 600

(a) In September, credit sales of previous June quarter = $550 000 × 10% = $55 000 commission.
(b) $80 000 × 20% = $16 000.
(c) $72 000 × 20% = $14 400.

Mark Ting Ltd is now in a position to prepare its overall cash budget. The business expects to begin the year with $80 000 cash and end it with $255 600. During the year, dividends of $200 000 will be paid in two instalments, one in December and one in June. An estimated income tax payment of $42 000, based on the income tax liability of $168 000 for 2012–13 profits, will be paid in each quarter. The cash budget shown in figure 12.10 is for use by internal management.

Figure 12.10 Cash budget for a service entity

MARK TING LTD
Cash Budget
for the year ending 30 June 2014

	Quarter				Annual total
	Sept.	Dec.	Mar.	June	
Cash at bank, beginning balance	$ 80 000	$159 900	$188 000	$283 300	$ 80 000
Collections from service income (figure 12.8)	524 800	528 400	494 000	468 000	2 015 200
Total cash available	604 800	688 300	682 000	751 300	2 095 200
Estimated cash payments					
Budgeted expense payments (figure 12.9)	352 900	342 300	347 700	348 700	1 391 600
Capital expenditure (figure 12.7)	50 000	16 000	9 000	5 000	80 000
Dividends		100 000		100 000	200 000
Estimated income tax payments	42 000	42 000	42 000	42 000	168 000
Total expected payments	444 900	500 300	398 700	495 700	1 839 600
CASH AT BANK, ENDING BALANCE	$159 900	$188 000	$283 300	$255 600	$ 255 600

BUSINESS KNOWLEDGE

Budget shift to buying habits

The company behind the world's most successful loyalty card scheme, Tesco's Clubcard, is predicting that within a decade half the global marketing budgets will be spent on ads directed at individuals based on their purchasing habits.

Ads sent via digital channels such as email or digitally-enabled TVs will account for half the $US450 billion ($545 billion) spent globally on advertising, said Martin Hayward, the director of strategy and futures at data analyst DunnHumby.

This week Woolworths unveiled the next plank in its Everyday Rewards loyalty program, rewarding its 3 million registered cardholders with frequent flyer points. The deal will generate large volumes of information on its customers' purchasing habits.

The supermarket chain signalled a shift in marketing budgets. Woolworths' general manager of customer engagement, Richard Umbers, said on Monday: 'This also represents an opportunity to reallocate some of the more traditional marketing spend.' He declined to give any details on the future allocation of its $30 million budget.

Already $6 of every $10 spent at Myer goes through its Myer One program, which has 2.6 million members. Chief executive Bernie Brookes recently said that more of its $50 million advertising is spent through its loyalty program than on mainstream ads.

Source: Excerpts from Julian Lee, 'Budget shift to buying habits', *The Sydney Morning Herald.*

Budgeted balance sheet

Because Mark Ting Ltd prepares the budget for the year ending 30 June 2014 *before* the end of the year ending 30 June 2013, the balance sheet as at 30 June 2013 is not yet prepared and so it must be estimated. It is shown in figure 12.11 and provides the beginning balances for the 2013–14 budgeting process. Once the actual results are known, the beginning balance sheet can be revised if significant differences occur. The budgeted balance sheet as at 30 June 2014 is presented in figure 12.11 (p. 506) and is the result of translating the beginning balances through the 2014 budgeting process into ending balances.

For example, the cash at bank balance comes from the cash budget (figure 12.10). The accounts receivable balance of $188 800 is 40% of income of $472 000 invoiced in the June quarter (figure 12.4) that has not been collected by year-end. Increases in office equipment are calculated

Figure 12.11 Budgeted balance sheet for a service entity

MARK TING LTD
Budgeted Balance Sheet
as at 30 June 2014
(with estimates as at 30 June 2013 shown)

	2013		2014	
CURRENT ASSETS				
Cash at bank (figure 12.10)	$ 80 000		$255 600	
Accounts receivable	220 000		188 800	
TOTAL CURRENT ASSETS		$300 000		$444 400
NON-CURRENT ASSETS				
Office equipment	560 000		640 000[a]	
Accumulated depreciation	(210 000)		(331 600)[b]	
TOTAL NON-CURRENT ASSETS		350 000		308 400
TOTAL ASSETS		650 000		752 800
CURRENT LIABILITIES				
Accounts payable (media)	14 400		17 000	
Commission payable (figure 12.5)	55 000		47 200	
Current tax liability (figure 12.6)	168 000		142 800	
TOTAL CURRENT LIABILITIES		237 400		207 000
NET ASSETS		$412 600		$545 800
EQUITY				
Share capital		$100 000		$100 000
Retained earnings		312 600		445 800[c]
TOTAL EQUITY		$412 600		$545 800

(a) Opening balance $560 000 + Purchases $80 000 = $640 000.
(b) Opening balance $210 000 + Depreciation expense $121 600 = $331 600.
(c) Opening balance $312 600 + Profit after tax $333 200 − Dividends $200 000 = $445 800.

by adding budgeted capital expenditure $80 000 (figure 12.7) to the opening balance for the year, and accumulated depreciation is the opening balance plus the depreciation expense from the expenses budget (figure 12.5). Accounts payable ($17 000) is 20% of the June quarter media expenses $85 000 that won't be paid until the following budget period (figure 12.5), and commission payable $47 200 reflects the June quarter commissions (figure 12.5) that will be paid in the following quarter. Current tax liability comes from the budgeted income statement (figure 12.6). Finally, budgeted retained earnings are calculated by adding the budgeted profit (figure 12.6) to the opening retained earnings and deducting the budgeted dividends as per the cash budget (figure 12.10). If the budgeted balance sheet is in balance, then this should indicate that the budgets are internally consistent.

Management must evaluate the budgeted balance sheet carefully to ensure it reflects the achievement of goals during the budget period. If the projected balance sheet does not reflect the desired financial position at the end of the budget period, the master budget needs to be revised.

Learning objective 8

Prepare and interpret a set of operating and financial budgets within a master budget for a retail or manufacturing entity

12.8 Operating and financial budgets for retail and manufacturing entities

Operating budgets for retail and manufacturing entities

To illustrate the preparation of a master budget for retail and manufacturing entities, we refer to K.Q. Lattor Ltd, which produces and sells two types of calculators, the XS Calculator (XS means 'extra special') and the Calculator Excite, a straightforward calculator with a name the marketing department believed would set it apart from its competitors.

K.Q. Lattor Ltd has the choice of either purchasing the calculators from another manufacturer for resale or manufacturing the calculators itself. This illustration is not to show how a company decides between these two alternatives; it is simply to show how a retail entity budgets for purchases whereas a manufacturing entity budgets for production.

The only budgets that differ significantly between a retail entity and a manufacturing entity are those that relate to budgeting for the cost of sales. A retail entity prepares budgets for purchases in units and in dollars and then a cost of sales budget. A manufacturing entity prepares production, direct materials, direct labour and factory overhead budgets and then a cost of sales budget.

Both retail and manufacturing entities prepare similar income, expenses, capital expenditure and cash budgets, budgeted income statement and budgeted balance sheet as per table 12.1 (p. 499).

In the following illustration, we are concerned with a summary of the steps that are taken by K.Q. Lattor Ltd in the preparation of the master budget. The master budget illustrated is prepared for the financial year and is subdivided into quarters. Work in process inventories are negligible for the company, so they are ignored here in order to concentrate on the basic principles of budgeting.

Sales budget for a retail or manufacturing entity

As noted earlier, virtually every phase of the master budget for retail and manufacturing entities depends on the sales volume forecast. The **sales budget** is prepared from the sales volume forecast. Detailed information concerning sales volume, selling prices and sales mix is presented in the sales budget. K.Q. Lattor Ltd has used the forecasting methods discussed earlier to develop the sales budget shown in figure 12.12. In addition, management has considered the influence of selling expenses such as advertising on the projected demand for the two products. The sales budget also furnishes the information required to prepare the cash receipts part of the cash budget shown later in figure 12.27 (p. 517). The sales budget will be the same regardless of whether K.Q. Lattor Ltd purchases or produces the calculators it sells.

Figure 12.12 Sales budget for a retail or manufacturing entity

K.Q. LATTOR LTD
Sales Budget
for the year ending 30 June 2014

	Quarter Sept.	Quarter Dec.	Quarter Mar.	Quarter June	Annual total
XS Calculator					
Budgeted sales units	4 000	6 000	6 500	5 000	21 500
Budgeted price per unit	$48	$48	$48	$48	$48
BUDGETED SALES	$192 000	$288 000	$312 000	$240 000	$1 032 000
Calculator Excite					
Budgeted sales units	6 000	8 000	8 500	7 000	29 500
Budgeted price per unit	$30	$30	$30	$30	$30
BUDGETED SALES	$180 000	$240 000	$255 000	$210 000	$ 885 000
TOTAL BUDGETED SALES	$372 000	$528 000	$567 000	$450 000	$1 917 000

To work through an example of budgeting for a manufacturing entity without going through an example of a retail entity, go direct to 'Production budget for a manufacturing entity' (p. 509).

Purchases budget for a retail entity

Once the sales budget has been prepared, the purchase requirements for the period are determined as:

$$\text{Purchase units required} = \text{Forecast sales units} + \text{Desired ending inventory} - \text{Beginning inventory}$$

K.Q. Lattor Ltd plans its inventory level for each type of calculator so as to have an adequate number of units available to satisfy the expected sales demand for the current quarter and have enough ending inventory for future sales. The desired ending inventory for a particular quarter is set equal to the expected sales for the *first month of the succeeding quarter*. For example, the desired ending inventory for XS Calculators at the end of the first quarter is set equal to the sales expected for October. This policy has enabled the company to maintain an adequate but not excessive ending inventory. Since the purchases budget is developed before the budget year starts, the beginning inventory has to be estimated. The purchases budget in units for the year ending 30 June 2014 is shown in figure 12.13.

Figure 12.13 Purchases budget in units for a retail entity

K.Q. LATTOR LTD
Purchases Budget in Units
for the year ending 30 June 2014

	Quarter				Annual total
	Sept.	Dec.	Mar.	June	
XS Calculator					
Forecast sales units (figure 12.12)	4 000	6 000	6 500	5 000	21 500
Desired ending inventory	3 000	2 150	1 650	1 950	1 950
Total units needed	7 000	8 150	8 150	6 950	23 450
Beginning inventory	1 350	3 000	2 150	1 650	1 350
PURCHASES REQUIRED — UNITS	5 650	5 150	6 000	5 300	22 100
Calculator Excite					
Forecast sales units (figure 12.12)	6 000	8 000	8 500	7 000	29 500
Desired ending inventory	2 500	3 000	2 500	2 400	2 400
Total units needed	8 500	11 000	11 000	9 400	31 900
Beginning inventory	2 000	2 500	3 000	2 500	2 000
PURCHASES REQUIRED — UNITS	6 500	8 500	8 000	6 900	29 900

Once the purchases requirements in units have been determined, they need to be converted to dollars. K.Q. Lattor Ltd can purchase calculators from a supplier for the following prices:

XS Calculator $35
Calculator Excite $19

Figure 12.14 Purchases budget in dollars for a retail entity

The purchases budget in dollars for the year ending 30 June 2014 is shown in figure 12.14.

K.Q. LATTOR LTD
Purchases Budget in Dollars
for the year ending 30 June 2014

	Quarter				Annual total
	Sept.	Dec.	Mar.	June	
XS Calculator					
Purchases required — units (figure 12.13)	5 650	5 150	6 000	5 300	22 100
Purchase price per unit	$35	$35	$35	$35	$35
	$197 750	$180 250	$210 000	$185 500	$ 773 500
Calculator Excite					
Purchases required — units (figure 12.13)	6 500	8 500	8 000	6 900	29 900
Purchase price per unit	$19	$19	$19	$19	$19
	$123 500	$161 500	$152 000	$131 100	$ 568 100
TOTAL PURCHASES	**$321 250**	**$341 750**	**$362 000**	**$316 600**	**$1 341 600**

Cost of sales budget for a retail entity

Having calculated the purchases of inventory for the budget period, it is now possible to construct a cost of sales budget for a retail entity as shown in figure 12.15.

Figure 12.15 Cost of sales budget for a retail entity

K.Q. LATTOR LTD
Cost of Sales Budget
for the year ending 30 June 2014

	XS Calculator	Calculator Excite	Total
Beginning inventory	$ 47 250[(a)]	$ 38 000[(b)]	$ 85 250
Add: Purchases (figure 12.14)	773 500	568 100	1 341 600
Less: Ending inventory	(68 250)[(c)]	(45 600)[(d)]	(113 850)
COST OF SALES	$752 500	$560 500	$1 313 000

(a) 1350 units (figure 12.13) × $35.
(b) 2000 units (figure 12.13) × $19.
(c) 1950 units (figure 12.13) × $35.
(d) 2400 units (figure 12.13) × $19.

To avoid working through an example of budgeting for a manufacturing entity, go to the section on 'Selling and distribution expenses budget for a retail or manufacturing entity' (p. 512).

Production budget for a manufacturing entity

A **production budget** for a manufacturing entity is prepared in exactly the same way as the purchases budget (in units) for a retail entity shown in figure 12.13. If K.Q. Lattor Ltd manufactures the calculators, the company needs to budget to produce 22 100 of the XS Calculator and 29 900 of the Calculator Excite. However, rather than simply preparing a purchases budget in dollars, as shown in figure 12.14, K.Q. Lattor Ltd has to prepare manufacturing budgets for direct materials, direct labour and factory overhead, as shown in figure 12.3 and table 12.1 (p. 499).

Before these budgets can be prepared, the costs of production need to be considered. The XS Calculator has more functions than the Calculator Excite and so requires more direct raw materials in terms of processing chips. It also takes longer for the direct labour to complete than a Calculator Excite. Specialised processing chips are purchased by K.Q. Lattor Ltd and converted into calculators with skilled labour and a highly automated manufacturing process. The following data represent the estimated direct costs for the production of each calculator:

	XS Calculator	**Calculator Excite**
Direct materials — processing chips	5 @ $3.00 each	3 @ $3.00 each
Direct labour	1 hour @ $12 per hour	$1/_2$ hour @ $12 per hour

The first of the manufacturing budgets is the direct materials budget.

Direct materials budget for a manufacturing entity

Once the production requirements have been determined, the **direct materials budget** can be developed. Inventory level decisions again must be made by management in the preparation of this budget. Budgeted direct materials purchases are calculated using the same approach as for the purchases budget as:

$$\begin{array}{c} \text{Budgeted} \\ \text{purchases in} \\ \text{units} \end{array} = \begin{array}{c} \text{Budgeted} \\ \text{direct materials} \\ \text{usage} \end{array} + \begin{array}{c} \text{Desired} \\ \text{ending direct} \\ \text{materials} \end{array} - \begin{array}{c} \text{Beginning} \\ \text{direct} \\ \text{materials} \end{array}$$

The direct materials are determined first in terms of processing chips required and then converted to dollars by multiplying by the appropriate costs. K.Q. Lattor Ltd requires five processing chips for the XS Calculator and three for the Calculator Excite. Each processing chip costs $3. The company also uses a 1-month supply for the estimate of desired ending direct materials inventory, which is approximately one-third of the following quarter's requirements. The total purchases of direct materials are $599 400 (110 300 processing chips @ $3 + 89 500 processing chips @ $3), as shown in figure 12.16.

Figure 12.16 Direct materials budget for a manufacturing entity

K.Q. LATTOR LTD Direct Materials Budget for the year ending 30 June 2014					
	Quarter				Annual total
	Sept.	Dec.	Mar.	June	
XS Calculator					
Production units required (figure 12.13)	5 650	5 150	6 000	5 300	22 100
Processing chips per unit	5	5	5	5	5
Processing chips required	20 250	25 750	30 000	26 500	110 500
Desired ending materials (assumed)	8 500	10 000	8 800	9 200	9 200
Processing chips needed	36 750	35 750	38 800	35 700	119 700
Beginning materials	9 400	8 500	10 000	8 800	9 400
Purchases required — processing chips	27 350	27 250	28 800	26 900	110 300
Cost per processing chip	$3	$3	$3	$3	$3
COST OF PURCHASES	$ 82 050	$ 81 750	$ 86 400	$ 80 700	$330 900
Calculator Excite					
Production units required (figure 12.13)	6 500	8 500	8 000	6 900	29 900
Processing chips per unit	3	3	3	3	3
Processing chips required	19 500	25 500	24 000	20 700	89 700
Desired ending materials (assumed)	8 500	8 000	6 900	6 500	6 500
Processing chips needed	28 000	33 500	30 900	27 200	96 200
Beginning materials	6 700	8 500	8 000	6 900	6 700
Purchases required — processing chips	21 300	25 000	22 900	20 300	89 500
Cost per processing chip	$3	$3	$3	$3	$3
COST OF PURCHASES	$ 63 900	$ 75 000	$ 68 700	$ 60 900	$268 500
TOTAL PURCHASES	**$145 950**	**$156 750**	**$155 100**	**$141 600**	**$599 400**

Direct labour budget for a manufacturing entity

The **direct labour budget** is also developed from the production budget and provides important information concerning the size of the labour force needed each quarter. The main objective is to maintain a labour force large enough to satisfy the production requirements but *not so large that it results in costly idle time*.

The first step in the development of the direct labour budget is to estimate the time needed to produce each type of calculator. For one XS Calculator, 1 hour is required, and half an hour is needed for a Calculator Excite. The total labour hours required are calculated by multiplying these hourly measures by the respective number of calculators to be produced. For the year, 37 050 direct labour hours are projected. Multiplication of the total direct labour hours by the hourly labour rate of $12 gives the budgeted total direct labour cost, which amounts to $444 600 for the year, as shown in figure 12.17.

Figure 12.17 Direct labour budget for a manufacturing entity

K.Q. LATTOR LTD
Direct Labour Budget
for the year ending 30 June 2014

	Sept.	Dec.	Mar.	June	Annual total
			Quarter		
XS Calculator					
Production units required (figure 12.13)	5 650	5 150	6 000	5 300	22 100
Direct labour hours per unit	1	1	1	1	1
Total hours required	5 650	5 150	6 000	5 300	22 100
Labour rate per hour	$12	$12	$12	$12	$12
DIRECT LABOUR COST	$ 67 800	$ 61 800	$ 72 000	$ 63 600	$265 200
Calculator Excite					
Production units required (figure 12.13)	6 500	8 500	8 000	6 900	29 900
Direct labour hours per unit	0.50	0.50	0.50	0.50	0.50
Total hours required	3 250	4 250	4 000	3 450	14 950
Labour rate per hour	$12	$12	$12	$12	$12
DIRECT LABOUR COST	$ 39 000	$ 51 000	$ 48 000	$ 41 400	$179 400
TOTAL DIRECT LABOUR COST	$106 800	$112 800	$120 000	$105 000	$444 600
TOTAL DIRECT LABOUR HOURS	8 900	9 400	10 000	8 750	37 050

Factory overhead budget for a manufacturing entity

K.Q. Lattor Ltd applies factory overhead to inventory on the basis of the 37 050 budgeted direct labour hours found in the direct labour budget. Total budgeted factory overhead is $296 400, so the predetermined overhead rate to be used for product costing purposes is $8 per direct labour hour ($296 400 ÷ 37 050). The company distinguishes between variable and fixed factory overhead. As seen in figure 12.18, variable factory overhead costs total $88 920 for the year, or $2.40 per budgeted direct labour hour ($88 920 ÷ 37 050). The total fixed factory overhead costs are $207 480 or $5.60 per budgeted direct labour hour ($207 480 ÷ 37 050). For every hour of direct labour recorded during actual production, $8 is applied for factory overhead.

The fixed portion of the **factory overhead budget** is determined by spreading the annual fixed costs equally over the four quarters, since we assume that K.Q. Lattor Ltd does not have any seasonal differences in its fixed costs. As a result, the fixed overhead costs are $51 870 per quarter. Cost behaviour analysis has shown that the variable costs fluctuate with the production level per quarter, based on the rates shown below.

Overhead item	Estimated variable rate per direct labour hour
Indirect labour	$0.30
Indirect materials	0.20
Employee benefits	1.50
Electricity	0.40
	$2.40

The direct labour hours of 8900, 9400, 10 000 and 8750 for the four quarters respectively are multiplied by the variable rates to determine the budgeted variable overhead costs per quarter as shown in figure 12.18 (p. 512).

Figure 12.18 Factory overhead budget for a manufacturing entity

K.Q. LATTOR LTD
Factory Overhead Budget
for the year ending 30 June 2014

	Quarter				Annual total
	Sept.	Dec.	Mar.	June	
Variable costs					
Indirect labour	$ 2 670	$ 2 820	$ 3 000	$ 2 625	$ 11 115
Employee benefits	13 350	14 100	15 000	13 125	55 575
Indirect materials	1 780	1 880	2 000	1 750	7 410
Electricity	3 560	3 760	4 000	3 500	14 820
TOTAL VARIABLE COSTS	21 360	22 560	24 000	21 000	88 920
Fixed costs					
Supervisors' salaries	22 000	22 000	22 000	22 000	88 000
Depreciation	9 600	9 600	9 600	9 600	38 400
Rates	3 250	3 250	3 250	3 250	13 000
Insurance	2 500	2 500	2 500	2 500	10 000
Maintenance	5 700	5 700	5 700	5 700	22 800
Electricity	5 160	5 160	5 160	5 160	20 640
Other	3 660	3 660	3 660	3 660	14 640
TOTAL FIXED COSTS	51 870	51 870	51 870	51 870	207 480
TOTAL FACTORY OVERHEAD	$73 230	$74 430	$75 870	$72 870	$296 400
Direct labour hours (figure 12.17)	8 900	9 400	10 000	8 750	37 050
FACTORY OVERHEAD RATE PER DIRECT LABOUR HOUR					$ 8.00

Cost of sales budget for a manufacturing entity

The **cost of sales budget** is shown in figure 12.19. The unit costs of $35 and $19 for the XS Calculator and the Calculator Excite respectively can be multiplied by the number of units sold to determine the cost of sales for each product. The budgeted sales units of XS Calculators are 21 500, so the cost of sales is $752 500, and 29 500 Calculator Excites are planned at a cost of $560 500. The total budgeted cost of sales is $1 313 000. The same result is obtained for each product by working through the traditional form of calculating the cost of sales as shown in figure 12.19.

Selling and distribution expenses budget for a retail or manufacturing entity

Having established the cost of sales for either a retail or manufacturing entity, the remainder of the budgeting process is similar regardless of whether K.Q. Lattor Ltd purchases or manufactures its goods for sale.

We noted earlier that the influence of selling and distribution expenses on the sales budget must be evaluated carefully. The management of K.Q. Lattor Ltd does this by preparing the **selling and distribution expenses budget** along with the sales budget, and the expected effect on sales from the selling effort is considered when the sales volume is forecast. We assume in our illustration that all selling and distribution expenses are fixed and amount to $128 600 spread evenly over the four quarters. The selling and distribution expenses budget shown in figure 12.20 is the same regardless of whether K.Q. Lattor Ltd is a retail or manufacturing entity.

Administrative expenses budget for a retail or manufacturing entity

The **administrative expenses budget** provides a listing of the administrative expense estimates for the period. The total administrative expenses for K.Q. Lattor Ltd of $100 004 are fixed and spread evenly among the quarters, as shown in figure 12.21 (p. 514).

Figure 12.19 Cost of sales budget for a manufacturing entity

K.Q. LATTOR LTD
Cost of Sales Budget
for the year ending 30 June 2014

	XS Calculator	Calculator Excite	Total
Beginning finished goods (fig. 12.15)	$ 47 250[(a)]	$ 38 000[(e)]	$ 85 250
Direct materials used			
Beginning materials	$ 28 200[(b)]	$ 20 100[(f)]	$ 48 300
Budgeted purchases (fig. 12.16)	330 900	268 500	599 400
Ending materials	(27 600)[(c)]	(19 500)[(g)]	(47 100)
Direct materials used	331 500	269 100	600 600
Direct labour (fig. 12.17)	265 200	179 400	444 600
Factory overhead			
(direct labour hours × $8)	176 800	119 600	296 400
Total manufacturing cost	773 500	568 100	1 341 600
Ending finished goods (fig. 12.15)	(68 250)[(d)]	(45 600)[(h)]	(113 850)
COST OF SALES	$752 500	$560 500	$1 313 000

Unit costs per product			
Direct materials	5 processing chips	3 processing chips	
	@ $3 = $15.00	@ $3 = $ 9.00	
Direct labour	1 hour @ $12 = 12.00	0.5 hours @ $12 = 6.00	
Factory overhead	1 hour @ $8 = 8.00	0.5 hours @ $8 = 4.00	
UNIT COST	$35.00	$19.00	

(a) 1350 calculators (figure 12.13) @ $35 = $47 250.
(b) 9400 chips (figure 12.16) @ $3 = $28 200.
(c) 9200 chips (figure 12.16) @ $3 = $27 600.
(d) 1950 calculators (figure 12.13) @ $35 = $68 250.

(e) 2000 calculators (figure 12.13) @ $19 = $38 000.
(f) 6700 chips (figure 12.16) @ $3 = $20 100.
(g) 6500 chips (figure 12.16) @ $3 = $19 500.
(h) 2400 calculators (figure 12.13) @ $19 = $45 600.

Figure 12.20 Selling and distribution expenses budget for a retail or manufacturing entity

K.Q. LATTOR LTD
Selling and Distribution Expenses Budget
for the year ending 30 June 2014

Selling and distribution expenses	Quarter Sept.	Dec.	Mar.	June	Annual total
Sales salaries	$23 450	$23 450	$23 450	$23 450	$ 93 800
Depreciation	1 200	1 200	1 200	1 200	4 800
Advertising	4 500	4 500	4 500	4 500	18 000
Travel	1 200	1 200	1 200	1 200	4 800
Entertainment	800	800	800	800	3 200
Insurance	320	320	320	320	1 280
Postage and freight	380	380	380	380	1 520
Electricity	200	200	200	200	800
Other	100	100	100	100	400
TOTAL SELLING AND DISTRIBUTION EXPENSES	**$32 150**	**$32 150**	**$32 150**	**$32 150**	**$ 128 600**

Finance and other expenses budget for a retail or manufacturing entity

The **finance and other expenses budget** provides a listing of the finance and other expenses such as discount allowed, interest expense and rent expense estimated to be incurred during the budget

Figure 12.21 Administrative expenses budget for a retail or manufacturing entity

K.Q. LATTOR LTD
Administrative Expenses Budget
for the year ending 30 June 2014

Administrative expenses	Sept.	Dec.	Mar.	June	Annual total
Management salaries	$21 441	$21 441	$21 441	$21 441	$ 85 764
Clerical salaries	2 500	2 500	2 500	2 500	10 000
Depreciation	500	500	500	500	2 000
Insurance	130	130	130	130	520
Postage and freight	160	160	160	160	640
Supplies	150	150	150	150	600
Other	120	120	120	120	480
TOTAL ADMINISTRATIVE EXPENSES	**$25 001**	**$25 001**	**$25 001**	**$25 001**	**$ 100 004**

period. Although this budget would normally be part of a master budget, it is assumed in our illustration that finance expenses expected for the budget period were negligible.

Budgeted income statement for a retail or manufacturing entity

The budgeted income statement shown in figure 12.22 is developed from the individual budgets discussed previously. Note that the budgeted income statement is the same for a retail entity as for a manufacturing entity.

Figure 12.22 Budgeted income statement for a retail or manufacturing entity

K.Q. LATTOR LTD
Budgeted Income Statement
for the year ending 30 June 2014

	XS Calculator	Calculator Excite	Total
Sales — units (figure 12.12)	21 500	29 500	51 000
Sales — dollars (figure 12.12)	$1 032 000	$885 000	$1 917 000
Cost of sales (figure 12.15 or 12.19)	752 500	560 500	1 313 000
GROSS PROFIT	279 500	324 500	604 000
Expenses:			
Selling and distribution expenses (figure 12.20)			128 600
Administrative expenses (figure 12.21)			100 004
			228 604
PROFIT BEFORE TAX			375 396
Income tax expense (30%)			112 619
PROFIT			$ 262 777

Management wanted to achieve a before-tax profit margin of 20% of sales and a before-tax return on average equity in the range of 23% to 25%. The before-tax profit is budgeted at $375 396, which is about 20% of sales and an approximate 46% before-tax return on average equity. An average equity is calculated from the balance sheet presented later by adding the beginning and ending balances of equity for the year and dividing the result by two.

Financial budgets for retail and manufacturing entities

With the preparation of the operating budgets now completed, the financial budgets within the master budget can be prepared. These budgets are illustrated on the following pages.

Capital expenditure budget for a retail or manufacturing entity

The **capital expenditure budget** (figure 12.23) included in the master budget shows the acquisition of facilities and equipment planned for the period. K.Q. Lattor Ltd will finance capital expenditure of $65 000 from internal sources during the year ending 30 June 2014.

Figure 12.23 Capital expenditure budget for a retail or manufacturing entity

K.Q. LATTOR LTD
Capital Expenditure Budget
for the year ending 30 June 2014

	Quarter				Annual total
	Sept.	Dec.	Mar.	June	
Manufacturing equipment — machines		$25 000		$25 000	$50 000
Office equipment — filing cabinets			$ 1 000		1 000
Sales equipment — motor vehicle			14 000		14 000
TOTAL CAPITAL EXPENDITURE	**$ 0**	**$25 000**	**$15 000**	**$25 000**	**$65 000**

Cash budget for a retail or manufacturing entity

The sales and expenses budgets must be translated into cash receipts and cash payments from operations for financial planning purposes. This process is similar regardless of whether the company purchases goods for resale or manufactures them, except for the cash flows relating to the cost of sales. If K.Q. Lattor Ltd manufactures the calculators, then it will need to budget for cash flows for direct materials, direct labour and factory overhead rather than simply purchases.

To simplify the preparation of the cash budget, it is useful to prepare schedules of estimated collections of sales and estimated payments for expenses. K.Q. Lattor Ltd has analysed its previous experience with cash receipts from sales and has decided that 70% of each quarter's sales should be collected in the current quarter and 30% in the following quarter. Bad debts are negligible, so they are ignored. Using this information, K.Q. Lattor Ltd can prepare a schedule of estimated collections of sales as shown in figure 12.24.

Figure 12.24 Schedule of estimated cash collections from sales for a retail or manufacturing entity

K.Q. LATTOR LTD
Schedule of Estimated Cash Collections from Sales
for the year ending 30 June 2014

Quarter	Sales	Cash collections			
		Sept.	Dec.	Mar.	June
June 2013	$586 666	$176 000			
September (figure 12.12)	372 000	260 400[a]	$111 600[b]		
December (figure 12.12)	528 000		369 600	$158 400	
March	567 000			396 900	$170 100
June	450 000				315 000
COLLECTIONS FROM SALES		**$436 400**	**$481 200**	**$555 300**	**$485 100**

(a) $372 000 × 70% = $260 400.
(b) $372 000 × 30% = $111 600.

The next step is to prepare a schedule of estimated payments for expenses. The company projects that 80% of its materials purchases will be paid for in the quarter in which they are incurred and the remaining 20% in the following quarter. All other expenses are paid for in the quarter in which they are incurred. Depreciation expense in factory overhead, selling and distribution, and administrative expenses is ignored in the cash budget since it is a non-cash expense. Figure 12.25 assumes K.Q. Lattor Ltd manufactures the calculators — if it purchases them, the schedule would include purchases of calculators rather than direct materials, direct labour and factory overhead. Using this information, K.Q. Lattor Ltd can now prepare a schedule of estimated payments for expenses as illustrated in figure 12.25 (p. 516).

Figure 12.25 Schedule of estimated cash payments for expenses for a manufacturing entity

K.Q. LATTOR LTD
Schedule of Estimated Cash Payments for Expenses
for the year ending 30 June 2014

	Sept.	Dec.	Mar.	June	Annual total
	Quarter				
Direct materials purchased in:					
Current quarter (80% of figure 12.16)	$116 760	$125 400	$124 080	$113 280	$ 479 520
Previous quarter (20% of figure 12.16)	33 000	29 190	31 350	31 020	124 560
TOTAL CASH FOR MATERIALS PURCHASES	149 760	154 590	155 430	144 300	604 080
Direct labour (figure 12.17)	106 800	112 800	120 000	105 000	444 600
Factory overhead (figure 12.18)[a]	63 630	64 830	66 270	63 270	258 000
Selling and distribution expenses (figure 12.20)[a]	30 950	30 950	30 950	30 950	123 800
Administrative expenses (figure 12.21)[a]	24 501	24 501	24 501	24 501	98 004
BUDGETED EXPENSE PAYMENTS	**$375 641**	**$387 671**	**$397 151**	**$368 021**	**$1 528 484**

(a) These expenses from figures 12.18, 12.20 and 12.21 have been reduced by the amount of depreciation; for example, $63 630 = $73 230 − $9600 (depreciation).

K.Q. Lattor Ltd is now in a position to prepare its overall cash budget. The business expects to begin the year with $62 000 cash and end it with $222 516 if it manufactures the calculators. Dividends of $100 000 will be paid during the year. An estimated income tax payment of $26 000, based on the income tax expense for 2012–13 profits, will be paid in each quarter. The cash budget shown in figure 12.26 is for use by internal management.

Figure 12.26 Cash budget for a manufacturing entity

K.Q. LATTOR LTD
Cash Budget
for the year ending 30 June 2014

	Sept.	Dec.	Mar.	June	Annual total
	Quarter				
Cash at bank, beginning balance	$ 62 000	$ 96 759	$ 89 288	$206 437	$ 62 000
Collections from sales (figure 12.24)	436 400	481 200	555 300	485 100	1 958 000
Total cash available	498 400	577 959	644 588	691 537	2 020 000
Estimated cash payments					
Budgeted expense payments (figure 12.25)	375 641	387 671	397 151	368 021	1 528 484
Capital expenditure (figure 12.23)	0	25 000	15 000	25 000	65 000
Dividends	0	50 000	0	50 000	100 000
Estimated income tax payments	26 000	26 000	26 000	26 000	104 000
Total expected payments	401 641	488 671	438 151	469 021	1 797 484
CASH AT BANK, ENDING BALANCE	**$ 96 759**	**$ 89 288**	**$206 437**	**$222 516**	**$ 222 516**

Budgeted balance sheet

Because the budget for the year ending 30 June 2014 is prepared by K.Q. Lattor Ltd *before* the end of the year ending 30 June 2013, the balance sheet as at 30 June 2013 must be estimated. It is shown in figure 12.27 and provides the beginning balances for the 2013–14 budgeting process. Once the actual results are known, the beginning balance sheet may be revised if significant differences occur. The budgeted balance sheet at 30 June 2014 also is presented in figure 12.27 and is the result of translating the beginning balances through the 2014 budgeting process into ending balances. For example, the cash at bank balance comes from the cash budget (figure 12.26). The accounts receivable balance of $135 000 is 30% of sales in the June quarter ($450 000) (figure 12.12) that have not been collected by year-end. Finished goods inventory of $113 850 comes from the cost of sales budget (figure 12.19), and the raw materials inventory of $47 100 comes from the raw materials purchases budget (figure 12.16). Increases in building and equipment are calculated by adding budgeted capital expenditure of $65 000 (figure 12.23) to the opening balance for the year, and accumulated depreciation is the opening balance plus the depreciation expense of $45 200 from the various expense budgets (figures 12.18, 12.20 and 12.21). Accounts payable of $28 320 is the 20% of the June quarter raw materials purchases that won't be paid until the following budget period (figure 12.16). The current tax liability of $112 619 comes from the income statement budget (figure 12.22). Finally, budgeted retained earnings are calculated by adding the budgeted profit of $262 777 (figure 12.22) to the opening retained earnings and deducting the budgeted dividends of $100 000 as per the cash budget (figure 12.26).

If K.Q. Lattor Ltd were to purchase the calculators rather than manufacturing them, the financial position would not include raw materials inventory. In most other respects the balance sheets would be very similar.

Figure 12.27 Budgeted balance sheet for a manufacturing entity

K.Q. LATTOR LTD Budgeted Balance Sheet as at 30 June 2014 (with estimates as at 30 June 2013 shown)				
	2013		2014	
CURRENT ASSETS				
Cash at bank (figure 12.26)	$ 62 000		$222 516	
Accounts receivable (figure 12.12)	176 000		135 000[a]	
Finished goods inventory (figure 12.19)	85 250		113 850	
Raw materials inventory	48 300		47 100[b]	
TOTAL CURRENT ASSETS		$371 550		$ 518 466
NON-CURRENT ASSETS				
Land	110 000		110 000	
Building and equipment	689 585		754 585[c]	
Accumulated depreciation	(280 000)	409 585	(325 200)[d]	429 385
TOTAL NON-CURRENT ASSETS		519 585		539 385
TOTAL ASSETS		891 135		1 057 851
CURRENT LIABILITIES				
Accounts payable	33 000		28 320[e]	
Current tax liability (figure 12.22)	104 000		112 619	
TOTAL CURRENT LIABILITIES		137 000		140 939
NET ASSETS		$754 135		$ 916 912
EQUITY				
Share capital		$100 000		$ 100 000
Retained earnings		654 135		816 912[f]
TOTAL EQUITY		$754 135		$ 916 912

(a) June sales $450 000 × 30% = $135 000.
(b) Ending raw materials units (9200 + 6500) (figure 12.16) × $3.00 = $47 100.
(c) Opening balance $689 585 + purchases (figure 12.23) $65 000 = $754 585.
(d) Opening balance $280 000 + depreciation $38 400 + $4800 + $2000 = $325 200 (figures 12.18, 12.20, 12.21).
(e) June purchases of direct materials $141 500 (figure 12.16) × 20% = $28 320.
(f) Opening balance $654 135 + profit $262 777 − dividends $100 000 = $816 912.

Management must evaluate the budgeted balance sheet carefully to ensure it reflects the desired financial position. If the projected financial position is unacceptable, revisions to the master budget should be made.

Computers play an extensive role in the planning phase of budget development. Spreadsheet packages are used to set up budgeting models and, once variables are entered, the package can generate budgeted financial statements like the ones shown in this chapter. Furthermore, variables can be altered (e.g. the sales price of a calculator) and the effects of such a change are monitored to see how sensitive financial data (e.g. profit) would be to a change in variables. Management can find the expected effect on profits and cash in a few minutes through the use of spreadsheet packages when 'what if?' questions are asked. The use of electronic spreadsheets is very common in the budgeting task, and is a powerful way of providing budget data, as information is gradually merged from lower chains of authority up to the requirements of top management. Integrated financial planning packages also exist for the purpose of preparing budgets.

Most computerised accounting packages integrate budgets into the accounting system, and will automatically prepare reports comparing actual results with the budget at any point of time. MYOB Accounting illustrated in chapter 7 incorporates this budgeting and reporting feature.

12.9 Financial control with budgeting

The control phase of budgeting consists of three steps:
- comparing the actual financial performance with the budget estimates
- identifying any significant variances
- deciding what management action should be taken.

Budget performance reports that show significant differences, or variances, between the actual and planned performance provide the feedback necessary to evaluate the financial results on the basis of management by exception. This is a part of the accountability objective of financial reporting.

Unfavourable variances are investigated to determine the cause and whether corrective action can be taken to improve the future performance. Even significantly large favourable variances should be evaluated to be sure the related estimates were correct. If they were too easy to attain, the estimates should be changed for the future. The variances may be due to increases in efficiency that can then be incorporated into future planning. The performance reports are prepared for the business as a whole and for its various segments on a responsibility accounting basis. Only controllable revenues and costs should be included in the performance reports; it would be unreasonable to hold managers accountable for uncontrollable items.

To illustrate the basic format of a performance report, figure 12.28 shows one prepared for the sales manager of K.Q. Lattor Ltd. The report includes the controllable costs of the sales department during the first quarter. The 'actual' column shows the actual costs incurred by the department, and the 'budget' column contains the budget estimates for each category. The *U* indicates an unfavourable variance, which results in a decrease in actual profit below budgeted profit, and the *F* refers to a favourable variance, which results in an increase in actual profit above budgeted profit. The department incurred expenses that exceeded its budget by $2535. Unless sales are substantially higher because of the increased spending, these results will have an adverse effect on overall profits and will require corrective action if the financial goals of future quarters are to be achieved.

Figure 12.28 Budget performance report

K.Q. LATTOR LTD
Sales Department
Budget Performance Report
for the quarter ending 30 September 2013

Controllable expenses	Budgeted	Actual	Variance
Advertising	$ 4 500	$ 5 200	$ 700 U
Sales salaries	23 450	24 550	1 100 U
Travel	1 200	1 750	550 U
Entertainment	800	980	180 U
Electricity	200	210	10 U
Other	100	95	5 F
	$30 250	$32 785	$2 535 U

Financial control with budgeting has improved considerably owing to the timeliness of information provided by budget performance reports prepared by computerised accounting systems. Feedback reports showing differences between actual and budgeted figures are processed very quickly and allow management to act more promptly to investigate significant exceptions. Consequently, management efficiency is increased, and appropriate corrective action can be taken.

KEY TERMS

Administrative expenses budget, p. 512
Budget, p. 494
Budget performance report, p. 518
Budgeting period, p. 494
Capital expenditure budget, p. 515
Cash budget, p. 503

Cost of sales budget, p. 512
Direct labour budget, p. 510
Direct materials budget, p. 509
Factory overhead budget, p. 511
Finance and other expenses budget, p. 513
Financial budgets, p. 498
Goal congruence, p. 496

Master budget, p. 497
Operating budgets, p. 498
Production budget, p. 509
Purchases budget, p. 499
Sales budget, p. 507
Selling and distribution expenses budget, p. 512
Service income budget, p. 501

DISCUSSION QUESTIONS

1. You are newly employed by Bonza Resources Ltd to promote its environmental approach to mining for minerals. In its annual report and promotional material, Bonza Resources Ltd states that protecting the environment while mining is one of its most important goals. This is what attracted you to your new position. Having completed an accounting subject during your marketing degree, rather than simply accepting the budget at face value you decide to scrutinise it to see what you can learn about your new employer. You find no resources budgeted for revegetating and regenerating old mine sites, and mining practices appear to be based on minimising costs rather than minimising damage to the environment. However, you do find budgeted expenditure for lobbying politicians to grant mining rights in national parks, and you are pleased to see a large amount of resources allocated to marketing the company's positive environmental image.

   Discuss whether what the budget communicates is consistent with the stated position on environmental issues of Bonza Resources Ltd and how this might affect your continuing employment with the company.

2. As a student, consider what assessment you would want for the course you are studying and what achievement levels you would set if you could participate in the assessment setting process. For example, how much continuous assessment would you set and how much of your assessment would be exams? Would you make it hard to meet the assessment criteria or would you set a low pass mark so that you did not have to dedicate much time to your study? Now consider whether your approach to participation in budgeting would be similar. What does this tell you about the risks to an organisation of such an approach to budgeting?

3. The cornerstone of any budgetary system is the sales or income forecast. The level of sales is extremely difficult to forecast with any degree of accuracy, and in that case it could be argued that the master budget which is based on this forecast is fundamentally flawed. Discuss.

4. The manager of a medium-sized business was heard to remark: 'My business is one that involves too many uncertainties for a budget to be of any use to me.' Is the stance taken by the manager reasonable? Discuss.

5. Because master budgets for service organisations are more straightforward than those for manufacturing entities, it is not as important to budget for service organisations. Discuss.

6. The manager of High Tech Industries Ltd made the following comment: 'In my business everything is computerised. Everything is online and I have at my disposal at all times up-to-date information. I know how we are going at any one time, therefore there is no need for a budgetary system.' Discuss.

7. 'A complete budgetary system can be costly. One solution to this problem is to prepare only a cash budget.' Would you agree? Explain your answer.

8. 'As I see it, budgeting boils down to taking the results of the last reporting period and adjusting the data for the new reporting period. Budgets based on past performance are of little value. Therefore I cannot justify the setting up of a budgetary system because costs would appear to exceed benefits.' Discuss.

9. 'The problem with budgets is if you achieve the budget targets in one year, top management then increases its expectations of you in the subsequent years.' In this context it is sometimes argued that budgets can act as a motivator or demotivator of management. Discuss the above comment.

EXERCISES

LO 7

Exercise 12.1   INCOME BUDGET FOR A LAW FIRM

Mason, Mason and Mason IR are three generations of the one family involved in providing industrial relations services for nearly 50 years. The firm is preparing its fees budget for the year ending 30 June 2014. They budget on a quarterly basis in a manner similar to figure 12.4 (p. 501). Craig Mason is the most senior member of the family and estimates that he will bill clients for 40 hours per week and have 2 weeks annual leave during January. Alexander Mason is Craig's son and intends to take 4 weeks leave during June and to bill clients for 42 hours per week. Craig's grandson, Samuel, is new to the firm and enjoys golfing on Friday afternoons and so usually bills clients for only 36 hours per week. Samuel intends to take 2 weeks leave beginning in April.

The charge-out rates per hour for each of the Masons are as follows:

Craig	$250 per hour
Alexander	$190 per hour
Samuel	$125 per hour

Required

Prepare the income budget for Mason, Mason and Mason IR for the year ending 30 June 2014, showing projected dollar service revenues by quarter as per the income statement. Assume there are 13 weeks in each of the four quarters of the year ending 30 June 2014.

LO 7

Exercise 12.2   BUDGETED CASH COLLECTIONS

Sporting Fixtures Pty Ltd, which develops and runs athletics training programs for primary schools, has budgeted revenue for the first 6 months of 2013 as follows:

Month	Budgeted revenue
January	$20 000
February	60 000
March	80 000
April	20 000
May	70 000
June	60 000

All revenue is provided on account and Sporting Fixtures Pty Ltd posts out the account statements on the last day of each month for that month's services. Schools are given 14 days to pay and 80% of schools pay within the month. The other 20% usually pay the following month. In December 2012 Sporting Fixtures Pty Ltd provided no training programs as the schools were preparing for the end-of-year break. The company also made sure that all outstanding balances owed by schools from November were paid before the end of December 2012.

Required

Prepare a schedule of estimated cash collections from revenue for the first 6 months of 2013 for Sporting Fixtures Pty Ltd.

Exercise 12.3 ESTIMATED CASH PAYMENTS

The following expenses budget has been prepared for PMI Travel Services for the year ending 30 June 2014:

PMI Travel Services
Expenses Budget
for the year ending 30 June 2014

| | Quarter | | | | Annual total |
	Sept.	Dec.	Mar.	June	
Salaries	$ 60 000	$ 80 000	$ 60 000	$ 60 000	$ 260 000
Secretarial wages	30 000	30 000	30 000	30 000	120 000
Commissions	40 000	70 000	30 000	40 000	180 000
Depreciation	18 000	18 000	18 000	18 000	72 000
Electricity	1 200	1 800	1 600	1 400	6 000
Insurance	4 000	4 000	4 000	4 000	16 000
Rent	24 000	24 000	26 000	26 000	100 000
Travel	42 000	28 000	56 000	46 000	172 000
TOTAL EXPENSES	$219 200	$255 800	$225 600	$225 400	$ 926 000

Salaries and secretarial wages are paid in the quarter in which they are incurred. Commissions, electricity and travel are paid in the quarter after they are incurred and in the June 2013 quarter were $35 000, $1500 and $42 000 respectively. Rent is paid in the quarter before it is incurred and for the September 2014 quarter is budgeted at $26 000. Insurance is paid annually at the beginning of January and is expected to remain at the same level for the next year.

Required
Prepare a schedule of estimated cash payments for expenses for PMI Travel Services for the year ending 30 June 2014.

Exercise 12.4 SALES BUDGET

Space Cadet Pty Ltd produces three toy space people, which are sold to local retail stores. The marketing department expects the following sales performance for the next year:

Toy	Selling price	Annual sales (units)
Space Boy	$50	80 000
Space Lady	60	60 000
Electric Space Man	90	40 000

The budgeted annual sales are distributed by month in the following percentages:

Month	Percentage of annual sales
January	2
February	3
March	4
April	4
May	5
June	12
July	6
August	6
September	8
October	12
November	16
December	22
	100%

The cash from sales is collected, 70% in the month of sale and the remainder in the following month.

Required

Prepare a monthly sales budget in units and dollars for all three space people combined for the months July to December. Show the receivables in the balance sheet at the end of July to December and the budgeted cash collections from sales for July to December.

Exercise 12.5 SALES BUDGET   LO 8

Lois Diaz, the marketing manager for Puerto Rico Pots Ltd, is preparing a sales budget for the year ended 30 June 2014. In reviewing the actual sales data for the previous year, the sales and marketing managers involved agree that the number of units of terracotta pots sold in the year ended 30 June 2014 should represent a 10% increase over the previous year's sales, plastic pots unit sales should increase 5%, and foam pots unit sales should decrease 4%. The managers' projections took into consideration the general economic conditions and expected changes in consumer preferences. The selling prices of terracotta and plastic pots will increase 10% and the selling price of foam pots will decline 5%. The percentages of each product's sales occurring in each quarter are as shown below:

	First quarter	Second quarter	Third quarter	Fourth quarter
Terracotta pots	25%	30%	15%	30%
Plastic pots	20%	25%	35%	20%
Foam pots	30%	20%	25%	25%

The actual product sales data for the year ended 30 June 2013 were:

	Unit selling price	Total sales
Terracotta pots	$25	$1 175 000
Plastic pots	15	540 000
Foam pots	12	504 000

Required

Prepare the marketing manager's sales budget for the year ended 30 June 2014, showing projected dollar sales by quarter. Round all calculations to the nearest dollar.

Exercise 12.6 PRODUCTION BUDGET   LO 8

Graham's Gardening Supplies grows two varieties of plants, Miniature and Standard. The projected operating data for the month of April are as follows:

	Miniature	Standard
Estimated beginning inventory (plants)	13 800	11 600
Estimated April sales (plants)	36 400	34 000
Desired ending inventory	15 200	10 800

Required

Prepare a production budget for April.

Exercise 12.7 PRODUCTION BUDGET   LO 8

Florida Motors Ltd produces two models of cars, Reliable and Luxury. The projected financial data for the month of January are as follows:

	Reliable	Luxury
Estimated beginning inventory (units)	2300	510
Estimated June sales (units)	8550	4320
Desired ending inventory (units)	2500	550

Required

Prepare a production budget for January.

Exercise 12.8 BUDGETED PURCHASES AND CASH PAYMENTS

The purchasing officer of Melbourne Department Store has prepared a purchases budget for the financial year ending 31 March 2014, based on the following data:

Purchases for February 2014		$320 000
Purchases for March 2014		340 320
Ending inventory — 31 March 2014		438 900
Budgeted sales:	April 2014	576 000
	May 2014	518 000
	June 2014	614 000
	July 2014	560 000

The cost of sales is 60% of sales, and the store's policy is to maintain a month-end inventory balance sufficient to meet the projected sales requirement for the following month. The store pays for 50% of its purchases in the month of purchase, 40% in the following month, and 10% in the second month following.

Required

A. Calculate the amount of purchases required for April and May of 2014.
B. Calculate the estimated cash payments in April and May for inventory purchased.

Exercise 12.9 DIRECT LABOUR BUDGET

Botton Manufacturing Pty Ltd has a policy of maintaining a finished goods inventory balance at the end of a month equal to 30% of the sales requirements of the following month. The ending inventory balance on 30 April included 1440 units, and the projected unit sales for May, June and July were 4800, 5200 and 5400 units respectively. The labour requirements per unit produced are as follows:

	Time required (hours)	Rate per hour
Welder	0.8	$25.00
Assembly labour	0.6	16.00
Painter	1.2	24.00

Required

Prepare a direct labour budget for May and June.

Exercise 12.10 DIRECT MATERIALS BUDGET

Wildfire Manufacturing Pty Ltd has a policy of maintaining a finished goods inventory balance at the end of a month equal to 40% of the sales requirements of the following month. The ending inventory balance on 31 July included 3200 units, and the projected sales for August, September and October were 8000, 9200 and 12 000 units respectively. The raw material requirements per unit produced are as follows:

	Quantity required	Cost per unit
Plastic	2.4 m²	$6 per m²
Motor	1	$12
Keyboard	1	$ 5

Required

Prepare a direct materials budget for August and September.

Exercise 12.11 DIRECT LABOUR AND FACTORY OVERHEAD BUDGET

Maximilian Ltd is in the process of preparing direct labour and factory overhead budgets for the year ending 30 June 2014. Relevant data are set out below:

Production: 12 000, 14 000, 14 500, 15 000 units per quarter
Direct labour: Hourly rate is $15 per hour. Each unit requires 1.5 hours of labour
Factory overhead:
   Fixed overhead costs per quarter —
     Salaries, $17 500
     Depreciation, $13 000
     Rent, $6000
   Variable overhead —
     Indirect materials, $1.50 per direct labour hour
     Indirect labour, $1.60 per direct labour hour
     Other, 30c per direct labour hour

Required

A. Prepare the direct labour budget by quarter for the year ending 30 June 2014.
B. Prepare the factory overhead budget by quarter for the year ended 30 June 2014.

Exercise 12.12 ESTIMATED CASH RECEIPTS

The budgeted monthly service revenues for KL Languages School for July to December are presented below. The firm's experience is that 80% of monthly invoicing for services is on a credit basis. All payments received from clients during the month of invoicing are subject to a 5% cash discount. Approximately 40% of the credit billings are collected in the month following the service, 35% are collected in the second month following, and 20% are collected in the third month after invoicing; 5% are never collected.

The projected service revenues by month are:

July	$36 000
August	48 000
September	48 000
October	52 000
November	36 000
December	24 000

Required

Calculate the forecast cash receipts from clients for October, November and December.

Exercise 12.13 ESTIMATED CASH RECEIPTS

The budgeted monthly service revenues for Sellit 2 M Pty Ltd marketing firm for January to June are as follows:

January	$84 000
February	76 000
March	82 000
April	86 000
May	90 000
June	96 000

All of the firm's invoicing for services is on a credit basis. All payments received from clients on time receive a 3% discount. All fees are due the month after the services are performed. Approximately 60% of the credit billings are collected in the month following the service, 25% are collected in the second month following, and 10% are collected in the third month after invoicing; 5% are never collected. Ignore GST.

Required

Calculate the forecast cash receipts from clients for April, May and June.

Exercise 12.14 BUDGET PERFORMANCE REPORT

Orlando International High School has used the following budgeted amounts for its controllable costs during 2014:

Cost items	Fixed amount	Variable cost per student enrolled
Administration salaries	$120 000	$ 2.40
Electricity	42 200	0.72
Maintenance	40 000	0.80
Supplies	36 600	3.20
Copying	12 000	20.00
Government charges	52 000	—

The actual enrolment for the school for the year was 1500 students. The actual costs incurred for the year were as follows:

Administration salaries	$125 800
Electricity	41 380
Maintenance	41 400
Supplies	43 200
Copying	45 200
Government charges	48 000

Required

Prepare a budget performance report for 2014 by preparing a budget for each cost item based on its fixed cost plus the variable cost per student multiplied by the actual number of students enrolled. Compare this budget for 1500 students with the actual costs incurred.

Exercise 12.15 BUDGET PERFORMANCE REPORT

D & M Holiday Cabins has prepared the following budgeted amounts for its costs for 2013:

Costs	Fixed amount	Variable cost per cabin night let
Wages	$128 000	$2.00
Electricity	24 000	1.00
Cleaning	32 000	5.00
Gas	8 400	0.50
Water	15 600	0.20
Maintenance	4 800	1.20

The number of cabin nights let for the year was 11 200. The actual costs incurred for the year were as follows:

Wages	$154 000
Electricity	33 000
Cleaning	88 000
Gas	12 000
Water	22 800
Maintenance	16 200

Required

Prepare a fixed budget performance report for 2013 by preparing a budget for each cost item based on its fixed costs plus the variable cost per cabin night multiplied by the actual number of cabin nights. Compare this budget for 11 200 cabin nights with the actual costs incurred.

LO 7

Problem 12.1 INCOME FORECAST ★

The Sporting Spa Resort has 100 residential villas to accommodate guests. The accountant for the resort has asked you, the marketing manager, to prepare a budget for expected relaxation treatment receipts for the month of September 2014.

The facilities are provided exclusively for the use of resort guests. The resort caters only for adults. Past records indicate that for the month of September the average adult occupancy for each of the villas is two persons, who stay an average of 5 days. The occupancy rate for the villas in the resort for September is approximately 90%.

The resort provides three types of relaxation treatments — a therapeutic massage for $120, a massage and facial treatment for $180, and a straight facial for $80.

Past records for September indicate that 60% of guests have a therapeutic massage, 20% have a massage and facial, and 20% have just a facial treatment.

Required

Prepare the budget for relaxation treatments for the month of September 2014.

LO 8

Problem 12.2 PREPARING A SALES FORECAST ★★

CleanAir Ltd manufactures exhaust fans designed for apartment use. The company markets this line in two geographic areas, one with a humid climate and the other with a dry climate. Approximately 60% of all new apartment blocks in the two areas will have an individual exhaust fan installed in each apartment. They have also projected that 5% of the existing apartments will install new individual exhaust fans to improve existing systems or replace old ones that cannot be repaired. Based on past experience, CleanAir Ltd expects to capture 30% of the new apartment block construction market and 10% of the replacement market.

The company sells two models of exhaust fans — the standard and the deluxe, a more energy-efficient unit. Builders will use the standard model in 70% of the apartments they construct and the deluxe model in 30%. When an existing block installs new exhaust fans, it will use the standard model in 25% of the apartments and the deluxe model in 75%.

The other information available is:

	Humid climate	Dry climate
Number of apartments to be constructed	4200	5100
Number of existing apartments	50 000	40 000
Selling price — standard	$750	$800
Selling price — deluxe	$1150	$1200

Required

Prepare a sales forecast for CleanAir Ltd by market area.

LO 8

Problem 12.3 BUDGETED FINANCIAL STATEMENTS FOR A QUARTER FOR A RETAIL FIRM ★★

High Street Grocers is preparing a quarterly budget covering the 3 months ending 30 September 2014. The information available for the budget is as follows:
1. Cash sales represent 60% of all monthly sales; 50% of all credit sales are collected in the month after sale and the remainder are collected in the second month following the sale.
2. Inventory purchases that are made on account equal 60% of the sales forecast for that month; 30% of the purchases are paid for in the month of purchase, and 70% are paid for in the following month.
3. Ending inventory on 30 September 2014 is projected to be $57 800.
4. Equipment purchases at the end of September are budgeted at $95 000.
5. Other quarterly expenses are budgeted as follows: electricity, $14 700; rent, $55 000; salaries, $154 000. These expenses are paid when incurred.

6. Depreciation for the quarter is $14 000.
7. The balance sheet as at 1 July 2014 will have the following account balances:

Cash at bank	$ 29 760	Accumulated depreciation	$ 94 000
Accounts receivable	98 460	Accounts payable	85 370
Inventory	60 400	Share capital	100 000
Equipment	290 000	Retained earnings	199 250

8. Budgeted sales are: July, $240 000; August, $227 000; September, $220 000.

Required

Prepare a budgeted income statement and balance sheet for the quarter ending 30 September 2014. Ignore income tax.

LO 8

Problem 12.4 BUDGETED FINANCIAL STATEMENTS FOR A QUARTER FOR A RETAIL FIRM ★★

Shopaholics is preparing a quarterly budget covering the 3 months ending 30 June 2013. The information available for the budget is as follows:

1. Cash sales represent 30% of all monthly sales; 50% of all credit sales are collected in the month of sale and the remainder are collected in the month following the sale.
2. Inventory purchases that are made on account equal 60% of the sales forecast for that month; 40% of the purchases are paid for in the month of purchase, and 60% are paid for in the following month.
3. Ending inventory on 30 June 2013 is projected to be $34 600.
4. Equipment purchases at the end of June are budgeted at $57 000.
5. Other quarterly expenses are budgeted as follows: electricity, $8800; rent, $33 000; salaries, $92 000. These expenses are paid when incurred.
6. Depreciation for the quarter is $8400.
7. The balance sheet as at 1 April 2013 will have the following account balances:

Cash at bank	$ 17 820	Accumulated depreciation	$ 56 300
Accounts receivable	58 960	Accounts payable	51 120
Inventory	36 200	Share capital	100 000
Equipment	172 500	Retained earnings	78 060

8. Budgeted sales are: April, $142 000; May, $136 000; June, $132 000.

Required

Prepare a budgeted income statement and balance sheet for the quarter ending 30 June 2013. Ignore income tax.

LO 8

Problem 12.5 PRODUCTION AND RELATED BUDGETS ★★

Burnt & Crisp Manufacturers produces barbecues for domestic use. The manager in charge of production has been asked to prepare a production budget, a direct materials budget and a direct labour budget for part of 2014 based on the company's sales forecast.

The materials and labour requirements per barbecue are:

	Quantity	Cost
Sheet metal	3 square metres	$24 per square metre
Enamel paint	1 litre	12 per litre
Cutting and welding labour	3 hours	16 per hour
Finishing labour	1 hour	12 per hour

The business requires a finished goods ending inventory for each quarter that equals 20% of expected sales for the next quarter. Also, the ending inventory balance of direct materials should equal 25% of the next quarter's production requirements. The inventory balances on 1 January 2014 are forecast as:

Sheet metal	6200 square metres
Enamel paint	1200 litres
Barbecues	240 units

The forecast quarterly sales in units are:

First quarter 2014	12 400
Second quarter 2014	6 200
Third quarter 2014	8 800
Fourth quarter 2014	14 200

Required

A. Prepare a quarterly production budget, in units only, for the first three quarters of 2014.

B. Prepare a direct materials budget for the first two quarters of 2014 in both units and dollars.

C. Prepare a direct labour budget for the first two quarters of 2014.

Problem 12.6 PRODUCTION AND RELATED BUDGETS ★★ **LO 8**

Water from Heaven Manufacturers Pty Ltd produces plastic rainwater tanks for household use. The following information has been gathered so that a production budget, a direct materials budget and a direct labour budget for part of 2014 can be prepared.

The materials and labour requirements per tank are as follows:

	Quantity	Cost
Plastic (weather resistant)	50 kilograms	$12 per kilogram
Plastic pipes	2.2 metres	2 per metre
Moulding and welding	2 hours	22 per hour
Finishing labour	0.5 hour	18 per hour

Management prefers a finished goods ending inventory for each quarter that equals 25% of expected sales for the next quarter. Also, the ending inventory balance of direct materials should equal 25% of the next quarter's production requirements. The inventory balances on 1 January 2014 are forecast as:

Plastic (weather resistant)	266 250 kilograms
Plastic pipes	11 715 metres
Tanks	5 100

The forecast quarterly sales in units are:

March 2014	20 400
June 2014	24 000
September 2014	22 800
December 2014	16 500

Required

A. Prepare a quarterly production budget, in units only, for the March, June and September quarters of 2014.

B. Prepare a direct materials budget for the March and June quarters of 2014 in both units and dollars.

C. Prepare a direct labour budget for the March and June quarters of 2014.

Problem 12.7 FACTORY OVERHEAD BUDGET AND OVERHEAD APPLICATION RATE ★★ **LO 8**

Hot U Up Manufacturers Ltd produces two types of heaters, a standard model and a deluxe model. The budgeted factory overhead costs for the production operation during 2014 are as follows:

Variable costs:	
Indirect materials	$8.00 per machine hour
Indirect labour	$0.60 per machine hour
Electricity	$0.20 per machine hour
Other	$0.20 per machine hour
Fixed costs:	
Production manager's salary	$120 000
Depreciation	$54 000
Insurance	$50 000
Miscellaneous	$17 920

Production of 36 000 standard heaters and 24 000 deluxe heaters is budgeted for 2014. Each standard heater requires 1.2 machine hours, and each deluxe heater requires only 1 machine hour because of the extensive use of component parts.

Required

A. Prepare a factory overhead budget for 2014 based on the estimated production level.
B. Calculate the predetermined overhead rate based on machine hours.

Problem 12.8 PREPARING PRODUCTION BUDGETS UNDER ALTERNATIVE STRATEGIES ★★   **LO 8**

Aldinga Pty Ltd is a small manufacturing business. For the year ending 30 June 2013, the company achieved sales of $2 772 000 and a gross profit margin of 30%. Although satisfied with this result, management was, however, keen to increase the company's performance in the following year. Management was considering adjusting the unit price of its product, currently $6, to achieve a better outcome. It is considering two alternative strategies.

Under Strategy One, the selling price would be increased by 50 cents, but it is expected that this increase would result in a decrease of 5% in sales volume (units) for the year, and inventory at 30 June 2014 would be equal to 4% of the units sold during the year. Strategy Two is to decrease the selling price by 50 cents, which is expected to lead to an increase in sales of 24 000 units, and result in 20 000 units being on hand at 30 June 2014. Inventory on hand at 1 July 2013 was 15 000 units.

Projected cost data for the year ended 30 June 2014 are:

Direct materials	$1.00 per unit
Direct labour	$0.80 per unit
Overheads — variable	$0.60 per unit
fixed	$600 000

Required

A. Prepare a sales budget and a production budget for the year ending 30 June 2014 under both strategies. (For unit calculations, round to the nearest 10 units.)
B. Which strategy should management adopt? Why?

Problem 12.9 PREPARING MASTER BUDGETS FOR A RETAILER ★★   **LO 8**

The following *actual* balance sheet was prepared for Northhampton Abbey Ltd as at 31 March 2013.

Cash at bank	$ 6 000	Accounts payable	$ 7 000
Accounts receivable (net)	12 000	Accrued wages	1 200
Inventory	21 800	Bank loan	48 000
Prepaid rent	1 000	Share capital	30 000
Furniture & equipment	27 000	Retained earnings	8 600
Accumulated depreciation	(4 600)		
Plant & machinery	54 000		
Accumulated depreciation	(22 400)		
	$ 94 800		$ 94 800

At 31 March you are also provided with the following information:

1. Sales forecasts available for 2013: April $25 000; May $27 000; June $20 000.
2. Cash sales account for 50% of sales. Credit sales are collected 40% in the month of sale and 60% in the following month.
3. Purchases are expected to be made at the rate of 55% of expected sales for each month and are purchased on credit.
4. Creditors are paid 20% in the month of purchase and 80% in the next month.
5. Dividends are paid by the business at the rate of $4000 per quarter.

6. Rent on premises is $3000 per quarter, paid on the last day of the first month of each quarter.
7. Wages are normally paid as incurred and this will occur in the quarter ended 30 June. In the quarter ended 31 March, pay day fell on 25 March so 6 days wages were outstanding at 31 March and are yet to be paid. Wages are normally incurred at the rate of $5000 per month.
8. The following are paid as incurred: electricity $400 per month, interest on loan $180 per month and cleaning contractor $200 per month. The loan principal is paid at the rate of $2000 per quarter.
9. Depreciation is charged at 10% p.a. on the cost of the furniture and equipment and 15% p.a. on the cost of the plant and machinery.
10. New machinery will be purchased for cash on 30 June 2013 for $10 000.
11. Inventory is projected to be $23 200 at 30 June 2013.

Required

Prepare a budgeted income statement, a cash budget and a budgeted balance sheet for Northampton Abbey Ltd for the quarter ended 30 June 2013.

LO 8

Problem 12.10 CASH BUDGET AND BUDGETED PROFIT ★★★

Brabham's Bathrooms buys and sells bathroom equipment. The firm's estimated sales and expenses for the first 4 months of 2013 are:

	Sales	Expenses
January	$500 000	$129 000
February	650 000	129 000
March	450 000	129 000
April	400 000	129 000

Actual sales for December 2012 were $450 000 and actual expenses were $129 000.

All sales are on credit, and the firm estimates that 40% of the accounts receivable will be collected in the month of sale with the other 60% collected the following month. The average selling price for the products sold is $300. The cash balance as at 1 January 2013 is expected to be $70 000.

The firm pays for 30% of its purchases in the month of the purchase and the balance is paid in the following month. Average gross profit margin is 40%. The firm plans to continue maintaining an end-of-month inventory equal to 10% of the next month's projected cost of sales. Depreciation amounting to $12 000 per month and wages of $57 000 are included in the monthly expenses of $129 000. Other expenses are paid during the month they are incurred.

Required

A. Prepare a monthly schedule of expected cash receipts for the first quarter of 2013.
B. Prepare a monthly purchases budget for the first quarter of 2013.
C. Prepare a monthly schedule of expected cash payments for the first quarter of 2013.
D. Prepare a monthly cash budget for the first quarter of 2013.
E. Prepare a monthly budgeted income statement for the first quarter of 2013.
F. Calculate the difference between the expected increase in cash and the expected profit or loss for the first quarter. Explain why the two amounts are different.

LO 8

Problem 12.11 CASH BUDGET AND BUDGETED PROFIT ★★★

I Can't Believe It's Not Grass purchases and installs plastic grass. The firm's estimated sales and expenses for the first 4 months of 2014 are:

	Sales	Expenses
January	$725 000	$190 000
February	940 000	190 000
March	650 000	190 000
April	580 000	190 000

Actual sales for November and December 2013 were $550 000 and $650 000 and actual expenses were $190 000 for each month.

All sales are on credit, and the firm estimates that 40% of the accounts receivable will be collected in the month after sale with the other 60% collected the second month following sale. The average selling price for the products sold is $5000. The cash balance as at 1 January 2014 is expected to be $100 000.

The firm pays for 30% of its purchases in the month after purchase and the balance is paid in the second month following purchase. Average gross profit margin is 50%. The firm plans to continue maintaining an end-of-month inventory equal to 20% of the next month's projected cost of sales. Depreciation amounting to $16 000 per month and wages of $82 000 are included in the monthly expenses of $190 000. Other expenses are paid during the month they are incurred.

Required
A. Prepare a monthly schedule of expected cash receipts for the first quarter of 2014.
B. Prepare a monthly purchases budget for the first quarter of 2014.
C. Prepare a monthly schedule of expected cash payments for the first quarter of 2014.
D. Prepare a monthly cash budget for the first quarter of 2014.
E. Prepare a monthly budgeted income statement for the first quarter of 2014.
F. Calculate the difference between the expected increase in cash and the expected profit or loss for the first quarter. Explain why the two amounts are different.

Problem 12.12 COMPREHENSIVE PROBLEM ★★★   LO 7

Prue Williamson Marketing Services is preparing a budget for the quarter year ended 31 December 2013. The information available for the budget is as follows:
1. Prue's hourly charge-out rate for the year ended 30 September 2013 was $160 but she intends to increase this by 5% for the budget period. Prue also employs Win Kee, a newly graduated marketing student, and charges his work out at $80 per hour and does not intend to increase this for the next year.
2. Prue estimates that the following hours will be billed to clients for the quarter:
   Prue   500 hours
   Win Kee   400 hours
3. The services are all provided on credit and are collected 60% in the same quarter and 40% in the following quarter.
4. The *monthly* expenses for the year ended 30 September are provided with Prue's estimates of how they will change for the budget period:

	Year ended 30 Sept. 2013	Year ended 30 Sept. 2014
Depreciation	$ 400	No increase
Electricity	500	Increase of 10%
Insurance	2 000	Increase of 20%
Long-service leave provision	300	2% of salaries
Rent	2 000	Increase of 5%
Salaries	15 000	Increase of 5%
Stationery	500	No increase
Telephone	1 000	Increase of 3%

5. Insurance is paid annually in October. Rent is paid 1 month in advance and electricity and telephone expenses are paid in the month after they are incurred. All other expenses are paid in the month they occur.
6. Prue intends to buy new office furniture at the end of December for $5200.
7. The balance sheet as at 1 October 2013 has the following account balances:

Cash at bank	$ 52 000	Accumulated depreciation	$ 14 400
Accounts receivable	75 600	Electricity payable	500
Prepaid rent	2 100	Telephone payable	1 000
Furniture and equipment	24 000	Provision for long-service leave	7 200
		Prue Williamson, Capital	130 600

Required

Prepare a budgeted income statement, a cash budget and a budgeted balance sheet for the quarter ending 31 December 2013.

Problem 12.13 COMPREHENSIVE PROBLEM ★★★ LO 8

Warner Manufacturing is preparing a master budget for the first quarter of the year ending 31 March 2014, and has compiled the following data:

1. The firm sells a single product at a price of $24 per unit. The sales forecast (in units) prepared by the marketing department for the quarter ending 31 March 2013 and the first 7 months of the next financial year is as follows:

	Number of units
January	12 000
February	12 000
March	12 500
April	13 000
May	14 000
June	14 000
July	15 500
August	16 000
September	18 000
October	24 000

2. 40% of the sales are collected in the month of sale, 40% are collected in the following month, and 20% are collected in the second month following the sale.
3. The beginning inventories on 1 April 2013 will be 4200 units of finished goods and no raw materials. The ending finished goods inventory should equal 20% of the sales requirements for the next 3 months, and the raw materials ending inventory should equal 40% of the next month's production.
4. 80% of the material purchases are paid in the quarter of purchase and 20% are paid in the following quarter. The amount owing for purchases at 1 April 2013 is $82 000.
5. Variable selling expenses are 5% of sales. Administrative expenses are $52 500 per quarter, of which $8200 represents depreciation expense and $40 000 is wages. Fixed selling expenses are $15 200 each quarter. All selling and administrative expenses are paid in the quarter in which they are incurred.
6. The production requirements are:

	Direct materials	Direct labour
Per unit	1 kg	0.4 hour

The direct materials are purchased for $4 a kilogram. The direct labour wage rate is $16 an hour. The factory overhead cost is $64 000 per month, and is paid in the month incurred (except for depreciation of $12 000).
7. The 1 April 2013 cash balance is expected to be $16 800.

Required

A. Prepare a sales budget by month for the period February to June 2013.
B. Determine estimated cash collections from receivables for the first quarter of the financial year starting 1 April 2013.
C. Calculate the number of units to be produced in the first quarter of the financial year starting 1 April 2013.
D. Prepare a direct materials budget for the first quarter of the financial year starting 1 April 2013.

E. Prepare a cash budget for the first quarter of the financial year starting 1 April 2013 including any necessary schedules.

F. Prepare a budgeted income statement for the first quarter of the financial year starting 1 April 2013.

G. Calculate the difference between the expected increase in cash and the profit or loss for the first quarter. Explain why the two amounts are different.

Problem 12.14   COMPREHENSIVE PROBLEM ★★★   **LO 8**

The following *actual* balance sheet was prepared for Jesam Foods Ltd as at 30 September 2012.

JESAM FOODS LTD
Balance Sheet
as at 30 September 2012

Cash at bank	$ 11 000	Accounts payable	$ 12 000
Accounts receivable (net)	20 000	Accrued wages	1 600
Inventory	32 000	Bank loan	34 000
Prepaid rent	1 600	Share capital	40 000
Furniture & equipment	40 000	Retained earnings	13 000
Accumulated depreciation	(20 000)		
Plant & machinery	64 000		
Accumulated depreciation	(48 000)		
	$100 600		$100 600

At 30 September, you are also provided with the following information:

1. Sales forecasts available: October $39 000, November $44 000, December $48 000.
2. Cash sales account for 40% of sales. Credit sales are collected 30% in the month of sale, 50% in the following month and 20% in the second month following the sale.
3. Purchases are expected to be made at the rate of 60% of expected sales for each month and are purchased on credit.
4. Creditors are paid 40% in the month of purchase and 60% in the next month.
5. Inventory is projected to be $37 600 at 31 December 2012.
6. Rent on premises increased to $4950 per quarter from 1 August 2012. This is paid on the last day of the first month of each quarter.
7. Wages of $12 000 per month are normally paid as incurred, although December wages of $2000 are expected be outstanding at 31 December 2012 as a result of the normal payday being a week after the end of the year.
8. The following are paid as incurred: electricity $600 per month, interest on loan $220 per month and cleaning contractor $400 per month. The loan principal is paid at the rate of $2000 per quarter.
9. Depreciation is charged at 10% per annum on the cost of the furniture and equipment and 15% per annum on the cost of the plant and machinery.
10. A new machine will be purchased for cash on 31 December 2012 for $16 000.

Required
A. Prepare a budgeted income statement for the quarter ended 31 December 2012.
B. Prepare a cash budget for the quarter ended 31 December 2012.
C. Prepare a budgeted balance sheet as at 31 December 2012.

Problem 12.15   COMPREHENSIVE PROBLEM ★★★   **LO 8**

Elliot & Morris Manufacturing is preparing a master budget for the quarter ending 30 September 2013, and has compiled the data shown overleaf.

1. The firm sells a single product at a price of $60 per unit. The sales forecast (in units) prepared by the marketing department for the quarter ending 30 June 2013 and the first 7 months of the next financial year is as follows:

	Number of units
April	28 800
May	28 800
June	30 000
July	31 200
August	33 600
September	33 600
October	37 200
November	38 400
December	43 200
January	57 600

2. 40% of the sales are collected in the month of sale, 40% are collected in the following month, and 20% are collected in the second month following the sale.

3. The beginning inventories on 1 July 2013 will be 10 800 units of finished goods and no raw materials. The ending finished goods inventory should equal 20% of the sales requirements for the next 3 months, and the raw materials ending inventory should equal 40% of the next month's production.

4. 80% of the materials purchases are paid in the quarter of purchase and 20% are paid in the following quarter. The amount owing for purchases at 1 July 2013 is $196 800.

5. Variable selling expenses are 5% of sales. Administrative expenses are $126 000 per quarter, of which $20 000 represents depreciation expense and $96 000 is wages. Fixed selling expenses are $36 000 each quarter. All selling and administrative expenses are paid in the quarter in which they are incurred.

6. The production requirements are:

	Direct materials	Direct labour
Per unit	1.1 kg	0.5 hour

The direct materials are purchased for $8.00 a kilogram. The direct labour wage rate is $24 an hour. The factory overhead cost is $154 000 per month, and is paid in the month incurred (except for depreciation of $28 000).

7. The 1 July 2013 cash balance is expected to be $40 320.

Required

A. Prepare a sales budget by month for the period May to September 2013.

B. Determine estimated cash collections from receivables for the quarter of the financial year starting 1 July 2013.

C. Calculate the number of units to be produced in the quarter of the financial year starting 1 July 2013.

D. Prepare a direct materials budget for the quarter of the financial year starting 1 July 2013.

E. Prepare a cash budget for the quarter of the financial year starting 1 July 2013, including any necessary schedules.

F. Prepare a budgeted income statement for the quarter of the financial year starting 1 July 2013.

DECISION ANALYSIS

Budget for a tourist venture

Deep Dive Adventures operates a boat taking tourists to an area off the south coast of Australia to watch the annual mating season of the cuttlefish from May to July. During this time, male cuttlefish, a large squid-like fish, change colour to trick other larger male cuttlefish so that they can sneak up on the female cuttlefish. This provides a spectacular colour display for divers. The breeding period is limited and the adult cuttlefish die soon after laying their eggs. The number of tourists gradually builds up from May and dwindles by the end of July. You have been asked by the operator of Deep Dive Adventures to prepare a budget for the 3-month period from May to July.

You have determined from the previous years financial information and discussions with the owner of the business that the following are reasonable projections for the 3 months operations:

Salaries: Three people are employed to run the boat and help passengers with their diving gear. The monthly salary is $12 000.

Expenses: Monthly fixed expenses for the business are expected to be $42 000, including $3000 depreciation on the boat. For each customer, food is provided at a cost of $10 and insurance of $24 is paid.

Collections: All customers book their cuttlefish tour in advance and pay a $20 deposit; the balance of the $200 fee is paid when the tour is taken. About 5% of customers who book a tour cannot take it and so lose their deposit. Approximately 20% of customers book 2 months in advance of their tour, 50% book a month in advance and 30% book in the actual month of their tour. No sales are made on account and all tours are paid in full before a customer is allowed on the boat.

Payments: All salaries are paid in the month in which the service is performed; 60% of the monthly cash operating expenses, food costs and insurance costs are paid in the same month, and 40% of them are paid in the next month.

Customers: The boat can take twenty passengers at a time and does two tours a day, seven days a week from May to July. From past experience it is estimated that the following percentage of capacity is booked for each month:

May	70%
June	90%
July	80%

Cash balance: Deep Dive Adventures expects to have a cash balance at the beginning of May of $20 000 including deposits paid in advance. The owner of the business takes out drawings of $40 000 for each of the 3 months as her income for the year. At the end of July, Deep Dive Adventures has to pay back a loan of $200 000.

Required

A. Prepare a budgeted income statement for each month during the May to July period. (Assume no expenses owing from the previous period.)

B. Prepare a cash budget for each month during the May to July period.

C. Based on the information in requirements A and B, can Deep Dive Adventures meet its loan repayment of $200 000 at the end of July, or will the owner need to reduce her drawings during the period? Explain your conclusion.

CRITICAL THINKING

Green strategy

Read the following article and answer the questions that follow.

Council's green strategy no longer a key area of failure

A South Australian council has overhauled its carbon reduction strategy and will install software from TechnologyOne to improve its reporting capability.

Campbelltown City council in Adelaide devised its strategy almost a decade ago but struggled to achieve its goals because it could not properly access data about emissions. In anticipation of federal government regulation of the national greenhouse reporting initiative, it will replace the web-based spreadsheet application to record emissions data.

'We've set targets and tried to do efficiency improvements but we haven't had the systems in place to let us track that. Even though we're doing the data-entry side, we haven't had a reporting platform that allows us to see that data easily and simply.'

The council is now using TechnologyOne financials and payroll systems to capture data about electricity, fuel and gas use, and waste output. It will install the enterprise budgeting and business intelligence modules to collate this information, apply the relevant formulas to calculate its emissions, and present the information in a meaningful way.

TechnologyOne's software allows reports to be published internally, Ms Sarac said.

'The other ones we looked at tended to be more externally based. They would take our data and manipulate it offsite and provide a report back to us... TechOne allows us to keep that internal control.'

She said the system gave specific information about the council's widely distributed operations. 'It makes for far more consistency in reporting,' she said. 'We can pool those and get a good picture at the large scale across the organisation on what's going on in any given year.'

Source: Excerpts from Mahesh Sharma, 'Council's green strategy no longer a key area of failure', *The Australian*.

Required

Explain how a system like TechnologyOne's software is likely to be integrated into the traditional budgeting system of the Campbelltown Council and how budgeting would assist in the reduction of greenhouse emissions.

ETHICS AND GOVERNANCE

Production budget for a car manufacturer

William Bill is the production manager for Cheetah Motors Ltd and is responsible for preparing the production budget for the Cheetah car that the company manufactures. During the previous year, new robots were installed on the production line that significantly increased fixed factory overheads but reduced the amount of labour involved in production and the amount of material wasted due to improved efficiency. In preparing the production budget for the next year, William decided to 'cut himself a bit of slack'. Because the cost structure of the production line had changed so much as a result of the new robots, William decided that in the first year of their introduction he would set a production budget that was easy to meet and management would not be able to recognise this as they couldn't compare it with previous production budgets. William received a bonus if positive production variances were greater than 10%. By not reducing the amount of labour or materials costs in the budget by the amount that the new robots should save, William believed he was in for an easy year with a guaranteed bonus at the end.

Required

A. Who are the stakeholders affected by William's budget?
B. What are the ethical issues involved, if any?
C. How could the company stop its managers padding their budgets?

FINANCIAL ANALYSIS

Refer to the latest financial report of JB Hi-Fi Limited on its website, www.jbhifi.com.au, and answer the following questions:

1. After examining the report, is it possible to conclude that there is a budgetary system in operation within JB Hi-Fi Limited?
2. What would be the key element driving a budgetary system for JB Hi-Fi Limited? What budgets might the company prepare?
3. Is there any evidence in the report that there is a performance evaluation system linked to a budgetary system? Explain your conclusion.

Chapter 13

Performance evaluation for managers

Concepts for review

Before studying this chapter, you should understand or, if necessary, revise:

- the difference between variable costs and fixed costs (pp. 463–5)
- the purposes and advantages of preparing a budget (pp. 494, 496–7)
- the importance of organisational structure in planning and control (pp. 494–5)
- the role of budgets in the control function of management (pp. 518–19).

Learning objectives

After studying this chapter, you should be able to:

1 explain responsibility accounting and describe its essential features (pp. 540–2)

2 describe the essential features of departmental (segmental) accounting, and be able to determine departmental gross profit for a retail business (pp. 543–5)

3 define direct and indirect expenses as they relate to departments, and explain the different bases for allocation of indirect expenses to departments (pp. 545–9)

4 prepare a departmental income statement (p. 549)

5 perform the analysis required to identify an unprofitable department (pp. 549–53)

6 prepare a flexible budget and explain how it is used in performance evaluation (pp. 553–7)

7 define standard costs, and understand how they are used in performance evaluation (pp. 557–8)

8 understand the balanced scorecard management system and how it is used for performance evaluation (pp. 559–61).

Skill is second to well-tuned feedback

Franklin sat in front of me lamenting he had been passed over for a promotion. In fact, as we talked, he became quite despondent. 'This is not the first time,' he said. He couldn't understand it because he thought that he had worked hard, kept his head down and done his work well. His performance appraisal reviews had always been positive. He always put in the effort, he said, and while others in the office might socialise and chat or gossip, he kept to the task in hand. He largely kept to himself. He said he didn't want to worry his boss unnecessarily and only ever talked to him if there was a problem. He missed a promotion about 18 months previously and now it had happened again. He was devastated when he found out and felt badly not only for himself but for his family in that he thought he'd let them down.

Franklin has overlooked a key to career success. The Stanford Research Institute in the US undertook a series of research projects and substantiated that both career and business success was attributable to two main factors — 'technical skills and knowledge' and 'interpersonal and communication skills'.

So what, you say. That's not hard to work out. However, the Stanford Institute went a step further. Through its research, it also allocated the percentage that was attributable to technical skills and knowledge and the percentage attributable to interpersonal skills and communication. Which would you say was the largest contributor of these two factors? What would you say they were in percentage terms?

How would you feel if I told you the institute found the percentage of career and business success attributable to technical skills and knowledge was only 12.5 per cent and the percentage attributable to interpersonal and communication skills was 87.5 per cent? But let's just say that even if it was 20:80 or whatever; the message is the same. It's not what you know that is important. It's how to communicate it and how you connect to others.

I'm not saying that knowledge is useless or that academic qualifications are superfluous because these are vital pieces of paper whereby you do learn material and personally develop and it gets you in the door for a job or a career but, beyond that, what is critical is how you interrelate and communicate with those around you. With Franklin, we devised a program whereby he got out of his office more, he went to the water cooler and made it his task to stop and chat to one person on the way. It was also his task to attend at least one social function a quarter. Most importantly, he was to keep his boss informed of what he was doing and where he was up to on his projects. Another job hasn't come up yet for him to go for, but Franklin is already reporting that he is enjoying work more and that others seem more friendly towards him and that he is getting on better with his boss.

Source: Dr Darryl Cross, 'Skill is second to well-tuned feedback', *The Advertiser*.

Chapter preview

In chapter 12, we discussed in detail the role of budgets in the planning function of management and how budgets are used by managers in the control of businesses. This chapter examines the use of budgets by managers in controlling an entity and evaluating the performance of both managers and employees in meeting budgetary and other targets. The scene setter suggests that interpersonal skills contribute at least 80% to a person's success at work. This chapter considers the use of accounting in making performance evaluation more objective and less subject to non-technical skills. The general concern is that performance of company employees must be linked to positive performance outcomes. In spite of this, most employees who succeed do so due to their interpersonal skills with little reference to their technical skills and knowledge or to actual company performance.

This chapter focuses on performance evaluation for managers. This entails an appreciation of the role of responsibility accounting used within the budgetary framework, an understanding of the importance of appropriate reporting by departments (segmental reporting), the use of flexible budgets and standard costs in evaluating the performance of employees at all levels, and an appreciation of the concept of the 'balanced scorecard' in the evaluation of performance.

13.1 Responsibility accounting

Learning objective 1

Explain responsibility accounting and describe its essential features

An important part of the organising function of management is dividing an entity into well-defined parts or specialised segments. This enables the organisation to accomplish more than it would otherwise. Many business entities are divided into segments or departments to differentiate between the products or services offered or organised on a geographical basis. Decision making is usually better since managers of the segments are closer to the day-to-day activities and can control them more effectively.

To evaluate the performance of a segment, the accounting system must provide detailed financial information for each segment. Managers are able to use this information to plan activities for each segment, allocate scarce resources, evaluate actual performance and take corrective action whenever necessary to improve the efficiency and effectiveness of the segments.

Responsibility accounting requires each manager to participate in the development of financial plans for his or her department or segment and to receive timely performance reports that compare actual results with those planned or budgeted. When responsibility accounting is used along with budgeting (discussed in chapter 12), the combination provides managers with an effective means of planning and controlling an entity's financial performance.

A number of things are essential for responsibility accounting to function effectively and efficiently:

- responsibility centres need to be determined
- the accounting system must be tailored to the organisational structure
- individual managers' ability to control activities should be a priority
- managers must participate in developing departmental plans and targets
- an effective and efficient responsibility reporting system must be established
- the principle of management by exception should be adopted.

These are discussed on the following pages.

Responsibility centres

A **responsibility centre** is a business segment such as a department that can be set up as a cost centre, a profit centre or an investment centre. The choice between the three depends on the answer to the question 'What aspect of financial performance can be controlled?'

If managers are responsible only for the costs incurred in a particular department, it is defined as a *cost centre*. Cost centres are the most popular form of responsibility centre since many departments do not produce income. For example, a retail business's accounting department could be established as a cost centre. If managers are concerned with income earned as well as with the costs incurred in a particular department, it is defined as a *profit centre*. A sales department of a retail business can be a profit centre because income from the segment's activity, as well as its expenses, can be measured.

The most complete form of responsibility centre, however, is an *investment centre*, in which senior managers are held responsible for the return on the resources (assets) used by the segment. The manager of an investment centre will be accountable for expenses, income and assets and is responsible for generating a satisfactory return on the assets invested in the segment. A department store operated by a retail organisation is an example of an investment centre.

Tailoring the accounting system to organisational structure

The accounting system must be designed to collect relevant financial data for each responsibility centre in the organisational structure. Hence, the accounting system itself is segmented to provide information for individual managers, as well as for the entity as a whole. This is achieved through the use of a numbering system in the chart of accounts to code the general ledger accounts. For example, the manager of the shoe department at a local department store needs accounting information to manage the department and to determine its profitability. This information is a subset of the accounting information used by the store manager to manage the overall store and its profitability. Information about the store is, in turn, a subset of accounting information for a geographical area, such as a state, used by the area manager to manage all the stores in a given geographical area. In turn, the accounting information of different geographical areas is compiled to produce national accounting information, which may even be a subset of international accounting information if the store is part of a multinational company.

Controllability of activities by individual managers

In evaluating the financial performances of responsibility centres, managers should be accountable only for the financial (and non-financial) items that they control, i.e. **controllable income, costs/expenses or investments**. At their individual level of management, they must be able to regulate or at least influence all expenses, income or invested resources classified as controllable during a given accounting period.

The two key dimensions of controllability in responsibility accounting are the specific level of management and the given time period. For example, a controllable cost is one that can be authorised by a particular manager during a specified time period. The manager of a sales department in a retail business usually is able to control the labour costs of the department but cannot influence the local government rates imposed on the property occupied by the business. The manager could be held accountable for the labour cost but not for the rates.

Participation of managers

The managers accountable for the performance of responsibility centres should participate actively in planning the centre's financial performance, which usually is expressed in terms of a budget. When managers participate in the preparation of financial estimates, the goals, which may be modified by senior management, are likely to be more realistic than ones established and imposed by senior management. This approach should motivate managers to achieve the planned performance.

Responsibility reporting

The reporting phase of responsibility accounting is based on the idea that the assignment of responsibility and authority flows from top to bottom in an organisation, whereas accountability flows from bottom to top. Consequently, performance reports start at the lowest level of management and build upwards, with managers receiving information concerning their own performance as well as that of any other manager under their control. Managers of responsibility centres are evaluated using performance reports that show the financial items for which they are responsible.

Performance reports should:
- be timely
- be based on relevant and reliable data
- highlight differences between actual and budgeted performance.

Figure 13.1 is an extract of a responsibility reporting system used to control the expenses of the motor vehicle dealership shown in figure 12.1 (p. 495). Cost centres have been established at three levels of management — departmental, sales or service manager, and the general manager. For illustrative purposes, we have restricted our attention to only three cost centres in the organisation in figure 12.1 (p. 495), although all segments would be included in a real-life situation.

Figure 13.1 Motor vehicle dealership responsibility reporting system, January 2013

		Budget	Actual	Variance
Level 1	*General manager's report*			
	General manager's office	$ 12 800	$ 13 900	$ 1 100U
	Sales departments	102 900	112 370	9 470U
	Service departments	92 500	98 600	6 100U
	Total	$208 200	$224 870	$16 670U
Level 2	*Sales manager's report*			
	Sales manager's office	$ 9 500	$ 9 900	$ 400U
	New car sales department	56 600	61 970	5 370U
	Used car sales department	28 200	32 100	3 500U
	Leasing department	8 600	8 400	200 F
	Total	$102 900	$112 370	$ 9 470U
Level 3	*New car sales manager's report*			
	Sales salaries	$ 18 200	$ 19 800	$ 1 600U
	Advertising	20 000	23 200	3 200U
	Light and power	4 400	4 850	450U
	Insurance	3 200	3 200	—
	Rent	10 000	10 000	—
	Other	800	920	120U
	Total	$ 56 600	$ 61 970	$ 5 370U

As the performance information flows from bottom to top, it is cumulative and less detailed. As figure 13.1 illustrates, the new car sales manager's (level 3) report is summarised and becomes a single line in the sales manager's (level 2) report. The report covering all departmental sales managers is summarised as one line in the general manager's (level 1) report.

At the top of the organisation — level 1 management — the general manager is accountable for one large responsibility centre representing the entire business. The expected expenses are shown in the 'budget' column and the actual expenses incurred are presented in the 'actual' column. The **variance** shown for each line item in the right-hand column is the difference between the budgeted and actual expense. Corrective action needs to be taken when variances are considered material or significant. The *U* indicates an unfavourable variance whenever the actual expenses are greater than those budgeted, because profits will be lower. A favourable variance, *F*, occurs when the actual expenses are less than those planned, and final profits will therefore be higher.

Management by exception

Only significant variances between the planned and actual performance of each responsibility centre should be emphasised in the performance reports so their causes can be determined and corrective action taken. This is known as **management by exception**. For example, in the dealership illustration, the unfavourable variances would be investigated to explain why the actual expenses reported are $16 670 higher than expected. The general manager can request detailed copies of the performance reports from all levels of responsibility and can trace the variances downwards through the performance reports to identify their sources so that corrective action can be taken to improve future operations. In turn, each accountable manager can do the same thing for his or her area of control.

13.2 Departmental/segmental accounting

Learning objective 2

Describe the essential features of departmental (segmental) accounting, and be able to determine departmental gross profit for a retail business

Departmental (segmental) accounting is used mostly by large businesses, which are more likely to have control problems and want to constantly evaluate the profitability of their different activities. However, even small businesses can use departmental accounting to determine where their resources can be used best. For example, a small accounting practice may account separately for its consultancy, audit and tax services so that senior managers can decide where the professional time of employees should be directed to achieve the best financial results.

Although segmental information is mainly for management use, there may be a need to disclose some segmental information in the general purpose financial reports of an entity. IFRS 8/AASB 8 *Operating Segments* require entities to disclose in their financial statements information on operating and other segments whenever it is significant to the understanding of those statements. Under the standards, entities are required to disclose a summary of segment revenues, segment expenses, segment profit and loss, segment assets and segment liabilities in relation to each reportable segment.

In this chapter, however, we direct our attention towards internal management reporting for responsibility centres organised as departments/segments.

The income statement is usually the only accounting statement used for departmental accounting, because the balance sheet/statement of financial position is common to the entire entity. In developing departmental accounting information, the accountant must decide how detailed the income statement should be for each of the departments. Some small businesses might segregate only revenue by departments. Many retail businesses restrict their attention to the gross profit on sales. Other businesses include certain direct expenses of the departments, and some prepare a complete income statement for each department by allocating indirect expenses among departments. Each of these approaches has certain advantages, but keep in mind that the managers of the various departments should be held accountable only for those financial items they can control. Comparison of actual performance with budgeted performance is also vital in assessing the accountability of departmental managers for their departments. Departmental accounting can be applied in all types of business entities, but attention is given here to a retail business. The same principles can be applied to service businesses and manufacturing businesses (e.g. production processes).

BUSINESS KNOWLEDGE

The Wesfarmers Limited story so far . . . (as at July 2010)

Founded: in 1914 as the Western Australian Farmers Cooperative.

Operates: a very diversified group employing about 200 000 people in Australia and New Zealand.

Ownership: is Australian-owned and is listed on the Australian Securities Exchange and has about 400 000 shareholders.

Turnover: in 2009, annual revenue of $50.98 billion, profit of $1.5 billion. The purchase of the Coles Group in November 2007 added supermarket businesses, liquor retailing, fuel and convenience outlets, an online pharmacy, Officeworks, Target and Kmart.

Business segments: 10 operating divisions: Coles; Home Improvement and Office Supplies; Target; Kmart; Resources; Insurance; Industrial and Safety; Chemicals and Fertilisers; Energy; and Other Businesses.

Geographical segments: Australia, New Zealand and Asia.

Source: Information from Wesfarmers Ltd website www.wesfarmers.com.au.

Departmental gross profit: retail business

Departmental gross profit (also called gross margin) is a key indicator of profitability that is watched closely by senior managers of retail businesses. If a retail business is to achieve its profit goals, the gross profit must be sufficient to cover expenses and produce the desired profit. The factors influencing departmental gross profit are:

- the number of units sold
- selling prices
- mix of inventory sold
- the cost of sales.

In most cases, all four factors are the responsibility of departmental managers and are controllable by them. Hence, the departmental gross profit receives a significant amount of attention.

Faster inventory turnover, higher prices, a more profitable sales mix and effective cost control are among the most important objectives of departmental managers. This does not mean that managers ignore expenses, since the ultimate measure of financial performance is profit. However, many of the expenses are beyond the control and responsibility of departmental managers.

In developing departmental gross profit information, the approach most often used is to establish a complete set of general ledger accounts for the items that contribute to the gross profit in each department. Such accounts as sales, purchases, inventory, sales returns and allowances, freight inwards, and purchases returns and allowances are used in each department (depending on the inventory system — perpetual or periodic) to record transactions as they occur.

With the use of bar coding or wireless tags, most goods, once scanned, are entered into the computer system under their appropriate departmental heading. Whenever a sale occurs, the sales record for the appropriate department is updated as well as the overall sales for the store. At the end of the month, a sales analysis by department can be printed so that the performance of each department can be reviewed. Figure 13.2 illustrates a sales analysis sheet used to track the monthly sales of a hardware store.

Figure 13.2 Sales analysis sheet

Sales Analysis
for the month ending 31 January 2013

Date	Tools	Department Hardware	Paint	Combined
1 (Store closed)	—			—
2	$ 905	$ 1 245	$ 310	$ 2 460
3	682	982	245	1 909
4	962	1 168	412	2 542
31	750	890	280	1 920
Totals — month	$24 440	$36 110	$16 405	$76 955

Income statement — departmental gross profits

Figure 13.3 shows an income statement prepared for Andrews Hardware Store, which operates three departments. The statement reveals departmental gross profits and their combined total. The statement provides managers with information from which the departmental performance can be evaluated and the sources of profit identified. The expenses are not assigned to the departments when this format is used but instead are subtracted in total from the total gross profit. The gross profit is presented as a dollar amount as well as a percentage of sales. The combination of the volume of inventory sold and the gross profit rate for each sales dollar must be considered because the same total gross profit can be achieved with a large volume of sales at a low gross profit rate or with a smaller volume of sales at a higher gross profit rate. However, note that the analysis is not complete because some of the expenses will be related to specific departments, and the ultimate objective is to earn a satisfactory amount of profit. Because the focus of the statement in figure 13.3 is on departmental gross profit, an itemised listing of the selling and distribution, and administrative and other expenses is omitted.

Figure 13.3 Departmental income statement — gross profit format

ANDREWS HARDWARE STORE
Income Statement
(Departmental gross profit format)
for the year ended 30 June 2013

	Tools department	Hardware department	Paint department	Combined departments
INCOME				
Sales revenue	$ 352 000	$448 000	$224 000	$1 024 000
Less: Sales returns	8 000	4 800	3 200	16 000
Net sales revenue	344 000	443 200	220 800	1 008 000
COST OF SALES				
Beginning inventory	68 800	88 640	36 800	194 240
Purchases	262 480	278 968	129 680	671 128
Freight inwards	4 800	5 600	3 200	13 600
Goods available for sale	336 080	373 208	169 680	878 968
Ending inventory	71 200	89 560	37 200	197 960
Cost of sales	264 880	283 648	132 480	681 008
GROSS PROFIT (%)	$ 79 120 (23.0)	$159 552 (36.0)	$ 88 320 (40.0)	326 992 (32.4)
EXPENSES				
Selling and distribution				146 400
Administrative and other				132 800
				279 200
PROFIT				$ 47 792

Departmental profit

Departmental profitability reporting can be extended beyond the gross profit calculation to show the profit of each department through the use of **expense allocation**. The justification for such an extension is that a department is merely a part of the entire business and could not function without the benefits provided by such expenses as advertising, rent, electricity, rates, insurance and salaries. Since revenues are generated by the sales departments, a share of the entity's total expenses must also be incurred by them.

Unfortunately, expense allocation problems are inevitable in determining departmental profit and affect the accuracy, and hence interpretation, of the results. When **departmental profit** is calculated, the reports must be interpreted and used carefully. They should not be used for responsibility accounting purposes if they contain expenses that the departmental managers cannot control. Instead, complete departmental income statements should be used by senior management only to assess the approximate profitability of departments as separate businesses. The allocation of expenses to departments to enable the determination of departmental profit is covered in the next section.

13.3 Direct and indirect expenses

To determine departmental profit a distinction must be made between the direct and indirect expenses. Management accountants often use the terms *direct* and *indirect* in relation to some **cost object**, which is defined as any activity for which separate cost measurement is performed. In general, a **direct cost** can be traced to a specific cost object, whereas an **indirect cost**, also called a common cost, is incurred for multiple cost objects. Although management accounting uses a

> **Learning objective 3**
>
> Define direct and indirect expenses as they relate to departments, and explain the different bases for allocation of indirect expenses to departments

wide range of other cost objects such as a product produced by a manufacturing business, a service performed by a bank, a consulting activity, or even a specialised item of equipment, in this chapter the cost object is a department in a retail business.

Direct expenses

Direct expenses can be traced to a particular department (cost object) since they are incurred solely for the benefit of that department. Examples are the sales salaries and commissions paid to salespeople who work exclusively in one department, or time charged to particular clients in a consulting business. The direct expenses are charged to separate departmental expense accounts when incurred unless the costs of doing so exceed any perceived benefits.

Indirect expenses

Indirect expenses are incurred for the benefit of the entity as a whole and cannot be traced directly to a particular department (cost object). An indirect expense is a common expense since it is incurred for the benefit of more than one segment. Rent, electricity, insurance, rates and senior management salaries are examples of indirect expenses. Another type of indirect expense is that incurred by a service department. A **service (or support) department** supports the sales departments in some specific way that enables the sales departments to function. A personnel department, an advertising department, a general office department, a finance department and a maintenance department are service departments. Although certain expenses such as salaries and supplies are directly related to the service departments, they are indirect expenses for the selling departments.

Because none of the indirect expenses can be traced to specific selling departments, they must be assigned to them using an allocation base. This means the indirect expenses are divided among the various departments that jointly benefit from them. A number of bases have been developed as potentially equitable ways to allocate indirect expenses. The selling departments ideally will be charged for indirect expenses on the basis of the benefits they receive. However, these benefits are often difficult to measure, and sound judgement rather than absolute rules may be the only approach possible. Managers and accountants will often disagree on the choice of the best allocation base for a specific indirect expense. As a result, extreme caution must be exercised in interpreting income statements in which indirect expenses have been allocated.

Bases for allocating expenses

To illustrate the allocation of indirect expenses to departments, we continue to use the example of Andrews Hardware Store. Assume that the direct expenses are charged to the departments at the end of the accounting period and the indirect expenses are allocated on bases that the accountant believes best represent the benefits received from the expenses. A departmental expense allocation worksheet is used to allocate the expenses to the three departments — tools, hardware and paint. Typical methods used for the allocation of the expenses are discussed on the following pages and shown in figure 13.4.

Sales salaries. Each salesperson employed by Andrews Hardware Store works exclusively in one department, so all sales salaries are *direct expenses*. Payroll records are departmentalised and show that the sales salaries are $36 960, $34 240 and $21 200 for the tools department, hardware department and paint department respectively.

If the people responsible for running departments are included as salespeople, then care must be taken when using the accounts for responsibility accounting purposes. Although these people may work exclusively in their particular department, they obviously do not control their own salary rates, as these are set by management. So although the salaries of the people running departments are a direct cost of each department, they should not be held accountable for their own salary levels or the associated expenses.

Advertising expense. Andrews Hardware Store relies mainly on newspaper and radio advertising. The department managers can authorise only a limited amount of advertising for their departments. Invoices received indicate that the direct departmental advertising amounted to $5200, $2400 and

Figure 13.4 Expense allocation worksheet

ANDREWS HARDWARE STORE Departmental Expense Allocation Worksheet for the year ended 30 June 2013					
Expenses	Amount	Allocation base — source	Tools	Hardware	Paint
Selling and distribution expenses					
Sales salaries	$ 92 400	Direct — payroll records	$36 960	$34 240	$21 200
Advertising	12 600	Direct — invoices	5 200	2 400	5 000
Advertising	17 640	Indirect — net sales	6 015	7 762	3 863
Inventory insurance	5 760	Direct — insurance policy	2 056	2 615	1 089
Sales supplies	3 800	Direct — requisitions	1 200	1 100	1 500
Depreciation — equipment	5 200	Direct — asset register	1 900	1 500	1 800
Sundry	9 000	Indirect — net sales	3 071	3 957	1 972
	$146 400		$56 402	$53 574	$36 424
Administrative and other expenses:					
Management salaries	48 000	Indirect — time	16 000	16 000	16 000
Building occupancy expenses	46 800	Indirect — space	11 700	23 400	11 700
Purchasing department	16 000	Indirect — purchases	6 240	6 656	3 104
General office	16 200	Indirect — employees	6 480	5 670	4 050
Sundry	5 800	Indirect — net sales	1 978	2 552	1 270
	$132 800		$42 398	$54 278	$36 124

$5000 for the three departments, or a total of $12 600. The remaining $17 740 was spent on store advertising that featured all three departments and is allocated on the basis of sales as the most realistic distribution based on related benefits. The indirect advertising expense of Andrews Hardware Store is allocated according to the following schedule:

	Tools	Hardware	Paint	Combined
2012–13 net sales	$344 000	$443 200	$220 800	$1 008 000
Percentage of combined sales	34.1%	44.0%	21.9%	100.0%
Allocation of $17 640	$6015	$7762	$3863	$17 640

An alternative treatment is to distribute the indirect advertising on the basis of the direct advertising expense or the relative number of departmental products presented in the indirect advertising.

Inventory insurance. The insurance premium paid to insure the store's inventory is treated as a direct expense since it is calculated on the basis of the average dollar amount of inventory maintained during the year. Hence, the total insurance expense is divided between the departments according to their average inventory balances. The calculation of the average departmental inventories as percentages of the average inventory of the store is as follows:

	Tools	Hardware	Paint	Combined
Beginning inventory	$68 800	$88 640	$36 800	$194 240
Ending inventory	$71 200	$89 560	$37 200	$197 960
Average inventory	$70 000	$89 100	$37 000	$196 100
Percentage of combined av. inventory	35.7%	45.4%	18.9%	100.0%
Allocation of $5760	$2056	$2615	$1089	$5760

Sales supplies. The sales supplies are treated as direct expenses for each of the departments. The dollar amounts per department are determined from the requisition forms used to order the supplies. The amounts recorded are $1200, $1100 and $1500 respectively for the three departments.

Depreciation expense. Depreciation on the equipment used in each department is calculated from the non-current assets records, which are maintained on a departmental basis. Hence, the depreciation expense can be directly charged to the departments and amounts to $1900, $1500 and $1800 respectively for the three departments.

Sundry selling expenses. Since the expenses listed in this category originated from a variety of sources, it is assumed that allocating them on the basis of sales provides the best overall measure of the benefits received by each department. Therefore, the distribution of sundry selling expense of $9000 is $3071, $3957 and $1972 respectively for the three departments.

Management salaries. These expenses are allocated on the basis of the approximate time devoted by senior managers of the store to each department. Considerations such as sales volume, personnel requirements, promotional effort and operating problems affect the time spent by managers on departmental activities. In the case of Andrews Hardware Store, it is estimated that managers devote about the same amount of time to each department, so the total of $48 000 is divided equally among the departments.

Building occupancy expenses. Building occupancy expenses including rent, cleaning, rates, electricity, maintenance and insurance are charged to one account — Building Occupancy Expenses — and allocated to the sales departments on the basis of square metres occupied. If the building is owned, its depreciation is allocated on the same basis. The tools, hardware and paint departments occupy a quarter, a half and a quarter of the total space respectively, so their charges are $11 700, $23 400 and $11 700. All space is of approximately the same value. If significant differences in value exist because of a department's location in a store, they should be taken into consideration in the allocation of any building expenses affected. For example, if management believes the space near the store entrance is worth twice as much as the same area on the second floor, resulting in higher sales, the building rent allocated should be twice as much for the more valuable space.

Purchasing department expenses. The purchasing department is one of two service or support departments used by Andrews Hardware Store. The department has the responsibility of finding the best suppliers for purchases required by the selling departments and for placing specific orders. A variety of service departments may provide support to the selling departments of retail businesses. Commonly used bases for allocating service department expenses to the selling departments are shown in table 13.1.

Table 13.1 Service department expense allocation bases

Service department	Expense allocation bases
Advertising	Sales or number of advertisements placed by each selling department
General office	Number of employees or sales in each selling department
Cleaning	Square metres of floor space in each selling department
Maintenance	Service rendered to each selling department
Personnel	Number of employees in each selling department
Purchasing	Dollar amounts of purchases by each selling department
Storeroom	Dollar amounts of purchases or merchandise handled for each selling department

Andrews Hardware Store uses the purchases of a given year to allocate the purchasing department's expenses, since this is considered the best approximation of the services rendered to the selling departments.

The resulting distribution is:

	Tools	Hardware	Paint	Combined
2012–13 purchases	$267 280	$284 568	$132 880	$684 728
Percentage of combined purchases	39.0%	41.6%	19.4%	100.0%
Allocation of $16 000	$6240	$6656	$3104	$16 000

General office expenses. The other service department of Andrews Hardware Store provides personnel, accounting and payroll services to the three selling departments. The number of employees per department is the basis used to allocate the general office expenses to the selling departments since it is considered the best approximation of the benefits provided. An evaluation of the personnel employed in each department indicates that the following allocation is appropriate:

	Tools	Hardware	Paint	Combined
Percentage of total employees	40%	35%	25%	100%
Allocation of $16 200	$6480	$5670	$4050	$16 200

Sundry expenses. The sundry expenses are allocated to the departments on the basis of sales for the same reason discussed earlier for the sundry selling expenses. Consequently, the distribution of the total amount of $5800 is $1978, $2552 and $1270 to the tools, hardware and paint departments respectively.

13.4 Departmental income statement

Learning objective 4

Prepare a departmental income statement

Once the allocation of expenses is completed, an income statement showing the profit by department, such as the one presented in figure 13.5 (p. 550), can be prepared. The results indicate that two of the departments, hardware and paint, were profitable with profits of $51 700 and $15 772 respectively, whereas the tools department incurred a loss of $19 680. However, remember that these results represent estimates of the 'bottom line' profit performances of the departments after they are assigned 'their share' of the indirect expenses. In turn, they represent estimates of the financial results of the departments as independent businesses and should be interpreted cautiously. As suggested earlier, however, 'their share' is subject to a great deal of judgement and depends on the choice of the bases used to allocate the indirect expenses. Different accountants may choose different allocation bases and thus may achieve different results.

The statements can also be criticised on the basis that the departments are not really separate businesses but segments of the same business. Therefore, their 'bottom line' evaluation should be concerned only with the expenses for which they are directly accountable and the indirect expenses should be a common pool that benefits the entire business rather than individual departments. Such a presentation would avoid arbitrary allocations and represent the contribution of each department to the united efforts of the business as a whole.

13.5 Departmental contribution

Learning objective 5

Perform the analysis required to identify an unprofitable department

Analysis of the profit results shown in figure 13.5 may lead to the conclusion that the tools department is so unprofitable that management should consider eliminating it. The loss of $19 680 may suggest to management that profits would have been $67 472 without the tools department instead of $47 792 with it. But is this an accurate conclusion? It is true that the tools department does not have enough gross profit to cover its direct expenses plus its allocated indirect expenses; however, it is making a contribution to the business's profit result.

Figure 13.5 Departmental income statement — profit format

ANDREWS HARDWARE STORE				
Income Statement				
(Departmental profit format)				
for the year ended 30 June 2013				
	Tools department	Hardware department	Paint department	Combined departments
INCOME				
Net sales revenue	$344 000	$443 200	$220 000	$1 000 000
Less: Cost of sales	264 880	283 648	132 480	681 008
GROSS PROFIT	79 120	159 552	88 320	326 992
EXPENSES				
Selling and distribution expenses:				
Sales salaries	36 960	34 240	21 200	92 400
Advertising	11 215	10 162	8 863	30 240
Insurance	2 056	2 615	1 089	5 760
Supplies	1 200	1 100	1 500	3 800
Depreciation	1 900	1 500	1 800	5 200
Sundry	3 071	3 957	1 972	9 000
	56 402	53 574	36 424	146 400
Administrative and other expenses:				
Management salaries	16 000	16 000	16 000	48 000
Building occupancy	11 700	23 400	11 700	46 800
Purchasing	6 240	6 656	3 104	16 000
General office	6 480	5 670	4 050	16 200
Sundry	1 978	2 552	1 270	5 800
	42 398	54 278	36 124	132 800
	98 800	107 852	72 548	279 200
PROFIT (LOSS)	$ (19 680)	$ 51 700	$ 15 772	$ 47 792

The **departmental contribution** is considered by many accountants and managers to be a more realistic assessment of a department's profitability performance than profit, which involves the allocation process described earlier. The advantage of the departmental contribution is that it usually consists of the income and expenses that would disappear if the department did not exist. Its use avoids the somewhat arbitrary allocation of indirect expenses required when an attempt is made to measure departmental profit.

The departmental contribution is found by subtracting only the direct expenses of a department from the departmental gross profit. In most cases, the direct expenses are controllable by the department managers, so the departmental contribution can be used effectively in responsibility accounting. However, sometimes direct expenses are not controllable expenses and should not be included in the departmental contribution if it is being used to assess the department manager. For example, if the insurance cover on inventory is negotiated by senior management, it may be a direct cost based on the level of inventory a department holds, but the insurer, level of insurance and cost are controlled by the senior managers. The salary of a department manager is also likely to be a direct expense but not a controllable cost of the department.

The results of Andrews Hardware Store have been restated in the departmental contribution format in figure 13.6, assuming all direct expenses are controlled by each department. Since the indirect expenses are outside the control of the department managers, they are deducted from the total departmental contribution. The departmental contributions of $31 804, $117 697 and $57 731 identify the controllable profit performances of the three departmental managers.

In figure 13.6, the tools department has made a contribution of $31 804 to cover indirect expenses. Consequently, rather than increasing the total profit by $19 680, the elimination of the tools department would cause a decrease in overall profit of $31 804. This decrease in profit would occur because the two remaining departments have a combined departmental contribution of $175 428 and will have to absorb all the indirect expenses, amounting to $159 440. Thus, the overall profit would be only $15 988 in contrast to the profit of $47 792 from a three-department operation. The difference is the $31 804 contributed by the tools department. An alternative way to evaluate the results of eliminating the tools department is to consider the gross profit of $79 120 given up versus the decreased direct expenses of $47 316. Again, the difference is $31 804 in favour of keeping the department. The most significant point in this analysis is that profitability measurement involving allocated expenses can generate misleading information when it is interpreted incorrectly.

Figure 13.6 Income statement showing departmental contributions

ANDREWS HARDWARE STORE
Income Statement
(Departmental contribution format)
for the year ended 30 June 2013

	Tools department	Hardware department	Paint department	Combined departments
INCOME				
Net sales revenue	$344 000	$443 200	$220 800	$1 008 000
Less: Cost of sales	264 880	283 648	132 480	681 008
GROSS PROFIT	79 120	159 552	88 320	326 992
DIRECT EXPENSES				
Sales salaries	36 960	34 240	21 200	92 400
Advertising	5 200	2 400	5 000	12 600
Insurance	2 056	2 615	1 089	5 760
Supplies	1 200	1 100	1 500	3 800
Depreciation	1 900	1 500	1 800	5 200
Total	47 316	41 855	30 589	119 760
DEPARTMENTAL CONTRIBUTION	$ 31 804	$117 697	$ 57 731	207 232
INDIRECT EXPENSES				
Advertising				17 640
Sundry selling				9 000
Management salaries				48 000
Building expenses				46 800
Purchasing				16 000
General office				16 200
Sundry				5 800
				159 440
PROFIT				$ 47 792

A complete analysis of the tools department would have to take into consideration alternative uses of the space currently occupied by it and any adverse effect on the sales of the hardware and paint departments that will occur as a result of its elimination. There may also be an interdependence between the sales of the three departments. Customers may want to shop at only one store with a complete line of hardware products, so the elimination of tools is likely to adversely affect the sales of the other two departments. Also, we have assumed that all the direct expenses are avoidable expenses and all the indirect expenses are unavoidable. **Avoidable expenses** are ones that can be eliminated by the termination of a department, but **unavoidable expenses** are those that cannot be eliminated. Consequently, only the direct expenses can be eliminated by disposing of the tools department, whereas the indirect expenses do not change since the store requires essentially the same amount of services to support the remaining departments. Certain indirect expenses also may be avoidable because they can be eliminated by reducing the size of the operation.

Demonstration problem

Mr Sharp operates a hardware store with three departments — hardware, plumbing and paint. The income statement for the year ended 30 June 2013 is shown below.

SHARP HARDWARE STORE
Income Statement
for the year ended 30 June 2013

	Hardware	Plumbing	Paint	Total
INCOME				
Sales revenue	$858 000	$462 000	$227 500	$1 547 500
Less: Cost of sales	399 250	215 750	68 250	683 250
GROSS PROFIT	458 750	246 250	159 250	864 250
EXPENSES				
Salaries	255 000	145 000	175 000	575 000
Office expenses	30 000	21 600	8 400	60 000
Telephone	13 750	9 900	3 800	27 450
Supplies	55 000	39 600	15 400	110 000
Rent	40 000	22 500	17 500	80 000
	393 750	238 600	220 100	852 450
PROFIT (LOSS)	$ 65 000	$ 7 650	$ (60 850)	$ 11 800

For the past 3 years, the paint department has shown a loss and the owner of the store has asked you to determine whether the paint department should be dropped. If Mr Sharp decides to eliminate the paint department, 75% of the space occupied by the paint department will be used by the hardware department and the remaining 25% will be used by the plumbing department. Neither sales nor gross profits of the hardware or plumbing departments will change if the paint department is eliminated.

The following information describes the expenses currently relating to the paint department:
1. The salary of a senior manager of $90 000 has been allocated equally among the three departments.
2. At present there are two salespeople and a manager in the paint department. If the paint department is eliminated, the manager would be transferred to the hardware department and the salespeople would be discharged. The salespeople's salary is $42 500 each.
3. Office, telephone and supplies expenses are allocated on the basis of sales. The supplies expense would decrease by $5000 if the paint department is eliminated, but the office expense and telephone expense would not change.
4. The rent expense is allocated on the basis of area and would not change if the paint department is eliminated.

Required

A. Should the paint department be dropped? Produce figures to support your answer.

B. Prepare a departmental income statement for the year ended 30 June 2013 showing the results if the paint department did not exist.

Solution to demonstration problem

A. The department should *not* be dropped because, as shown below, a fall in profits will occur.

	Transferred to hardware dept	Transferred to plumbing dept	Eliminated
Salaries: Senior manager*	$ 15 000	$15 000	—
Paint manager*	60 000		—
Salespeople*			$85 000
Office expense ($8400 allocated)	5 460	2 940	—
Telephone ($3800 allocated)	2 470	1 330	—
Supplies ($10 400 allocated)	6 760	3 640	5 000
Rent ($17 500 allocated)	13 125	4 375	—
	$ 102 815	$27 285	$90 000
Cost savings	$ 90 000		
Lost gross profit	(159 250)		
Net disadvantage	$ (69 250)		

* Paint department salaries of $175 000 represent $30 000 of allocated senior manager salary now reallocated $15 000 each to hardware and plumbing, $85 000 of salespeople's salary now eliminated, and $60 000 of paint manager's salary allocated to hardware.

B.

SHARP HARDWARE STORE
Income Statement
for the year ended 30 June 2013

	Hardware	Plumbing	Total
INCOME			
Sales revenue	$858 000	$462 000	$1 320 000
Less: Cost of sales	399 250	215 750	615 000
GROSS PROFIT	458 750	246 250	705 000
EXPENSES			
Salaries	330 000	160 000	490 000
Office expenses	35 460	24 540	60 000
Telephone	16 220	11 230	27 450
Supplies	61 760	43 240	105 000
Rent	53 125	26 875	80 000
	496 565	265 885	762 450
PROFIT (LOSS)	$ (37 815)	$ (19 635)	$ (57 450)

13.6 Flexible budgeting
Fixed (static) and flexible budgets

Learning objective 6

Prepare a flexible budget and explain how it is used in performance evaluation

The master budgeting procedures discussed in chapter 12 have a potential deficiency in many applications — all budgeted costs are estimated on the basis of a *single* level of activity for income, sales or production. A budget of this type is called a **fixed**, or **static**, **budget** because *only one* level of activity is considered and all other items in the master budget are based on this level. Provided the level of activity actually achieved is approximately the same as the one planned, the fixed budget serves as a useful managerial tool.

When significant differences between the actual and budgeted levels of activity (e.g. income, expenses) occur, however, the fixed budget has limitations (see below) and should be revised to reflect these differences. This can be done with the use of a **flexible budget**, which is a series of budgets taking into account different levels of activity. A flexible budget is particularly important for planning and controlling factory overhead costs.

Limitations of a fixed budget for performance evaluation

As discussed in chapter 12, the starting point in the development of a master budget is the income or sales forecast for the budget period. The planning phase of the management cycle is served efficiently by this approach since all the entity's activities are directed towards a common level of achievement. The production level and all budgets for manufacturing, selling and distribution, administrative, and finance and other activities are based on the single estimate of income/sales volume. This is an example of a fixed budgeting approach since cost and income estimates are developed for only one fixed level of activity.

A potential problem with a fixed budget for control purposes is that it does not take into consideration the possibility that the sales, production or profit goals of the business may not be achieved. If the actual level of activity differs *significantly* from that planned, it is difficult to evaluate performance with a fixed budget. For example, consider the comparison of the budgeted performance and the actual cost results achieved by the production department of Bendigo Manufacturing Ltd shown in figure 13.7.

Figure 13.7 Fixed budget performance report

BENDIGO MANUFACTURING LTD
Fixed Budget Performance Report
for the year ended 30 June 2013

	Budget	Actual	Variance
Units produced	25 000	20 000	5 000 U
Variable costs:			
Direct materials	$125 000	$110 000	$15 000 F
Direct labour	300 000	260 000	40 000 F
Indirect materials	12 500	11 400	1 100 F
Indirect labour	18 750	16 200	2 550 F
Light and power	31 250	24 600	6 650 F
Total variable costs	487 500	422 200	65 300 F
Fixed costs:			
Supervision	60 500	61 400	900 U
Rates	8 700	8 700	0
Insurance	5 200	5 300	100 U
Maintenance	4 700	4 450	250 F
Depreciation	15 300	15 300	0
Total fixed costs	94 400	95 150	750 U
Total manufacturing costs	$581 900	$517 350	$64 550 F

U indicates an unfavourable variance.
F indicates a favourable variance.

Can we really say that the production department's actual cost performance was $64 550 less than its budget, i.e. better than budget? This might be the conclusion based on the fixed budgeting approach used here, although it would be wrong. Because the department actually produced only 20 000 units and not the 25 000 units budgeted, all the budgeted variable costs *should have been* lower. The budget estimates in figure 13.7 simply do not reflect what costs should have been for the 20 000 units actually produced. We cannot compare the variable manufacturing costs of one production level with those of another production level and expect the results to be useful. Instead, a flexible budget should be used to provide a comparable basis for evaluating financial performance when the actual level of activity is different from the one budgeted. Actual performance should be measured against a flexible budget prepared on the basis of the same level of production and sales as those actually achieved.

Preparation of a flexible budget

A flexible budget is developed for a *range of activity levels* rather than for a single level. A flexible budget, in contrast to a static fixed budget, is said to be dynamic because it enables management to quickly adjust the budget figures based on the actual activity level achieved. The adjusted budget represents what costs should have been for the actual activity level achieved.

The initial step in the preparation of a flexible budget is to distinguish between fixed and variable costs. The cost behaviour of each cost item over past periods can be studied to see whether it changes as the activity level changes. As explained in a previous chapter, a variable cost varies in total amount proportionally with changes in volume. The variable cost rate is constant on a per-unit basis. A fixed cost remains constant in total amount over a wide range of activity but varies inversely on a per-unit basis. Procedures for analysing the cost behaviour of specific costs were presented in chapter 11.

In the case of Bendigo Manufacturing Ltd, three of the factory overhead items — indirect materials, indirect labour, and light and power — have been classified as variable costs along with the direct materials and direct labour. The business has established the variable cost rates for these costs as shown below:

Cost item	Variable cost rate per unit
Direct materials	$ 5.00
Direct labour	12.00
Indirect materials	0.50
Indirect labour	0.75
Light and power	1.25
	$19.50

The variable cost portion of the flexible budget will change for different levels of production, as we see in figure 13.8. The range of production activity is from 20 000 units to 30 000 units of production. The variable cost rates are multiplied by a specific number of units to determine the budgeted variable costs for that level of production. Figure 13.8 also shows that the five fixed

Figure 13.8 Flexible budget

BENDIGO MANUFACTURING LTD Flexible budget for the year ended 30 June 2013	Per unit	Levels of activity		
		20 000	25 000	30 000
Variable costs:				
Direct materials	$ 5.00	$100 000	$125 000	$150 000
Direct labour	12.00	240 000	300 000	360 000
Indirect materials	0.50	10 000	12 500	15 000
Indirect labour	0.75	15 000	18 750	22 500
Light and power	1.25	25 000	31 250	37 500
Total variable costs	$ 19.50	390 000	487 500	585 000
Fixed costs:				
Supervision		60 500	60 500	60 500
Rates		8 700	8 700	8 700
Insurance		5 200	5 200	5 200
Maintenance		4 700	4 700	4 700
Depreciation		15 300	15 300	15 300
Total fixed costs		94 400	94 400	94 400
Total manufacturing costs		$484 400	$581 900	$679 400

cost items remain constant over the entire range of activity. The variable costs are the costs that 'flex' over different levels of activity. It can now be seen that if 20 000 units are actually produced, the total of budgeted costs is $484 400, whereas if 30 000 units are actually produced, their total budgeted costs are $679 400.

Performance evaluation with a flexible budget

The use of a flexible budget for cost performance reporting makes the budget estimates and actual results comparable since both are based on the *same level of activity*. Figure 13.9 presents a flexible budget performance report for the production department of Bendigo Manufacturing Ltd. Instead of achieving favourable financial results that might be reported with the fixed budget shown earlier, the department actually incurred an unfavourable variance of $32 950. Both the budget column and the actual column in the report are based on the same production level of 20 000 units. The flexible budget performance report represents a much more realistic evaluation of the departmental cost performance than the fixed budget performance report.

Figure 13.9 Flexible budget performance report

BENDIGO MANUFACTURING LTD
Flexible Budget Performance Report
for the year ended 30 June 2013

	Budget	Actual	Variance
Production units	20 000	20 000	
Variable costs:			
Direct materials	$100 000	$110 000	$10 000 U
Direct labour	240 000	260 000	20 000 U
Indirect materials	10 000	11 400	1 400 U
Indirect labour	15 000	16 200	1 200 U
Light and power	25 000	24 600	400 F
Total variable costs	390 000	422 200	32 200 U
Fixed costs:			
Supervision	60 500	61 400	900 U
Rates	8 700	8 700	0
Insurance	5 200	5 300	100 U
Maintenance	4 700	4 450	250 F
Depreciation	15 300	15 300	0
Total fixed costs	94 400	95 150	750 U
Total manufacturing costs	$484 400	$517 350	$32 950 U

U indicates an unfavourable variance.
F indicates a favourable variance.

The variances shown in figure 13.9 have meaning because they relate to the cost performance only, since production volume differences have been eliminated by adjusting the flexible budget to the level of 20 000 units. The performance report gives management a realistic indication of the areas that should be investigated further in order to control the production costs. For example, direct materials cost and direct labour cost exceeded the budget estimates by $10 000 (10%) and $20 000 (8.3%) respectively. Corrective action is required if future profitability goals are to be achieved. Note also that it is possible for some fixed costs to differ from budget for various reasons, e.g. price changes.

The dynamic nature of a flexible budget permits management to adjust it to any level as long as the same cost behaviour patterns prevail. In the case of Bendigo Manufacturing Ltd, the actual level of activity was the same as one of the levels in the original flexible budget (20 000 units). Even if the actual activity level is not found in the flexible budget, management can easily prepare a revised budget for that level. For example, if Bendigo Manufacturing Ltd had produced 22 400 units, the budget would be adjusted to that level and the results would be compared with the associated actual costs. The variable cost rates (totalling $19.50 per unit) would be multiplied by 22 400 to determine the total variable costs, and the fixed costs would be the same as they were for the production of 25 000 units ($94 400). The total budgeted manufacturing costs for 22 400 units would be $531 200. Flexible budgeting can be applied in retail and service businesses in a similar manner as illustrated for a manufacturing business. Sales revenue and billable hours are appropriate activity levels.

13.7 Standard costs

Learning objective 7

Define standard costs, and understand how they are used in performance evaluation

Chapter 9 demonstrated how a cost accounting system can be used to determine the actual costs of producing a product. The cost data are also used to value inventory and to calculate profit in financial reporting. However, the results have serious limitations in measuring the efficiency of operations.

The limitation of historical or actual cost data is that they represent *what happened*, which is not necessarily what *should have happened*. Efficiency evaluations are limited to historical comparisons such as unit costs from month to month and to management's judgement about what costs should be. The problem with trend analysis is that there is no guarantee that the operation was efficient to begin with, so it may be meaningless to compare the costs of one period with those of another period. Hence, it is difficult to determine a reliable performance measurement base using historical cost data. Typical questions that are difficult to answer with historical cost data are:

- Are the costs too high?
- If so, who is responsible?
- How can costs be reduced?
- Are the costs representative of the future?

If an entity is to operate efficiently, it must be certain that economical amounts of resource inputs are used in the provision of its products and services. This is true also for both job order and process costing operations. **Standard costs** are carefully predetermined measures of what costs *should be* to produce a product or perform an operation in accordance with management's planned performance. Standard costs serve as benchmarks against which the actual performance can be evaluated realistically.

Although our example in this chapter is of standard costs typically used in manufacturing entities, they can also be used in a wide range of other business entities such as hospitals, restaurants, accounting practices, banks and service stations. In practice, standard costing is potentially applicable whenever the activities of a business are repetitive.

In a manufacturing operation, standards are used to plan and control direct materials, direct labour and factory overhead. The objective is to establish a standard cost for each unit of product by predetermining the cost of the direct materials, direct labour and factory overhead required to produce it. Total standard cost generally is determined by multiplying standard quantity per unit by standard price or rate per unit. Both the per-unit dollar amounts that should be incurred for the three manufacturing cost elements and the quantity of each that should be used are identified. In a service business, it is possible to establish a standard billing cost per hour and a certain number of standard hours for specific tasks and services.

Establishing standard costs

As noted previously, standard costs in production are made up of a quantity and a unit price. For example, the production of one finished product may require 5 kilograms of direct materials at a price of $2 per kilogram. The standard direct materials cost is thus $10 per finished unit. Product specifications must be considered carefully when establishing standard costs to ensure that desired quality levels are maintained. Standard costs are usually established with one or some combination of the following three methods: (1) an engineering approach, (2) analysis of historical performance data, and (3) management judgement concerning future operating conditions.

Time and motion studies, work sampling and simulation procedures are examples of engineering methods that can be used to develop standards. For example, a time and motion study may be performed to determine the most economic labour operations needed for a particular job.

Historical cost data should not be ignored in the development of standard costs even though they may have the deficiencies mentioned earlier. The most recent past, in particular, can provide valuable insights into what can be expected in the future.

Finally, managers' judgement concerning future performance must be weighed heavily. They are the people closest to the day-to-day operations, so their opinions and knowledge must be considered. This is particularly important whenever external influences such as union applications for wage rises and market conditions for materials prices are involved.

Managers also must decide what type of standards the business will use. **Ideal standards** require the highest possible level of effort if they are to be achieved. Consequently, they represent maximum efficiency and do not consider allowances for such factors as waste, spoilage, fatigue, work interruptions and human error. Few businesses use ideal standards.

Attainable standards are preferred because they represent targets that can be achieved with a reasonably efficient effort. As such, they are difficult but possible to attain and include allowances for departures from maximum efficiency. Once the standards are established, they should be reviewed regularly and revised whenever necessary to coincide with internal and external changes (e.g. inflation).

Benefits of standard costs

The most important benefits of standard costs are the following:

1. Standard costs provide *reliable estimates* for the planning phase of budgeting. Since standard costs are carefully predetermined costs, they provide the best bases for estimating future cost performance.
2. Standard costs serve as *targets* or performance benchmarks in the application of responsibility accounting to evaluate performance and to control costs. The standard costs represent measures of what costs *should be*, so any variances between them and the actual costs incurred can be investigated for potential corrective action. Responsible managers receive periodic reports that reveal any significant variances through the application of management by exception.
3. Standard costs may be used for inventory valuation in the record-keeping function with *cost savings*. The inventories are maintained on the basis of standard costs (only quantities need be recorded in inventory records) without the detailed accounting of the actual costs needed in an actual costing system.
4. Standard cost information is available on a *timely basis for management decision making*. Standard costs can be used in many cases without waiting for the results of the actual performance.
5. Standard costs make employees *more aware of costs* and their impact on the operation. Since the standard costs represent what costs should be, they make the employees more cost and time conscious, thus promoting an efficient use of resources.

Standard costs and performance evaluation

Standard cost variance analysis is used to determine the amount of any difference between actual costs and standard costs, as well as to discover what caused the deviation. **Standard cost variances** arise when total actual costs are different from total standard costs. The cost variances enable managers to evaluate the efficiency of operations and improve cost performance. An unfavourable variance arises when actual costs exceed standard costs as this will decrease profit. A favourable variance occurs when actual costs are less than standard costs as this will increase profit.

Standard costs can be used for analytical purposes only or can be incorporated into the formal accounting system. When they are used just for analytical purposes, standard cost variances are shown on management performance reports used to control manufacturing costs, and are not recorded in the general ledger. Alternatively, when cost variances are recorded in the general ledger, cost variance accounts are used to accumulate differences between actual cost performance and standard cost performance.

Accounting for the standard costs of materials, labour and factory overhead, and derivation and recording of standard cost variances are topics beyond the scope of this book. Readers wishing to pursue these topics further are referred to any book on cost accounting or management accounting.

13.8 Management systems and performance evaluation

Learning objective **8**

Understand the balanced scorecard management system and how it is used for performance evaluation

This chapter describes how organisations and accounting systems can be structured to provide managers with more useful information for decision making and control. The concept of responsibility accounting demonstrates how accounting systems can be used to evaluate the performance of individual managers at all levels of an organisation. The emphasis is on measurement systems that can be used by managers to evaluate and improve performance. These systems rely almost exclusively on the measurement of financial data, and therefore are subject to the criticism that the data on which future decisions are made relate to past or historical data, thus omitting non-financial data.

However, the focus of managers has now shifted away from measurement systems such as those provided by accounting to the design of total management systems. A number of such systems have been developed over the years. Some of the more well known include management by objectives (MBO), total quality control, total quality management (TQM), project management, business process improvement (BPI) and re-engineering, quality measurement procedures, and quality certification such as ISO-9000. The last few years have seen the development of a management planning and evaluation system known as the balanced scorecard (BSC), which incorporates many of the ideas and concepts of the various models of management systems that preceded its development. Following is a brief introduction to the balanced scorecard approach and its role in the context of performance evaluation.

The balanced scorecard — the basics

The **balanced scorecard** approach focuses on strategic management and appropriate measures that can be developed for evaluating the success or otherwise of these strategies within an organisation. The developers of the BSC approach, Robert Kaplan and David Norton, aimed at providing a system that gave clear directives as to what organisations should measure to evaluate the performance of managers in addition to the traditional financial measures. The BSC provides a 'balance' between the traditional financial perspective and non-financial measures.

Kaplan and Norton described the BSC approach as follows (see www.balancedscorecard.org):

> The balanced scorecard retains traditional financial measures. But financial measures tell the story of past events, an adequate story for industrial age companies for which investments in long-term capabilities and customer relationships were not critical for success. These financial measures are inadequate, however, for guiding and evaluating the journey that information age companies must take to create future value through investment in customers, suppliers, employees, processes, technology, and innovation.

Kaplan and Norton argue that an organisation should be viewed from four perspectives when determining measures to evaluate the performance of managers and the organisation. As well as the traditional financial perspective, they added the learning and growth perspective, the internal business process perspective, and the customer perspective. Under the BSC approach, appropriate measures ('metrics' in the original model) of outcomes or performance needed to be developed, data on these measures had to be collected, and the data had to be analysed. Any corrective actions needed are then taken. The view of an organisation where management has adopted the BSC approach to performance evaluation is summarised in figure 13.10.

Figure 13.10 (p. 560) emphasises that the BSC approach is a management system that requires the organisation adopting it to clearly define its vision and strategies, and focus all activities towards achieving them. Defining the vision and strategic planning become the keystones of the organisation's operations.

The learning and growth perspective focuses attention on the fact that in today's climate of continuous technological change, organisations have become knowledge-worker organisations where people are one of the main resources. In a successful organisation, therefore, the knowledge-workers must be in a state of continuous learning. Kaplan and Norton saw 'learning' as more than training. It includes the use of tutors and mentors within the organisation, and relies on ease of communication among all workers.

Figure 13.10 Perspectives of an organisation — balanced scorecard

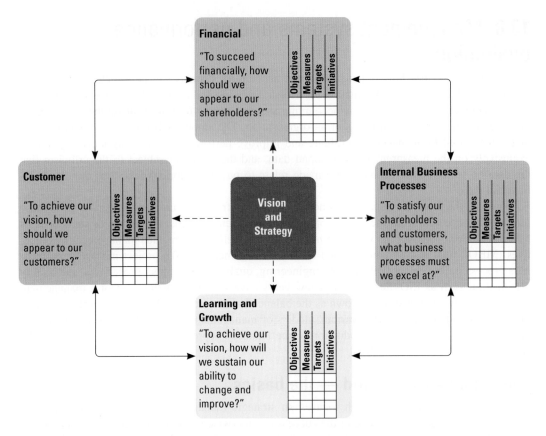

The business process perspective focuses on internal business processes, and appropriately developed measures allow managers to assess how well the business is functioning, and whether products and services are meeting customer expectations.

The customer perspective recognises the increasing emphasis on and importance of customer satisfaction. Poor performance in relation to this perspective is an indicator of the long-term demise of the business even though financial measures of performance are currently acceptable.

Kaplan and Norton acknowledged the importance of financial data, and that timely and reliable financial data are still a priority for managers. Their main concern was that the traditional emphasis on financial measures tended to give an unbalanced view of the organisation, given that the other essential perspectives of the business received insufficient, if any, attention.

The balanced scorecard and performance evaluation

A major requirement for the BSC management system is to develop appropriate measures for all four perspectives based on the priorities of the organisation's strategic plan. This plan should identify the key drivers and criteria that need to be measured for each of the organisational perspectives in order to gauge the success of all strategic outcomes.

The model requires the identification of both financial and non-financial measures of performance and outcomes. Managers can analyse the measures of performance, evaluate performance, and then take corrective action as a result of the feedback obtained. As in any system of management performance evaluation, the managers who are to be evaluated must be involved in developing the measures by which they will be evaluated. It is also essential that outcomes are capable of being measured quantitatively and that the measures are reliable.

In evaluating performance, feedback can be obtained from internal processes, learning and growth and internal business processes perspectives, and from external outcomes (sources) for the financial and customer perspectives. This provides a 'double-loop' feedback process covering both internal and external perspectives.

Implementing the BSC management system in a large organisation can cause many problems if not handled carefully. In practice, the BSC system is usually implemented in stages gradually throughout organisational units. Examples of companies that have adopted the BSC include Citibank, CSR Ltd, Brisbane City Council, BMW Financial Services, Deakin University and Philips Electronics.

BUSINESS KNOWLEDGE

Balanced scorecard

The range of industries that have adopted the balanced scorecard is extremely diverse and includes banking, retail, marketing, hospitality, higher education, insurance and government.

To view some examples of the different approaches various businesses have taken to implementing the balanced scorecard, go to the following website: www.balancedscorecard.org.

Click on an organisation's name to see its details. Some organisations provide a link to their own discussion of the balanced scorecard.

KEY TERMS

Attainable standards, p. 558

Avoidable expenses, p. 551

Balanced scorecard, p. 559

Controllable income, costs/ expenses or investments, p. 541

Cost object, p. 545

Departmental (segmental) accounting, p. 543

Departmental contribution, p. 550

Departmental gross profit, p. 544

Departmental profit, p. 545

Direct cost (expenses), p. 545

Expense allocation, p. 545

Fixed (static) budget, p. 553

Flexible budget, p. 553

Ideal standards, p. 558

Indirect cost (expenses), p. 545

Management by exception, p. 542

Responsibility accounting. p. 540

Responsibility centre, p. 540

Service (or support) department, p. 546

Standard cost variances, p. 558

Standard costs, p. 557

Unavoidable expenses, p. 551

Variance, p. 542

DISCUSSION QUESTIONS

1. 'The problem some people have distinguishing between direct cost, controllable cost and avoidable cost is hard to understand, since they all really mean the same except they are used in different contexts.' Discuss.

2. It is much more time-consuming to involve all managers accountable for responsibility centres in the planning process. Given the extra time and resources of this approach, what are some of the benefits of participation of all managers?

3. 'Although determining gross profit for departments in a department store has some merit, the idea of trying to determine departmental profit is questionable because of all the indirect costs usually involved. Allocation of these costs is so arbitrary that it makes the departmental income statement virtually useless.' Discuss.

4. The manager of a newly established department store asked the accountant to make recommendations regarding reports that should be produced for management use. The accountant was adamant that an income statement that disclosed departmental contributions was far superior to a fully departmentalised one that disclosed departmental profits. Do you agree with the accountant? What advice would you give to the manager? Explain.

5. When preparing department contribution income statements, all direct expenses are controllable by department managers. Discuss, giving examples.

6. What are two factors that need to be taken into account when determining whether a department should be maintained or closed down? Give examples to illustrate each factor.

7. 'Variable costs represent the "flex" in the flexible budget and fixed costs really are of no use in such a budget.' Discuss.

8. 'The only difference between fixed and flexible budgets is the number of fixed budgets — with a fixed budget there is one, with a flexible budget there are many fixed budgets.' Discuss.

9. In performance evaluation, is a fixed budget or a flexible budget more likely to provide a better measure of how well a manager has performed? Explain your answer by using examples.

10. 'The principles of responsibility accounting are just as relevant for the balanced scorecard management system as for an accounting system.' Discuss.

EXERCISES

Exercise 13.1 VARIANCE ANALYSIS   **LO 1**

Following is a performance report for Tamlin Trucking.

	Budget	Actual	Variance
Drivers' wages	$432 000	$464 000	
Fuel and oil	250 000	245 000	
Repairs and maintenance	80 000	105 000	
Registration and insurance	24 000	25 000	
Advertising	18 000	18 000	
Other	12 000	6 000	

Required
Calculate the variances, stating whether they are favourable or unfavourable, and suggest reasons for any variances that you consider significant.

Exercise 13.2 DEPARTMENTAL GROSS PROFIT   **LO 2**

Michael's Bookstore operates two departments, Reference Books and Fiction Books. During the year ended 30 June 2013, the store had the following financial results:

	Reference Books	Fiction Books
Sales	$176 800	$212 600
Sales returns	5 300	6 380
Direct expenses	35 200	67 400
Gross profit percentage of sales	30%	50%

In addition, indirect expenses that were not allocated to the departments amounted to $21 960.

Required
Prepare a departmental income statement for the year ended 30 June 2013, based on the departmental gross profit approach. (Use three columns headed Reference Book department, Fiction Book department, and Total store.)

Exercise 13.3 DEPARTMENTAL GROSS PROFIT AND DEPARTMENTAL CONTRIBUTION   **LO 2**

Wan Chai Meat Store operates two departments, Poultry and Seafood. During the year ended 30 June 2013, the store had the following financial results:

	Poultry	Seafood
Sales	$742 560	$892 900
Direct expenses	154 880	256 120
Gross profit percentage of sales	40%	30%

In addition, indirect expenses that were not allocated to the departments amounted to $55 894.

Required

Prepare departmental income statements for the year ended 30 June 2013, based on the departmental gross profit and the departmental contribution approaches. (Use three columns headed Poultry Department, Seafood Department, and Total Store.)

Exercise 13.4 INDIRECT EXPENSE ALLOCATION WITH SALES LO 3

Trina's Minimart allocates indirect expenses to its three departments on the basis of sales. For the year ended 30 June 2013, the following allocations were made:

	Groceries	Fruit and Vegetables	Meat and Smallgoods	Total
Sales	$711 000	$553 000	$316 000	$1 580 000
Indirect expenses	497 700	387 100	221 200	1 106 000

Assume that, during the year ended 30 June 2014, the Fruit and Vegetables and Meat and Smallgoods departments have the same sales they had in the previous year, but Groceries' sales increase to $741 000 because of the popularity of a new product line. Assume further that the total indirect expenses of $1 106 800 increase by 5%.

Required

A. Determine the allocation of indirect expenses for the year ended 30 June 2014, using the same approach taken in the previous year.
B. Are the results of requirement A logical for an equitable allocation of indirect expenses? Explain.

Exercise 13.5 ALTERNATIVE ALLOCATIONS OF INDIRECT COSTS LO 3

Ladies Luxuries is a women's clothing store and for management and control purposes is divided into three departments. For the year ended 30 June the following information has been collected to determine the best way to allocate rent expense to each department.

	Evening wear	Day wear	Shoes	Total
Sales	$480 000	$288 000	$192 000	$960 000
Floor area occupied (m²)	200	300	100	600
Profit before rent allocation	$96 000	$42 000	$38 000	$176 000

The rent for the year for the store is $60 000. The manager of each department is paid a bonus of 10% of any profit in excess of 10% of sales for the department. The owner of Ladies Luxuries is considering allocating the rent expense to each department using as the base either the percentage of total sales or the floor area occupied.

Required

Determine which method of allocating the rent would be preferred by the manager of each department.

Exercise 13.6 EFFECT OF UNAVOIDABLE COSTS LO 5

One of the Garden Guru Store's four departments has reported a loss of $45 000 after deducting $102 000 of expenses. Assume that only $65 000 of the expenses can be eliminated if the department is discontinued.

Required

A. Should the business keep operating the department reporting the loss when these facts only are considered? Explain.
B. Will the performance of the three other departments ever be considered in the decision to eliminate this department? Explain.

Exercise 13.7 INDIRECT EXPENSE ALLOCATION

Sleeping Beauty Ltd operates three selling departments. Certain indirect expenses are allocated to the selling departments as follows.

	Amount	Basis of allocation
Marketing	$156 000	Sales
Personnel department	96 800	Payroll
Building occupancy	72 200	Floor space
Insurance on inventory	36 800	Average inventory
Administration	64 400	Sales

The following information is obtained from store records for the last financial year:

	Beds	Mattresses	Bed linen
Wages and salaries	$111 600	$148 800	$111 600
Square metres of floor space	800	700	500
Sales	$588 000	$672 000	$420 000
Average inventory	$115 500	$122 100	$92 400

Required

Prepare a schedule allocating the indirect expenses to the three departments.

Exercise 13.8 INDIRECT EXPENSE ALLOCATION

Gentlemen's Clothing Ltd operates three selling departments. Certain indirect expenses are allocated to the selling departments as follows:

	Amount	Basis of allocation
Administration	$206 000	Sales
Personnel department	312 000	Number of staff
Marketing	148 000	Sales
Rent	232 000	Floor space
Insurance on inventory	118 000	Average inventory

The following information is obtained from store records for the last financial year:

	Clothes	Shoes	Accessories
Sales	$1 680 000	$480 000	$240 000
Number of staff	6	2	2
Floor Space	1 000 m^2	600 m^2	400 m^2
Average inventory	$192 000	$80 000	$48 000

Required

A. Prepare a schedule allocating the indirect expenses to the three departments.
B. Assuming all products are priced so that they provide a 50% gross margin, calculate the contribution of each department and comment on why the business may still choose to keep all three departments.

Exercise 13.9 AVOIDABLE VERSUS UNAVOIDABLE COSTS

Meagan's Budget Shop operates three departments, including a linen department that has consistently shown losses. For the year just ended, the linen department showed the following performance:

Sales	$176 000
Cost of sales	120 000
Gross profit	56 000
Expenses	112 800
Loss	$ (56 800)

The expenses include allocated indirect expenses amounting to $62 400, which will be incurred whether the department is operated or not. The remainder of the expenses are direct, but include $28 000 that will have to be reassigned to another department because that amount is the salary of the owner's daughter, who will be kept employed regardless of the decision made about the linen department.

Required

Should the linen department be eliminated? Support your answer with calculations showing the effect on storewide profits of eliminating the department.

Exercise 13.10 ELIMINATION OF A DEPARTMENT

LO 5

Dale's Emporium operates with three departments. The owner-manager wants to close Department B because it continually shows a loss. During the past year ending 30 June 2013, the departmental performances were as follows:

	Dept A	Dept B	Dept C
Sales	$468 000	$188 000	$280 000
Cost of sales	280 000	140 000	182 000
Gross profit	188 000	48 000	98 000
Direct expenses	(46 000)	(24 000)	(28 100)
Indirect expenses	(82 000)	(32 760)	(49 140)
Profit (loss)	$ 60 000	$ (8 760)	$ 20 760

In analysing these results, the accountant determines that insurance expense of $4680 is the only indirect expense that can be avoided if Department B is closed. All direct expenses are avoidable.

Required

What would the effect be on the store's overall profits of closing down Department B?

Exercise 13.11 FLEXIBLE BUDGET FOR SELLING EXPENSES

LO 6

Temby & Associates uses flexible budgets in order to control selling expenses.

Monthly sales range from $210 000 to $200 000. Budgeted fixed monthly expenses for the Sales Department are $36 000 for salaries of sales staff, $8000 for depreciation of delivery vans, and $5000 for insurance. Variable expenses expressed as a percentage of sales are: training expenses for sales staff, 5%; advertising, 8%; sales commissions, 4%; and sundry selling expenses, 2%.

Required

Prepare a flexible budget using increments of $20 000 over the expected range of sales.

Exercise 13.12 FLEXIBLE BUDGET

LO 6

Carol's Clutter Cleanup Pty Ltd wants to prepare flexible budget cost estimates for the following items within a range of 16 000 to 20 000 chargeable hours.

	Fixed cost	Variable cost per chargeable hour
Depreciation	$18 000	$0.10
Electricity	3 600	0.20
Insurance	8 600	0.60
Maintenance	7 400	0.30
Non-billable hours	16 920	—
Rent	14 400	—
Supplies	2 480	1.10

Required

A. Prepare a flexible overhead budget for 16 000, 18 000 and 20 000 chargeable hours.
B. Calculate the fixed, variable and total overhead rates if 17 000 hours are actually charged to clients during the budget period.

Exercise 13.13 FLEXIBLE BUDGET

Maximilian Marketing Pty Ltd is preparing flexible budget cost estimates for the following items within a range of 24 000 to 32 000 chargeable hours:

	Fixed cost	Variable cost per chargeable hour
Rent	$104 000	—
Electricity	7 200	$ 0.18
Insurance	8 000	0.40
Supplies	3 300	2.40
Temporary secretarial support	—	22.00
Non-billable hours	28 000	—
Sundry expenses	12 000	1.40

Required

A. Prepare a flexible overhead budget for 24 000, 28 000 and 32 000 chargeable hours.

B. Calculate the fixed, variable and total overhead rates if 25 000 hours are actually charged to clients during the budget period.

Exercise 13.14 FLEXIBLE BUDGET AND A PERFORMANCE REPORT

Bugis Bags uses an annual flexible budget based on standard direct machine hours for the following factory overhead items:

	Fixed cost	Variable cost per standard direct machine hour
Supplies	$16 000	$0.30
Electricity	19 600	0.20
Indirect labour	24 400	1.10

During the year, 15 000 direct machine hours were recorded for the production achieved. The following actual costs were incurred:

Variable costs:	
Supplies	$ 4 800
Electricity	2 900
Indirect labour	17 200
Fixed costs:	
Supplies	$16 500
Electricity	18 800
Indirect labour	24 400

Required

A. Why is a flexible budget performance report a better basis for assessing a manager's performance than a fixed budget performance report?

B. Prepare a flexible budget for the three cost items using 12 000, 15 000 and 18 000 direct machine hours.

C. Prepare a flexible budget performance report for the three cost items, based on the actual results for the year.

Exercise 13.15 BALANCED SCORECARD

The balanced scorecard goes beyond financial measures to provide a broader range of performance measures. Refer to The Balanced Scorecard Institute at the following website:
www.balancedscorecard.org.

Required

Suggest non-financial measures that could be used in performance management.

Problem 13.1   RESPONSIBILITY ACCOUNTING ★

★ Basic

★★ Moderate

★★★ Challenging

You are provided with the profit centre responsibility accounting reports for Bullseye Department Stores:

	Budget ($'000)	Actual ($'000)	Variance ($'000)
General manager's report			
Clothing department	$ 3 400	$ 3 450	$ 50 F
Homewares department	5 200	4 800	400 U
Electrical department	2 800	2 900	100 F
Furniture department	4 600	4 000	600 U
Total	$16 000	$15 150	$ 850 U
Homewares manager's report			
Linen	$ 1 200	$ 1 300	$ 100 F
Cookware	2 800	2 500	300 U
Cushions	600	550	50 U
Pictures and prints	600	450	150 U
Total	$ 5 200	$ 4 800	$ 400 U
Cookware manager's report			
Frying pans	$ 600	$ 620	$ 20 F
Cooking utensils	480	440	40 U
Crockery	720	600	120 U
Cutlery	600	620	20 F
Glassware	400	220	180 U
Total	$ 2 800	$ 2 500	$ 300 U

Required

A. Explain the relationship between the three profit responsibility reports for Bullseye Department Stores.

B. Explain to whom each of the three managers who receive the reports for Bullseye Department Stores are responsible.

C. Assuming Bullseye Department Stores investigates variances in excess of 5% of budget, outline which items each of the three managers shown are likely to focus on in their respective reports and suggest what non-financial information would also be useful in investigating these variances.

Problem 13.2   DEPARTMENTAL ACCOUNTING ★

Outback Lagoon Ltd specialises in luggage. The store operates two departments — Cases and Backpacks. The following information was obtained from the store's accounting records for the year ended 30 June 2013:

	Cases	Backpacks
Net sales	$588 000	$392 000
Purchases	339 660	214 800
Purchases returns	5 200	3 370
Freight inwards	740	530
Direct expenses	110 000	131 625
Inventory, 1 July 2012	63 800	56 650
Inventory, 30 June 2013	74 500	43 970

Indirect expenses are $84 800 per year.

Required

A. Prepare a departmental income statement showing the departmental gross profit for each department and the store's profit for the year.
B. Calculate the gross profit percentage for each department.
C. Prepare a departmental income statement that shows the profit of each department after the indirect expenses are allocated on the basis of sales.

Problem 13.3 DEPARTMENTAL ACCOUNTING ★   **LO 2**

Hungerford Books Ltd is a book retailer. Hungerford specialises in selling fiction and reference books. The following information was derived from the shop's accounting records for the year ended 30 June 2014:

	Fiction books	Reference books
Net sales	$982 000	$456 000
Purchases	589 200	328 320
Purchase returns	4 600	3 800
Direct expenses	165 000	87 500
Inventory, 1 July 2013	196 400	152 200
Inventory, 30 June 2014	202 600	148 900

Indirect expenses are $164 000 per year.

Required

A. Prepare a departmental income statement showing the departmental gross profit for each department and the store's profit for the year.
B. Calculate the gross profit percentage for each department.
C. Prepare a departmental income statement that shows the profit of each department after the indirect expenses are allocated on the basis of gross profit.

Problem 13.4 INDIRECT EXPENSE ALLOCATION ★   **LO 3**

Bishop's Electrical Store operates three departments — Computers, Televisions and Appliances. When preparing a departmental income statement, the store's accountant allocates indirect expenses using the following allocation bases:

Indirect expense	Allocation base	Total amount
Occupancy costs	Relative value of floor space	$280 000
Personnel overhead cost	Number of employees	60 000
Insurance	Value of inventory	90 000
Advertising	Sales	240 000

The following data were obtained for the three departments:

	Computers	Televisions	Appliances
Sales	$2 124 200	$3 431 400	$2 614 400
Floor space (m²)	340	408	204
Number of employees	3	4	3
Value of inventory	$430 000	$860 000	$860 000

The Television Department is located at the front of the store and the other two departments are at the back. For the purposes of the allocation of the rent expense, it is assumed that the front of the store is twice as valuable as the back.

Required

Prepare a schedule showing the allocation of the indirect expenses to the three departments.

LO 4

Problem 13.5 INCOME STATEMENT WITH DEPARTMENTAL CONTRIBUTIONS ★★

Beige Books Ltd operates a bookstore with two departments — a New Books department and a Second-hand Books department. The company's accountant has prepared an income statement for the year ending 30 June 2013.

BEIGE BOOKS
Income Statement
for the year ended 30 June 2013

INCOME		
Sales		$1 130 000
Cost of sales:		
Beginning inventory	$111 300	
Purchases	646 600	
Goods available for sale	757 900	
Ending inventory	97 520	
Cost of sales		660 380
GROSS PROFIT		469 620
EXPENSES		
Advertising	47 700	
Salaries	132 500	
Insurance	45 600	
Depreciation	18 000	
Supplies	27 500	
Interest	38 160	
Total expenses		309 460
PROFIT		$ 100 100

The beginning inventory of the New Books department was $65 520, and the ending inventory was $57 140. The beginning inventory for the Second-hand Books department was $45 780, and the ending inventory was $40 380.

The company's records indicate that the following percentages of each expense or revenue are directly chargeable to the departments. Any balance left in an expense account is an indirect expense.

	New Books	Second-hand Books
Sales revenue	55%	45%
Purchases	53%	47%
Advertising	43%	32%
Salaries	34%	21%
Insurance	36%	26%
Depreciation	19%	23%
Supplies	35%	33%

Required

Prepare a departmental income statement for the year ended 30 June 2013, showing the departmental contribution for each department.

Dressed to Kill Ltd operates two departments — Men's Clothes and Women's Clothes. The store's income statement for the year ending 30 June 2013 has been prepared from the accounting records.

DRESSED TO KILL LTD
Income Statement
for the year ended 30 June 2013

INCOME		
Sales		$1 600 000
Cost of sales:		
Beginning inventory	$142 000	
Purchases	510 000	
Goods available for sale	652 000	
Ending inventory	98 600	
Cost of sales		553 400
GROSS PROFIT		1 046 600
EXPENSES		
Sales salaries	431 250	
Advertising	74 000	
Depreciation	62 000	
Managerial salaries	140 000	
Rent	88 700	
Property rates	20 000	
Sundry expenses	54 000	
Total expenses		869 950
PROFIT		$ 176 650

The company's records indicate that the following percentages of each expense or revenue account are directly chargeable to the departments. (Any balance left in an expense account after allocation of direct charges is treated as an indirect expense.)

	Music	Movies
Sales	35%	65%
Purchases	40%	60%
Sales salaries	32%	68%
Advertising	25%	35%
Depreciation	20%	25%
Rent	30%	30%
Sundry expenses	28%	32%

The beginning inventory for the Men's Clothes department was $64 000 and the ending inventory was $44 000. The beginning inventory for the Women's Clothes department was $78 000 and the ending inventory was $54 600.

Required

Prepare a departmental income statement for the year ending 30 June 2013 that shows the departmental contribution for each department.

Ashcroft Ltd operates four departments. Management is concerned about the financial results of the Small Appliance Department, which has shown a loss for the past 3 years according to the company's income statement. Competition in small appliances is exceptionally strong in the area in which the company operates. The departmental income statement for the year ended 30 June 2013 was as follows:

ASHCROFT LTD
Income Statement
for the year ended 30 June 2013

	Small Appliance Department	All other departments
INCOME		
Sales	$375 800	$1 865 000
Less: Cost of sales	280 800	1 118 700
GROSS PROFIT	95 000	746 300
Direct expenses	(43 800)	(292 700)
Indirect expenses	(60 500)	(246 300)
PROFIT (LOSS)	$ (9 300)	$ 207 300

If the Small Appliance Department is closed, direct expenses amounting to $13 000 would be shifted to the other three departments. In addition, indirect expenses of $53 700 are unavoidable if the department is eliminated.

Required

A. Calculate the departmental margin for the Small Appliance Department.
B. Should the Small Appliance Department be closed down? Justify your answer.
C. Prepare an income statement for the three remaining departments, assuming the Small Appliance Department is dropped, to confirm your results in requirement B.

Problem 13.6 CLOSING DOWN A DEPARTMENT ★★

Wright Ltd operates three departments. The Phone Department has not been performing very well and has shown a loss for the past 3 years according to the company's income statement. Competition in phone equipment is strong and the margins are low. The departmental income statement for the year ended 30 June 2013 was as follows:

WRIGHT LTD
Income Statement
for the year ended 30 June 2013

	Phone Department	Other two departments
INCOME		
Sales	$488 000	$1 500 200
Less: Cost of sales	366 000	671 200
GROSS PROFIT	122 000	829 000
Direct expenses	(56 900)	(235 500)
Indirect expenses	(78 600)	(198 200)
PROFIT (LOSS)	$ (13 500)	$ 395 300

Indirect expenses of $5300 are unavoidable if the Phone Department is eliminated.

Required

A. Calculate the departmental margin for the Phone Department.

B. Should the Phone Department be closed down? Justify your answer.

C. Prepare an income statement for the three remaining departments, assuming the Phone Department is dropped, to confirm your results in requirement B.

Problem 13.9 PREPARING A FLEXIBLE BUDGET PERFORMANCE REPORT ★★

Macquire Manufacturing Ltd has prepared the following fixed budget performance report:

MACQUIRE MANUFACTURING LTD
Fixed Budget Performance Report
for the year ended 30 June 2013

	Budget	Actual	Variance
Units produced	50 000	56 000	6 000 F
Variable costs:			
Direct materials	$ 750 000	$ 924 000	$174 000 U
Direct labour	400 000	420 000	20 000 U
Indirect materials	60 000	61 600	1 600 U
Indirect labour	40 000	50 400	10 400 U
Electricity and gas	62 500	61 600	900 F
Total variable costs	1 312 500	1 517 600	205 100 U
Fixed costs:			
Supervisor's salary	80 000	84 000	4 000 U
Rent	120 000	120 000	0
Insurance	25 000	24 000	1 000 F
Maintenance	20 000	18 000	2 000 F
Depreciation	18 000	18 000	0
Total fixed costs	263 000	264 000	1 000 U
Total manufacturing costs	$1 575 500	$1 781 600	$206 100 U

U indicates an unfavourable variance.
F indicates a favourable variance.

The variable cost rates per unit for Macquire Manufacturing Ltd are as follows:

Cost item	Variable cost rate per unit
Direct materials	$15.00
Direct labour	8.00
Indirect materials	1.20
Indirect labour	0.80
Electricity and gas	1.25
	$26.25

Required

A. Prepare a flexible budget performance report for the actual level of activity.

B. Comment on the significant variances in the flexible budget performance report and explain why this is a better method of measuring variances than a fixed budget performance report such as the one above.

C. If the number of units produced is less than budget, what disadvantages does a flexible budget performance report have?

Problem 13.10   FLEXIBLE BUDGETS AND PERFORMANCE REPORTING ★★

Hossain Ltd has prepared the following fixed budget performance report for the production department's financial results during the year ended 30 June 2013:

HOSSAIN LTD
Fixed Budget Performance Report
for the year ended 30 June 2013

	Budget	Actual	Variance
Units of production:	72 000	62 400	9 600 U
Manufacturing costs:			
Direct materials	$ 648 000	$ 577 200	$ 70 800 F
Direct labour	504 000	430 560	73 440 F
Factory overhead:			
Variable costs:			
Indirect labour	36 000	32 760	3 240 F
Supplies	54 000	54 600	600 U
Repairs	27 000	28 080	1 080 U
Total variable overhead	117 000	115 440	1 560 F
Fixed costs:			
Depreciation	127 200	127 440	240 U
Insurance	2 400	1 920	480 F
Rent	12 000	12 000	—
Salaries	16 800	17 280	480 U
Total fixed overhead	158 400	158 640	240 U
Total factory overhead	275 400	274 080	1 320 F
Total manufacturing costs	$1 427 400	$1 281 840	$145 560 F

Required

A. Should the production department manager be rewarded for the significantly large favourable variance reported for the year? Explain.
B. Prepare a flexible budget performance report for the company's results. Comment on the manager's performance.

Problem 13.11   FLEXIBLE BUDGETING AND PERFORMANCE REPORTING ★★

The fixed budget performance report for the year ended 30 June 2014 for Lapierre Ltd is as follows:

	Budget	Actual	Variance
Units of production:	50 000	55 000	5 000 F
Factory overhead:			
Variable costs:			
Indirect labour	$115 000	$132 000	$17 000 U
Factory supplies	80 000	80 000	—
Repairs and maintenance	33 600	42 000	8 400 U
Total variable overhead	228 600	254 000	25 400 U
Fixed costs:			
Factory insurance	12 000	10 500	1 500 F
Rent expense	18 600	24 000	5 400 U
Depreciation	14 500	13 800	700 F
Management salaries	86 000	92 000	6 000 U
Total fixed overhead	131 100	140 300	9 200 U
Total factory overhead	$359 700	$394 300	$34 600 U

Required

Convert the fixed budget performance report prepared by Lapierre Ltd to a flexible budget performance report.

Problem 13.12 FLEXIBLE BUDGETING AND PERFORMANCE REPORTING ★★

Bartkowski's Bricks Ltd has prepared a fixed budget performance report for the year ended 30 June 2013 as follows:

	Budget	Actual	Variance
Units of production:	72 000	75 200	3 200 F
Factory overhead:			
Variable costs:			
Indirect labour	$108 000	$116 560	$ 8 560 U
Factory supplies	39 600	39 856	256 U
Repairs and maintenance	25 200	27 072	1 872 U
Total variable overhead	172 800	183 488	10 688 U
Fixed costs:			
Insurance of factory	16 600	24 600	8 000 U
Occupancy costs	24 000	25 400	600 U
Depreciation	20 700	20 700	—
Supervisory salaries	43 400	42 200	1 200 F
Total fixed overhead	105 500	112 900	7 400 U
Total factory overhead	$278 300	$296 388	$18 088 U

Required

A. Convert the fixed budget performance report prepared by Bartkowski's Bricks Ltd to a flexible budget performance report.
B. Why does a report based on a flexible budget provide a better means of evaluating performance as opposed to a fixed budget?

Problem 13.13 ELIMINATION OF A DEPARTMENT ★★★

Fillmore Furniture Ltd operates three departments — a Lounge Furniture department, a Dining Furniture department, and a Bedroom Furniture department. The store's accountant has prepared an income statement by department for the year ended 30 June 2013 and, for the third year in a row, the Bedroom Furniture department has shown a loss.

If the company decides to shut down the unprofitable department, 30% of the space occupied by the Bedroom Furniture department will be used by the Lounge Furniture department and 30% will be used by the Dining Furniture department. The other 40% of the space will no longer be rented by Fillmore Furniture Ltd. The company does not believe that eliminating the Bedroom Furniture department and at the same time enlarging the remaining two departments will change the sales or gross profits of the Lounge Furniture and Dining Furniture departments.

The accountant has also provided the following information.

1. At present, there are three salespeople and a manager in the Bedroom Furniture department. If the department is eliminated, the manager would be transferred to the Lounge Furniture department and the three salespeople's employment would be terminated. The manager's salary is $52 000 per year.
2. Electricity, rent and insurance are allocated on the basis of floor space. The insurance would decrease $4000 a year if the department is eliminated; the rent and electricity would decrease by 40% of Bedroom Furniture's expense in line with the area given up.
3. Indirect advertising expenses of $40 000 were allocated to the departments on the basis of sales. The direct advertising expenditures incurred by the Bedroom Furniture department would be eliminated.

4. The equipment in the Bedroom Furniture department would be transferred to the other departments — 40% to the Lounge Furniture department and 20% to the Dining Furniture department and the other 40% would be scrapped.
5. The managing director's salary of $60 000 p.a. has been allocated equally over the departments.

FILLMORE FURNITURE LTD
Income Statement
for the year ended 30 June 2013

	Lounge Furniture	Dining Furniture	Bedroom Furniture	Total
INCOME				
Sales	$766 000	$459 600	$306 400	$1 532 000
Less: Cost of sales	306 400	206 820	107 240	620 460
GROSS PROFIT	459 600	252 780	199 160	911 540
EXPENSES				
Salaries	144 990	74 410	80 950	300 350
Electricity	14 700	14 700	12 600	42 000
Advertising	126 280	78 470	86 590	291 340
Rent on building	28 700	28 700	24 600	82 000
Depreciation on equipment	31 570	23 450	19 840	74 860
Insurance	9 555	9 555	8 190	27 300
Total expenses	355 795	229 285	232 770	817 850
PROFIT (LOSS)	$103 805	$ 23 495	$ (33 610)	$ 93 690

Required

A. Should the Bedroom Furniture department be closed down? What would be the impact on company total profit if it is eliminated?
B. Prepare a departmental income statement that would result if the Bedroom Furniture department is dropped.

Problem 13.14 RESPONSIBILITY ACCOUNTING ★★★   LO 1

Carthew's Cars Pty Ltd is a motor vehicle dealership. In recent years, the company has experienced unsatisfactory profit results because of declining sales in the area. At the suggestion of the company's public accountant, responsibility accounting was implemented at the beginning of 2012. The following departments were organised as profit centres:

- new car sales
- used car sales
- service — mechanical
- service — body shop
- parts and accessories.

Monthly reports are prepared showing the profit results of each of the five departments. On 13 April 2012, the parts and accessories manager and the used car manager requested a meeting with the company's general manager to discuss the way responsibility accounting was being applied. In particular, they are protesting against two policies that currently are in effect:

1. The parts and accessories department must transfer all parts and accessories internally to other departments at their original invoice cost.
2. The used car sales department is charged the full dollar amount allowed by the new car sales department on a used car traded in for a new car. In many cases, this amount exceeds the ultimate selling price of the used car. The used car sales manager tells the general manager about a recent case that is typical. A vehicle with a wholesale market value of $19 000 was traded in on a new car with a list price of $48 000 and a dealer cost of $40 600. A trade-in allowance of $26 100 was given on the used car to promote the deal and the customer paid cash of $21 900. Consequently, a profit of $7400 (i.e. $26 100 + $21 900 − $40 600) was recognised by the new car sales department.

The retail market value of the used car was $22 080 and it was sold at that price 2 weeks later. Since the used car sales department was charged $26 100 when the used car was added to the inventory, it incurred a loss of $4020 on the ultimate sale.

Both managers (parts and accessories and used car) are upset by what they consider unfair practices and violation of the basic premise of responsibility accounting.

Required

A. Do you agree or disagree with the two managers?

B. What would you do to improve the situation, if anything?

Problem 13.15 FLEXIBLE BUDGETS AND PERFORMANCE EVALUATION ★★   **LO 6**

Dee Romm, sales manager of Easy Software Ltd, was given the following budget performance report for selling expenses in the Marketing Software Department for the month of April 2013.

The recently appointed managing director of the company was pleased that Dee had been able to increase her department's sales by 20% over the budgeted sales of 12 000 units. On the other hand, Dee came in for some severe criticism for the apparent blow-out of selling expenses in her department. Dee felt that the criticism she received was unfounded, because she believed that, given the level of sales volume achieved, the selling expenses were under control. She is unsure how to argue her case with the managing director, and approaches you as an accountant to help her.

EASY SOFTWARE LTD
Marketing Software Budget Report
for the month ended 30 April 2013

	Budget	Actual	Variance
Sales in units	12 000	14 400	2 400 F
Fixed expenses:			
Sales salaries	$ 1 800	$ 1 800	$ —
Office salaries	1 200	1 200	—
Rent	2 250	2 250	—
Depreciation — delivery vehicles	750	750	—
Total fixed expenses	6 000	6 000	—
Variable costs:			
Sales commissions	2 400	3 160	760 U
Advertising expense	1 200	1 200	— U
Free samples and promotions	1 440	2 016	576 U
Travel expense	6 000	6 912	912 U
Total variable expenses	11 040	13 296	2 256 U
Total expenses	$17 040	$19 296	$2 256 U

Required

A. Prepare a report based on flexible budget principles.

B. Does Dee deserve the criticism she received for not controlling selling expenses in her department?

C. Should the format of future budget reports be changed and, if so, why?

DECISION ANALYSIS

To open or not to open?

Penny Farthing, proprietor of the Healthy Holiday Resort, had generally been satisfied with the results of her resort in past years. However, she had felt for some time that business always seemed to be a little quiet towards the end of each financial year ending on 30 June. As a matter of curiosity, she had her accountant prepare an analysis of the last financial year's results by quarters. The analysis yielded the figures set out below:

HEALTHY HOLIDAY RESORT Income Statement for the year ended 31 December 2014 (total and by quarter)					
	Total	1st quarter	2nd quarter	3rd quarter	4th quarter
INCOME					
Sales revenue	$884 870	$226 990	$294 620	$237 600	$125 660
EXPENSES					
Advertising	26 390	6 330	8 450	7 390	4 220
Wages and salaries	476 250	120 380	142 560	125 660	87 650
Lease of land	126 720	31 680	31 680	31 680	31 680
Maintenance	12 650	3 160	4 220	3 160	2 110
Electricity	104 540	26 400	30 620	27 460	20 060
Insurance	21 120	5 280	5 280	5 280	5 280
Depreciation	16 880	4 220	4 220	4 220	4 220
Interest on loan	25 320	6 330	6 330	6 330	6 330
Total expenses	809 870	203 780	233 360	211 180	161 550
PROFIT (LOSS)	$ 75 000	$ 23 210	$ 61 260	$ 26 420	$ (35 890)

The analysis revealed what Penny had suspected. The resort was running at a loss for the final quarter of the year. She then reasoned that she could either stop trading for the unprofitable quarter and take her family on holiday to somewhere cooler, or earn some additional money by being a tour guide in the nearby national park.

Her accountant determined that, if the resort closed for the fourth quarter, fourth-quarter expenses would be affected in the following ways. Wages and salaries included an unavoidable $30 600 fixed component; interest on loan and lease payments would still need to be paid; 40% of advertising costs were fixed, Insurance premiums would reduce by $960; 60% of maintenance costs could be saved; a minimum electricity charge of $1050 would still apply; depreciation of $1680 would still need to be charged.

Required
A. Should Penny close her resort in the fourth quarter and take her family on holiday? Explain why.
B. Should Penny close her resort in the fourth quarter and seek employment as a tour guide? Explain your conclusion.

CRITICAL THINKING

Employee bonuses

Ellie works for a medium-sized family-owned firm and was employed on a low retainer with the majority of her income based on bonuses. Ellie is in charge of one of four responsibility centres and the bonuses were based on the final profit for each centre. Ellie was not satisfied with this arrangement and renegotiated her contract so that bonuses are now based on gross profit.

Required
A. Why was Ellie, who is accountable for a responsibility centre, not satisfied with bonuses based on final profit for the centre?
B. Why might it not be in the best interests of the owner-manager of the firm to base employee bonuses on the gross profit of the responsibility centre?
C. What would be the most effective way of determining employee bonuses that should satisfy the requirements of both employees and the owner-manager?

Personal human resources

Bill Robbie works for a human resource management firm, People 4 U (P4U), that searches for middle and senior managers for large businesses. The firm receives a fee equivalent to 80% of the salary package of the people the firm successfully finds for clients. Each job is allocated direct expenses, such as the time spent by staff looking for potential employees and interviewing them, stationery, advertising costs, phone calls and secretarial time.

As well as the direct costs, each job is allocated overhead costs determined by the accountant, Crea Tive, who estimates what proportion of total work done by the firm each year applies to each job. This estimate is very subjective. Bill regularly takes Crea out to lunch or for drinks after work at the local hotel. Crea believes Bill is interested in a relationship with her, but Bill has a steady partner and does not reciprocate Crea's feelings.

Each employee of P4U earns a base salary and a bonus equal to 10% of the profit on each job. The profit on each job is calculated by deducting the direct costs and allocated overhead costs from the fee charged to the client. Bill has borrowed a large amount to finance a new house, and is having difficulties meeting his repayments. At lunch one day, Bill intimated that it might be in Crea's interests if she allocated less of overhead costs to Bill's jobs and that some of the direct costs could easily be charged to other jobs that Bill was not involved with. Eager to please Bill, Crea agrees and charges some of the phone calls, stationery and secretarial costs for Bill's jobs to Nadia's, as she doesn't like Nadia anyway. Crea also reduces the amount of overhead costs allocated to Bill's jobs. In return, Bill takes Crea to lunch more often just to keep her on side, as he has no intention of developing a personal relationship with her.

Required
A. Who are the stakeholders?
B. What are the ethical issues, if any, involved?
C. How are the actions of Crea likely to affect the performance evaluations of Nadia?

Refer to the latest financial report of JB Hi-Fi Limited on its website, www.jbhifi.com.au, and answer the following questions:
1. Is JB Hi-Fi Limited segmented?
2. Could JB Hi-Fi Limited be described as a diversified economic entity? Explain why.
3. Describe how segmental information is presented in the report and comment on the degree of disclosure of segmental performance and position in the income statement and balance sheet.
4. Do you believe that the users of the annual report would be better served if segmental information was presented in the income statement? Explain.

Chapter 14

Differential analysis, profitability analysis and capital budgeting

Concepts for review

Before studying this chapter, you should understand or, if necessary, revise:

- the differences between variable, fixed and mixed costs (pp. 463–5)
- what a contribution margin is, and how it is calculated (pp. 467–8).

Learning objectives

After studying this chapter, you should be able to:

1 explain the basic characteristics of management decision making, and the major steps in the decision-making process (pp. 582–3)

2 use differential analysis to choose between alternative courses of action, including evaluation of a special order, evaluation of a make-or-buy decision, processing of joint products, and product mix decisions (pp. 583–7)

3 explain how to use return on investment analysis and residual profit analysis (pp. 587–9)

4 describe the nature and importance of capital budgeting decisions (pp. 590–2)

5 understand the role of cash flows and the time value of money in capital budgeting decisions (pp. 593–6)

6 evaluate investments using the time value of money (pp. 596–7)

7 evaluate investments using methods not based on the time value of money (p. 598).

Return on investment a goal for all industries

Profitability analysis is an important part of any business venture regardless of the industry in which an entity is involved. This is highlighted by the following extracts from recent newspaper articles that consider the return on investment within sporting investments and business.

Israel Folau may be costing Greater Western Sydney and the AFL a truckload of cash, but he seems to be delivering a strong **return on investment** before he plays a game.

AFL chief executive Andrew Demetriou said yesterday that Folau had generated more than $9 million worth of publicity for the game since his decision to cross codes from rugby league was announced last month.

The figures come from an independent media review, and assess how much it would cost to buy as much media coverage. 'If we had spent $2 million promoting AFL in NSW, it probably wouldn't have got a blip on the radar, to be quite truthful,' Demetriou said on SEN Radio.

'There's certainly a lot of awareness around GWS because of Folau, so from that perspective we're pleased. But we haven't won the battle. It's a long haul, we've always said it's a long haul.'

Source: Excerpt from Martin Blake, 'AFL has nine million reasons why their money was well spent at GWS — AFL', *The Sydney Morning Herald*

The company to operate the national broadband network would need to be adopted by 70 per cent of consumers to give the government a 6 per cent **return on investment**, according to the implementation study released yesterday.

It says winning that share of the market would call for the company to aggressively pursue Telstra's wholesale customers.

The study, released yesterday by McKinsey, forecasts that the government would spend $26 billion on the network, and receive returns of up to 7 per cent when NBN Co is fully privatised in 15 years.

To achieve those returns, McKinsey recommends NBN be biased towards 'achieving take-up rather than maximising revenue', and offer migration incentives to encourage Australians on to the network. It even recommends that NBN pay providers $300 for each household that moves from Telstra's network on to the fibre network.

But all fixed-line consumers would eventually migrate on to the fibre network as the copper network deteriorates, the study says.

Source: Excerpt from Lucy Battersby, 'NBN needs a high fibre diet', *The Age*.

This chapter explains how the return on investment is calculated and interpreted.

Chapter preview

We have seen in previous chapters that managers make decisions continuously as they plan activities, organise resources, direct operations and control performance. Topics covered in previous chapters help managers make decisions, either directly or indirectly. This chapter deals specifically with the subject of decision making and the accounting information required for the decision-making process. **Decision making** involves a choice between alternative courses of action, and the alternative chosen is usually selected on the basis of some measure of profitability or cost savings. What products to produce, how to produce them, how to sell them, what price to charge, how to allocate resources, what equipment to buy, and whether to expand the operating capacity of an entity are examples of business decisions.

Although all business decisions are future-oriented, some will have longer term implications than others. In the first part of this chapter we are concerned with short-term economic decisions. Managers must make good day-to-day decisions to use the existing capacity of the entity profitably. Many aspects of making such decisions are also useful to top management in strategic decision making. In the latter part of the chapter, we look at capital budgeting, which is an important long-term decision-making tool used by managers to establish, maintain and expand an entity's operating capacity. Examples of this are shown in the scene setter where companies have to determine the return on investment regardless of whether they are involved in sport or providing the internet.

The quality of decision making depends on the quality of the information available to the decision maker. Appropriate information should lead to correct decisions, whereas poor information usually leads to incorrect decisions. A basic understanding of the general decision-making process must precede any coverage of the role of accounting information in decision making.

14.1 Management decision making

Learning objective 1

Explain the basic characteristics of management decision making, and the major steps in the decision-making process

Business decisions range from the routine and repetitive to the complex and non-recurring. Management decision making is both instinctive and logical because a combination of qualitative (subjective) and quantitative (objective) factors are required. Such qualitative factors as public image, social responsibility, competitive reaction, management intuition and employee attitudes often have an important bearing on a decision. At the same time, management attempts to structure a decision-making situation in quantitative terms whenever possible so a choice can be made on a systematic basis. Accounting provides most of the quantitative information (income, costs, invested capital and operating statistics) required to evaluate alternative courses of action.

Although there is no universal way managers make decisions, the **decision-making process** in general consists of these four steps, as discussed in chapter 1:

1. *Establish goals and strategies, and then define the problems.* Managers should develop a complete understanding of the problems that must be solved and the goals they want to accomplish. If the goals are not identified and the problems are incorrectly defined, time and resources will be wasted by ineffective decision making.
2. *Gather information on alternative courses of action.* In some cases, only two alternatives are considered. For example, a human resources manager may have to decide whether to employ permanent staff or hire temporary staff. More complex decisions involve more than two alternatives, and here it is important to limit the analysis to a manageable number of alternatives, but still find a satisfactory solution. For example, a marketing firm trying to decide what kind of computer system to install for processing client data and preparing marketing proposals may consider only those suppliers known for their expertise in high-end graphics applications.
3. *Evaluate the outcomes of each of the alternatives.* Only *relevant* information, both qualitative and quantitative, should be considered — information useful in influencing the decision. Whenever the information collected is the result of past performance, it should be recast as a projection of what is expected or desired in the future so that future consequences can be assessed.
4. *Make a decision, i.e. choose a course of action.* The final choice among alternative courses of action is the one the decision maker believes will achieve the desired goals identified in the first step. In many cases, a **decision model** (a formalised method for evaluating alternatives)

is used as an aid in the selection process. The cost–volume–profit analysis methods discussed in chapter 11 are examples of decision models that can be used to evaluate the profitability of various alternatives. Other decision models based on mathematical or statistical procedures are also available for decision making in well-structured situations.

Computer packages such as an Excel spreadsheet package or corporate performance management systems can be useful tools in the decision-making process to perform the various analyses considered below. The costs and benefits of purchasing such packages must also be taken into consideration in the decision-making process.

14.2 Differential analysis

Learning objective 2

Use differential analysis to choose between alternative courses of action, including evaluation of a special order, evaluation of a make-or-buy decision, processing of joint products, and product mix decisions

Differential analysis, also called **incremental analysis**, is a decision model that can be used to evaluate the differences in revenue and costs for alternative courses of action. The costs considered are not necessarily those used in conventional financial reporting. There are different costs for different purposes. For decision-making purposes, relevant costs, differential costs, unavoidable costs, sunk costs and opportunity costs are important classifications. **Relevant costs** are expected future costs, which differ between the alternatives. The difference between the relevant costs of two or more alternatives is called a **differential cost**. For example, if a production manager is deciding which of two machines to buy, direct labour cost may or may not be relevant. If the same skilled labour with an hourly rate of $30 is required to operate either machine, then the labour cost is not relevant to this decision. However, if one machine requires less skill with a $20-per-hour operator, the labour cost is relevant and the differential cost is $10 per hour.

All costs are relevant in decision making except the unavoidable costs; they are the same regardless of the alternative selected. **Unavoidable costs** are either future costs that will not differ between alternatives (the $30 direct labour cost needed for both machines in the above example) or sunk costs. **Sunk costs** are not relevant in decision making because they have already been incurred and cannot be changed. An example is the carrying amount of an item of depreciable equipment a business is trying to decide whether to replace, assuming the equipment has no resale value. If the item is replaced, the recorded amount will be written off in the period of disposal. If it is kept, the same amount will be depreciated over the remaining life of the asset. Consequently, the carrying amount will be expensed in either case, and it is therefore a sunk cost.

An **opportunity cost** is the potential benefit forgone by rejecting one alternative and accepting another. Opportunity costs are not found in the general ledger but are considered either formally or informally as part of virtually every decision. For example, if a student decides to undertake a tertiary course instead of accepting a job that pays $40 000, the true cost of studying is more than the books, tuition and housing. An opportunity cost of $40 000 exists. As a business example, if a business is considering the investment of money in land to be held for future expansion, the profit that is lost from an alternative investment such as a bank deposit is an opportunity cost associated with the land acquisition.

Relevant income is income that will differ between alternatives; **differential income** is the difference between the relevant incomes of two or more alternatives. Whenever there is no relevant income (meaning that the differential income is zero) for a given decision, the selection between alternatives is made on the basis of the lowest cost. For example, assume that a business is considering the addition of a new product to make use of available production capacity. Two choices are being evaluated — water skis and snow skis. The projected income with water skis is $286 000, whereas that of snow skis is $326 000, or a differential income of $40 000. The related costs also are considered if they are relevant.

Differential analysis can help management in making several types of business decisions. We used differential analysis without identifying it as such in chapter 13 when we considered a department's contribution to indirect expenses in evaluating whether to close down a department. Other examples are: Should a one-off special order be accepted? Should a product or service be discontinued? Is it better to produce or to purchase a part needed in manufacturing? Does a product need further processing or is it ready to sell? Should a non-current asset be replaced? In the following sections, we consider the application of differential analysis to some of these types of decisions.

Evaluation of a special order

Business entities often must decide whether to accept a special order, usually at a price lower than its normal selling price. The long-term pricing policy of any business must be based on a consideration of all costs incurred if the business is to be profitable. However, when idle capacity exists, a special order may be attractive even though a lower-than-normal selling price is involved. Differential analysis can be applied to evaluate the differential revenue and costs associated with a special order. (Remember that a pricing decision based on differential analysis is valid for a one-time order but normally not for an entity's regular line of business.)

To illustrate a decision about a special order, consider Wattle Ltd, a manufacturer of tennis balls sold with a Wattle label to discount stores.

Current operations

Capacity to produce 100 000 balls per month
May sales forecast of 60 000 balls due to seasonal demand
Normal selling price is $2.50 per ball
Monthly fixed production costs are $84 000
Variable cost required to produce a ball is $0.80

The sales and marketing department has been approached by an exporter for distribution overseas.

Special order:

Number of balls in the special order is 10 000
Price the exporter is prepared to pay is $1.90 per ball
Set-up costs for a special design to be imprinted on each ball is $5000
No additional selling and distribution, administrative, and finance and other expenses will be required for the order

---

Should the offer be accepted? If the decision is made on the basis of the average production cost per ball with the order, the offer will be rejected because the $1.90 price is less than the average cost of $2.07 ($0.80 + $89 000/70 000). However, the average cost of production is irrelevant, as shown by the following differential analysis:

	Without order	With order	Differential analysis	
Sales 60 000 @ $2.50	$150 000	$150 000		
10 000 @ $1.90		19 000	$19 000	(Differential income)
Variable expenses				
60 000 @ $0.80	(48 000)	(48 000)		
10 000 @ $0.80		(8 000)	(8 000)	(Differential expenses)
Fixed expenses — regular	(84 000)	(84 000)		
— setup		(5 000)	(5 000)	(Differential expenses)
Gross profit	$ 18 000	$ 24 000	$ 6 000	

Profit will be $6000 higher with the special order even though the price is lower than normal. As long as the company does not have a better alternative use for the production capacity and is certain that the special order will not have an adverse effect on its regular business, the sales and marketing department should accept the order.

Evaluation of a make-or-buy decision

Most manufacturing entities use many component parts in the production of their finished products. These parts can be produced by the manufacturer or purchased from an outside source. A motor vehicle manufacturer may produce its own engines but purchase tyres. In turn, certain parts of the engine (such as nuts and bolts) may be acquired from other manufacturers.

Whenever a manufacturing entity has the production capacity and expertise to produce a given part, the decision to make it or buy the part is based on the relevant costs of each alternative. Differential analysis is used to evaluate the relevant costs of making or buying a part. For example, assume that Beetle Co. Ltd has been operating at 75% of capacity and has been paying $8 each to purchase a small gear used in its production process. A forecast indicates that regular production will remain at approximately 75% of capacity. As a means of using some of the unused capacity, the company is considering the possibility of producing 20 000 gears instead of purchasing them. Based on the company's normal product-costing approach, costs are estimated for 20 000 gears as shown below:

Direct materials	$ 42 000
Direct labour	73 000
Variable factory overhead	20 000
Fixed factory overhead	55 000
Total costs	$190 000
Cost of each gear (20 000 gears)	$ 9.50

At first glance, it may appear that the cost of producing a gear exceeds the purchase price by $1.50 ($9.50 less $8.00). However, differential analysis requires a review of costs to determine which are avoidable if the gears are purchased. Assume that this has been done and the direct materials, direct labour, variable factory overhead and fixed factory overhead of $5000 can be eliminated by purchasing the gears. Fixed factory overhead of $50 000 will be incurred whether the gears are produced or purchased, so it is not a relevant cost.

Differential analysis shows:

	Make the gears	Buy the gears	Differential analysis
Direct materials	$ 42 000		$ 42 000
Direct labour	73 000		73 000
Variable factory overhead	20 000		20 000
Fixed factory overhead	55 000	$ 50 000	5 000
Purchase costs (20 000 @ $8)		160 000	(160 000)
Total costs	$190 000	$210 000	$ (20 000)

The relevant costs of producing the gears are $140 000 ($42 000 + $73 000 + $20 000 + $5000), or $7 per unit. Therefore, a cost saving of $1 per unit ($8 less $7) will result if the company produces the gears — for a total cost saving of $20 000. The company also should consider any alternative uses of the unused capacity with a contribution margin in excess of $20 000, because they would generate even higher profits than the production of gears. Also, the desire to control the quality of the gears internally may be an important factor in the analysis. In addition, any potential adverse effect on the business relationship with the outside supplier of the gears — who may provide other components used in the production process — must be evaluated carefully.

Treatment of joint product costs

Many manufacturers produce several products from common raw materials or from the same production process. For example, an oil refinery may produce petrol, fuel oil, kerosene, lubricating oils, naphtha and paraffin from crude oil. Chemical, timber, mining and meatpacking industries are others in which it is possible to produce a number of products from common raw materials. These multiple products are called **joint products**; the common costs required to produce them before they are identifiable as separate units of output are termed **joint product costs**. The point in the production process at which the joint products become separate products is called the **split-off point**. Some of the products may be in saleable form at the split-off point but others may require further processing before they can be sold. The production flow of a manufacturing entity with two products (A and B) that are saleable at the split-off point and one product (C) that must be processed further to become a saleable product is shown in figure 14.1 (p. 586).

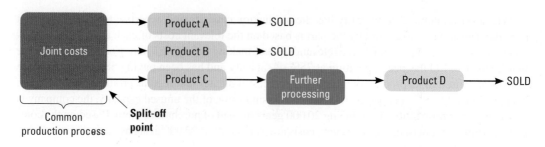

Figure 14.1 Production flows — three products

Joint costs → Product A → SOLD

Joint costs → Product B → SOLD

Joint costs → Product C → Further processing → Product D → SOLD

Common production process

Split-off point

In the treatment of joint product costs, a distinction must be made between recognising and valuing inventories and deciding when the products should be sold. Joint product costs are common costs that must be allocated to the individual products involved to value inventories. The most common practice is to allocate joint product costs on the basis of the product's relative sales value. Assume that a chemical company produces 24 000 litres of Alodane and 12 000 litres of Balodane while incurring joint product costs of $108 000. Alodane sells for $4 per litre and Balodane sells for $4.50 per litre. Therefore, the sales value of Alodane is $96 000 and the sales value of Balodane is $54 000, for total sales value of $150 000. Using the relative sales value method, the joint product costs of $108 000 would be assigned to the two products as follows:

Alodane	$\dfrac{\$96\,000}{\$150\,000} \times \$108\,000 = \$\ 69\,120$
Balodane	$\dfrac{\$54\,000}{\$150\,000} \times \$108\,000 = \$\ 38\,880$
Total joint costs	$108\,000

The allocation of joint product costs must be done so that the production costs can be divided between inventories and the cost of sales. However, like any cost allocation procedure, the results must be interpreted carefully since they are only approximations of the true costs of producing individual products.

Managers often must decide whether to sell a joint product at the split-off point or to process it further. Joint product costs are irrelevant in such decisions since they are *sunk costs* and should not be allocated to the joint products involved for decision-making purposes. Instead, differential analysis should be used to evaluate the relevant costs and income. For example, assume that the two products, Alodane and Balodane, can either be sold at the split-off point for $4 and $4.50 per litre respectively, or be processed further and subsequently sold. The following data are relevant:

Product	Selling price per litre at split-off point	Further processing costs per litre	Selling price per litre after further processing
Alodane	$4.00	$2.00	$7.00
Balodane	$4.50	$3.50	$7.75

The joint product costs (common to both products) of $108 000 are ignored because they are sunk costs. Alodane would be processed further and sold for $7 per litre and Balodane would be sold at the split-off point for $4.50 because of this differential analysis:

Product	Differential income per litre with further processing	Differential cost per litre of further processing	Profit (loss) per litre after further processing
Alodane	$3.00 ($7.00 less $4.00)	$2.00	$1.00
Balodane	$3.25 ($7.75 less $4.50)	$3.50	($0.25)

The gross profit earned by selling Alodane after further processing and Balodane at the split-off point would be $66 000 [(24 000 × $7) + (12 000 × $4.50) − (24 000 × $2) − $108 000]. This is $24 000 higher than the gross profit of $42 000 ($150 000 − $108 000) that would be earned by selling both products at the split-off point. The reason is the additional profit of $24 000 (24 000 × $1) earned by the further processing of Alodane.

Product mix decisions

Any business that sells more than one product must continuously evaluate the profitability of the various products to determine the most profitable product mix. In most cases, this cannot be done by simply selecting the products with the highest individual contribution margins because scarce resources and other limiting factors are characteristic of virtually every business. For example, a manufacturing entity will have a limited amount of production capacity as measured by direct labour hours or machine hours. In a department store, the limitation is the amount of floor space available. These limitations are called *constraints*, and management's job is to maximise the use of them.

The most profitable product mix should be determined by relating the contribution margin of each product to the constraints of the entity to give the contribution margin of each product per unit of scarce resource. For example, consider a company that produces and sells two types of furniture — tables and chairs — with these selling prices and variable expenses:

	Table	Chair
Selling price	$100	$80
Variable expenses	50	60
Contribution margin	$ 50	$20
Contribution margin ratio	50%	25%

At first glance, a table appears to be the most profitable and management might be tempted to produce as many tables as can be sold. Assume, however, that the same machines are used to produce both products and only 60 000 machine hours are available each month. Six machine hours are required to produce a table, two machine hours for each chair. If an unlimited number of either product can be sold, only chairs should be produced because they are more profitable on the basis of contribution margin per machine hour:

	Table	Chair
Contribution margin per machine hour	$\dfrac{\$50}{6} = \$8.33$	$\dfrac{\$20}{2} = \$10.00$

By producing a maximum of 30 000 chairs (60 000 ÷ 2), the total contribution margin earned will be $600 000 (30 000 chairs × $20 or 60 000 hours × $10). It is unlikely, however, that an unlimited number of chairs can be sold since the market usually imposes constraints that must be recognised in product mix decisions. For example, a minimum number of tables may have to be produced to satisfy the needs of customers who want to buy both tables and chairs. In addition, the maximum number of chairs that can be sold may be less than 30 000.

Other constraints such as limited raw materials and direct labour hours also may require consideration in the analysis. In most cases, more than two products must be evaluated, so the determination of the most profitable product mix is a complex decision. A mathematical tool that can be used to overcome the complexities of multiple constraints and multiple products is linear programming. This is a series of algebraic manipulations, and is described in most quantitative business analysis books.

14.3 Profitability analysis

Throughout this text, we have shown how managers need to constantly analyse and assess the performance of an entity in terms of its profitability. Various methods of analysing and assessing profitability have been covered already. In this section, two additional types of analyses — return on investment and residual profit analysis — are considered.

Learning objective 3

Explain how to use return on investment analysis and residual profit analysis

Return on investment analysis

The rate of return on certain measures of investment can be used as important evaluations of a business entity's profitability performance. When **return on investment (ROI) analysis** is combined with the business segmentation topics discussed in chapter 13, management has an effective way of deciding which segments of the business are using their resources most efficiently. Recall from chapter 13 that a responsibility centre can be established as an *investment centre* if the manager of that centre has control of the revenue, costs and resources invested.

Understanding ROI in this context requires an understanding of two ratios used to evaluate the performance and stability of the business as a whole over time. These ratios are the rate of return on assets and asset turnover. The rate of return on assets is calculated by expressing profit before tax and interest on borrowings over a time period as a percentage of the average total assets of the business held over that time. The interest expense is eliminated because it is considered a return to creditors for the assets they have provided and reflects how the firm is financed rather than how it has performed. Tax is eliminated because it reflects the government's political decisions rather than decisions of management. Total assets are usually defined as the average of the annual beginning and ending asset balances in the accounts for the investment centre concerned. All productive assets — cash at bank, accounts receivable, inventories and non-current assets — are included. The rate of return on assets is particularly useful for evaluating the profit performance of an entity over time.

Asset turnover measures the efficiency with which the assets of a business are used by management to generate income, e.g. sales, and is calculated by expressing sales (or service income) over a certain time period as a percentage of the total assets employed during that time. When ROI analysis is used for investment centres within a business, profit figures relate to profits attributed to the investment centre, income or sales are those of the investment centre, and the investment consists of the assets used in that investment centre.

ROI analysis can be applied to such investment centres as divisions, product lines, plants and retail stores with this formula:

$$\text{ROI} = \text{Profit margin} \times \text{Asset turnover}$$

$$= \frac{\text{Profit before income tax and interest}}{\text{Sales}} \times \frac{\text{Sales}}{\text{Total assets}}$$

Since sales cancel out in the ROI calculation, the same result can be found by dividing profit before tax and interest by total assets. The expanded version of ROI shown above is preferred by most managers because it emphasises the fact that ROI is actually a result of two variables, *profit margin* and *asset turnover*. To achieve a desired ROI, management must control both of these variables. Improvements in ROI can be achieved by increasing sales, reducing expenses, reducing assets, or some combination of these.

To illustrate the application of ROI analysis, assume G & P Co. Ltd operates two divisions as investment centres. Top management wants to know which of the two earned the highest ROI during the past year so it can decide which segment of the business to expand in the future. The data below indicate that the Personal Products Division has a higher ROI than the Cleaning Products Division, even though it is much smaller.

		Personal Products Division	Cleaning Products Division
Profit before tax	(a)	$ 420 000	$ 880 000
Interest expense	(b)	30 000	44 000
Profit before tax and interest	(c = a + b)	450 000	924 000
Sales revenue	(d)	3 600 000	8 400 000
Average total assets	(e)	2 400 000	6 000 000
Profit margin	(c ÷ d)	12.5%	11.0%
Asset turnover	(d ÷ e)	1.5	1.4
ROI	(c ÷ e)	18.75%	15.4%

The Cleaning Products Division has a lower profit margin and a lower asset turnover than the Personal Products Division. As a result, the Cleaning Products Division's ROI is only 15.4% compared with 18.75% for the Personal Products Division. Future expansion should take place in the Personal Products Division and resources might be moved to it from the Cleaning Products Division. If a higher ROI is to be achieved, the divisions will have to increase sales, reduce costs and/or reduce assets.

Residual profit analysis

Another way of evaluating the performance of an investment centre is by applying residual profit analysis. **Residual profit** is the profit earned in excess of a certain minimum rate of return on assets. This term is also referred to as **residual income**. When residual profit is used to evaluate performance, the aim is to maximise the amount of residual profit rather than the return on investment. The advantage of residual profit analysis is that it prevents the possibility of a segment manager rejecting an opportunity to earn a return on investment acceptable to the business as a whole but below the ROI of his or her investment centre.

For example, assume that G & P Co. Ltd has decided that a minimum ROI of 12% is acceptable. Since the Personal Products Division has an ROI of 18.75%, its manager may reject an opportunity to earn 15% with a new product even though it is acceptable to the business because the division's ROI will decrease. The residual profit approach would charge the division manager only 12% so all projects with a return in excess of 12% will be accepted.

The major limitation of the residual profit approach is that it is difficult to compare the performance of business segments of different sizes because the larger segments will have more residual profit than the smaller ones. Nevertheless, it is useful for evaluating the profitability of specific profit results. The following analysis illustrates the application of the residual profit approach to G & P Co. Ltd's performance:

		Personal Products Division
Average assets	(a)	$2 400 000
Minimum return at 12%	(b – 0.12a)	288 000
Profit	(c)	450 000
Residual profit	(c – b)	$ 162 000

BUSINESS KNOWLEDGE

Getting the green light

It seems almost trite to make mention of climate change and our personal finances and profits in the same sentence.

Renewable energy, while still perched on the high-cost side of the energy spectrum, is becoming more important for many planners and a commercial opportunity for business.

A raft of grants, loans and rebates from state and federal governments, as well as concessions from local governments, are fuelling a massive take-up of solar panels for both water heating and energy usage.

On the one hand, solar, which as a technology is well advanced, remains a high-capital cost renewable energy solution and one that takes years to offer the consumer a *return on investment*. Yet, on the other hand, it presents a cash saving in terms of the monthly energy bill.

A number of academics and building industry experts (not associated with the solar industry) assert that in the emerging new green economy, a home with solar equipped energy will command a premium in the market in terms of capital value.

At the household level, green grants are becoming hugely popular. These grants and loans, made available by the federal government, enable householders to buy the solar panels, the water systems (for example, brown-water systems).

These incentives are needed to overcome the complacency and the lack of available capital in the average household.

We all want to be green, but the costs remain high. Investment in green technology at the household level will produce dividends in time, just as investing in companies which will become tomorrow's green champions will produce long-term returns.

Source: Excerpt from Morris Kaplan, 'Getting the green light', *Sunday Tasmanian.*

14.4 Capital budgeting decisions

Nature and importance of capital budgeting decisions

The types of management decisions discussed so far have been mainly short-term oriented, with the major consideration being the best use of existing operating capacity. We now consider long-term decision making that is required to establish, maintain and increase an entity's long-term operating capacity. The expenditures made to generate operating capacity are referred to as *capital expenditures* because they involve investments in assets with long lives. Each year, businesses spend billions of dollars in capital expenditures, such as replacing equipment, expanding production facilities, opening new offices or stores, improving product quality, introducing new product lines and improving cost efficiency.

Capital budgeting is the process used to evaluate capital expenditures in a rational and systematic way. The main objective of capital budgeting is to add to the value of a business by selecting capital expenditures that are compatible with the goals of the organisation and that provide the highest rates of return. A capital budgeting decision is concerned with an expenditure that will pay for itself and provide an acceptable rate of return over its life. As such, capital budgeting decisions are vital to the long-term profitability of an entity.

Capital budgeting decisions must be carefully considered for several reasons:

1. They involve large sums of money and the success or failure of an entity may depend on a single decision.
2. The resources invested are committed for a long period of time.
3. They cannot be reversed easily since the investment becomes a sunk cost that can be recovered only by the productive use of the relevant assets, so reversal can be extremely difficult and costly.
4. Since they are long-term oriented, substantial risk is involved because of such uncertainties as local and global economic conditions, technological developments, consumer preferences and social responsibilities.

A number of methods are available to management for the evaluation of capital expenditures. In fact, entire books have been written about the subject of capital budgeting, which can involve many sophisticated techniques. Our coverage of capital budgeting is limited to three basic methods — *discounted cash flows* (net present value, net present value index, internal rate of return), *payback period*, and *return on average investment*.

Use of cash flows in capital budgeting

Most capital budgeting methods require information about future net cash flows (defined as periodic future cash inflows less periodic future cash outflows) to evaluate the return on an investment. The reason for using net cash flows instead of accounting profit to measure the return from an investment is the time value of money. The principle on which this concept is based is that cash received today from an investment is worth more than the same amount of cash received next month or next year.

Because profit is based on accrual accounting, it usually does not reflect the flow of cash in and out of a business. The cash flows involved with an accrual income statement may precede or follow the profit reported. Revenues or sales usually do not produce immediate cash receipts because of the time needed to collect accounts receivable. Expenses may require cash payments before they appear on the income statement (e.g. the depreciation on equipment and the inventory included in cost of sales) or after the income statement period (e.g. accrued salaries and income tax). Consequently, accrual accounting must be converted to cash accounting before the time value of money can be evaluated accurately in capital budgeting.

The most common future cash inflows considered in a capital budgeting decision are:

- expected cash flows from increased income resulting from an investment
- expected cost reductions from an investment that improves efficiency
- any residual value at the end of the useful life of the investment.

Typical cash outflows associated with capital budgeting decisions are the initial cost of the investment and the periodic expenditures incurred for the investment (including income tax on the earnings involved). In many cases, an additional cash outflow is the increased working capital (e.g. accounts receivable and inventory) required to support the investment. This incremental working capital is part of the initial investment. When the life of the investment is finished, the additional working capital can be eliminated, and the decrease treated as a cash inflow. The same dollar increase and decrease in working capital will not simply cancel out because of the time value of money.

Note that depreciation does not require a cash outlay when it is recorded each period, so it should not be included as a cash expenditure for capital budgeting purposes. The related cash outflow is recognised when the initial investment is made. As we shall see later, however, the impact of depreciation on income tax (cash outflows) must be considered in capital budgeting.

Time value of money: An overview

The basic principle of the time value of money is that a dollar held today is worth more than a dollar held at any time in the future. If we have the money today, it can be invested to earn interest and so will grow in amount as future periods pass. Consequently, 1 year from now we will have the original investment plus 1 year's interest. If we invest $1000 today at 6% compounded annually (the interest is calculated once a year), we will have $1060 in a year's time [$1000 + (0.06 × $1000)]. As a result, we can say that the $1060 in a year from now is worth only $1000 today. A more detailed coverage of the time value of money is available in the appendix at the back of this book.

The time value of money can be expressed in terms of its future value or its present value. The $1060 is the future value of the $1000, because of the interest earned for 1 year. In contrast, the $1000 is the present value of the $1060 if we discount the future value back to today's dollars. The process of converting a future value into what has to be a smaller present value is called *discounting*, and we use the term *discount rate* to indicate that a present value is being calculated, instead of a future value involving an interest rate. However, the interest rate and the discount rate are both the same in a given future value–present value relationship, i.e. 6% in the example described above.

In capital budgeting, we are concerned with **discounted cash flows** so we can compare the present cost of an investment with the present value of the net cash flows expected from it in the future. The expected future net cash flows from an investment can be compared with the investment only when both are measured in equivalent dollars. We do this by discounting the future dollars to their present value, which is the equivalent dollar value today of a known future amount (given a certain discount rate and time period for receipt or payment).

The concepts of the time value of money can also be applied to an annuity, which is a series of equal payments over a specified number of periods. The future value of an annuity is the sum of all payments made plus the interest accumulated on each payment. In contrast, the present value of an annuity is the amount that would have to be invested today at a certain interest rate to receive a series of future payments over a specified period of time. This means that the future payments are discounted to their present value by removing the amount of interest involved. If we consider a capital expenditure as an investment made today to receive a series of equal annual payments over the life of the investment that will recover the original amount invested and give a desired rate of return, we have an example of the present value of an annuity.

Tables are used to calculate the time value of money to avoid the complex mathematics that would otherwise be required. Capital budgeting decisions consist of present value applications, and tables 14.1 and 14.2 (p. 592) illustrate discounted cash flows. Table 14.1 provides factors for various combinations of discount rates and number of periods relating to the present value of a single amount; table 14.2 contains the factors for the present value of an annuity. When equal net cash inflows per year are involved, we can use table 14.2 for the discounting process. Otherwise, we consider the net cash inflow of each year separately, using table 14.1. Financial calculators, spreadsheets and computer programs can also be used to perform present value calculations quickly and accurately. The net present value method and the internal rate of return are two important discounted cash flow techniques used to evaluate capital budgeting decisions in the business world.

Table 14.1 Present value of $1

Periods	4%	5%	6%	8%	10%	12%	16%	20%
1	0.9615	0.9524	0.9434	0.9259	0.9091	0.8929	0.8621	0.8333
2	0.9246	0.9070	0.8900	0.8573	0.8264	0.7972	0.7432	0.6944
3	0.8890	0.8638	0.8396	0.7938	0.7513	0.7118	0.6407	0.5787
4	0.8548	0.8227	0.7921	0.7350	0.6830	0.6355	0.5523	0.4823
5	0.8219	0.7835	0.7473	0.6806	0.6209	0.5674	0.4761	0.4019
6	0.7903	0.7462	0.7050	0.6302	0.5645	0.5066	0.4104	0.3349
7	0.7599	0.7107	0.6651	0.5835	0.5132	0.4523	0.3538	0.2791
8	0.7307	0.6768	0.6274	0.5403	0.4665	0.4039	0.3050	0.2326
9	0.7026	0.6446	0.5919	0.5002	0.4241	0.3606	0.2630	0.1938
10	0.6756	0.6139	0.5584	0.4632	0.3855	0.3220	0.2267	0.1615
11	0.6496	0.5847	0.5268	0.4289	0.3505	0.2875	0.1954	0.1346
12	0.6246	0.5568	0.4970	0.3971	0.3186	0.2567	0.1685	0.1122
13	0.6006	0.5303	0.4688	0.3677	0.2897	0.2292	0.1452	0.0925
14	0.5775	0.5051	0.4423	0.3405	0.2633	0.2046	0.1252	0.0779
15	0.5553	0.4810	0.4173	0.3152	0.2394	0.1827	0.1079	0.0649
16	0.5339	0.4581	0.3936	0.2919	0.2176	0.1631	0.0930	0.0541
17	0.5134	0.4363	0.3714	0.2703	0.1978	0.1456	0.0802	0.0451
18	0.4936	0.4155	0.3503	0.2502	0.1799	0.1300	0.0691	0.0376
19	0.4746	0.3957	0.3305	0.2317	0.1635	0.1161	0.0596	0.0313
20	0.4564	0.3769	0.3118	0.2145	0.1486	0.1037	0.0514	0.0261
25	0.3751	0.2953	0.2330	0.1460	0.0923	0.0588	0.0245	0.0105
30	0.3083	0.2314	0.1741	0.0994	0.0573	0.0334	0.0116	0.0042

Table 14.2 Present value of an ordinary annuity of $1

Periods	4%	5%	6%	8%	10%	12%	16%	20%
1	0.9615	0.9524	0.9434	0.9259	0.9091	0.8929	0.8621	0.8333
2	1.8861	1.8594	1.8334	1.7833	1.7355	1.6901	1.6052	1.5278
3	2.7751	2.7232	2.6730	2.5771	2.4869	2.4018	2.2459	2.1065
4	3.6299	3.5460	3.4651	3.3121	3.1699	3.0373	2.7982	2.5887
5	4.4518	4.3295	4.2124	3.9927	3.7908	3.6048	3.2743	2.9906
6	5.2421	5.0757	4.9173	4.6229	4.3553	4.1114	3.6847	3.3255
7	6.0021	5.7864	5.5824	5.2064	4.8684	4.5638	4.0386	3.6016
8	6.7327	6.4632	6.2098	5.7466	5.3349	4.9676	4.3436	3.8273
9	7.4353	7.1078	6.8017	6.2469	5.7590	5.3282	4.6065	4.0310
10	8.1109	7.7217	7.3601	6.7101	6.1446	5.6502	4.8332	4.1925
11	8.7605	8.3064	7.8869	7.1390	6.4951	5.9377	5.0286	4.3271
12	9.3851	8.8633	8.3838	7.5361	6.8137	6.1944	5.1971	4.4392
13	9.9856	9.3936	8.8527	7.9038	7.1034	6.4235	5.3423	4.5327
14	10.5631	9.8986	9.2950	8.2442	7.3667	6.6282	5.4675	4.6106
15	11.1184	10.3797	9.7122	8.5595	7.6061	6.8109	5.5755	4.6755
16	11.6523	10.8378	10.1059	8.8514	7.8237	6.9740	5.6685	4.7296
17	12.1657	11.2741	10.4773	9.1216	8.0216	7.1196	5.7487	4.7746
18	12.6593	11.6896	10.8276	9.3719	8.2014	7.2497	5.8178	4.8122
19	13.1339	12.0853	11.1581	9.6036	8.3649	7.3658	5.8775	4.8435
20	13.5903	12.4622	11.4699	9.8181	8.5136	7.4694	5.9288	4.8696
25	15.6221	14.0939	12.7834	10.6748	9.0770	7.8431	6.0971	4.9476
30	17.2920	15.3725	13.7648	11.2578	9.4269	8.0552	6.1772	4.9789

14.5 Capital budgeting methods based on the time value of money

Learning objective 5

Understand the role of cash flows and the time value of money in capital budgeting decisions

Net present value method

To illustrate the **net present value (NPV) method** of capital budgeting, assume that Canberra Co. Ltd is considering the possibility of producing a new product that will require the acquisition of a new machine. The machine presently costs $81 000, including installation and transport charges. It has a useful life of 10 years and at the end of the 10 years a resale value (net of income tax effects) of $13 000.

The company estimates that the new product will increase its annual profit by $11 200, calculated as:

Estimated annual sales of new product		$48 000
Estimated annual costs and expenses:		
Manufacturing costs (including depreciation of $6800)	$27 000	
Selling and other expenses	5 000	32 000
Estimated profit before tax		16 000
Income tax at 30% (assumed)		4 800
Estimated annual profit		$11 200

For simplicity, we assume that Canberra Co. Ltd will receive the revenue from the new product in cash (cash inflow), and all costs other than depreciation will be paid in cash (cash outflows). When complete accrual accounting is involved, it is necessary to convert income, expenses and profit to net cash flows. In this case, net cash flows after income tax are obtained by adding back the non-cash depreciation of $6800 to the estimated profit of $11 200. The net cash flows after tax are therefore $18 000.

Canberra Co. Ltd is considering an investment of $81 000 in current dollars, which will yield estimated net cash inflows of $18 000 ($11 200 plus $6800 depreciation) for each of the next 10 years. In making any investment, the net cash inflows expected in the future must be compared with the amount of the investment required to obtain them. The objective is to return the amount invested, as well as to earn a satisfactory return on the investment. When the NPV method is used, the cash inflows and the cash outflows associated with an investment are discounted to their present values (note that when the investment is paid for at the time of acquisition, the amount involved is in present value form). The difference between the two present values — that is, the NPV — determines whether the investment is acceptable. The NPV of the proposed project is $8945 as set out in figure 14.2.

Year	Expected net cash inflow	Present value of $1 at 16%	Present value of net cash flows
1	$18 000	0.8621	$15 518
2	18 000	0.7432	13 377
3	18 000	0.6407	11 533
4	18 000	0.5523	9 941
5	18 000	0.4761	8 570
6	18 000	0.4104	7 387
7	18 000	0.3538	6 368
8	18 000	0.3050	5 490
9	18 000	0.2630	4 734
10	18 000	0.2267	4 080
10 (resale value)	13 000	0.2267	2 947
Total present value of cash flows			89 945
Cost of initial investment — cash outflow			(81 000)
Net present value			$ 8 945

Figure 14.2 NPV analysis of investment in machine

The net cash inflows expected in the future can be discounted by one of two approaches. They can be discounted year by year, using table 14.1 (p. 592), the *present value of $1* table. This approach was used in figure 14.2. However, since the amount received each year is the same, the net cash flows of $18 000 per year can be discounted more easily by using the *present value of an annuity of $1* table (16% and 10 periods), table 14.2 on page 592. The $13 000 resale value received in year 10 needs to be discounted using table 14.1.

The NPV under this alternative treatment is determined as follows:

Present value of expected annual net cash inflows ($18 000 × 4.8332)	$86 998
Present value of expected net cash inflow ($13 000 × 0.2267)	2 947
	89 945
Cost of initial investment	(81 000)
Net present value	$ 8 945

Since the NPV of this project is greater than $0, or positive, the investment is acceptable. If the NPV was negative, the investment would be unacceptable.

The discount rate chosen for the discounting process is the required rate of return, often called the cost of capital. The nature of cost of capital and the principle behind its calculation (at 16% in our example) are discussed briefly below.

Cost of capital

The **cost of capital** is the cost of obtaining funds in the form of debt and equity. The cost of capital is not the same as the interest rate at which money can be borrowed because the cost of *all means* of financing used by an entity must be considered. For example, a given entity may use three common types of financing — borrowings, preference shares and ordinary shares (ordinary share capital and retained earnings).

The concepts and calculations underlying a complete coverage of the cost of capital are complex and beyond the scope of this book, and can be obtained from any finance textbook. However, the basic principles involved can be illustrated with a simple example. Assume that the after-tax costs of Canberra Co. Ltd's borrowings, preference shares and ordinary shares are 16%, 12% and 17.6% respectively. Further, assume the capital structure of the company consists of the following:

Type of financing	Percentage of total capital
Borrowings	30
Preference shares	20
Ordinary shares	50

The cost of capital is a weighted average, calculated as the sum of the products of each financing source's cost multiplied by its percentage of the total capital, or in this case it is:

$$\text{Cost of capital} = (16\% \times 30\%) + (12\% \times 20\%) + (17.6\% \times 50\%)$$
$$= (0.16 \times 0.3) + (0.12 \times 0.2) + (0.176 \times 0.5)$$
$$= 0.048 + 0.024 + 0.088$$
$$= 0.16 \text{ or } 16\%$$

As long as an investment offers a rate of return higher than the cost of capital, it is potentially attractive because the return will exceed the cost of the funds used to pay for it. This will occur when the NPV is positive (the discounted cash inflows exceed the discounted cash outflows). A negative NPV indicates that an investment should be rejected because the discounted cash outflows exceed the discounted cash inflows, resulting in an inadequate return. If the net present value of an investment is zero, management will be indifferent about accepting or rejecting it because the true cost of the investment will be the same as the return earned from it.

Note in figure 14.2 that the annual net cash inflows of $18 000 are worth less and less in present value terms as time passes. If a discount rate higher than 16% had been used, the total present value of the net cash inflows would have been lower than $89 945. In contrast, a discount rate lower than 16% would have produced a total present value of the net cash inflows in excess of $89 945. Thus, an inverse relationship exists between the discount rate chosen and the present value of the net cash inflows. This means that a business will be willing to pay more for an investment when it requires a lower return on the investment.

BUSINESS KNOWLEDGE

Weighted average cost of capital unveiled

One of the more dreaded parts of fundamental analysis is the weighted average cost of capital.

You'll often see it mentioned in broker reports, especially if the broker is talking about discounted cash flows.

In short, the weighted average cost of capital is the cost of money for any particular business. It's that easy!

If you've just started a business, and you promise to pay 10 per cent of all your profits to the person that provided you with the start-up money, then you might view your 'cost of capital' as 10 per cent of your profits.

In a sense, this is how companies are funded by equity. Shareholders give them money, and then expect a proportion of the profits.

Of course, sophisticated companies like the ones we trade on the Australian stock market are funded not only by equity (like in the example above), but also debt.

So, the weighted average cost of capital — or WACC as it is commonly known — attempts to gauge how much it costs a company to fund itself with both equity and debt.

To discover a company's WACC, analysts only need a little information.

First, how much does it cost a company for equity, and how much for debt? . . .

Then, it's simply a case of multiplying the cost by the proportion for both equity and debt, and then adding the result.

Will you ever calculate this number? Probably not, but you'll often see it in broker reports, and it'll help you understand what exactly companies are trying to achieve by running businesses.

In short, they're trying to pay, for example, 10 per cent for the money to run the company, and then earn 20 per cent from doing business.

What WACC tells you is how much it costs the company to run its operations.

From there, you can look at how much of a return a company is making, through return on assets for example, to figure out whether a company's operations are in the black or the red.

So, while you might never calculate the WACC, it's good to know what it is.

Source: 'WACC', Herald Sun.

Depreciation as a tax shield

We emphasised earlier that depreciation expense should not be included as a cash outflow in capital budgeting, because it does not require a cash payment when it is recorded.

The cost of the asset is a cash outflow when it is paid for. As we have seen, depreciation is the process of spreading this cost over the life of the asset. However, depreciation *does* affect the amount of income tax paid because it is deductible for tax purposes. Consequently, depreciation has an impact on the cash flows used to evaluate a capital budgeting decision.

The net cash flow expected by Canberra Co. Ltd is $18 000 per year. Annual depreciation of $6800 has been calculated by the straight-line method ([$81 000 − $13 000] ÷ 10). Because the depreciation expense does not require a cash outlay, it must be added back to the profit after tax to determine the net cash flow of $18 000. Alternatively, the $18 000 net cash can be calculated as $48 000 (sales) − $20 200 (cash manufacturing costs) − $5000 (selling and other expenses) − $4800 (income tax). Although the depreciation expense does not involve a cash outflow, it is deductible in determining taxable income. Consequently, it reduces the cash outflow for income tax by the amount deducted multiplied by the tax rate ($6800 × 0.30 = $2040). The depreciation deduction is called a **tax shield** because it is a tax-deductible expense that saves the business $2040 in income tax. This means that the cash outlay for income tax would have been $2040 higher without depreciation because it would have been calculated as ($48 000 − $25 200) × 0.30, or $6840 instead of $4800.

The true impact of depreciation as a tax shield is also affected by the time value of money. That is, the tax deductions are worth more to a business in early years than in later years because of the time value of money. As a result, the present value of the net cash inflows involved with differences in the timing of depreciation deductions must be carefully considered. Generally, the diminishing-balance method of depreciation is used for tax purposes for this reason, because it allows greater deductions for depreciation in earlier years, thus saving more income tax cash outflows when the time value of money is greatest.

Net present value index

An extension of the NPV method, called the **net present value (NPV) index method** (sometimes referred to as a profitability index), can be used to compare investments that involve different amounts of money. The NPV of one investment cannot be compared directly with the NPV of another one, unless both are of equal size. For example, an NPV of $10 000 from an investment of $50 000 is more attractive than an NPV of $10 000 from an investment of $500 000. We can use a profitability index to provide the relative measurement needed to compare two or more competing investments. Competing investments are mutually exclusive, which means that the acceptance of one investment results in the rejection of the other. An NPV index is calculated by dividing the present value of the net cash inflows by the cost of the investment. In the case of Canberra Co. Ltd, the NPV index is determined as follows:

$$\frac{\text{Present value of net cash inflows}}{\text{Cost of investment}} = \frac{\$89\,945}{\$81\,000} = 1.11$$

The simple decision rule used with the NPV index is that the investment with the largest index is preferred over others with lower indexes. The NPV index can be used to rank investments in their descending order so that the entity's resources will be channelled into the most potentially profitable investments.

Internal rate of return method

The internal rate of return, another discounted cash flow technique, can be used to determine the actual rate of return. The **internal rate of return (IRR)**, also called the time-adjusted rate of return or the actual rate of return, is defined as the discount rate that will produce an NPV of zero for an investment. In other words, the discounted cash inflows will be equal to the discounted cash outflows when the IRR is used as the discount rate. An investment with an IRR that exceeds the cost of capital will be attractive to a business. A detailed treatment of the IRR is beyond the scope of this book. In practice, hand-held financial calculators, spreadsheet programs and other computer programs can calculate the IRR for management use quickly and accurately.

In the Canberra Co. Ltd example, we know that the actual rate of return from the machine must be higher than 16%, because the NPV is positive at that discount rate. If we discounted the net cash inflows at 20% in the same manner as was done in figure 14.2, the NPV would be −$3435. In other words, the investment does not return 20% since the NPV is negative. It can be concluded, therefore, that the actual IRR lies somewhere between 16% and 20%. In fact, the actual rate of return is close to 18.5%.

14.6 Other capital budgeting methods

Learning objective 6

Evaluate investments using the time value of money

Some other common methods of capital budgeting do not consider the time value of money. It could be argued that this constitutes their major limitation. Two very popular ones are the payback period and the return on average investment.

Payback period method

The **payback period** is the length of time required to recover the cost of an investment from the net cash flows (undiscounted) it generates; this is the period of time needed for an investment to pay for itself. The payback period is simple to calculate and easy to understand. Use of the shortest payback period possible is desirable for two reasons: (1) the sooner the cash outlay is recovered, the sooner it can be reinvested in other assets, (2) a quick payback period may reduce the risk of the investment because uncertainty usually increases over time. Disadvantages of the method are that it ignores the time value of money and the total life of the investment. An investment selected because of its short payback period may be less profitable over its entire life than an alternative investment with a longer payback period and total life. However, many businesses use the method to make a final choice among alternatives when other methods of evaluation indicate they are equally attractive. The payback period in Canberra Co. Ltd's decision is calculated as:

$$\text{Payback period} = \frac{\text{Initial cost of investment}}{\text{Annual net cash flows}}$$

$$= \frac{\$81\,000}{\$18\,000} = 4.5 \text{ years}$$

The analysis shows that it will take 4.5 years to recover the initial investment of $81 000.

Return on average investment method

The **return on average investment** is a rough approximation of an investment's profitability. It is calculated by dividing the average annual profit after tax from an investment by the average investment. When straight-line depreciation is used, the carrying amount of an asset decreases uniformly over its life. As a result, the average investment is calculated as:

$$\text{Average investment} = \frac{\text{Initial cost + Final resale value}}{2}$$

$$= \frac{\$81\,000 + \$13\,000}{2}$$

$$= \$47\,000$$

When the resale value is zero, the average investment is simply the initial cost divided by 2. The return on average investment for Canberra Co. Ltd's proposed machine is:

$$\text{Return on average investment} = \frac{\text{Average profit}}{\text{Average investment}}$$

$$= \frac{\$11\,200}{\$47\,000}$$

$$= 23.8\%$$

The 23.8% return would be compared with the returns of alternative investments and with the minimum return required by management to decide whether it should be accepted. In addition, the risk associated with each alternative must be evaluated carefully. Most businesses using the return on average investment method rank all of the investments according to their returns and risks. Available resources are committed to those investments with an acceptable combination of returns and risks.

Some people support the return on average investment method because it follows the income statement in measuring the return on an investment. The $11 200 used in the example is the estimate of annual accounting profit rather than the estimated net cash flows. Hence, it is commonly referred to as the accounting rate of return. The method is widely used to rank alternative investments because it is easy to use and understand.

Unlike the payback period method, the return on average investment method does consider the profitability of an investment over its useful life. However, it does not consider the time value of money. The use of the average annual profit ignores the timing of cash inflows and outflows. Consequently, the net cash flow from an investment's last year of life is valued the same as that of its first year. In addition, the method does not distinguish between an investment requiring an immediate payment of cash and one that will be paid for in the future.

14.7 Demonstration problem

Quick Brekkie Ltd is evaluating three comparable investments. Summary data for the three investments, each of which would be paid for in current dollars, are listed below.

Investment	Expected annual net cash inflows	Estimated life	Initial cost
X	$20 000	8 years	$99 352
Y	16 000	14 years	87 480
Z	15 000	18 years	72 183

The company's cost of capital is 12%.

Required

Rank the three investments using each of the following methods:
1. payback period
2. net present value
3. net present value index.

Solution to demonstration problem

1. *Payback period*

	X	Y	Z
Initial cost (a)	$99 352	$87 480	$72 183
Annual net cash inflows (b)	$20 000	$16 000	$15 000
Payback period [(a) ÷ (b)]	4.9676	5.4675	4.8122
Ranking	2	3	1

2. *Net present value (12%)*

	X	Y	Z
Discounted net cash inflows:			
4.9676 × $20 000	$99 352		
6.6282 × $16 000		$106 051	
7.2497 × $15 000			$108 746
Initial cost	99 352	87 480	72 183
Net present value	$ —	$ 18 571	$ 36 563
Ranking	3	2	1

3. *Net present value index*

	X	Y	Z
Discounted net cash inflows (a)	$99 352	$106 051	$108 746
Initial cost (b)	$99 352	$ 87 480	$ 72 183
Profitability index [(a) ÷ (b)]	1.0000	1.2123	1.5065
Ranking	3	2	1

Capital budgeting, p. 590
Cost of capital, p. 594
Decision making, p. 582
Decision-making process, p. 582
Decision model, p. 582
Differential analysis (incremental analysis), p. 583
Differential cost, p. 583
Differential income, p. 583
Discounted cash flows, p. 591

Internal rate of return (IRR), p. 596
Joint products, p. 585
Joint product costs, p. 585
Net present value (NPV) index method, p. 596
Net present value (NPV) method, p. 593
Opportunity cost, p. 583
Payback period, p. 596
Relevant costs, p. 583
Relevant income, p. 583

Residual profit (residual income), p. 589
Return on average investment, p. 597
Return on investment (ROI) analysis, p. 588
Split-off point, p. 585
Sunk costs, p. 583
Tax shield, p. 595
Unavoidable costs, p. 583

DISCUSSION QUESTIONS

1. Accountants may provide much of the quantitative information in the decision-making process outlined in this chapter. What quantitative and non-quantitative information could people working in marketing, human resources management, tourism and hospitality, and sports and recreation contribute to the decision-making process of an organisation such as a hotel chain?

2. This book indicates that one of the roles of managers is to make decisions about organising resources. How can a human resources manager use differential analysis in deciding the appropriate number and levels of staff in a large professional office such as a marketing, law or accounting firm?

3. A business manager was heard to remark: 'Quantitative analysis may be all right for some businesses but I'd rather make decisions based on my intuition and years of experience.' Do you agree? Explain.

4. How can the ideas of 'evaluation of a make-or-buy decision' be used in deciding whether to use existing staff expertise and existing resources in a new marketing campaign for a clothing brand name or whether to employ an external professional marketing firm's expertise? Other than costs, what factors should be taken into account in such a decision?

5. You are responsible for managing a large department store. Explain how the section on 'product mix decisions' in this chapter might be relevant to deciding which departments you would include in the store and where you might position such departments within the store.

6. On presenting your manager with the differential analysis of two possible uses for a piece of land that cost the company $2 million, your manager believes you have made a major error because you omitted the cost of the land. Explain the term 'sunk costs' and why you have not made an error.

7. An accounting student said, 'In making capital budgeting decisions it is necessary to determine the relevant cash flows from the proposal rather than the income and expenses based on normal accrual accounting.' Do you agree? Explain.

8. Calculation of present value and determining discounted cash flows are two techniques that are the same. Do you agree? Explain your stance.

9. The method of depreciation used has no effect on the capital budgeting decision. Discuss.

10. Comment on the following statement: 'Cost of capital is the cost of the capital raised to pay for a particular project. If the money is borrowed from the bank, then the interest rate charged on the loan by the bank is the cost of capital.'

Exercise 14.1   DECISION-MAKING PROCESS

LO 1

McQuade Marketing is considering employing another marketing consultant to help with managing its clients. The human resources manager of the firm is weighing up whether to employ a marketing graduate or a marketing manager with at least 5 years experience.

Required

Using the decision-making process outlined at the beginning of this chapter, describe the process the human resources manager would follow, including possible goals of employing someone, the type of information required on the alternatives, and how the manager could evaluate the outcomes and make a decision.

Exercise 14.2   DIFFERENTIAL ANALYSIS

LO 2

Adept Adventures Pty Ltd, operated by Alexander Adept a graduate of a sports and recreation course, offers customised adventures for business groups wanting to develop their staff. Two clients have approached Adept Adventures Pty Ltd to run an adventure in the first week of October but Alexander can run only one adventure at a time and has to choose which alternative will maximise profit. Both adventures will require a week of Alexander's time at a cost of $1600 and the use of the company's specially fitted-out SUV at a cost of $4000. One client wants a rock climbing adventure for 10 people and will pay up to $1200 per person. The cost per person for food and equipment is $250 and fixed setup costs are $3500. The other client wants a white water rafting adventure for 8 people and will pay up to $1500 per person. Alexander estimates the cost per person for food and equipment is $280 and the fixed setup costs are $3500.

Required

Using only the differential income and expenses, determine which adventure Alexander should provide.

Exercise 14.3   SPECIAL ORDER

LO 2

Quantum Music Ltd manufactures portable MP3 music players at a per-unit cost of:

Direct labour	$ 4
Direct materials	12
Variable factory overhead	24
Fixed factory overhead	20
Total unit cost	$60

The company sells each player for $199 and is presently operating at 80% of its capacity of 100 000 units per year. The company has received a special order at a price of $120 per unit from an e-retailer for 1000 units per month for 1 year only. The units sold to the e-retailer would have a different cover from the company's regular players that would add an extra $5 per unit to direct materials. Quantum Ltd would have to purchase a new machine for $120 000 to produce the new covers. The machine will have no alternative use or residual value at the end of the year. The sales by the e-retailer would have no impact on the company's regular sales, because of the different cover and markets involved.

Required

A. Should the company accept the special order? Explain.

B. What would be the impact on profits of accepting the order?

Exercise 14.4 MAKE-OR-BUY DECISION

Blubyu Ltd manufactures Blu ray players and has always produced in-house all necessary parts for them, including casings. The cost per unit of the casings at a production level of 80 000 units is as follows:

Direct labour	$ 6.00
Direct materials	3.00
Variable factory overhead	18.00
Fixed factory overhead	6.00
Total unit cost	$33.00

The fixed factory overhead cost is direct, and half of the direct fixed overhead cost could be eliminated if the casings are purchased rather than produced. An outside supplier has offered to produce and sell to Blubyu Ltd 80 000 casings at a price of $31 per unit.

Required

Should the offer be accepted if there are no alternative uses for the manufacturing capacity currently being used to produce the casings? Why?

Exercise 14.5 EMPLOY FULL TIME OR USE CASUAL STAFF

Highered Ltd is a private provider of diplomas in business studies and is currently deciding whether to employ a new full-time staff member or whether to use casual staff paid by the hour to cover the increased demand for its courses. The costs of employing a new staff member to teach five classes for 3 hours each per week for 40 weeks per year and to perform associated assessment and administration tasks is:

Direct salary	$ 72 000
Direct oncosts	21 600
Variable costs of extra office space	8 000
Fixed costs of office space	24 000
Total costs	$125 600
Cost per hour for casual staff	$ 62

For each hour of teaching, the casual staff are also paid an hour of marking and an hour of administration at a rate of $25 per hour.

Required

Calculate whether it is more cost-effective to employ a new permanent staff member or to employ casual staff on an hourly basis. What factors, other than costs, should be taken into consideration in making the final decision?

Exercise 14.6 DIFFERENTIAL ANALYSIS AND JOINT PRODUCTS

Silicon Ltd produces four joint products — A, B, C and D — at a total cost of $250 000. The company can sell the products immediately at the split-off point for $80 000, $30 000, $68 000 and $65 000 respectively. Alternatively, the products also can be processed further and sold as shown below:

Product	Further processing costs	Sales (excluding GST)
A	$ 72 000	$160 000
B	150 000	182 400
C	166 300	225 000
D	38 800	105 800

Assume that all costs after the split-off point can be avoided for any product that is not processed beyond the split-off point.

Required

Which products should be processed further and which should be sold at the split-off point? Show calculations to justify the decisions.

Exercise 14.7   PRODUCT MIX DECISIONS   LO 2

Yuan Ltd manufactures and sells four products — A, B, C and D. The selling prices, variable costs, and number of machine hours required to produce each product are as follows:

Product	Selling price	Variable costs	Machine hours per unit
A	$40	$24	3
B	55	30	2
C	60	42	1.5
D	48	30	4

Each of the four products is produced using a single machine. The machine has a maximum production capacity of 7300 hours per year.

Required

A. How many units of each of the four products can be produced in a year if the company produces only that product?
B. Assuming that the company can sell all units produced, which product or mix of products should be produced?
C. Assuming that the company must produce 1000 units of Product C, what additional products should be produced?

Exercise 14.8   PROFITABILITY PERFORMANCE   LO 3

Go Slow Ltd operates four departments, and data relevant to each are:

Department	Sales	Cost of sales	Other expenses	Assets Beginning	Assets End
Ladies' wear	$920 000	$765 000	$ 99 000	$380 000	$420 000
Men's wear	765 000	460 000	169 850	780 000	810 000
Kitchen	125 000	92 000	11 440	92 000	104 000
Manchester	55 300	21 500	14 040	112 000	96 000

Required

A. Rank the four departments based on return on assets.
B. What is the residual profit of each department, assuming that the company requires a minimum return on the average investment in assets of 16%?

Exercise 14.9   RETURN ON INVESTMENT ANALYSIS   LO 3

Veikko Ltd operates two divisions as investment centres: Television Screens and Computer Screens. Management wants to know which of the two earned the highest return on investment for the year ended 30 June 2014. The details for each division for the year ended 30 June 2014 were as follows:

	Television Screens	Computer Screens
Sales revenue	$2 000 000	$1 500 000
Interest expense	40 000	60 000
Profit before tax	240 000	180 000
Assets 1 July 2013	1 000 000	800 000
Assets 30 June 2014	1 500 000	1 200 000

Required

Calculate the return on investment for each division.

Exercise 14.10   RESIDUAL PROFIT ANALYSIS

Veikko Ltd, from exercise 14.9, requires a minimum return on investment of 16%.

Required

Calculate the residual profit for the Television Screens and the Computer Screens divisions of Veikko Ltd using the data from exercise 14.9

Exercise 14.11   CAPITAL BUDGETING METHODS

Coffee producers Caffeine Kick Ltd are evaluating the purchase of a new machine that will cost $725 000 and have no residual value. Annual net cash inflows (including tax payments) for each of the next 10 years are expected to be $130 000. The average annual profit is expected to be $65 250. The company has a cost of capital of 10%.

Required

A. Calculate the payback period.
B. Calculate the net present value.
C. Calculate the return on average investment.

Exercise 14.12   COST OF CAPITAL

Perez Ltd wants to determine its cost of capital to use in future capital budgeting decisions. The company's capital structure is as follows:

Source of capital	Amount	After-tax cost
Borrowings	$600 000	12%
Preference shares	100 000	9%
Ordinary shares	1 000 000	14%
Retained earnings	700 000	14%

Required

Calculate the company's cost of capital based on the information available.

Exercise 14.13   DISCOUNTED CASH FLOWS AND PAYBACK PERIOD

Jumbuck Ltd, technology consultants, is evaluating the purchase of a new machine that will cost $180 000 and be paid for in cash. The machine will be depreciated over 10 years with a resale value at the end of $20 000. Annual before-tax cash savings from better productivity are expected to be $40 000. The company has a cost of capital of 12%. Assume an income tax rate of 30%.

Required

A. Determine the annual after-tax cash savings from the machine.
B. What is the payback period for the investment?
C. What is the net present value of the investment?

Exercise 14.14   CAPITAL BUDGETING DECISION

Padovesi Pagolas is considering the purchase of equipment that will produce net after-tax cash savings over the useful life of the equipment of 5 years as follows:

Year	After-tax savings
1	$6200
2	6000
3	5800
4	5600
5	5400

Required

What is the maximum price the business should pay for the equipment, assuming a discount rate of 12%?

Exercise 14.15 CAPITAL BUDGETING EVALUATIONS

Trooper Manufacturing Ltd is evaluating investment alternatives for three machines and has compiled the following relevant information:

	Investment		
	Machine M1	**Machine M2**	**Machine M3**
Initial investment	$150 000	$216 288	$140 000
Net cash inflows:			
Year 1	$ 35 000	$ 60 000	$ 45 000
2	35 000	60 000	45 000
3	35 000	60 000	45 000
4	35 000	60 000	45 000
5	35 000	60 000	
6	35 000		

The company requires a 12% minimum return on new investments.

Required
A. Calculate the payback period for each investment.
B. Calculate the net present value for each investment.
C. Determine the net present value index for each investment.
D. Based on your analysis in requirements A, B and C above, which machine (if any) should be purchased?

PROBLEMS

★ Basic

★★ Moderate

★★★ Challenging

Problem 14.1 MAKE OR BUY DECISION ★

The screens for notebooks are currently purchased from an outside supplier at a cost of $200 each by Reliable Technologies Ltd. The company is concerned about the quality of the screens it is buying as one in a thousand is found to be faulty within a year of using them to make notebooks.

If the company decides to manufacture the screens, it would have to purchase new machines at a cost of $7 200 000. The new machinery would enable the company to produce its annual requirement of 10 000 screens and would have to be scrapped at the end of a 5-year useful life. The following costs per unit would be required to produce the screens (excluding the cost of the new machinery):

Direct materials	$36
Direct labour	6
Variable factory overhead	24
Fixed factory overhead – allocated	30
Total	$96

The allocated fixed factory overhead would be a reassignment of existing costs based on estimated sales volume.

Required
Should the company make or buy the screens for the notebooks? Explain why.

Problem 14.2 MAKE OR BUY DECISION ★

Manga Motors Ltd produces motor vehicles for the small-car market. The motors for the cars are currently purchased from an outside supplier at a cost of $5000 each. Some factory space that Manga Motors currently rents to another company for storage purposes could be used to produce the motors. The annual rental revenue from the factory space is now $2 500 000.

If the company decides to manufacture the motors, it will have to purchase new machines at a cost of $75 000 000. The new machinery will enable the company to produce its annual requirement of 60 000 motors and will have to be scrapped at the end of a 5-year useful life. The following costs per unit will be required to produce the motors (excluding the cost of the new machinery):

Direct labour	$1000
Direct materials	1400
Variable factory overhead	800
Fixed factory overhead — direct	400
Fixed factory overhead — allocated	500
Total	$4100

The direct fixed factory overhead will be required to start producing the motors, and the allocated fixed factory overhead will be a reassignment of existing costs based on estimated sales volume.

Required

Should the company make or buy the motors for the cars? Explain why.

Problem 14.3 DIFFERENTIAL ANALYSIS AND JOINT PRODUCTS ★   **LO 2**

Panaplay Ltd produces two products, A and B, at a joint cost of $148 000. The company can sell 20 000 units of product A for $9 per unit, or the units can be processed further at a cost of $50 000 to produce 5000 units of product X, 7000 units of product Y, and 8000 units of product Z. The unit selling prices for products X, Y and Z are $14, $10 and $12 respectively. The company can sell 7500 units of product B or they can be processed further to produce 3000 units of product C and 4500 units of product D. The additional processing to produce products C and D will cost $40 000. The per-unit selling prices are product B $18, product C $30, and product D $18.

Required

Which of the products should be sold at the split-off point and which processed further?

Problem 14.4 CASH FLOWS IN A CAPITAL BUDGETING DECISION ★   **LO 5**

Carlos Manufacturers Ltd is considering installing a computer controlled system to significantly reduce its manufacturing costs. The annual after-tax cost savings are expected to be $120 000 and the system will cost $450 000. Its useful life will be 6 years and its resale value at that time is estimated at $10 000, net of tax effects. However, a major upgrade costing $30 000 will be required at the end of the third year. The company's cost of capital is 12%.

Required

Using the net present value method, determine whether the computer controlled system should be purchased. Justify your conclusion.

Problem 14.5 SPECIAL ORDER ★★   **LO 2**

Austin Harmer is the owner of a small company, Harmer's Chips Pty Ltd, that produces communication chips for mobile phones. The company has two production lines, one for a standard communication chip that is also produced by several competitors and one for custom communication chips built to customer specifications. Financial results of the company for the previous year are as shown below.

	Custom chips	Standard chips	Total
Sales	$120 000	$90 000	$210 000
Direct materials	24 500	28 800	53 300
Direct labour	48 000	32 400	80 400
Rent	14 400	3 600	18 000
Depreciation	15 100	12 900	28 000
Electricity	1 800	450	2 250
Other fixed manufacturing costs	4 320	1 080	5 400
	108 120	$79 230	187 350
Profit	$ 11 880	$10 770	$ 22 650

The building has been leased for 10 years at $18 000 per year. The rent, electricity, and other fixed manufacturing costs are allocated based on the amount of floor space occupied by each production line. Depreciation is specifically allocated to the machines used on each line.

Austin recently received an order from one of his best customers to produce 5000 custom-built communication chips and is trying to decide whether he should accept the order. His company is currently working at full capacity and is required by contract to produce all specialty orders already received. He could reduce the production of standard chips by a third for the next year to accept the new special order. The customer has offered to pay $22.00 per chip with the new order. The direct costs will be $18 per chip, and Austin will have to buy a new tool costing $12 000 to produce the custom-built chips. The tool will be scrapped when this order has been delivered.

Required

Should Austin accept the order? In your answer, identify the unavoidable costs, differential income and costs, and opportunity costs.

Problem 14.6 SPECIAL ORDER WITH OPPORTUNITY COSTS ★★   `LO 2`

SpeedBurn Ltd manufactures DVD burners and is considering expanding production. A distributor has asked the company to produce a special order of 3000 DVD burners. The burners will be sold using a different brand name and will not influence SpeedBurn Ltd's current sales. The plant is currently producing 28 000 units per year. Total capacity is 30 000 units per year, so the company will have to reduce the production of units sold under its own brand name by 1000 units if the special order is accepted.

The company's income statement for the previous financial year ended 30 June 2014 is summarised below:

SPEEDBURN LTD Income Statement for the year ended 30 June 2014		
Sales (28 000 units)		$3 920 000
Cost of sales:		
Direct materials	$1 260 000	
Direct labour	560 000	
Factory overhead	1 250 000	3 070 000
GROSS PROFIT		850 000
Selling and distribution expenses	520 000	
Administrative expenses	300 000	820 000
PROFIT		$ 30 000

The company's variable factory overhead is $30 per unit, and the variable selling and distribution expenses are $10 per unit. The administrative expenses are completely fixed and will increase by $10 000 if the special order is accepted. There will be no variable selling and distribution expenses associated with the special order, and variable factory overhead per unit will remain constant.

The company's direct labour cost per unit for the special order will increase 5%, and direct materials cost per unit for the special order will decrease 5%. Fixed factory overhead and fixed selling and distribution expenses will not change.

Required

If the distributor has offered to pay $110 per unit for the special order, should the company accept the offer? Show calculations to support your conclusion.

Problem 14.7 MAKE OR BUY DECISION ★★   `LO 2`

Prenzel Ltd manufactures LCD television screens. Recently, the company has been producing slightly below 80% of capacity and management is considering how to use currently unused plant capacity. One proposal is to produce a component used in several of the company's products that is currently being purchased from a supplier for $100 per unit. The company uses 25 000 of these components per year. The estimated cost of producing each component is as follows:

Direct materials	$ 32.00
Direct labour (2 hours @ $25)	50.00
Factory overhead	36.00
Total	$118.00

Factory overhead is applied to all products on the basis of direct labour hours. The expected capacity for the year is 400 000 direct labour hours. Fixed factory overhead for the year is budgeted at $3 200 000.

Required

Should the company continue to purchase the component or produce it internally? What is the total cost differential involved?

LO 2

Problem 14.8 JOINT PRODUCT COSTS ★★

Green Gnome Ltd produces garden fertilisers. The fertilisers are made into pellets which are sold in 5-kilogram packets. The fertilisers are based on a basic mix of minerals and nutrients that make up 80% of each packet. To this basic mix are added special nutrients and minerals for special purpose fertilisers such as the lawn mix, the rose mix, the Australian native plant mix as well as a general mix, which is made up entirely of the basic mix.

Green Gnome Ltd can make up to 100 tonnes of the basic mix each year at a cost of $200 000 and it needs to decide how to divide this between its four product lines. To some extent this is determined by how many 5-kilogram packets the company can sell of each product line.

The following data is relevant:

Product	Cost of 1kg of special nutrients and minerals	Selling price per 5 kg packet	Estimated maximum number of packets can sell
General Mix	Same as basic mix	$20	15 000 packets
Lawn Mix	$3	$26	12 000 packets
Rose Mix	$4	$30	8 000 packets
Australian Native Mix	$3	$20	12 000 packets

Required

Determine the most profitable mix of products given the amount of basic mix that can be produced each year and the estimated market for each product.

LO 3

Problem 14.9 PROFITABILITY ANALYSIS ★★

SLO Delivery Co. Ltd operates a package delivery service and is planning the next year's operation. The company's assets are estimated to be $1 200 000 at the beginning of the financial year and $1 500 000 at the 30 June end of financial year. The company expects that it will deliver 150 000 packages during the year. The variable costs per package average $4, and total fixed costs are budgeted at $300 000.

Required

A. What price should the company charge to deliver a package to earn a 20% before-tax return on the estimated investment in assets?

B. Calculate the approximate profit margin earned and turnover of assets expected for the company's next financial year. The company will not have any interest expense. Use the price from requirement A.

C. If the company can reduce the variable costs needed to deliver a package by $0.40, what will be the effect on the return on the estimated investment in operating assets?

D. If the company actually delivers 160 000 packages at the price determined in requirement A, what is the company's rate of return on its budgeted average investment in assets?

E. Refer to requirement A. If the company requires a return on investment of 15%, how much residual profit can be expected for the next financial year?

LO 3

Problem 14.10   RETURN ON INVESTMENT ★★

Pierre Ltd is a catering business owned by well-known chef Pierre Boudin. It is organised as two divisions, each with its own manager. There is the Shop Division, managed by Louise Lane, that runs retail outlets in a number of shopping centres throughout the city, and the Catering Division, managed by Brett Spark, that provides food for corporate functions, parties and public events. Pierre is considering going into semi-retirement and wants one of the managers to run the overall business.

Pierre has decided to assess the return on investment of the two divisions and to hand over the management of Pierre Ltd to whichever manager runs the division with the higher return on investment. Relevant information for the divisions is as follows:

	Shop Division	Catering Division
Sales revenue	$2 400 000	$1 800 000
Selling & administrative expenses	1 600 000	1 200 000
Interest expense	60 000	80 000
Profit before tax	740 000	520 000
Tax expense	220 000	160 000
Profit	$ 520 000	$ 360 000
Average total assets	$2 200 000	$1 600 000

Required

Which manager should Pierre appoint to take over management of the company?

LO 6

Problem 14.11   CAPITAL BUDGETING EVALUATIONS ★★★

Selling IT 2 the Masses, marketing consultants, is considering a project requiring considerable expansion of its current operations. This will require the purchase of equipment at a cost of $560 000. The new equipment will have a 6-year life and then have no resale value. The new project would produce a net increase in cash inflows of $140 000 each year. The company has a cost of capital of 10%.

Required

A. What is the payback period for the equipment?

B. Calculate the net present value of the equipment.

C. What is the net present value index for the equipment?

D. Should the firm purchase the equipment? Why or why not?

LO 6

Problem 14.12   CAPITAL BUDGETING EVALUATIONS ★★★

Rocks Ltd is a diamond wholesaling company that commands a large share of the international diamond market. The company is looking at three alternative specialised machines to sort and prepare its diamonds for cutting by its jewellers. Data for each of the machines are as follows:

Machine	Expected annual profit increase	Estimated annual net cash inflows increase	Estimated life	Initial cost
Diamondo	$370 000	$250 000	10 years	$1 200 000
Divine Diamonds	320 000	200 000	12 years	1 000 000
Rough Diamonds	320 000	200 000	8 years	900 000

The company's cost of capital is 16%.

Required

A. Rank the three machines using each of the following methods:
   1. Net present value method
   2. Net present value index method
   3. Payback period
   4. Return on average investment.
B. Comment on the rankings under the four methods of evaluating the machines and explain which method will provide the best result for the firm and why payback period or return on average investment might be preferred by Rocks Ltd.

LO 6

Problem 14.13 CAPITAL EXPENDITURE DECISION ★★★

Encom Engineering is an engineering consulting firm specialising in the installation of electronic communications systems. The company is considering the purchase of testing equipment that will be used on jobs. The equipment will cost $158 400 and will have no residual value at the end of its 5-year life.

The firm's accountant projects revenue and expenses with the operation of the equipment that are equal to the cash inflows and cash outflows associated with it, except for depreciation. A summary of the cash flows expected from the equipment (without considering taxes) is as follows:

Year	Revenues	Expenses (excluding depreciation)
1	$124 488	$83 520
2	138 240	88 560
3	147 240	88 560
4	156 240	88 560
5	165 240	88 560

Assume the company's cost of capital is 12% and its expected tax rate is 30%.

Required

A. Calculate the return on average investment for the equipment.
B. Determine the annual net cash inflows (after tax) expected from the operation of the equipment
C. Calculate the net present value for the investment.
D. Determine the net present value index for the investment.
E. Should the testing equipment be purchased? Explain why.

LO 6

Problem 14.14 ALTERNATIVE CAPITAL BUDGETING METHODS ★★★

Flasher Freight Ltd is considering three investments for the new year. The company has a cost of capital of 12%. Summary information concerning the net cash inflows of the investments and their initial costs is shown below:

| Year | Investment | | |
	A	B	C
1	$ 48 000	$ 36 000	$ 24 000
2	48 000	36 000	24 000
3	48 000	36 000	24 000
4	48 000	36 000	24 000
5	48 000	36 000	24 000
6	48 000		24 000
7	48 000		24 000
8	48 000		24 000
9			24 000
10			24 000
11			24 000
12			24 000
Initial cost	$(198 493)	$(120 875)	$(124 730)

Required

A. Calculate the payback period for each investment.
B. What is the net present value for each investment?
C. What is the net present value index for each investment?
D. Should any of these investments be accepted? If so, in what order should they be accepted, given limited available funds?

Problem 14.15 COMPREHENSIVE EXAMPLE ★★★ LO 6, 7

Ben's Big BBQs Pty Ltd makes large barbecues and sells them through specialist barbecue stores and outdoor furniture stores. Ben's Big BBQs Pty Ltd has been approached by a national department store, DMart, to produce 2000 barbecues per year for the next 3 years on their behalf.

Ben's Big BBQs Pty Ltd has the capacity to produce 20 000 barbecues per year but is currently making and selling only 15 000 under its own brand name at a wholesale price of $300 per barbecue. DMart wants the barbecues made for them to have Dmart's brand name on them and to have special features not on the standard model produced by Ben's Big BBQs Pty Ltd. DMart is prepared to pay only $200 per barbecue. If Ben's Big BBQs Pty Ltd takes the order it will need a special machine that will cost $200 000 and last only the 3 years of the deal with DMart — it will then be scrapped for $20 000. This machine will be depreciated using straight-line depreciation.

Currently the variable cost per barbecue is $150, and this will be the same variable cost for the DMart barbecues. Fixed costs for Ben's Big BBQs Pty Ltd are $1 200 000 per year and this will not change if the special order is accepted, except for the depreciation costs of the new machine. Ben's Big BBQs Pty Ltd is taxed at the company rate of 30%.

The capital structure of Ben's Big BBQs Pty Ltd is as follows:

Type of financing	Percentage of total capital	After-tax cost of borrowings and shares
Borrowings	40%	12%
Preference shares	20%	18%
Ordinary shares	40%	19%

Required

A. Calculate the annual increase in cash flows if the special order for DMart is accepted. Assume all sales and variable expenses are eventually received and paid in cash.
B. Calculate the weighted average cost of capital for Ben's Big BBQs Pty Ltd.
C. Calculate the net present value of the new machine that Ben's Big BBQs Pty Ltd will have to purchase if the special order for DMart is accepted.
D. Calculate the net present value index for the new machine.
E. Calculate the payback period for the new machine.
F. Calculate the return on average investment for the new machine.
G. Comment on whether Ben's Big BBQs Pty Ltd should purchase the new machine based on your calculations above, and suggest factors other than financial ones that should be taken into consideration when making the final decision about whether to accept the special order from DMart.

DECISION ANALYSIS

Make or buy plastic casings

Fonus Ltd produces mobile phones. The machine used to manufacture the plastic casings for the phones is increasingly producing twisted and deformed casings and is in urgent need of replacement. You are the accountant for Fonus Ltd, and have investigated the possibility of either replacing the machine with an updated version or buying in the casings from an outside supplier that produces plastic parts for other manufacturers. You have summarised your findings thus far.

Make the plastic casings. The new machine required to manufacture the plastic casings costs $720 000 and has a useful life of 3 years. The equipment will have no final resale value. The machine can manufacture all the different-shaped casings needed for Fonus Ltd's range of mobile phones by simply changing the mould that is used. The cost of the various plastic casings is estimated to be the same regardless of the shape or size. Each year, Fonus Ltd makes 300 000 mobile phones that all require one plastic casing each. The company's costs incurred in producing a plastic casing with the old machine were:

Direct materials		$ 4.20
Direct labour		3.00
Factory overhead:		
Variable portion	$1.20	
Fixed portion	6.40	7.60
Total cost per unit		$14.80

Included in the fixed factory overhead costs is depreciation of the old plastic casings moulding machine of $0.75 per unit. The new equipment will be more efficient and will reduce direct labour costs and variable overhead cost by 30%. The direct materials cost will be reduced by $0.20 per unit but fixed factory overhead will not change, except for the depreciation, if the new equipment is purchased. The new plastic casings moulding machine has a capacity of 500 000 casings per year and Fonus Ltd has no other use for the space involved.

Buy the plastic casings. You have found a supplier who is prepared to produce the plastic casings for the company for $7.60 each. The supplier will sign a contract fixing that price for the next 3 years.

Required

A. Assuming that Fonus Ltd continues to produce 300 000 phones each year, should the plastic casings be made by Fonus or bought?
B. If Fonus Ltd produces 500 000 phones each year, would your decision be different? If so, why?
C. If the space involved in the production of the plastic casings can be leased for 3 years at an annual rent of $100 000, how would this affect your decision?
D. What non-financial considerations should be taken into account in the decision to make or buy the plastic casings?

COMMUNICATION AND LEADERSHIP

Capital budgeting decisions

The Hyupp Group runs five-star hotels in most major cities. The group is looking to build a six-star luxury resort in South-East Asia on a remote island. The chief financial officer prefers to use the payback method to evaluate the new investment. The senior accountant believes the return on average investment would be a better approach as it uses the accounting records of the firm. The assistant accountant paid attention in her lectures on discounted cash flow during her recent time at university and believes that is the superior method for analysing capital budgeting decisions. The three agree to make notes on their preferred method and then compare the three approaches.

Required

In groups of three, each person takes on the role of one of the finance staff and writes a page on the pros and cons of the method chosen by that character. Try to convince the other two people in the group that your method would be the most appropriate in this instance.

ETHICS AND GOVERNANCE

Conflict of interests

Creekside Cement Ltd is considering purchasing a new cement-mixing truck. The supplier of trucks, Sea Meant Trucks Ltd, sells its trucks for $350 000 cash *or* customers can purchase them by paying annual instalments of $60 000 per year over 10 years at a discount rate of 10%.

Di Shonest is the chief financial officer for Creekside Cement Ltd and her husband, Barry, works for the Loans & Savings Bank. Barry earns a 0.1% commission on any loans he makes. Barry has told Di that he can organise a loan for Creekside Cement Ltd to purchase the cement mixing truck with repayments of only $52 000 per year. This loan will be over 15 years with a discount rate of 12%.

Creekside Cement Ltd is experiencing some cash flow problems at the moment so it cannot afford to pay cash for a new cement truck, though it could afford annual payments of $60 000. Di has done all the relevant calculations and recommends to the board that Creekside Cement Ltd should borrow the $350 000 from the Loans & Savings Bank on the terms Barry suggested.

Required

A. Calculate the present value of the three finance options available to Creekside Cement Ltd.
B. Who are the stakeholders involved in the machine purchase decision?
C. What are the ethical issues, if any, involved?

FINANCIAL ANALYSIS

Refer to the latest financial report of JB Hi-Fi Limited on its website, www.jbhifi.com.au, and answer the following questions:

1. A perusal of the report clearly indicates that JB Hi-Fi Limited does make capital budgeting decisions of some magnitude. What evidence is there of these activities?
2. What method of capital budgeting would you expect JB Hi-Fi Limited to use? Explain your answer.
3. Does JB Hi-Fi Limited fund capital projects through special borrowings or through equity? Explain your answer.
4. What does the investing activity section of the statement of cash flows tell us about capital budgeting for the previous 12 months?

Part 4

Equity in business

Chapter

15

Partnerships: formation, operation and reporting

Learning objectives

After studying this chapter, you should be able to:

1 define a partnership and the major attributes of a partnership (p. 616)

2 state the advantages and main characteristics of the partnership structure of business (pp. 616–7)

3 explain the purpose of a partnership agreement and describe its typical contents (p. 618)

4 describe the special features applicable to accounting for partnerships (pp. 618–9)

5 explain the accounting entries for the formation of a partnership (pp. 619–21)

6 explain the accounting entries for the allocation of profits and losses of a partnership (pp. 621–6)

7 explain the accounting entries for drawings and advances or loans made by partners (pp. 626–8)

8 describe the content of the financial statements of a partnership (pp. 628–30).

Partnership — a global success story

The professional services firm PricewaterhouseCoopers (PwC) operates as a worldwide partnership. It is one of the world's largest partnerships, and came into being through the amalgamation of two worldwide accounting partnerships — Price Waterhouse and Coopers & Lybrand. The history of Price Waterhouse dates back to 1922, and the beginnings of Coopers & Lybrand can be traced as far back as 1874. PwC Australia is a member firm of the worldwide PwC organisation.

By 2010, PwC operated in 757 offices in 154 countries around the world, including most major cities in Australia. At 30 June 2010, PwC had a combined headcount of over 162 000 people globally, and over 4500 in Australia.

There were 8578 partners globally, 13% of whom are women.

PwC combines technical expertise with an industry-focused emphasis on providing an array of professional services. Broadly, these are assurance and business advisory services, corporate finance and recovery, business process outsourcing, and tax and legal services.

For the financial year ended 30 June 2010, PwC recorded global gross revenues of US$26.6 billion. Member firms performed services for 84% of the companies in the Fortune Global 500.

PwC is one of the current 'big four' professional services accounting firms operating worldwide.

Further information on PwC can be obtained from the firm's website www.pwc.com.

Chapter preview

Partnerships have always been a popular form of organisation for professionals and service businesses. PricewaterhouseCoopers, discussed in the scene setter, is one of the world's largest partnerships, offering professional services in consulting, assurance (audit), tax and corporate finance.

This chapter discusses the partnership structure of business organisations and the applicable accounting procedures. Many of the accounting principles and practices discussed so far are also appropriate for a partnership. Nevertheless, some aspects of partnership accounting are different. These unique aspects involve mainly accounting for equity transactions, allocation of profit or loss, the admission or retirement of a partner from the partnership, and winding up the partnership.

Before dealing with the accounting for partnerships, we shall look at some of the general characteristics of a partnership. Partnership law has a significant influence on accounting practice. All states in Australia have adopted a uniform Partnership Act to govern the formation, operation and winding up of partnerships. The main provisions of the Partnership Act are discussed briefly throughout this chapter where it is considered appropriate. More extensive study of the legal aspects of a partnership is part of most business law courses.

15.1 Partnership defined

Learning objective 1

Define a partnership and the major attributes of a partnership

A **partnership** is defined in the Partnership Act as the relationship that 'subsists between persons carrying on a business in common with a view to profit'. Because a written agreement is not necessary to form a partnership, it is sometimes difficult to determine whether a partnership does in fact exist. Three attributes are necessary for a business partnership to exist:

1. There must be an agreement (verbal or written) between two or more legally competent persons or entities to carry on a business.
2. The business must be operated with a view to earning a profit.
3. Members must be co-owners of the business.

Co-ownership (often the most difficult attribute to determine) involves the right of each partner to share in the profits of the business, to participate with the other partners in the management of the business, and to own jointly with the other partners the property of the partnership. The right to participate in management may be limited by an express agreement among the partners.

It is important to note that, in legal terms, a partnership is not a separate legal entity; hence it is not legally correct to talk of a partnership doing business. Legally, it is the partners who are carrying on a business. Nevertheless, in the normal commercial environment it is commonplace to treat a partnership as if it was a separate entity or enterprise. A partnership is regarded as a separate accounting entity for accounting purposes, distinct from each partner and other businesses conducted by them. Note that this is in contrast to the legal entity concept.

15.2 Advantages and characteristics of a partnership

Learning objective 2

State the advantages and main characteristics of the partnership structure of business

We have already noted that a business operating with a profit motive can be structured as a sole trader, a partnership or a company, and each structure has certain advantages and disadvantages. Some of the advantages of a partnership over other forms are:

- it permits the pooling of both capital resources and the multiple skills of the individual partners
- it is easier and less costly to establish than a company
- it is not subject to as much government regulation and supervision as companies
- partners may be able to operate with more flexibility because they are not subject to the control of a board of directors
- there may be certain tax advantages (see 'Business knowledge' on the next page).

Characteristics of a partnership

Prospective owners of a business should consider the tax and legal aspects of the various structural forms of business carefully before selecting the one that meets their organisational objectives and personal goals. The partnership form may turn out to be unattractive because of one or more of the following characteristics.

A taxing issue

The fact that a partnership has no legal entity status is confirmed by the approach taken by the Australian Taxation Office to the taxing of partnership income. A partnership is not liable for the payment of income tax on its profits. The profits of the partnership are taxed in the hands of the individual partners who must include their share of the partnership profits in their individual annual tax returns as assessable income. This applies regardless of the form (cash or otherwise) in which the profits are distributed.

Mutual agency

Normally, every partner acts as an agent for the partnership and for every other partner. This is known as **mutual agency**. Therefore, a partner can represent the other partners and bind them to a contract if he or she is acting within the apparent scope of the business. For example, a single partner can enter into contracts to buy and sell merchandise, hire employees and acquire office equipment. However, activities outside the normal course of the business, such as selling land owned by the partnership, must be authorised by all partners.

Unlimited liability

In a **general partnership**, the most common form, each partner is personally liable for the obligations of the partnership. This is termed **unlimited liability**. This means that if the creditors of the partnership are not paid fully from assets of the partnership, they can look to an individual partner's personal assets for full recovery of any unpaid claims. In contrast, a **limited partnership** exists when one or more of the partners have limited their liability for partnership debts to the amount of assets they have contributed. However, at least one of the partners must be a general partner and hence liable to meet claims on the partnership out of personal assets. Limited partnerships are uncommon in Australia and legislation for their formation does not exist in some states.

Limited life

A partnership is dissolved for a number of reasons, including the death of a partner, the bankruptcy of the partnership or an individual partner, the admission of a new partner or retirement of an old partner from the partnership, the expiration of the period specified in a contract, or a judgement by a court that a partner is of unsound mind and incapable of performing partnership duties. In some of these cases, the partnership business activities are terminated and the partnership ceases to exist.

Transfer of partnership interest

A capital interest in a partnership is a personal asset of the individual partner that can be sold or disposed of legally. However, partnership law recognises the highly personal relationship of partners and provides that the purchaser of a partner's interest does not have the right to participate in management unless accepted and agreed to by all the other partners. The new partner is entitled to the profit allocation acquired and, in the event of dissolution, to receive whatever assets the selling partner would have received had he or she continued in the partnership. Obtaining approval to participate in management from the other partners may make it difficult to transfer a partnership interest.

The above discussion emphasises the importance of careful selection of the individuals forming a partnership. The mutual-agency and unlimited liability characteristics could result in extensive personal liability resulting from the acts of other partners.

Because of these characteristics, it can be more difficult for a partnership to raise capital than it is for a company. Partnerships are thus most common in comparatively small businesses, professional organisations such as a medical practice or an accounting practice, and some limited projects undertaken to accomplish a single goal such as an oil and gas exploration project or a real estate development project.

Learning objective 3

Explain the purpose of a
partnership agreement
and describe its typical
contents

15.3 Partnership agreement

A partnership is a voluntary association based on the contractual agreement between legally competent people. The contract between the parties is called the **partnership agreement**. Although the partnership agreement may be verbal, it is good business practice to have the agreement in writing. The partners should clearly express their intentions and the document should cover all aspects of operating the partnership. If there are subsequent unresolved disputes, it may be necessary to resort to litigation. The court will attempt to interpret the partnership agreement and the intentions of the partners. To avoid as many conflicts as possible, the partners should seek professional legal guidance in drawing up the agreement.

The partnership agreement should be as explicit as possible and typically should include these important points:
- partnership name and identity of the partners
- nature and duration of the business
- location of the place of business
- how profits and losses are to be shared
- how the withdrawal of assets by a partner is to be handled
- conduct of the partnership affairs
- the accounting system and banking arrangements
- authority of each partner in contractual situations
- identification and valuation of initial asset contributions and specification of capital interest each respective partner is to receive
- accounting practices (e.g. depreciation method) to be used
- how disputes among the partners are to be resolved
- how day-to-day operations are to be conducted and how the various partners' interests are to be satisfied on the admission, death, retirement or expulsion of a partner, and the cessation of business.

Sometimes the partnership agreement may exclude particular rights or duties of the individual partners. In these cases, the Partnership Act (each Australian state has its own Act) sets down a number of rights and duties applicable to a partnership. Subject to any agreement to the contrary:
- partners are entitled to share equally in the capital and profits of the business, and must contribute equally towards partnership losses
- partners are liable for the debts of the partnership to the whole extent of their personal property; partners must contribute to those debts in the same proportions in which they share profits
- partners are entitled to take part in the management of the partnership business
- partners are not entitled, before the ascertainment of profits, to interest on the capital contributed by them
- partners are not entitled to any remuneration for conducting the business affairs of the partnership
- no person may be introduced as a partner or expelled from the partnership without the consent of all existing partners
- if a partner advances money to the partnership beyond the amount of his or her contributed capital, that partner is entitled to interest at the rate specified in the Act (interest rate varies from state to state in Australia)
- partnership records are to be kept at the place of business and may be inspected by any partner at any time.

Learning objective 4

Describe the special
features applicable to
accounting for partnerships

15.4 Accounting for a partnership

As already noted, a partnership is a separate accounting entity distinct from the partners. The transactions and events that affect the assets, liabilities and partners' equity accounts of the partnership are accounted for separately from the personal activities of the individual partners. For reporting purposes, however, a creditor may require information concerning the personal assets and debts of individual partners as well as financial reports of the business because a general partner has unlimited liability for the partnership debts.

Most partnerships are not reporting entities and hence do not have to comply with accounting standards. The accounting and reporting is determined entirely by the partners themselves and any financial reports are thus special-purpose reports. This book provides the accounting treatment appropriate if the partnership is a reporting entity.

Accounting for a partnership involves essentially the same procedures and accounting principles examined in preceding chapters. A major difference, however, is accounting for partners' equity. In a partnership, ownership interests generally are not equal because the capital investments and drawings of each partner vary over time. Also, the profit or loss reported each accounting period is distributed to the partners in accordance with the partnership agreement, or Partnership Act if there is no partnership agreement. Because the capital interest of each partner can vary, a separate Capital account and a separate Drawings account are maintained for each partner.

There are two commonly used methods for accounting for equity in a partnership:
- Method 1: use of Capital accounts for each partner that not only record capital contributed and withdrawn but also include each partner's periodic share of profits and/or losses
- Method 2: use of Capital accounts with fixed balances for each partner reflecting only the capital contributed and capital withdrawn. A partner's share of profits and/or losses and drawings from profits are recorded in a separate Retained Earnings (or Current) account for each partner.

Method 1: Capital accounts that include profits and losses

Under this method, the Capital account of each partner is credited when assets are invested in the partnership by that partner. During each accounting period, each partner's Drawings account is debited to record the withdrawal of assets or the payment of personal expenses by an individual partner from partnership assets. At the end of the period, the Drawings account of each partner is typically closed to his or her Capital account, and the balance in the Profit or Loss Summary account is transferred to a Profit Distribution account where profits/losses are allocated to the partners in an agreed ratio and closed to their respective Capital accounts. Except for the additional accounts and the need to divide the profit or loss, these are the same procedures as illustrated in previous chapters to account for the capital transactions of a sole trader.

Method 2: Fixed capital accounts

Under this method, the Capital account of each partner is credited when assets are invested in the partnership by that person. However, after this initial entry, very few adjustments are made to the Capital account. The only entries made in the account represent either (a) further contributions of capital by that partner or (b) withdrawals of capital (as opposed to drawings of profits).

Hence, each partner's Drawings account is debited only for withdrawals of assets or the payment of personal expenses by the partner out of his or her share of profits or expected profits. At the end of the accounting period, the balance in the Profit or Loss Summary account, representing the partnership profit or loss for the period, is transferred to a Profit Distribution account, which is then closed by allocating profits/losses to the respective Retained Earnings accounts of the partners. The Drawings account of each partner is closed to the Retained Earnings account for each partner. These procedures closely follow the procedures in accounting for the profits/losses of companies.

In this chapter, the procedures for both methods 1 and 2 are illustrated whenever they differ. However, in practice our preference is to use method 2.

15.5 Accounting for the formation of a partnership

Assets contributed to a partnership, liabilities assumed by a partnership, monetary amounts to be assigned to specific assets and liabilities, and the capital interest each partner is to receive should be agreed on and specified in the partnership agreement. Once the agreement is made, entries to record the formation of a partnership can be made.

Learning objective 5

Explain the accounting entries for the formation of a partnership

To illustrate, assume that Max Becker and Robyn Cook, operators of currently competing businesses, agree on 1 July 2012 to form the BC Partnership. The carrying amount and fair value of the assets being contributed and the liabilities assumed by the partnership are agreed on as follows:

	Carrying amount		Fair value	
	Becker	**Cook**	**Becker**	**Cook**
Cash at bank	$ 60 000	$ 20 000	$ 60 000	$ 20 000
Accounts receivable	—	22 000	—	20 000
Inventory	43 000	9 000	40 000	10 000
Equipment	80 000	42 000	50 000	20 000
Accumulated depreciation – equipment	(35 000)	(18 000)	—	—
Land	—	15 000	—	20 000
Building	—	110 000	—	50 000
Accumulated depreciation – building	—	(70 000)	—	—
Total assets contributed	148 000	130 000	150 000	140 000
Mortgage acquired	—	40 000	—	40 000
Assets and liabilities contributed	$148 000	$ 90 000	$150 000	$100 000

Fair value is defined in international accounting standards as the price that would be received to sell an asset or paid to transfer a liability in an orderly transaction between market participants at the measurement date. The fair values of the assets given above meet this definition.

Assuming that the partners agree to have capital balances equal to the fair value of net assets contributed and that GST is not applicable, journal entries to record the initial investment are:

2012				
July	1	Cash at Bank	60 000	
		Inventory	40 000	
		Equipment	50 000	
		M. Becker, Capital		150 000
		(Assets contributed by Becker to the partnership)		
	1	Cash at Bank	20 000	
		Accounts Receivable	20 000	
		Inventory	10 000	
		Equipment	20 000	
		Land	20 000	
		Building	50 000	
		Mortgage Payable		40 000
		R. Cook, Capital		100 000
		(Assets and liabilities contributed by Cook to the partnership)		

Note that the non-cash assets and liabilities are recorded at their fair values. Each partner's Capital account is credited with the fair value of the assets and liabilities contributed. The amounts recorded in the accounts of the partnership may differ from the carrying amounts recorded in the accounts of the separate businesses. For example, the equipment of Becker recorded at $50 000 in the journal entry shown above had a carrying amount of $45 000 ($80 000 − $35 000). The use of fair value provides a more equitable measure of the amount invested by each partner and is the appropriate measure of the cost paid by the partnership. Entries to record additional investments after the partnership is formed are based on the same principles.

One or more of the partners may negotiate a capital interest different from the total of the identifiable net assets contributed. For example, Becker and Cook may agree that their capital investment should be $175 000 and $125 000 respectively in the new partnership in recognition of the value of unidentifiable net assets contributed by them. These unidentifiable net assets are recorded as goodwill purchased by the partnership from each of the partners.

The term **goodwill** is used by accountants and others to mean various things. It is often thought of as the favourable reputation enjoyed by an entity among its customers. From an accounting standpoint, however, goodwill has a special meaning not limited to good customer relations. Goodwill arises from many factors, including customer confidence, quality management, favourable location, manufacturing efficiency, good employee relations and market share. A successful entity continually develops these factors, but the expenditures made in doing so cannot be specifically identified with each of these factors. Nor can these factors be separated from the business as a whole. The term 'goodwill' is therefore used to describe all these unidentifiable assets.

Goodwill may be generated internally or purchased in an exchange transaction. *Only purchased goodwill should be recorded in the accounts*, according to IAS 38/AASB 138 *Intangible Assets*, because purchased goodwill can be measured reliably on the basis of the amount paid for it, whereas internally generated goodwill is not usually capable of reliable measurement. When recorded, goodwill is classified as a non-current asset.

In the illustration below, both Becker and Cook mutually agree that the capital interest for each is greater than the fair value of the identifiable assets and liabilities being contributed by them to the new partnership entity. This difference represents goodwill, and since it is being purchased from each of the partners, it is recorded in the partnership accounting records.

The entries to record the identifiable assets and liabilities at fair values, the goodwill, and capital interests of the partners are:

2012				
July	1	Cash at Bank	60 000	
		Inventory	40 000	
		Equipment	50 000	
		Goodwill	25 000	
		M. Becker, Capital		175 000
		(Assets contributed by Becker to the partnership)		
	1	Cash at Bank	20 000	
		Accounts Receivable	20 000	
		Inventory	10 000	
		Equipment	20 000	
		Land	20 000	
		Building	50 000	
		Goodwill	25 000	
		Mortgage Payable		40 000
		R. Cook, Capital		125 000
		(Assets and liabilities contributed by Cook to the partnership)		

The same entries would be made for partnership formation whether the business had decided to use method 1 or method 2 in accounting for partners' equity, since the entries relate solely to capital contributed by the partners.

15.6 Allocation of partnership profits and losses

Learning objective 6

Explain the accounting entries for the allocation of profits and losses of a partnership

The partners may agree to any method of allocating profit or losses, and details of the allocation method should be included in the partnership agreement. In the absence of an agreement or if the partners are unable to reach an agreement, the Partnership Act provides that profits are to be divided equally, regardless of the amount invested by the partners. If a profit agreement is made but a loss agreement is not, any loss must be allocated in the same way as a profit.

In establishing an equitable way to allocate partnership profits and losses, the partners should consider the three distinct elements that make up partnership profits:
- a return for the personal services performed by the partners
- a return on the capital provided by the partners
- a return for the business risks assumed by the partners.

If profits are to be allocated equitably, the allocation method should take into consideration any difference in the amount of resources and services contributed. For example, if one partner is more actively involved in the management of the business or if his or her services are more valuable to the business, this fact should be recognised in the profit and loss agreement. Similarly, if the partners' capital investments are not equal, a statement to recognise these differences should be included in the agreement.

As noted, the objective of the profit and loss agreement is to reward each partner for resources and services contributed to the business. Some of the more common profit and loss sharing agreements are:

- a fixed ratio
- a ratio based on capital balances
- a fixed ratio established by the partners after allowing for interest on capital contributions and salaries to partners for services rendered to the partnership.

In the following illustrations, it is assumed that Max Becker and Robyn Cook formed the BC Partnership with capital investments of $150 000 and $100 000 respectively. At the end of the first year of operations, the Profit or Loss Summary account had a credit balance of $60 000 (final profit). Completion of the closing process depends on whether method 1 or method 2 is used.

Under method 1, the Profit or Loss Summary account is closed via a Profit Distribution account to the individual partners' Capital accounts. Under method 2, the Profit or Loss Summary account is closed via a Profit Distribution account to each partner's Retained Earnings account. The amount credited to each Capital account depends on the profit allocation method agreed to by the partners.

Fixed ratio

One of the simplest profit and loss agreements is for each partner to be allocated profits or losses based on some specified ratio. This method may be appropriate if the partners' contribution can be stated in terms of a fixed percentage. For example, assume that Becker and Cook agree to a 7:3 sharing of profits and losses respectively. The applicable closing entries to cover the profit distribution are:

		Method 1		Method 2	
2013		Dr	Cr	Dr	Cr
June 30	Profit or Loss Summary	60 000		60 000	
	Profit Distribution		60 000		60 000
	(Transfer of partnership profit to Profit Distribution account for distribution of profits to partners)				
30	Profit Distribution	60 000		60 000	
	M. Becker, Retained Earnings				42 000
	R. Cook, Retained Earnings				18 000
	M. Becker, Capital		42 000		
	R. Cook, Capital		18 000		
	(Distribution of profit to partners)				

The partners' equity accounts as shown in a balance sheet prepared on 30 June 2013 would appear as shown below.

	Method 1	Method 2
M. Becker, Capital	$192 000	$150 000
R. Cook, Capital	118 000	100 000
M. Becker, Retained Earnings		42 000
R. Cook, Retained Earnings		18 000
Total	$310 000	$310 000

Partnership losses are allocated using the same 7:3 ratio unless a separate loss-sharing arrangement is stated in the partnership contract.

Ratio based on capital balances

The allocation of profits based on the ratio of capital balances may result in an equitable allocation when invested capital is considered the most important factor and/or the partnership operations require little of the partners' time. Since the capital balances may change during the period whether method 1 or method 2 is in use, the agreement should specify whether the ratio is to be calculated from the original investment, the beginning-of-year balances, the end-of-year balances, or an average of the balances.

Assuming that the ratio is to be calculated from the beginning-of-year balances, the $60 000 profit is allocated as follows:

	Capital investment	Profit allocation
Becker	$150 000	($150 000/$250 000) × $60 000 = $36 000
Cook	100 000	($100 000/$250 000) × $60 000 = 24 000
Totals	$250 000	$60 000

The relevant closing entries are:

			Method 1		Method 2	
2013		Dr	Cr	Dr	Cr	
June 30	Profit or Loss Summary	60 000		60 000		
	Profit Distribution		60 000		60 000	
	(Transfer of partnership profit for distribution to partners)					
30	Profit Distribution	60 000		60 000		
	M. Becker, Retained Earnings				36 000	
	R. Cook, Retained Earnings				24 000	
	M. Becker, Capital		36 000			
	R. Cook, Capital		24 000			
	(Distribution of profit to partners' Capital or Retained Earnings accounts)					

In a computerised accounting system (including integrated accounting packages), the system is set up initially to record partnership equity accounts and profit/loss sharing ratios are inserted. The allocation of profits/losses to the partners' equity accounts, therefore, is done automatically.

Fixed ratio after allowing for interest and salaries

Often, individual partners make unequal capital contributions, and the amount of time and the nature of services performed in the management function are not the same. Unless provided for in the partnership agreement, a partner is not legally entitled to receive compensation for services performed for the partnership or interest on capital investments. Thus, if profit is to be allocated equitably to compensate the partners for unequal contributions, a profit allocation method that contains a provision for interest and/or salaries must be included in the partnership agreement. To illustrate, assume the partnership agreement of BC Partnership contains this profit agreement:
1. Each partner is to be allowed interest of 10% on the initial capital investment.
2. Max Becker and Robyn Cook are to receive salary allowances per year of $18 000 and $10 000 respectively.
3. Any residual profit or loss is to be shared equally. (Equal percentages are used here on the assumption that business risk is assumed equally by each partner.)

The allocation of $60 000 profit will be:

	Becker	Cook	Total
Interest on capital credited			
$150 000 × 10%	$15 000		
$100 000 × 10%		$10 000	$25 000
Salaries to partners credited	18 000	10 000	28 000
Total interest and salary credited	33 000	20 000	53 000
Residual to be divided equally	3 500	3 500	7 000*
Equity increase	$36 500	$23 500	$60 000

* The residual is the difference between the profit of $60 000 and the salary and interest allocation of $53 000. It is allocated equally to each partner as provided for in item 3 of the partnership agreement above.

The closing entries to allocate the balance in the Profit or Loss Summary account to the partners under methods 1 and 2 are:

			Method 1		Method 2	
2013			Dr	Cr	Dr	Cr
June 30	Profit or Loss Summary		60 000		60 000	
	Profit Distribution			60 000		60 000
	(Transfer of profit for distribution to partners)					
30	Profit Distribution		25 000		25 000	
	M. Becker, Capital			15 000		
	R. Cook, Capital			10 000		
	M. Becker, Retained Earnings					15 000
	R. Cook, Retained Earnings					10 000
	(Distribution of interest on capital to partners)					
30	Profit Distribution		28 000		28 000	
	M. Becker, Capital			18 000		
	R. Cook, Capital			10 000		
	M. Becker, Retained Earnings					18 000
	R. Cook, Retained Earnings					10 000
	(Distribution of salaries to partners)					
30	Profit Distribution		7 000		7 000	
	M. Becker, Capital			3 500		
	R. Cook, Capital			3 500		
	M. Becker, Retained Earnings					3 500
	R. Cook, Retained Earnings					3 500
	(Distribution of residual profit to partners)					

The T accounts to illustrate these entries are shown on the next page. Note that the salary and interest provisions are not accounted for as an increase in expenses of the partnership but are considered determinants in the allocation of profit.

A salary agreement is sometimes confused with an agreement that permits withdrawals of assets. Since the term *salary* is commonly understood to mean a cash payment for services rendered, it is important that the partners specify clearly their intentions as to whether the salary is part of the profit agreement or an agreement to permit drawings during the period. That is, the partners may agree that each is permitted to withdraw a certain amount of cash from the business at regular intervals for personal living expenses.

The partners may further agree that the drawings are salaries in expectation of profitable operations and are to be considered part of the profit allocation to be made at the end of the period. Or

Profit Distribution (Methods 1 and 2)

30/6/13	Interest — Becker	15 000	30/6/13 Profit or Loss Summary	60 000
	Interest — Cook	10 000		
30/6/13	Salary — Becker	18 000		
	Salary — Cook	10 000		
30/6/13	Residual profit — Becker	3 500		
	Residual profit — Cook	3 500		
		60 000		60 000

METHOD 1
M. Becker, Capital

			1/7/12	Assets	150 000
			30/6/13	Interest	15 000
			30/6/13	Salary	18 000
30/6/13	Bal. c/d	186 500	30/6/13	Residual profit	3 500
		186 500			186 500
			1/7/13	Bal. b/d	186 500

R. Cook, Capital

			1/7/12	Assets	100 000
			30/6/13	Interest	10 000
			30/6/13	Salary	10 000
30/6/13	Bal. c/d	123 500	30/6/13	Residual profit	3 500
		123 500			123 500
			1/7/13	Bal. b/d	123 500

METHOD 2
M. Becker, Capital

	1/7/12	Assets	150 000

R. Cook, Capital

	1/7/12	Assets	100 000

M. Becker, Retained Earnings

			30/6/13	Interest	15 000
			30/6/13	Salary	18 000
30/6/13	Bal. c/d	36 500	30/6/13	Residual profit	3 500
		36 500			36 500
			1/7/13	Bal. b/d	36 500

R. Cook, Retained Earnings

			30/6/13	Interest	10 000
			30/6/13	Salary	10 000
30/6/13	Bal. c/d	23 500	30/6/13	Residual profit	3 500
		23 500			23 500
			1/7/13	Bal. b/d	23 500

the partners may provide for a profit agreement that is independent of the drawings agreement. In the remainder of this chapter and in the end-of-chapter material, a salary agreement is considered as a distribution of profit or loss.

In the preceding example, the profit of $60 000 was greater than the interest and salary allocations of $53 000. The same method is used to allocate profit that is less than the interest and salary allocation or to allocate the residual loss if the partners fail to provide alternative allocations for these two possibilities in the partnership agreement. For example, assume that the profit for the period had been $41 000 rather than $60 000. The allocation to the partners would then be:

	Allocation of $41 000 profit		
	Becker	**Cook**	**Total**
Interest on capital credited	$15 000	$10 000	$ 25 000
Salaries to partners credited	18 000	10 000	28 000
Total interest and salary allocation	33 000	20 000	53 000
Residual loss allocation equally	(6 000)	(6 000)	(12 000)*
Equity increase	$27 000	$14 000	$ 41 000

* Profit minus interest and salary allocation: $41 000 – $53 000 = ($12 000).

If the Profit or Loss Summary account shows a partnership loss of $10 000, the allocation of $53 000 (interest and salary) still follows the procedures shown on the previous page, and the total loss allocation of $63 000 ($53 000 + $10 000) is allocated equally to the partners. Thus, Becker's equity is credited for $1500 and Cook's equity is debited for $11 500:

	Allocation of $10 000 loss		
	Becker	**Cook**	**Total**
Total interest and salary credited	$ 33 000	$ 20 000	$ 53 000
Residual loss allocation equally	(31 500)	(31 500)	(63 000)*
Equity increase (decrease)	$ 1 500	$(11 500)	$(10 000)

* Loss plus interest and salary allocation: $10 000 + $53 000 = $63 000.

To avoid the above allocations when the profit is insufficient to cover the interest and salary allocations, the partnership agreement may specify an alternative allocation arrangement.

BUSINESS KNOWLEDGE

Macphersons shakes off suburban roots

For its first 103 years, Melbourne firm Macpherson + Kelley traded as a traditional suburban partnership that made a living dealing with whatever legal problems walked in the door.

Today, two years after incorporating and appointing veteran Phil Clark as chairman, Macphersons is one of the nation's fastest-growing practices. Mr Clark is a former managing partner of Minter Ellison and Mallesons Stephen Jaques.

Within the space of five years, Macphersons says, gross revenue has jumped from $13 million to $42 million, profit is said to be growing at 20 per cent a year and the company is days away from unveiling the latest in a series of mergers.

According to national managing director Damian Paul, none of that would have been possible had the firm not abandoned the partnership structure and become a company.

He believes the ability to offer lawyers shares as well as profit participation is one of the key reasons for Macphersons' rapid growth.

'There are a number of firms where there is some dissatisfaction because some of the younger up-and-coming guns are delivering and would expect to be coming into equity (partnerships),' Mr Paul said. 'But the older equity partners are trying to hang on for dear life.

'If they were to adopt our model, where you get rewarded for performance, then it would be more difficult for underperforming partners to stay within those firms.

'As people — lawyers in particular — stay with the firm, they are eligible to participate in share ownership. So two years ago we had four owners and on July 1 we will have in excess of 30 shareholders.

'This time next year we will have in excess of 60 shareholders, as employees — senior lawyers in the firm — access their shares through the share ownership plan.'

Source: Excerpts from Chris Merritt, 'Macphersons shakes off suburban roots', *The Australian.*

Learning objective 7

Explain the accounting entries for drawings and advances or loans made by partners

15.7 Drawings and loans made by partners

Drawings

From time to time, partners may withdraw cash or other assets from the partnership to provide for their everyday living needs, or to provide for unexpected or emergency needs in their private family circumstances. Most of these drawings are viewed as withdrawals of future profits, but in particular cases the drawings may represent a part withdrawal of the partner's capital contribution.

To illustrate, assume that during the year ended 30 June 2013, Becker withdrew $14 000 cash on 31 December 2012, and Cook withdrew $8000 cash on 31 March 2013 in the expectation that the partnership would earn a profit. Assume as well that, owing to unforeseen circumstances, Cook decided to withdraw $6000 of his capital investment in cash on 31 May 2013.

The accounting treatment for these withdrawals depends on whether method 1 or method 2 is being used. Under method 1, no distinction is made between withdrawals of capital and withdrawals of profits, hence all withdrawals are debited to the Drawings account of the partners and credited to Cash at Bank. Under method 2, the withdrawal of capital by Cook is debited directly to his Capital account, and other drawings are taken to Retained Earnings. The necessary entries and subsequent closing entries for the Drawings accounts are:

2012		Method 1		Method 2	
		Dr	Cr	Dr	Cr
Dec. 31	M. Becker, Drawings	14 000		14 000	
	Cash at Bank		14 000		14 000
	(Cash drawings by Becker)				
2013					
Mar. 31	R. Cook, Drawings	8 000		8 000	
	Cash at Bank		8 000		8 000
	(Cash drawings by Cook)				
May 31	R. Cook, Drawings	6 000			
	R. Cook, Capital			6 000	
	Cash at Bank		6 000		6 000
	(Withdrawals of capital by Cook)				
June 30	M. Becker, Capital	14 000			
	M. Becker, Retained Earnings			14 000	
	M. Becker, Drawings		14 000		14 000
	(Closing entry for Becker's withdrawals)				
June 30	R. Cook, Capital	14 000			
	R. Cook, Retained Earnings			8 000	
	R. Cook, Drawings		14 000		8 000
	(Closing entry for Cook's withdrawals)				

Interest on drawings

Partnership agreements may sometimes contain clauses that state that interest is to be charged at a certain rate per annum on drawings of profits or capital or both made by partners during the year.

Such interest agreements act as an incentive for partners to retain their profits and capital in the business and as a disincentive to partners to withdraw excessive amounts from the partnership.

To illustrate interest on drawings, assume that the partnership agreement for the BC Partnership contained a clause stating that interest at the rate of 8% p.a. is to be charged against all withdrawals by partners of both profits and capital in the current year. Interest on drawings is not normally paid by the partners into the partnership but is added to the profit distribution account and deducted from the Capital (method 1) or Retained Earnings (method 2) accounts of each partner at the end of the year. The interest charged against each partner on 30 June 2013 is:

Interest on drawings	Becker	Cook
$14 000 × 8% × 6/12	$560	
$ 8 000 × 8% × 3/12		$160
$ 6 000 × 8% × 1/12		40
Equity increase	$560	$200

The entries to record interest on drawings are:

2013		Method 1 Dr	Method 1 Cr	Method 2 Dr	Method 2 Cr
June 30	M. Becker, Capital	560			
	R. Cook, Capital	200			
	M. Becker, Retained Earnings			560	
	R. Cook, Retained Earnings			200	
	Profit Distribution		760		760
	(Charging interest on drawings)				

The additional $760 credited to the Profit Distribution account is now available for distribution to partners as part of the residual profit to be divided between the two partners. In other words, assuming partnership profit is $60 000, the residual profit, after deducting $53 000 for salaries and interest on capital, equals $7760 ($60 000 − $53 000 + $760), which means that Becker and Cook are each allocated $3880. Total profit allocations to Becker and Cook are therefore:

	Becker	Cook	Total
Interest on capital credited	$15 000	$10 000	$25 000
Salaries to partners credited	18 000	10 000	28 000
Interest on drawings debited	(560)	(200)	(760)
	32 440	19 800	52 240
Residual profit divided equally	3 880	3 880	7 760
Equity increase	$36 320	$23 680	$60 000

Loans or advances by partners

Occasionally, a partner may lend or advance money to the partnership rather than investing the money in the business as a further capital contribution. Such an advance of money is correctly treated as a current and/or non-current liability of the partnership and is accounted for using the following entry (in general journal form):

Cash at Bank		x	
Advance from Partner A			x

Unless there is any agreement to the contrary, the Partnership Act states that any partner making advances to the partnership is entitled to interest at the rate of 7% p.a. from the date of the advance (the rate varies from state to state in Australia). To record interest on advances, the entry in general journal form is as follows:

Interest Expense		x	
Cash at Bank/Interest Payable			x

Because the advance is a liability of the partnership, the interest is regarded as an expense, and is transferred to the Profit or Loss Summary account at the end of the reporting period for the purpose of determining partnership profit or loss. This treatment is consistent with the accounting definition of an expense.

Learning objective 8

Describe the content of the financial statements of a partnership

15.8 Financial statements for a partnership

The internally prepared financial statements for a partnership are prepared in much the same manner as for other forms of business. The following items specifically related to partnership reporting should be noted:

1. If the partnership is not a reporting entity, it will prepare special-purpose financial statements, and this must be clearly stated. If the partnership is a reporting entity, then it must prepare general purpose financial reports complying with accounting standards — an income statement,

a statement of changes in partners' equity, a balance sheet/statement of financial position and a statement of cash flows.

2. Each partner's equity in the business is reported separately on the balance sheet or in a separate statement of changes in partners' equity.

3. Salaries authorised for each partner, interest on capital investments and interest on drawings are not reported as expenses but recognised as an allocation of profit.

4. There is no income tax expense since a partnership is not a legal entity and not subject to tax.

5. The profit or loss allocation for the period is normally disclosed in the financial statements in a separate statement of changes in partners' equity.

The income statement for a partnership should comply with the basic reporting requirements of accounting standards if the partnership qualifies as a reporting entity. A suitable partnership income statement is presented in figure 15.1.

BC PARTNERSHIP
Income Statement
for the year ended 30 June 2013

INCOME	$480 000
EXPENSES	420 000
PROFIT	$ 60 000

Figure 15.1 Income statement for a partnership

A **statement of changes in partners' equity** may appear as shown in figure 15.2 for the BC Partnership. Both method 1 and method 2 presentations are illustrated.

Figure 15.2 Statement of changes in partners' equity

BC PARTNERSHIP
Statement of Changes in Partners' Equity
for the year ended 30 June 2013

Method 1

	Becker	Cook	Total
Capital balances 1/7/12	$150 000	$100 000	$250 000
Add: Additional investment*	10 000	—	10 000
Profit allocation	36 320	23 680	60 000
	196 320	123 680	320 000
Less: Drawings	14 000	14 000	28 000
CAPITAL BALANCES 30/6/13	$182 320	$109 680	$292 000

Method 2

	Becker	Cook	Total
CAPITAL			
Capital balances 1/7/12	$150 000	$100 000	$250 000
Add: Additional investment*	10 000	—	10 000
Less: Withdrawals of capital	—	6 000	6 000
Capital balances 30/6/13	160 000	94 000	254 000
RETAINED EARNINGS			
Balances at 1/7/12	—	—	—
Add: Profit allocation	36 320	23 680	60 000
Less: Drawings	14 000	8 000	22 000
Balances at 30/6/13	22 320	15 680	38 000
TOTAL EQUITY	$182 320	$109 680	$292 000

* Additional capital investment is assumed for illustrative purposes.

In a balance sheet prepared for the partnership, the partners' equity accounts will appear as in figure 15.3, using method 2. Alternatively, partners' equity may be shown as a single figure of $292 000 and a separate statement of changes in partners' equity disclosing detail as in figure 15.2 can be presented.

Figure 15.3 Partnership balance sheet (extract) (method 2 only)

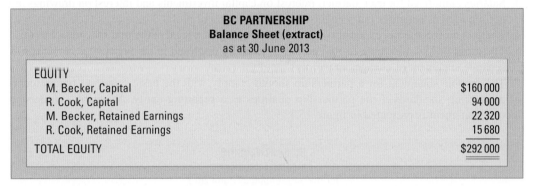

BC PARTNERSHIP Balance Sheet (extract) as at 30 June 2013	
EQUITY	
M. Becker, Capital	$160 000
R. Cook, Capital	94 000
M. Becker, Retained Earnings	22 320
R. Cook, Retained Earnings	15 680
TOTAL EQUITY	$292 000

Further discussion of financial statements suitable for external reporting purposes is provided in a later chapter.

KEY TERMS

Fair value, p. 620
General partnership, p. 617
Goodwill, p. 621

Limited partnership, p. 617
Mutual agency, p. 617
Partnership, p. 616

Partnership agreement, p. 618
Statement of changes in partners' equity, p. 629
Unlimited liability, p. 617

DISCUSSION QUESTIONS

1. 'The big disadvantage of a sole trader business is that the personal liability of the owner is unlimited — the owner could lose everything. I think I will take on a partner and convert my business to a partnership. That way I will certainly reduce the chances of losing my personal assets if the business fails.' Discuss.
2. 'There is really no need for a partnership agreement since all issues likely to arise among partners are adequately covered in the appropriate Partnership Act.' Discuss.
3. Which is likely to last longer and why: a partnership or a company?
4. Liam sold his partnership interest to Jason even though his other partners were unaware that Liam intended to do so. Does Jason have the right to be a partner? Does Jason have the right to take over Liam's position as manager of the business? Will Jason be entitled to share in the partnership profits and, if so, how much?
5. 'The accounting treatment of a partner's drawings differs when separate Retained Earnings accounts are kept for each partner as opposed to not having Retained Earnings accounts. Choice of method is immaterial.' Discuss.
6. A student of accounting was heard to remark: 'You really do not need a Profit Distribution account when accounting for profit distribution in a partnership. Everything can be done through the Profit or Loss Summary account.' Discuss.
7. 'Partners' advances and capital both represent money contributed to the partnership by the partners. Therefore the accounting treatment for interest paid on advances and capital should be the same.' Discuss.
8. Hannah and Jeremy set up a partnership to run a café. At the time of establishing the business, Hannah was in a better financial position than Jeremy and so contributed 60% of the capital required. Jeremy believes that he contributes as much effort to running the café as Hannah and therefore assumes that any profit made will be distributed evenly between Hannah and him. Is Jeremy correct, and what factors might determine how much profit each of the partners will receive?

9. Eduardo and Evanthia run a craft shop as a partnership. During the year Eduardo incurred an unusual amount of personal expenses in relation to his family and felt that his share of the partnership profit for the year would not cover these costs. Eduardo approached Evanthia to see whether he could get any extra cash out of the business just for the current year to cover the shortfall in his personal finances. What options are there for Eduardo to receive extra cash and what are some of the future implications of this?

10. Ethan and Amy, who have been friends for a long time, decide to go into partnership selling a range of pet accessories. They seek advice from an accountant regarding the best system, the generally accepted accounting principles to be used in the accounting records, and the format and contents of the financial statements. The accountant replies that since the partnership will be a non-reporting entity, they can account any way they like, and include whatever they like in the reports to suit their own requirements. The partners point out that they have other business interests and would like to have some comparability in accounting and statements. As the accountant, how would you advise the partners?

EXERCISES

LO 5

Exercise 15.1 PARTNERSHIP FORMATION

Sudjai and Sutrin, who were operating separate competing businesses, decided on 1 July 2012 to form a partnership by contributing cash, assets and liabilities of their respective businesses. At that date the fair values of the assets and liabilities were as set out below:

	Sudjai	Sutrin
Cash at bank	$80 000	$90 000
Accounts receivable	12 000	7 500
Inventory	45 000	40 000
Plant and equipment	90 000	70 000
Accounts payable	12 500	8 000

Required

A. Assuming that Sudjai and Sutrin agree that their capitals should be equal to the fair value of the net assets contributed, prepare general journal entries to record the formation of the partnership.

B. If Sudjai and Sutrin agree that their respective capital should be $220 000 each, show the general journal entries to establish the partnership.

LO 5

Exercise 15.2 PARTNERSHIP FORMATION

Bruce Becker and Darryl Dickson agree to combine their businesses and form a partnership. The fair value and the carrying amount of the assets contributed by each partner and the liabilities assumed by the partnership are shown below:

	Bruce Becker		Darryl Dickson	
	Carrying amount	Fair value	Carrying amount	Fair value
Cash at bank	$ 6 200	$ 6 200	$ 5 800	$ 5 800
Accounts receivable	12 800	12 800	11 400	11 400
Inventory	22 000	21 500	18 500	18 300
Equipment	72 000	48 000	75 000	32 000
Accumulated depreciation – equipment	(18 600)	—	(26 500)	—
Accounts payable	13 400	13 400	12 800	12 800

Required

Prepare separate general journal entries to record the initial investment of each partner, assuming assets are recorded by the business to reflect their purchase price, and the arrangement is GST-free.

Refer to the data presented in exercise 15.2. Assume further that Becker and Dickson agree that their opening capital balances in the new partnership should be the same and set the amount at $80 000.

Required

Prepare separate general journal entries to record the initial investment of each partner, assuming assets are recorded by the business to reflect their purchase price, and the arrangement is GST-free.

Exercise 15.4 PARTNERSHIP PROFIT DISTRIBUTION — FIXED RATIO

LO 6, 8

Gottsche and Gutteridge formed a partnership on 1 July 2012 with initial capital balances of $90 000 and $60 000 respectively. For the year ended 30 June 2013, the Profit or Loss Summary account disclosed a final credit balance of $96 000.

Required

A. Prepare the closing entry to transfer the profit disclosed in the Profit or Loss Summary account to the Profit Distribution account under method 1 and method 2.
B. Prepare the closing general journal entry to distribute the profit to Gottsche and Gutteridge assuming they have agreed to share profits in proportion to each partner's initial capital balance under both method 1 and method 2.
C. Show how the partners' equity accounts would appear in the balance sheet of the partnership at 30 June 2013.

Exercise 15.5 PARTNERSHIP PROFIT DISTRIBUTION — CAPITAL BALANCES

Leung and Lim formed a partnership on 1 July 2012 with initial capital balances of $180 000 and $120 000 respectively. For the year ended 30 June 2013, the Profit or Loss Summary account disclosed a final credit balance of $160 000.

Required

A. Prepare the closing entry to transfer the profit disclosed in the Profit or Loss Summary account to the Profit Distribution account under method 1 and method 2.
B. Prepare the closing general journal entry to distribute the profit to Leung and Lim, assuming they have agreed to share profits in the ratio of 3:2.
C. Show how the partners' equity accounts will appear in the balance sheet of the partnership at 30 June 2013.

Exercise 15.6 ALLOCATION OF PROFIT

LO 6, 7

Laing and Lowry's partnership had a final profit for the year of $40 500. When the partnership was formed at the beginning of the year Laing invested $120 000 and Lowry invested $90 000.

Required

A. Prepare the journal entries to record the allocation of profit under each of the following assumptions, using method 1 procedures:
   1. Laing and Lowry agree to a 55:45 sharing of profits.
   2. The partners agree to share profits in the ratio of their original capital investments.
   3. The partners agree to recognise $12 000 per year salary allowance to Laing and a $4500 per year salary allowance to Lowry. Each partner is entitled to 6% interest on his original investment, and any remaining profit is to be shared equally.
B. Repeat requirement A.3 above assuming the partnership has a profit of $27 000 for the first year.

Exercise 15.7 ALLOCATION OF PROFIT

LO 6, 7

Miller and Monterosa formed a partnership by investing $110 000 and $90 000 respectively. The partnership had a final profit of $72 000 in the first year.

Required

A. Prepare the journal entries to record the allocation of profit under each of the following assumptions, using method 1 procedures:

1. Miller and Monterosa agree to a 60:40 sharing of profits.
2. The partners agree to share profits in the ratio of their original capital investments.
3. The partners agree to recognise a $12 000 per year salary allowance to Miller and an $8000 per year salary allowance to Monterosa. Each partner is entitled to 8% interest on her original investment, and any remaining profit is to be shared equally.

B. Repeat requirement A.3 above assuming the partnership has a profit of $30 000 for the first year.

Exercise 15.8 INTEREST ON CAPITAL AND DRAWINGS LO 7

Zollo and Zoumboulis run a market stall together as a partnership. On 30 November 2013 Zollo withdrew $12 000 cash. Zoumboulis withdrew $8000 on 20 December 2013. On 31 March 2014 Zoumboulis withdrew $15 000 of her capital investment in cash to meet unexpected medical expenses for her son.

Required

Prepare the journal entries for the above transactions for the year ended 30 June 2014 using both method 1 and method 2.

Exercise 15.9 INTEREST ON CAPITAL AND DRAWINGS LO 7

Peter and Paula are in partnership, sharing profits equally. Provision exists in the partnership agreement for charging interest on capital at the rate of 8% p.a. and interest on drawings at 10% p.a. Capital and Drawings account balances are:

Peter, Capital	$ 96 000
Paula, Capital	108 000
Peter, Drawings	24 000
Paula, Drawings	30 000

Profit before allowing for interest was $144 000. All drawings were made in expectation of profits.

Required

Prepare journal entries to account for interest on capital and on drawings, and any necessary closing entries using:

1. method 1 — variable capital balances
2. method 2 — fixed capital balances.

Exercise 15.10 ALLOCATION OF PROFIT LO 6

Richards and Rogers share profits in the proportion of one-third and two-thirds respectively. On 1 July 2012 the equity accounts stood as follows:

	Richards	Rogers
Capital	$80 000	$120 000
Retained earnings	25 000	32 000

Partners were entitled to 8% interest on capital, and Richards, as manager, was entitled to a salary of $30 000 p.a. During the year, Richards withdrew $12 000 in cash and Rogers withdrew $17 000. The profits for the year ended 30 June 2013 were $68 000 before providing for interest on capital balances and for Richards' salary.

Required

Prepare the Profit Distribution account and partners' Retained Earnings accounts for the year ended 30 June 2013.

Exercise 15.11 ALLOCATION OF PROFIT

Matthew and Mark share profits on a 60:40 basis respectively. On 1 July 2013 the equity accounts were as follows:

	Matthew	**Mark**
Capital	$540 000	$460 000
Retained earnings	160 000	130 000

The partners were entitled to 12% interest on capital. Mark ran the business and received a salary of $80 000. During the year Matthew withdrew $48 000 in cash and Mark withdrew $12 000. The profits for the year ended 30 June 2014 were $460 000 before providing for interest on capital balances and Mark's salary.

Required

Prepare the Profit Distribution account and the partners' Retained Earnings accounts for the year ended 30 June 2014.

Exercise 15.12 ALLOCATION OF PROFIT — AVERAGE CAPITAL BALANCES

Trevor, Tammy and Tan are partners. The partnership agreement provides that partners will receive interest of 8% of their average capital balance and a salary allowance as follows:

Trevor	$50 000
Tammy	40 000
Tan	40 000

Trevor, who manages the business, will receive a bonus of 25% of the profit in excess of $90 000 after partners' interest and salary allowances. Residual profits will be divided:

Trevor $^1/_2$ Tammy $^1/_3$ Tan $^1/_6$

During the current year their average capital balances were as follows:

Trevor	$250 000
Tammy	150 000
Tan	90 000

Required

Prepare a schedule showing how profit will be divided among the three partners if the profit for the year before the above adjustments is $320 000.

Exercise 15.13 FORMATION AND ALLOCATION OF PROFITS OF PARTNERSHIP

Wing, Wen and Winnie are independent website developers who had been trading in active opposition to one another for some years. They decide to form a partnership, WWW Web Developers, as from 1 January 2012. The agreement set out the following basic arrangements:

Wing to contribute $7000 in cash, computers valued at $8000, and debtors of $12 000.
Wen to contribute a lease of premises used by her, such a lease to be regarded as having a capital value of $12 500, computers of $10 000 and $5000 in cash.
Winnie to contribute computers valued at $13 750 and to act as managing partner at a salary of $20 000 per year.
Interest for the period is to be allowed partners at the rate of 8% p.a. on beginning capital but is not charged on drawings.
Profits or losses to be shared in the same proportions as capital contributed.

Required

A. Prepare the journal entries necessary to open the records of the partnership. (Ignore GST.)
B. Assuming in the first year that the partnership makes a profit of $65 000, show how this profit would be allocated to partners. (Round amounts to nearest dollar — 50c is rounded down.)

Exercise 15.14 STATEMENT OF CHANGES IN PARTNERS' EQUITY

Jonathon and Daniel began their partnership on 1 July 2012 by contributing $320 000 and $280 000 respectively. During the first year of business, Daniel contributed another $40 000 and Jonathon withdrew $20 000 of his capital investment. The profit for the year ended 30 June 2013 of $160 000 was divided evenly between the partners. During the year Jonathon withdrew $25 000 from profits and Daniel withdrew $20 000 of his share of the profits.

Required

Prepare a statement of changes in partners' equity for the year ended 30 June 2013 using both method 1 and method 2.

Exercise 15.15 STATEMENT OF CHANGES IN PARTNERS' EQUITY

Anthony and Cleopatra have a partnership to run their human resource management services firm. Account balances related to their equity for the year ended 30 June 2013 are as follows:

Capital Balance 1 July 2012, Anthony	$120 000
Capital Balance 1 July 2012, Cleopatra	100 000
Additional investment, Anthony	32 000
Withdrawal of capital, Cleopatra	15 000
Drawings, Anthony	16 000
Drawings, Cleopatra	18 000

Profit of $124 000 for the year was distributed evenly between the partners.

Required

Prepare a statement of changes in partners' equity using both method 1 and method 2.

PROBLEMS

Problem 15.1 PARTNERSHIP FORMATION ★

★ Basic

★★ Moderate

★★★ Challenging

Ralph Hartwig and Alice Wisdom formed a partnership on 1 July 2012, agreeing to share profits and losses in the ratio of 60:40. Ralph contributed $30 000 in cash and land with a fair value of $180 000. Assets contributed to and liabilities assumed by the partnership from Alice's business at both carrying amount and fair value are shown below:

	Carrying amount	Fair value
Cash at bank	$22 500	$22 500
Accounts receivable	12 800	12 800
Inventory	24 600	23 800
Office equipment	76 000	62 000
Accounts payable	11 500	11 500
Bank loan	18 000	18 000

During the first year, Ralph contributed an additional $12 000 in cash. The partnership's profit was $56 000. Ralph withdrew $8000 and Alice withdrew $16 000 in expectation of profits (ignore GST).

Required

A. Prepare the journal entries to record each partner's initial investment.
B. Prepare the partnership's balance sheet as at 1 July 2012.
C. Prepare a statement of changes in partners' equity for the year ended 30 June 2013, using method 2 for recording partners' equity accounts.

Problem 15.2 PARTNERSHIP FORMATION ★

Conway Chan and Peter Papadopoulos formed a partnership on 1 January 2012, agreeing to share profits and losses equally. Conway contributed $80 000 in cash and plant and equipment with a fair value of $120 000. Assets contributed to and liabilities assumed by the partnership from Peter's business at both carrying amount and fair value are shown below.

	Carrying amount	Fair value
Cash at bank	$ 12 600	$ 12 600
Accounts receivable	22 500	22 500
Inventory	32 500	30 400
Building	220 000	480 000
Accounts payable	18 500	18 500
Bank loan	180 000	180 000

During the first year, Conway contributed an additional $24 000 in cash. The partnership's profit was $96 000. Conway withdrew $16 000 and Peter withdrew $18 000 in expectation of profits (ignore GST).

Required

A. Prepare the journal entries to record each partner's initial investment.
B. Prepare the partnership's balance sheet as at 1 January 2012.
C. Prepare a statement of changes in partners' equity for the year ended 31 December 2012, using method 1 for recording partners' equity accounts.

Problem 15.3 ALLOCATION OF PROFIT OR LOSS ★

Jong and Joy have decided to form a partnership by investing $90 000 and $60 000 respectively. The following plans for dividing profits and losses are under consideration:
(a) Sharing profits equally.
(b) A $20 000 salary to Jong, a $30 000 salary to Joy, and the remainder in the ratio of 6:4.
(c) A $25 000 salary to Joy, 8% interest on their original investments, and the remainder equally.
(d) In the ratio of their original investments.

Required

A. Determine the division of the profit or loss assuming a profit of $120 000.
B. Determine the division of the profit or loss assuming a profit of $60 000.
C. Determine the division of the profit or loss assuming a loss of $6000.

Problem 15.4 ALLOCATION OF PROFIT OR LOSS ★

A partnership is formed by Peter investing $150 000 and Wendy investing $100 000. The partners are considering the following plans for dividing profits and losses:
(a) According to the ratio of their original investment.
(b) Paying Peter a salary of $60 000 and Wendy a salary of $50 000 and the balance on the basis of their original investment.
(c) A $60 000 salary to Peter, 12% interest on their original investments, and the balance equally.
(d) Share the profits equally.

Required

A. Determine the division of the profit or loss assuming a profit of $200 000.
B. Determine the division of the profit or loss assuming a profit of $150 000.
C. Determine the division of the profit or loss assuming a loss of $10 000.

Problem 15.5 ALLOCATION OF PROFITS ★★

The partnership deed of Molika, Ming and Mengyao, partners trading as Triple M Traders, includes the following provisions:
1. Salaries are to be allowed: Molika, $30 000; Ming, $25 000; Mengyao, $20 000.
2. Mengyao is to receive a bonus of 20% of the profits after allowing for partners' salaries and interest.
3. Interest is to be allowed on advances by partners at 6% p.a.
4. Interest on drawings to be charged at 8% p.a.
5. Residual profits are to be divided: Molika, 3/8; Ming, 3/8; Mengyao, 1/4.

Account balances at 30 June 2012 before any adjustment in respect of provisions (1) to (5) include the following:

Capital:	
Molika	$160 000
Ming	80 000
Mengyao	200 000
Retained earnings:	
Molika	32 000
Ming	31 200
Mengyao	50 600
Advances:	
Ming (on 1 July 2011)	72 000
Mengyao (on 1 July 2011)	40 000
Drawings:	
Molika (on 1 March 2012)	12 600
Ming (on 1 January 2012)	7 900
Mengyao (on 1 October 2011)	5 900
Profit or Loss Summary	
(profit for the year ended 30 June 2012)	188 000

Required

Prepare a schedule showing the distribution of final profit to each partner (round to the nearest dollar).

Problem 15.6 FORMATION AND ALLOCATION OF PROFITS   METHOD I ★★

On 1 October 2012, Lucas Lloyd and Sami Schulz formed a partnership. Some business assets and the liabilities of Lloyd were assumed by the partnership, and these are listed below at both carrying amounts and fair value.

	Carrying amount	Fair value
Cash at bank	$ 28 000	$ 28 000
Marketable securities	24 000	26 800
Accounts receivable	47 000	47 000
Inventory	122 600	125 400
Equipment	38 500	230 000
Accounts payable	36 000	36 000

Schulz contributed a building worth $820 000, land worth $350 000, and a $456 000 mortgage was taken over by the partnership. They agreed to share profits and losses in the ratio of 6:4. During the first year of the partnership, Lloyd invested $60 000 in the business and withdrew $45 000. Schulz invested $115 200 and withdrew $17 200. The partnership had a profit of $88 460. Retained Earnings accounts are not used.

Required

A. Prepare the general journal entries to record the initial investments of both partners (ignore GST).
B. Prepare a balance sheet as at 1 October 2012.
C. Prepare a statement of changes in partners' equity for the year ended 30 September 2013.

Problem 15.7 FORMATION AND ALLOCATION OF PROFITS — METHOD 1 ★★

Sarah Salmon and Dean Davis formed a partnership on 1 July 2012. Some of Salmon's business assets and liabilities were assumed by the partnership, and these are listed below at both carrying amounts and fair value.

	Carrying amount	Fair value
Cash at bank	$ 62 000	$ 62 000
Accounts receivable	34 000	34 000
Inventory	98 600	96 000
Equipment	320 000	360 000
Accounts payable	24 000	24 000
Loan	80 000	80 000

Davis contributed a commercial property to the partnership that had a fair value of $460 000 which was financed by a mortgage of $280 000. They agreed to share profits and losses evenly. During the first year of the partnership, Salmon invested $80 000 in the business and withdrew $20 000. Davis invested $82 000 and withdrew $24 000. The partnership had a profit of $132 800. Retained Earnings accounts are not used.

Required

A. Prepare the general journal entries to record the initial investments of both partners (assume no GST).
B. Prepare a balance sheet as at 1 July 2012.
C. Prepare a statement of changes in partners' equity for the year ended 30 June 2013.

Problem 15.8 FORMATION AND ALLOCATION OF PROFIT — METHOD 2 ★★

Arnold, Omond and Edwards decided to enter into a partnership agreement as from 1 July 2012, some of the provisions of which were as follows:

1. Arnold to contribute $20 000 cash, inventory the fair value of which was $42 500, plant and machinery $78 600, accounts receivable totalling $12 700.
2. Omond to contribute $37 500 cash and act as manager for the business at an annual salary of $32 000 to be allocated to her at the end of each year.
3. Edwards to contribute $16 500 cash, land $120 000, premises $240 000, furniture and fittings $40 500, motor vehicles $31 500. A mortgage of $180 000 secured over the premises was out-standing and the partnership agreed to assume the mortgage.
4. Profits or losses of the firm to be divided between or borne by Arnold, Omond and Edwards in the proportion of 2:2:1 respectively.
5. Interest to be allowed at 8% p.a. on the capital contribution by the partners. Interest at 10% p.a. to be charged on partners' drawings.

During the year ended 30 June 2013, the income of the partnership totalled $120 800, and the expenses (excluding interest on capital and drawings, and Omond's salary) amounted to $43 000.

Arnold withdrew $12 000 on 1 October 2012 and $8000 on 1 January 2013; Omond withdrew $4000 only on 1 April 2013; Edwards withdrew $10 000 on 30 June 2013.

Required

A. Prepare general journal entries necessary to open the records of the partnership.
B. Prepare the balance sheet of the partnership immediately after formation.
C. Prepare a Profit Distribution account for the year ended 30 June 2013 using method 2.

Problem 15.9 ALLOCATION OF PROFITS — METHOD 2 ★★

Selected accounts from the trial balance as at 30 June 2013 of the partnership of Oscar, Patrick and Bruce are as follows:

	Debit	Credit
Oscar, Capital		$102 500
Oscar, Retained earnings		$ 26 000
Patrick, Capital		112 800
Patrick, Retained earnings		32 000
Bruce, Capital		108 000
Bruce, Retained earnings		24 500
Loan — Big Bank Ltd		85 000
Bruce, Salary	32 000	
Advance, Oscar (repayable in November 2014)		18 000
Profit or loss summary (after usual adjusting and closing entries for profit determination)		148 000

End-of-period adjustments for the financial year ended 30 June 2013 have yet to be made as follows:

1. The partnership accountant has duly paid cash for Bruce's agreed salary as part-time manager ($32 000 p.a.) but was uncertain how to charge it.
2. Interest accrued to Big Bank Ltd — $1800.
3. Partners have agreed to the following arrangements:
   (a) 6% p.a. interest on fixed capitals.
   (b) 10% interest on total drawings for the year, which were:

Oscar	$32 000
Patrick	28 000
Bruce	5 000

   (c) 8% p.a. interest on advance from Oscar.
   (d) Profits/losses to be shared 2:2:1 by Oscar, Patrick and Bruce respectively.

Required

A. Complete the Profit or Loss Summary account for the year ended 30 June 2013.
B. Prepare the Profit Distribution account.
C. Complete each partner's Retained Earnings account after all adjustments.

Problem 15.10 FORMATION AND ALLOCATION OF PROFIT — METHOD 2 ★★

On 1 July 2012, Warner and Ellis decided to amalgamate their businesses and to share profits equally. Financial information at that date was:

	Warner	Ellis
Capital	$101 380	$119 800
Accounts payable	41 470	55 300
Bank overdraft	18 430	
	$161 280	$175 100
Cash at bank		$ 59 900
Accounts receivable	$ 61 280	46 080
Inventory	46 080	69 120
Furniture and fittings	26 260	
Equipment	27 660	
	$161 280	$175 100

At 1 July 2012, Warner's accounts receivable and inventory had fair values of $61 280 and $48 380 respectively, and Ellis's accounts receivable and inventory had fair values respectively of $46 080 and $73 720. Warner's equipment was written down by 10%.

Warner and Ellis negotiated to have equal capital balances of $150 000.

After 1 year, the following were the only changes to the assets and liabilities, as compared with the position at the time of forming the partnership:

Net cash at bank had increased by	$23 040
Accounts receivable had decreased by	10 120
Inventory had increased by	36 860
Accounts payable had decreased by	27 650

Depreciation still has to be charged on the furniture and fittings and on equipment at the rates of 10% and 15% respectively for the year. Cash drawings for the year were: Warner, $28 800; Ellis, $36 240.

Required

A. Prepare journal entries to record the formation of the partnership.
B. Prepare a statement of changes in partners' equity as at 30 June 2013 showing each partner's share of profit/loss for the year.
C. Prepare the balance sheet of the partnership as at 30 June 2013.

Problem 15.11 ALLOCATION OF PROFITS — METHOD 2 ★★   **LO 5, 8**

McGowan and Whait share profits in a proportion of 60:40. McGowan is entitled to a salary allowance of $60 000 p.a., and Whait is entitled to $50 000 p.a. Capitals are fixed at McGowan $72 000 and Whait $48 000. Interest is to be calculated on partners' capital, advances, and drawings in excess of salary at 8% p.a. The trial balance after the determination of profit for the 6-month period is shown below.

McGowan had withdrawn $12 000 cash on 1 April; Whait's cash drawings included $24 000 on 1 March and $12 000 on 1 May.

Required

A. Prepare the Profit Distribution account for 6 months ended 30 June 2013.
B. Prepare the Retained Earnings accounts for each partner at 30 June 2013.
C. Prepare a balance sheet as at 30 June 2013.

McGOWAN AND WHAIT
Trial Balance
as at 30 June 2013

	Debit	Credit
McGowan, Capital		$ 72 000
Whait, Capital		48 000
McGowan, Advance (Balance at 1/1/2013)		24 000
McGowan, Retained earnings	$ 22 000	
Whait, Retained earnings	16 000	
McGowan, Salary	30 000	
Whait, Salary	25 000	
Cash at bank	3 200	
Accounts receivable	22 000	
Plant and equipment	106 000	
Accumulated depreciation – plant and equipment		47 800
Inventory	32 000	
Accounts payable		18 400
Profit or loss summary		46 000
	$256 200	$256 200

Problem 15.12 ALLOCATION OF PROFIT — METHOD 1 ★★★

At the end of the financial year ended 30 June 2012, the trial balance of Bedford, Belling and Broadbent is as shown below:

BEDFORD, BELLING AND BROADBENT
Trial Balance
as at 30 June 2012

	Debit	Credit
Cash at bank	$ 162 500	
Accounts receivable	248 620	
Inventory	178 460	
Equipment	1 430 800	
Accumulated depreciation – equipment		$ 462 600
Goodwill	360 000	
Accounts payable		345 780
Advance, Broadbent (due for payment 31 May 2013)		320 000
Capital, 30 June 2011		
Bedford		160 000
Belling		320 000
Broadbent		640 000
Drawings:		
Bedford	60 000	
Belling	60 000	
Broadbent	20 000	
Profit or loss summary		272 000
	$2 520 380	$2 520 380

Note: Partnership agreement does not specify profit-sharing ratios.

Broadbent made her advance before 1 July 2011. Bedford and Belling each withdrew $12 000 on 30 September 2011, $8000 on 31 December 2011, $5000 on 31 March 2012, and the remainder on 30 June 2012. Broadbent made her drawing on 30 June 2012.

The partnership agreement contains the following provisions in relation to the allocation of profits:

(a) A salary of $92 000 per year for Bedford and $56 000 per year for Belling.
(b) Interest of 6% p.a. on capital contributed at the start of each financial year.
(c) Interest on advances of 8% p.a.
(d) Interest on drawings at 8% p.a.

Required
A. Prepare the Profit Distribution account for the year ended 30 June 2012.
B. Prepare the capital accounts for each partner at 30 June 2012.
C. Prepare the balance sheet as at 30 June 2012.

Problem 15.13 COMPREHENSIVE PROBLEM ★★★

Clarke, Cooper and Cornish are partners in the consulting firm of Clarke and Associates. The balance sheet of the partnership as at 31 March 2012 is set out on the next page.

CLARKE AND ASSOCIATES
Balance Sheet
as at 31 March 2012

CURRENT ASSETS		
Cash at bank	$61 980	
Accounts receivable	59 500	
Advances — receivables from clients	6 880	$128 360
NON-CURRENT ASSETS		
Professional library	45 000	
Office furniture	66 500	111 500
		$239 860
CURRENT LIABILITIES		
Accrued expenses (office)		$ 15 200
EQUITY		
Partner's capital accounts: Clarke	$51 450	
Cooper	51 450	
Cornish	44 100	147 000
Partner's retained earnings: Clarke	29 500	
Cooper	25 500	
Cornish	22 660	77 660
		$239 860

It was agreed that all profits would be divided equally between the partners.

Business transactions for the year ending 31 March 2013 were as follows (ignore GST):

Invoices issued for services to clients	$450 000
Cash receipts:	
Accounts for fees collected	452 000
Advances made on behalf of clients repaid	45 000
	$497 000
Cash payments:	
Salaries	$ 92 800
Rent	18 000
Office expenses	19 500
Library maintenance	9 200
Advances made on behalf of clients	40 000
Insurance premiums	6 500
Drawings: Clarke	96 000
Cooper	72 900
Cornish	36 300
	$391 200

Accounts payable for office expenses at 31/3/13, $15 000.
Furniture to be depreciated at 15% p.a.

Required

A. Prepare the income statement for the year ended 31 March 2013.
B. Prepare the statement of changes in partners' equity for the year ended 31 March 2013.
C. Prepare the balance sheet as at 31 March 2013.

Pearson, Pelham and Perrin are partners in the consulting firm of PPP Partners. The balance sheet of the partnership as at 30 June 2012 is set out below.

<table>
<tr><td colspan="3" align="center">**PPP PARTNERS**
Balance Sheet
as at 30 June 2012</td></tr>
<tr><td>CURRENT ASSETS</td><td></td><td></td></tr>
<tr><td>Cash at bank</td><td>$30 200</td><td></td></tr>
<tr><td>Accounts receivable</td><td>32 600</td><td></td></tr>
<tr><td>Inventory</td><td>46 700</td><td>$109 500</td></tr>
<tr><td>NON-CURRENT ASSETS</td><td></td><td></td></tr>
<tr><td>Plant and Equipment</td><td>88 400</td><td></td></tr>
<tr><td>Office furniture</td><td>34 300</td><td>122 700</td></tr>
<tr><td></td><td></td><td>$232 200</td></tr>
<tr><td>CURRENT LIABILITIES</td><td></td><td></td></tr>
<tr><td>Accounts Payable</td><td></td><td>$ 22 600</td></tr>
<tr><td>EQUITY</td><td></td><td></td></tr>
<tr><td>Partner's capital accounts: Pearson</td><td>$62 000</td><td></td></tr>
<tr><td>Pelham</td><td>62 000</td><td></td></tr>
<tr><td>Perrin</td><td>42 000</td><td>166 000</td></tr>
<tr><td>Partner's retained earnings: Pearson</td><td>16 200</td><td></td></tr>
<tr><td>Pelham</td><td>12 800</td><td></td></tr>
<tr><td>Perrin</td><td>14 600</td><td>43 600</td></tr>
<tr><td></td><td></td><td>$232 200</td></tr>
</table>

It was agreed that all profits should be divided equally between the partners.

Business transactions for the year ending 30 June 2013 were as follows (ignore GST):

Sales	$472 800
Cash receipts:	
Sales collected	$474 800
Cash payments:	
Purchases	283 200
Salaries	62 900
Office expenses	24 500
Operating expenses	43 300
Drawings: Pearson	12 000
Pelham	12 500
Perrin	11 800
	$450 200

Inventory at 30 June 2013 was $45 000. Non-current assets are depreciated at 10% p.a.

Required

A. Prepare the income statement for the year ended 30 June 2013.

B. Prepare the statement of changes in partners' equity for the year ended 30 June 2013.

C. Prepare the balance sheet as at 30 June 2013.

Eton, Elgar and Erin are partners in the consulting firm of Triple E Partners. The balance sheet of the partnership as at 30 June 2012 is set out below.

TRIPLE E PARTNERS
Balance Sheet
as at 30 June 2012

CURRENT ASSETS			
Cash at bank		$25 900	
Accounts receivable		28 000	
Inventory		40 000	$ 93 900
NON-CURRENT ASSETS			
Plant and Equipment		76 000	
Office furniture		30 000	106 000
			$199 900
CURRENT LIABILITIES			
Accounts Payable (for purchases)			$ 19 500
EQUITY			
Partner's capital accounts:	Eton	$54 000	
	Elgar	50 000	
	Erin	52 000	156 000
Partner's retained earnings:	Eton	8 200	
	Elgar	8 200	
	Erin	8 000	24 400
			$199 900

It was agreed that all profits be divided equally between the partners.

Business transactions for the year were as follows (ignore GST):

Sales	$368 600
Cash receipts:	
Sales collected	$370 300
Cash payments:	
Purchases	220 000
Salaries	50 000
Office expenses	19 100
Operating expenses	34 000
Drawings: Eton	9 360
Elgar	9 750
Erin	9 200
	$351 410

Inventory at 30 June 2013 was $38 700 and Accounts Payable was $18 000.
Non-current assets are depreciated at 10% per annum.

Required

A. Prepare the income statement for the year ended 30 June 2013.
B. Prepare the statement of changes in partners' equity for the year ended 30 June 2013.
C. Prepare the balance sheet as at 30 June 2013.

A partnership without a partnership agreement

O'Malley and O'Reilly formed a partnership on 1 July 2012 to run an information systems consultancy business by investing $400 000 and $360 000 respectively. Both partners work similar hours in the business. O'Reilly has a Masters degree in information systems and 5 years experience in the workforce; O'Malley has an undergraduate degree and has worked for 3 years; she has invested money inherited from her parents. On 1 January 2013 O'Malley invested an additional $40 000 cash as a capital contribution. On 1 May 2013 O'Malley and O'Reilly withdrew $50 000 each in cash in expectation of profits for the current year ended 30 June 2013. They had not drawn up a partnership agreement and so are not sure how the profits of $120 000 should be distributed to each partner. You have been asked to decide the most appropriate way to divide the profit, and a number of alternative scenarios are provided for you to consider:

(a) no suggestions have been made by the partners
(b) the partners suggest distributing the profits in the ratio of the original capital balances
(c) the partners suggest that O'Malley receives a salary of $40 000 and O'Reilly receives a salary of $60 000 to reflect his greater qualifications and experience, with interest of 5% on ending capital balances, and the remainder distributed evenly between the partners.

Required

A. Calculate the amount of profit distribution to each partner under each scenario. Which scenario is most favourable to O'Malley? to O'Reilly?
B. Given the capital commitments and expertise of each partner, which scenario is the most appropriate for the partnership agreement?
C. What recommendations would you make for any proposed partnership agreement in the event that the partnership incurs a loss for the year?

Forming partnerships

Divide into groups of three or four according to students' major areas of interest — for example, a group of commerce students, a group of management students, a group of marketing students. Discuss the following and report back to the whole class:

1. If your group formed a partnership to carry out the business of your major area of study, how would you determine who was the senior partner?
2. On what basis can you agree to share profit? Would this be affected by the amount of capital each partner contributed or would you share profits evenly? Would you pay interest to the partners based on their capital contributions?
3. Would you consider paying each partner a salary that reflected their expertise, experience or ability to generate business for the partnership? If so, how would you determine the impact of such factors on the salary of each partner?
4. What other factors would you include in a partnership agreement?

Partnership concerns

Craig Fraser and Michelle Mason set up a partnership to run a small retail business. Craig contributed $60 000 to begin the business and Michelle's contribution was $50 000. Craig is confident with numbers and accounting whereas Michelle prefers to deal with people and to ignore anything requiring numbers. Michelle has put her trust in Craig to set up the financial side of the business. Craig has decided that all profits should be distributed according to the initial capital contribution by each of the partners.

During the second year of operation Craig bought a new house and to finance the deposit he withdrew $20 000 from his capital investment in the partnership. Michelle accepted that this was reasonable and did not even think about the implications for profit distribution. The following year Craig withdrew another $20 000 from his capital investment in the partnership to reduce his house mortgage. Michelle accepted that as Craig had put the money into the partnership it was only fair that he could take it out again.

Craig and Michelle both worked actively in the business, and generally worked well together as business partners. They both were entitled to a salary of $30 000 on the assumption that they would contribute equally to the management of the business.

Required

A. Who are the stakeholders in this situation?

B. Does Craig appear to be doing anything wrong? Explain your response.

C. Are there any ethical issues involved here? If so, identify them.

FINANCIAL ANALYSIS

Refer to the latest financial report of JB Hi-Fi Limited on its website, www.jbhifi.com.au, and answer the following questions using the consolidated income statement and balance sheet/statement of financial position and notes to the consolidated financial statements.

1. The JB Hi-Fi Limited income statement shows a deduction for income tax expense. Would this expense item be seen in the income statement of a partnership? Explain your answer.

2. In the statement of changes in equity regarding retained earnings, how is the total profit available appropriated? How does the allocation of the total profit available for appropriation in a partnership differ from that shown for JB Hi-Fi Limited? Explain the reasons for any differences.

3. Refer to the balance sheet/statement of financial position of JB Hi-Fi Limited. How does the 'equity' segment differ from that of a typical partnership? Explain.

4. JB Hi-Fi Limited is required to produce a statement of cash flows and include this in its annual financial statements. Would the typical partnership be *required* to prepare such a statement? Why or why not? Would a typical partnership prepare such a statement? Explain.

Companies: formation and operations

Learning objectives

After studying this chapter, you should be able to:

1 describe the different types of companies permitted to exist by law in the Australian business environment (pp. 650–2)

2 summarise the advantages and disadvantages of the corporate form of organisation (pp. 652–4)

3 describe the documentation required for forming a company (pp. 654–5)

4 identify the management structure commonly used for administering a company (pp. 655–6)

5 describe the three main categories of equity in a company (pp. 656–8)

6 account for the issue of shares (pp. 658–66)

7 account for the declaration and payment of cash dividends on shares, share dividends and share splits (pp. 667–71)

8 account for the creation and reduction of the different types of reserves that are included in equity (pp. 671–2)

9 prepare basic entries for income tax expense in a company (pp. 672–3)

10 prepare a company's income statement, statement of changes in equity and balance sheet for internal use (pp. 673–79).

Seek a house, find a job

In 1997, Paul Basset was frustrated in his search to buy a house through newspaper classifieds. There had to be a better way! Paul, in consultation with his brother Andrew, researched the main classified markets — real estate, cars and employment — and then developed a plan around an online job classified business. With little start-up capital, they sought money from old clients, friends and family. They named their new company 'Seek'. In 2005, Seek went public, offering investors shares at $2.20. A year later, the share price had climbed to $4.00 and the company's ordinary shares had a market value over $1 billion. Seek has experienced ups and downs as the economy has ebbed and flowed, but it is now Australia's leading employment web site.

Babcock & Brown is a different story. Founded in 1977 in San Francisco and opening a Sydney office in 1982, Babcock & Brown operated as a corporate consultancy specialising in aircraft and equipment leasing. With seed capital gained from a German bank the company's focus turned to investment banking and it became known globally for its structured finance deals. Buoyed by its success, Babcock & Brown sought to become a bigger global player, and management sold shares at $5 in an initial public offering in 2004. By the end of the first day the price had increased to $7.98 per share. However, for Babcock & Brown, life in the fast lane came to an abrupt halt with the onset of the global financial crisis. In 2007 its share price was $33.90; by the end of 2008 the share price was $0.14. On 24 August 2009 the creditors of Babcock & Brown voted to place the company in liquidation.

Both Seek and Babcock & Brown were initially funded with private capital but then turned to the public markets when private sources of capital were no longer adequate to fund their growth. While they ultimately experienced sharply different levels of success, Seek and Babcock & Brown obtained financing from comparable sources.

Source: Rebecca Martin, 'Seek a house, find a job', *Catapault.*

Chapter preview

The corporate form of business organisation is not as common as the sole trader or partnership. Nevertheless, the size of business activity conducted by companies far exceeds that of the other two combined. Companies or corporations control vast amounts of economic resources and therefore play a dominant role in the national economy of Australia. Most large businesses as well as many small ones are organised as companies, and it is important to have an understanding of companies and their accounting practices.

The domination of our economy by companies has led to increasing demands for information about them. Almost everyone is affected in their daily lives by the activities of companies. We all buy goods and services produced by them; many people work for companies, receive interest and dividends from them or sell goods and services to them. All segments of society — including investors and prospective investors, creditors, labour unions, government agencies and consumers — are necessarily interested in the financial strength and profitability of companies as a means of assessing the efficiency with which they have used resources. Many are also interested in the environmental and social impacts that companies have on the Australian way of life.

Because of the sizeable impact that companies have on our lives, all companies are required to comply with certain rules and regulations and accountability requirements established by government. All companies are formed, administered and wound up in accordance with the *Corporations Act 2001*, a uniform legal code throughout Australia. The administration of all companies is carried out by one federal body, the Australian Securities and Investments Commission (ASIC), with branches in each state.

16.1 Types of companies

Learning objective 1

Describe the different types of companies permitted to exist by law in the Australian business environment

Under the Corporations Act, a company is a legal entity or artificial person, separate and distinct from its owners. On registration or incorporation, each company is allocated an Australian company number (ACN) that helps to identify it (in addition to its Australian business number (ABN), issued when it registers for GST).

As a separate legal entity, a company has many of the rights, duties and responsibilities of a natural person. It can, through its agents, buy, own and sell property in its own name and engage in business activities by entering into contracts with others. It has legal status in a court and can sue and be sued, is legally responsible for its liabilities, and must pay income tax just as a natural person does. A company's money and other assets belong to the company, and must be used for the company's purposes.

A number of different types of companies exist under the Corporations Act, and may be classified broadly as:
1. limited companies
    (a) proprietary companies with a share capital
    (b) public companies with a share capital
    (c) companies limited by guarantee, without any shares
2. unlimited companies, which may be proprietary or public companies, both of which must have a share capital
3. no-liability companies
4. special companies
    (a) investment companies
    (b) banking companies
    (c) life insurance companies.

These different types are described briefly on the following pages.

Limited companies

One of the main reasons for setting up a company is that the corporate form of organisation permits individuals to have limited liability in relation to personal funds they are required to contribute to the company. Under corporate legislation, the shareholders in a **limited company** are liable only to the extent of the amount unpaid on their shares up to the full issue price of those shares. For example, if a company has issued 1000 shares with an issue price of $5, and the shares have been paid up to $3, the maximum liability each shareholder has to pay to the company if it cannot pay its debts is $2 per share. Contrast this with the partnership form of organisation in which each partner is personally liable for all partnership debts, i.e. unlimited liability. If one or more partners are insolvent, the remaining solvent partners must meet all losses and debts out of their private assets. This principle of unlimited liability also applies to a sole trader.

A limited company is required by corporate legislation to have the word 'Limited' or the contraction 'Ltd' at the end of its name.

Proprietary companies

A **proprietary company** may be formed by a minimum of one person and need have only one director; however, certain restrictions are placed on the company with regard to the maximum number of shareholders (namely, 50) and the right to raise capital — it cannot raise funds from the public. The company must have the word 'Proprietary' or the contraction 'Pty' as part of its name inserted before the word 'Limited' or the contraction 'Ltd'. Usually, a proprietary company is a family business that has been incorporated to obtain the benefits of limited liability for the family members who own the business.

A proprietary company must have a share capital, i.e. it cannot be limited by guarantee; but there are no restrictions placed on the transfer of its shares to others. The law also provides for proprietary companies to be classified as *large* and *small*, but a company's classification can change from one year to the next, as circumstances change. A small proprietary company is defined as one that satisfies at least two of the following tests:

- the consolidated gross revenue for the financial year of the company and the entities it controls (if any) is less than $25 million, or any other amount prescribed by the regulations
- the value of the consolidated gross assets at the end of the financial year of the company and the entities it controls (if any) is less than $12.5 million, or any other amount prescribed by the regulations
- the company and the entities it controls (if any) have fewer than 50 employees, or any other number prescribed by the regulations, at the end of the financial year.

If a proprietary company is not classified as 'small', then it is 'large' and is subject to additional reporting and auditing obligations under the Corporations Act. (Even small proprietary companies have to comply with additional reporting and auditing obligations in certain circumstances.) Determination of consolidated gross operating revenue and consolidated gross assets must occur in line with current accounting standards, and part-time employees must be counted as an appropriate fraction of a full-time equivalent in assessing whether a proprietary company is large or small.

Public companies

A business registered as a **public company** may have a minimum of only one member, but is required to have three directors, two of whom must ordinarily reside in Australia. Generally speaking, however, ownership of a public company is widely spread, with large numbers of people owning a relatively small number of shares each. The major advantage of a public company is that the company is entitled to raise capital by inviting members of the public to subscribe for any of its shares, debentures, unsecured notes or loans, and to have these shares, debentures, etc. listed for easy transferability on one or more of Australia's securities exchanges.

Because the activities of public companies can significantly affect the general public, much of the legislation has been passed to protect the 'public interest'. For example, public companies must issue a disclosure document known as a prospectus before issuing shares or debentures.

If a public company wishes to have its shares listed on the securities exchange in Australia, the company must comply with regulations issued by ASIC and the Listing Rules issued by the Australian Securities Exchange (ASX). See the ASIC website, www.asic.gov.au, for regulations related to public companies, and also the ASX website, www.asx.com.au, for information on the Listing Rules.

Companies limited by guarantee

A **company limited by guarantee** is also a public company, whose members undertake to contribute a guaranteed amount if the company is wound up. Companies of this type are commonly associated with special events such as an arts festival or sporting event. The Corporations Act, from 2010 onwards, also distinguishes between large and small companies limited by guarantee. Small companies of this type are exempted from having to comply with certain accounting standards.

Unlimited companies

In an **unlimited company**, members are liable for all debts of the company. The unlimited company is not common in Australia and exists to some extent among mutual funds, a type of investment company.

No-liability companies

A **no-liability company** is a public company that does not have a right to require shareholders to make any contribution towards the debts of the company; there is no liability on the part of shareholders to pay any calls on shares. Non-payment of a call leads to automatic forfeiture of shares. Such a company must engage solely in mining activities, and must have the words 'No Liability' or the abbreviation 'NL' at the end of its name.

Special companies

Investment companies

An investment company is a special type of company that is engaged mainly in the business of investment in marketable securities for the purpose of earning profits, and not for the purpose of exercising control. It is subject to certain restrictions on borrowing, on investment in other companies, on holding shares in other investment companies and on speculation.

Banking companies

A banking company is defined as any bank constituted under a law of a state or territory or as defined in the Banking Act. Under corporate legislation, banks are given certain privileges and special provisions regarding the issue of a prospectus for the purpose of subscribing for debentures and the presentation of financial statements.

Life insurance companies

A life insurance company is registered under the Life Insurance Act. It is subject to special requirements regarding the preparation and presentation of annual financial statements.

Learning objective **2**

Summarise the advantages and disadvantages of the corporate form of organisation

16.2 Advantages and disadvantages of the corporate entity

Advantages

The corporate form of business has several advantages over the sole trader and partnership forms. The main ones are discussed below.

Limited liability

As a separate legal entity, a company is responsible for its actions and liabilities. Creditors have claims only against the assets of the company, not against the personal assets of the shareholders. Because owners of a company are not personally liable for corporate debts, the maximum amount they can lose is the amount they have already invested, plus any money owing on shares. To investors, this is one of the most important advantages of the corporate entity, because under the alternative forms of business organisation, owners are personally liable for business debts if the business becomes insolvent. However, shareholders are generally separated from the day-to-day operations of the company and cannot participate in the daily management.

Broad source of capital

Ownership rights in companies are represented by transferable shares. By dividing ownership of the business into many shares, each with a relatively small value, both large and small investors are able to participate in the ownership of the business. Most large public companies can therefore draw on the savings of many people and other entities to obtain the capital they need.

For example, a company's capital of $100 000 000 may be divided into 10 000 000 shares issued at a price of $10 each, which thus allows small investors to buy small parcels of shares. (Telecommunications company Telstra has about 1.5 million different shareholders each having an average of 600 shares.)

Continuity of existence

A company has an indefinite life and continues in existence even if its shareholders change, i.e. a company has the attribute of perpetual succession. The transfer of shares from one owner to another has no effect on the continuity of a company. In contrast, the death, incapacity or retirement of an owner terminates the business of a sole trader or a partnership.

Ready transferability of shares

Company shares may be transferred easily without disrupting the activities of the company. Shares in public companies can be bought and sold through stock exchanges that exist in all state capital cities in Australia. Consequently, shareholders can readily convert their investments in shares into cash if the need arises.

Use of professional management

Although the shareholders own the company, they do not manage its daily activities. Shareholders elect a board of directors, consisting of professional managers, which has overall responsibility for administrative decisions. The board then hires a managing director or chief executive officer (CEO) and other officers to manage the business.

In contrast to a partnership, no mutual agency exists in a company. An individual shareholder does not have the right to bind the company to a contract unless he or she has been hired as a corporate officer. This separation of management and ownership permits the company to obtain the best managerial talent available.

Potential income tax savings

One of the major reasons for the formation of companies is the potential savings in income tax that flow to shareholders. Although a sole trader or a partnership is not subject to income tax as a separate business unit, any profit derived by sole traders and partners is taxed as personal income and is subject to marginal tax rates that may rise above 40%, excluding the Medicare levy. In contrast, a company pays income tax as a separate legal entity, at a flat tax rate, which at 30 April 2011 was 30%, and does not pay a Medicare levy. Hence, depending on the level of a person's income, there may be tax advantages in incorporation because of the potential difference in tax rates.

These tax advantages for companies are improved considerably by the dividend imputation scheme for the taxing of dividends received by shareholders. Before the dividend imputation scheme was introduced, when a company's after-tax profits were distributed to its shareholders as dividends the profit was taxed again as personal income of the shareholders receiving the dividends. However, under the dividend imputation scheme, shareholders are allowed a tax rebate for dividends received out of company profits on which the company has been fully taxed. These dividends are referred to as *franked* dividends. Dividends are discussed in more detail later in the chapter.

Disadvantages

The corporate entity also has some disadvantages when compared with the sole trader and partnership forms. The main disadvantages are described below.

Greater government regulation

Companies are created under an Act of Parliament and are subject to a much greater degree of control and supervision than are sole traders or partnerships. In addition, public companies must prepare regular financial statements for presentation to their members, to the securities exchanges on which their shares are traded, and to ASIC. These annual reports must be prepared in accordance with the disclosure requirements provided in accounting standards, and with the Listing Rules of the ASX. Satisfaction of these reporting requirements often can be very costly and time-consuming.

Separation of ownership and management

The use of professional managers was cited earlier as an advantage of the corporate entity. In some cases, however, this separation of ownership from management may prove to be a disadvantage because managers, even though they are employed as agents of the shareholders, sometimes operate companies for their own benefit rather than for the benefit of the shareholders. Considerable harm may be done before shareholders become aware of the situation and take action to change management. Many requirements in corporate legislation have been established to discourage management from acting in their own interests to the detriment of shareholders. Increased disclosure of corporate governance has been required as a means of providing a level of accountability to a company's shareholders.

Learning objective 3

Describe the documentation required for forming a company

16.3 Forming a company

Under the Corporations Act, any person may lodge an application with ASIC in order to register a company. One is the minimum number of people needed to form a company.

The application form must contain the following information:

- the type of company that is proposed to be registered under the Corporations Act
- the company's proposed name (unless the ACN is to be used in its name)
- the name and address of each person who consents to become a member
- full names, date and place of birth, and address of each person who consents in writing to become a director or a company secretary
- the address of the company's proposed registered office and proposed principal place of business (if it is not the address of the proposed registered office)
- for a public company — the proposed opening hours of its registered office
- for a company limited by shares or an unlimited company — the following:
  (i) the number and class of shares each founding member agrees, in writing, to take up
  (ii) the amount each founding member agrees, in writing, to pay for each share
  (iii) if that amount is not paid in full on registration, the amount each founding member agrees in writing to be unpaid on each share.
- for a public company that is limited by shares or is an unlimited company, if shares will be issued for a non-cash consideration — the prescribed particulars about the issue of the shares, unless the shares are issued under a written contract and a copy of the contract is lodged with the application
- for a company limited by guarantee — the proposed amount of the guarantee that each member agrees to in writing.

If the company is to be a public company and is to have a constitution on registration, a copy of the constitution must be lodged with the application. To register a company in accordance with these requirements, all of the details above must be provided on a single prescribed application form.

Replaceable rules and constitution

Rules for governing the internal affairs of a company, especially with respect to the dealings between management and shareholders, have been built into the Corporations Act and are called **replaceable rules**. A company can adopt the Act's replaceable rules as its own rules. These rules deal with the appointment, powers and remuneration of directors, directors' meetings, members' meetings, share transfers and inspection of the company's books by members. However, if a company wishes to adopt different rules from any of these replaceable rules, it needs to set up its own **constitution**, specifying the different rules that it wishes to have for operating its internal affairs. The company must then conduct its activities under both the replaceable rules it is happy to adopt and its own constitution.

If a public company decides to have a constitution to determine relationships between management and shareholders, and relationships between different classes of shareholders, then this constitution must be lodged with ASIC along with the application for registration. Alternatively, the company may decide to adopt a constitution by special resolution of its members after the company's registration. If so, a copy of the constitution and the special resolution must be lodged with ASIC within 14 days after it is passed. The company can also modify or repeal its constitution by a special resolution of members. If so, such information must also flow to ASIC.

In the interests of simplification, the Australian Government hopes that most proprietary companies will choose to abide by the replaceable rules in the Act instead of establishing their own constitutions. If a company is a public company listed on the ASX, however, it is required by the ASX Listing Rules to have its own constitution.

A company's constitution (if any) and any replaceable rules that apply to the company act as a contract between the company and each member, each director, and the company secretary, and between a member and each other member. Unless members of a company agree in writing, they are not bound by any of the following modifications to the constitution made *after* the date on which they became members:

- modifications that require the members to take up additional shares
- modifications to increase the members' liability to contribute to the share capital of, or otherwise pay money to, the company
- modifications to impose or increase restrictions on the right to transfer the shares already held by the members, unless the modifications are made in connection with the company's change from a public company to a proprietary company, or as part of a takeover arrangement.

The certificate of registration

In order to incorporate the company, ASIC issues a **certificate of registration** on approval of the company's application for registration. The company is also issued with its Australian company number (ACN). The company is considered to be registered as from the date on the certificate — it is able then to perform all the functions of a corporate body, and is capable of suing and being sued and of acquiring, holding and disposing of property.

The prospectus

When raising funds for the start of business or for future economic development, any offer or invitation by a company to issue shares, debentures or other securities must be accompanied by a disclosure document known as a **prospectus**. A prospectus contains all the information that potential investors and their professional advisers reasonably require and expect for the purpose of making an informed assessment of (a) the assets, liabilities, financial position, profits and losses, and prospects of the company, and (b) the rights attached to the securities being issued. In addition, the interests of every director or proposed director in any property that may be acquired with the money from the security issue must be disclosed in the prospectus.

The prospectus must be lodged with ASIC, and those who produce the prospectus may be subject to civil liability for the contravention of prospectus requirements under the law. ASIC has the power to restrain dealings in securities subject to a prospectus if it considers that there has been a breach of the requirements or that it contains any misleading information. A company may be required to issue supplements to the prospectus if there has been a significant change in items disclosed in the original prospectus.

16.4 Administering a company

Learning objective 4

Identify the management structure commonly used for administering a company

Although control of a company rests ultimately with its shareholders, that control is exercised only indirectly. Administration of the company is usually placed in the hands of a board of directors who set overall corporate policies and appoint a managing director or CEO and other officers to manage the company's day-to-day affairs.

The board of directors is responsible to the shareholders for the formulation of overall business policies in the running of the company. Duties of the board generally include:

- protecting the rights of shareholders
- setting officers' salaries
- recommending and declaring dividends
- authorising long-term borrowing, additional share issues and major capital projects
- reviewing the system of internal control.

The board of directors is normally composed of a chair, executives such as the managing director (or CEO), and directors appointed by large shareholders. In addition, the board normally includes several outside or part-time directors to ensure a more objective evaluation of management performance.

Official actions of the board are recorded in the minutes of its meetings. The *minutes book* is important to the accountant because it contains board decisions that serve as the basis for the authorisation of certain transactions and the recording of these.

A company's senior management team usually includes a managing director (or CEO) with responsibility to the board of directors for managing and controlling business activities. The CEO is normally supported by one or more general managers who are responsible to the CEO for specific functional areas. For example, a company may have a general manager of marketing and sales. Other officers are the chief financial officer, the treasurer and the secretary.

The *chief financial officer* (CFO) is generally responsible for maintaining the accounting records and an adequate internal control system, preparing financial statements, tax returns and other reports, developing the budget and financial plans, and ensuring the business activities are adequately financed. The CFO also often advises the board of directors about the accounting and tax consequences of proposed corporate actions. The *treasurer* is the main manager of cash. He or she normally has responsibility for the custody of the company's funds and is responsible for planning and controlling the company's cash position. The *secretary* maintains the minutes of meetings of the directors and shareholders, and represents the company in many legal and contractual matters. The secretary normally also maintains the register of shareholders and the amount of their share interests. Some companies, particularly smaller ones, combine the positions of secretary and treasurer.

Figure 16.1 illustrates a typical public company organisation chart. Lines of authority extend from the shareholders to the board of directors to the managing director to other officers.

Figure 16.1 Organisation chart — public company

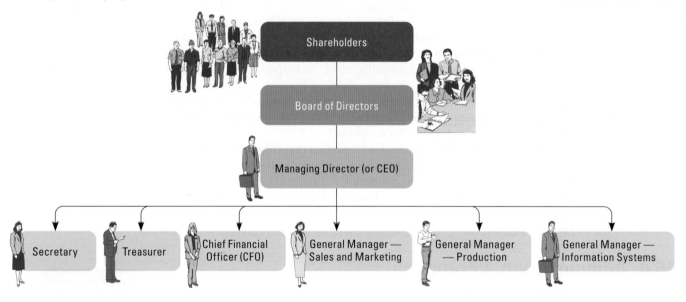

Learning objective 5

Describe the three main categories of equity in a company

16.5 Categories of equity in a company

Accounting for a company is similar in most respects to accounting for a sole trader or partnership. The income statement and the asset and liability sections of the balance sheet are essentially the same for all forms of business organisation. There is a major difference, however, in accounting for equity. The equity of a typical company is split into three major categories:

(a) share capital
(b) retained earnings
(c) other reserves.

Share capital

Share capital is an equity account representing the amount of assets invested in the company by its shareholders. Under the Corporations Act, a company can issue shares on the terms and with the rights and restrictions that the directors determine. Thus, a company can issue shares at any price, a determining factor being the marketplace. A company will issue its shares at the price it thinks will attract investors to buy the shares. For example, one company may issue shares at, say, 80 cents each; another company may issue its shares at $10 each.

Under the Act, a company is allowed to issue partly paid shares. For example, a share may be issued at $3.50, with $2.00 payable immediately and the balance payable in one year's time. This additional amount of $1.50 is referred to as **uncalled capital** until the company makes a **call** on the shares in one year's time, i.e. in accordance with the terms of the share issue. When the call is made, the shareholders are required to pay in the extra $1.50 per share to the company (unless the company is a no-liability company).

The practice of requiring a company's shareholders to pay by instalment has been used in Australia particularly for large public issues, e.g. Telstra. However, the issue of shares fully paid is more common. Both situations are covered in this text.

A company has the right to issue ordinary shares and preference shares (see later in this chapter) and can determine the terms on which these shares are issued. Generally, a company offers shares as the directors see fit for the effective management of the company. Some shares may be issued to the public whereas other shares are 'privately placed', i.e. sold to a specific person or other entity; however, a company can issue shares to the public only if it is a public company, and this must be done only after the issue of a prospectus. Sometimes shares are issued to the existing shareholders only (rights issues), and sometimes the shares may be bought back from existing shareholders. Share buybacks are discussed in Leo et al., *Company Accounting*, 9th edn (John Wiley & Sons, Brisbane, 2012) and are not considered in any detail here.

Retained earnings

Retained earnings is a special type of reserve account that reflects the amount of profits (after tax) earned by the company and retained in the business. When a company's income and expense accounts are closed at year end, the Profit or Loss Summary account is closed to Retained Earnings. For example, if profit for the year is $120 000, the Profit or Loss Summary account has a credit balance and is closed to Retained Earnings by the following entry:

June	30	Profit or Loss Summary	120 000	
		Retained Earnings		120 000
		(Closing the Profit or Loss Summary account)		

BUSINESS KNOWLEDGE

The sustainable accountant

We are witnessing a radical economic, political, social and business shift towards more sustainable practices. All businesses — regardless of size, sector or geographic location — face significant financial, strategic and operational challenges in adapting. Some businesses are more advanced than others in dealing with the issues related to sustainability. This is particularly the case for a number of companies that are at the vanguard of the sustainability movement in the UK and Europe, with fewer companies in Asia well prepared at present to deal with the issues. On average, Australian businesses probably occupy the middle ground.

Many accountants, in their role of 'strategic resource manager', will play a common and critical part in helping businesses to answer these new-found challenges. Although stakeholders increasingly have expectations that businesses will operate in a sustainable fashion, it is surprising that accountants are not necessarily top of mind for employers when it comes to working out a sustainable development strategy and reporting non-financial business information — particularly information that reflects a company's sustainability performance.

After all, accountants are skilled at capturing and interpreting vital corporate information which is used as a basis for organisational decision-making. This makes them fundamental to the development and reporting of sustainability practices

(continued)

and their various impacts. Our members' ability to contribute to a business's direction and development was a factor in determining our vision that CPA Australia be the global accountancy designation for strategic business leaders.

Recent research, commissioned by CPA Australia and carried out in Australia, Hong Kong, Singapore, Malaysia and New Zealand, shows there is a distinct lack of understanding in the marketplace about who has ownership of sustainability reporting. Most employers said they were better at practising sustainability than reporting on it. Yet, the same employers cited brand and reputation as a primary reason for reporting. This suggests that they are missing an opportunity if they are not actively or successfully communicating what they are doing in the sustainability space. Members of CPA Australia who were surveyed, and who have an opportunity to influence their employer, also indicated that building brand and reputation was the primary reason for sustainability reporting. However, only 37% who participated in the survey claimed to be undertaking some form of sustainability reporting. Encouragingly, 72% felt they should be doing so.

Awareness of what is involved in sustainability reporting might be one obstacle to more widespread reporting on sustainability. Many survey respondents claimed that their first sustainability report was produced following a 'trial and error' approach, and only a third of employers who took part in the survey said they had adapted their business systems for sustainability reporting. In time, this will change, but finding ways to accelerate the pace of change seems worthwhile. One way to speed things up is to achieve consensus on what to report, when to report, where to

report, and how to report. To this end, some useful work already has been done. The Global Reporting Initiative (GRI), in which CPA Australia is a stakeholder, has a clear framework on what to report. The GRI consulted widely on the development of its reporting framework, and CPA Australia advocates its use by businesses as well as using it to report on CPA Australia and its activities.

Although the GRI framework has been in existence for some years and is used by companies internationally, another player, the International Organization for Standardization, has entered the arena with a draft ISO 26000 – *Guidance on Social Responsibility*. Technically, ISO 26000 does not require anybody to do anything. Unlike other ISO standards, it is not designed for certification but guidance. It can be argued, however, that the GRI framework, along with the principles contained in the United Nations Global Compact, through providing sustainability reporting guidelines, already fulfils the aim of ISO 26000 to provide assistance for organisations in understanding and operationalising social responsibility. We caution against the proliferation of more standards in the environmental, social and governance domain where there is clear demand for greater convergence.

I believe that, just as the business world and the accounting profession jointly understand the benefit in having global accounting standards for financial information, the value to be obtained by reporting non-financial information will increasingly become clear and will result in a common global standard for sustainability reporting and other forms of non-financial reporting.

Source: Professor Richard Petty, 'The sustainable accountant', *InTheBlack*.

If the company incurred a loss for the year, the Profit or Loss Summary account has a debit balance and the closing entry consists of a debit to Retained Earnings and a credit to the Profit or Loss Summary account. A debit balance in the Retained Earnings account is called an **accumulated loss** and is deducted in arriving at total equity.

Other reserves

Reserves are another category of equity created as a result of the application of generally accepted accounting practice or under accounting standards. Retained earnings are regarded as a subcategory of reserves. Further discussion of reserves is provided later in the chapter.

Learning objective 6

Account for the issue of shares

16.6 Accounting for share issues

Directors have a number of choices when issuing shares. First, they may choose to issue ordinary shares, preference shares or both. Second, the shares may be issued (a) payable in full on application, (b) deposit payable on application and the remainder on allotment (i.e. when shares are allotted to applicants) or (c) part payment on application, part on allotment, and the remainder in one or more instalments or calls. As mentioned above, (a) has been the most common. Nevertheless, in this chapter we intend to illustrate all choices by considering the type and purpose of the accounts used in accounting for share issues.

Private share placements

Once a company has received its certificate of registration, it is able to raise money by issuing shares. Money may be raised privately by prospective shareholders contributing funds to the company. This is the practice used in proprietary companies. However, some public companies also make private placements to institutional investors such as insurance companies and superannuation funds. To illustrate a share issue to private investors, assume that, on 1 July 2013, Allan and Barbara Hume each contribute $50 000 in cash to buy shares in the proprietary company Hume Enterprises Pty Ltd (such raising of capital is free of GST). The appropriate journal entry (in general journal format) to record this event is:

July	1	Cash at Bank	100 000	
		Share Capital		100 000
		(Cash contributed to the company by its two shareholders)		

Public share issue, payable in full on application

Under corporate legislation, a public company is allowed to invite the public to subscribe for shares whereas a proprietary company cannot make any such invitation. First, the public company draws up a prospectus — an application form for shares cannot be issued unless a disclosure document such as a prospectus has been issued. The company specifies how many shares it would like to issue but at this stage no accounting entries are made. It is the subscriber or applicant who makes the offer to buy the shares by completing the application form. It is then up to the company to accept or reject the offer. Those people willing to apply for shares complete the application form and forward this, plus the application fee, to the company.

Assume that, on 30 September, Brazil Ltd received application forms for a total of 100 000 shares from prospective shareholders, receiving the issue price of $10 per share. The following entry is made:

Sept.	30	Cash Trust	1 000 000	
		Application		1 000 000
		(Receipt of cash of $10 per share on 100 000 shares)		

Until shares are allotted to applicants, the money received by the company must be held in a special Cash Trust account. The debit to the Cash Trust account represents money paid in by applicants before shares are allotted, the credit entry going to an **Application** account.

No further entries are made until the directors allot shares to successful applicants. Allotment of shares can occur only if a certain minimum subscription as specified in the prospectus has been reached. If the minimum subscription is not reached, all application money must be refunded out of the Cash Trust account. Once the minimum subscription has been attained, directors can allot the shares to applicants as they see fit. In some cases, the number of shares applied for may exceed the number being issued. Hence the directors may allot shares proportionally (pro rata) to each applicant or on a first-come-first-served basis, or some other basis. This could cause the directors to refund some cash to unsuccessful applicants, the entry being:

Sept.	30	Application	x	
		Cash Trust		x
		(Refund of excess application money to unsuccessful applicants)		

Once the directors have allotted the shares, the amount of money paid in by successful applicants is transferred from the Cash Trust account to the Cash at Bank account. The entry is made here in the general journal for illustrative purposes; however, it is usually made in the cash receipts journal of the company.

Oct.	1	Cash at Bank	1 000 000	
		Cash Trust		1 000 000
		(Transfer of application money into a general cash account)		

To complete the process, the balance remaining in the Application account is now regarded as the equity of the shareholders in the company. Hence, the balance is transferred to the Share Capital account, as shown below.

Oct.	1	Application	1 000 000	
		Share Capital		1 000 000
		(Funds contributed for 100 000 shares paid in full)		

Public share issue, payable by instalments

Alternatively, a company may decide to issue its shares on an instalment basis. Such a practice has become rare. Nevertheless, the practice is still available under the Act. Assume, for example, that Brazil Ltd decides on 15 September to issue 100 000 shares, payable in three instalments:

$4 initially on application,
then $3 payable on 15 October after allotment of shares,
and $3 payable on 1 December.

Assuming that, by 30 September, Brazil Ltd received application forms for a total of 100 000 shares, receiving $4 per share, the following entry is made:

Sept.	30	Cash Trust	400 000	
		Application		400 000
		(Receipt of cash of $4 per share on 100 000 shares)		

As in the previous case, if applications are received in excess of the 100 000 shares, the directors will refund this excess money out of the Cash Trust account by reversing the above entry for the amount of the refund. Also, as before, once the directors have allotted the shares on 1 October, the amount of money paid in by successful applicants is transferred from the Cash Trust account to the Cash at Bank account, and the following entry is made (in general journal format):

Oct.	1	Cash at Bank	400 000	
		Cash Trust		400 000
		(Transfer of application money into a general cash account)		

Both the Application account and an **Allotment** account can be set up to record the amounts of money now due and receivable from the shareholders after the shares have been allotted. The entries necessary are:

Oct.	1	Application	400 000	
		Share Capital		400 000
		(Application fee of $4 on 100 000 shares allotted)		
Oct.	1	Allotment	300 000	
		Share Capital		300 000
		(Allotment fee of $3 receivable on 100 000 shares allotted)		

The debit to the Application account closes that account since money due has already been received when applicants forwarded their application forms to the company. The debit to the Allotment account represents the amount due and receivable from those applicants who have been allotted shares, i.e. $3 on 100 000 shares. The credit to the Share Capital account in both journal entries recognises the fact that $7 ($4 + $3) has now been called up, and therefore constitutes the called-up capital of the company.

When the cash is received on 15 October for allotment money, the entry is:

Oct.	15	Cash at Bank	300 000	
		Allotment		300 000
		(Cash received on allotment)		

The Allotment account thus contains initially the balance of money receivable from the successful applicants on allotment of shares. On receipt of the money, the Allotment account is credited. At this stage, the share capital of the company consists of:

100 000 ordinary shares called and paid to $7 $700 000

Further amounts receivable on these shares can be called by the company as and when needed or in accordance with agreements set out in the prospectus. The directors are said to make a call on the shareholders. If the company makes a call of $3 per share on 15 November, the following entry is passed:

Nov.	15	Call	300 000	
		Share Capital		300 000
		(Call of $3 per share on 100 000 shares)		

The Call account is debited for the amount due to be received from shareholders in relation to the call. Share Capital is increased by a further $3 per share, to give a balance in the account of $1 000 000, since all money has now been called on the shares. Assuming that cash is received on 95 000 shares, the company makes the entry:

Dec.	1	Cash at Bank	285 000	
		Call		285 000
		(Receipt of call money on 95 000 shares)		

This means there is a debit balance of $15 000 left in the Call account, representing the calls unpaid by shareholders. These calls are sometimes referred to as *calls in arrears* when they are overdue. In order to determine the actual amount of capital paid in by shareholders, the balance of the Call account is deducted from Share Capital, to give the amount of capital received from shareholders, as reported in the company's balance sheet/statement of financial position:

Share capital (100 000 ordinary shares called to $10)	$1 000 000
Less: Unpaid calls (5000 shares @ $3)	15 000
Total share capital	$ 985 000

Note that all these transactions are exempt from GST. An example to illustrate all steps discussed so far is presented below.

Example

Colombia Ltd was incorporated on 1 July 2013. On this day a prospectus was issued calling for applications for 75 000 ordinary shares at an issue price of $7.50, payable $2.50 per share on application, $2.50 per share on allotment and the balance in calls as required.

Applications closed on 1 August 2013 with the receipt by the company of $187 500, representing 75 000 shares at $2.50 each. The shares were allotted on 15 August 2013. All allotment money was received by 31 August. A call of $2.50 per share was made on 1 October 2013. All call money except that payable on 1000 shares was received by 31 October 2013.

The journal entries in general journal form and general ledger accounts in respect of the above transactions are shown below, as well as a balance sheet/statement of financial position showing in detail the equity as at 31 October 2013.

COLOMBIA LTD
General Journal

2013				
Aug.	1	Cash Trust	187 500	
		Application		187 500
		(Money received on application)		
	15	Cash at Bank	187 500	
		Cash Trust		187 500
		(Transfer to general cash on allotment)		
	15	Application	187 500	
		Share Capital		187 500
		(Application fee of $2.50 on 75 000 ordinary shares)		
	15	Allotment	187 500	
		Share Capital		187 500
		(Allotment fee of $2.50 on 75 000 shares)		
	31	Cash at Bank	187 500	
		Allotment		187 500
		(Allotment money received on 75 000 shares)		
Oct.	1	Call	187 500	
		Share Capital		187 500
		(Call of $2.50 on 75 000 shares)		
	31	Cash at Bank	185 000	
		Call		185 000
		(Receipt of call on 74 000 shares)		

General Ledger

Share Capital

				15/8	Application	187 500
				15/8	Allotment	187 500
31/10	Balance c/d	562 500		1/10	Call	187 500
		562 500				562 500
				31/10	Balance b/d	562 500

Application

15/8	Share Capital	187 500	1/8	Cash Trust	187 500

Allotment

15/8	Share Capital	187 500	31/8	Cash at Bank	187 500

Call

1/10	Share Capital	187 500	31/10	Cash at Bank	185 000
			31/10	Balance c/d	2 500
		187 500			187 500
31/10	Balance b/d	2 500			

Cash Trust

1/8	Application	187 500	15/8	Cash at Bank	187 500

Cash at Bank

15/8	Cash Trust	187 500				
31/8	Allotment	187 500				
31/10	Call	185 000	31/10	Balance c/d		560 000
		560 000				560 000
31/10	Balance b/d	560 000				

COLOMBIA LTD
Balance Sheet
as at 31 October 2013

EQUITY	
Share capital (75 000 shares at $7.50 per share)	$562 500
Less: Unpaid calls (1 000 shares at $2.50 per share)	2 500
	$560 000
ASSETS	
Cash at bank	$560 000

Undersubscription and oversubscription

Undersubscription

If there are applications for fewer shares than the company would like to issue, i.e. the issue is undersubscribed but above the minimum subscription, the directors may simply issue the number of shares applied for by allocating them to applicants. Journal entries necessary are as per those shown previously *for the actual number of shares being issued*.

In order to avoid the possibility of undersubscription, it is common for a company to appoint an underwriter to any public share issue. The role of the underwriter is to take up any shares that are undersubscribed in any share issue. For this service, the underwriter charges an underwriting fee, which must be paid by the company even if the issue is fully subscribed or oversubscribed. The underwriter's fee is regarded as part of share issue costs, the accounting treatment of which is discussed later in this chapter.

Oversubscription

In many cases a public issue is oversubscribed, i.e. the company receives more than the required number of applications for its shares. The treatment of excess application money depends on the company's constitution and the terms of the prospectus. It is common for a company to have the right to retain excess application money to satisfy allotment and future calls when they fall due. If the amount paid in exceeds the issue price of the shares allotted to a shareholder, the excess is refunded to that shareholder.

For example, assume that on 15 September Brazil Ltd invited applications for 100 000 shares on the following terms:

$4 payable on application
$3 payable on allotment due on 15 October
$3 payable on call

Assume as well that applications were received for 300 000 shares and the directors decide to allot shares on a proportional basis, i.e. each applicant receives 1 share for every 3 applied for. Assume that the company has the power in its constitution to retain excess application money to satisfy future amounts payable on allotment and calls. If there is any surplus money that cannot be so retained, it must be refunded to the applicants before the money is available for general use by the company.

The journal entries (in general journal form) to record the issue of the shares by Brazil Ltd are:

Sept.	20	Cash Trust	1 200 000	
		Application		1 200 000
		(Receipt of $4 application money on 300 000 shares)		
Oct.	1	Application	400 000	
		Share Capital		400 000
		(Application of $4 per share)		
	1	Allotment	300 000	
		Share Capital		300 000
		(Allotment of $3 per share on 100 000 shares)		
	1	Application	800 000	
		Allotment		300 000
		Calls in Advance		300 000
		Cash Trust		200 000
		(Transfer of excess money on application to allotment, to calls in advance, and to refund surplus money)		
	1	Cash at Bank	1 000 000	
		Cash Trust		1 000 000
		(Transfer of money held in trust to general funds)		

Note that the Allotment account is closed in this case because all money has been received. The Calls in Advance account represents funds retained by the company in anticipation of the future call to be made on those shares. When the call is made on 15 November, the following entries are made:

Nov.	15	Call	300 000	
		Share Capital		300 000
		(Call of $3 per share on 100 000 shares)		
	15	Calls in Advance	300 000	
		Call		300 000
		(Transfer of call money previously received in advance)		

Any balance in the Calls in Advance account at the end of the reporting period should be reported in the balance sheet as a separate item of equity, as shown below:

EQUITY
Share capital	$x
Reserves	x
Calls in advance	x
Total equity	$x

Rights issue of shares

Another common method of raising equity is by way of a **rights issue**, which is an issue of new shares giving existing shareholders the right to an additional number of shares in proportion to their current shareholdings. If all the existing shareholders exercise their rights and take up the new shares, there is no change in each shareholder's percentage ownership interest in the company. Rights issues may be 'renounceable' or 'non-renounceable'. If renounceable, existing shareholders have three options:

1. They may exercise their rights and acquire more shares in the company.
2. They may decline to exercise the rights and let them lapse.
3. They may sell their rights on a stock exchange and allow other investors to acquire the company's shares.

If the rights issue is non-renounceable, shareholders are not allowed to sell their rights and must accept or reject the offer to acquire new shares in the company.

In offering the shares to existing shareholders, the company sets an issue price — this is often below the current market price of the company's shares in order to encourage shareholders to exercise their rights.

A major difference between an issue of shares to the public and a rights issue is that with the former, the offer comes from the applicant (the prospective shareholder) and it is for the company to accept or reject the offer. With a rights issue, the letter from the company to the shareholders informing them of their rights constitutes an offer. The acceptance by the shareholders of this offer seals the contract. The point of acceptance of the offer is then the point of allotment of the shares. As no money is received by the company before the allotment, there is no need for the company to raise a Cash Trust account.

To illustrate a rights issue, consider the information below, based on an actual case:

> Mexico Ltd planned to raise $4.2 million from existing shareholders through a renounceable 1-for-6 rights issue. The aim of the issue was to make the company financially stronger and to ensure future growth. The terms of the issue were: 6 478 611 shares to be issued at 65c each. At date of issue, the market price of the company's shares was 80c per share.

Assuming that the issue is fully subscribed, the journal entry to record the issue is illustrated below:

Cash	4 211 097	
Share Capital		4 211 097
(Receipt of 65c per share on rights issue of 6 478 611 shares)		

Bonus share issues

A **bonus share issue** is an issue of shares to existing shareholders in the proportion of their current shareholdings at no cost to the shareholders. The company uses one or more of its reserve balances (including retained earnings) to make the issue. For example, 5 bonus shares may be issued for every 100 shares presently held by shareholders. Several reasons have been advanced for issuing bonus shares:

* to provide a 'return' to shareholders without any cash outlays, thus protecting the company's current liquidity
* to capitalise the reserves of a company by converting such items into share capital
* to signal to the capital market that the company expects good future profitability levels for future cash dividends per share, as the number of shares issued increases under a bonus share issue.

Assuming that a bonus share issue of $60 000 is declared and paid out of a general reserve, the necessary accounting entry is:

General Reserve	60 000	
Share Capital		60 000
(Payment of bonus share issue out of general reserve)		

Bonus shares can be issued out of any reserve, including retained earnings. When a bonus issue is made out of retained earnings, it is sometimes referred to as a 'share dividend'.

Formation costs and share issue costs

The costs incurred in forming a company and that are paid from company assets are often called **preliminary expenses** or **start-up costs**. These include the registration fee, legal and accounting fees, and various other expenditures needed to establish the company. (GST may be payable on some of these costs.) In the past, it was common to treat such costs as non-current assets and amortise them over an arbitrary number of years, e.g. 20 years. However, this practice was questionable, as it was difficult to understand where the future economic benefits lay in some of these expenditures. Under current accounting standards, preliminary expenses cannot be treated as an asset, and must be written off to expense.

Share issue costs include stamp duty, broker's fees, underwriter's fees and professional adviser's fees, as well as printing costs associated with the issue of shares. Accounting standards argue that such costs should not be treated as either an asset or an expense. Instead, the standards regard these costs as a deduction from the equity of the entity. The issue of shares and the cost of such issue are regarded as one transaction. Therefore, whenever shares are issued, the amount credited to Share Capital is the gross proceeds received from the issue, less the applicable share issue costs. In other words, share issue costs result in a debit to Share Capital and a credit to Cash at Bank.

Preference shares

In addition to **ordinary shares**, many companies issue one or more types of preference shares. **Preference shares** are so called because shareholders receive preferential treatment over ordinary shareholders in one or more respects. Preference shareholders usually receive only a fixed rate of dividend, commonly expressed as a number of cents per share or as a percentage of the issued preference capital, and normally do not have a right to participate in any distribution of surplus profits made by the company. Consequently, if the company lists its preference shares on the stock exchange, the profit-making potential of these shares generally is less attractive than that of ordinary shares. Further discussion of the rights of preference shareholders in relation to dividends is provided later in the chapter.

In contrast, ordinary share capital is the residual equity in a company, which means that ordinary shareholders are commonly the last to receive asset distributions if the company is wound up. Ordinary shareholders take a greater risk of loss if the company is unsuccessful, but also have a greater potential for gain if the company is profitable. As a result, the market value of ordinary shares is closely related to profitability and increases or decreases as shareholders' expectations about future profits rise and fall.

Preference shareholders are normally given several preferences over ordinary shareholders. The most common is preference as to dividend distributions. Also, depending on the constitution of the company, they may receive preferential treatment as to distribution of assets on liquidation. In addition, preference capital is often redeemable at the option of the company and sometimes is convertible into ordinary shares. In exchange for these rights, preference shareholders normally relinquish the right to vote. Rights and other special features of preference shares vary widely and should be considered carefully because, under IAS 32/AASB 132 *Financial Instruments: Presentation*, certain preference shares may need to be classified as liabilities rather than as equity in external financial statements. The constitution must be read carefully to determine specific provisions applicable to preference shares.

The accounting treatment for the equity issue of preference shares is the same as that for ordinary shares. It is a common practice to have separate Share Capital, Application, Allotment and Call accounts for each class of share.

BUSINESS KNOWLEDGE

Survival in hard times

Independent expert Grant Thornton has labelled Port Bouvard's decision to sell a cornerstone stake to Queensland property developer FKP as "not fair" but vital to ensure the heavily indebted Perth group continues as a going concern.

Port Bouvard last night released Grant Thornton's report, which was commissioned to assess the merits of a proposal to sell a 29.5% stake to FKP as part of a broader, life-saving $60.2 million capital raising. The FKP investment, which should raise $22.8 million, will be priced at 13c per Port Bouvard share. A $17 million non-renounceable one-for-one rights issue and a $20.4 million institutional placement, which like the FKP investment will require Port Bouvard shareholder approval at a meeting next month, are also priced at 13c.

Port Bouvard shares have been suspended from trading since October, when they were worth 25c. But Grant Thornton said Port Bouvard was worth between 24c and 34c on a controlled-stake valuation, which meant the FKP investment 'is not fair to existing shareholders'.

The independent expert said FKP could use its stake to gain significant influence over Port Bouvard and deter future takeover bids. '(However,) if Port Bouvard is unable to resolve its immediate funding issues, it may have difficulty in continuing to operate as a going concern and is unlikely to have sufficient capital to undertake further development of any of the company's core projects,' Grant Thornton said in its report. 'It is our opinion that on balance the likely advantages of the FKP placement outweigh the likely disadvantages. Accordingly, we consider the FKP placement reasonable.'

Port Bouvard last month secured a $167.6 million loan from St George Bank, conditional on arranging an underwritten capital raising by June 30 and cutting debt by $20 million by July 15.

Source: Vivienne Ryan, 'Port Bouvard rescue "not fair" but reasonable', *The West Australian.*

16.7 Dividends

The nature of dividends and their accounting treatment were introduced very briefly in chapter 5. We now provide a more complete discussion of the appropriate treatment of the payment of dividends, and amend some aspects of the coverage in chapter 5.

Dividends are simply a distribution of cash or other assets, or of a company's own shares, to its shareholders. Cash dividends are the most common. The legal requirements in the Corporations Act (as amended in 2010) specify that a company must not pay a dividend unless:

(a) the company's assets exceed its liabilities immediately before the dividend is declared and the excess is sufficient for the payment of the dividend

(b) the payment of the dividend is fair and reasonable to the company's shareholders as a whole, and

(c) the payment of the dividend does not materially prejudice the company's ability to pay its creditors. The payment of a dividend is considered to materially prejudice the company's ability to pay its creditors if the company becomes insolvent as a result of the payment.

Assets and liabilities in (a) above are to be calculated in accordance with accounting standards in force at the relevant time.

In essence, the Act uses a solvency test for the payment of dividends whereas, in the past, a 'profits' test was used, i.e. dividends could only be paid out of 'profits'. Under the new approach adopted in June 2010, it appears that dividends can now be paid out of capital as well as out of retained earnings or other reserves. There seems to be little point, therefore, in making a distinction between classes of equity in a corporate entity, and the use of one account for all equity, similar to that in a sole trader entity, appears suitable.

In terms of the declaration and payment of dividends, the Act also includes a replaceable rule, which specifies that the directors may determine that a dividend is payable, and fix:

- the amount
- the time for payment
- the method of payment.

The replaceable rule further specifies that the methods of payment may include the payment of cash, the issue of shares, the grant of options and the transfer of assets, and that interest is not payable on a dividend.

However, a company can amend this rule in its own constitution. If a company has a constitution, it is common for the constitution to provide for the *declaration* of dividends by the directors. If so, the Act specifies that the company incurs a legal debt for dividends when the dividend is *declared*. However, *if there is no such provision in the company's constitution*, the Act states that a debt for dividends is incurred only when the time fixed for payment arrives, and the decision to pay the dividend may be revoked at any time before then. This avoids the difficulties that could arise if net assets (assets less liabilities) which were sufficient to cover the dividend when it was recommended, have diminished when the time comes to pay the dividend.

A common practice is for the constitution of companies to allow payment of two types of dividends — interim and final — although the power to declare dividends at any time rests with the directors. An interim dividend is a dividend that is declared and paid part way through the accounting period. A final dividend is payable after the end of the accounting period. It is a usual practice for the directors to recommend the payment of a final dividend, which is then disclosed by way of footnotes to the financial statements of the company at the end of the financial year. When the dividend is declared at the annual general meeting of shareholders, under the constitution, it becomes a legal debt; hence, no dividend liability can be recorded at the end of the financial year (see IAS 10/AASB 110 *Events after the Reporting Period*). On the rare occasion that the directors *declare* the dividend before the end of the reporting period, i.e. there is no discretion to change the dividend, it is a legal debt, and should be recognised and reported as a liability in the balance sheet.

Therefore, it is important that, for each company, the constitution is consulted in order to determine the rights of all classes of shareholders in relation to dividends. It is common for a company's constitution to allow for the issue of both preference and ordinary shares, and for preference shareholders to have special rights for the payment of dividends. These special rights must be followed carefully.

A dividend is usually expressed as a certain amount of money (cents) per share. For example, if a dividend of 18c per share is declared, then a shareholder with 1000 fully paid shares will receive a dividend of $180. Partly paid shares in listed companies receive their appropriate portion of the dividend. On occasions, dividends may be expressed as a percentage of the company's share capital; for example, if a final dividend of 10% is recommended, this means that the directors are recommending a dividend of 10% of the company's share capital to be paid. The practice of expressing dividends as a percentage is more common with preference shares.

Cash dividends

Cash dividends are normally stated as so many cents per share, and may consist of both interim and final dividends. A company's shareholders may change if the shares are traded on the stock market. To ensure that dividends are paid to the rightful owner of the shares, dividends are often declared on one date and are payable on some future date to shareholders on the register at a particular date between the declaration date and the payment date.

To illustrate, assume that on 25 August (the declaration date) the company at its annual general meeting declared a 20c per share final dividend on 400 000 ordinary shares, fully paid at $1, to be paid on 20 September (the payment date) to shareholders on the register on 10 September. (Note that investors buying shares between 25 August and 10 September will therefore have the ownership of their shares recorded before payment of the dividend.) The dividend is to be paid out of the retained earnings of the company.

A dividend liability account for the final dividend is recognised when it is declared. Hence, the entry for dividends is made on 25 August as follows:

Aug.	25	Retained Earnings	80 000	
		Final Dividend Payable		80 000
		(Declared a cash dividend of 20c per share		
		on 400 000 ordinary shares)		

When the dividend becomes payable on 20 September, it is common practice in Australia to open a special dividend bank account and to deposit an amount of money in the account. All dividend cheques or electronic transfers, when paid by the bank, are taken out of that special account.

For our purposes, however, it is sufficient to record (in general journal form) *payment* of the final dividend as:

Sept.	20	Final Dividend Payable	80 000	
		Cash at Bank		80 000
		(Payment of the dividend declared on 25 August)		

No entry is required on 10 September because that date is used only to determine the owners of the shares who are to receive the dividends.

Companies that normally declare interim dividends would debit an equity account and credit Interim Dividend Payable. If a company declares dividends on both ordinary and preference shares, it should use a separate Dividend Payable account for each type of share. The net effect of a cash dividend is to reduce both the Equity and Cash at Bank accounts for the amount of the dividend.

Preference dividends

If a company has preference shares as permitted by its constitution, the preference shareholders are entitled usually to some specified dividend before any dividend is paid to ordinary shareholders. The annual preference dividend is usually stated either as an amount of cents per share or as a percentage of the preference share capital. Because the obligation to pay a dividend arises only if one is declared, preference shareholders are not assured of receiving a dividend each year.

Although dividends must be paid on preference shares before any are paid on ordinary shares, the directors may decide not to declare a dividend on either preference or ordinary shares because the company has an insufficient amount of net assets, i.e. assets minus liabilities. In the constitutions of some companies, the dividend on preference shares may be **cumulative**, which means that undeclared dividends accumulate, and the accumulated amount plus the current year's preference dividend must be paid before any dividend can be paid to ordinary shareholders. Dividends on cumulative preference shares that are not declared in the year they are due are called **dividends in arrears**. Disclosure of arrears of dividends is generally made in a footnote to the financial statements.

To illustrate cumulative dividends, assume that a company has previously issued 500 000 10% cumulative preference shares fully paid at $1, on which no dividends were declared in the preceding year. In addition, assume there are 100 000 ordinary shares issued and fully paid for $1. If the company declares a $200 000 dividend, it will be distributed to preference and ordinary shareholders as follows:

	Preference	Ordinary
Dividends in arrears ($500 000 × 10%)	$ 50 000	
Current year's dividend	50 000	$100 000
	$100 000	$100 000

If the company declares a dividend of only $80 000, it will all be distributed to preference shareholders; ordinary shareholders will receive no dividends, and dividends in arrears on preference shares will still exist for the amount of $20 000. If preference shares are **non-cumulative**, any undeclared dividends at the end of any year are lost.

A further right that preference shareholders may have under the company's constitution is that of participating in extra dividends once a certain level of dividends has been paid to ordinary shareholders. **Participating preference shares** have the right to receive further dividends above their fixed rate once ordinary shares have received a dividend up to a stated percentage. To illustrate participating preference dividends, assume a company has issued 200 000 ordinary shares for $1 and 100 000 12% preference shares for $1, all shares being fully paid. Assume that on 31 August the company declares a total dividend of $45 000 at the annual general meeting, and that preference shares are entitled to participate in further dividends once ordinary shares have received 12 cents per share. The dividends are apportioned as shown below:

		Apportionment of dividend	
		Preference	Ordinary
1. Current rate of preference dividend (12%)		$12 000	
2. Ordinary dividend (12c × 200 000 shares)			$24 000
3. *Participation apportionment*			
Total distribution	$45 000		
Preference and ordinary dividend	36 000		
Balance for participation	9 000		
Number of shares issued = 300 000 shares			
Cents per share in participation = 3c			
Hence,			
to preference shareholders (100 000 × 3c)		3 000	
to ordinary shareholders (200 000 × 3c)			6 000
		$15 000	$30 000

Thus assuming that the dividend is paid out of the company's retained earnings, the following entry is made to record the dividends payable:

Aug.	31	Retained Earnings	45 000	
		Preference Dividend Payable		15 000
		Ordinary Dividend Payable		30 000
		(Recording of dividends declared)		

The dividend payable accounts are reported as current liabilities in the company's balance sheet until paid.

Share dividends

A **share dividend** is a pro rata distribution of additional shares by a company to its shareholders, normally consisting of the distribution of additional ordinary shares to ordinary shareholders. Share dividends should be distinguished from cash dividends.

Unlike cash dividends, which reduce corporate assets and equity, share dividends have no effect on corporate assets or on total equity. The only effect of a share dividend is a transfer of retained earnings or other reserves to contributed share capital. Share dividends often are declared by successful companies that have used their profitable resources to expand operations. These companies use their earnings received in cash to acquire additional plant and equipment in order to grow and therefore generally declare only minimal cash dividends. The declaration of a share dividend gives shareholders some additional shares as evidence of the increase in their equity in the company, without distributing cash or other assets to them. However, in effect, shareholders receive nothing more than the equity they already have.

Another reason for issuing share dividends is to reduce the market price of the shares by increasing the number of shares issued. When a company grows, the market price of its shares tends to increase. By reducing the market price of its shares, a company can encourage a broader ownership by both small and large investors. To accomplish this, the share dividend must be a relatively large one. Alternatively, the company may undertake a share split (discussed in the next section).

When share dividends are declared and paid, retained earnings or other reserves are transferred to share capital. The accounting impact of a share dividend is essentially the same as a bonus share issue. To illustrate, assume that a company has the following equity on 20 December:

Equity	
Share capital: 250 000 ordinary shares, fully paid at $1	$250 000
General reserve	300 000
Retained earnings	400 000
	$950 000

Assume further that, on 20 December, the board of directors declares out of the general reserve a share dividend of 1 share valued at $1 for every 20 shares held, to be distributed on 10 January to shareholders registered on 31 December. The entry to record the share dividend is:

Jan.	10	General Reserve	12 500	
		Share Capital		12 500
		(Distribution of a 1-for-20 share dividend on 250 000 ordinary shares, at a value of $1 each)		

The net effect of the entry on 10 January is to decrease retained earnings by $12 500 and to increase share capital by the same amount. Thus, total equity remains unchanged by the share dividend as demonstrated below:

	Before share dividend	After share dividend
Ordinary share capital	$250 000	$262 500
General reserve	300 000	287 500
Retained earnings	400 000	400 000
	$950 000	$950 000

Because total equity remains unchanged, each shareholder's interest in total equity also remains unchanged. For example, assume that Paul Dean owned 25 000 shares (10%) of the company before distribution of the share dividend. His share of the equity before and after the dividend is:

$$\text{Before:} \quad \frac{25\,000 \text{ shares}}{250\,000 \text{ shares}} = 10\% \times \$950\,000 = \$95\,000$$

$$\text{After:} \quad \frac{26\,250 \text{ shares}}{262\,500 \text{ shares}} = 10\% \times \$950\,000 = \$95\,000$$

Instead of paying the share dividend out of the General Reserve account, the company could have paid the dividend out of a different reserve account or out of the Retained Earnings account, in which case that account would have been debited instead.

A share dividend effectively converts a company's retained earnings and/or other reserves into share capital. This conversion is often referred to as a process of *capitalising the profits* of the company. As mentioned above, a share dividend may also be referred to as a bonus share issue. A bonus share issue is legally regarded as a 'dividend' when it is payable from the 'profits' of the company.

Share splits

A company may want to reduce the market price of its shares in order to make the shares available to a wider range of investors. One method of accomplishing this objective is to declare a share dividend as discussed previously. An alternative is to split or subdivide its shares into shares of smaller issue price, and at the same time proportionally increase the number of issued shares. To illustrate, assume that a company's equity is as follows:

Equity	
Share capital: 250 000 ordinary shares, fully paid at $1	$250 000
General reserve	300 000
Retained earnings	400 000
	$950 000

Assume further that the ordinary shares now have a current market price of $10 per share. In order to reduce the market price, the board of directors resolves to subdivide the shares 4 for 1, which should reduce the market price per share to about $2.50. When the shares are subdivided, the number of shares is increased to 1 000 000. Share ownership statements are recalled and new share ownership statements are issued, 4 new shares being given for each share recalled.

A **share split** does not change the balance of any of the equity accounts. Share capital remains the same — at $250 000 — because there are now 1 000 000 shares with an issue price of 25c each. Thus, no entry is necessary in the general ledger for a share split.

Comparison of share dividends and share splits

Share dividends are sometimes mistakenly called share splits. Although both have the same effect on the market price of the shares — a 2-for-1 share split and a 100% share dividend both result in a doubling of the number of shares issued and a market price of about half of the previous market price — they are legally different. All share dividends result in an increase in the amount of share capital and a decrease in retained earnings or other reserves; share splits do not.

16.8 Reserves

Reserves represent those items of equity other than capital contributed by owners. Retained earnings is one category of reserves, but many other reserves are created by transferring amounts out of the Retained Earnings account to set aside equity for particular purposes. Some reserves are created in order to comply with accounting standards. For example, if a non-current asset is revalued

Learning objective **8**

Account for the creation and reduction of the different types of reserves that are included in equity upwards in the company's accounts to reflect the asset's fair value, the revaluation increment is usually credited to a Revaluation Surplus account in order to comply with IAS 16/AASB 116 *Property, Plant and Equipment*.

Reserves are not defined in Australian legislation, accounting standards or in the *Conceptual Framework*. Since no official definition exists, companies have followed the practice of using the title 'reserve' for many different items, for example:

- general reserve
- options reserve
- plant replacement reserve
- currency fluctuation reserve.

Creation of reserves

The creation of (or transfer to) reserves in the accounting records is generally a simple matter. The basic journal entry format is:

June	30	Retained Earnings	x	
		Reserve		x
		(Creation of a reserve by appropriating profits)		

For example, a general reserve (created for no specific purpose) is established by debiting Retained Earnings and crediting General Reserve. Transfers to reserves of this type are simply regarded as appropriations of profit. They do not affect expenses.

When non-current assets are revalued upwards, the creation of a revaluation surplus is achieved by the following entry:

June	30	Asset	x	
		Accumulated Depreciation	x	
		Revaluation Surplus		x
		(Revaluation upwards of the carrying amount of a non-current asset to fair value)		

Notice that it is the carrying amount of the non-current asset that is revalued when the surplus is created. Any accumulated depreciation on the asset is written back against that asset and the Revaluation Surplus account is credited for the revaluation increase. The revaluation surplus is classified in equity as a reserve. The treatment of revalued non-current assets is expanded in a later chapter.

Disposal of reserves

Reserve accounts (including the revaluation surplus) may be written off or reduced either by paying a cash dividend or share dividend from the reserve or by transferring the reserve account back to the Retained Earnings account. The general journal entry for the latter method is:

June	30	Reserve	x	
		Retained Earnings		x
		(Transfer of reserve account back to retained earnings)		

Learning objective 9

Prepare basic entries for income tax expense in a company

16.9 Income tax

Once a company has determined its profits for the period, a further expense for income tax must be deducted before arriving at the company's final profit after tax. Income tax payable by a company is based on the company's **taxable income** as determined under the Income Tax Assessment Act and not on the company's accounting profit. Company tax is payable in Australia, for example, either in one lump sum or in quarterly instalments, as explained later in the chapter on the statement of cash flows.

At the end of the financial year, say 30 June 2013, the company normally makes an estimate of the income tax it is likely to pay, and makes an end-of-period adjustment entry to debit the Income Tax Expense account and to credit the Current Tax Liability account. When the tax is paid, either in a lump sum or in instalments, the company then debits Current Tax Liability and credits Cash at Bank.

Normally, a company is responsible for assessing its own income tax payable. Occasionally, however, the Australian Taxation Office (ATO) may conduct an audit of the company's tax payments, and if it assesses the tax to be more than the amount provided for, an Underprovision for Income Tax account is debited and treated as an expense in the current period, and Current Tax Liability is credited until paid. Similarly, if the income tax assessed after an audit is less than the amount provided for, an Overprovision for Income Tax account is credited and treated as income in the current period.

The issue of concern here is not the determination of tax actually payable under the Act to the Tax Commissioner, but the determination and reporting of income tax expense in the company's records and financial statements. There are, theoretically, two methods of determining a company's income tax expense for inclusion in the accounts of the company: the tax payable method, and the tax-effect accounting method.

Under the **tax payable method**, income tax expense for the period is measured as being equal to the current tax liability for income tax, payable to the ATO. In other words, income tax expense is viewed as related to the taxable income determined under the Income Tax Assessment Act. However, accounting standards have rejected this approach in favour of the tax-effect accounting method, as discussed in IAS 12/AASB 112 *Income Taxes*. In this book, only the tax payable method is used. A consideration of tax-effect accounting is found in more advanced texts.

16.10 Preparing the financial statements

Learning objective **10**

Prepare a company's income statement, statement of changes in equity and balance sheet for internal use

Once a company has determined all its assets, liabilities, equity (including dividends and reserves), income (including revenues) and expenses, and recognised them in its accounting records, it can prepare a set of financial statements at the end of the period in order to assess its financial performance and its financial position. This is done after all adjusting entries have been made at the end of the period, as discussed in chapter 4. Furthermore, worksheets can be prepared, as discussed in chapters 4 and 5, before preparing the financial statements. As with sole traders and partnerships, there are four main financial statements that are usually prepared:

- an income statement, (or statement of profit or loss), which shows all the relevant income (and revenues) and expenses so as to measure the company's profit performance for the period
- a statement of changes in equity, which shows movements in the company's retained earnings, other reserves and share capital for the period
- a balance sheet (or statement of financial position), which shows the company's assets, liabilities and equity on the last day of the period as a means of assessing the entity's financial position
- a statement of cash flows, showing the sources and uses of the entity's cash resources during the current period.

The following pages illustrate the first three of these financial statements for a company for *internal* purposes. Coverage of the statement of cash flows is provided in a later chapter.

Illustrative example: Preparation of financial statements

To illustrate the preparation of an income statement, statement of changes in equity and balance sheet, the unadjusted trial balance of Bolivia Ltd is shown in figure 16.2 (p. 674). Several adjusting entries are required in this example as a means of revising such entries from chapter 4.

Additional information

Bolivia Ltd is involved in the computer sales and services industry. Leased vehicles are used mainly for delivery and service of computers. The company's head office, which houses its administrative staff, is located on a prime piece of real estate in the local township.

Figure 16.2 Unadjusted trial balance of Bolivia Ltd

BOLIVIA LTD
Unadjusted Trial Balance
as at 30 June 2013

	Debit	Credit
Bank overdraft		$ 178 050
Vehicle rental expense	$ 72 000	
Cash at bank	7 500	
Investment in government bonds	180 000	
Interest revenue		4 800
Insurance expense	3 000	
Land	230 000	
Buildings	1 000 000	
Office furniture and equipment	127 000	
Retained earnings (1/7/12)		89 000
Accum. depr. – office furniture and equipment		23 000
Accum. depr. – buildings		100 000
Cost of sales	202 400	
Advertising expense	12 300	
Sales returns and allowances	8 700	
Sales		491 120
Mortgage payable		90 000
GST collections		22 000
GST outlays	7 000	
Inventory	106 000	
Share capital (called to $1 per share)		1 140 000
General reserve		33 000
Interest expense on overdraft	11 300	
Discount received		11 250
Discount allowed	12 000	
Fees revenue		17 900
Accounts payable		118 900
Accounts receivable	210 700	
Salaries of sales staff	60 000	
Administrative wages	68 620	
Calls in arrears (25c per share)	2 000	
Calls in advance (25c per share)		6 000
Interest expense on mortgage	4 500	
	$2 325 020	$2 325 020

At the beginning of the year, the company's share capital consisted of 1 140 000 shares called to 75c each. During the year, the company made a call of 25c per share on all issued shares. Some shareholders paid an additional call in advance and some calls were still unpaid at the end of the year.

The following adjustments are yet to be made to the trial balance before financial statements can be prepared.

1. Depreciation to be provided on buildings at 5% p.a. and on office furniture and equipment at 10% p.a.
2. Current income tax expense (and tax liability) for the year is estimated to be $8000.
3. Accrued wages to staff: sales, $1500; administrative, $2000.
4. Vehicle rental paid in advance at 30 June 2013 amounted to $30 000.
5. A dividend of 3c per share is to be recommended on shares, out of the company's retained earnings.
6. Transfer $10 000 from the general reserve to retained earnings.

Required

A. Prepare the journal entries (in general journal form) required by items 1 to 6 above.
B. Prepare the adjusted trial balance as at 30 June 2013.
C. Prepare the income statement, with expenses classified by function, for Bolivia Ltd for the year ended 30 June 2013.
D. Prepare the Retained Earnings account for the year. The beginning balance of Retained Earnings was $89 000. Prepare the company's statement of changes in equity for the year ended 30 June 2013.
E. Prepare the company's internal classified balance sheet as at 30 June 2013.

Solution

A. The journal entries in figure 16.3 illustrate the adjustments required before the financial statements at the end of June 2013 are prepared.

BOLIVIA LTD General Journal			
2013			
June 30 (1)	Depreciation Expense – Buildings	50 000	
	Accumulated Depreciation – Buildings		50 000
	(Depreciation at 5% p.a.)		
(1) 30	Depr. Expense – Furniture and Equipment	12 700	
	Acc. Depr. – Furniture and Equipment		12 700
	(Depreciation at 10% p.a.)		
(2) 30	Income Tax Expense	8 000	
	Current Tax Liability		8 000
	(Income tax expense)		
(3) 30	Salaries Expense – Sales Staff	1 500	
	Wages and Salaries Payable		1 500
	(Accrued salaries of sales staff)		
(3) 30	Administrative Wages Expense	2 000	
	Wages and Salaries Payable		2 000
	(Accrued wages of admin. staff)		
(4) 30	Prepaid Rent	30 000	
	Vehicle Rental Expense		30 000
	(Rent prepaid)		
(5) 30	No entry		
(6) 30	General Reserve	10 000	
	Retained Earnings		10 000
	(Transfer from general reserve)		

Figure 16.3 Adjusting entries for Bolivia Ltd

B. After the adjusting entries are posted to the ledger of Bolivia Ltd, the adjusted trial balance of the company appears as is shown in figure 16.4.

Figure 16.4 Adjusted trial balance for Bolivia Ltd

BOLIVIA LTD
Adjusted Trial Balance
as at 30 June 2013

	Debit	Credit
Bank overdraft		$ 178 050
Vehicle rental expense	$ 42 000	
Cash at bank	7 500	
Investment in government bonds	180 000	
Interest revenue		4 800
Insurance expense	3 000	
Land	230 000	
Buildings	1 000 000	
Office furniture and equipment	127 000	
Retained earnings		99 000
Accum. depr. – office furniture and equipment		35 700
Accum. depr. – buildings		150 000
Cost of sales	202 400	
Advertising expense	12 300	
Sales returns and allowances	8 700	
Sales		491 120
Mortgage payable		90 000
GST collections		22 000
GST outlays	7 000	
Inventory	106 000	
Share capital (called to $1 per share)		1 140 000
General reserve		23 000
Interest expense on overdraft	11 300	
Discount received		11 250
Discount allowed	12 000	
Fees revenue		17 900
Accounts payable		118 900
Accounts receivable	210 700	
Salaries of sales staff	61 500	
Administrative wages	70 620	
Calls in arrears (25c per share)	2 000	
Calls in advance (25c per share)		6 000
Interest expense on mortgage	4 500	
Depreciation expense – buildings	50 000	
Depreciation expense – furniture and equipment	12 700	
Income tax expense	8 000	
Current tax liability		8 000
Wages and salaries payable		3 500
Prepaid rent	30 000	
	$2 399 220	$2 399 220

C. The income statement of Bolivia Ltd based on the information in figure 16.4 is as shown in figure 16.5. Expenses are classified according to various functions carried on in the business, namely by the selling and distribution, administrative and finance functions.

Figure 16.5 Income statement for Bolivia Ltd

BOLIVIA LTD
Income Statement
for the year ended 30 June 2013

INCOME		
Revenue:		
Sales	$491 120	
Less: Sales returns	8 700	
Discount allowed	12 000	$470 420
Fees revenue		17 900
Total revenue		488 320
Cost of sales	202 400	
Less: Discount received	11 250	191 150
Gross profit		297 170
Other income:		
Interest		4 800
		301 970
EXPENSES		
Selling and distribution expenses		
Advertising	12 300	
Vehicle rent	42 000	
Sales staff salaries	61 500	
	115 800	
Administrative expenses:		
Insurance expense	3 000	
Administrative wages	70 620	
Depreciation of furniture and equipment	12 700	
Depreciation of buildings	50 000	
	136 320	
Finance and other expenses:		
Interest expense on overdraft	11 300	
Interest expense on mortgage	4 500	
	15 800	
Total expenses		267 920
PROFIT BEFORE INCOME TAX		34 050
Income tax expense		8 000
PROFIT		$ 26 050

D. Having determined the profit of the company, the Retained Earnings account (in T account format) for the year is as follows:

Retained Earnings

30/6/13	Balance c/d	125 050	1/7/12	Balance	89 000
			30/6/13	Profit	26 050
			30/6/13	Transfer from General Reserve	10 000
		125 050			125 050
			1/7/13	Balance b/d	125 050

The statement of changes in equity for Bolivia Ltd is shown in figure 16.6.

Figure 16.6 Statement of changes in equity for Bolivia Ltd

BOLIVIA LTD Statement of Changes in Equity for the year ended 30 June 2013	
Share capital	
Share capital at 1 July 2012	$ 855 000
Call on ordinary shares (25c per share)	285 000
	1 140 000
Less: Calls in arrears	(2 000)
Add: Calls in advance	6 000
Share capital at 30 June 2013	$1 144 000
Retained earnings	
Retained earnings at 1 July 2012	$ 89 000
Add: Profit	26 050
Transfer from general reserve	10 000
Retained earnings at 30 June 2013	$ 125 050
General reserve	
General reserve at 1 July 2012	$ 33 000
Transfer to retained earnings	(10 000)
General reserve at 30 June 2013	$ 23 000

The statement of changes in equity is a useful financial statement in that it provides an effective link between the income statement and the balance sheet in terms of any movements in equity accounts during the year. The statement shows how the Retained Earnings account was increased by profits and transfers from reserves, and decreased by losses (if applicable), transfers to reserves, and distributions to the owners usually in the form of dividends during the current period, leaving the closing balance of Retained Earnings, which also appears in the company's balance sheet. The statement also shows the movement in the general reserve account for the year and the movements in share capital during the year.

F. The balance sheet of a company lists all its assets, liabilities and equities as at the end of the reporting period. As discussed in earlier chapters dealing with sole traders, it is also common for a company to classify assets and liabilities on the basis of whether they are current or non-current. Such a classification is presented in figure 16.7 for Bolivia Ltd.

The balance sheet in figure 16.7 follows the format of the accounting equation expressed as Assets − Liabilities = Equity. Many other formats are acceptable, especially for internal management purposes, depending on the information to be emphasised in the statement. Information considered most relevant by management should be placed in the most prominent position. For example, if equities are to be emphasised, the balance sheet could begin with equities and follow the format Equity = Assets − Liabilities. Alternatively, it could be presented in the format Assets = Liabilities + Equity if this is suitable for management purposes.

Figure 16.7 Balance sheet for Bolivia Ltd, for internal use

BOLIVIA LTD
Balance Sheet
as at 30 June 2013

CURRENT ASSETS		
Cash at bank		$ 7 500
Accounts receivable		210 700
Inventory		106 000
Prepaid rent		30 000
TOTAL CURRENT ASSETS		354 200
NON-CURRENT ASSETS		
Government bonds		180 000
Land		230 000
Buildings	$1 000 000	
Accumulated depreciation	(150 000)	850 000
Office furniture and equipment	127 000	
Accumulated depreciation	(35 700)	91 300
TOTAL NON-CURRENT ASSETS		1 351 300
TOTAL ASSETS		1 705 500
CURRENT LIABILITIES		
Bank overdraft		178 050
Accounts payable		118 900
GST payable [$22 000 – $7000]		15 000
Wages and salaries payable		3 500
Current tax liability		8 000
TOTAL CURRENT LIABILITIES		323 450
NON-CURRENT LIABILITIES		
Mortgage payable		90 000
TOTAL NON-CURRENT LIABILITIES		90 000
TOTAL LIABILITIES		413 450
NET ASSETS		$1 292 050
EQUITY		
Share capital		
1 140 000 ordinary shares called to $1		$1 140 000
Less: Calls in arrears*		(2 000)
Add: Calls in advance*		6 000
		1 144 000
General reserve		23 000
Retained earnings		125 050
TOTAL EQUITY		$1 292 050

* These details may be omitted here as the information is contained in the statement of changes in equity.

Footnote: The directors have recommended a final dividend of 3c per share. This dividend is not reflected in the financial statements.

For external reporting, the formats of the income statement, statement of changes in equity and the balance sheet as presented in this chapter are unsuitable as they do not comply with the requirements of accounting standard IAS 1/AASB 101 *Presentation of Financial Statements*. External financial reporting for companies in accordance with accounting standards is considered in a later chapter.

Accumulated loss, p. 658
Allotment, p. 660
Application, p. 659
Bonus share issue, p. 665
Call, p. 657
Certificate of registration, p. 655
Company limited by guarantee, p. 651
Constitution, p. 654
Cumulative preference shares, p. 669
Dividends, p. 667
Dividends in arrears, p. 669

Limited company, p. 650
No-liability company, p. 652
Non-cumulative preference shares, p. 669
Ordinary shares, p. 666
Participating preference shares, p. 669
Preference shares, p. 666
Preliminary expenses (start-up costs), p. 665
Proprietary company, p. 651
Prospectus, p. 655
Public company, p. 651
Replaceable rules, p. 654

Reserves, p. 671
Retained earnings, p. 657
Rights issue, p. 664
Share capital, p. 657
Share dividend, p. 670
Share issue costs, p. 665
Share split, p. 671
Start-up costs (preliminary expenses), p. 665
Taxable income, p. 672
Tax payable method, p. 673
Uncalled capital, p. 657
Underwriter, p. 663
Unlimited company, p. 652

DISCUSSION QUESTIONS

1. Two partners in a business are discussing the possibility of incorporating their business as a proprietary company. Discuss the advantages and disadvantages of this move. Briefly discuss the impact the Corporations Act would have on their decision.
2. What is the difference between a small proprietary company, a large proprietary company and a public company?
3. What are the contents of an application form to register a company?
4. 'It is better for a company to have a constitution rather than rely on the replaceable rules in the Act.' Discuss.
5. Explain the purpose of each of the following accounts used in a public share issue: Share Capital, Application, Cash Trust, Allotment, Call, Calls in Advance.
6. Distinguish between a private placement, a public share issue and a rights issue. Distinguish also between a renounceable rights issue and a non-renounceable rights issue.
7. How should a company account for its start-up costs and its share issue costs? How should a company account for the fees paid to an underwriter?
8. 'Preference shares can offer security of dividends and other advantages over ordinary shares, and are therefore the best equity to have in a company.' Do you agree? Explain.
9. A well-established company, which wanted to raise finance for expansion, decided to issue some preference shares. The terms of the issue were that the shareholders did not have the right to vote at meetings, but were entitled to dividends of 12 cents per share each year, on a cumulative basis. Discuss the merits of issuing such shares. Where should they appear in the company's balance sheet? Explain your reasoning.
10. 'A company must have made sufficient profits before it can pay dividends to its shareholders.' Discuss.

EXERCISES

LO 6

Exercise 16.1 ISSUE OF SHARES PAYABLE IN FULL

The directors of Ecuador Ltd decided to issue 100 000 ordinary shares.

Required

A. Prepare journal entries (in general journal form) to record the issue of shares as a private placement to Good Times Ltd for $15 per share payable in full.
B. Prepare journal entries (in general journal form) to record the issue of shares to the public at $18 per share payable in full.

Exercise 16.2   DETERMINING EQUITY IN THE BALANCE SHEET

Jamaica Ltd was organised on 2 January 2013, and proceeded to issue 100 000 9% cumulative preference shares and 200 000 ordinary shares. The preference shares were issued privately at a value of $2 each and the ordinary shares were issued to the public at $5 each, payable in two instalments of $2.50 per share. The first instalment was payable on application and the remaining instalment was payable by 30 June 2014.

Required

Prepare the equity section of the balance sheet as at 30 June 2013.

Exercise 16.3   ISSUE OF SHARES BY INSTALMENTS AND UNDERSUBSCRIPTION

On 30 April, Argentina Ltd issued 50 000 shares for $6 each, payable $2 on application, $2 on allotment and the remainder due by two equal calls on 30 June and 31 August. Share issue costs of $4000 were paid on 31 May.

Required

Prepare journal entries (in general journal format) to record the share issue up to collection of allotment money assuming:

1. the shares were fully subscribed
2. the shares were undersubscribed by 8000 shares.

Exercise 16.4   SHARE ISSUE WITH OVERSUBSCRIPTION

On 1 July 2013, Chile Ltd issued a prospectus offering 160 000 of its ordinary shares, payable $1 on application, $1 on allotment and $2 to be called as and when required. When applications closed on 23 July, applications had been received for 240 000 shares, including one applicant for 20 000 shares who had paid in full. The directors allotted the shares on 24 July as follows:

1. The applicant for 20 000 shares, who paid in full, was allotted 20 000 shares.
2. Applications for 20 000 shares were rejected and the application money was refunded.
3. The remaining applicants were allotted 7 shares for every 10 applied for. The excess application money on these shares was to be applied in part payment of allotment money.

All allotment money was received by 7 August.

Required

Prepare journal entries in general journal form to record the share issue.

Exercise 16.5   PRIVATE PLACEMENT AND PUBLIC ISSUE OF SHARES

Paraguay Ltd was registered on 1 February 2013. The following events occurred in that year:

Feb.	1	25 000 ordinary shares were allotted to the original members. The shares were paid for in full at a price of $1 each.
		A prospectus was issued for 50 000 10% preference shares and 150 000 ordinary shares, payable in full on application. The issue prices of the preference shares and ordinary shares respectively were $2 and $1.
Mar.	15	Applications were received for 50 000 preference shares and 220 000 ordinary shares.
Mar.	18	The directors allotted the shares in terms of the prospectus, excess monies being returned to unsuccessful applicants.

Required

A. Prepare entries in general journal form to record the above transactions.
B. Show the equity section of the balance sheet as at 18 March 2013.

Exercise 16.6 LEDGER ACCOUNTS FOR PUBLIC ISSUE AND RIGHTS ISSUE

The following events occurred in the newly formed company, Honduras Ltd, which was registered on 31 January 2013:

2013

Feb. 1 Honduras Ltd issued a prospectus calling for applications for 600 000 ordinary shares to be issued at a price of $3, payable $2 on application, 50c on allotment and the balance as and when required.

Mar. 1 Applications closed with the issue oversubscribed by $1 800 000. The directors allotted shares on the basis of 1 share for every 3 applied for. Excess application money was applied against amounts owing on allotment and the balance was refunded.

Sept. 20 A final call on shares was made.

Oct. 20 Call money was received.

Nov. 1 Shareholders were offered a 1-for-5 rights issue at a price of $2.80, with rights to be exercised by 15 December. If rights are not exercised, they will lapse.

Dec. 15 Holders of 560 000 shares exercised their rights to take up new shares in accordance with the rights issue by paying in the appropriate money to the company.

Required

Prepare ledger T accounts to record the above events in the records of Honduras Ltd for 2013.

Exercise 16.7 ISSUE OF ORDINARY SHARES

The following is an actual case:

Fortescue raises $504m

Iron ore hopeful Fortescue Metals Group has raised $504 million to fund expansions to its emerging project in the Pilbara region of Western Australia. Fortescue said it had set a minimum raising target of US$300 million (A$344 million) for the much-anticipated capital raising, but decided to increase the target amount after strong demand. The company issued 14 million shares at $36 each to raise $504 million.

The project was initially slated to produce 45 million tonnes of iron ore on an annual basis...

Source: Excerpts from Ben Sharples, 'Fortescue raises $504m', *The Courier-Mail*.

Required

A. As the above share issue was a private placement with several well-known investors, prepare the journal entry, in general journal form, made by the company to record the share issue.

B. How would your answer to requirement A differ if the share issue had been a public share float?

Exercise 16.8 PARTICIPATING PREFERENCE SHARES

Cuba Ltd has issued 1 000 000 ordinary shares for $2 and 200 000 8% preference shares for $2, all shares being fully paid. On 30 September 2013 at the annual general meeting of the company, a dividend was declared for a total cash payout of $160 000. Preference shares are entitled to participate in further dividends once ordinary shares have received 8 cents per share. Assume that the dividends are taken out of retained earnings.

Required

A. Show how the total dividend would be apportioned between ordinary and preference shares.

B. Prepare journal entries in general journal form to record the dividend payments.

Exercise 16.9 JOURNAL AND LEDGERS FOR ISSUE OF SHARES

Nicaragua Ltd was registered as a new company on 2 January 2014. On that day a prospectus was issued inviting applications for 300 000 ordinary shares at $10, payable $2.50 on application, $2.50 on allotment and the balance due in one call on 15 June 2014. The issue was underwritten for a fee of $7000.

On 31 January, applications closed with the issue undersubscribed by 15 000 shares. Directors proceeded to allot the shares. Amounts due on allotment were received on 9 February, including the amount due from the underwriter less the underwriter's commission.

On 15 June, the amounts due on the call were received with the exception of the amount due on 12 000 shares.

Required

Prepare journal entries (in general journal form) and ledger accounts (in T-account format) to record the above transactions.

Exercise 16.10 DIVIDENDS, TAX AND RESERVE TRANSFERS

During the year ended 30 June 2013, the directors of Costa Rica Ltd paid a final dividend out of retained earnings of $60 000, which had been recommended at the end of the previous financial year. They also declared and paid an interim dividend of $75 000 on 1 February 2014. The balance of the Retained Earnings account at 1 July 2013 was $100 000.

At 30 June 2014, the ledger accounts showed that the company had made a total profit of $1 000 000 for the year. However, the directors determined that the following adjustments were still necessary to finalise the accounts:
1. Provide for an income tax liability of $300 000.
2. Recommend the payment of a final dividend of $100 000 out of retained earnings.
3. Transfer $150 000 to a general reserve and $120 000 to a plant replacement reserve.

Required

A. Prepare journal entries to record all transactions above for the year ended 30 June 2014.
B. Prepare the Retained Earnings account for the year ended 30 June 2014.

Exercise 16.11 SHARE DIVIDENDS

Peru Ltd's balance sheet, before a share dividend, is as follows:

PERU LTD
Balance Sheet
as at 30 June 2013

ASSETS		EQUITY	
Cash at bank	$ 20 000	Share capital	$100 000
Non-current assets	150 000	General reserve	40 000
		Retained earnings	30 000
	$170 000		$170 000

The company immediately declared a share dividend from the general reserve on the basis of 1 bonus share for every 5 shares held. All shares were issued at $1.

Required

Prepare any journal entries necessary to record the payment of this share dividend.

Exercise 16.12 PREPARATION OF INCOME STATEMENT

The following information relates to Uruguay Ltd. Profit before income tax for the year ended 30 June 2013 was $180 000. The following items were used in determining that profit:

Sales	$540 000
Cost of sales	234 000
Selling, administrative and finance expenses	72 000
Loss from flood	14 000
Interest revenue	18 000
Bad debts	36 000
Development costs written off	22 000

Assume the company's taxation rate is 30c in the dollar.

Required
Prepare the income statement for the year ended 30 June 2013.

Exercise 16.13 DIVIDENDS, RESERVES, RETAINED EARNINGS

During the year ended 30 June 2013, the directors of Venezuela Ltd declared and paid an interim dividend of $20 800 out of retained earnings. At the end of the year the financial statements showed a profit (before tax) of $400 000 out of which the directors made the following reserve transfers and tax liability.

Income tax expense	$160 000
Reserves:	
Plant replacement	38 000
General	100 000

The beginning balance of retained earnings was $12 500.

Required
A. Prepare journal entries relating to the above transactions.
B. Prepare the Retained Earnings account for Venezuela Ltd for the year ended 30 June 2013.

Exercise 16.14 DIVIDENDS, RESERVES, STATEMENT OF CHANGES IN EQUITY

A. Show the journal entries to record the following transactions for Guyana Ltd.
  1. Profit for the year was $1 750 000. Ignore income tax.
  2. Directors resolved to transfer the amounts specified below from retained earnings to:
    (a) contingencies reserve, $1 000 000
    (b) general reserve, $400 000.
  3. Some years ago, the company had established an exchange fluctuation reserve, $4 500 000, but now that it had withdrawn from international trade, this reserve was no longer required.
  4. Start-up costs $250 000 were to be written off. This has not been reflected in the profit in (1) above.
  5. An interim dividend of $200 000 had been paid and directors recommended a final dividend of $300 000 to be paid in 3 months time, after ratification by shareholders at the annual general meeting. Both dividends were paid out of retained earnings.
  Note: The beginning balance of the Retained Earnings account was $1 800 000.
B. Prepare the statement of changes in equity for Guyana Ltd.

Exercise 16.15 ISSUE OF SHARES, AND EQUITY IN THE BALANCE SHEET

On 1 July 2013, Panama Ltd was incorporated, and on 4 July a prospectus was issued inviting applications for 40 000 shares payable $4.50 on application, $2.50 on allotment and $2.50 on each of two calls to be made at intervals of 3 months after the date of allotment.

By 31 July, applications were received for 48 000 shares. On 3 August, the directors allotted 40 000 shares to the applicants in proportion to the number of shares for which application had been made. The surplus application money was offset against the amount payable on allotment. The balance of allotment money was received by 12 August.

The two calls were made on the dates stated in the prospectus, but the holders of 2400 shares did not pay either call. In addition, a holder of another 1200 shares did not pay the second call.

Required

A. Prepare journal entries to record the above transactions (in general journal format).
B. Prepare the equity section of the balance sheet of Panama Ltd on completion of the transactions.

PROBLEMS

Problem 16.1 LEDGER ACCOUNTS ON ISSUE OF ORDINARY SHARES ★   LO 6

★ Basic
★★ Moderate
★★★ Challenging

Scotland Ltd was incorporated on 1 July 2013. On 1 August, it was decided to issue 300 000 ordinary shares on the following terms:

Application	$2 per share
Allotment	$1 per share
Call as required	$1 per share

To the end of August, applications for 350 000 shares had been received together with the application money due on each share. One applicant for 5000 shares had forwarded $20 000 in full payment of the shares.

On 15 September, the directors proceeded to allot 300 000 shares on the following basis. Applicants for 30 000 shares were refunded their application money in full, 5000 shares were allotted to the applicant who paid for the shares in full, and the other successful applicants were allotted the remaining shares, excess application money being transferred to allotment.

On 7 October, all allotment money had been received.

A first and final call was made on 1 November, and all call money was received by 30 November with the exception of the amount due on 6000 shares.

Required

Prepare all ledger accounts (T account format) necessary to record the above transactions.

Problem 16.2 LEDGER ACCOUNTS FOR ISSUE OF SHARES, PREPARATION OF BALANCE SHEET ★   LO 6, 10

On 1 January 2013, Albania Ltd was registered and, on the same day, the company purchased the net assets (excluding cash) of a partnership for a consideration of 240 000 ordinary shares (fully paid) at a price of $2.40 per share. 1 000 000 ordinary shares were offered to the public at $2.40 per share on the following terms:

$1 on application (due 15 January)
70c on allotment (due 15 February)
balance on final call (due 15 May).

By 15 January, applications had been received for 1 200 000 ordinary shares of which applicants for 200 000 shares forwarded the full $2.40 per share.

At a directors' meeting on 16 January, it was decided:
1. to allot ordinary shares in full to applicants who had paid in full on application
2. to allot the remaining ordinary shares from this issue in proportion of 4 for every 5 applied for.

According to the prospectus, all surplus money from applications was to be transferred to allotment and/or call accounts.

The share issue costs were $5600 and were paid on 15 February.

By 31 May, all money was received except for the holder of 2000 shares who did not pay the final call.

Required

A. Prepare ledger accounts (running balance format) to record all the above transactions.

B. Prepare a balance sheet for Albania Ltd as at 31 May 2013.

Problem 16.3 ISSUE OF ORDINARY AND PREFERENCE SHARES ★ LO 6

Wales Ltd was registered on 1 July 2013. On 4 August a prospectus was issued inviting public subscriptions for an issue of 100 000 12% preference shares payable $2 in full on application, and 300 000 ordinary shares at a price of $1.60 per share, payable $1 on application, 20c on allotment and the balance as and when required.

Applications were to be made in multiples of 100 shares with a minimum of 200 preference shares or 500 ordinary shares. The directors reserved the right to allot the shares applied for in full or such lesser number as resolved and to apply excess money towards amounts due on allotment. All other money was to be refunded to applicants.

Applications were received for 120 000 preference shares and 400 000 ordinary shares by 16 August when the directors closed the issue. On 19 August, the directors allotted the shares as follows:

1. *Preference:* Three applications for a total of 20 000 shares were rejected, and the balance allotted in full.

2. *Ordinary:* Applications for 60 000 shares were rejected in full and the balance was allotted on a pro rata basis.

On 24 August, refunds were made to the respective applicants in accordance with the directors' resolutions. Share issue costs of $1500 were also paid on this date. Outstanding allotment money was received by 30 September.

On 8 November the directors resolved that a call of 30c per share was to be made on the 300 000 partly paid ordinary shares. The call is due and payable by 1 December.

Call money was received as follows:

    1 December on 260 000 shares

  15 December on 20 000 shares.

Required

Prepare entries in general journal form to record the above events in the accounts of Wales Ltd.

Problem 16.4 RIGHTS ISSUE, PRIVATE PLACEMENT, DIVIDENDS AND CHANGES IN EQUITY ★ LO 6, 7, 10

The following is the equity of Haiti Ltd at 30 June 2013:

Share capital (200 000 fully paid ordinary shares)	$400 000
General reserve	200 000
Retained earnings	10 000

The transactions below occurred during the year ended 30 June 2014:

2013

July	1	Prospectus issued inviting offers for 200 000 shares to be issued for $3 per share. These shares were offered to existing shareholders on the basis of 1 share for every 2 shares at present held. Shares were payable in full on application and rights to the issue were transferable. The prospectus provided that these shares were to rank equally with existing shares from 1 July 2013. The issue was underwritten for a commission of $5000. In addition, 200 000 shares were privately placed with QLM Insurance Ltd at $2.80 per share, and these shares were to rank for dividend purposes from 1 October 2013.
July	31	The issue closed fully subscribed, the holders of 40 000 shares having transferred their rights. Directors proceeded to allotment.
Aug.	1	Underwriting commission paid.
Sept.	22	At the annual general meeting, shareholders approved a final dividend of 15c per share for the year ended 30 June 2013. The dividend had not been recorded in the accounts for the year ended 30 June 2013. Dividends were paid by direct debit to shareholders after the close of the meeting. Dividends were paid from General Reserve.

Required

1. Prepare entries in general journal format to record the above transactions.
2. Prepare a statement of changes in equity for the period 1 July to 30 September 2013.

Problem 16.5   LEDGERS, STATEMENT OF CHANGES IN EQUITY ★★ LO 6, 7, 10

The following information relating to the year ending 30 June 2013 for Poland Ltd has been obtained from the company's records.

Profit for year before further adjustments and tax	$33 000
Retained earnings (1 July 2009)	5 500
General reserve	3 000
Revaluation surplus	2 500
Interim dividend paid	5 000
Development costs	3 500

On 30 June 2013, the directors decided to:

1. recommend a final cash dividend of $7000, to be ratified by shareholders at the annual general meeting
2. write off development costs
3. increase the general reserve by $1000
4. provide for an estimated tax expense and current tax liability of $7500 on 2012–13 profits.

Required

Record the above adjustments in ledger accounts and prepare a statement of changes in equity for Poland Ltd for the year ended 30 June 2013.

Problem 16.6   DIVIDENDS, RESERVES ★★ LO 7, 8, 9

Equity of Switzerland Ltd at 14 February 2013 consisted of:

Share capital:		
800 000 shares (fully paid for $1)	$800 000	
600 000 shares (paid to 50c, issued at $1)	300 000	$1 100 000
General reserve		100 000
Plant replacement reserve		50 000
Retained earnings		125 000

The following events occurred during 2013:

Feb.	15	Interim dividend of 5c per fully paid equivalent share declared and paid out of retained earnings.
April	2	Final call made on the 600 000 partly paid shares.
May	30	All call money received.
June	30	Profit before tax for the year was $700 000 out of which the following appropriations were made:

(a) Income tax expense	$250 000
(b) Transfers to reserves: General reserve	240 000
Plant replacement reserve	30 000

Aug.	15	Shareholders approved the final dividend of 5c per share out of retained earnings recommended by the directors, and a one-for-five bonus issue of shares at a price of $1 per share to be satisfied out of the general reserve.
Aug.	16	Payment of final dividend.
		Allotment of bonus shares.

Required

A. Prepare journal entries in general journal format to give effect to the above transactions.
B. Show the Retained Earnings account up to 17 August 2013.
C. Show the statement of changes in equity from 14 February 2013 to 17 August 2013.

Problem 16.7 ISSUE OF SHARES, DIVIDENDS AND STATEMENT OF CHANGES IN EQUITY ★★

Germany Ltd's equity at 30 June 2013 was as follows:

100 000 ordinary shares, issued at $3.20, fully paid	$320 000
250 000 ordinary shares, issued at $3.40, called to $2.40	600 000
90 000 redeemable preference shares, issued at $1, fully paid	90 000
Calls in advance (5000 ordinary shares)	5 000
Share issue costs	(4 850)
General reserve	30 000
Retained earnings	150 000

The following events occurred during the year ended 30 June 2014:

2013

July	15	The final call, due 31 August, was made on the partly paid shares.
Aug.	31	All call money was received.
Sept.	20	Paid the final dividends (ordinary: 20c per fully paid equivalent share, and preference: 9%) declared on 30 June 2013.
Dec.	10	Declaration and payment of a 6c per fully paid equivalent share interim dividend on ordinary shares.

2014

Jan.	3	A prospectus was issued, inviting applications for 80 000 ordinary shares at an issue price of $2.50, payable in full on application.
Jan.	31	The issue closed fully subscribed, with all money due having been received.
Feb.	5	The 80 000 shares were allotted.
June	30	The directors declared a final dividend of 12c per share (payable on 20 September 2014), and transferred $50 000 to the general reserve.

Required

A. Prepare journal entries (in general journal form) to record the above transactions.

B. Prepare a statement of changes in equity for the year ended 30 June 2014, assuming profit for the year was $180 000.

Problem 16.8 SHARE ISSUES AND STATEMENT OF CHANGES IN EQUITY ★★

Lithuania Ltd was incorporated on 30 June 2013. On 1 July 2013, the company issued a prospectus offering 300 000 ordinary shares at an issue price of $10, payable on the following terms:

$3 on application
$3 on allotment
$2 on first call
$2 on second call

A summary of the applications and allotments register follows:

Amount paid per share on application	Number of shares applied for	Number of shares allotted
$ 3	200 000	150 000
$ 6	100 000	100 000
$10	50 000	50 000

Shares were allotted to all applicants on 1 September 2013. All money received in excess of amounts due on application was applied to amounts due on allotment and calls. Where appropriate, refunds of application money were made. All allotment money was received by 30 September 2013.

On 1 November 2013, Lithuania Ltd's directors made a call of 42c per share, payable by 30 November 2013. By 31 December, call money had not been received from holders of 25 000 shares.

Required

A. Prepare general journal entries to record the above events.

B. Prepare the ledger accounts (running balance format) for the period 1 July to 31 December 2013.

C. Prepare the statement of changes in equity for the period ending 31 December 2013.

Problem 16.9 SHARE ISSUES AND DIVIDENDS ★★

At 30 June 2013, Ireland Ltd's equity was as follows:

Issued capital:	
200 000 ordinary shares issued at $1.20, fully paid	$240 000
40 000 7% preference shares issued at $1, fully paid	40 000
	280 000
Retained earnings	174 000
General reserve	35 000
Total equity	$489 000

The preference shares were non-participating. The following events occurred after 30 June 2013:

2013

Sept.	1	Final dividends out of retained earnings, as recommended in June, were paid in cash. This included the 7% preference dividend for the year ended 30 June 2013 and a final ordinary dividend of 10c per share.
Oct.	15	A prospectus was issued inviting subscriptions for 50 000 ordinary shares at an issue price of $1.40, payable 80 cents on application and 60 cents on allotment.
Nov.	18	Applications closed, with applications having been received for 50 000 shares. Applicants for 4000 shares had paid in full on application.
Nov.	20	Shares applied for were allotted, with excess application money being applied to allotment.
Dec.	11	The balance of allotment money due was received.
Dec.	31	In order to keep cash in the company to meet its ever-increasing need for liquidity, the directors decided not to pay an interim cash dividend. Instead, they made a bonus issue from the general reserve of one ordinary share (valued at $1.20) for every 10 ordinary shares held.

2014

June	20	The directors paid the preference dividend for the year.
June	30	The directors recommended a final dividend of 12c per ordinary share.

Required

Prepare the journal entries (in general journal form) necessary to record the above events in Ireland Ltd's accounting records.

Problem 16.10 SHARE ISSUES AND STATEMENT OF CHANGES IN EQUITY ★★

A trial balance taken from Hungary Ltd's accounting records at 30 September 2013 showed the following account balances:

HUNGARY LTD Trial Balance as at 30 September 2013		
Account	Debit	Credit
Share capital (700 000 shares fully paid)		$ 700 000
General reserve		240 000
Retained earnings		117 800
Current tax liability		30 000
Accounts payable		120 900
Mortgage payable		180 000
Bank overdraft (current)		60 600
Other liabilities (current)		3 300
Property, plant and equipment (net)	$ 890 800	
Accounts receivable	90 200	
Inventory	370 600	
Prepayments	1 000	
Patent	100 000	
	$1 452 600	$1 452 600

At a meeting of directors on 1 October, it was decided to issue additional shares to fund future operations. Accordingly a prospectus was issued on 10 October offering 400 000 ordinary shares at $1 each to the public, payable 50c per share on application, 25c per share on allotment and the remainder in one call when required.

By 30 November, applications were received from the public for 24 000 shares in excess of the number available, and the application money paid in on 24 000 shares was refunded to unsuccessful applicants. The rest of the shares were allotted to the successful applicants, including one who had paid in full on application for 4000 shares. The share issue had been underwritten for a fee of $8000.

By 15 December, all cash due on allotment had been received, and the underwriting fee was paid on this date.

On 31 January 2014, an interim dividend of 6c per share was paid out of retained earnings on all fully paid equivalent shares.

On 28 February, the remaining call on the shares was made, and all cash was received on the call by 31 March, except for the holder of 7000 shares.

Required

A. Prepare journal entries in general journal form to record the above transactions.
B. Prepare the following accounts in T-account format to show the effect of the above transactions: Share Capital, Application, Allotment, Call.
C. Prepare a statement of changes in equity for the 6 months ended 31 March 2014, assuming that the profit made by the company during that period amounted to $120 000.

Problem 16.11 SHARE ISSUES AND STATEMENT OF CHANGES IN EQUITY ★★ — LO 6, 7, 8, 10

In January 2012, the management of Austria Ltd decided on a program of expansion for the business. On 1 July 2012, the company had $900 000 in retained earnings, and another reserve totalling $600 000 had been set aside out of retained earnings for the acquisition of equipment. Share capital consisted of 2 800 000 shares issued for $1 each. The following events occurred in relation to the equity accounts of Austria Ltd over the next few years:

2013
June 30 Profit for the year amounted to $270 000. Interim dividends paid during the year amounted to $20 000, and $120 000 was added to the reserve for acquiring equipment. The directors recommended a final dividend of 2.5c per share to be approved at the annual meeting in September.

Sept. 21 The final dividend recommended in June was paid out of retained earnings.

Nov. 30 800 000 ordinary shares in Austria Ltd, with a fair market value of $1.20 each, were issued as payment for acquiring 1 000 000 ordinary shares in Vienna Ltd, a company that conducted activities complementary to those of Austria Ltd. The shares in Vienna Ltd had been issued originally for $1 each.

2014
June 30 Profit for the financial year was calculated to be $500 000. The directors recommended a final dividend of 3c per share out of retained earnings and $150 000 was added to the reserve for equipment acquisition.

Sept. 22 The dividend recommended in June was approved at the annual general meeting and paid in cash.

2015
June 30 Profit for the year amounted to $480 000. A dividend of 4c per share was recommended by directors and a further $130 000 was set aside to the reserve for acquisition of equipment.

Sept. 23 The dividend recommended on 30 June was approved and paid out of retained earnings.

Dec. 31 The contractor who had been employed by the company completed construction of new, technologically advanced equipment for the company's use. The total cost of construction amounted to $1 020 000. Cash was paid in full to the contractor for the equipment. The directors ruled that the reserve for acquisition of new equipment was to be eliminated from the accounting records. Profit for the half-year was determined as $300 000. An interim dividend of 2c per share was declared and paid out of retained earnings.

Required

A. Prepare journal entries to record all transactions and events across the 3-year period.

B. Show the equity section of the balance sheet of Austria Ltd as at 31 December 2015.

LO 6, 7, 8, 10

Problem 16.12 DIVIDENDS, RESERVES, BONUS ISSUE AND STATEMENT OF CHANGES IN EQUITY ★★

The equity of France Ltd at 30 June 2013 was:

Share capital	
50 000 10% cumulative preference shares — fully paid	$ 50 000
100 000 ordinary shares — fully paid	200 000
	250 000
Revaluation surplus	60 000
Contingencies reserve	20 000
Retained earnings	(40 000)
Total equity	$290 000

During the year ended 30 June 2014, the following transactions occurred:

2013

Sept. 1   France Ltd paid damages of $18 000 awarded in a lawsuit against it. In anticipation of this, the directors had authorised the appropriation for contingencies last year. The board now directs that the reserve is to be discontinued.

2014

March 1   The directors authorised payment of dividends of 10% on the preference shares and 10c per share interim on ordinary shares out of retained earnings. Preference dividends have not been paid for 2012 or 2013.

March 12   Dividends declared on 1 March were paid.

April 30   The directors authorised the issue to ordinary shareholders of a bonus share issue of 1 share for every 5 held, valued at $2.60. The shares do not rank for dividend until 2015. The issue is out of the revaluation surplus.

June 30   The profit before tax for the year was $370 000. The directors decided to recommend in the annual general meeting a final dividend of 10c per share on ordinary shares, to come out of retained earnings. Assume the taxation rate is 30%.

Required

A. Prepare general journal entries to record all transactions for the year.

B. Prepare a statement of changes in equity for France Ltd for the year ended 30 June 2014.

LO 6, 7, 8, 9, 10

Problem 16.13 COMPREHENSIVE PROBLEM ★★★

Belgium Ltd prepared the unadjusted trial balance as at 30 June 2013 shown on page 692.

The following information and events are yet to be recorded by the company on 30 June 2013:

1. Inventory on hand after a physical stocktake at 30 June 2013 amounted to $265 000.
2. Prepaid insurance at the end of the year amounted to $3000.
3. Wages accrued and unpaid were $1700.
4. Interest owing and unrecorded on debentures and bank overdraft was $15 000.
5. Depreciation to be recorded on delivery vehicles at the rate of 20% p.a., on buildings at the rate of 5% p.a., and on furniture at the rate of 10% p.a. All these assets have been on hand throughout the year.
6. Interest due on investments amounted to $6000.
7. Sales made on the last day of the financial year but not recorded were for $8000.
8. The directors have decided to transfer $20 000 to the general reserve from retained earnings.
9. Dividends of 5c per share were recommended. An interim dividend of $35 000 had been paid during the year, and this dividend had been debited to the Retained Earnings account.
10. The company issued 30 000 bonus shares valued at $1 each out of the revaluation surplus.

BELGIUM LTD
Unadjusted Trial Balance
as at 30 June 2013

Account	Debit	Credit
Share capital (700 000 shares fully paid)		$ 700 000
General reserve		200 000
Retained earnings		80 000
Revaluation surplus		30 400
Current tax liability		20 800
Accounts payable		50 300
Debentures		400 000
Bank overdraft (current)		30 700
Other liabilities (current)		30 300
Land	$ 400 000	
Buildings	620 000	
Accum. depr. – buildings		100 000
Furniture and equipment	160 000	
Accum. depr. – furniture and equipment		80 000
Delivery vehicles	60 400	
Accum. depr. – delivery vehicles		20 000
Accounts receivable	60 600	
Inventory (1 July 2012)	240 000	
Investments	200 000	
Prepaid insurance	10 000	
Sales		530 600
Purchases	240 000	
Sales returns and allowances	2 080	
Purchases returns and allowances		2 000
Freight inwards	10 080	
Freight outwards	9 060	
Wages expense	100 500	
Discount allowed	3 050	
Discount received		3 020
Interest expense	10 140	
Advertising expense	30 700	
Income tax expense	20 800	
Administrative expenses	100 710	
	$2 278 120	$2 278 120

Required

A. Prepare the adjusting entries necessary.
B. Prepare a detailed income statement for internal use for Belgium Ltd for the year ended 30 June 2013.
C. Prepare the statement of changes in equity for Belgium Ltd for the year ended 30 June 2013.
D. Prepare the balance sheet for Belgium Ltd as at 30 June 2013.

Problem 16.14 COMPREHENSIVE PROBLEM ★★★   LO 5,6,7,8,9,10

The accounts in the ledger of England Ltd as at 30 June 2014 had balances as shown on page 693.

The Share Capital account represents 30 000 000 shares fully paid at $1 and 50 000 000 shares issued at $1 but called to 75c per share. A call of 25c per share had been made on these 50 000 000 shares during the year, but 2 000 000 had failed to pay the call by 30 June 2014. An interim dividend of $1 500 000 has been paid during the year out of retained earnings.

Inventory on hand at 30 June 2014 was $16 000 000.

The following adjustments have to be made:

1. Provide for 10% p.a. depreciation on cost of fixtures and fittings and 5% p.a. on buildings for the whole year.

2. Unrecorded and unpaid expenses: travellers' salaries $100 000.
3. General expenses prepaid, $15 000.
4. Record income tax expense and current tax liability of $900 000.
5. Declare a final dividend, $1 500 000. No ratification of this dividend is needed.
6. Share issue costs to be written off against share capital.
7. An amount of $1 000 000 is to be transferred to a general reserve from retained earnings.

ENGLAND LTD		
	Debit ($000)	Credit ($000)
Share Capital		67 500
Second Call	500	
Retained Earnings		4 600
Mortgage Payable on Land and Buildings		20 000
Land	10 200	
Buildings	40 000	
Fixtures and Fittings	2 500	
Accumulated Depreciation – Buildings		4 000
– Fixtures and Fittings		500
Investments	40 000	
Share Issue Costs	500	
Accounts Receivable Control	5 495	
Inventory on hand (1 July 2013)	15 000	
Bank Overdraft		11 000
Accounts Payable Control		2 000
Sales Revenue		24 000
Interest from Investments		1 750
Purchases	11 850	
Freight Inwards	150	
Commission Expense	100	
Delivery Expense	200	
Salaries: Administrative	3 600	
Travellers	1 100	
Directors' Fees	200	
General Expenses	2 965	
Interest on Mortgage Expense	1 000	
	$135 350	$135 350

Required

Prepare an income statement for the year ended 30 June 2014, and a balance sheet as at 30 June 2014.

LO 5,6,7,8,9,10

Problem 16.15 COMPREHENSIVE PROBLEM ★★★

The trial balance of Italy Ltd at 30 June 2013 is shown on page 694.

There was no movement in share capital for the year.

The following adjustments are required:

1. Record income tax expense of $7500.
2. Transfer $1000 to general reserve.
3. Accrued expenses: sales staff's salary $650; office salaries $270; interest on bank loan $20.
4. Write off preliminary expenses $3000.
5. Rent prepaid $300.
6. Record depreciation: motor vehicles 10% on cost; office furniture 20% on cost; buildings 5%.
7. Recommend a dividend of 20c per share.

ITALY LTD
Trial Balance
as at 30 June 2013

	Debit	Credit
Share capital (50 000 shares issued at $1 called to 80c)		$ 40 000
Retained earnings 1/7/12		5 000
General reserve		4 700
Asset replacement reserve		10 000
Sales		150 000
Sales returns and allowances	$ 500	
Cost of sales	93 280	
Freight inwards	600	
Freight outwards	700	
Advertising expense	1 000	
Preliminary expenses	3 000	
Buildings	44 000	
Selling expenses	1 000	
Sales staff's salary expense	10 000	
Sales staff's car expenses	1 500	
Sales staff's entertainment expenses	1 200	
General expenses	1 250	
Insurance expense	2 000	
Rates expense	1 000	
Discount allowed	1 270	
Accounts receivable	16 500	
Accumulated depreciation – buildings		1 000
– motor vehicles		2 000
– office furniture		1 000
Accounts payable		6 000
Bank loan (repayable 1 July 2013)		1 000
Cash at bank	6 100	
Motor vehicles (at cost)	10 000	
Office furniture (at cost)	3 000	
Inventory	16 000	
Office salaries expense	5 300	
Interest on overdraft expense	50	
Rent expense	1 450	
	$220 700	$220 700

Required

Prepare an income statement and a statement of changes in equity for the year ended 30 June 2013 and a balance sheet for Italy Ltd as at 30 June 2013.

DECISION ANALYSIS

From partnership to company

Fifteen years ago, John Kerr worked as a production manager for a small manufacturing firm involved in the production of metal furniture. Owing to his keen interest in woodworking, he decided at that time to begin his own business, Woodworkers Anonymous, with the aim of manufacturing dolls' houses and other wooden toys to retail.

After moderate success in this venture over a period of 5 years, he decided to form a partnership with two good friends, Alexis Thompson and James Bentley, and to branch out into the manufacture of wooden garden furniture. This partnership traded under the name of The Garden Furniture Store, even though the construction of dolls' houses and other toys was to continue. John had a 60% interest in the partnership, and both Alexis and James had 20% interests. John took on the role of general manager in the partnership, with Alexis and James being responsible for production and sales respectively.

After further success in this venture, because of John's previous experience in the metal industry, the partners decided to expand the business into metal garden furniture and metal fencing. As part of these arrangements, they were thinking of applying to ASIC to be registered as a proprietary company. The proposed name for the new company was Relaxaquipment Pty Ltd, and each partner was to continue operating in a similar role.

Before registering the company, a trial balance of the partnership was as follows:

THE GARDEN FURNITURE STORE Trial Balance as at 30 June 2013	Debit	Credit
Cash at bank	$ 20 250	
Accounts receivable	43 650	
Inventories	71 250	
Prepaid insurance	1 500	
Land	45 000	
Building	225 000	
Accumulated depreciation – building		$ 37 500
Equipment	150 000	
Accumulated depreciation – equipment		30 000
Accounts payable		63 750
Accrued expenses		2 625
John Kerr, Capital		200 000
John Kerr, Retained Earnings		19 844
Alexis Thompson, Capital		70 000
Alexis Thompson, Retained Earnings		31 463
James Bentley, Capital		70 000
James Bentley, Retained Earnings		31 468
	$556 650	$556 650

It was agreed that the fair values of all assets and liabilities were equal to their carrying amounts, and that each partner would be issued with shares in the new company, valued at $1 each, in accordance with the values of their total equity in the partnership. In order to finance expansion into metal gates and fencing, the three partners decided that the new company would need to apply for a $60 000 loan, interest payable annually at 8%, from the Western Bank, with the principal repayable over a 10-year period. They also agreed that they could ask another friend, Simone Carey, to become a member of the company by taking up shares and contributing further cash requirements of $50 000, if necessary.

Before incorporation, however, they seek your advice on the following questions:

- What are the advantages and disadvantages of incorporation, compared with remaining a partnership?
- What is the legal relationship between the shareholders, directors and officers in a company?
- What portion of the total equity belongs to each partner in the new company? Will the partners be happy with this if they expect the same profit-sharing ratio as in the partnership?
- Given that it will cost $300 in legal fees to form the company, how should these legal fees be recorded in the company's accounts?
- How would the balance sheet of the company appear immediately after registering and taking up the loan from Western Bank?
- How much profit before income tax and interest would the company have to earn in the first year in order to achieve a rate of return on total assets (net of depreciation) of 15%?
- Assuming an income tax rate of 30% on profit, how much profit would this represent for the shareholders after interest and after tax?

Ignore GST in this situation.

Required

A. Answer the above questions for the three partners.

B. Should they proceed with incorporation? Are there other factors they should consider?

CRITICAL THINKING

Accounting for a donation

Recyclers Ltd was formed for the purpose of collecting and recycling household garbage in Australia's capital cities. The company has been in operation for 5 years and has managed to be profitable enough to survive. Nevertheless, it has come across a number of problems, especially related to the need for new technology to increase the amount of recyclable waste. Another problem has been in separating recyclable and non-recyclable material, which householders have been placing in their recycle bins.

The company has been seeking financial support from the local and international community in order to carry out its research program to improve the technology of the industry. Hearing of the company's need, the well-known environmentally conscious philanthropist, Richard Rich, decided to donate $1 000 000 to the company for the purpose of continuing its research activities. All that he asked was that the money was spent wisely, and that the company provided him with financial statements after each 6 months, showing how the money was spent and how the research was progressing.

The company accepted the money gratefully and was happy to comply with Rich's wishes; the managing director believed that Rich may be prepared to donate more money in future if technological progress could be shown to occur.

When Rich's cheque for $1 000 000 arrived, there was considerable disagreement among the accounting staff as to how this transaction should be recorded. One accountant believed that the money should be treated as revenue; another argued that it should be regarded as a type of capital account, and called 'donated capital'.

Required

Advise the managing director of Recyclers Ltd of the best accounting treatment. Present reasons for your answer.

COMMUNICATION AND LEADERSHIP

Companies — online resources

Assign one of the following websites to each group of 3 or more people:

- www.comlaw.gov.au: Investigate the procedures that are required under the *Corporations Act 2001* to establish a small proprietary company.
- www.asx.com.au: Investigate information about the role of the Australian Securities Exchange in society.
- www.asx.com.au: Investigate the ASX Listing Rules and what is required for a company to have its shares listed on the Australian Securities Exchange.
- www.asic.gov.au: Investigate the role played by the Australian Securities and Investments Commission in regulating company behaviour.

FINANCIAL ANALYSIS

Refer to the consolidated financial statements in the latest financial report of JB Hi-Fi Limited on its website, www.jbhifi.com.au, especially the statement of changes in equity, and answer the following questions:

1. How many ordinary shares have been issued by the company at financial year-end?
2. Are any of the company's issued shares not fully paid at the end of the financial year? If so, provide details.

3. Has the company issued any shares over the last 2 financial years? If so, provide details of those shares.
4. What is the amount of cash that has flowed to the company from share issues over the last 2 financial years (see the statement of cash flows)?
5. List the different types of reserves, and their amounts, recognised by JB Hi-Fi Limited in its consolidated statements at the end of the financial year.
6. Provide details of any movements in these reserves over the last financial year.
7. How much has been paid in dividends on all shares in the current financial year? Determine the amount of dividends recommended to shareholders at the end of the year.

Part 5

Accounting regulation of assets and liabilities

Chapter

17

Regulation and the *Conceptual Framework*

Concepts for review

Before studying this chapter, you should understand or, if necessary, revise:

- the nature and basic objectives of accounting (pp. 6–8)
- basic assumptions used by accountants in the preparation of financial statements (pp. 36–40)
- the importance of ethics in the exercise of an accountant's duties (pp. 20–1)
- the difference between financial accounting and management accounting (pp. 12–13).

Learning objectives

After studying this chapter, you should be able to:

1 describe the development of accounting regulation in Australia resulting in the issue of accounting standards (pp. 702–9)

2 explain the nature of the *Conceptual Framework for Financial Reporting*, and the history of the development of the framework (pp. 710–11)

3 describe the nature of a reporting entity under the *Conceptual Framework* (pp. 711–14)

4 describe the objectives of general purpose financial reporting under the *Conceptual Framework* (pp. 714–16)

5 identify the qualitative characteristics for the selection and presentation of financial information (pp. 716–20)

6 define assets, liabilities, equity, income and expenses, as established under the *Conceptual Framework* (pp. 720–4)

7 describe the recognition criteria, established in the *Conceptual Framework*, for assets, liabilities, income and expenses (pp. 724–30)

8 explain the importance of measurement in the preparation of financial statements (pp. 730–1).

An asset to be a liability

You will have noticed the latest military jargon . . . it is now *de rigueur* to describe military equipment and troops as 'assets' . . . In the military context, where you're sending people off to face the prospect of getting their heads shot off, calling them assets keeps it clinical.

They're no longer husbands, wives, sons, daughters, fathers, mothers, sweethearts, friends or even citizens. They're just assets, so that's all right then.

The process began with personnel — another military term that passed into civilian use. In the corporate world, personnel have long since degenerated into human resources . . . Once you start thinking of people as assets, it won't be long before your mind turns to the alternative, and it's pretty clear who the liabilities are in contemporary Australia.

The ABC is [a] well-known liability, which is why its budget has had to be slashed so savagely. Our universities are positively clogged with liabilities. All those fusty academics who persist in thinking there's some benefit to a society in the study of unproductive stuff like archaeology or classics or philosophy. How can that sort of pointless activity ever improve a university's balance sheet? Creative artists, eccentrics, dreamers, challengers of conventional wisdom . . . liabilities, the lot of them!

It almost makes you proud to be a liability.

Source: Excerpts from Hugh Mackay, 'An asset to be a liability', *The West Australian.*

Chapter preview

This chapter introduces the current regulatory arrangements in Australia for the development of accounting standards. Such standards are variously influenced by many interested parties, including the government, professional accounting bodies, representatives of those who prepare financial statements for publication (such as the Institute of Directors, the Group of 100), and international accounting standard-setting bodies. The chapter also discusses the basic accounting concepts such as assets and liabilities (consider the scene setter) developed as part of *The Conceptual Framework for Financial Reporting* (the *Conceptual Framework*). The *Conceptual Framework* has been the source of much discussion and controversy among preparers of financial statements, as it has heavily influenced the accounting standards issued by the International Accounting Standards Board (IASB), which have been adopted for use in Australia by the Australian Accounting Standards Board (AASB), a body established by the Australian Government.

At the time of writing, the IASB and the Financial Accounting Standards Board (FASB) in the United States are undertaking a joint project to amend the existing conceptual framework. This is a long-term project which will take several years to complete. Any amendments and suggested amendments to the conceptual framework made jointly by the IASB and FASB have a flow-on effect in Australia; hence, many of the amendments and suggested amendments to the current *Conceptual Framework* are incorporated into this chapter where necessary.

17.1 Regulation and development of accounting standards

Learning objective 1

Describe the development of accounting regulation in Australia resulting in the issue of accounting standards

Brief history of regulation

Accounting has evolved through time, changing with the needs of society. As new types of transactions evolved in business, accountants developed rules and practices for recording them. These accounting practices came to be known as *generally accepted accounting principles* (GAAP). GAAP consist of rules, practices and procedures, the authority of which stems from their general acceptance and use by the accounting profession and the business community. They have evolved from the experiences and thinking of members of the accounting profession and influential businesspeople.

In spite of the gradual development of GAAP in the profession, a need for the development of more rigid, compulsory accounting standards was recognised. This need had its beginnings with the growth of industrialised society in the nineteenth century. During this time, the company form of organisation was born and with it the separation of ownership from management. Management was appointed as an agent of the owners (shareholders) of the company to conduct the day-to-day operations with a view to earning profits for the owners.

As business organisation became more complex, different levels of management came into existence. Consequently, financial reporting became important, so that lower levels of management could report to higher levels (internal reporting) and top management could report on the entity's progress to the owners (external reporting). In particular, external users of information had to rely on the honesty and integrity of management in the use of the owners' money; but, for various reasons, corporate secrecy was considered to be acceptable behaviour. Consequently, share investments gained the reputation of being risky investments, and shareholders were, to some extent, at the mercy of potentially unscrupulous management.

To provide some protection for shareholders, governments began to legislate for the preparation of a balance sheet (statement of financial position) by companies in order to monitor the behaviour of managers as stewards of the shareholders' funds. The Victorian Government was particularly active and was the first in Australia to legislate for the presentation of both a balance sheet and an income statement for companies. It was not until the 1940s that the first attempt was made by the accounting profession in Australia to provide guidance as to the content of these statements, when the Institute of Chartered Accountants in Australia (ICAA) adopted a series of recommendations developed in the United Kingdom by the equivalent professional body in England and Wales. These recommendations were not compulsory, and were basically ignored by many entities.

After a series of company failures in the late 1950s and early 1960s, which caused many shareholders to lose considerable savings, much criticism was directed towards the content of externally reported financial statements. This led to the formation of the Australian Accounting Research Foundation (AARF) and the attempt by professional accounting bodies to establish a set of accounting standards for presenting external financial reports. However, compliance with these accounting standards was hard to achieve, as many companies chose merely to ignore them.

Consequently, in 1984, the Australian Government stepped into the standard-setting process to approve accounting standards and to ensure compliance with them. This was achieved by establishing an Accounting Standards Review Board (ASRB), which was replaced in 1991 by the Australian Accounting Standards Board (AASB). The Australian Government is active today in the standard-setting process and, in 1997, the responsibility for the development of accounting standards was handed to the Treasurer. In 2000, the Treasurer at the time reorganised the standard-setting process by establishing the Financial Reporting Council (FRC) to provide strategic directions for the AASB.

Thus, the development of accounting principles became a significant political program among members of the profession, business enterprises and their representatives, and the Australian Government. This has led to GAAP being formalised gradually as accounting standards. The Australian Government today, by way of the FRC, requires the AASB to adopt International Financial Reporting Standards (IFRSs) issued by the IASB for use in the general purpose financial statements and reports of Australian companies and other institutions. The IASB's standards, however, are directed solely towards profit-making enterprises; hence, the AASB, which is also responsible for issuing accounting standards for use in the public and not-for-profit sectors, is required to adapt the IASB's standards for use in these other sectors as well. **Accounting standards** in Australia therefore are issued for *all* types of entities — business, public sector entities and not-for-profit entities.

Following the election of the Labor government in late 2007, the responsibility for managing the standard-setting process in Australia was taken away from Treasury and passed to the Minister for Financial Services, Superannuation and Corporate Law, who is directly responsible for appointing the Chair of the AASB. This followed, in 2006, the establishment of the Accounting Professional & Ethical Standards Board Limited (APESB) as an initiative of the Institute of Chartered Accountants in Australia (ICAA) and CPA Australia. The Institute of Public Accountants (IPA) has subsequently become a member. The APESB is an independent body responsible for setting the code of ethics and the professional standards by which the members of these professional accounting bodies are required to abide. The APESB issues and reviews the professional and ethical standards and guidance notes for the benefit of practising accountants. The requirements of these standards are mandatory for all members of the professional accounting bodies. The standards of practice relate to ethical issues, compliance with accounting standards, quality control in accounting practices and aspects of tax practice, trust accounts, insolvency practice, forensic accounting and management advisory services. For additional information, visit the website of the APESB (www.apesb.org.au).

In summary, financial accounting practice in Australia is determined mainly by the application of accounting standards issued by the AASB, which are developed within the context of IFRSs issued by the IASB. Accounting standards in Australia are generated within a government institutional framework, which includes the FRC and the AASB. In addition, the APESB influences the ethical behaviour and integrity of professional accountants in this country. Finally, accounting and reporting practices are influenced by the Australian Securities and Investments Commission and the Australian Securities Exchange. These are discussed below.

Financial Reporting Council

The Australian Government, by way of the *Australian Securities and Investments Commission Act 2001*, established the Financial Reporting Council (FRC). The role of the FRC is to act as an overseer and advisory body to the accounting standard setter, the AASB, and to the auditing standard setter, the Auditing and Assurance Standards Board (AUASB). Membership of the FRC consists of representatives of professional, business and government organisations with an interest in the standard-setting process. The FRC's brief is to appoint members of the AASB and the AUASB, and approve and monitor the priorities, business plan, budget and staffing arrangements for both boards. In the context of accounting standards, the FRC is required to determine the

AASB's broad strategic directions and to encourage the AASB to issue and adopt accounting standards which represent internationally accepted best practices if doing so would be in the best interests of the Australian economy. The FRC is also required to monitor the operation of Australian accounting standards to ensure their continued relevance and effectiveness in achieving their objectives. Figure 17.1 shows the structure of institutional arrangements for accounting and auditing standard setting overseen by the FRC.

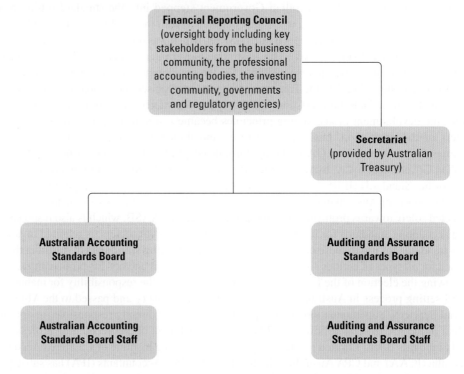

Figure 17.1 Structure of institutional arrangements for accounting and auditing standard setting overseen by the Financial Reporting Council (FRC)
Source: FRC, 'Structure of institutional arrangements for accounting and auditing standard setting', www.frc.gov.au.

In line with the FRC's main function of overseeing the process of setting accounting standards, the chairman of the FRC announced in July 2002 that, after 1 January 2005, the AASB was required to adopt IASB standards. This followed developments in the European Union (EU) which required EU listed companies that were preparing consolidated financial statements of the parent and subsidiary companies to adopt accounting standards and financial reporting standards issued by the IASB. Furthermore, company audits were to be performed in such a way as to comply with IASB standards. The FRC argued that a single set of high-quality accounting standards that are accepted in international capital markets would greatly help cross-border comparisons by investors, reduce the cost of capital, and help Australian companies wishing to raise capital or list their shares on overseas stock markets.

Australian Accounting Standards Board

In January 1984, the Australian Government established the Accounting Standards Review Board (ASRB). The role of the ASRB was to issue accounting standards applicable to companies in the private sector, and legislative backing was given to these standards. All companies were required to comply with accounting standards approved by the Board unless it could be shown that such compliance would not provide a true and fair view of the affairs of the company. Approval of standards by the Board was not restricted solely to those issued by the professional accounting bodies. The two major professional bodies, as well as providing resources through the AARF to the ASRB, were represented on the Board.

With the introduction of the Corporations Law in 1991 (now the *Corporations Act 2001*), the ASRB was replaced by the Australian Accounting Standards Board (AASB). It was then a requirement for companies to prepare their financial reports so as to comply with *all* applicable accounting standards issued by the AASB. If a company's directors felt that complying with all applicable accounting standards did not reflect a true and fair view of the company's state of affairs, then additional disclosures were required so that the company's financial statements did provide a true and fair view.

The AASB was responsible for developing accounting standards relating to the preparation of financial reports. The work of the AASB gave rise to the AASB series of accounting standards, or AASB standards.

The reorganisation of the AASB in 2000 and the formation of the FRC brought significant reforms to the standard-setting process in Australia. The aim of these reforms was to provide a standard-setting process that was economically efficient and beneficial to Australian business operating in a global environment. It was also expected that the standard-setting process would be more efficient in time, as the AASB had previously been taking up to 3 years before a standard was issued on a particular topic.

After the announcement by the FRC regarding adoption of IASB standards, the following occurred:

- The AASB began a program of developing a set of Australian accounting standards that, when applied by Australian entities, enabled those entities to assert that their financial statements comply with the IASB's accounting standards. The Australian accounting standards and their international counterparts are identical, with three exceptions:
  - Some Australian accounting standards require more information to be disclosed in the financial statements and in notes to those statements than is required by the equivalent IASB standard.
  - Australian accounting standards contain, where applicable, extra paragraphs relevant for entities in the public and not-for-profit sectors. IASB standards are written for application within the business profit sector only. The AASB has continued to issue additional accounting standards relevant to the public sector, as well as accounting standards where no equivalent IASB standard exists, e.g. AASB 1031 *Materiality*.
  - Other differences between Australian standards and the IASB's standards may arise as a result of the AASB's legal obligations that require the AASB to issue accounting standards that facilitate the Australian economy by reducing the cost of capital, and allowing Australian entities to compete effectively overseas. If the AASB amends IASB standards for issue in Australia to achieve these purposes, then the Australian standards will not comply with the IASB's standards, and statements to this effect need to be included in the amended standards.
- At the time of writing, the AASB is in the process of revising and adopting the *Conceptual Framework for Financial Reporting* (the *Conceptual Framework*) issued by the IASB in September 2010. The IASB, in a joint project with the US FASB, is continuing to revise its conceptual framework documents following extensive consultation with its constituents.

Meetings of the AASB are held in public, so that the process of standard setting is open for all to see. Further details on the AASB and its current work program are available from the AASB website, as illustrated in figure 17.2 (overleaf).

Australian Securities and Investments Commission

The Australian Securities and Investments Commission (ASIC) was established by the Australian Government in 1989, and in 1990 ASIC was given the task of administering company law throughout the nation. ASIC does not determine accounting standards, but is concerned with ensuring that companies comply with the requirements of AASB accounting standards when providing information in their financial reports.

According to the ASIC website (www.asic.gov.au), ASIC regulates and informs the public about Australian companies, financial markets, financial services organisations and professionals who deal and advise in investments, superannuation, insurance, deposit taking and credit. According to the ASIC website, www.asic.gov.au, the *Australian Securities and Investments Commission Act 2001* (the ASIC Act) requires ASIC to:

- maintain, facilitate and improve the performance of the financial system and entities in it
- promote confident and informed participation by investors and consumers in the financial system
- administer the law effectively and with minimal procedural requirements
- enforce and give effect to the law
- receive, process and store, efficiently and quickly, information that is given to it
- make information about companies and other bodies available to the public as soon as practicable

Figure 17.2 AASB website, www.aasb.com.au

Under the ASIC Act, ASIC also has the function of monitoring and promoting market integrity and consumer protection in relation to the Australian financial system. Hence, as part of its response to the global financial crisis, the Australian Government, in late 2010, required ASIC to take over the overseer role from the Australian Securities Exchange (ASX) in relation to Australia's securities markets. Unlike the ASX, which is a public company, ASIC, which is a government regulatory authority, now has the responsibility for supervising real-time trading on Australia's domestic licensed markets and for enforcing laws against misconduct on Australia's financial markets. This has allowed ASIC to investigate directly investors for misconduct in the market. As part of the takeover, ASIC has developed a set of Market Integrity Rules (MIR) and established a Market Disciplinary Panel to impose penalties and require remedial action, if necessary, for any breaches of these rules.

Australian Securities Exchange

The Australian Securities Exchange (ASX) also influences accounting. The ASX is concerned with improving disclosure in financial reports of companies listed on the various exchanges throughout Australia. It has included in its Listing Rules a number of disclosure requirements and other regulations with which a listed company must comply if it wishes to continue to have its shares traded on the stock exchange.

The ASX has played a very significant part in influencing the regulatory program for the development of accounting standards in Australia, especially in the late 1990s. In 1996, the ASX agreed to provide resources to the AASB on the assumption that the AASB would undertake a program of international harmonisation to bring Australian standards into line with international accounting standards so that compliance with Australian standards meant automatic compliance with those. The ASX's push towards the use of international standards was given strong support from companies in Australia, particularly large multinational companies, and the Group of 100 (G100), an organisation representing the top 100 companies in Australia.

International Accounting Standards Board (IASB)

In 1973, the International Accounting Standards Committee (IASC) was formed to develop a set of international accounting standards to be used by those countries that wished to do so. Membership of the IASC consisted of representatives of several professional accounting bodies throughout the world.

The IASC issued accounting standards over a 27-year period until it was replaced in 2001 by the IASB. The main reason for replacement was that the IASC's standards allowed too many alternatives and it was felt that international accounting standards should be of a higher quality if they were to be accepted and used for the purpose of listing a company's shares on securities exchanges around the world.

With the growth of the globalisation movement in the 1990s came the perceived need for a set of global accounting standards. The IASC was considered to be in the best position to undertake such a task, provided that membership of the IASC was representative of accounting standards boards, rather than of professional accounting bodies, across national borders. Consequently, the IASC Foundation (now the IFRS Foundation) was born with a new constitution (published in March 2000 and revised in 2002, 2005 and 2007) which established the International Accounting Standards Board (IASB) to replace the IASC. (The Constitution of the IFRS Foundation can be found on the IASB's website, www.ifrs.org.)

The IASB has members drawn from national standard setters across a wide geographical base: some must be practising auditors, others must be preparers of financial statements, and others must have a background as users of financial statements. Several of these members are expected to liaise with national standard setters in various countries. Refer to the IASB's website to view its mission statement.

Following the direction given by Australia's FRC in 2002, the AASB was required to adopt IFRSs issued by the IASB as from 1 January 2005. Hence, the financial statements prepared by Australian companies are in line with those prepared by entities in other countries which also have adopted IASB standards. This should allow for greater comparability and understanding of financial statements worldwide, and lead to a more efficient flow of capital resources across national boundaries.

The IFRS Interpretations Committee

Established in December 2001, the IFRS Interpretations Committee (formerly the International Financial Reporting Interpretations Committee (IFRIC)) is a subcommittee of the IASB. The committee has the task of periodically reviewing, within the context of existing international accounting standards and the *Conceptual Framework*, accounting issues that are likely to receive divergent or unacceptable treatment in the absence of authoritative guidance, in order to reach consensus on the appropriate accounting treatment. The IFRS Interpretations Committee handles issues of reasonably widespread importance, rather than issues of concern to only a small set of entities. The interpretations cover:

- newly identified financial reporting issues not specifically covered by international financial reporting standards (IFRSs) issued by the IASB
- issues where unsatisfactory or conflicting interpretations have developed, or are likely to develop in the absence of authoritative guidance, to try to reach consensus on the appropriate treatment.

Australia's AASB adopted the interpretations issued by the IFRS Interpretations Committee for use by companies in this country as from 1 January 2005.

As a result of adopting international standards, Australian accounting standards come, via the AASB, from three sources:

- Standards that are Australian equivalents of:
  - international accounting standards (IASs) — these standards were originally issued between 1973 and 2001 by the IASC, the forerunner of the IASB, and are now part of the IASB's standards; in Australia, these standards have titles beginning with the format AASB 101, AASB 102, etc.
  - International Financial Reporting Standards (IFRSs), which are the standards issued by the IASB since its inception in 2001; in Australia, the equivalent IFRS begins with AASB 1, AASB 2, etc.
  - interpretations issued by the IFRS Interpretations Committee.
- Other Australian accounting standards issued by the AASB, for which there are currently no equivalent standards issued by the IASB, e.g. AASB 1031 *Materiality*. Some of these standards apply exclusively to the not-for-profit sector.
- Interpretations issued by the old Urgent Issues Group (UIG) to the extent that there are no equivalent IFRS interpretations. The UIG was a subcommittee of the AASB established in 1994 to provide solutions relatively quickly to accounting problems which confronted practitioners from time to time. The UIG was dissolved in 2006 and the task of adopting IFRS interpretations is now part of the role of the AASB. However, some of the old UIG's interpretations dealt with issues peculiar to the legal environment in Australia, e.g. Interpretation 1031 *Accounting for the Goods and Services Tax (GST)*, and these interpretations have been retained and are now issued by the AASB, in accordance with accounting standard AASB 1048 *Interpretation of Standards*.

Financial Accounting Standards Board (FASB)

Since 1973, the most active and well-known accounting standard-setting board in the world has been the Financial Accounting Standards Board (FASB), the body responsible for issuing accounting standards in the United States. Because of the size and strength of the US capital market, the FASB has been arguably the most powerful and well-organised body in the standard-setting arena.

On 29 October 2002, the FASB announced that it had signed an agreement (known as the Norwalk Agreement) with the IASB. The Norwalk Agreement required both bodies to work together towards one set of compatible, global accounting standards. The aim was to agree on high-quality solutions to existing and future accounting issues and to converge their existing standards as soon as is practicable. Commitment to the principles of the Norwalk Agreement was reaffirmed in 2005 and again in 2008 when the FASB and IASB signed a Memorandum of Understanding regarding the convergence of US generally accepted accounting principles (GAAP) and the IFRSs. It is hoped that there will be one set of high-quality global accounting standards as the IASB and the FASB work towards achieving their long-term strategic priority.

The potential for achieving one set of global standards is high, because IFRSs have been adopted not only by Australia, but also by the European Union, Hong Kong, South Africa, and New Zealand. Other countries that have decided on convergence in the future include Canada, India, Korea, Japan, China and Brazil. Significantly, even the US Securities and Exchange Commission (SEC) has allowed non-US companies to issue financial statements in the United States without having to reconcile these financial statements to US GAAP (as reported in an IASB press release on 15 November 2007; see the IASB website).

The FASB is also subject to the directions of the SEC in the United States. In November 2008, the SEC proposed a 'roadmap' to evaluating the further role of IFRSs in the US capital markets. The roadmap proposed that the SEC could be in a position in 2011 to decide whether to require the use of IFRSs by US companies beginning in 2014. This followed requests by the leaders of the Group of Twenty nations (G20) that international accounting bodies redouble their efforts to achieve a single set of high-quality, global accounting standards through their independent standard-setting processes and complete their convergence project in June 2011. The FASB and IASB in June 2010 (see the FASB and IASB websites) reaffirmed their commitment to improving and converging their respective accounting standards.

The Asian-Oceanian Standard-Setters Group (AOSSG)

A further development towards the establishment of global accounting standards came in November 2009 when the Asian-Oceanian Standard-Setters Group (AOSSG) was formed. Initiated by China, Japan and Korea, the AOSSG was formed by a group of 21 standard-setting bodies which adopted a memorandum of understanding with the aim of taking agreed views to the IASB. As reported in 'New regional clout' (*InTheBlack* 2010), the memorandum specified the following objectives:

- promoting the adoption of and convergence with IFRS by jurisdictions in the region
- promoting consistent application of IFRS in the region
- coordinating input from the region to the technical activities of the IASB
- cooperating with governments and regulators and other regional and international organisations to improve the quality of financial reporting.

There was a feeling among members that the IASB was too influenced by the developed countries of Europe and the United States in the standard-setting process. The AOSSG is seen as an important new group which will influence the IASB to consider the issues of the Asia–Oceania region in the standard-setting process. With the growth of market economies in this region, the AOSSG will develop as an important influential voice in the future. Included in the inaugural 21 members of the AOSSG are not only the initiators, China, Japan and Korea, but also Australia, New Zealand, Indonesia, Malaysia, Singapore, Thailand, India, Sri Lanka, Saudi Arabia, Turkey and others.

As a result of the move towards global accounting standards, the standard-setting process around the world has been largely removed from national standard setters (such as the AASB in Australia) and is currently in the hands of the IASB, with significant influence from the FASB. Australia's AASB now has the role of adopting standards issued by the IASB, with minimal input to the development of such standards.

For further information, visit the various websites of the organisations involved in accounting regulation:

- Australian Accounting Standards Board: www.aasb.com.au
- International Accounting Standards Board: www.ifrs.org
- Financial Accounting Standards Board: www.fasb.org
- Australian Securities and Investments Commission: www.asic.gov.au
- Group of 100 Inc.: www.group100.com.au
- Australian Securities Exchange Ltd. www.asx.com.au
- Asian-Oceanian Standard-Setters Group: www.aossg.org

BUSINESS KNOWLEDGE

Convergence or adoption: resistance is futile

The International Accounting Standards Board (IASB), comprised of leading international thinkers on accounting theory and practice, has developed a single set of quality accounting standards called the IFRS, and countries are converting en masse to IFRS as their local generally accepted accounting principles (GAAP).

The intention of the IASB isn't to encourage hundreds of different local GAAPs to slowly morph into the IFRS, as the term 'global convergence' would imply. You either use IFRS as developed by the IASB, or you do not. So perhaps it's time to give up the term 'convergence', for a clearer way of saying that, although still evolving, the IFRS exist, and are indeed world GAAP.

Secondly, there is an underlying assumption in the US that 'convergence' means that the Financial Accounting Standards Board (FASB) is working towards moving the IFRS in the direction of US GAAP. The FASB and IASB are working together to bring the best possible insight to the IFRS through several 'convergence projects'.

However, this doesn't necessarily mean that the IFRS are eventually going to look more and more like US GAAP. FASB

chairman Bob Herz is firmly behind principles-based standards, and for all intents and purposes the FASB and IASB are behaving as one board, moving towards the goal of, as Herz calls it, 'a one-GAAP world'.

Semantics aside, how is it that Australia, Canada, Japan, China and the whole of Europe have either converted or are converting to IFRS now, while the US is still focusing on the outcome of a 'convergence' process?

Some observers as well as the US regulatory community have expressed concerns that if the US adopts the IFRS as they currently sit, the convergence projects of the FASB and IASB could come to a halt, leaving the US with an IASB-only solution to some pressing issues . . .

Such a scenario could only take place if the FASB somehow immediately loses interest in developing one set of global standards. Or the IASB will say, 'Now that you've adopted IFRS America, I think we'll take it from here'. The likelihood of either of those things happening is zero to none.

Source: Excerpts from Ramona Dzinkowski, 'Resistance is futile', *InTheBlack.*

Learning objective 2

Explain the nature of the *Conceptual Framework for Financial Reporting*, and the history of the development of the framework

17.2 The *Conceptual Framework*

Business managers, investors, creditors, government boards and agencies, and other outside parties use accounting information to make decisions concerning the allocation of scarce resources. These decisions have a significant effect on the whole of society since they affect the form and direction of the economy. The effectiveness of decision makers is enhanced if they have information that has several important characteristics. For example, is the information relevant for economic decision making? Do the users find the information about the entity understandable and comparable with previous periods as well as with other entities? Accountants need a framework or a theory to guide them in developing accounting standards for preparing financial statements and reports that contain information exhibiting important characteristics such as relevance, understandability and comparability.

Considerable emphasis has been given in the last 50 years to the development of accounting standards governing accounting and reporting practices used in preparing an entity's financial statements and reports. Until 1984, the development of these standards in Australia was chiefly in the hands of the accounting profession. However, since accounting standards have an impact on the decisions made by society as a whole, the task of issuing accounting standards for companies (and other entities) is now vested in the AASB, a government body, which has adopted accounting standards issued by the IASB.

Accounting standards are continually being reviewed and revised to keep up with the increasing complexity of economic activity, both in Australia and at international levels. Accounting standards are not fundamental natural laws like those of the physical sciences; they are requirements that attain their status through consensus among the accounting profession, government, preparers of financial reports (e.g. companies), user groups and other interested parties internationally. Sometimes, this consensus does not come easily, but is achieved through political compromise.

Given the increased regulation of the standard-setting process and the proliferation of standards, the need for an underlying theory or framework became evident. In order to provide a conceptual basis for the development of accounting standards, the AASB, along with similar developments at the FASB in the United States and at the IASB, worked towards the development of a conceptual framework for financial reporting. This development arose because accounting standards in the past were established on a problem-by-problem basis; and this basis was leading to inconsistent rules and regulations over time. It was hoped that development of a conceptual framework for financial reporting would enable regulators to:

- develop standards that were consistent and logically formulated
- provide guidance to accountants in areas where no standards exist
- enable users of financial reports to understand better the standards developed.

In essence, the conceptual framework project is an attempt to derive a theory for determining the information to be provided in financial reports.

Background to development of the *Conceptual Framework*

In developing the conceptual framework for financial reporting, there have been a number of important steps taken by the AASB in the Australian context. Step 1 was to delineate the boundaries of financial reporting in that the conceptual framework was to deal only with *general purpose* financial reporting (as explained later on pages 714–6). Step 2 was to define the reporting entity. This second step established the criteria by which a reporting entity is recognised to exist, in order to determine which entities should prepare general purpose financial reports. Step 3 was to establish the objectives of general purpose financial reporting. This step also identified the users of financial reports, their information needs, and the types of reports which best meet those needs.

Step 4 used the broad framework established in the first three steps to develop the qualitative characteristics of financial information (relevance etc.), the elements of the reporting processes (e.g. assets, liabilities, equities, income, expenses), and recognition and measurement of those elements.

The AASB developed four statements of accounting concepts (SACs) in the 1990s, namely:

- SAC 1 *Definition of the Reporting Entity* (issued 1990)
- SAC 2 *Objective of General Purpose Financial Reporting* (issued 1990)
- SAC 3 *Qualitative Characteristics of Financial Information* (issued 1990, withdrawn 2005)
- SAC 4 *Definition and Recognition of the Elements of Financial Statements* (issued 1992, withdrawn and reissued 1995, withdrawn 2005).

However, the AASB was not the only national standard setter to develop a conceptual framework for general purpose financial reporting. The FASB in the United States and other standard setters in Canada, New Zealand and South Africa, as well as the IASB, also devoted considerable resources to establishing such frameworks for their own use. There were several similarities and differences among the frameworks as developed by the AASB, the FASB and the IASB, which have contributed towards many similarities and differences among the accounting standards developed by these bodies.

Australia's adoption in 2005 of the IASB's international accounting standards meant that the AASB also rejected part of its own framework (namely SAC 3 and SAC 4) and adopted the IASB's *Framework for the Preparation and Presentation of Financial Statements*. In September 2010, the IASB reissued its framework document under the title *The Conceptual Framework for Financial Reporting* (the *Conceptual Framework*), following consultation with the FASB. Nevertheless, the AASB has retained both SAC 1 and SAC 2 for use in the Australian context, as these documents provide considerably more detail about the reporting entity concept and wider objectives than is evident in the *Conceptual Framework*. It is expected that, when the IASB makes further revisions to its framework in the future in cooperation with the FASB, these revisions will be adopted in Australia. This will lead eventually to the AASB also rejecting SAC 1 and SAC 2. In the following sections, we discuss the basic content of SACs 1 and 2 and the qualitative characteristics and elements as specified in the IASB's *Conceptual Framework*.

Proposed additional changes to the *Conceptual Framework* as a result of the IASB's joint project with the FASB are also referred to in this chapter. The overall objective of this joint project between the FASB and the IASB is to develop a common framework that is both complete and internally consistent. The boards want to develop a framework that will provide a sound foundation for developing future accounting standards that are principles based, internally consistent, internationally converged, and lead to financial reporting that provides the information needed for investment, credit and similar decisions. That framework, which will deal with a wide range of issues, will build on the existing IASB and FASB frameworks and consider developments since the boards issued their original framework documents.

17.3 The reporting entity

Learning objective 3

Describe the nature of a reporting entity under the *Conceptual Framework*

Questions have arisen in the past as to which entities need to publish financial reports and which do not. The purpose of SAC 1 *Definition of the Reporting Entity* is to define and explain the concept of a **reporting entity**, and to establish a benchmark for the minimum required quality for financial reporting by such an entity. A reporting entity is defined in SAC 1 as an entity in which it is reasonable to expect the existence of users who depend on general purpose financial reports for information to enable them to make and evaluate economic decisions. SAC 1 suggests a number of indicators to help assess when dependent users exist and hence when an entity is a reporting entity:

1. *Separation of management from economic interest.* The greater the spread of ownership and the greater the extent of the separation between management and owners, the more likely it is that there will be users who depend on general purpose financial reports for decision making.
2. *Economic or political importance/influence.* The greater the economic or political importance or influence of an entity, the more likely it is that dependent users will exist.
3. *Financial characteristics.* The larger the size of an entity, or the greater the indebtedness of or resources allocated to an entity, the more likely it is that users who depend on general purpose financial reports will exist.

The implications of these indicators are that judgement is necessary in distinguishing reporting entities from non-reporting entities. Nevertheless, it is expected that reporting entities include most government departments, statutory authorities and boards, most public companies, some large proprietary companies and listed investment trusts. Non-reporting entities include most sole traders, partnerships and small proprietary companies. Nevertheless, there will be exceptions to these generalities based on a consideration of the indicators.

The reporting entity concept in SAC 1 has been included in Australian accounting standards, for example AASB 1053 *Application of Tiers of Australian Accounting Standards;* hence, it has become a definition which must be applied in practice. Reporting entities are therefore required to prepare general purpose financial statements that comply with the accounting standards and interpretations issued and adopted by the AASB. However, applying the reporting entity concept has become a problem for some because of the qualitative nature of the criteria. Some people in business prefer that a reporting entity is determined by applying a quantitative test such as 'does the entity have annual income greater than (say) $25 million, and assets greater than $12.5 million?' Such quantitative criteria are easy to apply but also potentially easy to avoid, as entities have incentives not to prepare financial reports consistent with accounting standards because of the potential costs involved in doing so. Others believe that the reporting entity concept is working well in the Australian business environment.

In 2007, debate arose as to whether the AASB should abandon the reporting entity concept specified in SAC 1. This followed the release of the IASB's Exposure Draft of a proposed IFRS for small and medium-sized entities (SMEs), published in February 2007, a document subsequently issued in 2009 by the IASB as *International Financial Reporting Standards for Small and Medium-sized Entities (IFRS for SMEs).* In May 2007, based on the IASB's 2007 Exposure Draft, the AASB issued Invitation to Comment ITC 12, proposing to revise the differential reporting regime in Australia by switching the focus away from whether an entity is or is not a reporting entity to whether the entity (subject to a size test) is required to prepare a general purpose financial report and is publicly accountable. **Public accountability** is defined in the IASB's *IFRS for SMEs* as:

> Accountability to those existing and potential resource providers and others external to the entity who make economic decisions but are not in a position to demand reports tailored to meet their particular information needs. An entity has public accountability if:
> (a) its debt or equity instruments are traded in a public market or it is in the process of issuing such instruments for trading in a public market (a domestic or foreign stock exchange or an over-the-counter market, including local and regional markets), or
> (b) it holds assets in a fiduciary capacity for a broad group of outsiders as one of its primary businesses. This is typically the case for banks, credit unions, insurance companies, securities brokers/dealers, mutual funds and investment banks.

The proposed implications of ITC 12 were that if an entity was publicly accountable or satisfied a size test, then it would be required to apply Australian equivalents to IFRSs in its general purpose financial reports. If an entity was not publicly accountable, or did not meet the size test, then the entity needed to apply the Australian equivalents to the IFRS for SMEs only. Figure 17.3 is a flowchart showing the changes as proposed by ITC 12.

At the time of writing, the AASB had received negative comments on the proposals in ITC 12, particularly in relation to application of the size test, which was seen as arbitrary, and the fact that the public accountability test would appear to apply to all public sector entities irrespective of size. Hence, the AASB has tackled the problem differently by issuing AASB 1053 *Application of Tiers of Australian Accounting Standards* in June 2010, which has adopted a Tier 1 and Tier 2 system of financial reporting, to be applied on or after 1 July 2013. When preparing general purpose financial statements, those entities in Tier 1 shall apply full IFRSs as adopted in Australia, and those in Tier 2 can adopt Reduced Disclosure Requirements (RDRs). The RDRs involve compliance with the recognition and measurement requirements of IFRSs, as already adopted in Australia, but with disclosures substantially reduced compared with those that would be required under full IFRSs. Figure 17.4 illustrates the key elements of the standard.

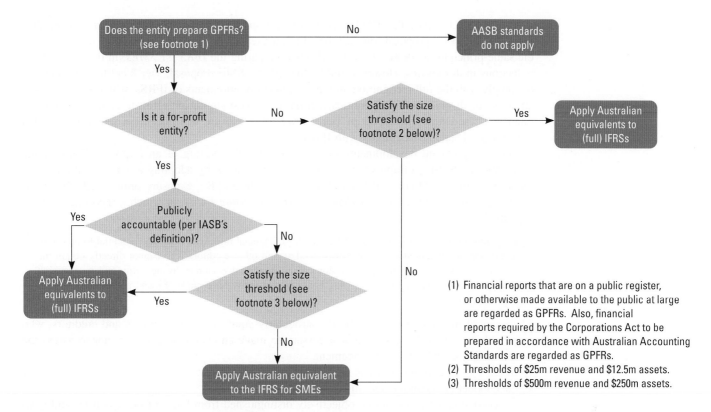

Figure 17.3 Proposed differential reporting regime

Source: Australian Accounting Standards Board, 2007, Invitation to Comment ITC 12, Request for Comment on a Proposed Revised Differential Reporting Regime for Australia and IASB *Exposure Draft of A Proposed IFRS for Small and Medium-sized Entities*, May, Appendix 1 to Preface, p. xxviii.

	Sector		
	For-profit private	**Not-for profit private**	**For-profit and not-for-profit public**
Tier 1 Full IFRSs as adopted in Australia	Publicly accountable (per IASB definition)		Federal, State and Territory Governments, Local Governments, and Universities
Tier 2 Reduced Disclosure Requirements	Non-publicly accountable unless, they elect to apply Tier 1	All NFP private sector entities apply Tier 2 requirements, unless the relevant regulator requires application of Tier 1	Entities other than Tier 1 entities above, unless the relevant regulator requires application of Tier 1, e.g. if AASB 1049 *Whole of government and General Government Sector Financial Reporting* applies

Figure 17.4 Tiers 1 and 2 differential reporting requirements

Source: Adapted from AASB, 'ED 192 *Revised Differential Reporting Framework*', as amended by 'AASB 1053 *Application of Tiers of Australian Accounting Standards*', www.aasb.com.au.

The AASB believes the RDRs are more appropriate for the Australian environment than the *IFRS for SMEs* proposal, on cost–benefit and user needs grounds. In essence, the RDRs use the same principles as those of the IASB when preparing the *IFRS for SMEs*, in determining the reductions in disclosures. However, unlike the IASB's SME proposal, Tier 2 entities are required to comply with the full recognition and measurement requirements of IFRSs, which is expected to attract some disquiet as Tier 2 entities will have to invest significant effort to achieve such compliance. Those entities which adopt Tier 2 levels of disclosure will not be permitted to state that their financial statements comply with IFRSs.

Further significant developments in 2010 included the issuing of an Exposure Draft by the IASB and the FASB to improve the *Conceptual Framework* by adopting a new definition of the reporting entity. In March 2010, the AASB issued the IASB's exposure draft as ED 193 *Conceptual Framework for Financial Reporting: The Reporting Entity*, in which a reporting entity is described as:

> a circumscribed area of economic activities whose financial information has the potential to be useful to existing and potential equity investors, lenders and other creditors who cannot directly obtain the information they need in making decisions about providing resources to the entity and in assessing whether management and the governing board of that entity have made efficient and effective use of the resources provided.

The focus of this definition is on users, particularly equity investors, lenders and creditors, who are unable to obtain the information necessary to make an economic decision, nor to assess the accountability of the entity's management.

In ED 193, a reporting entity is seen as having three features:
1. the conduct of economic activities;
2. the economic activities can be objectively distinguished from those of other entities and from the economic environment in which the entity exists; and
3. financial information about those economic activities is potentially useful in making economic decisions and in assessing whether the management have made efficient and effective use of the resources provided.

ED 193 also makes the point that these features are necessary — but not always sufficient — to identify a reporting entity. It states that the existence of a legal entity is neither necessary nor sufficient to identify a reporting entity. Even though a single legal entity is likely to qualify as being a reporting entity, a reporting entity can include more than one entity, or it can be a portion of a single entity, e.g. a branch or division of an entity.

The AASB, however, is responsible for setting standards and developing a conceptual framework not only for the private sector but also for the public and not-for-profit sectors, and ED 193 is directed only at the private sector. In its request for comments on ED 193, the AASB argues that, once the IASB has completed its project on the reporting entity, the AASB will then consider whether the reporting entity concept should apply only to Australian for-profit entities, with the potential of retaining the existing AASB *Framework* for not-for-profit entities, as an interim measure until pronouncements on other types of entities are made at an international level. In the meantime, AASB 1053, which has adopted Tier 1 and Tier 2 differential reporting requirements and the SAC 1 definition of the reporting entity, will apply.

Learning objective 4

Describe the objectives of general purpose financial reporting under the *Conceptual Framework*

17.4 Objectives of general purpose financial reporting

In addition to the reporting entity concept, another important step in developing the *Conceptual Framework* was to determine the objective of financial reporting. The IASB's *Conceptual Framework* and SAC 2 deal only with the objective of **general purpose financial reports**. There is no clear definition of general purpose financial reports in the IASB's *Conceptual Framework*. It does state, however, that general purpose financial reports are those on which existing and potential investors, lenders and other creditors must rely for much of the financial information they need, as they cannot require reporting entities to provide information directly to them. The primary users of general purpose financial reports are existing and potential investors and creditors.

On the other hand, SAC 2 defines general purpose financial reports as those intended to meet the information needs common to a range of users who are unable to command the preparation of reports tailored to meet their own particular needs. The SAC 2 definition implies that general purpose financial reports will satisfy users' needs, but this is not the case. The IASB's *Conceptual Framework* points out that general purpose financial reports do not and cannot provide all of the information needs of users. Users must consider pertinent information from other sources, e.g. general economic conditions and expectations, political events and political climate, and industry and company outlooks. Also, general purpose financial reports are not designed to show the value of a reporting entity, but they do provide information to help the primary users estimate the value of the reporting entity.

In 2010, both the IASB and the FASB amended the *Conceptual Framework* to specify the objective of general purpose financial reporting. The objective is contained in paragraph OB2 of the IASB's *Conceptual Framework*:

> to provide financial information about the reporting entity that is useful to present and potential equity investors, lenders and other creditors in making decisions about providing resources to the entity. Those decisions involve buying, selling or holding equity and debt instruments, and providing or settling loans and other forms of credit.

The boards have adopted the 'entity perspective', which is intended to convey that an entity — not its owners and others having an interest in the entity — is the object of general purpose financial reporting. In other words, the focus is placed on reporting the entity's resources (assets), the claims to the entity's resources (liabilities and equity) and the changes in them. Shareholders are seen not so much as owners of the entity but merely as providers of resources to the entity, in much the same way as lenders and other creditors. Both present and potential equity investors and creditors are seen as constituting the single primary user group. Other potential user groups, e.g. government and other regulatory bodies, customers, employees and their representatives, are not the focus of the IASB and FASB's objective. The *Conceptual Framework* states that other parties, such as regulators and members of the public other than investors, lenders and other creditors, may also find general purpose financial reports useful; however, such reports are not primarily directed to these other groups.

The IASB's direction towards a primary user group poses a problem for the AASB, which is required to develop accounting standards not only for the private sector, but also for the public and not-for-profit sectors. Hence, the IASB's narrow focus on serving the needs of present and potential equity investors, lenders and other creditors is not satisfactory for the AASB, and the AASB will be required to maintain aspects of SAC 2. At the time of writing, SAC 2 divides primary users of general purpose financial reports into three categories:

1. *Resource providers.* This category includes employees, lenders, creditors, suppliers and investors. In the case of non-business entities, the category includes donors, members of clubs, taxpayers and ratepayers.
2. *Recipients or consumers of goods and services,* i.e. customers, beneficiaries, taxpayers and ratepayers.
3. *Parties performing a review or overseeing function.* These include parliaments, governments, regulatory agencies, labour unions, employer groups, media, and special-interest community groups, e.g. environmental and conservation groups.

According to SAC 2, the main objective of general purpose financial reporting is to provide information useful to users for making and evaluating decisions on the allocation of scarce resources. A secondary objective is that the reports should be presented by management and governing bodies in such a manner as to discharge their 'accountability' for the resources entrusted to them. This objective is often referred to as one of reporting on the results of 'stewardship'.

The objective of accountability and/or stewardship, contained in SAC 2, is deliberately de-emphasised in the IASB's *Conceptual Framework*. This is unfortunate. In these times when environmental and social issues are of greater importance to society, and there is greater desire for sustainability reporting, why have these issues been ignored in the IASB's revised *Conceptual Framework*?

Regarding the types of information to be included in general purpose financial reports, the IASB's *Conceptual Framework* argues that the reports should provide information about the financial position of a reporting entity, which is information about the entity's economic resources and the claims against the reporting entity. The financial reports also provide information about the effects of transactions and other events that change a reporting entity's economic resources and claims. The *Conceptual Framework* argues that information about the nature and amounts of a reporting entity's economic resources and claims can help users to assess the entity's liquidity and solvency, its needs for additional financing, and how successful it is likely to be in obtaining that financing.

Information about a reporting entity's **performance** (in financial terms) is also useful. It helps users to understand the return that the entity has produced on its economic resources. Such information provides an indication as to how well management has discharged its responsibilities to make efficient and effective use of the reporting entity's resources. Information about a reporting entity's past financial performance and how its management discharged its responsibilities is usually helpful in predicting the entity's future returns on its economic resources and future cash flows. SAC 2 further argues that aspects of an entity's performance can be measured in financial and non-financial terms.

Before the objective of general purpose financial reporting can be implemented in practice, there is a need also to specify the basic qualitative characteristics that financial information should have. It is necessary to define as well the basic elements, e.g. assets, liabilities, equity, income and expenses, used in financial statements. Hence, these aspects of the *Conceptual Framework* are considered below.

Learning objective 5

Identify the qualitative characteristics for the selection and presentation of financial information

17.5 Qualitative characteristics of financial information

What characteristics should financial information have in order to be included in general purpose financial reports? The IASB's *Conceptual Framework* asserts that there are six main qualitative characteristics that financial information should have in order to be the subject matter of general purpose financial reports: *relevance*, *faithful representation*, *comparability*, *verifiability*, *timeliness* and *understandability*. Relevance and faithful representation are distinguished as 'fundamental' qualitative characteristics, and the others are viewed as 'enhancing' qualitative characteristics. The *Conceptual Framework* also specifies that there is a constraint on financial reporting, namely a *cost constraint*. The qualitative characteristics of financial information as contained in the *Conceptual Framework* can be expressed diagrammatically as shown in figure 17.5.

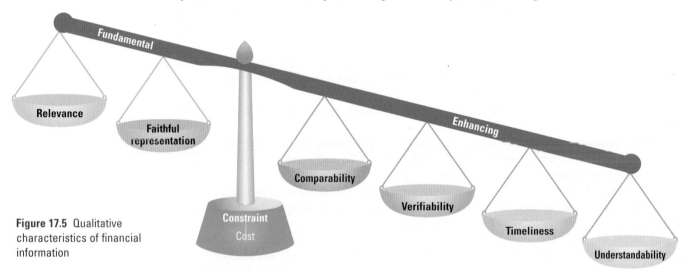

Figure 17.5 Qualitative characteristics of financial information

Fundamental characteristics

Relevance

To have **relevance**, financial information must have a quality which makes a difference in a decision of an economic nature made by users. Information may be capable of making a difference in a decision even if some users choose not to take advantage of it or are already aware of it from other sources. Information is relevant to a decision if it helps users to form predictions about the outcomes of past, present or future events, and/or confirms or changes their previous evaluations by providing suitable feedback. In other words, for information to be relevant, it must have *predictive value* and/or have *confirmatory value*. Note that having predictive value does not mean that the financial information must be in the form of an explicit forecast or budget. The *Conceptual Framework* provides an example of predictive and confirmatory values in that revenue information for the current year can be used as the basis for predicting revenues in future years, and can also be compared with past years' revenue predictions for the current year. The results of these comparisons can help a user to correct and improve the processes that were used to make those previous predictions.

Thus, relevant information about financial position and past performance is often used as the basis for predicting future financial position and performance and other matters in which users are directly interested, such as future dividends and wage payments, future share prices, and the ability of the reporting entity to pay its debts when they fall due. The predictive ability of information may be improved if unusual or infrequent transactions and events are reported separately in the financial reports.

Another aspect of relevance in the context of each specific entity is the **materiality** of the items reported by that entity. In some cases, the nature of the information alone is enough to determine its relevance, such as money lost through embezzlement by staff. In other cases, both the nature and magnitude are important. The *Conceptual Framework* states that information is material if omitting it or misstating it could influence decisions that users make on the basis of financial information about a specific reporting entity. AASB 1031 *Materiality* adds, in addition to omission and misstatement, that information may be material if its non-disclosure, i.e. it is not disclosed separately, has the potential to affect adversely the users' decisions, or the rendering of accountability by preparers. Any assessment of materiality needs to be made in relation not only to individual items but also to classes of similar items. For instance, errors in individual items may be immaterial by themselves, but material in aggregate. A practical aspect to materiality is the immediate expensing of small costs incurred for the purchase of assets on the grounds that the amount paid is not significant enough to affect decisions. Small expenditures for non-current assets, it is usual, are often expensed immediately, rather than depreciated over their useful lives, to save clerical costs of recording depreciation, and because the effects on performance and financial position measures over their useful lives are not large enough to affect decisions. Another example of the application of materiality is the common practice by large companies of rounding amounts to the nearest thousand dollars in their financial statements.

Materiality is a relative matter. What is material for one entity may be immaterial for another. A $100 000 error in the financial statements of a multimillion-dollar company may not be important, but it may be critical to a small business. The materiality of an item may depend not only on its relative size but also on its nature. For example, the discovery of a $10 000 bribe is a material event even for a large company. Judgements as to the materiality of an item or event are often difficult. Accountants make judgements based on their knowledge of the company and on past experience, and users of financial statements must generally rely on the accountants' judgements.

It is argued in the *Conceptual Framework* that materiality is an entity-specific matter and is therefore not a primary qualitative characteristic which information must have if it is to be useful. Materiality provides a threshold or cut-off point in determining whether information is relevant for inclusion in financial reports.

Faithful representation

According to the *Conceptual Framework*, for relevant information to be useful for the primary user group in making resource allocation decisions, the information reported must be a **faithful representation** of the real-world economic phenomena that it purports to represent. For a complete faithful representation, information must be *complete, neutral* and *free from material error.* Of course, perfection is seldom, if ever, achievable. The objective, therefore, is to maximise those qualities to the extent possible.

A *complete,* faithful representation of an item or event includes all necessary descriptions and explanations. For example, a complete depiction of an entity's assets would include, as a minimum, a description of the nature of the assets, a numerical amount for all of the assets, and a description of what the numerical amount represents (e.g. is the amount based on original cost, adjusted cost or fair value?). For some items, a complete faithful representation may also entail explanations of significant facts about the quality and nature of the items, factors and circumstances that might affect their quality and nature, and the process used to determine the numerical depiction.

According to the *Conceptual Framework*, information is *neutral* if it is determined without bias in its selection or presentation. A neutral representation of an item is not slanted, weighted, emphasised, de-emphasised or otherwise manipulated to increase the probability that the information will be received favourably or unfavourably by users. Neutral information does not mean information with no purpose or no influence on behaviour. On the contrary, relevant financial information is, by definition, capable of making a difference in users' decisions.

Freedom from material error in the *Conceptual Framework* does not mean the total absence of errors in the depiction of economic events, because economic events presented in financial reports are generally measured under conditions of uncertainty, and judgements are necessary. Freedom from material error means there are no errors or omissions in the 'description' of the item or event, and in the 'process' used to produce the information reported. To illustrate, it is not known whether an estimate of a price or value which cannot be observed in the marketplace is accurate or inaccurate. However, a representation of that estimate can be faithful if the amount is 'described' clearly and accurately as being an estimate, the nature and limitations of the estimating 'process' are explained, and no errors have been made in selecting and applying the process to determine the estimate.

To sum up, a faithful representation of an economic event must reflect the best available estimate of the real-world phenomenon being depicted. Completeness and neutrality of estimates are desirable, and the absence of material errors is also necessary for estimates to be faithful representations of economic events. Thus, adequate descriptions of the economic events, and disclosure of the processes used in handling uncertainty in measurement, are required.

In applying the fundamental qualitative characteristics, information must be both relevant and faithfully represented if it is to be useful. A faithful representation of an irrelevant transaction or event, or an unfaithful representation of a relevant transaction or event, does not help users make good decisions. According to the *Conceptual Framework*, the best process for applying the fundamental qualitative characteristics is usually as follows:

1. Identify an economic phenomenon that has the potential to be useful to users of the reporting entity's financial information.
2. Identify the type of information about that phenomenon that would be most relevant if it is available and can be faithfully represented.
3. Determine whether that information is available and can be faithfully represented. If so, the process of satisfying the fundamental qualitative characteristics ends at that point. If not, the process is repeated with the next most relevant type of information.

Somewhat surprisingly, there is no discussion in the IASB's *Conceptual Framework* about the importance of focusing on the economic substance of a transaction or event, rather than its legal form, when selecting information to be reported in general purpose financial reports. Furthermore, the concept of *prudence*, which is explained in terms of a desire to exercise care and caution when dealing with uncertainties in the measurement process, has been excluded from the *Conceptual Framework*.

Enhancing qualitative characteristics

According to the IASB's *Conceptual Framework*, *comparability*, *verifiability*, *timeliness* and *understandability* are qualitative characteristics that enhance the usefulness of information that is relevant and faithfully represented.

Comparability

Making a decision involves choosing between alternatives, e.g. selling or holding shares, or buying shares in one reporting entity as opposed to another. Consequently, the *Conceptual Framework* argues that information about a reporting entity is more useful if it can be compared with similar information about other entities and with similar information about the same entity for another period or another date. **Comparability** is the qualitative characteristic that enables users to identify and understand similarities in, and differences among, items. Unlike the other qualitative characteristics, comparability does not relate to a single item. A comparison requires at least two items.

Comparability is more effective when different entities use the same accounting practices. An important implication of the qualitative characteristic of comparability is that users will be informed of the accounting policies used in the preparation of the general purpose financial report, plus any changes to those policies and the effect of those changes. This implies the measurement and reporting of transactions and events with **consistency** over time and between entities. Consistency, although related to comparability, is not the same. Consistency refers to the use of the same methods for the same items, either from period to period within a reporting entity or in a single period across entities. Comparability is the goal; consistency helps to achieve that goal.

Alternative accounting practices and policies exist in the treatment of many items, such as inventories and cost of sales, non-current assets and depreciation, and intangible assets such as patents and copyrights. The standard setters have expressed their position regarding the consistency of accounting methods in accounting standard IAS 8/AASB 108 *Accounting Policies, Changes in Accounting Estimates and Errors*, which states that an entity must select and apply its accounting policies in a consistent manner from one period to another. Consistency of practices between entities is also desired. Any change made in an accounting policy by an entity must be disclosed by stating the nature of the change, the reasons the change provides reliable and more relevant information, and the effect of the change in monetary terms on each financial statement item affected. For example, a change in policies may be disclosed in a footnote such as this:

> During the year, the company changed from the first-in first-out to the weighted average cost method of accounting for inventory because the weighted average cost method provides a more relevant measure of the entity's financial performance. The effect of this change was to increase cost of sales by $460 000 for the current financial year.

Note that the need for consistency does not require a given accounting method to be applied throughout the entity. An entity may very well use different inventory methods for different types of inventory and different depreciation methods for different kinds of non-current assets. (Different inventory costing and depreciation methods are discussed in later chapters.) Furthermore, the need for consistency should not be allowed to become an impediment to better accounting. Consistency from year to year or entity to entity is not an end in itself, but a means for achieving greater comparability in the presentation of information in general purpose financial reports.

The *Conceptual Framework* also points out that the need for comparability should not be confused with uniformity. For information to be comparable, like things must look alike and different things must look different. Comparability of financial information is not enhanced by making unlike things look alike; nor is it enhanced by making like things look different. It is not appropriate for an entity to continue to apply an accounting policy if the policy is not in keeping with the qualitative characteristics of relevance and faithful representation.

Verifiability

According to the IASB's *Conceptual Framework,* verifiability helps assure users that information faithfully represents the economic phenomena it purports to represent. **Verifiability** means that different knowledgeable and independent observers could reach consensus, although not necessarily complete agreement, that a particular piece of information is a faithful representation of the economic phenomena. Numeric information need not be a single point estimate to be verifiable. A range of possible amounts and the related probabilities can also be verified.

The *Conceptual Framework* states that verification can be direct or indirect. Direct verification means verifying an amount or other representation through direct observation, e.g. by counting cash. Indirect verification means checking the inputs to a model, formula or other technique and recalculating the outputs using the same methodology. An example is verifying the carrying amount of inventory by checking the inputs (quantities and costs) and recalculating the ending inventory using the same cost flow assumption (e.g. using the first-in, first-out method).

The characteristic of verifiability has the consequence that an entity's future budgets are not disclosed in general purpose financial reports. It may not be possible to verify forward-looking financial information until a future period, if at all.

Timeliness

Timeliness simply means having information available to decision makers in time to be capable of influencing their decisions. Having relevant information available sooner than later can enhance its capacity to influence decisions, and a lack of timeliness can rob information of its potential usefulness. Generally, the older the information is the less useful it is. However, some information may continue to be timely long after the end of a reporting period because decision makers may need to establish trends in the data.

The need for timely reporting raises a question about the frequency of reports (yearly? half-yearly? quarterly? monthly?) and also the length of time that can be allowed between the reporting date and the publication of general purpose financial reports for users. Any delays in publication cause the information in these reports to be less relevant.

Understandability

When information is included in general purpose financial reports, there is an obvious need for the users of those reports to be able to comprehend their meaning; hence, the *Conceptual Framework* lists the final qualitative characteristic of financial reports to be **understandability**. Understandability, however, does not necessarily imply simplicity. It is assumed that readers of reports have a reasonable knowledge of business and economic activities, and that they are willing to study the information with reasonable diligence. The *Conceptual Framework* makes it clear that information about complex matters should still be included in the report if it is considered relevant to the decision-making needs of users, even if it is too difficult for some users to understand. If users find that the information is too complex for their understanding, it is expected that they will seek professional help and advice.

The cost constraint on relevant, faithfully representative information

Reporting financial information imposes costs, and it is important that those costs are justified by the benefits of reporting that information. The cost constraint requires the costs incurred in generating information do not outweigh the benefits to be obtained from having the information. Costs could include those of collection, storage, retrieval, presentation, analysis and interpretation, and loss of competitive position, most of which are incurred by the reporting entity. Nevertheless, these costs will generally flow in a number of direct and indirect ways to other parties, e.g. consumers. The benefits are enjoyed directly by parties external to the entity, namely shareholders, investors and creditors. There is little chance that the costs of preparation will be borne ultimately by all of those parties who enjoy the benefits.

The cost constraint is applied by standard setters when developing a proposed financial reporting standard. Unfortunately, determining expected costs and benefits is inherently subjective, as different individuals' assessments of the costs and benefits of reporting particular items of financial information will vary. Hence, standard setters have been prepared to adopt differential reporting, namely different levels of reporting requirements for different entities. Differential reporting requirements feature in current accounting standards; such standards apply mainly to those entities classified as reporting entities. In the case of external reporting by companies, accounting standards apply mainly to public companies and to large proprietary companies. In Australia, many small to medium-sized entities must also follow the recognition and measurement requirements of accounting standards, but are able to apply reduced disclosure requirements in accordance with AASB 1053 *Application of Tiers of Australian Accounting Standards*.

Learning objective 6

Define assets, liabilities, equity, income and expenses, as established under the *Conceptual Framework*

17.6 Definitions of elements in financial statements

The *Conceptual Framework* provides definitions of important elements underlying general purpose financial reports, namely assets, liabilities, equity, income and expenses. So far in this book, the definitions of these terms have been simplified. Here, we will expand our discussion of the terms in order to provide a greater appreciation of the issues considered in the *Conceptual Framework*.

Assets in the current *Conceptual Framework*

An **asset** is defined in the current *Conceptual Framework* as 'a resource controlled by the entity as a result of past events and from which future economic benefits are expected to flow to the entity'.

This definition identifies three essential characteristics:

1. The resource must contain future economic benefits, i.e. it must have the potential to contribute, directly or indirectly, to the flow of cash and cash equivalents to the entity. An asset can cause future economic benefits to flow to the entity in a number of ways:
   - it can be exchanged for another asset
   - it can be used to settle a liability
   - it can be used singly or in combination with other assets to produce goods or services to be sold by the entity.
2. The entity must have **control** over the resource in such a way that the entity has the capacity to benefit economically from the asset in the pursuit of the entity's objectives, and can deny or regulate the access of others to those economic benefits.
3. The event or events giving rise to the entity's control over the resource must have occurred.

An asset may have other characteristics, but the *Conceptual Framework* does not consider them essential for an asset to exist. For instance, assets are normally acquired at a cost incurred by the entity, but it is not essential that a cost is incurred in order to determine the existence of an asset. Similarly, it is not essential that an asset is tangible, as many assets (e.g. receivables, copyrights, patents) represent future economic benefits without the existence of any physical substance. Furthermore, assets can be exchanged normally for other assets, but this does not make exchangeability an essential characteristic of an asset. Finally, it is not essential that an asset is legally owned by the reporting entity. Control by the entity often results from legal ownership, but the absence of legal rights or ownership does not preclude the existence of control, e.g. a lease.

For an entity to have an asset, it must control the asset (as discussed in point 2 above). Mere possession of an asset is not enough. Agents who hold goods received on consignment cannot treat the goods as their own asset because they do not have control.

Assets in the proposed framework

Following discussions between the IASB and the FASB, several shortcomings were identified with the existing definition of an asset:

- The existing definition focuses on identifying future economic benefits, whereas it is believed that the focus should be on the existence of a present economic resource.
- The existing definition of 'control' has been misinterpreted and used in the same sense as control over subsidiaries for consolidation purposes. Hence, it is proposed that the new definition should focus on rights or privileged access to the economic resource.
- The focus on the existence of a past event has taken away the emphasis on whether the economic resource and rights to it exist at the end of the financial year.
- It is unclear how the existing definition applies to contractual promises.
- Any assessment of expectation or probability should be removed from the definition of an asset.

Therefore, it is proposed that the definition of an asset should be amended to the following:

An asset of an entity is a present economic resource to which the entity has a right or other access that others do not have. (FASB *Action Alert*, 20 October 2008 — updated on 15 March 2010).

This definition places emphasis not only on the existence of a present economic resource but also on the need for rights that limit the access of others to that resource. Thus, assets will be seen in future more in the context of legally enforceable rights to the resource.

Liabilities in the current *Conceptual Framework*

A **liability** is defined in the current *Conceptual Framework* as 'a present obligation of the entity arising from past events, the settlement of which is expected to result in an outflow from the entity of resources embodying economic benefits'. There are a number of important aspects concerning this definition:

- A legal debt constitutes a liability, but a liability is not restricted to being a legal debt. Its essential characteristic is the existence of a present obligation, being a duty or responsibility of the entity to act or perform in a certain way. A present obligation may arise as an obligation imposed by notions of equity or fairness (referred to as an 'equitable' obligation), and by custom or normal business practices (referred to as a 'constructive' obligation), as well as those resulting from legally enforceable contracts. For example, an entity may decide as a matter of policy to rectify faults in its products even after the warranty period has expired. Hence, the amounts that are expected to be spent in respect of goods already sold are liabilities.
- It is not sufficient for an entity merely to have an intention of sacrificing economic benefits in the future. A present obligation needs to be distinguished from a future commitment. A decision by management to buy an asset in the future does not give rise to a present obligation. An obligation normally arises when the asset is delivered, or the entity has entered into an irrevocable agreement to buy the asset, with a substantial penalty if the agreement is revoked.
- A liability must result in the giving up of resources embodying economic benefits which requires settlement in the future. The entity has little, if any, discretion in avoiding this sacrifice. This settlement in the future may be required on demand, at a specified date, or when a specified event occurs. Thus, a guarantee under a loan agreement is regarded as giving rise to a liability in that a sacrifice is required when a specified event occurs, e.g. default under the loan. Settlement of a present obligation may occur in a number of ways:
  - by paying cash
  - by transferring other assets
  - by providing services
  - by replacing that obligation with another obligation
  - by converting that obligation to equity
  - by a creditor waiving or forfeiting his or her rights.
- A final characteristic of a liability is that it must have resulted from a past transaction or event. For example, the acquisition of goods and the work done by staff give rise to accounts payable and wages payable respectively. Wages to be paid to staff for work they will do in the future is not a liability as there is no past transaction or event and no present obligation.

Liabilities in the proposed framework

In December 2007, the IASB and FASB announced (in IASB *Update*, December 2007, and FASB Project Update, 4 February 2008) that the definition of a liability should change by focusing on a liability as an enforceable 'economic obligation' or present 'economic burden' rather than an expected future sacrifice of economic benefits. The reference to past events is to be replaced by a focus on the present. The essential attributes of an enforceable obligation include the involvement of a separate party and the existence of a mechanism that is capable of forcing an entity to take a specified course of action.

At their meeting on 20 October 2008, the boards agreed that the current liability definition should be replaced by the following tentative definition:

> A *liability* of an entity is a present economic obligation for which the entity is the obligor (FASB Action Alert, 20 October 2008 — updated on 15 March 2010).

The boards also expanded on the meanings of certain terms in this definition as follows:

- *Present* means that on the date of the financial statements both the economic obligation exists and the entity is the obligor.
- An *economic obligation* is an unconditional promise or other requirement to provide or forgo economic resources, including through risk protection.
- An entity is the *obligor* if the entity is required to bear the economic obligation and its requirement to bear the economic obligation is enforceable by legal or equivalent means.

The boards agreed that the existence of a present obligation distinguishes a liability from a general risk. A present economic obligation conceptually exists when an entity is committed to a particular action(s) that is capable of resulting in an outflow of cash flows and there is a mechanism to enforce that economic obligation against the entity.

The IASB and FASB plan to develop and refine this working definition of a liability after they have considered the implications of another joint project, *Financial Instruments with Characteristics of Equity*. This project, begun in 2007, arose because of difficulties experienced by many companies in distinguishing between liabilities and equity, particularly in the context of financial instruments such as redeemable preference shares and derivatives.

Equity in the current *Conceptual Framework*

The *Conceptual Framework* defines **equity** as 'the residual interest in the assets of the entity after deducting all its liabilities'. Defining equity in this manner shows clearly that it cannot be defined independently of the other elements in the statement of financial position/balance sheet. The characteristics of equity are as follows:

- Equity is a residual, i.e. something left over. In other words:

Equity = Assets – Liabilities

- Equity increases as a result of profitable operations, i.e. the excesses of income over expenses, and by contributions by owners. Similarly, equity is diminished by unprofitable operations and by distributions to owners (drawings and dividends).
- Equity is influenced by the measurement system adopted for assets and liabilities and by the concepts of capital and capital maintenance adopted in the preparation of general purpose financial reports. (These aspects are discussed later in the chapter.)
- Equity may be subclassified in the statement of financial position/balance sheet, for example into contributed funds from owners, retained earnings, other reserves representing appropriations of retained earnings, and reserves representing capital maintenance adjustments.

At the time of writing, the IASB/FASB have not proposed a new definition of equity.

Income in the current *Conceptual Framework*

The *Conceptual Framework* defines **income** as:

increases in economic benefits during the accounting period in the form of inflows or enhancements of assets or decreases of liabilities that result in increases in equity, other than those relating to contributions from equity participants.

Note that this definition of income is linked to the definitions of assets and liabilities. The definition of income is wide in its scope, in that income in the form of inflows or enhancements of assets can arise from providing goods or services, investing in or lending to another entity, holding and disposing of assets, and receiving contributions such as grants and donations. To qualify as income, the inflows or enhancements of assets must have the effect of increasing the equity, excluding capital contributions by owners. Also excluded are certain increases in equity under various inflation accounting models that require the recognition of capital maintenance adjustments (see more advanced books on the subject).

Another important aspect of the definition is that, if income arises as a result of an increase in economic benefits, it is necessary for the entity to *control* that increase in economic benefits. If control does not exist, then no asset exists. Income arises once control over the increase in economic benefits has been achieved and an asset exists, provided there is no equivalent increase in liabilities. For example, in the case of magazine subscriptions received in advance, no income exists on receipt of the cash because an equivalent obligation also has arisen for services to be performed through supply of magazines in the future to clients.

Income can exist as well through a reduction in liabilities that increase the entity's equity. An example of a liability reduction is if a liability of the entity is 'forgiven'. Income arises as a result of that forgiveness, unless the forgiveness of the debt constitutes a contribution by owners.

Under the current *Conceptual Framework*, income encompasses both revenue and gains. A more complete definition of **revenue** is contained in accounting standard IAS 18/AASB 118 *Revenue* as follows:

the gross inflow of economic benefits during the period arising in the course of the ordinary activities of an entity when those inflows result in increases in equity, other than increases relating to contributions from equity participants.

Thus revenue represents income which has arisen from 'the ordinary activities of an entity', an idea which has been reinforced in the IASB/AASB Exposure Draft 198 *Revenue from Contracts with Customers*, issued in June 2010. On the other hand, **gains** represent income that does not necessarily arise from the ordinary activities of the entity, e.g. gains on the disposal of non-current assets or on the revaluation of marketable securities. Gains are usually disclosed in the income statement net of any related expenses, whereas revenues are reported at a gross amount. As revenues and gains are both income, there is no need to regard them as separate elements under the *Conceptual Framework*.

At the time of writing, no proposals have come from the IASB/FASB to amend the definition of income.

Expenses in the current *Conceptual Framework*

The definition of **expenses** in the *Conceptual Framework* is as follows:

> decreases in economic benefits during the accounting period in the form of outflows or depletions of assets or incurrences of liabilities that result in decreases in equity, other than those relating to distributions to equity participants.

To qualify as an expense, a reduction in an asset or an increase in a liability must have the effect of decreasing the entity's equity. The purchase of an asset does not decrease equity and therefore does not create an expense. An expense arises whenever the economic benefits in the asset are consumed, expired or lost. Like income, the definition of expenses is expressed in terms of changes in assets, liabilities and equity.

This concept of expense is broad enough to encompass items that have typically been reported in financial statements as 'losses', e.g. loss on foreign currency transactions, losses from fire, flood, etc., losses on the abandonment of a research project. Losses are expenses that may not arise in the ordinary course of the entity's activities.

At the time of writing, no proposals have come from the IASB/FASB to amend the definition of expenses.

17.7 Recognition of the elements

Learning objective 7

Describe the recognition criteria, established in the *Conceptual Framework*, for assets, liabilities, income and expenses

There are recognition criteria to be followed in the preparation and presentation of general purpose financial reports in practice. These criteria have been set down as part of the *Conceptual Framework*. **Recognition** means the process of incorporating in the statement of financial position/balance sheet or income statement an item that meets the definition of an element. In other words, it involves the inclusion of dollar amounts in the entity's accounting system. Note that an item must satisfy the definition of an element before it is 'recognised'.

Asset recognition in the current *Conceptual Framework*

The *Conceptual Framework* states that an asset should be recognised in the statement of financial position/balance sheet when it is probable that the future economic benefits will flow to the entity and the asset has a cost or other value that can be measured reliably.

Consideration of the definition of an asset, as discussed on page 721, helps to determine whether an asset exists. Here, emphasis is placed on criteria for determining *when to record* an asset in the entity's accounting records. An asset is to be recognised only when both the probability and the reliable measurement criteria are satisfied. The term 'probability' refers to the degree of certainty that the future economic benefits will flow to the entity. The benefits should be more likely rather than less likely. For example, some development costs are not recognised as an asset because it is not 'probable' that future economic benefits will eventuate.

Even if such probability of future benefits is high, no recognition of an asset can occur unless some cost or other value is capable of reliable measurement. Without such a measurement, the qualitative characteristic of 'reliability' will not be achieved. In practice, reliable measurement of internally generated goodwill has been difficult, and therefore such goodwill has not been recognised as an asset. Similarly, reliable measurement of an entity's mineral reserves is difficult. It is argued in the *Conceptual Framework* that assets that cannot be measured reliably may nevertheless be disclosed in notes to the financial statements, particularly if knowledge of the item is considered relevant to evaluating the entity's financial position, performance and cash flows.

Asset recognition in the proposed framework

At the time of writing, this issue has not been clarified. However, because 'reliability' has been replaced by 'faithful representation' and 'verifiability', asset recognition criteria will change. It is expected that the measurement of an asset will need to be a faithful representation of the economic phenomena, and that the measurement must be verifiable.

Liability recognition in the current *Conceptual Framework*

Once the existence of a liability has been established in accordance with the definition as discussed on pages 721–2, criteria must then exist for the recognition of a liability in an entity's accounting records. The *Conceptual Framework* states that a liability is recognised in the statement of financial position/balance sheet when it is probable that an outflow of resources embodying economic benefits will result from settling the present obligation and the amount at which the settlement will take place can be measured reliably.

As with the recognition of assets, 'probable' means that the chance of the outflow of economic benefits being required is likely. The additional need for reliable measurement is an attempt to measure, in monetary terms, the amount of economic benefits that will be sacrificed to satisfy the obligation. Any liabilities that are not recognised in the accounting records because they do not satisfy the recognition criteria may be disclosed in notes to the financial statements, if considered relevant. Further discussion of the recognition of liabilities is provided in the chapter on liabilities.

Liability recognition in the proposed framework

At the time of writing, this issue has not been clarified. However, because 'reliability' has been replaced by 'faithful representation' and 'verifiability', liability recognition criteria will change. It is expected that the measurement of a liability will need to be a faithful representation of the economic resources given up, and that the measurement must be verifiable.

The IASB and FASB in their deliberations to date (up to 15 March 2010) have suggested that the issue of uncertainty as to whether a liability exists should be considered in the definitional stage and not as part of the recognition criteria. The boards argue that, given uncertainty, if it is judged that a liability exists, the uncertainty about the amount of the liability would be taken into account in measurement of the liability.

Income recognition in the current *Conceptual Framework* and standards

In accordance with the *Conceptual Framework*, income is recognised in the income statement when an increase in future economic benefits relating to an increase in an asset or decrease of a liability can be measured reliably.

As with the recognition criteria for assets and liabilities, probability of occurrence and reliability of measurement are presented as the two criteria for income recognition. For many entities, the majority of income in the form of revenues results from the provision of goods and services during the reporting period. There is little uncertainty that the income has occurred since the entity has received cash or has an explicit claim against an external party as a result of a past transaction. However, the absence of an exchange transaction often raises doubts as to whether the income has achieved the required degree of certainty. In situations of uncertainty, the *Conceptual Framework* requires the income to be recognised as long as it is 'probable' that it has occurred and the amount can be measured reliably. It is essential to remove any GST which may be included in the cash received or receivable in order to measure the amount of income reliably.

As stated previously, income includes both revenues and gains. The standard setters have provided further requirements for the recognition of revenues in accounting standard IAS 18/AASB 118 *Revenue*, which deals with the recognition of different types of revenue that can arise in an entity.

The standard requires all revenue recognised in the entity's financial statements to be measured at the fair value of the consideration received or receivable. Separate recognition criteria are then provided for each different category of revenue.

Revenue from sale of goods

For revenue arising from the sale of goods, recognition as income can occur only when all the following conditions are satisfied:

(a) the entity has transferred to the buyer the significant risks and rewards of ownership of the goods

(b) the entity does not retain continuing managerial involvement to the degree usually associated with ownership or effective control of the goods sold

(c) the amount of the revenue can be measured reliably

(d) it is probable that the economic benefits associated with the transaction will flow to the entity

(e) the costs incurred or to be incurred in respect of the transaction can be measured reliably.

In most retail sales, criteria (a) and (b) will be satisfied when legal title to the goods has passed from the seller to the buyer; however, the standard requires only the risks and benefits of ownership, and effective control, to pass to the buyer, and this may be different from the point of transfer of legal title. These criteria appear consistent with the current definition of an asset, which requires an entity merely to have control over future economic benefits, rather than legal ownership, for an asset to exist. However, the *Conceptual Framework* does not require a sale to occur for revenue to exist, contrary to IAS 18/AASB 118, which implicitly assumes that revenue is to be earned in this context. Furthermore, IAS 18/AASB 118 requires a reliable measure of all costs associated with the sale.

Revenue from rendering services

IAS 18/AASB 118 requires that revenue from rendering services is recognised as income only on the satisfaction of four criteria:

(a) the amount of the revenue can be reliably measured (ex GST)

(b) it is probable that the economic benefits associated with the transaction will flow to the entity

(c) the stage of completion of the transaction at the end of the reporting period can be reliably measured

(d) the costs incurred for the transaction and the costs to complete the transaction can be measured reliably.

Under IAS 18/AASB 118, revenue from services is normally recognised as those services are performed or earned, provided that the amount of those services can be measured reliably. Criterion (c) is particularly appropriate for services rendered over a long period of time. For example, a company may have a contract to perform cleaning and maintenance services in an office building over a 5-year period. Revenue can be recognised by the company progressively (in stages) over the life of this contract. This stage-of-completion approach is sometimes referred to as the **percentage-of-completion method**. The method is also used by companies in the construction industry to recognise revenue progressively over the life of a large, long-term construction contract, in accordance with accounting standard IAS 11/AASB 111 *Construction Contracts*.

Nevertheless, some people have found IAS 18/AASB 118 confusing when recognising revenue under contractual arrangements. Hence, in June/July 2010, an Exposure Draft was issued by the IASB, FASB and the AASB, namely Exposure Draft 198 *Revenue from Contracts with Customers*, outlining major proposed principles for an entity to apply in order to report useful information about the revenue and cash flows arising from its contracts to provide goods or services to customers. The core principle requires an entity to recognise revenue for the transfer of goods or services to customers at an amount that reflects the consideration that it receives, or expects to receive, in exchange for those goods or services. To apply the principle, an entity is required to:

1. identify the contract(s) with a customer

2. identify the separate performance obligations in the contract

3. determine the transaction price

4. allocate the transaction price to the separate performance obligations

5. recognise revenue when the entity satisfies each performance obligation.

In regard to (2) identifying the separate performance obligations in the contract, a performance obligation is defined as an enforceable promise (whether explicit or implicit) in a contract with a customer to transfer a good or service to the customer. If an entity promises to provide more than one good or service, e.g. with the cleaning contract mentioned previously where several cleaning tasks would be undertaken, it must account for each promised good or service as a separate performance obligation if the good or service is distinct.

Regarding (3), the transaction price is the amount of consideration that an entity receives, or expects to receive, from a customer in exchange for transferring goods or services promised in the contract. In many contracts, the transaction price is easily determined because the customer promises to pay a fixed amount at or near the time of the transfer of the promised goods or services. But if the amount of consideration is variable (for instance, because of rebates, bonuses, penalties, or the customer's credit risk), an entity can recognise revenue from satisfying a performance obligation only if the transaction price can be reasonably estimated. In determining the transaction price, an entity considers the effects of the following:

(a) collectability
(b) the time value of money
(c) non-cash consideration
(d) consideration payable to the customer.

Having determined the transaction price, the entity must then allocate the price to all separate performance obligations in proportion to the stand-alone selling prices of the goods or services underlying each of those performance obligations at contract inception. The entity will then recognise revenue when it satisfies a performance obligation by transferring a promised good or service to a customer. According to ED 198, a good or service is transferred when the customer obtains control of that good or service. The entity will recognise revenue to the extent of the amount of the transaction price allocated to the satisfied performance obligation.

Revenue from interest, royalties and dividends

Recognition of revenue from interest, royalties and dividends can occur only when the following criteria are satisfied according to IAS 18/AASB 118:

(a) It is probable that the economic benefits associated with the transaction will flow to the entity
(b) the amount of the revenue can be measured reliably (AY GST if applicable)

In accordance with the standard, interest revenue must be recognised on a proportionate basis over the periods in which it is earned, as has been illustrated in previous chapters. The standard requires interest revenue to be recognised using the effective interest method, but the use of this method is beyond the scope of this book.

Royalties are rights of composers and authors to receive payments from publishing companies for the sale of their music or books. Royalties are also cash received by the owner of land (such as a pastoral company, the government or an Aboriginal community) from a mining company that has been given the right to mine mineral reserves on the owner's land. As an example of mining royalties, state governments, particularly in Queensland and Western Australia, receive considerable amounts of money annually from large companies as royalty payments for granting permission to the companies to extract mineral resources from land controlled by those governments. Under the standard, any entity entitled to royalty revenue must recognise it on an accrual basis according to the terms of the contract.

Dividends represent the return received by a person or entity holding share investments in another entity. In accordance with IAS 18/AASB 118, dividends can be recognised only when the holder of those shares has an established right to receive such payments. Unlike interest, dividends do not accrue on a time basis but are recognised only when an amount is clearly receivable from the entity paying those dividends.

Income from contributions

Income from the contributions of assets arises when an entity receives cash, or a right to receive cash or other assets, without having to give approximately equal value in return. This is sometimes referred to as a **non-reciprocal transfer**. Contributions of assets which constitute income under the *Conceptual Framework* exclude any contributions made by the owners to the entity. Examples of contributions that represent non-reciprocal transfers include:

(a) members' annual subscriptions to a club, such as a football club or social club
(b) cash donations received by entities for the purpose of future research
(c) cash donations received by charitable or relief organisations, or special-interest groups
(d) other assets received as donations.

To recognise income from contributions, AASB 1004 *Contributions*, which applies only to not-for-profit entities, states that the following criteria need to be satisfied:

(a) the entity obtains control of the contribution or the right to receive the contribution
(b) it is probable that the economic benefits comprising the contribution will flow to the entity
(c) the amount of the contribution can be measured reliably.

In other words, the recognition criteria for contributions income in AASB 1004 are similar to those for revenue from the sale of goods in IAS 18/AASB 118.

These criteria apply only to non-profit entities including not-for-profit government departments. If a government department is an entity created with a profit motive, the standard does not apply. Contributions to a government department or whole of government are received in the form of rates, taxes, fines, grants and donations. In the case of government departments, parliamentary appropriations, other than those that give rise to a liability or that are in the nature of a contribution by owners, may also be a type of contribution. AASB 1004 requires contributions, other than contributions by owners, to be recognised as income when the receiving entity obtains control over them, irrespective of whether restrictions or conditions are imposed on the use of the contributions. The income is measured at the fair value of the contributions received or receivable.

Liabilities forgiven

Another category of income for not-for-profit entities discussed in AASB 1004 is income from liabilities forgiven by a creditor of the entity. Sometimes a creditor may cancel or give up a claim to a debt that is owed by an entity. In this case, the entity is 'forgiven' the debt and must treat the gross amount of the cancelled or 'forgiven' debt as income. This is done by debiting the account of the creditor concerned and crediting the Income from Debts Forgiven account.

Government grants received

From time to time, a business entity may receive grants from a government department or agency for the purpose of conducting research, environmental protection, or other reasons. IAS 20/AASB 120 *Accounting for Government Grants and Disclosure of Government Assistance* specifically deals with this issue. Government grants received by an entity in the form of income tax benefits or subsidies for agricultural activities are excluded from the standard. (Agricultural subsidies are discussed in IAS 41/AASB 141 *Agriculture* and are not considered here.)

Under IAS 20/AASB 120, government grants are divided into two categories:

• **grants related to assets**, whose main condition is that an entity qualifying for them should purchase, construct or otherwise acquire long-term assets
• **grants related to income**, which are grants other than those related to assets.

According to the standard, government grants of both categories, including non-monetary grants at fair value, cannot be recognised until there is reasonable assurance that:

• the entity will comply with the conditions attaching to them
• the grants will be received.

Government grants related to income, when recognised, are to be recognised as income systematically over the periods necessary to match them with the related costs that they are intended to compensate, on a systematic basis. They are not to be credited directly to equity. Note that, under this policy, the recognition of the income depends on a knowledge of the related costs, and income recognition is then tied to cost and expense recognition. The process of requiring an association of costs with the income is evident as well in the recognition criteria for revenue from the sale of goods and the provision of services under IAS 18/AASB 118, as discussed above.

However, government grants related to assets are to be debited to assets but cannot be credited directly to income or to equity. Instead, they must be credited to an account called 'deferred income' and presented in the statement of financial position/balance sheet as such. Alternatively, a grant related to assets may be presented as a reduction of the carrying amount of the asset concerned. A 'deferred income' account has no conceptual place in the *Conceptual Framework*, as it appears to be neither income nor equity nor a liability. It is hoped that IAS 20/AASB 120 will be amended to eliminate this requirement in future. Furthermore, the required treatment of government grants by the recipient is contrary to the treatment of contributions receivable under AASB 1004.

Income recognition in the proposed framework

At the time of writing, this issue has not been clarified. However, because 'reliability' has been replaced by 'faithful representation' and 'verifiability', recognition criteria for all types of income including revenues and all contributions and government grants will change. It is expected that the measurement of an item of income will need to be a faithful representation of the appropriate economic phenomena, and that the measurement must be verifiable.

In addition, the IASB and FASB are continuing work on a joint project to clarify revenue recognition criteria. The objective of the project is to develop a single coherent asset and liability model for revenue recognition. In such a model, revenue is a function of changes in assets and liabilities and is not based on the notions of realisation and the completion of an earnings process. At the time of writing, the IASB and FASB are considering the implications of a model focusing on contract assets and contract liabilities, and this has resulted in the release of ED 198 *Revenue from Contracts with Customers* by the AASB in July 2010, as discussed previously.

Expense recognition in the current *Conceptual Framework*

Just as the income recognition criteria have been developed in the *Conceptual Framework* as a guide to the timing of income recognition, the expense recognition criteria have been developed to guide the timing of expense recognition. The formulators of the *Conceptual Framework* view expenses in terms of decreases in future economic benefits in the form of reductions in assets or increases in liabilities of the entity (see the definition of expenses on page 724). In addition to the probability criteria for expense recognition, the *Conceptual Framework* states that expenses are recognised in the income statement when a decrease in future economic benefits related to a decrease in an asset or an increase in a liability can be measured reliably.

This means that an expense is recognised simultaneously with a decrease in an asset or increase in a liability. An expense is also recognised in the income statement when the entity incurs a liability without the recognition of any asset, e.g. wages payable.

In years past, the process of recognising expenses was referred to as a 'matching process', whereby an attempt was made to associate each cost with the income recognised in the current period. Costs which were 'associated' with the revenue were then said to be 'matched' and written off to expenses. This idea of matching expenses with income has been dropped in the *Conceptual Framework* in favour of assessing the probability of a decrease in economic benefits which can be measured reliably. Matching is no longer the expense recognition criterion under the *Conceptual Framework*.

Expense recognition in the proposed framework

At the time of writing, this issue has not been discussed in any detail. However, because 'reliability' has been replaced by 'faithful representation' and 'verifiability', recognition criteria for all types of expenses will change. It is expected that the measurement of an expense will need to be a faithful representation of the appropriate economic phenomena, and that the measurement must be verifiable. In addition, it is expected that amendments to the definition and recognition of expenses will flow from the current IASB and FASB considerations of the definition and recognition of revenue, as referred to above, in due course.

Developing green industries with sun, wind, waves and water

In October 2009, the Australian Conservation Foundation (ACF) and the Australian Council of Trade Unions (ACTU) released a report outlining the potential benefits for Australia in developing green industries. It says that if Australia is proactive, its green sector could be worth US$243 billion and employ 847 000 people by 2030. The authors believe the opportunities for Australia are so vast they labelled the report 'Green Gold Rush'. They are not alone in predicting the possibilities of an amazing future. Australia is facing 'the perfect storm of opportunities', according to Dr James Bradfield Moody, the Commonwealth Scientific and Industrial Research Organisation's (CSIRO) Executive Director of Development.

But at the same time, the report's authors and other experts are warning that Australia needs to begin the hard task of investing in and creating businesses in the green sector right now, or face being left behind.

The good news is that Australia has excellent competitive advantages in six key areas: renewable energy, energy efficiency, bio-materials, green buildings, sustainable water systems, and waste management and recycling.

Australia has already made solid use of its wind and sun resources by developing solar and wind industries. The nation's renewable energy sector now employs 20 000 people and generates annual sales of US$1.4 billion. But most experts believe that the biggest opportunities in the next few years could come from one of its greatest weaknesses. 'Australia has got great sun, good wind and good waves ... but no water,' says John O'Brien, the founder of green industry consultancy and research company Australian CleanTech.

Source: Excerpts from Ben Power, 'Green profits', *InTheBlack.*

Learning objective 8

Explain the importance of measurement in the preparation of financial statements

17.8 Measurement

Because the concepts of equity, income and expenses are highly dependent on the concepts of assets and liabilities, measurement of the former depends on measurement of the latter. In other words, emphasis is placed on measuring assets and liabilities; the measurement of equity, income and expenses then follows. Measurement is very important in accounting in that it is the process by which valuations are placed on all elements reported in financial statements. Measurements thus have an important effect on the economic decisions made by users of those financial statements.

The current *Conceptual Framework* points out that a number of different measurement bases may be used for assets, liabilities, income and expenses in varying degrees and in varying combinations in financial statements. They include the following, the most common of which in practice is the historical cost basis:

- *Historical cost.* Under the **historical cost** measurement basis, an asset is recorded at the amount of cash or cash equivalents paid or the fair value of the consideration given to acquire it at its acquisition date. Liabilities are recorded at the amount of the proceeds received in exchange for an obligation, or at the amount of cash to be paid out in order to satisfy the liability in the normal course of business.
- *Current cost.* For an asset, **current cost** represents the amount of cash or cash equivalents that would be paid if the same or equivalent asset was acquired currently. A liability is recorded at the amount of cash or cash equivalents needed to settle the obligation currently.
- *Realisable or settlement value.* For an asset, the **realisable value** is the amount of cash or cash equivalents that could be obtained currently by selling the asset in an orderly disposal, or in the normal course of business. A liability is measured as the amount of cash or cash equivalents expected to be paid to satisfy the obligation in the normal course of business.
- *Present value.* The present value of an asset means the discounted future net cash inflows or net cash savings that are expected to arise in the normal course of business. The present value of a liability is the discounted future net cash outflows that are expected to settle the obligation in the normal course of business.

The measurement basis most commonly adopted by entities is the historical cost basis. Nevertheless, other bases are used from time to time. For example, in order to comply with IAS 2/AASB 102 *Inventories*, inventories are to be measured at the lower of cost and net realisable value. Non-current assets may be measured under the cost basis or revalued to **fair value**, defined, for assets, as the price that would be received to sell an asset in an orderly transaction between market participants at the measurement date, as per the requirements of IFRS 13/AASB 13 *Fair Value Measurement*. Fair value is basically a measure of an item's market exit price on a particular date in the normal course of business.

The topic of measurement is part of the joint project of the IASB and FASB to amend and expand the *Conceptual Framework*. Discussions on measurement are continuing but no decisions have been reached (see FASB Project Update: Phase C: Measurement, 23 November 2010).

Concepts of capital

Scant attention has been given to the concept of capital in accounting in the last 30 years, but it was a topic which received considerable focus during the current value debates of the 1960s to early 1980s. It was argued then, and now, that before an entity can determine its income for any period, it must adopt not only a measurement basis for assets and liabilities but also a concept of capital. Two main concepts of capital are discussed in the *Conceptual Framework*, namely financial capital and physical capital.

Financial capital

Under the **financial capital** concept, capital is synonymous with the net assets or equity of the entity, measured either in terms of the actual number of calculated dollars by subtracting the total of liabilities from assets, or in terms of the purchasing power of the dollar amount recorded as equity. Profit exists only after the entity has maintained its capital, measured as either the dollar value of equity at the beginning of the period, or the purchasing power of those dollars in the equity at the beginning of the period.

Physical capital

Under the **physical capital** concept, capital is seen not so much as the equity recorded by the entity but as the operating capability of the assets. Profit exists only after the entity has set aside enough capital to maintain the operating capability of its assets.

A number of different measurement systems have been devised in the past to provide alternatives to the conventional historical cost system, which is the system predominantly used in practice. These alternatives, which represent different combinations of the measurement of assets and liabilities and the concept of capital maintenance, include:

- the *general price level accounting system*, which had its origins in Germany after World War I when inflation reached excessive levels — this system modifies the conventional historical cost system for the effects of inflation and therefore follows a financial capital concept
- *current value systems*, which attempt to measure the changes in the current values of assets and liabilities — these systems include measures of the current buying or input prices of net assets, and/or measures of the current selling or realisable values of net assets. Capital may be measured as either financial or physical.

KEY TERMS

1. Outline the regulatory process in Australia in relation to accounting standard setting, and discuss the influence of international bodies in the standard-setting process.

2. What is meant by an entity's financial position and performance? To whom and for what purpose are the financial position and performance appropriate sources of information?

3. 'One of the major changes in both corporations legislation and accounting standards is the adoption of the reporting entity concept.'

   This comment was made in a presentation at an accounting conference. One of the directors of your entity, a Brisbane-based company that is a wholly owned subsidiary of a Sydney-based company, was at the presentation and was concerned at his lack of knowledge of this concept.

   Explain to the director what is meant by the 'reporting entity' concept, the steps the company needs to take to determine whether it is a reporting entity, and the potential impact of this concept on financial reporting. Discuss as well whether or not the reporting entity concept should be abandoned.

4. Briefly explain the nature of the *Conceptual Framework for Financial Reporting*, and discuss the perceived advantages and disadvantages of having a conceptual framework.

5. Specify the objectives of general purpose financial reporting, the nature of users, and the information to be provided to users in order to achieve the objectives as provided in the *Conceptual Framework*.

6. From the current *Conceptual Framework*, outline the qualitative characteristics of financial information to be included in general purpose financial reports.

7. The *Conceptual Framework* discusses 'essential' and 'non-essential' characteristics of an asset. Consider which characteristics of an asset are 'essential', explaining why you regard other characteristics as being non-essential. How would these characteristics change as a result of the proposed asset definition put forward by the IASB and FASB?

8. 'To determine whether an entity should classify its costs either as an asset or an expense, accounting standards must contain definitions of these terms.'

   With reference to the above statement, discuss the concept of an asset and an expense provided in the *Conceptual Framework*. Provide also a discussion of the IASB and FASB's alternative suggestion for amending the definition of an asset. Do you agree with the above statement? Why or why not?

9. Outline the definitions of a liability and equity as provided in the current *Conceptual Framework*. Provide and discuss examples of situations where there is confusion in determining whether a liability exists as opposed to equity.

10. 'Accounting profit is determined by recognising the income earned by the entity, and associating with that income the costs incurred in generating it.'

    This statement describes the way in which accountants have determined profit in practice for many years under the historical cost system. Is the statement an accurate reflection of the requirements of the *Conceptual Framework* for general purpose financial reporting? If not, explain any differences.

11. 'I find the distinction between income, revenue and gains confusing.' This is a student's statement overhead in a corridor. Help this student by discussing the major issues involved.

12. Outline and compare the revenue recognition criteria required by accounting standards for the sale of goods, the provision of services, contributions, and government grants. Are there any inconsistencies in these requirements? If so, discuss.

13. A major step in the framework project being undertaken by the regulators is the measurement of assets and liabilities. Some accountants argue that this will lead to a re-emergence of the current value debate.

    Why is measurement such an important issue? What alternatives for measurement have been put forward by the *Conceptual Framework*? What role does capital maintenance have in selecting an appropriate measurement system?

Exercise 17.1 VIOLATION OF REPORTING REQUIREMENTS

Several independent situations are described below:

1. The owner of the business included his personal dental expenses in the entity's income statement.
2. The company spent $40 000 on computer software development and recorded the cost as an asset. As yet it is impossible to predict whether this cost will result in future economic benefits.
3. Depreciation expense was not recorded because to do so would result in a loss for the period.
4. The cost of three books (cost $110 each) was charged to expense when purchased even though they had a useful life of several years.
5. A major lawsuit has been filed against the company for environmental damage, and the company's solicitors believe there is a high probability of losing the suit. However, nothing is recorded in the accounts.
6. Land was reported at its estimated selling price, which is substantially higher than its cost. The increase in value was included on the income statement.
7. The company received a government grant of $60 000 to continue its research program into finding a cure for diabetes. The company recognised the grant as an addition to capital.

Required

Indicate for each situation the accounting principle(s) or reporting characteristics (if any) that are violated.

Exercise 17.2 INCOME RECOGNITION

Described below are several transactions and events for Keswick Insurance Ltd for the year ended 30 June 2013.

1. The company issued a 1-year insurance policy to Sunshine Ltd on 1 March 2013, costing $6000, received in advance.
2. The company leased premises to Kingston Ltd for a period of 3 years, beginning on 1 January 2013. Kingston Ltd paid $40 000 on this date, and is required to pay further instalments of $40 000 in 2014 and 2015.
3. The company has been a generous sponsor of the Clean-Up Australia Campaign in past years. In recognition of its support, an anonymous donor sent the company a cheque for $10 000, with a letter stating, 'keep up the good work!'
4. On 30 January 2013, the company sold a non-current asset to another organisation for $16 000. The asset originally cost Keswick Insurance Ltd $40 000 and had been depreciated to a carrying amount of $10 000.

Required

For each transaction or event, determine the appropriate amount to be recognised as income in the current year. Ignore GST.

Exercise 17.3 ASSETS AND ASSET RECOGNITION

Explain whether you would recognise each item below as an asset, justifying your answer by reference to the *Conceptual Framework*'s asset definition and recognition criteria:

(a) a trinket of sentimental value only
(b) discovery (at insignificant cost) of evidence of mineral reserves
(c) specialised equipment with zero disposal value, which now, because of downsizing, is surplus to requirements and has thus been retired from use
(d) your staff
(e) goods held on consignment for another entity.

Exercise 17.4 ASSET DEFINITION AND RECOGNITION

Modbury Medical Laboratory Ltd, MMLL, a medical research entity, has discovered a cure for a previously incurable disease. MMLL is protecting the drug's formula by keeping it secure in the company vault, rather than by patenting it. MMLL shortly plans to start discussions with vitally interested pharmaceutical companies about producing the drug for commercial sale. Being the first of its kind and, therefore, unique, MMLL has no idea as to the formula's value. Costs incurred to date in developing the formula are impossible to identify, given that the cure was discovered as a by-product of another research project.

Required

Outline how MMLL should account for the formula, justifying your answer by reference to relevant definitions and recognition criteria.

Exercise 17.5 REVENUE AND REVENUE RECOGNITION **LO 6, 7**

Telecommunications company, Crafters Ltd, signed a 15-year deal to sell capacity on its cable network to a rival company for $200 million. The deal was completed on the last day of Crafters Ltd's financial year, 30 June. The company received an upfront payment of only $20 million from its competitor on that day, but decided to recognise 'revenue' of $200 million for the financial year just completed.

Required

Discuss fully how Crafters Ltd should account for the contract, justifying your answer by reference to relevant definitions and recognition criteria and relevant accounting standards.

Exercise 17.6 REVENUE AND REVENUE RECOGNITION **LO 6, 7**

State the amount of revenue that should be recognised by Blackwood Ltd in the year ended 31 December 2014 for each item below, justifying your answer by reference to the revenue definition and recognition criteria in IAS 18/AASB 118. Prepare any journal entries where necessary:

(a) Blackwood Ltd's net credit sales for 2014 were $400 000, 75% of which were collected in 2014. Past experience indicates that about 96% of all credit sales are eventually collected.

(b) Blackwood Ltd received $100 000 cash from a customer in December 2014 as payment for special-purpose machinery which is to be manufactured and shipped to the customer in February 2015.

(c) Blackwood Ltd started renting out its excess warehouse space on 1 October 2014, on which date it received $12 000 cash from the tenant for 6 months rent in advance. Ignore GST.

(d) Blackwood Ltd received 10 000 shares in Mitcham Ltd on 20 December 2014, on which date the shares were trading at $4.50 per share, as a gift from a grateful client.

(e) Blackwood Ltd received an item of equipment as settlement for goods sold on credit for $3000. On the date of the sale, the equipment had a fair value of $3200 and a carrying amount in the customer's records of $2200. Prepare also the journal entry to record the receipt of the equipment. Ignore GST.

Exercise 17.7 LIABILITIES AND LIABILITY RECOGNITION **LO 6, 7**

Outline whether you would recognise each item below as a liability, justifying your answer by reference to the *Conceptual Framework*'s liability definition and recognition criteria:

(a) Your parents have lent you $20 000 to buy a car and have told you to pay it back whenever you like.

(b) You are guarantor for your friend's bank loan:
  (i) You have no reason to believe that your friend will default on the loan.
  (ii) Your friend has been encountering serious financial problems and you think it is likely that he will default on the loan.

(c) The court has ordered you to repair the environmental damage your firm has caused to a park next to your firm's premises. You have no idea as yet how much this repair work will cost.

(d) Your firm has a 20-year history of donating $2000 each year to the Telethon Appeal. As yet, no amount has been paid in the current year and nothing has been recorded in the accounts.

Exercise 17.8 SUBSTANCE OVER FORM

Unley Ltd sold some property to Eastwood Ltd for $1 000 000 cash in June 2014, recording a profit of $200 000. A further element of the sale was that Unley Ltd gave Eastwood Ltd an option to sell the property back to Unley Ltd at any time after 30 June 2014, the end of Unley Ltd's reporting period, for $1 000 000. If Eastwood Ltd exercised the option, there would be no cash flow to Eastwood Ltd from Unley until 2 years had passed.

The land has a current fair value of $800 000 with no changes expected in this amount in the next 3 years.

Required

Discuss the appropriate accounting treatment of this transaction in the accounting records of Unley Ltd. Ignore GST.

Exercise 17.9 LIABILITIES

The following items occurred in Norwood Ltd for the year ended 30 June 2014:
(a) Some of Norwood Ltd's plant and equipment is situated in an area which, on average, is flooded every 15 years. The company has no flood insurance, but provides an amount each year as a liability in the accounts for uninsured flood losses.
(b) Norwood Ltd entered into a contract with Burnside Ltd to acquire some plant and equipment at a cost of $1 000 000. At the end of the reporting period, Norwood Ltd had paid a 10% deposit.
(c) Norwood Ltd has a regular program of maintenance for its plant and equipment. In order to provide for this program, the company has been in the habit of establishing a Provision for Plant Maintenance account and disclosing it as part of liabilities.

Required

Discuss how the above items should be treated in the general purpose financial reports of Norwood Ltd if the company were to comply with the provisions of the *Conceptual Framework*. Ignore GST.

Exercise 17.10 ASSETS AND ASSET RECOGNITION

For several seasons, Megan Gale and Jennifer Hawkins have been employed by David Jones Limited and Myer Limited respectively. In order to attract more fashion-conscious customers to their stores. This strategy has met with some success and their continued employment at fashion events in the future for their respective companies appears assured.

Required

Discuss whether Megan Gale and Jennifer Hawkins should be regarded as assets of David Jones Limited and Myer Limited respectively. Discuss also whether they should be recognised on the statement of financial position/balance sheet of the respective companies as assets.

Exercise 17.11 EXPENSES, LIABILITIES AND EQUITY

Hectorville Ltd is seeking your advice on how to account for the following transactions, in line with the *Conceptual Framework* and other relevant documents. Discuss and explain your recommended treatment of each of the situations below:
1. Hectorville Ltd spends $10 000 per year to have its head office cleaned and its gardens maintained. In order to continue this maintenance, the company established a Provision for Maintenance account and classified this provision as a liability on the statement of financial position/balance sheet.
2. Hectorville Ltd raised $1 000 000 by issuing 100 000 10-year redeemable preference shares. The company classified these shares as equity.
3. Hectorville Ltd is in the business of selling house and land packages to its customers. The current demand for these packages is extremely low and this is placing Hectorville Ltd in severe financial difficulties. The company has approached Lofty Finance Company Ltd (LFC), to provide special finance for the buyers of their house and land packages. LFC normally charges 13% interest but agrees to lower the interest rate by 3%. Customers of Hectorville Ltd will therefore

pay only 10% interest and Hectorville Ltd will then pay LFC a sum equal to 3% interest as soon as each package is sold. Hectorville Ltd wants to know how to treat the 3% payment to LFC in its accounting records.

LO 5

Exercise 17.12 QUALITATIVE CHARACTERISTICS

Assume that the IASB (and AASB) is in the process of writing an accounting standard on accounting for water resources, and has received submissions that can be divided roughly into two camps — measurement of the resources at cost, and measurement at fair value. The process has reached the stage of applying the following qualitative characteristics of financial information.

	Cost	Fair value
Tick which of the two measures has greater:		
relevance	_____	_____
materiality	_____	_____
consistency	_____	_____
prudence	_____	_____
substance over form	_____	_____
freedom from bias	_____	_____
neutrality	_____	_____
objectivity	_____	_____
reliability	_____	_____
timeliness	_____	_____
comparability	_____	_____
understandability	_____	_____
faithful representation	_____	_____
verifiability	_____	_____

Required

A. Place a tick in one of the columns against each characteristic.
B. On the basis of this analysis, discuss which measure should be chosen for water resources.

LO 6, 7

Exercise 17.13 ASSETS AND EXPENSES

Brompton Boutique Brewing Ltd (BBB) has suffered a significant reduction in profitability, as a result of the current economic downturn and doubts about the quality of certain boutique beers. The company's profit for the year ended 30 June 2014 was only $2 150 000.

The general purpose financial reports for the year disclosed a note regarding the company's policy on beer advertising as follows:

> *Advertising costs expecting to generate significant future economic benefits have been treated as an asset and carried forward to future years to be expensed against the future expected revenues. Management intends to review these deferred costs on a regular basis.*

The statement of financial position/balance sheet revealed that an amount of $10 million had been treated in this manner up to the end of 30 June 2014 as there was an item called Deferred Expenditure in the statement of financial position/balance sheet. This represented a change to the previous accounting policy of writing off advertising as it was incurred.

A finance report in the local newspaper commented that normally advertising is charged as an expense in the period it is incurred. The auditor of the company did not mention the deferred expenditure in the audit report.

Required

In light of the *Conceptual Framework*, evaluate BBB's treatment of the advertising expenditure carried forward.

Exercise 17.14 COSTS AND INCOME

Rosewood Housing Ltd (RHL) is a land development company trading in the construction of residential house and land packages in Brisbane's western suburbs. The company is currently developing a residential subdivision, and the total cost of the development has been estimated at $18 000 000. This is related to future house and land packages, none of which is yet available for sale. RHL treated these costs as an asset.

By 30 June 2014, RHL sold 40 house and land packages in a different subdivision for the financial year. The total value of these packages is $15 000 000. The funds have not been received by RHL because it was arranged that payments would be received from various finance companies by the end of July 2014. RHL recognised the revenue in its income statement for the year ended 30 June 2014.

Required

Discuss RHL's treatment of the development costs of $18 000 000 and the packages sold for $15 000 000. Are these treatments consistent with the *Conceptual Framework* and accounting standards? Explain.

Exercise 17.15 ORDERING AN ASSET

A well-known Australian airline has placed a non-cancellable order for a new Airbus A380. The price between the airline and the manufacturer is fixed, and delivery is to occur in 24 months with full payment to be made on delivery.

Required

A. Should the airline recognise an asset or liability at the time it places the order? Discuss in line with the *Conceptual Framework* definitions of assets and liabilities.
B. One year later, the price of the Airbus A380 has risen by 6%, but the airline had locked in its contract at a fixed, lower price. Under the *Conceptual Framework*, should the airline recognise any asset (and income) at the time of the price rise? If the price fell by 6% instead of rising, should the airline recognise a liability (and expense) under the *Conceptual Framework*?

PROBLEMS

Problem 17.1 CONCEPTUAL FRAMEWORK ★

★ Basic
★★ Moderate
★★★ Challenging

After conducting an audit of the accounts of Woodville Ltd, you discover that the following transactions and events were recorded during the current year. Woodville Ltd uses the historical cost system.

1. The company borrowed $500 000 from a bank at an interest rate of 10% to construct a new warehouse. At the completion of construction, the loan was repaid and the following entry was made:

Bank Loan	500 000	
Warehouse	50 000	
Cash at Bank		550 000

2. A patent with a cost of $160 000 was being amortised over its useful life of 8 years. The amortisation entry made at the end of the current year was:

Retained Earnings	20 000	
Patents		20 000

3. A speed-control device was installed on each of the company's 8 delivery trucks at a cost of $300 each plus GST. The transaction was recorded as follows:

Maintenance Expense	2 400	
GST Outlays	240	
Cash at Bank		2 640

4. At the beginning of the current year, a new vehicle was purchased for $36 000. The vehicle had an estimated useful life of 4 years. Depreciation expense for the year was recorded as follows in order to avoid reporting a loss:

Depreciation Expense	2 000	
Accumulated Depreciation – Vehicle		2 000

5. Inventory was acquired at $30 per unit throughout the current year until the last purchase was made in the last month of the year. At that time the company was able to negotiate a special deal and acquired 10 000 units at $25 per unit. Ignore GST. The purchase was recorded as follows:

Inventory	300 000	
Cash at Bank		250 000
Income		50 000

Required

For each item above, determine which accounting concept(s) (if any) is violated, and explain why. For each violation, indicate the correct treatment.

Problem 17.2 CONCEPTUAL FRAMEWORK ★   LO 5, 6, 7

Parafield Ltd uses the historical cost system. While reviewing the business activities of the company, you discover that the following transactions and events were recorded. Ignore GST.

1. Ending inventory for the current year had a cost of $115 200 and a selling price of $102 000. The inventory was valued at cost because the company's accountant believed that 'the selling price will probably increase again during the next year'.

2. On 28 December of the current year, Parafield Ltd signed a contract with a customer under which Parafield Ltd agreed to manufacture equipment for the customer during January of the following year at a price of $39 000. Parafield Ltd received a cheque for $7500 from the customer on 28 December and made the following entry:

Accounts Receivable	31 500	
Cash at Bank	7 500	
Sales		39 000

3. A new vehicle was purchased at an auction for cash of $32 000. If purchased from the company's normal supplier, the cash price of the machine would have been $38 000. The Vehicles account was debited for $38 000 and the following entry was made:

Vehicles	38 000	
Cash at Bank		32 000
Gain from Bargain Purchase		6 000

4. Ignition security locks were installed in each of Parafield Ltd's six delivery trucks at a cost of $180 each. The trucks had an average remaining useful life of 5 years. The transaction was recorded as:

Repairs Expense	1 080	
Cash at Bank		1 080

5. Building improvements with an estimated useful life of 20 years were completed early in the current year at a cost of $120 000. Parafield Ltd believed that the building to which the improvements were made could be used for only 15 years. To record depreciation for the current year, the accountant made the following entry:

Depreciation Expense	6 000	
Building Improvements		6 000

Required

For each of items (1) to (5), determine which accounting concept(s) (if any) is violated, and explain why. For each violation, indicate the correct treatment.

Problem 17.3 ASSETS AND INCOME ★

A legal wrangle developed between the Australian Taxation Office (ATO) and Glenelg Ltd concerning the treatment of certain disputed income tax payments. This prompted ASIC to seek a formal ruling on the dispute and call for full disclosure of the effects of tax disputes in the company's financial statements.

Glenelg Ltd and several other leading companies operated an in-house, tax-minimisation scheme which was unacceptable to the ATO. As a result, the ATO assessed Glenelg Ltd as owing $15 million in tax stemming from the use of the scheme. The company paid the tax to the ATO but then challenged the ATO in court and won its challenge to the assessment in the state Supreme Court. Since then, the ATO has appealed against the decision to the Federal Court, but no decision has yet been made.

In its financial statements at the end of the financial year, Glenelg Ltd included the amount of $15 million as an asset, refundable from the ATO. On reviewing the financial statements, ASIC expressed concern about the treatment of the money expected to be recovered from the ATO as an 'asset', as the amount appeared to affect materially the reported profits of the company. ASIC suggested that disputed taxation assessments do not qualify as items resulting from past transactions or to which a company has a definite legal right.

Required

Discuss whether the disputed amount should be recognised as an asset and as income in the financial statements of Glenelg Ltd.

Problem 17.4 ASSETS, EXPENSES AND LIABILITIES ★★

Land and Water Waste Disposal Ltd (LAWWD) is a public company providing waste disposal services to private homeowners and to customers in the commercial, industrial and public sectors. Because of its active research program, the company has built a fine reputation as the leading handler of waste products in Adelaide.

During the year ended 30 June 2014, LAWWD undertook an investigation on the feasibility of establishing a waste processing plant in one of Adelaide's eastern suburbs. Financial advisers, engineers, architects and lawyers were consulted to determine the economic and legal feasibility of establishing such a plant. As at 30 June 2014, the company had incurred costs of $600 000 but was still unable to determine clearly the feasibility of the project, these costs were deferred as assets in the company's financial statements.

LAWWD has several long-term contracts which specify that predetermined quantities of waste must be delivered to certain locations each year. The contracts specify that, if LAWWD is unable to deliver the predetermined quantities, shortfalls must be made up in equivalent cash payments. Unfortunately, LAWWD has not developed a system to keep track of exact quantities delivered to each location. It has become an acceptable practice for delivery requirements to be renegotiated during the life of any contract.

Shortly after the end of the financial year ending 30 June 2014, LAWWD was advised by one of its clients, Calm Ltd, that there was a shortfall in the tonnage of land waste delivered. The cash penalty for this deficiency was approximately $300 000. Because of the long-standing business relationship between the two parties, the management of Calm Ltd agreed to a future meeting with LAWWD to be held on 30 September 2014 to discuss waiving the penalty and reducing next year's delivery requirements. In the finalisation of its general purpose financial reports at the end of August 2014, LAWWD has not recognised any liability for penalties under this contract.

Required

In light of the *Conceptual Framework*, discuss LAWWD's treatment in the general purpose financial reports of the costs incurred for the feasibility study, and the penalty under the contract with Calm Ltd.

Problem 17.5 REPORTING ENTITY, REVENUES AND EXPENSES ★★

Magill Machinery Ltd (MML), a reporting entity which distributes heavy-duty equipment to industrial entities, has had a significant increase in sales over the last few years to government departments. By 30 June 2014, the percentage of sales to the government sector had risen to 40% of total sales.

The shareholders of MML are considering an offer to sell the company to Bigger Roads and Wider Ltd (BRAWL) and have agreed to an audit of the company by BRAWL's auditors, Fair, Fairer and Fairest (FFF). During their investigations, FFF questioned MML's accounting policies in relation to heavy equipment sales to the government. Sales to government departments were carried out under the following terms:

1. Sales are made at normal retail prices, and the sales price is payable at the date of delivery of the equipment. Ownership title transfers at the date of delivery.
2. MML guarantees to repurchase the equipment for a predetermined sum, either at the completion of a specified period of time (normally 2 years), or based on a specified equipment usage factor.
3. The purchaser is responsible for normal recurring maintenance on the equipment; however, MML is responsible for providing, at no cost to the purchaser, any maintenance above normal levels.
4. The purchaser bears the full risk of any loss on the sold equipment once title has passed and up to the date on which the equipment is repurchased by MML or sold to an independent third party.

MML has followed the policy of recognising revenue on government sales on the date of delivery. The auditors assess that MML's guaranteed price for repurchase of the equipment, as per (2) above, is quite high, and is likely to lead to 70% of all equipment subject to government sales being repurchased by MML. The auditors further assess that MML is likely to incur losses on resale of some of this repurchased equipment.

MML has also followed a policy of not accruing any future costs that may be incurred from its maintenance obligations above the normal level.

Required

A. Briefly discuss how a company such as MML determines whether it is a reporting entity.
B. In light of the *Conceptual Framework*, discuss MML's treatment in the accounting records of:
1. the revenue from government sales of heavy equipment, given the guaranteed repurchase option
2. the treatment of future costs for abnormal maintenance.

Problem 17.6 REVENUES AND EXPENSES ★★ LO 6, 7

Fashion World is a glossy monthly magazine that has been on the market for nearly 2 years. It currently has a circulation across several countries of 1.6 million copies per month. Currently, negotiations are under way for the company that produces the magazine, among other publications, to obtain a loan from a bank in order to upgrade production facilities. The company is currently producing close to capacity and expects to grow at an average of 15% over the next 3 years.

After reviewing the financial statements of the company, the bank loan officer, B. Honest, has indicated that a loan could be made if the company is able to improve its debt–equity ratio (non-current liabilities divided by equity) and current ratio (current assets divided by current liabilities) to a specified level.

The company's marketing manager, B. Quick, has devised a plan to meet these requirements. Quick indicates that an advertising campaign can be initiated immediately to increase the company's circulation. The campaign would include:

- an offer to subscribe to *Fashion World* at 75% of the normal price for 1 year
- a special offer to all new subscribers to receive another of the company's publications, *World Atlas*, at a guaranteed price of $8; the atlas usually sells for $15.95 and costs $11 to produce
- an unconditional guarantee that any subscriber will receive a full refund if dissatisfied with the magazine.

Although the offer for a full refund is risky, Quick claims that very few people ask for a refund after receiving half of their subscription issues. Quick also claims that other magazine companies have tried this sales campaign and have had great success, with an average cancellation rate of only 25%. Overall, these other companies increased their initial circulation threefold, and in the long run increased circulation to twice that which existed before the promotion. Furthermore, 80% of the new subscribers are expected to take up the atlas offer. Quick feels confident that the increased subscriptions from the campaign will increase the current ratio and reduce the debt–equity ratio to the required levels. The managing director agrees.

You are the accountant for the company, and must give your opinion of the accounting treatment for the proposed campaign.

Required

In light of the *Conceptual Framework*, explain:
1. how you would treat the costs of the advertising campaign
2. when revenue should be recognised from the new subscriptions
3. how you would treat the sales returns stemming from the unconditional guarantee
4. how the extra $8 received per atlas should be recorded.

Problem 17.7 CONCEPTUAL FRAMEWORK — INCOME, LIABILITIES AND EQUITY ★★ **LO 4, 6, 7**

Strathalbyn Leasing Ltd (SLL) is the owner–lessor of some high-quality apartment blocks, which have pleasant surroundings of parks and gardens and are only a short walk to a busy shopping centre and to public transport.

In order to achieve tax benefits, the company leased all units in the blocks to its customers for a period of 20 years, requiring all customers to pay for the lease with a lump sum in advance. All units have been leased and SLL has received approximately $30 million in cash.

Since the customers (lessees) were to receive the benefits of their lease over a 20-year period, SLL decided to account for the cash received in advance as deferred lease income, and to use a straight-line basis over 20 years in order to recognise revenue. In SLL's accounts at the end of the year, the deferred lease income was disclosed as a non-current liability.

ASIC objected to this treatment and argued that the item in question should be disclosed in the company's statement of financial position/balance sheet not as a liability but as a separate amount after total equity.

Required

Using the *Conceptual Framework* as a guide, discuss whether ASIC's proposed treatment of the $30 million in the financial reports of SLL is correct, stating your reasons. Consider also whether SLL's program for recognising revenue is appropriate.

Read the following extract:

Museum and art gallery annual general-purpose financial reports may amount to misrepresentations if they include heritage and art collections that are not assets, as defined by the Australian Accounting Standards.

The Australian accounting profession defined an asset in the conceptual framework so that when financial reports are prepared, only those things that meet the requirements can be included. There are two decisions: definition and recognition by valuation.

Defining an asset

... Accountants know that an asset is a representation of 'future economic benefits' that must be accruing to the organisation that prepares the financial reports. That is, for the purposes of the financial reports, any argument that there will be 'future economic benefits' to the community at large is irrelevant.

Certainly, public heritage collections have a number of future benefits for individuals and the community generally, but is there any future benefit deriving from the collections which is economic to the museum?

The 'future economic benefits' ... are the income received from admission fees, other user-pays fees, grants and sponsorship. However, these are discounted for various reasons, including the fact that the value of the receipts is a minimum and variable measure of the benefits flowing from the overall operation of a museum. The collections do not generate museums' net revenues — rather, it is a package of services offered by a museum or gallery that is the chief generator.

Even if a museum can argue that its collections are representations of 'future economic benefits' as per the definitions in the accounting standards, the question of whether it is probable that the 'future economic benefits' will eventuate must be asked. If museums can find any 'future economic benefits', can they list the 'future economic benefits' of their collections with any degree of certainty? Is it valid to use current or past data to provide evidence of a future benefit? Can conjecture be evidence? No, of course not.

Yet this is what the accounting profession seems to be encouraging as a result of the writing of the conceptual framework and accounting standards ...

The 'future economic benefit' is only an asset if the museum controls that 'future economic benefit'. Control 'means the capacity of the entity to benefit from the asset in the pursuit of the entity's objectives and to deny or regulate the access of others to that benefit'.

The conceptual framework is very clear that it is *control,* not ownership, which is a defining characteristic of an asset ...

Source: Helen Tyzack, 'Invisible assets?', *Charter.*

Required

Discuss whether museum and art collections should be recognised as assets on the statement of financial position/balance sheet of a public museum. Do you agree with Tyzack? Why or why not?

Problem 17.9 EXISTENCES OF ASSETS AND LIABILITIES — CONTRACTS ★★

Read the following extract from an article about Bob Jane's latest business venture:

He may have turned 80 but there's no stopping Bob Jane from wheeling and dealing. He recently signed a heads of agreement document with senior Chinese government officials to build three car-racing tracks within a single multi-purpose sports venue, car-warehousing facilities, an exhibition centre, accessory outlets and a finance house about 500 kilometres east of Beijing, in the Dalian Huay-uankou Economic Zone.

The company Bob Jane (China) is party to an agreement to build a car-racing track capable of hosting a Formula 1 Grand Prix, an oval-shaped speedway and a drag-racing strip. He expects work to start within the next 12 months. 'I refer to this centre as an automotive hub, and these multi-purpose facilities will be available to the public and Chinese government officials,' says Jane.

'Besides hosting domestic motorsport events, people will learn how to drive at this centre, and police, government chauffeurs and public officials will be able to do additional training to sharpen up their road skills.

'The centre will sell new cars, tyres, wheels and other accessories and will offer full-service repair workshops. This will be a state-of-the-art hub as China is committed to investing heavily in its automotive industry. China sees automotive growth as being tremendous, and I'm a small party to an investment which could grow to between US$20 billion and US$30 billion before it's finished. The Chinese are also proposing to build a tennis centre, soccer stadium, golf course and yacht club within the same zone. This is the most exciting venture I've ever been involved in after more than 50 years in business and I will be spending much more time in China. We've only just started — I've only just signed the deal in Australia with senior Chinese government officials.'

Jane stresses that the deal is between him and Chinese government officials and does not involve his mostly franchised T-Marts tyre empire. Jane remains chairman of Bob Jane T-Marts, but the day-to-day operations are left to his son Rodney, who is chief executive and, like his father, a racing-car driver. Jane, who has been importing tyres from Europe, the US and China for about 45 years, sees his latest deal as an extension of a long business career that began with a leather goods business more than 50 years ago.

Source: Anthony Black, 'Still on track', *InTheBlack*.

This article was written by the financial journalist Anthony Black who has extensive experience writing on corporate and financial matters. For enquiries on past articles refer to 'anthonyblack3@bigpond.com'

Required

By referring to the definitions and recognition criteria of the elements of financial reports as contained in the *Conceptual Framework*, discuss when and how Bob Jane's business should account for the deal signed with the Chinese government officials.

Problem 17.10 CONCEPTUAL FRAMEWORK ★★

Felixtow Ltd is a manufacturer of fuel injection systems for the automotive industry. At the beginning of the current financial year, Felixtow Ltd entered an agreement with Spare Parts Ltd to manufacture and to supply to Spare Parts Ltd 10 000 fuel injection systems at a stipulated price before the end of the financial year. The systems were to be made to the exact specifications required by Spare Parts Ltd. If Felixtow Ltd failed to perform as per the agreement, severe financial penalties were included as part of the contractual arrangements.

The agreement also provided that Spare Parts Ltd would make royalty payments to Felixtow Ltd after each batch of 2000 systems was delivered. Each royalty payment was to be $100 000, and was to be paid by Spare Parts Ltd for the use of Felixtow Ltd's patent rights attached to the fuel injection systems, and to help in supplying working capital to Felixtow Ltd during the manufacturing process. The royalty payments were considered to be a part payment of the ultimate selling price, which was receivable in full immediately on delivery of the final batch.

On delivery of the first batch of 2000 systems to Spare Parts Ltd, the batch was found not to comply with the exact specifications required, and the batch was returned to Felixtow Ltd. Spare Parts Ltd refused to pay the royalty payment attached to that batch until the appropriate modifications had been carried out. Furthermore, Spare Parts Ltd indicated that, unless the modifications were completed promptly, financial penalties under the contract would be instigated. Felixtow Ltd assessed that the modifications would delay completion of all batches by 6 months. Spare Parts Ltd was prepared to accept this delay without imposing penalties, but indicated that no further delays would be tolerated. If further delays occur, the contract would be cancelled.

Required

Discuss, with reference to the *Conceptual Framework*, the appropriate accounting treatment in the accounting records of Felixtow Ltd for its contract with Spare Parts Ltd. Pay particular attention to the timing of recognition of the appropriate financial statement elements.

Problem 17.11 LIABILITIES, EQUITY AND EXPENSES ★★★ LO 6, 7

Salisbury Ltd is a public company supplying different types of packaging for the food and beverage industry. Among its products are labels for beer bottles, soft-drink bottles and jam jars and tins, and packages for frozen foods, cheese, yoghurt, confectionery and snack foods.

Salisbury Ltd has reported sales of approximately $25 million for the year ended 30 June 2013. The directors of the company have been considering a public share offer and have contacted a merchant banker to investigate the possibility.

On 15 November 2013, the company made a private placement of 200 000 8% cumulative, redeemable, non-participating preference shares at an issue price of $5 per share. The share issue was made for the purpose of financing expansion of needed plant and equipment. Each preference share is convertible into two ordinary shares at the option of the holder, and is subject to mandatory conversion in the event of a public share issue or mandatory redemption in cash on 15 November 2018 for $8 per share, whichever occurrence is the earlier. It is expected that no cumulative preference dividends will be due when the preference shares are converted.

In preparing its draft general purpose financial reports for the year ended 30 June 2014, the chief accountant of Salisbury Ltd, L. Fingers, disclosed the preference shares in the equity section. Fingers did not adjust periodically the carrying amount of the preference shares for the difference between the issue price and the redemption price.

On examining the draft financial reports, Salisbury Ltd's auditor argued that the preference shares should be regarded as long-term debt financing and reported as non-current liabilities, and that the periodic adjustment, representing the difference between the issue price and the redemption price, should be reported over time as interest expense in the income statement.

Required

Discuss, with reference to the *Conceptual Framework*, the appropriate accounting treatment for these preference shares and for the potential increase in the redemption price.

Problem 17.12 INCOME AND LIABILITIES ★★★ LO 6, 7

Bartholomew Sampson owns 80% of the issued shares of Sampson Industrial and Commercial Cleaning Ltd (SICC), a distributor of cleaning equipment for industrial purposes. During the annual audit of SICC, the firm's auditors, Lane, Ingerson, Samuel and Adamson (LISA), noticed two irregularities in the accounts and asked Sampson to provide reasons for these irregularities.

First, SICC had, in error, been charging GST for the last year on certain equipment sales that were exempt from GST, under the government's roll-back scheme, as they had been sold to various not-for-profit institutions. Sampson, as managing director, claimed that it was impractical and costly to refund the GST collected (approximately $100 000) to these customers. These amounts had been transferred to current year's profits.

Second, LISA noticed that at the beginning of the current year Sampson had advanced $500 000 to SICC, at an interest rate of 8% per year. Because of the concerns of bank creditors as to the weak capital position of SICC at year's end, Sampson decided to regard these advances as further capital contributions to SICC, and the $500 000 was recorded as contributed equity. Interest for the current year, totalling $40 000, had been recorded as an expense.

Third, a number of years ago, Sampson had purchased and donated to SICC a collection of artworks, which had cost Sampson $300 000. SICC had recorded these works in its own records at that price. Sampson had these artworks valued by a licensed valuer on 30 June at $1 000 000. SICC passed a journal entry to revalue the artworks and recognise income of $700 000.

Required

In light of the *Conceptual Framework*, discuss SICC's treatment in the accounts of the GST over-charge, the treatment of Sampson's advance plus the interest on the advance, and the artworks.

Sand and Gravel Company Ltd (SGC) was floated by public subscription on 1 July 2014. The entity so formed engaged in a number of revenue-earning activities which had been previously administered by the government's Department of Waterways. However, the government, in order to generate much-needed cash flows, decided to sell these activities to private enterprise.

The two major revenue-earning activities acquired by SGC were:

1. Operation and maintenance of all shipping channels within the port of Osborne. After the company was formed, it acquired a number of dredges from the Department of Waterways, these being used to prevent silting of shipping channels.

    Constant dredging of the channels and creation of new channels has occurred since the city began, because only limited natural channels exist within the port. In return for undertaking these activities, SGC has the authority to charge shipping fees on all visiting cargo ships using the channels. Many other forms of shipping traffic such as pleasure craft, tourist boats, fishing trawlers, ferries, power boats and jet skis also use these shipping channels because of the shallowness of the port, but are not required to pay any formal shipping fees. No organisation other than SGC is permitted to dredge channels.

2. The basin of the Torrent River on which the port of Osborne is situated is very rich in gravel. Hence, as a result of the dredging operations, a very large tonnage of high-quality gravel is dredged by SGC. All gravel is sold under a fixed contract to Croydon Concrete Ltd. Gravel is also quarried by a number of other companies around the port of Osborne.

The general manager of SGC is having difficulty in clarifying a number of conceptual and practical issues about the entity he now controls. He is seeking answers to the following questions:

- What assets does SGC have?
- Are the river channels assets or are they a public good?
- Tons of gravel are lying on the river bed, just waiting to be dredged. Is it an asset now, or when it is 'floating gravel', or when it is delivered, or at some other time?
- As SGC is required by the government to keep the channels clean or face penalties, is there a liability here? Over how many years?
- Pleasure craft use SGC's channels. Does this affect the classification of the channels?

Required

As consultant to SGC, provide a report to the general manager to help him determine what items should be included in SGC's financial statements and how to account for the activities of the business.

DECISION ANALYSIS

Recognition of revenue

Paddy Hanlon has spent many years of his life panning for gold, with little success. On several occasions, he has found small traces of gold along the usual river banks that he is licensed to pan. However, on his last trip to the Bendigo River, almost by accident he managed to find a very promising piece of rock which he placed in his satchel. He took the rock into town to be examined and valued by experts, who assured him that the rock was a valuable gold nugget and that it was worth at least $50 000. Paddy was elated and opened a bottle of champagne to celebrate with his friends.

About 2 weeks later, he sold the nugget to a jeweller for $60 000 in cash.

Required

Based on the *Conceptual Framework* and IAS 18/AASB 118 *Revenue*, decide whether and when revenue exists and on the appropriate time for this revenue to be recognised in the accounts of Paddy Hanlon, Gold Prospector.

Accounting and politics

Visit the websites of the IASB (www.ifrs.org), the FASB (www.fasb.org) and the AASB (www.aasb.com.au).

Required

A. Discuss what influence politics has on the establishment of accounting standards?

B. Examine whether political factors have played a role in the development of accounting standards in Australia, and comment on whether you agree or disagree with the Australian Government's involvement in the standard-setting process.

Future considerations

Visit the websites of the IASB (www.ifrs.org) and the AASB (www.aasb.com.au).

Required

A. Find out the major issues currently on the agenda for consideration in future accounting standards, and present a report to the class on the basic requirements of those standards.

B. Determine and report to the class on the latest issues being discussed by the IASB and the FASB in their joint project of revising the conceptual framework.

Refer to the latest financial report of JB Hi-Fi Limited on its website, www.jbhifi.com.au, and answer the following questions:

1. From the nature of the report, JB Hi-Fi Limited is a reporting entity. Why is this so?

2. Who would you consider to be the main users of the JB Hi-Fi Limited financial report? What types of decisions would they make based on the information contained in the report?

3. Does JB Hi-Fi Limited use the historical cost system or some other method of valuing assets? Is there any evidence that the company has revalued any of its assets in the past 12 months? Explain.

4. In the report, a summary statistical analysis is often presented. What is the importance of the statement of accounting policies in interpreting these figures? Do you consider that the figures would be of benefit to users of the report?

5. What evidence is there of the application of the materiality concept in the report?

Receivables

Learning objectives

After studying this chapter, you should be able to:

1 describe the different types of receivables (pp. 750–1)

2 define accounts receivable, and state how accounting recognises and values them (pp. 751–2)

3 explain the nature of bad and doubtful debts and demonstrate how to account for them
   (pp. 752–61)

4 describe the principles involved in the management and control of accounts receivable (pp. 761–5)

5 discuss the nature of bills receivable and demonstrate how to account for them (pp. 765–71).

Money too slow coming in

Business owners remain under cash flow pressure as payment terms deteriorated in the December quarter, a survey shows.

The latest figures from credit reporting agency Dun & Bradstreet reveal South Australian businesses take an average of 54.1 days to pay their accounts — nearly double the standard 30-day term.

Firms based in New South Wales and the Australian Capital Territory are the slowest to settle outstanding accounts, both recording payment terms of 54.8 days. West Australian-based firms were the quickest to pay, averaging 52.2 days.

The survey, which includes more than nine million current accounts receivable records contained on the D&B database, puts the national average at 53.9 days — 2.1 days longer than the previous quarter.

Chief executive Christine Christian says access to cash from accounts receivable is critical to business survival as the economy emerges from the downturn.

'Businesses have begun to upgrade investment plans and confidence levels bode well for domestic demand in 2010,' she said. 'However, liquidity and access to cash are absolutely critical in an upturn. If payment terms

continue to deteriorate in the months ahead, firms may find themselves battling the cash flow pressures that impacted business growth and stability during the height of the credit crisis.'

Source: Excerpts from Frances Steward, 'Cashflow crisis for business owners', *The Advertiser.*

Chapter preview

Many economies today are credit economies. Manufacturers, wholesalers, retailers and service organisations regularly extend credit to buyers of their goods and services as a means of increasing sales. The willingness of entities to extend credit has been an important factor in the significant growth of the world economy over time. This extension of credit has given rise to accounts receivable or debtors. In addition, businesses make use of negotiable legal instruments, referred to as bills of exchange and promissory notes, which are an alternative means of extending credit and arranging finance. Other receivables arise when an entity lends money to owners and employees.

A common feature of all receivables is that they are regarded as highly liquid assets that are generally expected to convert into cash in the short term, and hence are classified as current assets in the financial statements. Any receivables not planned for collection within the operating cycle or within 12 months after the date of the financial statements are usually classified as non-current assets. Depending on the particular business entity, receivables can constitute a relatively large asset, and accurate accounting and control is important.

As the scene setter highlights, receivables management and cash collection are high-risk areas for businesses and are vital for their survival. The issues identified are disturbing because small businesses seem to be paying little attention to the management and control of receivables.

Accounting for, and control of, receivables are discussed in this chapter.

18.1 Types of receivables

Learning objective 1

Describe the different types of receivables

Receivables are categorised into three main types: (1) accounts receivable, (2) bills and notes receivable, and (3) other receivables. Important aspects of these categories are examined below.

Accounts receivable

In a broad sense, accounts receivable relate to all accounts for which a business expects to receive money in the near future. For accounting purposes, however, accounts receivable are specifically those accounts that arise from the sale of goods and services on credit in the ordinary course of business. Credit is often extended to customers, i.e. the buyer has a specified length of time, such as 30 or 60 days, before payment is due. These customers' accounts are called **accounts receivable** or **trade debtors** by the entity granting credit.

Chapter 7 illustrated the accounting procedures for accounts receivable. Sales of merchandise on credit, plus any applicable GST are entered into the sales journal, and debited to the individual customers' accounts in the subsidiary ledger. At the end of the period, the totals from the sales journal are posted to the appropriate general ledger accounts. The sum of all the debits to customer accounts is sent to the Accounts Receivable Control account, the GST is credited to the GST Collections account, and the Sales account is credited for the Sales Revenue, which excludes GST. The same procedures apply for the sale or provision of services. Accounts receivable are usually classified as current assets in the balance sheet because, by definition (as discussed in chapter 4), they are expected to be collected in cash within the entity's operating cycle.

Bills receivable

Sometimes credit is granted only on receipt of a formal legal instrument such as a bill of exchange or a promissory note. A **bill of exchange** is simply a written order made by a debtor to pay a certain amount of money on a predetermined date in the future, and a **promissory note** is a written promise made by a debtor to pay a certain amount of money on a predetermined date in the future. This predetermined date is called the maturity date. Since in both cases an entity expects to receive cash in the near future for these instruments, they are collectively referred to as **bills receivable** and are treated as such for accounting purposes.

Bills of exchange and promissory notes had their origins in the need to have an instrument that made it possible for the seller of goods to allow the buyer extended credit on sales and the payment for goods exported. Bills arising in this way are referred to as 'trade bills'. Trade bills should be accounted for in a similar manner to accounts receivable and should be amalgamated with accounts receivable for a number of important analyses of business performance.

The main use of bills today is as a means of obtaining finance. They are now an important feature of the capital market and these are referred to as 'commercial bills'. Commercial bills are freely traded in financial markets. Reporting practices do not classify bills receivable into trade bills and commercial bills for balance sheet purposes. Since the term of all bills receivable ranges up to a maximum of 180 days, bills receivable are classified as current assets in the balance sheet.

Other receivables

Other receivables can also arise, such as loans to directors, managers and employees of the business entity, interest and rent receivable, amounts receivable as a result of the sale of non-current assets, and short-term deposits. These are recorded for accounting purposes outside the Accounts Receivable Control account and its subsidiary ledger. A separate account can be opened for each of the other receivables accounts in the general ledger, or a control account can be established, e.g. Other Receivables, and details of each of the individual non-trade receivables can be recorded in a subsidiary ledger. These accounts are classified as current assets and reported as such in the balance sheet if they are expected to be collected within the entity's operating cycle or within 12 months. Otherwise, they are classified as non-current assets.

The above classification of accounts receivable and other receivables is important to allow proper analysis by both management and external users of accounting reports of the performance and financial position of the business entity. As discussed in a later chapter, certain analyses used in evaluating the performance of a business entity depend on this classification.

18.2 Accounts receivable (trade debtors)

Learning objective 2

Define accounts receivable, and state how accounting recognises and values them

Accounts receivable are assets because they represent resources controlled by the entity from which future economic benefits are expected to flow to the entity. Accounts receivable result from the sale of goods or services on credit. The future economic benefit is the cash that will be received from customers who have been extended credit. Although business entities prefer to collect the money owing at the time of sale, experience has shown that extending credit can increase income, and hence profit, significantly. To accomplish an increase in profit, however, the additional gross profit generated by credit sales must exceed the additional expenses incurred in extending credit. These expenses include investigation of the creditworthiness of prospective customers, additional record keeping and the cost of uncollectable accounts.

As with all assets, accounting is concerned with:

● when to recognise the account receivable (recognition)
● how to measure the value of accounts receivable for reporting purposes (valuation)
● assisting in the management and control of accounts receivable (control).

The first two of these are dealt with in the following subsections, and the third is discussed later in the chapter.

Recognition of accounts receivable

Recognition of accounts receivable presents few problems in accounting. For an entity providing services, accounts receivable are recognised when services are provided and invoices issued for the amount owing. For entities concerned with wholesaling and retailing goods, accounts receivable are recognised at the time of sale, evidenced by the issue of invoices detailing the amounts owing for the goods. If businesses are registered for the GST, the amount of GST is included in the amount of the account receivable. The only other accounting issue to be considered, apart from the subsequent receipt of cash, is the possibility of adjusting the amount to be received if the customer is offered a discount for payment in cash within a designated discount period or if the customer is given an allowance for returned or damaged goods. Accounting for cash discounts and sales returns and allowances is covered in previous chapters.

Valuation of accounts receivable

The valuation issue arises when accounts receivable have to be included in the financial statements at the end of the accounting period. Experience shows that not all amounts owing from receivables are collected — some debtors cannot, or will not, pay when the time comes. Therefore, the valuation of receivables becomes an important issue, because 100% will not normally be collected. The accounts receivable are said to be impaired, which means the carrying amount is greater than the amount that is expected to be recovered. A similar issue can arise for other non-current assets. This is discussed in detail in chapter 21. This uncollectable portion, or impairment, can be known as bad debts.

The accounts receivable should be reported in terms of their future economic benefits — their gross amount less an allowance for expected bad debts. The receivables are therefore reported at fair value. Remember also that the amounts of any receivables that will not be collected are an expense incurred as a result of the revenue earned from the initial sale. This bad debts expense (as it is called) will not be known with certainty until the next accounting period, but it is estimated in the current period as an expense of earning the current period's income. Therefore, estimating future bad debts has consequences for reporting bad debts expense in the current period's income statement.

A major accounting problem lies in estimating the amount of the receivables that will become bad. Accounting for bad debts and doubtful debts and estimating and allowing for such debts are examined below.

Learning objective 3

Explain the nature of bad and doubtful debts and demonstrate how to account for them

18.3 Bad and doubtful debts

As already mentioned, regardless of the diligence and care exercised in extending credit, there are almost always some customers who do not pay all or some of the amounts they owe. When businesses make the decision to sell goods and services on credit, they know that some of the resulting accounts receivable will eventually prove to be uncollectable. These uncollectable accounts are called bad debts and are considered an expense of extending credit to customers.

In accounting, **bad debts expense** is best recognised in the same accounting period in which the credit sales are recognised. There is no general rule for determining the time at which a receivable actually becomes bad. The fact that the debtor fails to pay on the due date does not by itself establish that the debt is bad. The debtor may simply have forgotten to pay or may be temporarily short of cash and cannot pay until later. The entity (creditor) normally makes a continued effort to collect overdue accounts through oral and/or written communication with the debtor. It may eventually turn the receivable over to a collection agency or begin legal action to recover the debt. This process may take many months to complete, with receivables arising in one accounting period being collected or written off in the following accounting period, or later. Because the specific debtors that will eventually become bad are unknown in advance (otherwise the business would not extend credit to that debtor), bad debts expense, as demonstrated below, is estimated at the end of the accounting period by what is known as the allowance method of accounting for bad debts.

Allowance method of accounting for bad debts

At the end of the accounting period, before the accounting records are closed and the financial statements prepared, an estimate is made of the amount of accounts receivable expected to be uncollectable, i.e. doubtful debts. An adjusting entry is prepared with a debit to the Bad Debts Expense account and a credit to an account called **Allowance for Doubtful Debts**. For external reporting purposes, this allowance is sometimes called an 'allowance for impairment of receivables'. If accounts receivable include GST, any GST included in a debt that becomes bad can be claimed as an adjustment (a write-back) of GST Collections recorded at the time of sale.

To illustrate, assume that Hannah Ltd began operations on 1 July 2012, made credit sales for $440 000 including GST during 2012–13, and collected $330 000 of these accounts during the year. The balance in the Accounts Receivable account at the end of the first year is therefore $110 000, including $10 000 GST. After a careful review of the accounts receivable, the management of Hannah Ltd estimates that $6600 of the accounts will be uncollectable. Since this amount includes $600 GST that will be recoverable from the ATO if and when any specific account is finally declared bad, the allowance for the doubtful debts is set at $6000.

An adjusting entry is made on 30 June 2013, the end of the financial year for Hannah Ltd, as follows:

2013 June 30	Bad Debts Expense	6 000	
	Allowance for Doubtful Debts		6 000
	(Estimated bad debts expense)		

The entry serves two important purposes. First, it records the estimated bad debts of $6000 as an expense of the period in which the income from credit sales was recognised, thereby relating expenses incurred to revenues earned. Note that the sales revenue recorded always excludes GST in accordance with accounting practice. Bad debts expense of $6000 is deducted on the income statement for the year ended 30 June 2013. Second, the entry establishes an allowance account that is deducted from accounts receivable on the balance sheet in order to report accounts receivable at their estimated fair (collectable) value as explained previously. Again, note that the GST component of $600 is recoverable in the future when debts are actually written off as bad.

Allowance for doubtful debts. Why credit an allowance account rather than crediting accounts receivable directly when recording the entry for estimated bad debts? Recall that the general ledger Accounts Receivable account is a control account supported by a subsidiary ledger that identifies the amounts owed by individual customers. Any debit or credit to the Accounts Receivable Control account requires an equivalent debit or credit to one or more of the subsidiary ledger accounts. But it is impossible to determine in advance which specific accounts will prove bad, otherwise (as already stated) credit would not be extended in the first place. A direct credit to the Accounts Receivable Control account will produce an imbalance between it and the accounts receivable subsidiary ledger, thereby destroying an important element of internal control. The alternative is to credit an allowance account (in the nature of a contra-asset account) that, when subtracted from accounts receivable on the balance sheet, results in reporting accounts receivable at the estimated amount expected to be collected (i.e. fair value), as shown in figure 18.1

Common usage has, in the past, seen this account described in accounting standards and legislation as the Provision for Doubtful Debts. Accounting standard IAS 37/AASB 137 *Provisions, Contingent Liabilities and Contingent Assets* defines provisions as liabilities for which the amount or timing of the future sacrifice of economic benefits is uncertain. To reduce confusion in the use of the term 'provision', now defined as a subset of liabilities, we have adopted the term 'allowance' when used in relation to bad debts.

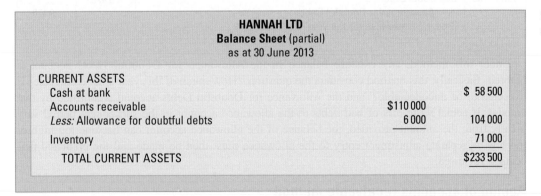

HANNAH LTD
Balance Sheet (partial)
as at 30 June 2013

CURRENT ASSETS		
Cash at bank		$ 58 500
Accounts receivable	$110 000	
Less: Allowance for doubtful debts	6 000	104 000
Inventory		71 000
TOTAL CURRENT ASSETS		$233 500

Figure 18.1 Reporting the allowance for doubtful debts

Estimating doubtful debts

A number of approaches can be used to estimate of the amount of doubtful debts, whatever method is used, accurate estimation will require a combination of past experience and forecasts of future economic and business conditions, with considerable personal judgement involved. The goal is to produce a reasonable estimate of the amount of accounts receivable for which the cash will actually be received. If the accountant underestimates doubtful debts, profit will be overstated in the current period, reducing the usefulness of the information provided to users, and profit will have to be reduced in future periods. However, the use of an overcautious approach to recording and reporting will produce a relatively low asset value for accounts receivable as well as an understated profit figure in the current period.

Two methods are widely used to estimate doubtful debts:
- percentage of net sales
- ageing of accounts receivable.

The first method determines the amount as a **percentage of net credit sales** for the period. Because this method uses net credit sales (credit sales less credit sales returns and allowances) as a base, it has traditionally been referred to as the 'income statement' approach. The method places emphasis on the relationship between credit sales and bad debts, and is therefore an attempt to record the expense in the same period as the sales were made. We noted earlier that the allowance for doubtful debts is calculated excluding GST; because the sales figure also excludes GST no adjustment needs to be made in this calculation.

The second method analyses the age and probability of collection of the individual accounts receivable and is called **ageing of accounts receivable**. Since this method bases doubtful debts on an analysis of accounts receivable, it has traditionally been referred to as the 'balance sheet' approach. Emphasis is placed on determining the fair value of accounts receivable on the balance sheet. Accounts receivable may include GST and therefore an adjustment must be made to ensure any GST is excluded from the amount of the allowance, and will only be considered in the event of the actual write-off of that account receivable. Most entities use one of these two methods, but not both.

Percentage of net credit sales method

An analysis of past accounting data usually establishes some predictable percentage relationship between the amount of bad debts and the amount of net credit sales (excluding GST). This percentage is then applied to net credit sales for the relevant period to estimate the amount that should be credited to doubtful debts. The logic of this method is that credit sales produce the accounts receivable that may become bad debts in the future. As an example, assume that past experience shows that about 1% of net credit sales each year has been written off as bad debts and that net credit sales for the current year (excluding GST) amount to $847 000. The year-end adjustment to recognise bad debts expense is as follows:

2013			
June 30	Bad Debts Expense	8 470	
	Allowance for Doubtful Debts		8 470
	(Bad debts expense for the year, 1% × $847 000)		

Under this method, any existing balance in the Allowance for Doubtful Debts account is ignored. Basically, this method considers the question, 'How much of this year's net credit sales is expected to be uncollectable?' and the Allowance for Doubtful Debts account is adjusted by that amount. If actual write-offs of bad debts to the allowance account in the subsequent period vary greatly from the amount provided, the balance of the allowance account can become too high or too low. A separate adjustment entry to the allowance must then be made and the predicted percentage reviewed.

Ageing of accounts receivable method

If the estimate of doubtful debts is based on an analysis of accounts receivable, the estimate is derived from a schedule that analyses and classifies accounts receivable by age (how many days overdue they are). This method calculates what the amount of the allowance *should be* and, depending on what is already in the allowance account, an *adjustment* is made. The preparation of the schedule is shown in figure 18.2. All amounts include GST.

It is known that the longer an account receivable is overdue, the greater the probability that it will never be paid, i.e. go 'bad'. Past accounting records are therefore analysed to determine the approximate percentage of each age group that will become bad debts. For example, the analysis of past accounting records presented underneath figure 18.2 shows the estimated percentages of accounts receivable that were written off as bad.

Figure 18.2 Ageing of accounts receivable method of measuring doubtful debts

Ageing of Accounts Receivable
as at 30 June 2013

| Customer | Balance | Not yet due | Number of days overdue | | | | |
			1–30	31–60	61–90	91–180	Over 180
Apex Ltd	$ 748		$ 748				
B. Brent	385	$ 385					
Carr Co. Ltd	649	264	385				
Darnett Ltd	946			$ 462	$ 484		
J. Evans	682						$ 682
S. Fox	236					$ 236	
E. Ware	814	814					
B. Yale	1 023	913			110		
Total	$91 960	$61 600	$11 660	$7 260	$4 620	$4 180	$2 640

Analysis of past accounting records

Age category	Percentage
Not yet due	1%
1–30 days overdue	5%
31–60 days overdue	10%
61 90 days overduc	20%
91–180 days overdue	30%
Over 180 days overdue	60%

With these data, the balance needed in the allowance for doubtful debts to reduce the accounts receivable to estimated fair value is calculated as follows:

| Age category | Amount | Estimated bad debts amount | |
		Percentage	Amount
Not yet due	$61 600	1	$ 616
1–30 days overdue	11 660	5	583
31–60 days overdue	7 260	10	726
61–90 days overdue	4 620	20	924
91–180 days overdue	4 180	30	1 254
Over 180 days overdue	2 640	60	1 584
	$91 960		$5 687

The total determined as doubtful and estimated to become bad of $5687 includes $517 (i.e. $1/11$ of $5687) of GST. This component is recoverable from the ATO in the event of an actual bad debt, and is therefore excluded from the allowance for doubtful debts amount.

The total determined, $5170 (i.e. $5687 − $517), is the balance needed in the Allowance for Doubtful Debts account. Consequently, any existing balance in the allowance account must be taken into consideration when determining the amount of the end-of-period adjustment to be made on 30 June. For example, if the Allowance for Doubtful Debts account already has a $1540 credit balance before adjustment, bad debts expense must be charged for the difference of $3630 (i.e. $5170 − $1540), and the following adjusting entry prepared:

June	30	Bad Debts Expense	3 630	
		Allowance for Doubtful Debts		3 630
		(Estimated bad debts expense for the year)		

After this entry is posted, the Accounts Receivable Control and Allowance for Doubtful Debts accounts appear as follows:

Accounts Receivable Control

30/6	Balance	91 960		

Allowance for Doubtful Debts

			30/6	Balance (before adjustment)	1 540
30/6	Balance c/d	5 170	30/6	Bad Debts Expense	3 630
		5 170			5 170
			1/7	Balance b/d	5 170

The Allowance for Doubtful Debts account may sometimes have a debit balance at year-end (before any adjustment entry is made) because more accounts than estimated actually went bad and were debited to the allowance account. If the Allowance for Doubtful Debts account had a debit balance (for example $260) before adjustment, that balance would be added to the $5170 and the total of $5430 would be debited to Bad Debts Expense and credited to the Allowance for Doubtful Debts account to produce the desired balance of $5170 in the allowance account.

Rather than preparing an ageing schedule as in figure 18.2, some entities simply analyse past data to determine a percentage relationship between estimated bad debts and accounts receivable. GST is taken into account in this percentage. The percentage is multiplied by the balance in accounts receivable at the end of the year to determine the balance needed in the Allowance for Doubtful Debts account after extracting any GST component present. The account is then adjusted to that balance by an entry similar to the one shown above.

BUSINESS KNOWLEDGE

Ageing analysis of receivables

In the manual system of accounting, the ageing analysis of debtors can be a laborious and time-consuming task. However, computerised accounts receivable accounting modules (as are available in MYOB Accounting and QuickBooks) can perform an ageing analysis of receivables on demand, even if thousands of accounts are involved. As indicated elsewhere, electronic spreadsheets can also be used to keep a record of accounts receivable, and programming the spreadsheet to perform an ageing analysis is relatively simple.

Polly's Plants Aged Receivables 30th November				
Name	Total Due	0–30	31–60	61–90
Thelma's Nursery	$ 550.00	$ 0.00	$ 550.00	$ 0.00
Roses R Red	$1,200.00	$1,200.00	$ 0.00	$ 0.00
Callam Gardens	$1,410.00	$1,410.00	$ 0.00	$ 0.00
Total	$3,160.00	$2,610.00	$ 550.00	$ 0.00

Writing off bad debts

When an account receivable is determined to be bad, it is written off by debiting the Allowance for Doubtful Debts account, writing back GST previously recognised on the sale or service by debiting GST Collections, and crediting Accounts Receivable Control. An adjustment note complying with GST legislative requirements must be issued in order to obtain an adjustment of GST previously recognised. Of course, the related account in the accounts receivable subsidiary ledger is also credited. For example, assume that on 31 July 2013, after an extended effort to collect, the $682 account of J. Evans is determined to be bad and the write-off of the account is authorised. The following entry is made:

2013			
July 31	Allowance for Doubtful Debts	620	
	GST Collections	62	
	Accounts Receivable Control – J. Evans		682
	(Write-off of the account receivable as bad)		

The first thing to note about this entry is that the write-off is debited to the Allowance for Doubtful Debts account not to the Bad Debts Expense account. The bad debts expense was recognised on an estimated basis at the end of the year in which the sale was made. To charge an expense account again at the time the account is written off results in a double recording of the expense, which leads to an understated profit. The second thing to note is that the net amount of accounts receivable is almost unchanged by the entry to write off a bad debt, being reduced only by the GST on the bad debt. After the write-off entry is posted, the general ledger accounts appear as shown below:

Accounts Receivable Control

2013			2013		
1/7	Balance (before write-off)	91 960	31/7	Allowance for Doubtful Debts and GST Collections	682
			31/7	Balance c/d	91 278
		91 960			91 960
1/8	Balance b/d	91 278			

GST Collections

2013				
31/7	Account Receivable Control – J. Evans	62		

Allowance for Doubtful Debts

2013			2013		
31/7	Account Receivable Control – J. Evans	620	1/7	Balance (before write-off)	5 170
31/7	Balance c/d	4 550			
		5 170			5 170
			1/8	Balance b/d	4 550

Note that the net amount of accounts receivable is reduced only by the adjustment to GST collections.

	Before write-off	After write-off
Accounts Receivable Control	$91 960	$91 278
Less: Allowance for Doubtful Debts	(5 170)	(4 550)
	$86 790	$86 728*

* The change in net Accounts Receivable is $62, which is the amount of GST now written off.

The fact that the write-off changed the net amount of accounts receivable only by the adjustment to GST demonstrates the notion that no expense results from the write-off of a bad debt itself. The reduction in the Accounts Receivable asset is exactly balanced by the reduction in the GST Collections liability. The expense from bad debts was effectively charged to the period in which the credit sale occurred rather than to the period in which the account is written off.

The total amount written off against the allowance account during a period seldom agrees with the amount in the allowance account at the beginning of the period. If write-offs during the period are less than the opening balance in the account, the account has a credit balance at the end of the period before adjustment. If this happens consistently over a number of periods the assumptions used to calculate Doubtful Debts should be reviewed. If write-offs exceed the opening balance, the account has a debit balance at the end of the period before adjustment. This situation is dealt with in the normal course of calculating the adjustment under the ageing method. However, under the percentage of sales method any debit balance should be written off against bad debts expense before providing for the current year's estimated bad debts. Again, if this happens consistently over a number of periods, the assumptions used should be reviewed. After the year-end adjustment to record bad debts expense, the Allowance for Doubtful Debts account must have a normal credit balance.

Alternative approaches

Many approaches are available when accounting for bad debts. Some treatments advocate the use of a Bad Debts Expense account to record debts actually written off and a Doubtful Debts Expense account to record doubtful debts at period end when establishing the allowance account. Taxation authorities normally require this distinction to be made. We believe that our approach provides the most consistent accrual-based accounting approach. Also, remember that the Allowance for Doubtful Debts account is a *monthly adjustment* in practice, and it may take several months for a bad debt allowed for to actually become bad. Writing off to the allowance account is appropriate under the balance sheet approach, as receivables will be reported at the appropriate net realisable value, or fair value, at each month-end (after adjusting for any GST in the allowance).

Recovery of an account written off

In some cases, an account that has been written off is collected in part or in full at a later date. If this occurs, the account receivable should be re-established in the accounts in order to maintain a complete history of the customer's activity. This could be important for future credit rating purposes. Assume, for example, that J. Evans underwent bankruptcy proceedings, at which stage his account receivable was written off as shown earlier. As part of the liquidation process, an attempt was made to recover money for the creditors, and in this case a final settlement of Evans' account was received on 4 November 2013 for $275. The entry to reinstate the account receivable previously written off, including its GST component, is:

2013				
Nov.	4	Accounts Receivable Control – J. Evans	275	
		GST Collections		25
		Bad Debts Recovered		250
		(Re-establish part of the account receivable written off as bad on 31 July)		

An account called Bad Debts Recovered is credited, and is shown as an item of other income in the entity's income statement. Note that any GST included is payable and hence the GST Collections account is credited for this amount.

After the receivable account is re-established, the cash collection is recorded so that there is a debit to the Cash at Bank account for $275, a credit to the Accounts Receivable Control account, and a credit to the account of J. Evans in the subsidiary ledger for $275.

Direct write-off method

Although the allowance method is the one that effectively relates expenses to income and is the method most widely used, some small business entities use the **direct write-off method**. With this method, no allowance is made for doubtful debts and only actual bad debts are charged to expense at the time an account is determined to be uncollectable. This is done by debiting Bad Debts Expense and crediting Accounts Receivable Control and the appropriate account in the subsidiary ledger. Using the previous example, if the account of J. Evans is written off as bad under this method, the following general journal entry is made:

2013 July	31	Bad Debts Expense	620	
		GST Collections	62	
		Accounts Receivable Control – J. Evans		682
		(Write-off of J. Evans' account as bad)		

Under this method, no attempt is made at the end of the reporting period to estimate future bad debts and therefore value total receivables at fair value. For this reason, the direct write-off method is not recommended in practice and its use is justified only on the basis of immateriality of the amounts normally involved. Many small business entities sell goods and services mainly on a cash or credit card basis and make only occasional sales on credit, and any bad debts written off will be small. In the event that an account previously written off is collected later, the collection is recorded in the same way used for the allowance method described above.

Although the allowance method is the one recommended for use in the entity's accounting system, the entity can claim as an allowable deduction for taxation purposes only those debts that have actually been written off during the year, i.e. the amount *debited* to the Allowance for Doubtful Debts account in the entity's accounting system if the allowance method is used.

Use of the direct write-off method produces the appropriate 'expense' for income tax purposes, but its use in the accounting records means that Accounts Receivable in the balance sheet is not shown at fair value, as there is no contra asset for estimated doubtful debts. This is contrary to the requirements of accounting standards, which require a company to make adequate allowance for impairment of receivables before the income statement is prepared.

Demonstration problem

Transactions affecting Bradford Ltd's accounts receivable for the year ended 30 June are presented below. On 1 July of the previous year, the opening balance of the Allowance for Doubtful Debts account was a credit of $1960. GST is 10%.

Aug.	3	Wrote off the $770 account of Gum Ltd as uncollectable.
Sept.	6	Received 50% of the $704 balance owed by J. Wiley and wrote off the remainder as a bad debt.
Oct.	16	Recorded the collection of $528 from G. Rhodes in full payment of her account, which had been written off earlier as a bad debt.
Jan.	15	Wrote off the accounts of Pauley Ltd, $1210, and R. Donley, $396, as bad debts.
March	9	Received $550 from E. Darkins in full payment of his account, which had been written off earlier as a bad debt.
April	8	Received 25% of the $2860 owed by North Ltd and wrote off the remainder as a bad debt.
June	30	Estimated bad debts expense for the year to be 1% of net credit sales of $503 500 (excluding GST).

Required

A. Prepare journal entries for each of the transactions in general journal format.

B. Prepare the Allowance for Doubtful Debts account showing the balance of the account after the 30 June adjustment.

C. Assume that, instead of basing the allowance on net credit sales, the allowance is based on an ageing of accounts receivable and that $8921 of the accounts receivable at 30 June were estimated to be uncollectable. Determine the adjustment necessary to bring the allowance account to the desired balance, and prepare the Allowance for Doubtful Debts account.

Solution to demonstration problem

A.

		BRADFORD LTD General Journal		
Aug.	3	Allowance for Doubtful Debts	700	
		GST Collections	70	
		Accounts Receivable – Gum Ltd		770
		(Write-off of uncollectable account)		
Sept.	6	Cash at Bank	352	
		GST Collections	32	
		Allowance for Doubtful Debts	320	
		Accounts Receivable – J. Wiley		704
		(Cash received and write-off of the remainder)		
Oct.	16	Accounts Receivable – G. Rhodes	528	
		GST Collections		48
		Bad Debts Recovered		480
		(Recovery of bad debt)		
	16	Cash at Bank	528	
		Accounts Receivable – G. Rhodes		528
		(Cash received from customer)		
Jan.	15	Allowance for Doubtful Debts	1 460	
		GST Collections	146	
		Accounts Receivable – Pauley Ltd		1 210
		Accounts Receivable – R. Donley		396
		(Write-off of bad debts)		
Mar.	9	Accounts Receivable – E. Darkins	550	
		GST Collections		50
		Bad Debts Recovered		500
		(Recovery of bad debt)		
	9	Cash at Bank	550	
		Accounts Receivable – E. Darkins		550
		(Cash received from E. Darkins)		
April	8	Cash at Bank	715	
		GST Collections	195	
		Allowance for Doubtful Debts	1 950	
		Accounts Receivable – North Ltd		2 860
		(Cash received and write-off of the balance of account)		
June	30	Bad Debts Expense	2 470	
		Allowance for Doubtful Debts		2 470
		(Write-off of under provision for bad debts)		
	30	Bad Debts Expense	5 035	
		Allowance for Doubtful Debts		5 035
		(End-of-period adjustment for estimated bad debts)		

B.

ACCOUNT   **Allowance for Doubtful Debts**

Date		Explanation	Debit	Credit	Balance
July	1	Balance			1 960
Aug.	3	Accounts Receivable – Gum Ltd	700		1 260
Sept.	6	Accounts Receivable – J. Wiley	320		940
Jan.	15	Accounts Receivable – Pauley Ltd/Donley	1 460		520 Dr
April	8	Accounts Receivable – North Ltd	1 950		2 470 Dr
June	30	Under provision for bad debts		2 470	0
June	30	Adjusting entry		5 035	5 035

C.

$$\text{Adjustment} = \text{Desired balance} - \text{Current balance}$$
$$= \$8921 - (-\$2470)$$
$$= \$11\,391 \text{ Cr}$$

ACCOUNT **Allowance for Doubtful Debts**

Date		Explanation	Debit	Credit	Balance
July	1	Balance			1 960
Aug.	3	Accounts Receivable – Gum Ltd	700		1 260
Sept.	6	Accounts Receivable – J. Wiley	320		940
Jan.	15	Accounts Receivable – Pauley Ltd/Donley	1 460		520 Dr
April	8	Accounts Receivable – North Ltd	1 950		2 470 Dr
June	30	Adjusting entry		11 391	8 921

18.4 Management and control of accounts receivable

Learning objective 4

Describe the principles involved in the management and control of accounts receivable

Accounts receivable arise by granting credit to customers. A number of important managerial decisions need to be made in this process — the entity has to decide (1) how it will determine which customers will be offered credit, (2) what the terms of the credit will be, and (3) how to communicate these terms to existing and potential customers. The entity must also determine (4) policies to ensure satisfactory collection of amounts owing, (5) methods to encourage debtors to pay on time, and (6) the methods to use to follow up slow-paying customers or clients.

A business entity also needs to constantly review the composition of its accounts receivable in terms of amounts presently owing and amounts overdue. The success or otherwise of the entity's credit and collection policies can be gauged by a number of techniques, including ratios.

An appropriate system of internal control needs to be in place. Management must be mindful of the costs of carrying a large volume of accounts receivable, and be aware of opportunities and methods that can be used to reduce these costs.

It is important that all matters relating to the control of credit policies and accounts receivable are properly organised and administered, and most organisations of any reasonable size establish a credit department, under the control of a credit manager. Some of the more important functions of a credit department (or, in its absence, management) are discussed in the next four subsections.

Credit policies

No business entity wants to extend credit to a customer or client who is unlikely to pay the account when due. The **credit department** is responsible for investigating the credit history and determining the debt-paying ability of customers who apply for credit.

- If the customer is a business entity, the credit department normally requests a set of its audited financial statements for use in judging its ability to pay.
- If the customer is an individual, the credit department asks for information about current earnings, current expenses, outstanding debts, general financial position and past experiences in handling obligations.

In addition, the credit department may obtain a credit report from a local or national credit-rating agency that accumulates data on the credit history of individuals and business entities.

The decision on the creditworthiness of potential customers/clients is an important one. If the entity is too generous in extending credit to risky customers, losses will be incurred. But if credit policies are too tight, existing customers will be lost and potential customers may go elsewhere. If approved credit customers do not prove worthy of credit, then credit can be withdrawn and future sales made only on a cash basis.

The credit department, having established the creditworthiness of a potential customer, must then communicate the established terms to the customer. Terms normally state the period after the date of the invoice by which the amount due should be paid, e.g. 30 days, and any cash discounts for prompt payment to which the customer is entitled. Cash discounts (discussed in chapter 6) are stated as a percentage of the invoice amount if paid within a certain period of time, e.g. 2/10, n/30 days. Credit terms may need to be reviewed from time to time both for receivables as a whole and for individual customers.

Monitoring credit policies

The best measure of success or otherwise of the credit policies of a business entity is receipt of cash collections within normal credit terms. Poor credit policies usually see a gradual rise in the number of accounts receivable exceeding the normal period for payment, and an increase in the number of accounts that have to be written off as bad. It is essential that overdue accounts are detected early, and steps are taken to encourage payment. This may entail reminder notices, letters, phone calls to discuss payment problems, and handing the debt over to a collection agency. If all these methods fail, a decision must then be taken to write the account off as a bad debt.

Ageing analysis of receivables

The longer an account is overdue, the more likely it will become bad, and thus discounts are offered to encourage early payment. An ageing analysis of accounts receivable is one way to find out the age of individual customers' balances and identify those accounts that require the attention of the credit department. Ageing analysis of receivables is covered on pages 754–6 in determining the amount of the allowance for doubtful debts. Such an analysis provides an important control mechanism in monitoring cash collections. An analysis should be done regularly, usually monthly, and follow-up action taken on overdue accounts. Computerised accounting systems can provide an up-to-date analysis on a daily basis if required, providing timely information for management action. An ageing analysis can also help management predict future cash inflows for cash planning purposes.

Calculating and analysing ratios

Management can also make use of ratios to assess credit control performance. One useful ratio, described as a credit risk ratio, is derived by dividing the amount of the allowance for doubtful debts by the amount of accounts receivable. The trend in this ratio over time indicates an improving or a worsening of credit policies. A comparison with industry averages, if available, also provides useful information for decision making. Two other common measures used by management in monitoring and controlling accounts receivable are the receivables turnover ratio and average collection period.

Receivables turnover

The **receivables turnover ratio** is a measure of how many times the average receivables balance is converted into cash during the year. It is also considered a measure of the efficiency of the credit-granting and collection policies that have been established, and is calculated as follows:

$$\text{Receivables turnover} = \frac{\text{Net credit sales revenue (income)}}{\text{Average receivables}}$$

The higher the receivables turnover ratio, the shorter the period of time between recording a credit sale and collecting the cash. So that an entity is competitive, its established credit policies are influenced by industry practices. Comparison of this ratio with industry norms can reveal deviations from competitors' financial results.

In calculating this ratio, credit sales (credit income), meaning cash sales are excluded, should be used in the numerator whenever the amount is available. However, such information is normally not available to external users of financial statements, so net sales revenue (income) is then used as a substitute. An average of monthly receivables balances (including any trade bills receivable) should be used in the denominator. In the absence of monthly information, the year-end balance, or an average of the beginning-of-year and end-of-year balances, or averages of quarterly balances are used in the calculation.

Many financial analysts prefer to use gross receivables in the calculation instead of net receivables as stated above. It is argued that a more accurate calculation of receivables turnover is provided by using average *gross* receivables in the denominator, i.e. before deduction of any allowance for doubtful debts. Gross receivables does represent the actual legal balances that an entity is attempting to collect. Using this argument, any GST included in the receivables balances is not deducted.

Average collection period

Frequently, the receivables turnover ratio is divided into 365 days to derive the average number of days it takes to collect receivables from credit sales. The new ratio so calculated is often called the **average collection period** for receivables and may be calculated as:

$$\text{Average collection period} = \frac{365 \text{ days}}{\text{Receivables turnover ratio}}$$

or, if expressed fully:

$$\text{Average collection period} = \frac{\text{Average receivables} \times 365}{\text{Net credit sales revenue (income)}}$$

If credit terms are 2/10, n/30, the amount of accounts receivable outstanding at any time should be less than the credit sales for the last 30 days, because many of the credit accounts will have been paid within the discount period. If allowance is made for slow-paying accounts, the receivables may represent 30–35 days sales. If the receivables exceed this range, a careful analysis of all the accounts should be made.

To illustrate the calculation of the receivables turnover per year and the average collection period, the following data for James Ltd are used:

	2015	2014	2013
Credit sales for year	$367 200	$331 200	$320 000
Accounts and bills receivable at end of year	$ 28 840	$ 34 400	$ 30 000

Only gross receivables (accounts and bills) (including GST) arising out of the sale of inventory or provision of services on credit are used.

	2015	2014
A. Net credit sales	$367 200	$331 200
B. Days in year	365	365
C. Average receivables [(balance at beginning of year + balance at end of year) ÷ 2]	$31 620	$32 200
D. Receivables turnover per year (A ÷ C)	11.61 times	10.29 times
Average collection period (B ÷ D)	31 days	35 days

Average collection periods vary with the nature of business activity. Wholesalers of footwear may average 40 days, compared with grocery wholesalers whose average may be 15 days. In the illustration above, assuming that credit sales are on terms of 2/10, n/30, both years show a healthy situation, since average collection periods are just in excess of the credit period, with 2015 showing an improved performance. For a benchmark of performance, the preceding year's rate or the industry rate may be used. An increasing turnover of receivables as exhibited above indicates an improvement from 2014 to 2015, and hence reflects a decreasing relative amount of investment in receivables.

Internal control of accounts receivable

As in the case of cash, adequate safeguards must be established for accounts receivable. It is important that people who maintain the accounts receivable records should not have access to cash receipts. Recording of sales returns and allowances, discounts allowed, and bad debt write-offs should be authorised by a responsible officer and separated from the cash receipts and cash payments functions. Monthly statements of account should be verified and forwarded to customers by someone other than the person in charge of the accounts receivable records. Another independent check should be made to ensure that the statements sent to customers are in agreement with the accounts receivable records.

Slow-paying accounts should be reviewed periodically by a senior official of the business. Adequate control over receivables begins with the receipt of an approved purchase order and continues through all the remaining stages in the credit sales process: approval of credit terms, shipment of goods, customer invoicing, recording of the account receivable and its ultimate collection.

Benefits from use of credit cards

In modern commerce, financial institutions offer advice on business management and the many methods by which cash can be received. The following statement from visa on the benefits of accepting credit cards is typical.

Reduce losses from errors or theft

Cashiers do not make errors in counting change when handling card payments. This is because payment is exact and there is no need for change. Thieves are more likely to target cash to steal since sales drafts cannot be spent. Cash may also be lost through refunds and unrecorded sales.

Reduce the time spent on managing cash

Less time is needed to count cash at the beginning and end of the day, and to deposit proceeds at a bank. When cash is the primary or only way to make a purchase, each sales staff has to count cash, and the entire store needs to monitor cash.

Receive and deposit your sales faster

Transaction data from sales can be sent automatically to your acquiring bank daily where you can earn interest. Cash that is held in a register does not earn interest for the merchant.

Benefit from larger transactions and higher sales

Visa has received feedback from its merchants indicating that the average value of a transaction made with a payment card is higher than a purchase made with cash.

Serve your customers better

Provide your customers with a convenient way to pay for their purchases.

Source: Excerpts from Visa, 'Merchant benefits', www.visa-asia.com.

Disposal of accounts receivable

Sale of accounts receivable

As many business transactions are conducted on credit, accounts receivable constitutes a large asset for many businesses. Entities not only forgo cash but also incur considerable costs in credit control, preparing and sending accounts, collecting debts, and incur losses through bad debts. It is therefore becoming common practice for businesses to sell their accounts receivable in order to:

- realise cash to finance trading operations
- provide a source of cash for other activities
- minimise the costs of credit control, collection expenses and bad debt losses.

Disposal of accounts receivable is referred to as the **factoring** of accounts receivable. The business entity or financial institution that buys the receivables for a fee and then collects the amounts receivable is known as a **factor**. There are businesses that specialise in factoring. Credit card companies such as American Express and Diners Club and financial institutions that issue MasterCard, Visa card and similar credit cards are, in effect, specialising in collection of accounts receivable. Businesses that offer EFTPOS facilities are, in effect, factoring potential accounts receivable to a financial institution.

Factoring arrangements differ from factor to factor, but normally a commission of 2–3% is charged. A typical journal entry to record the sale of accounts receivable to a factor is illustrated below. Assume that Ip Ltd factors $500 000 of receivables to Fast Factors Ltd, which imposes a service charge of 2% of the gross amount of the receivables being disposed of. A typical general journal entry to record such a sale is:

April	15	Cash at Bank	490 000	
		Service Charge Expense	10 000	
		Accounts Receivable Control		500 000
		(Sale of receivables)		

Note that any GST paid or payable to the ATO included in the receivables factored will be recovered in the amount received by Ip Ltd from Fast Factors Ltd.

Use of credit cards

Credit cards enable retail businesses and others to sell goods and services to customers where the customers obtain possession of the goods or have services performed immediately but do not have to pay for the goods or services for up to 55 days. A **credit card** enables the holder to obtain credit up to a predetermined limit from the issuer of the card for the purchase of goods and services. This arrangement amounts to the retail business transferring the detailed accounting for and collection of receivables to the issuer of the cards.

The accounting treatment for credit card sales depends on the type of organisation issuing the card. The major credit card issuers in Australia are the banks, which issue the well-known Visa card and MasterCard. Non-bank institutions also issue credit cards, e.g. American Express and Diners Club.

When a transaction occurs, the retail business retains a copy of the transaction recorded by the use of the card. Most systems are now via the EFTPOS (electronic funds transfer at point of sale) system, automating the transfer of funds from the card provider to the mechant's bank account. A typical general journal entry to cover, for example, MasterCard sales of $2000 plus GST on 22 April is:

April	22	Cash at Bank	2 200	
		GST Collections		200
		Sales		2 000
		(MasterCard sales)		

The bank issuing the credit card imposes a charge, normally referred to as a 'merchant's fee', on all credit card deposits recorded for the month, and deducts the appropriate fee from the Cash at Bank account of the business at month-end. This is revealed on the monthly bank statement, and the charge is debited to the Merchants' Fees Expense account. Assuming MasterCard deposits for the month of April of $15 400 and a credit card charge of 3%, the general journal entry to record the total charge is:

April	30	Merchants' Fees Expense	462	
		Cash at Bank		462
		(Fees on monthly MasterCard sales for April)		

The entry to record the above fee is recorded normally in the cash payments journal. Note that, in practice, merchant fees are subject to GST. However, GST in this context is ignored in this book.

Use of debit cards

Prevalent in the retail industry is the **debit card**. These cards are used in conjunction with the EFTPOS system. Use of a debit card by the cardholder results in an immediate transfer of funds from the cardholder's account at the bank to the account of the business selling the goods or services. The transaction is in essence a cash sale, and is recorded as such.

Electronic transfer of funds has increased dramatically in recent years and continues to grow. EFTPOS services are provided by 'merchants' of such services, and they levy a variety of charges on the business providing the EFTPOS service, including a start-up fee, a charge for the EFTPOS terminals, and transaction fees. Note that GST is payable on these fees as they are not considered to be of a financial nature for tax purpose.

18.5 Bills receivable

Learning objective 5

Discuss the nature of bills receivable and demonstrate how to account for them

Bills of exchange and promissory notes are instruments that can be used for extending credit on normal trading transactions, where they are referred to as 'trade bills'. Common examples of transactions involving trade bills are where a bill is received in exchange for an existing account receivable or, indeed, where a bill is received in payment for a sale at the time of sale. Credit can also be extended to customers where the credit is not based on normal trading transactions but purely on the basis of providing funds for a return of interest. These bills receivable are known as 'commercial bills'. The principles used for accounting for all bills are the same.

The law relating to bills of exchange and promissory notes is contained in the *Bills of Exchange Act 1909* (as amended), the most recent compilation at the time of writing having been prepared in 2008. A **bill of exchange** is defined in this Act as 'an unconditional order in writing, addressed by one person to another, signed by the person giving it, requiring the person to whom it is addressed to pay on demand, or at a fixed or determinable future time, a sum certain in money to or to the order of a specified person or to bearer'.

The definition identifies four essential features of a bill of exchange. It must be an order that is unconditional, i.e. no specific criteria can be attached to payment. It must be in writing, although there have been proposals to allow electronic communications but these amendments have not been accepted to date. It must involve three parties — the party issuing the order (the drawer) who must sign the bill, the person to whom the bill is addressed (the drawee and acceptor) and the person to whom payment is to be made (the payee). Finally, the date for payment must be fixed or be capable of being specifically determined.

Trade bills

Although format and presentation on the face of a bill of exchange can vary, a typical trade bill of exchange is illustrated in figure 18.3.

Figure 18.3 Trade bill of exchange

Here, DMF Ltd, the drawer of the bill, is the creditor owed $30 000 for equipment previously sold to Baker Wholesale Ltd on account. It is assumed that any interest involved is included in the $30 000 face value of the bill. DMF Ltd has drawn up the bill and forwarded it to Baker Wholesale Ltd for acceptance. In this form the bill is referred to as a *draft*, and becomes an *acceptance* when accepted by Baker Wholesale Ltd, which becomes the acceptor of the bill. Acceptance may involve Baker Wholesale Ltd writing the word 'accepted' on the face of the bill and attaching a signature. In figure 18.3, acceptance is effected when B. Baker signs for and on behalf of Baker Wholesale Ltd.

DMF Ltd in this example is the payee. Once the bill is accepted and the acceptance returned to DMF Ltd, it is regarded as a bill receivable by DMF Ltd since this business will ultimately receive cash for the bill on its maturity. Baker Wholesale Ltd, on the other hand, regards the accepted bill as a bill payable since, on the due date, Baker Wholesale Ltd is legally obliged to pay the face value of the bill to the holder of the bill.

Because the bill is made payable to DMF Ltd or order, it is possible for DMF Ltd to pass on or *negotiate* the bill to a third party for value received. Alternatively, DMF Ltd could cash the bill at a bank before the due date. This is referred to as discounting the bill and is discussed in more detail later in the chapter. Of course, DMF Ltd will receive less than the face value of the bill if it adopts this option, because of the discounting charge that will be deducted by the bank.

As already indicated, DMF Ltd could make use of a bill of exchange to obtain finance from a bank or other financier. Such an arrangement would lead to a liability for DMF Ltd, since such a bill would be a bill payable. Consideration of commercial bills is deferred until the chapter on liabilities.

Promissory notes

A **promissory note** is defined in the Bills of Exchange Act as 'an unconditional promise in writing made by one person to another, signed by the maker, engaging to pay, on demand or at a fixed or determinable future time, a sum certain in money, to or to the order of a specified person, or to bearer'. The essential features of a promissory note are: (1) there must be an unconditional promise in writing; (2) it must involve two parties — the maker of the promise and the payee (usually specified, or it may be the bearer); (3) it must be signed by the maker; (4) it must specify the sum of money to be paid on demand or on a specified date.

As with bills of exchange, promissory notes arise as a result of trading and financing transactions. To illustrate a trade promissory note, assume that Machinery Supplies Ltd sold machinery to R. Jensen on 1 May 2013 for $40 000. Machinery Supplies Ltd agrees to take a 180-day promissory note, payable on 28 October, for the amount due together with $2960 to cover interest for the extended credit. A sample promissory note appears in figure 18.4. Machinery Supplies Ltd regards the promissory note when received from Jensen as a bill receivable, whereas Jensen treats the note as a bill payable.

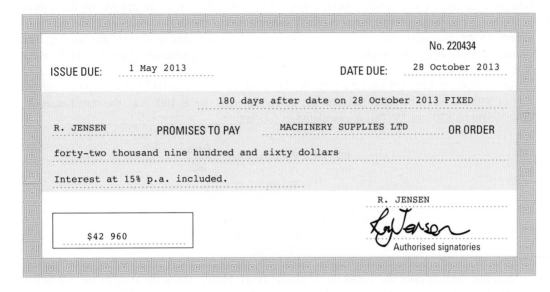

Figure 18.4 Promissory note

Bills and notes are normally taken out for periods of 30, 60, 90, 120 or 180 days. The bill and note illustrated were both for a period of 180 days. Implicit in most trade and commercial bills and notes is a rate of interest. **Interest** is a charge made for the use of money. To the payee, interest is revenue; to the acceptor of a bill or maker of a note, interest is an expense. The amount of money stated on the face of a bill or note, e.g. $42 960 in figure 18.4, is called the **maturity value** and is the amount that must ultimately be paid on the date of maturity of the bill or note. In figure 18.4, the maturity date is 28 October, and the maturity value is made up of the **principal** of the debt, $40 000, plus $2960 interest.

Because most bills and notes are interest-bearing, an interest factor is generally implicit in the maturity value. The amount of the interest depends on market interest rates prevailing at the time the bill or note is written. Some trade bills and notes, however, may be non-interest-bearing, in which case the maturity value is equal to the principal value of the debt being settled.

Determining due date

Bills and notes are issued for terms ranging from 30 to 180 days. The **maturity date** is determined as the number of days in the term after the issue date. To illustrate the calculation of a maturity date, assume that a 90-day promissory note was written on 14 February 2013. The maturity date is determined as shown below:

Term of the note in days		90
Number of days in February	28	
Date of note	14	
Number of days outstanding in February		14
Number of days remaining		76
Number of days in March		31
Number of days remaining		45
Number of days in April		30
Due date in May		15

Thus the maturity date is determined to be 15 May 2013. The Bills of Exchange Act states that if the maturity date as determined falls on a non-business day, then the bill or note becomes payable on the next business day. Non-business days are defined as Christmas Day, Good Friday, a Sunday or a bank holiday. The term of a bill or note cannot be extended and the bill or note has to be 'rolled over', i.e. a new bill or note has to replace the old one.

Calculating interest on bills and notes

Whenever an entity issues a bill or note, a number of different charges are payable by the drawer or maker. The most important charge is that of interest for the use of the money over the period of the bill. Other charges such as establishment and acceptance fees and legal costs are payable. The amount of interest payable depends on the market rate of interest prevailing at the time of the issue of the bill or note.

For example, if ABC Ltd issued a fixed 90-day promissory note to DMF Ltd to cover a current debt of $30 000 owed by ABC Ltd, and the agreed interest rate is 10% p.a., the stated maturity value would be $30 739.73. This is calculated as follows:

$$\text{Interest} = \text{Principal} \times \text{Rate} \times \frac{\text{Days}}{365}$$
$$= \$30\,000 \times 0.10 \times \frac{90}{365}$$
$$= \$739.73$$
$$\text{Maturity value} = \text{Principal} + \text{Interest}$$
$$= \$30\,000 + \$739.73$$
$$= \$30\,739.73$$

Note that interest rates are stated on an annual basis. Hence, when the term of the bill is for, say, 90 days, the interest charge must be determined by using the factor 90/365 in the formula (365 being the number of days in a calendar year). Although it is possible for the maturity value to exclude the interest charge, the practice of including interest in the maturity value of the bill is followed in this book.

Accounting for receipt and collection of bills receivable

For accounting purposes, both bills and notes are classified as either bills receivable or bills payable, depending on whether the bill or note represents a right to receive cash in the future (a bill receivable) or an obligation to pay cash in the future (a bill payable). For the purposes of the following discussion, a bill receivable exists when an accepted bill of exchange, called an acceptance, is received or when a promissory note is received. For illustrative purposes, accounting for the receipt, collection, disposal and dishonour of promissory notes is demonstrated. Identical entries are made for a bill of exchange. Bills payable are covered in the chapter on liabilities.

Examples of the use of promissory notes include the following:
- Manufacturing and wholesale businesses that sell in large quantities often request a note from a buyer who asks for credit.
- Retail businesses may receive notes only occasionally, although they may sell high-priced items on an instalment plan under which the buyer pays a deposit and gives a note (or a series of notes with different maturity dates) for the balance.
- Businesses that regularly sell goods on credit are sometimes asked for an extension of credit beyond the normal due date. In these cases, the company sometimes insists that the customer gives an interest-bearing note to replace the account receivable.

A single Bills Receivable account is normally maintained in the general ledger of the payee. The Bills Receivable account is a control account, with a subsidiary ledger consisting of a file of the actual notes and bills held, arranged in order of due date. The notes and bills themselves contain all the information needed — the name of the drawer or maker, the acceptor, maturity date and interest rate. No other records are needed.

To illustrate the accounting treatment for bills receivable, assume that Hannah Ltd has an account receivable from D. Mead for $1500 that is overdue. Mead requested a 90-day extension of the payment date, and Hannah Ltd agreed by accepting a 90-day, 15% promissory note in exchange for the account receivable. Note that transactions relating to bills and associated interest are exempt from the GST, because they are transactions of a financial nature. On receipt of the note, Hannah Ltd makes the following entry:

July	9	Bills Receivable	1 555.48	
		Accounts Receivable – D. Mead		1 500.00
		Unearned Interest		55.48
		(Receipt of a note in settlement of an account receivable)		
		[Interest = $1500 × 0.15 × 90/365]		

This entry simply substitutes a bill receivable for the account receivable. Interest is included in the maturity value of the note and is recorded in an Unearned Interest account, a contra account to Bills Receivable.

On 7 October, when Mead pays the note, the entry in general journal form is:

Oct.	7	Cash at Bank	1 555.48	
		Bills Receivable		1 555.48
		(Collection of promissory note from D. Mead)		
	7	Unearned Interest	55.48	
		Interest Income		55.48
		(Interest earned on note from D. Mead)		

In the event that the promissory note is not paid on the due date, the note is said to be a **dishonoured bill**. Hannah Ltd would then have to take action to recover the amount due by other means. This could involve the receipt of a new note for the amount due plus an additional interest charge.

Discounting bills receivable

One of the reasons bills receivable are popular with creditors is their ability to be converted into cash before maturity date. A bill receivable may be endorsed by the holder and sold to a bank in exchange for cash. The bank then holds the bill or note until its maturity date, when it expects to collect the maturity value from its drawer or maker. This process is called *discounting bills receivable* because the bank will deduct in advance an interest charge called a **discount**. The discount is based on (a) the maturity value of the bill for the period it is held by the bank, i.e the time between the date it is transferred to the bank and its due date, and (b) the discount rate used by the bank. In practice, the discount rate is based on the effective interest rate or yield. For our purposes we shall assume the discount rate given is the 'yield' rate. The maturity value less the discount deducted, called the **proceeds**, is then paid to the endorser by the bank.

To illustrate, assume that Hannah Ltd received a 90-day, 8% note dated 16 March from F. Morgan, to settle his debt of $2000. Hannah Ltd held the note until 15 April, on which date it was discounted at a bank at a discount yield rate of 10%. Since the maturity date of the note is 14 June (15 days in March, 30 days in April, 31 days in May and 14 days in June), the bank will hold the note for 60 days (15 days in April, 31 days in May and 14 days in June = 60 days). The period of time the bank holds the note before its collection is called the **discount period**, for which the bank will charge interest (discount) at 10%. The bank will deduct from the maturity value of the note 60 days interest at 10% and give Hannah Ltd the proceeds as follows:

Amount of debt	$2000.00
Interest on note at 8% ($2000 × 0.08 × 90/365)	39.45
Maturity value of the promissory note	2039.45
Less: Discount at 10% for 60 days ($2039.45 × 0.10 × 60/365)	33.53
Proceeds	$2005.92

The entry in general journal form to record discounting of the note by Hannah Ltd is:

April	15	Cash at Bank	2 005.92	
		Unearned Interest	33.53	
		Bills Receivable		2 039.45
		(Discounted F. Morgan's note at the bank at 10%)		

The difference between the proceeds received and the maturity value of the note is recorded as a reduction of the interest that is yet to be earned. It represents the amount of interest Hannah Ltd has to give up to the bank by way of the discount charge. Any balance remaining in the Unearned Interest account is then transferred to Interest Revenue to record the net interest earned after discounting the bill. The discount on the bill is effectively offset against the interest that would have been earned if the bill receivable had been held until maturity date.

April	15	Unearned Interest	5.92	
		Interest Revenue		5.92
		(Interest earned on discounted note from F. Morgan)		

Contingent liability

A discounted note must be endorsed by the holder, who then becomes contingently liable for payment of the note. This gives rise to a **contingent liability**, which refers to a potential or possible liability that can become an actual liability if a particular event occurs. In this case, a contingent liability exists in that the endorser (Hannah Ltd in our example) must pay the note on its maturity date *if* the maker (F. Morgan) fails to do so. The discounting of the note therefore creates a contingent liability for Hannah Ltd that continues until the due date of the note. If F. Morgan pays the note on its due date, the contingent liability ceases. If he defaults, Hannah Ltd's contingent liability becomes a real liability to the bank, which will debit the account of Hannah Ltd for the maturity value of the note.

The nature and amount of any contingent liability must be disclosed in financial statements in accordance with IAS 37/AASB 137 *Provisions, Contingent Liabilities and Contingent Assets*. Consequently, the contingent liability for bills receivable discounted must be disclosed if a balance sheet is prepared earlier than the maturity date of the notes. Disclosure is made by a note to the financial statements that explains the nature and amount of the contingent liability.

End-of-period adjustments for interest revenue

Interest is earned as time passes. When an interest-bearing bill receivable is held at the end of the accounting period, interest revenue should be calculated and recorded. For example, assume that Hannah Ltd received a 90-day, 10% promissory note on 1 May in settlement of the account of P. Edwards for $4000. The following entry is made on receipt of the note:

May	1	Bills Receivable	4 098.63	
		Unearned Interest		98.63
		Accounts Receivable – P. Edwards		4 000.00
		(Receipt of note from P. Edwards)		
		[Interest = $4000 × 0.10 × 90/365]		

As the term of the note expires, the unearned interest becomes interest revenue. At the end of the financial year on 30 June, 60 days of the term of the note have elapsed. An adjusting entry is therefore necessary at the end of the reporting period to give recognition of the interest revenue up to that date. The entry is:

June	30	Unearned Interest	65.75	
		Interest Revenue		65.75
		(Interest earned on note from P. Edwards)		
		[Interest = $4000 × 0.10 × 60/365]		

When the note is collected on 30 July in the new financial year, the following entries (in general journal form) are made:

July	30	Cash at Bank	4 098.63	
		Bills Receivable		4 098.63
		(Collection of note)		
	30	Unearned Interest	32.88	
		Interest Revenue		32.88
		(Interest earned on note)		

This entry removes the bill receivable and the unearned interest from the business records, and recognises the $32.88 interest revenue for the 30 days of the term of the note in the new financial year.

In computer-based accounting systems, calculations such as interest are performed quickly and accurately once the appropriate formula is programmed into the computer. Hand-held financial calculators also enable maturity date, interest and yields to be readily calculated.

KEY TERMS

Accounts receivable, p. 750

Ageing of accounts receivable, p. 754

Allowance for doubtful debts, p. 752

Average collection period, p. 763

Bad debts expense, p. 752

Bill of exchange, pp. 750, 765

Bill receivable, p. 750

Contingent liability, p. 770

Credit card, p. 764

Credit department, p. 761

Debit card, p. 765

Direct write-off method, p. 759

Discount (in relation to bills of exchange), p. 769

Discount period, p. 769

Dishonoured bill, p. 769

Factor, p. 764

Factoring, p. 764

Interest (in relation to bills of exchange), p. 767

Maturity date, p. 767

Maturity value, p. 767

Percentage of net credit sales, p. 754

Principal, p. 767

Proceeds, p. 769

Promissory note, pp. 750, 766

Receivables turnover ratio, p. 762

Trade debtors, p. 750

DISCUSSION QUESTIONS

1. Compare and contrast accounts receivable and bills receivable.
2. 'Having accounts receivable means by definition that there will be bad debts; therefore it makes no sense for an organisation to extend credit.' Discuss.
3. 'Determining the amount of the allowance for doubtful debts by simply using a percentage of net sales is the obvious way to do it — the alternatives are complicated and onerous.' Discuss.
4. In a reasonably run organisation the amount of doubtful debts should be immaterial and therefore make little difference on the accounts of the organisation. Why do accountants spend time estimating and disclosing this amount?
5. The two main ways of determining the allowance for doubtful debts are sometimes referred to as the 'balance sheet' and the 'income statement' approach. To which method does each term refer, why and which would be more appropriate under the IASB's *Conceptual Framework*?
6. A business student was heard to make the following remark: 'With the existence of credit cards it is now possible for business entities to offer extensive credit facilities to customers without having to worry about accounting for accounts receivable and all the problems that it brings. Carrying one's own accounts receivable will become a thing of the past.' Discuss.
7. Studies indicate that entities that rely on factoring their receivables have significant risk of financial distress. What are the benefits and disadvantages of factoring accounts receivable and what might be the cause of this correlation between factoring and business failure?

8. Several months ago, Slase Ltd, a trade debtor for $4620, had his account written off as a bad debt. A cheque has just been received in the post from Slase Ltd for $4620, and the assistant accountant made the following journal entry:

Cash at Bank	4 620	
GST Collections		420
Bad Debts Recovered		4 200

The assistant accountant asserted that there were more complicated ways of handling such a transaction, but his method is simple and direct and therefore better. Do you agree? Explain why or why not.

9. 'Control over receivables is not quite as important as control over cash.' Discuss.

10. When bills receivable are recorded in the accounts why do we recognise an unearned interest liability at inception even though no cash has been received, rather than accruing an interest receivable asset over the life of the receivable?

EXERCISES

Exercise 18.1   BAD DEBTS — ALLOWANCE METHODS   **LO 3**

The following information relates to the business of G. Thumb, a contract gardener. All work is performed on account and Ms Thumb uses the net credit sales method for estimating doubtful debts, assuming 3% will become uncollectable. The service revenue for the year ended 30 June 2014 was $130 000 and, at that date, accounts receivable amounted to $48 100. During the year, $3600 of accounts receivable was written off as bad. At 1 July 2013, the balance of Accounts Receivable was $37 000 and the Allowance for Doubtful Debts account was $4700. Ignore GST.

Required

A. Prepare and balance the Allowance for Doubtful Debts account for the year ended 30 June 2014.

B. Show how the above information would be disclosed in:
   1. the income statement for the year ended 30 June 2014
   2. the balance sheet as at 30 June 2014.

Exercise 18.2   BAD DEBTS — DIRECT WRITE-OFF AND ALLOWANCE METHODS   **LO 3**

EchoGnomics is a wholesaler of garden figurines, selling mainly to independent gardening shops in Australia. All sales are conducted on a 30-day credit basis and no early payment or cash discounts are given. Ignore GST. The following information has been extracted from the accounting records as at 30 June 2013:

Sales	$874 000
Sales returns and allowances	45 600
Cash collected from sales	549 600
Debts considered bad (not yet written off)	6 952

Required

A. Assuming that EchoGnomics uses the direct write-off method of accounting for bad debts:
   1. Show the general journal entry required to write off the bad debts.
   2. What amount would be shown for bad debts expense in the income statement at 30 June 2013?
   3. What amount would be shown for accounts receivable in the balance sheet at 30 June 2013?

B. Assuming that EchoGnomics uses the allowance method of accounting for bad debts and the following additional information was found after examination of the accounts:

Allowance for doubtful debts (1 July 2012)	$7920 Cr
Allowance calculated based on 1% of net credit sales for the year.	

1. Show the general journal entries required to write off the bad debts and recognise the required allowance for doubtful debts.
2. What amount would be shown for bad debts expense in the income statement at 30 June 2013?
3. What amount would be shown for accounts receivable in the balance sheet at 30 June 2013?

Exercise 18.3 BAD DEBTS — DIRECT WRITE-OFF AND ALLOWANCE METHODS **GST** **LO 3**

Refer to the information in exercise 18.2. Complete requirements A and B but this time include the impact of a 10% GST.

Exercise 18.4 DOUBTFUL DEBTS — NET CREDIT SALES METHOD **LO 3**

Alya's Agricultural Supplies Ltd uses the net credit sales method for estimating doubtful debts. It is estimated that 2% will be uncollectable. You have been provided with the following information. Ignore GST.

June	1	Balance in the Allowance for Doubtful Debts account is $2100 Cr.
June	5	After concerted effort to collect, an account receivable of $1125 for Z. Sufiya was written off as a bad debt.
June	15	Z. Sufiya unexpectedly paid $875 of the amount of her debt written off on 5 June.
June	30	An appropriate adjusting entry is made to the allowance for doubtful debts. Sales for the year ending 30 June were $800 000, 25% of which are for cash.

Required
A. Record the above transactions in general journal form.
B. What is the balance in the Allowance for Doubtful Debts account and the Bad Debts Recovered account? Where are these accounts shown on the financial statements?

Exercise 18.5 DOUBTFUL DEBTS — AGEING METHOD **LO 3**

On 30 June, the end of its financial year, Maarof Consulting completed an age analysis of its accounts receivable and determined that an allowance for doubtful debts of $6520 was needed in order to report accounts receivable at their estimated collectable amount in the balance sheet. Assume a 10% GST.

Required
A. Prepare the entry to record bad debts expense, assuming that the Allowance for Doubtful Debts account currently has a $1940 credit balance.
B. Prepare the entry to record bad debts expense, assuming that the Allowance for Doubtful Debts account currently has an $820 debit balance.
C. Prepare the entry to write off an account receivable from M. Hakeem for $682.
D. Prepare the entry to write off the account receivable in requirement C above if the business was not registered for the GST.
E. Assume that before the entry recorded in requirement C above, the net amount of accounts receivable was $99 000, including GST. What is the net amount of accounts receivable after recording the write-off of Hakeem's account? Explain.

Exercise 18.6 DOUBTFUL DEBTS — AGEING METHOD **LO 3**

The following details were obtained from the accounting records of Sanyam, Solicitor at the end of the 2013 financial year (all figures exclude GST).

Legal fees owing	$235 000
Allowance for doubtful debts	21 500
Fees owed determined to be uncollectable (not yet written off)	8 600

The firm uses a version of the ageing method that requires an allowance for doubtful debts of 10% of outstanding fees at 30 June. Ignore GST.

Required

A. Prepare the appropriate general journal entries.

B. Prepare and balance the Allowance for Doubtful Debts account at 30 June 2013.

C. Show the amount(s) to be charged as bad debts expense for the year.

Exercise 18.7 DOUBTFUL DEBTS — AGEING METHOD

Refer to the data in exercise 18.6. Assume that the company is registered for the GST.

Required

A. Prepare the appropriate general journal entries after adding in GST.

B. Prepare and balance the Allowance for Doubtful Debts account at 30 June 2013.

C. Show the amount(s) to be charged as bad debts expense for the year.

Exercise 18.8 ALLOWANCE FOR DOUBTFUL DEBTS OVER 2 YEARS LO 3

The information in the table below relates to the accounts receivable and allowance for doubtful debts of Easy-Credit Ltd. Ignore GST. The company policy is to provide an allowance for doubtful debts at the rate of 3% of accounts receivable at 30 June each year. The balance of the Allowance for Doubtful Debts account on 1 July 2012 was $10 000.

	June 2013	June 2014
Accounts receivable	$300 000	$320 000
Bad debts written off for past year	$8 000	$10 000
Required balance of Allowance for Doutbful Debts	(a)	(d)
Increase/decrease in allowance required	(b)	(e)
Allowance for doubtful debts at 30 June	(c)	(f)

Required

Determine the missing amounts in the table.

Exercise 18.9 DOUBTFUL DEBTS — AGEING METHOD OVER 2 YEARS LO 3

While accounting for accounts receivable for Games Galore Ltd, the following information became available to the accountant. At 1 July 2012, the Allowance for Doubtful Debts account balance was $16 200. To 30 June 2013, debts amounting to $33 120 were written off as bad, and at 30 June 2013, the required allowance for doubtful debts was calculated under the ageing method to be $25 000. To 30 June 2014, debts amounting to $23 380 were written off, and at 30 June 2014, the allowance for doubtful debts was calculated under the ageing method to be $21 690. Ignore GST.

Required

A. Prepare and balance the Allowance for Doubtful Debts account and the Bad Debts Expense account for the years ending 30 June 2013 and 30 June 2014.

B. Prepare the necessary general journal entries to bring the allowance for doubtful debts to the appropriate amount at 30 June 2013 and 30 June 2014.

Exercise 18.10 INTERPRETATION LO 3

While reviewing the accounts of Hannah Ltd, the auditor noticed that credit sales increased significantly in the last 2 months of the financial year. This had the effect of turning an almost certain overall loss in the income statement to a small profit. Why might this cause the auditor concern, and what further investigations should be undertaken in relation to this matter?

Exercise 18.11 CONTROL OF ACCOUNTS RECEIVABLE LO 4

Many retailers now extend various forms of credit to potential customers; this is particularly common in the home electrical market. What information do you think would be relevant to a retailer's credit department when assessing whether to extend credit to a customer? What action could a credit department undertake in the event that a customer then fails to meet their obligations?

Exercise 18.12   NOTE RECEIVED IN EXCHANGE FOR ACCOUNT RECEIVABLE

Carol's Catering Services has overdue fees receivable from D. McMahon for $12 000. On 26 May, McMahon requested a 60-day extension of the payment date, and the firm agreed to accept a 60-day, 8% promissory note in exchange for the account receivable. Carol's Catering Services' financial year ends on 30 June.

Required
A. Prepare a general journal entry to record the receipt of the promissory note.
B. Prepare general journal entries to record any adjustments necessary at 30 June.
C. Prepare general journal entries to record the cash received on the note on its maturity date.
D. What impact would GST have on this transaction, if any?

Exercise 18.13   BILLS RECEIVABLE

The following transactions relate to the business of Motor Mirrors Ltd:
1. A bill dated 4 April provided for payment after 120 days of $8000 plus interest at 12% p.a. was received on 4 April.
2. On 5 July, the company received a 60-day, 8% bill covering an account receivable owed by HK Holden, the acceptor, for $6000.
3. The company received a 90-day, 10% promissory note dated 10 July for a debt of $8000 from a customer, and discounted it at 12% at the bank after 30 days.

Required
A. What is the maturity value and maturity date of the bill in (1) above? Give the general journal entry to record the receipt of the bill.
B. Refer to the details provided in (2) above. Show the general journal entries to record receipt of the bill and its collection at its maturity date.
C. Refer to the details provided in (3) above. Show the general journal entries to record receipt of the bill and the discounting of the bill.

PROBLEMS

Problem 18.1   DOUBTFUL DEBTS — PERCENTAGE OF DEBTORS ★

★ Basic

★★ Moderate

★★★ Challenging

Adele Evans started business on 1 July 2012. On 30 June 2013, she found that she had written off debts amounting to $7500. In addition, she found it necessary to create an allowance for doubtful debts of $12 120. During the year to 30 June 2014, debts totalling $4800 proved to be bad and were written off, and $1320 was recovered in respect of bad debts previously written off. The total of debtors' balances at 30 June 2014 was $337 200 (after the bad debts had been written off) and it was decided to increase the allowance for doubtful debts to 4% of this figure. Ignore GST.

Required
A. Prepare general journal entries to record all the above transactions.
B. Prepare the Bad Debts Expense account and the Allowance for Doubtful Debts account for 2013 and 2014.

Problem 18.2   DOUBTFUL DEBTS — AGEING METHOD ★

On 1 June, Coffee Machine Clean had Accounts Receivable and Allowance for Doubtful Debts accounts as set out below. Ignore GST.

Accounts Receivable

1/6	Balance	356 756	

Allowance for Doubtful Debts

		1/6 Balance	5430

During June, the following transactions occurred.

1. Fees earned on credit, $562 500.
2. Fees refunded, $11 275.
3. Accounts receivable collected, $684 560.
4. Accounts written off as uncollectable, $7453.

Based on an ageing of accounts receivable on 30 June, the entity determined that the Allowance for Doubtful Debts account should have a credit balance of $6250 on the balance sheet as at 30 June. Ignore GST.

Required

A. Prepare general journal entries to record the four transactions above and to adjust the Allowance for Doubtful Debts account.

B. Show how accounts receivable and the allowance for doubtful debts would appear on the balance sheet at 30 June.

C. On 29 July, Chan Ltd, whose $1800 account had been written off as uncollectable in June, paid its account in full. Prepare general journal entries to record the collection.

Problem 18.3 DOUBTFUL DEBTS — AGEING METHOD ★

On 1 June, Novella Brothers and Associates had Accounts Receivable and Allowance for Doubtful Debts accounts as set out below. The firm is registered for the GST.

Accounts Receivable

1/6 Balance 1 848 770	

Allowance for Doubtful Debts

	1/6 Balance 50 421

During June, the following transactions occurred.

1. Fees earned on credit, $2 848 700 plus GST.
2. Fees refunded, $50 000 plus GST.
3. Accounts receivable collected, $2 420 220.
4. Accounts written off as uncollectable, $33 000.

Based on an ageing of accounts receivable on 30 June, the entity decided that the Allowance for Doubtful Debts account should have a credit balance of $50 000 on the balance sheet as at 30 June.

Required

A. Prepare general journal entries to record the four transactions above and to adjust the Allowance for Doubtful Debts account.

B. Show how accounts receivable and the allowance for doubtful debts would appear on the balance sheet at 30 June.

C. On 29 July, DeAngelis Ltd, whose $1870 account had been written off as uncollectable in June, paid its account in full. Prepare journal entries to record the collection.

Problem 18.4 CREDITOR MANAGEMENT ★★ LO 4

The owner of Victor's Property Maintenance has asked your advice on whether he should allow customers to pay on account. Explain the costs and benefits of extending credit to customers. Identify and discuss the key components of a comprehensive creditor management system for a small service organisation. In your discussion, consider both the decision to extend credit and how to manage credit once it is extended. In addition, Victor prepares simple accrual-based accounting statements for his wife, Kaye, to allow her to monitor the business's performance. What impact will extending credit have on these statements and what new issues would you advise Kaye to be conscious of when reviewing them?

Problem 18.5 DOUBTFUL DEBTS — NET CREDIT SALES AND AGEING METHODS ★★ LO 3

Aussi World Ltd sells outdoor furniture settings on credit. The accounting records at 30 June 2013 reveal the information shown on the next page. Ignore GST.

Credit sales (for year)	$1 070 000
Credit sales returns and allowances (for year)	90 000
Accounts receivable (balance 30 June 2013)	323 500
Allowance for doubtful debts (credit balance 30 June 2013)	1 500

In the past, the company's yearly bad debts expense had been estimated at 2% of net credit sales revenue. It was decided to compare that method with an ageing of the accounts receivable method. The following analysis was obtained with respect to the accounts receivable:

	Balance	% estimated uncollectable
Accounts not yet due	$173 600	½
Accounts overdue: 10–30 days	60 000	2
31–60 days	42 000	10
61–120 days	26 400	25
121 days and over	21 500	40
	$323 500	

Required

A. Prepare the journal entries to adjust the Allowance for Doubtful Debts at 30 June 2013 under:
   1. the net credit sales method
   2. the ageing of accounts receivable method.
B. Determine the balance in the Allowance for Doubtful Debts account under both methods.
C. Assume that the allowance account had a debit balance of $850 at 30 June 2012. Show the journal entries to record the allowance for doubtful debts at 30 June 2013 under:
   1. the net credit sales method
   2. the ageing of accounts receivable method.
D. Using the journal entries from requirement C, determine the balance in the allowance account under both methods.
E. Explain, with reference to requirements B and D, why the two different methods result in different balances.

Problem 18.6 ACCOUNTS RECEIVABLE AND BILLS RECEIVABLE ★★ **LO 3, 5**

Nola Nogovic, who trades as Nola's Nook, uses the following journals in her business: general, cash receipts, cash payments, sales and purchases. The control account for the accounts receivable in the general ledger at 1 June 2013 (with posting references omitted) is summarised below:

Accounts Receivable

2013			2013		
1/6		232 760	7/6		14 926*
19/6		14 916	16/6		1 496
30/6		264 000	28/6		14 916
			30/6		193 600

* (Promissory note due 16/10)

Set out below are the only two subsidiary ledger accounts for receivables affected by general journal entries during June:

E. Grete

Date	Post Ref	Debit	Credit	Balance
2013				
June 1				(1496)
10	S5	3 476		1980
16	GJ7		1 496	484

Tricky Ltd.

Date	Post Ref	Debit	Credit	Balance
2013				
June 1				14 872
8	GJ7		14 872	—
19	CP8	14 916		14 916
28	GJ7		14 916	—

Required

A. Complete the Accounts Receivable Control Account by inserting posting references and balancing.
B. How could the credit balance in the account of E. Grete have arisen?
C. What transaction would have led to the debit in the account of Tricky Ltd on 19 June?
D. Explain the transactions that would have led to the credit entries in the Accounts Receivable Control account on 8, 16 and 28 June.

Problem 18.7 DOUBTFUL DEBTS — NET CREDIT SALES AND
AGEING METHODS ★★

All transactions below relate to Parson's Builders Pty Ltd's uncollectable accounts for the financial
year ended 30 June 2013. The company is registered for GST.

July	18	Wrote off the $561 account of J. Brooks as uncollectable.
Oct.	19	Re-established the account of J. Fuller and recorded the collection of $1562 in full payment of his account, which had been written off previously.
Jan.	31	Received 40% of the $990 balance owed by W. Chan and wrote off the remainder as uncollectable.
Feb.	16	Wrote off as bad the accounts of Foxon Co. Ltd, $2640, and D. Ferres, $3465.
March	20	Received 25% of the $1716 owed by XL Painters and wrote off the remainder as a bad debt.
April	16	Received $1056 from D. Lowe in full payment of his account, which had been written off earlier as uncollectable.
June	30	Estimated bad debts expense for the year to be 1.5% of net credit sales of $631 000 (excluding GST).

The Accounts Receivable account had a balance at 30 June 2013 of $189 200, and the begin-
ning (1 July 2012) balance in the Allowance for Doubtful Debts account was $9300.

Required

A. Prepare journal entries for each of the transactions.
B. Determine (1) the balance in the Allowance for Doubtful Debts account after the 30 June adjustment, and (2) the expected collectable amount of the accounts receivable as at 30 June.
C. Assume that instead of basing the allowance for doubtful debts on net credit sales, the estimate
   of uncollectable accounts is based on an ageing of accounts receivable and that $11 630 of the
   accounts receivable as at 30 June was estimated to be uncollectable. Determine:
   1. the general journal entry to bring the allowance account to the desired balance
   2. the expected collectable amount of the accounts receivable as at 30 June.

Problem 18.8 AGEING OF ACCOUNTS RECEIVABLE AND ADJUSTMENT OF
ALLOWANCE ★★

The accountant for Mynn's Moving Pty Ltd provided the analysis of accounts receivable balances
at 30 June 2013 as set out below. The percentages expected to go bad are also provided and are
based on past experience. The company is registered for GST. The allowance method is used to
account for bad debts. On 30 June 2013 the credit balance of the Allowance for Doubtful Debts
account is $1150 before any adjustments.

Customer	0–30 days	31–60 days	61–90 days	90–180 days	Over 180 days
Alan	$ 9746				
Bill	11 055	$3 245			
Cathy				$12 353	
Derek	9 108				$2 596
Edward	13 112				
Fran			$9 746		

Estimated uncollectable:

Age	Estimated uncollectable
Current	1%
30–60 days outstanding	4%
61–90 days outstanding	10%
90–180 days outstanding	25%
180+ days outstanding	60%

Required

A. Use the ageing analysis of accounts receivable to estimate the bad debts amount.
B. Prepare the general journal adjusting entry to record estimated bad debts on 30 June 2013.
C. Give the entry to write off the account of Cathy in August 2013, $12 353.
D. Do you have any comments or observations on Mynn's Moving Pty Ltd's credit policies?

LO 5

Problem 18.9 BILLS RECEIVABLE, INCLUDING DISCOUNTING ★★

Adrienne Ltd received the following bills during the last 3 months of the financial year ended 30 June.

Date of bill	Amount of debt	Term of bill	Interest rate	Date of discount	Discount rate
1. April 1	$ 9 000	60 days	8%	May 1	10%
2. May 2	15 000	90 days	9%	June 11	11%
3. May 15	12 000	60 days	10%		
4. June 1	7 500	60 days	9%		
5. June 8	12 000	60 days	8%	June 24	10%
6. June 16	15 000	60 days	10%		

Required

A. Determine the due date and the maturity value for each bill; for bills 1, 2 and 5, determine also the discount period, the amount of discount, and the net proceeds.
B. Prepare journal entries to record the discounting of bills 1, 2 and 5 at the bank.
C. Prepare a general journal entry to accrue interest on bills 3, 4 and 6 on 30 June.
D. Prepare general journal entries to record the collection of bills 3, 4 and 6 in the next financial year.
E. Prepare journal entries, if any, to record the effect of bill 5 being dishonoured.

LO 4

Problem 18.10 MONITORING CASH COLLECTION ★★

The information below has been extracted from the financial statements of Ballina Beachwear Ltd.

	2013	2014	2015
Cash at bank	$ 44 000	$ 40 000	$ 36 000
Marketable securities	88 000	100 000	96 000
Accounts receivable	102 000	108 000	124 000
Sales revenue (all sales on credit)	1 108 000	1 120 000	1 130 000
Cost of sales	672 000	680 000	700 000

Required

A. Calculate the following for years 2014 and 2015:
   1. receivables turnover ratio
   2. average collection period of accounts receivable.
B. Using your calculations in requirement A, comment on the credit collection policies of the company. What additional information could be used to make an analysis of cash collection policies more meaningful?

LO 4

Problem 18.11 MONITORING CASH COLLECTIONS ★★

The following information has been extracted from the annual reports of Nani Ltd and Wani Ltd.

	Nani Ltd	Wani Ltd
Sales (net credit) revenue for the year	100 000	100 000
Allowance for doubtful debts, 1/7/2012	2 500	12 000
Allowance for doubtful debts, 30/6/2013	3 210	13 500
Accounts receivable (gross), 1/7/2012	24 000	9 500
Accounts receivable (gross), 30/6/2013	42 000	9 500

Required

A. Calculate the receivables turnover ratio and average collection period for both companies. Comment on the difference in their collection experiences.

B. Compare the success or otherwise of their cash collection policies, given that the average receivables turnover for the industry in which the companies operate is 7. Credit terms for both companies are 2/10, n/30.

Problem 18.12 USE OF CREDIT CARDS ★★★ LO 5

Sure Foot Shoes Ltd has traditionally made sales for cash and on credit only. Management has resisted accepting credit cards on the basis that the business would lose on average a credit card fee of 4% of the sale value, adversely affecting already low profit margins.

Management is concerned at negative customer reaction to the policy of not accepting credit cards and, indeed, suspects that sales are being lost because of this policy.

Management has asked you to provide a table showing credit and collection costs in dollars and as a percentage of net sales associated with credit sales and maintaining accounts receivable. The following data have been provided for the two most recent years which are expected to be representative of future operations.

	2013	2014
Net credit sales	$720 000	$600 000
Part-time salary — accounts receivable clerk	4 350	4 350
Collection agency fees for slow payers	3 250	3 200

Other collection and credit expenses expressed as percentages of net sales are:

Bad debts	1.5%
Invoicing and mailing costs	0.6%
Credit evaluation of new customers	0.14%

It is also estimated that the average accounts receivable balance during the year is approximately 6% of net credit sales, and that surplus cash can be invested at 14% p.a. The credit card company charges a fee of 4% at the end of each month.

Required

A. Prepare a table setting out for each year all the credit and collection expenses both in dollars and as a percentage of net sales.

B. Estimate, as a percentage of net credit sales, the cost of the interest forgone in carrying accounts receivable.

C. Explain how credit cards are a means of disposing of accounts receivable.

DECISION ANALYSIS

Credit cards or not?

Heidi's Homewares and Gifts Pty Ltd has been operating profitably for a number of years and has always sold merchandise on the basis of cash or credit. Heidi, the proprietor, had always resisted accepting credit cards as payment, as she has always had a dislike for them as a result of family upbringing where she was constantly reminded of the dangers of using personal credit cards. Although profits of the business have been satisfactory, they are declining, and it is becoming clear that sales are being lost because credit card facilities are not available to potential customers. Major competitors have been accepting credit cards for many years and appear to have an expanding customer base. Heidi is also mindful of the costs that are associated with offering credit card facilities.

Hans Aidsall, an accountant and personal friend, recently pointed out to Heidi that selling goods on credit also incurred considerable costs that were often overlooked. Examples of such costs include credit assessment of potential customers, invoicing and record keeping, bad debts, and credit collection costs. He pointed out that offering credit card facilities in some cases could be more financially attractive than selling on credit. He volunteered to prepare data to enable a comparative analysis to be made of the costs of selling on credit and carrying accounts receivable and the costs of accepting credit cards.

After analysing the past 3 years of accounting records, Hans produced the following figures based on a 3-year average of recorded results:

Annual credit sales	$1 350 000
Cost of accounting for accounts receivable (part-time clerk)	19 000
Collection costs paid to agencies	8 000

Other direct financial costs identified and expressed as a percentage of credit sales were:

Invoicing and collection costs	0.54%
Credit assessment of potential customers	0.10%
Bad debts	1.25%

Hans also established that credit card issuers impose, on average, a charge of 4% of credit sales and the cash is received approximately 5 days from the date of sale. The average monthly accounts receivable balance is $40 000, and any surplus cash arising from the use of credit cards (ignoring the 5 days delay period) can be invested at 7% p.a.

Required

A. Prepare a table setting out the average credit/collection costs both in total dollars and a percentage of net credit sales.

B. Prepare an analysis to show the cost of interest earnings forgone as a result of not being able to invest money that would become available if credit cards were introduced.

C. Prepare a table setting out the total cost in dollars and in percentage of credit sales of credit and collection costs of carrying accounts receivable.

D. Based on the analyses above, would you recommend that Heidi's Homewares Pty Ltd offers credit card facilities to its customers rather than selling on credit? Would your recommendation be the same if non-financial qualitative factors were considered? Explain.

CRITICAL THINKING

Fall in bad debts boosts ANZ result

A sharp fall in provisions for bad debts aided by a steadily improving domestic economy has helped ANZ Bank to a 36 per cent surge in its first-half profits which almost topped $2 billion.

Still cautious

While the bank acknowledged the better performance on its bad debt position, it sounded a note of caution about the global financial environment that is continuing to cause concern across the world and domestic economies.

The corporate, rural and small business sectors in Australia were still feeling the pinch, the bank said in a statement, which explained an overall growth in the total number of impaired assets on its loan books.

The bank still expects to be making provisions for bad debts well into the next financial and calendar year as its smaller institutional, middle market and better secured customers work through their credit problems. ANZ said it was 'prudent' to take a cautious approach to its exposures — but is planning for growth in new impaired loans to fall as they have done in recent months.

That caution was reflected in the comments by ANZ's CEO Mike Smith who, while welcoming the group's better overall performance, highlighted the difficulties still faced by the worldwide economy following the global financial crisis.

Source: Excerpts from Danny John, 'Fall in bad debts boosts ANZ result', *The Age*.

Required

Read the extract by Danny John. The determination of bad debts is particularly important yet difficult activity for an organisation. What economic factors would you expect an organisation to consider when assessing the appropriateness of its allowance for doubtful debts? How would you assess the current economic conditions with regards to bad and doubtful debts? Why do you think many analysts carefully monitor changes in the allowance for doubtful debts?

STRATEGIC MANAGING

Monitoring cash collections

Divide into groups and, under the guidance of a group leader, compare and contrast the credit policies and methods of monitoring cash collections appropriate for the following types of businesses:

1. an electronics retailer, extending credit to the general public to purchase large consumer goods
2. a relatively large manufacturer of leisure footwear, supplying shoes to many small indepen-dent footwear retailers operating mainly through large suburban shopping centres. There are a number of similar manufacturers supplying footwear in a very competitive market.

Required

After discussion as outlined above, each group should develop a written plan for managing the receivables appropriate for each of the above businesses.

ETHICS AND GOVERNANCE

Bad debts

Rachael Shock, assistant accountant for Bunbury Instruments Ltd, was finalising the balance sheet of the company as at 30 June 2013 with the accountant of the business, Olle Twist. Although both agreed that everything appeared to be in order, Rachael had noticed that a large loan had been taken out by the company with Bunbury Bank and that, as part of the loan agreement, Bunbury Instruments Ltd was to maintain a ratio of current assets (less inventories) to current liabilities of at least 1.25:1. She was concerned that the company would not be able to maintain this ratio given the fact that she had just learned that two of the company's largest customers had gone into liquidation and there was every likelihood that the company would recover no more than 10% of the debts owing. The current allowance for doubtful debts was grossly inadequate and thus the accounts receivable was overstated.

The relevant figures prepared for the balance sheet showed current assets (less inventories) standing at $1 250 000 and current liabilities standing at $1 000 000. Rachael raised her concerns with Olle Twist about the overstatement of accounts receivable and not being able to maintain the desired minimum ratio for the purpose of the loan agreement, if the accounts receivable figure was updated. Olle replied: 'Yes, I can appreciate your concerns. However, we don't know how much will be recovered from the liquidated companies, so let's leave things the way they are. The bank wants only the 30 June figures and, as it is, the ratio will be okay as far as the bank is concerned.' Olle thought about the problem a little further and then explained: 'We won't have to write off the additional bad debts until next year when they occur and are known with certainty, and by then things will have picked up. I am sure the directors of the company will agree with me, and be happy to leave the accounts as they are, so there is no need for you to worry any more.'

Required

A. Identify the stakeholders involved in this situation.
B. What are the main ethical issues involved?
C. What actions are available to Rachael to resolve the dilemma she faces?
D. What would you do if you were Rachael?

Refer to the latest financial report of JB Hi-Fi Limited on its website, www.jbhifi.com.au, and answer the following questions using the consolidated balance sheet and notes to the consolidated financial statements.

1. Have the trade receivables of JB Hi-Fi Limited increased or decreased over the year? By how much? Is the figure at the end of the year gross or net receivables? What was the balance of the allowance for doubtful debts on the same date?

2. What other receivables are recorded under the classification trade and other receivables?

3. Compare current assets and current liabilities as shown on the balance sheet and comment on the short-term solvency of the company.

4. What was the amount of bad debts actually written off during the financial year? How does this compare with the previous year?

5. Calculate the average collection period for trade receivables. Comment on any changes from the previous year.

Concepts for review

Before studying this chapter, you should understand or, if necessary, revise:

- how to record the sales transactions (including returns) of a retail business (pp. 234–8)
- how to determine cost of sales under the periodic and perpetual inventory systems (pp. 238–49)
- the differences in shipping terms (p. 238)
- how to prepare an income statement for a retail business (pp. 253–4)
- ratios used in analysing and controlling inventory (pp. 256–7)
- the bodies involved in the regulation of accounting standards (pp. 702–9).

Learning objectives

When you have studied this chapter, you should be able to:

1 describe how an entity determines its inventory on hand by way of a physical stocktake, and how the cost of inventory is determined (pp. 786–8)

2 determine cost of sales under alternative cost flow assumptions for the periodic inventory system (pp. 788–95)

3 determine the valuation of ending inventory and cost of sales under alternative cost flow assumptions for the perpetual inventory system (pp. 795–97)

4 compare the results of cost flow assumptions for the periodic and perpetual inventory systems (pp. 798–800)

5 apply the lower of cost and net realisable value rule, required by accounting standards, for the valuation of inventory (pp. 800–1)

6 understand how to record sales returns and purchases returns under the perpetual inventory system with different cost flow assumptions (pp. 801–3)

7 describe the effects on financial statements of errors made in determining inventory (pp. 803–5)

8 estimate the value for inventories using the retail inventory and gross profit methods (pp. 805–8)

9 present information on inventories in financial statements (p. 809)

10 discuss the effects of different cost flow assumptions on ratios used by decision makers (pp. 809–10).

New BlackBerry a response to rivals

Smartphone maker Research In Motion has unveiled a new version of its popular BlackBerry handset designed to take on Apple's iPhone and devices based on Google's Android operating system in the consumer market.

The BlackBerry Torch is RIM's first product to employ a slide-out keypad as well as a touch-screen interface. RIM is eager to become more relevant in the consumer market as its traditional corporate stronghold comes under increased pressure.

Apple earlier this month claimed more than 80 per cent of the Fortune 100 companies were planning for or evaluating the iPhone, up from 70 per cent six months ago.

In Australia, the company launched a business-targeted advertising campaign on the same day as the iPhone 4 launch.

Google has also begun to eat into the BlackBerry pie. A Nielsen poll of BlackBerry users earlier this year showed more than 40 per cent were considering a switch to either iPhone or Android.

Nielsen figures also showed Android share in the United States has skyrocketed over the last six months, from 6 per cent in quarter four 2009 to 27 per cent of the US market in the second quarter of 2010.

Even so, BlackBerry still has for 19 per cent of the total global smart-phone market, according to market research from Strategy Analytics.

Early US reviews of the Torch have been lukewarm, describing the software as 'sluggish' and bemoaning the screen resolution.

Telstra, Optus, Vodafone and 3 will all offer the Torch to customers when it launches in Australia. A date has not been set but it is expected before the end of the year.

Executive director for Telstra's mobility products Ross Fielding said the Torch 'elegantly' solved the dilemma over touch-screen versus keypad and customers would be impressed with the phone's speed.

But bloggers have ripped into the device, suggesting it was a step up for users of the BlackBerry 6, but was just playing catch-up with features such as tab browsing and social networking tools, which are already offered by the iPhone and Android products.

Analyst at research firm NPD, Ross Rubin, told the Associated Press that the Storm had been an 'exercise in differentiation', but had introduced more challenges than it

addressed. The phone is thick and heavy compared to the iPhone he said.

'It's not particularly flashy, but it should extend the company's reputation for solid, efficient, reliable products that have good battery life', Mr Rubin said.

Meanwhile, RIM executives had little to say at its product launch about a decision in the United Arab Emirates to ban its phones.

The ban is planned to start this Friday because data use cannot be monitored to censorship standards.

The UAE said access to instant messenger, email and the internet via BlackBerry smartphones would be suspended from October 11 as they 'allow individuals to commit violations' the country could not monitor.

RIM deliberately designs its security systems to prevent others, including the manufacturer, from monitoring data use. The security features inherent in the BlackBerry series is one of the reasons it has remained so popular in the business sector.

RIM said it was aware some customers were 'curious about the discussions that occur between RIM and certain governments' but that such talks were confidential.

Source: Rachael Bolton, 'New BlackBerry a response to rivals', *Australian Financial Review*.

Chapter preview

In chapter 6, the term *inventory* was used to designate all goods and property owned by a retail business and held for future sale to its customers in the ordinary course of business. Two inventory systems, perpetual and periodic, were described and illustrated assuming that the cost per unit was the same for the beginning inventory and for purchases made during the period. However, in today's markets the prices of most goods change frequently. When prices change, the business entity is confronted with the problem of determining what portion of the total cost of goods available for sale should be assigned to ending inventory and what portion to cost of sales. In this chapter, we consider a number of alternative methods used to assign the total cost of goods to ending inventory and cost of sales when prices are changing.

We also discuss some additional issues relating to accounting for and control of inventory. For example, what valuation should be placed on inventories at the end of the reporting period? If inventory is readily saleable (as is the product described in the scene setter), can the entity value its inventory at selling price?

19.1 Determining the cost of inventory on hand

Performing a stocktake

Learning objective 1

Describe how an entity determines its inventory on hand by way of a physical stocktake, and how the cost of inventory is determined

When a periodic inventory system is used, the cost of inventory purchased during the period is recorded in the Purchases account, as we saw in chapter 6. Throughout the period, the balance in the Inventory account represents the cost of the inventory on hand at the beginning of the period. To determine the cost of the ending inventory, the units on hand at the end of the period must be counted and costed. The cost of ending inventory is then reported usually as a current asset in the balance sheet and is also deducted from the cost of goods available for sale in the income statement to determine the cost of sales.

When a perpetual inventory system is used (manual or computerised), although the inventory on hand and the cost of sales balances are available in the accounts at all times, a physical stocktake is still done at least once a year to verify the balances recorded in the accounting records. In this way, any discrepancies from loss, theft or deterioration can be accounted for.

A stocktake must be carefully planned, and the procedure supervised to ensure that all units owned by the business entity are properly counted. Although the specific details vary, the following is a typical approach in a manual system:

1. An inventory ticket for each type of item in stock is prenumbered and issued to each department. A space is provided on the ticket to record a description or code number of the item, the number of units counted, the initials of the person making the count and the initials of the person verifying the count.
2. An employee counts the units of each item and enters on the inventory ticket the type of item counted and the number of units on hand, plus initials to identify the person performing the count. The inventory ticket is then attached to the units counted. Because conducting the physical count is often difficult, this step is often performed outside normal trading hours, or the business may close for a short time for stocktake.
3. A supervisor recounts a sufficient number of items to ensure the accuracy of the recorded count and initials the inventory ticket.
4. A supervisor examines the inventory in each department to be sure that an inventory ticket has been attached to all like items. Any group of like items without a ticket attached has obviously not been counted.
5. The inventory tickets are collected and forwarded to the accounting department, where the prenumbered tickets are all accounted for. The information on the inventory tickets is summarised on an inventory summary sheet.
6. The unit cost of each type of item in stock is determined from purchase invoices or other supplementary records.
7. The number of units of each type of item is multiplied by their cost and added together to calculate the total ending inventory value.

In a computerised inventory system, determining the cost of inventory is greatly simplified. Once the physical quantities are entered into the computer, the system automatically applies unit cost data to the quantities and produces the total cost of inventory and any other inventory analyses required. A computerised inventory system offers a high degree of accuracy and speed of calculation. Although computerised inventory systems were used in the past only by larger businesses with large inventories, the reduced cost of computers and the availability of inventory software for personal desktop computers have placed computerised inventory management within the reach of most small businesses.

In variety stores and supermarkets, the use of scanning devices with cash registers at checkouts has permitted fast and accurate entry of cost of sales data into the computerised perpetual inventory system, enabling immediate updating of inventory records for goods sold. In addition, such systems enable immediate recording of sales revenue information in the accounts, and customers' bank accounts also may be debited for the amounts owed when an EFTPOS system is in operation.

Transfer of ownership

During a stocktake, care must be taken to ensure that all goods that represent inventory assets of the business entity on the date of the stocktake are included in the ending inventory, regardless of where the inventory is located. To qualify as an asset of the business, the inventory need only be *controlled* by the business and not necessarily owned. Nevertheless, in most cases, control is synonymous with ownership. Transfer of ownership normally depends on the terms of the shipment. Recall from chapter 6 that when goods are sold EXW, freight is paid by the buyer and title ordinarily transfers when the goods are delivered to the carrier at the seller's warehouse. If the terms are DDP, the seller is responsible for paying the freight and title usually does not transfer until delivery is made to the buyer.

From an accounting point of view, at the time title to the goods transfers, the seller may record a sales transaction and the buyer a purchase of inventory. In practice, however, sales are normally recorded when shipment is made and purchases are recorded when the inventory is received irrespective of the shipping terms. To increase the accuracy of the financial statements at year-end, purchases and sales invoices for the last week or two of the current accounting period and for the first week or two of the next period should be reviewed to determine whether there were units in transit on the date of the stocktake that should be included with the units counted.

For example, goods purchased EXW and in transit at year-end should be recorded as a purchase and included in the physical count even though they were not on hand when the actual count was made. Although exclusion of this inventory will have no effect on profit (purchases, goods available for sale and ending inventory are all understated by an equal amount), total assets and total liabilities are understated if the purchase is not recorded. Similarly, goods sold DDP should be included in the seller's ending inventory if in transit at year-end since title to the goods has not transferred. The sale and related cost of sales are transactions to be recorded in the succeeding period.

In some cases, the seller may have received orders for goods but shipment may not have been made. In such situations, a sale is not recorded because the revenue has not been earned. However, an exception is made when an order for goods has been received and the goods are ready for shipment, but the buyer requests that the goods be held for later delivery. Such items should be excluded from the inventory of the seller and included in the inventory of the buyer. In still other cases, it may not be clear that title has transferred. The accountant must then use judgement and try to assess when the parties to the transaction intended to transfer the title.

Goods on consignment

Another problem sometimes encountered in conducting a stocktake is the treatment of goods held on **consignment**. A consignment is a selling arrangement whereby a business (the **consignor**) ships goods to a dealer or agent (the **consignee**) who agrees to sell the goods on behalf of the consignor for a commission. Although a transfer of goods has taken place, title to and control of the goods in this case remains with the consignor until the goods have been sold to a third party. Since title to the goods has not transferred, the shipment of consigned goods is not considered a sales/purchase transaction. Goods out on consignment are therefore part of the consignor's inventory even though physical possession of the goods is with the consignee. The goods are excluded from the inventory of the consignee since they remain under the control and ownership of the consignor.

The cost of inventory

Determination of the cost of inventory is governed by IAS 2/AASB 102 *Inventories*. In IAS 2/AASB 102, inventories are defined as assets held for sale in the ordinary course of business, and include goods purchased by a retailer, or land and other property held for resale. Inventories also include goods produced within an entity, work in progress, and raw materials and supplies awaiting use in the production process. (Thus, stationery supplies are excluded from inventory unless they are used in the production process.) In order to determine the profit of an entity by recognising income and expenses in the appropriate period, it is usually necessary to carry forward the costs related to the acquisition of inventories until the inventories are sold or consumed in the production process. In historical cost accounting, the main basis for stating inventories held at the end of the reporting period is cost.

In IAS 2/AASB 102, 'cost' in relation to inventories means the sum of all direct and indirect costs — costs of purchase, costs of conversion, and other costs — incurred in bringing the merchandise to a saleable condition and to its existing location. In a retail business, this includes the purchase price, import duties and taxes (other than those subsequently recoverable from tax authorities, such as GST), transport, handling charges such as insurance on the goods while in transit, and other costs directly incurred in acquiring the goods and bringing them to their present location and condition. However, any trade discounts or rebates received must be deducted. Furthermore, as discussed in chapter 6, settlement discounts received on the purchase of inventory are normally deducted from cost of sales.

For a manufacturing business, the cost of inventories under IAS 2/AASB 102 also includes the cost of conversion, which comprises all costs directly related to the units of production. Hence, the costs of direct labour, plus a systematic allocation of the entity's fixed and variable factory overhead costs incurred in converting raw materials into finished goods, are included in the cost of conversion. However, the following costs are excluded from the cost of inventories:

- the *abnormal* cost of wasted materials, labour and overhead
- storage costs, unless those costs are necessary before a further production stage
- administrative overhead costs that do not contribute to bringing the inventories to their present location and condition
- selling and distribution costs.

When several types of inventory are acquired in one shipment, it is often difficult to allocate the incidental costs, such as transport and insurance, to individual items in order to obtain a unit cost. In addition, storage costs and costs relating to purchasing and receiving departments need to be allocated arbitrarily across inventory categories, and this may not produce enough benefits to justify the additional cost of making the allocation. Many inventory costs are thus expensed in the period incurred as a matter of convenience rather than added to the cost of inventory. As a result, often only the invoice price is used in calculating a unit cost of goods purchased in a retail business.

19.2 Assignment of cost to ending inventory and cost of sales — periodic system

In chapter 6, it was assumed that the unit cost of the beginning inventory and the unit cost of additional units acquired during the period were the same. As is more often the case, however, units purchased at different dates have different unit costs. When this happens, the accountant must select the unit cost to determine cost of sales. The problem can be readily appreciated if it is related to an inventory of fluid in a container. For example, at the beginning of July the container held 10 litres that cost $10 per litre. Assume now that 12 litres were purchased at $11 per litre on 15 September and added to the container. If 8 litres are drawn off as a result of a sale on 20 September, the accountant is faced with a problem of measuring the cost of the 8 litres drawn from the container and the cost of the remaining 14 litres in the container at 20 September. Should the unit cost assigned to the litres removed and sold be $10, $11 or an average of the two? Since it is impossible to assign a specific cost to litres withdrawn, a cost assumption has to be made.

In order to measure the cost of sales expense, the allocation of total inventory cost between inventory and cost of sales must be based on some cost flow assumption. This is true whether a periodic or perpetual inventory system is being used. Several methods based on different cost assumptions have been suggested:

- specific identification
- first-in, first-out (FIFO)
- last-in, first-out (LIFO)
- average cost.

The terminology for the average cost method varies with the inventory system in use. The method is called the *weighted average* method when using a periodic system and the *moving average* method when using a perpetual system. When prices are changing, each method produces different ending inventory and cost of sales amounts. The cost flow assumption does not have to conform to the actual physical movement of goods. A business may rotate its inventory so that the oldest units are sold first. However, in determining the cost of units sold, the average cost of goods available for sale may be assigned to cost of sales.

To illustrate the effects of the inventory costing methods on the allocation of the total cost of goods available for sale to ending inventory and cost of sales, the inventory data in figure 19.1 for a single item are assumed for the accounting period. In figure 19.1, the problem is how to allocate the goods available for sale of $412 to ending inventory and cost of sales.

Date	Number of units	Unit cost	Total cost
1 July Beginning inventory	10	$10	$100.00
Purchases made during the current period:			
15 Sept. Purchase	12	11	$132.00
7 Dec. Purchase	15	12	180.00
Total purchases	27		312.00
Goods available for sale	37		$412.00
Sales made during the current period:			
20 Sept. Sales	8	?	?
12 Jan. Sales	10	?	?
Total cost of sales	18		?
30 June Ending inventory	19		?

Figure 19.1 Inventory cost problem

If a perpetual inventory system is in operation, the number of units purchased, sold and on hand is available from the inventory record. In a periodic inventory system, the 19 units on hand at 30 June must be determined by physical stocktake.

With a periodic inventory system, the number of units on hand at the end of the period must be counted and priced before the cost of goods available for sale of $412 can be allocated between the ending inventory and cost of sales. The portion of the total inventory cost assigned to the ending inventory depends on the cost flow assumption the entity adopts. Once the cost of the ending inventory is determined, the cost of sales is calculated by deducting the ending inventory cost from the cost of goods available for sale (beginning inventory plus purchases). Determination of the cost of sales is considered to be an important objective of accounting for inventory.

Specific identification method — periodic

The **specific identification** method requires each unit sold and each unit on hand to be identified with a specific purchase invoice. To do this, the entity must use some form of identification such as serial numbers, stock tags, or bar codes containing the cost recorded in some appropriate coding system, which are attached to the item. Obviously, this method is inappropriate where an entity sells high unit volumes with small unit prices, or liquids stored in large containers as discussed previously. Nevertheless, application of the specific identification method is a greater possibility when using a computerised inventory system, where the cost of each item may be identified in the bar code for that item. When the item is sold, the cost of that item is readily obtained from the computer's reading of the bar code.

To illustrate the specific identification method, assume that, after a stocktake, the 19 units in the ending inventory can be separately identified as 10 units from the 7 December purchase and 9 units from the beginning inventory. Costs are assigned as follows:

Cost of goods available for sale — 37 units				$412.00
Less: Cost of 19 units in the ending inventory:				

Date	Units	Unit cost	Total cost
1/7	9	$10	$ 90.00
7/12	10	12	120.00

Cost of ending inventory — 19 units	210.00
∴ Cost of sales — 18 units	$202.00

Although the cost of sales is a residual amount, the $202 figure can be verified as follows:

Cost of sales — 18 units	
1 unit from the beginning inventory at $10 per unit	$ 10.00
12 units from the 15 September purchase at $11 per unit	132.00
5 units from the 7 December purchase at $12 per unit	60.00
Total cost of sales	$202.00

Using the amounts calculated for the specific identification method, the cost allocation procedure is shown below:

$$
\begin{array}{c} \$100 \\ + \\ 312 \\ \hline \$412 \end{array}
\left. \begin{array}{c} \text{Cost of beginning} \\ \text{inventory} \\ + \\ \text{Cost of purchases} \end{array} \right\}
=
\begin{array}{c} \text{Cost of} \\ \text{goods} \\ \text{available} \\ \text{for sale} \\ \hline \$412^* \end{array}
=
\left. \begin{array}{c} \text{Cost of ending} \\ \text{inventory} \\ + \\ \text{Cost of sales} \end{array} \right.
\begin{array}{c} \$210 \\ + \\ 202 \\ \hline \$412 \end{array}
$$

*Allocation of the cost of goods available for sale to cost of ending inventory and cost of sales varies depending on the cost flow assumption used.

Under the periodic inventory system, the ending inventory of $210 is reported as a current asset in the balance sheet and as a deduction from cost of goods available for sale in the income statement. As shown in chapter 6, these amounts may be entered in the ledger accounts as part of the closing process. Recall that, in one closing entry, inventory is credited for $100 to remove the beginning inventory balance from the account and transfer it to the Profit or Loss Summary account. In a second closing entry, inventory is debited for $210 to record the ending inventory. These procedures are the same for the other three costing methods that follow, but the amounts vary with the cost flow assumption adopted.

First-in, first-out (FIFO) method — periodic

The **FIFO** method of determining the cost of sales is based on the *assumption* that the cost of the first units acquired is the cost of the first units sold. Therefore, the cost of the units on hand is assumed to be the cost of the most recent purchases. Once again, this is a cost flow assumption and *need not represent the actual physical movement of goods*. It should be emphasised that the name of the inventory method, in this case FIFO, refers to the flow of costs and the determination of cost of sales. That is, under FIFO, the cost of sales is assumed to consist of the cost of the *first units* purchased, and the ending inventory cost is assumed to consist of the cost of the *last units* purchased.

In the periodic inventory system, the ending inventory is generally calculated first after a stocktake and subtracted from the cost of goods available for sale to calculate the cost of sales as follows:

Cost of goods available for sale — 37 units					$412.00
Less: Cost of 19 units in the ending inventory:					

Date	Units	Unit cost	Total cost
7/12	15	$12	$180.00
15/9	4	11	44.00

Cost of ending inventory — 19 units	224.00
∴ Cost of sales — 18 units	$188.00

Note that the 19 units in the ending inventory are assumed to represent the cost of the last two purchases. In a periodic inventory system, the cost of sales is a residual amount, but in this simplified example it can be verified as follows:

Cost of sales — 18 units	
10 units from the beginning inventory at $10 per unit	$100.00
8 units from the 15 September purchase at $11 per unit	88.00
Total cost of sales	$188.00

The cost of the 18 units sold in this period consists of the cost of the beginning inventory and a portion of the cost of the first purchase made on 15 September. The other four units from the 15 September purchase are assumed to be still on hand.

Last-in, first-out (LIFO) method — periodic

Under the **LIFO** method, the cost of *last units* purchased is assumed to be the cost of first units sold. Consequently, the costs of the most recent purchases are transferred to cost of sales. The cost of the ending inventory is determined by the cost of the *earliest* purchases. The cost allocation is:

Cost of goods available for sale — 37 units					$412.00
Less: Cost of 19 units in the ending inventory:					

Date	Units	Unit cost	Total cost
1/7	10	$10	$100.00
15/9	9	11	99.00

Cost of ending inventory — 19 units	199.00
∴ Cost of sales — 18 units	$213.00

The cost of sales can be verified as follows:

Cost of sales — 18 units	
15 units from the 7 December purchase at $12 per unit	$180.00
3 units from the 15 September purchase at $11 per unit	33.00
Total cost of sales	$213.00

As with the FIFO method, the LIFO method *may have nothing to do with the actual physical flow of the merchandise*. It merely assumes a *cost* flow.

When the LIFO method is used with a periodic inventory system, no attempt is made after the stocktake to compare the dates of sales with those of purchases. Units sold during the period are identified with the most recent purchases. In other words, it is possible to expense the cost of units sold even though they were not on hand at the time of sale. For example, if a purchase had been made after 12 January, the date of the last sale, the costs of those units would be assumed to flow into cost of sales in applying the LIFO method.

Weighted average method — periodic

Under the **weighted average** method, an **average cost** per unit is calculated by dividing the total cost of goods available for sale, including the cost of the beginning inventory and all purchases, by the total number of units available for sale. This weighted average is then multiplied by the number of units available for sale to determine the cost of the ending inventory as shown below.

$$\frac{\text{Cost of goods available for sale}}{\text{Number of units available for sale}} = \frac{\$412.00}{37 \text{ units}} = \$11.14 \text{ per unit}$$

Ending inventory: 19 units × $11.14 per unit = $211.66

The cost of sales is:

Cost of goods available for sale — 37 units	$412.00
Less: Cost of ending inventory — 19 units	211.66
Cost of sales — 18 units	$200.34

The cost assigned to cost of sales is confirmed as follows:

18 units × $11.14 per unit = $200.52
(Difference is due to rounding the unit cost.)

The use of this method results in all units sold and on hand being costed at the average of $11.14 per unit.

Comparison of costing methods

In the preceding sections, the procedural aspects of each costing method were illustrated using a periodic inventory system. Let us now examine the justifications, features and disadvantages of each method. In doing so, it is helpful to compare the effects of the methods on the business's financial statements. The results obtained in applying the methods in the previous example are summarised in figure 19.2. It is assumed that the 18 units were sold for $360, and all other expenses were $120. The sales and other expenses are the same in all cases because the inventory method used does not affect these income statement items. The beginning inventory in each case is assumed to be 10 units costing $100. In the next period, the beginning inventory value will vary depending on the costing method selected and will be equal to the ending inventory calculated in the current period.

Note that the calculations in figure 19.2 are based on the assumption that the unit cost increased steadily from $10 to $12 during the period. If the unit cost had not changed during the period, cost of sales, profit and ending inventory values would be the same for all four methods. When costs change during a period, the costing method selected can have a significant effect on the entity's reported assets and profit figures. Even in our simple example of increasing prices and only one inventory item held for sale, FIFO profit was almost twice as much as LIFO profit.

The absolute difference between the methods is greater if the volume of purchases and sales and the variety of individual items held for sale are increased. However, keep in mind that all methods assume that inventory is valued at cost. Although cost of sales and profit may vary between accounting periods, the total cost of sales and total profit reported over the life of the entity are the same for all methods since only the actual cost incurred for inventory can be expensed over the long term.

Figure 19.2 Comparison of costing methods — periodic inventory system

Periodic Inventory System				
	Specific identification	FIFO	LIFO	Weighted average
Sales revenue — 18 units	$360	$360	$360	$360
Beginning inventory	$100	$100	$100	$100
Add: Purchases	312	312	312	312
Goods available for sale	412	412	412	412
Less: Ending inventory	210	224	199	212
Cost of sales	202	188	213	200
Gross profit	158	172	147	160
Less: Expenses	120	120	120	120
Profit	$ 38	$ 52	$ 27	$ 40
Ending inventory reported in the balance sheet	$210	$224	$199	$212

Specific identification

Under the specific identification method, when a sale is made the item sold is identified and the cost of that item is expensed against revenues. Thus, the method is based on the actual physical flow of goods. For most entities, this method is not practical and is too costly to apply. Its use is limited mainly to businesses that sell easily identified items that are not ordinarily interchangeable and with a high unit cost (jewellery stores, for example) or to businesses with sophisticated computer-based costing systems. Another disadvantage of the method is that if the inventory units are identical and have different costs, it is possible for management to manipulate profit by choosing to sell a unit with a low or high cost.

First-in, first-out (FIFO)

The FIFO method is widely used because it is easy to apply. It does not permit manipulation of profit, since management is not free to pick the cost of a certain item to be expensed against revenue, but must expense the oldest unit cost available for sale. During periods of consistently rising unit costs, this method results in reporting a lower cost of sales and higher profit than the LIFO and weighted average methods (see figure 19.2). In the balance sheet, the ending inventory reflects the higher cost of the most recent purchases, which could be seen as a more realistic measure of the current value of the inventory than is provided by the other methods. On the other hand, during a period of declining unit cost, FIFO produces the highest cost of sales, the lowest profit and the lowest ending inventory values.

Many accountants agree that using FIFO during periods of consistently rising prices could be seen as resulting in an overstatement of profit. To illustrate this point, consider the data used in our previous illustration.

1 July	Beginning inventory	10 units @ $10
15 September	Purchases	12 units @ $11
20 September	Sales	8 units @ $20
7 December	Purchases	15 units @ $12
12 January	Sales	10 units @ $20

On 20 September, the business sold 8 units for $20 per unit. Under FIFO, $10 per unit is charged to cost of sales, which resulted in a gross profit of $10 per unit. However, these units were replaced on 7 December with units costing $12. Therefore, some accountants have argued that $2

of the gross profit is used to replace the units sold and only $8 represents the 'real' gross profit to the business. Inclusion of the $2 in gross profit is considered misleading because it cannot be distributed to the owners or reinvested in other aspects of the business without reducing the ability to replace units sold. For this reason, it is sometimes called 'phantom profit' or 'illusory profit'. The same line of reasoning applies to the units sold on 12 January, which, if prices continue to rise, must be replaced with higher cost units.

Last-in, first-out (LIFO)

The basic assumption of the LIFO method is that the business must maintain a certain level of inventory to operate. When inventory is sold, it must be replaced at its current cost. Profit is not considered earned unless the sales price exceeds the cost to replace the units sold. It is often argued that LIFO provides a better measure of profit by expensing the more recent costs with current revenues. Since prices have generally moved upwards, the effect of this method is to produce a higher cost of sales and a lower profit than the other methods (see figure 19.2). However, balance sheet values soon become outdated because the oldest unit costs remain in the inventory. This creates some problems in evaluating the working capital position of an entity. Also, if there is a reduction in the inventory below its normal quantity, old costs are expensed against current income, which distorts profit in the year of the inventory liquidation. Another disadvantage of LIFO is that the possibility exists for management to manipulate profit by buying, or not buying, goods at the end of the year.

Weighted average

The average cost method is usually justified because it is simple to apply and is not subject to profit manipulation as are some of the other methods. In applying this method, the average unit cost is affected by the units and cost in the beginning inventory and all purchases made during the year. As a result, cost of sales, profit and ending inventory amounts reported under this method are between the extremes produced by FIFO and LIFO whether prices are rising or falling. Thus, the use of this method tends to smooth out profit and inventory values with neither the cost of sales nor the ending inventory reported at current values. This method is sometimes used when the units involved are homogeneous in nature and tend to be mixed together. Examples are grain in a silo or petrol in a storage tank.

Which method to select?

The selection of a cost method to use for a particular type of inventory depends on many factors such as the effect each method has on the entity's financial statements, income tax laws, information needs of management and statement users, the clerical cost of applying a costing method, and requirements of accounting standards. In practice, more than one of the methods may be considered appropriate in accounting for the same type of inventory. That is, accounting standards do not prescribe the use of a specific costing method as being 'best' for a particular set of inventory conditions. It is up to management and the accountant to decide which method provides the most useful information to statement users. Nevertheless, the standard insists that the same cost formula should be used for all inventories having a similar nature and use to the entity.

Under IAS 2/AASB 102, if an entity is required to prepare general purpose financial statements, some costing methods are acceptable and some are not. According to the standard, costs should be assigned by the specific identification method for goods not ordinarily interchangeable or goods produced and segregated for specific projects. For all other inventories, only the FIFO method or weighted average cost method is acceptable. The standard ignores, and therefore rejects, the use of the LIFO method, but no reasons are given in the standard as to why LIFO is not included as an acceptable inventory method.

Consistency in using a costing method

The costing method selected can have a significant impact on the entity's reported profit and asset figures. Thus, the method used to assign cost to inventory and cost of sales should be disclosed in general purpose financial statements. IAS 2/AASB 102 specifically requires this.

Once a costing method has been selected, management cannot indiscriminately switch to another. When alternative accounting methods or procedures are considered acceptable in a given situation, consistency becomes an important consideration. If an entity was allowed to switch from one accounting method to another indiscriminately, the accounting data produced in different accounting periods would not be comparable.

The need for consistency does not completely rule out switching to an alternative acceptable method if the new method results in improved financial reporting. However, if a change is approved and made and has a material effect on the financial results, the nature of the change, the effect of the change on the financial statements and the reasons for the change must be disclosed fully in notes accompanying the financial statements (as required by IAS 8/AASB 108 *Accounting Policies, Changes in Accounting Estimates and Errors*).

19.3 Costing methods in the perpetual inventory system

Learning objective 3

Determine the valuation of ending inventory and cost of sales under alternative cost flow assumptions for the perpetual inventory system

One or more of the costing methods discussed for the periodic inventory system may also be adopted if the entity uses a perpetual inventory system. Under the perpetual system, the cost of sales is determined at the time of sale rather than at the end of the period; as a result the two systems in some cases produce different profit and ending inventory figures. As noted before, with the availability of more versatile and less costly computers, most companies use the perpetual inventory system in their accounting records to achieve better inventory control.

Computerised accounting systems process transactions as closely as possible to the time the transaction takes place. The use of EFTPOS and electronic product scanners are examples where accounting and inventory records are updated at the time of sale, i.e. in *real time*. Cash registers are, in reality, computer terminals. Such systems instantaneously update inventory records, check stock levels, initiate purchase orders, identify time, place and responsibility for a sale, verify selling price and automatically adjust for discounts or specials. Other functions can also be performed.

In a perpetual inventory system, an inventory card or inventory record is maintained for each item in stock. An Inventory Control account is kept in the general ledger and the inventory records collectively constitute the subsidiary ledger for inventory. To provide a continuous and current record of inventory transactions, the appropriate inventory card or record and the Inventory Control account are adjusted as purchases and sales transactions occur. Inventory purchases are recorded at cost in the Inventory Control account and in the individual inventory cards or records. We saw in chapter 6 that the following two entries are made at the time of sale:

(1)	Accounts Receivable/Cash at Bank	22	
	GST Collections		2
	Sales		20
	(Sold one unit of inventory for $22 including GST)		
(2)	Cost of Sales	10	
	Inventory Control		10
	(Transferred cost of unit sold)		

The dollar amounts of the first entry are based on the sales price plus GST. If the per-unit cost varies, the dollar amount recorded in the second entry varies depending on the cost flow method used.

A perpetual inventory record using the same data presented earlier for the periodic inventory system is shown in figure 19.3 (p. 796) for three cost flow assumptions: FIFO, LIFO and moving average. Note that the perpetual inventory record shows the unit and dollar amounts on a continuous basis for goods on hand, goods purchased and goods sold. The calculations for the specific identification method are the same as those described earlier under a periodic inventory system and are not repeated here. The only difference is that an entry is made at the time of sale to record the transfer of cost from the Inventory Control account to the Cost of Sales account.

Figure 19.3 Inventory records, perpetual inventory system (FIFO, LIFO, moving average)

A. FIFO method

Item: Sandwich Toaster
Code: B1800 — Location: Store Display
Minimum Stock: 10
Maximum Stock: 30

Date	Explanation	Purchases Units	Unit cost	Total cost	Cost of sales Units	Unit cost	Total cost	Balance Units	Unit cost	Total cost
1/7	Beginning balance							10	10.00	100.00
15/9	Purchases	12	11.00	132.00				10	10.00	100.00
								12	11.00	132.00
20/9	Sales				8	10.00	80.00	2	10.00	20.00
								12	11.00	132.00
7/12	Purchases	15	12.00	180.00				2	10.00	20.00
								12	11.00	132.00
								15	12.00	180.00
12/1	Sales				2	10.00	20.00	4	11.00	44.00
					8	11.00	88.00	15	12.00	180.00 } 224

B. LIFO method

Item: Sandwich Toaster
Code: B1800 — Location: Store Display
Minimum Stock: 10
Maximum Stock: 30

Date	Explanation	Purchases Units	Unit cost	Total cost	Cost of sales Units	Unit cost	Total cost	Balance Units	Unit cost	Total cost
1/7	Beginning balance							10	10.00	100.00
15/9	Purchases	12	11.00	132.00				10	10.00	100.00
								12	11.00	132.00
20/9	Sales				8	11.00	88.00	10	10.00	100.00
								4	11.00	44.00
7/12	Purchases	15	12.00	180.00				10	10.00	100.00
								4	11.00	44.00
								15	12.00	180.00
12/1	Sales				10	12.00	120.00	10	10.00	100.00
								4	11.00	44.00
								5	12.00	60.00 } 204

C. Moving average method

Item: Sandwich Toaster
Code: B1800 — Location: Store Display
Minimum Stock: 10
Maximum Stock: 30

Date	Explanation	Purchases Units	Unit cost	Total cost	Cost of sales Units	Unit cost	Total cost	Balance Units	Unit cost	Total cost
1/7	Beginning balance							10	10.00	100.00
15/9	Purchases	12	11.00	132.00				22	10.55	232.00
20/9	Sales				8	10.55	84.40	14	10.55	147.60
7/12	Purchases	15	12.00	180.00				29	11.30	327.60
12/1	Sales				10	11.30	113.00	19	11.30	**214.60**

Calculations
15/9 ($100.00 + $132.00)/(10 units + 12 units) = $10.55 per unit
7/12 ($147.60 + $180.00)/(14 units + 15 units) = $11.30 per unit

First-in, first-out method

Under the FIFO method (part A of figure 19.3), the cost of units removed from inventory is assumed to be from the *first units available for sale* at the time of each sale. The cost of the units on hand, therefore, is composed of the most recent purchases. Thus, in figure 19.3, the cost of the 8 units sold ($80) on 20 September is calculated from the unit cost of the earliest units available, which are those in the beginning inventory. The 14 remaining unsold units are assumed to be from the beginning inventory (2 units) and from the 15 September purchase (12 units). The identification of units from separate purchases results in what are frequently called 'inventory cost layers'. For the next sale, the costs of 2 units from the beginning inventory ($20) and 8 units from the first purchase ($88) are transferred to cost of sales. This leaves an ending inventory of 19 units, valued at $224. The Cost of Sales account shows a total of $188 ($80 + $20 + $88) at the end of the period.

Last-in, first-out method

When the LIFO method (part B of figure 19.3) is used in conjunction with a perpetual inventory system, the cost of sales is determined at the point of each sale based on the assumption that the last costs acquired are transferred out first. Thus the cost of the units sold on 20 September consists of the cost of the most recent units purchased on 15 September. The inventory balance of 14 units consists of two inventory cost layers — 10 units from the beginning inventory and 4 from the 15 September purchase. Similarly, the units sold on 12 January are identified with the most recent costs acquired on 7 December. The cost of sales for the period is $208 ($88 + $120) and the ending inventory is $204 ($100 + $44 + $60).

Moving average method

Under the **moving average** method (part C of figure 19.3), a new average cost per unit is calculated after each purchase. The average is called a moving average because a new weighted average cost is calculated after each purchase rather than simply calculating a weighted average at the end of the period. The moving average cost, calculated after a purchase, is used to calculate the cost of sales and inventory on hand until additional units are acquired at a different unit price. The moving average cost is calculated as follows:

$$\frac{\text{Cost of goods available for sale currently}}{\text{Total number of units available for sale currently}} = \text{Moving average cost}$$

In our illustration, the average cost per unit after the 15 September purchase is:

($100 + $132)/(10 units + 12 units) = $10.55 per unit

Since there were no additional purchases made before the sale of 8 units on 20 September, the cost of these units sold is $84.40 (8 units × $10.55 per unit). The 14 units on hand are valued at $147.60 ($232.00 − $84.40). As a result of rounding, the ending inventory is approximately equal to the 14 units times the $10.55 per unit. This average cost of $10.55 is used to cost additional units sold until another purchase is made, at which time a new moving average cost is calculated, as shown in part C of figure 19.3, after the purchase transaction of 7 December.

Justifications for and disadvantages of using each method are the same as those discussed earlier for the periodic inventory system and are not repeated here. Furthermore, the relative dollar amounts of cost of sales, profit and ending inventory produced by the methods are also the same. That is, in periods of rising prices, LIFO produces a higher cost of sales, a lower profit and a lower ending inventory than the FIFO or average cost methods.

Consumers sever Bonds, change their underwear

Australian shoppers have fallen out of love with underwear brand Bonds, with sales falling about 4 per cent over the past year after owner Pacific Brands moved production to China.

PacBrands' reported sales plunged 11 per cent to $1.74 billion in 2009–10, but the company is back in the black after absorbing most of the costs associated with the restructure, which cost about 2000 factory jobs.

The turnaround helped the company's stock surge yesterday. It closed 11c, or 12 per cent, higher at 99.5c.

PacBrands chief executive Sue Morphett said the job losses, and associated bad publicity, had a 'negligible' effect on sales. She sheeted home the sales fall to the company's dumping of a raft of unprofitable brands and Kmart's decision to replace. PacBrands products with cheaper home-brand lines.

Ms Morphett promised that sales would improve this financial year, along with earnings.

PacBrands declared a full-year net profit of $52.7 million, a dramatic improvement on the previous year's $234 million loss, and said it might resume dividends in the first half...

PacBrands has slashed its brands from about 350 to about 100, accounting for about half the fall in sales. But underlying sales, which represent retained brands including King Gee, Slazenger, Hush Puppies, Berlei and Jockey, fell 5.9 per cent in 2009–10.

Ms Morphett said PacBrands had thrown more resources at its footwear, outerwear and sport division, where sales dived 18.7 per cent.

'We are actively working to turn this business around and, while I am far from happy with the result, there are some pockets of good news starting to appear,' she said.

Source: Excerpts from Ben Butler, 'Consumers sever Bonds, change their underwear', *The West Australian*.

Learning objective 4

Compare the results of cost flow assumptions for the periodic and perpetual inventory systems

19.4 Comparison of inventory systems

Application of the alternative cost flow assumptions has now been illustrated using the same data for both the periodic and perpetual inventory systems. For comparison, the results obtained for both methods are presented in figure 19.4, assuming that the 18 units were sold for $360 and other expenses were $120.

A comparison of the specific identification and the FIFO methods in figure 19.4 reveals that the same amount of cost is assigned to the ending inventory and to cost of sales under both the perpetual and the periodic inventory systems. Using FIFO, the same amounts are obtained because in calculating the cost of sales it is always the oldest units available for sale that are assumed to be the units sold. (Another way to say this is that the ending inventory cost under both systems is assumed to consist of the most recent purchases.) The values obtained with the specific identification method are the same because the units identified as sold are the same under both inventory systems.

When the LIFO method is used, both the ending inventory and cost of sales dollar amounts may vary between the perpetual and periodic systems. The periodic system with LIFO produces a cost of sales of $213 and an ending inventory of $199. The amounts for the perpetual inventory system are $208 and $204 respectively. The two methods produce different results because of the timing of the calculation of cost of sales. Under the periodic system, cost of sales is calculated at the end of the period and the dates of sale are ignored. With the perpetual system, cost of sales is calculated at the time of each sale. The cost of sales and ending inventory calculations for both inventory systems are shown underneath figure 19.4.

When the perpetual system is used and prices are rising, units with a lower cost (the more recent purchases at the time of sale) are charged to cost of sales, which in this example results in some units of the last purchase on 7 December being considered still on hand. Under a periodic system, these more expensive units are included in the cost of sales calculation; the lower-cost units in the beginning inventory and first purchase are considered still to be on hand in the ending inventory.

Although the calculation of average cost is essentially the same under both systems, the two systems produce different results when prices change during the reporting period. The results differ because, under the perpetual system, the cost transferred to cost of sales each time a sale is made is based on a moving average that changes whenever new goods are purchased. Under the periodic system, one weighted average cost for the entire period is used to cost all sales during the period.

Figure 19.4 Comparison of inventory systems and costing methods

Perpetual Inventory System
(from figure 19.3 for FIFO, LIFO and moving average)

	Specific identification	FIFO	LIFO	Moving average
Sales revenue — 18 units	$360	$360	$360	$360
Less: Cost of sales	202	188	208	197
Gross profit	158	172	152	163
Less: Expenses	120	120	120	120
Profit	$ 38	$ 52	$ 32	$ 43
Ending inventory	$210	$224	$204	$215

Periodic Inventory System
(from figure 19.2)

	Specific identification		FIFO		LIFO		Weighted average	
Sales revenue — 18 units		$360		$360		$360		$360
Beginning inventory	$100		$100		$100		$100	
Add: Purchases	312		312		312		312	
Goods available for sale	412		412		412		412	
Less: Ending inventory	210		224		199		212	
Cost of sales		202		188		213		200
Gross profit		158		172		147		160
Less: Expenses		120		120		120		120
Profit		$ 38		$ 52		$ 27		$ 40
Ending inventory		$210		$224		$199		$212

Periodic inventory system (LIFO) (see pages 791–2)				**Perpetual inventory system (LIFO)** (see figure 19.3)			

Cost of sales

Date acquired	Units	Unit cost	Total	Date acquired	Units	Unit cost	Total
15/9	3	$11	$ 33	15/9	8	$11	$ 88
7/12	15	12	180	7/12	10	12	120
Cost of sales			$213	Cost of sales			$208

Ending inventory

Date acquired	Units	Unit cost	Total	Date acquired	Units	Unit cost	Total
1/7	10	$10	$100	1/7	10	$10	$100
15/9	9	11	99	15/9	4	11	44
				7/12	5	12	60
Ending inventory			$199	Ending inventory			$204

When prices increase during a period, a moving average yields a lower cost of sales and a higher ending inventory than a periodic weighted average. This happens because the periodic weighted average is calculated at the end of the period and is affected by the higher unit cost of purchases made late in the period.

In summary, when prices are changing, the periodic and perpetual systems produce different profit figures under the LIFO and average costing methods. The extent of the variation is determined mainly by the rate of change in prices during the period and the frequency with which the inventory is purchased and sold.

19.5 The lower of cost and net realisable value rule

Learning objective 5

Apply the lower of cost and net realisable value rule, required by accounting standards, for the valuation of inventory

Cost is the main basis for recording and reporting most assets in current accounting practice. The inventory costing methods we have been discussing are alternatives for arriving at the cost of inventory when unit costs fluctuate during the period. When there has been a decrease in the selling price of inventory, however, it is considered appropriate in certain circumstances to report inventory at an amount below its cost. In essence, IAS 2/AASB 102 requires inventories to be valued at the **lower of cost and net realisable value**. The standard defines **net realisable value** as the estimated selling price in the normal course of business less the estimated costs of completion and the estimated costs necessary to make the sale.

A decline in value below cost could result from obsolescence, damage, deterioration or a decline in demand. At the end of the period, the cost of the inventory on hand is compared with its net realisable value. If the net realisable value of the inventory is less than its cost, the inventory is written down to net realisable value and the associated expense must be recognised in the period in which the write-down occurs. Application of this requirement ensures that inventory cannot be valued above cost; in other words, inventories cannot be revalued upwards above cost, but can be revalued downwards to net realisable value, if applicable.

In measuring inventories at the lower of cost and net realisable value, the standard suggests that this is usually performed on an item-by-item basis. However, in some cases, it may be appropriate to group together similar or related items, especially inventories relating to the same product line or inventories that have similar purposes or end uses.

Estimates of net realisable value at the end of the period must be based on the most verifiable evidence available of the net amount that the inventories are expected to realise. These estimates should take into consideration price fluctuations relating to events after the end of the period only when such events confirm conditions existing at the end of the period.

In a manufacturing entity, materials and other supplies held for use in the production process are not to be written down below cost if the finished goods to which they relate are expected to be sold at or above cost. However, if a drop in the price of materials indicates that the cost of the finished goods exceeds net realisable value, then the materials should be written down to net realisable value.

Net realisable value should be assessed at the end of each period and further decisions made. If there is clear evidence in a later period that net realisable value has increased because of improved economic circumstances, then IAS 2/AASB 102 requires any previous write-down to net realisable value to be reversed; but the reversal cannot exceed the previous write-down from cost. Cost is the maximum value to be placed on inventories.

In a not-for-profit entity, application of the lower of cost and net realisable value rule is inappropriate for any inventories held for the purpose of distribution rather than for sale (e.g. for distribution to needy people). Instead, AASB 102 (but not IAS 2, which deals only with business entities) requires inventories held for distribution to be valued at the lower of cost and current replacement cost. **Current replacement cost** is defined as the cost that the not-for-profit entity would incur to acquire the asset at the end of the reporting period. If a not-for-profit entity acquires inventories at no cost or at a nominal amount, AASB 102 requires these inventories also to be valued at current replacement cost.

If a business entity uses a valuation figure that is lower than cost, this is justified by the desire of accountants to be prudent in valuing assets in the preparation of financial statements. Hence, probable losses are recorded in the accounts in the period in which the loss is first noticed. Thus, application of the lower of cost and net realisable value rule results in a decrease in inventory value being recorded in the period in which the decrease in value occurs rather than in a subsequent period when the inventory is sold.

To illustrate the application of the rule, assume that 10 units of an item costing $180 per unit were priced to sell for $300 per unit excluding GST and 5 units were sold during the period. The expected gross profit is $120 per unit or 40% ($120 ÷ $300) of sales price. At the end of the period, net realisable value of the units declined to $135, 25% below cost. Gross profit on sales based on cost and the lower of cost and net realisable value for the year is shown below:

| | Ending inventory valued at | | |
	Cost	Lower of cost and net realisable value	Difference
Sales revenue (5 units × $300)	$1 500	$1 500	—
Cost of goods available for sale	$1 800	$1 800	—
Less: Ending inventory			
5 units × $180*	900		
5 units × $135		675	–$225
Cost of sales	900	1 125	+$225
Gross profit	$ 600	$ 375	–$225

* When the unit cost fluctuates, cost would be determined by using any of the cost flow assumptions.

Applying the lower of cost and net realisable value rule in this example results in the ending inventory being $225 [5 units × ($180 – $135)] less than the historical cost ending inventory figure. The reduction in the ending inventory value becomes a part of the cost of sales, reducing the gross profit by $225. In the next period, when the goods are sold at a price of $135 each, gross profit on sales based on cost and on the lower of cost and net realisable value is $(225) and zero respectively, as shown below:

	Cost	Lower of cost and net realisable value	Difference
Sales (5 units × $135)	$ 675	$675	—
Less: Beginning inventory	900	675	–$225
Gross loss on units sold	$(225)	$ 0	+$225

As shown in the cost column, if the write-down is not made in the preceding period, a loss of $225 is made in the year the units are sold. When the write-down of the inventory to the lower of cost and net realisable value in the preceding period is made, the gross profit in the current period is expected to be zero. Thus, applying the rule results in the $225 decline in inventory cost being recognised in the period in which it occurs rather than in the period in which the goods are sold. If, in a subsequent period, there is a reversal of this decline because of a rise in net realisable value, according to IAS 2/AASB 102 the reversal must be recognised in the period in which it occurs as a reduction of the expense relating to inventories, i.e. the cost of sales, for that period.

19.6 Sales returns and purchases returns

Sales returns and purchases returns, when inventory prices are rising or falling, are illustrated for the perpetual inventory system by modifying the sandwich toaster example. Assume now the data shown in figure 19.5, amended from figure 19.1.

Under the perpetual inventory system, details of the inventory record for this item under the alternative cost flow assumptions of FIFO and moving average are presented in figure 19.6. Note that purchases returns are recorded as negative items in the purchases column of the inventory record,

Figure 19.5 Data including sales returns and purchases returns

Date		Number of units	Unit cost	Total cost
1 July	Beginning inventory	10	$10	$ 100.00
15 Sept.	Units purchased	12	11	132.00
20 Sept.	Units sold	8	?	?
25 Sept.	Purchases returns	4	11	44.00
7 Dec.	Units purchased	15	12	180.00
12 Jan.	Units sold	8	?	?
14 Jan.	Sales returns	2	?	?

Figure 19.6 Sales returns and purchases returns in the perpetual inventory system under different cost flow assumptions

A. FIFO method
Item: <u>Sandwich Toaster</u>
Code: <u>B1800</u>   Location: Store Display

Minimum Stock: <u>10</u>
Maximum Stock: <u>30</u>

Date	Explanation	Purchases			Cost of sales			Balance		
		Units	Unit cost	Total cost	Units	Unit cost	Total cost	Units	Unit cost	Total cost
1/7	Beginning balance							10	10.00	100.00
15/9	Purchases	12	11.00	132.00				10	10.00	100.00
								12	11.00	132.00
20/9	Sales				8	10.00	80.00	2	10.00	20.00
								12	11.00	132.00
25/9	Purchases returns	(4)	11.00	(44.00)				2	10.00	20.00
								8	11.00	88.00
7/12	Purchases	15	12.00	180.00				2	10.00	20.00
								8	11.00	88.00
								15	12.00	180.00
12/1	Sales				2	10.00	20.00	2	11.00	22.00
					6	11.00	66.00	15	12.00	180.00
14/1	Sales returns				(2)	11.00	(22.00)	4	11.00	44.00
								15	12.00	180.00

B. Moving average method
Item: <u>Sandwich Toaster</u>
Code: <u>B1800</u>   Location: Store Display

Minimum Stock: <u>10</u>
Maximum Stock: <u>30</u>

Date	Explanation	Purchases			Cost of sales			Balance		
		Units	Unit cost	Total cost	Units	Unit cost	Total cost	Units	Unit cost	Total cost
1/7	Beginning balance							10	10.00	100.00
15/9	Purchases	12	11.00	132.00				22	10.55	232.00
20/9	Sales				8	10.55	84.40	14	10.55	147.60*
25/9	Purchases returns	(4)	11.00	(44.00)				10	10.36	103.60
7/12	Purchases	15	12.00	180.00				25	11.34	283.60
12/1	Sales				8	11.34	90.72	17	11.34	192.88
14/1	Sales returns				(2)	11.34	(22.68)	19	11.34	215.56

Calculations
15/9 ($100.00 + $132.00)/(10 units + 12 units) = $10.55 per unit
25/9 ($147.60 − $44.00)/10   = $10.36 per unit
7/12 ($103.60 + $180.00)/(10 units + 15 units) = $11.34 per unit

* Slight discrepancies because of rounding of figures.

and are recorded in accordance with the price as negotiated with the supplier/account payable. It is assumed in figure 19.5 that purchases returns on 25 September came from the purchases of 15 September, hence the purchases returns are recorded at $11 each. The price of $11 is used irrespective of the cost flow assumption adopted by the entity. Note, however, that the return of inventory to the supplier has an effect on the moving average cost calculated in part B of figure 19.6, as explained below. Sales returns are indicated on the inventory record as negative items in the cost of sales column. It is assumed that these returns on 14 January came from the sale of goods on 12 January. However, the cost price attached to the items returned varies in accordance with the cost flow assumption used.

Returns using the first-in, first-out method

For the FIFO method (part A of figure 19.6), purchases returns are shown on the inventory record at the negotiated price of $11. However, for sales returns, notice that they are costed back into inventory at the *most recent* cost price that had been attached to the sale of 12 January. In other words, under FIFO, goods returned are brought in at the latest price attached to the relevant sale, in order to ensure that cost of sales still reflects the first costs out of inventory. This, too, will cause the inventory account after the sales return to reflect the later costs inwards, and will ensure consistency with FIFO calculations under the periodic inventory system.

Returns using the moving average method

Under the moving average method (part B of figure 19.6), a new average cost per unit is calculated after each purchase and also after each purchase return in order to keep the moving average up to date. The purchase return is recorded on the inventory record at the actual price negotiated with the supplier and not at the moving average price. Hence, on 25 September, a new moving average cost is calculated at ($147.60 − $44.00)/10 = $10.36. This cost is then used for all sales and sales returns until the next purchase or purchase return occurs. Note that for the sales return on 14 January, the moving average cost at the time, $11.34, is recorded on the inventory record.

19.7 Inventory errors

Learning objective 7

Describe the effects on financial statements of errors made in determining inventory

Cost of sales is the largest expense item for retail entities. The inventory balance of unsold goods is often the largest current asset reported in the balance sheet. The determination of correct dollar amounts to be reported for these two financial statement items is therefore very important. Because of the large volume of inventory transactions and the necessity of making numerous calculations, errors can occur at various stages in accounting for inventory.

Perpetual inventory. If a perpetual inventory system is maintained, a physical stocktake is made at the end of the period to verify the balances shown in the individual inventory cards or records. Even if the inventory records and the physical count are in agreement, there may still be errors in the accounts. A common error is the failure to record goods in transit owned by the entity at the end of the period. As discussed earlier, such errors have no effect on profit, but inventory and accounts payable are both understated by the same amount.

Another common error is the failure to observe a proper cut-off for recording sales and the related cost of sales. For example, a sale made after the year-end may have been recorded before year-end. If this error occurs, sales, cost of sales, gross profit and profit are overstated. In the balance sheet, accounts receivable is overstated and inventory is understated — resulting in a net overstatement in total assets and equity equal to the amount of the gross profit on the sale.

Periodic inventory. Under a periodic inventory system, errors may occur in counting and pricing the inventory and in the failure to use the proper cut-off dates for recording purchases and sales. To illustrate the effects of errors in a periodic inventory system, it is helpful to consider the calculation of cost of sales. In figure 19.7, it is assumed that a $10 000 understatement in

Figure 19.7 Comparative income statements showing effects of inventory errors in two operating periods (all amounts are assumed)

	2013		2014	
	With a correct ending inventory	With an understated ending inventory	With an understated beginning inventory	With a correct beginning inventory
INCOME				
Sales revenue	$300 000	$300 000	$300 000	$300 000
Cost of sales:				
Beginning inventory	50 000	50 000	50 000	60 000
Purchases	190 000	190 000	200 000	200 000
Goods available for sale	240 000	240 000	250 000	260 000
Less: Ending inventory	60 000	50 000	80 000	80 000
Cost of sales	180 000	190 000	170 000	180 000
GROSS PROFIT	120 000	110 000	130 000	120 000
Other expenses	70 000	70 000	75 000	75 000
PROFIT	$ 50 000	$ 40 000	$ 55 000	$ 45 000

(Ending inventory for one period becomes beginning inventory for next period.)

Total profit for two periods	Correct	Incorrect	Difference
2013	$50 000	$40 000	$(10 000)
2014	45 000	55 000	10 000
	$95 000	$95 000	$ —

the ending inventory occurred while doing the stocktake at the end of 2013. As can be seen when compared with the 'correct' column, this error resulted in an overstatement in the cost of sales and an understatement in both gross profit and profit. Since the ending inventory is also reported as a current asset, this error will cause current assets, total assets and equity all to be understated by $10 000. The opposite happens if the ending inventory is overstated rather than understated.

The failure to discover the error in the ending inventory will also cause the income statement for the next period to be incorrect, since the ending inventory for one period becomes the beginning inventory for the next period. In the next year, cost of sales is understated by $10 000, and both gross profit and profit are overstated by $10 000. Again, the opposite is true if the beginning inventory had been overstated.

In the absence of any other errors, the balance sheet amounts are correct at the end of 2014. This results because inventory errors offset one another over two consecutive periods. That is, the profit in 2013 is understated by $10 000, but the profit in 2014 is overstated by $10 000. Thus, although each year is in error, the total profit for the two periods of $95 000 is correct and the equity accounts at the end of 2014 are also correct.

If the errors are discovered after 2014 and comparative financial statements are prepared, the appropriate amounts reported in the financial statements should be corrected even though the errors are offsetting. Failure to do so distorts the trend of the entity's profits. For example, in figure 19.7, the correct inventory amounts yield a declining profit trend, whereas the incorrect amounts show increasing profit amounts. Finally, if the error is discovered before the close of the 2014 year-end, a correcting entry should be made to increase the Inventory account. The offsetting credit is made to profit because the profit was understated by $10 000 at the end of 2013. Adjustments to profits must be reflected through the profits of the year in which the adjustment was recognised.

The effects of inventory errors on various financial statement items can be summarised as shown below:

	Income statement			Balance sheet	
	Cost of sales	Gross profit	Profit	Inventory balance	Equity
Year 1 — Ending inventory is understated	+	−	−	−	−
Year 2 — Beginning inventory is understated	−	+	+	0	0
Year 1 — Ending inventory is overstated	−	+	+	+	+
Year 2 — Beginning inventory is overstated	+	−	−	0	0

+ = Overstated   − = Understated   0 = Correct balance

BUSINESS KNOWLEDGE

Harvey Norman falls short

Australia's largest white goods and furniture retailer, Harvey Norman, posted worse than expected fourth-quarter sales as consumers continued to tighten spending, shunning computers and electronic goods.

Harvey Norman was a big beneficiary of the federal government's stimulus package last year. Without the extra help this year, some retailers are finding it harder to grow sales.

Analysts also suggested that Harvey Norman's decision not to sell Apple computers had probably hurt sales growth.

Sales fell 4 per cent to $1.44 billion in Australia, the company's key market, in the three months ended June 00. After eliminating the effect of new stores, sales were down 3.4 per cent.

The result was a significant turnaround from the first quarter when sales were up 5.8 per cent and in the second quarter when sales improved 6.8 per cent. Sales were flat in the third quarter.

Chief financial officer Chris Mentis said lead retail indicators in Australia showed a sharp decline in household disposable income and consumer sentiment for the last quarter.

He said sales in electrical and computers had softened in the last quarter, while furniture and bedding continued to take market share despite the industry experiencing a slowdown with the dampened housing market.

Sales for the full year from the franchised Harvey Norman complexes, commercial divisions and other sales outlets across Australia, New Zealand, Slovenia and Ireland totalled $6.08 billion, up just 0.8 per cent from $6.03 billion.

Like-for-like sales in the same period were essentially flat while sales in Australia for the year inched up 2.2 per cent.

Retail spending has slowed in 2010 and household consumption grew by a subdued 0.6 per cent in the first quarter. But most retailers now believe conditions are ripe for a return to solid sales growth in 2011.

Unemployment remains low and demand for commodities from countries such as China and India will continue to underpin economic growth.

There was no comment on Harvey Norman's plans for the recently acquired 32 Clive Peeters and Rick Hart retail stores and seven warehouses.

However, analysts said that with one less competitor in the market, the news was good for Harvey Norman.

Source: Excerpts from Carrie LaFrenz, 'Harvey Norman falls short', *Australian Financial Review*, www.afr.com.

19.8 Estimating inventories

Learning objective **8**

Estimate the value for inventories using the retail inventory and gross profit methods

When a perpetual inventory accounting system is used, the cost of sales and the dollar amount of the inventory on hand are readily determinable throughout the period from the accounting records. However, some small business entities often use a periodic inventory system. As we know, a periodic system needs a physical stocktake to determine the ending inventory balance. A stocktake is so time-consuming and expensive that it is usually performed only at the end of the financial year.

However, management and other statement users want interim financial statements at regular intervals during the accounting period in order to make economic decisions about the performance of the entity. If a periodic inventory system is used, the preparation of the income statement requires the inventory on hand to be determined for the calculation of the cost of sales. The *retail inventory method* and the *gross profit method* are two approaches that can be used to *estimate* the dollar amount of unsold goods without a stocktake.

In addition, the two methods are also useful for testing the accuracy of a stocktake done by the entity's employees, for providing some insights into the dollar amount of inventory shortages from such causes as theft and damage, and for estimating the goods on hand when a stocktake cannot be done, such as when the inventory has been destroyed by fire or flood. The retail inventory method is also used by a retail business to convert a physical stocktake valued at retail prices to an estimated cost amount.

Retail inventory method

The **retail inventory method** may be used in two ways. In one approach, no physical stocktake is performed and the cost of ending inventory is estimated. This is acceptable for interim reporting purposes (e.g. monthly) when a physical stocktake would be costly and inconvenient. Entities using this method normally perform an annual stocktake to ensure the accuracy of cost of sales and inventory figures for annual reporting purposes. With the second approach, a physical stocktake is carried out and valued at retail prices and this value is then converted to cost for financial statement purposes. Both methods are covered below.

To use the retail inventory method, the entity must maintain records of the beginning inventory and purchases made during the period at both cost and retail (selling price excluding GST). One method of achieving this is to add another column to the purchases journal in which to record the retail value. The goods available for sale at cost are divided by the goods available for sale at retail to calculate a relationship between cost and selling price called the *ratio of cost to retail* or simply the *cost ratio*. An estimate of the inventory at retail is then determined by subtracting the sales recorded during the period from the goods available for sale at retail. The ending inventory at retail is multiplied by the cost ratio to arrive at an estimate of the ending inventory at cost.

To illustrate, assume that the following information was accumulated in the accounts and supplementary records:

	Cost	Retail
Beginning inventory	$24 500	$40 000
Net purchases to date	35 500	60 000
Net sales	—	80 000

The ending inventory at cost is estimated as follows:

	Cost	Retail
Beginning inventory	$24 500	$ 40 000
Net purchases	35 500	60 000
Goods available for sale	$60 000	100 000
Ratio of cost to retail:		

$$\frac{\$60\,000}{\$100\,000} = 60\%$$

Less: Net sales (excluding GST)	80 000
Estimate of ending inventory at retail	20 000
Cost ratio	× 60%
Estimate of ending inventory at cost	$ 12 000

The cost of sales can now be determined as $48 000 ($60 000 cost of goods available for sale minus $12 000 ending inventory at cost). The ending inventory, as calculated above, is an estimate acceptable for interim statements. The entity should still conduct a stocktake at least once a year for control purposes and to ensure a proper measurement of the cost of sales and of inventory for financial statement purposes.

The retail inventory method is also a convenient means of converting a physical inventory taken at retail to a cost amount. In other words, in a retail store each item for sale is generally marked to indicate the sales price. Consequently, during a stocktake the units are listed at current retail prices as they are counted. This procedure eliminates the need to look up purchase invoices to determine the unit cost of each item. The retail dollar value of the ending inventory is converted to cost by applying the cost ratio calculated as shown above. Remember that the cost ratio is applied to the inventory value determined by a physical count. An estimate of the ending inventory at retail is still calculated as a control measure because significant differences between the actual retail value and the estimate may indicate problems in the accounting system or excessive losses from theft or other causes.

The accuracy of the ending inventory determined by the retail inventory method depends on the mix or composition of goods in the ending inventory in relation to the mix of goods used to calculate the cost ratio. The method assumes that the ending inventory consists of the same mix of goods at various cost percentages as was contained in the goods available for sale.

In practice, the originally established sales price of many items does not remain constant during the period but, in fact, changes frequently during the year as prices are reduced for special sales or are increased as the market value of the item increases. Several different types of adjustments between cost price and retail price can occur:

- **Additional mark-ups** — representing increases above original retail prices because of unusual demand, or rises in the general level of prices (but excluding GST).
- **Mark-up cancellations** — representing a downward revision of retail prices (excluding GST) because of lack of demand, or too high a mark-up in the first place because of competition.

Note that both additional mark-ups and mark-up cancellations are permanent alterations to retail prices and therefore affect both cost of sales and ending inventory and should be taken into account in determining the cost ratio.

- **Mark-downs** — a price cut to promote sales often for seasonal or slow-moving items.
- A **mark-down cancellation** — a price increase to cancel a mark-down and to adjust sale items back to normal retail prices.

Mark-downs also must come into the calculation of cost of sales and ending inventory by adjusting the retail figures. In other words, they affect calculation of the cost ratio. Employee or staff discounts are a particular type of mark-down.

To illustrate the effect of additional mark-ups and mark-downs, let us extend the previous example by assuming the following data:

Adjustments affecting both goods sold and ending inventory:

additional mark-ups	$1200
mark-up cancellations	800
mark-downs	1800
mark-down cancellations	300
staff discounts	3000

The ending inventory at cost is estimated as follows:

	Cost	Retail
Beginning inventory	$24 500	$ 40 000
Net purchases	35 500	60 000
		100 000
Add: Additional mark-ups		1 200
Less: Mark-up cancellations		(800)
Staff discounts		(3 000)
Mark-downs		(1 800)
Add: Mark-down cancellations		300
Goods available for sale	$60 000	95 900
Ratio of cost to retail:		
$\dfrac{\$60\,000}{\$95\,900} = 62.565\%$		
Less: Sales (excluding GST)		80 000
Ending inventory at retail		15 900
Cost ratio		× 62.565%
Ending inventory at cost		$ 9 948

In IAS 2/AASB 102, the retail inventory method is allowed to be used for convenience in general purpose financial statements if it results in an inventory valuation that approximates cost.

Gross profit method

Some business entities do not maintain a record of the retail price of beginning inventory and purchases. If this information is not available, the retail inventory method cannot be used. However, the goods on hand may be estimated without a stocktake by applying the **gross profit method**. This method is based on the assumption that the gross profit percentage remains approximately the same from period to period. If an estimated value for ending inventory for the current period is required, the gross profit percentage (gross profit to net sales) of the previous period is used.

To illustrate, assume that the inventory of a business was totally destroyed by fire. A review of the last 2 years operations revealed that the gross profit percentage was 40%. On the date of the fire, the ledger had been posted and was up to date. Selected account balances were:

	Dr (Cr) balance
Sales	$(140 000)
Sales returns and allowances	8 000
Purchases	83 100
Inventory — Beginning balance	16 300
Purchases returns and allowances	(2 500)
Freight inwards	700

The inventory on hand on the date of the fire can be estimated for insurance purposes by preparing a partial section of the income statement, using the available information:

INCOME			
Sales revenue		$140 000	
Less: Sales returns and allowances		8 000	
Net sales revenue		132 000	100%
Cost of sales:			
Beginning inventory		$16 300	
Purchases	$83 100		
Less: Purchases returns and allowances	(2 500)		
Add: Freight inwards	700		
Net purchases		81 300	
Goods available for sale		97 600	
Less: Estimated ending inventory		?	
Estimated cost of sales ($132 000 × 0.60)		79 200	60%
ESTIMATED GROSS PROFIT ($132 000 × 0.40)		$ 52 800	40%

It can be determined from the records that the business had $97 600 of goods available for sale up to the date of the fire. The cost of sales is estimated to be $79 200 by applying the cost percentage of 60% to the net sales. The goods that were available for sale but had not been sold must have been on hand; their cost is the difference between the estimated cost of sales ($79 200) and the cost of goods available for sale ($97 600), which is $18 400.

The above example presents a special case where the use of the gross profit method is necessary in order to make an estimate of inventory for, say, insurance claim purposes. As noted above, in the circumstances where inventory comprises a large number of rapidly changing items and where the cost of individual items may not be readily available, the retail inventory method was acceptable for the purposes of IAS 2/AASB 102. Under normal operating conditions and given inventories with these characteristics, the standard does not support the use of past gross profit percentages for determining values of inventory items, i.e. the gross profit method is not acceptable under the inventory standard for general purpose financial statements.

19.9 Presentation in financial statements

Learning objective 9

Present information on inventories in financial statements

The method used to account for inventory can affect significantly an entity's financial position and performance, thus affecting the information available for making economic decisions. Because of the importance of inventory, certain information should be provided in general purpose financial statements. For a retail business such as a supermarket, inventory consists of many hundreds of different inventory items such as canned foods, meats, fruit and vegetables, dairy products and pharmaceuticals. Since all these various inventory items are owned by the business and are in a saleable condition, only one inventory classification is necessary, simply described as inventory.

For a manufacturing business, however, all inventories held at a certain date may not be in a saleable condition. For example, a furniture manufacturer would have inventories of finished goods, partly finished goods, and raw materials (such as steel, timber, stores and supplies). A manufacturer therefore classifies inventories into three categories: finished goods, work in process, and raw materials. Under IAS 2/AASB 102, for disclosure in general purpose financial statements, inventories are required to be subclassified in a manner suitable to the entity's activities. The total value of each of these subclassifications should be shown. Further subdivisions of inventory categories into current and non-current assets are required for general purpose statement preparation for the information of users.

In addition, the general basis or bases (cost, net realisable value) must be disclosed for each subclassification of inventory. Note that one or more bases may be used within inventories of each subclassification. The methods (e.g. FIFO, weighted or moving average) used to assign costs to inventory items must also be disclosed. Readers should peruse the set of published financial statements on the JB Hi-Fi Limited website at www.jbhifi.com.au to see how that company discloses inventories. Most details are shown in footnotes, which form part of the statements.

19.10 Effect of costing methods on decision making

Learning objective 10

Discuss the effects of different cost flow assumptions on ratios used by decision makers

In chapter 6 on pages 256–7, we introduced four ratios that are useful indicators of the entity's performance in relation to retail operations. Three of these ratios are the gross profit ratio, which indicates the entity's overall mark-up on goods sold, the profit margin, which indicates the ability of the entity to convert its sales into profit, and the inventory turnover, which indicates the number of times an entity is able to turn over or sell its whole inventory during the accounting period.

Recall the formulas for these ratios:

$$\text{Gross profit ratio} = \frac{\text{Gross profit}}{\text{Net sales}}$$

$$\text{Profit margin} = \frac{\text{Profit}}{\text{Net sales}}$$

$$\text{Inventory turnover} = \frac{\text{Cost of sales}}{\text{Average inventory}}$$

To illustrate the effect of different inventory costing methods on these ratios, refer to figure 19.4 (p. 799) and consider the information available for the various costing methods under the perpetual inventory system. Calculations of the ratios for each costing method are contained in figure 19.8 (assuming that ending inventory is used as an approximation for average inventory in the turnover ratio):

	Specific identification	FIFO	LIFO	Moving average
Gross profit ratio	$\frac{\$158}{\$360} = 43.9\%$	$\frac{\$172}{\$360} = 47.8\%$	$\frac{\$152}{\$360} = 42.2\%$	$\frac{\$163}{\$360} = 45.3\%$
Profit margin	$\frac{\$38}{\$360} = 10.6\%$	$\frac{\$52}{\$360} = 14.4\%$	$\frac{\$32}{\$360} = 8.9\%$	$\frac{\$43}{\$360} = 11.9\%$
Inventory turnover	$\frac{\$202}{\$210} = 0.96$	$\frac{\$188}{\$224} = 0.84$	$\frac{\$208}{\$204} = 1.02$	$\frac{\$197}{\$215} = 0.92$

Figure 19.8 The effect of inventory costing methods on performance indicators

As can be seen from figure 19.8, an entity can influence significantly the ratios calculated as indicators of its performance merely by changing its costing methods for inventory. It is important that decision makers are aware of the costing methods used by the entity; thus, the costing methods applied should be disclosed to external users of information about the entity under IAS 2/AASB 102, as discussed above. Note that LIFO, which produced the lowest profit ratios and the highest turnover, is not included as an acceptable method by the standard.

Note that, in times of rising prices, the FIFO method produces the highest gross profit ratio and profit margin, and the lowest inventory turnover, and the LIFO method produces the lowest gross profit ratio and profit margin, and the highest inventory turnover. The moving average method lies between these two extremes. As for the specific identification method, the three ratios can be manipulated merely by careful selection of the specific item to be sold. In relation to the example used in this chapter, figure 19.8 also shows that the specific identification method gives results between the FIFO system and the LIFO system. It is important for a decision maker, therefore, to interpret the entity's performance in light of the costing method being used.

KEY TERMS

Additional mark-ups, p. 807
Average cost, p. 792
Consignee, p. 787
Consignment, p. 787
Consignor, p. 787
Current replacement cost, p. 800
First-in, first-out (FIFO), p. 790

Gross profit method, p. 808
Last-in, first-out (LIFO), p. 791
Lower of cost and net realisable value, p. 800
Mark-down cancellation, p. 807
Mark-downs, p. 807
Mark-up cancellations, p. 807

Moving average, p. 797
Net realisable value, p. 800
Retail inventory method, p. 806
Specific identification, p. 789
Weighted average, p. 792

DISCUSSION QUESTIONS

1. What costs should be included in the cost of an item of inventory?
2. 'With sophisticated computer equipment available these days, the controversy over cost flow assumptions is no longer an issue.' Discuss.
3. Must a company use the inventory costing method that best conforms to the actual physical movement of the goods? Explain.
4. Critically examine the following statement: 'During times of high inflation, the LIFO cost assumption should be permitted in financial statements because it allows the entity to show a more up-to-date profit figure.'
5. Cottesloe Ltd has been using the FIFO costing method to account for inventories for several years. The company also has a policy of paying out all of its profits in cash dividends. What are the likely effects, adverse or otherwise, of continuing these policies?
6. 'Estimating the value of inventory is not sufficiently accurate to justify using such an approach. Only a full physical stocktake can give full accuracy.' Discuss.
7. 'Now that we have adopted the perpetual inventory system, we no longer need to conduct a costly and time-consuming stocktake'. Discuss.
8. Why is the lower of cost and net realisable value rule required by accounting standards? Is it permissible to revalue inventories upwards? If so, when? Are there any limits to revaluation?
9. If the ending inventory is understated because of an error, what is the effect on profit in that reporting year and in the next reporting year? What is the effect on the value of assets as reported in the balance sheet at the end of each year?
10. Why must decision makers consider various inventory costing methods when interpreting ratios used in retail operations?

Exercise 19.1 DETERMINING ENDING INVENTORY

Emerald Ltd's ending inventory was assigned a cost of $55 200 by way of a physical inventory count on 31 December 2013. An audit of the company's records revealed the following information:

1. Emerald Ltd had recorded a $4500 invoice (net of GST) from a supplier for goods shipped EXW on 26 December 2014. The goods were not included in the physical inventory count because they had not yet arrived.
2. Emerald Ltd had recorded a $2000 tax invoice (net of GST) from a supplier for goods shipped DDP on 28 December 2013. The goods were not included in the physical inventory count because they had not yet arrived.
3. Emerald Ltd had goods valued at $6400 (net of GST) out on consignment on 31 December 2013 that were not included in the physical inventory count.
4. Emerald Ltd also acts as a consignee. Consigned goods on hand on 31 December 2013 totalled $6100 (net of GST), and were included in the physical inventory count.
5. Emerald Ltd purchased goods worth $5500 (net of GST), which were received on 30 December 2013 and included in the physical inventory count. The invoice from the supplier was not recorded until January.
6. Emerald Ltd sold goods costing $800 for $1200 plus GST on 27 December 2013, DDP. The buyer received the goods on 5 January 2014. The sale was on credit and was recorded in 2013, and the goods were excluded from the physical inventory count.

Required
A. For each of the above, determine the effects on Emerald Ltd's 31 December account balances.
B. What is the correct ending inventory?

Exercise 19.2 INVENTORY COST FLOW METHODS — PERIODIC INVENTORY SYSTEM

Inventories and purchases for the month of June for Go Ltd are as follows:

Date	Detail	Units	Cost per unit	Total
1-Jun	Inventory	8 000	$18	$144 000
3-Jun	Purchase	7 000	$19	133 000
15-Jun	Purchase	12 000	$20	240 000
20-Jun	Purchase	15 000	$21	315 000
30-Jun	Inventory	18 000	—	—

Required
Determine the cost of sales for the month under the cost flow assumptions, based on the periodic inventory system.
1. FIFO   2. weighted average.

Exercise 19.3 LOWER OF COST AND NET REALISABLE VALUE

The inventory of Slack Ltd contains the following items at 30 June 2013.

Item type	Quantity	Unit price Cost	Net realisable value
3011	70	$ 3.00	$ 2.60
2507	30	7.00	8.50
601	18	30.00	27.00
4500	52	3.50	2.50
2825	45	6.00	7.00

Required

A. Determine the ending inventory value at 30 June 2013, applying the lower of cost and net realisable value rule to the individual items.

B. What effect did application of the rule rather than cost have on the financial statements of the company?

Exercise 19.4 NET REALISABLE VALUE

Melbourne Motors is a car dealership. One of its models was used as a demonstrator during the year. Presented below is information relating to the demonstrator as of 30 June 2014, the end of the current financial year.

Normal sales price (net of GST)	$29 990
Original cost (net of GST)	22 000
Estimated sales value in existing condition	23 500
Estimated selling and disposal cost	1 800

Required

From the information above, determine the value at which the demonstrator should be reported in the 30 June 2014 financial statements. Is there any effect on profit reported for the current period? Explain.

Exercise 19.5 INVENTORY COST METHODS — PERPETUAL INVENTORY SYSTEM

The following information relates to the inventory of Open Ltd during May:

May	1	Beginning Inventory	80 units @ $6
	3	Purchased	90 units @ $7
	10	Sold	110 units
	12	Purchased	90 units @ $8
	17	Sold	80 units
	25	Sold	30 units

Open Ltd uses a perpetual inventory system. Ignore GST.

Required

Determine the cost of the ending inventory and the cost of sales, using the following three methods:

1. the moving average; round unit cost to the nearest cent
2. specific identification; assume that the ending inventory on 31 May consisted of 13 units from the beginning inventory, 24 units from the 3 May purchase, and the remainder from the 12 May purchase
3. FIFO.

Exercise 19.6 FIFO AND AVERAGE COST FLOW METHODS — PERIODIC AND PERPETUAL INVENTORY SYSTEMS

The following information relates to the inventory of a small electrical appliance in the records of Power Ltd, a company registered for GST. All unit prices below exclude GST.

July	1	Beginning Inventory	8 @ $35 = $280
Aug.	14	Purchased	11 @ $38 = $418
Sept.	25	Sold	9
Jan.	8	Purchased	10 @ $40 = $400
March	3	Purchased	5 @ $42 = $210
April	13	Sold	11
June	10	Sold	3

Required

A. Using a periodic system and the weighted average method, calculate the cost of the 11 items in inventory on 30 June and the cost of sales for the year.

B. Using a perpetual system and the moving average method, calculate the cost of the year-end inventory and the cost of sales.

C. Using a periodic system and the FIFO method, determine the cost of the 11 items in inventory on 30 June and the cost of sales for the year.

D. Using a perpetual system and the FIFO method, determine the cost of the year-end inventory and the cost of sales.

E. Compare the results obtained under requirements A, B, C and D above.

Exercise 19.7 FIFO AND MOVING AVERAGE METHODS — PERPETUAL INVENTORY SYSTEM `LO 3, 4`

Classy Cameras Ltd records its inventory of digital cameras by using a perpetual inventory system on a FIFO basis. The following details are supplied for one particular popular make and model for the month of November. Ignore GST.

Nov.	1	Inventory on hand consisted of 18 cameras costed at $150 each.

Purchases:

Nov.	2	10 cameras at $140 each
Nov.	20	20 cameras at $155 each
Nov.	25	30 cameras at $148 each

Sales:

Nov.	4	16 cameras at $280 each
Nov.	22	22 cameras at $280 each
Nov.	29	20 cameras at $300 each

Required

A. Prepare an inventory record showing the above transactions.

B. Assuming instead that the company uses the moving average method of recording cost of sales, calculate the cost of sales and ending inventory balance for the month of November and compare your answers with those from requirement A.

Exercise 19.8 PERPETUAL INVENTORY SYSTEM AND PHYSICAL STOCKTAKES `LO 3`

Speedy Cycles maintains inventory records under the perpetual inventory system. At 30 June 2013, the inventory balance determined by the system showed a value of $300 000. However, on conducting a physical stocktake, ending inventory was calculated as being only $260 000. An investigation revealed that the difference was due to two factors:
- bicycle theft, amounting to $32 000
- destruction of parts on bicycles exhibited in the shop, $8000.

Bicycle sales for the year amounted to $1 000 000, purchases were $560 000 and the balance of inventory on hand at the beginning of the year was $220 000.

Required

Prepare the Cost of Sales and Inventory Control ledger accounts for the year ended 30 June 2013.

Exercise 19.9 FIFO AND GROSS PROFIT RATIO — PERPETUAL INVENTORY SYSTEMS `LO 3, 10`

Super Soakers Ltd manufactures and sells soakwells for use in suburban and light industrial areas of Perth. Over the past year, the cost of manufacturing the soakwells has gradually risen and the company has been required to increase inventory levels to meet expected demand in the new year, which has been forecast to bring better-than-average rainfall. At 1 July 2013, the company had 35 soakwells on hand, which had cost $200 each to make. The selling price of each soakwell remained at $400 in 2013 but was raised to $470 in 2014. Ignore GST.

During the year ended 30 June 2014, details of soakwells completed and sold are as follows:

Soakwells manufactured:

2013
Aug. 31   40 at $220 each
Oct. 31   50 at $240 each

2014
Jan. 31   60 at $270 each
May 31   80 at $300 each

Soakwells sold:

2013
Sept. 30   45
Nov. 30   60

2014
Feb. 28   70
June 30   65

Required

A. Prepare the perpetual inventory record for soakwells for the year on the basis of FIFO.
B. How much gross profit has been generated for the year from the sale of soakwells?
C. What is the gross profit ratio achieved by the company in the year ended 30 June 2014?
D. What value is placed on the inventory of soakwells at 30 June 2014?

Exercise 19.10   EFFECTS OF INVENTORY ERRORS   **LO 7**

Water Tank Suppliers Ltd began operations in the south-east Queensland region in July 2010. During the annual audit for the year ended 30 June 2015, it was discovered that errors had been made in the annual physical stocktake. Further investigation revealed the following details for the years ended 30 June:

    2011: Ending inventory was undervalued by $60 000.
    2012: Ending inventory was overvalued by $15 000.
    2013: Ending inventory was undervalued by $40 000.
    2014: Ending inventory was correctly valued.
    2015: Ending inventory was overvalued by $30 000.

Required

Explain the effects that these errors would have on the profit figure and ending asset balances for each year, and determine the cumulative effect of these errors over the 5-year period.

Exercise 19.11   EFFECTS OF INVENTORY ERRORS   **LO 7, 9**

Orff Bros' income statements for the past 3 years are as shown:

	2013	2014	2015
Net sales	$68 000	$78 000	$70 000
Beginning inventory	16 000	14 000	20 000
Net purchases	30 000	36 000	22 000
Goods available for sale	46 000	50 000	42 000
Ending inventory	14 000	20 000	12 000
Cost of sales	32 000	30 000	30 000
Gross profit	36 000	48 000	40 000
Other expenses	16 000	14 000	19 000
Profit	$20 000	$34 000	$21 000

Because of errors, the 2013 ending inventory is understated by $2000 and the 2014 ending inventory is overstated by $6000. The 2015 ending inventory is correct.

Required

A. Determine the correct amount of profit for each of the 3 years.

B. Determine the total profit for the 3-year period as shown and as corrected.

Exercise 19.12 RETAIL INVENTORY AND GROSS PROFIT METHODS LO 8

Part A

Closed Ltd's inventory on 1 April 2013 had a cost of $100 000 and a retail value of $170 000. During April, the company's net purchases cost $216 000 and had a net retail value of $324 000. Net sales for April totalled $390 000. Ignore GST.

Required

A. Calculate estimated cost of inventory at 30 April 2013 using the retail inventory method.

B. What key assumptions underlie the validity of this estimate of inventory cost?

Part B

On 18 July, the warehouse storing the inventory of Dolly Ltd was destroyed by a fire. The insurance company asked the managing director to prove his inventory loss. Available records indicated that the beginning inventory was $320 000. Sales up to 18 July were $1 082 000, sales returns were $60 000, and it was company policy to mark up goods in such a way as to have a gross profit of 40%. Purchases totalled $920 000, purchases returns were $22 000, and freight inwards was $6800. Ignore GST.

Required

Determine the amount of Dolly Ltd's claim for the inventory loss.

Exercise 19.13 RETAIL INVENTORY METHOD LO 8

Gypsum Ltd, a retail business, took a physical stocktake of inventory at retail price at the end of the current year and determined that the total retail value of the ending inventory was $190 000. The following information for the year is available:

	Cost	Selling price
Beginning inventory	$108 000	$160 000
Net purchases	486 000	740 000
Sales		704 000

Management estimates its inventory loss from theft and other causes by comparing its physical ending inventory at retail prices with an estimated ending inventory at retail prices (determined by subtracting goods available for sale at selling prices from sales) and reducing this difference to cost by applying the proper cost ratio.

Required

A. Calculate the estimated cost of the ending inventory using the retail inventory method. This is the inventory amount that will appear in the balance sheet, and the calculation should be based on the physical inventory taken at retail prices.

B. Calculate the estimated inventory loss for the year from theft and other causes.

Exercise 19.14 COST OF SALES UNDER FIFO LO 2, 3

Tricky Ltd's inventory transactions for November 2014 were as shown below:

Date		Transaction	No.	Unit cost	Total cost
Nov.	1	Inventory on hand	50	$10.00	$ 500.00
Nov.	6	Purchase	170	11.00	1 870.00
Nov.	10	Sale	90		
Nov.	14	Purchase	90	12.00	1 080.00
Nov.	18	Purchase return	30	12.00	360.00
Nov.	23	Sale	135		
Nov.	28	Sale return (on 23 November sale)	15		

Required

A. Using the information shown and assuming no losses of inventory, if Tricky Ltd uses the periodic inventory system with the FIFO cost flow method, calculate the cost of sales for November 2014.

B. Using the information shown, if Tricky Ltd uses the perpetual system with the moving average cost flow method, what would be the unit cost of the 23 November sale?

Exercise 19.15 EFFECTS OF INVENTORY ERRORS

A. Explain the effect of each of the following errors in the ending inventory of a retail business.
   1. Incorrectly included 100 units of Commodity A, valued at $1 per unit, in the ending inventory; the purchase was recorded.
   2. Incorrectly included 200 units of Commodity B, valued at $2 per unit, in the ending inventory; the purchase was not recorded.
   3. Incorrectly excluded 300 units of Commodity C, valued at $3 per unit, from the ending inventory; the purchase was recorded.
   4. Incorrectly excluded 400 units of Commodity D, valued at $4 per unit, from the ending inventory; the purchase was not recorded.

B. In determining the unit cost for inventory purposes, discuss how the following items should be treated?
   1. Freight on goods and materials purchased
   2. Purchase returns
   3. Discount received

PROBLEMS

★ Basic

★★ Moderate

★★★ Challenging

Problem 19.1 INVENTORY COST FLOW METHODS — PERIODIC INVENTORY SYSTEM ★

The following information relates to the inventory of Moveit Ltd during December.

	Units	Unit cost	Total cost
1/12 Beginning inventory	700	$3.00	$2100
10/12 Purchase (excluding GST)	500	3.15	1575
15/12 Purchase (excluding GST)	300	3.30	990
23/12 Purchase (excluding GST)	500	3.50	1750
Totals	2000		$6415

Moveit Ltd uses the periodic inventory system. During the month, 1300 units were sold for $5525 plus GST. A physical count on 31 December verified that 700 units were on hand.

Required

A. Prepare an income statement down to gross profit for December, using each of the following costing methods:
   1. specific identification, assuming that 400 units were sold from the beginning inventory, 400 units from the first purchase, 200 units from the 15 December purchase, and the remainder from the 23 December purchase
   2. FIFO
   3. LIFO
   4. weighted average.

B. Which cost flow method(s) resulted in the highest gross profit on sales? the highest ending inventory? Explain your results.

C. Prepare an income statement down to gross profit for December, using FIFO and LIFO costing methods and assuming the 23 December purchase had been delayed until January.

D. The management of Moveit Ltd expects the unit cost to increase to $3.85 excluding GST early in the next period. In anticipation of the price increase, a purchase of 600 additional units was made on 29 December at a unit cost of $3.60 excluding GST. Prepare an income statement down to gross profit for December, using the FIFO and LIFO costing methods.

E. Compare your results obtained in requirements A, C and D. Explain why your results are or are not the same.

Problem 19.2 SPECIFIC IDENTIFICATION — PERIODIC INVENTORY SYSTEM ★ GST LO 2, 9

Race Ltd buys and sells brand-name refrigerators, which are identified by the manufacturer's initials and model number.

The inventory on 1 July 2013 is as follows:

Identification number	Quantity	Unit cost	Selling price
WES301	3	$880	$1150
EMA4256	4	920	1350
F&P111	4	800	1199
KEL633	3	700	900
MAL720	5	600	800

All cost and selling prices exclude GST of 10%. Purchases and sales for July follow:

July	1	Purchased 3 KEL633.
	5	Sold 2 EMA4256.
	8	Purchased 4 WES301.
	9	Sold 3 MAL720.
	11	Sold 1 F&P111.
	15	Purchased 6 EMA4256.
	20	Sold 2 KEL633.
	23	Sold 5 WES301.

Race Ltd uses the specific identification method to account for its inventory. All transactions were on credit and the unit cost of purchases and per unit selling price for July were the same as given for the beginning inventory.

Required

A. Prepare entries to record the 8 July purchase and the 20 July sale under the periodic inventory system method. Purchases and sales are subject to GST.

B. Calculate the cost of sales for July.

C. Calculate the cost of ending inventory on 31 July 2013.

D. Prepare an income statement for July based on the periodic inventory system.

Problem 19.3 RETAIL INVENTORY METHOD ★ LO 8

Boney Retailers provided the following information for the month of June 2014. The entity uses the retail inventory method for interim reporting purposes. Normal mark-up on cost is 60%. Ignore GST.

Beginning inventory (cost)	$ 7 000
Net purchases (cost)	9 800
Sales	20 000
Mark-downs (some items still in stock)	900
Mark-down cancellations (some items still in stock)	120
Additional mark-ups (some items affected still in stock)	260
Staff discounts (on items sold)	500

Required

Boney Retailers requests that an estimate be made of inventory on hand at cost at 30 June 2014. Provide this estimate.

Problem 19.4 GROSS PROFIT METHOD ★

LO 8

An explosion at Allstate Chemicals on the night of 11 April destroyed the entire inventory. The accounting records, which survived the explosion, contained the following account balances for the period 1 January to 11 April:

Sales	$330 700
Sales returns and allowances	4 200
Purchases	285 000
Purchases returns and allowances	3 150
Freight inwards	2 400
Inventory balance, 1 January	59 300

The gross profit margin has averaged 42% over the last 3 years. Ignore GST.

Required
Estimate the cost of inventory that was destroyed, for insurance purposes.

Problem 19.5 LOWER OF COST AND NET REALISABLE VALUE ★

LO 5

The following information applies to the inventory of Fast Foto Shop as at 30 June 2014:

		Unit price (excluding GST)	
Model number	Quantity	Actual cost	Net realisable value
Cameras:			
A-4	18	$ 90	$ 75
C-7	12	100	120
G-1	20	65	60
Z-8	6	40	55
Video equipment:			
BD-5	15	175	190
FY-9	10	230	220

Required
A. Calculate the ending inventory value as at 30 June 2014, applying the lower of cost and net realisable value rule to:
   1. individual inventory items
   2. major categories of cameras and video equipment
   3. total inventory.
B. What effect does application of the lower of cost and net realisable value rule have on the financial statements of the business?
C. Assume that at the end of the next financial year, 12 units of model A-4 are still on hand and the net realisable value is $80 per unit. How would this increase in net realisable value affect the inventory value of the 12 units?
D. How would the increase in net realisable value in requirement C be treated in the accounting records?

Problem 19.6 LOWER OF COST AND NET REALISABLE VALUE ★

LO 3, 4, 5

The information below relates to barrels of oil held in the inventory of Even Ltd during 2013.

		Barrels	Unit cost
1 January	Beginning inventory	30 000	$44
15 April	Purchases	40 000	44
13 May	Sales ($52 per barrel)	(50 000)	
9 August	Purchases	35 000	44
28 October	Sales ($52 per barrel)	(40 000)	

Owing to an oil glut, the net realisable value for a barrel of the same grade of oil was $40 per barrel on 31 December 2013. In 2014, the company disposed of the 15 000 barrels of oil in the ending inventory for $600 000. No additional purchases were made in 2014. Even Ltd uses a periodic inventory system and the average cost flow method. Ignore GST.

Required

Complete the partial income statements for 2013 and 2014 shown below under the average cost flow method and the lower of cost and net realisable value rule.

	Average cost		Lower of cost and net realisable value	
	2013	2014	2013	2014
Sales revenue				
Cost of sales:				
Beginning inventory				
Purchases				
Cost of goods available for sale				
Less: Ending inventory				
Cost of sales				
Gross profit				

Problem 19.7 FIFO METHOD — PERPETUAL INVENTORY SYSTEM ★   GST LO 3, 9

Rough Ltd is a company operating in the retail sector. The beginning inventory of Product EF5089 and information about purchases and sales made during June are shown below:

June	1	Inventory	6000 units	@ $2.20
	4	Purchases	4500 units	@ 2.25
	9	Sales	4000 units	
	12	Purchases	4000 units	@ 2.40
	21	Sales	3000 units	
	24	Sales	2800 units	
	26	Purchases	3000 units	@ 2.50
	30	Sales	2500 units	

Rough Ltd uses the perpetual inventory system, and all purchases and sales are on credit. Selling price is $5 per unit. GST is 10% and is not included in any of the costs and selling prices above.

Required

A. Using the FIFO method, prepare appropriate purchases and sales journals to record these events.
B. Prepare an appropriate inventory record for Product EF5089 for June, and post the journals prepared in requirement A above to the appropriate general ledger accounts (assuming that product EF5089 is the only product bought and sold by Rough Ltd).
C. Prepare an income statement for Rough Ltd for June.

Problem 19.8 COST OF SALES — FIFO AND MOVING AVERAGE ★★   LO 3, 9

The following information has been extracted from the records of Sammy's Stationery about one of its popular products. Sammy's Stationery uses the perpetual inventory system. Its annual reporting date is 31 December. Ignore GST.

			No. of units	Unit cost
2013				
Jan.	1	Beginning balance	900	$7.00
	6	Purchases	400	7.05
Feb.	5	Sales @ $12.00 per unit	1 000	
March 17		Purchases	1 100	7.35

(continued)

			No. of units	Unit cost
2013				
April	24	Purchases returns	80	7.35
May	4	Sales @ $12.10 per unit	700	
June	26	Purchases	8 400	7.50
Aug.	11	Sales @ $13.25 per unit	1 800	
Aug.	19	Sales returns @ $13.25 per unit	20	
Sept.	11	Sales @ $13.50 per unit	3 500	
Oct.	6	Purchases	500	8.00
Dec.	11	Sales @ $15.00 per unit	3 100	

Required

A. Calculate the cost of inventory on hand at 31 December 2013 and the cost of sales for the year ended 31 December 2013, assuming:
- the FIFO cost flow assumption
- the moving average cost flow assumption (round average unit costs to the nearest cent, and total cost amounts to the nearest dollar).

B. Prepare the income statement to gross profit for the year ended 31 December 2013, assuming:
- the FIFO cost flow assumption
- the moving average cost flow assumption.

Problem 19.9 COST OF SALES — PERIODIC INVENTORY SYSTEM ★★ LO 2, 4

The following information relates to the inventory of Welsh and Brown during the month of December:

			Units	Unit cost	Total cost
Dec.	1	Beginning inventory	400	$5.00	$2 000
	10	Purchases	400	5.30	2 120
	23	Purchases	500	5.60	2 800
			1300		$6 920

Welsh and Brown uses the periodic inventory system. During the month, 700 units were sold for $6300. A physical stocktake on 31 December verified that 590 units were on hand. Ignore GST.

Required

A. Prepare an income statement up to gross profit for December using each of the following costing methods:
1. specific identification, assuming that 300 units were sold from the beginning inventory and 400 units were sold from the first purchase
2. FIFO
3. LIFO
4. weighted average.

B. Which cost flow method resulted in the highest gross profit on sales? the highest ending inventory? Explain why your results differ.

C. Prepare an income statement to gross profit for December using the FIFO and LIFO costing methods and assuming the 23 December purchase had not been made.

D. Management of Welsh and Brown is expecting the unit cost to increase to $6.00 early in the next period. In anticipation of the price increase, a purchase of 600 additional units was made on 29 December at a unit cost of $5.80. Prepare an income statement to gross profit for December using the FIFO and LIFO costing methods.

E. Compare your results obtained in requirements A, C and D. Explain why your results are or are not the same.

Problem 19.10 CORRECTION OF INVENTORY ERRORS ★★

Charlie Angel, who operates a business as a toy retailer, was concerned about the end-of-year physical stocktake and 'cut-off' procedures.

The Inventory Control account balance at 30 June 2013, under the perpetual inventory system, was $77 200. The physical stocktake count, however, revealed the cost of inventory on hand at 30 June 2013 to be only $73 400. Although Charlie expected some inventory shortfall because of breakage and petty theft, he considered this shortfall to be excessive.

Net realisable value for each inventory item held for sale exceeds cost.

In investigating the reason for the inventory 'shortfall', Charlie discovered the following:

1. Goods costing $800 were sold on credit to E. Blythe for $1500 on 26 June 2013 on DDP terms. The goods were still in transit at 30 June 2013. Charlie had recorded the sale on 26 June 2013 and did not include these goods in the physical stocktake.
2. Charlie included $2200 of goods held on consignment in the physical stocktake.
3. Goods costing $910 were purchased on credit from Bear in There on 26 June 2013 and received on 28 June 2013. The purchase was unrecorded at 30 June 2013, but the goods were included in the physical stocktake.
4. Goods costing $400 were purchased on credit from CBA Supplies on 23 June 2013 on EXW shipping terms. The goods were delivered to the transport company on 27 June 2013. The purchase was recorded on 27 June 2013 but, as the goods had not yet arrived, Charlie did not include these goods in the physical stocktake.
5. At 30 June 2013, Charlie had unsold goods costing $3700 out on consignment. These goods were not included in the physical stocktake.
6. Goods costing $2100 were sold on credit to Fun Parlour for $3800 on 24 June 2013 on EXW shipping terms. The goods were shipped on 28 June 2013. The sale was unrecorded at 30 June 2013 and Charlie did not include these goods in the physical stocktake.

Required
Prepare any journal entries necessary on 30 June 2013 to correct any errors and to adjust inventory.

Problem 19.11 PERPETUAL INVENTORY SYSTEM AND
INVENTORY ERRORS ★★

Part A
Langer Ltd is registered for GST, balances its accounts at month-end, uses special journals, and uses the perpetual inventory system with the FIFO cost flow assumption. All purchases and sales of inventory are made on credit. End of the reporting period is 30 June. Sales and purchases (all net of GST) of product JINX-87 in May 2014 were:

Date	Transaction	No.	Unit cost
May 1	Inventory on hand	50	$10
May 7	Purchase	20	$11
May 11	Sale @ $35/unit	54	
May 17	Purchase	30	$12
May 21	Purchase return	10	$11
May 24	Sale @ $36/unit	30	
May 29	Sale return (on 24 May sale)	8	

Required
For product JINX-87, calculate May 2014's cost of sales and the cost of inventory on hand at 31 May 2014, using an inventory record.

Part B
The inventory ledger account balance at 30 June 2014 was $7650, and net realisable value for each product line exceeded cost. The cost of inventory on hand at 30 June 2014 determined by physical

count, however, was only $7578. In investigating the reasons for the discrepancy, Langer Ltd discovered the following:

- Goods costing $87 plus GST were sold for $100 plus GST on 26 June 2014 on DDP shipping terms. The goods were in transit at 30 June 2014. The sale was recorded on 26 June 2014 and the goods were not included in the physical count.
- Goods costing $90 plus GST were ordered on 24 June 2014 on EXW shipping terms. The goods were delivered to the transport company on 27 June 2014. The purchase was recorded on 27 June 2014 but, as the goods had not yet arrived, the goods were not included in the physical count.
- Goods costing $140 (excluding GST) held on consignment for Waffle Ltd were included in the physical count.

Required

Prepare any journal entries required on 30 June 2014 to correct error(s) and to adjust the inventory account. (Use the general journal.)

Problem 19.12 PERPETUAL INVENTORY SYSTEM WITH RETURNS ★★★   LO 3, 6

During the year ended 30 June 2014, TooBakko Ltd sold each unit of its goods at $9. Purchases and sales of the goods are shown below. Ignore GST.

2013			
July	1	Inventory on hand	200 units @ $5.00 each
	30	Sales	120 units
Aug.	25	Purchases	300 @ $5.25
	30	Sales	250 units
Sept.	3	Purchases	450 units @ $5.30
	10	Purchases returns	50 damaged units from 3 September purchase
	30	Sales	300 units
Oct.	5	Purchases	300 units @ $5.40
Dec.	8	Purchases	250 units at $5.45
	11	Sales	500 units
2014			
Feb.	21	Purchases	150 units @ $5.50
March	18	Purchases	100 units at $5.60
April	30	Sales	300 units
May	2	Sales returns	30 units from 30 April sales, goods returned to inventory
	4	Purchases	250 units @ $5.70
June	6	Purchases	300 units @ $5.85
	30	Sales	460 units

TooBakko Ltd uses a perpetual inventory system.

Required

A. Using dollars and cents in appropriate inventory records, determine the cost of the inventory at 30 June 2014 under the following inventory cost flow assumptions:
- FIFO
- moving average (round to the nearest cent).
B. Assuming that a physical count at 30 June 2014 determined that only 300 units remained in inventory, prepare the journal entry to record the fact that some units had gone missing.
C. Using the moving average method, prepare the Inventory Control, Cost of Sales and Sales accounts (T-account format), assuming that these accounts are balanced yearly on 30 June. Assume as well that the physical count of inventory was as mentioned in requirement B above.

Problem 19.13 INVENTORY COST FLOW METHODS — PERIODIC AND   LO 2, 3, 6
PERPETUAL — AND RETURNS ★★★

The purchases and sales of Green Gardening Pty Ltd of one brand of lawn fertiliser for the year ended 31 December 2014 are contained in the schedule on the next page.

The selling price up to 30 June was $12 per unit but was raised to $14 for the rest of the year. Ignore GST.

Required

A. Prepare the income statement up to the gross profit stage under the following cost flow assumptions:
  1. periodic inventory
     (a) FIFO (b) weighted average
  2. perpetual inventory
     (a) FIFO (b) moving average.
B. If 10 of the units sold on 9 October were returned and placed back into inventory, how would this affect profits calculated under requirements A2(a) and A2(b) above?
C. If 5 of the units purchased on 11 December were returned to the supplier, how would this affect profits calculated under requirements A2(a) and A2(b) above.

Date		Purchases			Sales			Balance		
	Units	Unit cost	Total	Units	Unit cost	Total	Units	Unit cost	Total
Jan. 1							80	$5.00	$400
Jan. 7				40					
Jan. 30	50	$5.10	$255						
Feb. 2				27					
Feb. 20	60	5.20	312						
Feb. 28				50					
Mar. 16	25	5.20	130						
Mar. 24	30	5.30	159						
Mar. 27				20					
Apr. 7				23					
Apr. 15	40	5.35	214						
Apr. 18				50					
May 4	30	5.30	159						
June 2	20	5.40	108						
June 20				40					
July 27	30	5.40	102						
Aug. 6				50					
Aug. 31	60	5.50	330						
Sept. 11				20					
Sept. 26	40	5.50	220						
Oct. 9				60					
Nov. 4	40	5.60	224						
Nov. 30				30					
Dec. 11	20	5.65	113						
Dec. 27				10					

LO 3, 7

Problem 19.14 COST OF SALES ★★★

Pedal Ltd balances its books at month-end, uses special journals, and uses the perpetual inventory system with the moving average cost flow assumption. All purchases and sales of inventory are made on credit. Reporting date is 31 December. Ignore GST.

Sales and purchases of product AZL-002 in October 2013 were:

Date		Transaction	No.	Unit cost	Total cost
Oct.	1	Inventory on hand	52	$12.00	$624
Oct.	8	Purchase	30	$13.00	$390
Oct.	10	Purchase return	10	$13.00	$130
Oct.	13	Sale @ $15/unit	36		
Oct.	16	Sale return (on Oct. 13 sale)	12		
Oct.	20	Purchase	50	$14.00	$700
Oct.	26	Sale @ $16/unit	42		

Accounts Receivable Control and Accounts Payable Control ledger account balances at 31 October 2013 were $86 600 Dr and $82 470 Cr respectively.

Transactions involving Pedal Ltd's customers and suppliers for November 2013 were:

Inventory sales	$112 930
Inventory purchases	137 440
Cash payments to suppliers	139 820
Cash receipts from customers	117 470
Discount received from suppliers	3 080
Discount allowed to customers	2 760
Nov. 13: Inventory (not yet paid for) returned by customer	8 100
Nov. 19: Inventory (paid for) returned to supplier	4 130
Nov. 22: Inventory (not yet paid for) returned to supplier	6 170
Nov. 26: Offset of accounts receivable and payable recorded	3 940
Nov. 29: Debt written off	5 160

The Inventory Control ledger account balance at 31 December 2013 was $85 590, and net realisable value for each product line exceeded cost. The cost of inventory on hand at 31 December 2013 determined by physical count, however, was only $83 510. In investigating the reasons for the discrepancy, Pedal Ltd discovered the following:

- Goods costing $1150 were ordered on 26 December 2013 on EXW terms. The transport firm took possession of the goods from the supplier on 28 December 2013. The purchase was recorded on 28 December 2013 but, as the goods had not yet arrived, the goods were not included in the physical count.
- $1860 of goods held on consignment for Collie Ltd were included in the physical count.
- Goods costing $980 were sold for $1130 on 29 December 2013 on DDP terms. The goods were in transit at 31 December 2013. The sale was recorded on 28 December 2013 and the goods were not included in the physical count.

Required

A. For product AZL-002, calculate October 2013's cost of sales and the cost of inventory on hand at 31 October 2013. (Round each average unit cost to the nearest cent, but round each total cost amount to the nearest dollar.)

B. Prepare the Accounts Receivable Control and Accounts Payable Control general ledger accounts (T-format) for the period 31 October to 30 November 2013.

C. Prepare any journal entries necessary on 31 December 2013 to correct error(s) and adjust inventory. (Use the general journal.)

Problem 19.15 EFFECTS OF INVENTORY ERRORS ★★★

Below are the income statements for Outdoors Ltd for the year ended 31 December for 2 years.

	2013	2014
Sales revenue	$325 000	$400 000
Cost of sales:		
Beginning inventory	68 000	100 000
Purchases	200 000	220 000
Goods available for sale	268 000	320 000
Ending inventory	100 000	90 000
Cost of sales	168 000	230 000
Gross profit	157 000	170 000
Other expenses	91 000	99 000
Profit	$ 66 000	$ 71 000

The following information has been discovered concerning 2013:

1. On 23 December, Outdoors Ltd recorded goods purchased at a cost of $1000 plus GST. The terms were EXW. The goods were delivered by the seller to the transport company on 27 December. The goods were not included in the ending inventory because they had not arrived.
2. Outdoors Ltd sells goods that it does not own on a consignment basis. Consigned goods on hand at year-end were included in inventory at a cost of $3500 (excluding GST).
3. A purchase of goods worth $2200 plus GST was made in December, but not recorded until January. The goods were received on 28 December and included in the physical inventory.
4. A sale of goods costing $1800 net of GST was made and recorded in December. Since the buyer requested that the goods be held for later delivery, the items were on hand and included in inventory at year-end.
5. Outdoors Ltd sold goods costing $1400 for $2000 plus GST on 26 December. The terms were DDP. The goods arrived at the destination in January. The sale was recorded in 2013, and the goods were excluded from the ending inventory.

Required
A. Determine the correct ending inventory figure for 31 December 2013.
B. Prepare revised income statements for 2013 and 2014.
C. Determine the total profit for the 2-year period, both before and after the revisions. Why are these figures similar or different?

DECISION ANALYSIS

Inventory and computer retailing

During January 2014, Ezy PC, a retailer of personal computers, began operations. The transactions for January were as shown below (ignore GST).

Jan.	5	Purchased eight computers for $1300 each.
	8	Sold three computers for $2500 each.
	11	Purchased three computers for $1400 each.
	13	Sold one computer for $2500.
	16	Sold four computers for $2500 each.
	22	Purchased four computers for $1500 each.
	25	Sold two computers for $2600 each.

Other expenses for the month were $1200.

Required
A. Record the information on a perpetual inventory record using each of the following methods:
   1. FIFO
   2. moving average
   3. LIFO.
B. Prepare an income statement based on each of the three methods of inventory cost flows.
C. Give reasons to the manager of Ezy PC for the variations in cost of sales and profit in the three statements.
D. What factors should be considered in choosing an inventory cost flow method? Make a recommendation to management on the appropriate cost flow method to use in this business.
E. Assume that the manager wants to purchase another computer before the end of the month, but asks you first (a) how that will affect the profit for the month, and (b) whether the purchase should be deferred until early February. The purchase price would not change. What would you recommend?

CRITICAL THINKING

Inventory values in financial statements

During an audit of the inventory records of Winthrop Ltd for the year ended 30 June 2014, the auditor discovered that the ending inventory balance was overvalued by $36 000. On further investigation, it was discovered as well that the ending inventory for the previous year was correctly counted and valued, but that the inventory balance as at 30 June 2012 was undervalued by $100 000. Spurred on by the concern for errors undetected in previous periods, a thorough investigation was carried out as to the inventory values shown in the company's financial statements during its 5-year history. The following additional errors were detected:

1. As at 30 June 2011, inventory was overvalued by $10 000.
2. As at 30 June 2010, inventory was undervalued by $60 000.

Required

A. Determine the effects that these errors have had on the company's profit figures in each year, beginning in the year ended 30 June 2010.
B. Determine the effect of the inventory errors on the balance sheet over the total time period. Show the cumulative impact on the company's retained earnings.

COMMUNICATION AND LEADERSHIP

Inventory errors

The manager of Big and Beautiful Clothing Ltd, importer and wholesaler of fashion clothing for women, has been investigating the inventory levels of the business at the end of the previous year ended 30 June 2012. She discovered, in consultation with the purchasing department, that an error had been made in the physical count on that date, which resulted in the inventory balance being overstated by $800 000. She also discovered that the inventory balance at 30 June 2013 had been correctly determined. She commented to the accountant that the profit figure for the year ending 30 June 2013 should also be correct, and that there is no point worrying about the error of $800 000 any more.

Required

Assume that you are the accountant for Big and Beautiful Clothing Ltd. In discussion with two or three other members of the 'accounting department' of the business (other students), draft a memo to the manager clarifying the situation and assessing the truth of the manager's remarks.

FINANCIAL ANALYSIS

Refer to the consolidated financial statements in the latest financial report of JB Hi-Fi Limited on its website, www.jbhifi.com.au, and answer the following questions:

1. What value is placed on the consolidated group's inventories at the end of the current year?
2. Determine the accounting policies used by JB Hi-Fi Limited for the valuation of inventories. Briefly outline the features of the system used.
3. Were any inventories valued using the lower of cost and net realisable value rule? If so, what value is placed on these inventories?
4. How much is reported as the cost of sales for the group of companies?

Chapter

20

Non-current assets: acquisition and depreciation

Concepts for review

Before studying this chapter, you should understand or, if necessary, revise:

- the concept and purpose of the accrual basis, going concern, and period assumptions (pp. 37–8)
- the nature of an expense (pp. 34, 724)
- how to prepare adjusting entries for depreciation (pp. 132–3).

Learning objectives

After studying this chapter, you should be able to:

1 identify the nature of property, plant and equipment (p. 830)

2 determine the cost of property, plant and equipment (pp. 830–3)

3 apportion the cost of a lump-sum payment for multiple asset acquisitions (pp. 833–4)

4 discuss the nature of depreciation and determine the amount of depreciation expense using several different cost allocation methods (pp. 834–41)

5 account for subsequent costs incurred in relation to property, plant and equipment (pp. 841–4)

6 record property and plant records in the property and plant subsidiary ledger (pp. 844–6)

7 determine the reporting requirements for property, plant and equipment and depreciation in an entity's financial statements (pp. 846–7)

8 analyse and interpret information on property, plant and equipment and discuss the critical nature and importance of management decisions in relation to property, plant and equipment (pp. 847–8).

Plant and equipment for a sustainable economy

Put out the trash bin, flush the toilet or shove something down the garbage disposal, and out of sight is out of mind. Thanks to our modern waste removal systems we barely have to see our waste, let alone smell or handle it.

In affluent consumer cultures, our relationship with waste is characterised by distance, denial and disposability, according to Gay Hawkins, author of *The Ethics of Waste* and professor in social theory at the University of New South Wales.

Tough economic times may curb excessive consumption, but a fundamental change in our relationship to waste is difficult when disposability is encouraged — when it's cheaper to buy a new product than get one fixed, when your computer or mobile phone is superseded every year, and when products are designed with built in obsolescence.

Distancing ourselves from the waste we create not only means that we shirk responsibility for the harm it can do to human health and the environment. It also means we can fail to recognise the regenerative power of waste.

No so in Lünen. This German town is the first in the world to be powered by poo. Cow and horse manure as well as other organic material from local farms will provide electricity for its 90 000 residents when it launches a biogas network this year.

This may seem amazing, but it's the way nature has been working for millions of years. In natural systems 'waste' is never removed because it's critical to sustaining life. Everything that lives dies; what dies decomposes into its constituent parts, which are then used to create something new. This is true of organic matter, but most industrial objects have been designed by a production system that takes, makes and wastes. Some businesses however, are embracing 'biomimicry', an innovation that seeks sustainable solutions by mimicking nature's strategies …

Alan Greenfield is the director and founder of Taylor Fry Consulting Actuaries, which has offices in Sydney and

Melbourne. Since founding the company in 1999 Greenfield has been committed to growing a sustainable business.

'Whatever business you are in, waste reduction is the first and most important step in becoming more sustainable,' says Greenfield. A recent fit-out of Fry's offices saw all but two of the old doors get reused. All of the glass in the new fit-out came from the previous one and rather than throw away their 15 workstations, they kept them and matched new stations with existing ones.

Computers, printers, phones, photocopiers and lights are basic electronic equipment for office-based businesses. With regular upgrades they also create a mountain of electronic waste. When thrown away, e-waste ends up in landfills where it leaches toxic heavy metals, such as lead, mercury, cadmium and beryllium into groundwater, contaminating soils and bringing significant risks to human health and the environment. 'We get as much use out of our computers as we can,' says Greenfield. 'When a computer dies, we don't just chuck it out but take it to a recycling centre. And when we no longer need a computer, we give it away.'

Extended producer responsibility (EPR) for electronic products has become law in the European Union, Japan, China, South Korea, the US, Canada and parts of South America. This means that manufacturers must take responsibility for the collection and recycling of their products after the consumer has used them.

Source: Extract from Thea O'Connor, 'What a load of rubbish', *InTheBlack*.

Chapter preview

The terms *property, plant and equipment* and *plant and machinery* and *plant assets* are used in accounting to describe the non-current assets with physical substance acquired by an entity for use in the production or supply of goods and services rather than for resale to customers. Examples include land, buildings, equipment, machinery, storage facilities and motor vehicles. The term *fixed assets* is sometimes used to describe this category of assets. In the scene setter, such assets are electricity generators and electronic equipment.

Learning objective 1

Identify the nature of property, plant and equipment

20.1 What is property, plant and equipment?

Management's intention to use 'property, plant and equipment' assets for the future production of goods or services over several accounting periods is the main factor that distinguishes them from other assets. Since they have value in use, they are said to represent a store of economic benefits available for the future operations of the entity. Buildings contain future housing benefits, vehicles contain future transport benefits, and computers contain future data processing benefits. All these assets are expected to be used in the future, directly or indirectly, in the production of goods or services for sale to customers. Assets that have physical characteristics similar to those of property, plant and equipment but are not intended for future use to produce goods or services should not be included in the category. For example, construction equipment held by an equipment dealer is inventory, but the same type of equipment held by a construction company represents property, plant and equipment. Similarly, land held for future expansion or as an investment should be excluded from property, plant and equipment and be regarded as a long-term investment. Furthermore, if an entity holds non-current assets which are held principally so that income will be earned through their sale, then these assets are not to be classified as property, plant and equipment; instead, they must be classified as non-current assets 'held for sale', according to IFRS 5/AASB 5 *Non-current Assets Held for Sale and Discontinued Operations*.

Under IAS 16/AASB 116 *Property, Plant and Equipment*, any asset with physical substance that is expected to be used over more than 1 year *must* be recognised at its cost when it is probable that the future economic benefits will flow to the entity, and the cost of the asset can be measured reliably. Because the future economic benefits contained in property, plant and equipment will be received over two or more accounting periods, the depreciable amount of these assets must be allocated in a systematic manner over their useful lives to measure depreciation, as would be the case with the new electricity generators using waste products which are being built in Germany (see the scene setter). As the assets are used to produce goods or services, their costs are transferred to depreciation expense to be deducted from the income produced by the sale of the goods or services.

Learning objective 2

Determine the cost of property, plant and equipment

20.2 Determining the cost of property, plant and equipment

Whenever an entity acquires an asset from an outside party, the accounting treatment for the acquisition is governed by IAS 16/AASB 116. According to the standard, in order to account for the acquisition of property, plant and equipment, the cost method must be used, whereby the assets acquired are initially recorded on recognition date at their **cost**, which is defined as the amount of cash or cash equivalents paid or the fair value of the other consideration given to acquire an asset at the time of its acquisition or construction.

There is an important principle here. In order to determine the acquisition cost of a plant asset, the entity must measure the fair value of the items it has *given up* to acquire the asset, and *not* the fair value of the asset being acquired. According to IFRS 13/AASB 13 *Fair Value Measurement* issued in May 2011, **fair value** means the price that would be received to sell an asset or paid to transfer a liability in an orderly transaction between market participants at the measurement date. If a not-for-profit entity acquires an asset at no cost, it shall be recorded in the accounts at fair value, as a measure of cost.

According to IAS 16/AASB 116, the cost of an item of property, plant and equipment comprises:

(a) its purchase price, including import duties and non-refundable purchase taxes, after deducting trade discounts and rebates; hence, GST is excluded because it is a refundable purchase tax

(b) any costs directly attributable to bringing the asset to the location and condition *necessary* for it to be used in the way management intended

(c) the initial estimate of the costs of dismantling and removing the item and restoring the site on which it is located, if the entity is obliged to do so.

Examples of directly attributable costs, item (b) above, are:

- costs of site preparation
- initial delivery and handling costs
- installation and assembly costs
- costs of testing whether the asset is functioning properly, after deducting the net proceeds of selling any items produced during the testing phase
- the costs of employee benefits, such as leave entitlements and superannuation, arising directly from constructing or acquiring the property, plant and equipment
- professional fees.

The inclusion of costs in the carrying amount of an item of property, plant and equipment ceases when the asset is in the location and condition ready for its intended use. Only those costs that are necessarily incurred should be included in the cost of the asset.

To illustrate, the acquisition cost of a machine includes its invoice price (minus trade discounts and any GST recoverable) plus directly attributable costs such as costs of site preparation, freight, insurance in transit, installation expenditures such as power connection, and any initial adjustments needed to make the machine function properly, including any spare parts that would be of no use if the asset were sold. Directly attributable costs also include any staff training costs to enable the asset to be used.

Assume, for example, the purchase of a machine at a list price of $22 000 including GST with trade discount of 10% and terms of 3/20, n/60. In addition, freight charges net of GST amount to $820, and installation expenditures net of GST amount to $675. The cost to be debited to the Machinery account is calculated as follows:

List price of the machine	$22 000
Less: Trade discount (10% × $22 000)	2 200
	19 800
Less: GST (1/11)	1 800
Purchase price	18 000
Freight inwards (net of GST)	820
Installation costs (net of GST)	675
Cost of machine	$19 495

The cost of an asset should not exceed the amount for which it could be acquired in a cash transaction plus the other expenditures necessary to get the asset ready for use. Any cash discounts received on terms should be credited to discount received (income) rather than deducted from the cost of the machine. The cost of a used or *second-hand* asset should include its purchase price net of GST plus initial expenditures made for repairs, new parts, paint and any other costs necessary to get the asset ready for use.

Care should be taken that only *reasonable* and *necessary* expenditures are included. Expenditures that could be avoided or that do not increase the future economic benefits of the asset should be excluded from its purchase price. For example, expenditures required to repair damage to an asset caused by carelessness during installation should be charged to an expense account rather than to the asset account.

When an item of property, plant and equipment is acquired, its cost must represent the cash price equivalent on the day it is recognised. Therefore, if the entity defers payment for the asset beyond normal credit terms, the difference between the cash price equivalent and the total payment is recognised as interest expense over the period. This interest expense is determined by using present value techniques to discount the deferred payment to its present value equivalent.

Whenever *land* is purchased, the cost of land includes the price paid to the seller (net of GST) plus the estate agent's commission and other necessary expenditures (net of GST) such as title-search and survey fees. If the buyer pays accrued rates and taxes on the property, they should also be included in the cost of the land. If the land contains a building that is to be demolished in order to construct a new building, the total purchase price plus the cost of removing the old building (less amounts received from the sale of salvaged materials) is included in the cost of the land. The cost of removing the old building is considered part of the land cost because it was incurred to get the land into condition for its intended use — the construction of a new building.

Although land is generally not depreciable because it has an unlimited life, some expenditures related to its acquisition and use, such as driveways, fences, parking lots and landscaping, do have limited lives and are properly depreciated. Consequently, these items are normally charged to a separate *land improvements* account and depreciated over their estimated useful lives. Some landscaping costs may create an asset with an indeterminate life. If so, these costs may be treated more appropriately as part of the cost of the land, rather than as land improvements.

When an entity *constructs an asset for its own use*, the acquisition cost includes all expenditures (net of GST) incurred directly for construction, such as labour, materials and insurance paid during construction. The cost of buildings also includes architectural fees, engineering fees, building permits and excavation for the foundations. In addition, a reasonable amount of manufacturing overhead for such things as power, management supervision during construction, and depreciation on machinery used for construction should be included.

Sometimes, when an entity is constructing an asset for its own use, the entity is required to borrow large sums of money in order to finance the construction costs. In this situation, a question arises as to whether the **borrowing costs** incurred, namely interest and other costs incurred in connection with the borrowing of funds, should be treated as part of the acquisition cost. The regulators have issued IAS 23/AASB 123 *Borrowing Costs* to deal with this problem. The standard states that borrowing costs must be recognised as an expense (usually a finance expense) in the year in which they are incurred.

However, if borrowing costs are directly attributable to the acquisition, construction or production of a qualifying asset, the standard requires these borrowing costs to be included as part of the cost of the asset. A **qualifying asset** is defined as an asset that necessarily takes a substantial period of time, i.e. usually longer than 1 year, to get ready for its intended use or sale. Thus, a qualifying asset may be part of the entity's property, plant and equipment, or part of its inventories, as long as such items take a considerable period of time to produce. Borrowing costs included as part of the cost of acquiring the qualifying asset are to be measured at the costs that would have been avoided if the expenditure on the qualifying asset had not been made, according to IAS 23/AASB 123. The type of electricity generators being constructed in the scene setter would satisfy the definition of a qualifying asset.

Certain items of property, plant and equipment may be acquired for safety or environmental reasons. Although the acquisition of these items does not directly increase the future economic benefits of existing property, plant and equipment, it may be necessary for an entity to acquire them in order to obtain the future economic benefits from its existing assets. Hence, under IAS 16/AASB 116, such items of property, plant and equipment qualify for recognition as assets because they enable an entity to derive economic benefits from related assets in excess of what could be derived had they not been acquired. These assets are measured at cost. As an example, a chemical manufacturer may install new chemical handling processes to comply with environmental requirements for the production and storage of dangerous chemicals. The cost of such installations is recorded as an asset because, without them, the entity is unable to manufacture and sell chemicals.

Another popular mechanism for an entity to acquire the benefits of property, plant and equipment is by leasing them. Many different types of assets are subject to lease agreements; for example, motor vehicles, land, buildings, machinery and storage space are assets commonly leased instead of purchased. The required accounting treatment for leased assets is beyond the scope of this book and is covered in more advanced texts.

Shopping centres rebound

The downturn in Australia's shopping centre sector may be nearing an end with a small rise in new projects, more refurbishments at existing centres and stronger demand from international retailers, according to Jones Lang LaSalle.

The real estate firm said the number of completed retail construction projects had slowed to a trickle this year but a recent rise in new construction projects indicated the market might be recovering.

Just seven retail projects were completed nationally in the second quarter, adding 52 700 sqm, while construction work started on 10 projects for 97 400 sqm. This lifted total retail space under construction in Australia to 590 300 sqm.

Jones Lang La Salle also said developers were looking at restarting refurbishment plans put on hold in the global financial crisis, with several big projects receiving developmental approval.

'Investors and owners are still very much focused on adding value to existing centres, rather than developing new centres. They are looking at core assets in premium locations and consequently the development pipeline is more focused on the CBD and regional centre markets than it has been over recent years,' Leigh Warner, Jones Lang LaSalle's national retail analyst, said.

'There is no doubt the development environment remains very challenging, particularly for smaller developers, but there is clear evidence that the tide is turning.'

The data also showed retail vacancies had stabilised in the first half and that an encouraging level of support came from overseas retailers.

'While some are feeling the pinch and winding back plans, there are still some retailers that are expanding rapidly' Tony Doherty, Jones Lang LaSalle's head of retail management, said. 'One very bright spot is demand from international retailers, many of whom are looking to increase their presence in Australia because of lower growth prospects in their home countries.'

Source: Extract from Marissa Lague, 'Shopping centres rebound', *The West Australian.*

20.3 Apportioning the cost of a lump-sum acquisition

Learning objective 3

Apportion the cost of a lump-sum payment for multiple asset acquisitions

In a **lump-sum acquisition**, several items of property, plant and equipment may be acquired for a lump-sum payment without an identification of the cost of each asset. In these cases, the total cost must be allocated in some systematic way to the assets purchased because they may have different useful lives, or they may not be depreciable at all. According to IFRS 3/AASB 3 *Business Combinations*, when the lump sum acquisition does not constitute a **business combination** (the bringing together of separate entities or businesses into one reporting entity), the cost of the acquisition must be allocated on the basis of the fair values on acquisition date of the assets acquired. For example, assume that a building, land and office equipment were acquired on 2 January for a lump-sum payment of $800 000 (plus GST). Fair values of the assets were determined by an independent appraisal as follows:

	Fair value
Building	$595 000
Land	170 000
Office equipment	85 000
	$850 000

The total cost of $800 000 (net of GST) is allocated to each asset on the basis of these fair values by use of the following formula:

$$\frac{\text{Fair value of specific asset}}{\text{Total fair value}} \times \text{Total cost} = \text{Cost allocated to the specific asset}$$

The allocation is as follows:

$$\text{Building} \quad = \frac{595\,000}{850\,000} \times \$800\,000 = \$560\,000$$

$$\text{Land} \quad = \frac{170\,000}{850\,000} \times \$800\,000 = \ 160\,000$$

$$\text{Equipment} = \frac{85\,000}{850\,000} \times \$800\,000 = \ 80\,000$$

$$\$800\,000$$

The acquisition is recorded with the following entry:

Jan.	2	Buildings	560 000	
		Land	160 000	
		Office Equipment	80 000	
		GST Outlays	80 000	
		Cash at Bank		880 000
		(Acquisition of property and equipment)		

Learning objective 4

Discuss the nature of depreciation and determine the amount of depreciation expense using several different cost allocation methods

20.4 Depreciation

The nature of depreciation

As described earlier, property, plant and equipment represent a store of future economic benefits that an entity intends to receive over the useful life of the assets in the production of goods and services. All such assets except land, whether purchased or leased, have limited useful lives, i.e. their economic benefits are consumed over time to a point where they are either used up or lost. Non-current assets with limited useful lives are often referred to as **depreciable assets**. IAS 16/AASB 116 discusses four factors that contribute to a depreciable asset having a limited useful life:

* *expected use* of the asset, as assessed by reference to the asset's expected output
* *expected wear and tear*, through physical use; wear and tear is affected by such things as frequency of use, climatic conditions under which the asset is used, and frequency of expected maintenance — for some assets such as construction equipment, these physical factors are the most important ones affecting useful life
* *technical and commercial obsolescence*, which arise from technological changes or improvements in production or the process of becoming redundant through a fall in the market demand for the goods or services that the asset is used to produce; obsolescence is an important factor affecting the decline in future economic benefits of assets such as computers — rapid improvements made in the design and performance of computers generally make them obsolete long before they wear out physically
* *legal or similar limits* on the use of an asset, such as the expiry dates of leases.

Accounting for **depreciation** represents the process whereby the decline in future economic benefits of an asset through use, wear and tear, and obsolescence is progressively brought to account as a periodic charge against income. There are two differing views as to how depreciation should be measured by accountants:

* One view suggests that depreciation should be calculated as the difference between an asset's market value (or fair value) at the beginning and end of a period. In other words, depreciation is measured as a value adjustment for each asset. If the market or fair value of asset A at the beginning of the period is $5000 and at the end of the period is $3000, then depreciation is equal to $5000 − $3000 = $2000, which represents the decline in the asset's market or fair value during the period — the valuation approach.
* The second view suggests that depreciation should be measured by allocating the asset's cost or depreciable amount over its estimated useful life, i.e. the period over which the future economic benefits embodied in the asset are expected to be consumed by the entity — the allocation approach.

This second view is favoured in IAS 16/AASB 116. In other words, depreciation in practice is measured and recorded using a process of allocation rather than of valuation. As the asset is used, its depreciable amount is said to expire gradually or be used up. The allocation method used must reflect the pattern in which the asset's future economic benefits are expected to be consumed or lost by the entity.

The meaning of depreciation as used by accountants is often misunderstood because the term is used generally by non-accountants to refer to a fall in the market value of property, plant and equipment. Although such assets are subject to changes in market values, accountants traditionally have not been concerned with recognising these changes in the accounts because property, plant and equipment are acquired for use, not for sale. Depreciation is therefore regarded as an allocation process, not a valuation process.

Determining the amount of depreciation

The depreciation of an asset begins when it is available for use, i.e. when it is in the location and condition necessary for it to be capable of operating in the manner intended by management. Depreciation ceases when an asset is classified as 'held for sale' or is derecognised, i.e. written off. Depreciation does not stop merely because an asset is idle or underused.

Factors needed to determine the amount of periodic depreciation for a depreciable asset are cost, useful life and residual value. Determination of the initial cost of property, plant and equipment was discussed earlier. A discussion of useful life and residual value follows.

Useful life

In order to allocate the **depreciable amount** (cost less residual value) of a depreciable asset to the periods benefiting from its use, an estimate must be made of its **useful life**. Useful life is defined in IAS 16/AASB 116 as:

(a) the period over which an asset is expected to be available for use by an entity; or
(b) the number of production or similar units expected to be obtained from the asset by an entity.

The useful life of an asset is most commonly assessed and expressed on a time basis. In assessing useful life, the accountant needs to consider not only the use of the asset and its physical wear and tear but also its technical and commercial life and its legal life. Physical wear and tear is assessed assuming adequate maintenance and a projected rate of use of the asset. Technical life is assessed in relation to the degree of technical obsolescence estimated to be experienced by the asset. Commercial life depends on the continued saleability of the asset's products or services.

Of course, technical and commercial obsolescence may cause the asset's useful life to be shorter than its physical life. For example, the physical life of a motor vehicle may be 15 to 20 years. Because it operates less efficiently as it becomes older, however, the owner may decide that its useful life is only 5 years for the entity, and that it should be traded in at the end of 5 years. The cost of the vehicle, less residual value, therefore, should be charged to depreciation expense over the 5-year period.

Residual value

The **residual value** of an asset is defined in IAS 16/AASB 116 as the estimated amount that an entity could currently obtain from disposal of the asset after deducting the estimated costs of disposal, if the asset were already of the age and in the condition expected at the end of its useful life. This estimate is based on the net amount (at acquisition date) to be recovered currently for similar assets that have already reached the end of their useful lives and have operated under conditions similar to those in which the asset will be used. Thus, residual value is a current value, not an estimated future value. Assets such as cars, trucks and buildings may have significant residual values; other assets such as specifically designed machinery and equipment may have value only as scrap metal at the end of their useful lives to the entity. The cost (or other value) of an asset less its residual value is the depreciable amount that should be charged to depreciation expense over the asset's useful life. If the residual value is expected to be an insignificant amount in relation to the asset's cost, it is often ignored in calculating depreciation. Residual value is sometimes referred to as *salvage value* or *trade-in value*.

IAS 16/AASB 116 requires an entity to review at least *annually*, and adjust if necessary, the useful lives and residual values of its depreciable assets. This enables the entity to calculate depreciation expense at the end of each current period based on up-to-date information. The standard points out that, in practice, the residual value of a depreciable asset is often insignificant and therefore immaterial in calculating the depreciable amount. However, it may be the case that an asset's residual value increases over time to an amount equal to or greater than the asset's **carrying amount** (cost less accumulated depreciation). If this happens, then the depreciation charge for the asset is zero unless or until the residual value subsequently falls to an amount below the asset's carrying amount.

Depreciation methods

Several methods can be used to allocate the cost of an asset over its useful life. The four most common are the straight-line, diminishing-balance, sum-of-years-digits, and units-of-production methods. All methods are acceptable under IAS 16/AASB 116 because they progressively write off the asset to expense by means of systematic depreciation charges against the periods that benefit from the asset's use. It is not necessary for an entity to use a single depreciation method for all of its depreciable assets. The methods chosen must reflect the pattern in which the asset's future economic benefits are consumed or lost by the entity, taking into account the underlying physical, technical, commercial and legal facts. In addition, the methods adopted by management for use in the accounts and financial reports may differ from those used in the preparation of income tax returns.

The standard requires the depreciation method applied to be reviewed at least at the end of each annual reporting period. If the expected pattern of consumption of the future economic benefits in the asset has changed, then the method should be changed to reflect the changed pattern.

Straight-line method

The **straight-line depreciation** method allocates an equal amount of depreciation to each full accounting period in the asset's useful life. The amount of depreciation for each period is determined by dividing the cost of the asset (or its revalued amount) minus its residual value, i.e. its depreciable amount, by the number of periods in the asset's useful life. For example, on 1 July, assume a machine has a cost of $33 000 (net of GST), a residual value of $3000, and a useful life of 4 years. Depreciation for each year is calculated as follows:

$$\frac{\text{Depreciable amount}}{\text{Useful life}} = \frac{\$33\,000 - \$3000}{4 \text{ years}} = \$7500 \text{ annual depreciation}$$

The entry to record the depreciation expense at the end of each year is:

June	30	Depreciation Expense – Machinery	7 500	
		Accumulated Depreciation – Machinery		7 500
		(Depreciation expense for the year)		

Annual depreciation expense is $7500. If the asset is acquired during the financial year, the depreciation amount for the first or last partial years of its use should be a proportion of the annual amount. For example, if the machine were purchased on 1 October, depreciation for the first year ended 30 June would be $9/12 \times \$7500$, or $5625. Although depreciation can be calculated to the exact day when an asset is acquired during a month, calculation to the nearest month is generally sufficient because depreciation is only an estimated amount.

Diminishing-balance method

The **diminishing-balance depreciation** method results in a decreasing depreciation charge over the useful life of the asset. This method is appropriate when the majority of the asset's benefits are consumed in the earlier years of its useful life. Depreciation expense for each period is calculated by applying a predetermined depreciation rate to the declining carrying amount of the asset. The annual depreciation rate is determined by the following formula:

$$\text{Depreciation rate} = 1 - \sqrt[n]{\frac{r}{c}}$$

n = useful life (in years)
r = residual value (in dollars)
c = original cost or gross revalued amount (in dollars)

To illustrate, assume the same asset as used in the previous example. On 1 July, the asset has a cost of $33 000 (net of GST), a residual value of $3000 and a useful life of 4 years. Using these figures in the formula:

$$\text{Depreciation rate} = 1 - \sqrt[4]{\frac{3\,000}{33\,000}}$$

$$= 45\% \text{ (approximately)}$$

The rate is then applied to the carrying amount of the asset at the beginning of the period to calculate depreciation expense for each period, as indicated in the following tabulation:

Year	Carrying amount at beginning of year		Rate	Annual depreciation expense	Carrying amount at end of year
1	$33 000	×	45%	$14 850	$18 150
2	18 150	×	45%	8 168	9 982
3	9 982	×	45%	4 492	5 490
4	5 490			2 490	3 000

There are three important things to note about this tabulation. First, the 45% depreciation rate is applied to the *carrying amount* of the asset. Estimated residual value is *not* deducted under the diminishing-balance method, because the residual value was used in calculating the 45% depreciation rate. Second, the amount of depreciation declines each period, because the carrying amount diminishes each period. Third, depreciation for the last period is *not* determined by multiplying $5490 by 45% (because this would result in a carrying amount ($3019.50) greater than the asset's residual value). Depreciation expense of $2490 is calculated for the last period by simply subtracting the residual value of $3000 from the carrying amount at the beginning of the period, $5490.

The entry to record depreciation in the first year is:

June	30	Depreciation Expense – Machinery	14 850	
		Accumulated Depreciation – Machinery		14 850
		(Depreciation expense for the year)		

It was assumed in the above illustration that the asset was acquired at the beginning of the financial year, which seldom occurs. When an asset is acquired during the year, the amount of depreciation for the first year should be a proportion of the annual amount. For example, if the asset was purchased on 1 October, the first year's depreciation would be 9/12 × $14 850, or $11 138. The method of calculating depreciation for subsequent years is unaffected, although the amounts will differ:

Year	Carrying amount at beginning of year		Rate	Annual depreciation expense	Carrying amount at end of year
1	$33 000	×	45% × 9/12	$11 138	$21 862
2	21 862	×	45%	9 838	12 024
3	12 024	×	45%	5 411	6 613
4	6 613	×	45%	2 976	3 637
5	3 637			637	(30 Sept.) 3 000

Since calculation of depreciation expense is at best an estimate, it has been a common practice when applying the diminishing-balance method not to use the above formula but to use a rate equal to some multiple of the straight-line depreciation rate allowable for income tax purposes. For example, given a motor vehicle with a cost of $40 000 and residual value of $5000 and the allowable straight-line rate for tax purposes of 15%, then a diminishing-balance depreciation schedule for this asset, using a rate of $22\frac{1}{2}\%$ ($1\frac{1}{2}$ times the straight-line rate), would appear as shown below:

Year	Carrying amount at beginning of year		Rate	Annual depreciation expense	Carrying amount at end of year
1	$40 000	×	$22\frac{1}{2}\%$	$9 000	$31 000
2	31 000	×	$22\frac{1}{2}\%$	6 975	24 025
3	24 025	×	$22\frac{1}{2}\%$	5 405	18 620
4	18 620	×	$22\frac{1}{2}\%$	4 190	14 430
5	14 430	×	$22\frac{1}{2}\%$	3 247	11 183
6	11 183	×	$22\frac{1}{2}\%$	2 516	8 667
7	8 667			3 667	5 000

Whatever technique is used to calculate diminishing-balance depreciation charges, the accountant must keep in mind that the method is justified only where the asset can be expected to yield more benefits in the earlier years than in the later years. In this way, the earlier years bear a larger allocation of the cost of the asset to reflect the economic benefits consumed in those years.

Sum-of-years-digits method

The **sum-of-years-digits depreciation** method is a different way of applying the diminishing-balance method and results in a decreasing depreciation charge over the useful life of the asset. Depreciation for each period is determined by multiplying the recorded cost less residual value, i.e. its depreciable amount, by successively smaller fractions. The denominator of the fractions, which is constant, is determined by adding the years in the asset's useful life. The numerators of the fractions, which change each year, are the years remaining in the asset's life at the beginning of the period.

To illustrate, assume that the sum-of-years-digits method is used to allocate depreciation on a machine with a cost of $33 000 (net of GST), a residual value of $3000, and a useful life of 4 years. The sum of the years digits (the denominator) is calculated as:

$$1 + 2 + 3 + 4 = 10$$

The depreciation charge for each year is then calculated as shown in the following tabulation:

Year	Depreciable amount		Fraction		Depreciation for the year	Total accumulated depreciation	Carrying amount
1	$30 000	×	4/10	=	$12 000	$12 000	$21 000
2	30 000	×	3/10	=	9 000	21 000	12 000
3	30 000	×	2/10	=	6 000	27 000	6 000
4	30 000	×	1/10	=	3 000	30 000	3 000

Note that the method results in a carrying amount equal to the asset's residual value at the end of its useful life. The journal entry for depreciation expense in the first year is:

June	30	Depreciation Expense – Machinery	12 000	
		Accumulated Depreciation – Machinery		12 000
		(Depreciation expense for the year)		

When the asset has a long useful life, the sum of the years digits can be calculated by using the formula:

$$S = n\left(\frac{n+1}{2}\right)$$

where $S =$ the sum of the years digits

$n =$ the number of years in the asset's useful life

The sum of the years digits for an asset with a 10-year useful life is therefore:

$$10\left(\frac{10+1}{2}\right) = 55$$

When an asset is acquired during the financial year, it is necessary to allocate each full year's amount to the years benefiting from the asset's use. Consequently, if the asset was acquired on 1 October, the depreciation recorded in the first year would be 9/12 × $12 000, or $9000. Depreciation for the second year would be:

3/12 × $12 000 (from year 1 above)	$3 000
9/12 × $9000 (from year 2 above)	6 750
Depreciation for second year	$9 750

Depreciation for each of the remaining years would be calculated in a similar manner.

Units-of-production method

The **units-of-production depreciation** method relates depreciation to use rather than to time. This method is particularly appropriate for assets where consumption of economic benefits varies significantly from one period to another. Accounting periods with greater production from the asset are charged with a greater amount of depreciation expense. A disadvantage of the method is that it requires additional record keeping to determine the units produced during each period by each asset.

Under the units-of-production method, the asset's depreciable amount is divided by the estimated number of production units expected from the asset during its estimated useful life. Production units might be expressed in several ways — kilometres, operating hours, units of product. The result of the division is a depreciation rate per production unit. The amount of depreciation for a period is then determined by multiplying the depreciation rate per production unit by the number of production units used or produced during the period.

To illustrate, assume that a machine with a cost of $33 000 (net of GST) and a residual value of $3000 is estimated to have a useful life of 15 000 operating hours. The depreciation rate per operating hour is:

$$\frac{\text{Depreciable amount}}{\text{Operating hours}} = \text{Depreciation per operating hour}$$

$$\frac{\$33\,000 - \$3000}{15\,000 \text{ hours}} = \$2 \text{ per operating hour}$$

If the machine is operated for 2500 hours during an accounting period, that period is charged with depreciation of $5000 (2500 hours × $2), and the following depreciation entry is prepared:

June	30	Depreciation Expense – Machinery	5 000	
		Accumulated Depreciation – Machinery		5 000
		(Depreciation expense for the year)		

Comparison of depreciation methods

The different methods allocate different amounts to depreciation expense over the life of an asset even though the cost of acquisition, residual value and useful life are the same. In practice, the straight-line depreciation method is the one most widely used. This method produces uniform charges to depreciation over the life of the asset. Depreciation under the straight-line method is considered a function of time. The benefits received from the use of the asset are assumed to be received evenly throughout the asset's life.

The units-of-production method produces depreciation charges that may vary significantly from one accounting period to another as the use of the asset varies. Thus, depreciation is considered a function of asset use.

Both the sum-of-years-digits and the diminishing-balance methods charge greater amounts of depreciation to the first year of an asset's life and gradually decrease charges thereafter. For that reason, these methods are often called **accelerated depreciation methods**. The methods are used when the benefits received from the asset are expected to be consumed in the early years of the asset's life. As the asset ages, it becomes less efficient and requires increasing expenditures for repairs and maintenance. The combination of decreasing depreciation expense and increasing repair and maintenance expense tends to equalise the total periodic expense of the asset (as illustrated in figure 20.1), thereby achieving a more even allocation of expense against revenue, and a smoothing of the profit figure.

Figure 20.1 Depreciation and maintenance expense

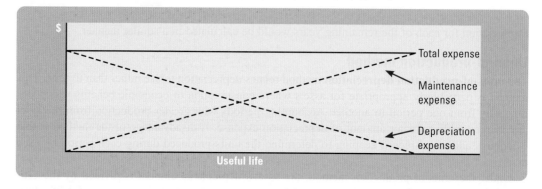

A comparison of the periodic depreciation charges under the straight-line and accelerated methods for the machine used in previous illustrations is presented below, based as before on a machine cost of $33 000, a residual value of $3000, and a useful life of 4 years. Management must choose the appropriate method based on an analysis of the consumption of expected economic benefits from the asset over time.

Year	Straight-line	Diminishing-balance	Sum-of-years-digits
1	$ 7 500	$14 850	$12 000
2	7 500	8 168	9 000
3	7 500	4 492	6 000
4	7 500	2 490	3 000
	$30 000	$30 000	$30 000

Revision of depreciation rates and methods

Two of the factors used to determine periodic depreciation — residual value and useful life — are based on estimates that are rarely precise. Small errors in estimates occur frequently and are generally ignored because their effects are not material. Nevertheless, residual values and useful lives should be assessed at least at the end of each annual reporting period, under IAS 16/AASB 116. Any large errors should be corrected when discovered. The usual procedure is to spread the remaining depreciable amount of the asset over its remaining useful life. Annual depreciation is increased or decreased enough in the current and future periods to offset the effect of the error in previous periods. For example, assume the following case:

Asset cost (net of GST)	$38 000
Useful life	6 years
Residual value	$ 8 000
Accumulated depreciation at the end of 4 years	$20 000

Early in the fifth year, it is decided that the asset's useful life will be extended for 4 more years and its residual value is revised accordingly to $4000. The amount of depreciation to be recognised in the fifth year and each of the remaining years is $2500, as calculated below:

Carrying amount at the end of the 4th year	
($38 000 – $20 000)	$18 000
Less: Residual value	4 000
Remaining depreciable amount	$14 000
Useful life remaining	4 years
Revised annual depreciation ($14 000 ÷ 4 years)	$ 3 500

Accumulated depreciation does not represent cash

Accumulated depreciation does not represent a cash reserve built up to replace assets when they wear out. The accumulated depreciation account is a contra-asset account with a credit balance, representing the portion of an asset's recorded cost that has been transferred progressively to depreciation expense since the asset was acquired. The Cash at Bank account is not directly affected by the periodic entries made to transfer the asset's cost to depreciation expense.

Depreciation expense, unlike most other expenses, is, in itself, only an internal transaction that does not involve a cash outflow. As a result, many entities have a net cash inflow from operations (cash receipts from revenues less cash payments for expenses) in excess of reported profits. To illustrate, assume that Beta Ltd sells services only in exchange for cash, and pays cash for all expenses with the exception of depreciation in the same period in which the expense is incurred. During 2014, Beta Ltd made cash sales of $230 000, paid cash expenses of $170 000, and recognised depreciation expense of $10 000 on equipment purchased at an earlier date. A comparison of cash flow from operations with profit reported for 2014 is:

	2014 Cash flow		2014 Profit	
Cash receipts from sales		$230 000		$230 000
Cash expenses	$170 000		$170 000	
Depreciation expense	—	170 000	10 000	180 000
Net cash flow		$ 60 000		
Profit				$ 50 000

Beta Ltd had a $10 000 greater net cash flow from operations than the amount of profit reported. This results because the depreciation expense deducted in arriving at profit was a non-cash item.

20.5 Subsequent costs

Learning objective 5

Account for subsequent costs incurred in relation to property, plant and equipment

Most entities incur additional costs after the original acquisition of property, plant and equipment. For example, a motor vehicle will require regular maintenance, including replacement of tyres; an aircraft may require all its seating and other internal fittings to be replaced four or five times over its useful life; escalators may be installed in a department store for the convenience of customers; a furnace may require relining after a specified number of hours of use. Should these subsequent costs be written off to expenses as incurred, treated as separate assets with their own useful lives, or added to the cost of the original asset, which would then be depreciated over a revised useful life?

Accounting for subsequent costs requires considerable judgement, using the requirements of IAS 16/AASB 116 as a base. According to the standard, the initial cost *and subsequent costs* of an item of property, plant and equipment should be recognised as an asset only under the following recognition principle, i.e. if:
(a) it is probable that the future economic benefits associated with the item will flow to the entity
(b) a faithful representation of the item's cost(s) can be measured.

The authors of this book recommend that, when subsequent costs meet this recognition principle, those costs should be added to the carrying amount of the asset (not to the original cost), or treated as a separate asset and thus subject to depreciation as a separate asset. The standard requires that if the subsequent cost of replacing part of an item of property, plant and equipment is added to the carrying amount of that asset, then the carrying amount of the part that is replaced must be 'derecognised', i.e. written off to expense. If the cost of the replacement part is regarded as a separate asset for depreciation purposes, then the carrying amount of the old part replaced must also be derecognised.

An example of a subsequent cost that is added to the carrying amount of the asset is the cost (net of GST) of a major overhaul to the asset that will extend its useful life or improve the quality of its outputs. However, a distinction should be made between a major overhaul and the replacement of an asset's major components.

If certain parts of an asset require regular replacement over the useful life of the asset, it may be best to treat these parts as separate assets with separate useful lives, and to depreciate them accordingly. For example, the costs of seating and additional fittings on an aircraft would be recorded in a separate account from the aircraft, and depreciated over their own useful life. Using the same principle, the tyres on a motor vehicle may be treated as an asset separate from the vehicle, if they are considered to be a separate part, and depreciated over their own useful lives of 2–3 years. This may apply particularly to the expensive tyres on heavy-duty trucks used in open-cut mining activities in remote areas of Australia.

However, the tyres on most vehicles are usually not regarded as separate parts but are included in the original cost of the vehicles, and are a necessary cost of providing each vehicle's original set of future economic benefits; thus, any replacement of such tyres is treated as an expense when incurred even though the useful lives of the tyres may extend well beyond the current accounting period. Similarly, day-to-day servicing, such as replacement of the oil filter (which does not have a long useful life) on a motor vehicle, is expensed as replaced because it does not extend the future economic benefits of the original asset. Costs of day-to-day repairs and maintenance do not increase the level of economic benefits that will flow to the entity in future periods and must be expensed. It is important to distinguish between day-to-day repairs and maintenance and costs of components or overhauls because improper treatment affects both the determination of periodic profit and the valuation of assets. The distinction between these costs will always be a matter of professional judgement.

Day-to-day repairs and maintenance

Day-to-day repairs and maintenance are those relatively small recurring outlays necessary to keep an asset in good operating condition. Buildings need painting and minor repairs to their electrical, airconditioning and plumbing systems. Machines must be lubricated, cleaned and reconditioned regularly. Engines require tune-ups and the replacement of small parts. Expenditures for these purposes do not materially add to the economic benefits or useful life of the asset. Rather, they are made to ensure that the original benefits from the asset are obtained over its useful life. Day-to-day repairs and maintenance expenditures are therefore treated as an expense of the current period.

For example, if on 6 June an entity spent $670 plus GST for a maintenance service, including a new battery and an engine tune-up for its delivery truck, the entry is:

June	6	Repairs and Maintenance Expense	670	
		GST Outlays	67	
		Cash at Bank		737
		(Repairs on delivery truck)		

Overhauls and replacement of major parts

Major reconditioning and overhaul expenditures are made to extend an asset's expected future benefits beyond the original estimate by adding materially to the asset's future capability to produce goods or perform services. For example, assume a delivery van was purchased for $34 000 (net of GST) and was estimated to have a useful life of 5 years with a residual value of $4000. At the end of the van's fourth year, its carrying amount is $10 000, as shown below:

Cost	$34 000
Accumulated depreciation (4 × $6000)	24 000
Carrying amount	$10 000

At the beginning of the fifth year, it is decided to replace the van's engine at a cost of $4500 plus GST, after which the van will last for 3 more years. The residual value is amended to $2000. The old engine was considered to have a carrying amount of $500, and was written off. The entries to record this capital expenditure are:

July	4	Accumulated Depreciation	24 000	
		Delivery Van		24 000
		(Reversing the accumulated depreciation)		
	4	Delivery Van	4 500	
		GST Outlays	450	
		Cash at Bank		4 950
		(Installation of a new engine)		
	4	Expense on Disposal	500	
		Delivery Van		500
		(Disposal of old engine)		

Depreciation expense for each of the remaining 3 years of the van's life is calculated as follows:

Delivery van carrying amount ($10 000 + $4500 − $500)	$14 000
Less: Residual value	2 000
New depreciable amount	$12 000
Annual depreciation expense ($12 000 ÷ 3 years)	$ 4 000

Since the overhaul of the asset is regarded as an addition or extension to that asset, the revised carrying amount should be depreciated over the remaining useful life of the asset; however, in some circumstances, the addition or extension may have a separate identity and be capable of being used even after the existing asset is sold. Such additions or extensions should be depreciated separately on the basis of their own useful lives.

Furthermore, where major parts of assets are recorded in separate accounts from the asset itself, these parts will be depreciated over their own useful lives using appropriate depreciation methods, as discussed previously.

Leasehold improvements

If an entity has leased an asset, particularly on a long-term basis, it is commonplace for the entity to incur additional costs to ensure that the asset is suitable for its own intended use. For example, the entity may incur the costs of constructing a road across land that it has leased, or install partitioning on the floor of a building it has leased. These additional costs are called **leasehold improvements** and are debited to a Leasehold Improvements account. For depreciation purposes, the depreciable amount of leasehold improvements should be allocated progressively over the unexpired period of the lease, or the useful lives of the improvements, whichever is the shorter.

To illustrate, if $10 000 plus GST was paid on 5 July to install partitions and permanent fixtures in a building leased for 5 years, the payment is recorded as shown below:

July	5	Leasehold Improvements GST Outlays	10 000	
		Cash at Bank	1 000	
		(Payment for improvements to leased building)		11 000

The leasehold improvements are then depreciated each year as shown below, assuming that the life of the lease is shorter than the useful life of the improvements, and residual value is zero:

June	30	Depreciation Expense – Leasehold Improvements	2 000	
		Accumulated Depreciation – Leasehold Improvements		2 000
		(Depreciation of leasehold improvements)		

Spare parts and service equipment

Consider an entity that purchases component spare parts or service equipment specifically for use with a particular asset. Sometimes, these parts and equipment may be sold separately by the entity after the entity has disposed of the asset itself. In this case, the parts and equipment should be recorded in their own separate account and be subject to treatment similar to that of supplies on hand; for example, as spare parts for repairs of a machine are used, the Spare Parts account is credited and Repairs and Maintenance Expense debited.

In certain cases, an entity's supply of spare parts and/or service equipment for an asset may become redundant if the asset is retired or discontinued; hence, the spare parts and/or service equipment do not have separate lives of their own. In this circumstance, the cost of these spare parts and equipment should be treated as a separate item of property, plant and equipment. As such, the depreciable amount of these parts and equipment must be depreciated over the useful life of the asset that they are expected to serve.

Learning objective 6

Record property and plant records in the property and plant subsidiary ledger

20.6 Property and plant records

Property, plant and equipment are normally divided into functional groups with a separate general ledger account and accumulated depreciation account provided for each group. For example, a retail furniture company has separate asset and accumulated depreciation accounts for delivery equipment, office equipment and store equipment. The company may have several delivery trucks and numerous items of office equipment. For example, the Office Equipment account may contain the cost of desktop computers, printers and fax machines, whereas the office chairs, desks and filing cabinets will be recorded in an Office Furniture account. These items may have been acquired on different dates and will have different useful lives and residual values. In addition, the composition of the group of assets will change over time as individual assets are disposed of and new ones acquired.

Because it is impossible to keep all of the detailed information needed for each asset in the general ledger accounts, each asset account and its related accumulated depreciation account become control accounts, with the detail about each item maintained in a subsidiary ledger. Although there are many variations in the form of subsidiary ledgers kept either manually or electronically, one commonly used manual method (which also may be computerised) consists of a file with a separate record for each item included in the control account. Each record contains a number that is also placed on the asset itself as a means of identification and to aid in internal control over the items. To illustrate, assume a simplified case of a company that has two delivery vans, both purchased on 1 October 2013. The general ledger Delivery Equipment and Accumulated Depreciation control accounts and subsidiary records for these assets are presented in figure 20.2.

Note that the account number on the subsidiary ledger records is the same as the general ledger account number for Delivery Equipment. Note also that the balance in the general ledger account Delivery Equipment is equal to the total of the balances of the asset section of the subsidiary ledger records. Similarly, the balance in the general ledger account Accumulated Depreciation – Delivery Equipment is equal to the sum of the balances of the accumulated depreciation section of the subsidiary ledger records. An inventory of property, plant and equipment is taken periodically to maintain control over the assets and to prove the equality of the general ledger accounts and subsidiary records.

It is a common practice in business for entities to attach a permanent sticker or label to each item of plant and equipment. This sticker usually contains its barcode plus details of the asset's type and serial number, and the account number in which it is recorded.

The subsidiary ledger records provide information for the preparation of income tax returns and for supporting insurance claims in the event of loss from theft and accident. The records also contain information for preparing year-end adjustments for depreciation and space for entries to record the disposal of the asset. When the asset is disposed of, the asset section of the subsidiary record is credited and the accumulated depreciation section is debited, thereby reducing both sections to zero. The record is then removed from the subsidiary ledger and filed in a permanent file for possible future reference.

Delivery Equipment — Account No. **216**

Date	Explanation	Post Ref	Debit	Credit	Balance
1/10/13		CP 18	76 800		76 800

Accumulated Depreciation – Delivery Equipment — Account No. **217**

Date	Explanation	Post Ref	Debit	Credit	Balance
30/6/14		GJ 12		9 300	9 300
30/6/15		GJ 29		12 400	21 700
30/6/16		GJ 41		12 400	34 100

Figure 20.2 Property and plant records

PROPERTY AND PLANT RECORD

Account No. _____216_____

Item ___³/₄ tonne van___ General Ledger Account ___Delivery Equipment___

Serial No. ___3AG64243321___

Purchased from ___Bextell Motors___

Useful Life ___5 years___   Residual Value ___$3200___

Depreciation per Year ___$6400___   Depreciation Method ___Straight-line___

Date	Explanation	Post Ref	Asset Dr	Asset Cr	Asset Bal.	Acc. Dep. Dr	Acc. Dep. Cr	Acc. Dep. Bal.
1/10/13		CP 18	35 200		35 200			
30/6/14		GJ 12					4 800	4 800
30/6/15		GJ 29					6 400	11 200
30/6/16		GJ 41					6 400	17 600

(continued)

Figure 20.2 *(continued)*

PROPERTY AND PLANT RECORD

Account No. _____216_____

Item ___One-tonne van___

General Ledger Account _____Delivery Equipment_____

Serial No. _____4SG7215B4312_____

Purchased from _____Bextell Motors_____

Useful Life _____6 years_____

Residual Value _____$5600_____

Depreciation per Year _____$6000_____

Depreciation Method _____Straight-line_____

Date	Explanation	Post Ref	Asset Dr	Asset Cr	Asset Bal.	Accumulated Depreciation Dr	Accumulated Depreciation Cr	Accumulated Depreciation Bal.
1/10/13		CP 18	41 600		41 600			
30/6/14		GJ 12					4 500	4 500
30/6/15		GJ 29					6 000	10 500
30/6/16		GJ 41					6 000	16 500

Learning objective 7

Determine the reporting requirements for property, plant and equipment and depreciation in an entity's financial statements

20.7 Disclosure of property, plant and equipment

For general purpose financial statements, IAS 16/AASB 116 require the disclosure of the depreciation methods used, the useful lives or the depreciation rates used, and the aggregate depreciation expense. Furthermore, both the cost of depreciable assets and their accumulated depreciation must be shown in the financial statements. Accumulated depreciation is disclosed as a deduction from the assets or class of assets to which it relates. Property, plant and equipment may be reported in the statement of financial position or in an accompanying schedule as follows:

Non-current assets:			
Property, plant and equipment:			
Land (at cost)		$164 000	
Buildings (at cost)	$849 000		
Less: Accumulated depreciation	231 500	617 500	
Plant and equipment (at cost)	236 400		
Less: Accumulated depreciation	172 600	63 800	$845 300

BUSINESS KNOWLEDGE

An electric car recharging network

Some may argue that Evan Thornley, chief executive of Better Place Australia, faces an uphill battle in convincing motorists to buy electric cars, which he freely admits can only travel 160 km before the battery is flat. After all, Australians enjoy their day trips and the freedom of being able to drive more than 500 kilometres on a tank of petrol. Thornley's answer is to build swap stations on the outer rims of major cities and connecting highways. He says motorists will drive into a swap-station lane that resembles a garage hoist, open the latches beneath the car and robots below will change a battery within three minutes. Simple ...

Thornley ... has no doubt in his ability to make his Better Place Australia project work.

Big-city motorists hold the key to its success, and Thornley will have to convince them they will be better off switching to electric cars. His sales pitch is that 'the electric car will be quieter, cheaper and greener' ...

The plug-in car will be promoted as convenient because motorists start every day with a 'full tank' and can recharge while in the office. Proponents also advocate that electric cars will be cheaper to run as renewable energy and battery costs fall, and fewer moving parts will save on repairs and maintenance. City air quality will improve with the shift to zero emissions cars, and the environmental risk of shipping crude oil across the globe will be significantly reduced by ditching petrol vehicles ...

He says Better Place Australia's plan to roll out a national recharging network is no pipe dream. The rollout will start in

20.8 Analysis, interpretation and management decisions

Analysis and interpretation

> **Learning objective 8**
>
> Analyse and interpret information on property, plant and equipment and discuss the critical nature and importance of management decisions in relation to property, plant and equipment

With information on property, plant and equipment disclosed in financial statements, the reader can determine the approximate age of the assets. If the assets are old, they are likely to be less efficient in producing future goods and services. In addition, knowledge of the age of assets is useful in judging the approximate time at which expenditures will be needed to replace them. For example, with the use of straight-line depreciation, the buildings presented in the previous section have been used for about 27% (i.e. \$231 500 ÷ \$849 000) of their useful lives. Financing the replacement of these assets will probably not be required in the near future.

However, the plant and equipment have been used for approximately 73% (i.e. \$172 600 ÷ \$236 400) of their useful life; thus, a decision to replace these assets will be necessary in the not-too-distant future.

Note that readers of financial statements can assess the average percentage of useful life expired of the entity's property, plant and equipment by calculating the following ratio:

$$\text{Average percentage of useful life expired} = \frac{\text{Accumulated depreciation}}{\text{Average recorded cost}}$$

This ratio is particularly useful for decision making when non-current assets have not been revalued. However, if revaluation has occurred, as discussed in the next chapter, this ratio is of limited usefulness as the Accumulated Depreciation account is often eliminated on revaluation.

Another ratio of benefit to readers of financial statements is one that shows the relationship between the average gross cost of property, plant and equipment and the current depreciation expense for the period, as an assessment of the assets' average useful life. Thus:

$$\text{Average useful life (in years)} = \frac{\text{Average recorded cost}}{\text{Depreciation expense}}$$

This ratio is helpful whenever an entity has failed to disclose the useful lives, or when the disclosure of useful lives is vague; for example, a company may state that the useful lives of its plant and equipment range from 2 years to 40 years!

Another ratio used in decision making assesses the entity's ability to turn over its assets during the current financial period. The asset turnover ratio is calculated as follows:

$$\text{Asset turnover (in number of times)} = \frac{\text{Net sales}}{\text{Average total assets}}$$

Average total assets is calculated as an average of the beginning and ending assets for the period. This ratio indicates the number of times average total assets have generated sales dollars. In other words, the ratio means that for every dollar invested in assets, the entity has been able to generate so many dollars or cents in sales. A refinement of this ratio relates net sales to investment in average property, plant and equipment. It is calculated as follows:

$$\frac{\text{Net sales}}{\text{Average property, plant and equipment}}$$

This ratio shows the revenue being generated by a certain level of investment in property, plant and equipment. A declining value of this ratio over time indicates a possible overinvestment in plant and equipment.

Ratios such as these are helpful to decision makers when used in conjunction with similar data for the same entity for previous years, and for different entities in the same year so as to assess comparative performance across time and between entities.

When interpreting these ratios, users must appreciate that since asset values are largely based on historical cost (albeit with some revaluations), changing technology, changing economic conditions and market price fluctuations affect these ratios. These factors can limit the usefulness of the ratios.

Management decisions

An entity's investment in property, plant and equipment varies depending on the nature of the business and its major types of activities. Entities engaged in the manufacturing and construction industries require a greater investment in plant and equipment than do those engaged in wholesaling and retailing activities. The relationship of plant and equipment to sales and total assets should be appropriate for the industry concerned. If investment in plant and equipment is too high, a smaller proportion of the entity's funds is available for working capital, and major operations may be curtailed as a result. Higher depreciation charges will result in lower profits, or higher prices for products sold. If the plant and equipment is financed by long-term borrowings, there will be additional demands on cash funds to meet interest payments and, ultimately, repayment of the loans. Thus management must make correct decisions regarding investment in plant assets.

The planning and financing of capital investments, such as the replacement of equipment, expansion of production facilities and introduction of a new product line, is an important area of management decision making. This function of management is known as **capital budgeting**. These decisions are concerned with a current expenditure that will pay for itself over time and yield an acceptable rate of return over a relatively long period of time. As such, capital budgeting decisions are vital to the long-term profitability of an entity, because they will determine its capacity to do business in the short and long term. Capital budgeting decisions must be considered carefully by top management for several reasons:

- They involve large sums of money.
- The resources invested are committed for a long period of time.
- They cannot be reversed easily since the investment becomes a sunk cost that can be recovered only through the productive use of the assets.
- Since they are long term in nature, substantial risk is involved because of such uncertainties as economic conditions, technological developments, consumer preferences and social responsibilities.

In many cases, the success or failure of an entity may depend on a single decision. Several methods are available to management for the evaluation of capital expenditures. In fact, entire books have been written about the subject of capital budgeting, which can involve many sophisticated techniques. Common methods are payback period, rate of return on average investment, and discounted cash flow techniques. Payback period is the number of years it takes for the investment to recover the funds initially outlaid. Rate of return on average investment relates the profits generated from the investment to the average investment in the assets over time. Discounted cash flow techniques relate the present value of projected future cash inflows to the initial outlay in the assets, and decisions are made based on this relationship. A detailed treatment of these techniques is not covered in this chapter; however, the importance of management decisions in relation to property, plant and equipment must be understood.

DISCUSSION QUESTIONS

1. Discuss which of the following should be included in the cost of equipment: (a) installation charges, (b) freight charges, (c) cost of building foundations, (d) new parts needed to replace those damaged while unloading, (e) borrowing costs incurred to finance the purchase of the equipment. What is the general principle to be followed in determining what should be included in the cost of property, plant and equipment?

2. 'According to IAS 16/AASB 116, an item of property, plant and equipment that qualifies for recognition must be recorded at cost, representing the fair value of any assets given up in order to acquire them. Would it not be better to record the assets acquired at their own fair values rather than at those of the assets given up?' Discuss this suggestion and explain the rationale behind the accounting standard. Do you agree with this rationale? Why or why not?

3. ABC Ltd acquired a piece of open land for speculation purposes. It is expected that the value of the land will increase so that it can be sold in the future at a profit. Where should this land be reported in the statement of financial position?

4. F. Murk acquired land, a building and office equipment for a lump sum payment of $2 800 000. Fair values of each asset as determined by an independent valuer are land, $840 000; building, $1 860 000; office equipment, $500 000. How much of the total payment of $2 800 000 should be allocated to each asset? Is the accounting treatment of lump-sum acquisitions appropriate if the assets acquired constitute a business? Explain.

5. Z Ltd depreciates its equipment using the straight-line method of depreciation. Y Ltd, which owns similar equipment and purchased the item on the same day from the same supplier as Z Ltd, uses the diminishing-balance method. Are the depreciation charges of these two companies non-comparable? Explain.

6. Should depreciation be recorded on a building for a year in which the market value of the building has increased? Discuss.

7. At a recent seminar, a managing director of a well-known company argued that the diminishing-balance method of depreciation was the best method to use because it had the effect of producing a 'nice, smooth income (profit) flow'. Discuss how this could occur, and consider the desirability of reporting smooth profit flows. What role does/should the accountant play in this respect?

8. (This is based on an actual case): A 'particularly aggressive' DVD rental store chain amended its depreciation charges for DVDs by extending their useful lives from 12 months to 48 months. This had the effect of adding $5 million to the company's profits, an increase of nearly 20% for the year! On publication of a report critical of this practice, the share price for the company fell dramatically.

   Critically examine the company's depreciation policy, and comment on the likely effects on shareholders, managers and customers of the consequences of the adverse report. Can the company justify its actions?

9. What is the distinction between an overhaul, replacement of a component, and day-to-day repairs and maintenance? Give an example of each and explain how the accounting treatment is different.

10. 'With proper maintenance, certain equipment will last almost indefinitely, in which case depreciation is not necessary.' Discuss.

Exercise 20.1 LUMP-SUM ACQUISITION

LO 3

Ace Ltd acquired a parcel of land, buildings and machinery on 10 July for a cash price of $1 300 000. Fair values of the assets on the acquisition date were appraised as:

Land	$ 400 000
Building	800 000
Machinery	150 000
	$1 350 000

The acquisition was not considered to be a business combination.

Required
Calculate the amount of cost that should be assigned to each of the assets and prepare a journal entry to record the acquisition. Ignore GST.

Exercise 20.2 COST AND ANNUAL DEPRECIATION

LO 2, 4

On 2 January 2013, Dexterous Ltd purchased a machine with a list price of $234 300 (including GST) and credit terms of 2/10, n/30. Payment was made within the discount period. Freight costs of $5400 plus GST and installation costs of $5280 plus GST were also paid. The machine has a useful life of 4 years and a residual value at the end of its useful life of $24 000.

Required
A. Determine the amount that should be debited to the machinery account and prepare a general journal entry to record the purchase, assuming a financial year ending 31 December.
B. Determine the amount of depreciation expense for each of the 4 years ending 31 December assuming use of:
   1. the straight-line depreciation method
   2. the diminishing-balance method of depreciation.
C. Prepare a journal entry to record depreciation expense for the year ending 31 December 2013 under the diminishing-balance method.

Exercise 20.3 DETERMINING COST

LO 2

The following data relate to the purchase of a machine by Ready Ltd for use in the manufacture of its products. Ignore GST.

Invoice price	$16 000
Purchase discount taken	320
Freight cost	400
Cost of transit insurance	100
Installation costs	1 200
Testing of machinery before use	150
Cost of repairing minor damage to the machine during testing	280

Required
Calculate the amount at which the machine should be recorded in the accounting records of Ready Ltd before it is put into full operation.

Exercise 20.4 DEPRECIATION METHODS

LO 4

Delightful Ltd purchased new equipment on 1 January 2013, at a cost of $420 000. The company estimated that the equipment has a residual value of $45 000. The equipment is expected to be used for 5 years.

Required

Assuming the year ends on 30 June, calculate the depreciation using the following methods for years 2013 to 2018:

1. straight-line
2. sum-of-years-digits
3. diminishing-balance.

LO 4

Exercise 20.5 DEPRECIATION METHODS

Dubious Ltd purchased a delivery van costing $32 000 net of GST. It is expected to have a residual value of $12 000 at the end of its useful life of 4 years or 200 000 kilometres.

Required

A. Assume the van was purchased on 2 July 2013 and that the accounting period ends on 30 June. Calculate the depreciation expense for the year 2013–14 using each of the following depreciation methods:
   1. straight-line
   2. sum-of-years-digits
   3. diminishing-balance
   4. units-of-production (assume the van was driven 78 000 kilometres during the financial year).

B. Assume the van was purchased on 1 October 2013 and that the accounting period ends on 30 June. Calculate the depreciation expense for the year 2013–14 using each of the following depreciation methods:
   1. straight-line
   2. sum-of-years-digits
   3. diminishing-balance
   4. units-of-production (assume the van was driven 60 000 kilometres during the financial year).

LO 4

Exercise 20.6 REVISION OF DEPRECIATION RATES

Chance Ltd purchased new equipment for $60 000 on 2 July 2013. The equipment was expected to have a $10 000 residual value at the end of its 8-year useful life. Straight line depreciation has been recorded. While reviewing the accounts in anticipation of adjusting them for the annual financial statements for the year ended 30 June 2016, Chance Ltd decided that the useful life of the equipment should be extended by 2 years, and that the residual value should be revised to $6000. Ignore GST.

Required

A. Give the general journal entry to record depreciation expense on the equipment for the year ended 30 June 2016.
B. Calculate the carrying amount of the equipment at 30 June 2016.

LO 4, 5

Exercise 20.7 OVERHAULS, REPAIRS AND REVISION OF DEPRECIATION

On 1 July 2010, Hopeful Ltd acquired a machine for $30 000. Its useful life was estimated to be 8 years with no residual value. Additional expenditures were made for transportation $500 and installation $900. The company plans to use the machine evenly over its useful life.

On 30 June 2017, repairs costing $8000 were made, increasing the efficiency of the machine and extending its useful life to 4 years beyond the original estimate. On 1 December 2017, some minor worn-out parts were replaced for $300. The company's reporting period ends on 31 December. Ignore GST.

Required

Prepare journal entries in general journal form to record:

1. the acquisition
2. the annual depreciation for 2010
3. the repairs on 30 June 2017
4. the repairs on 1 December 2017
5. annual depreciation for 2017.

Exercise 20.8 OVERHAULS, REPAIRS AND REVISION OF DEPRECIATION GST LO 4, 5

On 2 January 2013, Brilliant Ltd purchased a machine for $36 000 plus GST with a useful life of 5 years and a residual value of $6000. In order to keep the machine running properly, the company has performed regular maintenance and repairs each year since its acquisition. In the fourth year (2016), ordinary repairs amounted to $900 plus GST.

On 3 January 2017, Brilliant Ltd decided to completely overhaul the machine's major operating parts at a cost of $9600 (plus GST), after which the machine is expected to have a useful life of 4 more years and a revised residual value of $4000. Brilliant Ltd uses the straight-line depreciation method. The carrying amount of the parts replaced was considered to be $400.

Required

Prepare general journal entries to record:
1. the purchase of the machine on 2 January 2013
2. the day-to-day repairs on the machine in 2016
3. the overhaul of the machine on 3 January 2017
4. depreciation expense on the machine on 31 December 2017.

Exercise 20.9 OVERHAULS, REPAIRS AND REVISION OF DEPRECIATION LO 2, 4, 5

Heavy Ltd acquired a machine on 1 July 2012 at an invoice price of $15 000. Additional amounts were paid for transport, $250, and installation, $350. It was estimated the machine would have a useful life of 8 years, and no residual value. Heavy Ltd used the straight-line method.

On 1 July 2014, the company re-examined its estimates of useful lives and residual values, and decided that the remaining life of this machine was 4 years from that date with a residual value of $500.

On 1 July 2017, $4000 was paid for an overhaul of the machine, and it was estimated that the overhaul would result in a total useful life of 5 years from that date and an expected residual value of $2000 for the overhauled machine.

On 31 December 2018, the machine was sold for $3000 as it was found to be inefficient. Heavy Ltd's financial year ends 30 June. Ignore GST.

Required

Prepare general journal entries to record:
1. annual depreciation expense on 30 June 2014
2. annual depreciation expense on 30 June 2016
3. annual depreciation expense on 30 June 2018.

Exercise 20.10 ACQUISITION AND DEPRECIATION LO 2, 4

On 1 January 2014, Special Ltd acquired a wood lathe for $31 500, which included shipping charges of $500. The lathe has an estimated useful life of 5 years (or 30 000 machine hours of operation) and a residual value of $3000. Insurance on the lathe while in transit was $150; insurance against damage for 1 year amounted to $250. Finally, installation costs were $1000 and test runs before commissioning totalled $350.

During the first year of operation the machine was operated for 6200 hours.

Required

A. Calculate the cost of the lathe.
B. Calculate the depreciation for the year ending 31 December 2014 using each of the following methods:
   1. straight-line
   2. units-of-production
   3. diminishing-balance (use rate of 38%)
   4. sum-of-years-digits.
C. The nature of depreciation is discussed in IAS 16/AASB 116. Outline alternative views considered for the accounting treatment of depreciation and discuss the rationale for the treatment adopted in the standard.

Exercise 20.11 ACQUISITION, DEPRECIATION, AND SUBSEQUENT COSTS

Ferral Ltd incurred the following transactions for the year ended 31 December 2014. Ignore GST.

Jan.	6	Purchased for $38 200 cash a new delivery van, which is estimated to have a useful life of 3 years and a residual value of $20 000. Paid $600 in advance for 1 year's insurance and $400 for the annual vehicle registration.
Feb.	9	Installed a new set of rear-view mirrors for $300 cash.
June	10	Paid $250 for an engine tune-up, grease and oil change, and wheel balancing.
Aug.	25	Paid a repair bill of $350 for the uninsured portion of damages to the van caused by one of the company's drivers in a minor traffic mishap.
Dec.	1	Installed some new compartments in the back of the van to help improve the delivery of the company's products. Cost was $750. This was not expected to add any years to the useful life of the van nor add to its residual value.
	31	Recorded depreciation on the van for the year.

Ferral Ltd uses straight-line depreciation calculated to the nearest whole month.

Required

A. Prepare general journal entries to record all of the above transactions.

B. Justify your treatment of the following costs:
- insurance
- engine tune-up etc.
- vehicle registration
- compartments.
- mirrors

Exercise 20.12 IMPROVEMENTS AND REVISION OF DEPRECIATION

At 30 June 2012, the financial statements of Artistic Ltd showed a building with a cost of $300 000 and accumulated depreciation of $152 000. The business uses the straight-line method to depreciate the building. When acquired, the building's useful life was estimated at 30 years and its residual value at $60 000. On 1 January 2013, Artistic Ltd made structural improvements to the building costing $120 000. Although the capacity of the building was unchanged, it is estimated that the improvements will extend the useful life of the building to 40 years, rather than the 30 years originally estimated. No change is expected in the residual value. Ignore GST.

Required

A. Calculate the number of years the building had been depreciated to 30 June 2012.

B. Give the general journal entry to record the cost of the structural improvements on 1 January 2013.

C. Give the general journal entry to record the building's depreciation expense for the year ended 30 June 2013.

Exercise 20.13 DEPRECIATION, FINANCIAL POSITION AND MANAGEMENT DECISION MAKING

On 1 July 2013, Clandestine Ltd purchased a motor vehicle, which is estimated to have a $6000 residual value and a useful life of 4 years. On 1 July 2015, the company purchased plant and equipment estimated to have a residual value of $10 000 and a useful life of 4 years. The following is an extract from the statement of financial position showing the carrying amounts of these assets at 30 June 2016:

CLANDESTINE LTD
Statement of Financial Position (extract)
as at 30 June 2016

NON-CURRENT ASSETS		
Property, plant and equipment:		
Plant and equipment (at cost)	$90 000	
Less: Accumulated depreciation	20 000	$70 000
Motor vehicle (at cost)	30 000	
Less: Accumulated depreciation	18 000	12 000
		$82 000

Required

A. For each asset, calculate the percentage of useful life expired.
B. What decisions will management need to make in the next financial year?
C. Prepare the journal entries to record depreciation expense at 30 June 2017.
D. Prepare an extract from the statement of financial position at 30 June 2017 (assuming no new assets have been purchased).

Exercise 20.14 DEPRECIATION ENTRIES AND LEDGERS   LO 4, 5, 6

Jarrod Hill commenced operations on 30 March 2013 in the rubbish and recycling industry, trading as Enviro Services. The entity's end of the reporting period is 31 December.

The following events occurred during 2013 and 2014:

2013

Apr.	1	Paid $140 000 cash for a second-hand disposal truck.
Apr.	1	Paid $1500 cash to recondition the truck's engine.
June	30	Paid $12 000 cash for equipment. Jarrod estimated the equipment's useful life at 10 years and residual value at $1500.
Aug.	31	Paid $650 cash for the truck's transmission repairs and oil change.
Dec.	31	Recorded depreciation on the truck at 40% per annum on the diminishing balance, and on the equipment using the straight-line method.

2014

Mar.	13	Paid $700 cash to replace a damaged bumper bar on the truck.
June	30	Paid $2000 for a major refit of the equipment in order to improve its efficiency. This extended the useful life of the equipment by an extra year. Residual value is unchanged.
Dec.	31	Recorded depreciation on the truck and on the equipment.

Required

A. Prepare general journal entries to record the above events. Round amounts to the nearest dollar.
B. Prepare the following ledger accounts for the period 30 March 2013 to 1 January 2014:
- Truck
- Equipment
- Accumulated Depreciation — Truck
- Accumulated Depreciation — Equipment

Exercise 20.15 DEPRECIATION AND OVERHAULS   LO 2, 4, 5

Dashing Ltd commenced business on 1 July 2013. On 5 July 2013 a printing machine was purchased for $35 000 plus GST, payable in two equal instalments due on 1 August and 1 October 2013. Transport costs of $1200 plus GST were paid in cash to deliver the machine to Dashing Ltd's premises. The machine was expected to have a useful life of 5 years and a residual value of $3000.

On 22 September 2013 the business purchased a second-hand truck for $26 000 plus GST. Stamp duty amounted to $700 (GST does not apply). The truck dealer also fitted four new tyres at a cost of $1200 plus GST and spray-painted the business logo on the truck doors at a cost of $500 plus GST. All amounts were paid in cash. The truck was expected to have a useful life of 3 years and a residual value of $5000.

On 1 March 2014, extensive repairs were carried out on the printing machine at a cost of $18 230 plus GST, paid in cash. The company expects these repairs to extend the machine's useful life by 2 years. The residual value was revised to $4000. The carrying amount of the parts replaced in the machine was considered to be equal to $14 000.

The company uses the straight-line depreciation method, recording depreciation to the nearest month. The end of reporting period is 30 June.

Required (round all amounts to the nearest dollar)

A. Prepare general journal entries (narrations are not required, but show all workings) to record the above transactions and to record depreciation adjustments necessary for the year ended 30 June 2014.
B. Justify the value you recognised as the cost of the second-hand truck purchased on 22 September 2013 by reference to the requirements of IAS 16/AASB 116.

Golden Ltd owns two delivery vehicles (each with a residual value of $5000 and useful life of 4 years) and uses the straight-line method of depreciation. The business closes its accounting records annually on 30 June. The events and transactions recorded below occurred during the first 3 financial years. Ignore GST.

2013–14

July	1	Purchased a delivery truck from Midland Motors for $60 000 cash plus stamp duty of $620, and registration and third-party insurance of $840.
June	1	Made minor repairs to the truck for cash at a cost of $420.
June	30	Recorded annual depreciation.

2014–15

July	1	Purchased a delivery van from Such Motors for cash, $45 000. This van was a used vehicle which was expected to last 4 years from the date of purchase. Fitted four new tyres to the van at a cash cost of $1320.
June	30	Recorded depreciation on both truck and van.

2015–16

July	1	Paid $3700 for an overhaul of the motor of the delivery truck. This expenditure is expected to extend the useful life by 1 year. The parts replaced in the truck were considered to have a carrying amount of $2000. Installed a two-way radio in the delivery van at a cost of $1600 to improve efficiency. This expenditure will not increase the useful life.
June	30	Recorded depreciation on both truck and van.

Required

Prepare entries (in general journal form) to record the transactions of Golden Ltd as they relate to both vehicles to 30 June 2016.

On 1 July 2013, Wonderful Ltd purchased the following two machines to use in its factory:

Machine A: The list price of this machine was $96 250

Related expenditures included:	
Freight costs	$ 2 800
Insurance in transit	$ 150
Installation costs	$ 250
Fuel and oil costs for the machine in its first year of operations	$ 350

Wonderful Ltd estimates that the useful life of the machine is 6 years with a $9000 residual value.

Machine B: The cost of this machine was $200 000. It is expected to have a useful life of 4 years with a $16 000 residual value.

Required

A. Prepare the following for Machine A:
  (i) The journal entry (in general journal form) to record its purchase on 1 July 2013.
  (ii) The journal entry to record annual depreciation at 30 June 2014, assuming the straight-line method of depreciation is used.
B. Calculate the depreciation expense that Wonderful Ltd would record for Machine B for each year of its useful life under the following assumptions:
  (i) The company uses the straight-line method of depreciation.
  (ii) The company uses the diminishing-balance method of depreciation. The rate used is twice the straight-line rate.

(iii) Wonderful Ltd uses the units-of-production method and estimates the useful life of the machine is 50 000 units. Actual usage in units is as follows:

2014	17 000	2016	10 000
2015	14 000	2017	9 000

C. Which depreciation method for Machine B reports the highest amount of depreciation expense in 2014? The highest amount in 2015? The lowest total amount over the 4-year period?

LO 4

Problem 20.3 DEPRECIATION METHODS AND PARTIAL YEARS ★

Terrific Ltd operates four types of equipment. Because of their varied functions, management has decided that four different depreciation methods will be used to determine depreciation charges. Information on the equipment is summarised as follows:

Equipment type	Date acquired	Cost (net of GST)	Residual value	Useful life	Depreciation method
1	1/7/14	$ 95 400	$10 000	8 years	Diminishing-balance
2	1/7/14	148 000	15 000	6 years	Sum-of-years-digits
3	1/1/15	27 500	5 500	10 years	Straight-line
4	15/4/15	39 700	4 600	20 000 hours	Units-of-production

Use of equipment type 4 was 1200 hours in the year ended 30 June 2016; 3200 hours in 2017; and 2600 hours in 2018.

Required

Assuming the financial year ends on 30 June and that depreciation is recorded to the nearest month, calculate the depreciation charges for 2015, 2016, 2017 and 2018 by preparing a schedule with the following headings:

	Depreciation expense for year ended 30 June			
Equipment type	2015	2016	2017	2018

LO 2

Problem 20.4 DETERMINATION OF COST ★

Magnificent Ltd purchased land and buildings on 1 January 2013 for $1 500 000. The buildings were demolished and a new building was completed and machinery installed on the site by November 2013. The new machinery was placed into production on 1 December 2013. All expenditure relating to the new buildings and machinery was charged to a single account — Property. Entries in the account for 2013 included:

1.	Cost of land and old buildings purchased (1/1/13) as the construction site (appraised value of buildings $150 000)	$1 500 000
2.	Legal fees to secure title to property	3 000
3.	Cost of demolishing old buildings	127 000
4.	Proceeds from sale of materials from old buildings demolished	60 000
5.	Contract price of new building $4 450 000 paid for by delivery to contractor of $4 500 000 government bonds, which had cost the company $4 700 000 and had a market value at date of delivery to contractor of $4 450 000	4 700 000
6.	Cost of machinery badly damaged by fire while awaiting installation in new building; not insured	400 000
7.	Proceeds from sale of fire-damaged machinery	190 000
8.	New machinery for the building, including units to replace those damaged by fire	1 160 000
9.	Cost of installing machinery in building	60 000
10.	Landscaping of grounds	40 000
11.	Office equipment	210 000
12.	Retaining walls and fences	140 000
13.	Payment to architect for design and construction supervision	190 000
14.	Insurance on building during construction	20 000
15.	Repairs to building damaged by storm on 15 December 2013	35 000

Required

A. Reclassify all these items by recording them in their correct accounts, clearly indicating by account titles those (if any) that are to be expensed during the current period.

B. List and briefly explain the criteria for distinguishing between expenditure treated as an asset and those treated as an expense.

Problem 20.5 COST OF VARIOUS ASSETS AND DEPRECIATION ★★ LO 2, 4

Tops Ltd began operations during 2013. The company had a building constructed and acquired manufacturing equipment during the first 6 months of the year. Manufacturing operations began early in July 2013. The company's accountant, who was unsure how to treat property, plant and equipment transactions, opened a Property, Plant and Equipment account and debited (credited) that account for all the expenditures and receipts involving assets as shown below (all costs are net of GST).

1.	Cost of real estate purchased: Land	$ 453 600
	Old building	140 000
2.	Paid for the demolition of the old building to prepare the site for a new one.	60 000
3.	Paid for taxes in arrears on the property in (1)	26 800
4.	Paid fee for title search on property in (1)	2 400
5.	Received for sale of salvaged materials from old building	(18 400)
6.	Paid architect for designing new building	160 000
7.	Paid for a temporary fence around the construction site	93 200
8.	Paid excavation costs for new building	330 000
9.	Partial payment to building contractor	900 000
10.	Paid for construction of parking spaces and installation of parking area lights	62 800
11.	Paid interest on building loan during construction	78 000
12.	Made final payment to building contractor	1 100 000
13.	Paid for manufacturing equipment	336 000
14.	Paid freight on manufacturing equipment	6 400
15.	Paid installation costs of manufacturing equipment	11 600
16.	Paid for removal of temporary fencing around construction site	5 200
17.	Received for temporary fencing materials salvaged	(2 000)
18.	Paid for repair of manufacturing equipment that was damaged during installation	3 200
	Property, Plant and Equipment account balance	$3 748 800

Required

A. Prepare a schedule similar to the one below. Analyse each transaction and enter the payment (receipt) in the appropriate column. Total the columns.

Item no.	Land	Land improvements	Building	Manufacturing equipment	Other

B. Prepare a general journal entry to close the $3 748 800 balance in the Property, Plant and Equipment account and allocate the amounts to their appropriate accounts.

C. Prepare an entry to record depreciation expense for half the year to 31 December 2013 on land improvements, building and manufacturing equipment using straight-line depreciation. Useful lives and residual values are:

	Useful life	Residual value
Land improvements	10 years	—
Building	20 years	$184 400
Manufacturing equipment	8 years	30 000

Problem 20.6 DETERMINATION OF COST AND DEPRECIATION ★★

Your examination of the records of Lucky Ltd, which was established on 1 March 2013, reveals that the accountant debited the Land, Buildings and Equipment account with the following items (ignore GST):

Purchase price of land and building	$ 650 000
(An independent valuation was obtained, showing land being valued at $600 000 and the building at $80 000)	
Legal and transfer costs	3 500
Cost of demolition of building	25 000
Earthmoving on property	15 000
Architect's and other professional fees in respect of the erection of new buildings on the property	160 000
Cost of erection of new building	2 100 000
Layout of parking area	75 000
Lighting of parking area	18 000
Cost of machinery and equipment (including $9000 for a machine which was dropped from one of the company's vehicles during off-loading and irreparably damaged)	1 267 000
Installation cost of machinery	85 000
Cost of replacement of damaged machine	9 000
	$4 407 500

Examination of the wage records shows that the salary of the manager, $4000 per month, was debited to the Salaries Expense account. From 1 March to 31 August 2013, he supervised the erection of the factory buildings, and from 1 September to 31 October 2013 he supervised the installation of the machinery.

The accountant credited sundry income with $8400, being $7000 received for scrap building material from the demolished building and $1400 for the damaged machine.

Required

A. Show journal entries to transfer the amounts to three different accounts, i.e. Land account, Buildings account and Machinery account.
B. Assuming that the company started operations on 1 November 2013 and that its financial year ends on 31 March, journalise the following depreciation entries using the straight-line method:
   1. buildings: useful life 40 years, $20 000 residual value
   2. machinery: useful life 12 years and residual value amounting to 10% of cost.

Problem 20.7 DEPRECIATION METHODS AND RATIONALE ★★

Futuristic Ltd has investigated the history of its specialised machines, with a view to determining whether a change in their depreciation method is desirable. The following case history has been selected as being typical of all of its machines:

Machine no. 98
Installation: Installed 1 January 2012 for $125 000.
Expected useful life: 4 years.
Residual value $7500.

Operating record:

Year	Units of output	Maintenance cost
2012	28 600	$2 800
2013	29 000	$3 000
2014	29 000	$2 500
2015	33 400	$3 200

Depreciation record:

Depreciation actually recorded in the accounts:

2012	$47 000
2013	$35 250
2014	$23 500
2015	$11 750

The company has decided that, irrespective of its past practice, it will limit its investigation of methods to the following:
(a) straight-line
(b) units-of-production
(c) diminishing-balance.

Required

A. Specify the method actually used by Futuristic Ltd for machine no. 98. Show your calculations.
B. Prepare a comparative statement showing the yearly depreciation charge according to each of the three methods (a), (b) and (c) above, using the actual history of the machine and adopting a rate of 55% for the diminishing-balance method.
C. Which method would you advise the company to adopt? Give reasons.

LO 4, 5

Problem 20.8 MAJOR OVERHAULS AND DEPRECIATION REVISIONS ★★

The non-current asset transactions of Innovative Ltd are as given below. Straight-line depreciation is used for all depreciable assets except forklifts, which are depreciated using the sum-of-years-digits method. Depreciation is recorded (rounded to the nearest dollar) to the nearest month, and the end of the reporting period is 31 December.

2013

Jan.	3	Bought a new machine for of $114 000 cash. Freight charges of $880 and installation costs of $3500 were paid in cash. The useful life and residual value were estimated at 5 years and $8000.
June	22	Bought a used forklift for $70 000 cash. Repainting costs of $800 and 4 new tyres costing $700 were paid for in cash. The forklift has an expected useful life of 5 years and $10 000 residual value.
Dec.	31	Recorded depreciation.

2014

Jul.	30	Paid for repairs and maintenance on the machine and forklift at a cash cost of $530.
Dec.	31	Recorded depreciation expense.

2015

Jun.	26	Installed a fence around the property at a cash cost of $11 000. The fence has an estimated useful life of 10 years and zero residual value. (The cost of the fence is recorded in the Land Improvements account.)
Dec.	31	Recorded depreciation.

2016

Jan.	5	Completely overhauled the machine at a cash cost of $24 000, after which the remaining useful life was estimated at 1 additional year and the residual value was revised to $10 000.
Dec.	31	Recorded depreciation.

2017

June	10	Bought a delivery van for $30 500 cash. Stamp duty of $500 and registration and third-party insurance of $800 were paid for in cash. Useful life was 8 years and expected residual value was $1800.
Dec.	31	Recorded depreciation.

Required

A. Prepare journal entries to record the above transactions.
B. Prepare the machinery and accumulated depreciation ledger accounts for the period 1 January 2013 to 31 December 2017.
C. Justify your treatment of the repairs and maintenance costs and the overhaul costs.

On 2 January 2013, Superlative Ltd purchased, by exchanging $300 000 cash and a $180 000, 12%, 18-month finance company loan, assets with the following independently determined appraised values:

	Appraised value
Building	$320 000
Land	80 000
Machinery and equipment	100 000
	$500 000

The estimated useful life of the building is 30 years and its residual value is $20 000.

The $100 000 machinery and equipment amount consists of three machines independently valued at $30 000 each and some office equipment valued at $10 000. The estimated useful lives and residual values for these assets are:

	Useful life	Residual value
Machine 1	6 years	$3 000
Machine 2	9 years	3 000
Machine 3	4 years	4 000
Office equipment	5 years	500

Superlative Ltd uses the straight-line depreciation method. Ignore GST.

Required

A. Prepare journal entries (in general journal form) to record:
   1. the purchase of the assets
   2. the accrual of interest expense on the loan on 31 December 2013
   3. depreciation expense for the year 2013
   4. the payment of the loan on 2 July 2014.
B. Show how the assets would be reported in the 31 December 2013 statement of financial position.

Stupendous Ltd completed the following transactions during 2014. The company uses sum-of-years-digits depreciation and records depreciation to the nearest month.

Jan.	5	Purchased a used machine (No. 1) for $8000 cash (net of GST). The machine was painted and reconditioned at a cost of $900. During installation, one of the major components was dropped and had to be repaired at a cash cost of $300, net of GST. The machine is expected to have a useful life of 4 years and a residual value of $500.
March	7	Purchased land and a building with the intention of tearing down the building and constructing a new office complex. Stupendous Ltd paid $140 000 for the property, plus an agent's commission of $8000 and title search fees of $2500. All costs were net of GST.
March	20	Paid Brown Demolition Services $9000 to demolish the building acquired on 7 March. The cost is net of GST.
April	10	The company's parking area was paved at a cost of $28 000 (net of GST). The parking area has a useful life of 8 years with no residual value.
June	23	Purchased for cash a machine (No. 2) with a list price including GST of $16 500. The seller granted a 4% trade discount. GST is to be deducted. Transportation and freight charges of $1236 (net of GST) were also paid. The machine's useful life is estimated to be 5 years and its residual value $1600 (excluding GST).
Nov.	1	Purchased for $29 000 cash (plus GST) a machine (No. 3) with a useful life of 8 years and a residual value of $1000.

Required

A. Prepare general journal entries to record all the transactions of Stupendous Ltd.
B. Prepare an entry to record depreciation expense on 31 December 2014.

Problem 20.11 PROPERTY AND PLANT RECORDS ★★

Selected transactions of Ethical Ltd are given below. The company uses straight-line depreciation and calculates depreciation expense to the nearest whole month.

2013

Jan. 4 Purchased from Fair Ltd a bottle washer (Serial No. 17538X) for $44 000 cash (net of GST). The useful life of the machine is 5 years and its residual value is expected to be $8000.

April 10 Purchased from Good Ltd a dryer (Serial No. PY43121) for $39 000 cash (net of GST). The machine has a useful life of 6 years and a residual value of $9000.

Required

A. Prepare journal entries to record the purchase of the assets and to record depreciation expense on 30 June 2013 and 2014, the end of the company's reporting periods.

B. Open a Machinery account (No. 230) and an Accumulated Depreciation — Machinery account (No. 231), and prepare subsidiary property and plant records for the two assets. Post the journal entries to the general ledger accounts and to the subsidiary property and plant records.

Problem 20.12 DEPRECIATION AND OVERHAULS ★★

On 1 March 2012, Welcome Ltd purchased a new delivery van. Costs associated with the transaction were as follows (ignore GST):

Invoice price	$28 000
Special vehicle extras	1 400
On-road costs	800
Registration fee for 2009–10	500

The van will be used for 4 years and depreciated on a straight-line basis. It has an estimated residual value of $12 000. End of the reporting period for Welcome Ltd is 30 June.

Required

Prepare journal entries for each of the following transactions:

1. The van purchased for cash.
2. Depreciation on the van for the year ended 30 June 2012.
3. On 1 July 2013, a $1200 airconditioning unit was added to the van. Although the van's estimated useful life was not affected, its estimated residual value was increased by $1000.
4. On 1 September 2013, the van was given a full service and safety inspection at a cost of $800. Neither the useful life nor the residual value was affected.
5. Depreciation on the van for the year ended 30 June 2014.
6. Depreciation on the van for the year ended 30 June 2015.
7. On 2 January 2016, the van received a $2600 major overhaul. The overhaul is expected to extend the van's useful life by 1 year, at which time the revised residual value is estimated to be $14 000.
8. Depreciation on the van for the year ended 30 June 2017.

Problem 20.13 DEPRECIATION AND OVERHAULS ★★

Part A

Powerful Ltd purchased a printing machine on 18 October 2011 for $50 000. It is expected to have a useful life of 4 years or 20 000 hours of use and a residual value of $12 000 at the end of that time.

Required

A. Calculate the depreciation expense for the first two financial years (ending 30 June 2012 and 30 June 2013) using the following methods:

1. straight-line
2. diminishing-balance
3. units-of-production, assuming 3000 hours of use in the year ended 30 June 2012 and 11 000 hours of use in the year ended 30 June 2013.

B. The CEO of Powerful Ltd is trying to decide which method of depreciation should be used for the printing machine for financial reporting purposes. She anticipates that printing demand will fluctuate considerably from year to year. Which method would you advise the CEO to use?

Part B

On 1 July 2013, the printing machine had a serious breakdown. The CEO was faced with the following two options:

(a) Have a major overhaul done of the machine at a cost of $15 000, after which the machine will last for 4 years from date of overhaul. There will be no effect on the residual value of the machine.

(b) Have repairs done to the machine at a cost of $5000, which will ensure the benefits from the machine are obtained over its original estimated useful life.

Required

A. Prepare journal entries to record each option available to the CEO of Powerful Ltd, assuming a straight-line method of depreciation has been used to 1 July 2013.

B. Prepare journal entries to record depreciation at 30 June 2014 under each option, using the straight-line method.

Problem 20.14 COMPREHENSIVE PROBLEM ★★   **LO 2, 4, 5**

Over a 5-year period, Dodgy Ltd completed the transactions affecting non-current assets in the reporting periods ending 31 December shown below. The company uses straight-line depreciation on all depreciable assets and records depreciation to the nearest month.

2013

Jan.	3	Purchased a new machine for a cash price of $30 000 (net of GST). Freight charges of $700 (net of GST) and installation expenditures of $3200 (net of GST) were paid in cash. The machine has a useful life of 5 years and a residual value of $5000.
June	25	Purchased a used delivery van for $19 000 cash (net of GST). The van was repainted at a cost of $400 (net of GST) and a new battery (net cost: $100) and tyres (net cost: $800) were installed. The van has a useful life of 3 years and a residual value of $1300.
Dec.	31	Recorded depreciation expense on the assets.

2014

July	30	Paid for day-to-day repairs and maintenance on the machine and van at a cost of $520, net of GST.
Dec.	31	Recorded depreciation expense on the assets.

2015

April	2	Installed a fence around the company property at a cost of $8000 (net of GST). The fence has a useful life of 12 years with no residual value.
Dec.	31	Recorded depreciation expense on the assets.

2016

June	30	Recorded the final depreciation on the delivery van.
June	30	The company completed construction of a new warehouse. Construction costs incurred (all paid in cash, net of GST) were: labour, $18 000; materials, $33 000; building permits, $1500; architect fees, $2300; and overhead, $4000. The warehouse is expected to have a residual value of $7000 and a useful life of 30 years.
Dec.	27	Completely overhauled the machine purchased on 3 January 2006, at a cost of $5000 (net of GST), after which the useful life was estimated to be 4 additional years, and residual value was revised to $6000. The parts replaced were considered to have zero carrying amount.
Dec.	31	Recorded depreciation expense on the assets.

2017

Dec.	31	Recorded depreciation expense on the assets.

Required

A. Prepare general journal entries to record all the transactions of Dodgy Ltd.

B. Prepare a schedule showing the cost and accumulated depreciation of each asset after recording depreciation on 31 December 2017.

C. Post the journal entries in requirement A to the appropriate non-current asset accounts from 3 January 2013 to 31 December 2017.

At the end of Trustworthy Ltd's financial year, 30 June 2014, the following items must be resolved before adjusting entries and financial statements are prepared. Ignore GST.

1. On 1 July 2013, Trustworthy Ltd purchased a used machine for $48 000 cash. The cost was debited to the Machinery account. Prior to use, additional cash expenditures were made for painting and repairing the machine, $4200, and installing and testing the machine, $3000. These additional expenditures were debited to Repairs and Maintenance Expense. The repairs and installation were completed on 1 October 2013, and the machine was put to use. The machine has a useful life of 5 years with a residual value of $4000. Trustworthy Ltd uses straight-line depreciation and records depreciation to the nearest month.

2. A building and land were purchased on 2 July 2013 for $180 000 cash, debited to the Land account. The appraised values of the building and land were $100 000 and $60 000, respectively. The building has a useful life of 20 years with a residual value of $6000. Trustworthy Ltd uses straight-line depreciation for buildings.

3. A new truck was purchased on 1 March 2014. Trustworthy Ltd paid cash of $55 500 and also obtained a 12-month loan payable for the amount of $30 000. The Trucks account was debited for $85 500. The truck has a useful life of 4 years with a residual value of $20 000 and is to be depreciated by the diminishing-balance method. However, due to an oversight, the business used the straight-line method.

Required

A. Prepare journal entries on 30 June 2014 to correct the accounts.

B. Prepare journal entries as necessary to record depreciation expense after the corrections in requirement A have been made.

DECISION ANALYSIS

Depreciation of machinery

In early July 2013 Admirable Ltd is considering the acquisition of some machinery for $1 200 000 plus GST to be used in the manufacture of a new product. The machinery has a useful life of 10 years, during which management plans to produce 500 000 units of the new product. The residual value of the machinery is $100 000.

The following projections were made in order to select a depreciation method to be used for the machinery:

Year ended 30 June	Units of output	Repairs and maintenance	Profit before depreciation
2014	50 000	$ 70 000	$350 000
2015	45 000	60 000	340 000
2016	55 000	90 000	355 000
2017	58 000	95 000	360 000
2018	60 000	100 000	380 000

In calculating the profit before depreciation, all expenses have been deducted, including the repairs and maintenance expense.

Required

A. As the accountant for Admirable Ltd, prepare separate depreciation schedules for the machinery for the 5-year period, using the following depreciation methods: (a) straight-line, (b) diminishing-balance, (c) sum-of-years-digits, and (d) units-of-production. Use the following headings for each schedule: 'Year ending 30 June', 'Annual depreciation expense', 'Accumulated depreciation', 'Carrying amount at end of year'.

B. Prepare a report for management, stating the advantages and disadvantages of each depreciation method. Include in the report your recommendations on the choice of method consistent with the requirements of IAS 16/AASB 116. Support your recommendations with schedules showing the total annual cost of operating the machinery, and the profit after depreciation.

CRITICAL THINKING

Purchase price of land, building and furniture

Investments Plus Ltd has acquired a two-storey office building on a large piece of land. The land also includes a fully established car park and landscaping. The offices have recently been fitted out with new carpets, curtains and office furniture, which are all included in the purchase price.

As the accountant of Investments Plus Ltd you have been asked to work out the cost of the office building, the land, and the furniture and fittings so that they can be entered into the accounts of the company. You have gathered the following information (ignore GST):

- The advertised purchase price of the office building and land was $1.5 million. Investments Plus Ltd issued the owner of the land with 200 000 shares in Investments Plus Ltd that had been trading on the share market for $7.50 before the issue of the new shares but had subsequently fallen to $7 as a result of the share issue being made.
- A piece of vacant land next to the one purchased, and of equal size, recently sold for $800 000.
- The vendor of the office building has shown you the value of the furniture and fittings in their accounts as being $300 000.
- A builder has estimated that to build an office building similar to the one acquired would cost about $700 000.
- You want to maximise the cost of the furniture and fittings and the buildings as these are depreciable for taxation purposes.

Required
A. What is the fair value of the office buildings and the land?
B. How would you divide the purchase price between the land, buildings and office furniture?
C. Show the journal entry to record the acquisition of these assets in the accounts of Investments Plus Ltd.

ETHICS AND GOVERNANCE

Changing depreciation methods

Jason Domes Ltd is a large department store that has used the straight-line depreciation method since the company was first formed. For the year ended 30 June 2013, the company made a record profit and management expected these high profits to continue at least into 2014 and 2015, although economists were generally predicting an economic slowdown and a subsequent fall in profits in 2016 and 2017.

The general manager, Jason Domes, approached the accountant, Megan Mild, and asked her if she could find a way to reduce the profit in the next couple of years and transfer it to 2016 and 2017 when things may not be going so well. 'This would give us consistent profits over the next few years and keep our shareholders happy,' said Jason.

Although Megan did not feel that Jason's reason for the change was justified, she was concerned that her contract with the company would not be renewed if she upset the general manager. After some consideration, Megan decided to change the depreciation method from the straight-line method to the sum-of-years-digits method. Megan did not disclose this change in the notes to the financial statements as she felt that the reason given by Jason would not give a good impression.

Required
A. Who are the stakeholders in this situation?
B. What ethical issues, if any, arise in this situation?
C. How does the change in accounting methods by Megan meet the objectives set out by Jason?
D. Do Megan's actions comply with the requirements of IAS 16/AASB 116?

Refer to the consolidated financial statements and their notes in the latest financial report of JB Hi-Fi Limited on its website, www.jbhifi.com.au, and answer the following questions:

1. How is property, plant and equipment reported in the consolidated statement of financial position/balance sheet? What is the total carrying amount for property, plant and equipment as disclosed at the end of the financial year?

2. What was the composition of JB Hi-Fi's property, plant and equipment at the end of the reporting period? How have these assets been valued?

3. What methods of depreciation have been used for the various categories of property, plant and equipment?

4. Has the group disclosed the rates of depreciation or the useful lives of these assets?

5. What was the amount of depreciation charged on these assets for the current and previous years?

6. Were any items of property, plant and equipment purchased during the year? Were any such items constructed or under construction? Has the company treated any borrowing costs incurred as part of the cost of properties under development? Does the company have any commitments for future capital expenditure not provided for in the financial statements? Provide details (if any) of any financial amounts involved.

Non-current assets: revaluation, disposal and other aspects

Concepts for review

Before studying this chapter, you should understand or, if necessary, revise:

- the nature of non-current assets, especially property, plant and equipment (p. 830)

- how to record the acquisition of property, plant and equipment (pp. 830–2)

- the nature of depreciation in accounting (pp. 834–6)

- how to record depreciation expense under alternative depreciation allocation methods (pp. 836–40)

- the treatment of costs subsequent to acquisition of non-current assets (pp. 841–4)

- the accounting for the sale of inventory under a perpetual inventory system (pp. 238–44)

- the closing entries needed at the end of a reporting period (pp. 179–98).

Learning objectives

After studying this chapter, you should be able to:

1   account for the revaluation of non-current assets, both upwards and downwards (pp. 868–73)

2   account for the write-down of an impaired non-current asset to recoverable amount (pp. 873–4)

3   account for the derecognition of non-current assets by scrapping, by sale, or by exchange (pp. 874–8)

4   account for depreciation using composite rates (pp. 878–80)

5   describe the accounting for the acquisition and depletion of mineral resources (pp. 880–2)

6   describe the nature of biological assets and agricultural produce and how to account for them (pp. 882–3)

7   describe the nature of intangible assets and the problems of accounting for them (pp. 883–7)

8   describe the nature of goodwill and how to account for goodwill acquired by an entity (pp. 887–8).

Strike up the brand

Among the broad Texan accents and even broader cowboy hats milling around a San Antonio conference held in February this year were 35 Australian franchise executives. The Antipodeans were in town with the International Franchise Association, rubbing shoulders with executives from more than 40 countries.

Australia really packs a punch when it comes to franchising. It's not only our franchising execs who are heading overseas, but our businesses themselves — in droves. Australia is the world's second biggest exporter of franchising concepts, after the US.

Many of the Australian brands venturing offshore are household names: Cartridge World, Gloria Jean's Coffees, Bakers Delight and Cookie Man. Steve Wright, executive director of the Franchise Council of Australia, says the A$130 billion franchising sector has a strong export track record, earning A$200 million-plus abroad.

'Australians seem to have the entrepreneurial 'can do' attitude which is an important ingredient in successful franchising,' Wright says. 'We also have a sophisticated regulatory system in Australia, possibly the most comprehensive of anywhere in the world, which encourages good practice in franchising, so our franchisors are well training and equipped to do well in overseas markets.'

Cartridge World is perhaps the most conspicuous success. Born in Adelaide's trendy Norwood, the business opened its first overseas franchise in 2001 in Harrogate, in the United Kingdom's North Yorkshire. Just nine years later it has more than 1650 stores in 52 countries, and was brought by Wolseley Private Equity in 2007.

Other notable successes include Pack & Send, The Coffee Club and newcomer Hire A Box.

'The Coffee Club has partnered with a Thai investor and hotel owner for further regional expansion. I expect this to be a growing trend, where Australian owners partner with others overseas to find the best route to sustained successful penetration of offshore markets,' says Wright.

George Yammouni, the chairman of the Franchise Council of Australia, says franchising is at a peak. 'We had 9 per cent growth in 2009. By comparison, the US had a 1 per cent contraction,' he points out.

Franchising is a good way for small to medium enterprises to get into export, says Austrade chief economist Tim Harcourt. 'Australian SME franchises are going very well in Asia, particularly in India because of the young, middle class population,' he says.

After nearly 30 years in the business, Bakers Delight now has 700 bakeries worldwide, including 61 in Canada where it operates as COBS Bread. General manager Chris Caldwell has bullish growth plans and hopes to add another 150 franchisees across Australia, New Zealand and Canada this year. Fifty of those are earmarked for Canada. Caldwell is banking on the lingering effects of the global financial crisis, hoping it will encourage people to take control of their own destiny and start their own business …

Another major success is the Gloria Jean's Coffees chain of cafes …

Gloria Jean's Coffees currently has 917 stores and 38 master franchise agreements across 37 countries.

Source: Extract from Carolyn Boyd, 'Strike up the brand', *InTheBlack*.

Chapter preview

The previous chapter focused on accounting procedures for the initial and subsequent costs of property, plant and equipment, as well as on the nature of depreciation and the procedures for depreciation, as specified in accounting standard IAS 16/AASB 116 *Property, Plant and Equipment*. In this chapter, we introduce the accounting aspects for a range of topics associated with the broader category of non-current assets. The revaluation, impairment and derecognition (disposal) of property, plant and equipment completes the discussion of such property and plant begun in the previous chapter. We then look at other types of non-current assets, namely mineral resources, biological assets and intangible assets such as franchises and brand names (several franchises are mentioned in the scene setter). Finally, we consider the accounting treatment of goodwill acquired in a simple business combination.

21.1 The revaluation model

Learning objective 1

Account for the revaluation of non-current assets, both upwards and downwards

Following the initial acquisition of property, plant and equipment, an entity is required by IAS 16/AASB 116 to adopt either a cost model or a revaluation model for accounting for these assets. The previous chapter illustrated the cost model, where an item of property, plant and equipment is carried in the accounting records at cost less any accumulated depreciation.

If an entity chooses the revaluation model, then an asset must be revalued to its fair value, which, for an asset, is defined as the price that would be received to sell an asset in an orderly transaction between market participants at the measurement date (IFRS 13/AASB 13 *Fair Value Measurement*). Fair values must be capable of verifiable measurement and revaluations must be made, either upwards or downwards, with sufficient regularity to ensure that the carrying amount of each asset does not differ materially from its fair value. The **carrying amount** of an asset (also referred to as book value) refers to the amount at which an asset is recorded in the entity's accounts after deducting accumulated depreciation and accumulated impairment losses (see later in the chapter for a discussion of impairment). Any revaluation above the asset's existing carrying amount is referred to as a **revaluation increase**; any revaluation below the existing carrying amount is referred to as a **revaluation decrease**.[1]

IAS 16/AASB 116 states the general policy that, whenever a non-current asset is to be revalued, the entire class of assets to which that asset belongs must be revalued to fair value, so that all assets of the same class are stated at amounts that are determined at the same date. Thus, a revaluation to fair value of one item of plant and machinery leads to a revaluation of all plant and machinery; a revaluation of one block of land means that all blocks are to be revalued, provided that the land in question is treated by the entity as a non-current asset and not inventory. Once assets have been revalued to fair value, the revaluations must be kept at fair value at the end of each subsequent reporting period.

Note carefully that the standard *does not require* an entity to revalue its assets, but if revaluations *are* made, the measurement method to apply is fair value. The main aim of the standard is to prescribe the accounting entries to use if an entity decides to revalue classes of its non-current assets to fair value.

Initial revaluation increases

According to IAS 16/AASB 116, when each non-current asset of a particular class is initially revalued upwards to fair value, the revaluation increase shall be recognised in other comprehensive income and accumulated in equity under the heading of 'revaluation surplus'. The important point about the revaluation increase is that it is not included in the entity's profit for the year, but appears as part of an entity's comprehensive income, and is then directly accumulated into equity as a revaluation surplus which is a type of reserve. As discussed more fully in

---

1. In this book, the tax effect of revaluations is ignored on the grounds of simplicity. Under IAS 16/AASB 116, the tax effect of revaluations must be considered, thus creating a deferred tax liability associated with the change in the carrying amount of the asset revalued, as per IAS 12/AASB 112 *Income Taxes*. More complete coverage of the tax effect of revaluation is found in advanced accounting texts.

chapter 23 on disclosure in general purpose financial statements, a statement of profit or loss and other comprehensive income discloses not only the entity's profit or loss for the period but also **other comprehensive income**, which is defined in IAS 1/AASB 101 *Presentation of Financial Statements* as comprising items of income and expense that are not recognised in profit or loss, as required or permitted by other accounting standards. The components of other comprehensive income are described as including:

- changes in revaluation surpluses
- actuarial gains and losses on defined benefit superannuation plans
- gains and losses arising from translating the financial statements of a foreign operation
- gains and losses on remeasuring certain financial assets.

Hence, when preparing general purpose financial statements for the use of external parties, any increase or decrease in the revaluation surplus must be disclosed separately, below the profit figure, in the entity's statement of profit or loss and other comprehensive income, prepared in accordance with the requirements of IAS 1/AASB 101. When disclosed as part of other comprehensive income (OCI), the revaluation increase is usually described as a 'gain on revaluation'.

For any depreciable non-current asset which is revalued upwards, the existing accumulated depreciation account must be written off against the asset account to give the asset's carrying amount. The asset account should then be increased to reflect the revalued amount.

To illustrate, assume that Garden Landscaping has two non-current assets on 31 December 2013, namely:

Land		$150 000
Motor vehicle	$65 000	
Less: Accumulated depreciation	25 000	40 000

A decision is made on 31 December 2013 to adopt the revaluation model, and to revalue both classes of assets: the land to a fair value of $170 000 and the motor vehicle to a fair value of $45 000. The journal entries necessary for each asset are:

2013			
Dec. 31	Land	20 000	
	Gain on Revaluation – Land (OCI)		20 000
	(Revaluation increase on land)		
31	Accumulated Depreciation – Motor Vehicle	25 000	
	Motor Vehicle		20 000
	Gain on Revaluation – Motor Vehicle (OCI)		5 000
	(Revaluation increase on motor vehicle)		

The entry for the motor vehicle above may be a little clearer if split into two entries:

2013			
Dec. 31	Accumulated Depreciation – Motor Vehicle	25 000	
	Motor Vehicle		25 000
	(Write back accumulated depreciation)		
31	Motor Vehicle	5 000	
	Gain on Revaluation – Motor Vehicle (OCI)		5 000
	(Revaluation increase on motor vehicle)		

At the end of the reporting period, if the entity is required to prepare general purpose financial statements, the two gains on revaluation are reported as part of other comprehensive income (OCI). The authors recommend that, in addition to the Profit or Loss Summary account, another account called the Other Comprehensive Income Summary account (OCI Summary) be used as part of the closing process (for earlier discussion of the closing process, see chapter 5). The two gains on revaluation can then be transferred to the Revaluation Surplus account as shown below, assuming that 31 December 2013 is the end of the reporting period:

2013			
Dec. 31	Gain on Revaluation – Land (OCI)	20 000	
	Gain on Revaluation – Motor Vehicle (OCI)	5 000	
	Other Comprehensive Income Summary		25 000
	(Transfer of OCI gains)		
31	Other Comprehensive Income Summary	25 000	
	Revaluation Surplus		25 000
	(Transfer of OCI to appropriate reserve)		

The OCI Summary account is used as part of the closing process to accumulate every item which is included in the OCI as required by accounting standards. It is then cleared by transferring the balance to appropriate reserve accounts. In this case the appropriate reserve is entitled Revaluation Surplus in accordance with IAS 16/AASB 116.

After the revaluation, the asset accounts appear as follows:

Land	$170 000
Motor vehicle	45 000

Note the carrying amount of the motor vehicle before the revaluation was equal to $40 000 ($65 000 − $25 000). The revaluation increase of $5000 has then been added to the carrying amount after the accumulated depreciation has been written off. Any future depreciation charges on depreciable assets such as the motor vehicle in the example will then be based on the revalued carrying amounts. Thus, if the motor vehicle is now assessed to have a useful life of 3 years and its residual value is $3000, the entry for depreciation on a straight-line basis for the year ending 31 December 2014 (end of the reporting period) is:

2014			
Dec. 31	Depreciation Expense – Motor Vehicle	14 000	
	Accumulated Depreciation – Motor Vehicle		14 000
	[($45 000 − $3000) × 1/3]		

In relation to the write-back of existing accumulated depreciation balances, the standards permit an alternative treatment where an entity revalues a depreciable asset by reference to current prices for assets newer than those being revalued. For example, an entity may revalue its fleet of 2-year-old motor vehicles by using the current market buying prices of similar new vehicles, and adjusting those current prices to reflect the present condition of the fleet of vehicles held. In this situation, the entity may restate separately the gross amount and the related accumulated depreciation of the vehicle fleet.

To illustrate, assume that an entity acquires a non-current asset for a cost of $10 000 on 1 July 2012. The asset is expected to have a useful life of 10 years with no residual value and depreciation is to be determined on a straight-line basis. On 30 June 2014, when the carrying amount of the asset is $8000 ($10 000 cost less accumulated depreciation of $2000), the entity decides to adopt the revaluation model for this class of non-current asset. Fair value in this case is determined by reference to the current price of an equivalent brand-new asset, which has a current market price of $15 000. Since the asset held by the entity has been owned for 2 years and has been depreciated by a total of 20%, the amount of the asset after the revaluation must reflect an accumulated depreciation balance equal to 20% of the current market price of the new asset, namely 20% of $15 000, or $3000. The general journal entry to record the revaluation is:

2014				
Dec. 31	Asset		5 000	
	Accumulated Depreciation			1 000
	Gain on Revaluation of Asset (OCI)			4 000
	(Revaluation of the asset upwards to fair value as reflected by reference to current prices for a new asset)			

The asset will then be reflected in the financial statements at the fair value of $12 000, i.e. the gross price of $15 000 less accumulated depreciation of $3000.

Initial revaluation decreases

Under IAS 16/AASB 116, downward revaluations by an entity of assets within a *class* of non-current assets can occur only when the carrying amounts of those assets exceed their fair values. In other words, a revaluation decrease represents a write-down of a class of non-current assets from carrying amount to fair value. According to the standard, if an asset's carrying amount is decreased as a result of a revaluation, the decrease must be recognised in profit or loss, and not as a reduction in other comprehensive income. Thus, the standard requires a revaluation decrease to be treated as an expense, which reduces profit in the current period. The expense will therefore be transferred to the Profit or Loss Summary account at the end of the reporting period.

As with revaluation increases, any accumulated depreciation on the assets should be written off against the assets.

To illustrate, assume as before that on 31 December 2013 Garden Landscaping has two non-current assets, namely:

Land		$150 000
Motor vehicle	$65 000	
Less: Accumulated depreciation	25 000	40 000

The business learns on 31 December 2013 that the fair values for the land and motor vehicle have fallen to $140 000 and $34 000 respectively. The general journal entries (ignoring the tax effect of revaluation decreases) to record the revaluation decreases are:

2013				
Dec. 31	Expense on Revaluation of Land (P/L)		10 000	
	Land			10 000
	(Revaluation decrease on land)			
31	Accumulated Depreciation – Motor Vehicle		25 000	
	Expense on Revaluation of Motor Vehicle (P/L)		6 000	
	Motor Vehicle			31 000
	(Revaluation decrease on motor vehicle)			

As with revaluation increases, depreciation charges in future for the motor vehicle must now be based on the newly established fair value of $34 000.

Reversals of increases and decreases

In a future period or periods, the initial revaluation adjustments accounted for may reverse. If so, the revaluation increase (decrease) should be offset against the previous revaluation decrease (increase) for that class of asset.

Reversal of an initial increase

For reversal of an initial revaluation increase credited to revaluation surplus, according to IAS 16/AASB 116, the decrease in an asset's carrying amount shall be recognised in other comprehensive income to the extent of any credit balance existing in the revaluation surplus in respect of that asset. The decrease recognised in other comprehensive income is debited to a Loss on Revaluation (OCI) account, which is transferred to the Other Comprehensive Income Summary account at the end of the reporting period. The OCI Summary is then closed to reduce the amount accumulated in the Revaluation Surplus for that asset. However, the Revaluation Surplus for that asset can only be written down to the extent that it has been previously written up. To illustrate, consider the motor vehicle owned by Garden Landscaping on 31 December 2014 after the revaluation increase and depreciation charge:

Motor vehicle	$45 000	
Less: Accumulated depreciation	14 000	$ 31 000

On 31 December 2014, it is discovered that the carrying amount of the vehicle ($31 000) exceeds its fair value ($25 000). The revaluation decrease of $6000 reverses the previous revaluation increase ($5000) recognised on 31 December 2013 as well as recognising an expense for the additional $1000 decrease. The entry to record the reversal is:

2014			
Dec. 31	Accumulated Depreciation – Motor Vehicle	14 000	
	Loss on Revaluation of Motor Vehicle (OCI)	5 000	
	Expense on Revaluation of Motor Vehicle (P/L)	1 000	
	Motor Vehicle		20 000
	(Reversal of revaluation increase by writing down other comprehensive income and recognising an expense on motor vehicle)		

In general purpose financial statements, the expense on revaluation of the motor vehicle ($1000) is reported as a reduction of profit, but the loss on revaluation of the motor vehicle ($5000) is reported in the statement of profit or loss and other comprehensive income below the profit figure, in accordance with the requirements of IAS 16/AASB 116. The expense on revaluation ($1000) is transferred to the Profit or Loss Summary account, and the OCI loss ($5000) is then transferred to OCI Summary, at the end of the reporting period. The OCI Summary account is then closed off to Revaluation Surplus by $5000 to reduce the surplus balance to zero for the motor vehicle.

Reversal of an initial decrease

According to IAS 16/AASB 116, any increase in an asset's fair value which reverses a previous revaluation decrease must be recognised in profit or loss, but only to the extent that it reverses any previously recognised revaluation expense on the same asset. Any reversal in excess of the previous write-down should then be credited to the Gain on Revaluation. This Gain on Revaluation is then transferred to the OCI Summary and is reported in the statement of profit or loss and other comprehensive income below the profit figure as an increase in equity. The OCI Summary account is closed to Revaluation Surplus at the end of the reporting period.

To illustrate, consider the motor vehicle owned by Garden Landscaping that was revalued downwards to its fair value of $34 000 on 31 December 2013, as discussed above. Assume now that on 31 December 2014, the fair value of the vehicle is assessed at $30 000. Before the revaluation adjustment, depreciation for the year must be recognised, based on a useful life of 3 years and a residual value of $3000, as shown below. This will record the vehicle at a carrying amount of $23 667 on 31 December 2014 before the revaluation adjustment.

2014				
Dec.	31	Depreciation Expense – Motor Vehicle	10 333	
		Accumulated Depreciation – Motor Vehicle		10 333
		(Depreciation of the vehicle: [$34 000 – $3000] × 1/3)		
	31	Accumulated Depreciation – Motor Vehicle	10 333	
		Gain on Revaluation of Vehicle (P/L)		6 000
		Gain on Revaluation of Vehicle (OCI)		333
		Motor Vehicle		4 000
		(Revaluation upwards to fair value after a previous revaluation decrement of $6000)		

At the end of the reporting period, as part of the closing process, the Gain on Revaluation (OCI) ($333) is closed to OCI Summary and the Gain on Revaluation (P/L) ($6000) is closed to Profit or Loss Summary. From the OCI Summary, the amount of $333 is then credited to Revaluation Surplus and reported in equity as a reserve.

21.2 The impairment test

Learning objective 2

Account for the write-down of an impaired non-current asset to recoverable amount

In relation to non-current assets, an entity is also subject to the requirements of accounting standard IAS 36/AASB 136 *Impairment of Assets* to be applied whenever the carrying amount of a non-current asset is greater than its recoverable amount.

Whenever an asset's carrying amount exceeds recoverable amount, the asset is said to suffer an **impairment loss** and must be written down to recoverable amount. The write-down must be *recognised as an expense in that period if the cost model is used, or accounted for as a revaluation decrease if the revaluation model is used* (as discussed in the previous section). To illustrate, assume that Garden Landscaping Ltd has two non-current assets valued under the cost model on 31 December 2013:

Land		$150 000
Motor vehicle	$65 000	
Accumulated depreciation	25 000	40 000

On 31 December 2013 an estimate is made of the assets' recoverable amounts: the land has a recoverable amount of $160 000 and the motor vehicle $35 000. Because the carrying amount of the land is less than the recoverable amount, no entry is necessary; however, for the motor vehicle, the following journal entry is required:

2013				
Dec.	31	Impairment Loss on Motor Vehicle	5 000	
		Accumulated Depreciation and Impairment Losses		5 000
		(Impairment of vehicle to recoverable amount)		

Note that the accumulated depreciation recognised by the entity is increased by the size of the impairment loss on the asset when the asset is written down to recoverable amount. The contra-account to the asset is retitled 'Accumulated Depreciation and Impairment Losses'. If the vehicle was considered to have a residual value of $5000 and a further useful life of 2 years, depreciation on a straight-line basis per annum would then be based on the recoverable amount and be equal to $15 000 (i.e. [$35 000 – $5000] ÷ 2).

The write-down of non-current assets to recoverable amount occurs only if the asset has satisfied an 'impairment test', a test developed in IAS 36/AASB 136. Under the standard, an asset is 'impaired' whenever its recoverable amount is less than its carrying amount. **Recoverable amount** is defined as the higher of an asset's fair value less costs to sell and its value in use. **Value in use** is based on present value calculations of future net cash flows expected from the continuing use of an asset and from its disposal at the end of its useful life. In the standard, the impairment test must be applied to an individual asset, but if this is not possible, it must be applied to a **cash-generating unit**, which is defined as the smallest identifiable group of assets that generates cash inflows that are largely independent of the cash inflows from other assets or groups of assets. An example of a cash-generating unit provided in IAS 36/AASB 136 is where an entity has a contract with a city council to operate five separate bus routes. Even though it may be possible to identify the assets devoted to each route and the cash flows from each, the council will not permit the entity to drop a route even if that route is operating at a loss. Hence, the cash-generating unit is not each individual route, but the combination of all five bus routes, in accordance with the terms of the contract with the council.

Under IAS 36/AASB 136, an impairment loss occurs for a cash-generating unit when the recoverable amount of the group of assets as a whole is less than the carrying amount of that group. The recoverable amount determined is for the group of assets in combination rather than for the sum of the recoverable amounts of the individual assets in the group. Whenever a cash-generating unit is impaired, the entity must write down the group of assets and recognise an impairment loss either as an expense or as a revaluation decrease. Coverage of the impairment of cash-generating units is provided in advanced accounting texts.

The entity is also required to make an assessment at the end of each reporting period for impairment. If it subsequently finds that the group of assets previously written down for impairment is no longer so impaired, the entity is required to reverse the impairment loss to the extent that the loss no longer exists.

21.3 Derecognition of non-current assets

Learning objective 3

Account for the derecognition of non-current assets by scrapping, by sale, or by exchange

Scrapping non-current assets

When a non-current asset is no longer useful to the entity and *has no sales value*, it is discarded or scrapped and must be derecognised (written off) in the accounting records in accordance with IAS 16/AASB 116. If the asset is fully depreciated, there is no expense on disposal. For example, if a machine that has been fully depreciated by $7000 is discarded because it is worthless, the entry to scrap the machine is:

July	2	Accumulated Depreciation – Machinery	7 000	
		Machinery		7 000
		(Scrapped a fully depreciated machine)		

Sometimes a non-current asset is scrapped as worthless before it is fully depreciated, in which case the carrying amount of the asset represents an expense on disposal, and this expense must be recognised in the current period under IAS 16/AASB 116. If the machine above is discarded when it has an accumulated depreciation balance of $6500, a $500 expense is recorded when the asset is removed from the accounts:

July	2	Accumulated Depreciation – Machinery	6 500	
		Expense on Disposal of Machinery	500	
		Machinery		7 000
		(Scrapped a partially depreciated machine)		

If expenditures are incurred for the removal of the asset, they increase the expense on disposal. Assuming the company had to pay $400 plus 10% GST to have the machine dismantled and hauled away, the entry is:

July	2	Accumulated Depreciation – Machinery	6 500	
		Expense on Disposal of Machinery	900	
		GST Outlays	40	
		Machinery		7 000
		Cash at Bank		440
		(Scrapped a partially depreciated machine and incurred disposal costs of $400)		

In the illustrations above, it is assumed that the asset is disposed of at the beginning of the financial year. When non-current assets are disposed of during the year, an entry should be made to record depreciation expense for the fractional portion of the year before disposal, regardless of the method of disposal. If the monthly depreciation on the machine above was $100, for example, and the machine was discarded on 1 September, the entry to record depreciation for the 2 months before disposal is:

Sept.	1	Depreciation Expense – Machinery	200	
		Accumulated Depreciation – Machinery		200
		(Depreciation on scrapped machine to date of disposal)		

The entry to record the scrapping of the machine in accordance with the standard is:

Sept.	1	Accumulated Depreciation – Machinery	6 700	
		Expense on Disposal of Machinery	300	
		Machinery		7 000
		(Scrapped a partially depreciated machine)		

Sale of non-current assets

A second way of disposing of a non-current asset is to sell it. This could happen at the end of the asset's useful life when the asset has been depreciated down to its residual value, or at some time during the asset's useful life, as illustrated below. If the selling price exceeds the carrying amount of the asset, there is a gain on disposal. This gain is reported in the income statement as part of income, but not as revenue under IAS 16/AASB 116. If the selling price is less than the carrying amount, there is a loss on disposal, which is reported as an expense.

To illustrate, assume that a machine with a cost of $22 000, a residual value of $2800 and a useful life of 8 years was acquired on 3 July 2009. After the adjusting entry for depreciation was made on 30 June 2014, the accounts showed the following balances:

Machinery	$22 000
Accumulated Depreciation – Machinery	12 000*
	$10 000

$$* \ (\$22\,000 - \$2800) \div 8 = \$2400$$
$$\$2400 \times 5 \text{ years} = \$12\,000$$

The machine was sold on 1 February 2015.

Before recording the sale, 7 months depreciation should be recorded for the period of July 2014 to January 2015:

Feb.	1	Depreciation Expense – Machinery	1 400	
		Accumulated Depreciation – Machinery ($2400 × 7/12)		1 400
		(Depreciation to the date of sale)		

After recording depreciation to the date of sale, the carrying amount of the machine is $8600 ($22 000 – $13 400). Entries to record the sale of the machine under three different assumptions as to selling price are presented below.

1. The machine is sold for $8600 (ignoring GST)

The entry that traditionally has been used to record the sale is presented below:

Feb.	1	Cash at Bank	8 600	
		Accumulated Depreciation – Machinery	13 400	
		Machinery		22 000
		(Sold a machine for its carrying amount)		

Because the machine was sold for its carrying amount, no gain or loss is recognised. The cash received is recorded and the cost of the machine and its related accumulated depreciation are removed from the accounts. However, such an entry does not clearly show the gross proceeds and expenses involved in the disposal. Hence an alternative treatment is recommended in this book.

For the purpose of recording gross proceeds and of preparing cash flows from investing activities in line with IAS 7/AASB 107 *Statement of Cash Flows*, any proceeds on sale of a non-current asset should be shown at the *gross amount received*. Similarly, the carrying amount of an asset sold should be written off and treated as an expense from sale of the asset. This is similar to the treatment under the perpetual inventory system where the cost of inventory sold is debited immediately on sale to the Cost of Sales account as an expense from sales.

Therefore, we recommend that the following journal entries (in general journal format) should be made instead of the previous entry:

Feb.	1	Cash at Bank	8 600	
		Proceeds from Sale of Machinery		8 600
		(Gross proceeds from sale)		
	1	Carrying Amount of Machinery Sold	8 600	
		Accumulated Depreciation – Machinery	13 400	
		Machinery		22 000
		(Recognition as an expense of the carrying amount of the machine sold)		

The first entry records the proceeds on sale of the machine in terms of the gross amount received. The second entry records the elimination of the carrying amount of the machine sold from the accounting records. Any gain or loss on sale of the non-current asset for disclosure purposes in the income statement can be calculated as the difference between the Proceeds from Sale of Machinery account and the Carrying Amount of Machinery Sold account. In this case, because the sale amount exactly equals the carrying amount, there is neither a gain nor a loss.

2. The machine is sold for $9300 (ignoring GST)

Feb.	1	Cash at Bank	9 300	
		Proceeds from Sale of Machinery		9 300
		(Gross proceeds from sale)		
	1	Carrying Amount of Machinery Sold	8 600	
		Accumulated Depreciation – Machinery	13 400	
		Machinery		22 000
		(Recognition as an expense of the carrying amount of the machine sold)		

Since the machine was sold for more than its carrying amount, the Proceeds from Sale of Machinery $9300 exceeds the Carrying Amount of Machinery Sold $8600 by $700. For external reporting purposes under IAS 1/AASB 101 *Presentation of Financial Statements*, the gain on sale, $700, is disclosed separately in the statement of profit or loss and other comprehensive income or the notes thereto.

3. The machine is sold for $8200 (ignoring GST)

Feb.	1	Cash at Bank	8 200	
		Proceeds from Sale of Machinery		8 200
		(Gross proceeds from sale)		
	1	Carrying Amount of Machinery Sold	8 600	
		Accumulated Depreciation – Machinery	13 400	
		Machinery		22 000
		(Recognition as an expense of the carrying amount of the machine sold)		

Because the machine was sold for less than its carrying amount ($8200 − $8600), a loss of $400 is included as part of the entity's profit for the year.

Note that in all three cases for the sale of the machine, the second entry is exactly the same, because it is recording the expense of the carrying amount of the asset sold. Furthermore, in all three cases, the first entry is the same except for the amount of the proceeds (GST has been ignored for reasons of simplicity). Any gain or loss on sale of the non-current asset is determined by taking the difference between the Proceeds from Sale account and the Carrying Amount of Asset Sold account. Use of these two accounts allows for the easier generation of information for disclosure in an entity's general purpose financial reports, especially the statement of cash flows, as will be seen in a later chapter.

Derecognition of revalued assets

If an asset that has been revalued previously either upwards or downwards is disposed of, the gain or loss recognised on disposal should be included in the current period's profit. Any gain or loss is determined as the difference between the carrying amount of the revalued asset at the time of disposal (including depreciation up to the date of disposal) and the proceeds from disposal. Accounting for such cases is identical to that shown previously for the sale of non-current assets.

What is to happen to the Revaluation Surplus account whenever a revalued asset has been derecognised? According to IAS 16/AASB 116, the account cannot be transferred back to current profits. The standard does not clearly tell us what to do with it; nor are we told the reason it is created on the initial revaluation. The following alternative treatments of the surplus account (a reserve) are possible:

- The standard indicates that an entity *may* transfer the Revaluation Surplus account to Retained Earnings, or to the owner's Capital account, either at the date of derecognition or before that date.
- Alternatively, an entity could transfer the Revaluation Surplus account to a General Reserve account on date of disposal, or let the Revaluation Surplus account remain untouched in the entity's accounting records, or pay out the surplus in the form of a cash or share dividend to owners of the entity.

Detailed discussion of these alternatives is beyond the scope of this book. Further consideration of the implications of any transfers out of the Revaluation Surplus account and of the tax effects can be found in more advanced texts.

Exchanging non-current assets

Another way of derecognising a non-current asset is to trade it in on another asset. Such exchanges often occur with machinery, motor vehicles and equipment. A trade-in allowance for the old asset is deducted from the price of the new asset, and the balance is paid in accordance with the normal credit terms. Accounting procedures used for the exchange of assets are illustrated in the following example. GST is ignored.

Assume that a machine with a recorded cost of $22 000 and accumulated depreciation to date of exchange of $15 000 is traded in on a new machine. A fair trade-in allowance of $4000 is received for the old machine and $26 000 is paid in cash. The excess of the carrying amount of the old machine ($7000) over the trade-in allowance received ($4000) results in a loss of $3000, and the exchange is recorded in two entries as shown below:

Feb.	1	Machinery [new]	30 000	
		Cash at Bank		26 000
		Proceeds from Sale of Machinery [old]		4 000
		(Exchange of new machine for trade-in of $4000 and payment of $26 000)		
	1	Carrying Amount of Machinery Sold [old]	7 000	
		Accumulated Depreciation – Machinery [old]	15 000	
		Machinery [old]		22 000
		(Recognition as an expense of the carrying amount of the machine traded in)		

These entries record the new machinery at its cost of $30 000, i.e. the fair value of the assets given up in exchange for the new asset. The trade-in price of $4000 represents the fair value given up for the old machine. The first entry records the fact that the new machine was paid for by a trade-in allowance of $4000 plus $26 000 cash. In the second entry, the carrying amount of the old machine is removed from the records by transferring the carrying amount (i.e. cost of $22 000 less accumulated depreciation of $15 000) to expense. Note that any gain or loss made on the trade-in of the old machine is the difference between proceeds from sale and the carrying amount:

Proceeds from Sale of Machinery	$4 000
Carrying Amount of Machinery Sold	7 000
Loss on trade-in (sale) of machine	$3 000

Exchanging dissimilar assets

Sometimes assets that perform different functions in an entity are exchanged. Examples are the exchange of machinery for land or the exchange of a building for equipment. In these circumstances, the carrying amount of the old asset, i.e. the asset and related accumulated depreciation accounts, are removed from the records, and the asset purchased is recorded at its cost, represented by the fair value of assets given up to acquire it. To illustrate, assume that Dell Ltd exchanged a building with a cost of $125 000 and accumulated depreciation of $60 000, and a fair value of $90 000, for construction equipment. The exchange is recorded as follows (ignoring GST):

Jan.	5	Construction Equipment	90 000	
		Proceeds from Sale of Building		90 000
		(Exchange of building for new construction equipment)		
	5	Carrying Amount of Building Sold	65 000	
		Accumulated Depreciation – Building	60 000	
		Building		125 000
		(Recognition as an expense of the carrying amount of building sold)		

Note that the cost of acquiring the construction equipment is the fair market value ($90 000) of the building, which is regarded as sold for $90 000. The cost of the building ($125 000) and its related accumulated depreciation ($60 000) are removed from the accounts. A gain is calculated at $25 000, which is the difference between the proceeds on sale of the building ($90 000) and its carrying amount ($65 000).

If the fair value of the building is $50 000 rather than $90 000, the entries are:

Jan.	5	Construction Equipment	50 000	
		Proceeds from Sale of Building		50 000
		(Exchange of building for new construction equipment)		
	5	Carrying Amount of Building Sold	65 000	
		Accumulated Depreciation – Building	60 000	
		Building		125 000
		(Recognition as an expense of the carrying amount of building sold)		

Note in this case that a loss of $15 000 results because the fair value from sale of the building ($50 000) is less than the carrying amount ($65 000) of the building.

21.4 Composite-rate depreciation

Learning objective 4

Account for depreciation using composite rates

In previous illustrations, depreciation was calculated on each individual asset. An alternative approach, called **composite-rate depreciation**, is often used in practice by business entities with many similar assets in the one class of assets. Under this approach, a single average depreciation rate is applied to the cost of a functional group of assets such as office furniture or store equipment. The average depreciation rate is calculated by dividing the sum of the annual depreciation charges for each asset in the group by the total cost of the assets. For example, the calculation of the composite rate for office furniture might be made as follows:

Asset	Cost	Residual value	Depreciable amount	Useful life (years)	Annual depreciation
Chair	$ 150	$22	$128	8	$ 16
Desk	470	70	400	10	40
Filing cabinet	390	70	320	10	32
	$9 750				$731

$$\text{Composite rate} = \frac{\$731 \text{ annual depreciation}}{\$9750 \text{ cost}} = 7.5\%$$

Although the total cost of office furniture will change as new assets are added and old assets are derecognised, the general mix is assumed to remain relatively the same. Additions and retirements are assumed to occur uniformly throughout the year; the composite rate is therefore applied to the average of the beginning and ending balances in the account for the year. If the Office Furniture account has a $9750 balance at the beginning of the period and a $12 500 balance at the end of the period, the end-of-period adjustment for depreciation is $834 ($9750 + $12 500 = $22 500 ÷ 2 = $11 125 × 0.075), and the following depreciation entry is prepared:

June	30	Depreciation Expense – Office Furniture	834	
		Accumulated Depreciation – Office Furniture		834
		(Depreciation on office furniture)		

When assets within the composite group are disposed of, no gain or loss results. The cost of the asset is credited to the asset account and accumulated depreciation is debited for the difference between the asset's cost and the amount realised from the sale. For example, assume a desk with a cost of $470 is sold for $100. The following entry is made to record the disposal (ignoring GST):

July	10	Cash at Bank	100	
		Proceeds from Sale of Office Furniture		100
		(Sale of desk)		
	10	Carrying Amount of Office Furniture Sold*	100	
		Accumulated Depreciation – Office Furniture	370	
		Office Furniture		470
		(Recognition as an expense of the carrying amount of desk sold)		

* Since no gain or loss can arise in this situation, the carrying amount of the furniture must equal the proceeds. The accumulated depreciation amount is therefore a residual.

When an asset in the group is traded in on a new one, the transaction is recorded in a similar manner. If the desk above is traded in on a new one with a cost of $600, i.e. a trade-in allowance of $200 and $400 paid in cash, the entry is (ignoring GST):

July	10	Office Furniture	600	
		Cash at Bank		400
		Proceeds from Sale of Office Furniture		200
		(Sale of desk traded in on new desk)		
	10	Carrying Amount of Office Furniture Sold	200	
		Accumulated Depreciation – Office Furniture	270	
		Office Furniture		470
		(Recognition as an expense of the carrying amount of desk traded in on new desk)		

Thus, Accumulated Depreciation – Office Furniture is adjusted in this case to $270 in order to make the proceeds from the sale of the old desk ($200) equal to its carrying amount. Hence no gain or loss results.

Learning objective 5

Describe the accounting for the acquisition and depletion of mineral resources

21.5 Mineral resources

Mineral resources include mineral deposits, and oil and gas reserves. In their natural state they represent inventories that will be consumed in the future by mining or pumping to convert them into various products. For example, a copper mine is a deposit of unmined copper ore and an oilfield is a pool of unpumped oil. When mined or pumped they are converted into products for sale to customers. Until they are converted, they are assets shown on the balance sheet under such titles as Mineral Deposits and Oil and Gas Reserves.

Accounting for mineral resources is a somewhat complicated process governed by the requirements of several accounting standards. Any purchased mineral deposit, mine, or oil or gas reserve is to be accounted for as are other items of property, plant and equipment under IAS 16/AASB 116, the accounting procedures for which have been considered in the previous chapter and early in this chapter. Furthermore, as the mineral deposit, mine, or oil or gas reserve is used up, the entity must charge depreciation on the item as per the requirements of IAS 16/AASB 116.

Exploration and evaluation costs

If an entity engages in exploration for mineral resources, including their evaluation, the costs of such activities are to be accounted for under IFRS 6/AASB 6 *Exploration for and Evaluation of Mineral Resources*. In Australia particularly, where AASB 6 applies, an entity's accounting policy for the treatment of exploration and evaluation expenditures is to be assessed according to each area of interest. An **area of interest** refers to an individual geological area whereby the presence of a mineral deposit or oil or natural gas field is considered favourable or has been proven to exist.

For each area of interest, AASB 6 requires an entity to expense the exploration and evaluation costs as incurred. However, the initial costs may be partially or fully capitalised and recognised as an 'exploration and evaluation asset' if:
- the rights to tenure of the area of interest are current
- at least one of the following conditions is met:
  - the costs are expected to be recovered through successful development and exploitation of the area of interest, or by its sale
  - at the end of the reporting period, the continuing exploration and evaluation activities have not yet reached a stage where a reasonable assessment can be made of the existence of economically recoverable mineral reserves.

After initial recognition, the exploration and evaluation asset is then subject to the requirements of IAS 16/AASB 116. The entity can apply either the cost model or the revaluation model to the asset, and the requirements for eventual depreciation of the asset. Irrespective of the model adopted, the entity must then apply the impairment test under IAS 36/AASB 136. When facts and circumstances indicate that the carrying amount of the asset exceeds its recoverable amount, the entity must recognise an impairment loss. See further details of the impairment test earlier in this chapter.

Development costs, construction costs and inventories

After an entity has assessed that a mineral deposit or an oil or gas reserve is suitable for development, any costs of development are to be treated in accordance with IAS 38/AASB 138 *Intangible Assets*. Further discussion of development costs follows later in the chapter under the heading 'Intangible assets'.

Once construction has begun in the area of interest, the entity is required to account for construction costs under IAS 16/AASB 116. Construction costs include the erection of buildings on-site and installation of equipment useful for extraction of the mineral resources. These assets should be recorded initially at cost and depreciated over their useful lives or over the life of the mineral resource, whichever is shorter. The entity can then continue to apply the cost model to these assets, or can choose the revaluation model.

As soon as the entity has inventories of mineral ore, oil or gas from its activities, these inventories must then be accounted for under IAS 2/AASB 102 *Inventories*, which was covered in a previous chapter.

Amortisation

When a mineral resource becomes a viable proposition, and the production of inventories of ore or natural gas or oil begins, the exploration and evaluation asset recognised under AASB 6 should then be amortised. So, too, should any mineral resource purchased from an external party. **Amortisation** of mineral resources is calculated in a similar way to depreciation under the units-of-production method. The cost of the mineral resource (minus residual value) is divided by the estimated number of units available, such as tonnes of copper ore, to arrive at an amortisation rate per unit. This amortisation rate is then multiplied by the number of units removed during the period to determine the total amortisation charge for the period. If the exploration and evaluation asset for a copper mine at 1 July, the beginning of production, is $100 000 000, or if the copper mine is purchased on that date for $100 000 000 and the mine has a residual value of $10 000 000, and contains an estimated 4 500 000 tonnes of copper ore, the amortisation rate per tonne is $20 ($100 000 000 − $10 000 000 = $90 000 000 ÷ 4 500 000 tonnes). If 400 000 tonnes of ore are mined during the first year, the amortisation charge for the year is $8 000 000, and is recorded as follows:

June	30	Amortisation of Copper Mine	8 000 000	
		Accumulated Amortisation – Copper Mine		8 000 000
		(Amortisation for the year)		

On the balance sheet at the end of the first financial year, the copper mine is shown as follows:

Exploration and evaluation costs (copper mine)	$100 000 000	
Less: Accumulated amortisation	8 000 000	$92 000 000

Amortisation represents a part of the cost of the resource extracted or product produced. It is possible that a mineral resource extracted in one year may not be sold until a later year. In that case, the unsold portion represents inventory and should be reported as a current asset. For example, if only 300 000 tonnes of the copper ore in the illustration are actually processed and sold during the year, $6 000 000 is recorded as amortisation expense (included in cost of ore sold) and the remaining $2 000 000 is included as part of the cost of Inventory of Copper Ore on the balance sheet/statement of financial position. In other words, amortisation is recorded in the year in which the copper ore is mined and is then allocated to cost of sales and inventory, based on the number of units sold and the number of units retained in inventory, by the following entry:

June	30	Cost of Sales	6 000 000	
		Inventory of Copper Ore	2 000 000	
		Amortisation of Copper Mine		8 000 000
		(Allocation of amortisation of copper mine)		

Of course, the cost of the inventory on hand at year-end also would include labour costs and other extraction costs.

Depreciation of related construction assets

Depreciation of assets constructed at the area of interest is calculated on a similar basis to amortisation by use of the units-of-production method.

To illustrate, assume that mining equipment with a cost of $4 500 000 and a normal useful life of 15 years is installed at the copper mine in the preceding illustration. The copper ore is being mined at a rate that will exhaust the mine in approximately 10 years. At the end of that time, the equipment will be abandoned. Thus, to the entity, the useful life of the equipment is only 10 years. In this case, depreciation on the equipment should be based on the life of the mine. The depreciation rate per tonne would be $1 ($4 500 000 ÷ 4 500 000 tonnes), and the depreciation charge for mining equipment in the first year would be $400 000 ($1 × 400 000 tonnes).

The depreciation entry is:

June	30	Depreciation of Equipment	400 000	
		Accumulated Depreciation – Equipment		400 000
		(Depreciation for the year)		

Like amortisation, depreciation is allocated to expense and inventory based on the number of units sold and the number of units retained in inventory.

BUSINESS KNOWLEDGE

Rio's faith in China

Rio Tinto expects to resume big ticket expansion of its flagship Pilbara iron ore business, potentially worth US$10 billion ($11.3 billion), within months as the world's second-biggest producer of the steel-making commodity regains confidence in the China growth story.

Chief executive Tom Albanese said yesterday he was 'quite keen' to boost Rio's Pilbara output and was hopeful a 50 million tonne a year expansion would start by the middle of this year to boost the unit's capacity to 280 mtpa by 2013.

A second 50 mtpa push, to take Rio's Pilbara capacity to 330 mtpa by 2015, would follow thereafter.

The expansion is not included in Rio's US$5 billion to US$6 billion capital expenditure budget for this year and Rio is yet to discuss costs.

'I hope to see them move ahead in the first part of this year to proceed towards first 280 mtpa and 330 mtpa, driven off the strength of our infrastructure,' Mr Albanese said.

Mr Albanese's comments yesterday publicly confirm for the first time Rio's changed expansion strategy of pursuing two 50 mtpa projects rather than a one-hit 100 mtpa plan. *The West Australian* flagged the strategy change in October.

Rio is already working on two small expansions to boost Pilbara capacity from 220 mtpa to 230 mtpa by 2012.

But Mr Albanese's expectation that the big expansion push could happen by mid-year is the most bullish move by the mining giant since it was forced to axe the costly plan — analysts expect a 100 mtpa expansion to cost close to US$10 billion — as the global financial crisis hit in late 2008.

Although Rio yesterday warned of more volatility in global metals markets as worldwide stimulus packages were being wound down, a 'secular uplift' in commodities demands should ensure strong, long-term demand for the miner's products.

'Our long-term outlook remains strong as China, followed by India, continues to urbanise and industrialise over the next two decades,' Mr Albanese said.

Source: Extract from Peter Klinger, 'Rio faith in China revives $10 bn Pilbara expansion', *The West Australian.*

Learning objective 6

Describe the nature of biological assets and agricultural produce and how to account for them

21.6 Biological assets and agricultural produce

Other important categories of assets, particularly in primary-producing countries such as Australia, are biological assets and agricultural produce. **Biological assets** are defined in IAS 41/AASB 141 *Agriculture* as living animals or plants, and **agricultural produce** is defined as the harvested product of the entity's biological assets. Biological assets and agricultural produce include:

- livestock such as sheep, from which are harvested wool and meat, cattle for dairy products and beef, chickens for eggs and meat, pigs for meat, and fish and other marine life as part of the industry of aquaculture
- vines, which produce berries, grapes and wine
- trees in a forest, which produce logs and timber
- bushes and other plants, which produce tea, coffee, sugar cane, fruit and vegetables
- exotic animals such as angora goats and alpacas for wool, and emus, crocodiles and kangaroos for meat.

IAS 41/AASB 141 requires all biological assets and agricultural produce controlled by an entity to be recognised in the accounting records when their fair values or costs can be determined with a faithfully representative, verifiable measure and it is probable that the future economic benefits associated with the assets will eventuate. The basis for measurement of *biological assets* is the fair value less estimated point-of-sale costs (hereafter referred to as **net fair value**). However, if a faithfully representative measure of fair values is not possible, then biological assets are to be measured at cost less any accumulated depreciation and any impairment losses only until fair values can be estimated.

882 **Part 5** Accounting regulation of assets and liabilities

Agricultural produce harvested from the entity's biological assets is also measured at net fair value. This measurement is regarded as the cost of the produce for the purpose of applying IAS 2/AASB 102 *Inventories*; consequently, the value cannot be increased above this deemed cost, but can be written down in applying the lower of cost and net realisable value rule.

A gain or loss arising from *initial* recognition of a biological asset or agricultural produce at net fair value must be included in the entity's profit or loss for the period in which it arises. Similarly, for any change in the net fair value of a biological asset in *subsequent* periods, the entity must recognise this change as a gain or loss in the income statement for the period in which the change arises. This is done by debiting (crediting) the asset and crediting (debiting) an appropriately titled gain (loss) account, depending on the nature of the biological asset. However, as soon as the produce of a biological asset becomes non-living (e.g. the fruit picked from the trees) or the asset itself becomes non-living, either through harvest, felling or slaughter, the non-living agricultural produce must be accounted for as inventory. The initial net fair value of the agricultural produce is then regarded as its cost immediately after it becomes non-living.

The treatment of biological assets and agricultural products on a net fair value basis is considered to provide more relevant information to the users of financial statements, because the historical cost of these assets may have very little to do with their value. For example, it is more useful to determine the net fair value from a successful lambing season than to measure the historical cost of the birth of lambs. Assigning historical costs to natural increase and to budding trees is a meaningless activity.

21.7 Intangible assets

Learning objective 7

Describe the nature of intangible assets and the problems of accounting for them

There are certain assets that appear to have no physical substance but derive their value from the future economic benefits that may eventuate for the entity that controls them. These types of assets are often referred to as 'intangibles'.

An **intangible asset** is defined in IAS 38/AASB 138 *Intangible Assets* as an identifiable non-monetary asset without physical substance. They are usually held for use in the production or supply of goods or services, for rental to others, or for administrative purposes. Some assets that lack physical substance, such as accounts receivable, are not regarded as intangible assets because they are monetary in nature, i.e. their future benefits are measured by a fixed number of dollars receivable.

Assets may be further classified as *identifiable* or *unidentifiable*. **Identifiable assets** are those that are 'separable', that is, capable of being separated or divided from the entity and sold or transferred or rented or exchanged or licensed. Some intangibles, such as patents, trademarks, brand names, franchises, licences, copyrights and mastheads, are often called identifiable intangibles. If any assets cannot be separated from the entity, they are regarded as 'unidentifiable assets' and are referred to as 'goodwill'. Goodwill is discussed in a later section of this chapter.

Separately acquired intangibles

The basic principles followed in IAS 38/AASB 138 to account for intangible assets are similar to those used to account for property, plant and equipment. Those intangibles that are purchased by an entity are recorded initially at their cost (without GST). Accounting for intangibles is somewhat more difficult, however, because the apparent lack of physical substance makes their identification and valuation more difficult.

Consequently, IAS 38/AASB 138 requires an intangible asset acquired externally to be recognised only if the 'cost' of the asset can be measured, assuming that the future economic benefits from the asset will probably flow to the entity. As with property, plant and equipment, the cost of an intangible asset comprises its purchase price, including import duties, any non-refundable GST and any directly attributable expenditure on preparing the asset for its intended use, including professional fees for legal services.

Intangible assets may also be acquired as a result of a business combination, where one entity acquires the net assets of another entity. The accounting treatment of intangibles acquired in a business combination is covered in more advanced texts.

Internally generated intangibles

The fact that many intangibles are internally generated and not acquired in an arm's-length transaction causes valuation problems, and the standard states that any internally generated intangible can be recognised only if its 'cost' can be measured. It is argued in IAS 38/AASB 138 that certain internally generated items will never satisfy the criteria for recognition (namely brand names, mastheads, publishing titles, customer lists and items similar in substance) and therefore should not be recorded in the accounts. Hence, any of the internally generated brand names described in the scene setter could not appear in the entity's statement of financial position under IAS 38/AASB 138.

Nevertheless, for other internally generated intangibles (e.g. patents, copyrights), the entity must determine whether the intangible is in the 'research' phase or the 'development' phase. In this context, **research** is defined as an original and planned investigation undertaken with the prospect of gaining new scientific or technical knowledge and understanding. **Development** is the application of research knowledge to a plan or design for the production of new materials, products, processes, systems or services before commercial production. It is argued in IAS 38/AASB 138 that no internally generated intangible asset arising from the research phase should be recognised and that all expenditure on the research phase should be recognised as an expense when incurred.

However, an intangible asset arising from development can be recognised as an asset, but only if the entity can demonstrate *all* of the following:

- the technical feasibility of completing the intangible asset so that it will be available for use or sale
- its intention to complete the asset and use or sell it
- its ability to use or sell the asset
- how the asset will generate probable future economic benefits, including a demonstration that a market exists for the asset or its products
- the availability of adequate resources to complete the development and to use or sell the asset
- its ability to measure the expenditure on the asset in the development phase.

These tests are more stringent than for internally generated property, plant and equipment, and it is expected that few internally generated intangibles will satisfy such criteria, even though they may be quite valuable and information as to their existence may be relevant for the decision making of user groups.

Intangibles subsequent to initial recognition

The treatment of any additional costs incurred on an intangible asset after its purchase or its completion is similar to the treatment of subsequent costs on property, plant and equipment, as provided in IAS 16/AASB 116 (discussed in the previous chapter). In other words, subsequent costs must be added to the cost of the intangible asset only if they will enable the asset to generate future economic benefits.

IAS 38/AASB 138 establishes that intangible assets, after initial recognition, should be carried in the accounting records at cost less any accumulated amortisation (explained below) and impairment losses (explained earlier). However, IAS 38/AASB 138 also permits an alternative treatment, allowing intangible assets to be revalued provided that:

- the revaluation is to its fair value, as determined by reference to an active market
- revaluations are made with sufficient regularity so that the carrying amount does not differ materially from fair value at the end of the reporting period
- all other assets of the same class are revalued
- any increase in the valuation of the intangible is credited directly to equity as a revaluation surplus, and any decrease is recognised as an expense.

As there are limited active markets for intangible assets, it is expected that revaluations will be rare and that most intangibles will be recorded at cost, and amortised if required.

Whenever intangible assets are retired, disposed of or sold, the accounting treatment is the same as that for other non-current assets, as discussed earlier in this chapter.

Amortisation

The allocation of the depreciable amount of intangibles to the periods benefiting from their use is called **amortisation**. Amortisation is therefore similar to depreciation of property, plant and equipment. For many years accountants supported the view that some intangible assets had unlimited lives and therefore should not be amortised. IAS 38/AASB 138 accepts this view and requires the entity to assess each intangible asset to see whether its useful life is finite or indefinite. If the intangible asset arises from contractual or other legal rights, the useful life cannot exceed the period of those rights, but may be shorter, depending on the period of time over which the entity plans to use the asset. An intangible asset with a finite useful life must be amortised on a systematic basis over that useful life. Residual values for such intangibles are assumed to be zero unless there is an active market for the asset and residual values can be determined from that market, or there is a commitment by a third party to buy the asset at the end of its useful life.

The amortisation method used must reflect the pattern in which the asset's future economic benefits are consumed by the entity. If the pattern cannot be determined with a faithfully representative measure, the straight-line method must be used. An Accumulated Amortisation account should be used, with the amortisation entry consisting of a debit to Amortisation Expense and a credit to Accumulated Amortisation.

For an intangible asset with an indefinite useful life, amortisation must not occur. Furthermore, the useful life of the asset must be reviewed each period to determine whether events and circumstances still continue to support the indefinite life assumption. The entity is also required to test such an intangible asset for impairment under IAS 36/AASB 136. This is achieved annually by comparing the asset's carrying amount with its recoverable amount, or during a period if there is an indication that the asset may be impaired.

Patents and research and development costs

A **patent** is an exclusive right to produce and sell a particular product or to use a specific process for a period of 20 years. The reason for issuing patents is to encourage the invention of new machines, processes and mechanical devices.

Entities spend millions of dollars yearly on research and development for new products and new processes. These expenditures are vital in contributing to economic growth and increasing productivity. For many years, some business entities charged research and development costs to expense when incurred, and other businesses carried such expenditures forward as assets and amortised them over future periods. Because of this lack of uniformity, IAS 38/AASB 138 does not allow research costs to be recognised as an intangible asset. Research expenditure must be recognised as an expense when incurred. Only development costs that satisfy all the requirements discussed on page 884 can be carried forward as an asset.

Consequently, most research and development expenditures are charged to expense as incurred. The only additional costs involved in a patent developed internally are the legal fees paid to obtain the patent. Because these fees are usually relatively small, they too are generally charged to expense as incurred.

When a patent is *purchased* from its inventor or holder, rather than developed internally, the purchase price should be debited to the Patents account. For example, if a patent is purchased for $80 000 on 4 July, the entry is:

July	4	Patents	80 000	
		Cash at Bank		80 000
		(Purchase of a patent)		

Alternatively, this patent may have been *internally generated*. Some of the development costs incurred, $30 000, were considered to be associated directly with this patent, and had been carried forward previously as an asset. The entry to record this patent on 4 July, consistent with IAS 38/ AASB 138 is:

June	4	Patents	30 000	
		Development Costs		30 000
		(The cost of an internally generated patent)		

Although a patent grants exclusive rights to the holder for 20 years, new inventions often make the patent obsolete earlier. The valuation of a patent should therefore be amortised over its useful life with a maximum of 20 years. If the patent recorded above is expected to have a useful life of 10 years, the following adjusting entry is made each year to record amortisation:

June	30	Amortisation Expense – Patents	3 000	
		Accumulated Amortisation – Patents		3 000
		(Amortisation of patents)		

Amortisation expense is reported as an expense and accumulated amortisation is shown as a deduction from patents as follows:

Patents	$30 000	
Accumulated amortisation	3 000	$27 000

Copyrights

A **copyright** is an exclusive right to reproduce and sell an artistic or published work. The exclusive right exists for the life of the author plus 70 years. Currently, if a copyright is *purchased* from its holder, the purchase price is debited to a Copyrights account and amortised over its useful life. Under IAS 38/AASB 138, any *internally generated* copyrights are accounted for in the same way as patents. Because it is difficult to determine how long benefits will be received, most copyrights are amortised over a relatively short period. A copyright is an asset, as it may have significant future economic benefits to its holder. If no faithfully representative value can be determined for a copyright, then the copyright cannot be recognised as a separate asset, but becomes part of the entity's goodwill (see later in this chapter).

Trademarks and brand names

The exclusive right to trademarks and brand names can be obtained by registering them with a government agency. The main cost of developing trademarks and brand names lies in advertising, which should be charged to expense in the period incurred. Nevertheless, if the promotional or advertising expenditure is incurred in the current period in connection with the introduction of a new product or new model, it may give rise to income in a future period that can be directly attributable to that promotional expenditure. In this case, it is argued that such costs could be regarded as an asset, i.e. as a cost of developing the trademark or brand name. However, under IAS 38/ AASB 138, any *internally generated* trademark or brand name cannot be recognised as an asset. If a trademark or brand name is *acquired externally*, its cost should be debited to the appropriate intangible asset account and amortised over its useful life.

Franchises

A **franchise** is a right granted by a company or government body to conduct business at a specified location or in a specific geographical area. Examples are the right to operate a fast-food operation such as McDonald's and Hungry Jacks or a menswear store such as Roger David and Lowes, and the right to operate a municipal or suburban bus service. Franchises are very common in Australia and represent a significant export business, as discussed in the scene setter to this chapter. The initial cost of a franchise may be substantial and should be capitalised and amortised over the term of the franchise or useful life, whichever is shorter. If initial franchise costs are immaterial, they may be expensed when incurred. Periodic annual payments under a franchise agreement should be expensed.

Wheeling and dealing in a business combination

For some people, acquiring a business adds up to 'buying a job'. Others have it in their blood to run their own enterprise or see it as a good pre-retirement investment option. However, when it comes to either buying or selling a business, many still miss some fundamental knowledge that can financially make or break the experience. For instance, most vendors possess an unrealistic belief about how much their business is worth. And it's no surprise that sellers are often disappointed by the extent to which they have to temper expectations in order to do a deal — particularly in tighter credit markets.

On the flip side are the business buyers who fail to check a vendor's claims against the actual financial statements only to find that promises of a 'magical' cash component fail to materialise. Many of them have no clear idea of what type of business they want to buy, just that they want to work for themselves.

So, what are the golden rules in such transactions?

What business can learn from the dealmakers

- Be realistic about price when selling a business. Find out what the market is prepared to pay for a similar business.
- When selling a business, arrive at a fair price — and be satisfied with it — to reflect revenue and profit growth. Buyers will pay a premium for good operating businesses. But don't expect buyers to pay top dollar for ordinary or disappointing performers.

- A vendor who has built a strong business should not sell for a big discount just to get out. Such a business decision will probably be regretted later.
- If selling, seriously consider the first offer because it's often the best. Be a tough, reasonable and fair negotiator. Buyers can start to question if there is something wrong with a business that's been on the market for a long time.
- When buying a business, don't pay for potential. Why should you?
- Don't buy a business on word-of-mouth figures. 'Don't buy what you can't see.' A vendor must be able to prove revenue and profit growth in income statements before consideration is given to buying the business.
- Aim for at least a 30 per cent annual return on capital. Focus on buying businesses with strong recurring income and a growing client base. Fall in love with profit potential, not the product.
- Check how long a business has been established and conduct market research to establish continuing demand for products and services.
- Consider the pros and cons before buying a franchise business. Benefits include training and support, marketing and brand recognition.

Source: Extract from Anthony Black, 'Wheeling and dealing', *InTheBlack*. *This article was written by the financial journalist Anthony Black, who has extensive experience writing on corporate and financial matters. For enquiries on past articles refer to 'anthonyblack3@bigpond.com'.*

21.8 Goodwill in a business combination

Learning objective 8

Describe the nature of goodwill and how to account for goodwill acquired by an entity

The term **goodwill** is used by accountants and the public to mean various things. It is often thought of as the favourable reputation of an entity among its customers. From an accounting standpoint, however, goodwill has a special meaning not limited to good customer relations. Goodwill is defined in IFRS 3/AASB 3 *Business Combinations* as the 'future economic benefits arising from assets that are not capable of being individually identified and separately recognised'. Goodwill is to be regarded by the acquiring entity in a business combination as a non-current asset. It arises from many factors, including customer confidence, superior management, favourable location, manufacturing efficiency, good employee relations and market penetration. A successful entity continually develops these factors, but the expenditures made in doing so cannot be individually identified with each of these factors. The term 'goodwill' is therefore used to describe all these unidentifiable assets that cannot be separately measured.

Goodwill may be purchased in an exchange transaction or generated internally by an entity. From an accounting viewpoint, under IAS 38/AASB 138 *only purchased goodwill is to be recorded in the accounts*. The reason for this is that purchased goodwill can be measured on the basis of the amount paid for it in a business combination, whereas internally generated goodwill is not capable of such measurement.

Goodwill cannot be purchased or sold as a separate item, hence the recognition of purchased goodwill in the entity's accounts occurs only when the entity has acquired another entity or part of such an entity in a business combination. The consideration transferred by the acquiring entity to purchase another entity is assigned firstly to the fair values of the identifiable assets and liabilities acquired, and any remainder is recorded as goodwill.

To illustrate, assume that Entity A acquires the business of Entity B on 1 July 2014. At acquisition date, the carrying amounts of Entity B's identifiable net assets and their fair values are as listed on the next page.

	Carrying amounts	Fair values
Accounts receivable	$ 10 000	$ 10 000
Allowance for doubtful debts	(500)	(700)
Inventory	21 000	24 000
Machinery (net)	60 000	53 000
Motor vehicles (net)	35 000	40 000
Land	25 000	34 000
Buildings	45 000	49 000
Accounts payable	(9 000)	(9 000)
Mortgage payable	(20 000)	(20 000)
	$166 500	$180 300

The consideration transferred by Entity A in acquiring Entity B is $200 000 in cash. Hence, Entity A has also purchased from Entity B something in excess of the fair value of the identifiable net assets which is equal to $180 300. This additional asset is goodwill of $19 700 ($200 000 – $180 300). The entries (in general journal form) made by Entity A to take over Entity B's assets are as shown below (note that generally, when existing businesses are acquired, no GST is payable):

2014				
July	1	Accounts Receivable	10 000	
		Inventory	24 000	
		Machinery	53 000	
		Motor Vehicles	40 000	
		Land	34 000	
		Buildings	49 000	
		Goodwill	19 700	
		Allowance for Doubtful Debts		700
		Accounts Payable		9 000
		Mortgage Payable		20 000
		Payable to Entity B		200 000
		(Acquisition of net assets from Entity B)		
	1	Payable to Entity B	200 000	
		Cash at Bank		200 000
		(Payment of consideration transferred to Entity B)		

Note carefully that the assets brought into the records of Entity A are valued at fair value, as fair value represents the cost paid by Entity A for these assets on acquisition date. The carrying amounts of the assets in Entity B's records are of little interest to Entity A. Entity A wants to measure the cost of the assets to itself rather than the cost to somebody else. Note also the use of a Payable account to record the consideration payable to the creditor, Entity B. The Payable account is then closed when the consideration is paid or transferred. Goodwill of $19 700 is recorded as the difference between the consideration transferred and the fair value of the identifiable assets and liabilities acquired. In accordance with IFRS 3/AASB 3, the goodwill must remain in the accounts at cost less any accumulated impairment losses. Any impairment of goodwill under IAS 36/ AASB 136 is recognised as an expense.

If the entity believes that the value assigned to goodwill ($19 700) exceeds the value of the unidentifiable assets acquired, the difference does not constitute goodwill and should be written off immediately to expense.

In rare circumstances, the consideration transferred by the acquirer may be less than the sum of the fair values of the identifiable assets and liabilities acquired. If so, the acquirer (Entity A) must first *reassess the measurement* of the fair value of the consideration transferred and the fair values of the assets and liabilities acquired. If the entity is satisfied with the measurement, then the difference between the consideration transferred and the sum of fair values is to be recognised immediately as a gain in profit, because the entity has made a 'bargain purchase'.

Agricultural produce, p. 882
Amortisation, pp. 881, 885
Area of interest, p. 880
Biological assets, p. 882
Carrying amount, p. 868
Cash-generating unit, p. 873
Composite-rate depreciation, p. 878
Copyright, p. 886

Development, p. 884
Fair value, p. 868
Franchise, p. 886
Goodwill, p. 887
Identifiable assets, p. 883
Impairment loss, p. 873
Intangible assets, p. 883
Net fair value, p. 882

Other comprehensive income, p. 869
Patent, p. 885
Recoverable amount, p. 873
Research, p. 884
Revaluation decrease, p. 868
Revaluation increase, p. 868
Value in use, p. 873

DISCUSSION QUESTIONS

1. Discuss whether and how a company should account for a revaluation increase and a revaluation decrease on property, plant and equipment. Discuss also the accounting treatment if such an increase or decrease is reversed.

2. What is meant by 'recoverable amount'? When are assets to be written down to recoverable amount? What must an entity do if it is unable to determine the recoverable amount of an individual asset?

3. The following statement was included in the annual report of a company: 'All research, advertising and promotion costs are charged to expense in the year in which they are incurred. This enables the company to begin each new year with a 'clean slate'. Each new year benefits from the future earnings generated from new products developed and advertised in previous periods, and there is no offsetting by amortisation of introductory costs.' Discuss whether this treatment of research, advertising and promotion costs complies with requirements of current accounting standards and the definition of an asset.

4. Discuss whether internally generated intangible assets should be treated in the same way as acquired intangible assets.

5. In order to comply with IAS 38/AASB 138 *Intangible Assets*, how must an entity handle goodwill on the acquisition of the net assets of another entity? Is this treatment consistent with the principle of recording all assets acquired at cost? Explain why or why not.

6. 'Machinery is an asset. It may be disclosed as a tangible asset, an intangible asset, or as part of goodwill.' Discuss.

7. Aquarium Ltd has been developing specialised computer software for its own use. At the end of the reporting period, the company has spent $260 000 on the project. The final date for full implementation of the software is scheduled to be in 6 months time. However, the management accountant believes that the project will not be ready on time and that the company will have to acquire a commercial package instead, which will not be as efficient as the specialised software, but will be better than having no operational software at all. Others in the software department agree with her. In the financial statements, how should Aquarium Ltd account for the development costs of $260 000? Why?

8. Several years ago, Baxter Ltd acquired for $160 000 a patent for the manufacture of special 'seal-tight' plastic containers. After 5 years, the manufacture of these containers was discontinued because of the development of a new, more environmentally friendly container by a competitor. Baxter Ltd is continuing to deduct amortisation expense of $8000 per year based on the patent's life of 20 years. Discuss whether this treatment is in accord with accounting standards.

9. What are biological assets? How should they be accounted for in a company's accounting records?

10. Outline the treatment of exploration, evaluation and development costs on a mineral reserve in accordance with the latest accounting standards.

LO 1

Exercise 21.1 REVALUATIONS (INCREASE AND DECREASE)

Coogee Ltd has disclosed the following non-current asset classes as at 30 June 2013:

Machinery	$200 000	
Less: Accumulated depreciation	100 000	$100 000
Buildings	$300 000	
Less: Accumulated depreciation	120 000	$180 000

At 1 July 2013, the directors of Coogee Ltd decide to adopt the revaluation model and revalue the non-current asset classes to the following fair values:

Machinery	$ 85 000
Buildings	200 000

Required

Prepare general journal entries to record the revaluations, including any closing entries at the end of the reporting period.

LO 3

Exercise 21.2 DERECOGNITION OF ASSETS

Bankstown Pty Ltd scrapped the following machines as worthless:

Machine	Cost	Accumulated depreciation 2 Jan. 2010	Removal expense paid	Date of purchase	Date of disposal
1	$ 9 600	$ 9 600	—	2/1/09	2/1/13
2	15 000	13 500	$900	30/6/08	2/1/13
3	32 000	28 000	—	30/6/09	1/4/13

Depreciation expense was recorded last on 31 December 2012.

Required

Prepare separate entries to record the disposal of the machines by Bankstown Pty Ltd.

LO 3

Exercise 21.3 SALE OF NON-CURRENT ASSETS

On 3 January 2011, Bondi Ltd paid $33 000 for a machine with a useful life of 10 years and a residual value of $3000. On 31 December 2015, accumulated depreciation on the machine was $15 000. The machine was sold on 31 May 2016. Ignore GST.

Required

A. Prepare a general journal entry to record depreciation expense on the machine for the 5 months in 2016. Use the straight-line depreciation method.
B. Prepare an entry to record the sale of the machine on 31 May 2016, assuming a selling price of:
  1. $16 000
  2. $17 800.

Exercise 21.4 NON-CURRENT ASSET DERECOGNITION

Granville Ltd acquired a tractor with a cost of $100 000, an estimated useful life of 8 years and a residual value of $20 000. Sum-of-years-digits depreciation was used. Ignore GST.

Required

Prepare journal entries for each of the following events:
1. Sell the tractor for cash of $60 000 after 2 years of use.
2. Trade in the tractor for a $50 000 allowance after 4 years on another tractor with a cash price of $110 000.
3. Scrap the tractor after 7 years of usage. The tractor is given to a scrap dealer who pays $500 to remove it.

Exercise 21.5 EXCHANGE OF SIMILAR ASSETS

On 3 January 2013, Parramatta Ltd exchanged a machine with a cost of $65 000 and accumulated depreciation of $40 000 for a new similar machine with a cash price of $60 000. Ignore GST.

Required
A. Prepare general journal entries to record the exchange of the machines, assuming a trade-in allowance of $20 000 was received for the old machine and $40 000 was paid in cash.
B. Prepare general journal entries to record the exchange of machines, assuming a trade-in allowance of $27 000 for the old machine and $33 000 was paid in cash.

Exercise 21.6 EXCHANGE OF DISSIMILAR ASSETS

Penrith Ltd exchanged machinery with a cost of $350 000 and accumulated depreciation of $180 000 for a parcel of land. There were no other assets given in exchange. Ignore GST.

Required
Prepare general journal entries to record the exchange assuming:
1. the trade-in value of the machinery was $190 000
2. the trade-in value of the machinery was $150 000.

Exercise 21.7 REVALUATION AND DERECOGNITION

On 1 January 2010, Lidcombe Ltd acquired two identical pieces of equipment for a total cost of $440 000 plus GST. It was estimated that each item would have a useful life of 10 years and a residual value of $50 000. The company uses the straight-line method of depreciation and its end of reporting period is 30 June.

On 1 July 2016, the company changed its accounting policy and revalued each item of equipment upwards by a total of $80 000, based on an independent valuer's report, to fair value. There was no need to revise useful lives or residual amounts. On 31 December 2017, one of the items of equipment was sold for $90 000 cash plus GST.

Required
Prepare entries (in general journal format) in relation to the equipment from acquisition date to 31 December 2017.

Exercise 21.8 MINERAL RESOURCES

Maroubra Ltd, which operated a silver, lead and zinc mine, was purchased by Woolloomooloo Ltd for $63 000 000 (residual value $5 000 000). It is estimated that the mine will produce 15 million tonnes of ore. Mining equipment with a useful life of 16 years was installed at a cost of $3 200 000. Extraction of ore will exhaust the mine in about 10 years, after which time the equipment will be abandoned.

Required
A. Prepare entries for Woolloomooloo Ltd to record amortisation of the mine and depreciation of the mining equipment for the first year, assuming that 600 000 tonnes of silver, lead and zinc ore were mined and sold.
B. Prepare a partial statement of financial position for Woolloomooloo Ltd showing how the mine and the mining equipment would be reported at the end of the first year of operations.

Manly Ltd uses the composite-rate method to record depreciation of its store equipment. On 1 January 2013, the company owned the following store equipment (ignore GST):

Item	Cost	Residual value	Useful life
Display cases	$ 73 000	$3 000	10 years
Cash registers	28 000	8 000	5 years
Shopping trolleys	30 000	6 000	6 years
Shelving	30 000	2 000	7 years
Display racks	12 000	1 800	4 years
	$173 000		

Required

A. Calculate the composite rate for depreciating the store equipment.
B. Prepare the entry to record depreciation expense on 31 December 2013, assuming the store equipment account had a balance of $190 000 at year-end.
C. Prepare general journal entries to record the sale of a display case for $1500. The case had an original cost of $2600.
D. Prepare general journal entries to record the exchange of a cash register with an original cost of $3200 for a new cash register with a cash price of $5000. The company received a trade-in allowance of $1400 for the old register and paid the balance of $3600 in cash.

Richmond Ltd is considering the purchase of Windsor Ltd, which produces a product that Richmond Ltd uses in its manufacturing process. Relevant data for Windsor Ltd are:

Fair value of identifiable assets	$2 400 000
Fair value of identifiable liabilities	700 000

Required

A. Determine the price Richmond Ltd would pay for goodwill in acquiring Windsor Ltd if the total consideration transferred in the business combination was $2 000 000, in cash.
B. Prepare entries for Richmond Ltd in general journal form to record the acquisition of Windsor Ltd for $1 500 000 cash.

During 2013, Randwick Ltd disposed of four different non-current assets. On 1 January 2013 the accounts showed the following:

Asset	Cost	Residual value	Useful life	Accumulated depreciation
Van No. 4	$38 000	$8 000	5 years	$18 000
Van No. 6	44 000	4 000	4 years	15 000
Machine A	64 000	8 000	10 years	34 800
Machine B	78 000	6 000	15 years	38 400

Randwick Ltd depreciates its vans and machines by the straight-line method and records depreciation to the nearest month. Assets were disposed of as follows:

Van No. 6, which was not insured, was completely destroyed by fire on 6 January 2013. A towing company was paid $600 to remove the van and to clean up any debris.
Van No. 4 was traded in on a new van on 3 July 2013. The new van had a cash price of $46 000. The old van plus cash of $28 000 were given in exchange.

Machine A was sold for $27 000 cash on 1 October 2013.

Machine B was traded in on a new machine with a cash price of $81 000 on 22 December 2013. The old machine plus cash of $40 000 were given in exchange.

Required

Prepare all general journal entries needed to account for the above transactions. Ignore GST.

LO 3

Exercise 21.12 LEDGER ACCOUNTS FOR NON-CURRENT ASSET ACQUISITION AND DERECOGNITION

On 1 July 2013, Hornsby Pty Ltd owned several delivery vehicles that had cost a total of $155 000. Accumulated depreciation on these vehicles to 1 July 2013 amounted to $73 000.

On 30 September 2013, Hornsby Pty Ltd acquired a new delivery vehicle and traded in one vehicle that had cost $32 000 and which had accumulated depreciation of $14 400 up to 1 July 2013. The full price of the new vehicle was $29 500 and the trade-in value of the old vehicle was agreed at $18 400. Ignore GST.

On 31 December 2013, an additional delivery vehicle was purchased for $34 000 cash.

Depreciation is calculated at the rate of 20% p.a. on the diminishing balance.

Required

Prepare the following accounts for the year ended 30 June 2014:

1. Delivery Vehicles
2. Accumulated Depreciation – Delivery Vehicles.

LO 1, 2, 3

Exercise 21.13 NON-CURRENT ASSET REVALUATION MODEL

On 30 June 2013, Clovelly Ltd reported the following information for equipment in its statement of financial position:

Equipment (at cost)	$1 000 000
Accumulated depreciation	300 000
	$ 700 000

Investigation of the property and plant records showed that the equipment consisted of two items: a machine (no. 1) that cost the company $600 000 and had a carrying amount of $360 000 at 30 June 2013, and another machine (no. 2) that originally cost $400 000 and had a carrying amount at 30 June 2013 of $340 000. Both machines are depreciated on a straight-line basis over 10 years.

On 1 January 2014, the directors of Clovelly Ltd decided to switch the valuation method from the cost model to the revaluation model. Machine no. 1 was revalued to its fair value of $420 000, with an expected future useful life of 6 years, and machine no. 2 was revalued to $350 000, with an expected remaining useful life of 7 years.

On 30 June 2014, the fair value of machine no. 1 was assessed at $400 000, and the future useful life was estimated as 5 years. For machine no. 2, fair value was assessed to be only $280 000, and its future useful life to be 4 years because of a certain degree of commercial obsolescence.

Required

Prepare general journal entries for Clovelly Ltd for the equipment during the period from 1 July 2013 to 30 June 2014.

Drummoyne Ltd acquired the business of Mascot Ltd for a cash outlay of $4 400 000 on 1 July 2013. The summarised balance sheet of Mascot Ltd on that date was as follows:

MASCOT LTD
Summarised Balance Sheet
As at 1 July 2013

Assets	
Cash at bank	$ 165 000
Accounts receivable	330 000
Inventories	770 000
Land	660 000
Plant and equipment (net)	2 500 000
Total assets	$4 425 000
Liabilities and equity	
Accounts payable	460 000
Bank loan payable	1 200 000
Share capital	2 000 000
Retained earnings	765 000
Total liabilities and equity	$4 425 000

Most of the assets were recorded at fair value except for inventories and land, which were assessed to have fair values of $800 000 and $900 000 respectively.

Required

A. Determine the amount that Drummoyne Ltd should record as goodwill or bargain purchase on 1 July 2013.

B. Prepare journal entries in the records of Drummoyne Ltd to acquire the business of Mascot Ltd on 1 July 2013.

C. Discuss how your answer would differ if Drummoyne Ltd had paid $3 800 000 cash to acquire the business of Mascot Ltd.

Exercise 21.15 NON-CURRENT ASSET DEPRECIATION AND DERECOGNITION

LO 3

The following information was obtained from the accounting records of Chatswood Ltd.

	Vehicle A	Vehicle B	Vehicle C
Acquisition date	1 July 2012	1 July 2013	1 July 2014
Cost	$30 800	$28 800	$39 600
Residual value	$2 000	$2 400	$4 400
Useful life (in years)	5	6	8
Depreciation method	Straight-line	Straight-line	Sum-of-years-digits

On 1 July 2013, vehicle A was traded in for vehicle B. The trade-in price for vehicle A was determined to be $21 000.

Required

Prepare the general journal entries for all vehicle transactions from 1 July 2012 to 30 June 2015 in the accounting records of Chatswood Ltd.

Problem 21.1   METHODS OF DERECOGNISING A NON-CURRENT ASSET ★   **LO 3**

Balmain Ltd acquired two new machines for cash on 1 January 2011. The cost of machine A was $40 000, and of machine B, $100 000. Each machine was expected to have a useful life of 10 years, and residual values were estimated at $2000 for machine A and $5000 for machine B.

Because of technological advances, Balmain Ltd decided to replace machine A. It traded in machine A on 31 March 2015 for a new machine, C, which cost $64 000. $28 000 trade-in was allowed for machine A, and the balance of machine C's cost was paid in cash. Machine C was expected to have a useful life of 8 years and a residual value of $8000.

On 2 July 2015, extensive repairs were carried out on machine B for $66 000 cash. Balmain Ltd expected these repairs to extend machine B's useful life by 4 years and it revised machine B's estimated residual value to $13 450. Machine B was eventually sold on 1 April 2017 for $115 000 cash.

Balmain Ltd uses the straight-line depreciation method, recording depreciation to the nearest whole month. The end of the reporting period is 30 June.

Required

A. Prepare general journal entries to record the above transactions and depreciation journal entries required at the end of each reporting period up to 30 June 2017.

B. Prepare the following ledger accounts for the period 1 January 2011 to 1 July 2017:
  1. Machinery
  2. Accumulated Depreciation – Machinery.

Problem 21.2   METHODS OF DERECOGNISING A NON-CURRENT ASSET ★   **LO 3**

On 2 January 2012, Mosman Ltd purchased a machine for $39 000. The machine had a useful life of 5 years and a residual value of $4000. Straight-line depreciation is used. The machine is to be disposed of on 1 July 2016. Ignore GST. Mosman balances its books on 31 December.

Required

A. What entry should be made to record depreciation before the disposal?

B. Prepare journal entries to record the disposal of the machine under each of the following assumptions:
  1. The machine is sold for $20 000 cash.
  2. The machine is sold for $11 500 cash.
  3. The machine and cash of $20 000 are exchanged for a new machine with a cash price of $33 000.
  4. The machine was completely destroyed by fire and cash of $11 000 was received from the insurance company.
  5. The machine and cash of $20 000 are exchanged for a new machine with a cash price of $40 000.

Problem 21.3   REVALUATION, REVERSALS AND DEPRECIATION ★   **LO 1**

Ryde Ltd has a policy of revaluing its motor vehicles to fair value. The details at 30 June 2014 relating to Ryde Ltd's motor vehicles, which had previously been revalued upwards by $7000, are as follows:

Motor vehicles	$88 000	
Less: Accumulated depreciation	22 000	$66 000

At the date of the revaluation increase (1 July 2013) the vehicles had a zero residual value and a useful life of 4 years. Depreciation has been calculated using the straight-line method. On 31 December 2014, Ryde Ltd was informed that the fair value of the vehicles was $50 000. The useful life and residual value have not changed. At 30 June 2015, the carrying amounts are not materially different from fair values.

Required

A. Prepare the necessary general journal entries at 31 December 2014.

B. Calculate depreciation expense at 30 June 2015.

C. How would the motor vehicles be shown in financial statements at 30 June 2015?

Problem 21.4 DERECOGNITION OF ASSETS ★★ LO 3, 5

Wollongong Ltd reported the following non-current assets at 30 June 2013:

Land		$ 6 000 000
Buildings	$53 000 000	
Less: Accumulated Depreciation – Buildings	24 200 000	28 800 000
Equipment	80 000 000	
Less: Accumulated Depreciation – Equipment	10 000 000	70 000 000
Total non-current assets		$104 800 000

During the year 2013–14, the following transactions occurred:

Oct. 1   Purchased land for $4 400 000.

Nov. 1   Sold equipment that cost $1 500 000 when purchased on 1 July 2010. The equipment was sold for $900 000.

Dec. 1   Sold land purchased on 30 April 2004 for $4 000 000. The land's original cost was $600 000.

Jan. 1   Purchased equipment for $5 000 000 cash.

May 1   Scrapped equipment that had cost $1 000 000 when purchased on 30 June 2005. No residual value was received.

Required

A. Prepare journal entries to record the above transactions. Wollongong Ltd uses straight-line depreciation for buildings and equipment. The buildings are estimated to have a 50-year life and no residual value. The equipment is estimated to have a 10-year useful life and no residual value.

B. Record adjusting entries for depreciation for the year ended 30 June 2014.

C. Prepare the non-current assets section of Wollongong Ltd's statement of financial position as at 30 June 2014.

Problem 21.5 EXCHANGES AND DERECOGNITION ★★ LO 3, 5

Cronulla Ltd entered into the following transactions during the year ended 31 December 2013. Ignore GST.

Jan. 4   Scrapped a machine that cost $15 000 and had accumulated depreciation of $13 000. Disposal costs of $300 were incurred.

Mar. 30   Sold for $8000 a machine that had cost $16 000 on 2 January 2008. The machine's useful life and residual value were 5 years and $6000 respectively. Accumulated depreciation on the machine to 31 December 2012 was $8000.

April 1   Exchanged a machine with a cost of $42 000 and accumulated depreciation to the date of exchange of $28 000 for a new similar machine. A trade-in allowance of $14 000 was received for the old machine and $30 000 was paid in cash.

July 1   Exchanged a block of land that had cost $90 000 for machinery. The fair value of the land given up was $100 000.

Sept. 1   Exchanged a building with a cost of $125 000 and accumulated depreciation to the date of exchange of $90 000 for a machine. The fair value of the building at this date was $40 000.

Oct. 31   Sold for $20 000 cash a machine that cost $48 000 on 1 November 2008. The machine had a useful life of 6 years and a residual value of $6000 when purchased. On 31 December 2012, straight-line depreciation of $7000 p.a. was recorded. No depreciation has yet been recorded for 2013.

Dec. 31   Recorded amortisation of the company's natural gas reserve. The reserve was purchased on 1 January 2013 for $40 000 000. On the date of purchase, the reserve was estimated to contain 16 000 000 units of natural gas and to have a residual value of $4 000 000. One million units of gas were extracted and sold during 2013.

Required

Prepare entries in general journal form to record the above transactions.

Problem 21.6 EXCHANGES OF ASSETS ★★★

The beginning balance in the Machinery control account and Accumulated Depreciation account, and dates in the accounts for various machinery acquisitions and disposals during the year by Epping Ltd are presented below:

Machinery

1/1/13	Balance	93 500			
11/1/13			11/1/13		
25/1/13			25/1/13		
28/4/13			28/4/13		
31/8/13			31/8/13		
			31/12/13	Balance	

Accumulated Depreciation

11/1/13			1/1/13	Balance	69 700
25/1/13			11/1/13		
28/4/13			25/1/13		
31/8/13			28/4/13		
31/12/13	Balance		31/8/13		
			31/12/13		

Epping Ltd records depreciation to the nearest month.

At 1 January 2013, the company held only four items of machinery, and four exchange transactions took place during 2013 as indicated below:

Jan. 11 Exchanged an old machine and $13 000 cash for a similar machine (No. P) with a list price of $16 000. The old machine had a cost of $10 000 and accumulated depreciation of $7000 at the time of the exchange.

Jan. 25 An old machine with a cost of $24 000 and accumulated depreciation at 31 December 2012 of $19 200 was traded in on a new machine (No. Q) having a cash price of $36 000. Depreciation on the old machine for the month of January was $800. A trade-in allowance of $3000 was received and the balance was paid in cash.

April 28 A machine with an original cost of $54 000 and accumulated depreciation on 31 December 2012 of $40 000 was exchanged for a new machine (No. R) with a cash price of $75 000. A trade-in allowance of $10 000 was received and the balance paid in cash. Monthly depreciation on the old machine was $500.

Aug. 31 A machine with a cost of $5500 and a carrying amount at the date of the exchange of $1600 was traded in on a new machine (No. S) with a list price of $7000. A trade-in allowance of $2000 was received and $5000 was paid in cash. The old machine has been depreciated at $50 per month during 2013.

At the dates of acquisition, the useful lives and residual values of the new machines were as follows:

Machine no.	Useful life	Residual value
P	4 years	$ 2 000
Q	5 years	6 000
R	10 years	15 000
S	3 years	1 500

Straight-line depreciation is used by the entity.

Required

A. Prepare in Epping Ltd's accounting records the journal entries (in general journal format) for the acquisition, disposal and depreciation charges for the period 1 January to 31 December 2013.

B. Prepare the Accumulated Depreciation account for the period 1 January 2013 to 31 December 2013.

C. Provide reasons, by referring to appropriate accounting standards, for an entity adopting the straight-line method for depreciating its machinery.

Problem 21.7 DISPOSAL AND REVALUATION INCREASES AND DECREASES ★★

On 1 January 2011, Punchbowl Ltd bought a machine for $33 000 cash; its useful life was 12 years and its residual value was $3000. It was decided to depreciate the machine by the straight-line method. On 30 September 2013, the machine was traded in to Leichhardt Ltd for a new model, the total cost being $25 000. Leichhardt Ltd allowed $17 000 for the old machine. It was decided to depreciate the new machine at the rate of 45% p.a. by the diminishing-balance method. Residual value of the new machine was $7000.

On 1 July 2014, Punchbowl Ltd decided to adopt the revaluation model and revalue its machine upwards to reflect fair values. This represented a 15% increase in the carrying amount of the machine. The diminishing-balance method of depreciation was continued at the same rate. The accounting period ended on 30 June each year. At 30 June 2015, the carrying amount of the machine was approximately equal to fair value.

Required

A. Prepare relevant ledger accounts to record the above transactions up to 30 June 2015. Ignore GST.

B. Show how the asset would appear in the financial statements of Punchbowl Ltd as at 30 June 2012, 30 June 2014 and 30 June 2015.

C. Show the Machinery account and Accumulated Depreciation – Machinery account if the revaluation on 1 July 2014 had been downwards instead of upwards.

Problem 21.8 CORRECTING ERRORS ★★

The following errors were discovered during the current year.

1. Depreciation of machinery, $2140, was incorrectly credited to Accumulated Depreciation – Buildings.

2. A machine with a cost of $22 500 and accumulated depreciation to the date of sale of $16 000 was sold for $8000. The sale was recorded by a debit to Cash at Bank and a credit to Machinery for $8000.

3. Land taxes of $6420 were paid and debited to Land Tax Expense. Of this, $3600 was back taxes from previous years on land purchased during the current year.

4. Delivery equipment, purchased on 1 July for $7900, was debited to the Purchases account. The equipment has a useful life of 4 years and an estimated residual value of $900. The straight-line depreciation method is used for delivery equipment.

5. The cost of installing lighting in the company car park, $12 000, was charged to Maintenance Expense on 4 January. The lights have a useful life of 8 years and no residual value. Assume straight-line depreciation.

6. A machine with a cost of $26 000 and accumulated depreciation to the date of exchange of $19 000 was exchanged on 23 December for a new machine with a cash price of $35 000. A trade-in allowance of $9000 was allowed on the old machine. The following entry was made:

Machinery	33 000	
Accumulated Depreciation – Machinery	19 000	
Machinery		26 000
Cash at Bank		26 000

Required

Prepare general journal entries to correct the errors, assuming the accounting records have not been closed for the current year ending 31 December.

Problem 21.9 REVALUATION AND DISPOSAL ★★

Opposite are extracts from the financial reports of Willoughby Traders Ltd for the years ended 30 June 2013 and 30 June 2014.

WILLOUGHBY TRADERS LTD
Statement of Financial Position (extract)
as at 30 June 2013

NON-CURRENT ASSETS			
Land		$720 000	
Building	$450 000		
Less: Accumulated depreciation	120 000	330 000	
TOTAL NON-CURRENT ASSETS			$1 050 000
EQUITY			
Revaluation surplus		180 000	
Capital at 1 July 2012	140 000		
Add: Profit for year	37 000		
Capital at 30 June 2013		177 000	
TOTAL EQUITY			$ 357 000

WILLOUGHBY TRADERS LTD
Statement of Financial Position (extract)
as at 30 June 2014

NON-CURRENT ASSETS			
Land		$630 000	
Building		280 000	
TOTAL NON-CURRENT ASSETS			$910 000
EQUITY			
Revaluation surplus		90 000	
Capital at 1 July 2013	$177 000		
Add: Profit for year	20 000		
Capital at 30 June 2014		197 000	
TOTAL EQUITY			$287 000

WILLOUGHBY TRADERS LTD
Income Statement (extract)
for the year ended 30 June 2014

EXPENSES	
Supplies expense	$ 3 000
Wages expense	36 540
Depreciation expense – building	30 000
Bad debts expense	8 200
Insurance expense	15 160
Expense on revaluation of building	20 000
Total expenses	$112 900

Additional information

(a) The revaluation surplus at 30 June 2013 was raised entirely as the result of a previous revaluation increase in relation to the land.

(b) No land or buildings were acquired or disposed of during the year ended 30 June 2014.

(c) A revaluation of the land and buildings was carried out on 30 June 2014 after all adjusting entries had been entered and posted. The revaluation adjustment was entered into the accounts on 30 June 2014, and the statement of financial position at that date reflects the fair values in accordance with the revaluation.

(d) After the revaluation, the building was reassessed to have a residual value of $38 000 and a remaining useful life of 15 years. The building is to be depreciated using the straight-line method of depreciation.

(e) The land and buildings were sold on 31 December 2014. A lump sum of $850 000 was received. The proceeds were allocated to the land and buildings at $600 000 and $250 000 respectively. Ignore GST.

Required

A. Calculate the balance of the Accumulated Depreciation – Building account immediately before the revaluation on 30 June 2014.

B. Prepare the general journal entries to record:
   1. the revaluation of the building on 30 June 2014
   2. the revaluation of the land on 30 June 2014
   3. the disposal of the land on 31 December 2014
   4. the disposal of the building on 31 December 2014.

Problem 21.10   REVALUATION, DEPRECIATION, DISPOSAL ★★   LO 1, 3

On 1 January 2011, Cabramatta Ltd purchased two identical new trucks at a total cost of $500 000 plus GST. It was estimated that the trucks would have a useful life of 8 years and a residual value of $100 000 each. Cabramatta Ltd uses the straight-line method of depreciation for all of its equipment. The company's end of reporting period is 31 December.

Required

A. Record the purchase of the trucks on 1 January 2011.

B. Record the depreciation expense on the trucks for 2016.

C. Assume that early in 2017 the company revalued the trucks upwards by $50 000 each and assessed that the trucks would last 4 more years instead of 2 but that they would still have the same residual value. Record all journal entries for the trucks in 2017.

D. Make the necessary entries to record the sale of one of the trucks on 31 December 2017. The truck was sold for $120 000 plus GST. (Assume that the two trucks had the same carrying amount, which equalled their fair values at this date.)

E. How much depreciation expense would be recorded on the second truck during 2021 if it were still being used and if its residual value were still $100 000? Why?

Problem 21.11   INTANGIBLES AND MINERAL RESOURCES ★★   LO 5, 7

The following transactions and events affected the accounts of Narrabeen Ltd for the current year (ignore GST):

1. A patent with a useful life of 10 years was purchased for cash of $900 000 on 3 January last year.

2. On 6 January of the current year, Narrabeen Ltd paid $75 000 in legal fees for the successful defence of a patent infringement suit against the patent purchased in (1) above.

3. On 31 January, a valuable copyright held by the company and internally generated was valued independently at $90 000 — $40 000 of this had been previously included in the asset 'Development Costs'. It is expected that the copyright has a useful life of 6 years.

4. On 6 February of the current year, Narrabeen Ltd purchased a copper mine for $30 000 000. Of the total purchase price, $23 000 000 was assigned to the copper mine and the remaining amount was assigned to mining machinery. The mine has a residual value of $3 000 000 and contains an estimated 40 000 000 tonnes of copper ore. The mining machinery is expected to be useful for the entire life of the mine and will be abandoned when the copper deposits are depleted. During the current year, 5 000 000 tonnes of copper ore were mined.

Required

A. Prepare general journal entries to record the events occurring in the current year.

B. Prepare general journal entries to record amortisation and depreciation for the current year. Record to the nearest whole month.

Problem 21.12 GOODWILL ★★

Glen Brook, who recently won a major prize in a lottery, left his coaching job to invest in a business of his own. He found what he believed was an ideal business for his background, Gladesville Gym, which had been earning an average profit of $70 000 per year over the last 4 years.

Glen has a copy of Gladesville's current balance sheet, which discloses the following:

GLADESVILLE GYM
Balance Sheet

CURRENT ASSETS			
Cash at bank		$ 20 000	
Inventory		90 000	$110 000
NON-CURRENT ASSETS			
Land		50 000	
Building	$170 000		
Less: Accumulated depreciation	46 000	124 000	
Equipment	136 000		
Less: Accumulated depreciation	42 000	94 000	268 000
TOTAL ASSETS			$378 000
LIABILITIES			
Accounts payable			$ 20 000
Mortgage payable			100 000
			120 000
EQUITY			
Carl Ingford, Capital			258 000
TOTAL LIABILITIES AND EQUITY			$378 000

Glen Brook and Carl Ingford (the owner of Gladesville Gym) agree that the carrying amount of assets and liabilities are equal to their fair values with the exception of land, which has a fair value of $80 000, and inventory, which has a fair value of $85 000. Glen proposes to purchase the assets (except cash) and to assume the liabilities of Gladesville Gym.

Required
A. Determine the fair value of the identifiable assets and liabilities of Gladesville Gym.
B. Assuming that Glen is prepared to pay $310 000 cash for Gladesville Gym, determine the goodwill figure. Provide reasons Glen would be prepared to pay this amount.
C. Prepare general journal entries to acquire the business of Gladesville Gym.

Problem 21.13 INTANGIBLES ★★

Vaucluse Ltd has four different intangible assets at the end of 2013. Facts concerning each are:
1. *Copyright.* On 3 January 2013, the company purchased a copyright for $87 000. The remaining legal life of the copyright was 12 years, and it is expected to have a useful life of 8 years to Vaucluse Ltd with no residual value.
2. *Franchise.* On 2 April 2013, Vaucluse Ltd purchased a franchise to distribute a new product for a 10-year period with no right of renewal. Cost of the franchise was $120 000.
3. *Patent.* Vaucluse Ltd purchased a patent on 1 July 2013 from Kirribilli Ltd for $182 000. The patent had been registered initially on 1 January 2009 and is expected to be useful to Vaucluse Ltd for another 10 years.
4. *Goodwill.* Vaucluse Ltd began operations on 2 January 2009 by purchasing another company for a total cash payment of $470 000. Included in the purchase price was a payment of $90 000 for goodwill. The managing director of Vaucluse Ltd believes that 'the goodwill is such an important non-current asset of the company that it should last for 100 years'.

Required

A. Prepare journal entries to record the acquisition of intangible assets during 2013.

B. For each intangible asset, prepare journal entries that are necessary at the end of the annual accounting period on 31 December 2013.

Problem 21.14 OVERHAULS AND DISPOSALS ★★★　　LO 3

Campbelltown Ltd, which started operations on 1 October 2010, prepared the following account balances as at 30 June 2013:

Machinery (at cost)	$ 98 000
Accumulated Depreciation – Machinery	47 886
Vehicles (at cost; purchased 20 February 2011)	160 000
Accumulated Depreciation – Vehicles	89 440

Details of machines owned at 30 June 2013 were:

Machine	Purchase date	Cost	Useful life	Residual value
1	2 October 2010	$25 000	4 years	$2 500
2	27 December 2010	42 000	5 years	4 000
3	29 July 2011	31 000	4 years	3 000

Additional information

(a) Campbelltown Ltd calculates depreciation to the nearest month and balances its accounts at month-end. Recorded amounts are rounded to the nearest dollar, and end of the reporting period is 30 June.

(b) The company uses straight-line depreciation for all depreciable assets except vehicles, which are depreciated using the diminishing-balance method at a rate of 30% p.a.

(c) The Vehicles account balance reflects the total paid for four identical delivery vehicles, each of which cost $40 000.

The following transactions occurred from 1 July 2013 onwards:

2013

Aug.　3　Purchased a new machine (Machine 4) for a cash price of $36 000. Installation costs of $1800 were also paid. The company estimated the useful life and residual value at 5 years and $3500 respectively.

Nov.　15　Paid vehicle repairs of $600.

Dec.　30　Exchanged one of the vehicles for items of fixtures that had a fair value of $17 000 at the date of exchange. The fair value of the vehicle at the date of exchange was $16 000. The fixtures originally cost $50 000 and had been depreciated by $31 000 to the date of exchange in the previous owner's accounting records. Campbelltown Ltd estimated the fixtures' useful life and residual value at 5 years and $2000 respectively.

2014

March　5　Paid $8000 to overhaul Machine 1, after which Machine 1's useful life was estimated at 3 remaining years and its residual value was revised to $4000.

June　30　Recorded depreciation expense.

Sept.　20　Traded in Machine 3 for a new machine (Machine 5). A trade-in allowance of $10 000 was received for Machine 3 and $34 000 was paid in cash. The company estimated Machine 5's useful life and residual value at 6 years and $5000 respectively.

Required

Prepare journal entries in general journal form to record the above transactions.

Problem 21.15 BUSINESS COMBINATION, GOODWILL, REVALUATION, IMPAIRMENT ★★★

On 1 July 2013, Liverpool Ltd acquired the assets and liabilities of Eastwood Ltd. The assets and liabilities of Eastwood Ltd consisted of:

	Carrying amount	Fair value
Plant A (cost $840 000)	$620 000	$600 000
Plant B (cost $680 000)	362 000	350 000
Furniture (cost $160 000)	120 000	100 000
Land	200 000	260 000
Liabilities	(300 000)	(300 000)

In exchange for the business of Eastwood Ltd, Liverpool Ltd provided the following to Eastwood Ltd:
- 400 000 shares in Liverpool Ltd, these having a fair value of $2.00 per share
- cash of $360 000.

The acquisition went ahead as planned. The plant acquired was considered by Liverpool Ltd to have a further 10-year life with benefits being received evenly over that period; the furniture had an expected life of 5 years.

During the first year after the acquisition, the management of Liverpool Ltd decided to measure, at 30 June 2014, the plant at fair value (both plant assets being in the same class) and the furniture at cost.

At 30 June 2014, Liverpool Ltd assessed the fair values of its assets:
- Plant A was valued at $552 000, with an expected remaining useful life of 8 years.
- Plant B was valued at $320 000, with an expected remaining useful life of 8 years.

At 30 June 2014, the furniture's recoverable amount was assessed to be $70 000, with an expected useful life of 4 years.

Required
Prepare the journal entries in the records of Liverpool Ltd for the year ending 30 June 2014.

DECISION ANALYSIS

Selling price and goodwill

The summarised statements of financial position for two business entities are presented below:

	Framers & Son	Developers & Co.
ASSETS		
Cash at bank	$ 10 000	$ 13 000
Accounts receivable	12 000	19 000
Inventory	15 000	17 000
Property and plant (net)	40 000	60 000
Intangibles	25 000	—
TOTAL ASSETS	102 000	109 000
LIABILITIES		
Current liabilities	11 000	16 000
Non-current liabilities	20 000	25 000
TOTAL LIABILITIES	31 000	41 000
NET ASSETS	$ 71 000	$ 68 000
EQUITY		
A. Teake, Capital	$ 40 000	—
S. Teake, Capital	31 000	—
D. Pitcher, Capital	—	68 000
TOTAL EQUITY	$ 71 000	$ 68 000

Sharp Photographics is considering the possibility of acquiring the businesses of Framers & Son and Developers & Co., and is interested in establishing an appropriate purchase price for making offers to the two entities. An assessment of the fair values of the entities' assets is as follows:

	Fair values	
	Framers & Son	Developers & Co.
Receivables	$12 000	$18 000
Inventory	20 000	25 000
Property and plant (net)	60 000	70 000
Intangibles	40 000	15 000

The owners of Framers & Son are prepared to sell their firm at a price of 160% of the carrying amount of the entity's net assets, and the owner of Developers & Co. is prepared to sell at 180% of the carrying amount of the net assets of his business.

The owners of Sharp Photographics examined the earnings records and financial positions of the two entities over a number of years, and offered to pay the price required by Framers & Son, but offered to pay only 120% of the fair value of Developers & Co.'s net assets.

Required

A. Calculate the selling price being asked by each business and the purchase price offered by Sharp Photographics. Should each business sell out to Sharp Photographics?
B. The sale between Sharp Photographics and Framers & Son went ahead at the negotiated price; and the eventual sale price of Developers & Co. was $121 300. How much goodwill (if any) should be recognised by Sharp Photographics? Calculate the total valuations for all assets acquired from both businesses. Explain.

CRITICAL THINKING

Accounting for revaluations

On 1 January 2013, Good Ltd acquired a block of land for $100 000 cash, and on the same day Better Ltd purchased the adjacent block, which was virtually identical to the block purchased by Good Ltd, also for $100 000 cash. Both companies intended to construct industrial warehouses on these properties. For the next 2 years, the property market went through a boom period and, by coincidence, on 30 June 2015, both companies obtained independent valuations of $180 000 for their blocks of land.

Good Ltd has decided to adopt the revaluation model for land in the accounts on the last day of the year ended 30 June 2015 by following the requirements of IAS 16/AASB 116. Better Ltd decided to use the cost model.

On 30 April 2016, each company sold its block of land for $200 000 cash.

Required

A. In relation to the land, how much profit would each company report for the years ended 30 June 2015 and 30 June 2016?
B. Give reasons for the discrepancy in profit figures between the two companies. Does the existence of the discrepancy make sense? What message is being conveyed to users about the performance of both companies? Discuss fully. How can the discrepancy be avoided?
C. What profit would Good Ltd have made for the year ended 30 June 2016 if the revaluation of land had occurred on 29 April 2016, instead of on 30 June 2015? Compare this with the profit made by Better Ltd in the same year, and explain whether you regard the differences as satisfactory reporting.

Research and development costs

GeneTech Ltd is a biological research company that is developing gene technology in the hope of finding a vaccine for skin cancer. During the last financial year, GeneTech Ltd spent $1.2 million on research. The scientists involved in the project believe they may be on the right track with the research, although many other companies are claiming the same thing and as yet no one has patented a vaccine.

Required

In groups of three or four, discuss the options under IAS 38/AASB 138 *Intangible Assets* for the accounting treatment of the $1.2 million. What impact will each of these options have on the company's profit? Prepare a one-page letter to the managing director of GeneTech Ltd advising her of your preferred treatment for the research and development costs.

Refer to the consolidated financial statements and their notes in the latest financial report of JB Hi-Fi Limited on its website, www.jbhifi.com.au, and answer the following questions:

1. Were any items of property, plant and equipment revalued by the entity during the current financial year? during previous years? If so, give details.
2. Were any items of property, plant and equipment derecognised during the year? If so, how has the entity disclosed any gains or losses made on derecognition of such assets? Provide details of any financial amounts involved.
3. From the latest statement of financial position (balance sheet), provide details of the types and amounts of assets regarded by JB Hi-Fi Limited as 'intangible'. What accounting treatment is adopted in accounting for the acquisition of goodwill?
4. Have there been any instances where the group's non-current assets were revalued upwards/downwards? If so, provide details.

Liabilities

Concepts for review

Before studying this chapter, you should understand or, if necessary, revise:

- how to account for credit purchases (pp. 238–49)

- how and why adjusting entries are made (pp. 126–40)

- the nature and use of bills of exchange and promissory notes (pp. 765–70).

Learning objectives

After studying this chapter, you should be able to:

1 define liabilities (pp. 908–9)

2 describe when liabilities are recognised (pp. 909–10)

3 explain the nature of provisions and contingent liabilities (pp. 910–12)

4 discuss why and how liabilities are classified, and distinguish between current and non-current liabilities (p. 912–13)

5 explain the nature of the major categories of current liabilities, and how to account for them (pp. 913–21)

6 explain the nature of the major categories of non-current liabilities and how to account for them (pp. 922–8)

7 analyse liabilities for decision-making purposes (pp. 928–32).

$200bn debt bomb ticking for Australian corporations

Corporate Australia is sitting on a $200 billion debt bomb that needs to be refinanced over the next three years, with analysts warning some infrastructure and small companies will collapse under the mountain of debt.

Available information suggests companies face $38.5bn of debt maturities next year, another $97.3bn maturing in 2011 and $64.7bn in 2012, *The Australian* reports.

But the problem could be even worse. Data on corporate debt in Australia is based on publicly accessible databases and does not include private deals companies do with banks, so the real debt figure could be much higher than $200bn.

Infrastructure is the biggest worry, with more than $31bn in refinancing due at a time when asset prices are crashing amid funding pressures, tight credit markets and carbon tax uncertainties.

Property is also vulnerable, with more than $26bn of near-term debt due, and finance companies have $17bn of debt due in two years and another $3.4bn maturing in 2012.

Construction is next, with a total of $15bn of debt coming up in the next three years, then telecommunications, mining, and healthcare, which together have more than $31bn of debt sitting on their balance sheets requiring a debt rollover within three years ...

Infrastructure companies and utilities, including AGL Energy, listed toll road group Connect-East, SPI (Australia) Assets, LaTrobe Power Partnerships, Transfield Services Infrastructure, Envestra and APT Pipelines, will require bank co-operation to roll over debt facilities, and those with questionable business models will struggle.

Hundreds of small to mid-sized companies, yet to raise equity but close to tripping loan covenants, will also battle.

Marla Heller, head of debt at Deutsche Bank, said that based on recent transactions, bank debt could not be viewed as a commodity, and companies needed to actively manage their capital structure through the next phase of refinancing.

Source: Excerpts from Adele Ferguson, '$200bn debt bomb ticking for Australian corporations', *The Daily Telegraph*.

Chapter preview

One of the most important decisions owners and managers have to make is how to finance their business operations. Such decisions are also important to external users such as shareholders and fixed interest investors. Many of these decisions are reflected in the statement of financial position/balance sheet as liabilities. Liabilities are important because they represent past sources of cash and other assets, but they also represent obligations to give up cash and other resources at some time in the future. As highlighted in the scene setter, debt can be a significant percentage of a company's statement of financial position/balance sheet. Liabilities are a necessary part of the financing of a business entity, and the appropriate mix and level of different liabilities is essential to the continuing success of any business.

Regardless of the nature and size of the operations of any business or government entity, they all will incur liabilities. Liabilities arise from operating, investing and financing activities. As part of operating activities, the entity will incur liabilities for the purchase of goods and services on credit, for the wages of employees, for bills of exchange, for normal expenses, and for such items as warranties on products sold. Investment decisions regarding the purchase of property, plant and equipment will also give rise to obligations to outlay cash and resources in the future. Financing activities, such as borrowing over long periods of time using, for example, mortgage loans and debentures, also create liabilities. Finally, liabilities can arise from profit distributions such as the declaration of dividends to shareholders under certain conditions.

Many students will already be familiar with financing their lifestyles via the use of liabilities. For many, the most common types of liabilities are debts related to studying at university, possibly in the form of a loan from the government or parents. Some students may have bought a computer or car using some form of credit provider such as a bank or credit union. Others may have borrowed money to finance the purchase of a unit or house. It is also common for many students to incur liabilities for such things as mobile phone accounts.

Recognising, valuing, recording, reporting and analysing liabilities are discussed in this chapter.

22.1 Liabilities defined

Learning objective 1

Define liabilities

As previously noted, **liabilities** are defined in accounting standards and in the *Conceptual Framework for Financial Reporting (the Conceptual Framework)* as 'a present obligation of the entity arising from past events, the settlement of which is expected to result in an outflow from the entity of resources embodying economic benefits'. From the definition, it is clear that there are three essential characteristics of a liability:

- the entity must have a *present obligation* to an external party
- the obligation must have resulted from *past events*
- the entity must have a future *outflow of resources embodying economic benefits*, which represents a sacrifice of economic resources.

Present obligation

A primary characteristic of a liability is that the entity is presently obliged to act in a certain manner in the future, such as outlaying cash or other resources to a party external to the entity. Although the external party normally would be identified, e.g. a supplier for goods purchased, a financial institution for a loan, or an employee for wages, it is not essential for the identity of the external party to be known at the present point in time for a liability to exist. A liability can exist for the warranty on goods sold, such as computers or mobile phones; but because it is not known at the time of sale which goods will be faulty during their warranty period, who will make a warranty claim cannot be known at the time the liability is recognised.

Liabilities generally arise from contractual arrangements voluntarily entered into by the entity. Obligations to supply goods paid for in advance, for borrowings, for services provided by employees and other award benefits owing to them, and for plant and equipment purchased are all examples of transactions arising from contractual property arrangements. Most obligations are evidenced by formal documentation such as contracts or other documents which establish a present obligation. An entity can also have obligations imposed on it by external factors such as when it becomes liable for damages under a lawsuit or for employee or customer compensation claims, or when government taxes and charges are assessed or imposed.

As well as a **legal obligation** that arises from contracts, legislation or other operations of the law, such as those just discussed, a constructive obligation may give rise to a liability. A **constructive obligation** is when the past practices of an entity, its published policies or a specific current statement indicate that it will accept responsibility for certain actions, and so it becomes reasonable for others to assume the entity will fulfil those responsibilities. For example, a department store may have had a practice of exchanging damaged returned goods for new replacements, even when the customer had no proof of purchase and could not demonstrate that the goods were originally purchased from that store. If it could be shown that this practice had taken place over an extended period of time and that customers could reasonably assume that the exchange of damaged goods for new goods would continue without proof of purchase, then the store could have a present constructive obligation to replace the damaged goods for anyone who returned them to the store, regardless of the place of purchase. The store should therefore make a provision for the expected future cost of such returns.

Past event

For a present obligation to be a liability, it must have arisen from past events, such as the purchase of goods and services, or entering into a loan arrangement. An intention to borrow money in the future does not constitute a liability since no event giving rise to an obligation has occurred at the current point in time.

Future outflow of resources embodying economic benefits

A liability must involve an outflow of economic resources in the future. These future outflows of economic resources do not need to be in cash, and can take the form of transfer of other assets, the provision of services, replacement of that obligation with another, or conversion to equity. Discharge of an obligation can be required on demand (such as a bank overdraft), on a specific future date, or on the happening of some future event. Usually, a high degree of certainty is associated with liabilities — suppliers expect to be paid within 30 days of the invoice date, and a financial institution expects its loans to be repaid on specific dates over a period of time.

22.2 Recognition of liabilities

Learning objective 2

Describe when liabilities are recognised

Having established that a liability exists, it is then necessary to decide whether it is appropriate at the time to recognise the liability in the accounts and what the dollar amount of the liability is. Recognition of a liability simply means that the liability is recorded in the formal accounts of the entity, and disclosed in financial statements. The preceding section described the characteristics which must be present for a liability to exist, but it did not cover conditions to be met in deciding whether and when to recognise a liability and how to measure it.

Why recognition is important

If liabilities are not recognised and expressed in dollar terms as soon as possible, the liabilities of the entity will be understated, and the entity's equity will be overstated, as equity equals assets minus liabilities. Also, many expenses incurred and assets acquired, which result from transactions giving rise to liabilities, will be understated if such liabilities are not recognised. The relationship between expenses and liabilities is evident when end-of-period adjustments are made to the unadjusted accounts in the general ledger. An example is the recording of accrued wages, resulting in an increase in wages expense and an increase in wages payable to record the liability for amounts owing to employees. Coverage of end-of-period adjustments such as these was provided in chapter 4.

Criteria for recognition

Accounting standards and the *Conceptual Framework* specify two criteria which must be met before liabilities are recognised. Liabilities should be recognised when, and only when:
- it is *probable* that an outflow of resources embodying economic benefits will result from the settlement of a present obligation
- the *amount* at which the settlement will take place can be *measured reliably*.

Given the nature of most liabilities, which involve an agreement with an external party, these criteria are usually easy to verify.

In relation to the first criterion, 'probable' in this context simply means that the outflow of economic benefits is more likely than less likely to occur, i.e. higher than a 50% probability as required by IAS 37/AASB 137 *Provisions, Contingent Liabilities and Contingent Assets*. The outflow of resources from the entity can be paid:

- *on demand* — the amount of the liability is presently due and the payment is not subject to any conditions, e.g. a debt to a supplier for goods received
- *on a specified date* — only the passage of time is required to make the liability payable, e.g. repayment of a loan at set dates in the future
- *on the occurrence of a specified event* — requires that an event occurs before the liability becomes payable, e.g. a warranty claim on a faulty product previously sold.

The second criterion for recognition is that the outflow of economic benefits can be measured reliably. The amount recorded as a liability is the monetary measure of the obligation to sacrifice economic benefits. Reliable measurement requires adequate evidence to be available to support the dollar measurement assigned to the future outflow of economic benefits. Generally, the condition of reliable measurement is satisfied by the existence of source documents such as purchase orders, supplier invoices, wage agreements, and loan contracts resulting from transactions which give rise to the liabilities. In some circumstances, measurement of the liability requires estimates, and even discounting of future cash outflows back to present value.

Learning objective 3

Explain the nature of provisions and contingent liabilities

22.3 Provisions and contingent liabilities

Nature of provisions

Provisions are defined in IAS 37/AASB 137 as liabilities of uncertain timing or amount. Although the standard notes that the term 'provision' is used elsewhere in accounting and auditing standards to refer to items such as accumulated depreciation and the allowance for doubtful debts, these items are not covered by IAS 37/AASB 137. Such items are adjustments to the carrying amount of assets and therefore do not meet the definition of a liability. Because provisions are defined as liabilities of uncertain timing or amount, it seems that items such as accumulated depreciation and allowance for doubtful debts should not be referred to as 'provisions', since they do not meet the definition.

A provision exists when an entity is presently obliged to make a future outflow of economic benefits as a result of past events. In other words, a provision is a liability but the *amount* or *timing* of the outflow of economic benefits is *uncertain*. IAS 37/AASB 137 argues that the degree of uncertainty of the amount and timing of liabilities such as trade payables and accruals clearly contrasts with that applicable to provisions.

Provisions can arise from a number of situations or events. Examples of provisions include provision for long-service leave (from hiring labour), provision for warranties expense (providing a warranty on goods sold), provision for personal indemnity claims (accident on business premises), provision for environmental damages (legal action by external entities), and provision for onerous contracts (where future payments under a contract exceed benefits).

With these examples, the need to recognise expenses and their associated liabilities arises from the requirement to record expenses in the year in which it is probable that the consumption or loss of economic benefits occurs and can be reliably measured. The cost arising from warranties given with products sold is a good example of this. Warranty costs (i.e. costs associated with rectifying or replacing faulty products) result in future costs after the product has been sold. Sales revenue can be recorded in one accounting period, but the outflow of resources associated with meeting warranty claims can be incurred in the next or later reporting periods. It is appropriate to record the warranty expense and the warranty liability in the accounting period when the sales are made and the revenue is recognised, as the sale represents an obligating event. IAS 37/AASB 137 defines an **obligating event** as an event that results in an entity having no realistic alternative to settling that obligation. It is probable, from past experience, that a certain percentage of goods sold will be returned for repair or replacement during the warranty period.

As with liabilities, a provision is recognised when an entity has a present obligation (legal or constructive) as a result of a past event that will probably result in an outflow of economic benefits, and a reliable estimate can be made of the amount of the obligation. The measurement of the provision must be the best estimate, at the end of the reporting period, of the cash flows or other consideration required to settle the provision. When a provision is measured using estimated future cash flows, then these must be shown at the present value of those cash flows at the end of the reporting period where the effect of the time value of money is material. When providing for warranties, the amount of future costs related to the reporting period's sales can be estimated from past experience and is considered reliable enough to make a provision for warranty.

Items excluded from provisions — future costs

Given that a provision must satisfy the definition of a liability, items which do not satisfy the definition should not be labelled as a 'provision' in the financial statements. A common practice was for some entities at the end of the reporting period to credit in the accounts a provision for future repairs and maintenance whenever plant and equipment required a major overhaul in the coming financial period. By establishing such a provision, repairs and maintenance expense was debited on the grounds that it recorded the expense in the period that the economic benefits of the plant and equipment were used. However, under the definition of 'provision' given in IAS 37/AASB 137, the provision for future repairs and maintenance on plant and equipment does not satisfy the definition of a liability, as there is no present obligation to an external party at the end of the reporting period.

A further example of a commonly established provision which does not satisfy the definition is in the circumstance where an entity credits a provision for self-insurance against possible natural disasters. Entities have often 'insured themselves', instead of taking out insurance with an external party, by transferring to a provision the cost of the insurance premium that would be paid if such a policy existed. However, such a provision does not satisfy the definition of a liability, as there is no present obligation resulting in an outflow of economic resources in the future.

Contingent liabilities

Further confusion in the financial statements of an entity has occurred because of the treatment of circumstances which, although they exist at the end of the reporting period, depend on uncertain events for their existence or valuation. For example, an entity may be the subject of a legal dispute at the end of the reporting period, which may or may not lead to the entity having to pay significant damages as a result of past events. What should the entity disclose in its financial statements? This example is often described as a contingent liability and is covered by IAS 37/AASB 137. A **contingent liability** is defined in the standard as a possible obligation arising from a past event that will be confirmed only by the occurrence or non-occurrence of one or more uncertain future events that are not wholly within the control of the entity. A liability or provision that does not meet the recognition criteria of probable outflow of resources embodying economic benefits and/or reliable measurement is also defined as a contingent liability. The standard states that contingent liabilities are not to be included in the financial statements but are to be disclosed in the notes to the financial statements, but not if the possibility of an economic outflow is 'remote'. In the case the event is remote, no disclosure is required to be made. Figure 22.1 illustrates the distinction between a provision and a contingent liability.

It can be argued that information about contingent liabilites is useful to external users of financial statements in assessing the current financial position of an entity. One example of a contingent liability is a lawsuit brought against the entity for breach of environmental laws where, at the end of the reporting period, the probability that future economic resources will flow out of the entity is very high, but the amount cannot be measured reliably until damages are determined by the relevant court. Another example is where an entity has acted as guarantor for another entity's borrowings. Here, at the end of the reporting period, the liability can be reliably measured, but the probability that a future outflow of economic resources will be required is often less than 50%.

Figure 22.1 Decision tree from AASB 137, Appendix B, summarising the main recognition and disclosure requirements for provisions and contingent liabilities

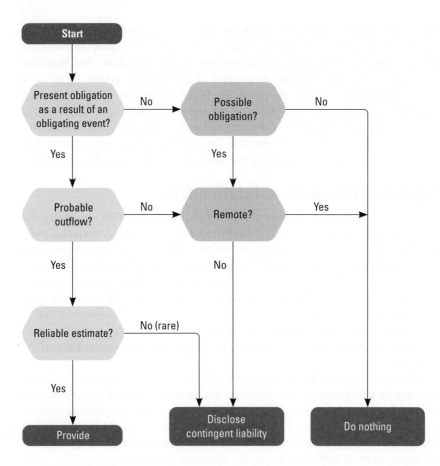

Contingent liabilities are characterised by the requirement that a future event does not have to be wholly within the control of the entity before any liability can be recognised and disclosed within the financial statements, e.g. the court determines the amount of damages to be paid by the entity, or the entity whose debt is guaranteed defaults on its loan repayments.

22.4 Classification of liabilities

Need for classification

Learning objective 4

Discuss why and how liabilities are classified, and distinguish between current and non-current liabilities

The previous discussion has indicated that liabilities originate from a wide variety of transactions and events, and hence the nature of liabilities varies greatly. When liabilities are reported in the statement of financial position/balance sheet, they need to be presented in relevant and comparable categories. This means that they should be classified into appropriate groups so that users of financial statements are able to analyse and interpret the role and significance of liabilities in the short-term and long-term activities of the entity. Decision makers want to be able to assess the entity's capacity to (1) meet its recurring commitments arising as part of the operating cycle, (2) pay interest and (3) repay long-term borrowings.

Basis of classification

Unlike assets, which are classified according to their nature (current and non-current), liquidity and function within the entity, IAS 1/AASB 101 *Presentation of Financial Statements* suggests that liabilities are classified according to their amount, nature and timing. Since the nature of liabilities varies considerably, there is a wide choice of classification. The nature of liabilities can relate to the timing of settlement, their liquidity, whether they are secured by assets or guarantees, whether they are unsecured, and their source (trade creditors as opposed to employee benefits). A perusal of company reports, such as the JB Hi-Fi Limited financial statements that can be found on its website, www.jbhifi.com.au, will indicate that companies generally provide a classification of liabilities that attempts to reflect the diverse nature of liabilities.

Categories

In practice, classifying liabilities is based on the timing of the expected outlays of economic resources to discharge the liabilities. This results in a classification of liabilities based on the time that is expected to elapse between the end of the reporting period and the expected date of settlement. Liabilities that are expected to be settled within the entity's normal operating cycle, or are held mainly for the purpose of being traded, or will be settled within 12 months of the end of the reporting period are classified as **current liabilities**. If the entity does not have an unconditional right to defer settlement of a liability for at least 12 months after the end of the reporting period, then that liability is also classified as current (IAS 1/AASB 101). All other liabilities are classified as **non-current liabilities**.

A secondary classification of liabilities is based on the uncertainty of the amount and timing of the future outflows. IAS 1/AASB 101 requires the statement of financial position/balance sheet to show, as a minimum, trade and other payables, provisions, financial liabilities, and liabilities for current and deferred tax. A major difference between these items is the degree of uncertainty surrounding the amount and timing of the future outflows of economic resources.

For reporting to the internal users of an entity, each entity can determine the appropriate categories which suit the needs of those users. The entity may report many different categories, such as accounts payable, bills payable, bank overdraft, wages and salaries payable, loans payable, telephone account payable, GST payable, and provision for warranties.

22.5 Current liabilities

Learning objective 5

Explain the nature of the major categories of current liabilities, and how to account for them

Current liabilities are liabilities that are expected to be settled during the entity's normal operating cycle (or within 12 months of the end of the reporting period), are held mainly to be traded, or that the entity does not have an unconditional right to delay settlement of for at least 12 months after the end of the reporting period. They include accounts payable, bills payable, interest-bearing liabilities (e.g. bank overdraft), employee benefits, accrued expenses, and provisions. Accounting for these major types of current liabilities is covered in this section.

Accounts payable (trade creditors)

Accounts payable are amounts owed to creditors for the purchase of inventory, supplies and services as part of the business operating cycle. Because they are not evidenced by a formal debt instrument such as a specifically written contract or raised note, they are often referred to as *open accounts*. Each time inventory, supplies or services are purchased on credit, the appropriate asset or expense account is debited and the Accounts Payable account is credited. Accounting for accounts payable has been covered in previous chapters, particularly chapter 7. These accounts are also commonly referred to as **trade creditors**.

Bills payable

Bills payable differ from accounts payable in that the liability is evidenced by a bill of exchange or a promissory note. In some industries it is normal practice for the purchaser of inventory to give an accepted bill of exchange or promissory note to the seller at the time of purchase. Bills are often issued when a business borrows money from a bank or other financial institution. Another transaction that results in bills payable is the substitution of a bill for an overdue account payable.

The similarity with bills receivable is obvious. A bill payable can arise by acceptance of a draft bill of exchange or the giving of a promissory note. The same principles regarding maturity value, maturity date, interest and so on, discussed when dealing with bills receivable, apply to bills payable. Accounting for bills payable is illustrated below. Bills payable can be classified into:

(1) 'trade' bills payable (used for the settlement of business transactions)
(2) 'commercial' bills payable (used for obtaining short-term finance from banks and other financial institutions).

Trade bills

Trade bills payable can arise from transactions in the normal course of business, e.g. the conversion of accounts payable to bills payable. For illustration purposes, assume BD Ltd had previously purchased inventory from R. Smith on credit for $4000 including GST. On 1 August, Smith agreed to accept a 90-day (due date fixed) bill of exchange from BD Ltd to cover the amount of the account payable together with interest at 10% p.a. The entry in the general journal of BD Ltd on issue of the bill is:

Aug.	1	Accounts Payable – R. Smith	4 000.00	
		Unexpired Interest	98.63	
		Bills Payable		4 098.63
		(Receipt of bill from R. Smith for account payable)		
		[Interest = $4000 × 0.10 × 90/365]		

The debit to a contra-liability account, Unexpired Interest, represents the interest expense which is not yet incurred, but will be with the passage of time.

On the maturity date, which is 30 October, BD Ltd is expected to pay the liability existing on the bill. When the bill is paid, the unexpired interest has expired and should therefore be charged to Interest Expense. The entries in general journal form are:

Oct.	30	Bills Payable	4 098.63	
		Cash at Bank		4 098.63
		(Payment of bill)		
	30	Interest Expense	98.63	
		Unexpired Interest		98.63
		(Interest expense on bill)		

Note that, if the end of the financial year falls within the term of the bill, an adjusting entry is necessary at the end of the reporting period to bring to account the interest expense incurred on the bill up to that time.

Commercial bills

Apart from their use as trade bills, a more common use for bills of exchange is to obtain short-term finance. These bills are known as **commercial bills** and, in some cases, are referred to as **accommodation bills**. If bills of exchange are used to obtain finance from a bank or through entities specialising in bill finance, the bills are referred to as *bank bills* and *finance bills* respectively.

These bills are bought and sold on a bills market, which is similar to a stock exchange. The market in bills requires that they must be for an amount of at least $100 000 and drawn for a maximum period of 180 days. If the financing arrangement is to exceed 180 days, then the bill expiring at the end of 180 days must be 'rolled over', i.e. replaced by a new bill.

The arrangements whereby an entity obtains finance from a bank, for example, can vary depending on circumstances. To illustrate, assume that DMF Ltd wished to obtain $100 000 by means of a 180-day bill of exchange, with the accommodation of the bill provided by an arrangement with Hometown Merchant Bank. DMF Ltd would draw up a draft bill and present this to the bank for acceptance. Once accepted, DMF Ltd could sell the accepted bill to another entity for the face value less a discounting fee. The entity discounting the bill feels secure because of the financial backing provided by the Hometown Merchant Bank's acceptance. On the maturity date, DMF Ltd would pay the face value of the bill to Hometown Merchant Bank, which in turn would pay the entity which presented the bill to the bank on the due date.

Alternatively, the bank (after its acceptance of the bill) could **discount** the bill and pay DMF Ltd the face value less the discounting fee (to cover interest). The bank could retain the bill until the due date and receive the face value from DMF Ltd, or the bank could sell the bill on the bill market. On the due date, DMF Ltd would pay the bank $100 000, and the bank would honour the bill when presented by the current holder of the bill.

Regardless of the particular financing arrangements, and who the ultimate holder of the bill is at its due date, the bill is a bill payable by DMF Ltd and, on the due date, DMF Ltd becomes liable to pay the face value of the bill to Hometown Merchant Bank. Even though the interest rate on the bill is 10% p.a., initial recording of the financing by DMF Ltd is as follows:

July	1	Cash at Bank	95 068	
		Unexpired Interest	4 932	
		Bills Payable		100 000
		(Arranged finance by a 180-day, $100 000 bill at 10%)		
		[Interest = $100 000 × 0.10 × 180/365]		

The Unexpired Interest account, representing the discount, is deducted as a contra-liability to the current liability as shown below:

CURRENT LIABILITIES
Accounts payable		$ 46 500
Bills payable	$100 000	
Less: Unexpired interest on bills	4 932	95 068
Accrued expenses		6 700
		$148 268

Instead of using an Unexpired Interest account, some accountants use a Discount on Bills Payable account to record the interest (discount). The discount account is then treated in exactly the same manner as the Unexpired Interest account, i.e. as a contra-liability to the Bills Payable account. Because the unexpired interest on bills payable represents interest deducted in advance, it is transferred to interest expense over the term of the bill.

In our illustration, assume that the maturity date of the bill falls within the same financial year as the issue date. Thus the discount is charged to interest expense when the bill is paid on 28 December by DMF Ltd and recorded in general journal format as follows:

Dec.	28	Bills Payable	100 000	
		Cash at Bank		100 000
		(Payment of bill to bank)		
		Interest Expense	4 932	
		Unexpired Interest		4 932
		(Interest expense on discounted bill)		

End-of-period adjustments for interest expense

When a bill payable is issued in one accounting period and matures in another, an adjusting entry must be made at the end of the first period to allocate interest expense properly. For example, assume that the $100 000, 180-day, 10% bill of DMF Ltd in the previous illustration was issued on 1 June rather than on 1 July. An adjusting entry is needed on 30 June to accrue interest expense for 30 days as follows:

June	30	Interest Expense	822	
		Unexpired Interest		822
		(Interest for 30 days on discounted bill: $100 000 × 0.10 × 30/365)		

The entry to record payment of the bill on 28 November is:

Nov.	28	Bills Payable		100 000	
		Cash at Bank			100 000
		(Payment of bill to bank)			
		Interest Expense		4 110	
		Unexpired Interest			4 110
		(Interest expense on bill: $100 000 \times 0.10 \times 150/365$)			

In either case, the total amount of interest expense, $4932, is the same, with $822 allocated to the period in which the bill was issued and $4110 allocated to the following period.

Employee benefits

One of the most important recurring expenses for business entities is compensating employees for services rendered under employment contracts. The combined costs of labour and fringe benefits, referred to collectively as employee benefits, are a major business expense. For each of the expenses generated, corresponding liabilities are generated. The entity owes employees wages and salaries earned until paid, and owes various external parties for deductions withheld from employees, e.g. income tax instalments. Other liabilities arise from such benefits as sick leave, long-service leave, workers compensation premiums, and superannuation. This section of the chapter covers aspects of both expenses and liabilities associated with employee benefits from the employer's point of view.

Employee benefits defined

Accounting standard IAS 19/AASB 119 *Employee Benefits* defines employee benefits, sets out criteria for the recognition and measurement of expenses and liabilities that arise in relation to employee benefits, and prescribes disclosure requirements for employee benefits.

Employee benefits are defined as all forms of consideration given by an entity in exchange for services rendered by employees and include wages and salaries (including all monetary and non-monetary fringe benefits), annual leave, sick leave, long-service leave, maternity leave, superannuation, and post-employment benefits. An employer is an entity that consumes the services of employees in exchange for providing employee benefits.

The principles for recognition of expenses and liabilities that arise out of employee benefits are based on the definitions of these elements of financial statements that are given in the standards and are consistent with those contained in the *Conceptual Framework*. For example, if an employee benefit meets the definition of an expense, then the item is recognised as such in the accounts. If the benefit meets the definition of a liability, then a liability is recorded and disclosed in the financial statements.

Two measurement methods are required for liabilities arising from employee benefits. Wages and salaries, annual leave and sick leave, which are expected to be settled within 12 months of the end of the reporting period, and deductions from wages expected to be made within the next 12 months of the end of the reporting period are to be recorded at their nominal amounts, i.e. undiscounted. Any long-term employee benefits are to be measured at **present value** if material, which is defined as the future cash flows to be paid to these employees discounted back to the present time using a suitable discount rate. The discount rate required to be used is the market yield on high-quality corporate bonds or national government bonds at the end of the reporting period. (Discussion of measurement techniques to determine present value is provided in the appendix at the back of this book.) It is important to note that GST is not payable on employee benefits.

Gross pay

The first step in calculating the amount paid to a particular employee during a given period is determining his or her **gross pay** (also called **gross earnings**) in the form of wages or salary. The term **wages** is used for remuneration paid to an employee on the basis of an hourly rate and hence varies in amount depending on the hours worked and hourly rate of pay applied. **Salary** refers to remuneration paid on a weekly, fortnightly or monthly basis and is determined using a fixed annual salary as the base. Both wages and salaries may be supplemented by bonuses, loadings, commissions and fringe benefits.

Gross pay depends on a number of considerations in addition to the rate paid per hour and the hours worked. Often, governments prescribe minimum rates of pay and standard hours of work, together with a number of other allowances relating to working conditions and pay rates. Allowances may be made for such items as overtime hours worked, travel, clothing, danger money for hazardous occupations, and dirt money in an occupation such as mining. These allowances are added to and form part of an employee's gross pay.

Deductions from gross pay

The net pay or take-home pay which is paid to an employee will be less than gross pay because of certain deductions that must be made. These deductions arise out of a statutory requirement to deduct income tax instalments, and out of agreements entered into whereby the employee authorises the employer to deduct certain amounts to cover items such as superannuation contributions, life assurance premiums and medical insurance. The **net pay** will therefore equal gross pay less deductions.

Employer's liability for deductions

The amounts deducted from an employee's gross pay are *liabilities* of the employer, who performs the duties of a collection agent. Various deductions must be paid when due to the government (tax instalments), and to other organisations where authorised by the employee (e.g. medical insurance). After the deductions are made but before they are remitted to the appropriate organisation, the amounts are *liabilities* of the employer. In turn, the employer is responsible for maintaining adequate records that provide the basis for filing any reports concerning the deductions and for making payments on time. The liabilities for the deductions are classified as current liabilities on the employer's balance sheet/statement of financial position until they are paid.

We now illustrate the recording of the expense of wages and salaries for an entity in a period, the liabilities that result from the wages and salaries earned, and the subsequent payment of those liabilities. Assume the following information, extracted from payroll records, covering all employees of Five Star Ltd for a period of 1 week ending 28 June:

Gross pay		$3650
Deductions:		
Income tax instalments	$748	
Superannuation contributions	191	
Insurance premiums	90	
Medical insurance	178	1207
Net pay		$2443

The general journal entry to record the week's payroll is:

June	28	Wages and Salaries Expense	3 650	
		Taxation Office		748
		AB Superannuation Fund		191
		XY Insurance Ltd		90
		FM Medical Fund		178
		Wages and Salaries Payable		2 443
		(Payroll for the week ending 28 June)		

Note that this entry records the $3650 expense incurred by the entity for hiring its employees, and $3650 in liabilities to be paid in the future. The net pay, $2443, is paid to employees on

28 June, and all the liabilities for deductions will be paid at various times, depending on arrangements with outside bodies — most likely in the following month. The entry to pay employees their net pay is recorded in the cash payments journal on 28 June, and examples of such entries have appeared in previous chapters.

In a statement of financial position/balance sheet prepared at 30 June, all the outstanding credits above except net pay are recorded as current liabilities. The above amounts are, of course, added to any unpaid amounts previously recorded as liabilities in the same accounts. Note also that, at 30 June, 2 days pay has accrued to all employees and an end-of-period adjustment for accrued wages and salaries has to be made, as discussed in chapter 4.

To illustrate the payment on 15 July of liabilities for deductions in June, assume that records show that amounts owing for deductions are: Taxation Office $1976, AB Superannuation Fund $670, XY Insurance Ltd $296, FM Medical Fund $427. The entry in the cash payments journal to record the payment of these liabilities is:

Cash Payments Journal					
			Chq.	Post	Credits
Date	Account		no.	ref	Cash at Bank
July 15	Taxation Office		054		1 976
	AB Superannuation Fund		055		670
	XY Insurance Ltd		056		296
	FM Medical Fund		057		427

Payroll ancillary costs

The expense of hiring employees can be considerably more than a fixed salary or simply multiplying the number of hours worked by the rate per hour. There are a number of other benefits that must be taken into account. These other costs may be mandatory on the employer as they are required by government legislation, or are specifically set down in the various wage and salary agreements and contracts. These additional benefits arise because of the existence of benefits to employees which must be borne by the employer, such as annual leave, sick leave, maternity leave, workers compensation, public holidays and long-service leave. A brief introduction to some of these expenses is given below, together with a suggested accounting treatment to record such benefits.

Annual leave. Under employee awards and employment contracts, employees are generally entitled to a few weeks paid **annual leave**. The annual leave benefit usually accrues to an employee on a day-by-day basis throughout the year. Since annual leave is a right, employees are entitled to receive pro rata benefit for annual leave if they resign or are dismissed or retrenched during a period. Since the expense of annual leave usually accrues on a day-to-day basis, annual leave should be accrued on a regular basis throughout the year, and an appropriate liability recognised for leave unpaid.

To illustrate how this is done, let us suppose that Five Star Ltd estimates that the gross wages and salaries payable for annual leave for the year is $28 200. At the end of each month, therefore, one-twelfth of this amount ($2350) should be set aside. Annual leave benefits arising from services rendered by employees throughout the reporting period that remain unpaid at the end of the reporting period meet the criteria for recognition as a liability. The general journal entry to recognise the expense and liability in each month is:

Annual Leave Expense	2 350	
Annual Leave Payable		2 350
(Annual leave liability for the month)		

When annual leave is paid, an entry is made in the cash payments journal to debit the Annual Leave Payable account (a current liability) and credit the Cash at Bank account.

Sick leave. Many agreements provide for paid sick leave as an employee benefit. The period of sick leave to which an employee is entitled varies, but paid sick leave of 10 working days per year is common. Like annual leave, sick leave usually accrues to an employee on a day-to-day basis throughout the year. Any sick leave benefits owing to an employee and unpaid at the end of the entity's reporting period satisfy the recognition criteria for a liability. Accounting for sick leave is largely determined by the conditions attaching to the leave.

The accounting entries for sick leave are similar to those for annual leave. To illustrate, assume that Five Star Ltd estimates that the cost of sick leave benefits for each month of the coming year is $1400. The general journal entry to be made each month is set out below. Note that the Sick Leave Payable is a current liability.

Sick Leave Expense	1 400	
Sick Leave Payable		1 400
(Sick leave liability for the month)		

When sick leave is actually taken by an employee, an entry is made in the cash payments journal to debit the Sick Leave Payable account and credit the Cash at Bank account. Sick leave has to be paid at rates prevailing at the time of the leave; adjustments to the liability should be made if changes occur in wages and salary rates.

Unlike annual leave, unused sick leave is not usually paid to employees when they resign or are dismissed or retrenched. For this reason, most employers do not account for sick leave separately and simply treat it as a part of wages expense. Usually, no expense or liability is recorded for sick leave. IAS 19/AASB 119 requires an entity to estimate the amount of sick leave that is expected to be paid out in the future.

Workers compensation. **Workers compensation** relates to an insurance scheme whereby employees are compensated for injuries, loss of limbs and loss of life while at work. Under legislation, it is often compulsory for all employers to take out workers compensation insurance. This involves a cost to the employer in the form of the yearly premium payable to obtain the insurance cover. The premium is payable in advance and is based on a percentage of the estimated wages and salaries for the forthcoming year. The percentage rates of premium are variable and are set in such a manner as to reflect the relative occupational risks to which employees are exposed on the job.

Accounting for workers compensation is similar to the payment of any insurance premium. To illustrate, assume that Five Star Ltd paid $8400 at the beginning of a year for workers compensation insurance. An entry is made in the cash payments journal resulting in a debit to Prepaid Workers Compensation Insurance and a credit to the Cash at Bank account. At the end of each month, the following general journal entry is made to reflect the workers compensation insurance expense for the month:

Workers Compensation Insurance Expense	700	
Prepaid Workers Compensation Insurance		700
(Workers compensation insurance expense for month)		

Public holidays. In any year, employees are typically entitled to at least 10 public holidays, which is the equivalent of 2 weeks work. Although there is a substantial expense involved to employers, there is no need for any special accounting treatment. Employees are simply paid in the normal way for public holidays. Unlike annual leave, there is no need to accrue the expense of public holidays or establish a liability.

Long-service leave. Another substantial expense of employment is paid **long-service leave**. Long-service leave represents paid leave granted to employees who have remained with the one employer over an extended period of time. Although leave benefits accrue over a long period, all the leave is paid at the rate of pay applicable when the leave is taken.

It is important to note that although the employee starts to accrue long-service leave from the beginning of employment, the employer is not liable to grant paid leave until the required period of employment has been completed, i.e. normally after 10 years. The general journal entry to record the expense and liability is:

Long-service Leave Expense	xxx	
Provision for Long-service Leave		xxx
(Liability of long-service leave)		

Provision for long-service leave has an element of current liability but is largely non-current and is measured by the present value of expected future cash outlays. Because of the uncertainty in timing and amount, it seems this liability should be recorded and reported as a provision, rather than a payable. If material, the future amounts should be discounted to present value. When the employee is paid his or her leave benefit, an entry is passed debiting the Provision for Long-service Leave account and crediting the Cash at Bank account.

Warranties

IAS 37/AASB 137 suggests that establishing a provision for any warranty given on the sale of inventory is appropriate, as there is no doubt that an obligation to sacrifice future economic resources exists, but there is uncertainty as to the timing and the amount of the liability. Reasonably accurate estimates can be made of warranty costs from past experience with the same or similar products, or the experience of other entities in the industry concerned. Accounting for warranties involves establishing a liability called Provision for Warranties in the year the products are sold, and recognising an equivalent expense against the provision.

To illustrate, assume that No Risk Computers Ltd sells a particular brand of computer for $2860 (including GST), with a 1-year labour and parts warranty. Accounting records reveal that the average cost of repairing defective computers is $350, and that about 10% of computers sold require warranty repairs. Thus, if 2000 computers were sold in the year ending 30 June, it is necessary to establish a provision to cover future warranty costs. The estimate of the future warranty expense is $70 000 (2000 × 10% × $350).

The adjusting general journal entry to record the warranty expense associated with sales in the year ended 30 June and the provision for warranties is:

June	30	Warranty Expense	70 000	
		Provision for Warranties		70 000
		(Provision for warranty expense related to sales made in the year ended 30 June)		

Warranty expense is regarded as a selling and distribution expense, and the Provision for Warranties is shown as a current liability. On each occasion that warranty costs are incurred during the following year, the following journal entry (in general journal format) is made (note that the amount will differ depending on the circumstances of each claim):

July	15	Provision for Warranties	350	
		Cash at Bank		350
		(Warranty costs incurred on a faulty computer)		

Onerous contracts

An **onerous contract** is a contract in which the unavoidable costs of meeting the obligations under the contract exceed the economic benefits expected to be received under it. Where a contract has become onerous, it falls under IAS 37/AASB 137 and the standard requires the onerous contract to be recognised and measured as a provision. The unavoidable costs are the lower of the cost of fulfilling the contract and the cost of penalties involved in exiting the contract. For example, a business moves to new premises but still has some time to run on the lease on its old premises — the unavoidable costs are the lower of the cost of exiting the lease agreement and simply paying the rent on the old premises until the lease runs out.

GST collections

Whenever entities in Australia sell goods and services that are subject to the GST, the entities must collect GST on behalf of the Australian Taxation Office (ATO). They thus have a liability to pay the GST they have collected to the ATO. To facilitate this, entities need to include a liability account for GST collections in their general ledger. The GST Collections account is a current liability because entities are required to submit GST collections, less any GST outlays, to the ATO on at least a quarterly basis.

To illustrate, consider No Risk Computers Ltd, which sells computers for $2860 each, including GST, on credit. Whenever a computer is sold, the following journal entry is made:

May	20	Accounts Receivable	2 860	
		Sales		2 600
		GST Collections		260
		(Sale of computer, including 10% GST)		

No Risk Computers Ltd purchases the computers from its supplier for $1540 each, including GST. Whenever No Risk purchases a computer, the following journal entry is made:

May	10	Purchases/Inventory	1 400	
		GST Outlays	140	
		Accounts Payable		1 540
		(Purchase of computer, including 10% GST)		

No Risk Computers Ltd pays GST to the ATO in the month following each quarter. Assume that for the quarter ended 30 June, the balance in the GST Collections account is $130 000 and the balance in the GST Outlays account is $110 000, so the following journal entry is made on the date of payment:

July	28	GST Collections	130 000	
		GST Outlays		110 000
		Cash at Bank		20 000
		(June quarter payment of GST)		

Note that the two accounts are offset and the balance is paid to the ATO, thus discharging the liability for the June quarter. In practice, some businesses may combine the two GST accounts into one clearing account which is called the GST Payable account. The journal entries are:

June	30	GST Collections	130 000	
		GST Outlays		110 000
		GST Payable		20 000
		(June quarter liability for GST)		
July	28	GST Payable	20 000	
		Cash at Bank		20 000
		(June quarter payment of GST)		

22.6 Non-current liabilities

Non-current liabilities generally include long-term borrowings such as debentures, unsecured notes, mortgage loans, unsecured long-term loans, and long-term commitments under a finance lease. They may also include provisions for long-service leave and warranty costs payable beyond the 12 months or operating cycle, as well as any long-term accounts payable. Note that the part of the non-current liabilities which comes due for payment within 1 year of the end of the reporting period or within the operating cycle is classified and reported as a current liability. This section deals with the accounting treatment of major types of non-current liabilities.

Entities obtain funds needed to operate a business by borrowing from a variety of lending sources. The method of financing depends on several factors, one of which is the length of time required to convert the assets acquired with the borrowed funds back into cash. Inventories that will be sold in the near future, for example, are usually financed through short-term credit. Cash needed to finance seasonal activities is generally borrowed through short-term bills or loans because current operations are expected to produce sufficient cash to repay the loan.

On the other hand, when an entity finds it necessary to obtain funds for long-term purposes such as the acquisition of non-current assets, the funds are often obtained by long-term borrowing. Deferring the payment for an extended period will allow time for the acquired assets to generate sufficient cash to cover interest payments and accumulate the funds needed to repay the loan.

The repayment of long-term debt can take up to 20 or more years. The agreement between the lender and the borrower usually provides for periodic interest payments on specified dates as well as the repayment of the amount borrowed. The borrower receives current dollars in exchange for a promise to make payments to the lender at specified intervals into the future. Dollars received and paid at different times are made comparable by considering the time value of money. (If you have not been exposed to present value concepts before, refer to the coverage in the appendix at the back of this book, and study the concepts and calculations presented.)

The types of non-current liabilities

Typical non-current liabilities are:

- **Term loans**: a liability which arises by borrowing from banks, life insurance companies, and other financial institutions for periods up to 10 years. The interest rate, which is usually higher than the bank overdraft interest rate, may be fixed or may vary in accordance with general market interest rate levels. Some form of security, such as the assets being financed, is usually required against the loan, which requires repayment of interest and capital.
- **Mortgage payable**: a liability in which specific property of the borrower serves as collateral (security) for the loan. **Collateral** is something of value acceptable to the lender that can be converted into cash to satisfy the debt if the borrower defaults.
- **Debentures or bonds**: a form of liability, either secured or unsecured, generally issued when a large amount is borrowed from many lenders. Under Australia's Corporations Act, the term 'debenture' is given the general meaning of a document that evidences indebtedness of a company in respect of money borrowed by the company, whether constituting a charge on property of the company or not, other than:
  (a) a cheque, or order for the payment of money on a bill of exchange
  (b) a promissory note having a face value of not less than $50 000
  (c) a document acknowledging a debt where the transaction occurs in the ordinary course of business between a borrower and a lender.

Normally, debentures represent a long-term secured liability borrowed from many lenders, who receive regular interest payments for the funds provided. Term loans and mortgages are normally used when money is borrowed from one or several lending institutions such as banks or insurance companies. Often, however, a few lenders may not be able or willing to lend the total amount of money needed. In such situations, long-term funds may be obtained by issuing debentures to many lenders drawn from the investing public at large.

Other types of non-current liabilities are lease contracts, superannuation liabilities, certain types of redeemable preference shares, and liabilities for long-service leave. GST is not payable on financial instruments.

BUSINESS KNOWLEDGE

In bonds we trust

Although bond issues are normally associated with companies and governments, for a second time now in Australia, a university has made an offer to the public. The University of Wollongong has issued $42.5 million of consumer price index-linked annuity bonds, for which credit agency Standard & Poor's has assigned a AA long-term rating. The bond funds will help the university build its innovation campus and will mature in 2038. This source of finance is a cheaper alternative for the university than bank finance. Consumer price index-linked bonds also enable the University of Wollongong to hedge against inflation.

Source: Based on information from Jill Rowbotham, 'Gong says in bonds we trust', *The Australian*.

Debentures

In general terms, a debenture is a written promise to pay a principal amount at a specified time and interest on the principal at a specified rate per period. Once issued (sold), the debenture becomes a non-current liability to the issuer and an investment to the buyer. When a debenture is issued, a certificate is given to the buyer as evidence of the company's indebtedness.

The company borrowing money must establish a **trust deed** and appoint a trustee under the deed. The trust deed indicates the interest rate to be paid, the dates interest is to be paid, the maturity date, the principal amount, and other features included in this particular issue such as the debenture holders' right to convert the debentures into ordinary shares. The trust deed may include covenants which are designed to provide protection to the debenture holders and prevent the borrowing company from borrowing beyond certain limits. Examples of covenants are the requirement that total secured creditors cannot exceed 40% of total tangible assets and that total borrowings cannot exceed 60% of total tangible assets.

Debentures are generally issued by companies in denominations of $100, which is called the **nominal value**, **face value** or **principal**. On the **maturity date**, the borrower must repay the nominal value to the debenture holder. Maturity dates vary, but most debentures are issued by finance companies and usually range from 1 month to 5 years.

A total debenture issue of $4 000 000 would generally consist of 40 000 debentures each of $100 nominal value. The division of the total issue into relatively small units permits more investors to participate in the issue.

Before a company issues debentures, it must issue a prospectus, which in Australia must be lodged with the Australian Securities and Investments Commission. The prospectus is an important document in that it is a marketing aid for a company to attract investors and also provides information to potential investors about the securities being purchased. Under the Corporations Act, a prospectus must contain all such information that investors and their professional advisers would reasonably require in order to assess:
- the assets and liabilities, financial position, profits or losses, and prospects of the issuing company
- the rights and liabilities attaching to the securities.

In so doing, a company must have regard for the type of investors being sought, e.g. many small investors or a small number of large institutional investors.

A copy of the full prospectus (or a short-form prospectus, if appropriate) must be attached to an application form for the issue of debentures. Any interested person may then fill out the application form and forward it to the issuing company for further action. Directors of the company can, after a certain specified time, allot debentures based on applications received.

Because the debentures may be held by numerous individual investors, a corporate body is usually appointed as a **trustee** by the issuing company to represent the debenture holders. In most cases, the trustee is a large bank, insurance company or trust company whose main duty is to ensure that the issuing company fulfils the terms and covenants of the trust deed. The borrowing company then has certain obligations to the trustee, including giving the trustee quarterly reports on the progress of the company during the life of the debentures.

A specified rate of interest is paid on the nominal value throughout the life of the debentures. The rate, called the **coupon rate**, **nominal rate** or **stated rate**, is expressed as a percentage of nominal value. Interest payments are normally made quarterly or half-yearly, although the stated rate of interest is expressed as an annual rate.

Debenture prices are quoted as a percentage of nominal value. For example, the price of a $100 nominal value debenture quoted at 104 is $104 ($100 × 104%). Debentures may be sold at nominal value, which means that the debenture price is 100. If the debenture price is below 100, e.g. 98, the debentures are said to sell at a **discount**; if the price is above 100, e.g. 104, the debentures are said to sell at a **premium**. The amount of the discount or premium is the difference between the issue price and the nominal value of the debenture. For example, a debenture quoted at 104 is selling at a $4 ($104 − $100) premium. Alternatively, if the company received $92 for a $100 debenture, there is an $8 discount.

Types of debentures

A trust deed is written to satisfy the financial needs of the borrower, but the agreement also must be attractive to a sufficient number of investors. Consequently, individual debenture issues with a variety of features have been created:

- *Mortgage debentures.* A **mortgage debenture** is one in which no more than 60% of the value of land controlled by the company is mortgaged as security for the debenture. If the entity fails to satisfy its obligations as specified in the trust deed, the land may be sold and the proceeds used to satisfy the indebtedness.
- *Debentures.* Holders of debentures are secured by a charge over the whole or any sufficient part of the tangible property of the company. This charge may be fixed on a particular asset, or floating generally over all of the entity's tangible assets.
- *Unsecured notes.* If the loan cannot be described as a mortgage debenture or debenture, as above, it must be described as an unsecured note. Thus, **unsecured notes** are, in effect, borrowings with no claim over any of the company's assets, and rank with ordinary creditors for repayment of debt in the event of the liquidation of the company.

A debenture issue may contain other special features. For instance, debentures may be irredeemable except at maturity date, or redeemable earlier than maturity at the option of the issuing company. Early redemption is commonly made at a price above nominal value, i.e. at a premium. Alternatively, the debentures may be convertible into ordinary shares after a certain period of time.

Although debenture and note issues may contain different features, accounting for the various issues is similar. Because the features of long term debt are important to potential investors, they are disclosed in the company's financial statements, usually in footnotes. The disclosure contains the interest rate, interest payments, maturity date, and any assets pledged as security. Examples of such disclosures can be seen in the annual reports of most public companies.

Accounting for debentures

When debentures are issued at nominal value, payable in full on application, money received from applicants who have sent in their application forms from the prospectus must be held in trust until directors have allotted the debentures to successful applicants. No formal journal entries are made when the prospectus is issued. To illustrate, assume that on 15 May 2013, Jordan Ltd's board of directors authorised the issue of 1000 $100 8% debentures for 5 years, payable in full on application. The date of allotment was 1 July 2013. Interest is payable half-yearly on 30 June and 31 December. There are no other special features in the trust deed. All debentures were applied for and allotted on 1 July. The entries to record the issue are (in general journal form):

2013				
July	1	Cash Trust	100 000	
		Application – Debentures		100 000
		(Money received on application for debentures)		
	1	Application – Debentures	100 000	
		Debentures		100 000
		(Allotment of 1000 $100 debentures)		
	1	Cash at Bank	100 000	
		Cash Trust		100 000
		(Transfer to cash at bank on allotment)		

Note that, for legal reasons, all money received on application is held in a Cash Trust account until the debentures are allotted to applicants. On allotment, the money in the Cash Trust account is then transferred to the company's normal Cash at Bank account and is available for use by the company.

In this example, interest of $4000 ($100 000 × 8% × 6/12) is due each 30 June and 31 December until the debentures mature. The entry to record the first half-yearly interest payment is:

Dec.	31	Debenture Interest Expense	4 000	
		Cash at Bank		4 000
		(Paid half-yearly interest on 8% debentures)		

During the 5-year period until the debentures mature, total interest expense of $40 000 is reported.

When a business has made a number of different debenture issues, the Debentures account represents a control account, and a subsidiary ledger is kept that records details of each separate issue.

Some debentures may be traded on the open market. Depending on a number of factors, such as current interest rates and the financial position of the borrower, the price of the debentures will fluctuate above or below their nominal value. Changes in the market price of the debentures are not entered in the entity's accounts because such changes do not alter the entity's commitment to make the stated half-yearly interest payments and to pay the nominal value when the debentures mature.

Redemption of debentures

When the debentures are issued, the entity undertakes to pay to debenture holders the interest payable at regular intervals, and eventually to repay the principal. As noted above, debenture holders' rights are protected by the existence of a trust deed, with security for the debt covered by a fixed or floating charge over some or all of the entity's assets. The entity can be released from its obligations under a trust deed in a number of ways — by redemption in cash, by redemption with cash accumulated in a sinking fund, or by defeasance.

When debentures are redeemed in cash at maturity, the entity can pay the nominal value of the debentures, pay an amount higher than the nominal value (redeem at a premium), or pay an amount less than nominal value (redeem at a discount). In this book, the redemption at nominal value only is illustrated. Assume that $100 000 of Jordan Ltd's debentures are redeemed on 30 June 2018 by the cash payment of $100 000.

The journal entries (in general journal format) to redeem debentures are:

2018				
June	30	Debentures	100 000	
		Debenture Holders		100 000
		(Redemption of $100 000 8% debentures)		
	30	Debenture Holders	100 000	
		Cash at Bank		100 000
		(Payment to debenture holders)		

Other methods of redemption are by sinking fund and by defeasance. **Redemption by sinking fund** means that the entity has established a fund into which it puts resources over the term of the debentures to buy assets such as government bonds. These investments are then used to redeem the debentures on maturity. **Defeasance** is an arrangement whereby the obligations under the trust deed are avoided by replacing each obligation for a cash payment with some other arrangement. Redemption by sinking fund and defeasance are beyond the scope of this book and are covered in more advanced books on accounting and finance.

Other non-current liabilities

Usually, a balance sheet/statement of financial position contains a number of different kinds of non-current liabilities other than debentures. Other common types of non-current liabilities are unsecured notes, mortgage payable, term loans, lease obligations, superannuation liabilities and liabilities for long-service leave.

Unsecured notes

The issue and redemption of unsecured notes are treated in the same way as debentures, except for the use of an Unsecured Notes account rather than a Debentures account.

Mortgage payable

A company may borrow money or finance the purchase of non-current assets on credit by giving the lender or seller a note secured by a legal document which is called a mortgage. A **mortgage** is a lien on specific property of the borrower (i.e. the lender, in effect, 'owns' the debtor's property until the debt is paid). If the debt is not paid, the mortgage holder (lender) may have the specific property sold, and the proceeds of the sale go towards reducing the debt.

Mortgage contracts generally require the borrower to make equal periodic payments that include both accrued interest and a reduction in principal. Each payment is applied first to the accrued interest; the remainder of the payment reduces the principal. As the principal balance declines over time, the portion of each payment assigned to interest decreases and the portion assigned to a reduction of principal increases.

To illustrate, assume that Central Airlines purchased a passenger plane for $2 500 000 on 1 September 2013. Central Airlines gave the seller a 12% mortgage that provided for a $252 250 deposit and 60 monthly payments of $50 000 each to begin on 1 October 2013. The division of the first five and last two monthly payments between interest and principal is shown in figure 22.2.

Figure 22.2 Monthly payment schedule

Monthly payment number	(A) Payment date	(B) Unpaid balance at beginning of month	(C) Cash payment	(D) Interest for one month (col. B × 1%)	(E) Reduction in principal (col. C – col. D)	(F) Principal balance at end of month
	2013					
	1 Sept.	$2 500 000	$252 250	$ —	$ 252 250	$2 247 750
1	1 Oct.	2 247 750	50 000	22 478	27 522	2 220 228
2	1 Nov.	2 220 228	50 000	22 202	27 798	2 192 430
3	1 Dec.	2 192 430	50 000	21 924	28 076	2 164 354
	2014					
4	1 Jan.	2 164 354	50 000	21 644	28 356	2 135 998
5	1 Feb.	2 135 998	50 000	21 360	28 640	2 107 358
	2018					
59	1 Aug.	98 520	50 000	985	49 015	49 505
60	1 Sept.	49 505	50 000	495	49 505	—

The entry to record the 1 October 2013 payment is:

Oct.	1	Interest Expense	22 478	
		Mortgage Payable	27 522	
		Cash at Bank		50 000
		(Monthly mortgage payment)		

For reporting purposes, the part of the unpaid principal balance to be paid during the next year is classified as a current liability, with the balance of the principal classified as a non-current liability.

Term loans

Term loans are similar to mortgages payable but there is no mortgage as such. Other security or guarantees are usually required. The accounting is the same as for mortgages payable.

Lease obligations

A **lease** is a rental agreement in which the lessee obtains from the lessor (the owner) the right to use property for a stated period of time in return for a series of rental payments. Many entities lease much of their equipment rather than purchase it, for one or more of the following reasons:

- The full lease payment, even for land, is deductible for tax purposes.
- Lease contracts may be more flexible and contain fewer restrictions than most debt agreements.
- The risk of obsolescence is shifted to the lessor.

Because of these advantages, the use of leasing has grown rapidly in the last 50 years. As a result, the accounting profession has devoted a great deal of effort to the establishment of accounting standards for lease reporting.

Accounting for leases by the lessee is similar to that described earlier for a mortgage payable. The lessee records the leased property as a non-current asset and credits a non-current liability for the future lease payments. The asset and liability are recorded at an amount equal to the present value of the future lease payments. Part of each lease rental payment is recorded as interest expense, and the remainder is a reduction in the principal balance. In addition, the leased asset is depreciated over the period that it is expected to be used in the normal manner for charging depreciation.

Accounting for leases is a specialist topic, and is covered in more advanced accounting books.

Why finance through long-term debt?

One function of management is to select the types of finance that are most advantageous to the entity. The major advantages and disadvantages of issuing long-term debt rather than owners' equity result from the legal distinction between creditors and owners.

The *advantages* of issuing long-term debt from the point of view of the owners include:

- Creditors do not have voting rights and therefore cannot participate in the management of the entity. This avoids diluting the control of the existing owners.
- Creditors do not share in any excess profits of the entity as they are due only the interest on the debt.
- Owners can earn a greater return than if more shares are issued.

The *disadvantages* of issuing long-term debt from the point of view of the owners include:

- Interest payments to creditors must be made each period as specified in the debt instrument regardless of whether the entity is profitable, whereas if funds are raised through the issue of shares, dividends do not have to be paid. This makes long-term debt a more risky option for the owners of an entity than a new share issue.
- Default on the interest commitment could result in a forced winding-up of the entity.
- If the entity is wound up, creditors must be paid in full before any asset distribution is made to owners.

Even though an entity may be able to raise funds by selling shares, long-term debt is often issued because of the gearing provided and the income tax treatment of interest payments. **Gearing (or leverage)** is the use of borrowed funds to earn a return greater than the interest paid on the debt. The use of debt has the additional advantage of interest expense being deductible in calculating taxable income, whereas dividends on shares are not tax-deductible.

To illustrate the effect of debt financing versus equity financing (raising money by selling shares), assume that a company with $2 000 000 in shares is currently earning $400 000 a year profit before income tax. The company needs to raise $1 000 000 in additional funds to finance a planned expansion of the plant. Management estimates that, after the expansion, $700 000 will be earned annually before interest and income tax. The $1 000 000 can be obtained from one of the two plans that are proposed for consideration:

- Plan 1 — issue 1 000 000 shares at $1 each
- Plan 2 — issue 8% debentures.

It is assumed that each security is issued at its total value of $1 000 000. Income tax is assumed to be 30%. The effect of these two plans on the profit available to shareholders is shown in figure 22.3.

Figure 22.3 Illustration of two plans to finance expansion

	Existing operations	Plan 1: shares	Plan 2: debentures
Shares currently issued	2 000 000	2 000 000	2 000 000
Additional shares issued	—	1 000 000	—
Total	2 000 000	3 000 000	2 000 000
Profit before debenture interest and income tax	$ 400 000	$ 700 000	$ 700 000
Less: Debenture interest expense	—	—	80 000
Profit before income tax	400 000	700 000	620 000
Less: Income tax (30%)	120 000	210 000	186 000
Profit	$ 280 000	$ 490 000	$ 434 000
Number of shares issued	2 000 000	3 000 000	2 000 000
Earnings per share	14c	16.3c	21.7c

Using earnings per share (profit ÷ number of issued shares) as the sole criterion for making the decision, Plan 2 is the most attractive to the existing shareholders despite the payment of $80 000 in interest each period. This results from a combination of two factors. First, the entity is predicting that profit will increase by $210 000 [$300 000 − (30% × $300 000)] before debenture interest expense is deducted. Second, because interest is a tax-deductible expense, the cost of borrowing is considerably less than the $80 000 paid to the debenture holders. In other words, the after-tax cost of borrowing is $56 000, which is the $80 000 expense minus the $24 000 (30% × $80 000) tax saving (reduction in income tax expense). The net increase in profit after tax of $154 000 ($210 000 − $56 000) accrues to the existing shareholders. Although Plan 1 shows an increase in profit of $210 000 ($490 000 − $280 000), the increase is divided over 50% more shares.

This analysis was based on the effect of the alternative plans on earnings per share and on a favourable gearing assumption. In financial planning, however, management cannot ignore the fact that the debentures will eventually mature and require repayment and that the fixed interest cost must be paid each period. At lower levels of profit, Plan 1 becomes more attractive. For example, if the company were to earn $80 000 before interest and taxes, the entire amount would be offset by the interest cost. At lower earnings levels, the company may be unable to generate sufficient cash to satisfy the interest payments and could be forced into liquidation.

Whether an entity relies on long-term debt or a share issue to finance long-term expansion, there is a risk–return trade-off for the owners. Long-term debt provides the potential for a greater return for the owners but also greater risk. Issuing shares involves less return for the owners but also less risk of going into liquidation.

22.7 Analysing liabilities for decision making

Learning objective 7

Analyse liabilities for decision-making purposes

In this chapter, we have seen that liabilities involve an outflow of resources embodying economic benefits that an entity is *presently obliged to make* as a result of past events. To ensure a continuing capacity to meet current or short-term liabilities, the operating cycle has to be managed to make sure that cash inflows are sufficient to cover current or short-term liabilities as they come due for payment. Sufficient cash also has to be generated in the operating cycle to provide the entity with the capacity to meet periodic interest payments and other charges associated with non-current liabilities. In the longer term, cash reserves have to be built up to provide the entity with the capacity to repay the principal on non-current liabilities. Creditors, both current and non-current, have a particular interest in an entity's liquidity and financial stability.

Cash management is a very important function of management, and external users are interested in how well the entity's short-term liquidity and its long-term financial stability are managed. Most entities, both large and small, that go into liquidation (i.e. are wound up) do so because of failure to successfully achieve an adequate level of liquidity and financial stability. Apart from evaluating absolute amounts of cash inflows and cash outflows, a number of common ratios can be used to analyse liabilities and their effect on liquidity and financial stability. These ratios can highlight areas of concern, and appropriate decisions can be taken to remedy any undesirable aspects and trends in liquidity and financial stability. These ratios are discussed below.

Liquidity ratios

Liquidity ratios provide a measure of an entity's ability to pay its short-term obligations and meet unexpected demands on its cash resources.

Current ratio

Perhaps the most commonly used measure of liquidity is the current ratio, which is calculated as:

$$\text{Current ratio} = \frac{\text{Current assets}}{\text{Current liabilities}}$$

The current ratio, a measure of the entity's ability to satisfy its obligations in the short term, measures a margin of safety for the creditors. It indicates how much current assets exceed current liabilities on a dollar-for-dollar basis. A low ratio may indicate inability to meet short-term debts in an emergency. A high ratio is considered favourable to creditors, but may indicate excessive investment in current assets that may not be contributing to profits.

Analysts often suggest as a rule of thumb that the current ratio should be at least 1.5:1; in other words, an entity should maintain $1.50 of current assets for every dollar of current liabilities. Although such rules may be one standard of comparison, they are arbitrary and subject to exceptions and numerous qualifications in the modern approach to statement analysis. Deviations from the rule, nevertheless, highlight an area that deserves further investigation.

Quick ratio or acid test ratio

One of the limitations of the current ratio is that it includes inventory and prepaid assets in the numerator. These items are not as liquid as cash, marketable securities (e.g. shares), current bills receivable and accounts receivable. In the normal course of business, inventories must first be sold, and then the cash collected, before cash is available. Also, most prepaid assets are to be consumed and cannot be readily converted back to cash. A ratio used to supplement the current ratio that provides a more rigorous measure of liquidity is the quick ratio, or acid test ratio as it is sometimes called. The quick ratio is calculated as follows:

$$\text{Quick ratio} = \frac{\text{Cash at bank} + \text{Marketable securities} + \text{Net receivables}}{\text{Current liabilities}}$$

The higher the ratio, the more liquid the entity is considered. A rule of thumb used by some analysts is that a 0.9:1 ratio is adequate. A lower ratio would indicate that, in an emergency, the entity may be unable to meet its immediate obligations.

Although a single measure of the above ratios can be the basis for making decisions, the trend in these ratios over time is more informative.

The current ratio and quick ratio are used to measure the adequacy of the current assets to satisfy current obligations at one point in time, the end of the reporting period. These ratios do not consider the movement of items making up the current assets. An important aspect of the entity's operations affecting liquidity is how long it takes to convert receivables and inventories into cash. Since receivables and inventories normally make up a large percentage of current assets, a quick ratio and a current ratio may be misleading if there is an extended interval between purchasing inventory, selling it, and collecting cash from the sale. The receivables turnover and inventory turnover ratios are two other measures of liquidity that can provide additional information and that should be used together with the quick and current ratios. (These ratios were covered in previous chapters.)

Financial stability ratios

Financial stability ratios are used to analyse the ability of an entity to continue its activities in the long term, to satisfy its long-term commitments, and still have sufficient working capital to operate successfully. Two such ratios are covered below.

Debt ratio

The proportion of total assets financed by creditors is important to long-term investors since the creditors have first claim to assets in the event of liquidation — the creditors must be paid before assets are distributed to owners. The greater the percentage of assets contributed by owners, the greater the protection for the creditors. The debt ratio is a measure of the relationship between total liabilities and total assets and is calculated as:

$$\text{Debt ratio} = \frac{\text{Total liabilities}}{\text{Total assets}}$$

Since this ratio is a measure of the margin of safety to the creditors in the event of liquidation, the lower the ratio, the greater the asset protection for the creditors.

Equity ratio

Another ratio that attempts to assess long-term stability and is sometimes used in place of the debt ratio is the equity ratio. This ratio is also referred to as the proprietorship ratio. The equity ratio examines the relationship between equity and total assets and is calculated as:

$$\text{Equity ratio} = \frac{\text{Total equity}}{\text{Total assets}}$$

As with the debt ratio, the equity ratio is a measure of the margin of safety to creditors in the event of liquidation. The higher the equity ratio, the greater the asset protection for creditors.

Note the following relationship between the debt ratio and equity ratio — one is the complement of the other. This is because total assets are financed by either debt or equity.

$$\text{Debt ratio} + \text{Equity ratio} = 1 \text{ or } 100\%$$

A further variation of the debt ratio and the equity ratio that is sometimes used is the capitalisation ratio (or gearing ratio), which is calculated as:

$$\text{Capitalisation ratio} = \frac{\text{Total assets}}{\text{Total equity}}$$

As with the debt and equity ratios, the capitalisation ratio points out the extent to which assets are financed by equity. It is usually expressed as a ratio, e.g. 2:1, which indicates that the equity structure of the entity is 50% equity and 50% debt. The capitalisation ratio is the reciprocal of the equity ratio and is simply another method of determining the amount of gearing in existence in the entity. It does not tell us anything about the desirability or otherwise of the gearing level in the entity. Trends in the ratio over time and comparison with the ratios of similar entities provide useful information regarding long-term stability and the degree of risk management has undertaken by financing assets with long-term debt.

Illustration of ratios

To illustrate the above ratios, the comparative balance sheets of Fletcher Pty Ltd are shown below. Calculate the following ratios — current ratio, quick ratio, debt ratio, equity ratio and capitalisation ratio for the years 2014 and 2013. Analyse the ratios, given that the industry averages for the above ratios are: current ratio 2.5:1, quick ratio 1.3:1, debt ratio 40%, and capitalisation ratio 2.5:1.

FLETCHER PTY LTD
Comparative Balance Sheets
as at 30 June 2014 and 2013
$'000

	2014	2013
CURRENT ASSETS		
Cash	$ 612	$ 880
Marketable securities	150	125
Accounts receivable	1 900	1 750
Inventory	3 250	3 300
TOTAL CURRENT ASSETS	5 912	6 055
NON-CURRENT ASSETS		
Plant and equipment	7 960	7 300
TOTAL ASSETS	$13 872	$13 355
CURRENT LIABILITIES		
Accounts payable	$ 2 600	$ 2 730
Accrued expenses and other	75	125
TOTAL CURRENT LIABILITIES	2 675	2 855
NON-CURRENT LIABILITIES		
Fixed term loans	400	300
Mortgage payable	4 200	4 200
TOTAL LIABILITIES	7 275	7 355
EQUITY		
Share capital	3 850	3 850
Retained earnings	2 747	2 150
TOTAL EQUITY	6 597	6 000
TOTAL LIABILITIES AND EQUITY	$13 872	$13 355

Using the formulas given previously, the ratios are (industry averages are in parentheses):

		2014	2013	
Current ratio	$\dfrac{\text{Current assets}}{\text{Current liabilities}}$	$\dfrac{5\,912}{2\,675} = 2.21{:}1$	$\dfrac{6\,055}{2\,855} = 2.12{:}1$	(2.5:1)
Quick ratio	$\dfrac{\text{Cash + Marketable securities + Receivables}}{\text{Current liabilities}}$	$\dfrac{2\,662}{2\,675} = 1{:}1$	$\dfrac{2\,755}{2\,855} = 0.97{:}1$	(1.3:1)
Debt ratio	$\dfrac{\text{Total liabilities}}{\text{Total assets}}$	$\dfrac{7\,275}{13\,872} = 0.524$ or 52%	$\dfrac{7\,355}{13\,355} = 0.55$ or 55%	(0.4) or 40%
Equity ratio	$\dfrac{\text{Total equity}}{\text{Total assets}}$	$\dfrac{6\,597}{13\,872} = 0.475$ or 48%	$\dfrac{6\,000}{13\,355} = 0.449$ or 45%	(0.6) or 60%
Capitalisation ratio	$\dfrac{\text{Total assets}}{\text{Total equity}}$	$\dfrac{13\,872}{6\,597} = 2.1{:}1$	$\dfrac{13\,355}{6\,000} = 2.23{:}1$	(2.5:1)

The company's liquidity is not convincing since, in both years, the current ratio and the quick ratio are both below the industry average. The liquidity position needs to be carefully monitored by management to assess why the ratios are below the industry averages. The trend from 2013 to 2014 is positive, but further improvement is necessary.

The financial stability ratios also are not strong. All ratios are below the industry average. As disclosed by the debt ratios, the company is relying heavily on debt financing (over 50%) of its assets in both years. This is well in excess of the policies on asset financing of the businesses in the industry, which average 40%. The equity ratios also confirm this heavier than normal reliance on debt financing. However, the trend is positive and needs to be maintained in future years. The capitalisation ratios of 2.23:1 and 2.1:1 are well below the industry average of 2.5:1.

Management needs to review its credit and financing policies and take remedial action as soon as possible, in an effort to get the company's financial position more in line with that of the industry in which it operates. If the current position is not improved, the company will have problems in the future obtaining credit and debt financing.

KEY TERMS

Accommodation bills, p. 914

Accounts payable, p. 913

Annual leave, p. 918

Bills payable, p. 913

Collateral, p. 922

Commercial bills, p. 914

Constructive obligation, p. 909

Contingent liability, p. 911

Coupon rate (nominal or stated rate), p. 924

Current liability, p. 913

Debentures (or bonds), p. 922

Defeasance, p. 926

Discount (in relation to bills of exchange), p. 915

Discount (on debentures), p. 924

Employee benefits, p. 916

Financial stability ratios, p. 930

Gearing (or leverage), p. 927

Gross pay (gross earnings), p. 916

Lease, p. 927

Legal obligation, p. 909

Liabilities, p. 908

Liquidity ratios, p. 929

Long-service leave, p. 920

Maturity date, p. 923

Mortgage, p. 926

Mortgage debenture, p. 924

Mortgage payable, p. 922

Net pay, p. 917

Nominal value (face value, principal), p. 923

Non-current liability, p. 913

Obligating event, p. 911

Onerous contract, p. 921

Premium (on debentures), p. 924

Present value, p. 916

Provisions, p. 910

Redemption by sinking fund, p. 926

Salary, p. 917

Term loan, p. 922

Trade creditors, p. 913

Trust deed, p. 923

Trustee, p. 924

Unsecured note, p. 924

Wages, p. 917

Workers compensation, p. 919

DISCUSSION QUESTIONS

1. 'Classification of liabilities is based on the same principles as the classification of assets.' Do you agree with this? Why or why not?
2. 'Classification of liabilities as current or non-current is not that important. The money is paid out eventually anyway, so what's the big deal?' Discuss.
3. 'A provision and a contingent liability are the same.' Discuss.
4. 'Employees often fail to appreciate the true cost of their employment.' Discuss.
5. Your accounting lecturer remarked: 'The journal entries necessary to record the expense and liability in accounting for long-service leave can be easily and logically derived. However, deciding when to record such entries and the dollar amount involved is problematic.' Discuss.
6. With reference to the *Conceptual Framework*, explain why future warranty costs should be recognised as a liability in the balance sheet/statement of financial position in the current period.
7. A family company, which had been operating successfully for five generations, continues to maintain a policy of raising money only through equity finance and never through debt. Discuss the advantages and disadvantages of adopting this policy. Would you recommend a continuation of this policy?

8. If a company is regarded as solvent, then it can be concluded that the company has no liquidity problems. Discuss.
9. A company issues debentures at 10%, the market rate at that time. What effect would an interest rate rise have?

EXERCISES

Exercise 22.1 CLASSIFICATION OF LIABILITIES

LO 4

How would each of the following liabilities be classified (current, non-current, or both) at the end of the financial year?

Unearned revenue	Provision for long-service leave
Accrued expenses	Bills payable
Provision for warranty repair costs	Fixed interest loan — 3-year
10-year debentures (after 5 years)	Accounts payable (trade)
Mortgage loan (15-year)	Dividend payable
Annual leave payable	10-year debentures (after $9^1/_2$ years)

Exercise 22.2 JOURNAL ENTRIES FOR BILL FINANCING

LO 5

The following were among transactions of Morissette Telecommunications during the financial years ending 30 June 2013 and 30 June 2014.

2013

March	1	Morissette Telecommunications discounted its own 90-day bill of exchange made out to the International Bank. The face value of the bill was $360 000 and the bill was discounted at 9% p.a.
May	30	Paid the International Bank the amount due on the bill.
June	1	Morissette Telecommunications discounted a further 60-day bill, made out to BankNorth for $200 000 at a discount rate of 8% p.a.
July	31	Morissette Telecommunications honoured its bill drawn on BankNorth.

Required
Record in general journal form all the above transactions, including any end-of-period adjustments required at 30 June 2014.

Exercise 22.3 DEBENTURES ISSUED AT NOMINAL VALUE

LO 6

The following information relates to a debentures issue of JLP Ltd dated 1 July 2013:

Date issued	1 January 2013
Nominal value	$1000
Stated interest rate	9%
Interest payment dates	30 June and 31 December
Term to maturity	10 years
Cash received from the issue	$800 000

The company's financial year-end is 30 June.

Required
A. Prepare general journal entries to record:
1. the issue of the debentures
2. the 31 December 2013 interest payment
3. the 30 June 2014 interest payment.
B. Calculate the interest expense for the year ended 30 June 2014, and prepare the entry to close the Interest Expense account to the Profit or Loss Summary account.
C. Show how the debentures will be reported at 30 June 2014.

Exercise 22.4 ANNUAL LEAVE PAYABLE

At 30 June 2014, the accountant for Jet Plane Ltd, Don Jenver, is preparing the financial statements for the year ended on that date. To calculate the annual leave payable, the accountant had gathered the following information on employee annual salary weeks leave outstanding:

Employee	Annual salary	Weeks leave outstanding
Don Jenver	120 120	6
Alicia Mae	83 200	4
Palao Marx	71 760	3
Vanessa Michael	67 600	4
George Moore	56 160	1
Richard Nutini	52 000	5

Required

A. Calculate the annual leave payable liability for Jet Plane Ltd as at 30 June 2011 based on a 52-week year.

B. The balance of the annual leave payable liability before the above calculation was $4310. Show the general journal entry to record the appropriate balance in the Annual Leave Payable account.

Exercise 22.5 EMPLOYEE BENEFITS

On 16 July, the weekly payroll register of Hammond Industries showed gross wages and salaries of $78 000. The organisation withheld $16 380 for income tax, $1760 for life insurance, $2100 for medical insurance premiums, and $8580 for superannuation deductions made on behalf of employees.

Required

A. Prepare the general journal entry to record the payroll and payroll deductions.

B. Prepare the general journal entry to record the employer's contributions to the employees' superannuation fund at the rate of 9% of gross payroll.

C. Prepare entries in the cash payments journal to record payment of the above liabilities.

Exercise 22.6 WARRANTIES

At 30 June 2014, Peacemaker Ltd adjusted its Provision for Warranties so that it would be equal to 4% of sales for the year ended on that date. Sales for the year ended 30 June 2014 were $1 600 000 and the Provision for Warranties before the adjustment was $45 000. On 6 October 2014, a successful claim for warranty on faulty goods to the cost of $600 was made on Peacemaker Ltd.

Required

A. Prepare the general journal entry at 30 June 2014 to adjust the Provision for Warranties to the required level.

B. Record the payment of the warranty claim on 6 October 2014 in general journal format.

Exercise 22.7 ISSUE OF DEBENTURES

On 1 June, Cooper Ltd received authorisation from its board of directors to issue $1 000 000 of 8% 10-year debentures dated 1 July. Interest is payable half-yearly on 31 December and 30 June each year.

Required

A. Record the issue of the debentures in general journal entry form, assuming allotment of all debentures on 1 July.

B. Record interest payments for 31 December and 30 June in the first financial year of issue.

Exercise 22.8 LIQUIDITY ANALYSIS

The following information has been extracted from the financial statements of Cold Ethyl Ltd.

	2014	2013
Cash at bank	$ 145 000	$ 160 000
Marketable securities	350 000	320 000
Accounts receivable	390 000	370 000
Inventory	940 000	960 000
Prepaid expenses	45 000	70 000
Plant and equipment	1 650 000	1 600 000
Accounts payable	879 000	823 500
Bills payable	50 000	47 000
Accrued expenses	6 000	3 500

Required

A. Calculate the following for 2013 and 2014:
   1. current ratio
   2. quick ratio.
B. Comment on the liquidity and trend in liquidity, given that the industry average for these ratios are: current 2.3:1 and quick 1.3:1.

Exercise 22.9 FINANCIAL STABILITY ANALYSIS

The following information is available for Keys Ltd.

	2014	2013
Total assets	$830 000	$725 000
Total liabilities	455 000	435 000
Share capital	310 000	260 000
Retained earnings	65 000	30 000

Required

A. Calculate the following ratios for 2013 and 2014:
   1. debt ratio   2. equity ratio   3. capitalisation ratio.
B. What do these ratios indicate about the company's gearing?

Exercise 22.10 CALCULATION OF LONG-SERVICE LEAVE LIABILITY

GoAhead Holiday Planner Pty Ltd has three employees. Their employment contracts entitle them to 13 weeks leave after 10 years of service. Refer to the following information about each employee at 30 June 2014:

Employee	Current salary	Years service
Albert	80 000	3
Alice	120 000	7
Alanis	150 000	9

Assume salaries are not expected to change, and ignore the effect of inflation. The employees are committed to the organisation and do not plan to resign but will take long-service leave as soon as available. You have found out the following information on current high-quality bond interest rates:

Period to maturity	Bond rate
3 years	6%
5 years	7%
8 years	8%

Required

Calculate the value of the provision for long-service leave for GoAhead Holiday Planner Pty Ltd at 30 June 2014.

Problem 22.1 CALCULATIONS AND JOURNAL ENTRIES FOR A PAYROLL ★

LO 5

The following information is used to calculate Ventura Highway Construction Ltd's payroll for the week ending 30 June 2014.

Employee	Gross pay	Salary sacrifice — donations
A. Beckley	832	20
B. Bunnell	1 140	50
C. Leacox	1 950	10
D. Woods	1 200	30

Employees' superannuation contribution is 9% of their gross pay. PAYG tax is taken out at 30% after subtracting the donations and superannuation. All employees also have the following deductions from their after-tax pay: 2.5% life insurance and 11% medical insurance.

Required

A. Calculate 'take-home' pay for each employee.
B. Prepare a general journal entry to accrue the payroll and associated deductions.
C. Prepare a cash payments journal entry to record the payment of wages.
D. Assume that, on 6 July 2014, the company forwarded cheques to cover amounts withheld from employees' wages for the month of June. Total income tax deductions were $6540. Other deduction liabilities were four times the total weekly deductions. Prepare a cash payments journal entry to record these payments.

Problem 22.2 PAYROLL TRANSACTIONS AND LIABILITIES ★★

LO 5

The following accounts and balances appeared in the ledger of Winehouse Enterprises Pty Ltd on 30 April 2016:

Annual Leave Payable	$14 400 Cr
Sick Leave Payable	6 640 Cr
Provision for Long-Service Leave	59 625 Cr
Taxation Office	12 210 Cr
Superannuation Fund	3 600 Cr
Medical Insurance Payable	1 580 Cr

The following transactions occurred during May and June:

May 3 Issued cheque payable to the Taxation Office in payment of employees' tax instalment deductions. Also forwarded cheques to other organisations to cover liabilities for deductions made on behalf of employees.

31 Prepared a general journal entry to record payroll for the period:

Gross wages	$58 200
Income tax instalments	12 100
Superannuation contributions	7 970
Medical insurance	1 760

Issued a cheque to cover the net amount of the monthly payroll.
Accrued long-service leave expense for May, $1000.
Accrued annual leave expense for May, $7680.
Accrued sick leave expense for May, $3690.

June 3 Issued cheque payable to Taxation Office for amount due.
Paid other deduction liabilities from May payroll.

27 Prepared journal entry to record payroll for June:

Gross wages	$55 400
Income tax instalments	12 000
Superannuation	3 510
Medical insurance	1 450

28 Drew cheque to pay fringe benefits tax instalment of $480.
30 Drew cheque to pay June wages to employees.
Accrued long-service, annual and sick leave for month (see 31 May entry above).

Required

Prepare entries in general journal form for Winehouse Enterprises Pty Ltd to record the above transactions.

Problem 22.3 PROVISION FOR WARRANTY CLAIM EXPENSES ★★

Back2Black Services has been operating a successful business for many years specialising in the servicing and reconditioning of high-end mobile phones. Servicing costs $200, while reconditioning costs $450. The business has a reputation for good customer service, an important feature of which is the 12 months parts and labour written warranty provided with each service.

On 30 June 2013, the owners decided to introduce the practice of providing for warranty expenses at year-end, thereby establishing a warranty expense in the year the phones are serviced or reconditioned, and setting up a provision to cover future warranty expenses as they occur. Past records have been examined, and it has been established that, on average, one in ten phones are subject to a claim under the warranty offered. The costs of warranty have amounted to $40 for serviced units and $160 for reconditioned units. During the year ended 30 June 2013, 2500 phones were serviced and 4000 phones were reconditioned.

During the year ended 30 June 2014, 310 serviced phones and 290 reconditioned phones were repaired under the warranty. The costs of warranty work carried out by Back2Black Services were all paid in cash. During the year, 3230 phones were serviced and 4120 phones were reconditioned. At 30 June 2014, it was decided that warranty costs in the following year would increase by 5%. (Ignore GST.)

Required

A. Show the general journal entries to record the services/reconditioning for the year, and to establish the Provision for Warranty at 30 June 2013.
B. Show the general journal entries to record sales and the actual warranty costs incurred during the year ended 30 June 2014.
C. Show the general journal entry to adjust the Provision for Warranty at 30 June 2014.
D. Show how the above transactions would affect the financial statements for the 2 years.

Problem 22.4 ALTERNATIVE FINANCING — SHARES VERSUS DEBENTURES ★★

A&J Stone Ltd, which has been trading profitably for many years, is planning to expand the business to meet the increasing demand for its products. The issue price of all shares is $2. It plans to invest $4 000 000 to finance this expansion, and as a result achieve an increase in profit before interest on debt and income tax of $1 200 000. A summary of financial results for the financial year ended 30 June 2014 is presented below:

Income	$12 770 000
Expenses (excluding interest and income tax)	(9 650 000)
Interest expense	(154 000)
Profit before income tax	2 966 000
Income tax (30%)	889 800
Profit	$ 2 076 200
Earnings per share	0.52

Management is considering whether to finance the expansion by selling 2 000 000 shares at $2 per share or by issuing 7% 10-year debentures at a nominal value of $100 each.

Required

A. Assuming that the company achieves the expected increase in profit from the expansion, what will be the earnings per share for each of the alternative methods of financing proposed?
B. Discuss the disadvantage(s) of the method that produces the highest earnings per share.
C. What other factors might be considered by management in making its decision on the preferred financing method?

Problem 22.5 MORTGAGE LOAN TO FINANCE NON-CURRENT ASSETS ★★

Bella Properties Ltd has decided to purchase a new office building. It purchased land and a building for $1 394 600 on 1 December 2014. Agreed financing arrangements included payment of an initial deposit of 10% of the purchase price and the signing of a 10% p.a. mortgage contract which provided for quarterly payments of $50 000 over 10 years. The first quarterly payment was made on 1 March 2015. The company's financial year ends on 30 June.

Required

A. Prepare a quarterly payment schedule for payments made in the years ended 30 June 2015 and 2016. Head the columns with the following titles: Payment Date, Unpaid Balance at Beginning of Quarter, Cash Payment, Interest for One Quarter, Reduction in Principal, Principal Balance at End of Quarter.

B. Prepare journal entries associated with the land and building on 1 December 2014 for the financial year ended 30 June 2015. (The building was allocated 80% of the purchase price.) (Ignore GST.)

Problem 22.6 RATIOS FOR ANALYSING LIABILITIES ★★

Several potential investors have been studying the affairs of Art Ltd to decide whether to invest in the company by purchasing unsecured notes which the company was proposing to issue. The comment had been made that the company was experiencing liquidity problems. The statements of financial position at 30 June 2014 and 2015 follow:

ART LTD
Statements of Financial Position
as at 30 June

	2015	2014
CURRENT ASSETS		
Cash at bank	$ 3 264	$ 2 832
Marketable securities	1 519	1 775
Accounts receivable (net)	1 178	930
Inventories	2 619	1 848
Other current assets	3 094	3 605
TOTAL CURRENT ASSETS	11 674	10 990
NON-CURRENT ASSETS	19 960	16 276
TOTAL ASSETS	$31 634	$27 266
CURRENT LIABILITIES		
Accounts payable	$ 4 880	$ 4 300
Bills payable	1 574	2 555
Current maturities of long-term debt	978	450
Accrued expenses	720	728
Provisions	3 420	2 345
TOTAL CURRENT LIABILITIES	11 572	10 378
NON-CURRENT LIABILITIES		
Long-term debt	5 800	4 160
Accrued expenses (payroll)	5 425	4 730
Other non-current liabilities	2 390	2 055
TOTAL NON-CURRENT LIABILITIES	13 615	10 945
TOTAL LIABILITIES	25 187	21 323
TOTAL EQUITY	6 447	5 943
TOTAL LIABILITIES AND EQUITY	$31 634	$27 266

Required

A. Calculate appropriate liquidity and financial stability ratios for the years ended 30 June 2014 and 2015. Research reveals that typical ratios in the industry for the current and quick ratios are 1.7:1 and 1.0:1 respectively. For financial stability ratios, industry averages are 2.5:1 for the capitalisation ratio and 60% for the debt ratio.

B. Comment on the liquidity and financial stability of the company, given the information available.

C. Would you, as one of the potential purchasers of the unsecured notes, lend money to the company? Explain why or why not.

Problem 22.7 JOURNAL ENTRIES FOR VARIOUS LIABILITIES ★★★   **LO 5, 6**

Ringo Ltd completed the following selected transactions during 2014 and 2015. The financial year for the company ends on 31 December. (Ignore GST.)

2014

Jan.	6	Issued a 7% 60-day promissory note to Rigby Pty Ltd in settlement of an account for $8000 for goods supplied in the previous year.
Feb.	5	Paid Rigby Pty Ltd $4000 on the 6 January promissory note and accepted a new 10%, 30-day bill of exchange for the balance still owing.
March	7	Paid Rigby Pty Ltd for the 5 February bill.
April	23	The company paid warranty costs of $200 in cash to make good warranty conditions on a product sold in 2010. The company had an established Provision for Warranty Costs.
June	15	Discounted at a discount rate of 10% its own $75 000, 30-day, non-interest bearing note, made out to the Bank of Liverpool.
July	15	Paid the Bank of Liverpool the amount due.
Aug.	29	The company agreed to act as guarantor for a loan of $150 000 taken out by an associated business.
Sept.	10	Purchased $12 000 worth of inventory from Rita Ltd, on credit terms of 2/10, n/30.
Sept.	19	Paid Rita Ltd the amount due.
Nov.	1	Issued to Lucy Supplies a 9% 90-day bill for $12 000 in settlement of account owing.
Dec.	10	Discounted at a discount rate of 9% its own $100 000 60-day bill made out to the Diamond Bank.

2015

Jan.	29	Paid the Diamond Bank the amount due.
Feb.	8	Paid the amount due to Lucy Supplies for the bill issued on 10 December.

Required

Show how the above transactions, including any necessary adjusting entries on 30 June 2015, would be recorded in the general and cash journals of the company.

Problem 22.8 JOURNAL ENTRIES FOR DEBENTURE ISSUE AND MORTGAGE ★★★   **LO 5, 6**

Newave Ltd wishes to raise $2 500 000 to carry out construction work as part of a major expansion of its shopping mall operations. The directors decide to issue 10 000 $100 8% debentures, fully payable on application, with interest payable 6-monthly on 1 July and 1 January, and to borrow another $1 500 000 with a mortgage signed against other assets currently unencumbered. The terms of the mortgage loan include a deposit of $150 150, repayment over 60 months and an interest rate of 10% p.a.

All application money for the debentures was received on 1 April 2014 and the debentures were allotted on that date. The mortgage arrangements were finalised also on the same date.

Required

A. Prepare entries (in general journal form) to record the mortgage loan and the receipt of the application money on the debentures on 1 April 2014.

B. Prepare a loan repayment schedule for the mortgage for the first 5 months.

C. Show general journal entries to record all interest payments, and any necessary adjustments, up to 31 December 2014, assuming the end of the financial year is 30 June.

To provide or not to provide for warranties?

Rosy Lynch and Jose Manzanares have been conducting business for a few years selling mobile phones. As part of its contract of sale, the business offers a 1-year labour and parts warranty on all phones. The business has recently introduced a new product line in the form of 3G video phones. The 1-year warranty cover was also stated on the sales invoice for these phones.

Jose had recently read an accounting text from which he learned that it would be good accounting practice to recognise, at the end of the period, a liability for future warranty costs on sales made during the period. This was justified on the basis of the definition of 'provisions'.

Rosy was a little concerned in that, although she could recognise that an obligation for future warranty costs existed at the end of the period, she had difficulty in accepting that the future costs could be reliably measured. She pointed out that this was also a requirement of accounting standards.

Jose responded that he had examined past records and was able to determine that warranty costs which were incurred in the period following the sale averaged about 3% of net sales of phones. Rosy then remarked: 'Yes, but what about our new 3G phones? We've only just begun to sell these. We have no way of knowing exactly what our warranty costs will be. I think we should be consistent in our approach to handling warranty costs.'

Rosy and Jose decided to approach you as an accountant for your view.

Required

A. Would you support Rosy in her approach to not providing for warranty costs on the 3G phones, and hence no provision at all for all products? Explain why or why not.
B. Would you support Jose in his decision to set up a provision for warranty costs on the mobile phones? How would you justify your decision?
C. Summarise your decision on whether a provision for warranty should be recognised at period-end in Rosy and Jose's business.

Recognition of liabilities

It has been argued that many companies' profits are overstated because they fail to take into account the full cost of their operating activities. This is particularly relevant when considering the potential future environmental impact of both production and ultimate disposal of the items they manufacture. Consider the current approach to accounting for liabilities.

Required

A. What are the shortfalls of the current definition for liabilities when applied to potentially negative environmental situations?
B. How might this lead to profits being overstated?
C. Does it matter that accounting often fails to capture this information?
D. Should we change the definition of liability, and if so how?
E. What would be the broader ramifications for accounting and businesses if we were able to more accurately capture these liabilities?

The road to liquidation

In recent years a number of companies have gone into liquidation (been 'wound up') because they have not been able to meet their liabilities when they fell due. In Australia, there are some well-publicised examples such as ABC Learning, HIH Insurance, One.Tel phone company, Sons of Gwalia and Westpoint.

Required

In groups of three or four, find (via electronic journals) an example of a listed company that has gone into liquidation in the past 5 years. Present a report to the class outlining a brief history of the company and its activities, and the events that led to the liquidation. Obtain the company's latest annual report (your librarian should be able to help you find the best source for this) and calculate and discuss, in light of the liquidation, the company's liquidity and financial stability ratios for the preceding 2 years. Is there any indication of financial distress in the management discussion in the annual report? Consider the usefulness of the annual report in identifying potential sources of concern about corporate survival.

ETHICS AND GOVERNANCE

Loan agreement

Sharon Rock, assistant accountant for Brady Industrial Products, was discussing the finalisation of the financial statements of the business as at 30 June 2011 with the accountant of the business, Tim O'Shea. Both agreed that everything appeared to be in order. Sharon, however, had noticed that a large loan had been taken out by the owner with Localtown Bank and that, as part of the loan agreement, Brady Industrial Products was to maintain a ratio of current assets (less inventories) to current liabilities of at least 1.2:1. The relevant figures prepared showed current assets (less inventories) standing at $1 100 000, whereas current liabilities stood at $1 000 000. Sharon raised her concerns with Tim O'Shea about not maintaining the desired minimum ratio for the purpose of the loan agreement. Tim replied: 'Yes, I can see the potential problem here. We could, I suppose, sell some inventory or put pressure on some trade debtors to pay up, but we may not have the time to get the ratio right for the bank's information. The bank will want the 30 June figures.'

Tim thought about the problem a little further and then explained: 'I have a better solution. There is a large loan of $120 000 which the business has made to the owner. This is currently classified as a non-current receivable as the loan is not due for repayment for another 14 months. This is probably close enough to be a current receivable, so let us simply reclassify the loan to the owner as a current receivable and this will overcome the potential problem with the bank's ratio requirement. I am sure the owner will agree with me on this.'

Required

A. Identify the stakeholders involved in this situation.
B. What are the main ethical issues involved?
C. What actions are available to Sharon to resolve the dilemma she faces?
D. What would you do if you were Sharon?

FINANCIAL ANALYSIS

Refer to the consolidated financial statements and notes in the latest financial report of JB Hi-Fi Limited on its website, www.jbhifi.com.au, and answer the following questions:

1. Have the current liabilities of JB Hi-Fi Limited increased or decreased over the year? By how much? What classes of liabilities are recorded under the classification 'Current liabilities'?
2. What are the major liabilities of JB Hi-Fi Limited at the end of the financial year?
3. What items are included under the heading 'Provisions' in the 'Current liabilities' section of the statement of financial position (balance sheet)? Explain the nature of these items. Do these satisfy the definition of provisions as contained in IAS 37/AASB 137? By how much have liabilities for employee benefits increased over the year?
4. How much cash has been raised by interest-bearing loans in the most recent financial year? How much of such loans has been repaid? How do these amounts compare with the previous year?
5. Determine whether any of the non-current liabilities are secured.
6. How much of the non-current borrowings are due to be repaid within 2 years? between 2 years and 5 years? beyond 5 years?
7. Are there any non-current provisions? If so, what, in very general terms, do these represent?

Part 6

External reporting and performance evaluation

Concepts for review

Before studying this chapter, you should understand or, if necessary, revise:

- the different components of equity in a company (pp. 656–8)
- the declaration and payment of dividends on shares (pp. 667–71)
- the preparation of an internal income statement and balance sheet for a company (pp. 673–79)
- the creation and disposal of reserves (pp. 671–2).

Learning objectives

After studying this chapter, you should be able to:

1 discuss the general reporting requirements imposed by the *Corporations Act 2001* and accounting standards (pp. 946–50)

2 demonstrate the external reporting requirements for a statement of profit or loss and other comprehensive income for a company in line with a suggested format (pp. 950–2)

3 demonstrate the external reporting requirements for a statement of financial position for a company in line with a suggested format (pp. 952–5)

4 demonstrate the external reporting requirements for a statement of changes in equity for a company in line with a suggested format (p. 955)

5 prepare the financial statements as required for general purpose financial reports (pp. 955–60).

Making financial reporting simpler and more useful

There is no doubt that, broadly, the idea of principles-based, or objectives-based, financial reporting standards has won the day. There are arguments about where on the spectrum between pure principles and a mass of rules they should fall. But that is detail. What is accepted is that a financial reporting process based, to a greater extent, on principles and judgement would make the whole process simpler. The challenge is in generating the necessary leadership, commitment and actions to achieve this in practice.

There is also a consensus that the current levels of complexity in financial reporting cannot be allowed to continue. Again, the real question is how to achieve this. No single compelling course of action was identified which would speed the demise of complexity. The answer which emerged was that, unlike much in financial reporting, this was not wholly a technical issue.

There was unavoidable complexity, which related to the growing complexity of business and the accounting which underpinned it. And there was avoidable complexity, the simple accretion of unnecessary detail. Accepting one while ridding reports and accounts of the other has to be the aim.

There would also be changes leading through from the gradual move towards principles-based standards. The current problems, which often stem from financial reporting being dominated by the objective of compliance, would change as the objective of communication slowly gained the upper hand.

It is a question of human behaviour. The continual urge to add more and more refinements and additions to the financial reporting process has to be curtailed. There has to be an active effort to remove elements which are now either unnecessary or have been found wanting.

Source: Excerpt from Global Accounting Alliance, 'Making Financial Reporting Simpler and More Useful: The Way Forward', www.globalaccounting alliance.com.au.

Chapter preview

In a previous chapter, details were presented on different types of companies and on accounting for company formation and issue of shares. Once funds have been raised through share issues, the directors of the company must then proceed with the task of fulfilling the company's objectives. Businesses hope to generate profits. The accounting for income and expenses and the determination of profit or loss for a company closely parallel those activities for a sole trader or a partnership. At the end of the reporting period, income and expense accounts are closed off to the Profit or Loss Summary account in the normal manner. One notable difference, however, arises from the fact that a company is liable to pay income tax on its final profit. Income tax is an expense in the year in which the profits are earned, and companies provide for the future liability for income tax at the end of the financial year. A general journal entry is made debiting Income Tax Expense and crediting Current Tax Liability. The Income Tax Expense account is closed off to the Profit or Loss Summary, and the final balance of this account, which represents the profit, is transferred to the credit of the Retained Earnings account for appropriation by the directors.

Profits, represented by the balance in the Retained Earnings account, are used by the directors to pay dividends to the shareholders and to establish reserves. The Retained Earnings account is debited for the dividends paid or declared during the year and for any reserves set aside by the directors. Sometimes, previously established reserves that are no longer required are transferred back to the Retained Earnings account by crediting that account, and therefore become available for future appropriation. The year-end balance of the Retained Earnings account is included as part of the entity's equity.

The major differences between the final financial statements of a company and those of a sole trader or partnership, therefore, concern the accounting for income tax, dividends and reserves. Reporting requirements for companies are also subject to requirements of corporate legislation, accounting standards and the concept of corporate social responsibility. This chapter focuses on the impact of legal requirements and the external reporting requirements in accounting standards for the presentation of the financial statements. More detailed discussion of social and environmental accounting and disclosure are left for more advanced texts.

23.1 External reporting requirements

Annual financial report

Learning objective 1

Discuss the general reporting requirements imposed by the *Corporations Act 2001* and accounting standards

For presentation of *general purpose financial statements*, which aim to provide information useful to people making economic decisions, and for the purpose of company managements discharging their accountability to shareholders, the *Corporations Act 2001* requires companies to prepare **annual financial reports** for presentation to users. The annual financial report must include the following items: a set of financial statements, notes to those financial statements, a directors' declaration, an annual directors' report and an annual auditor's report. The contents of the directors' declaration, directors' report and auditor's report are discussed in detail in the Corporations Act and are not discussed any further in this book.

The financial statements to be included in the annual financial report of a company are specified by the Corporations Act as those required by the accounting standards.

IAS 1/AASB 101 *Presentation of Financial Statements* defines a complete set of financial statements as comprising:

(a) a statement of financial position as at the end of the period;
(b) a statement of profit or loss and other comprehensive income for the period;
(c) a statement of changes in equity for the period;
(d) a statement of cash flows for the period;
(e) notes, comprising a summary of significant accounting policies and other explanatory information.

The current version of the standard goes on to note that a company may use other titles for these statements and so a few annual reports may still use the titles 'balance sheet' and 'income statement'. It is implied in the accompanying commentary to the standard, however, that the International Accounting Standards Board (IASB) would prefer the new titles to be used. This is the position adopted in this chapter, which will focus on the first three of the listed statements. The statement of cash flows is covered in the next chapter.

It has been proposed that the statement of comprehensive income may change its title to a statement of profit or loss and other comprehensive income. Part of this proposal would require this title to be used by entities presenting financial statements in accordance with the accounting standards. At the time of writing, this proposal has been the subject of significant debate, and even if accepted should not substantially change the presentation shown in this chapter. However, we have decided to adopt the proposed title statement of profit or loss and other comprehensive income throughout this book.

Included in the financial statements must be a set of notes providing disclosure of several different aspects of the company. The financial statements and notes must contain all information necessary to ensure that they provide a true and fair view of the entity's performance for the reporting period and its financial position at the end of the reporting period.

In 2010 the Australian Accounting Standards Board (AASB) introduced AASB 1053 *Application of Tiers of Australian Accounting Standards*, also referred to as the **Reduced Disclosure Requirements**, which will be mandatory from 2014. Under this framework all **disclosing entities** will be classified as either Tier 1 or Tier 2 disclosers. A disclosing entity is one which must lodge its annual reports under various corporate legislation, and in effect means all entities other than small proprietary companies, although occasionally a small proprietary company may be directed to prepare an annual financial report if requested by at least 5% of its shareholders. If so, the company will have to comply with certain accounting standards unless the shareholders issue a direction specifying that the financial report does not have to comply with those standards. The shareholders of a small proprietary company also may direct that the financial report should be audited.

AASB 1053 is meant to lessen the reporting burden on the majority of disclosing entities by introducing a second tier of reporting requirements into the Australian financial reporting framework. Only **publicly accountable** entities, being those with publicly traded shares or falling into a few narrowly defined categories, are required to report using full Australian accounting standards. All other disclosing entities will be classed as Tier 2 and be given relief from providing certain information in accordance with defined paragraphs, thus substantially reducing their financial reporting burden. The AASB also expects that Tier 2 requirements would apply to all not-for-profit private sector entities and most public sector entities, though regulators might require the application of Tier 1 requirements by the entities they regulate.

The subtleties of difference between Tier 1 and Tier 2 disclosure requirements will be discussed in more advanced accounting courses. This text will focus on broad principles, which, for the most part, apply equally to all disclosing entities.

The Corporations Act clearly indicates that the overriding purpose of the annual financial report is to provide a true and fair view of the operations of the company. It is conceivable, although the AASB considers it 'extremely rare', that even if a company has complied with accounting standards in preparing its financial report, it may not provide a true and fair view of its performance and financial position. In these circumstances, in addition to complying with the accounting standards, the company should provide supplemental disclosures required to achieve a fair presentation.

Concise report

One of the significant features of the Corporations Act is that it permits concise financial reporting to a company's shareholders. Instead of providing each shareholder with a full set of financial statements and notes, the directors' report and the auditor's report, a company has the right to provide a **concise report** for the financial year. This concise report consists of:

- a concise financial report drawn up in accordance with accounting standards
- the directors' report for the year
- a statement by the auditor that the financial report has been audited, and whether, in the auditor's opinion, the concise financial report complies with accounting standards
- a copy of any qualification in the auditor's report on the financial report
- a statement that the report is a concise financial report and that a full financial report and auditor's report will be sent to the shareholder free of charge if the shareholder asks for them.

Accounting standard AASB 1039 *Concise Financial Reports* (there is no equivalent international accounting standard) was issued with the purpose of specifying in more detail the minimum contents of a concise financial report. According to AASB 1039, a concise financial report must include the following financial statements:

- a statement of profit or loss and other comprehensive income for the annual reporting period
- a statement of financial position as at the end of the annual reporting period
- a statement of cash flows for the annual reporting period
- a statement of changes in equity for the annual reporting period.

Each of these statements must be presented as in the full financial report in accordance with accounting standards, except that cross-references to the detailed notes may be omitted. Although the notes themselves are not included, AASB 1039 states that, for entities other than listed companies, each financial statement must be accompanied by some *discussion and analysis* to help shareholders understand the message told by the statements. (Under the Corporations Act, listed companies must also provide such discussion and analysis as part of the directors' report.) It is suggested that this discussion and analysis covers such items as follows:

(a) *For the statement of profit or loss and other comprehensive income:*
- trends in revenues
- the effects of significant events on the company's operations
- the main influences on the costs of operations
- measures of financial performance such as return on sales (profit margin), return on assets, and return on equity.

(b) *For the statement of financial position:*
- changes in the composition of assets
- the relationship between debt and equity
- significant movements in assets, liabilities, and equity items.

(c) *For the statement of cash flows* (discussed in more detail in the next chapter):
- changes in cash flows from operations
- the financing of capital expenditure programs
- the repayment and servicing of any borrowings.

(d) *For the statement of changes in equity:*
- changes in the composition of the components of equity
- causes of significant changes in issued capital, such as rights issues, share buy-backs or capital reductions.

According to AASB 1039, in order to provide clear information to the company's shareholders, the concise financial report must also disclose:

- the amount of sales revenue recognised in accordance with IAS 18/AASB 118 *Revenue*
- the amount of dividends paid and dividends proposed, and the expected date of payment, as well as the dividends per share
- the earnings per share
- details of any events occurring *after* the end of the reporting period that do not relate to conditions at the end of the reporting period
- details of any changes in accounting policies or estimates that have affected the current financial statements.

The concise financial report must clearly indicate that it is an extract from the financial report and that it cannot be expected to provide a full understanding of the company's financial performance, financial position, and financing and investing activities. Shareholders who wish to obtain the full financial report can ask for one to be made available, and it must be provided free of charge.

Interim financial report

If an entity is a 'disclosing entity' as defined in the Corporations Act, it is required also to prepare an **interim financial report**. The interim financial report is defined in IAS 34/AASB 134 *Interim Financial Reporting* (as amended by changes to IAS 1/AASB 101) as a financial report containing either a complete set of financial statements or a set of condensed financial statements prepared for an interim period, which is specified as each half-year for a disclosing entity in Australia.

However, an interim period can be any period shorter than a full reporting period, and therefore an interim financial report applies to any period shorter than the full period. In Australia, a disclosing entity, which may or may not be incorporated, is an entity that has 'enhanced disclosure' securities; that is, it is an entity that:

- has its shares listed on the Australian Securities Exchange, or
- is raising funds pursuant to a prospectus, or
- is offering its securities as consideration for the acquisition of shares in another company under a takeover scheme, or
- is issuing shares under a compromise or scheme of arrangement, or
- is a borrowing corporation.

Each disclosing entity is required to follow the requirements of IAS 34/AASB 134 in the presentation of its interim financial report. If an entity does not make the content of an interim financial report exactly the same as the full annual report, then the content, as specified in IAS 34/AASB 134, must include, as a minimum:

- a condensed statement of financial position
- a condensed statement of profit or loss and other comprehensive income
- a condensed statement of changes in equity
- a condensed statement of cash flows
- selected notes.

BUSINESS KNOWLEDGE

Pendulum swings back to the balance sheet wonks

In business, there are only two basic types: income statement groupies and balance sheet wonks. It is the classic duel of perspectives that characterizes many human activities. In football it is strength vs. speed. Baseball has its batting vs. pitching. And in education it is knowledge vs. thinking process.

The push-me, pull-you quality never ends. There is no now-and-forever winner. There are periods of time, though, when one view prevails and for a time the other perspective is obscured and sometimes even forgotten.

In business, we have been in one of those periods for quite a few years. The income statement groupies had been flying the business models and strategies while the balance sheet wonks were carried along as checked baggage.

There are at least two reasons for that. The first is the pervasive influence of Wall Street on business thinking. And Wall Street rewards performance, meaning income, right now. In normal times it rarely rewards a strong balance sheet. That comes only when fear overtakes greed, and even then the Wall Street focus is on earnings potential, mostly in the short run.

The second reason seems almost trivial, but is related to how business strategies, plans and forecasts are produced in today's world. In times past, the predicted sales, goals and broad outlines were worked out and then sent to the pencil-pushers in finance to sweat the math and actually come up with the forecast's numbers on a month-by-month, quarter-by-quarter basis.

Source: Excerpts from James McCusker, 'Pendulum swings back to the balance sheet wonks', www.snohomishcountybusinessjournal.com.

General requirements for the annual report

In presenting a set of financial statements as part of the financial reports under the Act, IAS 1/AASB 101 sets down some general requirements:

- In Australia, the financial statements must be presented in English. (This is not a requirement of IAS 1, but is an additional paragraph in AASB 101.)
- The financial statements must be presented in a 'presentation currency', but if this currency differs from the local currency, e.g. the Australian dollar, the entity must state the reason and justification for not using the local currency.
- Each component of the financial report must be clearly identified and the following information must be displayed prominently:
  - the name of the entity and, if appropriate, any change in its name
  - whether the financial statements cover the individual entity or a group of entities
  - the date of the end of the reporting period or the period covered by the set of financial statements and notes, whichever is appropriate
  - the presentation currency
  - the level of rounding used in presenting amounts in the financial statements.

- The financial statements must provide comparative and corresponding financial disclosures for the previous reporting period, except in a few limited cases.
- If the financial statements are for a period other than 12 months, the period covered and the reasons for using a different time period must be stated. The fact that amounts for the previous period are not comparable because of the different lengths of reporting periods must also be stated.
- Notes in the annual report must be presented in a systematic manner, with appropriate cross-referencing to directly related information in the financial statements. The notes must disclose additional explanatory information not presented in the financial statements if relevant to a user's understanding of them. The first note to the financial statements contains information about the accounting policies adopted by the entity in preparing the statements.
- There must be consistency of presentation and classification of items in the financial statements from one period to the next, unless there has been a significant change in the entity's operations, or a change in accounting policies is warranted to provide more relevant information.
- The entity must disclose the following, somewhere in the financial report:
  - the domicile and legal form of the entity, its country of incorporation, the address of its registered office and principal place of business (if different)
  - a description of the entity's operations and its principal activities
  - the name of the parent entity and ultimate parent entity, if any.
- If the entity has reclassified financial information in the financial statements, comparative information must also be reclassified, if practicable, and the nature of the classification, the amount and the reason must be disclosed.

23.2 Statement of profit or loss and other comprehensive income

Learning objective 2

Demonstrate the external reporting requirements for a statement of profit or loss and other comprehensive income for a company in line with a suggested format

This chapter provides only an introduction to the disclosure requirements for a company's statement of profit or loss and other comprehensive income as they currently stand. For more advanced coverage of the topic, consult the accounting standards and more advanced textbooks. Further helpful guidance is provided by specimen presentations of financial reports published regularly by accounting firms, e.g. Endeavour (International) Ltd by Ernst & Young.

Disclosure requirements for a company's statement of profit or loss and other comprehensive income are contained in IAS 1/AASB 101. Total **comprehensive income** is defined by the standard as the change in equity during a period resulting from transactions and other events, other than those changes resulting from transactions with owners in their capacity as owners. These non-owner changes have two components — those that contribute to the company's profit or loss (income less expenses), and **other comprehensive income**, which comprises items of income and expense that are not recognised in profit or loss because of the requirements of other accounting standards. Although it is not immediately obvious, the standard has taken an all-inclusive approach to the determination of a company's profit or loss. This means that all income (including revenues) and all expenses must be included in the company's profit or loss for the year. The only exclusions to this are provided by other accounting standards and these must be included in other comprehensive income. The main exclusions include adjustments arising from:

- the revaluation upwards or downwards of an entity's non-current assets, requiring adjustments to a revaluation surplus as per IAS 16/AASB 116 *Property, Plant and Equipment*
- adjustments from translation of the financial statements of a foreign operation, as per IAS 21/AASB 121 *The Effects of Changes in Foreign Exchange Rates* (the accounting treatment of foreign operations is not presented in this book)
- gains or losses on remeasuring investments in equity instruments, as per IAS 39/AASB 139 *Financial Instruments: Recognition and Measurement*, which is not considered further in this book.

IAS 1/AASB 101 allows for two possible approaches to presenting the required information. The first approach is to present a single statement of profit or loss and other comprehensive income, with profit or loss and other comprehensive income presented together, but in separate sections. The second approach is to present two statements, the first being a statement of profit or loss outlining the items of profit or loss and the second being a statement of profit or loss and other comprehensive income, beginning with profit or loss and displaying the items of other comprehensive income. The International Accounting Standards Board has indicated a preference for the single statement and this is the approach demonstrated in this chapter. The standard does not set down a specifically required format for the presentation of a statement of profit or loss and other comprehensive income for external reporting purposes; nevertheless, the Implementation Guidance accompanying IAS 1/AASB 101 provides examples of possible presentations. The simplest format, with minor modifications, which provides all the detail required in the statement, is shown in figure 23.1.

Figure 23.1 Suggested format of statement of profit or loss and other comprehensive income to satisfy requirements of IAS 1/AASB 101

ABC LTD
Statement of Profit or Loss and Other Comprehensive Income
for the year ended 30 June 2014

	Note*	2014	2013
Revenue	2	$ x	$ x
Other income	2	x	x
Expenses, excluding finance costs	3	(x)	(x)
Finance costs	3	(x)	(x)
Share of profit of associates**	4	x	x
Profit (loss) before income tax		x	x
Income tax expense	5	(x)	(x)
Profit (loss) from continuing operations		x	x
Profit (loss) from discontinued operations†	7	x	x
PROFIT (LOSS) FOR THE PERIOD		x	x
Other comprehensive income:			
Items that will not be reclassified to profit or loss:‡			
Gains on asset revaluations	8	x	x
Income tax relating to items that will not be reclassified‡		(x)	(x)
Other comprehensive income for the period, net of tax		x	x
TOTAL COMPREHENSIVE INCOME FOR THE PERIOD		$ x	$ x

* Note numbers are illustrative only.
** This line appears only if the company has associates or joint ventures, which require the preparation of information in line with the equity method of accounting. The equity method is not covered in this book.
† This means profit (loss) from discontinued operations after tax in accordance with IFRS 5/AASB 5 *Non-current Assets Held for Sale and Discontinued Operations*.
‡ Reclassification of items of other comprehensive income is not covered in this book.
‡ The income tax relating to each component of other comprehensive income must be separately disclosed; in this case it would be done in the notes.

Total income and total expenses may be shown in the statement of profit or loss and other comprehensive income with details of the company's individual income and expenses included in notes to the statement. Alternatively, details of income and expenses can be shown in the statement. Note the importance given to the separate disclosure of a company's finance costs, which have been treated as an expense in accordance with IAS 23/AASB 123 *Borrowing Costs*. The general requirement of IAS 23/ AASB 123 (as amended in 2007) is that borrowing costs must be recognised as an expense in the financial year in which they are incurred. However, if borrowing costs are directly attributable to the acquisition, construction or production of a 'qualifying asset', the standard requires these borrowing costs to be treated as part of the cost of that asset. Hence, such borrowing costs do not appear in the statement of profit or loss and other comprehensive income. A **qualifying asset** is defined as an asset that necessarily takes a substantial period of time, usually longer than 1 year, to get ready for its intended use or sale. Thus a qualifying asset may be part of the entity's property, plant and equipment, or part of its inventories, as long as such items take a considerable period of time to produce, and are included in the company's statement of financial position.

Disclosure of income and expenses

In a previous chapter, we discussed the nature of income (including revenues) as outlined in the *Conceptual Framework* and in IAS 18/AASB 118 *Revenue*. Furthermore, we discussed the alternative criteria developed for the recognition of revenue in accordance with IAS 18/AASB 118.

This accounting standard also requires disclosure of the accounting policies used for recognising revenue and disclosure of all categories of revenue. The following categories of revenue must be disclosed under IAS 18/AASB 118:

- the sale of goods
- the rendering of services
- interest
- royalties
- dividends
- the amount of any revenue arising from exchanges or swaps of goods and services.

In relation to expenses, their definition and recognition criteria have been discussed in detail in a previous chapter. Disclosure of expenses under IAS 1/AASB 101 may occur in the statement of profit or loss and other comprehensive income, but it is more usual to find detailed disclosure in the notes. The standard requires each entity to present an analysis of expenses based on either the *nature* of the expenses or their *function* within the entity, whichever provides the more relevant and reliable information.

If expenses are classified by nature, a listing of disclosed expenses may appear as shown in figure 23.2.

Figure 23.2 Classification of expenses by nature

	2014	2013
Raw materials and consumables used*	$ x	$ x
Net purchases of inventory*	x	x
Change in inventories of finished goods and work in progress*	x	x
Employee benefits expense	x	x
Depreciation and amortisation expense	x	x
Impairment expense	x	x
Rent expense	x	x
Loss on the disposal of property, plant and equipment	x	x
Research expense	x	x
* These items together constitute the total of cost of sales.		

There is no need to allocate expenses across the different functions of the entity. Thus, depreciation expense can be presented as a total amount rather than being allocated across the selling function and the administrative function.

Alternatively, *expenses may be classified by function*, in which case they would be disclosed, for example, as in figure 23.3.

Figure 23.3 Classification of expenses by function

	2014	2013
Cost of sales	$ x	$ x
Selling and distribution expenses	x	x
Administrative expenses	x	x
Finance expenses	x	x
Other expenses	x	x

A retail entity is expected to disclose cost of sales separately, and to use classifications similar to those introduced in chapter 6. Furthermore, all expenses need to be allocated across the different functions; for example, wages and salaries and other employee benefits must be split into those for the selling function, those for the administrative function, and so on.

Nevertheless, separate disclosure of many categories of expenses is also required by several accounting standards. For example, various standards require disclosure of expense items, such as depreciation, amortisation and impairment expenses on non-current assets, rent expense, loss on disposal of property, plant and equipment, and expenses incurred in relation to bad and doubtful debts.

Learning objective 3

Demonstrate the external reporting requirements for a statement of financial position for a company in line with a suggested format

23.3 Statement of financial position

This chapter provides only an introduction to the disclosure requirements for a company's statement of financial position. Coverage of detailed notes to the statement is provided in more advanced texts. Further helpful guidance is provided by specimen presentations of financial statements published regularly by public accounting firms, e.g. Endeavour (International) Ltd by Ernst & Young.

IAS 1/AASB 101 does not insist on a prescribed format for the statement of financial position but the standard provides examples in its Implementation Guidance. The standard requires all assets and liabilities in the statement to be classified either as current or non-current, unless a liquidity presentation is more appropriate to provide relevant and reliable information. Distinctions between current and non-current assets and liabilities are discussed in earlier chapters and are not pursued further here.

Detailed disclosures of certain asset and liability categories and subcategories are required by IAS 1/AASB 101. A basic format to achieve these disclosures is illustrated in the Implementation Guidance accompanying the standard. Figure 23.4 is based on this illustration, and shows a current/non-current presentation of assets and liabilities. Figure 23.5 (overleaf) illustrates a liquidity presentation. In this book, the current/non-current classification is used for all exercises and problems, unless a liquidity presentation is specifically requested.

Figure 23.4 Current/ non-current format of statement of financial position to satisfy requirements of IAS 1/AASB 101

ABC LTD
Statement of Financial Position
as at 30 June 2014

	Note	2014	2013
ASSETS			
Non-current assets			
Property, plant and equipment	11	$ x	$ x
Goodwill	12	x	x
Other intangible assets	13	x	x
Investments in associates	14	x	x
Other financial assets	15	x	x
		x	x
Current assets			
Inventories	16	x	x
Trade receivables	17	x	x
Other current assets	18	x	x
Cash and cash equivalents	19	x	x
		x	x
Total assets		$ x	$ x
EQUITY AND LIABILITIES			
Equity			
Share capital	20	$ x	$ x
Retained earnings		x	x
Other components of equity	21	x	x
Total equity		x	x
Non-current liabilities			
Long-term borrowings	22	x	x
Deferred tax	23	x	x
Long-term provisions	24	x	x
Total non-current liabilities		x	x
Current liabilities			
Trade and other payables	25	x	x
Short-term borrowings	26	x	x
Current portion of long-term borrowings	27	x	x
Current tax payable	28	x	x
Short-term provisions	29	x	x
Total current liabilities		x	x
Total liabilities		x	x
Total equity and liabilities		$ x	$ x

ABC LTD
Statement of Financial Position
as at 30 June 2014

	Note	2014	2013
ASSETS			
Cash and cash equivalents	11	$ x	$ x
Trade receivables	12	x	x
Inventories	13	x	x
Other financial assets	14	x	x
Property, plant and equipment	15	x	x
Investments in associates	16	x	x
Goodwill	17	x	x
Other intangible assets	18	x	x
Other assets	19	x	x
Total assets		x	x
LIABILITIES			
Trade and other payables	20	x	x
Short-term borrowings	21	x	x
Current portion of long-term borrowings	22	x	x
Short-term provisions	23	x	x
Current tax payable	24	x	x
Long-term borrowings	25	x	x
Long-term provisions	26	x	x
Deferred tax	27	x	x
Total liabilities		x	x
Net assets		$ x	$ x
EQUITY			
Share capital	28	$ x	$ x
Retained earnings		x	x
Other components of equity	29	x	x
Total equity		$ x	$ x

A few observations can be made from figures 23.4 and 23.5:

- In presenting the statement of financial position of a particular company, it is helpful if the headings and subheadings are followed to the extent that the items exist in the company under consideration. Additional subheadings can be provided, e.g. a subheading for biological assets, or for development costs capitalised, depending on the disclosure policies of the company concerned. References to various notes in figures 23.4 and 23.5 (e.g. Note 11 in relation to property, plant and equipment and Note 16 in relation to inventories in figure 23.4) are followed up in the detailed notes for each type item to comply with accounting standards. These notes are not presented in this book.

- Details of appropriation items, such as transfers to or from reserves, and dividends declared or paid, do not appear in either the statement of profit or loss and other comprehensive income or the statement of financial position. Hence, there is no clear link between the two statements for external disclosure purposes. Instead, movements in the retained earnings balance are shown in the statement of changes in equity as discussed in the next section.

- An entity's statement of financial position shows the accounting equation in one form or another, for instance:

$$\text{Assets} - \text{Liabilities} = \text{Equity}$$

or

$$\text{Assets} = \text{Equity} + \text{Liabilities}$$

In the statement of financial position for external reporting, there is no requirement in IAS 1/AASB 101 to begin the statement with the assets. The statement could begin with equity and show, as an alternative, the accounting equation as follows:

$$\text{Equity} = \text{Assets} - \text{Liabilities}$$

23.4 Statement of changes in equity

Learning objective 4

Demonstrate the external reporting requirements for a statement of changes in equity for a company in line with a suggested format

IAS 1/AASB 101 requires each entity to supply in its financial reports a statement of changes in equity, showing the movements in each major equity item during the annual reporting period. The statement must disclose:

(a) total comprehensive income for the period
(b) the amounts of transactions with owners in their capacity as owners, showing separately contributions by and distributions to owners
(c) for each component of equity, a reconciliation between the carrying amount at the beginning and the end of the period, separately disclosing each change.

A suggested format for a simple statement of changes in equity is presented in figure 23.6, based on the Implementation Guidance accompanying IAS 1/AASB 101.

Figure 23.6 Statement of changes in equity — based on the Implementation Guidance accompanying IAS 1/AASB 101

ABC LTD
Statement of Changes in Equity
for the year ended 30 June 2014

	Share capital	Retained earnings	Revaluation surplus	Total equity
Balance at 1 July 2012	$ x	$ x	$ x	$ x
Changes in equity for year				
Dividends		(x)		(x)
Total comprehensive income for the year		x	x	x
Balance at 30 June 2013	x	x	x	x
Changes in equity for the year				
Issue of share capital	x			x
Dividends		(x)		(x)
Total comprehensive income for the year		x	x	x
Transfer to retained earnings		x	(x)	
Balance at 30 June 2014	$ x	$ x	$ x	$ x

23.5 Demonstration problem

Learning objective 5

Prepare the financial statements as required for general purpose financial reports

The internal financial statements of Mars Ltd are shown in figures 23.7 and 23.8 (pp. 956 and 957). Expenses are classified according to function, i.e. selling and distribution, administrative and finance. Note that cost of sales is classified as a selling expense in figure 23.7, but does not have to be, as per figure 23.3.

Figure 23.7 Internal income
statement for Mars Ltd

MARS LTD
Income Statement (internal)
for the year ended 30 June 2014

INCOME			
Revenues			
Sales		$1 545 000	
Less: Sales returns		5 000	$1 540 000
Services revenue			260 000
Total revenues			1 800 000
Other income: Gain on sale of office furniture			3 000
Total income			1 803 000
EXPENSES			
Selling and distribution expenses			
Cost of sales		942 800	
Freight inwards		6 000	
Total cost of sales		948 800	
Freight outwards		7 000	
Advertising expense		22 500	
Sales staff's salaries expense		205 000	
Sales staff's vehicle expenses		15 000	
Depreciation of motor vehicles		30 000	
Depreciation of store equipment		12 000	
Depreciation of retail store		25 000	
Total selling expenses		1 265 300	
Administrative expenses			
Rates expense		15 000	
Insurance expense		16 000	
Administrative staff salaries expense		197 000	
Impairment of goodwill		7 000	
Amortisation of development costs		10 000	
Depreciation of office furniture		18 000	
Total administrative expenses		263 000	
Finance expenses			
Rent expense		16 500	
Discount allowed		10 000	
Interest expense		1 500	
Bad debts expense		7 900	
Total finance expenses		35 900	
Total expenses			1 564 200
Profit before income tax			238 800
Income tax expense (30%)			71 640
Profit			$ 167 160

Additional information

(a) Assume that Mars Ltd had revalued its retail store upwards by $60 000, resulting in an increase in the revaluation surplus during the current period.

(b) Assume there were no interim dividends paid during the year, and that $15 000 was transferred to the general reserve from retained earnings.

(c) Assume that 50c per share was received as a payment for a call on all ordinary shares during the year.

(d) Assume that $3000 of the loan payable is due within 12 months.

Figure 23.8 Internal balance sheet for Mars Ltd

MARS LTD
Balance Sheet (internal)
as at 30 June 2014

CURRENT ASSETS		
Cash		$ 64 000
Accounts receivable	$ 218 000	
Allowance for doubtful debts	(10 900)	207 100
Inventory		250 000
Prepaid insurance		4 000
Prepaid rent		2 000
TOTAL CURRENT ASSETS		527 100
NON-CURRENT ASSETS		
Land (at cost)		100 000
Retail store (at fair value)		435 000
Motor vehicles (at cost)	300 000	
Accumulated depreciation	(180 000)	120 000
Store equipment (at cost)	60 000	
Accumulated depreciation	(27 000)	33 000
Office furniture (at cost)	90 000	
Accumulated depreciation	(38 000)	52 000
Goodwill (at cost)	140 000	
Accumulated impairment losses	(7 000)	133 000
Development costs	100 000	
Accumulated amortisation	(10 000)	90 000
TOTAL NON-CURRENT ASSETS		963 000
TOTAL ASSETS		1 490 100
CURRENT LIABILITIES		
Accounts payable		60 000
Salaries payable		9 000
Interest payable		300
Current tax liability		71 640
GST payable [collections less outlays]		8 000
Ordinary dividend payable		80 000
Preference dividend payable		40 000
TOTAL CURRENT LIABILITIES		268 940
NON-CURRENT LIABILITIES		
Loan payable		12 000
TOTAL NON-CURRENT LIABILITIES		12 000
TOTAL LIABILITIES		280 940
NET ASSETS		$1 209 160
EQUITY		
Share capital		
40 000 ordinary shares issued and paid to $1		$ 400 000
50 000 preference shares issued and paid to $1		500 000
		900 000
Less: Share issue costs (ordinary)		(13 000)
Net share capital		887 000
Reserves		
Revaluation surplus	$ 160 000	
General reserve	75 000	
Retained earnings	87 160	322 160
TOTAL EQUITY		$1 209 160

Required

A. Prepare the statement of profit or loss and other comprehensive income, the statement of financial position and the statement of changes in equity for external disclosure in the annual financial report for Mars Ltd, following the formats used in figures 23.1, 23.4 and 23.6 respectively.

B. Prepare a note showing expenses classified by nature, assuming that the beginning balance of inventory was $244 000.

Solution

A. Figure 23.9 illustrates the statement of profit or loss and other comprehensive income, figure 23.10 illustrates the statement of financial position, and figure 23.11 illustrates the statement of changes in equity for Mars Ltd. Note the following points:

1. To be complete, comparative (previous years) figures should be shown.
2. Expenses excluding finance costs equal total expenses of $1 564 200 less interest expense of $1500.
3. GST payable is treated as part of payables, not current tax liabilities, in the statement of financial position, as per the requirements of UIG Interpretation 1031. Salaries, interest and dividends are also treated as payables.
4. Property, plant and equipment includes land, retail store, motor vehicles, and store and office equipment.
5. Many additional note disclosures would be required for income, expenses, assets, liabilities and equity, but these are beyond the scope of this book.

Figure 23.9 Statement of profit or loss and other comprehensive income of Mars Ltd for external reporting purposes

MARS LTD		
Statement of Profit or Loss and Other Comprehensive Income		
for the year ended 30 June 2014		
	*Note**	
Revenue	2	$ 1 800 000
Other income	2	3 000
Expenses, excluding finance costs	3	(1 562 700)
Finance costs	3	(1 500)
Profit (loss) before income tax		238 800
Income tax expense	4	(71 640)
PROFIT (LOSS) FOR THE PERIOD		167 160
Other comprehensive income:		
Gains on asset revaluations	5	60 000
Income tax relating to components of other comprehensive income**	5	(0)
Other comprehensive income for the period, net of tax		60 000
TOTAL COMPREHENSIVE INCOME FOR THE PERIOD		$ 227 160

* Note numbers are illustrative only.
** The tax effect of an asset revaluation is beyond the scope of this book.

MARS LTD
Statement of Financial Position
as at 30 June 2014

	Note	
ASSETS		
Non-current assets		
Property, plant and equipment	6	$ 740 000
Goodwill	7	133 000
Other intangible assets	8	90 000
		963 000
Current assets		
Inventories	9	250 000
Trade receivables	10	207 100
Other current assets	11	6 000
Cash and cash equivalents	12	64 000
		527 100
Total assets		$1 490 100
EQUITY AND LIABILITIES		
Equity		
Share capital	13	$ 887 000
Retained earnings		87 160
Other components of equity	14	235 000
Total equity		1 209 160
Non-current liabilities		
Long-term borrowings	15	9 000
Total non-current liabilities		9 000
Current liabilities		
Trade and other payables	16	197 300
Current portion of long-term borrowings	17	3 000
Current tax payable	18	71 640
Total current liabilities		271 940
Total liabilities		280 940
Total equity and liabilities		$1 490 100

Figure 23.10 Statement of financial position of Mars Ltd for external reporting purposes

MARS LTD
Statement of Changes in Equity
for the year ended 30 June 2014

	Share capital	Retained earnings	Revaluation surplus	General reserve	Total equity
Balance at 30 June 2013*	$700 000	$ 55 000	$100 000	$60 000	$ 915 000
Changes in equity for the year					
Issue of share capital	200 000				200 000
Share issue costs	(13 000)				(13 000)
Dividends		(120 000)			(120 000)
Total comprehensive income for the year		167 160	60 000		227 160
Transfer to general reserve		(15 000)		15 000	
Balance at 30 June 2014	$887 000	$ 87 160	$160 000	$75 000	$1 209 160

* These amounts are found by working backwards from the final balances in the question.

Figure 23.11 Statement of changes in equity for Mars Ltd

B. A suitable note prepared by the company to classify expenses *by nature* is as shown in figure 23.12. (Expenses classified *by function* have appeared in the internal income statement shown in figure 23.7, although several of these expenses do not need to be disclosed separately. For example, in the selling and distribution expenses, depreciation on motor vehicles, store equipment and retail store can be added together and shown as one amount.)

Figure 23.12 Classification of expenses by nature

Note 3: Expenses (excluding finance costs) classified by nature

Net purchases of inventory	$ 954 800
Increase in inventories of finished goods*	(6 000)
Salaries, wages and other employee benefits**	402 000
Depreciation and amortisation expense†	95 000
Impairment expense	7 000
Rent expense	16 500
Bad debts expense	7 900
Other‡	85 500
Total expenses excluding finance costs	$1 562 700

* This is calculated by deducting from the total of cost of sales $948 800 the change to the value of inventory during the period ($6000 = $250 000 – $244 000).
** The sum of sales staff salaries and administrative staff salaries.
† The sum of depreciation on motor vehicles, store equipment, retail store, office furniture and amortisation of development costs.
‡ The sum of freight outwards, advertising, rates, insurance and discount allowed.

BUSINESS KNOWLEDGE

Continuous disclosure, corporate governance and the ASX

If companies are listed on the Australian Securities Exchange (ASX), they are required to provide additional information to their shareholders and to the ASX.

First, they must comply with the ASX's Listing Rules, which require additional disclosures above the requirements of accounting standards. Chapter 3 of the Listing Rules requires a listed company to provide disclosures referred to as 'continuous disclosures'. For example, a company is required to keep the stock market informed of events and developments as they occur, particularly if they are likely to have a material effect on the company's share price.

Second, following several notable collapses in the early 2000s, e.g. HIH Insurance, the ASX Corporate Governance Council developed the *Corporate Governance Principles and Recommendations* (2nd edition, amended 2010), which can be accessed in full from the ASX website, www.asx.com.au. Eight principles specified in this document for good corporate governance by an entity are:
1. Lay solid foundations for management and oversight.
2. Structure the board to add value.
3. Promote ethical and responsible decision making.
4. Safeguard integrity in financial reporting.
5. Make timely and balanced disclosure.
6. Respect the rights of shareholders.
7. Recognise and manage risk.
8. Remunerate fairly and responsibly.

KEY TERMS

DISCUSSION QUESTIONS

1. What statements comprise a set of financial statements and how does this differ from an annual report?
2. Distinguish between an annual financial report, a concise report and an interim financial report. Discuss the reason for having each.

3. A financial statement must include 'comparative figures'. What does this mean, why are they useful and can a company change these comparative figures in the following year?

4. A number of the financial statements have had various name changes over the past decade, which statements have changed, and what have the changes been? Discuss the risks and benefits of these names changes.

5. What is the purpose of separating other comprehensive income out from the profit or loss for the period in the statement of profit or loss and other comprehensive income?

6. What is meant by the all-inclusive concept of profit? Does IAS 1/AASB 101 *Presentation of Financial Statements* follow this concept in presenting a statement of profit or loss and other comprehensive income? Explain.

7. The basic format for a statement of financial position/balance sheet in the implementation guidance accompanying IAS 1/AASB 101 differs from the presentation of the balance sheet in earlier sections of the text. How does it differ and why do you think the IASB has presented the statement in this way?

8. What is the purpose of the statement of changes in equity?

EXERCISES

Exercise 23.1 STATEMENT OF PROFIT OR LOSS AND OTHER COMPREHENSIVE INCOME **LO 2**

Explain how the following would be treated in the statement of profit or loss and other comprehensive income:

(a) A bad debt of $50 000 written off in a previous period was recovered in the current period to the extent of $30 000.

(b) As a result of a fall in share prices in a recession, directors decided to write down the value of the company's investment, Shares in Pluto Ltd, by $80 000.

(c) Land costing $200 000 was acquired 20 years ago for redevelopment purposes. Unfortunately, the company was unsuccessful in obtaining rezoning approval and the property was sold in the current year for $600 000.

(d) Owing to developments in technology, a significant portion of the company's inventory has become obsolete. The company managed to dispose of the inventory in a sale for $100 000 less than its original cost.

Exercise 23.2 STATEMENT OF PROFIT OR LOSS AND OTHER COMPREHENSIVE INCOME AND STATEMENT OF CHANGES IN EQUITY **LO 2, 4**

The following information relates to Azerbaijan Ltd at 30 June 2015:

Share capital:	
Preference shares (100 000 fully paid at $2 each)	$200 000 Cr
Ordinary shares (80 000 shares called to $1.50, issued at $2)	120 000 Cr
Interim dividends — preference shares	7 000 Dr
— ordinary shares	8 000 Dr
General reserve (balance 1/7/14)	87 000 Cr
Retained earnings (balance 1/7/14)	24 000 Cr
Profit before income tax (and before the items listed below)	140 000 Cr
Interest Expense	14 000 Dr
Gain on sale of plant	80 000 Cr
Loss on sale of a business	6 000 Dr
Damages in a lawsuit	16 000 Dr

The following details are necessary also before preparing the final statements:

1. Declaration of final dividends liability:
   - Preference shares — 4% of preference share capital
   - Ordinary shares — 20c per share.

2. General reserve to be increased by $13 000.

3. Revenue from sales for the year ending 30 June 2015 amounted to $1 200 000.

4. Assume a tax rate of 30%.

5. There were no movements in share capital during the year.

Required

A. Prepare the statement of profit or loss and other comprehensive income for external reporting purposes for the year ended 30 June 2015 for Azerbaijan Ltd.

B. Prepare the statement of changes in equity for the year ended 30 June 2015.

Exercise 23.3 STATEMENT OF FINANCIAL POSITION [LO 3]

The summarised balance sheet of Burundi Ltd at 30 June 2015 for presentation to management is:

BURUNDI LTD
Balance Sheet
as at 30 June 2015

CURRENT ASSETS			CURRENT LIABILITIES		
Cash at bank	$126 000		Accounts payable	$ 75 000	
Accounts receivable (net)	50 000		Dividends payable	15 000	
Inventory	85 000		Current tax liability	10 000	$100 000
Prepayments	3 000	$264 000			
			NON-CURRENT LIABILITY		
			Loan payable		20 000
NON-CURRENT ASSETS			EQUITY		
Land (revaluation)	364 000		Share capital	600 000	
Fixtures	190 000		Revaluation surplus	25 000	
Accumulated depreciation	(30 000)		General reserve	43 000	
Goodwill	44 000		Retained earnings	33 000	701 000
Accumulated impairment	(11 000)	557 000			
		$821 000			$821 000

Required

Prepare the statement of financial position for external reporting purposes of Burundi Ltd at 30 June 2015 in accordance with the format illustrated in figure 23.4.

Exercise 23.4 STATEMENT OF PROFIT OR LOSS AND OTHER COMPREHENSIVE INCOME, INCOME AND EXPENSES CLASSIFIED BY FUNCTION [LO 2]

The following information was obtained for Cyprus Ltd for the year ended 30 June 2015:

Administrative expenses	$ 200 000
Cost of sales	880 000
Dividends declared	100 000
Gain on asset revaluation	40 000
Gain on sale of machinery	60 000
Income tax expense for current year	220 000
Losses on investments in equity instruments	8 000
Net sales revenue	1 800 000
Retained earnings (1/7/14)	120 000
Selling and distribution expenses	250 000
EPA Fine	30 000

Required

A. Prepare a statement of profit or loss and other comprehensive income for Cyprus Ltd for the year ended 30 June 2015 so as to comply with the requirements of IAS 1/AASB 101.

B. Prepare an appropriate note for the disclosure of income.

C. Prepare an appropriate note for expenses classified by function.

Exercise 23.5 STATEMENT OF PROFIT OR LOSS AND OTHER COMPREHENSIVE INCOME AND RETAINED EARNINGS ACCOUNT [LO 2, 4]

The information on the next page relates to Dominica Ltd for the year ended 30 June 2015.

Required

Prepare a statement of profit or loss and other comprehensive income for external reporting and prepare the Retained Earnings T account for the year ended 30 June 2015.

1.	Profit before tax	$ 345 000
	(This figure is before adjustments for points 4 and 5 are made.)	
2.	Retained earnings 1 July 2014	26 250
3.	Revenues for the year	1 290 000
4.	Interest expense	34 500
5.	Impairment of goodwill	16 500
6.	Transfer to general reserve	7 500
7.	Estimated income tax expense for year ended 30 June 2015	103 500
8.	Interim dividend paid	
	Preference	24 000
	Ordinary	30 000
9.	Final dividend declared	
	Preference	24 000
	Ordinary	60 000

Exercise 23.6 STATEMENT OF PROFIT OR LOSS AND OTHER COMPREHENSIVE INCOME AND NOTE FOR INCOME **LO 2**

The ledger of Ethiopia Ltd at 30 June 2015 contained the following information:

Sales revenue	$1 125 000
Gain on revaluation of building (not sold)	50 000
Interest revenue	30 000
Donations received	15 000
Cost of sales	650 000
Selling and distribution expenses	120 000
Administrative expenses	150 000
Finance expenses	30 000

(The finance expenses included $12 000 interest expense.)

Assume a tax rate of 28.5%.

You discover the following additional information, not reflected in the above figures:

1. No tax expense has yet been accounted for. Donations received are tax exempt.
2. One division of business for the company had been discontinued on 1 June 2015. The assets associated with this division were sold for $1 000 000, at a loss of $150 000 before income tax.
3. On 6 January 2015, certain items of company property were resumed by the government for upgrading of the interstate highway, which ran past the company's warehouse. The government paid sufficient compensation for the company to realise a $100 000 before-tax profit on the deal.

Required

A. Prepare a statement of profit or loss and other comprehensive income for the year ended 30 June 2015 to comply with the requirements of IAS 1/AASB 101.
B. Prepare an appropriate note for income in order to comply with accounting standards.

Exercise 23.7 DIVIDENDS AND STATEMENT OF CHANGES IN EQUITY **LO 4**

On 1 July 2014, the equity of France Ltd was as follows:

600 000 ordinary shares issued at $2.20	$1 320 000
General reserve	50 000
Retained earnings	500 000

During the year ended 30 June 2015, the following events affecting the company's equity occurred:

2014

Aug.	1	Declared and paid a cash dividend of 20c per share.
Oct.	1	Announced a share split of 4 shares for every 1 share held. This was eventually carried out on 5 October.

2015

Jan.	3	Declared and paid an interim cash dividend of 5c per share.
June	30	Declared a final dividend of 8c per share. Profit (after tax) was determined to be $300 000. Transferred $10 000 to the general reserve.

Required

A. Prepare journal entries (in general journal format) for the listed transactions and events for France Ltd for the year ended 30 June 2015.

B. Prepare a statement of changes in equity for the year ended 30 June 2015 to comply with IAS 1/AASB 101.

LO 1, 4

Exercise 23.8 DIVIDENDS

The equity of Guyana Ltd at 30 June 2014 is as follows:

Equity	
8% preference shares, cumulative and participating, issued at $5	$1 000 000
180 000 ordinary shares, fully paid	900 000
Revaluation reserve	250 000
General reserve	100 000
Retained earnings	650 000
	$2 900 000

Required

Based on the above information, answer the following questions:

1. What is the issue price per share of the ordinary shares?
2. If the directors decide to declare a final dividend of 20c per share on the ordinary shares, what journal entry would be necessary on 30 June 2014, assuming no ratification of the dividend is required by shareholders?
3. If the total dividend to be paid on all shares is to equal $200 000, how much money would be paid to the preference shareholders and to the ordinary shareholders assuming:
   (a) there are no accumulated dividends owing to preference shares and the preference shares are entitled to participate in additional dividends once the ordinary shareholders have received 20c per share?
   (b) there is 1 year of dividends in arrears on the preference shares?
   (c) there are no accumulated dividends owing to preference shares, and preference shares can participate only after ordinary shareholders have received 25c per share?
4. What are the necessary journal entries to provide for the dividends in questions 3(a), (b) and (c) respectively?
5. Assume that the market price of each ordinary share is currently $6. If a bonus dividend is to be provided out of the revaluation surplus to ordinary shareholders on the basis of 1 share for every 5 shares held, what is the journal entry required on 30 June 2014?
6. Assuming the existence of items in questions 3(a) and 5 and no other changes to issued capital for the year, and that the balance of retained earnings at the beginning of the year was $300 000, prepare a statement of changes in equity for the year ended 30 June 2014 for external reporting purposes to comply with current accounting standards.

LO 4

Exercise 23.9 RESERVES, DIVIDENDS, STATEMENT OF CHANGES IN EQUITY

The following was obtained from the ledger of Hungary Ltd as at 30 June 2014:

Share capital	
100 000 ordinary shares paid to 75c, but issued for $1	$75 000
40 000 10% preference shares fully paid at $1	40 000
Calls in advance	500
General reserve	20 000
Retained earnings 1/7/13	16 000
Profit for year (before tax)	30 000
Interim dividend paid on ordinary shares (1/1/14)	4 000

End-of-year adjustments

1. Income tax expense of $7000 is to be recognised. The company pays tax in one instalment annually.

2. Declare a dividend on the preference shares for the current year.
3. Declare a final dividend on ordinary shares of $3000. No ratification is required at the annual meeting.
4. Transfer $4000 from the general reserve to retained earnings.

Required
Prepare a statement of changes in equity for Hungary Ltd for the year ended 30 June 2014.

Exercise 23.10 GENERAL JOURNAL, STATEMENT OF CHANGES IN EQUITY **LO 4**

The following information relating to the year ending 30 June 2015 for Iran Ltd has been obtained from the company's records.

General reserve	$ 6 000
Goodwill	5 000
Income tax expense	16 000
Interim dividends paid	10 000
Profit for year before further adjustments and income tax	125 000
Retained earnings (1/7/14)	20 000
Revaluation surplus	20 000
Share capital — 50 000 ordinary shares issued at $1	50 000
Share issue costs	2 000

There were no shares issued during the year. The revaluation surplus related only to a block of land that had been previously revalued from a cost of $100 000. It is now fair valued at $75 000.

On 30 June 2015, the directors decided to:
1. declare a final dividend payment of 8c per share — this dividend does not have to be ratified by the annual meeting
2. write-off goodwill
3. increase general reserve by $10 000.

Required
A. Record the above adjustments in the general journal.
B. Prepare a statement of changes in equity complying with IAS 1/AASB 101 (ignore comparatives).

Exercise 23.11 DIVIDENDS, EQUITY SECTION OF STATEMENT OF FINANCIAL POSITION **LO 1, 4**

The equity of Jordan Ltd at 14 February 2014 consisted of:

Share capital:	
800 000 shares (fully paid for $1)	$800 000
600 000 shares (paid to 50c, issued at $1)	300 000
General reserve	100 000
Plant replacement reserve	50 000
Retained earnings	125 000

The following events occurred during 2014:

Feb.	15	Interim dividend of 5c per share declared and paid.
April	2	Final call made on the 600 000 partly paid shares.
May	30	All call money received.
June	30	Profit before tax for the year was $700 000 out of which the following adjustments were made (if appropriate):
		(a) Income tax expense was determined as $250 000.
		(b) Final dividend of 5c per share on all issued shares was recommended.
		(c) Transfers to reserves: General reserve $40 000
		Plant replacement reserve $30 000
		(d) Directors revalued the company's properties by $300 000.
Aug.	15	Shareholders approved the final dividend and a 1-for-5 bonus issue of shares at a price of $1 per share to be satisfied out of the surplus arising from revaluation of properties.
Aug.	16	Payment of final dividend and allotment of bonus shares.

Required

A. Prepare journal entries (in general journal format) to give effect to the above transactions.

B. Show the Retained Earnings account up to 17 August 2014.

C. Show the equity section of the statement of financial position as at 17 August 2014.

PROBLEMS

★ Basic

★★ Moderate

★★★ Challenging

LO 2, 4

Problem 23.1 RESERVES, DIVIDENDS, STATEMENT OF PROFIT OR LOSS AND OTHER COMPREHENSIVE INCOME, STATEMENT OF CHANGES IN EQUITY ★★

The equity of Kyrgyzstan Ltd at 30 June 2014 was:

Share capital

500 000 10% cumulative preference shares issued at $1 each	$ 500 000
1 000 000 ordinary shares issued at $1 each	1 000 000
Total share capital	1 500 000
General reserve	450 000
Retained earnings	(300 000)
	$1 650 000

Additional information

During the year ended 30 June 2015, the following transactions occurred:

2014

Oct. 1 Kyrgyzstan Ltd settled a long standing civil lawsuit for $75 000 (significantly less than had been expected). The directors had previously placed $450 000 into a general reserve in anticipation of the potential costs. The board has now decided that the general reserve can be discontinued.

Dec. 1 The directors had not paid the preference shareholders their dividend for 2014, given the lack of retained earnings. They now declare and pay the dividend.

2015

Feb. 1 The profits for the half year were such that the directors declare and pay 12c per share interim dividend for ordinary shareholders.

June 30 The profit before tax for the year was $3 264 000. The directors decided to recommend a final dividend of 27c per share for ordinary shareholders. Assume the tax rate is 30% for estimating income tax expense.

In determining the profit before tax of $3 264 000 the following items were taken into account:

Sales	$9 810 000
Cost of sales	5 760 000
Selling, distribution and administrative expenses	81 000
Damages on lawsuit	75 000
Revaluation down of land	243 000
Profit on sale of investment in government bonds	270 000
Bad debts expense	117 000

Required

A. Prepare general journal entries for all dated transactions in the additional information.

B. Prepare a statement of profit or loss and other comprehensive income for the reporting period ended 30 June 2015 in accordance with current accounting standards.

C. Prepare a statement of changes in equity for Kyrgyzstan Ltd for the reporting period ended 30 June 2015.

D. Discuss the nature and purpose of the contingency reserve.

LO 2, 3, 4

Problem 23.2 ANNUAL FINANCIAL STATEMENTS — LIQUIDITY PRESENTATION ★★

Refer to the information in problem 16.14 for England Ltd on page 692.

Required

A. Prepare a statement of profit or loss and other comprehensive income for England Ltd in accordance with the requirements of IAS 1/AASB 101.

B. Prepare a statement of financial position for England Ltd in accordance with IAS 1/AASB 101. Use the liquidity presentation format.

C. Prepare a statement of changes in equity for England Ltd in accordance with IAS 1/AASB 101.

LO 2, 3, 4

Problem 23.3 ANNUAL FINANCIAL STATEMENTS ★★

Refer to the information in problem 16.15 for Italy Ltd on page 693.

Required

A. Prepare a statement of profit or loss and other comprehensive income for Italy Ltd in accordance with the requirements of IAS 1/AASB 101.

B. Prepare a statement of financial position for Italy Ltd in accordance with IAS 1/AASB 101. Use the current/non-current presentation format.

C. Prepare a statement of changes in equity for Italy Ltd in accordance with IAS 1/AASB 101.

LO 2, 4

Problem 23.4 DIVIDENDS, RESERVES, FINANCIAL STATEMENTS ★★

Luxembourg Ltd commenced trading many years ago. Equity at 30 June 2014 comprised:

Share capital, 20 000 ordinary shares fully paid at $10	$200 000
General reserve	115 000
Retained earnings	21 500
	$336 500

During the financial year ended 30 June 2015, the following transactions with respect to capital and dividends took place:

2014

Sept. 30 Final dividend of $1 per share for year ended 30 June 2014 was ratified and paid.

Nov. 30 Issued 15 000 shares, fully paid at $10, in payment for assets with a fair value of $150 000.

2015

Mar. 31 Interim dividend of 50c for the half-year ended 31 December 2014 paid on all shares.

June 30 The company made a profit before tax of $200 000 for the financial year. Revenue for the year was $900 000 and interest expense was $15 000. The directors decided:

(a) to provide for income tax expense and current liability at 30% of profit before tax.

(b) to transfer $20 000 to general reserve.

(c) to recommend a final dividend of $1 per share on all issued shares

(d) to revalue plant with a cost of $100 000 and a carrying amount of $80 000 to $90 000.

Required

A. Prepare entries in general journal format to record the above transactions. Ignore closing entries.

B. Prepare the statement of profit or loss and other comprehensive income for the reporting period ended 30 June 2015 to comply with IAS 1/AASB 101.

C. Prepare a statement of changes in equity for the year ended 30 June 2015.

LO 3

Problem 23.5 TAKEOVER OF EXISTING BUSINESS, ISSUE OF ORDINARY SHARES, STATEMENT OF FINANCIAL POSITION ★★

Morocco Ltd was formed on 1 March 2014 for the purpose of purchasing the business of Norway Ltd whose assets and liabilities at that date were as shown below.

Assets	
Freehold land	$ 30 000
Buildings	180 000
Machinery	70 000
Supplies	45 000
Accounts receivable	120 000
Inventory	190 000
Liabilities	
Mortgage payable	70 000
Bank overdraft	25 000
Accounts payable	85 000

Morocco Ltd agreed that the fair values of all assets and liabilities taken over were equal to carrying amounts with the exception of the following:

Freehold land was to be valued at $50 000, buildings to be valued at $150 000, accounts receivable to be taken over at $110 000 and inventory to be valued at $180 000.

The purchase price was $450 000 and, in satisfaction thereof, the vendors were to receive $300 000 in fully paid ordinary shares and the balance in cash. The fair value of each ordinary share is $2.

The company offered for public subscription 250 000 ordinary shares on the following terms:

31 March:	60c per share on application
30 April:	60c per share on allotment
31 May:	40c per share on first call
and a final call:	40c per share as and when required.

Applications were received for 260 000 shares. The directors allotted 250 000 shares and any excess application money received was returned to unsuccessful applicants.

All money due was received on allotment, but holders of 2000 shares failed to pay the first call. Norway Ltd was paid, according to the agreement, on 15 May 2014.

Required

A. Record all the above transactions in general journal form in the accounts of Morocco Ltd up to 30 June 2014.
B. Prepare the statement of financial position for Morocco Ltd as at 30 June 2014 in accordance with the requirements of IAS 1/AASB 101.

Problem 23.6 CONVERSION OF PARTNERSHIP INTO COMPANY, ISSUE OF SHARES, STATEMENT OF FINANCIAL POSITION ★★ **LO 3**

Poland and Oman, the proprietors of a consulting business, decided to convert their business into a limited company known as Qatar Ltd. The following was the balance sheet for internal purposes at the date of the proposed conversion, 1 July 2014:

POLAND AND OMAN
Balance Sheet
as at 30 June 2014

CURRENT LIABILITY			NON-CURRENT ASSETS (NET)		
Accounts payable		$ 15 000	Freehold premises	$ 40 000	
NON-CURRENT LIABILITY			Equipment	18 000	
Mortgage payable		20 000	Fixtures and fittings	12 000	$ 70 000
EQUITY					
Oman, Capital	$45 000		CURRENT ASSETS		
Poland, Capital	45 000	90 000	Accounts receivable	22 000	
			Cash at bank	5 000	
			Inventory	28 000	55 000
		$125 000			$125 000

Qatar Ltd was registered on 1 July 2014. The purchase agreement provided that the assets other than cash at bank were to be taken over at the following fair values:

Freehold premises	$60 000
Equipment	18 000
Accounts receivable less 5%	
Inventory	25 000
Fixtures and fittings	10 000

Poland and Oman were to pay the accounts payable and discharge the mortgage payable. As consideration for the sale they were to receive $40 000 in cash 7 days after the allotment of shares issued to the public and on 31 August 60 000 fully paid ordinary shares and 40 000 fully paid 10% preference shares, valued at $1 per share.

The company offered for public subscription 80 000 preference shares and 100 000 ordinary shares payable 50c per share on application, 25c per share on allotment and 25c per share 1 month after allotment. The subscription lists closed on 31 July and application money was received for 65 000 preference shares and 120 000 ordinary shares.

On 4 August the directors proceeded to allotment, and forwarded letters of regret enclosing refund of application money to unsuccessful applicants. By 31 August all the allotment money was received except that due on 1400 ordinary shares. The purchase price was paid to Poland and Oman as per agreement. Share issue costs paid on 31 August amounted to $3500.

The company purchased additional freehold property on 1 September 2014 for $95 000, satisfied by the issue of 40 000 fully paid ordinary shares, valued at $1 each, $30 000 on long-term loan, and the balance in cash.

Required

A. Prepare journal entries (in general journal form) for Qatar Ltd up to and including 1 September 2014.

B. Show the statement of financial position of the company as at 1 September 2014. Follow the requirements of IAS 1/AASB 101.

Problem 23.7 STATEMENT OF PROFIT OR LOSS AND OTHER COMPREHENSIVE INCOME, STATEMENT OF FINANCIAL POSITION AND RETAINED EARNINGS ★★ **LO 2, 3, 4**

The trial balance of Russia Ltd at 30 June 2015 was as shown below.

RUSSIA LTD Trial Balance as at 30 June 2015	Debit	Credit
Share capital (ordinary shares issued at $2, fully paid)		$ 200 000
General surplus		25 000
Retained earnings		73 400
Revaluation surplus		85 000
Mortgage loan (secured over land and buildings)		250 000
Bank overdraft (at call)		70 900
7% debentures		80 000
Interest payable		2 800
Accounts payable		69 500
Dividend payable		10 000
Employee benefits payable		34 200
GST payable		18 400
Allowance for doubtful debts		12 800
Accumulated depreciation – plant and equipment		42 500
Accumulated impairment losses – goodwill		10 000
Cash at bank	$ 500	
Accounts receivable	67 800	
Inventory	87 700	
Prepaid insurance	7 000	
Plant and equipment	222 500	
Land	220 000	
Buildings	380 000	
Goodwill	50 000	
Government bonds (long-term)	35 000	
Shares in Slovenia Ltd	20 000	
Sales revenue		825 000
Cost of sales	450 000	
General expenses	265 000	
Loss on sale of plant	10 000	
Interest received		2 500
Dividends received		3 500
	$1 815 500	$1 815 500

Additional information
(a) General expenses for the year include the following items:

Depreciation – plant and equipment	$17 200
Depreciation – buildings	15 000
Employee benefits	11 600
Bad debts	10 000
Interest expense	28 700
Inventory losses	6 200
Discount allowed	4 200
Council rates	16 120
Superannuation contributions	7 000

(b) The company tax rate is 30%, to be applied to profit before tax.
(c) The opening balance of the allowance for doubtful debts was $15 250.
(d) All assets are carried at cost, except for land and buildings, which are carried at fair value.
(e) During the year, 50 000 shares were issued at an issue price of $2 each, payable in full on application.
(f) On 30 June 2015, the directors revalued land and buildings based on fair values. The carrying amounts of land and buildings before the revaluation were $195 000 and $350 000 respectively.
(g) The mortgage loan is repayable in annual instalments of $50 000 starting on 1 March.
(h) The debentures are to be redeemed on 31 March 2016. There is no plan to refinance these debentures in the future.
(i) The employee benefits payable consist of:

Annual leave	$18 400
Long-service leave	15 800

(j) No employee is eligible for long-service leave until 2019.
(k) Goodwill is not considered to be impaired.
(l) During the year, Russia Ltd sold an item of plant for $38 000. The carrying amount of the plant at the date of sale was $48 000.
(m) During the year, an interim dividend of $20 000 was paid, and a final dividend of $10 000 was declared. $25 000 was also transferred to the general reserve.

Required
A. Prepare a statement of profit or loss and other comprehensive income for Russia Ltd for the year ended 30 June 2015, according to the requirements of IAS 1/AASB 101.
B. Prepare a statement of financial position at 30 June 2015 to comply with IAS 1/AASB 101.
C. Prepare the Retained Earnings account for the year ended 30 June 2015.

Problem 23.8   COMPREHENSIVE PROBLEM ★★★   LO 2, 3

The ledger balances of Tuvalu Ltd as at 30 June 2016 are shown opposite.
The following adjustments are yet to be taken into the accounts:
1. Inventory on hand at 30 June 2016 valued at $94 250.
2. Allowance for doubtful debts to be increased to $1625, which was the balance of the account on 1 July 2015.
3. It was discovered that $780 for office equipment had been charged in error to the purchases account on 1 July 2015.
4. Depreciation of delivery vehicles and office equipment for the current year to be at the rate of 20% p.a. on cost, and on buildings at 5% on cost.

5. Interest expense accrued, $325.
6. Unexpired insurance, $130.
7. Declare a dividend to shareholders of $22 750 for the current year.
8. Transfer $6500 to general reserve and reduce goodwill by $13 000 because of impairment.

TUVALU LTD Trial Balance as at 30 June 2016	Debit	Credit
Accounts receivable	$ 81 250	
Accounts payable		$ 40 700
Advertising expense	4 875	
Stationery expenses	585	
Share capital		325 000
Bills receivable	6 175	
Bank overdraft		10 650
Delivery vehicles (at cost)	30 875	
Directors' fees	8 125	
Discount allowed	3 250	
First call (25c per share)	6 500	
General expenses	5 070	
Goodwill (at cost)	39 000	
Income from investments		5 000
Insurance expense	625	
Interest expense	3 120	
Investments (at cost)	104 000	
Land (at cost)	26 650	
Buildings (at cost)	100 000	
Electricity expense	1 075	
Maintenance of vehicles expense	4 375	
Office equipment (at cost)	3 250	
Petty cash advance	130	
Retained earnings (1/7/15)		34 585
Accumulated depreciation – delivery vehicles		5 850
– buildings		4 550
Allowance for doubtful debts		975
Current tax liability		27 650
Purchases	124 870	
Sales		227 500
Income tax expense	27 650	
Salaries expense – administrative	11 245	
Salaries expense – selling	15 015	
Inventory (1/7/15)	74 750	
	$682 460	$682 460

Required

A. Prepare the statement of profit or loss and other comprehensive income for the year ended 30 June 2016 in accordance with the requirements of IAS 1/AASB 101.

B. Prepare the statement of financial position as at 30 June 2016 in accordance with the requirements of IAS 1/AASB 101.

The following unadjusted trial balance is for the year ended 30 June 2015:

URUGUAY LTD
Unadjusted Trial Balance
as at 30 June 2015

	Debit	Credit
Bank overdraft		$ 178 050
Vehicle rental expenses	$ 72 000	
Cash at bank	7 500	
Investment in government bonds	150 000	
Goodwill	30 000	
Interest revenue		4 800
Insurance expense	3 000	
Land	230 000	
Buildings	1 000 000	
Office furniture and equipment	127 000	
Retained earnings (1/7/14)		89 000
Revaluation surplus		15 000
Accumulated depreciation – office furniture and equipment		23 000
Accumulated depreciation – buildings		100 000
Accumulated impairment losses – goodwill		6 000
Allowance for doubtful debts		14 700
Cost of sales	197 400	
Advertising expense	12 300	
Sales returns and allowances	8 700	
Sales		478 120
Mortgage payable		90 000
GST payable		15 000
Inventory	106 000	
Share capital (issued and paid to $1 per share)		1 140 000
General reserve		18 000
Interest expense on overdraft	11 300	
Discount received		11 250
Discount allowed	12 000	
Fees revenue		17 900
Proceeds on sale of furniture		13 000
Carrying amount of furniture sold	5 000	
Accounts payable		118 900
Accounts receivable	225 400	
Salaries of sales staff	60 000	
Administrative wages	70 620	
Interest expense on mortgage	4 500	
	$2 332 720	$2 332 720

Additional information

(a) Uruguay Ltd is involved in the computer services industry. Leased vehicles are used mainly for delivery and service of computers. The company's head office, which houses its administrative staff, is located on a prime piece of real estate in the local township.

(b) There have been no share issues during the year.

(c) The following adjustments are required before preparation of Uruguay Ltd's financial statements for the year:

    1. Depreciation to be provided on a straight-line basis on buildings at 5% p.a. and on office furniture and equipment at 10% p.a. The sale of office furniture occurred at the beginning of the current financial year.

2. Goodwill is considered to have fallen in value through impairment by 10% of its original cost.
3. Management was informed that a particular debtor was bankrupt and the full account of $12 000 needs to be written off.
4. The Allowance for Doubtful Debts account needs to be adjusted to 8% of accounts receivable, after considering the adjustment in (3) above.
5. Current income tax expense (and tax liability) for the year is estimated to be $8000.
6. Accrued wages to staff: sales $1500, administrative $2000.
7. Vehicle rental paid in advance at 30 June 2015 amounted to $30 000.
8. A dividend of 3c per share is to be declared on shares.
9. Land is to be revalued to its fair value of $250 000.
10. Transfer $10 000 from the general reserve to retained earnings.

Required

A. Prepare the journal entries (in general journal form) required by items 1–10 above.
B. Prepare the adjusted trial balance as at 30 June 2015.
C. Prepare the statement of profit or loss and other comprehensive income, with expenses classified by function, for Uruguay Ltd for the year ended 30 June 2015 in accordance with the requirements of IAS 1/ AASB 101.
D. Prepare the statement of changes in equity for the year ended 30 June 2015 in accordance with the requirements of IAS 1/AASB 101.
E. Prepare the company's classified statement of financial position as at 30 June 2015 in accordance with the requirements of IAS 1/AASB 101, using the current/non-current classification.

DECISION ANALYSIS

Treatment of events for a construction company

Terrific Town Houses Ltd is a large company registered in South Australia for the purpose of constructing blocks of home units and town houses. The company conducts its activities in all states. The managing director, Richard Townsend, who is keen to show favourable profit figures, especially profit from operations, is confronted with a number of doubtful issues. He has asked you, the accountant, to clarify the accounting treatment for each of these issues in order to finalise the accounts for the year ended 30 June 2015.

1. Last year, the company acquired land at Kalamunda on the Darling Ranges behind Perth, and had begun construction of 15 town houses on this land. The construction work was three-quarters finished when a bushfire swept through the area on the weekend of 24–25 March 2015. The company had a policy of self-insurance, and estimated that the loss incurred was approximately $2.5m. Fire danger in the locality of Kalamunda is extremely high during the late summer months every year.
2. Many years ago, the company purchased a large tract of land at Nambucca Heads in New South Wales for $1.5m, for the purpose of erecting home units. Because of a recession, construction work was delayed. Last November, the company received an offer for the land for $3m. The offer was considered too good to refuse, and the land was sold at this price to the offeror on 30 November 2014.
3. The company also holds land at Ipswich in Queensland, which it had purchased some years ago for $600 000. Unfortunately, part of the land subsided because of old coalmines that had not been recorded in the government's records because the mines were closed before records were kept. Consequently, the land was regarded as unsuitable for building purposes. The company believes that the land is worth only $300 000 at the end of the reporting period, and it intends to revalue the land down to this recoverable amount.

   However, in the Mount Lofty Ranges behind Adelaide, other land held by the company has jumped considerably in value from cost of $800 000 to an estimated $1.2m. Townsend intends to revalue this land to offset the loss on the downward valuation of the land at Ipswich.

4. Land costing $200 000 was purchased some years ago at Anglesea in Victoria. An application to have the land rezoned for the purpose of constructing town houses was unsuccessful, and the company sold the land for $350 000 on 16 April 2015.

5. The company had acquired, for $2.5m, a piece of land for construction of an international hotel and casino on the banks of the Tamar River. At that time (2012), the local council was enthusiastically pro-development and the company was given all necessary approvals to commence construction. Construction began in 2013, and costs of $3m had already been incurred when lobbying by conservationists caused the state government to halt the company's work on the project in May 2014. The subsequent court case did not favour the company's arguments for continuation of the project, and the project had to be abandoned in February 2015. The company lost $4m in sunk costs and legal fees. Townsend suggested that the loss should be written off against retained earnings on the grounds that it was really a loss incurred in the previous financial year when work ceased.

Required

Advise Townsend on the most appropriate treatment in the financial statements for each of the above circumstances.

CRITICAL THINKING

Coca-Cola Amatil backs out of Golden Circle takeover

Read the extract below and answer the questions that follow.

Coca-Cola Amatil yesterday said it has ended buy-out talks with Golden Circle and wasn't considering revising higher its takeover offer terms.

Its statement came after the Golden Circle board on Thursday rejected a $1-a-share offer for all of its 82 million issued shares.

For CCA, buying Golden Circle was a way to further diversify from carbonated drinks into the booming market for health drinks and food brands.

Golden Circle executive chairman Ern Pope yesterday said CCA's offer was inadequate given Golden Circle's net asset value was about 92c a share excluding a revaluation of excess land now up for sale.

On the books at a value of $5.6 million, the company has had offers in the region of $25 million for the land.

The Golden Circle board kept its recommendation with a proposal from private equity firm Anchorage Capital Partners which will be put to a shareholder vote on October 29.

The Anchorage deal will give the private equity firm a controlling 35 per cent stake.

Golden Circle has said the Anchorage deal will also ease the company's debt burden, interest payments for which have been savaging its bottom line and frustrating efforts to return to profitability.

Anchorage will buy out Golden Circle's convertible notes, issued by Babcock & Brown in an earlier rescue operation, and then have Golden Circle redeem them for $67.15 million. Anchorage will then subscribe for 44.35 million shares at 80c each.

CCA had made its offer conditional on receiving support from all Golden Circle directors.

It yesterday said it was ending those talks, given the board decision, and 'isn't considering a revised offer at this time'.

CCA said it was disappointed at the board recommending an offer that doesn't provide 'immediate returns' to shareholders and dilutes their holding through a large share issue at a price 20 per cent below that offered by CCA.

Source: Excerpts from Kerrie Sinclair, 'Coca-Cola Amatil backs out of Golden Circle takeover', *The Herald Sun.*

Required

A. Based on the information provided, summarise and compare the rival bids for Golden Circle.

B. Discuss the relationship between share value and the financial statements.

C. Discuss the impact of a land revaluation on the financial statements of Golden Circle.

D. How do you think the issues to do with the value of land would have affected CCA's decision about how much to offer for the shares?

Corporate governance in action

Refer to the 'Business Knowledge' on page 960 dealing with continuous disclosure, corporate governance and the ASX. Elaborate on the eight principles of corporate governance by consulting the website of the ASX, www.asx.com.au.

Refer to the latest consolidated financial statements of JB Hi-Fi Limited on its website, www.jbhifi.com.au, and answer the following questions:

1. Provide details of the consolidated entity's income and expenses for the current year. In percentage terms, how much has total income changed from the previous period?
2. Do the consolidated financial statements follow the suggested formats, as illustrated in figures 23.1 and 23.4 in this chapter? If not, how do they differ?

Statement of cash flows

Learning objectives

After studying this chapter, you should be able to:

1 explain the reasons for preparing a statement of cash flows (p. 978)

2 describe the general format of the statement of cash flows (pp. 978–80)

3 define the concept of cash in accordance with IAS 7/AASB 107 *Statement of Cash Flows* (pp. 980–1)

4 classify cash inflows and cash outflows into operating, investing and financing activities (pp. 981–3)

5 prepare a statement of cash flows for a sole trader using the direct method by analysing cash records and other financial statements (pp. 983–94)

6 determine the notes to the statement of cash flows (pp. 994–9)

7 identify and explain some of the more advanced issues involved in the preparation of the statement of cash flows (pp. 999–1009)

8 prepare and analyse the statement of cash flows for a company after consideration of the more advanced issues (pp. 1009–18)

9 identify the limitations of the statement of cash flows (p. 1018).

Lessons from the crisis

Australia's stunted listed debt market is hindering the efforts of companies to diversify their sources of funding.

When the global financial crisis (GFC) hit, a number of Australia's largest companies were forced to raise money on the share market to repay debt that the banks refused to roll over.

Some A$100 billion of equity was raised in 2009 — most of it to repay debt in a highly dilutive and expensive exercise for shareholders. Accessing a range of debt-funding options should not be difficult for Australia's largest companies but, prior to the GFC, no more than one-third of Australia's top 200 ASX-listed companies had a credit rating. And without a credit rating, it is very difficult to access debt markets.

Given the experiences of the GFC, and the possibility of restricted or rationed bank lending over the next few years, is corporate Australia changing the way it goes about funding its debt requirements?

The short answer is yes: corporate Australia is diversifying its sources of debt as well as going back to textbook good practice when it comes to diversifying the term of that debt. But the lack of a listed debt market remains a huge impediment to efficient debt raising.

'Incitec Pivot's debt funding needs are largely denominated in US dollars, so accessing the domestic corporate bond market is not a priority,' says Frank Micallef, CFO of the chemical manufacturer. However, he observes that 'the domestic market does not appear to be as comfortable with providing long-term debt, which makes raising such debt in large volume very difficult'.

The corporate debt market in Australia is an unlisted market whose investors are almost exclusively institutional investors. The average term to maturity of debt issued in this market is just over 2.5 years, an average that has actually shortened over the past 10 years.

Alternatives to short-term debt

Australian CFOs do have alternatives to this short-term debt, and Anthony Flintoff, managing director, Standard & Poor's Australia, says he is seeing much more appraisal going into debt-raising strategies in the wake of the funding crises of 2008 and 2009.

'Many Australian companies recognise that they dodged a bullet in the GFC,' he comments. 'They realise that they have been too beholden to the banks for their debt funding and are now looking to broaden their funding sources and potentially lengthen their debt maturity profiles at the same time.'

Flintoff says Brambles, Asciano, Incitec Pivot and APA Group had all recently obtained Standard & Poor's credit ratings. Incitec Pivot raised US$800 million for 10 years at 265 basis points over US Treasury bonds, with a yield of 6.09 per cent in December 2009. Incitec Pivot had a specific US dollar funding requirement after its acquisition of Dyno Nobel, said Micallef.

And there is anecdotal evidence that company directors are less likely to penny pinch when it comes to pricing. They just want to get the deals done, even if the price may be a bit more expensive than necessary.

Boards do not want any nasty surprises, such as banks refusing to roll over debt facilities, and have been stung by investor criticism of the deeply discounted equity issues undertaken last year. Boards also seem keen to get a second opinion in the form of an independent assessment of the credit quality of their companies. S&P reports that demand for confidential ratings has increased since the GFC.

It wasn't just corporate Australia that was caught out in this respect; so, too, were the country's major banks. The banks entered the GFC very reliant on short-term borrowings from international wholesale debt markets. This was one reason the government guarantee of their wholesale borrowings became essential to their survival.

Even now, concerns are being expressed by investors that Australia's four major banks have become the largest borrowers in global bond markets, relative to their size, and that they may find it difficult to continue over the next few years to borrow at the rates that they have.

Source: Extract from Philip Bayley, 'Lessons from the crisis', *InTheBlack*.

Chapter preview

As indicated in chapter 23, a statement of profit or loss and other comprehensive income, a statement of financial position, a statement of changes in equity and a statement of cash flows must be included in a set of annual financial statements to comply with the *Corporations Act 2001* (s. 295) and/or accounting standards. The first three statements are presented in chapter 23. The amounts presented in these statements are a result of applying accrual accounting.

The statement of cash flows is important to users of general purpose financial statements because it identifies the cash inflows and cash outflows from operating, financing and investing activities of the entity that have occurred during the reporting period. An analysis of comparative statements of financial position for successive periods will identify the total changes that have taken place in asset, liability and equity accounts, but will not provide details of the cash flows associated with those changes. The statement of changes in equity shows movements in equity from owner sources, including details of dividends, share issues and reserve movements, but does not show cash flows. The statement of profit or loss and other comprehensive income summarises the income, revenue and expense activities over the period from sources other than owners, but does not provide details of the cash flows associated with such activities, because the statement is based on accrual accounting principles and not on the cash basis of accounting. Details of the purpose and content of the statement of cash flows are contained in IAS 7/AASB 107 *Statement of Cash Flows*.

24.1 Purpose of the statement of cash flows

The purpose of a statement of cash flows is to provide information about the changes to an entity's cash and cash equivalents over a period of time. It is designed to enable users of general purpose financial statements to assess the ability of the entity to generate cash and to predict future cash requirements. According to the accounting standard, the statement of cash flows, when used in conjunction with the other financial statements, will enable users to:

- evaluate the entity's financial structure, including its liquidity and solvency
- assess the entity's ability to generate cash in the future and predict future cash flows
- check the accuracy of past assessments of future cash flows
- examine the relationship between profitability and net cash flow
- evaluate the changes in net assets of the entity
- compare the performance of this entity with other entities, because it eliminates the effects of using different accounting treatments (e.g. depreciation methods) for the same transactions and events
- evaluate the entity's ability to adapt to changing circumstances and opportunities.

The statement of cash flows can also provide useful information to internal users such as managers in their planning and controlling operations. For example, from the scene setter at the beginning of this chapter, the global financial crisis has had considerable impact on managements' abilities to raise cash in order to fund their companies' operations. Hence, they have needed to plan how and where they will obtain their cash requirements in order to continue business operations.

24.2 General format of the statement of cash flows

IAS 7/AASB 107 specifies the items to be disclosed in a statement of cash flows, and examples of acceptable formats are given in Appendixes A and B (which do not constitute a part of the standard). There are several ways in which the statement can be presented; a typical format of the statement of cash flows for a company is presented in figure 24.1.

The standard specifies that the statement must contain separate disclosure of cash inflows and outflows, classified as arising from operating, investing or financing activities, as appropriate. The international (IASB) standard and the Australian (AASB) standard allow the use of either the direct method of reporting cash flows or the indirect method; however, the use of the direct method is encouraged by both the IASB and the AASB. The difference between the direct and indirect methods is explained later (p. 986). The direct method is illustrated in figure 24.1.

Figure 24.1 Typical format for statement of cash flows using the direct method (based on Appendix A accompanying IAS 7/ AASB 107)

HAWKESBURY LTD Statement of Cash Flows for the year ended 30 June 2014		
Cash flows from operating activities		
Cash receipts from customers	$ x	
Cash paid to suppliers and employees	(x)	
Cash generated from operations	x	
Interest paid	(x)	
Income taxes paid	(x)	
Net cash from operating activities		$ x
Cash flows from investing activities		
Purchase of property, plant and equipment	(x)	
Proceeds from sale of equipment	x	
Interest received	x	
Dividends received	x	
Net cash used in investing activities		x
Cash flows from financing activities		
Proceeds from issue of share capital	x	
Proceeds from long-term borrowings	x	
Repayments of borrowings	(x)	
Dividends paid	(x)	
Net cash used in financing activities		x
Net increase (decrease) in cash and cash equivalents		x
Cash and cash equivalents at beginning of period		x
Cash and cash equivalents at end of period		$ x

The net cash flows for each classification are then totalled to provide the net increase (decrease) in cash over the reporting period. Cash at the beginning of the reporting period is added to disclose the amount of cash at the end of the reporting period. In practice, comparative statements — current year and previous year — are produced, but in this book 1-year statements only are illustrated. However, as is discussed later, comparative statements are essential for interpreting the information contained in the statement.

Even though subclassification of cash flows is not required, IAS 7/AASB 107 requires disclosure of specific information in the statement, provided that these items are material, as defined in AASB 1031 *Materiality*. Certain cash flows must be disclosed as separate items, and classified consistently from period to period regardless of the classification of cash flows used. The items (illustrated in figure 24.1) that must be separately disclosed under the standard are:

- interest received
- dividends received
- interest paid
- dividends paid, classified as either a financing cash flow or an operating cash flow
- income tax paid.

IAS 7/AASB 107 requires cash flows from income tax to be disclosed separately and classified as part of cash flows from operating activities, unless such payment can be *specifically* identified with investing or financing activities. If cash flows from income tax have been allocated to more than one category, the total amount must be disclosed separately.

Gross flows must be reported, and netting (e.g. setting off interest received against interest paid to determine a 'net' interest amount) is not allowed. Exceptions under the standard to this general principle are rare, but transactions that represent holdings and disbursements of cash on behalf of customers, and items where the turnover is quick, the amounts are large and the maturities are short, may be reported on the net basis. The standard provides examples of cash flows that can be reported on a net basis:

- the acceptance and repayment of demand deposits of a bank (but not if they are included within the definition of cash — see the next section in this chapter)
- funds held for customers by an investment entity
- rents collected on behalf of and paid over to the owners of properties
- provided that the turnover is quick, the amounts are large and the maturities are short, advances and repayments of:
  - principal amounts relating to credit card customers
  - the purchase and sale of investments
  - other short-term borrowings with maturity periods of 3 months or less (but not if they are included in the definition of cash — see the next section).

Cash flows may also be reported on a net basis for a financial institution for each of the following activities:

- receipts and payments for deposits with a fixed maturity date
- deposits placed with and withdrawn from other financial institutions
- cash advances and loans and the repayments of those advances and loans.

For the purposes of this chapter, the gross flows approach is followed with no amounts being netted.

Additional explanatory notes are usually required to fulfil all disclosure requirements of the standard, which are extensive. These are generally provided as notes to the statement of cash flows and include:

- a comment disclosing the components of 'cash and cash equivalents', and a reconciliation of the amounts in the statement of cash flows to items reported as cash assets in the statement of financial position
- a reconciliation of the net cash provided by operating activities to profit or loss (this note is not required if the indirect method is used in the statement of cash flows)
- details of cash flows from the acquisition and disposal of subsidiaries and other business units
- details about transactions and other events that affect assets and liabilities but do not result in cash flows, referred to as non-cash financing and investing transactions (these are discussed in more detail later in the chapter)
- details of cash balances that are not available for use and the reasons.

Details of an entity's unused loan facilities may also be disclosed if considered relevant to users in understanding the entity's financial position and liquidity.

Note that not all the above are covered or included in exercises and problems in this chapter.

24.3 Concept of cash

Learning objective 3

Define the concept of cash in accordance with IAS 7/ AASB 107 *Statement of Cash Flows*

The concept of cash adopted by IAS 7/AASB 107 covers cash and cash equivalents. The concept is important since all transfers among items within the concept are not reported in the statement of cash flows. In other words, an item included in the definition of cash and cash equivalents cannot generate a cash flow in the context of preparing a statement of cash flows. **Cash** comprises cash on hand and demand deposits. **Cash equivalents** are short-term highly liquid investments that are readily convertible into known amounts of cash, and that are subject to an insignificant risk of changes in value. Examples of cash equivalents include bank and non-bank bills, and money market deposits close to maturity. As a general rule, investments with a term of 3 months or less also fall within the definition of cash equivalents, provided that the investments are readily convertible into known amounts of cash and are subject to an insignificant risk of changes in value.

IAS 7/AASB 107 recognises that not all highly liquid investments will fall into the definition of cash equivalents, and each entity needs to identify which highly liquid investments are subject to an insignificant risk of changes in value and which are not. Normally, certain items are excluded from the definition of cash, and these include accounts receivable and equity securities (shares). An entity preparing a statement of cash flows is required to disclose, by way of note, the policy adopted for determining which items are classified as cash and cash equivalents in the statement of cash flows. The definition of cash used in the standard is summarised in figure 24.2.

Figure 24.2 Concept of cash and cash equivalents in IAS 7/AASB 107

	Form	Examples	Conditions
CASH ON HAND	**Cash** **Demand deposits**	Notes Coins Demand deposits held at financial institutions	None
CASH EQUIVALENTS	**Short-term highly liquid investments**	Bank bills Non-bank bills Deposits on short-term money market	Readily convertible to cash *and* Short-term investments (normally 3 months or less) *and* An insignificant risk of changes in value

With respect to bank borrowings, the standard suggests that such borrowings are generally reported as financing activities; nevertheless, in some countries, such as Australia, bank overdrafts may be repayable on demand and form an integral part of an entity's cash management. In these circumstances, bank overdrafts are included as a component of cash and cash equivalents. The important characteristic of such banking arrangements is that the bank balance often fluctuates from being positive to overdrawn, i.e. from 'the black into the red'. In this book, a bank overdraft is treated as a financing activity unless it is stated that such an overdraft is repayable on demand and is part of the entity's short-term cash management activities.

Having defined the concept of cash for the statement of cash flows, it is possible to summarise those activities resulting from transactions with parties external to the entity that led to increases and decreases in cash and cash equivalents.

In presenting the statement, the standard requires an entity to classify activities. Classification is based on different functions, and this helps users to identify the effect on cash of the major activities of the entity.

24.4 Classification of cash flow activities

Learning objective 4

Classify cash inflows and cash outflows into operating, investing and financing activities

IAS 7/AASB 107 requires the entity's statement of cash flows to report the cash inflows and cash outflows associated with each of the entity's major activities for the reporting period. The items disclosed in the statement in accordance with the standard should provide users with relevant information of the cash flows classified into the broad categories of:

- cash flows from operating activities
- cash flows from investing activities
- cash flows from financing activities.

Items that typically fall into the classification of operating, investing and financing activities are illustrated in the discussion below.

Cash flows from operating activities

Operating activities are defined in the standard as the 'principal revenue-producing activities of the entity and other activities that are not investing or financing activities'. The results of operating activities are therefore typically reflected in the statement of profit or loss and other comprehensive income. Transactions reflected in income are, of course, recorded on the basis of accrual accounting and do not necessarily reflect the cash flows associated therewith. The cash flows generated from operating activities generally include receipts from the sale of goods and rendering of services; cash payments to suppliers for goods and services; payments for wages and salaries; cash premiums to an insurance company for insurance cover; cash receipts from royalties, fees, commissions and other revenue; interest and other borrowing costs paid in cash; cash advances and loans made by financial institutions that relate to the main revenue-producing activities of the entity; and income tax paid or refunded. Note, however, that IAS 7/AASB 107 does not specify any particular categories of cash flows from operating activities apart from the suggestions above and the Appendixes accompanying the standard.

Depreciation of non-current assets, bad debts expense, and the gain/loss on disposal of non-current assets are non-cash items, all of which are included in profit but do not represent cash flows. They are therefore excluded from cash from operating activities. The gain/loss on the sale of non-current assets, which appears as income/expense in the statement of profit or loss and other comprehensive income, usually involves cash inflows in the form of proceeds from sale, which are classified as cash flows from investing activities under IAS 7/AASB 107.

Cash flows from operating activities are regarded as very important because they represent cash flows generated by the entity's major business operations. A high level and constant stream of these cash flows generally indicate an entity's capacity to generate cash in order to carry on as a going concern and its flexibility to change even the nature of its activities.

Cash flows from investing activities

The standard defines **investing activities** as those that relate to the acquisition and disposal of long term assets and other investments (such as other entities' shares and debentures) that are not included in cash equivalents. Typical examples of investing activities that generate cash inflows and cash outflows include the purchase and sale of property, plant and equipment, intangibles and other long-term assets, the purchase and sale of shares and debentures in other entities, and cash flows from advances and loans made to parties other than financial institutions. (See additional examples in the standard.)

In Appendix A that accompanies the standard, the cash inflows for interest and dividends generated by investing activities are also classified in the illustrations as cash inflows from investing activities along with the cash flows associated with the purchase and sale of the shares and securities that generate the interest and dividends.

Cash flows from financing activities

Activities that relate to changes in the size and composition of the equity and borrowings of an entity give rise to cash flows from **financing activities**. Examples of such activities include cash proceeds from a share issue, cash drawings by a sole trader, cash dividends paid, cash proceeds from issuing debentures, loans, notes, bonds, mortgages and other borrowings (such as a bank overdraft not repayable on demand and not part of the entity's cash management activities), cash repayment of a mortgage loan, and cash redemption of debentures and/or preference shares. With respect to dividends paid, IAS 7/AASB 107 permits such dividends to be classified as part of cash flows from operating activities in order to help users determine the ability of the entity to pay dividends out of operating cash flows.

Some cash flows resulting from financing activities, such as interest paid on debentures and loans, may be classified as cash outflows from operating activities, as shown in Appendix A accompanying the standard, and in figure 24.1 (p. 979). However, the treatment of interest paid as an operating activity may be quite inappropriate for some entities. In any one entity, there appears to be little reason for classifying borrowing costs paid from financing activities differently from dividends paid. Both are either financing activities or operating activities.

Refer back to the scene setter at the beginning of the chapter. Here you will see that one of the major focuses by companies as a result of the global financial crisis has been on cash flows from financing activities, namely the raising of funds through shares and the repayment of long-term debt.

Summary of classification

A summary of the typical items that generate cash inflows and cash outflows is shown in figure 24.3, based on the Appendixes accompanying the standard.

Figure 24.3 Typical cash inflows and cash outflows classified by activity

	OPERATING ACTIVITIES	
Operating activities (generally associated with revenues and expenses)	*Cash inflows* From sale of goods or services From cash advances and loans made by *financial institutions* relating to the entity's main revenue-producing activities	*Cash outflows* To suppliers for goods To employees for services To other persons/entities for expenses To lenders for interest and other borrowing costs To government for income tax, GST, and other fees and charges To other persons/entities for materials and contracts
	INVESTING ACTIVITIES	
Investing activities (generally movements in non-current assets)	*Cash inflows* From sale of property, plant and equipment From sale of shares and debentures of other entities From repayment of advances and loans to other entities From interest received [or operating activity] From dividends received [or operating activity]	*Cash outflows* To purchase property, plant and equipment To purchase shares and debentures of other entities To lend money to other entities
	FINANCING ACTIVITIES	
Financing activities (generally movements in non-current liabilities and equity)	*Cash inflows* From issue of shares From issuing debentures, notes From borrowings (loans, mortgages) From grants	*Cash outflows* To shareholders for share buy-backs and redemption of preference shares To owners for dividends paid [or operating activity] or cash drawings To debenture holders for redemption of debt To lenders to repay borrowings

24.5 Preparing the statement of cash flows — direct method

Learning objective 5

Prepare a statement of cash flows for a sole trader using the direct method by analysing cash records and other financial statements

Figure 24.1 (p. 979) illustrates that the preparation of a statement of cash flows requires information to be obtained about the cash inflows and cash outflows of an entity over the financial year. This information can be obtained in two ways:

- Analyse, summarise and classify the *cash* transactions of the entity together with an analysis of *other* transactions to determine the non-cash transactions that affected the assets and liabilities over the period. The other transactions would need to be reported in note form as part of the statement of cash flows.
- Analyse the other financial statements — the income statement and/or statement of profit or loss and other comprehensive income, the statement of financial position/balance sheet and the statement of changes in equity — to determine the cash flows. With this second approach, an analysis of the accounting records is also necessary to identify (a) the transactions that affected assets and liabilities during the reporting period but that did not affect cash, and (b) other information that needs to be disclosed.

Both approaches should produce the same cash inflows and cash outflows. To illustrate, consider the example below for the sole trader business, York Enterprises, which conducts business in the retail industry. Even though the business is small and is not a reporting entity, the owner, B. York, likes to prepare financial statements in accordance with IAS 7/AASB 107.

Analysis of cash and other records

Under this approach the information is obtained from a detailed analysis and summary of the cash records (cash receipts and cash payments journals) of the business over the year. Figure 24.4 illustrates this information source.

1. Cash received from accounts receivable	$471 000
2. Cash paid to accounts payable	328 000
3. Interest received on investments	1 050
4. Wages and salaries paid	63 000
5. Insurance paid	6 000
6. Other expenses paid	12 000
7. B. York, cash drawings	20 000
8. New equipment purchased	40 000
9. Proceeds from sale of equipment	3 000
10. Investments purchased	10 000
11. Cash at 1 July 2013	25 000
12. Cash at 30 June 2014	21 050

The statement of cash flows can be prepared from the summarised cash records shown in figure 24.4 by following these steps:

Step 1: Work out net cash from operating activities using the cash inflows and cash outflows identified as coming from operating activities, grouped according to the requirements of the standard.

Step 2: Work out net cash used in investing activities.

Step 3: Work out net cash used in financing activities.

Step 4: Work out net cash and cash equivalents increase (decrease) for the period.

Step 5: Reconcile cash and cash equivalents at the end of the period to that at the beginning of the period.

Operating activities are represented by summary items 1, 2, 4, 5 and 6 in figure 24.4, investing activities by items 3, 8, 9 and 10, and financing activities by item 7.

The statement of cash flows prepared in accordance with IAS 7/AASB 107 is presented in figure 24.5.

Additional disclosures required by way of notes to the statement of cash flows are introduced and illustrated later in the chapter.

Figure 24.5 Statement of cash flows for York Enterprises

YORK ENTERPRISES
Statement of Cash Flows
for the year ended 30 June 2014

Cash flows from operating activities		
Cash receipts from customers (Item 1)	$ 471 000	
Cash paid to suppliers and employees (Items 2, 4, 5, 6)	(409 000)	
Net cash from operating activities		$ 62 000
Cash flows from investing activities		
Purchase of investments (Item 10)	(10 000)	
Payment for equipment (Item 8)	(40 000)	
Proceeds from sale of equipment (Item 9)	3 000	
Interest received (Item 3)	1 050	
Net cash used in investing activities		(45 950)
Cash flows from financing activities		
B. York, Drawings	(20 000)	
Net cash used in financing activities		(20 000)
Net increase (decrease) in cash and cash equivalents		(3 950)
Cash and cash equivalents at beginning of period (Item 11)		25 000
Cash and cash equivalents at end of period (Item 12)		$ 21 050

Analysis of financial statements

A statement of cash flows can be prepared also by using comparative statements of financial position/balance sheets for successive periods, the income statement and/or statement of profit or loss and other comprehensive income and the statement of changes in equity of the entity, together with additional information extracted from the accounting records of the entity. The internal financial statements prepared by an entity, as illustrated in chapter 4, are used in this book as the basis for preparation of the statement of cash flows.

Comparative statements of financial position (or balance sheets) for 2013 and 2014, and the income statement and statement of changes in equity for the year ended 30 June 2014, as prepared for internal purposes, are shown in figure 24.6.

Figure 24.6 Internal financial statements of York Enterprises

YORK ENTERPRISES
Income Statement
for the year ended 30 June 2014

INCOME		
Revenue:		
Sales revenue		$480 000
Interest revenue on investments		1 000
		481 000
EXPENSES		
Cost of sales	$336 000	
Wages and salaries expense	65 000	
Insurance expense	8 000	
Loss on sale of equipment	2 000	
Depreciation expense – plant and equipment	20 000	
Other expenses	11 000	442 000
PROFIT		$ 39 000

YORK ENTERPRISES
Comparative Statements of Financial Position

	30 June 2013	30 June 2014
ASSETS		
Cash at bank	$ 13 000	$ 11 000
Accounts receivable	43 000	57 000
Inventory	52 000	50 000
Prepaid insurance	5 000	3 000
Interest receivable	150	100
Investments	10 000	20 000
Plant and equipment	180 000	200 000
Accumulated depreciation – plant and equipment	(45 000)	(50 000)
	$270 150	$296 150
LIABILITIES AND EQUITY		
Accounts payable	$ 32 000	$ 38 000
Wages and salaries payable	4 000	6 000
Other expenses payable	3 000	2 000
B. York, Capital	231 150	250 150
	$270 150	$296 150

YORK ENTERPRISES
Statement of Changes in Equity
for the year ended 30 June 2014

	Capital
Balance at 1/7/13	$231 150
Profit for the period	39 000
Drawings	(20 000)
Balance at 30/6/14	$250 150

In addition, an analysis of the year's activities reveals that the following events took place (ignore GST):

- Equipment that had cost $20 000 and was written down to a carrying amount of $5000 was sold for $3000 cash. New equipment purchased during the year for cash amounted to $40 000.
- All additional investments purchased were paid for in cash.
- B. York withdrew $20 000 in cash for the year, as shown in the statement of changes in equity. Income tax is ignored in this illustration as it is a sole trader, but such tax paid is discussed in more detail later in the chapter. Assume the business rents the premises but owns the plant and equipment used on the premises.

The cash flows derived by analysing financial statements should be the same as for those obtained by direct analysis and summation of the entity's cash flows. In preparing the statement of cash flows from an analysis of financial statements of York Enterprises, these steps are followed:

Step 1: Work out net cash from operating activities, disclosed according to the requirements of IAS 7/AASB 107. This requires separate calculations of the following items under the direct method, as encouraged by IAS 7/AASB 107:
   (a) cash receipts from customers
   (b) cash paid to suppliers and employees
   (c) other expense items affecting cash flows.

Step 2: Work out net cash used in investing activities. As with step 1, each item must be calculated individually.

Step 3: Work out net cash used in financing activities. Individual calculations of each item are needed.

Step 4: Work out net cash and cash equivalents increase (decrease) for the period.

Step 5: Reconcile cash and cash equivalents at the end of the year to that at the beginning of the period.

Note that, under the direct method, each individual item in the statement of cash flows must be generated from the information available.

The data provided in figure 24.6 in relation to York Enterprises are now used to illustrate the preparation of the statement of cash flows from financial statements and other information.

Step 1: Cash flows from operating activities

Step 1 requires the net cash flows resulting from the cash inflows and cash outflows generated by operating activities to be determined. Generally there are two methods that can be used — the direct method and the indirect method.

Under the *direct method*, major classes of revenues are shown as gross cash inflows from operations, and major classes of expenses are reported as gross cash outflows from operations. The difference between the cash inflows from revenues and cash payments for expenses represents the net cash flow from operating activities. The information necessary to determine the operating cash flows is obtained by adjusting sales, cost of sales and other items in the income statement for non-cash items and items that are not related to operating activities. The main advantage of the direct method is that it presents a summary of the major categories of operating cash inflows and outflows that can be traced to the cash records of the entity. Knowledge of operating cash flows in past periods may be useful in estimating future operating cash flows.

The *indirect method* does not show the major classes of operating cash inflows and cash outflows. Under this method, the accrual-basis profit is adjusted to a cash-basis profit by making adjustments for non-cash items used in the determination of profit. Added back to profit are the effects of all deferrals of cash inflows and outflows, and deducted are all accruals of expected future cash inflows and outflows. The deferrals and accruals of future cash flows are reflected in the changes in the balance of assets and liabilities relating to operating activities. The indirect method is also referred to as the *reconciliation method*, and is similar to preparing the reconciliation note required by AASB 107 when the direct method is used in the statement. The indirect method is illustrated later in the chapter.

The direct method is the approach favoured by IAS 7/AASB 107 in the statement of cash flows, although either method is permitted. The direct method is favoured because it is argued that it provides information not otherwise available in the other financial statements and a more reliable basis for estimating future cash flows from operations, whereas the indirect method provides only the net cash flow figures, with no indication of inflows/outflows of individual items of operating activities.

In order to determine net cash from operating activities under the direct method, it is necessary to convert items used in determining profit under the accrual basis to a cash basis. To make the conversion, the relationship between the effect of operating transactions on accrual-basis profit and cash movements within the entity must be considered. Thus, the different classes of accrual-basis revenues are adjusted to reflect the resulting cash inflows. Accrual-basis sales and other revenues are adjusted to provide cash receipts from customers. Accrual-basis expenses such as cost of sales, wages and salaries, and other expenses for services are adjusted to reflect the cash outflows for various classes of operating activities such as:

- cash paid to suppliers for inventory purchases, cash paid to employees for labour, and cash paid to suppliers for other goods and services such as office supplies, advertising, electricity and similar services
- cash paid to lenders for interest
- cash paid for income tax.

Note that in the conversion of accrual-basis revenues and expenses, certain items, such as depreciation, amortisation and impairment of non-current assets (which represent 'book' entries with no effects on cash flows) and gains (losses) on non-current assets disposed of, are excluded.

The difference between cash inflows from most revenue transactions and cash outflows for most expenses represents the net cash flow from operating activities. Having introduced the principles on which the conversion process is based, the direct method is now illustrated using the information supplied for York Enterprises in figure 24.6 (p. 985), including the additional information.

Cash receipts from customers

Under accrual accounting, credit sales are accompanied by a debit to accounts receivable and a credit to sales revenue at the time each sale is made. Under the cash basis, revenue is not recognised until cash is received. The conversion of accrual-basis sales revenues to cash received from customers is made by considering the beginning and ending balances in accounts receivable as follows:

Accrual-basis sales	+ Beginning accounts receivable − Ending accounts receivable	= Cash receipts from customers

Alternatively, this general principle can be stated in terms of changes in the balances of accounts receivable over the period and is:

Accrual-basis sales	+ Decrease in accounts receivable or − Increase in accounts receivable	= Cash receipts from customers

York Enterprises' comparative statements of financial position data show that accounts receivable on 30 June 2013 and 2014 were $43 000 and $52 000 respectively. Thus, cash receipts from customers can be determined as follows:

Accrual-basis sales	$480 000
Add: Beginning accounts receivable	43 000
Total cash collectable from customers	523 000
Less: Ending accounts receivable	52 000
Cash receipts from customers	$471 000

Alternatively, since there was an increase in accounts receivable of $9000, cash received is less than accrual-basis sales. Therefore, cash receipts from customers are calculated as:

$$\$480\,000 - \$9000 = \$471\,000$$

As a further alternative, cash receipts from customers can be calculated by reconstructing the Accounts Receivable account:

Accounts Receivable

1/7/13	Beginning Balance	43 000	30/6/14	Cash	**471 000**
30/6/14	Sales	480 000	30/6/14	Ending Balance	52 000
		523 000			523 000

Cash paid to suppliers and employees

Under the standard, the cash outflows for purchases, labour and other services are grouped under the broad heading of 'Cash paid to suppliers and employees' (*except* for items that must be specifically disclosed — interest paid and income tax paid). To determine this outflow, it is necessary to make separate calculations for payments made for purchases and other expenses. The results, except for the special items mentioned above, are then combined into one figure to be disclosed in the statement of cash flows. Each of these components is determined from the information in figure 24.6 (p. 985) for York Enterprises.

Cash paid to suppliers for purchases. Under accrual accounting, purchases of inventory on credit are recognised by a debit to the Inventory account (in a perpetual system) and a credit to the Accounts Payable account at the time of purchase. Under the cash basis, purchases are not recognised until cash is paid. To ascertain cash paid for purchases, the accrual-basis cost of sales is adjusted for the change in inventory over the period to determine the accrual-basis purchases. This figure is then adjusted for the change in the balance of accounts payable to arrive at the cash-basis purchases for the period. Thus, to convert from accrual-basis cost of sales to cash paid to suppliers for purchases, two adjustments must be made for the changes during the period in the Inventory account and Accounts Payable account as follows:

Accrual-basis cost of sales	− Beginning inventory	+ Ending inventory	= Accrual-basis purchases

Accrual-basis purchases	+ Beginning accounts payable	− Ending accounts payable	= Cash paid to suppliers for purchases

Again, these general formulas can be stated in terms of changes in the balances of inventory and accounts payable over the period:

Accrual-basis cost of sales	+ Increase in inventory *or* − Decrease in inventory	= Accrual-basis purchases

Accrual-basis purchases	+ Decrease in accounts payable *or* − Increase in accounts payable	= Cash paid to suppliers for purchases

York Enterprises' comparative statements of financial position in figure 24.6 show that, on 30 June 2013 and 30 June 2014, inventory balances were $52 000 and $50 000 respectively, and accounts payable balances were \$32 000 and \$38 000 respectively. Thus, cash paid to suppliers for purchases during the year ended 30 June 2014 can be calculated as follows:

Accrual-basis cost of sales	\$336 000
Less: Beginning inventory	52 000
Add: Ending inventory	50 000
Accrual-basis purchases for the year	334 000
Add: Beginning accounts payable	32 000
Less: Ending accounts payable	38 000
Cash paid to suppliers for purchases	\$328 000

The same result is obtained using changes in balances over the period. The conversion process can be seen clearly by reconstructing the Inventory and Accounts Payable accounts:

Inventory

30/6/13	Beginning Balance	52 000	30/6/14	Cost of Sales	336 000
30/6/14	Purchases	334 000	30/6/14	Ending Balance	50 000
		386 000			386 000

Accounts Payable

30/6/14	**Cash Payments**	**328 000**	30/6/13	Beginning Balance	32 000
30/6/14	Ending Balance	38 000	30/6/14	Purchases	334 000
		366 000			366 000

Cash paid to suppliers of services and labour. Under accrual accounting, expenses are recognised when resources are consumed. Some expenses are prepaid, some are paid during the current financial year as they are incurred, and some are accrued (payable) at the end of the financial year. Under the cash basis, expenses are recognised only when they are paid for. The relationship between various expenses and cash payments depends on the related changes in prepaid expenses and/or accrued expenses. Thus, the conversion of accrual-basis expenses to cash-basis expenses may be made as follows:

Accrual-basis expenses	− Beginning prepaid expense + Ending prepaid expense *and* + Beginning accrued expense − Ending accrued expense	= Cash paid for services

Alternatively, the above conversion process can be expressed in terms of changes to the balances of prepaid and accrued expenses, as follows:

Accrual-basis expenses	+ Increase in prepaid expense *or* − Decrease in prepaid expense	= Cash paid for services
	+ Decrease in accrued expense *or* − Increase in accrued expense	

York Enterprises' comparative statements of financial position (figure 24.6, p. 985) show that the 30 June 2013 and 30 June 2014 balances in the Prepaid Insurance account were \$5000 and

$3000 respectively. The income statement shows accrual-basis insurance expense as $8000. Thus, the conversion of accrual-basis insurance expense to cash paid for insurance is:

Accrual-basis insurance expense	$ 8000
Less: Beginning prepaid insurance	(5000)
Add: Ending prepaid insurance	3000
Payment for insurance	$ 6000

The same result is obtained if the change in the balance of prepaid insurance is adjusted against the accrual-basis insurance expense, as follows:

$$\$8000 - \$2000 \text{ (decrease in prepaid insurance)} = \$6000$$

The income statement of York Enterprises (figure 24.6, p. 985) reveals that wages and salaries expense was $65 000, and other expenses were $11 000. Reference to the comparative statements of financial position of the entity shows liabilities for two accrued expenses: wages and salaries payable and other expenses payable. Accrued wages and salaries payable on 30 June 2013 and 30 June 2014 amounted to $4000 and $6000 respectively; the amounts of accrued other expenses payable on those dates were $3000 and $2000 respectively. Thus, the conversion of accrual-basis wages and salaries expense and other expenses to cash paid for expenses is made as follows:

	Wages and salaries expense	Other expenses
Accrual-basis expense	$65 000	$11 000
Add: Beginning accrued expense	4 000	3 000
Less: Ending accrued expense	(6 000)	(2 000)
Cash paid for services	$63 000	$12 000

The same result is achieved if changes in the balance of accrued expenses are used:

	Wages and salaries expense	Other expenses
Accrual-basis expense	$65 000	$11 000
Add: Decrease in accrued expense		1 000
Less: Increase in accrued expense	(2 000)	
Cash paid for services	$63 000	$12 000

At this point, it is possible to summarise the items to appear in the cash flows from operations as 'Cash paid to suppliers and employees'. This is determined by summarising payments to suppliers for purchases, and payments for services as set out below:

Cash paid to suppliers and employees	
Cash paid to suppliers for purchases	$328 000
Cash paid for insurance	6 000
Cash paid for wages and salaries	63 000
Cash paid for other expenses	12 000
	$409 000

You should now realise that, in the process of converting accrual-basis expenses used in determining profit, all the cash flows associated therewith are reported as one item — cash paid to suppliers and employees. The only exception to this general aggregation process is the requirement to disclose certain individual items of cash flows in the statement. These were mentioned previously and included cash paid for interest and cash paid for income tax. Note, again, that although interest and other borrowing costs are paid for a financing 'service', they are reported in the income statement as an expense (or as part of the cost of a qualifying asset under IAS 23/ AASB 123 *Borrowing Costs*), and treated separately because they need to be disclosed separately under the standard. Interest paid and income tax paid do not apply in this simple illustration for York Enterprises. Further discussion of cash flows from other revenues and expenses is provided below.

Note that the income statement of York Enterprises includes the item depreciation expense. This item is not relevant for the cash flows from operating activities because depreciation of non-current assets is a book entry and does not represent a cash flow.

The calculations necessary for step 1 are now complete. It is possible to present the cash flows from operating activities section of the statement of cash flows (based on the direct method) as shown in figure 24.7.

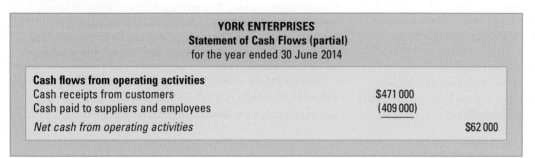

YORK ENTERPRISES
Statement of Cash Flows (partial)
for the year ended 30 June 2014

Cash flows from operating activities		
Cash receipts from customers	$471 000	
Cash paid to suppliers and employees	(409 000)	
Net cash from operating activities		$62 000

Figure 24.7 Cash flows from operating activities (direct method)

Other revenue and expense items. Apart from the sale of goods and rendering of services, IAS 7/ AASB 107 mentions examples of other revenue items that are generally regarded as cash flows from operating activities if they are derived primarily from the main revenue-producing activities of the entity. The standard also provides examples of cash flows from expenses incurred in determining the entity's profit or loss. These revenue and expense items that result in cash flows from operating activities include:

- cash receipts from royalties, fees, commissions
- cash receipts of an insurance entity for premiums and cash payments for claims, annuities and other policy benefits
- cash payments and refunds of income tax
- cash receipts and payments from contracts held for dealing or trading purposes.

Not included in this list are the cash receipts and payments from interest and dividends. Further discussion of these items is provided in the standard, which requires separate disclosure of interest received, interest paid, dividends received and dividends paid. The standard permits a choice of classification as operating, investing or financing activities, but requires the classification to be consistent from period to period.

In Appendix A accompanying the standard (refer to figure 24.1, p. 979), cash flow for interest paid is treated as an operating activity, whereas interest received and dividends received are treated as investing activities (even though they do not satisfy the definition of investing activities). Presumably this classification is used because interest and dividends received represent the results of financing and investing activities. Paragraph 33 of the standard explains:

> Interest paid and interest and dividends received are usually classified as operating cash flows for a financial institution. However, there is no consensus on the classification of these cash flows for other entities. Interest paid and interest and dividends received may be classified as operating cash flows because they enter into the determination of net profit or loss. Alternatively, interest paid and interest and dividends received may be classified as financing cash flows and investing cash flows respectively, because they are costs of obtaining financial resources or returns on investments.

In the exercises and problems attached to this chapter, interest paid is treated as an operating activity and disclosed separately, and interest received and dividends received are shown as investing activities, consistent with Appendix A. For dividends paid by a company, or drawings paid by a sole trader business or a partnership, the standard allows the alternative of showing them separately either as a financing cash flow or as an operating cash flow.

Although not specifically mentioned in the cash flow standard, cash flows received and paid under leases are to be treated as operating cash flows in accordance with the standard on leases.

BUSINESS KNOWLEDGE

The wolf at the door

Phil Bevan needed $100 000 to start a training company. In 2002, the bank gave Bevan and his two co-founders $30 000 and took the homes of all three as security.

'It's a common story — we needed more than we had and in that first year we had about $25 000 on credit cards,' he says.

Today, Esset Group — on track for annual growth of 42 per cent and to reach $7.5 million in revenue by June next year — employs 55 staff and 15 contractors and has blue-chip customers such as Qantas Airways and St George Bank.

As the unexpected economic upturn dawns across Australia, clever business leaders with the ability to garner cash, retain profits, woo banks and find investors are poised to grow fast, outstrip rivals and pick up market share.

Esset Group, already 72nd on the *BRW Fast 100* list, is among them. Bevan raised capital from three private individuals — business angels — in February last year and another four in May this year. His balance sheet looks so good, the bank is knocking on his door, offering cash.

The Fast 100 use various tactics to raise cash, at the start-up stage and beyond, to stay in front of the pack.

Source: Excerpt from Kath Walters, 'The Wolf at the Door', *BRW.*

Step 2: Cash flows from investing activities

Acquisition and disposal of non-current assets

Step 2 requires a determination of the cash inflows and cash outflows from investing activities relating to the acquisition and disposal of non-current assets. This step involves an examination of any changes in these long-term assets in the light of relevant transaction data to determine the effects on cash flows.

In the illustration for York Enterprises, an analysis of the statement of financial position (figure 24.6, p. 985) reveals that the following changes in long-term assets occurred — investments increased by $10 000 and plant and equipment increased by $20 000. Transaction data on the investment increase indicate that additional investments of $10 000 were paid for in cash. Additional transaction data on plant and equipment indicate that new equipment was purchased for $40 000 cash during the reporting period. Old equipment costing $20 000 with a carrying amount of $5000 was sold for $3000 cash. This information can be obtained from reconstructing the Plant and Equipment account as follows:

Plant and Equipment

30/6/13	Beginning Balance	180 000	30/6/14	Cost of Plant Sold	20 000
30/6/14	**Purchases**	**40 000**	30/6/14	Ending Balance	200 000
		220 000			220 000

The only cash flow resulting from the disposal of the equipment is the $3000 proceeds received. Loss on sale of the equipment of $2000 (see the income statement in figure 24.6) is a non-cash book entry and therefore excluded when preparing the statement of cash flows.

Interest and dividends received

As previously mentioned, cash inflows from revenue items (such as interest received and dividends received from investments in other entities) generally need to be disclosed separately, either as an operating activity or as an investing activity. For purposes of the current illustration, the income statement of York Enterprises (figure 24.6) shows a revenue item of 'interest received from investments' that must be disclosed separately. The conversion of accrual-basis revenue received to cash-basis revenue received for both interest revenue receivable or unearned interest revenue is done as follows:

Accrual-basis revenue	+ Beginning revenue receivable − Ending revenue receivable *or* − Beginning unearned revenue + Ending unearned revenue	= Cash-basis revenue

The formula can be expressed also on the basis of changes to the balances of revenue receivable and unearned revenue, i.e. revenue received in advance, as follows:

Accrual-basis revenue	+ Decrease in revenue receivable − Increase in revenue receivable *or* + Increase in unearned revenue − Decrease in unearned revenue	= Cash-basis revenue

The income statement of York Enterprises (figure 24.6, p. 985) shows accrual-basis interest revenue as $1000. The comparative statements of financial position show that interest receivable at 30 June 2013 and 30 June 2014 was $150 and $100 respectively. Thus, the conversion of accrual-basis interest revenue to cash-basis interest received is as follows:

Accrual-basis interest revenue	$1 000
Add: Beginning interest receivable	150
Less: Ending interest receivable	(100)
Cash-basis interest received	$1 050

Using the approach based on changes in the balances of the interest receivable, the cash-basis interest received would be $1000 + $50 (decrease in interest receivable) = $1050.

Those investing activities that resulted in cash flows during the period are then disclosed separately as inflows and outflows and the net cash used in investing activities is determined. The statement of cash flows to this point, including the net cash flows from operating activities and investing activities, appears in figure 24.8. Step 2 has now been completed.

Figure 24.8 Statement of cash flows (showing cash flows from operating activities and investing activities)

YORK ENTERPRISES
Statement of Cash Flows (partial)
for the year ended 30 June 2014

Cash flows from operating activities		
Cash receipts from customers	$ 471 000	
Cash paid to suppliers and employees	(409 000)	
Net cash from operating activities		$ 62 000
Cash flows from Investing activities		
Purchase of investments	(10 000)	
Purchase of equipment	(40 000)	
Proceeds from sale of equipment	3 000	
Interest received	1 050	
Net cash used in investing activities		(45 950)

Step 3: Cash flows from financing activities

Step 3 involves a determination of cash flows from financing activities, i.e. those activities that relate to changes in the composition and size of the equity capital and borrowings of the entity. The initial step is to analyse the comparative statements of financial position and the statement of changes in equity for changes in non-current liabilities and equity items. These changes are then assessed in light of additional relevant transaction data to determine changes that resulted in cash flows.

An examination of the comparative statements of financial position and the statement of changes in equity of York Enterprises (figure 24.6, p. 985) reveals that there were no non-current liabilities and that capital has increased by $19 000. Profit shown in the income statement would have caused an increase of $39 000, but the statement of changes in equity also reveals that drawings of $20 000 are paid in cash. These two items affect capital by the amount of the change. This can be seen by reconstructing the Capital account, as follows:

B. York, Capital

	Drawings Paid	**20 000**	1/7/13	Beginning Balance	231 150
30/6/14	Ending Balance	250 150		Profit	39 000
		270 150			270 150

Furthermore, no additional capital was contributed by the owner. The only cash flow resulting from this analysis is the cash drawings paid. Cash flows and net cash from financing activities can then be added to the statement of cash flows (see figure 24.9). This completes step 3.

Step 4: Ascertain net cash and cash equivalent increase (decrease)

Step 4 involves determining the net cash flow for the reporting period, which is obtained by adding the net cash flows from each category of operating, investing and financing activities. Figure 24.9 shows that the net cash and cash equivalent flow for the year was a decrease of $3950.

Step 5: Reconcile cash and cash equivalents at end with that at beginning

Step 5 involves reconciling the cash and cash equivalents at the beginning and at the end of the period. This change in cash is accounted for by the net cash flows for the year. The final statement of cash flows after completing steps 1 to 5 is now as shown in figure 24.9.

Figure 24.9 York Enterprises — statement of cash flows

YORK ENTERPRISES
Statement of Cash Flows
for the year ended 30 June 2014

Cash flows from operating activities		
Cash receipts from customers	$ 471 000	
Cash paid to suppliers and employees	(409 000)	
Net cash from operating activities		$ 62 000
Cash flows from investing activities		
Purchase of investments	(10 000)	
Purchase of equipment	(40 000)	
Proceeds from sale of equipment	3 000	
Interest received	1 050	
Net cash used in investing activities		(45 950)
Cash flows from financing activities		
Drawings paid	(20 000)	
Net cash used in financing activities		(20 000)
Net increase (decrease) in cash and cash equivalents held		(3 950)
Cash and cash equivalents at beginning of period		25 000
Cash and cash equivalents at end of period		$ 21 050

Learning objective **6**

Determine the notes to the statement of cash flows

24.6 Notes to the statement

Attached to the statement of cash flows as illustrated in Appendix A accompanying IAS 7/AASB 107 is a series of notes providing further explanatory material, reconciling the cash flow data to information in the other financial statements.

Preparation of the following notes is illustrated in three steps:

Step A: Note to disclose the items included in the cash and cash equivalents balance at the end of the period and to reconcile this balance to cash assets in the statement of financial position.

Step B: Note to reconcile the net cash used in operating activities to profit or loss. (This note is required by AASB 107 only if the direct method is used in the statement of cash flows.)

Step C: Notes to discuss non-cash financing and investing activities.

Items included in cash and cash equivalents

Step A involves the preparation of a note reconciling all items included in the concept of cash and cash equivalents used in the preparation of the statement of cash flows to the appropriate cash assets total in the statement of financial position. In York Enterprises, this simply indicates the cash assets included in cash and cash equivalents, which together add to the ending balance of cash. The method of presentation is illustrated in figure 24.10.

Note 1. Cash and cash equivalents consist of cash on hand and balances with banks, and investments in money market instruments (if any). Cash and cash equivalents included in the statement of cash flows comprise the following statement of financial position amounts:

	2014	2013
Cash on hand and balances with banks	$25 000	$21 050
Short-term investments	—	—
Cash and cash equivalents	$25 000	$21 050

Figure 24.10 Reconciliation of cash and cash equivalents to cash in the statement of financial position

Reconciliation note of profit and cash flows from operating activities (indirect method)

Step B: The other major reconciliation required under the standard consists of a note to the statement reconciling the net cash used in operating activities to profit for the period as shown in the income statement. This reconciliation is much more involved than the one in step A and is explained in detail below. In essence, the process consists of determining net cash flows from operating activities using the *indirect method*, which is briefly explained on page 986.

The reconciliation process begins with profit for the period determined under the accrual basis of accounting, adjusting for any non-operating items (e.g. gains and losses on sale of non-current assets) and all non-cash expenses and revenues to convert it to cash flows from operating activities. The principles involved in adjusting accrual-basis profit are the same as those performed on sales, cost of sales, revenues, expenses and other profit or loss items under the *direct method* already illustrated, *except* that the adjustments are applied in terms of their effects on profit and not on the individual items that together determine the profit. The conversion process is essentially a four-stage process:

Stage 1: Subtract from (add to) profit the gains (losses) on sale of any non-current assets disposed of (these relate to investing activities and are therefore eliminated).

Stage 2: Add back to the profit items used in determining profit that represent write-downs of non-current assets. These include depreciation and amortisation of non-current assets.

Stage 3: Make adjustments for investment revenues such as interest and dividends received (which are reported as cash flows from investing activities).

Stage 4: Add back to or subtract from profit any changes in balances that occurred over the period to accounts receivable, inventory, accounts payable, prepaid expenses, accrued expenses and unearned revenues. Changes to current assets and current liabilities are included *except* those items included in cash and cash equivalents and items that are unrelated to the provision of goods and services, e.g. a non-trade receivable such as cash loans to employees and those items representing prepayments and accruals on interest and dividends regarded as investment income.

A suggested format for the reconciliation note is set out below:

Profit for the period	$ x
Subtract: Gains on sale of non-current assets (Stage 1)	(x)
Add: Depreciation and other write-downs (Stage 2)	x
Subtract: Investment income (Stage 3)	(x)
Add/subtract: Changes in current assets and liabilities (Stage 4)	x
Net cash from operating activities	$ x

The changes in current assets and liabilities have already been referred to when converting accrual-basis activities such as sales revenue and cost of sales to cash-basis activities. In the reconciliation process, the effect of the changes in balances must be evaluated in terms of their impact on converting accrual-basis profit to a cash basis.

Figure 24.11 summarises how accrual profits are adjusted for changes in balances of current assets and current liabilities.

Figure 24.11 Adjustment of non-cash current assets and current liabilities

Current items in statement of financial position	Adjustments to accrual profit to give cash from operating activities	
	Add to profit	*Deduct* from profit
Accounts receivable	decrease	increase
Inventories	decrease	increase
Prepaid expenses	decrease	increase
Accounts payable	increase	decrease
Accrued expenses	increase	decrease
Unearned revenue	increase	decrease

Why particular changes in balances are added back or deducted from profit in the reconciliation note is explained below.

Accounts receivable changes

If the accounts receivable balance decreases over the financial year, revenues recorded on an accrual basis (e.g. sales) are lower than cash receipts from sales. Since revenues on an accrual basis used to determine accrual-basis profit are lower than cash-basis revenues, and revenues have the effect of increasing profit, then profit must be increased to arrive at cash from operating activities. Conversely, if the accounts receivable balance shows an increase over the period, revenues recorded on an accrual basis are higher than cash receipts from sales. The accrual-basis revenue is used in arriving at profit, and therefore profit is higher than the cash receipts from revenue. Therefore, the profit must be decreased for the increase in accounts receivable. The principle used above can be seen readily from the hypothetical Accounts Receivable account below.

Accounts Receivable

Beginning Balance	1 000	**Cash Receipts**	**8 000**
Accrual Revenue	9 000	Ending Balance	2 000
	10 000		10 000

If the balance increases by $1000 as shown, accrual-basis revenue must exceed cash receipts from sales. Conversely, if the accounts receivable balance decreases over time, the accrual-basis revenue is less than cash receipts. Similar arguments can be made to cover changes in balances for prepaid expenses and revenue receivable.

Inventory changes

A change in the balance of inventories is explained by its effect on the calculation of accrual-basis purchases and cash-basis cost of sales. This is covered in the next section.

Accounts payable changes

Accounts payable balances refer to changes in the balance of accounts payable for purchases, as well as accrued expenses and unearned revenue. As previously discussed, the role of inventory changes in this process is as shown below:

Accrual-basis cost of sales	+ Increase in inventory or − Decrease in inventory	= Accrual-basis purchases

Accrual-basis purchases	+ Decrease in accounts payable or − Increase in accounts payable	Cash paid to = suppliers for purchases

The cash paid to suppliers represents the cash-basis cost of sales. Assuming no change occurs in accounts payable, an increase in inventory has the effect of making accrual-basis cost of sales less than cash-basis cost of sales. Therefore, the inventory increase must be deducted from accrual-basis profit to calculate the cash basis. Similar reasoning establishes that if inventory decreases over a period, the decrease is added back to accrual-basis profit to obtain cash from operations.

If accounts payable relate to purchases of goods, the effect of a change on the balances over a period can be seen readily by referring to the previous paragraph on inventory changes. Assuming inventory did not change, an increase in accounts payable indicates that accrual-basis cost of sales is higher than cash paid to suppliers or cash-basis cost of sales. Therefore, the increase in accounts payable must be added to accrual-basis profit to determine cash from operating activities. When an entity also has other expenses and unearned revenue, the analysis is the same. If the accounts payable balance increased over the reporting period, accrual-basis expenses must be higher than cash-basis expenses since some expenses incurred during the period have not been paid for. This becomes evident from the hypothetical Accounts Payable account shown below.

Accounts Payable

Cash Paid	4 500	Beginning Balance	1 000
Ending Balance	1 500	Accrual Expenses/Purchases	5 000
	6 000		6 000

Since accounts payable have increased by $500 over the period, accrual-basis expenses/purchases ($5000) must be greater than cash-basis expenses ($4500). Accrual-basis profit therefore would be lower than cash-basis profit.

In summary, if accounts payable increase, profit for the period needs to be adjusted by adding back the increase in accounts payable, and decreases in accounts payable balances must be deducted from profit to arrive at cash flows from operating activities.

Using figure 24.11, it is now possible to prepare the reconciliation of net cash from operating activities to profit for York Enterprises. The reconciliation is shown in figure 24.12 (overleaf).

Note that the first four items in the reconciliation are obtained from the income statement, and changes in assets and liabilities are obtained from the comparative statements of financial position. Note also that the net cash from operating activities ($62 000) in figure 24.12 agrees with the amount in the statement of cash flows in figure 24.9 (p. 994).

Because the indirect method of calculating cash flows from operating activities is also permissible in Australia, the contents of this reconciliation note could be disclosed in the statement of cash flows instead of in the notes. If the note is presented in the statement, however, it will require some minor modifications so that such items as interest paid and interest received (if included in operating activities) could be disclosed separately as cash flows. The same applies to income tax paid, which must be disclosed separately (see later in the chapter). To accomplish this, simply begin the note with 'profit before tax' rather than with 'profit for the period', and then disclose interest paid/received and tax paid at the end to arrive at net cash from operating activities. In the above example for York Enterprises, interest paid and tax paid did not occur. Interest received was treated as an investing activity; hence, interest revenue is eliminated in the reconciliation note in figure 24.12 by deducting it from profit. The indirect method is shown in more detail in the comprehensive example later in the chapter.

Figure 24.12 Reconciliation of net cash from operating activities to profit — indirect method

	2014
Profit for the period	$39 000
Gain on sale of equipment (Stage 1)	—
Depreciation – plant and equipment (Stage 2)	20 000
Loss on sale of equipment (Stage 2)	2 000
Interest revenue (Stage 3)	(1 000)
Changes in assets and liabilities (Stage 4)	
Increase in accounts receivable	(9 000)
Decrease in inventories	2 000
Decrease in prepayments (insurance)	2 000
Increase in accounts payable	6 000
Increase in wages and salaries payable	2 000
Decrease in other expenses payable	(1 000)
Net cash from operating activities	$62 000

Other notes

Step C requires an examination of the accounting records to identify other transactions and events that are relevant to an assessment of the financing and investing activities of an entity. Such transactions or events include non-cash financing and investing activities, and cash flows presented on a net cash flows basis. Such details must be disclosed under the standard.

A statement of cash flows has, as one of its major objectives, the provision of relevant information on cash flows to users about the operating, financing and investing activities of the entity. However, since the statement of cash flows reports only the effects of transactions on cash and cash equivalents as defined by the standard, some material financing and investing activities may be omitted from the statement if such transactions do not affect cash flows. Examples of non-cash transactions and events that do not result in cash flows include the conversion of long-term debt to equity, the acquisition of other entities by means of a share issue, the acquisition of non-current assets by means of debt financing (mortgage), and the acquisition of assets by entering into a finance lease. Although these types of transactions do not affect current cash flows, they are significant because their disclosure provides more complete current information about the financing and investing activities of the entity because future cash flows will be affected, such as payment of interest on debt and repayment of mortgage.

IAS 7/AASB 107 requires disclosure of non-cash financing and investing transactions and events in order to provide all relevant information about these activities. As demonstrated in Appendix A to the standard, such transactions and events are disclosed by way of note to the statement of cash flows. An analysis of the entity's transactions and other records is necessary to obtain the information to include in this note.

No disclosure of these items is required in the case of York Enterprises. Total disclosure required under the standard in the case of the illustrated example is therefore the statement of cash flows shown in figure 24.9 (p. 994), together with the notes to the statement as illustrated in figure 24.13.

Figure 24.13 Notes to York
Enterprises' statement of
cash flows

Note 1. Cash and cash equivalents consist of cash on hand and balances with banks, and investments in money market instruments (if any). Cash and cash equivalents included in the statement of cash flows comprise the following statement of financial position amounts:

	2014	2013
Cash on hand and balances with banks	$25 000	$21 050
Short-term investments	—	—
Cash and cash equivalents	$25 000	$21 050

Note 2. Reconciliation of net cash from operating activities to profit for the period:

	2014	2013
Profit for the period	$39 000	$ x
Depreciation – plant and equipment	20 000	x
Loss on sale of equipment	2 000	x
Interest revenue	(1 000)	(x)
Changes in assets and liabilities		
Increase in accounts receivable	(9 000)	x
Decrease in inventories	2 000	x
Decrease in prepayments	2 000	x
Increase in accounts payable	6 000	x
Increase in wages and salaries payable	2 000	x
Decrease in other expenses payable	(1 000)	(x)
Net cash from operating activities	$62 000	$ x

24.7 Advanced issues

Learning objective 7

Identify and explain some
of the more advanced
issues involved in the
preparation of the
statement of cash flows

The previous discussion has concentrated on the basic concepts and principles followed in the preparation of a statement of cash flows for a sole trader. In practice, if the preparation of cash flows is to be based largely on financial reports, the process is more complex. There are many involved adjustments that may need to be made in the conversion process from accrual basis reports to the statement of cash flows. This section covers some of the more common of those adjustments.

Impact of the GST

The GST has an impact on many sole traders and companies. According to the AASB's Interpretation 1031 *Accounting for the Goods and Services Tax (GST)*, all receivables and payables are to be stated in financial reports at amounts inclusive of the GST, as has been shown in earlier chapters. Interpretation 1031 also concludes that there is no need for separate disclosure of any cash receipts or payments of GST in the statement of cash flows. Hence, the outlays and collections of GST made by an entity are included as part of the entity's calculations of receipts from customers and payments to suppliers and employees. Nevertheless, Interpretation 1031 requires cash flows from operating activities to be reported at gross amounts, including GST.

According to Interpretation 1031, the GST Outlays and GST Collections accounts are to be regarded as affecting operating activities in the statement of cash flows even though the original transactions on which the GST is paid or collected may have resulted in investing activities. For example, an acquisition of office furniture on which GST is paid is treated as an investing activity in the statement of cash flows as far as the office furniture is concerned and as an operating activity as far as the GST is concerned. The reason for treating GST outlays and collections, as well as the payment of GST to the ATO, as operating activities is that most assets acquired are recognised in the accounting records net of GST. Hence, the balances of inventory, office furniture and other plant and equipment, and prepayments such as prepaid insurance and prepaid rent are recorded net of GST and the cash flows from investing activities are to be reported net of GST. It is only receivables and payables that include GST, according to Interpretation 1031.

In order to calculate gross cash flows from operating activities including GST, the entity needs to adjust the calculation of cash receipts from customers for the additions to the GST Collections account arising during the period (this information is available from the net credits recorded in the GST Collections account during the year), plus the GST refund from the ATO (if any). GST collections usually arise from the sale of goods and services to customers. The calculation becomes:

Accrual-basis sales and services revenue	+ Beginning accounts receivable − Ending accounts receivable **+ Additions to the GST Collections** **account during the period** **+ Any GST refunds from the ATO**	= Cash receipts from customers

Alternatively, cash receipts from customers may be calculated by combining the effects of the Accounts Receivable account with GST collections data, as follows (using hypothetical figures and assuming no refund of GST from the ATO):

Accounts Receivable adjusted for GST Collections

Beginning Balance (receivable)	10 000	**Cash**	**299 350**
Sales	300 000	Ending Balance (receivable)	43 650
GST Collections (from the account)	33 000		
	343 000		343 000

As a result of these calculations, the cash receipts from customers is shown *at a gross figure as required by Interpretation 1031*. This contrasts with the cash flows from investing activities, which are shown at amounts *net* of GST; the GST on investing activities is included in operating activities.

If there are any unearned revenue balances (from fees not yet earned) at the beginning and end of the reporting period, they too must be adjusted in the above formula, as discussed previously on pages 991–3.

The GST Outlays account is increased not only for purchases of inventory but also for many other transactions, including purchases of supplies, electricity and gas, telephone and telecommunications services, insurance, plant and equipment, and so on. However, GST is not paid on wages or on most financial services. When calculating the cash paid to suppliers and employees for the statement of cash flows using an analysis of financial statements at the end of the reporting period, it is impossible to split the GST Outlays account into its various components based on source. Hence, as a compromise, the additions to the GST Outlays account in the current period should be adjusted totally in the calculation of payments to suppliers of inventory. The figure so calculated, when added to payments to suppliers for other goods and services excluding GST, will give the correct overall figure. Note that even GST outlays resulting from purchases of property, plant and equipment are included in the calculation of cash payments to suppliers of inventory. The formula for calculation is as follows:

Accrual-basis cost of sales	− Beginning inventory	+ Ending inventory	= Accrual-basis purchases

Accrual-basis purchases	+ Beginning accounts payable − Ending accounts payable	**+ Additions to GST Outlays account** **in the current period** **+ GST paid to the ATO (if any)**	Cash paid to = suppliers for purchases

For those who prefer account reconstruction in order to determine cash payments to suppliers, the calculation can be made by adding to the Accounts Payable account the necessary GST outlays information from the account as shown at the top of the next page (using hypothetical figures).

Accounts Payable with GST Outlays

Cash Paid	246 300	Beginning Balance (payable)	17 000
Ending Balance (payable)	53 700	Purchases	250 000
		Payment of GST to ATO	5 000
		GST Outlays (from the account)	28 000
	300 000		300 000

The cash payment calculation ($246 300) is then added to payments to employees and for other services to determine cash paid to suppliers and employees. Hence, cash paid to suppliers and employees is shown at a gross amount, as per the requirements of Interpretation 1031.

In reconciling net cash from operating activities to profit, the profit needs to be adjusted for the changes in the GST Outlays (asset) account and the GST Collections (liability) account, based on the same reasons as those discussed in relation to figure 24.11 (p. 996).

Trade accounts receivable

Under the direct approach to determining cash flows from operating activities, the Accounts Receivable account is used in determining cash receipts from customers. Note, however, that only trade receivables should be used for this purpose. Previous discussion indicated that accrual-basis sales reflected in the income statement are converted to cash receipts from customers by adjusting for the change in the balance of receivables over the reporting period. This approach assumes that the only transactions affecting accounts receivable are sales and cash received. However, other items can affect the change in the balance of receivables. These include the allowance for doubtful debts, an actual bad debt written off, and other credit entries such as discount allowed and interest charged on overdue accounts. Note that accrual-basis sales shown on the income statement are normally net sales, i.e. net of returns and allowances. In the conversion process, the net sales figure used includes both cash sales and credit sales. How the existence of an allowance for doubtful debts and bad debts written off is handled in the conversion process is now discussed. Discount allowed is then considered.

The illustration of York Enterprises' statement of cash flows assumed that no bad debts were written off during the reporting period and no allowance for doubtful debts existed. When preparing the statement of cash flows, additional adjustments must be made to account for these items when included in the financial reports. These items must be handled carefully to ensure accurate calculations of cash flows. Two conditions are discussed below:

- where bad debts are written off under the direct write-off approach (no allowance account is raised)
- where an Allowance for Doubtful Debts account is raised and bad debts are written off against the allowance.

Bad debts (direct write-off)

When bad debts are written off under the direct write-off approach, bad debts expense is reported in the income statement and accounts receivable is reduced. This reduction is reflected in the ending balance of accounts receivable. In determining the cash received from customers, an adjustment to the normal conversion approach has to be made, and the process becomes:

Accrual-basis sales	+ Beginning accounts receivable − Ending accounts receivable − **Bad debts written off (excluding GST)**	= Cash receipts from customers

When GST is considered, the bad debts written off against the accrual-basis sales and services revenue is the amount excluding GST, because the adjustments for the GST Collections in the formula on page 1000 cater for the GST effect.

The need for the bad debts adjustment can readily be seen by reconstructing the Accounts Receivable account for York Enterprises. If it is assumed that $1000 of bad debts have been written off during the period, the other expenses in the income statement in figure 24.6 (p. 985) are increased by the bad debts expense of $1000, and the ending balance of accounts receivable in the statement of financial position in figure 24.6 is $51 000. The reconstructed Accounts Receivable account is therefore:

Accounts Receivable

Beginning Balance	43 000	**Cash Receipts**	**471 000**
Sales	480 000	Bad Debts Written Off	1 000
		Ending Balance	51 000
	523 000		523 000

Note that cash receipts from customers of $471 000 is calculated only after consideration of the bad debts. The bad debts of $1000 represent non-cash items and their effects must be removed before calculating cash received from customers. In the note reconciling net cash used in operating activities to profit, the bad debts written off is a non-cash expense, but it does *not* need to be added back to profit in order to arrive at cash flow from operations. Profit is $38 000 (previously $39 000) after deducting the bad debts written off, and the balance of accounts receivable is now $51 000 (previously $52 000). Consequently, the bad debts adjustment is reflected in the change in balances of accounts receivable ($8000, previously $9000). As a general principle, the effect of the bad debts in the reconciliation process is taken into account when the change in accounts receivable balances is added back to the profit.

Allowance for doubtful debts

If an allowance account is used, it is a contra account to accounts receivable in the statement of financial position, and actual bad debts are debited to the allowance account as they are written off. The expense recorded in the income statement therefore represents the end-of-period adjustment upon assessment of the recoverability of the accounts receivable. Again, this situation needs to be carefully handled in calculating cash flows from operating activities and in the reconciliation of cash flows from operating activities to profit.

In determining cash receipts from customers under the direct method, the balance of the Allowance for Doubtful Debts account must *not* be netted off against the accounts receivable balance, because both cash received from customers and cash paid for expenses will be misstated. To calculate the cash flow from customers, the actual bad debts written off must be determined (as in the direct write-off approach described above) and the bad debt expense is ignored, since it is a book entry only and cannot be converted to a cash-basis expense. The calculation of bad debts written off by reconstructing the allowance account is shown in the comprehensive example beginning on page 1009.

In the note showing reconciliation of net cash from operating activities to profit (the indirect method), both the bad debts write-off and the increase/decrease in allowance for doubtful debts are taken into account automatically by the increase/decrease in the gross accounts receivable balance and the increase/decrease in the allowance for doubtful debts, which can be disclosed separately. (In the reconciliation process, however, it is possible to net the allowance accounts against the Accounts Receivable account and use the increase/decrease in net receivables for reconciliation purposes.) The approach that does not net off the allowance described above is used in the comprehensive example beginning on page 1009.

Discount allowed

If discounts have been allowed to customers during the financial year, the discount allowed must also be adjusted in the conversion process. Discount allowed is a non-cash item that, like bad debts written off, appears in the Accounts Receivable account. If both bad debts and discount allowed are recorded in the accounts of an entity, the conversion of accrual-basis sales to cash receipts from customers becomes:

Accrual-basis sales and services revenue	+ Beginning accounts receivable – Ending accounts receivable – Bad debts written off (excluding GST) **– Discount allowed (excluding GST)**	= Cash receipts from customers

Discounts allowed are not considered in the note showing reconciliation of net cash from operating activities to profit because the effect of the discount will be reflected in the adjustment made for changes in balances of current receivables.

Trade accounts payable and discount received

Under the direct method of deriving cash flows from operating activities, the conversion of accrual-basis expenses and services costs using the change in balances of the appropriate payables accounts is usually straightforward, as illustrated to date. In deriving cash paid to suppliers, however, only trade payables should be used, and the starting point of accrual-basis purchases is usually taken as credit purchases (net of returns and allowances) and cash purchases. If discounts received have arisen on payments to accounts payable, this amount, which represents a non-cash entry (debit) to accounts payable, must be adjusted to convert accrual-basis cost of sales to cash payments to suppliers. This process is:

Accrual-basis cost of sales	− Beginning inventory + Ending inventory	=	Accrual-basis purchases

Accrual-basis purchases	+ Beginning accounts payable − Ending accounts payable − **Discount received (excluding GST)**	=	Cash payments to suppliers

As with discount allowed, the discount received (revenue) account is recorded net of GST and the amount to be deducted from accrual-basis purchases is the net-of-GST figure. The adjustment for the GST Outlays account in the formula on page 1000 caters automatically for the GST adjustment on discount received.

In reconciling net cash from operating activities to profit, the profit is not adjusted for discount allowed as the impact of this item is incorporated into the adjustment for the change in balances of accounts payable.

Non-trade receivables and payables

Most discussions on the preparation of a statement of cash flows imply that all receivables and payables are trade receivables and payables and therefore are used in determining cash receipts from customers and cash paid for purchases. In preparing a statement of cash flows, an analysis must also be made for any non-trade receivables and payables that need to be included when determining cash flows. Examples of these include loans to employees, and amounts receivable or payable on the non-current assets sold and purchased. Non-trade receivables and payables may not be included in the calculation of cash flows from operating activities. They are treated as cash flows from investing activities if such items involve investments, or cash flows from financing activities if they are akin to borrowings.

Bills receivable and bills payable

Bills of exchange and promissory notes are classified into trade bills and commercial bills. Trade bills receivable and trade bills payable are essentially another form of accounts receivable or accounts payable respectively, and therefore must enter into the calculation of cash flows from operating activities. To illustrate the impact of trade bills receivable, consider the following simple illustration.

Suppose that comparative statements of financial position contain the following information:

Comparative Statements of Financial Position		
	2015	2014
Current assets		
Accounts receivable	$170 000	$150 000
Bills receivable	15 000	10 000

Accrual sales for the year were $500 000, and trade bills received from trade accounts receivable amounted to $25 000. Assuming no other items (e.g. bad debts, discount allowed, discount on bills) were involved, the Accounts Receivable account and Bills Receivable account appear as under:

Accounts Receivable

Beginning Balance	150 000	**Cash**	**455 000**
Sales	500 000	Bills Receivable	25 000
		Ending Balance	170 000
	650 000		650 000

Bills Receivable

Beginning Balance	10 000	**Cash**	**20 000**
Accounts Receivable	25 000	Ending Balance	15 000
	35 000		35 000

The cash received from accounts receivable is $455 000 and from bills receivable $20 000, i.e. a total of $475 000. This total amount of cash represents cash received from customers for sales of goods and services. Therefore, when arriving at cash receipts from customers by converting accrual-basis sales to cash receipts from customers, changes in balances of *both* accounts receivable and trade bills receivable (gross balance) must be considered. The conversion process is as shown below — other items such as bad debts require further adjustment.

Accrual-basis sales and services revenue	+ Beginning accounts receivable − Ending accounts receivable **+ Beginning bills receivable** **− Ending bills receivable**	= Cash receipts from customers

The calculation for the above example is:

$$\$500\,000 + \$150\,000 - \$170\,000 + \$10\,000 - \$15\,000 = \$475\,000$$

The change in the balances of bills receivable also is adjusted when reconciling net cash from operating activities to profit for the period.

Similarly, changes in the balances of trade bills payable are incorporated into the conversion process for arriving at cash payments to suppliers. The change in the balance of trade bills payable also is an item of adjustment in the process of reconciling net cash from operating activities to profit.

Note that, for both bills receivable and payable, these accounts are stated at a gross amount, including unearned interest. Hence, taking the difference in the gross balances causes an amount of interest to be recognised as part of cash received from customers. This interest element may be separated out if considered material and shown as part of interest received and borrowing costs paid. (In this circumstance, the interest is more appropriately classified as an operating cash flow.)

Commercial bills receivable and payable normally are regarded as relating to the investing and financing activities of the entity and as such not used in the process of converting accrual-basis expenses to cash-basis expenses. Hence, any interest received on such bills may appropriately be regarded as an investing activity, but interest paid on such bills is regarded as an operating activity under the standard.

Short-term investments

Short-term investments can appear in the current assets and current liabilities section of a balance sheet. Some short-term investments could qualify as cash equivalents, and others generally are classified as an investing activity of an entity. Therefore, these short-term investments are not included in the process of converting accrual-basis expenses to cash-basis expenses to arrive at cash flows from operating activities. In addition, changes in the balances of short-term investment accounts are not included in the process of reconciling net cash from operating activities to profit.

Dividends

Companies commonly pay cash dividends. Several steps and accounts can be involved in the process. For example, a company may pay an interim dividend during the reporting period, declare a final dividend at the end of the reporting period, and pay such dividend declared in the following reporting period. For the purpose of a statement of cash flows, only cash payments for dividends are considered — dividends declared are not considered. The cash payment in the current financial year usually consists of the interim dividends paid during the year plus the final dividends declared in the immediately preceding financial year and paid in the current year. The payment of cash dividends is usually reported in the statement of cash flows as a financing activity but may be shown as an operating activity.

To illustrate the handling of cash dividends, the following information is extracted from the records of Insider Ltd.

Comparative Statements of Financial Position		
	30 June 2015	30 June 2014
Final dividend payable	$60 000	$50 000
Retained earnings	55 000	70 000

The statement of changes in equity shows that an interim dividend of $25 000 was paid in cash for the year ended 30 June 2015. The dividend payable at the end of June 2014 was paid in cash on 30 October 2014. The relevant accounts in ascertaining cash dividends for the reporting period are shown below.

Retained Earnings

31/1/15	Interim Dividend Paid	25 000	1/7/14	Beginning Balance	70 000
30/6/15	Final Dividend Declared	00 000	30/6/15	Profit	00 000
30/6/15	Transfer to Reserve	10 000			
30/6/15	Ending Balance	55 000			
		150 000			150 000

Final Dividend Payable

30/10/14	Cash	50 000	1/7/14	Beginning Balance	50 000
			30/6/15	Retained Earnings	60 000

The cash paid for dividends during 2014–15 is $75 000 ($25 000 interim dividend for the current year and $50 000 final dividend declared at 30 June 2014).

A dividend paid other than in cash, for example a share dividend, does not appear as part of the statement of cash flows but needs to be shown in the note to the statement that covers non-cash activities.

Income tax

Companies are regarded as separate legal entities and are therefore required to pay income tax. For the purposes of preparing the statement of cash flows, it is only the income tax *paid* in cash that is reported normally as a cash outflow from operating activities. Income tax is reported in the financial statements by showing income tax expense in the income statement/statement of profit or loss and other comprehensive income, and recording the liability for tax as a current tax liability in the statement of financial position.

The cash crash

Coins and notes are becoming obsolete as payment systems go digital or even virtual. But is the cashless society just a pipe dream?

As long ago as 2005 the researcher ACNielsen predicted that by 2020 only 10 per cent of transactions in the US will be cash. Futurist Richard Watson thinks that figure could be even higher. He believes small change may eventually be phased out, noting that some people already throw small coins away. 'I think in five to 10 years money will be 95 per cent digital,' he says.

But despite reports of its imminent death, cash is still the most widely used payment method in Australia, especially for small items. The latest figures from the Reserve Bank of Australia bear this out, reporting that 70 per cent of payments are in cash, representing 30 per cent of the value. Cash is used for 95 per cent of transactions under $10 and 74 per cent of transactions under $25.

What is edging cash out are plastic cards and contactless payment systems using cards, mobile phones and key fobs, ideas that are new to Australia but old hat in Asia, the US and Europe.

Such is the rise of plastic that Watson cites an urban myth of a beggar in San Francisco taking American Express. The story isn't so fanciful with the arrival of peer-to-peer cash transfers on mobile phones, such as MasterCard's MoneySend, or iCCPay's application, available from the Apple iTunes Australia site, that allows individuals to take credit card payments on an iPhone.

With such systems coming online with increasing speed, analysts predict that the financial battlegrounds of the future will be very different as astute entrepreneurs work out just how lucrative shifting digital money can be. The European Commission recently calculated that total cost of all payment methods including cash, cheques and cards is equal to 3 per cent of Europe's GDP — larger than the entire European agricultural sector.

Watson sees banks moving more out of the money game and into wealth management, while supermarkets are moving in on the game and actually making money on each cash withdrawal.

Source: Excerpt from Ed Charles, 'The Cash Crash', *InTheBlack.*

Introduction to the tax payment system

The current system for paying company income tax was introduced by the Australian Government on 1 July 2000 as part of the legislation introducing the GST. The effect of this system for many companies is that income tax is paid, under the PAYG (pay-as-you-go) system, in quarterly instalments, thus smoothing out the cash flow requirements for tax payments throughout the year. Under the PAYG system, a company may pay income tax either in quarterly instalments or in one annual payment. An annual payment system is available only for companies that satisfy certain conditions. For companies permitted to pay only one annual instalment, the amount is due for payment on 21 October.

If a company is required to pay quarterly instalments of tax, it will do so at the amount specified on its quarterly business activity statement (BAS). A company with an annual reporting period ending on 30 June 2014 is required to make quarterly cash payments as follows:

Quarter ended	Due date of instalment
30 September 2013	28 October 2013
31 December 2013	28 February 2014
31 March 2014	28 April 2014
30 June 2014	28 July 2014

A company required to submit a BAS monthly for GST purposes, e.g. a company with an annual turnover of $20 million or more, still pays income tax by PAYG instalments on a quarterly basis. Note, however, that the PAYG instalments for companies that pay GST monthly are due on 21 October, 21 January, 21 April and 21 July.

Most companies that are PAYG instalment payers use the following formula to determine their quarterly income tax payments:

$$\text{Instalment income} \times \text{Instalment rate}$$

Instalment income is determined each quarter and represents the total actual ordinary assessable income as determined in accordance with income tax law for the period for which the instalment is being paid. For example, instalment income for the September quarter is the assessable income for that period, which is the basis of the tax payment made on 28 October. The instalment income is then multiplied by the instalment rate to determine the income tax payment. The instalment rate is a percentage figure worked out by the ATO based on the ATO's most recent assessment for the most recent income year. It is calculated by dividing the company's 'notional tax' by its 'base assessment instalment income' and multiplying by 100:

$$\text{Instalment rate} = (\text{Notional tax/Base assessment instalment income}) \times 100$$

'Notional tax' represents the equivalent tax that would have been payable on business and investment income, excluding capital gains, for the most recent income year for which an assessment has been made. 'Base assessment instalment income' represents that portion of the company's latest tax assessment that the ATO deems to be the company's instalment income.

To illustrate, assume that in the 2013–14 tax return, Outsider Ltd had assessable income of $375 000. This is adopted by the ATO as the base assessment instalment income. Assume as well that, after allowing for deductions and expected changes in tax rates, the notional tax is determined by the ATO as $78 750. The initial instalment rate is determined by the ATO as follows:

$$\text{Instalment rate} = (\$78\,750/\$375\,000) \times 100 = 21\%$$

Assuming that the instalment income for Outsider Ltd for the September 2014 quarter is $102 000, the first tax payment due on 28 October 2014 is determined by multiplying the instalment income by the instalment rate:

$$\text{September quarter tax payment} = \$102\,000 \times 21\% = \$21\,420$$

This amount of $21 420 is then listed on the company's BAS and paid on or before 28 October, along with other taxes as listed on the BAS, including the GST, PAYG withholdings from employees' wages, and fringe benefits tax.

A company is able to vary the instalment rate determined by the ATO in any quarter if it believes that the total instalments determined by the ATO's rate are likely to result in total tax payments being higher than the company's total expected current tax liability for the year. However, there are penalties (in the form of additional interest payments) if the company's varied instalment rate is less than 85% of the instalment rate that would have covered the actual current tax liability for the year. For example, Outsider Ltd may lower its instalment rate for the second instalment from 21% to 15% if it believes that it has suffered a downturn in its market for goods sold resulting in lower assessable income. This may result in Outsider Ltd's BAS for that quarter showing either a smaller tax payment or even a tax credit.

Assuming that a company's end of reporting period is 30 June, the end-of-period adjustment entry for income tax is based on the expected current tax payable as a percentage of the company's taxable income for the full year. This taxable income is likely to be different from the estimates made for the calculation of quarterly tax instalments. Furthermore, the company's calculation on 30 June for current income tax and the amount of tax paid to the ATO may differ depending on the outcome of any audit procedures carried out by the ATO.

As a result of these differences, the company will be left with either an overprovision or underprovision for tax when the current tax liability is fully paid. This overprovision or underprovision for tax normally is recognised as an item of income or expense of the company in the current period.

Example of tax payments by four instalments

Assume that Toodyay Ltd, for the year ended 30 June 2014, pays quarterly PAYG income tax instalments as follows:

$8000 on 28 July 2014
$4000 on 28 October 2014
$11 000 on 28 February 2015
$12 000 on 28 April 2015

On 30 June 2015, Toodyay Ltd determines its total current tax liability for the year to be $33 000 on an estimated taxable income of $110 000 (tax rate is 30%). As a result, the company pays a final tax payment for the year on 28 July 2015 as follows:

$$\text{Final tax instalment} = \$33\,000 - \$4000 - \$11\,000 - \$12\,000 = \$6000$$

As a result of an audit by the ATO, the ATO notified Toodyay Ltd on 1 October 2015 that its taxable income for the year ended 30 June 2015 was assessed as $115 000, requiring a total tax payment for that year of $34 500. In other words, there is an underprovision for income tax of $1500 (i.e. $34 500 − $33 000), which is recognised as an expense in the year ended 30 June 2016.

Toodyay Ltd paid the additional tax on 10 October 2015. Journal entries to record all payments of tax and the adjustment from the underprovision for tax in Toodyay Ltd's records are shown in figure 24.14.

Figure 24.14 Journal entries for income tax payments

2014				
July	28	Current Tax Liability	8 000	
		Cash		8 000
		(Payment of final PAYG instalment for year ended 30 June 2014)		
Oct.	28	Income Tax Expense	4 000	
		Cash		4 000
		(Payment of first PAYG instalment for year ended 30 June 2015)		
2015				
Feb.	28	Income Tax Expense	11 000	
		Cash		11 000
		(Payment of second PAYG instalment for year ended 30 June 2015)		
April	28	Income Tax Expense	12 000	
		Cash		12 000
		(Payment of third PAYG instalment for year ended 30 June 2015)		
June	30	Income Tax Expense	6 000	
		Current Tax Liability		6 000
		(End-of-period adjustment recording the final tax instalment of $6000)		
July	28	Current Tax Liability	6 000	
		Cash		6 000
		(Payment of final PAYG instalment for year ended 30 June 2015)		
Oct.	1	Underprovision for Tax (expense)	1 500	
		Current Tax Liability		1 500
		(Adjustment for income tax underprovided)		
	10	Current Tax Liability	1 500	
		Cash		1 500
		(Payment of additional tax)		

Thus, for the purpose of preparing a statement of cash flows, the cash paid for income tax for Toodyay Ltd in the year ended 30 June 2015 equals:

Final instalment for year ended 30 June 2014	$ 8 000
Any underprovision/overprovision for tax paid in the year	—
First instalment for year ended 30 June 2015	4 000
Second instalment for year ended 30 June 2015	11 000
Third instalment for year ended 30 June 2015	12 000
	$35 000

Alternatively, a simple way of calculating the cash flow by analysis of financial statements is to reconstruct the current tax liability as follows:

Current Tax Liability

30/6/15	Overprovision (if any)	—	30/6/14	Beginning Balance	8 000
	Cash	**35 000**	30/6/15	Income Tax Expense	33 000
30/6/15	Ending Balance	6 000	30/6/15	Underprovision (if any)	—
		41 000			41 000

As a further alternative, the following formula can be used:

Accrual-basis tax expense (including over/ underprovision)	− Increase in current tax liability *or* + Decrease in current tax liability	= Cash paid for income tax

The cash paid for income tax can be calculated in these two ways *irrespective of whether the tax is paid in one instalment or four instalments.*

For the purpose of preparing the note reconciling cash flow from operating activities to profit, the profit needs to be adjusted for the change in the current tax liability as reported in the comparative statements of financial position.

24.8 Comprehensive example

Learning objective 8

Prepare and analyse the statement of cash flows for a company after consideration of the more advanced issues

The example below shows a more complex statement of cash flows prepared from a company's financial reports, and follows the same step-by-step process outlined previously. The example introduces some of the more advanced aspects of the preparation of the statement. Both the direct method and indirect method are illustrated.

The comparative statements of financial position of Brookton Ltd as at 30 June 2014 and 2015 and the statement of profit or loss and other comprehensive income and statement of changes in equity for the year ended 30 June 2015, presented in figures 24.15(a), (b) and (c) (pp. 1010–11), are used in this illustration.

Additional information

During the year, Brookton Ltd entered into the following transactions relevant to the preparation of the statement of cash flows:
(a) Building additions were completed at a cost of $600 000 cash.
(b) New equipment was purchased at a cost of $337 000; $87 000 was paid in cash and the balance was covered by arranging a long-term mortgage loan with RCA Finance Ltd.
(c) Equipment with a cost of $211 000 and a carrying amount of $100 000 was sold for $92 000 cash.
(d) Shares in Bright Prospects Ltd were sold for $274 000 cash.
(e) Debentures (8%) were issued at nominal value for cash.
(f) The company pays tax in four quarterly instalments, the balance in the Current Tax Payable account representing the final instalment payable for the year. For the year ended 30 June 2014, income tax was assessed by the Tax Office to be $250 000. This has caused tax expense of $300 000 in the current year to include a $20 000 underprovision for tax.

Calculations for each of the steps required are presented on pages 1011–6 for the direct method.

Figure 24.15(a) Brookton Ltd
— comparative statements of
financial position

BROOKTON LTD
Comparative Statements of Financial Position
as at 30 June

	2015	2014
CURRENT ASSETS		
Cash at bank	$ 190 000	$ 95 000
Bank bills	50 000	43 000
Deposits at call	32 000	25 000
Accounts receivable	246 500	189 000
Less: Allowance for doubtful debts	(12 500)	(9 500)
Inventory	471 000	483 000
Prepaid expenses	54 000	21 000
TOTAL CURRENT ASSETS	1 031 000	846 500
NON-CURRENT ASSETS		
Shares in Bright Prospects Ltd	250 000	400 000
Buildings (cost)	1 800 000	1 200 000
Accumulated depreciation – buildings	(522 000)	(472 500)
Equipment (cost)	900 000	774 000
Accumulated depreciation – equipment	(289 500)	(348 000)
Land (cost)	350 000	350 000
TOTAL NON-CURRENT ASSETS	2 488 500	1 903 500
TOTAL ASSETS	3 519 500	2 750 000
CURRENT LIABILITIES		
Accounts payable	440 000	471 500
Trade bills payable	10 000	7 000
Expenses payable	31 500	24 000
Interest payable	20 000	15 000
Dividend payable	174 000	160 000
Current tax liability	70 000	60 000
TOTAL CURRENT LIABILITIES	745 500	737 500
NON-CURRENT LIABILITIES		
Mortgage loan	250 000	—
Debentures 10%	900 000	750 000
TOTAL NON-CURRENT LIABILITIES	1 150 000	750 000
TOTAL LIABILITIES	1 895 500	1 487 500
NET ASSETS	$1 624 000	$1 262 500
EQUITY		
Share capital (ordinary shares)	$1 177 000	$ 924 500
Retained earnings	447 000	338 000
TOTAL EQUITY	$1 624 000	$1 262 500

Figure 24.15(b) Brookton Ltd
— statement of profit or loss
and other comprehensive
income

BROOKTON LTD
Statement of Profit or Loss and Other Comprehensive Income
for the year ended 30 June 2015

INCOME			
Sales revenue	$6 930 000		
Less: Discount allowed	4 750	$6 925 250	
Dividends received on investments		36 000	
Gain on sale of shares		124 000	$7 085 250
EXPENSES			
Cost of sales	3 660 000		
Less: Discount received	10 500	3 649 500	
Selling and administrative expenses		2 619 750	
Loss on sale of equipment		8 000	
Depreciation expense – equipment		52 500	
Depreciation expense – buildings		49 500	
Interest expense		92 000	
Bad debts expense		11 000	6 482 250
Profit before income tax			603 000
Income tax expense			320 000
PROFIT FOR THE PERIOD			283 000
Other comprehensive income			0
TOTAL COMPREHENSIVE INCOME FOR THE PERIOD			$ 283 000

Figure 24.15(c) Brookton
Ltd — statement of changes
in equity

BROOKTON LTD
Statement of Changes in Equity
for the year ended 30 June 2015

	Share capital	Other reserves	Retained earnings	Total
Balance at 1/7/14	$ 924 500		$338 000	$1 262 500
Total comprehensive income for the period			283 000	283 000
Dividend declared			(174 000)	(174 000)
Issue of share capital	252 500			252 500
Balance at 30/6/15	$1 177 000		$447 000	$1 624 000

Step 1: Cash from operating activities — direct method
Cash receipts from customers

Receipts from customers = Sales + beginning accounts receivable
− ending accounts receivable − bad debts written off
− discount allowed − sales returns and allowances
= $6 930 000 + $189 000 − $246 500 − $8000 − $4750 − 0
= $6 859 750

To determine bad debts written off, the Allowance for Doubtful Debts account could be reconstructed as follows:

Allowance for Doubtful Debts

	Bad Debts Written Off	8 000	30/6/14	Beginning Balance	9 500
30/6/15	Ending Balance	12 500	30/6/15	Bad Debt Expense	11 000
		20 500			20 500

Note that, in calculating the cash flow, the allowance for doubtful debts balances are not netted against accounts receivable balances, i.e. the gross balances of receivables are used in determining receipts from customers.

Cash paid to suppliers for purchases

Cash payments to suppliers is determined by adjusting accrual-basis cost of sales for changes in inventory and accounts payable balances together with any other adjustments that may have affected the changes in balance. Here, trade bills payable (from the statements of financial position) and discounts received (from the statement of profit or loss and other comprehensive income) must be considered. Therefore:

$$
\begin{aligned}
\text{Cash payments for purchases} = {} & \text{Cost of sales} - \text{beginning inventory} + \text{ending} \\
& \text{inventory} + \text{beginning accounts payable} - \text{ending} \\
& \text{accounts payable} + \text{beginning bills payable} - \text{ending} \\
& \text{bills payable} - \text{discount received} \\
= {} & \$3\,660\,000 - \$483\,000 + \$471\,000 + \$471\,500 - \\
& \$440\,000 + \$7000 - \$10\,000 - \$10\,500 \\
= {} & \$3\,666\,000
\end{aligned}
$$

Cash paid to suppliers for services

Payments for services include items disclosed in the statement of profit or loss and other comprehensive income as selling and administrative expenses, together with other items that relate to expenses involved in acquiring services. The expenses of $2 619 750 must be adjusted for prepaid expenses and accrued expenses (expenses payable). Therefore:

$$
\begin{aligned}
\text{Cash paid to suppliers for services} = {} & \text{Selling and administrative expenses} - \text{beginning} \\
& \text{prepaid expenses} + \text{ending prepaid expenses} + \\
& \text{beginning expenses payable} - \text{ending expenses} \\
& \text{payable} \\
= {} & \$2\,619\,750 - \$21\,000 + \$54\,000 + \$24\,000 - \$31\,500 \\
= {} & \$2\,645\,250
\end{aligned}
$$

Hence, total payments to suppliers and employees = $3 666 000 + $2 645 250 = $6 311 250.

Interest paid

Another item in the statement of profit or loss and other comprehensive income that relates to cash payments for services is the interest expense of $92 000. Even though this interest relates mainly to the mortgage loan, a financing activity, it is a common practice to classify the interest paid as an operating cash flow (see IAS 7/AASB 107 for further discussion). Interest paid must be determined and disclosed irrespective of whether the direct method or the indirect method is used to calculate the cash from operating activities.

To determine the cash paid for borrowing costs during the period, interest expense is adjusted for changes in the balance of the Interest Payable account. Therefore, cash paid for borrowing costs is calculated as:

$$
\begin{aligned}
\text{Cash paid for borrowing costs} = {} & \text{Interest expense} + \text{beginning interest} \\
& \text{payable} - \text{ending interest payable} \\
= {} & \$92\,000 + \$15\,000 - \$20\,000 \\
= {} & \$87\,000
\end{aligned}
$$

Cash paid for income tax

The only other item from the statement of profit or loss and other comprehensive income that results in a cash flow is income tax, and it is necessary to determine the cash paid for tax during the last financial year. For the statement of cash flows, the income tax payment for this company for the year ended 30 June 2015 is found by subtracting the final tax payable ($70 000) from the income tax expense including the underprovision ($320 000), and adding the final tax instalment payable at the end of the previous year ($60 000) and paid in the current year. This gives an amount of cash paid in the current year of $310 000. Alternatively, the cash paid can be found by preparing the Current Tax Liability account on the assumption that all tax instalments and tax expense are passed through the liability account, as shown below.

Current Tax Liability

	Total Cash Payment	**310 000**	1/7/14	Beginning Balance	60 000
30/6/15	Ending Balance	70 000	30/6/15	Income Tax Expense	300 000
				Underprovision for Tax	20 000
		380 000			380 000

Alternatively, cash paid for income tax can be determined by the formula shown on page 1009, which adjusts accrual-based tax expense (including the underprovision) for changes in the balances of the current tax liability as follows:

$$\text{Cash paid} = \$320\,000 - (\$70\,000 - \$60\,000) = \$310\,000$$

All elements of cash flows from operating activities have now been considered and therefore step 1 is complete. Net cash from operating activities equals $151 500 and details are presented in the statement of cash flows in figure 24.17 (p. 1016).

Step 2: Cash from investing activities

Investing activities for Brookton Ltd are determined by examining the comparative statements of financial position and analysing changes in the light of the additional information available as presented on page 1009. Note that the analysis is concerned only with ascertaining cash inflows and cash outflows. Gains and losses on the sale of non-current assets are ignored.

The balance of the *long-term investment*, Shares in Bright Prospects Ltd, has decreased by $150 000. Additional information provided indicates that $274 000 cash was received for these shares. These proceeds may also be disclosed separately in the statement of profit or loss and other comprehensive income. The relevant cash flow is the cash inflow of $274 000 that resulted from the sale, and this appears in the statement of cash flows shown in figure 24.17.

Buildings in the statements of financial position shows an increase of $600 000 over the financial year. From the additional information, it is known that cash outflows of $600 000 occurred to pay for the building additions.

The *equipment* balances over the period show an increase of $126 000. This again needs to be analysed to determine the cash flows, if any, which are associated with this increase. The statement of profit or loss and other comprehensive income and additional information provided indicate that new equipment was purchased and old equipment disposed of during the year. Although the relevant cash flows can be determined easily from this information, it may be useful to reconstruct the Equipment account and other accounts affected by the changes. The accounts, when reconstructed, appear as shown in figure 24.16 (overleaf).

The items shown in bold type in figure 24.16 appear in the body of the statement of cash flows. The new equipment purchased of $337 000 results in a cash outflow of $87 000, and this appears in the statement, whereas the remainder, $250 000 (covered by the mortgage loan), needs to be disclosed in notes attached to the statement, because this represents a non-cash transaction (see note 3 in figure 24.17). The proceeds from the sale of the old equipment were received in cash and this cash inflow of $92 000 appears in the statement of cash flows. All other entries in relation to the equipment are internal 'book' entries and do not result in cash flows.

As part of the calculation of cash flows from investing activities, one other item in the statement of profit or loss and other comprehensive income needs to be examined — dividends revenue of $36 000. Since no receivable account exists in the statement of financial position for dividends to be received, it can be concluded that all of the $36 000 was received in cash.

The task of determining the cash inflows and cash outflows from investing activities has now been completed. These are summarised and the net cash used in investing activities of $285 000 is shown in the statement of cash flows in figure 24.17.

Figure 24.16 Equipment
account and other selected
accounts

Equipment					
30/6/14	Beginning Balance		774 000	Carrying Amount of	
	Purchase:			Equipment Sold	100 000
	Cash	**87 000**		Accum. Depreciation	111 000
	Mortgage	250 000	337 000	30/6/15 Ending Balance	900 000
			1 111 000		1 111 000

Accumulated Depreciation – Equipment				
	Equipment	111 000	30/6/14 Beginning Balance	348 000
30/6/15	Ending Balance	289 500	30/6/15 Depreciation Expense	52 500
		400 500		400 500

Carrying Amount of Equipment Sold				
	Equipment	100 000	30/6/15 Profit or Loss Summary	100 000
		100 000		100 000

Proceeds from Sale of Equipment				
30/6/15	Profit or Loss Summary	92 000	**30/6/15 Cash**	**92 000**
		92 000		92 000

Step 3: Cash from financing activities

To determine cash flows from financing activities, reference is made to the financial statements and other relevant information available. From this information, it is possible to determine the following items as financing activities:

- share capital increased by $252 500 (statement of changes in equity and statements of financial position)
- debenture debt increased by $150 000 (statements of financial position)
- dividend declared at end of period was $174 000 (statement of changes in equity)
- cash dividend paid was $160 000 (statement of financial position of previous period).

The first item indicates that the 30 000 *shares issued* raised $252 500 in cash. This cash inflow must be recorded in the statement of cash flows.

Since the *debentures* were issued for cash, the cash inflow resulting must have been $150 000.

Cash paid out for *dividends* of $160 000 could be ascertained by reconstructing the Dividend Payable account if the cash amount had not been given. The account appears as follows:

Dividend Payable			
Cash	**160 000**	30/6/14 Beginning Balance	160 000
		30/6/15 Retained Earnings	174 000

As can be seen from the account, the dividends paid during the year ended 30 June 2015 represent the amount declared and appearing as a liability in the statement of financial position as at 30 June 2014. Note that, although not relevant in this illustrative example, any interim dividend paid in cash during the year is taken into account as well.

Step 3 is now complete and the detailed cash inflows and outflows resulting from financing activities have been determined. Details of these and the resulting net cash used in financing activities of $242 500 appear as shown in the statement of cash flows in figure 24.17 (p. 1016).

Step 4: Net cash increase/decrease

After completion of steps 1 to 3, the net cash flow for the financial year can be determined by summing the net cash from operating activities, net cash used in investing activities, and net cash used in financing activities. Reference to figure 24.17 reveals a net increase in cash held of $109 000.

Step 5: Cash and cash equivalents at beginning and end

Cash and cash equivalents at the end of the period of $272 000 is reconciled to the amount of $163 000 at the beginning as below:

Net increase in cash and cash equivalents	$109 000
Cash and cash equivalents at beginning of period	163 000
Cash and cash equivalents at end of period	$272 000

This reconciliation is shown on the statement of cash flows in figure 24.17.

Notes to the statement

Step A: Note to reconcile cash balance

The reconciliation of the cash at end of year in the statement of financial position to the items defined as cash is shown in note form to the statement of cash flows (see Note 1 in figure 24.17).

Step B: Note reconciling profit and operating cash flow

The reconciliation of net cash from operating activities to profit is shown in note 2 to the statement of cash flows in figure 24.17. This process consists of adjusting the profit by removing the effects of depreciation of non-current assets, other items affecting non-current assets and income from investments, and adjusting for changes in the balances of current assets and current liabilities. Note that changes in balances of both receivables and the allowance for doubtful debts are shown. Note also that the increase in the balances of trade bills payable must be included as these have an impact on operating activities.

Step C: Non-cash financing and investing

An analysis of information provided and the workings above indicate that there was one transaction affecting assets that did not result in a cash flow. This was the part payment by way of a mortgage loan of $250 000 for the new equipment purchased. This non-cash transaction for Brookton Ltd is shown in note 3 in figure 24.17.

Steps 1 to 5 and A to C performed above will enable the preparation of the complete statement of cash flows together with the required notes thereto. The statement of cash flows for Brookton Ltd is as shown in figure 24.17 (overleaf).

The indirect method of determining net cash from operating activities

Figure 24.17 illustrates the statement of cash flows for Brookton Ltd using the direct method for calculating net cash from operating activities. As discussed previously, the accounting standard permits an entity to use the indirect method as an alternative, even though the direct method is preferred by standard setters. The authors of this book also prefer the direct method as the one that provides better information for users of general purpose financial reports. Nevertheless, the indirect method of calculating net cash from operating activities is presented in figure 24.18 (p. 1017). The similarities between the indirect method in figure 24.18 and the reconciliation note 2 in figure 24.17 are immediately obvious.

Figure 24.17 Statement of cash flows — Brookton Ltd

BROOKTON LTD
Statement of Cash Flows
for the year ended 30 June 2015

Cash flows from operating activities		
Cash receipts from customers	$6 859 750	
Cash paid to suppliers and employees	(6 311 250)	
Cash generated from operations	548 500	
Interest paid	(87 000)	
Income taxes paid	(310 000)	
Net cash from operating activities (Note 2)		$151 500
Cash flows from investing activities		
Building additions	(600 000)	
Purchase of new equipment	(87 000)	
Proceeds from sale of equipment	92 000	
Proceeds from sale of shares	274 000	
Dividends received	36 000	
Net cash used in investing activities		(285 000)
Cash flows from financing activities		
Proceeds from issue of ordinary shares	252 500	
Proceeds from issue of debentures	150 000	
Dividends paid	(160 000)	
Net cash used in financing activities		242 500
Net increase in cash and cash equivalents		109 000
Cash and cash equivalents at beginning of period		163 000
Cash and cash equivalents at end of period (Note 1)		$272 000

Notes to statement of cash flows

1. *Reconciliation of cash*
   Cash and cash equivalents consist of cash at bank, bank bills, and deposits at call with financial institutions. Cash and cash equivalents included in the statement of cash flows comprise the following statement of financial position amounts:

	2015	2014
Cash at bank	$190 000	$ 95 000
Bank bills	50 000	43 000
Deposits at call	32 000	25 000
Cash and cash equivalents	$272 000	$163 000

2. *Reconciliation of net cash from operating activities to profit*

Profit for the period	$283 000
Depreciation – equipment	52 500
Depreciation – buildings	49 500
Dividends received	(36 000)
Gain on sale of shares	(124 000)
Loss on sale of equipment	8 000
Changes in assets and liabilities:	
Increase in current tax liability	10 000
Increase in accounts receivable	(57 500)
Allowance for doubtful debts	3 000
Decrease in inventories	12 000
Increase in prepaid expenses	(33 000)
Decrease in accounts payable	(31 500)
Increase in trade bills payable	3 000
Increase in expenses payable	7 500
Increase in interest payable	5 000
Net cash from operating activities	$151 500

3. *Non-cash financing and investing activities*
   During the period, new equipment was purchased, part of which amounting to $250 000 was financed by means of a long-term mortgage loan.

Because the standard requires an entity to disclose separately interest paid and income tax paid as part of operating activities, the beginning point for the indirect method is profit *before* income tax, unlike the reconciliation note that begins with profit for the period. Profit before tax is then adjusted to eliminate non-cash expenses and income, as well as items that appear in investing and financing activities; for example, eliminate gains and losses on the sale of property, plant and equipment, and interest and dividends income if included in investing activities. The complete calculation of net cash from operating activities using the indirect method appears in figure 24.18.

Figure 24.18 Net cash from operating activities — indirect method

BROOKTON LTD
Statement of Cash Flows (partial)
for the year ended 30 June 2015

Cash flows from operating activities	
Profit before income tax	$ 603 000
Adjustments for:	
Depreciation – equipment	52 500
Depreciation – buildings	49 500
Dividends received	(36 000)
Gain on sale of shares	(124 000)
Loss on sale of equipment	8 000
Interest expense	92 000
Increase in accounts receivable	(57 500)
Allowance for doubtful debts	3 000
Decrease in inventories	12 000
Increase in prepaid expenses	(33 000)
Decrease in accounts payable	(31 500)
Increase in trade bills payable	3 000
Increase in expenses payable	7 500
Cash generated from operations	548 500
Interest paid	(87 000)
Income tax paid	(310 000)
Net cash from operating activities	$ 151 500

Analysing the statement of cash flows

The statement of cash flows prepared for Brookton Ltd in figure 24.17 can be used to evaluate cash position and cash flows in five main ways:
1. explain the change that took place in the cash and cash equivalents balance
2. explain the effects of operating activities on the cash and cash equivalents balance
3. explain the effects of other activities, generally investing and financing
4. evaluate the possible effects of non-cash transactions and events disclosed in notes on future cash flows
5. evaluate the statement of cash flows for the current period against those of previous periods in terms of trends in relation to items (1) to (4).

In terms of item (1), the overall balance of cash and cash equivalents as defined in Note 1 to the statement of cash flows has increased over the period by $109 000. Based on the information given and the lack of comparative figures, this appears to be satisfactory. In terms of item (2), the operating activities of the company generated a positive cash flow of $151 500. This also indicates a satisfactory position. Analysis in terms of item (3) indicates that considerable capital expansion for buildings and equipment was funded by cash outlays of $687 000. There was a sell-off of shares in Bright Prospects Ltd that realised $274 000, together with a share issue that realised $252 500, and a debenture issue that increased cash by $150 000. Capital expansion, therefore, was not covered by using cash generated from operating activities.

Examining the statement for non-cash transactions (4) reveals that a mortgage loan of $250 000 was used to partly finance the purchase of new equipment. This will require the future commitment of cash to cover repayment of principal and interest. This item, when reviewed in conjunction with the debenture issue and the statement of financial position, indicates that debt has risen a significant amount, placing future demands on cash resources.

It is not possible in this demonstration to carry out an analysis of trends in cash flows for the company, which is highly desirable.

Learning objective 9

Identify the limitations of the statement of cash flows

24.9 Limitations of the statement of cash flows

In the introduction to this chapter, the usefulness of a statement of cash flows to the users of general purpose financial reports was emphasised. However, a number of limitations and deficiencies associated with the statement of cash flows should be borne in mind when assessing an entity's cash position. The more important of these are set out below.

Past cash flows reported. The statement of cash flows is, in essence, based on past cash flows. The statement is useful to the extent that the past cash flow information helps predict the future cash flow position. Heavy reliance on the statement of cash flows for any one reporting period can be dangerous, but this is overcome to some extent by the requirements in the standards to produce comparative figures for the current and previous financial years. Trends in cash flows can then be examined, but remember that the information in the statement of cash flows is only a part of the total analysis necessary in determining an entity's likely cash position.

Non-cash transactions and events. A large number of important investing and financing activities may not affect cash flows in the financial year covered by the statement. Significant transactions/ events such as debt–equity swaps, the financing of non-current asset purchases by long-term debt, the use of finance leases, and barter transactions do not appear in the statement but are appendages by way of note. Even the disclosure in a note of non-cash transactions gives no indication of the impact on future cash flows of such transactions.

Disclosures in notes to the statement. In addition to the non-cash transactions mentioned above, other important information relevant to cash position and future cash flows does not appear in the statement of cash flows. The accounting standard makes it mandatory to disclose some of this information in notes to the statement. Such matters as details of any business entities acquired and disposed of must be disclosed in note form. In evaluating an entity's future cash flows, careful attention must be given to information contained in the notes to the statement.

Liquidity/solvency. The statement of cash flows as required under IAS 7/AASB 107 goes only some of the way to enabling users to establish the liquidity/solvency position of an entity. The entity is solvent when the assets of the entity, when realised, are sufficient to pay off all debts as they fall due. This information is not provided by the statement of cash flows. Perhaps in future, standard setters will issue additional documents that deal with solvency.

Management manipulation. Management may for a number of reasons wish to make cash flows appear better or worse than they actually were during a reporting period. Cash flows can be manipulated in various ways, including prepayment, delaying cash payments, postponing acquisition of large investments, deferring debenture issues, barter, and finance leasing. The effect of such practices in one reporting period will be felt in subsequent periods. It is essential, therefore, not to place too much emphasis on the statement of cash flows for one period. Comparative figures are necessary to offset possible management manipulation.

Costs. The direct method of converting accrual-basis revenues and expenses to cash flows from operating activities requires additional costs to produce the information required. Under IAS 7/ AASB 107, entities are able to choose between the direct and indirect methods of arriving at cash flows from operating activities. The direct method is encouraged by the standard because it provides additional information. It is believed, however, that many entities opt for the indirect method because it is less costly to implement than the direct method.

Cash, p. 980

Cash equivalents, p. 980

Financing activities, p. 982

Investing activities, p. 982

Operating activities, p. 981

1. What are the purposes of the statement of cash flows?
2. What is the concept of cash used in the preparation of the statement of cash flows? Why is defining cash important?
3. Explain why cash flows from operating activities are important to users of a statement of cash flows.
4. A recently graduated accountant made the following observation: 'For the purposes of preparing a statement of cash flows, cash includes 'cash equivalents'. It is therefore difficult to see why accounts receivable is not included in the concept of cash. After all, money owed to the business by the short-term money market (a receivable) is included in the definition of cash. So let us be consistent and include all receivables.' Discuss.
5. Distinguish between cash flows from operating activities, investing activities and financing activities. Identify three separate cash flows where the accounting standard appears to allow classification under more than one activity. Explain why such choice of classification is allowed.
6. A student of accounting, after studying Appendix A to AASB 107, was confused. Long-term borrowings are recognised as a financing activity of an entity, yet interest paid is included in cash flow from operations. After some consideration the student concluded, 'Interest paid should be regarded as part of the financing activities of an entity, and be classified in the statement of cash flows accordingly.' Would you support the conclusion reached by the student? Explain why or why not.
7. Distinguish between the direct and indirect methods of preparing the cash flows from operating activities in a statement of cash flows. Why does the accounting standard encourage the use of the direct method?
8. Laura Ferguson, the owner-manager of a small business, had carefully monitored her cash position over the past financial year, and was pleased to note at the end of the year that the cash position was strong, and had shown a healthy 50% increase over the year. When presented with the income statement for the year, she was dismayed to note that the profit earned in the last year had deteriorated significantly and had become a loss for the current period. In her anger, she accuses you of having made errors in the accounting since 'such a silly situation could not possibly exist'. How would you respond to Laura?
9. The statement of cash flows purports to provide a summary of cash inflows and cash outflows over a reporting period and to provide information on the financial strength of the company. Yet many important and substantial transactions, which potentially have significant consequences for the cash position of a company even though they do not affect the current cash position, are not included in the statement. This causes the statement to have limited value. Discuss.
10. What are the limitations of a statement of cash flows?

Exercise 24.1 EFFECTS OF TRANSACTIONS ON STATEMENT OF CASH FLOWS **LO 4**

Below is a list of transactions completed by Fashion Enterprises during 2014. Ignore GST. For each transaction, indicate (a) the section (i.e. operating, investing or financing) of the statement of cash flows (SCF) in which the cash effect is reported (if the effect is not reported in any of the sections, place NA on the line); (b) the amount; and (c) whether the effect would be an inflow (+) or outflow (−).

Transaction	(a) Section of SCF	(b) Amount	(c) Inflow (+) Outflow (−)
1. Accounts receivable increased by $60 000 during the year	_____	_____	_____
2. Sold for $44 000 cash a plant asset with a carrying amount of $33 000	_____	_____	_____
3. The owner contributed cash of $90 000	_____	_____	_____
4. Purchased a plant asset for $87 000, giving $27 000 cash and by borrowing $60 000	_____	_____	_____
5. Borrowed $30 000 with a 3-month bill	_____	_____	_____
6. Exchanged a machine for land with a fair value of $120 000	_____	_____	_____
7. Purchased government bonds for $50 000 cash	_____	_____	_____
8. Repaid fixed-term loan principal of $80 000	_____	_____	_____
9. Accounts payable increased by $25 000 during the year	_____	_____	_____
10. Paid $40 000 in cash to the owner for personal use	_____	_____	_____

Exercise 24.2 CONVERSION FROM ACCRUAL-BASIS ITEMS TO CASH BASIS **LO 5**

The information below was taken from the general ledger accounts of Anne Davidson, who uses the accrual basis of accounting.

Required

A. Calculate the amount of cash collected from customers during 2015.
B. Calculate the amount of cash paid to suppliers for purchases during 2015.
C. Calculate the amount of cash paid to suppliers of services (including employees) during 2015.

ANNE DAVIDSON		
	30 June	
	2015	2014
Accounts receivable	$115 800	$78 600
Inventory	48 360	52 200
Prepaid insurance	2 200	2 700
Accounts payable	35 500	37 700
Wages payable	3 200	4 700
Sales	270 000	
Cost of sales	148 000	
Expenses (including $47 000 depreciation)	88 000	

Exercise 24.3 CASH FLOW FROM OPERATING ACTIVITIES, INDIRECT METHOD

The simple income statement for Bruce's Paints is shown below:

BRUCE'S PAINTS
Income Statement
for the year ended 30 June 2014

Sales		$870 000
Less: Cost of sales		
Beginning inventory	$137 000	
Purchases	320 000	
Goods available for sale	457 000	
Ending Inventory	117 000	
Cost of sales		340 000
GROSS PROFIT		530 000
Expenses		
Selling expenses	150 000	
Administrative expenses	183 000	333 000
Profit		$197 000

Additional information
1. Accounts receivable increased $16 500 during the year.
2. Accounts payable to suppliers of inventory increased by $6500 during the year.
3. Wages payable decreased by $12 500 during the year (including selling expenses).
4. Administrative expenses include depreciation expense of $63 000.

Required
Prepare the net cash flows from operating activities for the year ended 30 June 2014 for Bruce's Paints using the indirect method.

Exercise 24.4 INVESTING AND FINANCING ACTIVITIES

The following transactions were undertaken by Ochre Ltd during the financial year ended 30 June 2014. Ignore GST.
1. Issued ordinary shares for cash, $500 000.
2. Purchased land to be held for future expansion for $450 000 cash.
3. Paid off a long-term $180 000 loan plus interest of $16 000.
4. Sold for $240 000 used machinery with a carrying amount of $100 000.
5. Paid cash dividends of $110 000.
6. Purchased machinery, giving $60 000 cash and signing a mortgage loan for $200 000.
7. Purchased shares in A Ltd to be held as an investment for $200 000 cash.
8. Sold a long-term government bond, with a carrying amount of $50 000, for $86 000, including $6000 accrued interest.
9. Purchased shares in Rouge Ltd to be held as a long-term investment, paying $190 000 cash.
10. Issued 7% debentures for $700 000.

Required
A. Prepare the net cash flow used in investing activities section of the statement of cash flows using the classification shown in Appendix A of IAS 7/AASB 107.
B. Prepare the net cash used in financing activities section of the statement of cash flows using the classification shown in Appendix A of IAS 7/AASB 107.

Exercise 24.5 RECONCILING CASH FROM OPERATING ACTIVITIES TO PROFIT

Following are the descriptions of changes in selected accounts and other events for Shiny Pty Ltd.

1. Decrease in accounts receivable   _____
2. Increase in inventory   _____
3. Cash proceeds from sale of shares   _____
4. Depreciation expense   _____
5. Increase in accounts payable   _____
6. Decrease in accrued expenses   _____
7. Increase in trade bills receivable   _____
8. Cash dividends paid   _____
9. Increase in interest receivable   _____

Required

Indicate whether each item should be added (A) to or deducted (D) from profit when reconciling cash from operating activities. If the item should be neither added nor deducted, indicate with an (N).

Exercise 24.6 STATEMENT OF CASH FLOWS FOR SOLE TRADER, DIRECT METHOD

Louise Martin has been in business as a sole trader for the past 5 years. The comparative statements of financial position for the years 2013 and 2014 and a summarised income statement for the year ended 30 June 2014 are shown below:

LOUISE MARTIN **Comparative Statements of Financial Position** as at 30 June		
	2013	2014
CURRENT ASSETS		
Cash	—	$ 540
Accounts receivable	$ 4 290	3 150
Inventory	6 000	6 600
Prepaid insurance	300	360
NON-CURRENT ASSETS		
Equipment	19 200	25 500
Accumulated depreciation – equipment	(6 000)	(7 500)
Land	20 400	24 000
Motor vehicles	14 550	15 600
Accumulated depreciation – motor vehicles	(5 490)	(6 300)
TOTAL ASSETS	53 250	61 950
CURRENT LIABILITIES		
Bank overdraft	300	—
Accounts payable	6 150	7 950
NON-CURRENT LIABILITIES		
Long-term mortgage	14 100	18 900
TOTAL LIABILITIES	20 550	26 850
NET ASSETS	$32 700	$35 100
EQUITY		
Louise Martin, Capital	$32 700	$35 100
TOTAL EQUITY	$32 700	$35 100

<table>
<tr><td colspan="2" align="center">**LOUISE MARTIN**
Income Statement
for the year ended 30 June 2014</td></tr>
<tr><td>Sales</td><td align="right">$16 800</td></tr>
<tr><td>*Less:* Cost of sales</td><td align="right">5 100</td></tr>
<tr><td>GROSS PROFIT</td><td align="right">11 700</td></tr>
<tr><td>*Less:* Expenses (including depreciation)</td><td align="right">8 610</td></tr>
<tr><td>PROFIT</td><td align="right">$ 3 090</td></tr>
</table>

Additional information

Louise had contributed capital during the year for $6000 cash and had made cash withdrawals during the year. The bank overdraft was considered to be part of the entity's everyday cash management activities.

Required

Prepare a statement of cash flows using the direct method for Louise Martin's business for the year ended 30 June 2014.

Exercise 24.7 STATEMENT OF CASH FLOWS AND GST GST LO 5

The business owned by Rhys Muller made the following cash transactions during the reporting period. GST of 10% was applicable on all transactions:
1. Purchased equipment for $11 000 (including GST).
2. Purchased inventory for $22 000 (including GST).
3. Sold inventory for $55 000 (including GST).
4. Purchased office supplies for $4400 (including GST).
5. Sold an item of plant for $33 000 (including GST).
6. A net amount of $4500, representing GST collections and outlays, excluding the above transactions, was paid to the Australian Taxation Office.

Required

Prepare a statement of cash flows using the direct method for the business for the period. Treat all GST items as part of operating activities.

Exercise 24.8 DIRECT AND INDIRECT METHODS LO 8

The comparative statements of financial position of Copper Ltd as at 30 June 2013 and 2014 and the income statement for the year ended 30 June 2014 are shown overleaf.

Additional information

• Other expenses include $55 500 depreciation expense.
• All sales and purchases of inventory are on credit.

Required

A. Prepare a statement of cash flows from operating activities only for Copper Ltd for the year ended 30 June 2014 using the direct method.
B. Repeat requirement A using the indirect method.

COPPER LTD
Comparative Statements of Financial Position
as at 30 June

	2013	2014
ASSETS		
Cash at bank	$ 22 500	$ 69 000
Accounts receivable	82 500	70 500
Inventory	165 000	216 000
Prepaid insurance	7 500	1 500
Property	190 500	172 500
Plant and equipment	757 500	1 072 500
Accum. depreciation – plant and equipment	(102 000)	(154 500)
TOTAL ASSETS	**$1 123 500**	**$1 447 500**
LIABILITIES AND EQUITY		
Accounts payable	$ 64 500	$ 75 000
Interest payable	7 500	4 500
Other accrued expenses	13 500	18 000
Mortgage payable	367 500	442 500
Share capital	500 000	750 000
Retained earnings	170 500	157 500
TOTAL LIABILITIES AND EQUITY	**$1 123 500**	**$1 447 500**

COPPER LTD
Income Statement
for the year ended 30 June 2014

Sales		$1 047 000
Less: Cost of sales		780 000
GROSS PROFIT		267 000
Add: Other income:		
Rent income	$ 9 000	
Gain on sale of property	20 000	29 000
		296 000
Less: Expenses:		
Interest expense	34 500	
Loss on sale of plant	6 500	
Other expenses	231 000	272 000
PROFIT		$ 24 000

LO 5

Exercise 24.9 STATEMENT OF CASH FLOWS FOR SOLE TRADER AND ANALYSIS

The financial statements for the business of Brett's Bait Supplies for the past two years are as shown on the next page.

Additional information

(a) All purchases and sales of inventories are on credit. All purchases of office supplies are for cash.

(b) The bank overdraft is considered to be part of the entity's cash management function.

(c) During the year ended 30 June 2014, the owner, B. Fish, withdrew $25 600 in cash for personal use.

(d) The entity sold some fixtures for $2400 cash during the current year. These fixtures initially cost $8400 and had been written down to a carrying amount at the date of sale of $4000.

(e) Depreciation of fixtures has been included in 'other expenses' for the year ended 30 June 2014. All remaining other expenses were paid in cash.

BRETT'S BAIT SUPPLIES
Comparative Income Statements
for the year ended 30 June

	2013	2014
Sales	$800 000	$1 000 000
Cost of sales	700 000	916 000
GROSS PROFIT	100 000	84 000
Proceeds on sale of fixtures	—	2 400
Interest income	2 000	4 000
	102 000	90 400
Office supplies used	20 000	22 000
Carrying amount of fixtures sold	—	4 000
Other expenses	58 000	58 000
	78 000	84 000
PROFIT	$ 24 000	$ 6 400

BRETT'S BAIT SUPPLIES
Comparative Statements of Financial Position
as at 30 June

	2013	2014
ASSETS		
Cash at bank	$ 8 800	—
Accounts receivable	84 000	$120 000
Inventory	160 000	80 000
Office supplies	4 000	10 000
Freehold property	120 000	160 000
Fixtures	80 000	92 000
Accumulated depreciation – fixtures	(32 000)	(40 400)
Investments	12 000	32 000
	$436 800	$453 600
LIABILITIES AND EQUITY		
Bank overdraft	—	$ 8 000
Accounts payable	$ 52 000	80 000
B. Fish, Capital	384 800	365 600
	$436 800	$226 800

Required

A. Prepare the statement of cash flows for Brett's Bait Supplies for the year ended 30 June 2014, using the direct method.

B. Comment on the cash flow position of the entity as shown in the statement of cash flows.

The following comparative statements of financial position and income statement are for the business of Eucalyptus Camping Supplies Pty Ltd:

EUCALYPTUS CAMPING SUPPLIES PTY LTD
Comparative Statements of Financial Position
as at 30 June

	2013	2014
ASSETS		
Cash at bank	$ 20 000	$ 30 000
Accounts receivable	74 000	52 000
Inventory	60 000	88 000
Prepaid expenses	44 000	36 000
Plant and equipment	600 000	648 000
Accumulated depreciation – plant and equipment	(180 000)	(230 000)
	$ 618 000	$ 624 000
LIABILITIES AND EQUITY		
Accounts payable	$ 96 000	$ 60 000
Expenses payable	22 000	40 000
Current tax liability	50 000	44 000
Share capital	300 000	300 000
Retained earnings	150 000	180 000
	$ 618 000	$ 624 000

EUCALYPTUS CAMPING SUPPLIES PTY LTD
Income Statement
for year ended 30 June 2014

INCOME		
Sales revenue		$800 000
EXPENSES		
Cost of sales	$408 000	
Wages and salaries	160 000	
Depreciation – plant and equipment	50 000	
Other expenses	78 000	
Income tax expense	44 000	740 000
PROFIT		$ 60 000

Additional information
(a) All sales and purchases of inventory are on credit.
(b) Income tax is paid in one instalment during the year.
(c) A dividend had been paid to shareholders.
(d) Additional plant had been acquired for a cash outlay.

Required
A. Prepare the statement of cash flows for the company for the year ended 30 June 2014. Use the direct method.
B. Repeat requirement A using the indirect method.

Exercise 24.11 STATEMENT OF CASH FLOWS FOR SOLE TRADER AND ANALYSIS

The financial statements for the business of Jet's Ski Equipment are shown below:

JET'S SKI EQUIPMENT
Comparative Statements of Financial Position
as at 30 June

	2013	2014
ASSETS		
Cash at bank	—	$ 27 000
Accounts receivable	$ 42 000	51 000
Inventory	144 000	168 000
Store equipment	90 000	108 000
Accumulated depreciation – store equipment	(27 000)	(45 000)
Land	120 000	60 000
Buildings	180 000	180 000
Accumulated depreciation – buildings	(9 000)	(15 000)
	$540 000	$534 000
LIABILITIES AND EQUITY		
Accounts payable	$ 72 000	$ 78 000
Bank overdraft	30 000	—
J. Waters, Capital	438 000	456 000
	$540 000	$534 000

JET'S SKI EQUIPMENT
Income Statement
for year ended 30 June 2014

INCOME		
Sales revenue		$270 000
EXPENSES		
Cost of sales	$144 000	
Depreciation – store equipment	21 000	
Depreciation – buildings	6 000	
Other expenses	60 000	
Loss on sale of land	12 000	
Loss on sale of equipment	9 000	252 000
PROFIT		$ 18 000

Additional information
(a) All purchases and sales of inventories are on credit.
(b) On 1 July 2013, J. Waters injected a further capital contribution of $21 000 cash into the business.
(c) During the year, store equipment costing $18 000 with a carrying amount of $15 000 was sold for $6000 cash.
(d) Half the land on hand at the beginning of the year was sold for $48 000 cash.
(e) During the year, the owner withdrew $6000 from the business bank account in order to pay his personal income tax bill and $300 per week for 50 weeks for private consumption.

Required
A. Prepare the statement of cash flows for Jet's Ski Equipment for the year ended 30 June 2014, using the direct method.
B. Comment on the cash flow position as shown in the entity's statement of cash flows.

Exercise 24.12 STATEMENT OF CASH FLOWS FOR SOLE TRADER

Comparative statements of financial position as at 31 December 2014 and 2013 and the income statement for 2014 for W. Yu are set out below.

W. YU
Comparative Statements of Financial Position
as at 31 December

	2014	2013
ASSETS		
Cash on hand and at bank	$111 600	$134 400
Accounts receivable	161 400	151 200
Inventory	196 200	208 800
Plant and equipment	408 000	300 000
Accumulated depreciation – plant and equipment	(180 000)	(162 000)
	$697 200	$632 400
LIABILITIES AND EQUITY		
Accounts payable	$140 400	$132 600
Expenses payable	77 400	83 400
Long-term loan payable	60 000	—
W. Yu, Capital	419 400	416 400
	$697 200	$632 400

W. YU
Income Statement
for the year ended 31 December 2014

Sales	$592 200
Less: Cost of sales	350 000
GROSS PROFIT	242 200
Less: Expenses (Including depreciation)	209 200
PROFIT	$ 33 000

No plant and equipment was sold during the year. W. Yu withdrew $30 000 in cash during the year.

Required

Prepare a statement of cash flows for the year ended 31 December 2014 in accordance with the direct method.

Exercise 24.13 CASH FLOW FROM OPERATING ACTIVITIES

Opposite are the comparative statements of financial position of Zinc Ltd as at 30 June 2013 and 2014, and the income statement and statement of changes in equity for the year ended 30 June 2014.

Additional information
(a) Other expenses include $22 000 depreciation expense on machinery and insurance expense of $3500.
(b) All sales and purchases are on credit.
(c) Rental income is earned as a result of renting part of the property that is in excess of the company's needs.

Required

Prepare the cash flows from operating activities *only* for Zinc Ltd for the year ended 30 June 2014, using the direct method. Ignore taxes.

ZINC LTD
Comparative Statements of Financial Position
as at 30 June

	2013	2014
ASSETS		
Cash at bank	$ 6 500	$ 23 000
Accounts receivable	37 500	33 500
Inventory	66 000	82 000
Prepaid insurance	3 500	2 500
Property	44 800	40 000
Machinery	300 000	360 000
Accumulated depreciation: machinery	(67 000)	(81 000)
	$391 300	$460 000
LIABILITIES AND EQUITY		
Accounts payable	$ 22 000	$ 25 000
Interest payable	3 400	3 000
Other accrued expenses	4 500	7 000
Mortgage payable	120 000	145 000
Share capital	100 000	170 000
Retained earnings	141 400	110 000
	$391 300	$460 000

ZINC LTD
Income Statement
for the year ended 30 June 2014

Sales		$420 000
Less: Cost of sales		281 000
GROSS PROFIT		139 000
Add: Other income:		
Lease income	$ 7 500	
Gain on the sale of machinery	9 000	16 500
		155 500
Less: Expenses:		
Interest expense	11 500	
Loss on the sale of property	10 000	
Other expenses	107 000	128 500
PROFIT		$ 27 000

ZINC LTD
Statement of Changes in Equity
for the year ended 30 June 2014

	Share capital	Other reserves	Retained earnings	Total
Balance at 1/7/13	$100 000		$141 400	$241 400
Total comprehensive income for the period			27 000	27 000
Dividends	70 000		(58 400)	(58 400)
Issue of share capital				70 000
Balance at 30/6/14	$170 000		$110 000	$280 000

Some of the most recent financial statements for Barium Pty Ltd are shown below:

BARIUM PTY LTD
Comparative Statements of Financial Position
as at 30 June

	2014	2015
ASSETS		
Cash at bank	—	$ 18 000
Accounts receivable	$ 28 000	34 000
Inventory	96 000	112 000
Sales equipment	60 000	72 000
Accumulated depreciation – sales equipment	(18 000)	(30 000)
Land	80 000	40 000
Buildings	120 000	120 000
Accumulated depreciation – buildings	(6 000)	(10 000)
	$360 000	$356 000
LIABILITIES AND EQUITY		
Accounts payable	$ 48 000	$ 52 000
Bank overdraft	20 000	—
Equity	292 000	304 000
	$360 000	$356 000

BARIUM PTY LTD
Income Statement
for the year ended 30 June 2015

Sales revenue			$180 000
Expenses:			
Cost of sales:			
Beginning inventory	$ 96 000		
Purchases	112 000		
	208 000		
Ending inventory	112 000	$96 000	
Depreciation – sales equipment		14 000	
Depreciation – buildings		4 000	
Other expenses (paid in cash)		40 000	
Loss on sale of land		8 000	
Loss on sales of equipment		6 000	168 000
Profit			$ 12 000

Additional information
(a) All purchases and sales of inventories are on credit.
(b) On 1 July 2014, the shareholders injected a further capital contribution of $14 000 cash into the business.
(c) During the year, sales equipment costing $12 000 and written down to a carrying amount of $10 000 was sold for $4000 cash.
(d) Half of the land on hand at the beginning of the year was sold for $32 000 cash.
(e) During the year, the company withdrew cash from the business bank account in order to pay cash dividends to its shareholders.

(f) The bank overdraft in the company is considered to be an integral part of the company's cash management arrangements.

(g) Ignore income tax.

Required

Prepare the statement of cash flows for Barium Pty Ltd for the year ended 30 June 2015, using the direct method.

LO 8

Exercise 24.15 STATEMENT OF CASH FLOWS FOR A COMPANY

Below are the comparative statements of financial position of Lithium Ltd.

LITHIUM LTD Comparative Statements of Financial Position as at 30 June				
	2014		2015	
ASSETS				
Petty cash		$ 200		$ 400
Cash at bank		24 200		30 600
Bank bills		10 000		12 000
Accounts receivable	$102 960		$127 400	
Allowance for doubtful debts	(6 960)	96 000	(11 400)	116 000
Inventory		74 600		70 800
Motor vehicles	42 000		50 400	
Acc. depr. – motor vehicles	(10 000)	32 000	(12 800)	37 600
Office furniture	16 000		18 400	
Acc. depr. – off. furn.	(7 600)	8 400	(8 400)	10 000
		$245 400		$277 400
LIABILITIES AND EQUITY				
Accounts payable		$ 45 000		$ 47 200
Current tax liability		3 200		4 200
Share capital		165 000		196 000
Retained earnings		32 200		30 000
		$245 400		$277 400

Additional information

(a) Income statement details were: sales revenue $750 000; cost of sales $603 000; expenses $116 360 (excludes depreciation and carrying amount of vehicle sold); bad debts expense $14 440; and tax expense $4200.

(b) A dividend was paid during the year.

(c) A vehicle that cost $5600 originally was sold during the year for $3000. The vehicle had been depreciated by $3200 at date of sale.

(d) The company pays tax in one instalment. The single instalment of $3200 due by 21 October 2014 was paid.

Required

Prepare a statement of cash flows for the year ended 30 June 2015 in accordance with the direct method. Include any appropriate notes.

LO 5, 6

★ Basic

★★ Moderate

★★★ Challenging

Problem 24.1 STATEMENT FOR SOLE TRADER ★

Financial statements for the years ended 30 June 2014 and 30 June 2015 for A. Smith follow:

A. SMITH
Comparative Statements of Financial Position
as at 30 June

	2014	2015
ASSETS		
Cash at bank	$ 6 000	$ 15 000
Accounts receivable	10 000	14 000
Inventory	30 000	28 000
Plant	300 000	350 000
Accumulated depreciation – equipment	(100 000)	(120 000)
Furniture	20 000	10 000
Accumulated depreciation – furniture	(6 000)	(4 000)
	$ 260 000	$293 000
LIABILITIES AND EQUITY		
Accounts payable	$ 60 000	$ 70 000
A. Smith, Capital	200 000	223 000
	$ 260 000	$293 000

A. SMITH
Income Statement
for the year ended 30 June 2015

Sales revenue		$146 000
Less: Cost of sales		60 000
GROSS PROFIT		86 000
Proceeds from sale of furniture		6 000
		92 000
Expenses:		
Selling and general expenses	$30 000	
Carrying amount of furniture sold	4 000	
Depreciation of equipment	20 000	
Depreciation of furniture	4 000	58 000
PROFIT		$ 34 000

Additional information

Smith withdrew $21 000 for private use during the year ended 30 June 2015. Furniture which had cost $10 000 and had a carrying amount of $4000 was sold for $6000 cash. No furniture was purchased during the year.

Required

A. Prepare a statement of cash flows for the year ended 30 June 2015 in accordance with the direct method.

B. Prepare a note to the statement reconciling cash flows from operating activities to profit.

Problem 24.2 STATEMENT OF CASH FLOWS FOR A SOLE TRADER ★

Financial figures of the business of L. Mitchum for the last 2 years are shown below.

L. MITCHUM
Comparative Statements of Financial Position
as at 30 June

	2014		2015	
ASSETS				
Cash at bank				$ 11 280
Accounts receivable		$ 16 800		20 400
Inventory		57 600		67 200
Plant and equipment	$36 000		$43 200	
Accumulated depreciation – plant and equipment	16 800	19 200	18 000	25 200
Land		48 000		24 000
Buildings	48 000		48 000	
Accumulated depreciation – buildings	2 400	45 600	3 360	44 640
		$187 200		$192 720
LIABILITIES AND EQUITY				
Accounts payable		$ 28 800		$ 31 200
Bank overdraft		12 000		—
Mitchum, Capital		146 400		161 520
		$187 200		$192 720

The income statement for the business for the year ended 30 June 2015 reveals the following details:

L. MITCHUM
Income Statement
for the year ended 30 June 2015

INCOME		
Sales revenue		$ 72 000
Proceeds from sale of land		33 600
Proceeds from sale of plant		2 880
		108 480
EXPENSES		
Cost of sales	$38 400	
Depreciation of plant and equipment	4 800	
Depreciation of buildings	960	
Other expenses (including carrying amount of land and plant sold)	38 160	82 320
PROFIT		$ 26 160

Additional information

(a) During the year ended 30 June 2015, Mitchum withdrew $120 per week in cash for 52 weeks for private purposes.

(b) Mitchum also withdrew $4800 on her business bank account to pay her personal income tax.

(c) Land, shown in the accounts at $24 000, was sold during the year for $33 600.

(d) Plant costing $7200 and written down to $3600 was sold for $2880.

(e) Ignore GST.

Required

A. Prepare a statement of cash flows for the year ended 30 June 2015 using the direct method.

B. Prepare the note to the above statement reconciling cash flows from operating activities with profit.

Problem 24.3   STATEMENT OF CASH FLOWS FOR A PARTNERSHIP ★★

The comparative statement of financial position of the partnership of Murray and Darling as at 30 June 2013 and 30 June 2014 were as follows:

MURRAY AND DARLING
Comparative Statements of Financial Position
as at 30 June

	2013		2014	
CURRENT ASSETS				
Cash at bank	$ 100		$ 300	
Accounts receivable (net)	83 400		90 000	
Bills receivable	5 200		3 800	
Inventory	56 300	$145 000	64 700	$158 800
NON-CURRENT ASSETS				
Furniture and equipment	42 000		47 500	
Accumulated depreciation	(6 400)		(7 200)	
Motor vehicles	36 800		27 600	
Accumulated depreciation	(8 200)	64 200	(8 500)	59 400
		$209 200		$218 200
CURRENT LIABILITIES				
Bank overdraft	$26 000		$ 4 000	
Accounts payable	23 600		25 500	
Murray, Advance	10 000	$ 59 600	8 000	$ 37 500
EQUITY				
Murray, Capital	80 000		92 000	
Darling, Capital	60 000		65 000	
Murray, Retained earnings	6 400		14 400	
Darling, Retained earnings	3 200	149 600	9 300	180 700
		$209 200		$218 200

Additional information

(a) Each partner's retained earnings account has been credited with a salary of $12 000 as part of their profit distribution.

(b) Drawings in cash for each partner in anticipation of profits amount to:

Murray	$ 9 900
Darling	10 400

(c) A motor vehicle that cost $9200 and had been written down to $3100 was sold for $3750.

(d) Expenses involving a flow of cash amounted to $75 000.

(e) Sales for the year were $300 000 and cost of sales was $184 050.

Required

Prepare a statement of cash flows for the partnership for the year ended 30 June 2014 using the direct method.

Problem 24.4 STATEMENT OF CASH FLOWS FOR A PARTNERSHIP ★★

K & L Hardware is operated by Ken and Len in partnership. Financial data for the partnership follow.

K & L HARDWARE
Comparative Statements of Financial Position
as at 30 June

	2013	2014
ASSETS		
Cash	$ 16 400	$ 19 000
Inventory	40 000	52 000
Accounts receivable	16 400	15 000
Prepaid insurance	600	700
Long-term investments	14 000	20 000
Motor vehicles	84 000	90 000
Accumulated depreciation – motor vehicles	(26 000)	(36 000)
	$145 400	$160 700
LIABILITIES AND EQUITY		
Accounts payable	$ 20 000	$ 14 000
Accrued sundry expenses	350	275
Long-term loan	35 000	25 000
Ken, Capital	20 000	30 000
Retained earnings	7 000	30 350
Len, Capital	40 000	40 000
Retained earnings	23 050	21 075
	$145 400	$160 700

K & L HARDWARE
Income Statement
for the year ended 30 June 2014

INCOME	
Sales	$450 000
Gross proceeds from sale of motor vehicle	3 000
	453 000
EXPENSES	
Cost of sales	320 000
General expenses (including depreciation)	68 000
Carrying amount of motor vehicle sold	2 000
	390 000
PROFIT	$ 63 000

Additional information

All profits/losses are shared equally by Ken and Len who also withdrew cash during the year. The vehicle that was sold had originally cost $10 000 (second-hand).

Required

A. Prepare a statement of cash flows for the year ended 30 June 2014 using the direct method.

B. Comment on the statement of cash flows with respect to the operating, investing and financing activities of K & L Hardware.

Problem 24.5 STATEMENT OF CASH FLOWS, DIRECT AND INDIRECT METHODS ★★

The simplified financial statements of Titanium Ltd appear below:

TITANIUM LTD
Statement of Financial Position
as at 30 June

	2014	2015
ASSETS		
Cash	$ 37 200	$ 15 600
Accounts receivable	33 600	16 800
Inventory	30 000	42 000
Plant and equipment	72 000	93 600
Accumulated depreciation – plant and equipment	(26 400)	(28 800)
	$146 400	$139 200
LIABILITIES AND EQUITY		
Accounts payable	$ 32 400	$ 27 600
Current tax liability	6 000	9 600
Loan payable	32 400	37 200
Share capital	41 600	41 600
Retained earnings	34 000	23 200
	$146 400	$139 200

TITANIUM LTD
Income Statement
as at 30 June

Sales		$264 000
Cost of sales		216 000
GROSS PROFIT		48 000
Selling expenses	$16 800	
Administrative expenses	9 600	
Interest expense	1 200	27 600
Profit before tax		20 400
Income tax expense		4 800
PROFIT		$ 15 600

Additional information
1. Dividends declared and paid were $26 400.
2. During the year equipment was sold for $10 200 cash. The equipment cost $21 600 and had a carrying amount of $10 200 at the time of sale.
3. Depreciation expense is included as a selling expense in the income statement.
4. All sales and purchases are on credit.

Required
A. Prepare a statement of cash flows using the indirect method.
B. Prepare a statement of cash flows using the direct method.

The following data relate to Silver Ltd:

SILVER LTD
Income Statement
for the year ended 30 June 2014

INCOME		
Sales revenue		$810 000
EXPENSES		
Cost of sales	$480 000	
Depreciation – machinery	20 000	
Depreciation – buildings	10 000	
Other expenses	221 000	731 000
PROFIT		$ 79 000

SILVER LTD
Comparative Statements of Financial Position
as at 30 June

	2013	2014
ASSETS		
Cash at bank	$ 37 000	$ 26 000
Accounts receivable	96 000	90 000
Inventory	80 000	100 000
Investments	10 000	12 000
Machinery (net)	150 000	200 000
Buildings (net)	100 000	160 000
Land	45 000	100 000
	$518 000	$688 000
LIABILITIES AND EQUITY		
Accounts payable	$ 65 000	$ 75 000
Expenses payable	4 000	3 000
Mortgage payable	88 000	150 000
Share capital	250 000	300 000
Retained earnings	111 000	160 000
	$518 000	$688 000

Additional information
(a) Dividends were paid during the year.
(b) The increases in investments and machinery were from cash purchases.
(c) The increases in land and buildings were from purchases but were partly funded by an increase in the mortgage with the bank.
(d) Share capital was issued during the year for cash.

Required
A. Prepare the statement of cash flows for Silver Ltd for the year ended 30 June 2014, using the direct method.
B. Prepare the note reconciling cash flows from operating activities to profit.
C. Prepare a note to disclose non-cash financing and investing activities.

Problem 24.7 STATEMENT OF CASH FLOWS AND GST ★★

Philippa Hayes set up a small business from her home by contributing $8000 cash to the business. The business is registered for GST. For the year ended 30 June 2015, the following transactions occurred:

1. Philippa contributed $8000 cash to the business.
2. Inventory was purchased on credit for $3000 plus GST of 10%. Philippa decided to adopt the perpetual inventory system.
3. Sales revenue of $4500 was earned, plus GST, for the sale of inventory on credit. Cost of sales was $3000.
4. Inventory was acquired for $2800 plus GST on credit.
5. Credit sales for $3000 plus GST were recorded, the cost of sales being $2100.
6. $3200 cash was received from accounts receivable.
7. $10 000 was borrowed from a bank under a long-term loan.
8. Equipment was purchased for $6000 plus GST, using the money borrowed.
9. GST owing was paid to the ATO.
10. Wages of $800 were paid to a part-time assistant.
11. $3300 cash was paid on accounts payable.
12. Inventory costing $2500 plus GST was purchased on credit.
13. Credit sales of $3000 plus GST were made, the cost of sales being $1500. The terms of the sale were 2/10, n/30.
14. The customer in (13) paid for the goods within the discount period.

Required
A. Prepare journal entries (in general journal form) for the business of Philippa Hayes.
B. Prepare the income statement and statement of financial position of the business after all transactions have been recorded.
C. Prepare the statement of cash flows under the direct method for the business using the analysis of cash records.
D. Prepare the statement of cash flows under the direct method for the business by analysing financial statements.
E. Prepare a note reconciling the cash flows from operating activities to profit.

Problem 24.8 STATEMENT OF CASH FLOWS FOR A COMPANY ★★

The comparative statements of financial position of Lead Ltd as at 30 June 2013 and 2014, the statement of profit or loss and other comprehensive income and the statement of changes in equity for the year ended 30 June 2014 are shown on pages 1039–40.

Additional information
(a) Other expenses include $54 000 depreciation expense on plant and insurance expense of $8000.
(b) All sales and purchases of inventory are on credit.
(c) Plant which had cost $60 000 and had a carrying amount of $34 000 was sold for $52 000 cash.
(d) Ignore taxes.

Required
A. Prepare the statement of cash flows for Lead Ltd for the year ended 30 June 2014 using the direct method.
B. Prepare the note reconciling cash flows from operating activities to profit.

LEAD LTD
Comparative Statements of Financial Position
as at 30 June

	2013	2014
ASSETS		
Cash at bank	$ 13 000	$ 46 000
Accounts receivable	70 000	60 000
Lease income receivable	5 000	7 000
Inventory	132 000	164 000
Prepaid insurance	7 000	5 000
Property	180 000	80 000
Plant	600 000	720 000
Accumulated depreciation – plant	(134 000)	(162 000)
	$ 873 000	$ 920 000
LIABILITIES AND EQUITY		
Accounts payable	$ 64 000	$ 40 000
Interest payable	12 000	10 000
Other expenses payable	9 000	10 000
Mortgage payable	240 000	250 000
Share capital	250 000	340 000
General reserve	—	50 000
Retained earnings	298 000	220 000
	$ 873 000	$ 920 000

LEAD LTD
Statement of Profit or Loss and Other Comprehensive Income
for the year ended 30 June 2014

Sales		$840 000
Less: Cost of sales		562 000
GROSS PROFIT		278 000
Add: Other income:		
Lease income	$15 000	
Profit on the sale of plant	18 000	33 000
		311 000
Less: Expenses:		
Interest expense	23 000	
Loss on the sale of property	20 000	
Other expenses	214 000	257 000
PROFIT		$ 54 000

LEAD LTD
Statement of Changes in Equity
for the year ended 30 June 2014

	Share capital	Other reserves	Retained earnings	Total
Balance at 1/7/13	$250 000	—	$298 000	$548 000
Total comprehensive income for the period			54 000	54 000
Dividends			(82 000)	(82 000)
Issue of share capital	90 000			90 000
Transfer to general reserve		$50 000	(50 000)	—
Balance at 30/6/14	$340 000	$50 000	$220 000	$610 000

Problem 24.9 STATEMENT OF CASH FLOWS, DIRECT AND INDIRECT METHODS ★★   LO 8

Comparative information as at 30 June 2014 and 30 June 2015 for Molybdenum Ltd is as follows:

MOLYBDENUM LTD
Comparative Statements of Financial Position
as at 30 June

	2014	2015
ASSETS		
Cash at bank	$ 124 000	$ 86 000
Accounts receivable	152 000	169 000
Inventory	248 000	227 000
Land	125 000	50 000
Buildings	275 000	530 000
Accumulated depreciation – buildings	(170 000)	(200 000)
Plant and equipment	80 000	80 000
Accumulated depreciation – plant and equipment	(10 000)	(20 000)
	$ 824 000	$ 922 000
LIABILITIES AND EQUITY		
Accounts payable	$ 121 000	$ 134 000
Interest payable	1 500	500
Other expenses payable	17 500	6 000
Mortgage loan payable	90 000	132 500
Share capital	250 000	250 000
Retained earnings	344 000	399 000
	$ 824 000	$ 922 000

Additional information
(a) Gross profit for the year ended 30 June 2015 was $321 000, and consisted of:

    Sales $887 000
    Cost of sales   566 000

(b) Purchases of inventory for the year were $545 000.
(c) All purchases and sales of inventories were on credit.
(d) Profit for the year ended 30 June 2015 was $62 500, after deducting expenses of $258 500 from the gross profit figure.
(e) Expenses of $258 500 include depreciation on buildings, and on plant and equipment, a loss on sale of land, and $10 000 in interest expense.

(f) During the year ended 30 June 2015, cash dividends were paid.

(g) Building extensions were paid for during the year, and a block of land, costing $75 000, was sold for $62 500 cash.

(h) No plant was purchased or sold during the year.

Required

A. Prepare the statement of cash flows for Molybdenum Ltd for the year ended 30 June 2015 using the direct method.

B. Show how cash flows from operating activities in the statement would be presented under the indirect method.

Problem 24.10 STATEMENT OF CASH FLOWS FOR A COMPANY ★★

The financial statements for Nickel Ltd are shown below.

Additional information

(a) Office furniture that had originally cost $11 000 and had accumulated depreciation of $2000 was sold during the year for $9500 cash.

(b) Plant and machinery costing $50 000 was paid for by the issue of 50 000 shares at a price of $1 each.

(c) The company pays tax in one instalment. Income tax expense as reported ($27 430) consists of the tax expense for the year ($40 000) less an overprovision for tax from the previous year ($12 570).

(d) The bank overdraft facility is considered part of the day-to-day cash management operations.

Required

Prepare a statement of cash flows in accordance with IAS 7/AASB 107 using the direct method. Also show any notes to the statement that are necessary.

NICKEL LTD
Comparative Trial Balance
as at 30 June

	2014 Debit	2014 Credit	2015 Debit	2015 Credit
Accounts payable		$ 48 320		$ 43 080
Bills payable (trade)		14 210		16 080
Bank overdraft		13 900		84 320
Current tax liability		30 000		40 000
Share capital		300 000		450 000
General reserve		50 000		75 000
Retained earnings		43 820		54 710
Petty cash	$ 250		$ 250	
Accounts receivable	57 810		104 320	
Allowance for doubtful debts		5 000		10 000
Bills receivable (trade)	7 560		5 430	
Inventory	182 580		302 890	
Plant and machinery	249 000		392 000	
Accumulated depreciation – plant and machinery		27 450		55 700
Furniture and equipment	50 000		39 000	
Accumulated depreciation – furniture and equipment		14 500		15 000
	$547 200	$547 200	$843 890	$843 890

NICKEL LTD
Statement of Profit or Loss and Other Comprehensive Income
for the year ended 30 June 2015

INCOME		
Sales revenue		$1 000 000
Gain on sale of furniture		500
		1 000 500
EXPENSES		
Cost of sales	$350 000	
Depreciation expense	30 750	
Bad debts expense	17 000	
Other expenses	499 430	897 180
Profit before income tax		103 320
Income tax expense		27 430
PROFIT		$ 75 890

NICKEL LTD
Statement of Changes in Equity
for the year ended 30 June 2015

	Share capital	Other reserves	Retained earnings	Total
Balance at 1/7/14	$300 000	$50 000	$ 43 820	$393 820
Total comprehensive income for the period			75 890	75 890
Dividends paid			(40 000)	(40 000)
Issue of share capital	150 000			150 000
Transfer to reserve		25 000	(25 000)	0
Balance at 30/6/15	$450 000	$75 000	$ 54 710	$579 710

Problem 24.11   STATEMENT OF CASH FLOWS FOR A COMPANY ★★   **LO 6, 8**

Comparative statements of financial position for Gold Ltd on 30 June 2014 and 2015 are presented below.

Examination of the company's statement of profit or loss and other comprehensive income and general ledger accounts disclosed the following:

1. Profit (after tax) for the year ending 30 June 2015 was $80 000.
2. Depreciation expense was recorded during the year on buildings, $13 800, and on equipment, $22 900.
3. An extension was added to the building at a cost of $300 000 cash.
4. Long-term investments with a cost of $90 000 were sold for $125 000.
5. Vacant land next to the company's factory was purchased for $129 000 with payment consisting of $39 000 cash and a loan payable for $90 000 due on 30 June 2018.
6. Debentures of $100 000 were issued for cash at nominal value.
7. 30 000 shares were issued at $3.80 per share.
8. Equipment was purchased for cash.
9. Net sales for the period were $875 600; cost of sales amounted to $525 300; other expenses (other than depreciation, carrying amount of investments sold, interest, and bad debts written off, $3500) amounted to $149 400.
10. Income tax paid during the year amounted to $73 700, and interest paid on liabilities amounted to $40 000.

GOLD LTD
Comparative Statements of Financial Position
as at 30 June

	2015	2014
CURRENT ASSETS		
Cash at bank	$ —	$ 74 600
Accounts receivable	127 200	111 300
Inventory	275 000	221 200
Prepaid expenses	22 800	23 000
	425 000	430 100
NON-CURRENT ASSETS		
Buildings	639 000	339 000
Accumulated depreciation – buildings	(111 400)	(97 600)
Equipment	361 200	331 200
Accumulated depreciation – equipment	(89 900)	(67 000)
Land	168 000	39 000
	966 900	544 600
Long-term investments	70 000	160 000
	$1 461 900	$1 134 700
CURRENT LIABILITIES		
Bank overdraft	$ 16 700	$ —
Bills payable (trade)	45 000	50 000
Accounts payable	170 000	168 000
Accrued expenses	10 500	14 000
Current tax liability	26 000	24 000
	268 200	256 000
NON CURRENT LIABILITIES		
Loan payable	240 000	150 000
Debentures due 1/9/20	300 000	200 000
	540 000	350 000
	$ 808 200	$ 606 000
EQUITY		
Share capital	$ 502 100	$ 388 100
Retained earnings	151 600	140 600
	$ 653 700	$ 528 700

Required

A. Prepare a statement of cash flows for the year ended 30 June 2015 using the direct method, and assuming that bank overdraft is part of the entity's cash management activities.

B. Prepare any notes required to be attached to the statement.

<hr />

LO 8

Problem 24.12 STATEMENT OF CASH FLOWS FOR A COMPANY ★★★

Strontium Ltd's comparative statements of financial position and statement of profit or loss and other comprehensive income for the year ended 30 June 2015 are shown on pages 1050–1.

Additional information

(a) New equipment was purchased at a cost of $67 400, paid in cash.

(b) Equipment that cost $42 200 and had a carrying amount of $20 000 was sold for cash.

(c) Additions to buildings were partly funded by a mortgage loan.

(d) Debentures were issued at nominal value ($100) for cash.

<hr />

(e) Share investments with a carrying amount of $32 200 were sold for cash at a profit.

(f) The company was given permission to pay income tax in one instalment.

(g) No interim dividends were paid during the year.

Required

A. Prepare the statement of cash flows for Strontium Ltd for the year ended 30 June 2015 in accordance with AASB 107, using the classifications shown in Appendix A to the standard.

B. Prepare the note showing the reconciliation of net cash from operating activities to profit for the year ended 30 June 2015.

STRONTIUM LTD
Comparative Statements of Financial Position
as at 30 June

	2015	2014
ASSETS		
Cash at bank	$ 70 000	$ 42 000
Bank bills	10 000	8 600
Deposits at call	6 400	5 000
Accounts receivable	49 300	37 800
Allowance for doubtful debts	(2 500)	(1 900)
Inventory	94 200	96 600
Prepaid expenses	10 800	4 200
Interest receivable	1 600	1 800
Share investments	35 600	67 800
Land	70 000	70 000
Buildings	360 000	240 000
Accum. depreciation – buildings	(104 400)	(94 500)
Equipment	180 000	154 800
Accum. depreciation – equipment	(57 900)	(69 600)
Patents (indefinite life)	14 400	12 200
	$737 500	$574 800
LIABILITIES AND EQUITY		
Accounts payable	$ 98 520	$ 92 560
Trade bills payable	2 000	1 400
Expenses payable	9 780	8 340
Interest payable	4 000	3 000
Current tax liability	14 400	15 000
Final dividend payable	34 800	32 000
Mortgage loan	40 000	—
Debentures (10%)	193 000	170 000
Share capital (ordinary shares, issued at $1)	295 440	184 900
Retained earnings	45 560	67 600
	$737 500	$574 800

STRONTIUM LTD
Statement of Profit or Loss and Other Comprehensive Income
for year ended 30 June 2015

INCOME		
Sales		$1 386 000
Interest income		4 360
Dividend income		7 200
Discount received		2 100
Gain on sale of share investments		22 600
		1 422 260
EXPENSES		
Cost of sales	$932 000	
Bad debts expense	2 800	
Loss on sale of equipment	1 600	
Depreciation – equipment	10 500	
Depreciation – buildings	9 900	
Discount allowed	950	
Interest expense	18 400	
Other expenses	418 950	1 395 100
Profit before income tax		27 160
Income tax expense		14 400
PROFIT		$ 12 760

Problem 24.13 CASH FLOW FROM OPERATING ACTIVITIES AND INCOME
TAX ENTRIES ★★★

The information overleaf relates to Cadmium Ltd.

Additional information in relation to the year ended 30 June 2015

(a) A loan payable of $45 000 was satisfied by conversion into 45 000 ordinary shares, valued at $1 each.
(b) The sold equipment cost $41 000.
(c) The company pays tax in four instalments on the normal due dates throughout the year. The first three instalments paid in cash were for $15 000, $12 750 and $16 000 respectively.

Required

A. Prepare *only* the cash flows from operating activities section of Cadmium Ltd's statement of cash flows for the year ended 30 June 2015 in accordance with IAS 7/AASB 107, using the direct method.

B. Reconstruct all journal entries in relation to income tax for the year ended 30 June 2015.

CADMIUM LTD
Comparative Statements of Financial Position
as at 30 June

	2015	2014
ASSETS		
Cash at bank	$ 52 700	$ 57 000
Accounts receivable	73 500	32 000
Allowance for doubtful debts	(7 000)	(6 000)
Inventory	54 000	10 000
Prepaid insurance	5 000	7 000
Land (at cost)	45 000	70 000
Buildings (at cost)	200 000	100 000
Accumulated depreciation – buildings	(21 000)	(11 000)
Equipment (at cost)	193 000	68 000
Accumulated depreciation – equipment	(28 000)	(10 000)
	$567 200	$317 000
LIABILITIES AND EQUITY		
Accounts payable	$ 75 200	$ 56 000
Interest payable	2 000	—
Other expenses payable	10 000	—
Current tax liability	11 800	15 000
Final dividend payable	19 800	4 800
Loan payable	75 000	130 000
Share capital (ordinary shares, issued at $1, fully paid)	220 000	60 000
General reserve	45 000	20 000
Retained earnings	108 400	31 200
	$567 200	$317 000

CADMIUM LTD
Statement of Profit or Loss and Other Comprehensive Income
for the year ended 30 June 2015

INCOME		
Sales		$890 000
Proceeds – sale of land		25 000
Proceeds – sale of equipment		34 000
		949 000
EXPENSES		
Cost of sales	$465 000	
Bad debts expense	10 000	
Carrying amount of land sold	25 000	
Carrying amount of equipment sold	36 000	
Depreciation	33 000	
Insurance expense	2 000	
Interest expense	12 000	
Salaries and wages	134 000	
Other expenses	42 000	759 000
Profit before income tax		190 000
Income tax expense		65 000
PROFIT		$125 000

Problem 24.14 STATEMENT OF CASH FLOWS AND ANALYSIS ★★★

The financial statements of Iron Ltd are provided below and overleaf.

IRON LTD
Comparative Statements of Financial Position
as at 30 June

	2014	2013	Changes
CURRENT ASSETS			
Bank bills (due 31 July)	$ 15 000	$ —	$ 15 000
Deposits at call	83 000	41 000	42 000
Accounts receivable	262 000	208 000	54 000
Allowance for doubtful debts	(14 500)	(11 500)	(3 000)
Trade bills receivable	15 000	12 000	3 000
Inventory	503 000	477 600	25 400
Prepaid expenses	40 000	45 000	(5 000)
	903 500	772 100	131 400
NON-CURRENT ASSETS			
Shares in Tin Ltd	225 000	375 000	(150 000)
Buildings (cost)	1 950 000	1350 000	600 000
Accumulated depreciation – buildings	(505 000)	(469 000)	(36 000)
Equipment (cost)	890 500	760 500	130 000
Accumulated depreciation – equipment	(289 500)	(348 000)	58 500
Land (cost)	500 000	500 000	0
	2 771 000	2 168 500	602 500
	3 674 500	2 940 600	733 900
CURRENT LIABILITIES			
Bank overdraft	63 000	107 000	(44 000)
Accounts payable	426 500	448 000	(21 500)
Trade bills payable	7 000	9 600	(2 600)
Expenses payable	33 750	29 500	4 250
Interest payable	25 000	22 500	2 500
Dividend payable	180 000	195 000	(15 000)
Current tax liability	77 300	64 500	12 800
	812 550	876 100	(63 550)
NON-CURRENT LIABILITIES			
Mortgage loan	180 000	100 000	80 000
Debentures	800 000	600 000	200 000
	980 000	700 000	280 000
	1 792 550	1 576 100	216 450
NET ASSETS	$1 881 950	$1 364 500	$ 517 450
EQUITY			
Share capital	$1 129 500	$ 889 500	$ 240 000
Retained earnings	752 450	475 000	277 450
	$1 881 950	$1 364 500	$ 517 450

IRON LTD
Statement of Profit or Loss and Other Comprehensive Income
for the year ended 30 June 2014

INCOME		
Sales revenue (net)	$6 580 000	
Dividends received	43 000	
Proceeds from sale of share investment	245 000	
Proceeds from sale of equipment	94 000	
Discount received	12 750	
Total income		$6 974 750
EXPENSES		
Cost of sales	3 475 000	
Carrying amount of shares sold	150 000	
Carrying amount of equipment sold	15 000	
Depreciation expense – equipment	46 500	
Depreciation expense – buildings	36 000	
Interest expense	73 000	
Bad debts expense	14 650	
Discount allowed	5 250	
Other expenses	2 411 100	6 226 500
Profit before income tax		748 250
Income tax expense		290 800
PROFIT		$ 457 450

IRON LTD
Statement of Changes in Equity
for the year ended 30 June 2014

	Share capital	Other reserves	Retained earnings	Total
Balance at 1/7/13	$ 889 500		$ 475 000	$1 364 500
Total comprehensive income for the period			457 450	457 450
Dividends declared			(180 000)	(180 000)
Issue of share capital	240 000			240 000
Balance at 30/6/14	$1 129 500		$ 752 450	$1 881 950

Additional information
During the year ended 30 June 2014, Iron Ltd entered into the following transactions relevant to the preparation of the statement of cash flows:
(a) Building additions were completed at a cost of $600 000 cash.
(b) New equipment was purchased at a cost of $250 000; $150 000 was paid in cash and the balance covered by arranging a long-term mortgage loan with Regal Finance Ltd.
(c) Equipment with a cost of $120 000 and accumulated depreciation of $105 000 was sold for $94 000 cash.
(d) Shares in Tin Ltd were sold for $245 000 cash.
(e) Debentures (9%) were issued at nominal value for cash, $200 000.
(f) An additional 40 000 ordinary shares were issued for cash for $6 per share.
(g) A cash dividend of $195 000 was paid during the year.
(h) $20 000 of mortgage due 30 June 2014 was repaid during the year.
(i) The company pays tax in four instalments, and the first three instalments have been paid in relation to the current year.

(j) The bank overdraft facility is used as part of the company's everyday cash management facilities.

Required

A. Prepare a statement of cash flows in accordance with accounting standards using the direct method.

B. Prepare notes to the statement to (1) reconcile cash at end shown in the statement of cash flows to the figures in the statement of financial position and (2) reconcile the net cash from operating activities to profit.

C. Comment on the company's cash flows during the year ended 30 June 2014 and cash position at 30 June 2014.

Problem 24.15 STATEMENT OF CASH FLOWS AND REPORT TO MANAGEMENT ★★★ **LO 6, 8**

The management of Aluminium Ltd is worried because the bank overdraft has increased by a substantial amount over the financial year ended 30 June 2015 despite a large profit and the introduction of additional capital. The internal comparative statements of financial position at 30 June 2014 and 2015 were as follows:

ALUMINIUM LTD Comparative Statements of Financial Position as at 30 June		
	2014	2015
EQUITY		
Share capital	$300 000	$385 000
Revaluation surplus	—	15 000
General reserve	50 000	85 000
Retained earnings	49 000	78 500
	$399 000	$563 500
NON-CURRENT ASSETS		
Land	$ 10 000	$ 25 000
Buildings	60 000	60 000
Accumulated depreciation – buildings	(30 000)	(35 000)
Plant and equipment	207 000	300 000
Accumulated depreciation – plant and equipment	(27 000)	(55 500)
	220 000	294 500
CURRENT ASSETS		
Petty cash	200	300
Accounts receivable	107 500	200 000
Allowance for doubtful debts	(10 000)	(20 000)
Inventory	182 500	305 500
	280 200	485 800
LESS: CURRENT LIABILITIES		
Accounts payable	36 200	29 300
Current tax liability	6 000	15 000
Bank overdraft	59 000	172 500
	101 200	216 800
Working capital	179 000	269 000
TOTAL NET ASSETS	$399 000	$563 500

The statement of profit or loss and other comprehensive income for the year ended 30 June 2015 for Aluminium Ltd, prepared for management purposes, is shown overleaf.

ALUMINIUM LTD
Statement of Profit or Loss and Other Comprehensive Income
for the year ended 30 June 2015

INCOME		
Sales revenue (net)		$550 000
Cost of sales	$277 000	
Less: Discount received	(750)	276 250
GROSS PROFIT		273 750
Proceeds from sale of plant and equipment		47 500
		321 250
EXPENSES		
Carrying amount of plant and equipment sold	$ 45 000	
Salaries and wages expense	60 250	
Depreciation on buildings	5 000	
Depreciation on plant and equipment	38 500	
Electricity expense	3 000	
Bad debts expense	30 000	181 750
Profit before tax		139 500
Income tax expense	50 000	
Underprovision for income tax	2 500	52 500
PROFIT FOR THE PERIOD		87 000
Other comprehensive income:		
Gain on revaluation of land		15 000
TOTAL COMPREHENSIVE INCOME FOR THE YEAR		$102 000

Additional information

(a) The land was revalued upwards during the year by $15 000.

(b) During the year, a dividend of $22 500 had been paid.

(c) Plant and equipment which had originally cost $55 000 and had been depreciated by $10 000 was sold during the year for $47 500.

(d) The company pays income tax in four instalments and the first three instalments have been paid. For the year ended 30 June 2014, the ATO issued an amended assessment of $8500 resulting in an underprovision of $2500 being recorded in 2015.

Required

A. Prepare a statement of cash flows as per current accounting standards using the direct method.

B. Prepare a note reconciling cash flows from operating activities to profit.

C. Prepare a brief report to management explaining the flow of cash and cash equivalents.

DECISION ANALYSIS

Analysing a statement of cash flows

The following statement of cash flows was produced by the trainee accountant for Grey Ltd for the year ended 30 June 2014, the company's first year of operations.

The trainee accountant was quite excited that the company's statement of cash flows had shown an excellent result. However, the accountant for the company was not so sure, and was quite surprised by the result. The accountant thought that the company had performed poorly during the year and suspected that the statement of cash flows had been prepared incorrectly. The cash balance at the beginning of the year was $70 000.

SOURCES OF CASH	
Sales of inventory	$185 000
Sale of ordinary shares in the company	210 000
Sale of investments	40 000
Depreciation of plant and equipment	27 500
Issue of a bill payable for purchase of delivery vehicle	10 000
Interest on investments	3 000
TOTAL SOURCES OF CASH	475 500
APPLICATIONS OF CASH	
Purchase of inventory	129 000
Operating expenses (including depreciation)	80 000
Purchase of plant and equipment	170 000
Purchase of investments (details of sale above)	37 500
Purchase of delivery vehicle by issuing a bill payable	10 000
Buyback of the company's shares	5 000
Interest on bill payable	1 500
TOTAL APPLICATIONS OF CASH	433 000
NET INCREASE IN CASH	$ 42 500

Required

A. Using the information provided, prepare a statement of cash flows in good format using the direct method. The only non-cash items are depreciation and the gain from sale of the investments.

B. Has the company performed well or poorly? Justify your conclusion.

COMMUNICATION AND LEADERSHIP

Reporting on cash flows

In groups of three, obtain the latest statement of cash flows for a company (other than JB Hi-Fi Limited). Financial reports are available from company websites, and usually from internet sites subscribed to by university libraries.

Required

For the statement of cash flows you have obtained, prepare a report of at least one page in length outlining the strengths and weaknesses of the company's cash flows from operating, investing and financing activities. Does your group believe the company is in a sound position in terms of its ability to generate positive cash flows? Explain your position to the class.

ETHICS AND GOVERNANCE

Reeling in the bank

Reel Estate Pty Ltd is a real estate company that specialises in selling holiday homes in the seaside resort of Bygone Bay to customers from the nearby city of Darwin. The company owned an office building overlooking the beach but during the year it sold this building and rented an office in the central business district of Bygone Bay. The owner of Reel Estate Pty Ltd, Bob Budgie, has a domineering personality — fortunately for his staff, he spends most of his time fishing.

Natascha Nitschke prepares the accounts for Reel Estate Pty Ltd each year and has just completed the draft version of the statement of cash flows. When Bob saw the draft statement, he was outraged as the cash flows from operating activities and the cash at the end of the year were both very low. The cash flow from investing activities was very good because of the sale of the company's office, which had been purchased many years earlier and had realised a very large positive cash inflow and profit on sale.

Bob was hoping to borrow a large amount of money from the bank to buy a piece of land with a good view of the beach on which to build an office with a boat shed attached so he could go fishing more often. He was concerned that the low cash flow from operating activities would deter the bank from lending him the money he wanted. Bob ordered Natascha to transfer the sale of the building out of cash flows from investing activities and into cash flows from operating activities — Reel Estate Pty Ltd was in the business of buying and selling properties anyway, so it would be reasonable to classify the sale of the office building as part of its normal activities. Natascha did not think this was correct but did as she was told.

Required

A. Who are the stakeholders in this situation?

B. Are there ethical issues involved here? If so, what are they?

C. What would you do if you were Natascha Nitschke?

FINANCIAL ANALYSIS

Refer to the latest financial report of JB Hi-Fi Limited on its website, www.jbhifi.com.au, and answer the questions below using the consolidated statement of comprehensive income (income statement), statement of financial position (balance sheet), statement of changes in equity, statement of cash flows, and notes to the consolidated financial statements.

1. For the purposes of the statement of cash flows, how is cash defined?

2. Were there any non-cash financing or investing transactions that occurred during the last financial year? If so, explain the nature of such transactions. Were there any non-cash transactions in the previous year? If so, explain the nature of these transactions.

3. What was the net increase/decrease in cash for the current financial year? How does this compare with the previous year?

4. How does JB Hi-Fi Limited classify dividends and interest received and paid in the statement of cash flows?

5. Identify the major investing and financing activities undertaken in the last financial year. How do these major activities compare with the previous year's activities?

6. Comment on the changes over the past year in JB Hi-Fi Limited's cash position.

Chapter 25

Analysis and interpretation of financial statements

Learning objectives

After studying this chapter, you should be able to:

1. identify the major sources of information about entities for the purpose of analysing their performance and financial position (p. 1056)

2. outline the various analytical techniques commonly used to assess an entity's performance and financial position (pp. 1056–9)

3. carry out horizontal, trend and vertical analyses of an entity's financial statements and be able to interpret these analyses (pp. 1059–61)

4. conduct ratio analysis to assess an entity's profitability (pp. 1061–6), liquidity (pp. 1066–9), and financial stability (pp. 1069–71)

5. analyse and interpret the ratio information provided by a statement of cash flows (pp. 1071–6)

6. describe the limitations of traditional financial statement analysis (pp. 1076–7)

7. explain the impact of capital markets research on the role of financial statement analysis (p. 1077).

Don't be fooled by illusory numbers

So often investors and entrepreneurs look at the wrong financial numbers and ratios when analysing companies. They focus obsessively on the latest year's pre-tax profits, or perhaps post-tax earnings. But these can often be manipulated, or temporary. What matters much more are underlying sales, strong gross margins and free cash flow. Study these numbers over several years to see if a business really owns a solid franchise.

When an enterprise enjoys consistently solid sales as a percentage of capital employed, and high gross margins, then it should by rights make a decent bottom line and an attractive return on investment. And by high gross margins, I mean 60 per cent or more. Companies that enjoy this scale of margins — and keep their fixed costs within reasonable boundaries — should prosper.

Of course, companies with huge mark-ups over their raw costs are more vulnerable to being undercut by discounters. But it is always better to start with a lot of margin than a low gross margin…

Decades ago, shares were valued on a multiple of post-tax earnings — a P/E ratio. More recently, acquirers have adopted the private equity model using the ratio of enterprise value to earnings before interest depreciation and amortisation (EV/EBITDA).

A surprising proportion of companies never really shows a genuine free cash return — they are essentially a charity for their staff and customers. I used to feel that about the nightclub business: even though you could make juicy profits for a few years, there needed to be a complete reinvention every three years or so — new lighting, sound and so on — just to compete with newcomers. That investment typically represented three years' profits. Effectively the whole undertaking just stood still. I fear the industry has become even tougher in recent times.

So my advice is to search out industries where you can capture at least a 60 per cent gross margin. And when examining a company's accounts, focus on actual cash flow after cash costs, rather than illusory numbers such as earnings or EBITDA.

Source: Excerpts from Luke Johnson, 'Don't be fooled by illusory numbers', *Financial Times.*

Chapter preview

The general purpose financial reports issued by entities, in both the private and the public sectors, are used by various parties to evaluate, among other things, the entity's financial performance and financial position. In the previous chapter, we demonstrated how the statement of cash flows could be used to supplement the traditional financial statements in analysing the operating, financing and investing activities of an entity. In this chapter we focus on the basic techniques commonly used to analyse an entity's financial statements so that interested parties can make economic decisions, e.g. to buy or sell shares, or to lend money to the entity. General purpose financial reports are emphasised because they are the main source of financial data for most outside users.

The scene setter highlights the importance of understanding the numbers reported in the financial statements and including an analysis of cash flow when analysing financial performance. The techniques of financial analysis are covered in this chapter.

25.1 Sources of financial information

Learning objective 1

Identify the major sources of information about entities for the purpose of analysing their performance and financial position

An entity's financial statements, with their schedules and explanatory notes, are the main means by which management communicates information about the entity to users of general purpose financial reports. In addition to data published by an entity, a wealth of information is available from other sources. Financial advisory services publish financial data for most companies, and details of company reports are generally available in most public libraries and libraries of universities. Much information is also available on the internet, e.g. see the website of the Australian Securities Exchange (ASX) at www.asx.com.au and individual company websites. Economic and financial newspapers and journals are also useful sources of information.

It is also useful to compare data of the entity under study with that of similar or competing entities. Industry data are available from Dun & Bradstreet, and from databases such as the ASX. Individual company and industry analyses are also available from stockbroking firms.

25.2 The need for analytical techniques

Learning objective 2

Outline the various analytical techniques commonly used to assess an entity's performance and financial position

The annual reports of most public companies contain a huge amount of information, which can be difficult to interpret and understand. Since the published financial statements are frequently the only source of financial information on which users base their decisions, such as whether to invest in the company, advance credit to the company, or accept employment with the company, it is useful to have tools available to assist with the analysis and interpretation of the financial information.

Much of the information contained in the various sources of financial data is expressed in monetary terms. Although dollar amounts are important, they tend to be of limited usefulness when viewed in isolation. This is because individual dollar amounts do not reveal relationships that exist between items in the financial statements, nor do they provide an indication of whether a specific number is good or bad. For example, if a business reports a profit of $1 000 000 for the current year, how could the user assess whether this profit figure is good or bad? The number itself must be compared with other information, such as (1) last year's profit, (2) the current year's sales, (3) the profits of other businesses in the same industry, or (4) some benchmark figure established by the statement user.

To assist in the analysis of the dollar amounts reported and make the numbers more meaningful, dollar values reported are frequently converted into percentages or ratios.

Percentage analysis and *ratio analysis* are two tools that have been developed to provide an efficient means by which a decision maker can identify important relationships between items in the same statements and trends in financial data. These tools are examined in more detail later in this chapter. The information produced by the analyses is used both to analyse past performance, and to forecast an entity's ability to pay its debts in the future, as well as to operate at a satisfactory level of profitability.

The specific percentages and ratios selected by each user of the financial information will differ depending on the purpose of their analysis and evaluation. For example, some users may be concerned with the entity's ability to generate sufficient cash to pay its immediate liabilities and fund ongoing operations, and will focus on ratios that measure this, while others may be more concerned with the entity's ability to meet longer term obligations and finance business growth in the future, and will therefore focus on different ratios and trends.

To facilitate a discussion and demonstrate the use of the analytical techniques, the income statement, statement of financial position, statement of changes in equity and some additional data are presented for Gordon Ltd during a 2-year period (2013–14) in the first two columns of figures 25.1, 25.2 and 25.3 (p. 1058). To enable the calculation of certain ratios for the 2013 financial year, a 30 June 2012 statement of financial position is also included in figure 25.1. Relevant information contained in the notes to the financial statements is included in figure 25.4 (p. 1059). As discussed previously, for the statement analysis of an individual entity to be useful, the percentages and ratios must be compared with other data or standards. In the following discussion, specific calculations and interpretations will be presented. Rather than stating the need for comparison every time a particular analysis is performed, it will be assumed that this additional step is taken by the user in forming an opinion about the information revealed by the analysis.

Entities who report financial information in accordance with accounting standards are required to include in their annual report financial statements for the current year and the preceding financial year (**comparative statements**). Many annual reports also include selected summary data for 5 years or more.

Figure 25.1 Comparative statements of financial position, horizontal change during the year, and common size statements

GORDON LTD
Comparative Statements of Financial Position
as at 30 June 2014, 2013 and 2012

	Year ended 30 June			Horizontal change during the year 2013–14		Common size* statements	
	2014 ($000)	2013 ($000)	2012 ($000)	Dollar amount ($000)	Per cent	2014	2013
Current assets							
Cash and cash equivalents	$ 770	$ 740	$ 750	$ 30	4.1	10.4	11.7
Trade and other receivables	1 460	1 290	1 320	170	13.2	19.6	20.5
Inventories	2 010	1 770	1 860	240	13.6	27.0	28.1
Other current assets	100	100	100	—	—	1.3	1.6
Total current assets	4 340	3 900	4 030	440	11.3	58.3	61.9
Non-current assets							
Other financial assets	400	500	500	(100)	(20.0)	5.4	7.9
Property, plant and equipment	2 600	1 800	1 770	800	44.4	35.0	28.6
Other non-current assets	100	100	100	—	—	1.3	1.6
Total non-current assets	3 100	2 400	2 370	700	29.2	41.7	38.1
Total assets	7 440	6 300	6 400	1 140	18.1	100.0	100.0
Current liabilities							
Trade and other payables (Note 14)	1 702	1 528	1 835	174	11.4	22.9	24.3
Current tax payable	58	72	65	(14)	19.4	0.8	1.1
Total current liabilities	1 760	1 600	1 900	160	10.0	23.7	25.4
Non-current liabilities							
Long-term borrowings	1 900	1 700	1 800	200	11.8	25.5	27.0
Total non-current liabilities	1 900	1 700	1 800	200	11.8	25.5	27.0
Total liabilities	3 660	3 300	3 700	360	10.9	49.2	52.4
Net assets	$3 780	$3 000	$2 700	$ 780	26.0	50.8	47.6
Equity							
Share capital (Note 23)	$2 302	$1 900	$1 900	$ 402	21.2	30.9	30.2
Retained earnings	1 478	1 100	800	378	34.4	19.9	17.4
Total equity	$3 780	$3 000	$2 700	$ 780	26.0	50.8	47.6

*Calculations are explained on pages 1059–61.

Figure 25.2 Comparative income statements, horizontal change during the year, and common size statements

GORDON LTD
Comparative Income Statements
for the years ended 30 June 2014 and 2013

	Year ended 30 June		Horizontal change during the year		Common size statements (per cent of revenues)	
	2014 ($000)	2013 ($000)	Dollar amount ($000)	Per cent	2014	2013
Revenue (Note 2)	$10 320	$9 582	$ 738	7.7	100.0	100.0
Expenses, excluding finance costs (Note 4)	9 366	8 425	941	11.2	90.8	87.9
Finance costs	252	230	22	9.6	2.4	2.4
Profit before income tax	702	927	(225)	(24.3)	6.8	9.7
Income tax expense	226	287	(61)	(21.3)	2.2	3.0
Profit	$ 476	$ 640	$(164)	25.6	4.6	6.7

Figure 25.3 Comparative statements of changes in equity, horizontal change during the year, and common size statements

GORDON LTD
Comparative Statements of Changes in Equity
for the years ended 30 June 2014 and 2013

	Year ended 30 June		Horizontal change during the year		Common size statements	
	2014 ($000)	2013 ($000)	Dollar amount ($000)	Per cent	2014	2013
Share capital (Note 23)						
Ordinary:						
Balance at start of period	$1 600	$1 600	—	—	69.5	84.2
Issue of share capital	402	—	$ 402	—	17.5	—
Balance at end of period	2 002	1 600	402	25.1	87.0	84.2
Preference:						
Balance at start of period	300	300	—	—	13.0	15.8
Balance at end of period	300	300	—	—	13.0	15.8
Total share capital	$2 302	$1 900	$ 402	21.2	100.0	100.0
Retained earnings						
Balance at start of period	$1 100	$ 800	$ 300	37.5	74.4	72.7
Total comprehensive income for the year*	476	640	(164)	(25.6)	32.2	58.2
Dividend paid — ordinary	(68)	(310)	(242)	(78.1)	(4.6)	(28.2)
Dividend paid — preference	(30)	(30)	—	—	(2.0)	(2.7)
Balance at end of period	$1 478	$1 100	$ 378	34.4	100.0	100.0

* There are assumed to be no items of other income for the periods and therefore profit and comprehensive income are the same.

Figure 25.4 Notes to the financial statements and additional information

Notes to the financial statements

		2014 ($000)	2013 ($000)	2012 ($000)
Note 2:	**Revenue**			
	Sales revenue (net)	$10 320	$9 582	
Note 4:	**Expenses, excluding finance costs**			
	Cost of sales	$7 719	$6 975	
	Selling and distribution expenses	1 030	800	
	Administration expenses	617	650	
Note 14:	**Trade and other payables — current**			
	Trade payables	$1 660	$1 500	$1 800
	Other	42	28	35
Note 23:	**No. of shares issued at end of year**			
	Ordinary shares	1 500 000	1 200 000	
	Preference shares	100 000	100 000	

Additional information

The Directors' Report disclosed that for the year 2014 the dividend paid to ordinary shareholders was $68 000, and the dividend paid to preference shareholders was $30 000.

The information presented for Gordon Ltd in figure 25.1 (p. 1057) includes two columns showing changes in individual line item figures between 2014 and 2013. This is referred to as **horizontal analysis**. It shows the difference between the preceding year's figure (the base year — in this example 2013) and the current year's figure (in this example 2014), both in dollars and as a percentage of the base year figure. Horizontal analysis is discussed in more detail later in this chapter.

The information for Gordon Ltd also shows **common size statements** for both 2014 and 2013. Common size statements are a type of **vertical analysis**, in which the individual line item dollar amounts are restated as a percentage of another line item in the same financial year (the base amount). Vertical analysis is discussed in more detail later in this chapter.

25.3 Percentage analysis

Horizontal analysis

As mentioned previously, horizontal analysis compares individual line items across two or more financial years. Placing comparative financial statements side by side (as shown in figures 25.1, 25.2 and 25.3) facilitates a logical presentation of the horizontal analysis.

Because it is difficult to compare absolute dollar amounts, the difference between the figures for 2 separate years is calculated in dollar amounts and percentage change. In calculating the increase or decrease in dollar amounts, the earlier statement is used as the base year. The percentage change is calculated by dividing the increase or decrease from the base year in dollars by the base-year amount. For example, from 2013 to 2014 the cash and cash equivalents of Gordon Ltd increased by $30 000, from $740 000 to $770 000 (figure 25.1). Whether a change of $30 000 is significant or not is difficult to assess since it is an absolute amount. The percentage change from 2013 to 2014 is 4.1%, calculated as follows:

$$\text{Percentage increase} = \frac{30\,000}{740\,000} \times 100 = 4.1\%$$

This percentage is easier to interpret by the user — perhaps a 4.1% change would not be considered to be a significant change. Note that a percentage change can be calculated only when a positive amount is reported in the base year; the amount of change cannot be stated as a percentage if the item in the base year is reported as a negative or a zero amount.

Learning objective 3

Carry out horizontal, trend and vertical analyses of an entity's financial statements and be able to interpret these analyses

The objectives of performing a horizontal analysis are to determine whether there are changes that have occurred that are significant, and therefore warrant further investigation. Note that changes could be favourable or unfavourable — both should be investigated to establish the cause of the movements, and to consider whether the trends revealed are expected to continue in the future.

Scanning the horizontal percentage changes shown in figure 25.1, the user may focus on, for example, property, plant and equipment, which shows a 44.4% (or $800 000) increase from 2013 to 2014. It appears that the company has purchased additional assets, possibly to expand its operations. At this stage, it may be useful to ask questions related to this, such as: How did the company finance the asset acquisition? This should direct the user's attention to other areas of the financial statements to seek clarification. Since the cash and cash equivalents assets have increased from 2013 to 2014, it seems unlikely that all of the new assets were purchased with cash (although some cash may have been used). Long-term borrowings have increased by $200 000 from 2013 to 2014 — it is likely that this was part of the source of finance for the new assets. Share capital increased by $402 000 — the proceeds from the additional shares issued are also likely to have been at least partly utilised in the purchase of the new assets.

The horizontal analysis presented with the comparative income statements in figure 25.2 show some interesting trends. Although revenue increased by 7.7%, expenses increased by a greater percentage (note 4 in figure 25.4 reveals that both cost of sales and selling and distribution expenses increased from 2013 to 2014). As a result of the expenses increasing by a greater percentage than revenue, the company was unable to maintain its profit level   the profit before tax decreased by 24.3%. This may show that the company was unable to control its expenses as well as it should have, or possibly that suppliers increased their prices (reflected in the relative increase in cost of sales) and Gordon was unable to pass these increases on to its customers through higher selling prices.

Trend analysis

When financial data are available for 3 or more years, trend analysis is a technique commonly used by financial analysts to assess the entity's track record and growth prospects. In this analysis, the earliest period is the base period, with all subsequent periods compared with the base. It is assumed that the base year selected is fairly typical of an entity's operations. For example, assume that revenue and profit for a business were reported for the last 5 years as shown below:

	2010	2011	2012	2013	2014
Revenue	$1 000 000	$1 050 000	$1 120 000	$1 150 000	$1 220 000
Profit	200 000	206 000	218 000	222 000	232 000

It is clear that the dollar amounts of both sales revenue and profit are increasing. However, the relationship between the change in sales and profit can be more easily interpreted if the changes are expressed in percentages (with the base year 2010 being 100%) by dividing the amount reported for each subsequent year by the base year amount, thus producing:

	2010	2011	2012	2013	2014
Revenue	100	105	112	115	122
Profit	100	103	109	111	116

Now it can be seen that profit is growing more slowly than revenue. The level of profit is affected not only by revenues, but also by expenses. It is possible that the entity's cost of sales is increasing faster than selling prices. Or the increase in revenues may be a result of granting more liberal credit terms that are resulting in larger bad debt expenses. The point is that other revenue and expense data must also be reviewed before drawing conclusions about the significance of one particular item. The overall objective is to evaluate various related trends and try to assess whether the trend can be expected to continue.

Although the previous example covered only two items in the financial statements, trend analysis could be carried out on all items in the income statement, statement of financial position and statement of changes in equity for which figures for 3 or more years are available.

Vertical analysis

Vertical analysis involves restating the dollar amount of each item reported in an individual financial statement as a percentage of a specific item in the same statement, referred to as the base amount. The analysis is done within the same year, and it is also useful to compare common size statements across different years to identify trends in the relationships.

Figures 25.1, 25.2 and 25.3 show common size statements for Gordon Ltd for 2014 and 2013. A review of the common size statement of financial position, for example, shows all figures as a percentage of the total assets (the base amount). The 2014 statement shows that property, plant and equipment represented 35% of total assets ($2 600 000 / $7 440 000), whereas in 2013 it represented 28.6% of total assets. From the previous discussion, we already know that Gordon invested $800 000 in new property, plant and equipment, so the increase in the relative percentage of total assets is expected.

Vertical analysis is useful for comparing data from one year to another, from one entity to another, or comparing an entity's percentages to averages that exist within the industry in which the entity operates.

25.4 Ratio analysis

Learning objective 4

Conduct ratio analysis to assess an entity's profitability, liquidity, and financial stability

The analysis tools discussed so far have focused on trends and relationships within a single financial statement. Ratio analysis provides an additional dimension to the interpretation of financial statements, by enabling the comparison of numbers and relationships between different financial statements as well as within single financial statements. A financial statement **ratio** is calculated by dividing the dollar amount of one or more items reported in the financial statements by the dollar amount of one or more other items reported.

As with the other analysis tools discussed in this chapter, ratio analysis is only useful if the ratios calculated are compared with others (such as the same entity over time, other entities within the same industry, or a benchmark ratio set by the user).

In performing a ratio analysis, it is often useful to classify the ratios that are calculated according to the primary purpose of the analysis, i.e. those commonly used to evaluate *profitability, liquidity* and *financial stability*. There are several alternative calculations used in practice for the same ratios. The key is to use the same calculation method consistently to identify a trend.

The discussion that follows illustrates ratio analysis using information for Gordon Ltd given in figures 25.1 to 25.4 and is presented in the categories mentioned above. Note that all figures used in the calculations are in $000s.

Profitability ratios

Profitability analysis is important to most users of financial statements. Investors (or potential investors) evaluate profitability to assess the likelihood of a positive return from their investment. Creditors (long-term and short-term) and suppliers use profitability to assess the risk of the entity not being able to pay its debts. Employees and unions are interested in assessing whether the entity is financially sound and in a position to meet its commitments.

The results of a profitability analysis are used to evaluate past profits, identify trends in profitability, and to consider how past results may be useful in predicting future profits.

When assessing profitability, relationships between items in the income statement that result in profits are analysed, as well as relationships between profits reported in the income statement and related items in the statement of financial position.

Poor profits can result from many factors, such as inadequate sales volumes, escalating costs (cost of sales and other expenses), poor product quality and increased competition in the industry. A profitability analysis also involves assessing the adequacy of profits generated from the assets the entity has invested in.

Profit margin

Profit margin (also called return on sales or profit ratio) is calculated during a vertical analysis of the income statement. It reflects the portion of each dollar of revenue that results in profit and is calculated by dividing profit from continuing operations by revenues:

$$\text{Profit margin} = \frac{\text{Profit (after income tax)}}{\text{Revenues}}$$

For Gordon Ltd the ratios are:

2014	2013
$\dfrac{476}{10\,320} \times 100 = 4.6\%$	$\dfrac{640}{9\,582} \times 100 = 6.7\%$

What do these results reveal? For 2014, each dollar of sales revenue produced 4.6 cents in profits. This is considerably lower than the 2013 profit ratio, and should be investigated further to establish the reason for the decline — note that in 2014 the revenue increased, but the expenses increased by more than revenue, resulting in a lower profit margin. The ratio could be compared with competing entities. If, for example, other entities in the industry are achieving profit ratios of around 4%, then the 4.6% achieved by Gordon appears fairly good even though it is less than the previous year.

Gross profit margin

Gross profit is calculated as sales less cost of sales. It represents the difference between what a business sells its goods or services for, and what it cost the business to buy the goods or provide the services. The bigger the gross profit, the greater the markup the business adds to its costs to arrive at its selling price. Presenting the gross profit as a ratio or percentage is a useful way to assess the size and adequacy of this markup. The gross profit ratio (or gross profit margin) is calculated as:

$$\text{Gross profit margin} = \frac{\text{Gross profit}}{\text{Net sales}}$$

For Gordon Ltd the ratios are:

2014	2013
$\dfrac{2\,601^*}{10\,320} \times 100 = 25.2\%$	$\dfrac{2\,607}{9\,582} \times 100 = 27.2\%$

*Calculated as sales revenue ($10 320) less cost of sales ($7719) given in notes 2 and 4 in figure 25.3. The 2013 calculation is done on the same basis.

The 2014 ratio reveals that every dollar of sales generated by Gordon earns the company 25.2 cents of gross profit. Another way to interpret this is that every dollar of sales costs the company 74.8 cents ($1 − 25.2 cents). The gross profit margin of Gordon has declined from 2013 to 2014, which may indicate that the costs of goods have increased and the increased costs were not passed on to its customers in full, or that there were more returned sales (due perhaps to faulty goods being sold) in 2014 which increased costs but not revenue. A declining gross profit may also indicate that there has been theft of goods, and for this reason gross profit should be carefully monitored by retailers, particularly small retailers that use a periodic inventory system. Note also that a declining gross profit margin is likely to result in a lower profit margin — this has been the case for Gordon as illustrated in the previous ratio.

The gross profit margins achieved by entities vary from one industry to another. For example, in general, a supermarket chain would have a relatively low gross profit margin as the turnover of goods is very quick, and the markup tends to be low, whereas a jewellery store generally would have a high gross profit margin with low turnover of sales and higher markup on costs.

Return on total assets

The return on total assets measures the amount of profit generated by the assets that are employed in the business. It reflects the efficiency with which management uses the resources at their disposal. Funds invested in assets are used to generate profits. The greater the profits earned from the asset base, the more efficiently the assets are being used. One word of caution: the results shown by this ratio are dependent on the valuation method chosen by management to value some of their assets. Before comparing or concluding on the strength of this ratio, therefore, it is important to consider the valuation methods used.

The ratio is determined as follows:

$$\text{Return on total assets} = \frac{\text{Profit before income tax} + \text{Finance costs}}{\text{Average total assets}}$$

Note that finance costs (interest expenses) are added back to profit before tax in the numerator (the top line in the ratio calculation) to remove the effect of the method of financing the acquisition of the assets. If the assets were acquired with debt (such as a loan), then the entity would have to pay interest on the debt, which reduces its profits, but does not affect the efficiency with which the assets are used in the operations of the business. Profit before tax is used rather than the after-tax figure, so that the ratio is not affected by external taxing policies. Average total assets is used in the denominator because the profits were produced by using assets employed throughout the period rather than at one point in time.

The management of Gordon Ltd produced a rate of return on average total assets of 13.9% in 2014 and 18.2% in 2013 as calculated below:[1]

2014	**2013**
$\dfrac{702 + 252}{(6300 + 7440)/2} \times 100 = 13.9\%$	$\dfrac{927 + 230}{(6400 + 6300)/2} \times 100 = 18.2\%$

During 2014, management through its ordinary activities produced 13.9 cents in profit before tax for every dollar invested in assets, compared with 18.2 cents in 2013. The decrease in rates is significant and results from a combination of decreased profit and an increased investment base. The horizontal analysis performed previously highlighted the increase in property, plant and equipment during 2014 — this was the major reason for the increase in total assets from 2013 to 2014. It may be that the new assets had not yet been fully employed by the end of 2014, resulting in a lower return on total assets ratio.

Return on equity

The return on equity (also called rate of return on ordinary equity or return on shareholders' funds) measures the rate at which profits are earned from funds invested by ordinary shareholders. The return is affected by the extent of use of **gearing** or **leverage** by the entity. Gearing or leverage refers to the amount of debt finance that is used relative to equity finance. Debt finance consists predominantly of borrowed funds (such as loans) or other fixed-return securities issued by the entity (such as preference shares). The amount that has to be paid to providers of debt finance (in the form of interest and preference dividends) is fixed, and has to be paid before the ordinary shareholders can receive a dividend. Ordinary shareholders are interested in assessing whether management of the entity have utilised debt finance effectively — be earning a return on the debt funds greater than the cost of those funds.

The return may be calculated as:

$$\text{Return on equity} = \frac{\text{Profit} - \text{Preference dividends}}{\text{Average ordinary equity}}$$

The preference dividend (which is disclosed in the statement of changes in equity) is subtracted from profit to calculate the profits to which ordinary shareholders are entitled. Some of these profits may be paid out as dividends, and some are generally retained to finance growth and earn a return in the future — this is discussed in a later ratio.

---

1. In the denominator, the sum of the beginning and ending total assets is divided by 2 to determine the average of these two amounts. If sufficient information were available, a monthly or quarterly average would be preferred to minimise the effects of seasonal fluctuations.

Ordinary equity is total equity less equity of preference shareholders (note that retained earnings are also part of ordinary equity — these are profits earned in the past which were not paid out in dividends but are still available to ordinary shareholders).

The calculations for Gordon Ltd are:

2014

$$\frac{476 - 30}{(2700 + 3480)/2} \times 100 = 14.4\%$$

2013

$$\frac{640 - 30}{(2400 + 2700)/2} \times 100 = 23.9\%$$

Preference share capital of $300 000 is removed from the calculation of average equity figures (see figure 25.3). Both these rates are higher than the returns calculated on total assets because the company earned a return on the assets financed by the debt providers and preference shareholders greater than the interest or dividends paid to them. However, the percentage decreased from 23.9% to 14.4%, a decrease worthy of further investigation. An examination of the figures shows that profits decreased in 2014, and long-term borrowings increased. The combination of these two factors will have contributed to the decrease in the return on equity.

Earnings per share

Earnings per share (EPS) on ordinary shares is a commonly quoted ratio, can be obtained from the notes of a listed company's financial statements, and is frequently quoted in newspapers in the stock exchange reports. This ratio calculates the amount of profit that has been earned per issued ordinary share, and is calculated as:

$$EPS = \frac{Profit\ (after\ income\ tax) - Preference\ dividends}{Weighted\ average\ number\ of\ ordinary\ shares\ issued}$$

For Gordon Ltd, the EPS for the two years is:

2014

$$\frac{476 - 30}{(1500 \times 6/12) + (1200 \times 6/12)} = 33.0c$$

2013

$$\frac{640 - 30}{1200} = 50.8c$$

The weighted average number of shares in 2014 is calculated assuming that 300 000 additional shares were issued in the middle of the year (see note 23 in figure 25.3). This ratio shows that for the year ended 30 June 2014, the company earned a profit of 33.0 cents per ordinary share issued, as opposed to 50.8 cents per share in 2013. The significant drop in EPS is due to a combination of the decline in profits, and the increase in the number of ordinary shares in issue in 2014 compared with 2013.

BUSINESS KNOWLEDGE

Profit and revenue — the key difference

ONE of the biggest lessons every small business owner needs to understand is the difference between profit and revenue.

Revenue is all the money a business earns before expenses such as taxes, wages and rent are taken into consideration.

Profit, on the other hand, is the money the business earns after all its expenses have been paid.

While it's important to have a handle on the revenue the business earns to make sure incomings cover outgoings, it's the profit figure that really matters.

The best business owners are focused on consistently trying to improve their profit margins.

How do they do this?

There are two main steps.

The first step is to try to reduce business costs. Cost reduction means constantly looking at ways to reduce every day expenses such as wages, utilities and phone bills.

The second step is to increase the amount the business charges for its products and services. Increasing prices is something that can be harder to achieve than cost reduction — especially if you operate in a commoditised market.

Although you won't be able to raise your prices as frequently as you can monitor your expenses, it's a good idea to regularly review your pricing structure to see if there are opportunities to make some changes to help increase your profits.

The worst thing you can do from a profit perspective is maintain your prices at the same level for years on end, while at the same time absorb rising costs. Why not look at the relationship between your costs and your prices to see if you can make some changes to increase your profit margin this year?

Source: News.com.au, 'Profit and revenue — the key difference', www.news.com.au.

Price–earnings ratio and earnings yield

The price–earnings ratio (P/E ratio) is calculated by dividing the market price of an ordinary share by the earnings per share:

$$P/E \text{ ratio} = \frac{\text{Market price per ordinary share}}{\text{Earnings per ordinary share}}$$

This ratio can only be calculated for companies that are quoted on the stock exchange and have a market price, and indicates how much an investor would have to pay in the market for each dollar of earnings. It enhances a statement user's ability to compare the market value of one ordinary share relative to profits with that of other entities.

Assuming an average market price of $1.20 per share for Gordon Ltd ordinary shares in 2014, the P/E ratio is:

$$\frac{\$1.20}{33.0c} = 3.6 \text{ times}$$

The ordinary shares of Gordon Ltd are said to be selling for 3.6 times current earnings.

P/E ratios vary widely between industries and reflect investors' expectations for a company. High P/E ratios are generally associated with growth companies or financially strong 'blue chip' companies that have good future prospects.

The reciprocal of the P/E ratio is known as earnings yield. Earnings yield indicates the average rate of return available to a prospective investor if an investment is made in the company's shares at the current market price, and is calculated as follows:

$$\text{Earnings yield} = \frac{\text{Earnings per ordinary share}}{\text{Market price per ordinary share}}$$

For Gordon Ltd, earnings yield (assuming a market price of $1.20 per share for 2014) is:

$$\frac{33.0c}{\$1.20} \times 100 - 27.5\%$$

Thus, if an investor buys one share in Gordon Ltd at a market price of $1.20, the investor can expect to receive an average return of 27.5% at current levels of profitability. Note that the P/E ratio and earnings yield would change every time the quoted share price changes.

Dividend yield and dividend payout ratio

Dividend yield is calculated as:

$$\text{Dividend yield} = \frac{\text{Annual dividend per ordinary share}}{\text{Market price per ordinary share}}$$

Cash dividends of $68 000 (4.5c per share) were paid during 2014 to the ordinary shareholders of Gordon Ltd (see figure 25.3). Assuming a market price of $1.20 per share, the dividend yield is calculated as follows:

$$\frac{4.5c}{\$1.20} \times 100 = 3.75\%$$

This ratio is normally calculated by an investor who is acquiring ordinary shares mainly for cash dividends rather than for appreciation in the market price of the shares (a capital gain). The percentage yield indicates a rate of return on the dollars invested and permits easier comparison with returns from alternative investment opportunities. Dividend yield is often quoted in daily newspapers as part of stock exchange price reports.

Investors interested in dividend yields may also calculate the percentage of ordinary share earnings distributed as dividends to the ordinary shareholders each period. This ratio is referred to as the dividend payout ratio:

$$\text{Dividend payout} = \frac{\text{Total dividends to ordinary shareholders}}{\text{Profit} - \text{Preference dividends}}$$

For Gordon Ltd, the 2014 ratio is:

$$\frac{68}{476 - 30} \times 100 = 15.2\%$$

This ratio gives an investor an insight into management's dividend policy with dividends expressed as a percentage of profits available to the ordinary shareholders. A low payout ratio indicates that management is reinvesting earnings internally, desirable for those investors seeking growth in the market price of the shares.

Liquidity ratios

Liquidity ratios look at various aspects of an entity's working capital. Working capital is the difference between an entity's current assets and current liabilities. Assessing an entity's **liquidity** is an important factor in financial statement analysis since it measures the entity's ability to meet its short-term obligations. An entity should be able to convert its current assets (such as inventory and accounts receivable) into cash within the time frame required to settle its short-term obligations (current liabilities). Some of the more commonly used liquidity ratios are discussed below.

Current ratio

The current ratio is calculated as:

$$\text{Current ratio} = \frac{\text{Current assets}}{\text{Current liabilities}}$$

The current ratio, a measure of the entity's ability to satisfy its obligations in the short term, measures a margin of safety to the creditors. It indicates the gap between current assets and current liabilities. A ratio below 1 indicates that current liabilities exceed current assets, and that the entity would therefore not be able to meet its current obligations with its current assets. Even though it is unlikely that all its current liabilities would have to be settled at the same time, a ratio below 1 indicates a risk that the entity may be forced into liquidation if the situation persisted or deteriorated further.

A high ratio is considered favourable to creditors, but may indicate excessive investment in current assets that may not be producing profits (such as inventory and accounts receivable).

Analysts often contend as a rule of thumb that the current ratio should be at least 1.5:1; in other words, an entity should maintain $1.50 of current assets for every $1 of current liabilities.

Although such rules may set a general benchmark, they are arbitrary and don't take into account norms for the industry in which the entity competes, or the economic environment in which it operates.

The current ratios for Gordon Ltd for 2014 and 2013 are:

2014	2013
$\frac{4340}{1760} = 2.5{:}1 \text{ (or } 247\%)$	$\frac{3900}{1600} = 2.4{:}1 \text{ (or } 244\%)$

Gordon Ltd shows a slight improvement in its liquidity position in 2014. However, a ratio of 2.4:1 or higher may signify excessive investment in current assets. The statements of financial position (see figure 25.1) show an increase in inventories and accounts receivable during 2014. There is a possibility that Gordon may have inventory on hand that it cannot sell, or may have accounts receivable that cannot pay their debts — if this is the case, an increasing current ratio is not necessarily a positive indication, and would warrant further investigation.

Quick ratio or acid test ratio

One of the limitations of the current ratio is that it includes inventory and prepaid assets in the numerator. However, these items are not as liquid as cash, marketable securities, current bills receivable and accounts receivable. In the normal course of business, inventories must be sold and cash collected before cash is available. Also, most prepaid assets are to be consumed and cannot be readily converted into cash. A ratio used to supplement the current ratio that provides a more rigorous measure of liquidity is the quick ratio, or acid test ratio. The quick ratio is calculated as follows:

$$\text{Quick ratio} = \frac{\text{Cash assets} + \text{Receivables}}{\text{Current liabilities}}$$

The higher the ratio, the more liquid the entity is considered. A rule of thumb used by some analysts is that a 0.9:1 ratio is adequate. A lower ratio may indicate that, in an emergency, the entity would be unable to meet its immediate obligations.

The quick ratio for Gordon Ltd is calculated as:

2014	2013
$\dfrac{770 + 1460}{1760} = 1.3\text{:}1 \text{ (or } 130\%)$	$\dfrac{740 + 1290}{1600} = 1.3\text{:}1 \text{ (or } 130\%)$

A ratio of 1.3:1 in both years may indicate high liquidity. However, this observation depends somewhat on the collectability of the receivables included in the numerator.

The current ratio and quick ratio are used to measure the adequacy of the current assets to satisfy current obligations at one point in time, the date of the statement of financial position. These ratios do not consider the movement of items making up the current assets. An important aspect of the entity's activities affecting liquidity is how long it takes to convert receivables and inventories into cash. Since receivables and inventories normally make up a large percentage of current assets, a quick ratio and a current ratio may be misleading if there is an extended interval between purchasing inventory, selling it, and collecting cash from the sale. The receivables turnover and inventory turnover ratios are two other measures of liquidity that can yield additional information and which should be used in conjunction with the quick and current ratios.

Receivables (or debtors) turnover

The receivables (or debtors) turnover ratio is a measure of how many times the average receivables balance is converted into cash during the year. It is also considered a measure of the efficiency of the credit-granting and collection policies that have been established and is calculated as follows:

$$\text{Receivables turnover} = \frac{\text{Net sales revenue}}{\text{Average receivables balance}}$$

The higher the receivables turnover ratio, the shorter the period of time between recording a credit sale and collecting the cash. To be competitive, the credit policies established by an entity are influenced by industry practices. Comparison of this ratio with industry norms can reveal deviations from competitors' operating results.

In calculating this ratio, only credit sales should be used in the numerator whenever the amount is available. However, such information is normally not available in general purpose financial statements, so net sales revenue is then used as a substitute. Also, an average of monthly receivables balances (including any trade bills receivable) should be used in the denominator. In the absence of monthly information, the year-end balance, or an average of the balances at the beginning and end of the year, or averages of quarterly balances are used in the calculation. The calculations for Gordon Ltd are:

2014	2013
$\dfrac{10\,320}{(1290 + 1460)/2} = 7.5 \text{ times}$	$\dfrac{9582}{(1320 + 1290)/2} = 7.3 \text{ times}$

Strictly speaking, a more accurate calculation of receivables turnover is provided by using average *gross* receivables in the denominator, i.e. before deduction of any allowance for doubtful debts. Gross receivables represent the actual legal balances that an entity would be attempting to collect; hence, many financial analysts prefer to use gross receivables in the calculation instead of net receivables as illustrated above. The gross receivables are available in the notes to the financial statements. Note that the receivables include GST whereas net sales revenue excludes GST. Provided the ratio is calculated consistently from period to period, this should not be a problem with this ratio.

Frequently, the receivables turnover ratio is divided into 365 days to derive the average number of days it takes to collect receivables from credit sales. The new ratio so calculated is called the average collection period for receivables and may be calculated as:

$$\text{Average collection period} = \frac{365 \text{ days}}{\text{Receivables turnover ratio}}$$

or, if expressed fully,

$$\text{Average collection period} = \frac{\text{Average receivables balance} \times 365}{\text{Net sales revenue}}$$

The average collection period for Gordon Ltd is:

2014	**2013**
$\dfrac{365 \text{ days}}{7.5} = 48.7 \text{ days}$	$\dfrac{365 \text{ days}}{7.3} = 50.0 \text{ days}$

During 2014, the company collected the average receivables balance 7.5 times; or, expressed another way, it took 48.7 days to collect sales — a slight improvement over 2013. These measures are particularly useful if one knows the credit terms extended to customers. Assuming credit terms of 60 days, the average collection period of 49 days provides some indication that the credit policy is effective and that the entity probably is not burdened by excessive amounts of bad debts that have not been written off. A collection period significantly in excess of 60 days (assuming credit terms of 60 days) usually indicates a problem with either the granting of credit, collection policies, or both.

Inventory turnover

Control over the amount invested in inventory is an important part of managing a business. The size of the investment in inventory and inventory turnover depend on such factors as the type of business and time of year. A supermarket has a higher inventory turnover than a motor vehicle dealer, and the inventory level of a seasonal business is higher at certain times in the operating cycle than at others.

The inventory turnover ratio is a measure of the adequacy of inventory and how efficiently it is being managed. The ratio is an expression of the number of times the average inventory balance was sold and then replaced during the year. The ratio is calculated as follows:

$$\text{Inventory turnover} = \frac{\text{Cost of sales}}{\text{Average inventory balance}}$$

Cost of sales (rather than sales) is used in the numerator because it is a measure of the cost of inventory sold during the year, and is consistent with the cost basis used to measure inventory in the denominator. Cost of sales is disclosed in the notes to the financial statements (see figure 25.3). Ideally, an average of monthly inventory balances should be calculated, but this information is generally not readily available. A half-yearly average can be calculated if interim reports are available for the entity.

The inventory turnover for Gordon Ltd is:

2014	**2013**
$\dfrac{7719}{(1770 + 2010)/2} = 4.1 \text{ times}$	$\dfrac{6975}{(1860 + 1770)/2} = 3.8 \text{ times}$

As with the receivables turnover, the average days per turnover can be calculated by dividing 365 days by the turnover ratio:

	2014		2013

$$\frac{365 \text{ days}}{4.1 \text{ times}} = 89.0 \text{ days} \qquad \frac{365 \text{ days}}{3.8 \text{ times}} = 96.1 \text{ days}$$

The 2014 turnover ratio indicates that the average inventory was sold 4.1 times during the year compared with 3.8 times in 2013. In terms of days, average inventory was held approximately 89 days in 2014 before it was sold, compared with 96 days in 2013. Essentially this means Gordon has about three month's worth of sales in inventory on average.

The increased turnover in 2014 would generally be considered a favourable trend. Inventory with a high turnover is less likely to become obsolete and decline in price before it is sold. A higher turnover also indicates greater liquidity since the inventory is converted into cash in a shorter period of time. A very high turnover, however, may indicate that the company is carrying insufficient inventory and is losing a significant amount of sales.

Financial stability ratios

We now focus on several ratios used to analyse an entity's financial stability. **Financial stability** (sometimes referred to as solvency) relates to the entity's ability to continue operations in the long term, to satisfy its long-term commitments, and still have sufficient working capital left over to operate successfully on a day to day basis.

Debt ratio

Entities can finance their assets with either debt (borrowings) or equity (shareholders funds), but commonly will use a combination of the two sources of finance. The proportion of total assets financed by debt is important to long-term investors since the debt providers (creditors) have first claim to assets in the event of liquidation — creditors must be paid before remaining assets are distributed to shareholders. The greater the percentage of assets financed by shareholders, the greater the protection to the creditors. The debt ratio is a measure of the relationship between total liabilities and total assets, or the proportion of assets financed by debt, and is calculated as:

$$\text{Debt ratio} = \frac{\text{Total liabilities}}{\text{Total assets}}$$

Since this ratio is a measure of the margin of safety to the creditors of the entity in the event of liquidation, the lower the ratio, the lower the proportion of assets financed by liabilities (and therefore the greater the proportion of assets financed by equity), and therefore the less risk creditors have to bear.

For Gordon Ltd, the ratio is:

	2014		2013

$$\frac{3660}{7440} = 0.492 \text{ or } 49.2\% \qquad \frac{3300}{6300} = 0.524 \text{ or } 52.4\%$$

Thus, for both years, approximately 50% of the assets were financed by the company's creditors (long-term and current creditors).

The fair value of the assets would have to decline to 50% below their carrying amount before the creditors would not be protected in liquidation. (Note that this ratio can also be found in the common size statements in figure 25.1 where all figures are stated as a percentage of total assets.)

Equity ratio

As discussed above, an entity's assets are financed with a combination of debt and equity. The equity ratio is closely related to the debt ratio, as it examines the relationship between total equity and total assets, or the proportion of assets financed by equity. The ratio is calculated as:

$$\text{Equity ratio} = \frac{\text{Total equity}}{\text{Total assets}}$$

Since the debt and equity ratios are related, if 49.2% of assets are financed through debt (as indicated in the debt ratio), the remaining 50.8% of assets must have been financed through equity. The calculations for Gordon Ltd's equity ratio below confirm this:

2014	2013
$\dfrac{3780}{7440} = 0.508$ or 50.8%	$\dfrac{3000}{6300} = 0.476$ or 47.6%

The relationship between the debt and equity ratios can therefore be stated as:

$$\text{Debt ratio} + \text{Equity ratio} = 1 \text{ or } 100\%$$

In the case of Gordon Ltd for 2014:

$$49.2\% + 50.8\% = 100\%$$

Leverage ratio

The leverage ratio (also called gearing ratio or capitalisation ratio) is a further variation on the debt and equity ratios discussed previously. This ratio calculates the extent to which assets are financed by shareholders equity — it is the reciprocal of the equity ratio, calculated as:

$$\text{Leverage ratio} = \frac{\text{Total assets}}{\text{Total equity}}$$

It can be expressed as a ratio (for example, a leverage ratio of 2:1 indicates that equity is 50% of total assets, and therefore that the entity's assets are financed 50% by equity and 50% by debt). The higher the leverage ratio, the greater the use of debt. As mentioned previously, the amount of debt versus equity finance is a relative measure of riskiness, but there is no generally accepted ideal level of gearing. This ratio is useful as a comparison over time and with other similar entities as a measure of longer term stability and risk management. For Gordon Ltd, the ratio is:

2014	2013
$\dfrac{7440}{3780} = 1.97{:}1$	$\dfrac{6300}{3000} = 2.1{:}1$

In 2014, a slightly smaller proportion of assets were financed by equity than in 2013. The change in leverage is not significant, however, and should be compared with the norm in the industry to assess the relative riskiness of Gordon.

Times interest earned

Current interest charges disclosed as borrowing costs are normally paid from funds provided by current activities. In recognition of this, analysts frequently calculate the relationship between profits and interest:

$$\text{Times interest earned} = \frac{\text{Profit before income tax} + \text{Finance costs expensed}}{\text{Finance costs expensed} + \text{Finance costs capitalised}}$$

This ratio (sometimes called the interest coverage ratio) is an indication of the entity's ability to satisfy periodic borrowing costs (interest payments) from current profits. Finance costs and income tax are added back to profit in the numerator because the ratio is a measure of profits available to pay finance costs. If any finance costs are included in the cost of an asset (i.e. are capitalised), those costs must also be included in the formula as shown.

For Gordon Ltd, the ratio (assuming no finance costs were capitalised), is (see figure 25.2):

2014	2013
$\dfrac{702 + 252}{252} = 3.8$ times	$\dfrac{927 + 230}{230} = 5.0$ times

In 2013, profit before income tax and finance costs was 5.0 times greater than finance costs. This ratio declined to 3.8 in 2014, which, although lower, is probably still an adequate coverage by most standards. A rough rule of thumb is that profits should be 3 to 4 times finance costs. Again, the 3.8 times should be considered in relation to other trends in the entity's financial stability and comparison with other benchmarks.

Asset turnover ratio

As a general indicator of long-term stability, an analysis of the entity's ability to use its assets during a period to generate revenues may be expressed in the asset turnover ratio, which is measured by:

$$\text{Asset turnover ratio} = \frac{\text{Revenues}}{\text{Average total assets}}$$

This ratio measures the effectiveness with which all assets have been used by assessing the number of revenue dollars generated for each dollar of average assets used during the period. For Gordon Ltd, the ratio is calculated as follows:

2014	**2013**
$\dfrac{10\,320}{(7440 + 6300)/2} = 1.5 \text{ times}$	$\dfrac{9582}{(6300 + 6400)/2} = 1.5 \text{ times}$

Thus, assets have been turned over an average of 1.5 times in both 2014 and 2013, or around $1.50 of revenue is generated for every $1 of assets held. Trends in this ratio over a number of years may be significant in assessing the entity's long-term stability. The ratio expresses the entity's ability to use its assets in the generation of revenue.

25.5 Analysis using cash flows

Learning objective **5**

Analyse and interpret the ratio information provided by a statement of cash flows

Entities are required to include, as part of their annual financial statements, a statement of cash flows, disclosing cash flows from operating, investing and financing activities. Preparation of this statement is dealt with in a previous chapter. In this section, we discuss how information contained in the statement of cash flows can be analysed and interpreted in order to provide the analyst (and user) with additional insight into the performance and financing and investing activities of the entity. (Our analysis draws on the helpful work of Don E. Giacomino and David E. Mielke, 'Cash flows: Another approach to ratio analysis', *Journal of Accountancy*, March 1993, pp. 55–8, and on the work of Divesh Sharma, 'Analysing the statement of cash flows', *Australian Accounting Review*, vol. 6, no. 2, 1996, pp. 37–44.)

Ratios derived from the statement of cash flows can help the analyst evaluate the **cash sufficiency** of the entity, i.e. the adequacy of the cash flows to meet the entity's cash needs, and the **cash flow efficiency** of the entity, i.e. how well the entity generates cash flows relative both to other periods and to other entities. The overall aim of these ratios is to evaluate the entity's performance relative to other periods, and to other entities in the same industry. The ratios are not useful in themselves, but must be compared with the same ratios in previous periods and for the industry in order to assess trends over time and the entity's relative performance. Furthermore, predictions of these ratios for the future, based on past trends and on other economic information, should be helpful in forecasting the entity's performance and financial position and in assessing strategies for the future. The author of the article included in the scene setter of this chapter holds the view that cash flow is the most important aspect to focus on.

In order to discuss additional relationships provided by a statement of cash flows, figure 25.5 (overleaf) presents the summarised statements of cash flows for 2013 and 2014 for Gordon Ltd.

Cash sufficiency ratios

The purpose in calculating these ratios is to assess the entity's relative ability to generate sufficient cash to meet the entity's cash flow needs. All ratios are based on the entity's cash flows from operations, and attempt to assess whether these cash flows are sufficient for the payment of debt, acquisitions of assets and payment of dividends. Giacomino and Mielke (see above) present the ratios discussed on the following pages for assessing cash sufficiency.

Figure 25.5 Statements of cash flows for Gordon Ltd

GORDON LTD
Statements of Cash Flows
for the years ended 30 June 2014 and 2013

	2014 Inflows (Outflows) ($000)	2013 Inflows (Outflows) ($000)
Cash flows from operating activities		
Cash receipts from customers	$10 150	$9 612
Cash paid to suppliers and employees	(9 349)	(8 542)
Cash generated from operations	801	1 070
Interest paid	(252)	(230)
Income taxes paid	(240)	(280)
Net cash from operating activities	309	560
Cash flows from investing activities		
Purchase of property, plant and equipment	(883)	(330)
Proceeds from sale of property and plant	—	200
Proceeds from sale of investments	100	—
Net cash used in investing activities	(783)	(130)
Cash flows from financing activities		
Preference dividends paid	(30)	(30)
Ordinary dividends paid	(68)	(310)
Proceeds from issue of ordinary shares	402	—
Proceeds from long-term borrowings	200	—
Repayment of long-term borrowings	—	(100)
Net cash used in financing activities	504	(440)
Net increase (decrease) in cash and cash equivalents	30	(10)
Cash and cash equivalents at beginning of year	740	750
Cash and cash equivalents at end of year	$ 770	$ 740

Cash flow adequacy ratio

Cash flow adequacy assesses the entity's ability to generate sufficient operating cash flows to cover its main cash requirements, namely, the payment of debt, the acquisition of assets, and the payment of dividends:

$$\text{Cash flow adequacy} = \frac{\text{Cash flows from operating activities}}{\text{Repayment of long-term borrowings} + \text{Assets acquired} + \text{Dividends paid}}$$

Assets acquired refers only to non-current assets, because acquisition of inventories is already included in the cash flow from operating activities. For Gordon Ltd, the cash flow adequacy ratios are:

2014	2013
$\dfrac{309}{0 + 883 + 98} = 0.31$	$\dfrac{560}{100 + 330 + 340} = 0.72$

The ratio calculations indicate that the company's ability to generate sufficient cash flow from operating activities to cover its dividends, debt and acquisition of assets has fallen from 0.72 (72%) in 2013 to 0.31 (31%) in 2014. As a guide, a value of 1 (100%) or more over a period of several years would seem to indicate an adequate ability to generate the entity's main cash requirements. The fall in the ratio in Gordon Ltd's case indicates the need for further investigation, and for the development of strategies to reverse the trend.

Overall coverage of the company's cash obligations is then examined more closely by the following three ratios — repayment of long-term borrowings, dividend payment, and reinvestment. These three ratios provide additional insight into the entity's ability to cover its cash outflows.

Repayment of long-term borrowings ratio

This ratio assesses the entity's ability to generate cash from operating activities for the purpose of covering its long-term debt commitments in the current year. The ratio is calculated as follows:

$$\text{Repayment of long-term borrowings} = \frac{\text{Repayment of long-term borrowings}}{\text{Cash flows from operating activities}}$$

For Gordon Ltd, the repayment of long-term borrowings ratios are:

2014	2013
$\dfrac{-}{309} = \text{n/a}$	$\dfrac{100}{560} = 0.18$

The ratio in 2013 indicates that 18% of the company's cash from operating activities was used for the repayment of long-term borrowings, whereas, in 2014, no debt was repaid. More borrowing occurred in 2014, thus requiring further drains on cash flows in the future.

Dividend payment ratio

This ratio assesses the entity's ability to generate cash from operating activities for the purpose of covering its dividend commitments to both ordinary and preference shareholders. The ratio is calculated as follows:

$$\text{Dividend payment} = \frac{\text{Dividends paid}}{\text{Cash flows from operating activities}}$$

For Gordon Ltd, the dividend payment ratios are:

2014	2013
$\dfrac{98}{309} = 0.32$	$\dfrac{340}{560} = 0.61$

The fall in the ratio from 0.61 in 2013 to 0.32 in 2014 indicates that the company is paying out a smaller portion of its cash from operating activities in dividend payments in the current year. This shows that the company's fall in cash flow from operating activities has been followed by an even greater reduction in its dividend payments.

In some cases preference shares may be more in the nature of long-term debt rather than equity. If preference shares are to be regarded as debt, then the dividend payment ratio should exclude preference dividends, and the repayment of borrowings ratio should include any redemption of preference shareholders' funds in the numerator.

Reinvestment ratio

This ratio assesses the entity's ability to generate cash from operating activities for the purpose of covering its asset acquisition payments. The ratio is calculated as follows:

$$\text{Reinvestment} = \frac{\text{Purchase of property, plant and equipment}}{\text{Cash flows from operating activities}}$$

For Gordon Ltd, the reinvestment ratios are:

2014	2013
$\dfrac{883}{309} = 2.85$	$\dfrac{330}{560} = 0.59$

The ratio indicates that the company has increased significantly its proportional use of cash from operating activities in payments for asset acquisitions in 2014. An examination of industry trends and the company's expected capital expenditure commitments, which must be disclosed in notes to the financial statements under AASB 101 *Presentation of Financial Statements*, is worthwhile to assess future trends in this ratio for the company.

When examined together, these last three ratios reflect an entity's use of cash from operating activities to make discretionary and non-discretionary payments in the current year. If the three ratios are expressed as a percentage and added together, the analyst is able to see whether the entity's cash flow from operating activities has been sufficient (less than 100%) or insufficient (more than 100%) to cover these payments. (In fact, the addition of these three ratios provides the reciprocal of the cash flow adequacy ratio, expressed as a percentage.)

Debt coverage ratio

This ratio assesses the entity's ability to generate cash from operating activities for paying its long-term debt commitments. The ratio uses information provided by the statement of cash flows and the statement of financial position. It is calculated as follows:

$$\text{Debt coverage} = \frac{\text{Non-current liabilities}}{\text{Cash flows from operating activities}}$$

For Gordon Ltd, the debt coverage ratios are:

2014	2013
$\dfrac{1900}{309} = 6.15$	$\dfrac{1700}{560} = 3.0$

The ratios provide an approximate measure of how many years it would take for the company to repay its long-term debt commitments, given its current cash flows from operating activities. In this sense, it provides the analyst with a crude measure of the debt payback period. Because additional borrowings have occurred in 2014, Gordon Ltd's debt coverage ratio (payback period) has jumped from 3.0 (years) in 2013 to 6.15 (years) in 2014. Once again, this information should not be used in isolation but must be examined with other data to assess the entity's relative performance.

Cash flow efficiency ratios

Analysts, and the investors and creditors they represent, are always interested in an entity's efficiency in generating profits. With the statement of cash flows, it is possible as well to analyse an entity's performance in terms of its efficiency for generating operating cash flows. Cash flow efficiency ratios assess the relationship between items in the income statement and cash flows as disclosed in the statement of cash flows, in an attempt to assess the efficiency of an entity in turning accrual-based profits into actual cash flows. The entity's performance in generating cash flows can be just as important as the entity's profitability. The following ratios are calculated by Giacomino and Mielke (see p. 1071) in assessing cash flow efficiency.

Cash flow to revenues ratio

This ratio, expressed as a percentage, assesses the proportion of an entity's revenues which are eventually realised as cash flow from operating activities. The ratio uses information provided by the statement of cash flows and the income statement. It is calculated as follows:

$$\text{Cash flow to revenues} = \frac{\text{Cash flows from operating activities}}{\text{Revenues}}$$

For Gordon Ltd, the cash flow to revenues ratios are:

2014	2013
$\dfrac{309}{10\,320} \times 100 = 3.0\%$	$\dfrac{560}{9582} \times 100 = 5.8\%$

This ratio can be compared with the profit margin ratio calculated earlier in assessing an entity's profitability. Over time, the cash flow to revenues ratio should be approximately equal to the profit margin. Any significant discrepancies indicate the efficiency with which the entity is or is not turning its accrual-based profits into operating cash flows.

Operations index

This ratio compares the entity's profit with the entity's cash flow from operating activities, and provides an index of the cash-generating productivity of the entity's operations. The ratio uses information provided by the statement of cash flows and the income statement. It is calculated as follows:

$$\text{Operations index} = \frac{\text{Cash flows from operating activities}}{\text{Profit}}$$

For Gordon Ltd, the operations indexes are:

2014	**2013**
$\frac{309}{476} = 0.65$	$\frac{560}{640} = 0.88$

The index shows that Gordon Ltd has been less efficient in 2014 in turning profits on an accrual basis into actual cash flows, as indicated by the fall from 0.88 in 2013 to 0.65 in 2014. Comparisons over time and with other entities in the industry are essential before any decisions are made and action taken.

Cash flow return on assets

This ratio measures the entity's return on assets in terms of the cash flow generated from operating activities. In order to compare this with the entity's accrual-based rate of return on total assets, the cash flow return must be calculated on a consistent basis with the accrual-based return. Hence, the cash flow from operating activities must be before any payments for interest and tax, and the total assets must reflect the average assets for the period. The ratio uses information provided by the statement of cash flows and the statement of financial position. It is calculated as follows:

$$\text{Cash flow return on assets} = \frac{\text{Cash flows from operating activities} + \text{Income tax paid} +}{\text{Average total assets}}$$
Interest paid (finance costs) in numerator

For Gordon Ltd, the cash flow return ratios are:

2014	**2013**
$\frac{309 + 240 + 252}{(6300 + 7440)/2} = 11.6\%$	$\frac{560 + 280 + 230}{(6400 + 6300)/2} = 16.9\%$

Comparison of this ratio and the rate of return on assets on an accrual basis shows that Gordon Ltd's cash flow return is lower than the accrual-based return in both years, and that both rates of return have fallen from 2013 to 2014. Analysis of trends over a longer period and comparison with other entities in the same industry must be conducted in order to assess the cash flow performance of Gordon Ltd.

Many other ratios can be calculated using cash flow information, e.g. operating cash flow per share, which can then be compared with earnings per share; price–cash flow ratio, which can then be compared with the price-earnings ratio. Divesh Sharma, in 1996 (see p. 1071), suggested the use of several different ratios based on cash flow information as better indicators of an entity's liquidity than the ratios discussed above from page 1071 on, which were based on the income statement and statement of financial position. Suggestions made include the ratio of cash from operating activities to current liabilities as a short-term indicator of liquidity, and cash flow from operating activities to total liabilities as an indicator of long-term liquidity. Further suggestions were made for the assessment of an entity's financial structure using cash flow information. Interested readers are referred to Sharma's paper for a full discussion of these points. However, the cash flow ratios presented in this book are considered to be helpful tools for analytical purposes at an introductory level.

BUSINESS KNOWLEDGE

Payouts trail the good times

Leading listed companies are taking a parsimonious approach to boosting dividend payout ratios, or returning surplus cash to holders.

Having collectively raised more than $100 billion last year — most of which they didn't end up needing — ASX200 companies are now on historically low gearing ratios. But the GFC experience is still too raw to allow them to become dependent once again on their bankers.

According to Macquarie Equities Australian strategist Tanya Branwhite, industrial stocks are expected to pay out an average of 71 per cent of their earnings in 2009–10, a marked contraction on the 80 per cent payout ratio in 2007–08, a trend which is currently forecast to continue into 2010–11, where the payout ratio is forecast to decline further to 65 per cent.

Citi forecasts the median dividend at 15c a share, compared with last year's 12.5c (this is based on 135 ASX200 stocks covered by the firm).

'I would imagine a slight increase in dividend payouts but certainly not a rapid reversion back to historical levels,' says Citi equities strategist Richard Schellbach.

Bell Potter head of research Peter Quinton says pressure will grow on boards either to deploy surplus funds or return them to holders.

'In effect, the corporate sector has recapitalised now and it has no reason to retain earnings. A lot of companies are attracting the attention of institutions who are critical they are sitting on a lot of money,' he said.

Morningstar head of strategy Ross Bird expects 'conservatism and austerity' to remain the order of the day.

'Companies are saying 'maybe we had better not be as highly geared as two or three years ago'. This will be in the psyche of companies and they will be cautious with their dividend payout ratios.'

Source: Excerpts from Tim Boreham, 'Payouts trail the good times', *The Australian.*

Learning objective 6

Describe the limitations of traditional financial statement analysis

25.6 Limitations of financial analysis

The analytical techniques introduced in this chapter are useful for providing insights into the financial position and financial performance of a particular entity. There are, nevertheless, certain limitations that should be kept in mind:

1. Financial analysis is performed on historical data mainly for the purpose of forecasting future performance. The historical relationships may not continue because of changes in the general state of the economy, the business environment in which the entity must operate, or internal factors such as change in management or changes in the policies established by management.

2. The measurement base used in calculating the analytical measures is historical cost. Failure to adjust for inflation or changes in fair values may result in some ratios providing misleading information on a trend basis and in any comparison between entities. The return on total assets includes profit in the numerator, which is affected by the current year's revenues and expenses measured in current dollars. Non-current assets and other non-monetary items, however, are measured in historical dollars, which are not adjusted to reflect current price levels. Thus, the ratio divides items measured mainly in current dollar amounts by a total measured mainly in terms of historical dollars. This limitation is partly overcome if entities report inflation-adjusted data or current value data as supplementary information to the historical cost statements.

3. Year-end data may not be typical of the entity's position during the year. Knowing that certain ratios are calculated at year-end, management may attempt to improve a ratio by entering into certain types of transactions near the end of the year. For example, the current ratio can be improved by using cash to pay off short-term debt. Also, if the financial year-end coincides with a low point of activity in the operating cycle, account balances such as receivables, payables and inventories may not be representative of the balances carried in these accounts during the year.

4. Lack of disclosure in general purpose financial reports may inhibit the extent of the analysis. Specific ratios and related tends may therefore be difficult to determine.

5. The existence of one-off, or non-recurring, items in an income statement, e.g. losses through floods, may inhibit the determination of trends to assess business efficiency. Hence, many analysts may exclude such items from all ratios. Nevertheless, in determining profitability these items must inevitably be considered in calculating the rate of return to ordinary shareholders.

6. Sometimes the information contained in the general purpose reports may be subject to modifications, supplementations and/or qualifications expressed in accompanying documents such as directors' reports and auditors' reports. Any analysis and interpretation should take into consideration such matters.

7. Entities may not be comparable. Throughout this chapter it has been emphasised that one important comparison is between competing entities. However, because of factors such as different accounting methods, size, and the diversification of product lines, data may not provide meaningful comparisons.

25.7 Capital markets research and statement analysis

Learning objective 7

Explain the impact of capital markets research on the role of financial statement analysis

A financial analysis as presented in this chapter is used for many purposes. Some analysts believe that by studying all the published information in relation to an entity and performing a fundamental analysis on this information, they can determine whether the entity's shares are under- or overvalued. These analysts assume that share markets are inefficient and that abnormal profits can be made by investing in shares which are shown by the analysis to be undervalued and by selling shares shown to be overvalued.

Considerable research into the efficiency of share markets has questioned the reality of the assumptions of this fundamental analysis. Research into the behaviour of share prices has assumed that share markets are efficient in terms of incorporating all publicly available information into the share price of an entity. Thus, the share price is seen to reflect the entity's value at a point in time, and it is impossible for any analyst to generate abnormal profits by studying publicly available information. Instead, the investor is encouraged to invest in shares in accordance with the extent of the risk that he or she is prepared to take. Investors are encouraged, by this research, to diversify their portfolio of investments, in order to spread the risk in the event that any investment should fail.

Even though capital markets research has pushed the view that the fundamental analysis of an entity's shares has been misguided, there are, nevertheless, many analysts who still engage in the practice of fundamental analysis. Why? There are several reasons:

- Some may not be convinced that the analysis is futile.
- Many people still believe that they can make a 'killing' in the stock market, and are prepared to consult analysts to help them in their quest.
- If the share market is efficient, this may have come about because of the existence of many analysts who are prepared to study publicly available information very closely. If these analysts ceased to do this work, the share market may become less efficient.
- The evidence from capital markets research is not conclusive, as some researchers appear to have developed strategies which suggest that abnormal profits can still be made by analysing publicly available information.

To conclude, the findings of capital markets research are not beyond question in spite of considerable research efforts. Hence, it is premature and perilous to discard fundamental analysis, as presented in this chapter, for analysing and interpreting the performance of an entity in the market. Further discussion of capital markets research is left to more advanced courses in accounting and finance.

Although there are other limitations of the techniques illustrated, those above should provide sufficient evidence that a user of general purpose financial statements must exercise caution in interpreting trends and ratios calculated.

A summary of the ratios discussed in this chapter is presented in figure 25.6.

Figure 25.6 Summary of ratios

Ratio	Method of calculation	Significance of each ratio
Profitability ratios		
Profit margin	$\dfrac{\text{Profit (after income tax)}}{\text{Revenues}}$	Measures net profitability of each dollar of sales
Gross profit margin	$\dfrac{\text{Gross profit}}{\text{Net sales}}$	Measures the costs of goods and services relative to their selling price
Return on total assets	$\dfrac{\text{Profit before income tax} + \text{Finance costs}}{\text{Average total assets}}$	Measures rate of return earned through operating total assets provided by both creditors and owners.
Return on equity	$\dfrac{\text{Profit} - \text{Preference dividends}}{\text{Average ordinary equity}}$	Measures rate of return earned on assets provided by owners.
Earnings per share	$\dfrac{\text{Profit (after income tax)} - \text{Preference dividends}}{\text{Weighted average number of ordinary shares issued}}$	Measures profit earned on each ordinary share.
Price–earnings ratio	$\dfrac{\text{Market price per ordinary share}}{\text{Earnings per ordinary share}}$	Measures the amount investors are paying for a dollar of earnings.
Earnings yield	$\dfrac{\text{Earnings per ordinary share}}{\text{Market price per ordinary share}}$	Measures the return to an investor purchasing shares at the current market price.
Dividend yield	$\dfrac{\text{Annual dividend per ordinary share}}{\text{Market price per ordinary share}}$	Measures the rate of return to shareholders based on current market price.
Dividend payout	$\dfrac{\text{Total dividends to ordinary shareholders}}{\text{Profit} - \text{Preference dividends}}$	Measures the percentage of profits paid out to ordinary shareholders.
Liquidity ratios		
Current ratio	$\dfrac{\text{Current assets}}{\text{Current liabilities}}$	A measure of short-term liquidity. Indicates the ability of an entity to meet its short-term debts from its current assets.
Quick ratio	$\dfrac{\text{Cash assets} + \text{Receivables}}{\text{Current liabilities}}$	A more rigorous measure of short-term liquidity. Indicates the ability of the entity to meet unexpected demands from liquid assets.
Receivables turnover	$\dfrac{\text{Net sales revenue}}{\text{Average receivables balance}}$	Measures the effectiveness of collections; used to evaluate whether receivables balance is excessive.
Average collection period	$\dfrac{\text{Average receivables balance} \times 365}{\text{Net sales revenue}}$	Measures the average number of days taken by an entity to collect its receivables.
Inventory turnover	$\dfrac{\text{Cost of sales}}{\text{Average inventory balance}}$	Indicates the liquidity of inventory. Measures the number of times inventory was sold on average during the period.
Financial stability ratios		
Debt ratio	$\dfrac{\text{Total liabilities}}{\text{Total assets}}$	Measures percentage of assets provided by creditors and extent of using gearing.
Equity ratio	$\dfrac{\text{Total equity}}{\text{Total assets}}$	Measures percentage of assets provided by shareholders and the extent of using gearing.
Leverage ratio	$\dfrac{\text{Total assets}}{\text{Total equity}}$	The reciprocal of the equity ratio and thus measures the same thing.

Figure 25.6 *(continued)*

Ratio	Method of calculation	Significance of each ratio
Financial stability ratios *(cont.)*		
Times interest earned	$$\frac{\text{Profit before income tax} + \text{Finance costs expensed}}{\text{Finance costs (expensed and capitalised)}}$$	Measures the ability of the entity to meet its interest payments on borrowings out of current profits.
Asset turnover ratio	$$\frac{\text{Revenues}}{\text{Average total assets}}$$	Measures the effectiveness of an entity in using its assets during the period.
Cash sufficiency ratios		
Cash flow adequacy	$$\frac{\text{Cash flows from operating activities}}{\text{Repayment of long-term borrowings} + \text{Assets acquired} + \text{Dividends paid}}$$	Measures the entity's ability to cover its main cash requirements.
Repayment of long-term borrowings	$$\frac{\text{Repayment of long-term borrowings}}{\text{Cash flows from operating activities}}$$	Measures the entity's ability to cover its long-term debt out of cash from operating activities.
Dividend payment	$$\frac{\text{Dividends paid}}{\text{Cash flows from operating activities}}$$	Measures the entity's ability to cover its dividend payments.
Reinvestment	$$\frac{\text{Purchase of property, plant and equipment}}{\text{Cash flows from operating activities}}$$	Measures the entity's ability to pay for its non-current assets out of cash from operating activities.
Debt coverage	$$\frac{\text{Non-current liabilities}}{\text{Cash flows from operating activities}}$$	Measures the payback period for coverage of long-term debt.
Cash flow efficiency ratios		
Cash flow to revenues	$$\frac{\text{Cash flows from operating activities}}{\text{Revenues}}$$	Measures ability to convert revenue into cash flows.
Operations index	$$\frac{\text{Cash flows from operating activities}}{\text{Profit}}$$	An index measuring the relationship between profit and operating cash flows.
Cash flow return on assets	$$\frac{\text{Cash flows from operating activities} + \text{Income tax paid} + \text{Interest paid (finance costs)}}{\text{Average total assets}}$$	Measures the operating cash flow return on assets before interest and tax.

KEY TERMS

Cash flow efficiency, p. 1071
Cash sufficiency, p. 1071
Common size statements, p. 1059
Comparative statements, p. 1057
Financial stability, p. 1069
Gearing (leverage), p. 1063
Horizontal analysis, p. 1059
Liquidity, p. 1066
Ratio, p. 1061
Vertical analysis, p. 1059

DISCUSSION QUESTIONS

1. After calculating the quick ratio for an entity and finding that the ratio's value was 0.9, a student analyst decided that the company was in a sound position for paying its liquid liabilities. Discuss the shortcomings of making such a conclusion.

2. Discuss how, in choosing the accounting methods below, the following ratios can be affected — rate of return on assets, quick ratio, profit margin, asset turnover:
   (a) a change in accounting method for depreciation from straight-line to diminishing-balance
   (b) revaluation of a non-current asset upwards at the beginning of the current year
   (c) recognising a loss through obsolescence of certain items of inventory.

3. In analysing the financial statements of an entity, the following ratios were calculated:

	2013	2014
Current ratio	2:1	1.3:1
Quick ratio	1:1	0.7:1
Receivables turnover	30 days	45 days
Inventory turnover	3 times	4 times
Profit margin	10%	7%

Discuss any potential weaknesses that these ratios may reveal in the overall performance of the entity, and discuss possible causes for these results.

4. Discuss the role(s) that an entity's cash flow data can play in analysing the entity's financial performance.

5. Discuss the general limitations of financial statement analysis.

6. Some accountants believe that financial statement analysis is of little benefit as it contradicts the findings of capital markets research. Discuss the findings of capital markets research and its implications for financial statement analysis.

EXERCISES

Exercise 25.1 TREND ANALYSIS LO 3

Preston Ltd reported the following financial data over a 5-year period.

	2010	2011	2012	2013	2014
Income	$748 000	$770 440	$789 140	$811 580	$822 800
Gross profit	298 000	309 920	315 880	324 820	333 760
Other expenses	202 000	207 050	210 080	217 150	220 180

Required
A. Prepare a trend analysis of the data using 2010 as the base year.
B. Do the trends signify a favourable or unfavourable situation? Explain.

Exercise 25.2 HORIZONTAL ANALYSIS LO 3

The asset section of the statement of financial position of DC Electrics Ltd is shown below:

	2012	2013
Cash assets	$ 247 500	$ 264 900
Receivables	417 000	444 090
Inventories	1 126 200	1 071 390
Prepaid advertisting	14 400	13 260
Plant and equipment	616 800	675 480
Land and buildings	975 000	1 050 600

Required
Calculate the changes in dollar amounts and percentages for the company.

Exercise 25.3 COMMON SIZE INCOME STATEMENTS LO 3

Comparative figures from the income statement of Ruby Ltd are shown on the next page.

Required
Prepare common size statements for the company for both years.

	2012	2013
Revenues (all sales)	$360 000	$460 000
Cost of sales	222 200	245 000
Gross profit	137 800	215 000
Expenses (including tax)	91 860	143 000
Profit	$ 45 940	$ 72 000

Exercise 25.4 COMMON SIZE STATEMENT OF FINANCIAL POSITION

Comparative figures from the statement of financial position for Morris Ltd are shown below:

	2012	2013
Current assets		
Cash at bank	$ 45 000	$ 37 500
Accounts receivable	78 000	81 000
Inventory	126 000	129 000
	249 000	247 500
Non-current assets		
Term deposit	75 000	60 000
Plant and equipment (net)	270 000	240 000
	345 000	300 000
Total assets	594 000	547 500
Current liabilities		
Accounts payable	72 000	78 000
Mortgage	30 000	30 000
	102 000	108 000
Non-current liabilities		
Mortgage	180 000	150 000
	180 000	150 000
Total liabilities	282 000	258 000
Net assets	$312 000	$289 500
Equity		
Share capital	$150 000	$150 000
Retained earnings	162 000	139 500
	$312 000	$289 500

Required

Prepare common size statements for the company for both years.

Exercise 25.5 LIQUIDITY ANALYSIS

The information on the next page has been extracted from the financial statements and notes of Cedar Ltd.

Required

A. Calculate the following for 2013 to one decimal place:
1. current ratio
2. quick ratio
3. receivables turnover ratio
4. average collection period of accounts receivable
5. inventory turnover ratio
6. average period for inventory turnover.

B. What conclusions can you come to in relation to Cedar Ltd's liquidity?

	2013	2012
Cash assets	$ 66 200	$ 71 800
Marketable securities	214 000	200 600
Accounts receivable	145 000	147 800
Inventories	364 000	333 600
Prepaid insurance	8 400	12 600
Property, plant and equipment	600 000	517 400
Accounts payable	356 400	321 000
Revenue (sales on credit)	1 901 200	1 805 800
Cost of sales	1 141 400	1 065 600

Exercise 25.6 PROFITABILITY AND FINANCIAL STABILITY ANALYSIS **LO 4**

The following information has been extracted from the financial statements and notes of Jack and Jill Pty Ltd, consultants.

	2013	2012
Services revenue	$870 000	$862 500
Interest expense	34 500	39 750
Income tax expense	66 900	79 500
Profit	78 750	84 150
Preference dividends	4 200	4 200
Total assets	810 000	832 500
Total liabilities	450 000	495 000
Preference share capital	93 000	93 000
Ordinary share capital	165 000	150 000
Retained earnings	102 000	94 500

Required
A. Calculate the following ratios for 2013:
  1. return on total assets
  2. return on ordinary equity.
B. Calculate the following ratios for 2012 and 2013:
  1. profit margin
  2. debt ratio
  3. times interest earned.
C. What do these ratios show in relation to the company's profitability and financial stability?

Exercise 25.7 PROFITABILITY ANALYSIS **LO 4**

The following information relates to the operations of Shore Mining Ltd. The profit was $1 500 000. The company distributed preference dividends of $45 000, and ordinary dividends of $750 000. Over the year, issued ordinary shares were 1 000 000. Ordinary shares are currently selling for $9 per share.

Required
Calculate the following ratios:
1. earnings per share
2. price–earnings ratio
3. dividend yield
4. dividend payout.

Exercise 25.8 EFFECT OF TRANSACTIONS ON CURRENT RATIO

Tindall Toys Ltd's statement of financial position (extract only) on 30 June 2012 is set out below:

TINDALL TOYS LTD
Statement of Financial Position
as at 30 June 2012

CURRENT ASSETS		CURRENT LIABILITIES	
Cash	$ 360 000	Payables	$360 000
Receivables	251 200	Other liabilities	416 000
Inventories	540 800		
Prepaid expenses	49 600		
	$1 201 600		$776 000

Required
A. Calculate the current and quick ratios.
B. A loan agreement entered into by the company in 2010 requires the company to maintain a minimum current ratio of 1.5:1. Management is concerned that this requirement will not be met and is considering entering into one or more of the following transactions before the end of the financial year, 30 June. Calculate the current and quick ratios after each of the following transactions and indicate whether the ratio would be increased, decreased or unaffected by the transaction.
1. Purchase $16 000 worth of inventory on credit.
2. Pay $100 000 on payables.
3. Give existing creditors a $80 000 bill to settle some payables.
4. Borrow $120 000 using a long-term bank loan.
5. Give existing creditors a $80 000 long-term loan to settle some payables.

Exercise 25.9 CASH SUFFICIENCY RATIOS

You are provided with the following information from the statement of cash flows for Flack Ltd:

	2013	2014
Cash flow from operating activities	$ 960 000	$1 020 000
Repayment of long-term borrowings	180 000	202 500
Assets acquired	1 230 000	420 000
Dividends paid	330 000	330 000

Required
Calculate the following cash sufficiency ratios for Flack Ltd for 2013 and 2014:
1. cash flow adequacy ratio
2. repayment of long-term borrowings ratio
3. dividend payment ratio.

Exercise 25.10 LIMITATIONS OF RATIO ANALYSIS

Pine Ltd and Bark Ltd both began operations on 1 January 2012. For illustrative purposes, assume that at that date their statements of financial position were identical and that their operations during 2012 were also identical. The only difference between the two companies is that they elected to use different accounting methods as can be seen below:

	Pine Ltd	Bark Ltd
Inventories	FIFO	Weighted average cost
Property, plant and equipment	Straight-line depreciation	Diminishing-balance depreciation

Summary financial information for both companies at the end of 2012 is presented below.

Income Statement
for the year ended 31 December 2012

	Pine Ltd	Bark Ltd
Revenues	$500 000	$ 500 000
Less: Cost of sales	276 000	300 000
GROSS PROFIT	224 000	200 000
Other expenses*	86 000	106 000
PROFIT	$138 000	$ 94 000

* Includes finance costs of $16 000 for both companies. Depreciation expense was $20 000 for Pine Ltd and $40 000 for Bark Ltd. Assume no income tax.

Statement of Financial Position
as at 31 December 2012

	Pine Ltd	Bark Ltd
Cash	$ 40 000	$ 40 000
Receivables	100 000	100 000
Inventories	104 000	80 000
Property, plant and equipment (net)	110 000	90 000
	$354 000	$310 000
Current liabilities	$ 60 000	$ 60 000
Non-current liabilities	90 000	90 000
Equity	204 000	160 000
	$354 000	$310 000

Required

A. Calculate the following ratios for each company:
   1. rate of return on total assets
   2. rate of return on ordinary equity
   3. profit margin
   4. gross profit margin
   5. current ratio
   6. receivables turnover
   7. inventory turnover
   8. debt ratio.
B. Comment on the impact that different accounting methods can have on the calculation of ratios.

PROBLEMS

★ Basic

★★ Moderate

★★★ Challenging

LO 3

Problem 25.1 TREND ANALYSIS ★

Comparative data extracted from the general purpose financial statements and notes of Fiddly Origami Ltd are presented on the next page.

Required

A. Prepare a trend analysis of the data.
B. Comment on any trends revealed by the analysis which you consider should be reported to managers.

FIDDLY ORIGAMI LTD
Comparative Income Statements
for the years ended 31 December
($000)

	2009	2010	2011	2012	2013	2014
Sales revenue	$550	$578	$577	$594	$715	$759
Less: Cost of sales	220	227	220	229	255	297
GROSS PROFIT	330	351	357	365	460	462
Expenses	210	221	212	258	290	294
Profit	$120	$130	$145	$107	$170	$168

FIDDLY ORIGAMI LTD
Comparative Statements of Financial Position
as at 31 December
($000)

	2009	2010	2011	2012	2013	2014
ASSETS						
Cash	$ 30	$ 32	$ 30	$ 43	$ 42	$ 23
Receivables	45	54	50	77	94	133
Inventories	100	114	120	159	203	216
Property, plant & equipment	250	270	290	483	477	473
Total assets	$425	$470	$490	$762	$816	$845
LIABILITIES						
Payables	$120	$146	$157	$216	$263	$283
Non-current liabilities	80	77	73	166	161	159
EQUITY						
Share capital	150	150	150	225	225	225
Retained earnings	75	97	110	155	167	178
Total liabilities & equity	$425	$470	$490	$762	$816	$845

Problem 25.2 PERCENTAGE ANALYSIS ★   LO 3, 4

Certain items taken from the financial statements, the notes thereto and other records of Caul Wu Ltd have been expressed as percentages of net revenue:

	Percentage of net revenue	
	2013	2012
Revenues (net)	100	100
Beginning inventories	30	32
Purchases (net)	60	61
Ending inventories	26	33
Selling and distribution expenses	14	12
Administrative expenses	9	10
Income tax expense	3.9	5.4

Net revenues were $1 200 000 in 2012; they increased by 12% in 2013. Average trade accounts receivable were $138 000 in 2013 and $132 000 in 2012. Credit sales were 80% of total revenues in both years.

Required

A. By what percentage did the entity's profit increase or decrease in 2013 compared with 2012? Prepare a comparative income statement (showing relevant items) including common size figures to support your answer.

B. Calculate the average collection period for the company's trade accounts receivable for both years, showing the basis for your calculation.

Problem 25.3 EFFECT OF TRANSACTIONS ON RATIOS ★ LO 4

Elm and Oak Ltd completed the following transactions during a given year:

Transaction	Ratio
1. Sold obsolete inventory at cost	Gross profit margin
2. Redeemed debentures by issuing ordinary shares	Return on equity
3. Issued a share dividend on ordinary shares	Earnings per share
4. Declared a cash dividend on ordinary shares	Dividend payout
5. Paid the cash dividend	Dividend yield
6. Purchased inventory on credit	Quick ratio
7. Sold inventory for cash	Current ratio
8. Wrote off a bad debt against Allowance for Doubtful Debts	Current ratio
9. Collected an account receivable	Receivables turnover
10. Sold inventory on credit	Inventory turnover
11. Issued additional ordinary shares for cash	Debt ratio
12. Paid trade accounts payable	Rate of return on total assets

Required

State whether each transaction would cause the ratio listed with the transaction to increase, decrease or remain unchanged.

Problem 25.4 RATIO ANALYSIS AND REPORT ★★ LO 4

The following information relates to the business of Claudia's Catering. The owner is concerned about the profitability and financial structure of the business at 30 June 2013, especially since the bank requires repayment of the business's overdraft.

	30 June 2012	30 June 2013
Revenues (sales on credit)	$ 55 000	$ 71 000
Cost of sales	35 200	49 500
Other expenses	15 000	19 020
Cash and cash equivalents	38 000	(40 000)
Inventories	19 000	24 000
Trade accounts receivable (net)	36 000	59 000
Non-current assets (net)	60 000	87 000
Trade accounts payable	27 000	29 000
Claudia, Capital	126 000	100 000
Non-current liabilities	0	1 000

Inventory at 1 July 2011 was $20 000.

Required

A. Calculate the following ratios for 2012 and 2013:
1. profit margin
2. gross profit margin
3. rate of return on proprietor's capital
4. current ratio
5. quick ratio
6. equity ratio
7. inventory turnover.

B. Write a short report to the owner in relation to the profitability and financial stability of the business.

The following financial statements were prepared for the management of Kim Lee Ltd. The statements contain some information that will be disclosed in note form in the general purpose financial statements to be issued.

KIM LEE LTD
Income Statement
for the year ended 30 June 2014

Revenues (Note 2)	$1 701 000
Expenses, excluding finance costs (Note 4)	1 373 400
Finance costs	12 600
Profit before income tax	315 000
Income tax expense	126 000
Profit	$ 189 000

KIM LEE LTD
Statement of Financial Position
as at 30 June 2014

Current assets		
Cash and cash equivalents		$ 75 600
Trade receivables	$598 500	
Less: Allowance for doubtful debts	37 800	560 700
Inventories		504 000
Total current assets		1 140 300
Non-current assets		
Land		126 000
Building	378 000	
Less: Accumulated depreciation	75 600	302 400
Store equipment	94 500	
Less: Accumulated depreciation	44 100	50 400
Total non-current assets		478 800
Total assets		1 619 100
Current liabilities		
Trade payables		541 800
Preference dividends payable		7 560
Ordinary dividends payable		50 400
Other current liabilities		25 200
Total current liabilities		624 960
Non-current liabilities		
Long-term borrowings (Note 5)		126 000
Total non-current liabilities		126 000
Total liabilities		750 960
Net assets		$ 868 140
Equity		
Share capital		$ 630 000
Retained earnings		238 140
Total equity		$ 868 140

KIM LEE LTD
Statement of Changes in Equity
for the year ended 30 June 2014

Share capital
Ordinary:

Balance at start of period	$504 000
Balance at end of period	504 000

Preference (Note 6):

Balance at start of period	126 000
Balance at end of period	126 000
Total share capital	$630 000

Retained earnings

Balance at start of period	$107 100
Total comprehensive income for the period	189 000
Dividend paid — preference	(7 560)
Dividend paid — ordinary	(50 400)
Balance at end of period	$238 140

Notes to the financial statements

Note 2: Revenue

Sales revenue (net)	$1 701 000

Note 4: Expenses

Cost of sales	1 134 000
Selling and distribution expenses	178 000
Administration expenses	61 400

Note 5: Long-term borrowings

10% mortgage payable	126 000

Note 6: Preference shares

6% preference shares	126 000

Additional information
1. The balances of certain accounts at the *beginning* of the year are:

Trade receivables	$630 000
Allowance for doubtful debts	(52 700)
Inventories	441 000

2. Total assets and total equity at the beginning of the year were $1 512 000 and $737 100 respectively.

Required

A. Name the ratios that a financial analyst might calculate to analyse the following:
1. a company's earning power
2. the extent to which internal sources have been used to finance acquisitions of assets
3. rapidity with which trade accounts receivable are collected
4. the ability of a business to meet quickly unexpected demands for working capital
5. the ability of the entity's earnings to cover its interest commitments
6. the length of time taken by the business to sell its inventories.

B. Calculate and briefly discuss any limitations of the ratios mentioned for *each* of the above analyses.

The following selected financial data of two companies operating in the same industry, Kirra Ltd and Banzai Ltd, are presented below for the year ended 30 June 2013:

	Kirra Ltd ($000)	Banzai Ltd ($000)
	Income Statement data	
Net sales	$ 260 000	$ 415 000
Cost of sales	(161 000)	(311 000)
Gross profit	99 000	104 000
Selling and administration expenses	(50 000)	(65 000)
Interest expense	(22 000)	(10 000)
Other expenses	(2 000)	(4 000)
Net profit before tax	25 000	25 000
Income tax expense	(7 500)	(7 500)
Net profit after tax	$ 17 500	$ 17 500
	Statement of Financial Position data	
Current assets		
Cash	$ 8 000	$ 15 000
Accounts receivable	41 000	30 000
Inventory	24 000	25 000
	73 000	70 000
Non-current assets		
Property, plant and equipment (net)	$ 90 000	$ 110 000
Total assets	$ 163 000	$ 180 000
Current liabilities		
Accounts payable	$ 20 000	$ 24 000
Non-current liabilities		
Interest-bearing loans	$ 120 000	$ 80 000
Total liabilities	$ 140 000	$ 104 000
Equity		
Total shareholders' equity	$ 23 000	$ 76 000

The following balances were recorded as at 30 June 2012 for each company:

	Kirra Ltd ($000)	Banzai Ltd ($000)
Accounts receivable	$ 35 000	$ 24 000
Inventory	30 000	20 000
Total assets	$ 170 000	$ 195 000

Required

A. Calculate the following ratios for 2013 for each company using a worksheet:

1. Gross profit margin
2. Profit margin
3. Return on total assets
4. Current ratio
5. Quick ratio
6. Receivables turnover
7. Inventory turnover

B. Compare the profitability and liquidity of the two entities based on the calculations performed in part A.

The comparative financial statements of Korma Ltd are shown below.

KORMA LTD
Comparative Income Statements
for the years ended 30 June 2014 and 2013
($000)

	Note	2014	2013
Revenue	2	$32 000	$27 500
Expenses, excluding finance costs	4	27 410	23 930
Finance costs		—	—
Profit before income tax expense		4 590	3 570
Income tax expense		1 756	1 070
Profit		$ 2 834	$ 2 500

KORMA LTD
Comparative Statements of Financial Position
as at 30 June 2014 and 2013
($000)

	2014	2013
Current assets		
Cash and cash equivalents	$ 160	$ 200
Trade and other receivables	760	670
Inventories	1 540	1 440
Total current assets	2 460	2 310
Non-current assets		
Other financial assets	280	320
Property, plant and equipment	6 800	5 570
Total non-current assets	7 080	5 890
Total assets	9 540	8 200
Current liabilities		
Trade and other payables (Note 14)	1 010	1 000
Total current liabilities	1 010	1 000
Non-current liabilities		
Long-term borrowings	3 500	3 500
Total non-current liabilities	3 500	3 500
Total liabilities	4 510	4 500
Net assets	$5 030	$3 700
Equity		
Share capital	$3 200	$3 000
Retained earnings	1 830	700
Total equity	$5 030	$3 700

KORMA LTD
Statement of Changes in Equity
for the years ended 30 June 2014 and 2013
($000)

	2014	2013
Share capital		
Ordinary:		
Balance at start of period	$ 3 000	$ 3 000
Issue of share capital	200	—
Balance at end of period	3 200	3 000
Retained earnings		
Balance at start of period	700	400
Total comprehensive income for the period	2 834	2 500
Dividend paid — ordinary	(1 704)	(2 200)
Balance at end of period	$ 1 830	$ 700

Notes to the financial statements ($000)		
	2014	**2013**
Note 2: **Revenues**		
Sales revenue (net)	$32 000	$27 500
Note 4: **Expenses**		
Cost of sales	18 000	17 700
Selling and distribution expenses	4 300	3 460
Administration expenses	5 110	2 770
Note 14: **Payables**		
Trade creditors	790	720
Other creditors and accruals	220	280

Required

A. Calculate the changes in the financial statements from 2013 to 2014 in both dollar amounts and percentages

B. Prepare common size financial statements for 2013 and 2014.

C. Comment on any relationships revealed by the horizontal and vertical analyses.

Problem 25.8 RATIO ANALYSIS ★★★

LO 4

Financial statements for Norco Ltd are presented on the following pages.

Additional information
Payables includes $11 240 000 (2013) and $11 460 000 (2012) trade accounts payable; the remainder is accrued expenses.
Market prices of issued shares at year-end (2013): Ordinary, $12.00

NORCO LTD
Comparative Statements of Financial Position
as at 31 December 2012 and 2013
($000)

	2013	2012
Current assets		
Cash and cash equivalents	$ 3 290	$ 4 220
Receivables (all trade)	8 200	7 350
Inventories	14 000	13 860
Total current assets	25 490	25 430
Non-current assets		
Property, plant and equipment	34 380	30 660
Total non-current assets	34 380	30 660
Total assets	$59 870	$56 090
Current liabilities		
Payables	$11 560	$11 980
Total current liabilities	11 560	11 980
Non-current liabilities		
Interest-bearing liabilities	19 880	18 900
Total non-current liabilities	19 880	18 900
Total liabilities	$31 440	$30 880
Equity		
Share capital	$15 400	$15 400
Retained earnings	13 030	9 810
Total equity	$28 430	$25 210

NORCO LTD
Income Statement
for the year ended 31 December 2013
($000)

Revenues (net sales)	$110 000
Less: Cost of sales	70 200
Gross profit	39 800
Less: Expenses	
Selling and distribution expenses	14 200
Administrative expenses	9 940
Finance costs	3 120
Total expenses	27 260
Profit before income tax	12 540
Income tax expense	3 816
Profit	$ 8 724

NORCO LTD
Statement of Changes in Equity
for the year ended 31 December 2013
($000)

Share capital	
Ordinary (14 400 000 shares):	
Balance at start of period	$14 400
Balance at end of period	14 400
Preference (500 000 shares):	
Balance at start of period	1 000
Balance at end of period	1 000
Total share capital	$15 400
Retained earnings	
Balance at start of period	$ 9 810
Total comprehensive income for the period	8 724
Dividend paid — ordinary	(5 404)
Dividend paid — preference	(100)
Balance at end of period	$13 030

Required

A. Calculate the following ratios for 2013. The industry average for similar businesses is shown.

	Industry average
1. rate of return on total assets	22.0%
2. rate of return on ordinary equity	20.0%
3. profit margin	4.0%
4. earnings per share	45c
5. price–earnings ratio	12.0
6. dividend yield	5.0%
7. dividend payout	70%
8. current ratio	2.5:1
9. quick ratio	1.3:1
10. receivables turnover	13.0
11. inventory turnover	6.0
12. debt ratio	40.0%
13. times interest earned	6.0
14. asset turnover	1.8

B. Given the above industry averages, comment on the company's profitability, liquidity and use of financial gearing.

Problem 25.9 PREPARATION OF FINANCIAL STATEMENTS FROM RATIOS ★★★ LO 4

The following values relate to various ratios determined for a sole trader, G. Heath, for the year ended 30 June 2014. At that date, the total assets in the statement of financial position were $900 000. The ratios relate to the accounts either in respect of the 12-month period or at the date of the statement of financial position for the end of the period.

1. Profit to total assets	15%
2. Current ratio	2.5:1
3. Acid test ratio	2:1
4. Credit sales to trade accounts receivable	7.5:1
5. Gross profit to total sales	25%
6. Trade accounts payable to purchases	40%

7. Credit sales to total sales   75%
8. Profit margin   10%
9. Profit to equity (commencement of year)   30%
10. Non-current assets to current assets   10%

Required

Assuming there are no prepaid expenses and that trade accounts payable are the only liability, and rounding answers to the nearest dollar, prepare:

1. a detailed income statement for the year ended 30 June 2014, including an itemised cost of sales calculation (assuming a periodic inventory system)
2. the business's statement of financial position as at 30 June 2014.

Problem 25.10 RATIO ANALYSIS COMPARING TWO ENTITIES ★★★   **LO 4, 6**

The statement of financial position and other information below relate to Pebble Ltd and Beach Ltd.

Statements of Financial Position as at 30 June 2013		
	Pebble Ltd	**Beach Ltd**
Current assets		
Cash and cash equivalents	$ 27 000	$ 30 240
Receivables (net trade)	129 600	134 190
Inventories	109 350	107 730
Other	2 700	5 670
Total current assets	268 650	277 830
Non-current assets		
Property, plant and equipment	446 850	527 310
Total non-current assets	446 850	527 310
Total assets	$715 500	$805 140
Current liabilities		
Payables	$108 000	$113 400
Total current liabilities	108 000	113 400
Non-current liabilities		
Long-term borrowings	162 000	189 000
Total non-current liabilities	162 000	189 000
Total liabilities	$270 000	$302 400
Equity		
Share capital	$270 000	$270 000
Retained earnings	175 500	232 740
Total equity	$445 500	$502 740

Additional information

1. The income statements for the two entities for the year ended 30 June 2013 reveal the following information:

	Pebble Ltd	**Beach Ltd**
Sales revenue	$ 975 000	$1 010 880
Cost of sales	653 100	672 870
Profit	70 470	59 670

2. The totals of certain items as at 1 July 2012 were:

	Pebble Ltd	Beach Ltd
Inventories	$ 101 250	$ 96 390
Total assets	688 500	782 460
Retained earnings	159 300	72 900
Trade accounts receivable (net)	118 800	124 740

Required
A. Calculate the following ratios for both companies:
1. current ratio
2. quick ratio
3. inventory turnover
4. average collection period for receivables.

Which company do you think is the better short-term credit risk? Give reasons for your answer.

B. Calculate the following ratios for both companies (ignore income tax):
1. rate of return on total assets
2. rate of return on equity (there were no changes in contributed equity during the year).

Which company do you think is the better investment? Why?

C. What other analysis may be carried out to help in decision making?

Problem 25.11 CASH SUFFICIENCY AND EFFICIENCY RATIOS ★★★   LO 5

The following is the statement of cash flows for Knodo Ltd for the year ended 30 June 2013:

KNODO LTD Statement of Cash Flows for the year ended 30 June 2013		
Cash flows from operating activities	$	$
Cash receipts from customers	3 430 000	
Cash paid to suppliers and employees	(3 150 000)	
Cash generated from operations	280 000	
Interest paid	(42 000)	
Income taxes paid	(150 000)	
Net cash from operating activities		88 000
Cash flows from investing activities		
Purchases of property, plant and equipment	(280 000)	
Dividends received	18 000	
Net cash used in investing activities		(262 000)
Cash flows from financing activities		
Proceeds from issue of ordinary shares	350 000	
Repayment of long term borrowings	(100 000)	
Dividends paid	(90 000)	
Net cash from financing activities		160 000
Net decrease in cash and cash equivalents		(14 000)
Cash and cash equivalents at beginning of period		160 000
Cash and cash equivalents at end of period		146 000
Additional information in relation to the year ended 30 June 2013:		
Total revenue		4 400 000
Average total assets		1 800 000
Total non-current liabilities		250 000

Required

A. Calculate the following cash sufficiency and efficiency ratios for Knodo for the year ended 30 June 2013 on the worksheet:

1. Cash flow adequacy
2. Dividend payment
3. Reinvestment ratio
4. Debt coverage
5. Cash flow to revenues
6. Cash flow return on assets

B. Briefly comment on the cash sufficiency and efficiency of Knodo at 30 June 2013 based on the calculations performed in part A.

DECISION ANALYSIS

Financial position of Killian Ltd

Killian Ltd has issued convertible notes under an agreement to maintain net assets, defined in the agreement as assets minus all liabilities except the convertible notes, at an amount not less than 2 times the amount of the convertible notes issued. Also under the agreement, working capital is to be maintained at not less than 100% of the convertible notes issued. Certain financial information for Killian Ltd is presented below:

KILLIAN LTD
Adjusted Trial Balance
as at 30 June 2014

	Debits	Credits
Cash at bank	$ 200 000	
Marketable securities	1 500 000	
Accounts receivable	1 480 000	
Allowance for doubtful debts		$ 60 000
Inventories	1 600 000	
Prepaid expenses	120 000	
Land	360 000	
Buildings	3 120 000	
Accumulated depreciation – buildings		420 000
Equipment	3 680 000	
Accumulated depreciation – equipment		840 000
Accounts payable		1 380 000
Loan payable (due 30 June 2015)		1 500 000
Accrued expenses payable		120 000
Convertible notes		4 000 000
Share capital — ordinary		2 400 000
Retained earnings		1 340 000
	$12 060 000	$12 060 000

Additional information

1. Killian Ltd had recorded, as at 30 June 2014, $320 000 of collections from its customers that were not received until 2 July 2014 on the basis that such collections were probably in the mail before midnight on 30 June 2014.
2. In the afternoon of 2 July 2014, Killian Ltd issued cheques to its creditors, dating and recording the cheques as at 30 June 2014. The cheques amounted to $320 000, which is equal to the collections in transit.
3. Killian Ltd is considering a 1-day extension on the due date of the loan payable to 1 July 2015.

Required

A. Contrast, by means of comparative ratios, the reported conditions with those that you believe more appropriately represent the financial position of the company. Limit your comparison to the convertible note holders' agreement.

B. Has the company met the conditions of the agreement? Explain.

Inventory methods

Wentworth Wholesalers Ltd began operations on 28 June 2013 by purchasing $1 000 000 of inventory. There were no sales up to the end of the financial year ending 30 June 2013. For the year ended 30 June 2014, additional inventory of $5 000 000 was purchased. Expenses, excluding cost of sales and incentive bonuses to management, totalled $500 000. Total sales for the year were $8 000 000. The company had in existence a management incentive scheme which provided bonuses, totalling 1% of profit (after income tax but before the bonuses), to be paid to management. Assume a company income tax rate of 30%.

The company was undecided as to whether it should select the FIFO or weighted average method of accounting for inventories. If the FIFO method was selected, the ending inventory balance would be $1 000 000, whereas if the weighted average method was chosen, the inventory would be valued at $1 400 000.

Required

A. What effect would the alternative inventory methods have on the profit margin and gross profit margin ratios? Based on these ratios, which method would be chosen by management. Why?
B. Assuming an efficient capital market, discuss the effect (if any) that the alternative inventory methods would have on the company's share price.
C. Discuss the advantages and disadvantages of management incentive schemes such as the one above.

Turbocharged: ethical investments beat the market

Read the extract from the article by John Collett, and answer the questions that follow.

Can you invest successfully without harming the environment or others? Or better still, make the world a better place?

It may come as a surprise to investors that ethical funds have outperformed the sharemarket over the past five years, meaning people who go down this path don't need to forgo returns.

A co-founder of Australian Ethical Investment, James Thier, says more and more people are thinking about what their money is doing and whether it could be supporting personal values.

Clean technology, healthcare, efficient transport, recycling and waste management are some of the industries that can make a difference while rewarding their investors with good returns, Thier says.

Grouped together, 'ethical' funds are outperforming their mainstream counterparts. According to Morningstar, Australian share funds that invest ethically produced an average annual return of 4.65 per cent over the five years to July 31, 2010, compared with 4.21 per cent for mainstream share options.

Only a fraction of people's savings is invested ethically, mainly because financial planners aren't supportive of such funds.

People interested in such investments will be confronted by an array of labels that are more confusing than illuminating, with terms such as 'green', 'sustainable' and 'responsible'. What you think those terms mean and what the fund manager thinks they mean may differ.

This underlines the importance of going behind the fund labels to check that you are comfortable with their approach.

There are three broad approaches taken by ethical fund managers.

Deep-green managers tend to apply a negative screen that rejects companies involved in industries considered 'dirty' and favours companies that make a positive difference, for example renewable energy.

The most widely used approach, though, is 'best-of-sector' or 'sustainable' investing. The manager selects companies with the best environmental and social records of all available companies. It is favoured by most super funds that offer 'sustainable' investment options.

The third approach — which has attracted only a small amount of money — is taken by the few funds that invest with a theme. These include climate change, water resources and clean energy.

Source: Excerpts from John Collet, 'Turbocharged: ethical investments beat the market', www.smh.com.au.

Required

A. What do you understand by the term 'ethical investment'? Which aspects of organisational behaviour and values would you be interested in when deciding whether investing in their shares constitutes an ethical investment?

B. What do you understand by the terms 'green', 'sustainable' and 'responsible' in the context of organisational behaviour, and how could the meaning of these terms differ among people and over time?

C. If you were interested in investing in ethical shares, would you be prepared to accept a rate of return lower than the average market rate? Why or why not?

FINANCIAL ANALYSIS

Refer to the latest financial report of JB Hi-Fi Limited on its website, www.jbhifi.com.au. Conduct a financial analysis of the company, assuming that you are interested in investing in JB Hi-Fi shares. The following analyses must be carried out:

(a) a 5-year trend analysis of consolidated net sales, and profit after income tax

(b) an evaluation of the company's profitability, liquidity and financial stability

(c) a discussion of any limitations of the analysis carried out.

Time value of money

Everyone is familiar with the concept of interest. Interest is the payment made for the use of money. As such, interest is the measure of the time value of money. A dollar expected some time in the future is not equivalent to a dollar held today because of the time value of money. The dollar available today can be invested to earn interest so it will increase in value to more than one dollar in the future. We would consequently rather receive a dollar now than the same amount in the future even if we are certain of receiving it at the later date. Businesses often invest and borrow large sums of money, so the time value of money is an important topic. Fluctuations in interest rates in recent years have had a corresponding impact on the time value of money. For example, the average interest rates on short-term loans in the late 1980s exceeded 20% at times. In the early 1990s, short-term interest rates fell considerably, and by 2010, interest rates were in the range of 6%–8%. We begin the examination of the time value of money with a discussion of simple and compound interest.

Simple and compound interest

Simple interest is interest earned on an original amount invested (the *principal*). The amount of principal and the interest payments remain the same from period to period since interest is calculated on the original principal amount only as:

$$\text{Interest (in dollars)} = \text{Principal (in dollars)} \times \text{Rate (\% per year)} \times \text{Time (in years)}$$

To illustrate the calculation of simple interest, assume that Brown Supplies Ltd invests $2000 for a 2-year period at 12% per year simple interest. The amount of interest received by Brown Supplies Ltd is:

$$\begin{aligned}\text{Interest} &= \text{Principal} \times \text{Rate} \times \text{Time} \\ &= \$2000 \times 0.12 \times 2 \\ &= \$480\end{aligned}$$

Compound interest is interest earned on the original amount invested (principal) plus previously earned interest. As interest is earned during any period, it is added to the principal; interest is calculated on the new balance (often called the compounded amount) during the next period. Interest can be compounded in a number of ways such as daily, monthly, quarterly, half-yearly or yearly. As an illustration of compound interest, assume the investment by Brown Supplies Ltd is the same as that described above except the interest is compounded annually. The total interest earned for the 2-year period can be calculated:

(1) Year	(2) Beginning balance	(3) Compound interest [Column (2) × 0.12]	(4) Ending balance
1	$2000.00	$240.00	$2240.00
2	2240.00	268.80	$2508.80

In the second case, the total interest earned is $508.80, compared with the $480.00 calculated using simple interest. The difference of $28.80 represents interest earned in the second year on the first year's interest ($240 × 0.12) and is the product of using compound rather than simple interest. In most cases involving the time value of money, compound interest is applicable, so we will consider only compound interest in the discussion that follows.

The time value of money is used in a wide variety of accounting applications, including the valuation of debentures, valuation of liabilities, accounting for instalment sales, valuation of leases and capital budgeting. Four cases must be considered in developing an understanding of the time value of money:

Case I   Future value of a single amount

Case II   Future value of an ordinary annuity

Case III   Present value of a single amount

Case IV   Present value of an ordinary annuity.

Case I: Future value of a single amount

A single amount of money invested today will have a higher future value than the original principal because of interest earned. The *future value of a single amount* invested today can be determined as follows:

$$FV = PV(1 + i)^n$$

where: FV = Future value

PV = Present value of single amount invested (principal)

i = Interest rate per period

n = Number of periods

Schematically, the future-value calculation can be shown as:

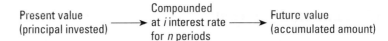

Present value (principal invested) $\longrightarrow$ Compounded at i interest rate for n periods $\longrightarrow$ Future value (accumulated amount)

Normally, the interest rate is expressed as an annual rate. However, interest often is compounded more frequently — daily, monthly, quarterly or half-yearly. In such cases, the interest rate and number of periods must coincide with the compounding schedule. For example, if 12% per year interest is earned over a 2-year period with quarterly compounding, the interest rate and number of periods used in the future-value formula are 3% and 8, respectively. This means that the annual interest rate (12%) is divided by the number of times compounding takes place (4) within a year, giving 3%, and the number of years (2) is multiplied by the number of compounding periods (4), giving 8 periods.

To illustrate the use of the future-value formula with annual compounding, consider again the Brown Supplies Ltd case with compound interest. The future value of the investment is found as follows:

$$FV = \$2000(1 + 0.12)^2$$
$$= \$2508.80$$

As we see, the total amount receivable by Brown Supplies Ltd at the end of 2 years ($2508.80) is the same as we calculated earlier by adding the compound interest to the principal. If the investment involves quarterly compounding, we must revise the formula by dividing the 12% interest rate by 4 and multiplying 2 years by 4 as:

$$FV = \$2000(1 + 0.03)^8$$
$$= \$2533.60$$

The amount of interest earned with quarterly compounding will be $24.80 more than it was with annual compounding. Note that the mathematics involved with the future value formula becomes more tedious as we increase the number of periods involved. Fortunately, tables have been developed for various combinations of interest rates and periods to avoid the necessity of using the formula each time a future value of a single amount of money must be calculated. Table A.1 shows the future value of $1 for various interest rates and various periods.

Suppose we want to know how much a dollar invested today at 12% interest compounded annually will be worth 10 years from now. We simply find the amount (called a *factor*) in the 12% column and 10-periods row of table A.1 — 3.1058. Thus, the dollar invested now will become approximately $3.11 in 10 years because of the compound interest earned. Note that the left-hand column of table A.1 (and the other tables discussed later) refers to periods instead of years. This enables us to use the table even if interest is compounded more frequently than once a year. As we noted earlier for such cases, the number of years is multiplied by the number of times compounding occurs to determine the number of periods that must be considered. In addition, an annual interest rate is divided by the number of compounding periods to convert it to the appropriate interest rate.

For example, assume the dollar invested earlier will earn 12% interest compounded half-yearly instead of yearly. We need to multiply 10 years by 2 (20 periods) and divide 12% by 2 (6%) to determine the appropriate factor in table A.1. The factor is 3.2071 — located in the 6% interest rate column and 20-periods row. Therefore the dollar will grow to approximately $3.21 over the 10-year period. This same adjustment is required with the later tables whenever interest is compounded more frequently than once a year.

Table A.1 Future value of $1

Periods	2%	3%	4%	5%	6%	8%	10%	12%	16%	20%
1	1.0200	1.0300	1.0400	1.0500	1.0600	1.0800	1.1000	1.1200	1.1600	1.2000
2	1.0404	1.0609	1.0816	1.1025	1.1236	1.1664	1.2100	1.2544	1.3456	1.4400
3	1.0612	1.0927	1.1249	1.1576	1.1910	1.2597	1.3310	1.4049	1.5609	1.7280
4	1.0824	1.1255	1.1699	1.2155	1.2625	1.3605	1.4641	1.5735	1.8106	2.0736
5	1.1041	1.1593	1.2167	1.2763	1.3382	1.4693	1.6105	1.7623	2.1003	2.4883
6	1.1262	1.1941	1.2653	1.3401	1.4185	1.5869	1.7716	1.9738	2.4364	2.9860
7	1.1487	1.2299	1.3159	1.4071	1.5036	1.7138	1.9487	2.2107	2.8262	3.5832
8	1.1717	1.2668	1.3686	1.4775	1.5938	1.8509	2.1436	2.4760	3.2784	4.2998
9	1.1951	1.3048	1.4233	1.5513	1.6895	1.9990	2.3579	2.7731	3.8030	5.1598
10	1.2190	1.3439	1.4802	1.6289	1.7908	2.1589	2.5937	3.1058	4.4114	6.1917
11	1.2434	1.3842	1.5395	1.7103	1.8983	2.3316	2.8531	3.4785	5.1173	7.4301
12	1.2682	1.4258	1.6010	1.7959	2.0122	2.5182	3.1384	3.8960	5.9360	8.9161
13	1.2936	1.4685	1.6651	1.8856	2.1329	2.7196	3.4523	4.3635	6.8858	10.6993
14	1.3195	1.5126	1.7317	1.9799	2.2609	2.9372	3.7975	4.8871	7.9875	12.8392
15	1.3459	1.5580	1.8009	2.0789	2.3966	3.1722	4.1772	5.4736	9.2655	15.4070
16	1.3728	1.6047	1.8730	2.1829	2.5404	3.4259	4.5950	6.1304	10.7480	18.4884
17	1.4002	1.6528	1.9479	2.2920	2.6928	3.7000	5.0545	6.8660	12.4677	22.1861
18	1.4282	1.7024	2.0258	2.4066	2.8543	3.9960	5.5599	7.6900	14.4625	26.6233
19	1.4568	1.7535	2.1068	2.5270	3.0256	4.3157	6.1159	8.6128	16.7765	31.9480
20	1.4859	1.8061	2.1911	2.6533	3.2071	4.6610	6.7275	9.6463	19.4608	38.3376
25	1.6406	2.0938	2.6658	3.3864	4.2919	6.8485	10.8347	17.0001	40.8742	95.3962
30	1.8114	2.4273	3.2434	4.3219	5.7435	10.0627	17.4494	29.9599	85.8499	237.3763

The factors in table A.1 were determined by using the future-value formula with a principal of $1. By multiplying a specific factor found in the table for the appropriate combination of interest rate and number of periods by the single amount of money involved, the future value of that amount can be calculated. To illustrate the use of table A.1 when the amount involved is more than $1, assume again that the 2-year investment by Brown Supplies Ltd has a 12% interest rate compounded annually. The factor in table A.1 for 12% interest and 2 years is 1.2544, so the investment's future value is:

$$FV = \$2000(1.2544)$$
$$= \$2508.80$$

This is the same result we obtained earlier with the future-value formula. If interest is compounded quarterly, the factor from the table is 1.2668 (3% and 8 periods) so the future value is:

$$FV = \$2000(1.2668)$$
$$= \$2533.60$$

Again, the future value is the same as the one calculated earlier with the formula approach.

Case II: Future value of an ordinary annuity

In contrast to the single amount of money considered in Case I, an *annuity* consists of a series of payments over a specified number of periods, with compound interest on the payments. An *ordinary annuity* is a series of equal payments that occur at the end of each time period involved. We consider here ordinary annuities only and defer the subject of annuities due (in which the payments occur at the beginning of the time periods) to more advanced accounting courses.

The future value of an ordinary annuity is the sum of all payments plus the compound interest accumulated on each. For example, if a business makes a deposit of $5000 to an investment account at the end of each of 3 consecutive years with each deposit earning 12% interest compounded annually, the total amount accumulated over the 3-year period is the future value of an ordinary annuity. One way to calculate the future value of the series of deposits is to treat each deposit separately and determine the amount of interest earned:

(1) Year	(2) Beginning balance	(3) Annual interest [Column (2) × 0.12]	(4) Deposit	(5) Ending balance
1			$5 000	$ 5 000
2	$ 5 000	$ 600	5 000	10 600
3	10 600	1 272	5 000	16 872

It can be seen from these calculations that interest is earned for only two periods even though three deposits were made, because the first deposit was made at the end of the first year. As the number of deposits increases, this approach obviously becomes more time-consuming.

A formula can be used also to calculate the future value of an ordinary annuity. The formula is more complicated than the one used for the future value of a single amount, however, so it is not normally used. Instead, a table such as table A.2 is used because it contains factors for various combinations of interest rates and number of periods as calculated with a *future value of an ordinary annuity* formula when payments of $1 are involved.

Table A.2 Future value of an ordinary annuity of $1

Periods	2%	3%	4%	5%	6%	8%	10%	12%	16%	20%
1	1.0000	1.0000	1.0000	1.0000	1.0000	1.0000	1.0000	1.0000	1.0000	1.0000
2	2.0200	2.0300	2.0400	2.0500	2.0600	2.0800	2.1000	2.1200	2.1600	2.2000
3	3.0604	3.0909	3.1216	3.1525	3.1836	3.2464	3.3100	3.3744	3.5056	3.6400
4	4.1216	4.1836	4.2465	4.3101	4.3746	4.5061	4.6410	4.7793	5.0665	5.3680
5	5.2040	5.3091	5.4163	5.5256	5.6371	5.8666	6.1051	6.3528	6.8771	7.4416
6	6.3081	6.4684	6.6330	6.8019	6.9753	7.3359	7.7156	8.1152	8.9775	9.9299
7	7.4343	7.6625	7.8983	8.1420	8.3938	8.9228	9.4872	10.0890	11.4139	12.9159
8	8.5830	8.8923	9.2142	9.5491	9.8975	10.6366	11.4359	12.2997	14.2401	16.4991
9	9.7546	10.1591	10.5828	11.0266	11.4913	12.4876	13.5795	14.7757	17.5185	20.7989
10	10.9497	11.4639	12.0061	12.5779	13.1808	14.4866	15.9374	17.5487	21.3215	25.9587
11	12.1687	12.8078	13.4864	14.2068	14.9716	16.6455	18.5312	20.6546	25.7329	32.1504
12	13.4121	14.1920	15.0258	15.9171	16.8699	18.9771	21.3843	24.1331	30.8502	39.5805
13	14.6803	15.6178	16.6268	17.7130	18.8821	21.4953	24.5227	28.0291	36.7862	48.4966
14	15.9739	17.0863	18.2919	19.5986	21.0151	24.2149	27.9750	32.3926	43.6720	59.1959
15	17.2934	18.5989	20.0236	21.5786	23.2760	27.1521	31.7725	37.2797	51.6595	72.0351
16	18.6393	20.1569	21.8245	23.6575	25.6725	30.3243	35.9497	42.7533	60.9250	87.4421
17	20.0121	21.7616	23.6975	25.8404	28.2129	33.7502	40.5447	48.8837	71.6730	105.9306
18	21.4123	23.4144	25.6454	28.1324	30.9057	37.4502	45.5992	55.7497	84.1407	128.1167
19	22.8406	25.1169	27.6712	30.5390	33.7600	41.4463	51.1591	63.4397	98.6032	154.7400
20	24.2974	26.8704	29.7781	33.0660	36.7856	45.7620	57.2750	72.0524	115.3797	186.6880
25	32.0303	36.4593	41.6459	47.7271	54.8645	73.1059	98.3471	133.3339	249.2140	471.9811
30	40.5681	47.5754	56.0849	66.4388	79.0582	113.2832	164.4940	241.3327	530.3117	1181.8816

To illustrate the use of table A.2, consider again that the company makes three annual deposits of $5000 at the end of each year and earns 12% interest, compounded annually. The factor for 12% interest and 3 periods in table A.2 is 3.3744. Since the factor represents the future value of three payments of $1 at 12% interest, it is used to determine the future value of the actual payments made as:

$$FV = \$5000(3.3744)$$
$$= \$16\,872$$

This is the same answer we found earlier by treating each deposit separately. The three deposits of $5000 (total of $15 000) will increase in value to $16 872 over the 3-year period. The difference between the $16 872 future value and the deposits totalling $15 000 is interest amounting to $1872. If half-yearly deposits of $2500 had been involved during the 3-year period, the appropriate factors from table A.2 would be for 6 periods and 6%. Again, this adjustment is required because of half-yearly compounding. The factor for 6 periods and 6% from table A.2 is 6.9753, so the future value of the ordinary annuity is:

$$FV = \$2500(6.9753)$$
$$= \$17\,438.25$$

As we see, the future value of $17 438.25 with half-yearly payments and compounding is higher than the $16 872.00 calculated with yearly compounding because additional interest is earned.

Case III: Present value of a single amount

In Case I, we were concerned with the determination of the future value of a single amount of money. Many accounting applications of the time value of money involve the reverse of the future-value consideration: the concern with calculating the present value of some future amount of money. As noted earlier, money held today is worth more than the same amount of money received in the future because of the time value of money. Consequently, the present value of a given amount to be received in the future will be less than the future value.

To determine the present value of a specific future amount, the future value must be discounted with an appropriate interest rate to the present. The interest rate involved often is called a *discount rate*. Future value and present value have a reciprocal relationship — as can be seen by comparing the formulas for the future value and present value of a single amount of money. Recall that the future value is calculated as:

$$FV = PV(1 + i)^n$$

In contrast, the *present value of a single amount* of money is calculated as:

$$PV = \frac{FV}{(1 + i)^n}$$

where: PV = Present value (principal)
FV = Future value of amount to be accumulated
i = Interest rate per period
n = Number of periods

Schematically, the present-value calculation can be shown as:

Present value ← Discounted at ← Future value
(amount to be ← i interest rate ← (amount to be
invested now) for n periods accumulated)

To illustrate the use of the formula for the present value of a single amount of money, consider again the investment made by Brown Supplies Ltd. We determined earlier that the future value of the investment was $2508.80 when interest was compounded annually. By discounting the $2508.80 for 2 years at 12%, we can determine its present value, which should be $2000, as:

$$PV = \frac{\$2508.80}{(1 + 0.12)^2}$$
$$= \$2000.00$$

If the interest is compounded quarterly, we determined earlier that the future value of the investment is $2533.60. However, the present value of the investment should remain at $2000 when it is discounted for 8 periods at 3% interest per period, or:

$$PV = \frac{\$2533.60}{(1 + 0.03)^8}$$
$$= \$2000.00$$

As another example of calculating the present value of a single amount of money, assume that Holt Ltd has a liability of $23 958 that must be paid in 3 years time. The company wants to know how much it must invest today to have $23 958 in 3 years if the amount earns 10% interest, compounded annually. The amount to be invested would be determined as:

$$PV = \frac{\$23\,958}{(1 + 0.10)^3}$$
$$= \$18\,000$$

Consequently, the $18 000 (present value) investment will increase in value to $23 958 (future value) by the end of the third year because interest amounting to $5958 will be earned. Like the future-value formulas, the maths involved in the calculation of present value with a formula can be tedious, so a table or business calculator is normally used. Table A.3 shows factors for various combinations of interest rates and number of periods when the present value of $1 is calculated. By multiplying an appropriate factor from the table by the single amount of money involved, its present value can be determined. For example, in the Brown Supplies Ltd case with annual compounding, a value of 0.7972 is found in table A.3 for 12% interest and 2 periods. The present value of the investment is thus:

$$PV = \$2508.80(0.7972)$$
$$= \$2000.02^*$$

* A small rounding difference may occur as a result of using the factors from the tables.

Table A.3 Present value of $1 at the end of future periods

Periods	2%	3%	4%	5%	6%	8%	10%	12%	16%	20%
1	0.9804	0.9709	0.9615	0.9524	0.9434	0.9259	0.9091	0.8929	0.8621	0.8333
2	0.9612	0.9426	0.9246	0.9070	0.8900	0.8573	0.8264	0.7972	0.7432	0.6944
3	0.9423	0.9151	0.8890	0.8638	0.8396	0.7938	0.7513	0.7118	0.6407	0.5787
4	0.9238	0.8885	0.8548	0.8227	0.7921	0.7350	0.6830	0.6355	0.5523	0.4823
5	0.9057	0.8626	0.8219	0.7835	0.7473	0.6806	0.6209	0.5674	0.4761	0.4019
6	0.8880	0.8375	0.7903	0.7462	0.7050	0.6302	0.5645	0.5066	0.4104	0.3349
7	0.8706	0.8131	0.7599	0.7107	0.6651	0.5835	0.5132	0.4523	0.3538	0.2791
8	0.8535	0.7894	0.7307	0.6768	0.6274	0.5403	0.4665	0.4039	0.3050	0.2326
9	0.8368	0.7664	0.7026	0.6446	0.5919	0.5002	0.4241	0.3606	0.2630	0.1938
10	0.8203	0.7441	0.6756	0.6139	0.5584	0.4632	0.3855	0.3220	0.2267	0.1615
11	0.8043	0.7224	0.6496	0.5847	0.5268	0.4289	0.3505	0.2875	0.1954	0.1346
12	0.7885	0.7014	0.6246	0.5568	0.4970	0.3971	0.3186	0.2567	0.1685	0.1122
13	0.7730	0.6810	0.6006	0.5303	0.4688	0.3677	0.2897	0.2292	0.1452	0.0925
14	0.7579	0.6611	0.5775	0.5051	0.4423	0.3405	0.2633	0.2046	0.1252	0.0779
15	0.7430	0.6419	0.5553	0.4810	0.4173	0.3152	0.2394	0.1827	0.1079	0.0649
16	0.7284	0.6232	0.5339	0.4581	0.3936	0.2919	0.2176	0.1631	0.0930	0.0541
17	0.7142	0.6050	0.5134	0.4363	0.3714	0.2703	0.1978	0.1456	0.0802	0.0451
18	0.7002	0.5874	0.4936	0.4155	0.3503	0.2502	0.1799	0.1300	0.0691	0.0376
19	0.6864	0.5703	0.4746	0.3957	0.3305	0.2317	0.1635	0.1161	0.0596	0.0313
20	0.6730	0.5537	0.4564	0.3769	0.3118	0.2145	0.1486	0.1037	0.0514	0.0261
25	0.6095	0.4776	0.3751	0.2953	0.2330	0.1460	0.0923	0.0588	0.0245	0.0105
30	0.5521	0.4120	0.3083	0.2314	0.1741	0.0994	0.0573	0.0334	0.0116	0.0042

With quarterly compounding, the value in table A.3 is found for 3% interest and 8 periods (0.7894) and used as follows:

$$PV = \$2533.60(0.7894)$$
$$= \$2000.02$$

Table A.3 also can be used to determine the amount Holt Ltd must invest today to have $23 958 in 3 years with the same factors discussed earlier. The factor in table A.3 for 10% interest and 3 periods is 0.7513, so the present value of $23 958 is:

$$PV = \$23\,958(0.7513)$$
$$= \$17\,999.65$$

Note that each of the factors shown in table A.3 for a particular combination of interest rates and number of periods is one (1) divided by the corresponding factor found in table A.1. This must be true because of the reciprocal relationship between the formulas for future value and present value of a single amount. For example, the factor in table A.3 for 12% interest and 2 periods is 0.7972, which is the same as one (1) divided by 1.2544 (table A.1). Consequently, you can always determine the appropriate table A.3 factor from table A.1 and vice versa if both tables are not available.

Case IV: Present value of an ordinary annuity

In Case II, we considered how to determine the future value of an ordinary annuity — a series of equal payments made at the end of each time period involved. Our final concern with the time value of money is the reverse of Case II — that is, the present value of a series of equal future payments representing an ordinary annuity. The present value of an ordinary annuity is the amount that would have to be invested today at a certain compound interest rate to enable the investor to receive the series of future payments over a specified period of time. Assume that Briden Ltd has obligations of $6000 that must be repaid at the end of each of the next 3 years, including the current one. The company wants to know how much it would have to invest today to repay each of the obligations if the amount invested earns 10%, compounded annually.

One way to determine the amount of the required investment is to treat each $6000 payment as a single amount. Each payment is discounted to its present value (using table A.3), and the results are added to determine the total amount needed to be invested. If this approach is taken, the following calculations are necessary:

(1) Year	(2) Payment	(3) Factor	(4) Present value
		(Table A.3 — 10%)	[Column (2) × Column (3)]
1	$6000	0.9091	$ 5 454.60
2	6000	0.8264	4 958.40
3	6000	0.7513	4 507.80
			$14 920.80

The company would have to invest $14 920.80 today to have the money available to make payments of $6000 at the end of each of the next 3 years. If numerous payments are involved, this approach obviously is quite time-consuming. Because the $6000 payments can be viewed as an annuity since the three annual payments are the same, an easier way to discount them to their present value is to use table A.4 (p. 1106). The factors in table A.4 have been derived from a formula representing the *present value of an annuity of $1*. In the table, factors for various combinations of interest rates and number of periods are presented for the determination of the present value of an annuity of $1. Again, a given factor must be multiplied by the actual amount of each payment involved. The factor is 2.4869 for 10% and 3 periods. Therefore, the present value of the $6000 payments can be calculated as:

$$PV = \$6000(2.4869)$$
$$= \$14\,921.40$$

As we see, the results are essentially the same as those obtained by discounting each payment and adding the individual present values. If half-yearly payments of $3000 were made to satisfy the company's obligations, the present value calculation would require an adjustment of the number of periods and the annual interest rate. Six periods (3 years × 2) and an interest rate of 5% (10% ÷ 2) would be used to determine the factor of 5.0757 from table A.4, and the present value of the annuity would be:

$$PV = \$3000(5.0757)$$
$$= \$15\,227.10$$

Note that the present value with half-yearly payments is more than it was with yearly payments. The reason for this is that the amount invested will not have as much time to earn interest because payments are made every 6 months rather than at the end of the year.

Table A.4 Present value of an ordinary annuity of $1 at the end of future periods

Periods	2%	3%	4%	5%	6%	8%	10%	12%	16%	20%
1	0.9804	0.9709	0.9615	0.9524	0.9434	0.9259	0.9091	0.8929	0.8621	0.8333
2	1.9416	1.9135	1.8861	1.8594	1.8334	1.7833	1.7355	1.6901	1.6052	1.5278
3	2.8839	2.8286	2.7751	2.7232	2.6730	2.5771	2.4869	2.4018	2.2459	2.1065
4	3.8077	3.7171	3.6299	3.5460	3.4651	3.3121	3.1699	3.0373	2.7982	2.5887
5	4.7135	4.5797	4.4518	4.3295	4.2124	3.9927	3.7908	3.6048	3.2743	2.9906
6	5.6014	5.4172	5.2421	5.0757	4.9173	4.6229	4.3553	4.1114	3.6847	3.3255
7	6.4720	6.2303	6.0021	5.7864	5.5824	5.2064	4.8684	4.5638	4.0386	3.6016
8	7.3255	7.0197	6.7327	6.4632	6.2098	5.7466	5.3349	4.9676	4.3436	3.8273
9	8.1622	7.7861	7.4353	7.1078	6.8017	6.2469	5.7590	5.3282	4.6065	4.0310
10	8.9826	8.5302	8.1109	7.7217	7.3601	6.7101	6.1446	5.6502	4.8332	4.1925
11	9.7868	9.2526	8.7605	8.3064	7.8869	7.1390	6.4951	5.9377	5.0286	4.3271
12	10.5753	9.9540	9.3851	8.8633	8.3838	7.5361	6.8137	6.1944	5.1971	4.4392
13	11.3484	10.6350	9.9856	9.3936	8.8527	7.9038	7.1034	6.4235	5.3423	4.5327
14	12.1062	11.2961	10.5631	9.8986	9.2950	8.2442	7.3667	6.6282	5.4675	4.6106
15	12.8493	11.9379	11.1184	10.3797	9.7122	8.5595	7.6061	6.8109	5.5755	4.6755
16	13.5777	12.5611	11.6523	10.8378	10.1059	8.8514	7.8237	6.9740	5.6685	4.7296
17	14.2919	13.1661	12.1657	11.2741	10.4773	9.1216	8.0216	7.1196	5.7487	4.7746
18	14.9920	13.7535	12.6593	11.6896	10.8276	9.3719	8.2014	7.2497	5.8178	4.8122
19	15.6785	14.3238	13.1339	12.0853	11.1581	9.6036	8.3649	7.3658	5.8775	4.8435
20	16.3514	14.8775	13.5903	12.4622	11.4699	9.8181	8.5136	7.4694	5.9288	4.8696
25	19.5235	17.4131	15.6221	14.0939	12.7834	10.6748	9.0770	7.8431	6.0971	4.9476
30	22.3965	19.6004	17.2920	15.3725	13.7648	11.2578	9.4269	8.0552	6.1772	4.9789

Exercises

Exercise A.1 Simple interest

On 1 March Hinkle Ltd borrowed $4000 at 10% simple interest for 3 years. Calculate the amount of interest payable over the 3 years.

Exercise A.2 Compound interest

Refer to exercise A.1. How much interest would be due if compound interest were involved?

Exercise A.3 Future value of a single amount

Using table A.1, calculate the following future values:
1. $10 000 invested at 8% for 5 years, compounded yearly
2. $10 000 invested at 8% for 5 years, compounded half-yearly
3. $10 000 invested at 8% for 5 years, compounded quarterly.

Exercise A.4 Future value of a single amount

An investor wants to know how much a $5000 investment made today will amount to in 15 years if it earns 10% interest, compounded yearly.

Exercise A.5 Future value of an annuity

Using table A.2, determine the following future values:
1. $10 000 invested at the end of each year for 5 years at 12%, compounded yearly
2. $5000 invested at the end of each 6 months for 5 years at 8% per year, compounded half-yearly
3. $2500 invested at the end of each 3 months for 5 years at 10% per year, compounded quarterly.

Exercise A.6 Future value of an annuity

An investor wants to know how much she will have if she makes annual payments of $5000 at the end of the year for 10 years assuming the money will earn 8%.

Exercise A.7 Present value of a single amount

Using table A.3, determine the present values of the following situations:
1. $10 000 in 5 years at 12%, compounded yearly
2. $10 000 in 5 years at 10%, compounded half-yearly
3. $10 000 in 5 years at 8%, compounded quarterly.

Exercise A.8 Present value of a single amount

Donna wants to establish an investment fund for her only daughter, who currently is 8 years old. She wants to know how much she must invest today for the amount to accumulate to $50 000 in 10 years at 12% per annum compounding annually. Ignore income tax.

Exercise A.9 Present value of an annuity

Using table A.4, calculate the present values of the following situations:
1. $10 000 to be paid at the end of each year for 5 years, assuming 10% interest and yearly compounding
2. $5000 to be paid at the end of each 6 months for 5 years, assuming 10% yearly interest and half-yearly compounding
3. $2500 to be paid at the end of each 3 months for 5 years, assuming 8% yearly interest and quarterly compounding.

Exercise A.10 Present value of an annuity

An investor wants to receive $5000 at the end of each year for the next 5 years (including the current year). How much must he invest today to achieve his objective assuming the money earns 8%?

Glossary

Absorption costing: An inventory valuation method in which all manufacturing costs are charged as product costs regardless of whether they change with production levels, i.e. both variable and fixed costs are charged to inventory (p. 346).

Accelerated depreciation methods: Any depreciation methods that result in greater depreciation expense in the early years of an asset's life than in later years (p. 840).

Accommodation bills: *See* **Commercial bills**.

Account: A device used to record increases and decreases for each item that appears in a financial statement (p. 69).

Account balance: The difference between the sum of the monetary amounts of debits and credits recorded in a particular account (p. 69).

Accounting: The process of identifying, measuring, recording and communicating economic information to permit informed judgements and economic decisions by users of the information (p. 7).

Accounting cycle: The sequence of accounting procedures (from transactions to financial statements) that takes place during each accounting period (p. 69).

Accounting entity assumption: The assumption that a business entity is separate and distinct from its owners and from other business entities (p. 37).

Accounting equation: An algebraic expression of the equality of assets to liabilities and equity: Assets = Liabilities + Equity (p. 32).

Accounting manual: A guide to the accounting policies and procedures used by the accounting staff of an entity (p. 77).

Accounting periods: Periods of time covered by a set of financial statements (p. 68).

Accounting standards: Standards issued for recording and communicating transactions and other economic events in all types of entities (p. 703).

Accounting system: A collection of source documents, records, procedures, management policies and data-processing methods used to transform economic data into useful information (p. 276).

Accounts payable: Amounts owed to creditors for the purchase of merchandise, supplies and services in the normal course of business; also commonly referred to as creditors or trade creditors (pp. 33, 913).

Accounts receivable: Amounts due from customers for sale of goods or services performed on credit; also commonly referred to as debtors or trade debtors (pp. 34, 750).

Accrual basis: The effects of transactions and events are recognised in accounting records when they occur, and not when the cash is received or paid (p. 37).

Accruals: Expenses that have been incurred but not recorded, or revenues that have been earned but not recorded (p. 127).

Accumulated depreciation: The amount of depreciation that has been recorded and accumulated on an asset since it was acquired; it is usually recorded in a contra account (p. 132).

Accumulated losses: Losses incurred by the company in previous periods, represented by a debit balance in the Retained Earnings account (pp. 205, 658).

Activity-based costing (ABC): A cost accounting system in which costs are assigned to products based on cost drivers for the various production activities required to produce the product (p. 396).

Additional mark-ups: Increases above original retail prices (excluding GST) because of unusual demand or rises in the general level of prices (p. 807).

Adjusted trial balance: A trial balance taken from the ledger after the adjusting entries have been posted (p. 140).

Adjusting entries: Journal entries made at the end of an accounting period to update or correct the account balances (p. 127).

Adjustment (GST): An increase or decrease in the net GST payable or refundable for a given tax period as a result of goods returned, a refund, an allowance made, or an amount written off a debt (p. 233).

Adjustment note: A source document evidencing that an amount owing has been adjusted (also referred to as a credit note). For a GST-registered business, it also takes into account any GST included in the amount adjusted. The adjustment note must be in a format complying with GST legislative requirements (p. 233).

Administrative expenses: Expenses associated with the operations of the general, accounting and personnel offices (p. 231).

Administrative expenses budget: Estimates of the administrative expenses for the budget period (p. 512).

Ageing of accounts receivable: The process of classifying accounts receivable on the basis of the length of time they have been outstanding and probability of collection; also a basis for determining the amount of the allowance for doubtful debts (p. 754).

Agricultural produce: The harvested product of an entity's biological assets (p. 882).

Allotment: The process whereby directors of the company allocate shares to those who have applied. Alternatively, an account recording an amount receivable on shares once allotment has been made (p. 660).

Allowance for doubtful debts: The estimated amount of accounts receivable expected to be uncollectable (p. 752).

Amortisation: The periodic allocation of the cost of intangible assets and natural resources to the periods benefiting from their use (pp. 881, 885).

Annual financial report: The statement of profit or loss and other comprehensive income/income statement, statement of financial position/balance sheet and statement of cash flows, appropriate notes and a directors' declaration presented to a company's shareholders at the end of the financial year. Also includes a statement of changes in equity to comply with accounting standards (p. 946).

Annual leave: Paid leave per year granted to all employees under industrial awards and employment contracts (p. 918).

Annual report: A complete set of financial statements issued at the end of an entity's accounting period (p. 68).

Application: The process whereby prospective shareholders apply to the company for an allocation of shares. Alternatively, an account recording an amount of money receivable by the company on application for shares (p. 659).

Area of interest: An individual geological area whereby the presence of a mineral deposit or oil or natural gas field is considered favourable or has been proven to exist (p. 880).

Assets: Resources controlled by the entity as a result of past events and from which future economic benefits are expected to flow to the entity (pp. 32, 721).

Assurance services: Independent professional review services that improve the quality of information, or its context, for decision makers (p. 14).

Attainable standards: Performance targets that can be achieved with a reasonably efficient effort (p. 558).

Audit: An examination by an independent accountant of the financial statements and supporting documents of an entity (p. 14).

Australian business number (ABN): An eleven-digit number given to each business entity that has registered for the goods and services tax (GST) in Australia (p. 68).

Average collection period: Number of days taken to collect amounts due from receivables for credit sales (p. 763).

Average cost: An inventory costing method in which an average unit cost is calculated by dividing the total cost of goods available for sale by the total number of units available for sale. Moving average (perpetual inventory system) and weighted average (periodic inventory system) are variations of the average cost method (p. 792).

Avoidable expenses: Expenses or costs that can be eliminated if a department or a product is discontinued (p. 551).

Bad debts expense: The expense resulting when allowance is made for estimated uncollectable accounts (p. 752).

Balance sheet (statement of financial position): A financial statement listing the assets, liabilities and equity of a business entity as at a specific date (p. 31).

Balanced scorecard: A measurement-based management system that aligns business activities with the vision and strategies of an organisation, and that uses measures to monitor performance in achieving these strategies over time (p. 559).

Bank reconciliation statement: A statement prepared to reconcile the balance reported on the bank statement with the bank balance as shown in the entity's records (p. 424).

Bank statement: A statement prepared by the bank that provides the detail of activity that has taken place in a current account for the period covered by the statement (p. 423).

Beginning inventory: Goods or stock on hand at the beginning of an accounting period that are available for sale to customers in the normal course of business (p. 245).

Bill of exchange: An unconditional order in writing, addressed by one person or entity to another, requiring the person or entity to whom it is addressed to pay a certain sum of money to a designated person or order on a determinable future date (pp. 750, 765).

Bill receivable: A receivable evidenced by a formal written promise or order to pay (p. 750).

Bill payable: Obligation evidenced by a formal written promise or order to pay a certain amount on a set date (p. 913).

Biological assets: Living animals and plants (p. 882).

Bonus share issue: An issue of shares to existing shareholders in the proportion of their current shareholdings at no cost to the shareholders (p. 665).

Book of original entry: *See* **Journal**.

Book value: *See* **Carrying amount**.

Borrowing costs: Interest costs and other costs incurred in connection with the borrowing of funds (p. 832).

Break-even point: The sales volume at which total income and total costs are equal resulting in no profit or loss (p. 469).

Budget: A quantitative plan showing how resources are expected to be acquired and used during a specified time period (p. 494).

Budget performance report: A report showing a comparison of the actual and budgeted performance with an emphasis on variances (p. 518).

Budgeting: Preparing a plan for the future operating activities of a business entity (p. 16).

Budgeting period: The time period a budget covers; this is typically 1 year but can be up to 5 years (p. 494).

Business combination: The bringing together of separate entities or businesses into one reporting entity (p. 833).

Call: An amount of money receivable on shares that have been allotted but not fully paid up (p. 657).

Capital budgeting: The planning and financing of capital investments, such as replacement of equipment, expansion of production facilities, and introduction of new products (pp. 590, 848).

Capital expenditure budget: A budget detailing the acquisition of non-current assets planned for a future period (p. 515).

Carrying amount (book value): The amount at which an asset is recorded in the accounts at a particular date. For a depreciable asset, carrying amount means the net amount after deducting accumulated depreciation from cost or revalued amount (pp. 133, 836, 868).

Cash: Money and any negotiable instrument such as a cheque, postal note, credit card duplicate or electronic transfer that a bank will accept for immediate deposit in a bank account (p. 418), i.e. cash on hand and cash equivalents (p. 980).

Cash budget: A projection of future cash receipts and cash payments over a period of time disclosing cash position at the end of that time (pp. 433, 503).

Cash discount: An incentive offered to the buyer to induce early payment of a credit sale; also known as a settlement discount (p. 235).

Cash equivalents: Short-term highly liquid investments that are readily convertible to cash at an entity's option and that are subject to an insignificant risk of changes in value (p. 980).

Cash flow efficiency: The efficiency with which the entity generates cash from its income, profits and assets (p. 1071).

Cash-generating unit: The smallest identifiable group of assets that generates cash inflows from continuing use, which are independent of cash inflows from other groups of assets (p. 873).

Cash movements: The cash inflows and outflows of an entity (p. 30).

Cash payments journal: A special journal used to record all cash payments by an entity (p. 294).

Cash receipts journal: A special journal used to record transactions involving the receipt of cash by an entity (p. 290).

Cash sufficiency: The adequacy of the cash flows to meet the entity's cash needs for long-term debt payments, dividends, and acquisition of non-current assets (p. 1071).

Certificate of registration: The initial legal document registering a company (p. 655).

Certified practising accountant (CPA): An accountant who has met the qualifications and experience requirements for membership of CPA Australia (p. 14).

Chart of accounts: A schedule listing the titles of all accounts contained in the ledger together with an appropriate numbering system for the accounts (p. 75).

Chartered accountant (CA): An accountant who has met the qualifications and experience requirements for membership of the Institute of Chartered Accountants in Australia (p. 14).

Closing entries: Journal entries made at the end of an accounting period to reduce income, expense and drawings accounts to a zero balance and transfer the net balance to the capital account in a sole trader or partnership business or, in the case of a company, to the retained earnings account (p. 179).

Collateral: Something of value that is acceptable to a lender as security for a loan (p. 922).

Commercial bills: Bills of exchange used in obtaining short-term finance; also known as accommodation bills (p. 914).

Committed fixed costs: Fixed costs that are required even if the operation is shut down temporarily (p. 464).

Common size statements: Financial statements in which the amount of each item reported in the statement is stated as a percentage of some specific base amount also reported in the same statement (p. 1059).

Company (or corporation): A form of business structure incorporated to operate as a business entity under the *Corporations Act 2001* throughout Australia (p. 18).

Company limited by guarantee: A public company whose members undertake to contribute a guaranteed amount if the company is wound up (p. 651).

Comparability: The quality of financial information that enables users to discern and evaluate similarities and differences between transactions and events, at one time and over time, for one entity or a number of entities (pp. 39, 719).

Comparative statements: Financial statements for the current year and previous years presented together to facilitate the analysis of changes in statement items (p. 1057).

Composite-rate depreciation: A depreciation method under which a single average depreciation rate is applied to the cost of a functional group of assets (p. 878).

Compound journal entry: A journal entry involving three or more accounts (p. 80).

Comprehensive income: The change in equity during a period resulting from transactions and other events, other than those changes resulting from transactions with owners in their capacity as owners (p. 950).

Concise report: A summarised set of financial reports plus directors' and auditor's reports sent to shareholders as an alternative to the full annual financial report (p. 947).

Consignee: An entity or individual holding goods on consignment; does not own the goods held (p. 787).

Consignment: A marketing arrangement whereby merchandise is transferred from one entity (the consignor) to another (the consignee or agent) in order that the consignee may sell the goods on behalf of the consignor; however, title and control of the goods remain with the consignor (p. 787).

Consignor: An individual or entity that ships goods on consignment. Title to the goods is retained by the consignor until the goods are sold by the consignee, at which time title passes to the purchaser (p. 787).

Consistency: The notion that once a particular accounting policy or procedure is adopted, it should not be changed from period to period unless a different method provides more useful information (pp. 39, 719).

Constitution: A document containing the rules for managing a company, particularly in terms of relationships and dealings between directors and shareholders, which are adopted by a company as an alternative to the replaceable rules in the *Corporations Act 2001* (p. 654).

Constructive obligation: When the past practices of an entity, its published policies or a specific current statement indicate that it will accept responsibility for certain actions, so it becomes reasonable for others to assume the entity will fulfil those responsibilities (p. 909).

Contingent liability: A possible liability arising from a past event that will become an actual liability by the occurrence or non-occurrence of one or more uncertain future events that are not completely within the control of the entity, or a liability that does not satisfy the recognition criteria (pp. 770, 911).

Contra account: An account that is deducted from a related account (p. 132).

Contribution margin: The sales revenue less all variable costs (or unit selling price less unit variable cost) (p. 467).

Contribution margin ratio: The contribution margin expressed as a percentage of sales (p. 467).

Contribution margin variance analysis: A technique used to evaluate the difference between the actual contribution margin for a period and the budgeted contribution margin for the same period (p. 476).

Control: In relation to an asset, the capacity of an entity to receive future economic benefits in pursuing its objectives and to deny or regulate the access of others to those benefits (p. 721).

Control account: A general ledger account that is supported by the detail of a subsidiary ledger (p. 284).

Controllable income, costs/expenses or investments: Income, costs/expenses or investments that can be regulated or influenced at a particular level of management during a specified time period (p. 541).

Conversion costs: The combined costs of direct labour and factory overhead incurred by a job or processing centre in the process of converting raw materials into finished goods (pp. 346, 387).

Copyright: An exclusive right to reproduce and sell an artistic or published work (p. 886).

Corporation: *See* **Company**.

Cost: An economic sacrifice of resources made in exchange for a product or service (p. 340); the amount of cash or cash equivalents paid or the fair value of the other consideration given to acquire an asset at the time of its acquisition or construction (p. 830).

Cost accounting: The aspect of accounting that deals with the collection, allocation and control of the cost of producing a product or providing a service (p. 16); a specialised form of accounting that enables an entity to measure, record and report product costs using a perpetual inventory system (p. 378).

Cost accounting system: An accounting system that records cost data in separate ledger accounts that are integrated into the general ledger (p. 378).

Cost behaviour: How a cost will react to changes in the level of some activity, e.g. production or sales, within an entity (pp. 346, 462).

Cost driver: A measure of business activity that incurs overhead costs (p. 386).

Cost function: The relationship between a cost as a dependent variable and some measure of the level of business activity as an independent variable (p. 462).

Cost object: Any activity for which separate cost measurement is performed; examples are a department or segment, or a product (p. 545).

Cost of capital: An entity's cost of obtaining funds in the form of borrowings or equity (p. 594).

Cost of goods manufactured statement: A detailed statement of manufacturing costs reported on the income statement of a manufacturing entity (p. 347).

Cost of production report: The control document used in process costing to account for the manufacturing costs of units in a processing centre (p. 390).

Cost of sales: An amount that is deducted from sales in the income statement and is a measure of the cost of the inventory sold during the accounting period (p. 231).

Cost of sales budget: An estimate of the cost of sales required for the budget period (p. 512).

Cost–volume–profit (CVP) analysis: A management analysis technique used to evaluate how costs and profits are affected by changes in the level of business activity (p. 462).

Cost–volume–profit chart: A graphic display of the break-even point as well as the profit or loss for a range of activity (p. 470).

Coupon rate (nominal or stated rate): The interest rate stated as a percentage of nominal value and used to determine the interest paid periodically to the debenture holder (p. 924).

Credit: An amount entered on the right-hand side or in the credit column of an account (p. 69).

Credit card: A plastic card that enables the holder to obtain credit up to a predetermined limit from the issuer of the card for the purchase of goods and services (p. 764).

Credit department: The organisational unit responsible for the credit and collection policies of the business (p. 761).

Credit period: The period of time granted for the payment of an account (p. 235).

Credit terms: The agreement made between buyer and seller concerning the sale of goods on credit (p. 235).

Creditors: People or business entities to whom debts are owed; alternatively, another name for the Accounts Payable account (pp. 33, 72).

Crossadding: Adding or subtracting horizontally across a worksheet (p. 150).

Cumulative preference shares: Preference shares on which undeclared dividends accumulate before any dividend can be paid to ordinary shares (p. 669).

Current assets: Cash and other types of assets that are held mainly for sale, or are reasonably expected to be converted to cash, sold or consumed by a business entity within its operating cycle (if this is discernible) or are expected to be realised within 12 months after the end of the entity's reporting period (p. 146).

Current cost: For an asset, the amount of cash or cash equivalents that would be paid if the same or equivalent asset was acquired currently (p. 730).

Current liabilities: Obligations of the entity that are reasonably expected to be settled in the entity's normal operating cycle, or are held for the purpose of being traded, or are

due to be settled within 12 months of the end of the reporting period (pp. 147, 913).

Current replacement cost: The cost that an entity would incur to acquire an asset at the end of the reporting period (p. 800).

DDP (delivered duty paid): A shipping/delivery term meaning the seller bears all the costs of delivering the goods to the buyer (p. 238).

Debentures (or bonds): A liability representing a written promise to pay a principal amount at a specified time, as well as interest on the principal at a specified rate per period (p. 922).

Debit: An amount entered on the left-hand side or in the debit column of an account (p. 69).

Debit card: A plastic card used in the electronic funds transfer point of sale (EFTPOS) system, where funds are debited to the card user's account at the bank and transferred instantaneously to the credit of the account of the seller of the goods or services (p. 765).

Debtors: People or business entities from whom debts are owed; alternatively, another name for the Accounts Receivable account (pp. 34, 72).

Decision: The making of a choice between two or more alternatives (p. 4).

Decision making: Making a choice among alternative courses of action (p. 582).

Decision-making process: Involves four main steps: (1) establish goals, (2) gather information on alternatives, (3) evaluate outcomes of alternatives, (4) choose a course of action (p. 582).

Decision model: A formalised method for evaluating alternative courses of action (p. 582).

Defeasance: An arrangement whereby the terms and conditions of a debt are avoided or defeated (p. 926).

Deferrals: Assets that represent expenses paid in advance, and revenues received in advance that represent liabilities until the revenues can be recognised as earned (p. 127).

Departmental (segmental) accounting: Accounting procedures required to evaluate the financial performance of individual segments or departments within an organisation (p. 543).

Departmental contribution: The revenues of a department less its cost of sales and direct expenses (p. 550).

Departmental gross profit: The revenues of a department less its cost of sales (p. 544).

Departmental profit: The revenues of a department less its cost of sales, its direct

expenses, and an allocated portion of indirect expenses (p. 545).

Depreciable amount: The historical cost of a depreciable asset, or other revalued amount substituted for historical cost in the accounting records, less, in either case, the residual value (p. 835).

Depreciable asset: A non-current asset having a limited useful life (p. 834).

Depreciation: An allocation of a depreciable asset's depreciable amount to reflect the consumption or loss of its future economic benefits through use, wear and tear, and obsolescence (pp. 132, 834).

Development: The application of research knowledge to a plan or design for the production of new materials, products, processes, systems or services before commercial production (p. 884).

Differential analysis (incremental analysis): A decision model used to evaluate the differences in relevant incomes and costs between alternative courses of action (p. 583).

Differential cost: The difference between the relevant costs of two alternatives (p. 583).

Differential income: The difference between the relevant incomes of two alternatives (p. 583).

Diminishing-balance depreciation: A depreciation method that results in a decreasing depreciation charge over the useful life of the asset, by applying a predetermined depreciation rate to the carrying amount of the asset (p. 836).

Direct cost (expenses): Cost or expenses traceable to a specific cost object (p. 545).

Direct costing: An inventory valuation method where only variable manufacturing costs are charged as product costs (compare **Absorption costing**) (p. 346).

Direct labour budget: A projection of the direct labour needs of a budget period based on the expected production level (p. 510).

Direct labour cost: Represents the wages paid to employees whose time and costs can be traced to specific products (p. 344).

Direct materials budget: A projection of the direct materials that must be purchased to satisfy the production requirements of a budget period (p. 509).

Direct materials cost: The cost of raw materials directly traceable to the finished product (p. 344).

Direct write-off method: The recognition of bad debts expense at the time an account receivable is deemed to be uncollectable (p. 759).

Disclosing entity: An entity, which may or may not be incorporated, that has 'enhanced disclosure' securities (p. 947).

Discount (in relation to bills of exchange): Interest deducted in advance, in practice at the effective interest rate or yield (pp. 769, 915).

Discount (on debentures): The amount by which the issue price of a debenture is below the nominal value (p. 924).

Discount allowed: An expense that results from cash discounts taken by customers on the sale of inventory (p. 235).

Discount period: The period of time in which a cash discount may be subtracted from the invoice price before payment or receipt (p. 235); the period of time for which interest on a discounted bill is charged (p. 769).

Discount received: Income that results from cash discounts taken by an entity on goods purchased for resale (p. 235).

Discounted cash flows: Capital budgeting method used to compare the cost of an investment with the present value of the net cash flows from it in the future (p. 591).

Discretionary fixed costs: Fixed costs that can be changed or discontinued by management if enough time is available (p. 464).

Dishonoured bill: A bill the drawer has failed to pay on its maturity date (p. 769).

Dishonoured cheques: Cheques that are included in a customer's deposit but are not paid by the drawer's bank because of lack of sufficient funds or some other irregularity (p. 424).

Dividends: Distributions of cash or other assets or a company's own shares to its shareholders (pp. 205, 669, 727).

Dividends in arrears: Dividends on cumulative preference shares that are not declared in the year in which they are due (p. 669).

Double-entry accounting: The accounting system where every transaction affects two (or more) components of the accounting equation (p. 44).

Drawings: The withdrawal of assets from the business entity by its owner(s) (p. 34).

Economic resources: Resources that are scarce and that are traded in the marketplace at a price (p. 5).

Economic substance: Accounting transactions and events are reported on the basis of economic reality rather than legal form (p. 38).

Effectiveness: A measure of how well an entity attains its goals (p. 19).

Efficiency: Maintaining a satisfactory relationship between an entity's resource inputs and its outputs of products or services (p. 19).

Electronic spreadsheet: A spreadsheet used to analyse business data and solve everyday business problems (p. 307).

Employee benefits: All forms of consideration that employees accumulate as a result of rendering services to their employer; these considerations include wages and salaries (including all monetary and non-monetary fringe benefits), annual leave, sick leave, maternity leave, long-service leave, superannuation, and post-employment benefits (p. 916).

Ending inventory: Goods or stock on hand at the end of an accounting period that are available for sale to customers in the ordinary course of the business (p. 245).

Entering or **journalising:** The process of recording a transaction in the journal (p. 80).

Equity: The residual interest in the assets of the entity after deducting all its liabilities (pp. 33, 723).

Equivalent units: A measure in process costing of how many equivalent whole units of output are represented by the units finished plus the units partly finished (p. 389).

Expense allocation: A systematic and rational process used to apportion indirect costs or expenses to departments (p. 545).

Expenses: Decreases in economic benefits during the accounting period in the form of outflows or depletions of assets or incurrences of liabilities that result in decreases in equity, other than those relating to distributions to equity participants (pp. 34, 74, 340, 724).

Expenses to sales ratio: A ratio that reflects the portion of each sales dollar needed to meet expenses (p. 256).

Expired cost: The cost of an asset used up in producing revenue; an expense (p. 125).

External transactions: Transactions involving parties outside the business entity (p. 66).

EXW (ex works): A shipping/delivery term meaning freight costs incurred from the point of shipment are paid by the buyer (p. 238).

Factor: A business or financial institution that buys accounts receivable for a fee, and then collects the cash from those accounts (the receivables) (p. 764).

Factoring: The selling (purchase) of accounts receivable to (by) a factor business (p. 764).

Factory overhead budget: A projection of the factory overhead cost items required to support the expected production level (p. 511).

Factory overhead cost: All factory costs except direct materials and direct labour required in the production process (p. 344).

Fair value: The price that would be received to sell an asset or paid to transfer a liability in an orderly transaction between market participants at the measurement date (pp. 620, 730, 830, 868).

Faithful representation: To be useful to the main user group in making resource allocation decisions, information must be a faithful representation of the real-world economic phenomena that it purports to represent. This requires information to be verifiable, neutral and complete (pp. 39, 717).

Finance and other expenses budget: Estimates of financial and other expenses for a budget period (p. 513).

Finance expenses: Expenses incurred in relation to the financing of the entity, collecting debts and running the credit department (p. 231).

Financial accounting: The area of accounting that provides information to external users to help them assess the entity's financial performance, financial position, financing and investing activities, and solvency (p. 12).

Financial budgets: The parts of the master budget that show the funding and financing needed for the planned operations (p. 498).

Financial capital: Capital is synonymous with the net assets or equity of the entity, measured either in terms of the actual number of calculated dollars by subtracting the total of liabilities from assets, or in terms of the purchasing power of the dollar amount recorded as equity. Profit exists only after the entity has maintained its capital, measured as either the dollar value of equity at the beginning of the period or the purchasing power of those dollars in the equity at the beginning of the period (p. 731).

Financial performance: The ability of an entity to utilise its assets efficiently and effectively to generate cash flows in the conduct of its activities, whether for profit or not for profit (p. 30).

Financial position: The economic condition of a reporting entity, with regard to its control over economic resources, financial structure, capacity for adaptation, and solvency (pp. 30, 716).

Financial stability: An entity's ability to continue operating in the future and to satisfy its long-term cash obligations (p. 1069).

Financial stability ratios: Ratios used to analyse the ability of an entity to continue operations in the long term and to satisfy long-term commitments while having sufficient working capital (p. 930).

Financing activities: Activities relating to the raising of funds for an entity to carry out its operating and investing activities, i.e. equity and borrowings that are not part of the definition of cash (pp. 31, 982).

Finished goods: The cost of the products that have been manufactured completely and are ready for sale (p. 342).

First-in, first-out (FIFO): A cost flow assumption in inventory costing that assumes the first units purchased were the first units sold. The cost of ending inventory is assumed to be the cost of the most recently purchased units (p. 790).

Fixed (static) budget: A budget prepared for only one level of activity (p. 553).

Fixed costs: Production costs that remain constant in total amount over a wide range of production levels (p. 346).

Flexible budget: A series of budgets prepared for a range of activity levels (p. 553).

Franchise: A right granted by a company or government body to conduct a franchised business at a specified location or in a specific geographical area (p. 886).

Freight inwards (transportation-in): A cost incurred by the buyer in transporting inventory purchases (p. 240). *See also* **EXW (ex works)**.

Freight outwards: Transport (delivery) expense incurred by the seller to deliver goods to customers (p. 238). *See also* **DDP (delivered duty paid)**.

Gains: Income that does not necessarily arise from the ordinary activities of the entity (pp. 74, 724).

Gearing (leverage): The use of borrowed funds to earn a return greater than interest or dividends paid to creditors and preference shareholders respectively (pp. 927, 1065).

General journal (two-column journal): A record book containing a chronological listing of transactions (p. 80).

General ledger: A collection of accounts maintained by an entity to enable the preparation of that entity's financial statements (p. 69).

General ledger software: Computerised accounting systems consisting of modular programs covering each of the major funtional areas of accounting (p. 307).

General partnership: Where each partner is individually liable for the partnership liabilities (p. 617).

General purpose financial reports: Financial reports intended to meet the information needs of a range of users who are unable to command the preparation of reports tailored to satisfy, specifically, all of their information needs (pp. 10, 714).

Goal congruence: The reconciliation of the goals of individual managers with those of the organisation (p. 495).

Going concern assumption (continuity): The assumption that a business will continue to operate in the future unless there is evidence to the contrary (p. 37).

Goodwill: Future benefits from unidentifiable assets (pp. 621, 887).

Grants related to assets: Government grants to an entity to purchase, construct or otherwise acquire long-term assets (p. 728).

Grants related to income: Government grants to an entity other than those related to assets (p. 728).

Gross pay (gross earnings): The total amount of an employee's wages or salary before any payroll deductions (p. 916).

Gross profit method: A method used to estimate ending inventory value based on the assumption that the gross profit percentage is approximately the same from period to period (p. 808).

Gross profit (or gross margin) on sales: Net sales less cost of sales (p. 231).

Gross profit ratio: A ratio that represents the portion of sales reflected in gross profit (p. 256).

GST Collections: The account recording the GST received or receivable by a GST-registered entity from its customers and clients (p. 73).

GST Outlays: The account recording the GST paid or payable by a GST-registered entity to its suppliers (p. 73).

Historical cost: An asset is recorded at the amount of cash or cash equivalents paid or the fair value of the consideration given to acquire it at its acquisition date (p. 730).

Horizontal analysis: That part of an analysis based on the comparison of amounts reported for the same item in two or more comparative statements with an emphasis on the change from year to year (p. 1059).

Ideal standards: Performance targets achievable only with best performance (p. 558).

Identifiable assets: Those assets that are capable of being both individually identified and specifically brought to account (p. 883).

Impairment loss: As applied to an individual asset, the situation where the

asset's recoverable amount is less than its carrying amount (p. 873). As applied to a cash-generating unit, the situation where the fair value of the group of assets as a whole is less than the carrying amount of that group (p. 873).

Imprest system: A system of petty cash fund operation where a fixed amount of cash can always be accounted for by a count of cash plus the value of expenditure vouchers issued (p. 432).

Income: Increases in economic benefits during the accounting period in the form of inflows or enhancements of assets or decreases of liabilities that result in increases in equity, other than those relating to contributions from equity participants; includes revenues and gains (pp. 34, 74, 723).

Income statement (or profit or loss statement or operating statement): A financial statement listing the income, expenses and profit/operating surplus or loss/deficit of an entity for a certain time period (p. 33).

Indirect cost (expenses): Cost or expenses incurred for the common benefit of multiple cost objects (p. 545).

Insolvent: Unable to pay debts as they fall due (p. 15).

Intangible assets: Identifiable non-monetary assets that usually do not have a physical existence and derive value from the rights that possession confers on their holders (pp. 147, 883).

Interest (in relation to bills of exchange): A charge made for the use of money, calculated as Principal × Rate × Time (p. 767).

Interim financial report: A set of half-yearly statements, including an income statement/statement of profit or loss and other comprehensive income, a statement of financial position/balance sheet, a statement of cash flows and selected explanatory notes, to be prepared by a disclosing entity (p. 948).

Interim statements: Financial statements prepared between the annual reports, usually half-yearly or quarterly (pp. 69, 179).

Internal audit: The ongoing investigation of compliance with established procedures and policies of an entity by its internal audit staff (p. 16).

Internal control system: The overall procedures adopted by a business to safeguard its assets, promote the reliability of accounting data, and encourage compliance with management policies (p. 280).

Internal rate of return (IRR): The interest rate that discounts the net cash flows from an investment so their present value is equal to the cost of the investment (p. 596).

Internal transactions: Business activities in which only the single business entity participates, such as the use of supplies by an employee (p. 66).

Inventory: Goods or property acquired by a retail business for the purposes of resale in the ordinary course of operations (p. 230).

Inventory turnover: A ratio that indicates the number of times average inventory has been sold during a period (p. 257).

Investing activities: Activities associated with the acquisition and sale of an entity's non-current assets (p. 31), and with the purchasing and selling of investments (e.g. shares) that are not part of the definition of cash (p. 982).

Investments: Assets held for investment purposes rather than for use in the normal activities of the entity (p. 147).

Job cost order: A control account used in job order costing to provide a detailed listing of the costs relating to the completion of a particular job (p. 380).

Job order costing: A cost system in which costs are accumulated by job (p. 379).

Joint product costs: Common costs required to produce joint products before they are identifiable as separate units (p. 585).

Joint products: More than one product produced from common raw materials or the same production process (p. 585).

Journal (book of original entry): A record in which transactions are initially recorded (p. 79).

Journal entry: The format in which a transaction is entered in the general journal (p. 80).

Just-in-time (JIT) processing: A system of manufacturing designed to eliminate the holding of inventories by putting raw materials directly into production when received and shipping finished goods immediately to customers (p. 395).

Last-in, first-out (LIFO): A cost flow assumption in inventory costing that assumes the most recent units purchased were the first units sold. The cost of ending inventory is assumed to be the cost of the earliest units purchased (p. 791).

Lease: A rental agreement in which the lessee obtains from the lessor the right to use property for a stated period of time (p. 927).

Leasehold improvements: Permanent improvements to leased property made by the lessee (p. 843).

Legal obligation: Obligation evidenced by formal documentation such as a contract, legislation or other operations of the law that establish a present obligation (p. 909).

Liabilities: Present obligations of an entity arising from past events, the settlement of which is expected to result in an outflow from the entity of resources embodying economic benefits (pp. 33, 721, 908).

Limited company: A company whose members are liable only to the extent of the amount of issue price unpaid on their shares, or to the extent of a guaranteed amount (p. 650).

Limited liability: In a company, shareholders are liable to contribute to the assets of a company only to the extent of amounts unpaid on their shares (p. 18).

Limited partnership: Where one or more of the partners have limited their liability for partnership debts to the amount of their investment. However, at all times at least one partner must have unlimited liability (p. 617).

Linearity assumption: A key assumption of CVP analysis that all revenue and costs will behave as straight-line functions in the relevant range of activity (p. 463).

Liquidation: The process of winding up the affairs of a company so that it ceases to exist (p. 15).

Liquidity (solvency): The ability of an entity to satisfy its short-term financial obligations; also refers to the average length of time it takes to convert a non-cash asset into cash (pp. 144, 1066).

Liquidity ratios: Ratios that provide a measure of an entity's ability to pay its short-term obligations, and meet unexpected demands on cash resources (p. 929).

Long-service leave: Paid leave granted to employees who have remained with the same employer over an extended period of time (p. 920).

Loss: The excess of expenses over total income (revenues and gains) (pp. 34, 74).

Lower of cost and net realisable value: Inventory valuation method where inventory is valued at lower of original cost and net realisable value at the end of the reporting period (p. 800).

Lump-sum acquisition: The purchase of a group of assets for one total payment (p. 833).

Management accounting: The area of accounting that provides information to management for planning, controlling and decision making (p. 12).

Management by exception: The concentration only on performance results that deviate significantly from those planned (pp. 20, 542).

Management functions: The planning, organising, directing and controlling required to manage an organisation (p. 19).

Manufacturing business: A business that converts raw materials into saleable products (p. 340).

Manufacturing cost elements: The direct materials, direct labour and factory overhead required to produce a saleable product (p. 343).

Manufacturing worksheet: Working papers used to organise financial data, including the manufacturing costs, and to prepare financial statements (p. 351).

Margin of safety: The excess of actual or expected sales over break-even sales (p. 471).

Mark-down cancellation: Reversal of a mark-down whereby inventory not sold at a sales promotion reverts to its normal retail price (p. 807).

Mark-downs: Price reductions to promote sales (p. 807).

Mark-up cancellations: Reversal of mark-ups. A downward revision on retail prices because of lack of demand or an excessive mark-up (p. 807).

Master budget: A set of interrelated budgets representing a comprehensive plan of action for a specified time period (p. 497).

Materiality: The extent to which information can be omitted, misstated or grouped with other information without misleading the users of that information when they are making their economic decisions (pp. 39, 717).

Materials requisition: A record of the amount of raw materials requisitioned from the storeroom for a job or as indirect materials (p. 381).

Maturity date: The date on which a bill or debenture is due for payment (pp. 767, 923).

Maturity value: The amount of a bill due on its maturity date; it includes principal as well as interest (p. 767).

Mixed cost: A cost that has both a variable component and a fixed component (p. 462).

Mortgage: A legal document setting forth the specific assets serving as collateral for a loan (p. 926).

Mortgage debenture: A debenture in which land held by the company is mortgaged as security for the debenture (p. 924).

Mortgage payable: A liability in which specific property of the borrower serves as collateral for a loan (p. 922).

Moving average: An inventory costing method by which an average unit cost is calculated after each purchase. The method applies only where a perpetual inventory system is being used (p. 797).

Mutual agency: A characteristic whereby each partner is an agent for the partnership and can bind the partnership to a contract if acting within the normal scope of the business (p. 617).

Net assets: Total assets minus total liabilities (as in the narrative form of the balance sheet/statement of financial position) (p. 32).

Net fair value: Fair value less estimated point-of-sale costs (p. 882).

Net pay (net earnings): Gross pay of an employee less deductions (p. 917).

Net present value (NPV) index method: A method of evaluating investments where an index is derived by relating the net present values of future cash flows to initial cost (p. 596).

Net present value (NPV) method: A capital budgeting method used to discount future net cash flows into present value terms with the entity's cost of capital (p. 593).

Net realisable value: The market value based on estimated proceeds of sales less, where applicable, GST and all further costs of production, marketing, selling and distribution to customers (p. 800).

No-liability company: A company, being a mining company, that does not have the right to require shareholders to pay calls to the company (p. 652).

Nominal value (face value, principal): The amount due to a lender when a debt under debentures or unsecured notes matures (p. 923).

Non-cumulative preference shares: Preference shares on which the right to receive dividends is lost in any year in which dividends are not declared (p. 669).

Non-current liabilities: Obligations of the entity that do not require payment within the operating cycle or within 12 months of the end of the reporting period (pp. 147, 913).

Non-reciprocal transfer: A transfer of assets in which the entity receives assets or services without giving approximately equal value in exchange for the assets or services received (p. 727).

Normal account balance: The side or column of the account on which increases are recorded (p. 78).

Obligating event: An event that results in an entity having no realistic alternative to settling the obligation (p. 911).

Onerous contract: A contract in which the unavoidable costs of meeting the obligations under the contract exceed the economic benefits expected to be received under it (p. 921).

Operating activities: Activities associated with the provision of an entity's goods or services, and other activities that are neither financing nor investing activities (pp. 31, 981).

Operating budgets: The components of the master budget that describe the income, costs and expenses required to achieve a satisfactory financial performance (p. 498).

Operating cycle: The average period of time it takes for an entity to purchase or manufacture inventory or perform services, and then receive cash from the sale (p. 146).

Operating statement: *See* **Income statement**.

Opportunity cost: The potential benefit forgone by rejecting one alternative while accepting another (p. 583).

Ordinary shares: A class of share that has no preferences relative to other classes (p. 666).

Organisation: A group of people who share common goals with a well-defined division of labour (p. 18).

Other comprehensive income: Items of income and expense that are not recognised in profit or loss because of the requirements of other standards (pp. 869, 950).

Overapplied factory overhead: The excess of the factory overhead applied to work in process with a predetermined rate during a given period over the actual factory overhead incurred (p. 385).

Overhead application rate: A predetermined rate used to assign factory overhead costs to products (p. 345).

Participating preference shares: Preference shares that have the right to receive further dividends above their fixed rate after ordinary shares have received dividends up to a stated percentage for the period (p. 669).

Partnership: A form of business structure under which a business entity is owned by two or more people as partners sharing profits and losses (pp. 17, 616).

Partnership agreement: The contract or agreement made among the partners to form and operate a partnership (p. 618).

Patent: An exclusive right to produce and sell a particular product or process for a period of 20 years (p. 885).

Payback period: The length of time required to recover the cost of an investment from the net cash flows it generates (p. 596).

Percentage-of-completion method: A method of accounting for service contracts and long-term construction contracts under which revenue is recognised in proportion to the services or work completed during the period (p. 726).

Percentage of net credit sales: A method used to determine the amount of the allowance for doubtful debts (p. 754).

Performance: The entity's ability to operate its assets efficiently and effectively in the conduct of its activities (p. 716).

Period assumption: The assumption that the economic life of an entity can be divided into arbitrary equal time intervals for reporting purposes (p. 38).

Period costs: Costs reported in the income statement of the period in which they are incurred rather than being costed to inventories as product costs (p. 343).

Periodic inventory system: A system of accounting for inventory in which the goods on hand are determined by a physical count and the cost of sales is equal to the beginning inventory plus net purchases less ending inventory (p. 244).

Permanent (real) accounts: Accounts reported in the balance sheet/statement of financial position (p. 126).

Perpetual inventory system: A system of accounting for inventory that provides a continuous and detailed record of the goods on hand and the cost of sales (p. 238).

Petty cash fund: A specified amount of cash placed under the control of an employee (petty cashier) for use in making small cash payments (p. 430).

Petty cash voucher or receipt: A form used as a receipt for payments from a petty cash fund (p. 431).

Physical capital: Capital is seen as the operating capability of the entity's assets. Profit exists only after the entity has set aside enough capital to maintain the operating capability of its assets (p. 731).

Physical inventory count (stocktake): The process of counting and pricing the goods on hand (p. 244).

Post-closing trial balance: A trial balance taken after the adjusting and closing entries have been posted to the accounts and the permanent accounts balanced (p. 198).

Posting: The process of transferring information recorded in a journal to the individual accounts in the ledger (p. 81).

Predetermined overhead rate: The rate determined by dividing estimated factory overhead or service costs for a period by some measure of the estimated activity and used to apply overhead to work in process/services provided (p. 384).

Preference shares: Shares that receive preferential treatment over ordinary shares such as a preference in dividend distributions, and/or a preference in asset distributions if the company is wound up (depending on the constitution) (p. 666).

Preliminary expenses (or start-up costs): The expenditures made to form a company. They include incorporation fees, legal fees, and promoters' and underwriters' fees (p. 665).

Premium (on debentures): The price in excess of nominal value on issue of debentures (p. 924).

Present value: The single value at the present time of cash flows expected to be received or paid in the future that have been discounted at an appropriate rate (p. 916).

Prime cost: The cost of direct materials plus the cost of direct labour (p. 344).

Principal: The base figure (face amount) of an amount owing (a bill) (p. 767).

Proceeds: The maturity value of a bill less discount (p. 769).

Process costing: A cost accounting system in which costs are accumulated by processing centres during a specified period (p. 387).

Processing centre: A segment of the manufacturing operation in which a particular process takes place and for which costs are accumulated in process costing (p. 387).

Product costs: Costs assigned to inventories during production and reported in the income statement when the related finished goods are sold (p. 343).

Production budget: An estimate of the number of units that will be manufactured during the budget period (p. 509).

Production departments: Departments engaged directly in the manufacturing operation required to convert raw materials into finished goods (p. 344).

Profit: When total income (revenues and gains) exceeds total expenses (pp. 34, 74).

Profit or loss statement: *See* **Income statement**.

Profit margin: A ratio that represents the portion of sales that ends up as profit (p. 256).

Promissory note: An unconditional written promise to pay a sum certain in money on demand or at a future determinable date (pp. 750, 766).

Property, plant and equipment: Resources of the entity that are physical in nature, have a relatively long useful life, and are used in the activities of the entity (p. 147).

Proprietary company: A company having a share capital in which the right to transfer shares is restricted as is the right to raise capital from the public (p. 651).

Prospectus: A legal document representing an approach by a company to raise funds in order to carry on business (p. 655).

Provisions: Liabilities of uncertain timing or amount (p. 910).

Public accountability: Accountability of an entity to present and potential resource providers and others external to the entity who make economic decisions but who are not in a position to demand reports tailored to meet their particular information needs. An entity has public accountability if:

(a) it has issued (or is in the process of issuing) debt or equity instruments in a public market

or

(b) it holds assets in a fiduciary capacity for a broad group of outsiders, such as a bank, insurance company, securities broker/dealer, pension (or superannuation) fund, mutual fund or investment bank (p. 712).

Public company: A company entitled to raise capital from the public and to have its shares listed on a securities exchange (p. 651).

Publicly accountable: An entity that has public accountability (p. 947).

Purchases: An account used in a periodic inventory system to record the cost of goods acquired for resale to customers (p. 245).

Purchases budget: An estimate of the number of units that will be purchased by a retail entity during the budget period (p. 499).

Purchases journal: A special journal used to record all purchases of inventory on credit (p. 288).

Purchases returns and allowances: An account used in the periodic inventory system to record the return by an entity of inventory or adjustments made to the purchase price (p. 246).

Qualifying asset: An asset that necessarily takes a substantial period of time (i.e. usually longer than 1 year) to get ready for its intended use or sale (pp. 832, 951).

Ratio: Division of the amount reported for one financial statement item by the amount reported for another. Ratio analysis is the

evaluation of the relationship indicated by this division (p. 1061).

Raw materials: The cost of the basic materials that have been purchased by a manufacturing entity and are available for conversion into saleable products (p. 342).

Realisable value: The amount of cash or cash equivalents that could be obtained currently by selling the asset in an orderly disposal or in the normal course of business (p. 730).

Receivables turnover ratio: A ratio that measures the number of times average receivables are converted into cash during a period (p. 762).

Recognition: The process of incorporating in the statement of financial position/ balance sheet or income statement an item that meets the definition of an element (p. 724).

Recoverable amount: The higher of an asset's net selling price and its value in use (p. 873).

Redemption by sinking fund: The redemption of long-term debt by way of establishing a fund that will be used to pay the debt's obligations on maturity (p. 926).

Reduced Disclosure Requirements: A reduced disclosure regime introduced as a result of AASB 1053 *Application of Tiers of Australian Accounting Standards* (p. 947).

Relevance: A quality of financial information that influences economic decisions by helping users to form predictions, to confirm or correct past evaluations and to assess the rendering of accountability by preparers (pp. 38, 716).

Relevant costs: Expected future costs that will differ between alternatives (p. 583).

Relevant income: Expected future income that will differ between alternatives (p. 583).

Relevant range: The range of activity within which a business expects to operate and incur variable costs with constant slopes as well as fixed costs that are constant in total amount (p. 463).

Reliability: A quality of financial information that assures the user that information in financial reports represents faithfully, without bias or undue error, the transactions and events being reported (p. 38).

Replaceable rules: Rules contained in the *Corporations Act 2001* relating to dealings between management and shareholders. If the company wishes to reject such rules, it must adopt a constitution (p. 654).

Reporting entity: Any entity where it is reasonable to expect the existence of users depending on general purpose financial reports for information used in economic decision making (p. 711).

Research: An original and planned investigation undertaken with the prospect of gaining new scientific or technical knowledge and understanding (p. 884).

Reserve: A category of equity created either by common business practice or in accordance with accounting standards (p. 671).

Residual profit (residual income): The profit earned in excess of a certain minimum rate of return on assets (p. 589).

Residual value: The estimated amount that an entity could currently obtain from disposal of an asset, after deducting the estimated costs of disposal, if the asset were already of the age and in the condition expected at the end of its useful life (p. 835).

Responsibility accounting: The accounting procedures used to evaluate the financial performance of responsibility centres (p. 540).

Responsibility centre: A business segment organised as a cost centre, a profit centre or an investment centre so responsibility accounting can be performed (p. 540).

Retail inventory method: A method used to estimate the ending inventory value based on the relationship of cost to retail prices (excluding GST) (p. 806).

Retained earnings: The accumulated profits of a company that have been retained in the company rather than distributed to shareholders as dividends (pp. 205, 657).

Return on average investment: A capital budgeting method that provides a measure of an investment's profitability by dividing the average profit after tax from an investment by average investment; also referred to as the accounting rate of return (p. 597).

Return on investment (ROI) analysis: A technique used to evaluate the profitability of segments of a business (p. 588).

Revaluation decrease: The amount by which the fair value of a non-current asset within a class at revaluation date is less than the asset's carrying amount (p. 868).

Revaluation increase: The amount by which the fair value of a non-current asset within a class at revaluation date exceeds the asset's carrying amount (p. 868).

Revenue: The gross inflow of economic benefits during the period arising in the course of the ordinary activities of an entity when those inflows result in increases in equity, other than increases relating to contributions from equity participants (pp. 74, 723).

Reversing entries: Entries made to reverse the effects of certain adjusting entries (p. 200).

Rights issue: An issue of new shares giving existing shareholders the right to an additional number of shares in proportion to their current shareholdings (p. 664).

Royalties: Rights of composers and authors to receive payments from publishing companies for the sale of their music or books. Also money received by the owner of land from a mining company that has been given the right to mine mineral reserves on the owner's land (p. 727).

Running balance account: An account format that enables the balance of the account to be calculated after each transaction affecting that account (p. 70).

Salary: Remuneration on a weekly, fortnightly or monthly basis paid to an employee, usually a fixed amount regardless of hours worked (p. 917).

Sales: Income (revenue) of a retail business represented by the sales price of goods sold (p. 231).

Sales budget: A translation of the sales forecast for a budget period into detailed information concerning the products that are expected to be sold (p. 507).

Sales journal: A special journal used to record all sales of inventory on credit (p. 286).

Sales returns and allowances: The selling price of inventory returned by customers or adjustments made to the sales price (p. 235).

Selling and distribution expenses: Expenses that result from efforts to store, sell and deliver goods to customers (p. 231).

Selling and distribution expenses budget: Estimates of the selling expenses needed to generate the expected sales volume for the budget period (p. 512).

Service (or support) departments: Departments that provide supporting services such as personnel, advertising, accounting, maintenance, production control, stores, or purchasing (pp. 344, 546).

Service income budget: A translation of the service income forecast for a budget period into detailed information concerning the services that are expected to be provided (p. 501).

Share capital: The amount of cash or other assets invested in the company by its shareholders (or members) (pp. 205, 657).

Share dividends: A pro rata distribution of a company's own shares to its shareholders (p. 670).

Share issue costs: The costs directly associated with the issue of shares, including stamp duty, broker's fees, underwriter's fees, professional adviser's fees and printing costs (p. 665).

Share split: A decrease in the issue price of shares with a proportionate increase in the number of shares (p. 671).

Shareholders: Persons or entities owning shares in a company (p. 18).

Single proprietorship (sole trader): A form of business structure in which the business entity is owned by an individual (p. 17).

Slide: An error in which the decimal point is shifted to the left or right (p. 101).

Solvency: The ability of an entity to pay its debts as and when they fall due (p. 437).

Source document: A paper, form or computer record that provides evidence that a transaction has occurred (p. 67).

Special journal: Book of original entry used for such repetitive transactions as sales, purchases, cash receipts and cash payments (p. 285).

Special-purpose financial reports: Reports prepared for users who have specialised needs and who possess the authority to obtain information to meet those needs (p. 9).

Specific identification: An inventory costing method by which the cost of a specific item sold can be separately identified from the cost of other units held in the inventory (p. 789).

Split-off point: The point in the production process at which joint products become separate products (p. 585).

Standard cost variances: The differences between standard costs and actual costs that can be used in the application of management by exception (p. 558).

Standard costs: Carefully predetermined costs that should be incurred to produce a product or perform a service. They are used to plan and control an entity's financial performance and are especially important in a manufacturing entity (p. 557).

Start-up costs: *See* **Preliminary expenses**.

Statement of cash flows: A financial statement that reports the cash flows in and out of an entity. The cash flows are classified into operating, investing and financing activities (p. 35).

Statement of changes in partners' equity: A financial statement that shows the changes in each partner's equity interest during the period (p. 629).

Statement of financial position: *See* **Balance sheet**.

Stocktake: *See* **Physical inventory count**.

Straight-line depreciation: A depreciation method that allocates an equal amount of an asset's depreciable amount to each period in its useful life (p. 836).

Subsidiary ledger: A group of individual accounts, the total of all balances of which should equal the balance of a related control account in the general ledger (p. 284).

Substance over form: A characteristic of information where the economic substance of a transaction takes precedence over its legal form (p. 717).

Sum-of-years-digits depreciation: A depreciation method under which the depreciable amount of an asset is allocated to depreciation on a fractional basis. The denominators of the fractions are the sum of the digits in the asset's useful life. The numerators of the fractions are the years remaining in the asset's useful life at the beginning of the period (p. 838).

Sunk costs: Costs that are not relevant in decision making because they already have been incurred and cannot be changed (p. 583).

Systems analysis: The initial stage in the development of an accounting system through which an understanding of a business's information requirements and sources of information is provided (p. 277).

Systems design: The second stage in the development of an accounting system through which the specific means to be used for input, processing and output are determined (p. 278).

Systems implementation and review: The final stage in the development of an accounting system through which the system is made operational (p. 278).

T account: An account format shaped like the letter T, in which the left-hand side of the account is the debit side and the right-hand side is the credit side (p. 69).

Taxable income: The amount of profit as determined by the Australian Taxation Office on which the current income tax liability is calculated (p. 672).

Tax invoice: A source document issued by a GST-registered business evidencing the sale of a taxable supply, and that complies with GST legislative requirements (p. 232).

Tax payable method: An accounting method whereby income tax expense is calculated as the tax rate times taxable income (p. 673).

Tax shield: The savings in cash outflows that result from a tax-deductible expense such as depreciation (p. 595).

Temporary (nominal) accounts: Accounts (income, expense and drawings accounts) that are reduced to a zero balance at the end of an accounting period (p. 126).

Term loan: A borrowing from a bank, life insurance company, and other financial institutions for periods of 1 to 10 years, usually at a fixed interest rate (p. 922).

Timeliness: Information must be available to decision makers before it loses its capacity to influence decisions, i.e. before the information loses its relevance (p. 720).

Trade creditors: Another name for the Accounts Payable account (pp. 72, 913).

Trade debtors: Another name for the Accounts Receivable account (pp. 72, 750).

Trade discount: A reduction in the suggested list price granted to certain customers. Trade discount is not recorded in the accounts but appears as a deduction from the list price shown on the invoice (p. 237).

Transactions: The events that are identified as making up the economic activities of an entity (p. 7).

Transportation-in: *See* **Freight inwards**.

Transposition: An error in which the order of the digits of a number is altered (p. 101).

Trial balance: A statement listing all the accounts in the general ledger and their debit or credit balances. A trial balance is prepared to verify the equality of debits and credits made to the accounts (p. 99).

Trust deed: A document setting down the terms of a debenture agreement and the appointment of a trustee (p. 923).

Trustee: A third party appointed to represent debenture holders (p. 924).

Two-column journal: *See* **General journal**.

Unavoidable costs: Future costs that will not differ between alternatives (p. 583).

Unavoidable expenses: Expenses that will not be eliminated if a department or a product is discontinued (p. 551).

Uncalled capital: The amount of issued share capital that has not yet been called by the company (p. 657).

Underapplied factory overhead: The excess of actual factory overhead incurred over the factory overhead applied during a particular period (p. 385).

Understandability: Does not necessarily mean simplicity. It is assumed that readers of reports have a reasonable knowledge of business and economic activities and accounting, and that they are willing to study the information with reasonable diligence (pp. 39, 720).

Underwriter: Takes up any shares that are undersubscribed in a share issue; is paid an underwriting fee regardless of whether the issue is fully subscribed or oversubscribed (p. 663).

Unexpired cost: A cost that has not been used to produce revenue and has future economic benefits to the entity; unexpired costs are initially recorded as assets (p. 125).

Units-of-production depreciation: A depreciation method under which the depreciable amount of an asset is allocated to depreciation expense based on the number of production units produced during the period (p. 839).

Unlimited company: A company in which shareholders are fully liable for all debts of the company (p. 652).

Unlimited liability: A characteristic of a partnership whereby each general partner is responsible for all debts of the partnership from personal assets if necessary (p. 617).

Unpresented cheques or outstanding cheques: Cheques written by a depositor that have not been presented to the bank for payment (p. 426).

Unsecured note: A borrowing with no security against the general assets of the borrower (p. 924).

Useful life: The estimated time period over which the future economic benefits embodied in a depreciable asset are expected to be consumed by the entity; or the estimated total service, expressed in terms of production or similar units, that is expected to be obtained from the asset by the entity (pp. 132, 835).

Value in use: The present value of future net cash flows expected from the continuing use of an asset and from its disposal at the end of its useful life (p. 873).

Variable costs: Production costs that vary in total amount directly with the volume of production (p. 346).

Variance: The difference between actual and planned results. A favourable cost variance occurs when the actual cost is less than the amount budgeted. In contrast, an unfavourable cost variance exists when the actual cost exceeds the amount budgeted (pp. 476, 542).

Verifiability: That quality of information whereby different independent observers would reach general agreement that a particular piece of information represents the economic phenomena that it purports to represent without material error or bias, or that the measurement method used has been applied without material error or bias (p. 719).

Vertical analysis: That part of an analysis in which the focus of the study is on the proportion of individual items expressed as a percentage of some specific item reported in the same statement (p. 1059). *See also* **Common size statement**.

Wages: Remuneration calculated on an hourly rate paid to an employee (p. 917).

Weighted average: An inventory costing method by which an average cost per unit is calculated by dividing the total cost of units available for sale by the total number of units available for sale. It is used in the periodic inventory system (p. 792).

Work in process: Inventory that has been partly converted into finished goods (p. 342).

Workers compensation: An insurance scheme imposed by law whereby the employer purchases insurance that may be used to compensate employees for job-related injuries and consequential loss of wages through loss of work (p. 919).

Working capital: The excess of current assets over current liabilities (p. 144).

Worksheet: A spreadsheet, prepared either manually or electronically, used by accountants to gather and organise information to enable preparation of the financial statements, and/or for use in the adjusting and closing processes of the accounting cycle (p. 148).

Index